Lecture Notes in Computer Science

Lecture Notes in Artificial Intelligence 14162

Founding Editor

Jörg Siekmann

Series Editors

The series Lecture Notes in Artificial Intelligence (LNAI) was established in 1988 as a topical subseries of LNCS devoted to artificial intelligence.

The series publishes state-of-the-art research results at a high level. As with the LNCS mother series, the mission of the series is to serve the international R & D community by providing an invaluable service, mainly focused on the publication of conference and workshop proceedings and postproceedings.

Ngoc Thanh Nguyen · János Botzheim ·
László Gulyás · Manuel Núñez · Jan Treur ·
Gottfried Vossen · Adrianna Kozierkiewicz
Editors

Computational Collective Intelligence

15th International Conference, ICCCI 2023
Budapest, Hungary, September 27–29, 2023
Proceedings

Springer

Editors
Ngoc Thanh Nguyen
Wrocław University of Science and Technology
Wrocław, Poland

László Gulyás
Eötvös Loránd University
Budapest, Hungary

Jan Treur
Vrije Universiteit Amsterdam
Amsterdam, The Netherlands

Adrianna Kozierkiewicz
Wrocław University of Science and Technology
Wrocław, Poland

János Botzheim
Eötvös Loránd University
Budapest, Hungary

Manuel Núñez
Universidad Complutense de Madrid
Madrid, Spain

Gottfried Vossen
Universität Münster
Münster, Germany

ISSN 0302-9743 ISSN 1611-3349 (electronic)
Lecture Notes in Artificial Intelligence
ISBN 978-3-031-41455-8 ISBN 978-3-031-41456-5 (eBook)
https://doi.org/10.1007/978-3-031-41456-5

LNCS Sublibrary: SL7 – Artificial Intelligence

This Springer imprint is published by the registered company Springer Nature Switzerland AG
The registered company address is: Gewerbestrasse 11, 6330 Cham, Switzerland

Preface

This volume contains the first part of the proceedings of the 15th International Conference on Computational Collective Intelligence (ICCCI 2023), held in Budapest, Hungary between 27–29 September 2023. The conference was organized in a hybrid mode which allowed for both on-site and online paper presentations. The conference was hosted by the Eötvös Loránd University (ELTE), Hungary and jointly organized by Wrocław University of Science and Technology, Poland in cooperation with IEEE SMC Technical Committee on Computational Collective Intelligence, European Research Center for Information Systems (ERCIS), International University-VNU-HCM (Vietnam) and John von Neumann Computer Society (NJSZT).

Following the successes of the 1st ICCCI (2009), held in Wrocław - Poland, the 2nd ICCCI (2010) in Kaohsiung - Taiwan, the 3rd ICCCI (2011) in Gdynia - Poland, the 4th ICCCI (2012) in Ho Chi Minh City - Vietnam, the 5th ICCCI (2013) in Craiova - Romania, the 6th ICCCI (2014) in Seoul - South Korea, the 7th ICCCI (2015) in Madrid - Spain, the 8th ICCCI (2016) in Halkidiki - Greece, the 9th ICCCI (2017) in Nicosia - Cyprus, the 10th ICCCI (2018) in Bristol - UK, the 11th ICCCI (2019) in Hendaye - France, the 12th ICCCI (2020) in Da Nang - Vietnam, the 13th ICCCI (2021) in Rhodes - Greece, and the 14th ICCCI (2022) in Hammamet, Tunisia, this conference continued to provide an internationally respected forum for scientific research in computer-based methods of collective intelligence and their applications.

Computational collective intelligence (CCI) is most often understood as a subfield of artificial intelligence (AI) dealing with soft computing methods that facilitate group decisions or processing knowledge among autonomous units acting in distributed environments. Methodological, theoretical, and practical aspects of CCI are considered as the form of intelligence that emerges from the collaboration and competition of many individuals (artificial and/or natural). The application of multiple computational intelligence technologies such as fuzzy systems, evolutionary computation, neural systems, consensus theory, etc. can support human and other collective intelligence, and create new forms of CCI in natural and/or artificial systems. Three subfields of the application of computational intelligence technologies to support various forms of collective intelligence are of special interest but are not exclusive: the Semantic Web (as an advanced tool for increasing collective intelligence), social network analysis (as a field targeted at the emergence of new forms of CCI), and multi-agent systems (as a computational and modeling paradigm especially tailored to capture the nature of CCI emergence in populations of autonomous individuals).

The ICCCI 2023 conference featured a number of keynote talks and oral presentations, closely aligned to the theme of the conference. The conference attracted a substantial number of researchers and practitioners from all over the world, who submitted their papers for the main track and 9 special sessions.

The main track, covering the methodology and applications of CCI, included: collective decision-making, data fusion, deep learning techniques, natural language processing, data mining and machine learning, social networks and intelligent systems, optimization, computer vision, knowledge engineering and application, as well as Internet of Things: technologies and applications. The special sessions, covering some specific topics of particular interest, included: cooperative strategies for decision making and optimization, artificial intelligence, speech communication, IOT applications, natural language processing, deep learning, intelligent systems, machine learning, collective intelligence in medical applications, and computer vision.

We received 218 papers submitted by authors coming from 41 countries around the world. Each paper was single-blind reviewed by at least three members of the international Program Committee (PC) of either the main track or one of the special sessions. Finally, we selected 63 papers for oral presentation and publication in one volume of the Lecture Notes in Artificial Intelligence series and 59 papers for oral presentation and publication in one volume of the Communications in Computer and Information Science series.

We would like to express our thanks to the keynote speakers: Loo Chu Kiong from Universiti Malaya (Malaysia), A.E. Eiben from Vrije Universiteit Amsterdam (The Netherlands), Aleksander Byrski from AGH University of Science and Technology (Poland), and Diego Paez-Granados from ETH Zürich (Switzerland).

Many people contributed toward the success of the conference. First, we would like to recognize the work of the PC co-chairs and special sessions organizers for taking good care of the organization of the reviewing process, an essential stage in ensuring the high quality of the accepted papers. The workshop and special session chairs deserve a special mention for the evaluation of the proposals and the organization and coordination of the work of eleven special sessions. In addition, we would like to thank the PC members, of the main track and of the special sessions, for performing their reviewing work with diligence. We thank the Local Organizing Committee chairs, Publicity chairs, Web chair, and Technical Support chairs for their fantastic work before and during the conference. Finally, we cordially thank all the authors, presenters, and delegates for their valuable contribution to this successful event. The conference would not have been possible without their support.

Our special thanks are also due to Springer for publishing the proceedings and to all the other sponsors for their kind support.

It is our pleasure to announce that the ICCCI conference series continues to have a close cooperation with the Springer journal Transactions on Computational Collective Intelligence, and the IEEE SMC Technical Committee on Transactions on Computational Collective Intelligence.

Finally, we hope that ICCCI 2023 contributed significantly to the academic excellence of the field and will lead to the even greater success of ICCCI events in the future.

September 2023

Ngoc Thanh Nguyen
János Botzheim
László Gulyás
Manuel Núñez
Jan Treur
Gottfried Vossen
Adrianna Kozierkiewicz

Organization

Organizing Committee

Honorary Chairs

László Borhy	Rector of Eötvös Loránd University, Hungary
Arkadiusz Wójs	Rector of Wrocław University of Science and Technology, Poland

General Chairs

Ngoc Thanh Nguyen	Wrocław University of Science and Technology, Poland
János Botzheim	Eötvös Loránd University, Hungary

Program Chairs

László Gulyás	Eötvös Loránd University, Hungary
Manuel Núñez	Universidad Complutense de Madrid, Spain
Jan Treur	Vrije Universiteit Amsterdam, The Netherlands
Gottfried Vossen	University of Münster, Germany

Steering Committee

Ngoc Thanh Nguyen	Wrocław University of Science and Technology, Poland
Piotr Jędrzejowicz	Gdynia Maritime University, Poland
Shyi-Ming Chen	National Taiwan University of Science and Technology, Taiwan
Kiem Hoang	VNU-HCM University of Information Technology, Vietnam
Dosam Hwang	Yeungnam University, South Korea
Lakhmi C. Jain	University of South Australia, Australia
Geun-Sik Jo	Inha University, South Korea
Janusz Kacprzyk	Polish Academy of Sciences, Poland
Ryszard Kowalczyk	Swinburne University of Technology, Australia
Yannis Manolopoulos	Open University of Cyprus, Cyprus
Toyoaki Nishida	Kyoto University, Japan

Manuel Núñez	Universidad Complutense de Madrid, Spain
Klaus Söilen	Halmstad University, Sweden
Khoa Tien Tran	VNU-HCM International University , Vietnam

Organizing Chairs

Udo Bub	Eötvös Loránd University, Hungary
Marcin Pietranik	Wrocław University of Science and Technology, Poland

Special Session Chairs

Adrianna Kozierkiewicz	Wrocław University of Science and Technology, Poland
Paweł Sitek	Kielce University of Technology, Poland
András Lőrincz	Eötvös Loránd University, Hungary
Ellák Somfai	Eötvös Loránd University, Hungary

Doctoral Track Chair

Marek Krótkiewicz	Wrocław University of Science and Technology, Poland

Publicity Chairs

Attila Kiss	Eötvös Loránd University, Hungary
Marcin Jodłowiec	Wrocław University of Science and Technology, Poland
Rafal Palak	Wrocław University of Science and Technology, Poland

Webmaster

Marek Kopel	Wrocław University of Science and Technology, Poland

Local Organizing Committee

Kaan Karaköse	Eötvös Loránd University, Hungary
Márk Domonkos	Eötvös Loránd University, Hungary
Natabara Gyöngyössy	Eötvös Loránd University, Hungary

Patient Zihisire Muke	Wrocław University of Science and Technology, Poland
Thanh-Ngo Nguyen	Wrocław University of Science and Technology, Poland
Jose Fabio Ribeiro Bezerra	Wrocław University of Science and Technology, Poland

Keynote Speakers

Loo Chu Kiong	Universiti Malaya, Malaysia
Agoston E. Eiben	Vrije Universiteit Amsterdam, The Netherlands
Aleksander Byrski	AGH University of Science and Technology, Poland
Diego Paez-Granados	ETH Zürich, Switzerland

Special Session Organizers

AISC 2023: Special Session on AI and Speech Communication

Ualsher Tukeyev	al-Farabi Kazakh National University, Kazakhstan
Orken Mamyrbayev	Institute of Information and Computational Technologies, Kazakhstan

EIIOT 2023: Special Session on Edge Intelligence for IOT Applications

Suresh Sankaranarayanan	King Faisal University, KSA
Pascal Lorenz	University of Haute Alsace, France

CCINLP 2023: Special Session on Computational Collective Intelligence and Natural Language Processing

Ismail Biskri	University of Québec at Trois-Rivières, Canada
Nadia Ghazzali	University of Québec at Trois-Rivières, Canada

DISADA 2023: Special Session on Deep Learning and Intelligent Systems for Arabic Document Analysis

Mounir Zrigui	University of Monastir, Tunisia
Sadek Mansouri	University of Monastir, Tunisia
Nafaa Haffar	University of Monastir, Tunisia

Dhaou Berchech	DB Consulting, France

CSDMO 2023: Special Session on Cooperative Strategies for Decision Making and Optimization

Piotr Jędrzejowicz	Gdynia Maritime University, Poland
Dariusz Barbucha	Gdynia Maritime University, Poland
Ireneusz Czarnowski	Gdynia Maritime University, Poland

MLRWD 2023: Special Session on Machine Learning in Real-World Data

Jan Kozak	University of Economics in Katowice, Poland
Artur Kozłowski	Łukasiewicz Research Network, Poland
Przemysław Juszczuk	Polish Academy of Sciences, Poland
Barbara Probierz	University of Economics in Katowice, Poland
Tomasz Jach	University of Economics in Katowice, Poland

AIIMTH 2023: Special Session on AI and Internet of Medical Things in Healthcare

Octavian Postolache	ISCTE-University Institute of Lisbon, Portugal
Madina Mansurova	al-Farabi Kazakh National University, Kazakhstan

DICV 2023: Special Session on Recent Advances of Deep Learning and Internet of Things in Computer Vision- Related Applications

Wadii Boulila	Prince Sultan University, KSA
Jawad Ahmad	Edinburgh Napier University, UK
Maha Driss	Prince Sultan University, KSA
Anis Koubaa	Prince Sultan University, KSA
Mark Elliot	University of Manchester, UK

Innov-Healthcare 2023: Special Session on Innovative use of Machine Learning and Deep Learning for HealthCare Empowerment

Yassine Ben Ayed	University of Sfax, Tunisia
Wael Ouarda	Ministry of Higher Education and Scientific Research, Tunisia

Senior Program Committee

Plamen Angelov	Lancaster University, UK
Costin Badica	University of Craiova, Romania
Nick Bassiliades	Aristotle University of Thessaloniki, Greece
Maria Bielikova	Slovak University of Technology in Bratislava, Slovakia
Abdelhamid Bouchachia	Bournemouth University, UK
David Camacho	Universidad Autónoma de Madrid, Spain
Richard Chbeir	University of Pau and Pays de l'Adour, France
Shyi-Ming Chen	National Taiwan University of Science and Technology, Taiwan
Paul Davidsson	Malmo University, Sweden
Mohamed Gaber	Birmingham City University, UK
Daniela Godoy	ISISTAN Research Institute, Argentina
Manuel Grana	University of the Basque Country, Spain
William Grosky	University of Michigan, USA
Francisco Herrera	University of Granada, Spain
Tzung-Pei Hong	National University of Kaohsiung, Taiwan
Dosam Hwang	Yeungnam University, South Korea
Lazaros Iliadis	Democritus University of Thrace, Greece
Mirjana Ivanovic	University of Novi Sad, Serbia
Piotr Jedrzejowicz	Gdynia Maritime University, Poland
Geun-Sik Jo	Inha University, South Korea
Kang-Hyun Jo	University of Ulsan, South Korea
Janusz Kacprzyk	Systems Research Institute, Polish Academy of Sciences, Poland
Ryszard Kowalczyk	Swinburne University of Technology, Australia
Ondrej Krejcar	University of Hradec Kralove, Czech Republic
Hoai An Le Thi	University of Lorraine, France
Edwin Lughofer	Johannes Kepler University Linz, Austria
Yannis Manolopoulos	Aristotle University of Thessaloniki, Greece
Grzegorz J. Nalepa	AGH University of Science and Technology, Poland
Toyoaki Nishida	Kyoto University, Japan
Manuel Núñez	Universidad Complutense de Madrid, Spain
George A. Papadopoulos	University of Cyprus, Cyprus
Radu-Emil Precup	Politehnica University of Timisoara, Romania
Leszek Rutkowski	Częstochowa University of Technology, Poland
Tomasz M. Rutkowski	University of Tokyo, Japan
Ali Selamat	Universiti Teknologi Malaysia, Malaysia
Edward Szczerbicki	University of Newcastle, Australia

Program Committee

Aleksander Byrski	AGH University of Science and Technology, Poland
Alberto Cano	Virginia Commonwealth University, USA
Frantisek Capkovic	Institute of Informatics, Slovak Academy of Sciences, Slovakia
Roberto Casadei	Università di Bologna, Italy
Raja Chiky	Institut Supérieur d'Electronique de Paris, France
Amine Chohra	Paris-East Créteil University, France
Kazimierz Choros	Wrocław University of Science and Technology, Poland
Robert Cierniak	Częstochowa University of Technology, Poland
Mihaela Colhon	University of Craiova, Romania
Antonio Corral	University of Almería, Spain
Rafal Cupek	Silesian University of Technology, Poland
Ireneusz Czarnowski	Gdynia Maritime University, Poland
Camelia Delcea	Bucharest University of Economic Studies, Romania
Konstantinos Demertzis	Democritus University of Thrace, Greece
Shridhar Devamane	Global Academy of Technology, India
Muthusamy Dharmalingam	Bharathiar University, India
Tien V. Do	Budapest University of Technology and Economics, Hungary
Márk Domonkos	Eötvös Loránd University, Hungary
Abdellatif El Afia	ENSIAS-Mohammed V University in Rabat, Morocco
Nadia Essoussi	University of Tunis, Tunisia
Rim Faiz	University of Carthage, Tunisia
Marcin Fojcik	Western Norway University of Applied Sciences, Norway
Anna Formica	IASI-CNR, Italy
Bogdan Franczyk	University of Leipzig, Germany
Dariusz Frejlichowski	West Pomeranian University of Technology in Szczecin, Poland
Mauro Gaspari	University of Bologna, Italy
K. M. George	Oklahoma State University, USA
Janusz Getta	University of Wollongong, Australia
Chirine Ghedira	Jean Moulin Lyon 3 University, France
Daniela Gifu	Romanian Academy - Iasi Branch, Romania
Arkadiusz Gola	Lublin University of Technology, Poland
László Gulyás	Eötvös Loránd University, Hungary
Natabara Gyöngyössy	Eötvös Loránd University, Hungary
Petr Hajek	University of Pardubice, Czech Republic
Kenji Hatano	Doshisha University, Japan

Marcin Hernes	Wrocław University of Economics, Poland
Huu Hanh Hoang	Hue University, Vietnam
Jeongky Hong	Yeungnam University, Korea
Frédéric Hubert	Laval University, Canada
Zbigniew Huzar	Wrocław University of Science and Technology, Poland
Agnieszka Indyka-Piasecka	Wrocław University of Science and Technology, Poland
Dan Istrate	Université de Technologie de Compiegne, France
Fethi Jarray	Gabes University, Tunisia
Joanna Jedrzejowicz	University of Gdansk, Poland
Gordan Jezic	University of Zagreb, Croatia
Ireneusz Jóźwiak	Wrocław University of Science and Technology, Poland
Przemysław Juszczuk	University of Economics in Katowice, Poland
Arkadiusz Kawa	Poznań School of Logistics, Poland
Zaheer Khan	University of the West of England, UK
Attila Kiss	Eötvös Loránd University, Hungary
Marek Kopel	Wrocław University of Science and Technology, Poland
Petia Koprinkova-Hristova	Bulgarian Academy of Sciences, Bulgaria
Szilárd Kovács	Eötvös Loránd University, Hungary
Ivan Koychev	University of Sofia "St. Kliment Ohridski", Bulgaria
Jan Kozak	University of Economics in Katowice, Poland
Dalia Kriksciuniene	Vilnius University, Lithuania
Stelios Krinidis	Centre for Research and Technology Hellas (CERTH), Greece
Dariusz Krol	Wrocław University of Science and Technology, Poland
Marek Krotkiewicz	Wrocław University of Science and Technology, Poland
Jan Kubicek	VSB - Technical University of Ostrava, Czech Republic
Elzbieta Kukla	Wrocław University of Science and Technology, Poland
Marek Kulbacki	Polish-Japanese Academy of Information Technology, Poland
Piotr Kulczycki	Polish Academy of Science, Systems Research Institute, Poland
Kazuhiro Kuwabara	Ritsumeikan University, Japan
Halina Kwasnicka	Wrocław University of Science and Technology, Poland

Mark Last	Ben-Gurion University of the Negev, Israel
Nguyen-Thinh Le	Humboldt-Universität zu Berlin, Germany
Philippe Lemoisson	French Agricultural Research Centre for International Development (CIRAD), France
Florin Leon	"Gheorghe Asachi" Technical University of Iasi, Romania
Mikołaj Leszczuk	AGH University of Science and Technology, Poland
Doina Logofatu	Frankfurt University of Applied Sciences, Germany
Aphilak Lonklang	Eötvös Loránd University, Hungary
Juraj Machaj	University of Zilina, Slovakia
George Magoulas	Birkbeck, University of London, UK
Bernadetta Maleszka	Wrocław University of Science and Technology, Poland
Marcin Maleszka	Wrocław University of Science and Technology, Poland
Adam Meissner	Poznań University of Technology, Poland
Manuel Méndez	Universidad Complutense de Madrid, Spain
Jacek Mercik	WSB University in Wrocław, Poland
Radosław Michalski	Wrocław University of Science and Technology, Poland
Peter Mikulecky	University of Hradec Kralove, Czech Republic
Miroslava Mikusova	University of Zilina, Slovakia
Jean-Luc Minel	Université Paris Nanterre, France
Javier Montero	Universidad Complutense de Madrid, Spain
Anna Motylska-Kuźma	WSB University in Wrocław, Poland
Manuel Munier	University of Pau and Pays de l'Adour, France
Phivos Mylonas	Ionian University, Greece
Laurent Nana	University of Brest, France
Anand Nayyar	Duy Tan University, Vietnam
Filippo Neri	University of Napoli Federico II, Italy
Linh Anh Nguyen	University of Warsaw, Poland
Loan T. T. Nguyen	VNU-HCM International University, Vietnam
Sinh Van Nguyen	VNU-HCM International University, Vietnam
Adam Niewiadomski	Lodz University of Technology, Poland
Adel Noureddine	University of Pau and Pays de l'Adour, France
Alberto Núñez	Universidad Complutense de Madrid, Spain
Mieczysław Owoc	Wrocław University of Economics, Poland
Marcin Paprzycki	Systems Research Institute, Polish Academy of Sciences, Poland
Isidoros Perikos	University of Patras, Greece
Elias Pimenidis	University of the West of England, UK

Constantin-Bala Zamfirescu	"Lucian Blaga" University of Sibiu, Romania
Katerina Zdravkova	University of Ss. Cyril and Methodius, Macedonia
Haoxi Zhang	Chengdu University of Information Technology, China
Jianlei Zhang	Nankai University, China
Adam Ziebinski	Silesian University of Technology, Poland

Contents

Cooperative Strategies for Decision Making and Optimization

Computational Intelligence for Digital Content Understanding

Collective Intelligence and Collective Decision-Making

Hybrid Genetic Algorithms to Determine 2-Optimality Consensus for a Collective of Ordered Partitions

Dai Tho Dang[1(✉)], Hai Bang Truong[2,3], and Ngoc Thanh Nguyen[4(✉)]

[1] Vietnam - Korea University of Information and Communications Technology, The University of Da Nang, Da Nang, Vietnam
ddtho@vku.udn.vn

[2] Faculty of Computer Science, University of Information Technology, Ho Chi Minh City, Vietnam
bangth@uit.edu.vn

[3] National University, Ho Chi Minh City, Vietnam

[4] Faculty of Information and Communication Technology, Wrocław University of Science and Technology, Wrocław, Poland
Ngoc-Thanh.Nguyen@pwr.edu.pl

Abstract. Determining consensus for a set of ordered partitions (or a collective) is used for making decisions. Ordered partitions are a helpful structure for representing the opinions of experts or agents. Algorithms to determine 1-Optimality consensus were introduced in the literature. However, no algorithm has yet to be proposed for determining the 2-Optimality consensus. Determining 2-Optimality consensus for a collective of ordered partitions is an NP-hard problem. In this study, first, we present a mathematical formula for determining such a collective. Then, three hybrid genetic algorithms are proposed to solve this problem. The simulation results show that the HG3 algorithm finds the best quality consensus in an acceptable time.

Keywords: Consensus · 2-Optimality · Ordered Partitions · Hybrid Genetic Algorithm

1 Introduction

The problem of determining the representation or consensus for a set of objects arises only when it is necessary to make a unanimous decision based on different experts' opinions. This study focuses on the case when experts' opinions, the results of measurements, or the analyses are ordered partitions, i.e., partitions of a finite set of elements with a fixed number of classes. Given a set of ordered partitions, a consensus of this set should represent the major tendency in the set [1].

Many postulates are used for determining consensus. The two most essential postulates are 1-Optimality and 2-Optimality. Postulate 1-Optimality demands the consensus to be as near as possible to collective members. Postulate 2-Optimality requires the sum

N. T. Nguyen et al. (Eds.): ICCCI 2023, LNAI 14162, pp. 3–15, 2023.
https://doi.org/10.1007/978-3-031-41456-5_1

of the squared distances between a consensus and the collective members to be minimal. One consensus satisfying one of these two postulates is the best representation of a collective. Besides, postulate 2-Optimality gives a consensus that distances between it to the collective members are more uniform than one generated by postulate 1-Optimality consensus [2].

There are algorithms for finding 1-Optimality consensus for a collective of ordered partitions in the literature. However, an algorithm for determining 2-Optimality consensus has yet to be proposed. Finding 2-Optimality consensus for such a collective type is complex and challenging because it is an NP-complete problem. Thus it is helpful to propose efficient algorithms to solve this task.

In this study, we focus on solving this problem. The study's significant contributions are shown as the followings:

- We present a mathematical formula for 2-Optimality for a collective of ordered partitions.
- We propose one local search and three hybrid algorithms for determining 2-Optimality for a collective of ordered partitions.
- We evaluate the efficiency of proposed algorithms, both consensus quality and running time.

The remainder of this paper is organized as follows. Section 2 provides a short review of related works. In Sect. 3, we introduce a collective of ordered partitions. Section 4 presents a mathematical formula for 2-Optimality and proposes algorithms for determining this type of consensus. Section 5 evaluates the algorithms' consensus quality and running time. Finally, conclusions and future directions are provided in Sect. 6.

2 Related Works

Consensus problems have an endurable history in computer science [3]. The consensus problem is the grounds of distributed computing [4]. In current years, it has become a fascinating research field. In IoT, many consensus problems need to be solved, such as task allocation, resource allocation, and service-oriented decision-making [5, 6]. Consensus algorithms are fundamental for maintaining blockchain [7, 8].

Three approaches for defining consensus choice functions have been proposed to solve the consensus problem. In the axiomatic approach, ten postulates are used to define consensus choice: Reliability, Simplification, Unanimity, Consistency, Quasi-unanimity, Condorcet consistency, Proportion, General consistency, 1-Optimality, and 2-Optimality. No consensus choice functions to fulfill all ten postulates contemporaneously [2]. The constructive approach solves the problem in two respects: the relation between elements and the structure of elements. The relation between these elements is often a preference relation or a distance function between elements [9–13, 21]. The optimization approach uses optimality rules to define consensus choice functions, such as global optimality and Condorcet's optimality [2]. Postulates 1-Optimality and 2-Optimality are the most important because if a consensus satisfies one of these, it satisfies most of the remaining postulates.

Let U be a finite set of objects representing all potential knowledge states for a given problem. In the set U, elements can contradict each other. Let $\Pi_b(U)$ denote the set of all b-element subsets with repetitions of set U for $b \in N$, and let

$$\Pi(U) = \cup_b \Pi_b(U) \tag{1}$$

Thus, $\Pi(U)$ is the finite set of all nonempty subsets with repetitions of set U. A set $X \in \Pi(U)$ is considered a collective, where each element $c \in X$ represents the consensus of a collective member [4, 6]. It is understood as a representative of this collective. For a given collective $X \in \Pi(U)$, the consensus of X is found by the following:

- Postulate 1-Otimality if

$$d(c^*, X) = \min d(y, X) \tag{2}$$

- Postulate 2-Otimality if

$$d^2(c^*, X) = \min d(y, X) \tag{3}$$

  where c^* is the consensus of X, $d(c^*, X)$ is the sum of distances from consensus c^* to members of the collective X and $d^2(c^*, X)$ is the sum of squared distances from the c^* to elements of the collective X.

Algorithms for determining 1-Optimality consensus for a collective of ordered partitions have been proposed [14, 22]. However, a formula for a 2-Optimality consensus for such a structure has yet to be proposed. Of course, there have not been algorithms for determining the 2-Optimality for this structure.

Holland introduced Genetic Algorithms called GAs in 1975. He applies the principles of natural evolution to optimization problems. GAs have been developed and have become a robust tool for resolving optimization problems [15, 16].

The elitism strategy has been regarded as a practical approach to enhance the efficiency of GAs for a long time. This strategy ensures that in each generation, the best individuals are passed on to the next generation without changing. In an algorithm using the elitism strategy, the solution quality does not decrease from generation to generation. For each generation, the quality of the best individual monotonically grows over time [17].

Exploration and exploitation are critical problems in problem-solving by searching. The population's diversity is one crucial factor in GAs. Increasing diversity means that GAs is in the exploration phase, and decreasing such a factor means that GAs is in the exploitation phase. One approach to reaching a good balance between exploration and exploitation is to maintain a diverse population [18, 19].

3 Ordered Partitions

Ordered partitions are a helpful structure for representing the opinions of experts or agents. In this section, we present cover some basics knowledge of order partitions.

Definition 1 [14]*: A K-class ordered partition of a finite set* $X = \{x_1, x_2, \ldots, x_N\}$ *is any sequence* $C = (C_1, C_2, \ldots, C_K)$*, where* $C_i \subseteq X$ *for* $i = 1, \ldots, K$*,* $C_i \cap C_j = \varnothing$ *for* $i \neq j$ *and* $\bigcup_{i=1}^{K} C_i = X$*.*

Example 1: Let $X = \{x_1, x_2, x_3, x_4\}$. The samples of 3-class ordered partitions of set X are $P = (\{x_1\}, \{x_2\}, \{x_3, x_4\})$, $Q = (\{x_2\}, \{x_1, x_3\}, \{x_4\})$.

A K-class ordered partition $P = (P_1, P_2, \ldots, P_N)$ can be represented as a vector $p = (p_1, p_2, \ldots, p_N)$ where p_i is an index of the class which includes the element x_i [14].

Example 2: Let $X = \{x_1, x_2, x_3, x_4\}$, $P = (\{x_1\}, \{x_2\}, \{x_3, x_4\})$. Then, P is represented as vector $p = (1, 2, 3, 3)$.

By $U_K(X)$, we denote the set all K-class ordered partitions of set X. By $V_K(X)$, we denote the set of all vectors $p = (p_1, p_2, \ldots, p_N)$, where $p_i = 1, 2, \ldots, K$ for $i = 1, \ldots, N$. Each vector $p \in V_K(X)$ corresponds to one partition $P \in U_K(X)$.

Any partition P can be transformed into another partition Q by subsequently moving those elements, which in the partitions P and Q belong to classes of different indexes.

Definition 2 [14]*: Let* $P = (P_1, \ldots, P_k, \ldots, P_l, \ldots, P_K) \in U_K(X)$ *and* $x_n \in P_k$*. A move* M_n^l *of an element* x_n *to the class* P_l *is a transformation*

$$M_n^l(P) = (P_1, \ldots, P_k \backslash \{x_n\}, \ldots, P_l \cup \{x_n\}, \ldots, P_K) \tag{4}$$

Example 3: Let $X = \{x_1, x_2, x_3, x_4\}$, $P = (\{x_1\}, \{x_2\}, \{x_3, x_4\})$. We have

$$M_1^3(P) = (\{\emptyset\}, \{x_2\}, \{x_1, x_3, x_4\})$$

$$(\{x_1\}, \{x_2\}, \{x_3, x_4\}) \xrightarrow{M_1^3} (\{\emptyset\}, \{x_2\}, \{x_1, x_3, x_4\})$$

Definition 3 [14]*: Distance* $d(P, Q), P, Q \in U_K(X)$ *is the minimum number of elements moves indispensable to transform a partition P into partition Q.*

Example 4: Let $X = \{x_1, x_2, x_3, x_4\}$, $P = (\{x_1\}, \{x_2\}, \{x_3, x_4\})$, $Q = (\{x_4\}, \{x_1, \}, \{x_2, x_3\})$. We have

$$P = (\{x_1\}, \{x_2\}, \{x_3, x_4\}) \xrightarrow{R_4^1} (\{x_1, x_4\}, \{x_2\}, \{x_3\})$$

$$(\{x_1, x_4\}, \{x_2\}, \{x_3\}) \xrightarrow{R_1^2} (\{x_4\}, \{x_1, x_2\}, \{x_3\})$$

$$(\{x_1, x_4\}, \{x_2\}, \{x_3\}) \xrightarrow{R_2^3} (\{x_4\}, \{x_1\}, \{x_2, x_3\}) = Q$$

Thus, $d(P, Q) = 3$.

Theorem 1 [14]*: Let* $P, Q \in U_K(X)$ *and* $p, q \in V_K(X)$ *be their corresponding vectors, then the distance between p and q is computed as follows*

$$d(P, Q) = \sum_{i=1}^{N} (p_i + q_i) \tag{5}$$

where $p_i + q_i = \begin{cases} 1 & \text{if } p_i \neq q_i \\ 0 & \text{if } p_i = q_i \end{cases}$

Let set $UP = \{P^{(1)}, \ldots, P^{(M)}\}$, then $UP \subseteq U_K(X)$.

Definition 4: A 2-Optimality consensus of UP is partition $P \in U_K(X)$ *that satisfy*

$$\sum_{i=1}^{M} d^2(P, P^{(i)}) = \min_{Q \in U_K(X)} \sum_{i=1}^{M} d^2(Q, P^{(i)}) \quad (6)$$

In other words, P is a 2-Optimality consensus of collective UP if $d^2(P, UP) = \min_{Q \in U_K(X)} d^2(Q, UP)$

From Theorem 1, we have

$$d^2(P, Q) = \sum_{i=1}^{N} (p_i + q_i)^2 \text{ where } p_i + q_i = \begin{cases} 1 & \text{if } p_i \neq q_i \\ 0 & \text{if } p_i = q_i \end{cases}$$

$VP = \{p^{(1)}, \ldots, p^{(M)}\}$ is the presentation of UP in $V_K(X)$.

Determining the 2-Optimality consensus P for UP corresponds to determining the consensus c^* for VP

$$d^2(c^*, VP) = \min_{c \in V_K(X)} d^2(c, VP)$$

The state space has K^N elements. Determining a 2-Optimality consensus for a collective of ordered partitions is an NP-complete problem. Determining a 2-Optimality consensus for VP is a discrete optimization problem. The objective function is shown as follows.

$$\min_{c \in V_K(X)} d^2(c, VP) \quad (7)$$

4 Proposed Approaches

This section first introduces one local search algorithm to find the best solution in the neighborhood. Then three hybrid genetic algorithms are proposed to find a 2-Optimality consensus for collectives of ordered partitions. Besides, a new mutation operator called K-operator is presented.

- **Local Search Algorithm (LS)**

Algorithm 1. LS

```
Input:  c_cur
Output: the best solution c_bes;
BEGIN
min=Computing d^2(c_cur, VP)
con=c_cur;
For each neighbour c_nei of c_cur do
   Begin
      Computing d^2(c_nei, VP);
      If min < d^2(c_nei, VP) then
         Begin
            min = d^2(c_nei, VP);
            c_best=c_nei;
         End
   End
Return c_bes;
END.
```

Given the input solution c_{cur}. If c_{nei} is a neighbor of c_{cur}, they have one and only one different component. This algorithm finds the best solution in neighbors of the solution c_{cur}. The set of neighbors of the solution c_{cur} has KN members. This algorithm sequentially computes $d^2(c_{nei}, VP)$ for each solution c_{nei}. The solution c_{nei} with a minimum value of $d^2(c_{nei}, VP)$ is the best solution (denoted c_{bes}). The LS algorithm is shown above.

- **Hybrid Genetic Algorithm 1 (HG1)**

Inspired by natural selection, genetic algorithms are used to solve optimization problems. It is a population-based search algorithm and employs the concept of survival of the fittest. New populations are generated by repeating the use of genetic operators on individuals. In genetic algorithms, critical components are chromosome representation, fitness function, selection, crossover, and mutation.

In this study, each chromosome is represented as a string over $Z = \{1, 2, ..., K\}$ where K is the number of classes. This study combines the genetic algorithm and the LS algorithm. The process of HG1 is shown in Fig. 1.

- Fitness function: We use

$$f(x) = d^2(c, VP) \tag{8}$$

- Initialization: Random initialization and heuristic initialization are two main approaches for initializing a population. Initializing by heuristics can lead to the population containing similar solutions and little diversity. Random initialization obtains a population with high diversity. The diversity of the solutions leads to optimality [16].

This algorithm uses random initialization to generate the initial population.

- Selection: Selection attempts to apply pressure upon the population, like that of natural selection seen in biological systems. This selection is randomly performed with a probability relying on the individuals' fitness value. The solutions with high fitness values are often selected for reproduction rather than solutions with low fitness values. Tournament selection is widely used because of its effectiveness. This technique randomly picks k individuals from the population and selects the best one of these individuals to become a parent. It repeats to determine the next parent [16].

  This algorithm applies tournament selection with a size of three ($k = 3$).
- Crossover: A Crossover combination of the chromosomes creates offspring from parents. The offspring have the genetic information of their parents. This operator influences the search process for getting good chromosomes directly. There are many crossover operators, such as single-point, two-point, partially matched, uniform, and shuffle [20]. For example, in a single-point operator, firstly, a crossover point is randomly chosen. Finally, the two parents' genetic information, which is beyond this point, is swapped.

  The two-point operator is applied in this study. It randomly chooses two of the parent chromosomes. Afterward, it exchanges the genes between these two points in order to generate two offspring.
- Mutation: We consider the case that parents hold the same allele at the same gene. It is clear that the gene's allele does not change after doing the crossover operator. Especially the population has the same allele at the same gene; the population holds the same allele perpetually. The most important function of the mutation operators is maintaining the population's diversity and preventing premature convergence. Displacement, scramble mutation, and simple inversion are popular mutation operators [16, 20].

This study propose a new mutation operator called K-value operator. This operator acts as follows.

- First, it randomly chooses an individual.
- Second, it alters one random gene of this individual with one of the $Z = \{1, 2, \ldots K\}$.

K-value operator is shown in Fig. 1.

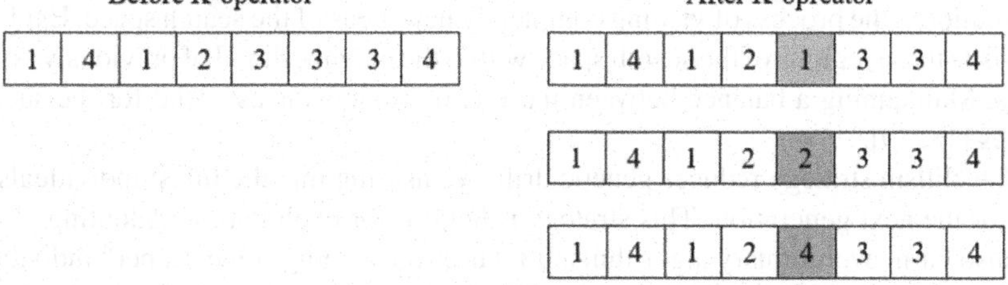

Fig. 1. K-operator.

- **Hybrid Genetic Algorithm 2 (HG2)**

The elitism strategy has been regarded as a practical approach to enhance the efficiency of GAs for a long time. Nowadays, the elitism strategy has been widely used in evolutionary algorithms or GAs. If one genetic algorithm uses this approach, elitist individuals are transferred to the next generation. Otherwise, the best individual can be lost in the next generation.

The elitism strategy ensures that the best solutions are always preserved. Therefore, each generation's best solution quality is unchanged or decreased over time [19]. Thus, we propose a hybrid genetic algorithm, combining the elitism strategy and the LS algorithm, to find the 2-Optimality consensus for ordered partitions.

This algorithm transfers the best elitist individual to the next generation. Figure 2 shows elitism acting over generations in this algorithm. In this algorithm, the LS algorithm is used to determine the best solution in the neighbors of the best solution of the final population. The schema of the EGA algorithm is shown in Fig. 3.

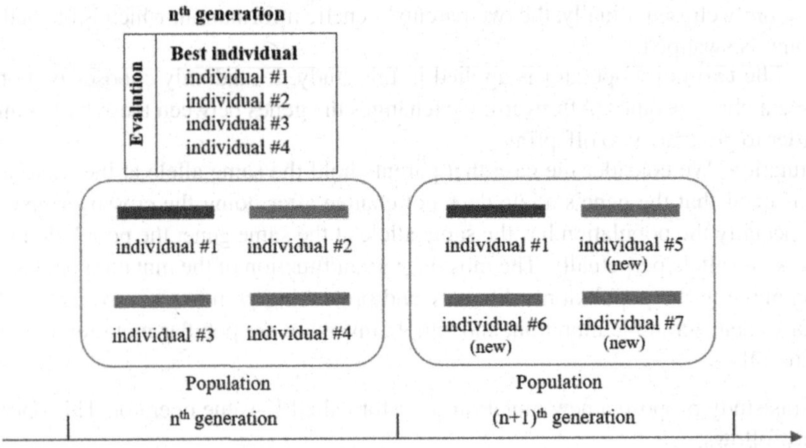

Fig. 2. The best elitist individual is transferred to the next generation.

- **Hybrid Genetic Algorithm 3 (HG3)**

Exploration and exploitation are critical problems in problem-solving by searching. Exploration is the process of visiting completely new areas of the search space. Exploitation visits those regions of the search space within the neighborhood of previously visited points. Maintaining a balance between these two problems is essential for the success of GAs [18, 19].

The elitism strategy reduces genetic drift by ensuring that the fittest individuals are kept for the next generation. This strategy is helpful for exploitation. Adopting elitism may also harm evolutionary algorithms. It focuses on keeping some "super" individuals but decreases the population's diversity. The low diversity of a population leads to a decrease in the algorithm's capacity to explore the search space. Adopting elitism does not maintain a balance between exploration and exploitation [18].

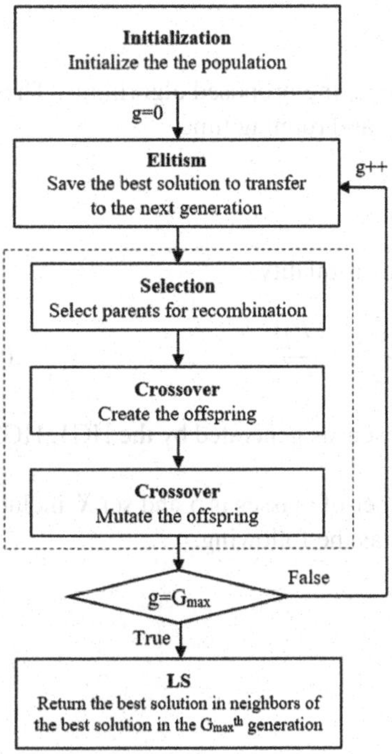

Fig. 3. The schema of HG2 algorithm.

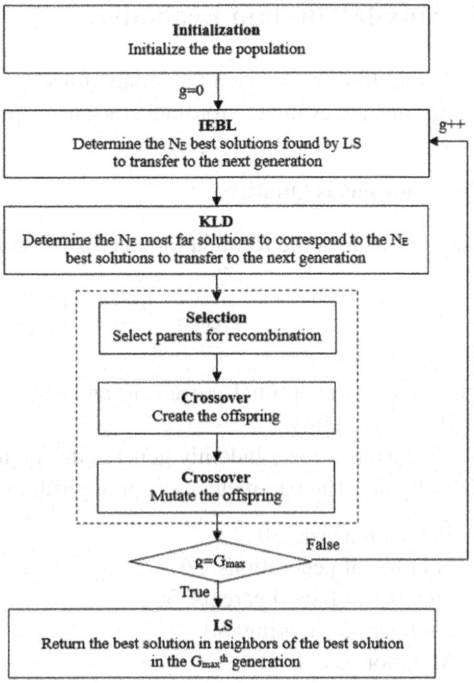

Fig. 4. The schema of HG3 algorithm.

Nowadays, the elitism strategy has been widely used in evolutionary algorithms or GAs. An improvement can be better for balancing exploration and exploitation. Based on the above motivation, in [16], we propose a new approach, including an elitism strategy named IEBL and a longest-distance strategy called the KLD strategy. HG3 algorithm applies this approach. Besides, the LS algorithm is used to increase the efficiency of the proposed algorithm.

The schema of this algorithm is presented in Fig. 4.

- IEBL: It includes two stages. The first stage determines set E, containing N_E elites. The second stage creates set *EB* by improving the quality of all elites in set E. LS algorithm is used for this task. It determines the best neighbor of each element in set E. If the best neighbor is better than the corresponding element in set E, it replaces this corresponding element. This set is passed to the next generation.
- KLD: The longest-distance strategy keeps individuals that are far from elites. For each element b_i in *EB*, it determines the element l_i in the offspring and parents with the farthest distance to the element b_i. The set *EL* is formed by elements l_i. This set is passed on to the next generation.

Both set E and set *EB*, including $2N_E$ individuals, are passed to the next generation. In this study, N_E is chosen as 1. Thus, there are two individuals to pass on to the next generation. One is an element of set E, and one individual is one of set B.

5 Simulations and Evaluation

In this section, we present the simulations to evaluate the proposed algorithms. These algorithms are evaluated for both consensus quality and running time.

5.1 Consensus Quality

The following is the formula for calculating consensus quality:

$$Qu = \frac{\left|d^2(c^*, VP) - d^2\left(c_{opt}, VP\right)\right|}{d^2(c^*, VP)} \tag{9}$$

where c_{opt} is the optimal consensus, and c^* is a consensus generated by the HG1, HG2, or HG3 algorithms.

The dataset was randomly generated. The number of classes is 5 and set X include 11 elements. The parameters set for algorithms are as the following.

- Population size: 30
- Number of generations: 26
- Number of paired parents: 30
- Number of offspring: 90
- Mutation rate: 0.01

For each algorithm, we run the dataset 42 times. Each time, both consensus and its quality are determined. Table 1 presents three consensus-quality samples of algorithms HG1, HG2, and HG3.

The significance level of this study is 0.05 ($\alpha = 0.05$). The Shapiro-Wilk test was applied to determine whether these consensus quality samples arrived from a normal distribution. The *p-value* of these algorithms are showed as the following. The *p-value* of HG1 is 0.0009515, that of HG2 is 7.624e−05, and that of HG3 is 0.00102. They were less than 0.05. These consensus quality samples are not normally distributed.

The following hypotheses are used to compare these consensus qualities.

- H_0: These consensus qualities are equal.
- H_1: These consensus qualities are unequal.

Because three consensus quality samples are not a normal distribution, the Kruskal–Wallis test is applied. The *p-value* is 0.00001. Thus, it can reject hypothesis H_0, or the three algorithms' consensus quality is unequal.

We compare each pair with the median values of the consensus-quality samples. The consensus quality found by the HG3 algorithm was 1.95% and 2.14% higher than that found by algorithms HG2 and HG1. The consensus quality found by the HG2 algorithm was 0.19% higher than that found by HG1.

5.2 Running Time

We compared the running times of the algorithms. The dataset was randomly generated. The number of classes is 5 and set X include 12 elements.

Table 1. The consensus qualities of the proposed algorithms.

ORD	HG1	HG2	HG3	ORD	HG1	HG2	HG3
1	0.9601	0.9767	1.0000	22	0.9667	0.9717	0.9851
2	0.9576	1.0000	0.9888	23	0.9570	1.0000	1.0000
3	0.9602	0.9612	0.9857	24	0.9648	0.9654	0.9873
4	1.0000	0.9871	0.9812	25	0.9762	0.9656	0.9861
5	0.9545	0.9628	1.0000	26	0.9928	0.9644	0.9816
6	0.9576	0.9612	0.9876	27	0.9783	0.9792	1.0000
7	0.9602	0.9689	0.9905	28	1.0000	0.9821	0.9834
8	0.9792	1.0000	1.0000	29	1.0000	0.9652	0.9954
9	0.9656	0.9711	1.0000	30	0.9642	0.9688	0.9881
10	0.9715	0.9635	0.9835	31	0.9677	1.0000	1.0000
11	1.0000	0.9626	0.9922	32	0.9708	0.9938	0.9900
12	0.9415	0.9638	0.9938	33	0.9679	1.0000	1.0000
13	0.9626	1.0000	1.0000	34	0.9587	0.9845	0.9831
14	0.9657	0.9510	0.9734	35	0.9735	0.9632	1.0000
15	0.9638	1.0000	0.9746	36	1.0000	0.9693	0.9877
16	0.9692	0.9670	0.9782	37	0.9766	0.9674	1.0000
17	1.0000	0.9715	1.0000	38	0.9677	0.9635	0.9835
18	0.9856	0.9800	0.9900	39	0.9708	0.9671	1.0000
19	0.9712	1.0000	0.9848	40	0.9679	0.9698	0.9939
20	1.0000	0.9716	1.0000	41	0.9587	0.9627	0.9872
21	0.9754	0.9738	0.9865	42	0.9735	0.9745	1.0000

The Shapiro-Wilk test was applied to determine whether running time samples came from a normal distribution. The *p-value* of these algorithms is shown as the following. The *p-value* of HG1 is 0.591, that of HG2 is 0.5497, and that of HG3 is 0.47.5. They were larger than 0.05. Thus, These consensus-quality samples are normally distributed.

The following hypotheses are used to compare these running time samples.

- H_0: The algorithms' running times are equal.
- H_1: The algorithms' running times are unequal.

We used the one-way ANOVA for this examination. The *p-value* is 0.156, thus; H_0 was rejected or the algorithms' running times were unequal.

The post-hoc Tukey HSD was applied. It shows that the running time samples of the HG1 and HG2 algorithms were 55.7% and 91.6% of the HG3 algorithm, respectively.

Table 2. The running times of the proposed algorithms.

Number of classes	HG1 (second)	HG2 (second)	HG3 (second)
2	0.201	0.337	0.376
3	0.273	0.462	0.493
4	0.391	0.604	0.641
5	0.469	0.796	0.878
6	0.675	1.072	1.173
7	0.892	1.499	1.667
8	1.018	1.676	1.901
9	1.213	2.036	2.199
10	1.407	2.347	2.506

6 Conclusions

This study presents a mathematical formula for 2-Optimality for a collective of ordered partitions. One local search algorithm was introduced to find the best neighborhood solution. We also proposed three hybrid genetic algorithms to determine 2-Optimality for such type collective. These algorithms are evaluated for both consensus quality and running time. The consensus quality found by the HG3 algorithm was 1.95% and 2.14% higher than that found by algorithms HG2 and HG1. The running time samples of the HG1 and HG2 algorithms were 55.7% and 91.6% of the HG3 algorithm, respectively. The HG3 algorithm gives the highest consensus quality and acceptable running time.

In future work, we will investigate increasing consensus quality for the HG3 algorithm.

Acknowledgement. This research is funded by Vietnam National University Ho Chi Minh City (VNU-HCM) under grant number DS2021-26-03.

References

1. Mirkin, B., Fenner, T.I.: Distance and consensus for preference relations corresponding to ordered partitions. J. Classif. **36**(2), 350–367 (2019)
2. Nguyen, N.T.: Advanced Methods for Inconsistent Knowledge Management. Springer, London (2008). https://doi.org/10.1007/978-1-84628-889-0
3. Dang, D.T., Nguyen, N.T., Hwang, D.: Multi-step consensus: an effective approach for determining consensus in large collectives. Cybern. Syst. **50**(2), 208–229 (2019). https://doi.org/10.1080/01969722.2019.1565117
4. Olfati-Saber, R., Fax, J.A., Murray, R.M.: Consensus and cooperation in networked multi-agent systems. Proc. IEEE **95**(1), 215–233 (2007)
5. Zhao, L., Wang, J., Liu, J., Kato, N.: Optimal edge resource allocation in IoT-based smart cities. IEEE Netw. **33**(2), 30–35 (2019)

6. Li, X., Tan, L., Li, F.: Optimal cloud resource allocation with cost performance tradeoff based on Internet of Things. IEEE Internet Things J. **6**(4), 6876–6886 (2019)
7. Wang, W., Hoang, D.T.: A survey on consensus mechanisms and mining strategy management in blockchain networks. IEEE Access **7**, 22328–22370 (2019)
8. Xiao, Y., Zhang, N., Lou, W., Hou, Y.T.: A survey of distributed consensus protocols for blockchain networks. IEEE Commun. Surv. Tutorials **22**, 1432–1465 (2020)
9. Nguyen, N.T.: Consensus-based timestamps in distributed temporal databases. Comput. J. **44**(5), 398–409 (2001). https://doi.org/10.1093/comjnl/44.5.398
10. Jansson, J., Shen, C., Sung, W.-K.: Improved algorithms for constructing consensus trees. J. ACM **63**(3), 1–24 (2016). https://doi.org/10.1145/2925985
11. Jansson, J., Rajaby, R., Shen, C., Sung, W.K.: Algorithms for the majority rule (+) consensus tree and the frequency difference consensus tree. IEEE/ACM Trans. Comput. Biol. Bioinform. **15**(1), 15–26 (2018)
12. Hernes, M., Nguyen, N.T.: Deriving consensus for hierarchical incomplete ordered partitions and coverings. J. Univers. Comput. Sci. **13**(2), 317–328 (2007)
13. Dang, D.T., Nguyen, N.T., Hwang, D.: A quick algorithm to determine 2-optimality consensus for collectives. IEEE Access **8**, 221794–221807 (2020). https://doi.org/10.1109/ACCESS.2020.3043371
14. Danilowicz, C., Nguyen, N.T.: Consensus-based partitions in the space of ordered partitions. Pattern Recognit. **21**(3), 269–273 (1988). https://doi.org/10.1016/0031-3203(88)90061-1
15. Holland, J.H.: Adaptation in Natural and Artificial Systems: An Introductory Analysis with Applications to Biology, Control, and Artificial Intelligence. Michigan Press, Ann Arbor (1975)
16. Dang, D.T., Nguyen, N.T., Hwang, D.: Hybrid genetic algorithms for the determination of DNA motifs to satisfy postulate 2-optimality. Appl. Intell. (2022). https://doi.org/10.1007/s10489-022-03491-7
17. Dulebenets, M.A.: Archived elitism in evolutionary computation: towards improving solution quality and population diversity. Int. J. Bio-Inspired Comput. **15**(3), 135 (2020). https://doi.org/10.1504/IJBIC.2020.107488
18. Črepinšek, M., Liu, S.-H., Mernik, M.: Exploration and exploitation in evolutionary algorithms. ACM Comput. Surv. **45**(3), 1–33 (2013)
19. Du, H., Wang, Z., Zhan, W., Guo, J.: Elitism and distance strategy for selection of evolutionary algorithms. IEEE Access **6**, 44531–44541 (2018)
20. Katoch, S., Chauhan, S.S., Kumar, V.: A review on genetic algorithm: past, present, and future. Multimed. Tools Appl. **80**(5), 8091–8126 (2021)
21. Nguyen, N.T.: Metody wyboru consensusu i ich zastosowanie w rozwiązywaniu konfliktów w systemach rozproszonych. Oficyna Wydawnicza Politechniki Wrocławskiej (2002)
22. Sliwko, L., Nguyen, N.T.: Using multi-agent systems and consensus methods for information retrieval in Internet. Int. J. Intell. Inf. Database Syst. **1**(2), 181–198 (2007). https://doi.org/10.1504/IJIIDS.2007.014949

From Fragmented Data to Collective Intelligence: A Data Fabric Approach for University Knowledge Management

Lan T. K. Nguyen[1], Hoa N. Nguyen[2(✉)], and Son H. Nguyen[3]

[1] VNU University of Social Sciences and Humanities, Hanoi, Vietnam
lanntk@vnu.edu.vn
[2] VNU University of Engineering and Technology, Hanoi, Vietnam
hoa.nguyen@vnu.edu.vn
[3] VNU Digital Knowledge Hub, Hanoi, Vietnam
sonnh@vnu.edu.vn

Abstract. Liberal education-especially in universities-requires knowledge management. It soon becomes a trend, improving corporate performance and employee retention. In nine institutions and hundreds of departments and majors, Vietnam National University in Hanoi has around 2,500 researchers. Thus, knowledge management manages massive amounts of fragmented data and knowledge from many departments, disciplines, multidisciplines, geographies, and unevenly distributed systems. We propose a data fabric strategy for managing university knowledge by integrating and harmonizing fragmented data across systems and sources. Data-driven decision making promotes collective intelligence by creating a unified and complete picture of institutional knowledge. The data fabric technique powers vDFKM, a knowledge management platform that goes beyond metadata and the knowledge graph paradigm in integrating, exploiting, and reusing knowledge. The paradigm includes KM-based Applications, KM Coordinator, and Runtime and Data Infrastructure. A VNU Digital Knowledge Hub (VNU-DKH) prototype promotes the vDFKM technique. Initial experimental findings show that VNU-DKH can model knowledge representation of learning resources more efficiently and improve knowledge integration across universities.

Keywords: Data Fabric · Knowledge Management · Knowledge Integration · Knowledge Graph · Active Metadata

1 Introduction

The amount of data generated by universities is expanding at an unprecedented rate, including research papers, student records, and administrative data. However, this data is frequently compartmentalized across systems and departments, resulting in fragmented knowledge and lost chances for collaboration and innovation. As data may arise from multiple and diverse sources and be distributed and

N. T. Nguyen et al. (Eds.): ICCCI 2023, LNAI 14162, pp. 16–28, 2023.
https://doi.org/10.1007/978-3-031-41456-5_2

mined for new purposes, meanings, and interpretations, the difficulties of designing effective data management systems could be triple or quadruple more difficult [1]. In many instances, if data is managed poorly in accordance with technical challenges, the situation could result in self-inflicted systems [2]. When it comes to academic data, it is often delicate scientific information that demands additional ability, understanding, theory, and management techniques. To address this challenge, a data fabric approach to knowledge management (KM) can be utilized to seamlessly connect and integrate disparate data sources, allowing for a holistic view of institutional knowledge. The result is a more efficient and effective system for managing data and facilitating collaboration, leading to the emergence of collective intelligence.

This paper discusses data fabric technique for university knowledge management, its benefits, drawbacks, and potential uses. We will examine how a data fabric strategy might help colleges overcome fragmented data, improve decision-making, and foster collaboration and innovation. Data fabric allows access to and integration of multiple data types and remote data storage and location. Data fabric can drive employees to search for, access, and share information by providing a single platform for data solutions from storage to access. A well-designed data fabric can help organizations overcome knowledge management issues like data integration, quality, security, and privacy [6,7]. Data fabric improves teamwork, productivity, and decision-making by managing and using knowledge assets. Corporate success depends on knowledge management competition. Human-machine power generates and shares knowledge. Despite the limits of AI, knowledge graphs, and NLP, knowledge management is projected to make a quantum leap to enhance knowledge donation, creation, and sharing, maximizing human potential in work and scientific study.

It has been estimated that Trends in Data and Analytics for 2021 has pointed out that *"By 2023, artificial intelligence in the data fabric will be capable of reducing data quality and data mastering ongoing operations costs up to 65%"* [10]. It faces numerous barriers to employee adoption of knowledge management systems for monetary value and scientific outputs. Researcher workflow integration is difficult. Maintaining employee engagement and knowledge management investment over time is a challenge to retain staff. Most users will struggle to ensure correctness, currency, and relevance. Leaders must conserve and transmit departing employees' expertise to protect grey materials and scale the knowledge management system for a growing firm and information users. Making knowledge easily accessible to those who need it, regardless of geography, device, or location, to ensure and encourage internal collaboration and sharing, overcome resistance to new technologies, and gain and create new interpretations in any situation is another challenge to consider [17,23]. Many companies use their knowledge exchange and management. Diverse tacit and implicit knowledge challenges them. Data can be converted from knowledge. Companies utilizing hybrid and multi-cloud architectures to establish centralized data management systems risk burying knowledge and losing massive amounts of data. Many organizations face these challenges due to their knowledge management system being overwhelmed by data and information.

Research Challenges: It can be shown that the management of knowledge and data in large companies is typically extremely difficult and fraught with obstacles.

1. Modeling knowledge from unprocessed member unit information systems does not standardize. Different systems reflect operational knowledge. Research modeling is different from university knowledge modeling. First, huge enterprises/state-owned entities must address knowledge management research.
2. Data exchange is cumbersome and unneeded because university federation members control business data domestically. Training management systems require learner tuition expenditures, not financial data. Business system data must be aggregated and provided proactively.
3. Large firms lack knowledge management systems, limiting knowledge extraction and dissemination. Due to their organizational structures, VNU University of Science and University of Social Sciences and Humanities use engineering and technology less. Organizations can't share knowledge either.

Contribution: From the aforementioned challenges, this study focuses on investigating and developing a data fabric architecture-based knowledge management model for large-scale enterprises. The principal contributions are:

1. Proposing a method for modelling knowledge using the metadata and knowledge graph methodology.
2. Large-scale data and knowledge management data fabric architecture. This model analyzes and synthesizes raw business data into metadata for integration, sharing, and exploitation by other systems and units on the centralized management platform vDFKM. Data, knowledge graphs, integration, coordination, and exploitations are processed by the platform.
3. Testing the approach at VNU-DKH with a centralized problem in knowledge management using the vDFKM platform.

This paper's innovation is that the data fabric strategy can assist businesses tackle the problem of unevenly distributed knowledge by offering a centralized repository for storing, organizing, and accessing all data and information. Enforcing consistent data norms and standards promotes data governance, security, and confidentiality and helps teams and departments interact. Better search and analytics help organizations find data.

The remainder of this paper is organized as follows. Section 2 introduces some fundamental theory and related works in knowledge integration and management. Section 3 presents our proposed method. In Sect. 4, we discuss and evaluate our proposed work. Finally, Sect. 5 concludes our contributions and describes some future works.

2 Background and Related Works

Data fabric is a large-scale data architecture approach that enables efficient end-to-end data management between sub-units in a large organization through the use of intelligent and automated systems with a combination of cloud and edge computing [14,19]. Data fabric manages, integrates, and secures data across systems, platforms, and locations. Data must be accessible, secure, and governed. Hybrid multi-cloud data fabric ensures endpoint consistency. Deeply developed knowledge management methods like Nonaka and Hirotaka Takeuchi's SECI Model focus on "the process of transforming tacit knowledge into explicit knowledge" [18] based on four stages, data fabric approaches play an important role in establishing "adaptive manufacturing contexts" [19]. The American Productivity and Quality Center's (APQC) Knowledge Management Maturity Model, which has six levels and provides guidance on how to move from one level to the next, was developed in the 1990s s to assess an organization's knowledge management maturity [5], facilitating access and sharing knowledge as well as optimizing "the effectiveness of existing knowledge management" [20].

In [12], the authors explore how information-seeking tactics can be used and whether different sorts of information-seeking behavior with different search circumstances could cause academic problems for undergraduates and postgraduates. Digital libraries struggle to manage and offer content to users due to this issue.

Approaching data fabric technology has been analyzed in the way data has been managed traditionally, from data collection to retrieval in scaling IT infrastructures and architects while enriching data with knowledge graphs toward centralized and structured data in the journey from managing data to managing knowledge [15]. In [9,11], the writers discussed diverse data management systems and sources. They also explored how semantic data fabric supports and consolidates insights, generates internal views, and engineering modeling methodologies. "Enriching data assets with knowledge and semantics, unifying governance and compliance, integrating intelligence as well as orchestra and life cycle" are additional instant benefits [13]. AI technology and methods have made managing complex and siloed data easier. However, integrating data storage, data lake, and data hub has relied on technology that can handle and simplify complex and diverse data types. Data fabric could be used as flexible tools in adaptive environments to improve decision-making and data and knowledge exchange to create a more sustainable, reproductive, verifiable, and provenance system for information users and the knowledge-sharing industry [4,19].

3 Proposed Method: vDFKM Platform

3.1 Overview

The data fabric system proposes a holistic approach to the present system and a new way to include new materials. The Vietnam National University-Digital Knowledge Hub in Hanoi was chosen as the case study to explore and redesign a data fabric framework to solve the organization's "concrete, in-depth knowledge and real-world problems" [27].

Data fabric should rationally handle knowledge. To identify which data should be preserved, formatted, and most crucially, accessed, organizations must examine their knowledge management needs. The second step is to design the data fabric architecture to support the knowledge management system with the right technologies and tools. Sharing data, information, and expertise is necessary for data fabric integration. Establishing the new system, maintaining the data fabric to meet users' expectations, and updating its functions can increase the knowledge management system's scalability, data, accessibility, and security.

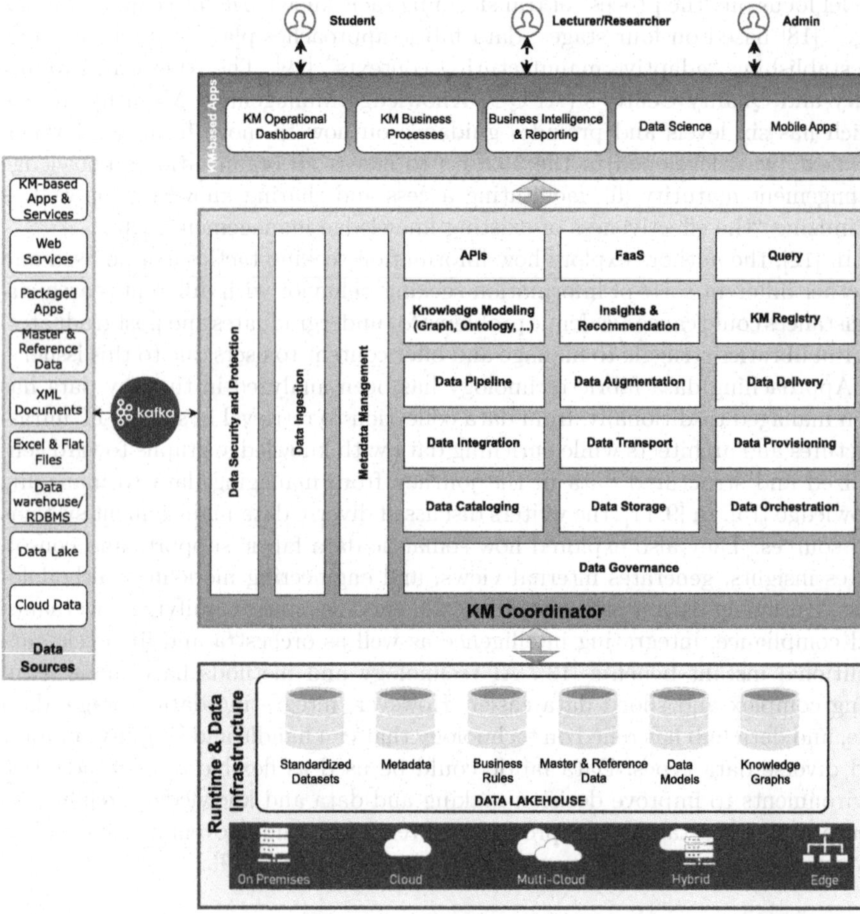

Fig. 1. General Architecture of vDFKM - Data Fabric-based Knowledge Management Platform

3.2 Data Fabric-Based Knowledge Management Architecture

Our data fabric-based knowledge management approach is illustrated in Fig. 1. The latter is considered as a distributed knowledge management platform, namely **vDFKM**. Three suggested components show vDFKM. The data lakehouse stores navigation and data if the first component handles several data types. A decentralized data management system runs the data lakehouse's multi-cloud and hybrid data blocks. Data fabric technology could sustain the system by establishing a technical relationship between implicit and tacit knowledge by recognizing identities using knowledge graphs and active metadata.

The second component of the proposed system may include data security and metadata management to address the organization's data provenance, a current data management issue, and help find useful and meaningful data and knowledge. Thus, authorized users-such as students, researchers, and administrative officials-could seek, match, link, or promote data.

To understand clearly our knowledge management with a data fabric approach shown Fig. 1, we describe the knowledge modelling method and the main components of vDFKM in the following sections.

3.3 Knowledge Modelling Based on Metadata and Knowledge Graph

Knowledge graph "is a combination of two things: business data in a graph, and an explicit knowledge" [22]. Modeling knowledge based on active metadata which is "is dynamic and not static" [24] and the knowledge graph entails the creation of a structured representation of data and its interactions with other data. Active metadata is metadata that is "dynamic" and subject to change "depending on the context of the material it describes" [21]. A knowledge graph is a searchable network of concepts, entities, and connections. Active metadata adapts knowledge modeling to data changes. Data analytics and real-time monitoring necessitate this. Knowledge graphs organize knowledge. Graph databases speed knowledge graph storage and querying. Active metadata and knowledge graphs assist interpret and analyze complex material. They support NLP, machine learning, and data analytics.

3.4 Data Sources

As one of the primary responsibilities of the VNU-DKH is to administer a wide variety of remotely accessible and ideally decentralized resources, based on the current content of VNU. The data sources depicted in Fig. 1 may include DL applications and services, web services to data from data lakes and cloud data, as well as other forms of content. Data management solutions should organize, store, and retrieve digital content. The library's and system's software can be adjusted to encourage users to find and use digital goods. Data integration and management are complicated by data silos. VNU universities, schools, and departments store data in databases, data warehouses, clouds, files, and buildings. According to a poll by Forrester Analytics [25], "Future-fit technology"-including "flatforms, practices, and partners"-could help organizations create new decision-making services. For new mobile and digital device apps, data and data-analytics decision makers need real-time data. Traditional centralized data architecture typically fails to fulfill these new data requirements, delaying insights and leading to incorrect decisions. Stakeholders should easily access corporate data with technology. The data fabric architecture makes data accessible to authorized users' systems. Technology shouldn't prevent interested parties from accessing organizational data. The data fabric design lets authorized user systems access data.

3.5 KM Coordinator

Data orchestration distributes data for knowledge sharing and system infrastructure management. Keep legalizing users' access rights. Data delivery and transportation transmit data from a data lakehouse to a target system in the correct format and structure, on schedule, consistently, and securely. Data integration requires indexing and describing data from numerous sources into a coherent framework. What's the point? While evaluating many sources, this method helps consumers discover hidden information. Knowledge hubs assist customers. Data pipelines visualize huge datasets. It can assist the company fix tech challenges and boost data credibility. Thus, Data augmentation will model and express data in ontology and knowledge graphs using Data lakehouse data. Data insights can help analyze data and predict future occurrences, boosting the knowledge-driving environment by revealing customer information behavior and authorizing knowledge source access. KM registry and Data Fabric manage and share knowledge assets and let stakeholders and information users reuse knowledge models, including platform-integrated files and models. Thus, new KM services may evaluate their clients to improve decision-making, cut costs, and boost efficiency.

3.6 Runtime and Data Infrastructure

Data can be well-formed and tidy, but raw, sparse, unevenly distributed, and incompatible. This is one of the biggest issues of modern data provenance. A data lakehouse consolidates and provides a consistent flat platform for the above data types to save time and obtain insight while maintaining data lake flexibility and scalability. Data governance includes master and reference data for organizational units. The digital knowledge center should focus on consumers, their personal profiles, products with materials, and other reference resources being mastered to ensure workflow consistency and integrity. Knowledge graphs now add "semantics to textual information" [8,16]. Knowledge graphs are successful, but they need current data. Knowledge graphs and active metadata show complex interactions between items and information, helping users understand and learn more. Thus, one graph cannot satisfy user needs [3,26]. Once data and information are indexed and actively described, various embedded knowledge graphs could help users make better-informed decisions based on their insights. This established the intended architecture.

3.7 KM-Based Apps

All apps might be created to provide a link between users and the system, where a functional interface could supply users with information, but access to the system must be based on the user's level. The current mobile application (Bookworm) could be upgraded to retrieve knowledge and data. A KM operation dashboard can depict knowledge management KPIs, allowing managers, leaders, information users, and other stakeholders to track progress and opportunities for improvement. It provides a graphical depiction of key performance indicators (KPIs) associated with knowledge management, enabling managers and stakeholders to track progress and identify areas for improvement. By monitoring these areas, an organization can ensure that its knowledge assets correspond with its overarching objectives, strategic visions, and missions. In the meanwhile, users such as students and teachers can utilize their right of access to acquire benefits from the organizations' tangible knowledge delivery.

4 Evaluation and Discussion

In order to prove the ability and efficiency of our proposed method, we carry out a prototype of vDFKM at VNU-DKH to respond to the following research questions:

- RQ1: Is the knowledge graph-based method of modeling data from the business systems of member units adequate and effective for enhancing the performance of knowledge modeling in large-scale organizations?
- RQ2: How does the vDFKM platform with its data fabric design enhance the efficacy of knowledge aggregation, sharing, and mining operations based on active metadata from business systems in various organizational units?
- RQ3: What ethical and legal factors must VNU-DKH consider when utilizing data fabric for data and knowledge management, and how can these be addressed?

The following sections will describe our experimental results and evaluation.

4.1 Context of KM at VNU

VNU (Vietnam National University) is the premier institution of higher education in Vietnam, housing more than 25,000 academic experts, lecturers from nine universities, four schools, six research institutes as well as other departments, and enrolling more than 16,000 graduates annually. Due to VNU's organizational structure, the operations of each member university are somewhat autonomous, and it is not viable to implement a uniform model for business information system solutions across all units. Nonetheless, each member institution has fundamental business systems, such as human resource management systems HM Apps, Formation Apps, Research Apps, Student Apps, and learning and knowledge management systems in particular. Learning Resources and KM-based applications (LR+KM Apps) in quantity. Due to the operational autonomy of each university under VNU, these types of systems are typically deployed on a wide variety of operating systems, utilizing distinct development environments and data management strategies. Therefore, a basis for the integration, sharing, and exploitation of knowledge between these systems and among VNU's member institutions is crucial.

KM is a key area of concentration for VNU, which seeks to increase its research capacity, foster innovation, and establish a knowledge-based economy in Vietnam. Additionally, the university may have a hierarchical culture that makes it difficult to share knowledge freely or encourage collaboration across departments and faculties. In addition, institutions frequently have siloed systems, with information and knowledge maintained within specific departments or disciplines. The second aspect that could be addressed is the fact that VNU is a huge, complex institution with established traditions and procedures. The installation of a new KM system or procedure may be met with opposition from professors and staff members who are resistant to change or unsure of the benefits of KM, particularly with regard to scientific values and financial gains. In addition, because the university is so large, its scientific activities may generate and collect voluminous amounts of information and data that are difficult to manage and arrange. There may also be difficulties in determining which information is pertinent and essential for certain parties.

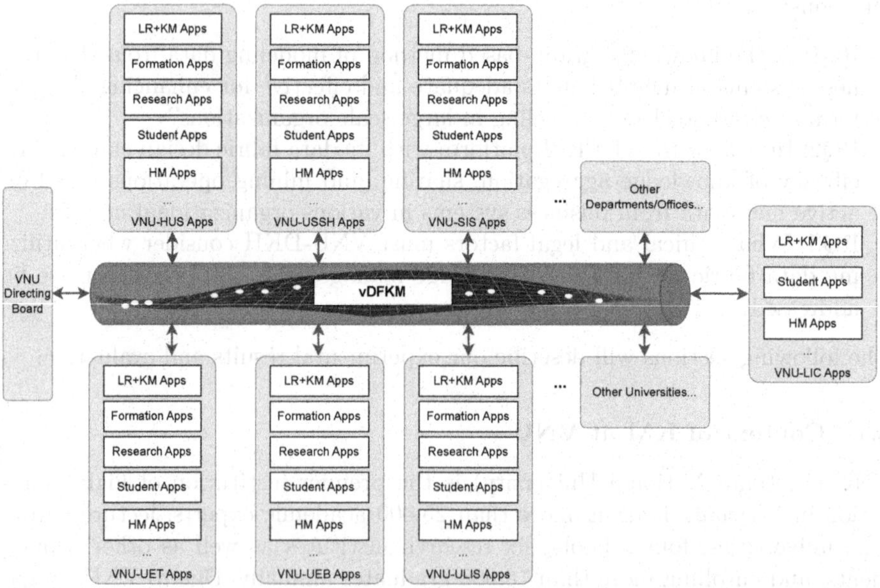

Fig. 2. vDFKM-based Knowledge Management for VNU

4.2 Deployment Model of vDFKM

To answer the aforementioned research issues, a prototype of the vDFKM platform has been implemented at VNU. With the knowledge management requirements described in Sect. 4.1, vDFKM was piloted with VNU-DKH as the management focal point. Here, we have experimentally installed this open-source platform. Specifically, the complete Runtime&Data Infrastructure component is deployed via Kubernetes (runtime - https://kubernetes.io/) and Delta Lakehouse (https://delta.io). The coordination of knowledge management operations is based on the expansion of functions from the open-source framework Kamu-Data (https://github.com/kamu-data). All vDFKM knowledge management functions are delivered as microservices through Rest APIs. Moreover, we offer these functions as a FaaS (Function as a Service) service via the Serverless open-source platform (https://github.com/serverless/serverless).

Figure 2 depicts the vDFKM deployment model at VNU. Based on the vDFKM platform, operational systems at each member university can integrate and share data and knowledge. In the data lakehouse of vDFKM, all aggregated data from business systems of VNU member units will be centrally handled. The vDFKM platform handles data gathering, integration, knowledge modeling, sharing, coordination, and administration for all active metadata.

4.3 Results and Discussion

The VNU-DKH is still in its early stages of deploying and sharing knowledge within universities. This suggests that the present system, which is responsible for spreading and exchanging knowledge among colleges, is not yet completely established or mature. It is still in its initial or early stages, indicating that there is considerable work to be done to improve and expand the system. As a result, the process of sharing information, ideas, and research findings within the academic community is still relatively young and may not be functioning optimally. There is undoubtedly still opportunity for growth, progress, and refinement in the way that knowledge is communicated and utilized inside colleges (http://digitalknowledgehub.vnu.edu.vn/).

The data fabric-based knowledge management system could be applied to the digital knowledge hub or any other organization to leverage knowledge management, knowledge sharing, and learning and decision-making in a workflow. A data fabric system helps businesses identify knowledge gaps by promoting the sharing of expertise and in-depth knowledge related to each role. The centralized system that could disseminate data/knowledge at the right time should reduce time-consuming searching for the right content and business cases, advancing digital learning and personal experience platforms that collective intelligence should help with. In a time when data literacy and knowledge literacy are no longer distinct, producing, gathering, understanding, and acting on data/knowledge-driven insights that enhance decision-making is crucial. Data fabric and AI-driven technologies would improve the connection between people and information. Fostering a knowledge-sharing culture in firms and using a built-in system to prioritize knowledge contributions from others is difficult. However, it would be easier to curate knowledge in action to increase work performance and productivity, even if people left the firm, and keeping collective intelligence may benefit owners, organizations, and other stakeholders the most.

All firms want to convert, share, and construct product layers and services from implicit to explicit knowledge to obtain seamless knowledge.

As a result of our analysis for our RQs (1,2), the suggested vDFKM design, we have determined that this model is suitable and adequate for VNU in terms of boosting the performance of knowledge modeling through the use of data fabric. In addition, it is crucial for enhancing the efficacy of information aggregation, sharing, mining, and distribution-related activities and operations that passive metadata and active metadata are managed appropriately. When managing and disseminating knowledge, the University must also address ethical and legal concerns in order to protect intellectual and property rights, thereby enhancing the organization's overall performance.

Regarding ethical and legal considerations (RQ3), in order for the proposed vDFKM to function properly, VNU must prioritize data privacy by ensuring that data stored in the data fabric is protected from unauthorized access and use and that users obtain consent from individuals whose data is being collected. Moreover, data security, data ownership, and intellectual property, as well as bias and discrimination, must be addressed to prevent the perpetuation of current disparities. VNU should take the initiative to interact with relevant stakeholders such as data subjects, regulators, and industry groups to ensure that their usage of the data fabric adheres to ethical and best practices.

5 Conclusions

In response to diverse changes in information technologies and digital transformation, the approach of implementing data fabric into managing knowledge from the organizational perspectives to solve the current issues of data provenances and knowledge sharing, and most importantly, how to put semantics into data to generate information and gain insights in order to acquire knowledge and wisdom, is still difficult. Nevertheless, we believe that, in the future, leveraging modern technologies such as machine learning and artificial intelligence to connect data to knowledge and wisdom will become the norm, with each organization finding its own way to suit the demands of its people. In the real world, when it comes to concerns of data and knowledge management, the majority of scientific societies discuss how to develop knowledge and adopt new technology. To completely develop data fabric and its application, a proposed platform such as this one must have all features that can cast a net across the entire organization's data model in order to keep up with the organization's ever-increasingly complicated data scales. In addition, the paper aims to construct a variety of new services to foster trust between the organization and its stakeholders, ensuring that knowledge is supplied to the right people at the right time in order to improve not just organizational performance but also scientific outputs.

In future works, we aim to involve technological advancements such as the integration of AI and machine learning and the use of blockchain technology methods in vDFKM to improve the ability of decision-making supports in the core activities of university. It is becoming increasingly important to assist our organization in gaining an understanding of these technologies, such as the in-context use of data visualization tools, greater emphasis on data governance and provenance, and cloud-based technologies, and solutions. In conclusion, the future of data fabric and knowledge management is expected to be defined by increased automation, intelligence, and security, as well as an emphasis on ensuring that data is handled responsibly and compliantly.

References

1. Borgman, C.L.: Big Data, Little Data, No Data: Scholarship in the Networked World. MIT Press, Cambridge (2017)
2. Borgman, C.L., Darch, P.T., Sands, A.E., Wallis, J.C., Traweek, S.: The ups and downs of knowledge infrastructures in science: implications for data management. In: IEEE/ACM Joint Conference on Digital Libraries, pp. 257–266. IEEE (2014). https://doi.org/10.1109/JCDL.2014.6970177
3. Cai, H., Liu, Z., Wang, C.: Intelligent recommendation system based on knowledge graph for scientific research teams. In: 2021 13th International Conference on Intelligent Human-Machine Systems and Cybernetics (IHMSC), pp. 204–207 (2021). https://doi.org/10.1109/IHMSC52134.2021.00054
4. Castelluccio, M.: Data fabric architecture. Strateg. Finance **103**(4), 57–58 (2021)
5. Cindy, H., Darcy, L.: APQC's levels of knowledge management maturity (2023). https://www.apqc.org/resource-library/resource-listing/apqcs-levels-knowledge-management-maturity
6. Du, P.-H., Pham, H.-D., Nguyen, N.-H.: An efficient parallel method for optimizing concurrent operations on social networks. In: Nguyen, N.T., Kowalczyk, R. (eds.) Transactions on Computational Collective Intelligence XXIX. LNCS, vol. 10840, pp. 182–199. Springer, Cham (2018). https://doi.org/10.1007/978-3-319-90287-6_10
7. Duan, R., Xiao, Y.: Enterprise knowledge graph from specific business task to enterprise knowledge management. In: Proceedings of the 28th ACM International Conference on Information and Knowledge Management, CIKM 2019, pp. 2965–2966. Association for Computing Machinery, New York (2019). https://doi.org/10.1145/3357384.3360314
8. Duan, Y., Shao, L., Hu, G., Zhou, Z., Zou, Q., Lin, Z.: Specifying architecture of knowledge graph with data graph, information graph, knowledge graph and wisdom graph. In: 2017 IEEE 15th International Conference on Software Engineering Research, Management and Applications (SERA), pp. 327–332 (2017). https://doi.org/10.1109/SERA.2017.7965747
9. Duong, S.N., Du, H.P., Nguyen, C.N., Nguyen, H.N.: A red-bet method to improve the information diffusion on social networks. Int. J. Adv. Comput. Sci. Appl. **12**(8) (2021). https://doi.org/10.14569/IJACSA.2021.0120898
10. Garner: Top trends in data and analytics for 2021: Data fabric is the foundation (2021). https://www.gartner.com/en/documents/3996983
11. Ghiran, A.-M., Buchmann, R.A.: The model-driven enterprise data fabric: a proposal based on conceptual modelling and knowledge graphs. In: Douligeris, C., Karagiannis, D., Apostolou, D. (eds.) KSEM 2019. LNCS (LNAI), vol. 11775, pp. 572–583. Springer, Cham (2019). https://doi.org/10.1007/978-3-030-29551-6_51

12. Hoeber, O., Storie, D.: Information seeking within academic digital libraries: a survey of graduate student search strategies. In: Proceedings of the 22nd ACM/IEEE Joint Conference on Digital Libraries, JCDL 2022. Association for Computing Machinery, New York (2022). https://doi.org/10.1145/3529372.3533286
13. IBM: Data fabric architecture delivers instant benefits (2021). https://www.ibm.com/downloads/cas/V4QYOAPR
14. Jahns, V.: Data fabric and datafication. ACM SIGSOFT Softw. Eng. Notes **47**(4), 30–31 (2022). https://doi.org/10.1145/3561846.3561854
15. Kuftinova, N., Ostroukh, A., Filippova, N., Gaevskii, V., Podgorny, A.: Integration of scalable it architectures on the basis of data fabric technology. Russ. Eng. Res. **42**(11), 1199–1202 (2022). https://doi.org/10.3103/S1068798X22110144
16. Lijuan, R., Jun, L., Wei, G.: Multi-source knowledge embedding research of knowledge graph. In: 2019 IEEE 3rd International Conference on Circuits, Systems and Devices (ICCSD), pp. 163–166 (2019). https://doi.org/10.1109/ICCSD.2019.8842938
17. Manesh, M.F., Pellegrini, M.M., Marzi, G., Dabic, M.: Knowledge management in the fourth industrial revolution: mapping the literature and scoping future avenues. IEEE Trans. Eng. Manag. **68**(1), 289–300 (2020). https://doi.org/10.1109/TEM.2019.2963489
18. Nonaka, I., Takeuchi, H.: The Knowledge-Creating Company: How Japanese Companies Create the Dynamics of Innovation, 1st edn. Oxford University Press, New York (1995)
19. Östberg, P.O., Vyhmeister, E., Castañé, G.G., Meyers, B., Van Noten, J.: Domain models and data modeling as drivers for data management: the assistant data fabric approach. IFAC-PapersOnLine **55**(10), 19–24 (2022). https://doi.org/10.1016/j.ifacol.2022.09.362
20. Rivai, M.A., Sfenrianto: Examining the impact of knowledge management capability on organizational performance: a study case at one of the international school in South Tangerang, Indonesia. In: 2020 International Conference on Information Management and Technology (ICIMTech), pp. 376–381 (2020). https://doi.org/10.1109/ICIMTech50083.2020.9211120
21. Rockley, A., Cooper, C.: Managing Enterprise Content: A Unified Content Strategy, 2nd edn. New Riders, Berkeley (2012)
22. Martin, S., Szekely, B., Allemang, D.: The rise of the knowledge graph (2021). https://info.cambridgesemantics.com/hubfs/The_Rise_of_the_Knowledge_Graph.pdf
23. Tiwari, S.P.: Emerging technologies: factors influencing knowledge sharing. World J. Educ. Res. (2022)
24. Tozer, G.V.: Metadata Management for Information Control and Business Success. Artech Print on Demand, Boston (1999)
25. Wilson, K., Bonde, A., M, B.: Forrester infographic: The state of services in 2021 - partners are key to your future fit strategy (2021)
26. Yang, K., Gao, H., Yang, Y., Qin, K.: Entities and relations aware graph convolutional network for knowledge base completion. In: 2021 IEEE 9th International Conference on Information, Communication and Networks (ICICN), pp. 71–75 (2021). https://doi.org/10.1109/ICICN52636.2021.9673867
27. Yin, R.: Case Study Research and Applications: Design and Methods. SAGE Publications (2017). https://books.google.com.vn/books?id=uX1ZDwAAQBAJ

An Architecture for Enabling Collective Intelligence in IoT Networks

Tapio Frantti[1(✉)] and Ilgın Şafak[2]

[1] University of Jyväskylä, Jyväskylä, Finland
tapio.k.frantti@jyu.fi

[2] Fibabanka R&D Center, Istanbul, Turkey
ilgin.safak@fibabanka.com.tr

Abstract. Proliferation of the Internet of Things (IoT) has fundamentally changed how different application environments are being used. IoT networks are prone to malicious attacks similar to other networks. Additionally, physical tampering, injection and capturing of the nodes are more probable in IoT networks. Therefore, conventional security practices require substantial re-engineering for IoT networks. Here we present an architecture that enables collective intelligence for IoT networks via smart network nodes and blockchain technology. In this architecture, various security related functionalities are distributed to network nodes to detect tampered, captured and injected devices, recognize their movements and prevent networks' use as an attack surface. Nodes interact with signaling, security information and data traffic. Security information aids to distribute cyber-security functionalities across the IoT network based on the device and/or application type. Every node in the proposed IoT network does not need to have all the cyber-security functionalities, but the network as a whole needs these functionalities.

Keywords: Distributed IoT networks · architecture · blockchain · AI · network security

1 Introduction

The Internet of Things (IoT) is one of the most important technologies of the last decades enabling data collection, data exchange, communication and control actions between people, processes, and things. We can connect to the Internet and control industrial and everyday objects. According to forecasts, the use of IoT devices will continue to increase with time. For example, Cisco estimates 500 billion devices to be connected to the Internet by 2030, [4]. IoT Analytics counts the number of IoT devices to exceed 30.9 billion units in year 2025, [11]. Statista forecasts that end-user spending on IoT solutions worldwide in 2025 will be 1567 billion US$ [15]. However, the number of security threats targeting IoT devices and the occurrence of cyber security incidents have also increased. The susceptibility to cyber threats is a serious concern for IoT networks and

N. T. Nguyen et al. (Eds.): ICCCI 2023, LNAI 14162, pp. 29–42, 2023.
https://doi.org/10.1007/978-3-031-41456-5_3

overlaid complex systems and forces the IoT actors to take countermeasures against hostile cyber actions and attacks. Adversaries may penetrate networks, disrupt or defeat the system defense using exploits available on the Internet, hang on systems for a long time, and utilize data available on the systems. Therefore, the growth of IoT usage will increase the need of new cyber security solutions.

Artificial intelligence (AI) could be used in enabling IoT networks and devices to become smarter and ensure the IoT network's security autonomously. AI-based IoT applications with continuous machine learning (ML) algorithm are capable of continually learning, interacting, and enhancing real-time cognition capabilities of devices.

IoT edge networks do not yet formalize and exploit collective intelligence (CI). CI encompasses task and information distribution, computational load balancing, code offloading, as well as instructing how and where to run CI. However, there are also several significant challenges that must be addressed in CI. These include the quality of data, the distribution of the computational workload and functionalities, mathematical models of the CI, and the scalability and portability of the solution.

Another critical cyber-security concern is related to the deployment of large-scale IoT systems. The centralized architecture of existing IoT systems have weaknesses such as single point of failure, high-cost of transmission and computation, and data loss. Additionally, due to the massive number of devices that can belong to several users, the IoT systems need to ensure data ownership, so that they can exercise complete control over the shared data. The coexistence and collaboration of different technologies and the open standards and protocols employed by the IoT may pose additional security risks. Despite the heterogeneity and inherent computational power constraints of the IoT devices and large scale of the IoT network, there is an increasing interest in autonomic computing for device management, where each device is allowed to make significant decisions without the consent of others. In this case, sensors and devices need to communicate with each other in a distributed way. This in turn leads to many design challenges including limited scalability and high latency. These challenges can be addressed by a secure and supervised distributed architecture where the security platform intelligently divides processing load among the nodes of the network. For this purpose, distributed ledger technology (DLT), such as blockchain, may be utilized. According to [8] blockchain provides advantages including decentralization, transparency, immutability, enhanced security, anonymity, cost reduction and autonomy. DLT transactions are validated using trust-free consensus algorithms that allow every node to participate in the consensus, which increases the robustness and reliability of transactions compared to absolute consensus methods used in centralized methods. Usage of DLT in IoT networks eliminates the need of a single trusted authority, thereby enhancing the potential for scalability and reliability.

Here we present a distributed IoT security architecture, SENTIENCE[1], that enables collective intelligence for IoT networks. The problem statement may be

[1] EPO patent number EP23155296.9 pending.

formulated as *Can we and how do we embed satisfactory security controls for computationally restricted heterogeneous network nodes to enable reliable, secure and resilient platforms for rich ecosystems by applying computational intelligence?*. The main contributions of the paper are as follows.

- A private-by-design and scalable blockchain-based collective intelligence system with distributed blacklisting and trust scoring protocol.
- An AI-based signaling protocol that enables collective intelligence.
- A security analysis of the presented architecture.

The organization of the rest of the paper is as follows. Section 2 presents an overview of AI-based distributed IoT security solutions available in the literature. Section 3 presents the proposed system architecture, blacklisting and signaling protocol. Section 4 provides a discussion on advantages and disadvantages of the presented solutions. Section 5 presents the conclusions of the paper.

2 Literature Review

Mohamudally [12] provides a comparative study of mathematical models for CI and a discussion of their suitability for implementation on mobile devices. Additionally, a framework for modeling CI systems using graph theory and artificial neural networks is proposed. Radanliev et al. [14] proposes a dynamic and self-adaptive cyber risk analytics system using AI/ML as well as real-time intelligence. The usage of edge computing nodes and AI/ML technology migrated to the periphery of the Internet, along with local IoT networks, enables a comprehensive and systematic understanding of the opportunities and threats. Joseph et al. [6] proposed a self-organizing IoT system architecture that relies on blockchain and its related features in order to achieve aspects of end-to-end IoT security.

Konstantinos et a. [9] propose a design method and cognitive platform that incorporate various technologies including Public Key Infrastructure (PKI), block-chain, and AI to support a unified and integrated approach towards data privacy, security and safety of Industrial IoT systems. The proposed system analyzes the IoT topology and signal metadata in relation to the relevant safety profiles. The aim is to exploit the cyber-physical representation of the system-of-systems in conjunction with security and safety policies to provide real-time risk mapping for static analysis and continuous monitoring to assess safety issues and take appropriate response actions.

An et al. [1] proposes a novel blockchain based anomaly detection architecture and method for IoT networks to overcome the problems of data resource sharing and collective learning in IoT. IoT devices with abnormal HTTP traffic are detected efficiently and accurately using the proposed clustering and autoencoder methods. This architecture allows detection models to be shared among users, effectively solving the problem of collective learning. Multiple joint detection methods can also be effective in improving the ability to detect anomalies.

Li et al. [10] examines network architectures that may be utilized in future 6G networks to support intelligent IoT. Furthermore, in order to facilitate the sharing of learning and training results in the intelligent IoT, the authors introduce and adopt a novel method called collective reinforcement learning (CRL) that is inspired by the collective learning of humans. Blockchain, mobile edge computing and cloud computing are applied to enhance data security and computing efficiency.

An et al. [1] provide a mechanism for sharing detection models and Li et al. [10] sharing training models. None of the aforementioned works study collective intelligence by AI signaling, distributed blacklisting via anomaly detection and blockchain network, the mitigation of security threats, or the disaster recovery, which are addressed in this paper.

3 An Architecture for Collective Intelligence

3.1 System Architecture

Here we propose a secure, blockchain-based architecture for enabling collective intelligence in zero-trust IoT networks. In the proposed system, resource constrained nodes combine jointly cyber-security information and defend against cyber threats. Intelligent security related computing, detection, and prevention algorithms are distributed to network nodes. Nodes interact with signaling, AI and data traffic (see Fig. 1).

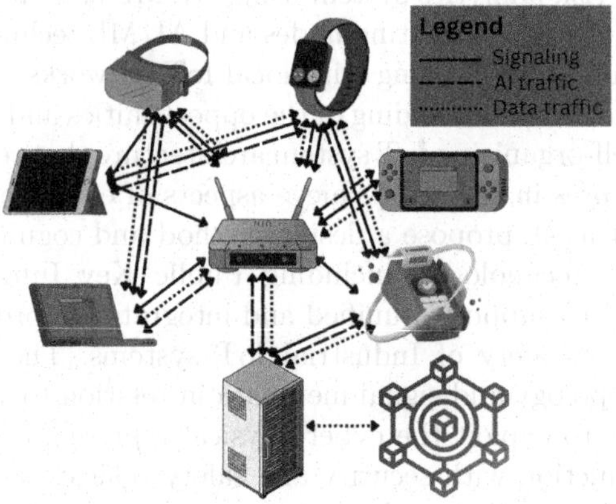

Fig. 1. Network nodes with signaling, data and AI traffic.

Data traffic refers to the actual payload, such as sensor readings, being transmitted over the network. Signaling refers to the exchange of control information between network elements to establish, maintain, or modify communication. AI traffic consists of information analyzed from received traffic and information from security algorithms. Analysis of the traffic is performed in the cloud servers, routers and IoT nodes. Solid lines in Fig. 1 describe signaling traffic. Signaling traffic of the external connections is not shown. Dashed and dotted lines describe AI and data traffic, respectively.

The usage of IoT and blockchain with AI enable collective intelligence and allow real-time decision making. This facilitates the identification and mitigation of cyber-security threats, reduction of system failures, optimization of data flow, and provides re-routing options for disaster recovery. This is achieved with the *IoT device registration to the network, collection of data from devices, detection of threats from the data anomalies, security incident publication to blockchain,* and *collective actions on detected threats.* Collective action on detected security threats includes, *e.g.*, blacklisting and removing malicious IoT devices from the network, applying load balancing rules to divide computation, retrieving back-up data and re-routing the data flow.

The main components of the system architecture include IoT clients, communication and blockchain network, distributed monitoring, threat detection/prevention, blockchain, CI, zero-trust, load balancing and recovery systems. The system architecture is designed in according to the Zero-Trust Architecture (ZTA) and the National Institute of Standards and Technology (NIST) Cybersecurity Framework. ZTA requires users of the network to be authenticated, authorized, and validated before being granted access to applications and data. Here this is achieved by *identity and access management, network segmentation, least priviledge principle, microsegmentation, continuous monitoring and analytics, endpoint security, data encryption, zero-trust access, device behavior analytics,* and *incident response.* The NIST Cybersecurity Framework was used to assist risk identification, secure delivery of services, and detection of and response to incidents.

The layers of the system architecture with the main functionality of the each layer is depicted in Fig. 2. Security algorithms and computational load are distributed between AI-blockchain nodes, routers and IoT clients to decentralize the computational load. Distribution is guided by time, computational capability and energy principles. Traffic monitoring and detection is distributed to different network nodes by time and energy division based scheduling. Nodes receive alarm information by the AI traffic.

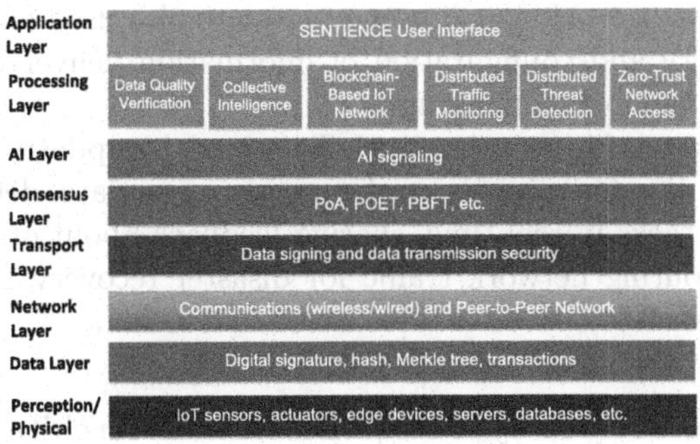

Fig. 2. Layered architecture.

3.2 AI Information Signaling and AI Layer

In the SENTIENCE architecture, intelligent security related functionalities are distributed to different network nodes, where each node has one or more cyber-security functionalities. The aim is to avoid each node requiring to have unnecessarily all the functionalities, but the network as a whole has the functionalities. The network awareness, collective intelligence, is distributed among the nodes. The AI layer handles AI messages between IoT devices and the cloud. It defines how AI messages are sent and received by nodes, as well as the cyber-security functionalities each device possesses, where these functionalities and the device status are kept track of in the cloud.

AI plays a critical role in improving the security and reliability of IoT networks through the data analysis. This allows IoT networks to proactively identify and respond to abnormal behavior or potential security threats. In order to detect anomalies and assign trust scores to devices, AI algorithms can learn from historical data, adapt to changing conditions, and continuously enhance their accuracy with time.

AI messages include device fingerprint, battery level, feedback about interactions with other network nodes, average processor load, tampering information, misuse and anomaly detection information, port scanning information, traffic latency, nodes responsiveness, smart contract information, network configuration information, location data, error logs, and optional fields for forthcoming use.

A device fingerprint may include device specific information such as device type, supported security and communications protocols, and MAC address. It is required for AI level topological device grouping and work load distribution. Battery level and processor(s) load are needed for work load distribution. Tampering information note if the node is on the target of side channel attack, tampering or movement. Nodes detect intrusions by misuse and anomaly detection techniques and they report all the security events in AI messages. IoT nodes have also built-in feature to do port scanning and they report all the unnecessary open ports. Latency and nodes responsiveness are included to the traffic information fields of the AI message. AI signaling messages are also used for smart contract information delivery and configuration of information delivery. There are also reserved fields for the forthcoming use.

AI messages are used in securing the IoT network by updating network access rules, keeping the disaster recovery configuration up-to-date, detecting and mitigating security attacks in real-time, sharing feedback about other nodes in the network, and re-routing network traffic for disaster recovery. AI messages are encrypted and hashed.

3.3 A Scalable, Private by Design Blockchain Architecture

Blockchain is an attractive option for the decentralized secure architecture. Its' transactions are validated by trust-free consensus algorithms that allow every node to participate in the consensus, which increases the robustness and reliability of transactions as well as scalability and reliability compared to absolute consensus methods.

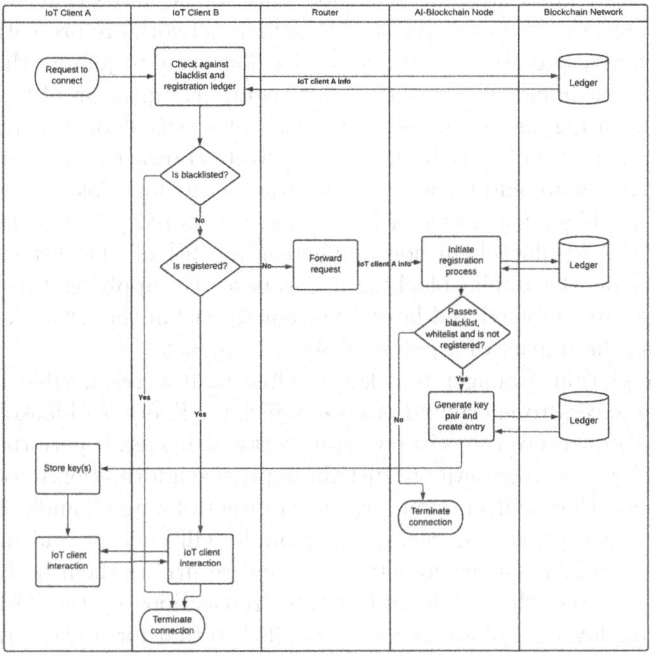

Fig. 3. Sequence chart of AI traffic for an injected IoT client.

The two most popular consensus algorithms, Proof of Work (PoW) and Proof of Stake (PoS), are computationally intensive and not suitable for IoT scenarios. Therefore, lightweight consensus algorithms are required for IoT-blockchain integration. A simple voting mechanism, *e.g.*, Proof of Authority (PoA), Practical Byzantine Fault Tolerance (PBFT), or Proof of Elapsed Time (PoET) could be used as the consensus algorithm for the block validation and transactions creation, where public-key cryptography is used as an encryption mechanism. The Lightning Network, a "layer 2" payment protocol designed to be layered on top of a blockchain-based cryptocurrency, such as bitcoin, could also be utilized to meet resource and power constraints of IoT networks, [13]. It has several desirable properties by design and was conceived to enable scalability and high transaction rates.

The SENTIENCE utilizes the private-by-design blockchain architecture based on [7] that ensures the intelligent supervision of all the necessary events in the consensus protocol distributed across the IoT network. This traceability is necessary to guarantee reliability and robustness of the system. Smart contracts are used in enabling and automating interactions between the system and the

IoT devices. A separate virtual database is used for logging interactions between IoT devices and the blockchain.

The consensus mechanism classifies the IoT device transactions as public and private. Public transactions are visible to every node in the IoT network, whereas private transactions are accessible only to the nodes that are a part of the transactions. Nodes in the private blockchain network are pre-authenticated using the security protocol described in Sect. 3.5 prior to joining the network. Therefore, maintaining consensus does not require complex proof to be carried out. A simple voting mechanism is used as the consensus algorithm for the block validation and creation for both public and private transactions. Network traffic and device data that could be used by malicious actors for exploiting weaknesses of the network, like trust scores of IoT nodes, are stored privately in a private database in the AI-blockchain nodes, whereas the list of blacklisted devices is kept publicly on the public blockchain database. By applying this approach, strict controls are enforced and lateral movement within the network is limited, thus reducing the impact of a potential security breach.

The Transaction Manager is a key module mainly responsible for storing and allowing access to encrypted transaction data. Every AI-blockchain node, whether sender or receiver, has its own transaction manager. It performs anomaly detection and acts as a gateway to distribute private information to other nodes in the network that will encrypt private transactions and handle IoT transactions. The encryption and decryption module will encrypt and decrypt the payload by generating the asymmetric keys and returning them to Transaction Manager. To process the public and private transactions by the AI-blockchain nodes, working layers of blockchain are modified so that for private transactions only the allowed authorized node takes part in communication. Similarly, block validation and block generation logic are modified so that instead of using global root check, it uses global public state root in the blockchain header. For private transaction block validation and creation, logic is altered to handle private transactions. However, still each node is able to demonstrate that it has the same set of transactions as other nodes, since the block validation process also includes a check of the global transaction hash, namely, the hash of all transactions in a block, both public and private ones (Fig. 4).

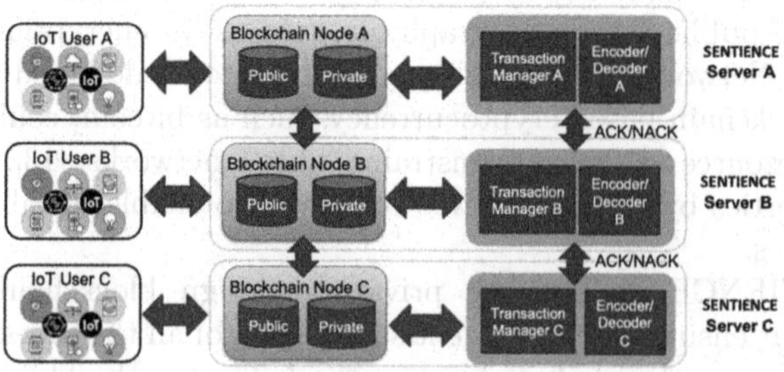

Fig. 4. A private-by-design blockchain architecture based on [7]

For scalability purposes, a sharding mechanism, such as the one proposed in [3], could be utilized. Blockchain sharding refers to the division of the entire blockchain network into several smaller sub-networks, known as shards. Each shard contains data that is unique to it, as well as being independent of other shards on the network. Each sub-network has its own consensus process for creating blocks. Due to the multiple shards in the network, blocks are generated faster than they would be in a network without shards. The number of shards can be increased as demand for the application grows, thereby allowing the system to allocate resources dynamically.

3.4 Zero Trust, Blacklisting, Trust Scoring and Anomaly Detection

Once an IoT client is registered in the IoT network, it can communicate with other IoT clients. Based on our previous work in [16] and [2], malicious IoT clients are blacklisted in a distributed way by AI-blockchain nodes via the blockchain-based IoT network security system using anomaly detection techniques and the blockchain network.

Figure 3 describes a case when a malicious client is injected to the IoT network. The malicious client (client A) requests to connect to a registered neighboring IoT client (client B). The client B checks whether the malicious IoT client is blacklisted or registered to the IoT network against the ledger via the blockchain network. If the client A is blacklisted, client B terminates the connection. If the client A is already registered, client B connects and interacts with it. If the client A is not blacklisted and is not registered to the IoT network, client B forwards the request to the AI-blockchain node via the router. After receiving the registration request from the registered client B, the AI-blockchain node initiates the registration process of client A. Firstly it performs a blacklist and registration check. If the client A is not blacklisted and is not registered, it then performs a whitelist check. If the client A passes the device whitelist check, it adds the client A to the IoT network by assigning a public key pair and creating an entry in the ledger. The AI-blockchain node shares the key pair with client A and completes the registration process. After registration is completed, the malicious IoT client can access the IoT network.

All network traffic is continuously monitored by AI-blockchain nodes. If any AI-blockchain node detects an anomalous behavior of the malicious IoT node, it publishes its finding on the ledger via the blockchain network. If and when AI-blockchain nodes have consensus on the anomalous behavior, then the malicious IoT client is added to the blacklist via the blockchain network. Similarly, AI-blockchain nodes may detect an IoT client to be offline, *e.g.*, due to a physical attack or battery depletion. If this client is not detected for a predefined period, then it is added to a list of compromised clients. Therefore, it is required that clients inform the AI-blockchain server about their presence in the network.

A malicious client may stay silent without advertising itself and eavesdrops communication. Therefore, the data traffic is encrypted for confidentiality reasons and to prevent eavesdropping and man in the middle (MitM) attacks. Additionally, in order to prevent registered malicious IoT clients from adding new malicious IoT clients, the AI-blockchain node also performs regular blacklist and registration checks. Power deprivation attacks are also possible by increased radio interference. The malicious client may also attempt to detect the topology of the networks by listening to the signaling traffic. The network depicted in Fig. 1 is assumed to consists of the trusted clients. The network itself can be analyzed using a trust metric to rate individual clients as well as AI-blockchain nodes.

3.5 Threat Detection

The SENTIENCE architecture provides distributed threat and incident detection solution for misuses, malware and anomalies. In traditional host-based anomaly detection systems, a system call sequence is analyzed in order to model normal behavior of an application. Using the model, the current sequence is examined for anomalous behavior, which may indicate an attack. However, it is shown that sequence-based systems are susceptible to evasion. As a mitigation method, multiple anomaly detection methods, including host-based event anomaly detection, signature-based anomaly detection, and network traffic-based anomaly detection could be jointly used.

4 Security Analysis of the SENTIENCE Architecture

Blockchain threat models relevant to IoT network security can be categorized as identity-based, manipulation-based, cryptanalytic, reputation-based and service-based attacks [5]. The SENTIENCE architecture is potentially resilient to all attack types based on the security analysis provided in Table 1. The channel model is depicted in Fig. 5.

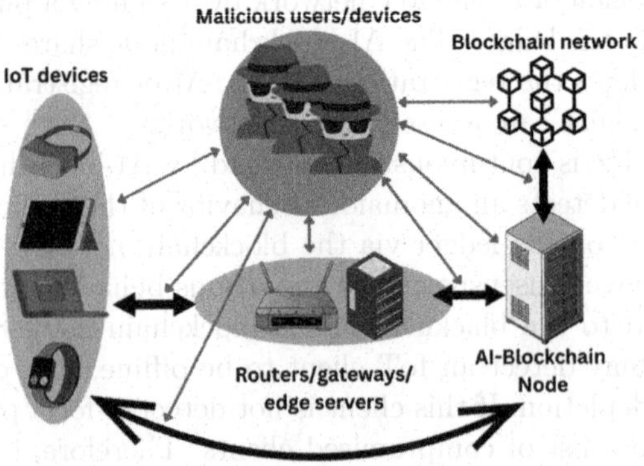

Fig. 5. Channel model

Table 1. Security analysis of the SENTIENCE architecture

Threat	Description	Guarantee	Proof	Assumptions
Identity	Forged identities masquerading as authorized users to gain access to the system and manipulate it. Includes key, replay, Sybil and impersonation attacks.	1. Immutable device identity. 2. Secure identity verification. 3. Strong access controls. 4. Resilience against Sybil attacks.	1. A PUF session key: authentication and non-repudiation. 2. Device's public key is linked to its identity. 3. Access control through the ZTNA, blacklisting, cryptography, and PUF keys. 4. Only authorized participants can reach consensus.	1. Each device is assigned a cryptographic identity (public-private key pair). 2. A PUF session key cannot be cloned. 3. ZTNA system assigns appropriate access levels. 4. The blockchain network withstands Sybil attacks.
Manipulation	False-Data Injection, Tampering, Overlay, Modification, and MitM attacks.	1. Immutable identity. 2. Identity verification. 3. Strong access controls. 4. Immutable transaction history	Proofs of guarantees 1–3 are the same as above. 4. A block cannot be modified after being added to the blockchain.	Assumptions of guarantees 1–3 are the same as above. 4. IoT data transmitted and stored on the blockchain is cryptographically secured and cannot be tampered with.
Cryptanalytic	Uncover the private key. Includes Side-Channel and Quantum attacks.	1. Secure Cryptographic Algorithms 2. Key management 3. Randomness generation 4. Side-channel mitigation	1. Strong cryptographic algorithms. 2. Robust key management. 3. Cryptographically secure random number generators. 4. PUF key to prevent key theft.	1. Cryptographic algorithms are secure. 2. Robust key management. 3. The RNGs are cryptographically secure. 4. Copying the session key generation function is not possible.
Reputation	Agents manipulate their reputations. Includes Hiding Block and Whitewashing attacks.	1. Robust Reputation Scoring 2. Transparent Trust Evaluation	1. Nodes with high trust scores have more impact on decisions. 2. Only authorized users access the trust scores. 3. Blacklisting decisions are on the blockchain.	1. Trust scoring is performed for all nodes. 2. The blacklist and the trust scores is stored on the public and the private blockchain database.
Service attacks	The purpose is either to disable or to alter the service. DoS/DDoS, Refusal to Sign, Double Spending, and Collusion attacks.	1. DDoS Mitigation 2. Scalability and Load Balancing 3. Resource Monitoring and Management 4. Secure Communication Channels 5. Intrusion Detection and Prevention	1. Traffic monitoring and analysis for DDoS mitigation. 2. Sharding for scaling the blockchain. Load balancing for high traffic loads. 3. Detection of resource exhaustion and abnormal usage by anomaly detection. 4. Data protection by encryption. 5. Traffic monitoring to detect malicious activity.	1. Services to mitigate DDoS attacks. 2. Traffic loads are handled by scalability. 3. Prevention of disruptions through proactive resource management. 4. Encryption, handshake protocol, ZTNA and key management protects the communication channels. 5. IDS/IPS monitor traffic, logs, and behavior.

5 Discussion About SENTIENCE Architecture

The presented architecture enables a cyber-secure IoT ecosystem. The intelligent IoT network nodes collectively detect malicious IoT devices, monitor traffic, detect and prevent threats, secure transactions, protect data and deliver awareness information among the nodes. The system also prevents its' use as an attack surface and performs disaster recovery.

The architecture has the several advantages. It *enhances security* with strong access control and real-time identification of malicious or suspicious activities. Its' blacklisting decisions are *fair, transparent and reliable. The immutability and tamper-resistance of transactions and device identities* are ensured by leveraging blockchain technology and device fingerprinting based on Physical Unclonable Functions (PUFs). The use of consensus algorithms, such as PoA and PoET strengthens the network's *resilience to Sybil attacks.* Network node provides feedback about other nodes in the network by monitoring and evaluating *QoS* metrics, such as latency, throughput, reliability, and availability.

The architecture also has some challenges. Despite the distributed load, increased activities of the IoT nodes increase *energy consumption.* As a mitigation technique, energy harvesting may be an option. Collective decision making, consensus protocols and inter-device communications, particularly with the blockchain network, introduces *latency.* Blockchain-based systems have also higher *computational costs* due to consensus and cryptographic operations. As traditional systems do not involve distributed consensus, their computational cost is generally lower. Lightweight consensus algorithms, such as PoA and POET, and sharding can be used to reduce the complexity. *Security and privacy* issues may arise as a result of increased interaction of IoT devices in the blockchain. This could be mitigated by developing new standards for blockchain-based IoT communications and security protocols. Blockchain-based systems may incur a higher *storage cost.* Nodes participating in the blockchain network maintain a copy of the entire blockchain, resulting in data redundancy. The *governance and administration* of SENTIENCE, including distribution of cyber-security functionalities across the network, trust scoring and blacklisting decisions, require careful management. Therefore, it is essential to establish governance policies, dispute resolution mechanisms, as well as ensuring transparency and accountability.

6 Conclusions

This paper presents an architecture to enable collective intelligence in distributed IoT networks. The architecture is based on the zero-trust and NCSF guidelines. In the presented solution, various intelligent security functionalities are distributed amongst nodes, where each node has one or more cyber-security functionalities. Nodes interact not only with signaling and data traffic but also with the AI traffic, to transfer security information in the network.

The architecture introduces networking and processing overheads for inter-device communications and collective decision making with AI signaling and the blockchain network. Challenges may arise from managing and optimizing the distribution of tasks amongst nodes and minimizing power consumption and latency.

Future work includes the creation of performance and accuracy metrics for the architecture and the validation of the architecture, as well as contributing to the standardization of blockchain-based IoT communications and improved security protocols that are suitable for IoT devices.

References

1. An, Y., et al.: An HTTP anomaly detection architecture based on the internet of intelligence. IEEE Trans. Cogn. Commun. Netw. **8**(3), 1552–1565 (2022)
2. Baykara, C.A., Şafak, I., Kalkan, K.: SHAPEIOT: secure handshake protocol for autonomous IoT device discovery and blacklisting using physical unclonable functions and machine learning. In: 13th International Conference on Network and Communications Security (NCS 2021), Toronto, Canada (2021)
3. Chow, Y.-W., et al.: Visualization and cybersecurity in the metaverse: a survey. J. Imaging **9**(1), 11 (2023). ISSN 2313-433X
4. Cisco. Cisco IoT Solutions. https://cisco.com/c/en/us/solutions/internet-of-things/overview.html. Accessed 07 Sept 2022
5. Ferrag, M.A., et al.: Blockchain technologies for the internet of things: research issues and challenges. IEEE Internet Things J. **6**(2), 2188–2204 (2019). https://doi.org/10.1109/JIOT.2018.2882794
6. Joseph, A.O., et al.: Securing self-organizing iot ecosystem: a distributed ledger technology approach. In: 2019 IEEE 5th World Forum on Internet of Things (WF-IoT), pp. 809–814 (2019). https://doi.org/10.1109/WF-IoT.2019.8767182
7. Kashif, M., Kalkan, K.: BCPriPIoT: BlockChain utilized privacy-preservation mechanism for IoT devices. In: 2021 Third International Conference on Blockchain Computing and Applications (BCCA), pp. 201–209 (2021). https://doi.org/10.1109/BCCA53669.2021.9657016
8. Khan, M.A., Salah, K.: IoT security: review, blockchain solutions, and open challenges. Futur. Gener. Comput. Syst. **82**, 395–411 (2018)
9. Loupos, K., et al.: Cognition enabled IoT platform for industrial IoT safety, security and privacy - the CHARIOT project. In: 2019 IEEE 24th International Workshop on Computer Aided Modeling and Design of Communication Links and Networks (CAMAD), pp. 1–4 (2019)
10. Li, M., et al.: Intelligent resource optimization for blockchain-enabled IoT in 6G via collective reinforcement learning. IEEE Network **36**(6), 175–182 (2022)
11. Lueth, K.: State of the IoT 2020: 12 billion IoT connections, surpassing non-IoT for the first time. https://iot-analytics.com/state-of-the-iot-2020-12-billion-iot-connections-surpassing-non-iot-for-the-first-time/. Accessed 07 Sept 2022
12. Mohamudally, N.: Paving the way towards collective intelligence at the IoT edge. In: Procedia Comput. Sci. **203** (2022). ISSN 1877-0509. 17th International Conference on Future Networks and Communications/19th International Conference on Mobile Systems and Pervasive Computing/12th International Conference on Sustainable Energy Information Technology (FNC/MobiSPC/SEIT 2022), 9–11 August 2022, Niagara Falls, Ontario, Canada, pp. 8–15. ISSN 1577-0509
13. Poon, J., Dryja, T.: The Bitcoin Lightning Network. Technical report, Lightning Network (2010)

14. Radanliev, P., et al.: Cyber risk at the edge: current and future trends on cyber risk analytics and artificial intelligence in the industrial internet of things and industry 4.0 supply chains. Cybersecurity **3** (2020)
15. Statista. Forecast end-user spending on IoT solutions worldwide from 2017 to 2025. https://www.statista.com/statistics/976313/global-iot-marketsize/. Accessed 07 Sept 2022
16. Tarlan, O., Şafak, I., Kalkan, K.: DiBLIoT: a distributed blacklisting protocol for IoT device classification using the hashgraph consensus algorithm. In: The 36th International Conference on Information Networking (ICOIN) 2022, Jeju Island, Korea (2022)

Self-Organizing Maps for Data Purchase Support in Data Marketplaces

Denis Mayr Lima Martins[1(✉)] and Gottfried Vossen[2]

[1] Machine Learning and Data Engineering, ERCIS, University of Münster, Leonardo-Campus 3, 48149 Münster, Germany
denis.martins@wwu.de

[2] European Research Center for Information Systems, University of Münster, Leonardo-Campus 3, 48149 Münster, Germany
vossen@wwu.de

Abstract. Data marketplaces have become popular in recent years, in particular for enterprises who want to enrich their own data with novel data from outside in order to improve their decision-making. A data marketplace is a platform that brings data producers and data consumers together; the platform itself provides the necessary infrastructure. Since producers want to maximize their revenue, while consumers want to minimize their spending, data pricing is among the central problems for a data marketplace. This paper investigates an approach in which the amount of data purchased is potentially minimized due to an indication of redundancy within the data or similarities between parts of the data. Thus, it is difficult for a buyer to decide whether all or just parts of the data should be paid for. The approach described utilizes Self-Organizing Maps and shows how they can be used to support a purchase decision.

Keywords: Data purchase · Data marketplace · Decision support · Self-organizing maps · Computational intelligence

1 Introduction

The need for highly optimized operations and decision-making has lead to an emergence of digital marketplaces specialized in the commercialization of data sets and data-related services, such as data integration, cleaning, aggregation, and analytics. Such data marketplaces connect a plethora of consumers to data providers interested in monetizing their data [5,13]. Examples of data marketplaces include Snowflake Marketplace[1] and Datarade[2]. Despite recent developments in pricing mechanisms for data products [10,15] and efficient market operations [3], little progress has been made in supporting a consumer's interest in purchasing data. More specifically, current data marketplaces give potential buyers no support for an advance evaluation of the intrinsic value of a data product

[1] https://www.snowflake.com/data-marketplace.
[2] https://about.datarade.ai.

N. T. Nguyen et al. (Eds.): ICCCI 2023, LNAI 14162, pp. 43–55, 2023.
https://doi.org/10.1007/978-3-031-41456-5_4

offered. In this work, we address this problem by leveraging the Self-Organizing Map (SOM) approach to support an informed data purchase decision.

Since data marketplaces adopt query-based pricing approaches [1,10], where the overall price depends on issued queries and the amount of data they return, customers may want to avoid buying redundant or duplicate data, i.e., paying twice for the same product. However, when inspecting data sets offered on data marketplaces, customers have little knowledge of the data that is actually provided. Indeed, to avoid disclosing the actual data for no monetary compensation, data providers obfuscate data values and provide data summaries or metadata only to the interested customer. In this scenario, there is no guarantee that customers would pay for uninformative data such as linear combinations of data attributes.

Example 1. As a first example, consider a supermarket that is interested in doing a sophisticated association-rule analysis on customer data, in order to find out what people generally tend to buy together in one stroke, at what prices and in which quantities. To this end, the supermarket is offered a huge data set of consumer and purchase data from a foreign supermarket chain. Initial inspection of the data set reveals that the data representing the quantity of items purchased looks similar to the data on item prices, besides the fact that quantities go up when prices are low. Assuming that demand is generally pretty stable and consumers just like to take advantage of bargains or special offers, the supermarket will not spend money on the entire data set, but only on either fraction of it. □

Example 2. As another example, consider a recycling company that is configuring its fleet of trucks for garbage collection. The company is interested in buying data from the nearby city on residual waste as well as on organic waste. The city sells its data together with data on plastic and paper waste, but allows obtaining the data in fractions. As it turns out, the volume produced by residual waste is almost the same as that of organic waste, so buying one of them together with the rest is sufficient to fulfill the company needs. □

To avoid situations in which the purchase of a full data set does not bring much additional information over the purchase of a part of the data set, data marketplaces would benefit from mechanisms of data inspection that would empower buyers to decide whether to invest in buying a particular data set.

The remainder of this paper is organized as follows: In Sect. 2 we summarize related work. In Sect. 3 we introduce the concept of data selection via self-organizing maps. Section 4 is about our experiments and the results obtained, and Sect. 5 concludes the paper and outlines further research.

2 Background and Related Work

2.1 Data Marketplaces

Data Marketplaces are digital platforms, often running on cloud environments, as depicted in Fig. 1. On data marketplaces, data providers and data consumers negotiate over data products (e.g., data sets) and services (e.g., integration and analytics). Data providers collect and offer data for a monetary compensation [13], whereas consumers pose several queries or system (e.g., API) calls to acquire suitable data, where each query or call incurs a monetary cost, depending on the pricing scheme adopted by the marketplace platform.

Besides the collection of data products and services offered, a central component of a data marketplace is a database management system (DBMS) that manages data sets, maintains catalogs and useful statistics, and can process incoming user queries efficiently.

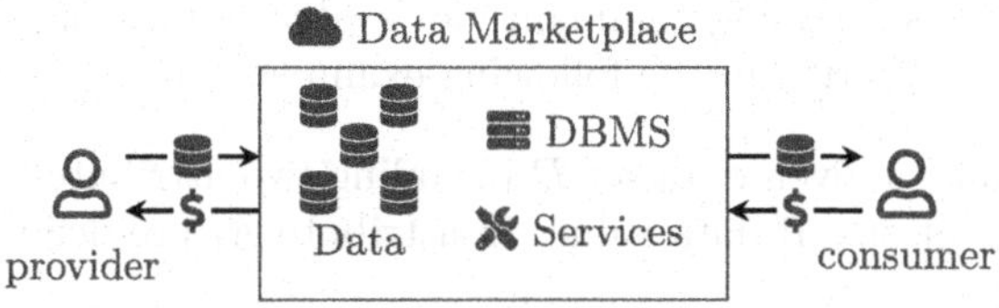

Fig. 1. Simplified structure of a data marketplace, including its main participants. Providers offer data sets for a monetary compensation, whereas consumers search for valuable data and/or data-related services (e.g., analytics and data integration). The DBMS manages all available data sets and processes incoming user queries.

Recent research on data marketplaces has focused on the design of flexible pricing models [10], especially targeting the issues of arbitrage, fairness violations, and revenue maximization. Heckman *et al.* [4] introduce a simple linear model inspired for pricing data sets as follows:

$$P(D) = \rho + \sum_{A \in attr(D)} w_A size(A) \tag{1}$$

where D is a data set and $P(D)$ its price, $attr(D)$ is a set of attributes (e.g., columns in a tabular form) in D, i.e., $attr(D) = \{A_1, A_2, \ldots, A_m\}$, $size(A)$ is the amount of data in A (e.g., number of non-*null* values), w_A is a weighting factor set by the data provider[3], and ρ is a base price factor.

Evaluating a data product for purchase involves multi-criteria decision-making that requires the consumer to understand the underlying data set (or at least what he or she is looking for). Stahl and Vossen [14] introduce the concept of a data quality score, in which a weighted sum model is employed to assess a quality-price trade-off of a data product. Under their approach, the quality score of a data set D is computed as $QS(D) = \sum_{c \in C} w_c \cdot c(D)$, where $c \in C$ is a data quality criterion function (e.g., completeness or timeliness), and w_c is a preference weight defined by the consumer over each quality criterion c such

[3] Such weighting factor can be automatically defined by leveraging available metadata (e.g., statistics, value distribution) or external aspects such as the effort of collecting the actual data.

that $\sum_{c \in C} w_c = 1$. The authors introduce a quality-for-money ratio $QM(D)$ of a data set D of price $P(D)$ as follows:

$$QM(D) = \frac{QS(D)}{P(D)}$$

The major drawback of this approach is the strong assumption that consumers do *a priori* have a complete set of quality preferences. In reality, such preferences are usually incomplete and consumers tend to learn that while inspecting data products. Even worse, many data quality criteria are just intuitive, without a formal foundation or an algorithm for efficient testing. Furthermore, such a quality score conveys insufficient guidance for evaluating which parts of the data to purchase, as we describe in the following example.

Example 3. Assume a given data set D including two attributes A_1 and A_2 and a thousand observations. If data values in attribute A_1 are defined as

$$V(A_1) = \{-1 \times a_i \mid a_i \in A_2\}$$

(similar to what we saw in Example 1), then paying for both A_1 and A_2 does not bring any new information to the customer. However, since the data provider may not disclose this relationship between A_1 and A_2 (perhaps for unfair reasons), customers may be led to purchase both attributes in hope for useful insights. □

Example 3 illustrates a case where paying for linear combinations of data attributes might harm customers. Note that leveraging data quality scores such as those proposed by Stahl and Vossen [14] does not help in situations like the one just described. For instance, quality aspects such as completeness and timeliness might be fulfilled by attribute A_1, and therefore by A_2 as well.

We argue that a visualization tool that can distinguish underlying patterns of the data can help consumers to have a better notion about data products, which may lead to a more informed purchase decision.

2.2 Self-Organizing Maps

Self-Organizing Maps or SOM for short are an early form of unsupervised neural networks introduced by Kohonen [6] for automatic data analysis and visualization. Its inspiration is derived from the structural behavior of the cerebral cortex, in which neurons located at specific regions form groups to react together to a particular type of stimuli, such as visual or auditory.

SOM is often represented as a two-layer neural network, where the first layer receives multidimensional data as input, and the output layer is organized as a two-dimensional lattice as shown in Fig. 2.

In contrast to other neural networks, such as the well-known multi-layer perceptron, SOM does not employ an error propagation learning for its training. Instead, it performs a learning procedure in which neurons compete for training data instances by adjusting their connection weights. More specifically, for each

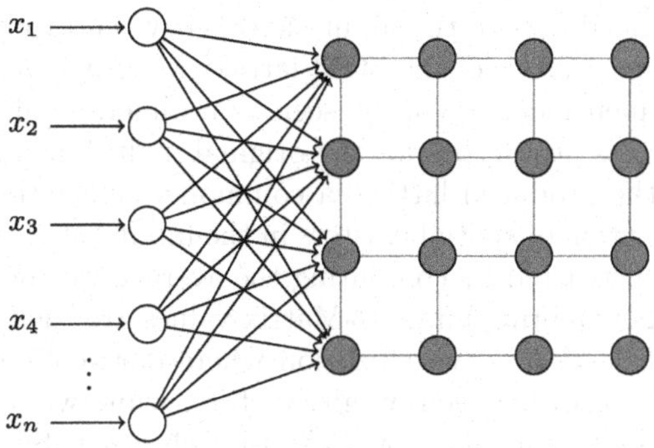

Fig. 2. General structure of a Self-Organizing Map. Multidimensional input data is organized into a lower dimensional output lattice (often in 2D). The lattice preserves the topological structure of the input data, i.e., spatial neighbors in the input space are located in spatially neighboring units in the SOM lattice.

training iteration t a data instance $\mathrm{x}(t)$ is presented to the SOM, and the neuron which provides the best match to it, with regard to a given distance metric (i.e., Euclidean distance), wins the competition. The winner neuron is referred to as *Best Matching Unit* (BMU) and has its connection weights adjusted towards $\mathrm{x}(t)$. This adjustment aims to move the BMU towards the input data in order to serve as its prototype in the SOM lattice. The learning procedure propagates such a weight adjustment to neurons surrounding the BMU via a spatial neighborhood function. In this way, nearby neurons are more likely to react to data instances similar to $\mathrm{x}(t)$, which leads to the emergence of regions in the SOM specialized to represent regions of the input space.

The original Kohonen's SOM introduced a weight adjustment function that affects both the BMU and its neighborhood towards the input data $\mathrm{x}(t)$:

$$w_i(t+1) = w_i(t) + \alpha(t) h_{c,i}(t)[\mathrm{x}(t) - \mathrm{w}_i(t)] \tag{2}$$

where w_i represents the weights of neuron i, $0 < \alpha(t) < 1$ is a monotonically decreasing learning rate function, and $h_{c,i}(t)$ is a neighborhood function centered on BMU c of training instance $\mathrm{x}(t)$. Finding the BMU c involves searching for the neuron whose weights have the smallest Euclidean distance from $\mathrm{x}(t)$, that is, $c = \arg\min_i ||\mathrm{x}(t) - \mathrm{w}_i(t)||_2$.

The spatial neighborhood function of BMU c is often defined as follows:

$$h_{c,i}(t) = e^{\frac{||r_c - r_i||_2^2}{2\sigma^2(t)}} \tag{3}$$

where r_c and r_i are, respectively, the coordinates of c and i in the SOM lattice, and $\sigma(t)$ is a monotonically decreasing function representing the wideness of the spatial neighborhood radius centered in c.

The main advantage of SOM in comparison to other unsupervised learning methods is its topographic preservation property. Indeed, the SOM lattice preserves the underlying topographic structure of the input data. That is, if two data instances are neighbors in the input space, they tend to be represented by spatially neighboring neurons of the SOM lattice. Moreover, since the SOM lattice is often two-dimensional, it can be seen as a dimensionality reduction tool where the BMU act as prototypes for the original multidimensional input data. To make sense of the produced lattice, a common visualization technique that enables the identification of spatial clusters in the input data is the *U-Matrix* [9]. The U-Matrix is constructed by computing the average weight distances among neurons and their neighboring units. U-Matrix values are then used to color the SOM lattice, which leads to a visualization where dark-colored neurons represent a large distance gap between weight vectors, while white-colored neurons correspond to weight vectors that are close to each other. Such a visualization highlights potential cluster boundaries when considering the entire input data dimensionality. Figure 3 shows the U-Matrix visualization for the well-known Iris[4] flower data set.

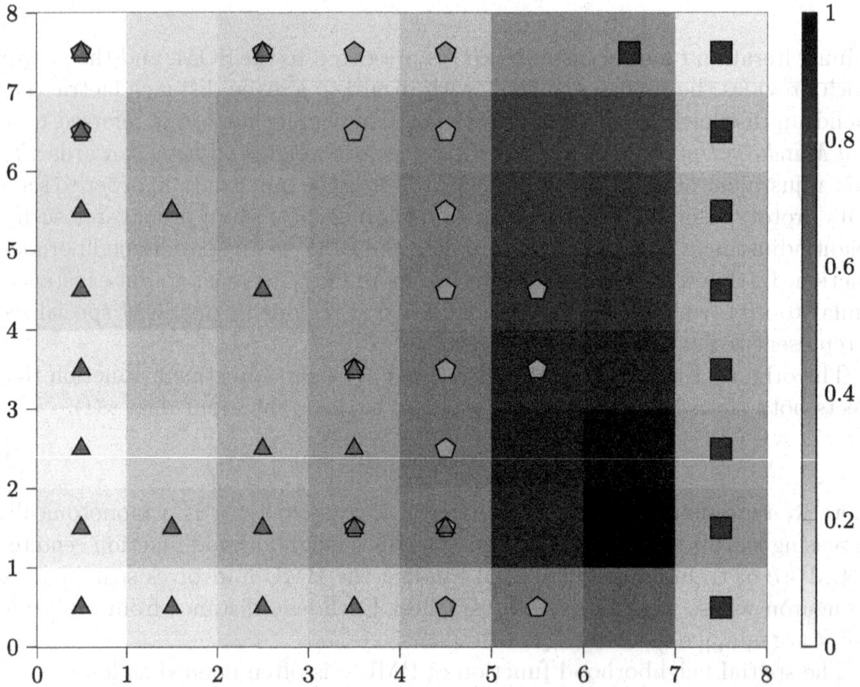

Fig. 3. U-Matrix visualization of a trained SOM over the classic Iris flower data set. The data set includes three classes: setosa (square), versicolor (pentagon), and virginica (triangle). Note that data instances of similar classes are clustered in nearby regions of the SOM lattice.

[4] Extracted from: https://archive.ics.uci.edu/ml//datasets/Iris.

Another useful visualization technique is the so-called *component plane* [6,9], which consists of plotting weight components related to each data attribute (i.e., feature) in a separate lattice. Since the BMU set is fixed after the training phase, data instances are located in the same place on each component plane. This facilitates visualizing the distribution of weight values per feature and enables an uncovering of patterns in the data, such as a potential correlation among features (i.e., by inspecting similar component planes visually). Figure 4 shows component planes for the Iris flower data set, where flowers of class *setosa* (square) tend to have high values in feature *sepal width (cm)* and low values for all the remaining features.

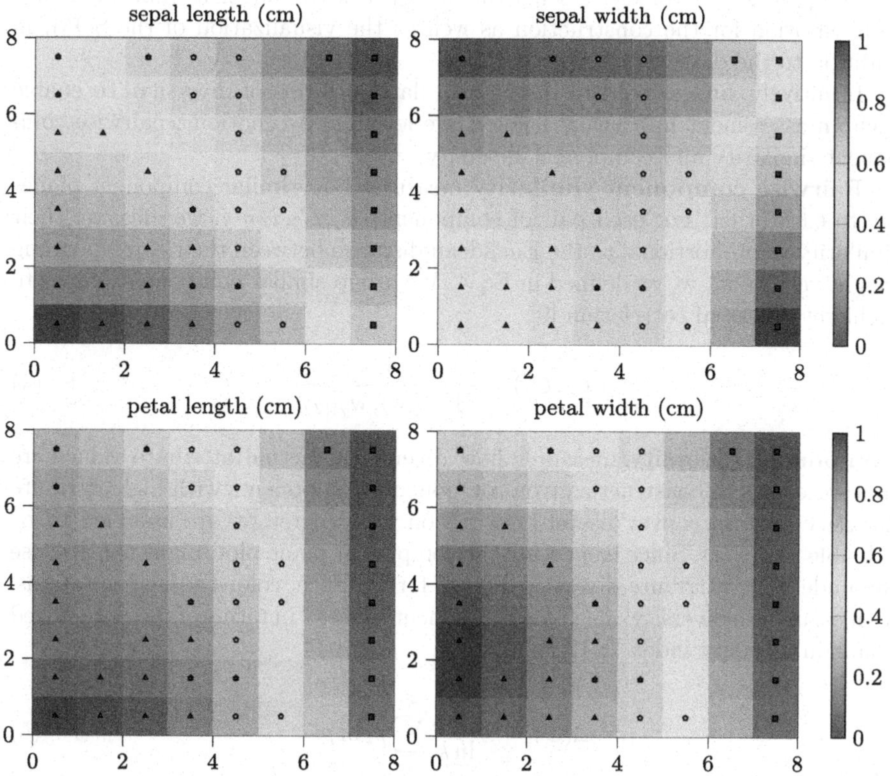

Fig. 4. SOM component planes and BMU set over the Iris flower data set.

3 Data Selection via SOM

We now exploit the SOM approach in the context of data marketplaces, in order to enable better buying decisions. We make two simplifying assumptions to leverage the central idea in this work. First, we do not consider data preprocessing tasks such as cleaning, transformation, and integration. We assume those tasks to be the responsibility of the data marketplace platform and that data sets constitute meaningful data products to be offered on the platform. Second, we assume our SOM-based approach as an additional service data providers are willing to offer as a means to attract buyers, without revealing sensitive information on the data offered for purchase.

With the preliminaries from the previous section, we can be more precise w.r.t. a buyer's goal. In terms of a SOM, a buyer could demand to be sold just the data clustered in the upper-left corner of the SOM lattice (see Definition 1). Even more to the point, a buyer could request to just get features with diverse component planes, which requires deriving a series of indicators to differentiate the planes. Conversely, a seller might now ask the buyer a small monetary compensation for the construction as well as the visualization of the SOM, in addition to the data set of interest.

Intuitively, buyers tend to distinguish data in terms of diversity. To enable such an assessment in a visual fashion, we leverage two notions: pairwise component similarity and component diversity:

Pairwise component similarity measures how similar component planes are to each other. For each pair of components $C_i, C_j, i \neq j$, we measure their similarity as proportional to the Euclidean distance between their corresponding weight vectors $\mathrm{w}_i, \mathrm{w}_j$ as defined in Eq. 4. We group similar component planes to highlight potential correlation [9].

$$\delta(C_i, C_j) = \frac{1}{(1 + ||\mathrm{w}_i, \mathrm{w}_j||_2)} \tag{4}$$

Component diversity measures how diverse the actual attribute values are that were used to construct a given component. Components with high attribute diversity tend to convey useful information and, therefore, are assumed to be valuable to buyers. Since inspecting the component plane plot might not disclose the underlying attribute diversity due to, for instance, color-coding limitations, we measure the diversity of a given component plane C in terms of the normalized Shannon diversity index [2,12]:

$$\Delta(C) = -\frac{1}{\ln k} \sum_{i}^{k} p_i \ln p_i \tag{5}$$

where k is the number of unique attribute values in the data attribute corresponding to component C, and p_i is the probability of each attribute value i.

Additionally, buyers are likely to focus on a particular *region of interest*, where weight values show a particular pattern or distribution (see Fig. 6 for an example):

Definition 1 (Region of Interest). *Given a SOM lattice with M neurons, a region of interest is a set $R = \{u_i | 1 \leq i \leq M\}$, where u_i represents a neuron.*

Naturally, training and visualizing a SOM involves additional computation costs that the seller (either the data provider or the data marketplace orchestrator) intends to be compensated for. Training cost depends on (1) the number of observations in the data, (2) the number of training epochs, and (3) the number of neurons in the output lattice (see Eq. 2), whereas visualization costs vary with the number of attributes in the data (e.g., the number of component planes to be produced).

SOM Training and Visualization Cost. For a given data set D, the cost of training and visualizing a two-dimensional SOM network S composed by M neurons over T training epochs is:

$$P_S(D, T, M) = w_D \cdot \log(size(D)) + \log(T \cdot M) \tag{6}$$

where $size(D)$ is the number of observations in the data, and w_D is a weighting factor that accounts for the part of the data that is revealed by the component plane visualization. For the sake of fairness, we envision data marketplaces to set $w_D \in [0.01, 0.05]$.

We now accommodate this into the original pricing scheme of Eq. 1 to obtain an enhanced pricing scheme for SOM-based data purchase decision-making support. Hence, the price of data within a region of interest $R \subseteq D$ over a set $\mathcal{C}$ of component planes is computed as:

$$P(R, \mathcal{C}, T, M) = \rho + \sum_{A \in \mathcal{C}} w_A \cdot size(R) + P_S(D, T, M) \tag{7}$$

4 Experiment and Result

In this section, we describe our experimental design to show how our approach can be applied to data marketplaces to support buyers. We use the 1994 US Census[5] data set extracted from the UCI Machine Learning Repository. The data set is publicly available and includes 48,842 data observations and 14 attributes.

In order to apply SOM on the data set, we transform categorical values into numerical ones using the one-hot encoding technique. That is, given a categorical attribute A with n unique values, we construct a sparse vector of size n where all elements are set to zero, except the one corresponding to the n-th attribute value. For simplicity, we discard data observations with missing values, which results in a data set including 32,561 observations and 90 numerical features.

Moreover, since SOM training requires computing the Euclidean distance between data vectors and weight vectors, we normalize attribute values such that all input values fed to the network are within the range $[0, 1]$.

We use the SOM implementation provided by the Python library MiniSOM [17]. For both data sets, we use a rectangular topology and set the horizontal and vertical dimensions of the SOM lattice as the lengths of the two largest principal components, as described in [7]. This leads to 1056 neurons distributed

[5] Extracted from: https://archive.ics.uci.edu/ml/datasets/Adult.

over a rectangular lattice of dimension 24×44. We also use the principal components to initialize neuron weights. We train the network in batch mode [6] during 10,000 epochs, with a starting learning rate of 0.5 and a neighborhood radius as half of the highest lattice dimension. The source code and analysis used in this work is available at https://github.com/denmartins/som4datapurchase.

Following the pricing scheme introduced in Sect. 3, and setting parameter $w_D = 0.01$, training and visualization costs amount to:

$$P_S = 0.01 \cdot \log(32,561) \cdot \log(10,000 \cdot 1056) \approx 1.68.$$

Figure 5 shows component planes produced for the data set. Due to the large dimensionality of the preprocessed data (i.e., 90 features) we only show a few component planes. Above each component, we show the corresponding data attribute (i.e., feature) along with its diversity index. Similar components are shown close to each other to facilitate visual analysis. Purple dots denote the BMU of the data observations, as described in Sect. 2.

By inspecting the component planes produced, buyers directly find that attributes `capitalgain` and `capitalloss` have very low diversity, which means that data values are expected to contain similar values along all data observations. This situation occurs similarly in component plane `raceOther`. Moreover, comparing components of the *race* attribute, one can clearly see that data observations of `raceWhite` tend to dominate. Buyers may find this information useful, in particular when their target application involves training Machine Learning models, since underrepresenting minorities in the data tend to yield biased[6] and unfair models [16]. As a result, buyers may avoid buying these attributes or even search for another data set.

Additionally, buyers can readily spot a few potential correlations that might be interesting for their target applications. For instance, a particular region of interest shown in Fig. 6 depicts data observations where high education level (i.e., `educationnum`) tend to be clustered at medium to high values of `age`.

[6] Bias and fairness issues in data systems have serious societal impact. A recent study [8] over US hospitals revealed that black patients are less likely to be selected by software-based decisions for medical care.

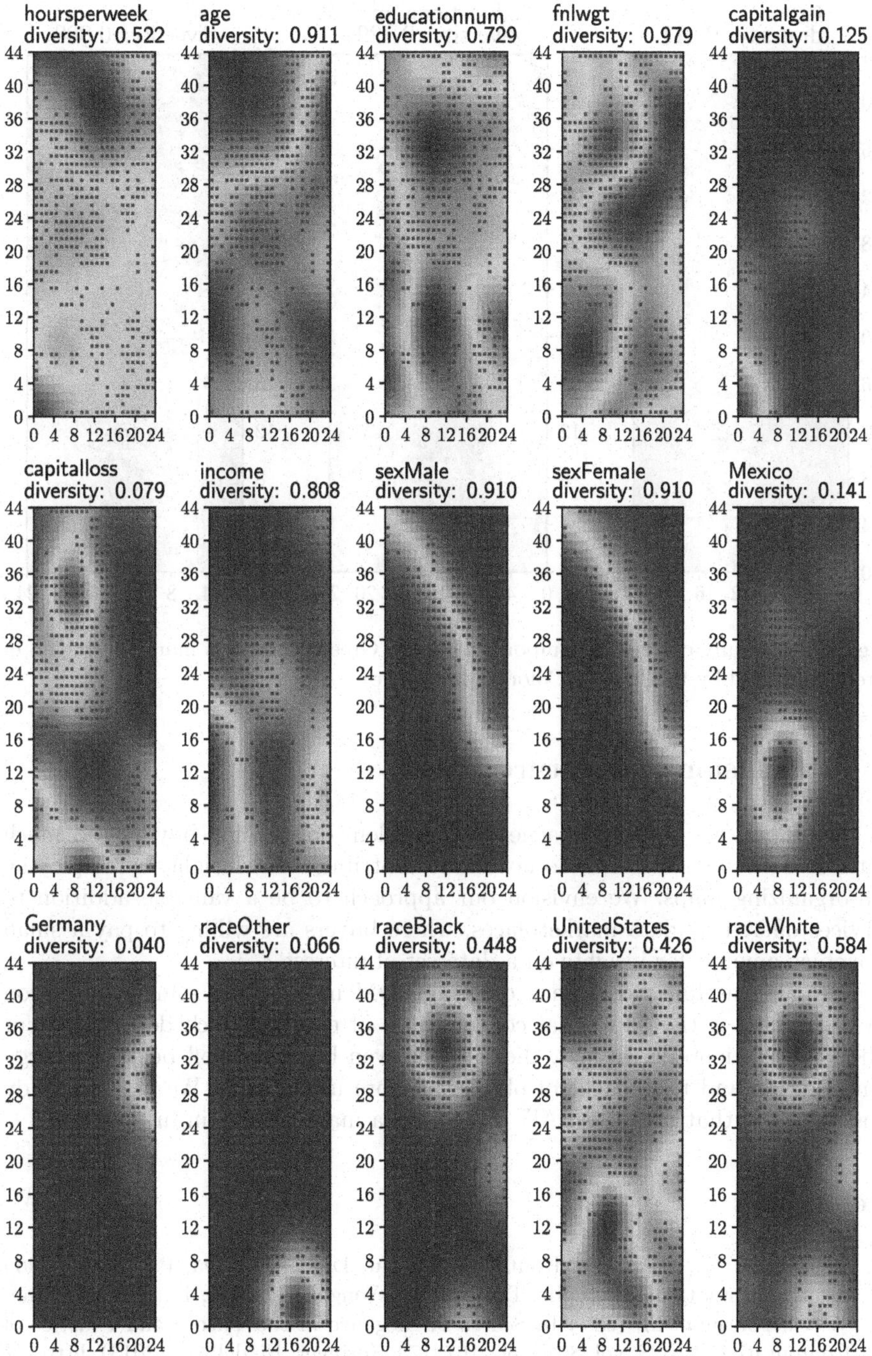

Fig. 5. Component planes over the 1994 US Census data set. Similar components are grouped using the Euclidean distance between their vectors of neuron weight. The diversity above each plot is computed as in Eq. 5. The produced SOM lattice is rectangular with dimensions 24×44.

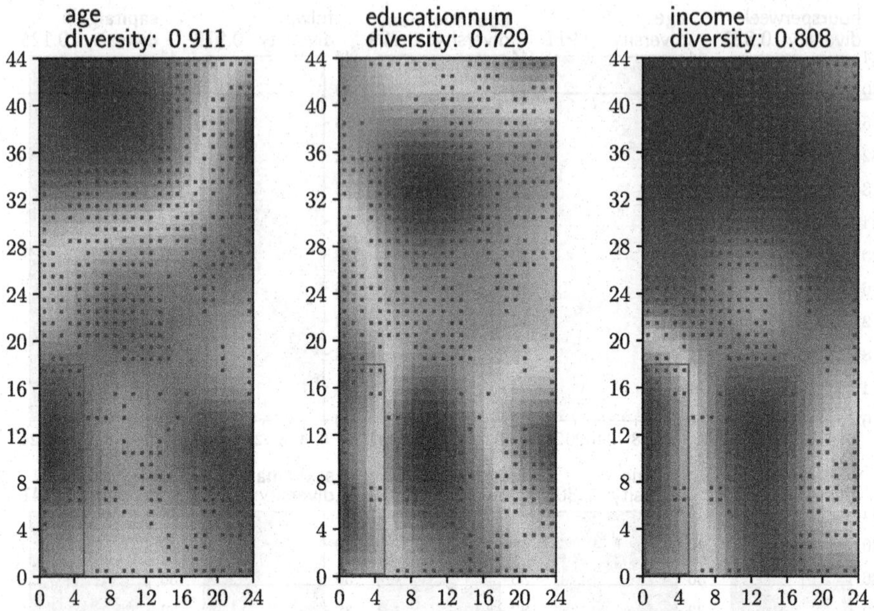

Fig. 6. Potentially correlated component planes. Green rectangles mark the region of interest selected by the buyer. (Color figure online)

5 Conclusion and Future Work

In this paper, we have approached the problem of avoiding buying too much data, or data parts of which do not really contribute new insight, by employing self-organizing maps. We envision our approach to be a valuable addition to services offered by data marketplaces, where buyers are willing to pay a small monetary amount for insights on a data set of interest.

Although useful, a drawback of using SOM in revealing some information on a data set is the additional consumption of energy, which does not occur when SOM is ignored. In fact, there might even be a trade-off between energy consumption and the benefit of obtaining more useful data. We plan to study this issue and that of "Green AI" [11] for data marketplaces in future work.

References

1. Balazinska, M., Howe, B., Koutris, P., Suciu, D., Upadhyaya, P.: A discussion on pricing relational data. In: Tannen, V., Wong, L., Libkin, L., Fan, W., Tan, W.-C., Fourman, M. (eds.) In Search of Elegance in the Theory and Practice of Computation. LNCS, vol. 8000, pp. 167–173. Springer, Heidelberg (2013). https://doi.org/10.1007/978-3-642-41660-6_7
2. Del Core, L., et al.: Normalization of clonal diversity in gene therapy studies using shape constrained splines. Sci. Rep. **12**(1), 3836 (2022)

3. Fernandez, R.C., Subramaniam, P., Franklin, M.J.: Data market platforms: trading data assets to solve data problems. Proc. VLDB Endow. **13**(12), 1933–1947 (2020). https://doi.org/10.14778/3407790.3407800
4. Heckman, J.R., Boehmer, E.L., Peters, E.H., Davaloo, M., Kurup, N.G.: A pricing model for data markets. In: iConference 2015 Proceedings (2015)
5. Kennedy, J., Subramaniam, P., Galhotra, S., Castro Fernandez, R.: Revisiting online data markets in 2022: a seller and buyer perspective. SIGMOD Rec. **51**(3), 30–37 (2022). https://doi.org/10.1145/3572751.3572757
6. Kohonen, T.: Self-Organizing Maps. Springer Series in Information Sciences, 3rd edn. Springer, Heidelberg (2001). https://doi.org/10.1007/978-3-642-56927-2
7. Kohonen, T.: Essentials of the self-organizing map. Neural Netw. **37**, 52–65 (2013). https://doi.org/10.1016/j.neunet.2012.09.018
8. Ledford, H.: Millions of black people affected by racial bias in health-care algorithms. Nature **574**(7780), 608–610 (2019)
9. Nagar, D., Ramu, P., Deb, K.: Visualization and analysis of pareto-optimal fronts using interpretable self-organizing map (iSOM). Swarm Evol. Comput. **76**, 101202 (2023). https://doi.org/10.1016/j.swevo.2022.101202
10. Pei, J.: A survey on data pricing: from economics to data science. IEEE Trans. Knowl. Data Eng. **34**(10), 4586–4608 (2022). https://doi.org/10.1109/TKDE.2020.3045927
11. Schwartz, R., Dodge, J., Smith, N.A., Etzioni, O.: Green AI. Commun. ACM **63**(12), 54–63 (2020). https://doi.org/10.1145/3381831
12. Shannon, C.E.: A mathematical theory of communication. Bell Syst. Tech. J. **27**(3), 379–423 (1948). https://doi.org/10.1002/j.1538-7305.1948.tb01338.x
13. Stahl, F., Schomm, F., Vomfell, L., Vossen, G.: Marketplaces for digital data: Quo Vadis? Comput. Inf. Sci. **10**(4), 22–37 (2017). https://doi.org/10.5539/cis.v10n4p22
14. Stahl, F., Vossen, G.: Data quality scores for pricing on data marketplaces. In: Nguyen, N.T., Trawiński, B., Fujita, H., Hong, T.-P. (eds.) ACIIDS 2016. LNCS (LNAI), vol. 9621, pp. 215–224. Springer, Heidelberg (2016). https://doi.org/10.1007/978-3-662-49381-6_21
15. Stahl, F., Vossen, G.: Fair knapsack pricing for data marketplaces. In: Pokorný, J., Ivanović, M., Thalheim, B., Šaloun, P. (eds.) ADBIS 2016. LNCS, vol. 9809, pp. 46–59. Springer, Cham (2016). https://doi.org/10.1007/978-3-319-44039-2_4
16. Tolan, S.: Fair and unbiased algorithmic decision making: current state and future challenges. CoRR abs/1901.04730 (2019). http://arxiv.org/abs/1901.04730
17. Vettigli, G.: Minisom: minimalistic and numpy-based implementation of the self organizing map (2018). https://github.com/JustGlowing/minisom/

Agent Based Model of Elementary School Group Learning – A Case Study

Barbara Wędrychowicz(✉) and Marcin Maleszka

Wroclaw University of Science and Technology, st. Wyspianskiego 27, 50-370 Wroclaw, Poland
{barbara.wedrychowicz,marcin.maleszka}@pwr.edu.pl

Abstract. The paper described an agent-based model that simulate group work of elementary school children. It imitates students' characteristics and behaviours most frequently found in pedagogical literature about active and group learning. The model main objective is to forecast the change in the student's knowledge. We simulated and compared knowledge changes during individual learning and cooperative learning with different group composition. The observation of real students was carried out and compared to the outcomes of the simulations. The results are discussed in the context of improving the model by adding previously not included students' characteristics and behaviours.

Keywords: Agent based modeling · Teaching model · Group modeling · Multi-agent simulation

1 Introduction

Working in group is a very popular method used in school as it is a simple way to introduce active learning to a larger group of students. There are indications that the appropriate selection of members in the group can affect the increase and speed of acquisition of student's knowledge [1].

The education system – students behaviours, collaboration among peers and cooperation between students and teacher creates complex and changeable environment. Each student can be described with a similar set of features, yet to reflect this domain reliably, the small differences between individual students should be taken into account. Each of the students is an individual that has its own characteristics and a specific goal to pursue - in most cases it is the acquisition of as much knowledge as possible [2]. Students form groups and use their individual characteristics and skills to achieve a common goal – knowledge acquisition.

Multi-agent systems consist of individual agents existing in a common environment and interacting with each other to solve a specific problem or achieve a given goal [3]. Agents, like physical students, are able to independently decide what actions to take to achieve the specified goal. Since the operations of agents works in a similar way to the operation of the real students, the multiagent system is a suitable tool to present the model and conduct the simulation of student's behaviour during dividing into group and cooperative learning.

N. T. Nguyen et al. (Eds.): ICCCI 2023, LNAI 14162, pp. 56–67, 2023.
https://doi.org/10.1007/978-3-031-41456-5_5

The work described here expands earlier related work [4] – study of the impact of group composition based on students' characteristics and group size on the increase in their knowledge based on multiagent simulation. Furthermore, it describes an attempt to apply the model in a real school environment.

The rest of this paper is organized in the following way: next section presents the literature overview of active learning, group learning and student's characteristic that have impact on the students learning. Then the model of elementary school group learning, and its simulations are described. Next sections present the new results and the outline of future work.

2 Related Works

2.1 Active Learning

Currently, interest in different methods of learning and teaching is very high. In schools, it is recommended to abandon teaching in form of traditional lectures and instead adapt teaching methods to individual classes and specific groups of students. The process of learning and knowledge acquisition is the research field in various fields of science. Pedagogical literature contains different theories of human learning and knowledge acquisition. The term active learning is very popular among the pedagogical researchers. Most of them acknowledge that the active learning is a very efficient way for knowledge acquisition [5, 6]. Learning process where students become active participants allow them to develop their skills, knowledge, and personal values more efficiently [7].

According to Prince [6], one of the types of active learning is group learning, which, in most cases, is efficient, as provides the opportunities to cooperate with peers. Two types of group learning can be distinguished: collaborative learning and cooperative learning. Both terms describe the process of learning together in small groups to achieve common goal. While the key element in the collaborative learning is the interaction between learners, the main part of cooperative learning is the effect of the result of cooperation where each student is assessed individually. Based in these definitions and the specifics of school environment, these terms will be used interchangeably.

Slavin's [8] approach to cooperative learning suggest that through working together, debate and discussions, students motivate one another to increase their knowledge. Also, the collaboration during group learning could create higher quality solutions than those created by individuals.

The pattern of correlated relationships between each of the elements of the model (see Fig. 1) starts with focusing attention on group and individual goals, and then encouraging students to cooperate. This means that the model assumes that the motivation to work in a group and to encourage and help others in learning strengthens one's own motivation to improve and acquire new knowledge. The resulting motivation includes both the motivation to perform tasks (learning) and the motivation to interact in a group. In this model, the motivation to cooperate leads directly to increased learning, and supports behaviours and attitudes that lead to better cooperation in the group, which in turn facilitates interaction within the group [8].

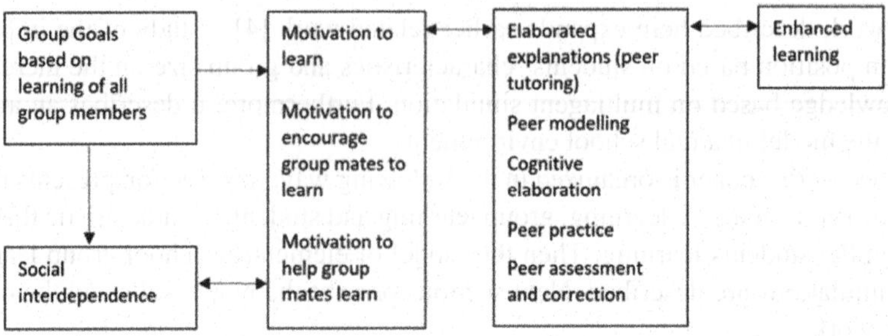

Fig. 1. Functional relationship among the major interaction components of group learning [8]

2.2 Three Phases of Learning

According to Shuell [9], just as the learning environment is complex and consists of many elements, the learning process itself is extensive. At the beginning, the student relies only on the information obtained. Usually, new facts are separated from the rest of the student's knowledge, and only over time are connections made to combine the new knowledge with the one student already have. The more time student devotes to learning and the more active it is, the faster associations are formed, and new knowledge is better absorbed. Only later the student is ready to use the newly acquired knowledge to expand and use it to gain and assimilate further new information. Shuell describes this phenomenon as three phases of learning:

- Initial Phase - the phase that student gain new facts and information.
- Intermediate Phase – the phase that student creates connections and relations between new information and knowledge he already possesses.
- Terminal Phase – the phase where student has understood and assimilated the data and is ready to use them as a knowledge.

2.3 Peers Tutoring

It seems that the most optimal way of knowledge transfer is a meeting of two people: more and less competent in the subject of a given task, and thus the creation of a student-teacher relationship. A professional teacher has the competence and the necessary knowledge to consciously transfer knowledge. However, it turns out that asking a teacher for assistance is far more challenging for a student than asking a peer whose level of knowledge is not much higher than his own [10].

It is also found that children do not have specific expectations regarding to the effectiveness of knowledge sharing. They also have more patience in interacting with students who are struggling to understand the content [11].

The transfer of knowledge in the student-student relationship is referred to as tutoring, which according to Topping can be defined as: "more able students helping less able students to learn in co-operative working pairs or small groups carefully organised by a professional teacher" [12].

According to Schaffer [13], student's interactions in the field of sharing and acquiring knowledge can take two different forms:

- collaborative learning - children who are at the same level work together in pairs or in larger groups,
- peer tutoring – children with more knowledge begin to give advice and guidance to other children – thanks to such activities, they are able to bring other students closer to a similar level of knowledge.

2.4 Student's Characteristic

According to some experts [14], dividing students according to their skills typically has a weak but beneficial effect on the level of cooperation and the growth of their knowledge. Compared to many other elements, such as active learning or learning with new technology, the influence is much lower but still exist. The quality and speed of learning might occasionally even decrease as a result of improper group structure.

Luttmer [15] assumes that some people acquire new knowledge easier than others. During working in group, it sometimes turns out that recognizing who is the most knowledgeable is obvious but learning from this person is more difficult and requires more time and effort than learning from a person with less knowledge but higher communication skills. His approach also assumes that individuals with high knowledge and high interest in the subject learn faster. At the same time, a high interest in the subject increases the probability of sharing the knowledge with other students.

Varying degrees of these students' characteristics result in various possible methods for approaching group work and creating groups. Groups can be formed by dividing students based on their characteristics. Different levels of these attributes of different students lead to different approaches to groupwork. Selecting students by these parameters could be a basis for group formation. Currently the most common methods of dividing students into groups are to let them get into groups on their own or done it randomly.

3 Proposed Group Model

The model uses the characteristics and behaviours of students that are most commonly found in pedagogical literature about learning and cooperating in a group. As the previous sections suggest, the school system is very complex, therefore the implementation only takes into account the main parts related to the acquisition of knowledge during group work. The model consists of the two elements – environment and agents.

The environment represents a classroom where students can cooperate and learn. Students are allowed to divide into groups, gain new knowledge, and share their existing knowledge. In this model, the learning action illustrates the second phase - the Intermediate Phase of learning, in which students try to make connections and relationships between the information and the knowledge they already possess, leading to an increase in their knowledge.

The moment of transferring knowledge between the teacher and the student (Initial Phase of learning) was intentionally omitted. In the case of the described model, the characteristics of the teacher do not affect the student's knowledge. It is assumed that students who started dividing into groups has participated in the introduction to the lesson, where the basic facts and tasks for working in groups were presented When students begin the process of finding and forming groups, they have some, varying levels of knowledge. Learning in a group usually begins with some, in most cases, a small level of prior knowledge. However, according to [16], there may be students whose level of knowledge is high from the very beginning.

In the described model there is only one type of agents - agents representing students. According to the cited literature, each agent is described by a set of features that have been indicated in the pedagogical literature as having an impact on the acquisition of knowledge, transfer of knowledge and interactions with peers. The following features have been selected:

- Communicativeness (C) – a rating of student's communication skills;
- LeaderPotential (L) – a rating of student's ability to lead the group in some tasks;
- Interest (I) – a rating of student's interest in the topic;
- Ease (E) – a rating of student's ease of learning for the specific topic.

The previous described model has been adapted to the real group of students. Some more characteristics have been added:

- Group (G) – the code of student's group. Identify the students who worked together;
- KnowledgeBeforeTeacher (KBT) – a rating of student's knowledge after theoretical introduction, before working in group rated by teacher;
- KnowledgeAfterTeacher (KAT) – a rating of student's knowledge after working in group rated by teacher.

The students were described by those attributes subjectively by their teacher, sample data can be found in Table 1. Then, based on the observed data, formulas describing actions performed by agents were adapted – Eqs. (1) and (2). In the previous related paper [4], a more detailed description of that model could be found.

Increase of knowledge of the student [4]:

$$knowledgelevel = 0.866 \cdot easy\_learning + 1.096 \cdot interest \tag{1}$$

Knowledge that the student could share with others [4]:

$$\begin{aligned} &extra\_knowledge = \\ &-1.375 - 0.398 \cdot knowledgelevel + 0.966 \cdot communicativeness\_other \\ &+1.096 \cdot interest\_other \end{aligned} \tag{2}$$

Table 1. Selected data of Students' characteristics during working in groups.

C	*L*	*I*	*E*	*KBT*	*KAT*
2	5	5	1	4	8
4	5	1	3	4	8
5	4	4	3	4	8
0	5	3	0	1	4
1	2	4	2	4	6
5	4	0	0	0	2
2	3	3	3	3	6
3	3	2	2	2	4
4	0	2	4	4	7
4	0	3	3	3	8
4	1	4	2	2	7
4	4	1	5	4	7
5	5	5	2	2	6
0	5	0	5	0	4
2	2	1	3	3	8
2	5	2	3	2	4
3	1	1	2	2	3
1	2	2	4	1	4
2	2	2	3	5	6
5	4	1	1	1	9
3	0	3	5	7	8
3	5	2	4	5	7
4	3	2	3	1	5
3	4	2	3	5	8
5	3	5	3	5	9

4 Simulation

Discrete simulation is used to execute and analyse the simulation, with each simulation corresponding to one minute of classroom time (in Polish elementary school, a single class between periods lasts 45 min). When working in group, the group formation lasts between the 17th and 20th min (cycle) of class time, after that the students start learning [4]. The GAMA platform, which is an environment for agent-based simulations, was used. It enables both the presentation of the results in numerical form as well as the graphic display of the simulation.

During the simulation, agents, like real students move around the environment (classroom) to form a group. Depending on the size of the target group, the agents move around the environment to find another agent in close proximity - they form a pair, and then start moving again looking for the next unpaired agent to join their group. When a group or a pair meet another group, and the number of people in both groups does not exceed the set number of people in the group, they merge into one group. Only after the groups are created, students start learning.

Therefore, the current simulation represents the second hour of the lesson (the second 45 min) - it is assumed that during the first hour the students were provided with the basic information and facts and the division into groups took place. Thus, the second hour of lesson represents the learning process itself. Students start the second stage of learning with the initial knowledge and belonging to a given group.

Based on that model, the series of simulations were conducted to try to determine the best group composition for students' knowledge increase. Then the obtained results were compared with the previously observed real description of the students. Afterwards the simulation results were compared to the real student description (Table 2).

Table 2. Example of the students' characteristics within one group. The group consist of the students with similar characteristics medium ease of learn, interest, and communicativeness level.

	easy_learning(E)	group_name(G)	interest(I)	leadership(L)	communicativeness(C)
student0	3	1	3	3	2
student1	2	1	2	3	3
student2	4	1	2	0	4
student3	3	1	3	0	4

Table 3 shows the results of the simulation comparing student's knowledge increase during individual learning, learning in group of 4 students and observations of real student. Additional table attributes show:

- KBT – a rating of real student's knowledge after theoretical introduction, before working in group, rated by teacher;
- KBS - a rating of student's knowledge after theoretical introduction, before working in group, calculated in the model;
- KAT - a rating of real student's knowledge after working in group rated by teacher after 45 min of lesson;
- KAS0 - a rating of student's knowledge after 25 min (25 cycles) of individual working, observe in the simulation.
- KAS1 - a rating of student's knowledge after 45 min (45 cycles) of individual working, observe in the simulation.
- KAS2 - a rating of student's knowledge after working in group for 25 min (25 cycles), observe in the simulation.

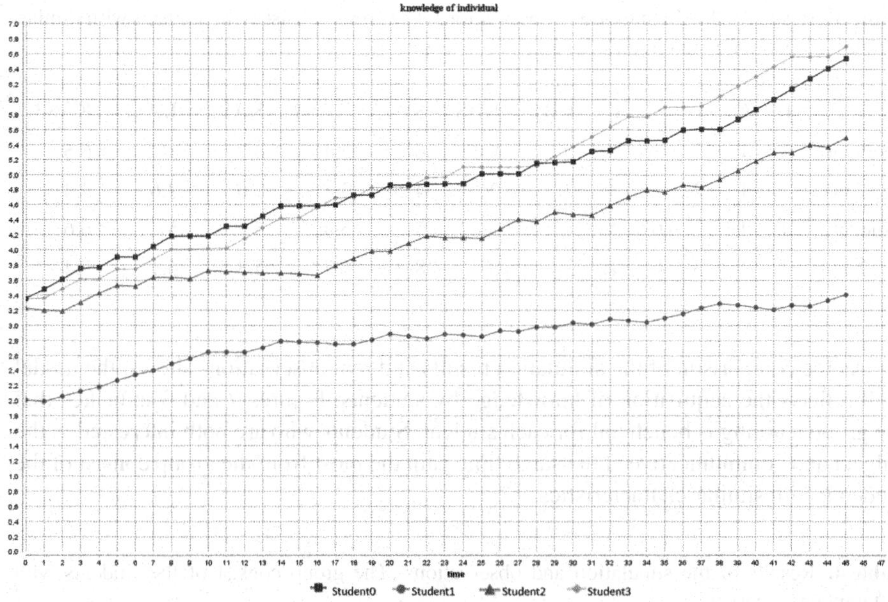

Fig. 2. Increase of knowledge during individual learning.

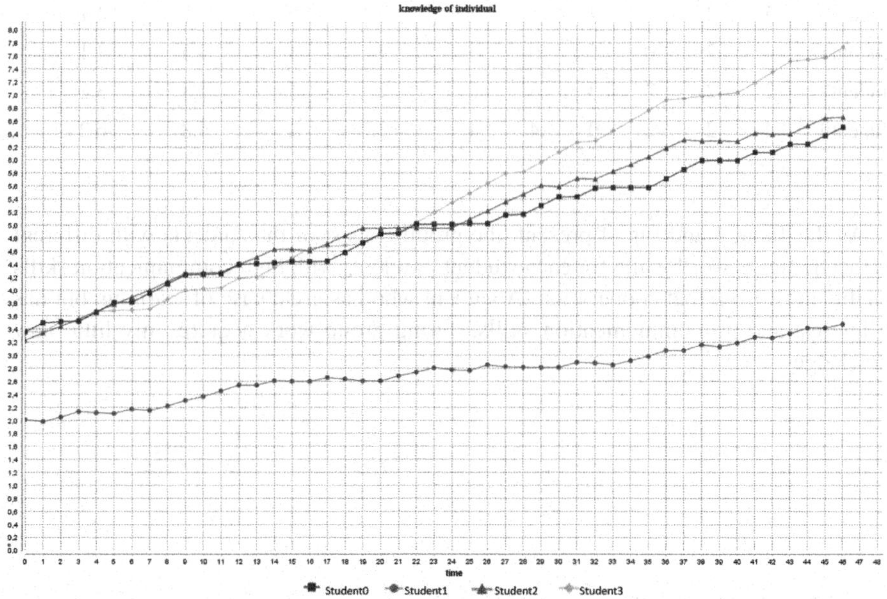

Fig. 3. Increase of knowledge during learning in group of 4. Students with similar characteristics.

- KAS3 - a rating of student's knowledge after working in group for 45 min (45 cycles), observe in the simulation.

Table 3. Results of the simulation and observations. The group consist of the students with similar, medium ease of learn and interest level.

	E	G	I	L	C	KBT	KBS	KAT	KAS0	KAS1	KAS2	KAS3
student0	3	1	3	3	2	3	3.2	6	5.4	4.7	4	6.5
student1	2	1	2	3	3	2	2	4	3.4	2.6	2.6	3.4
student2	4	1	2	0	4	4	3.4	7	6.4	5	5	6.6
student3	3	1	3	0	4	3	3.4	8	6.7	5.3	5.1	7.4

As the comparison of the simulation results and real observations shows, the model well reflects the acquisition of knowledge by students. Figures 2 and 3 indicates that the group learning is beneficial for each student. Students who are both interested in the subject and communicative at the same time gain the most from the group consist of the students with similar characteristics.

Table 4. Results of the simulation and observations. The group consist of the students with different characteristics.

	E	G	I	L	C	KBT	KBS	KAT	KAS2	KAS3
student0	5	2	1	4	4	3	3.1	4	3.7	4.1
student1	6	2	0	5	0	3	3	4	3.5	4.1
student2	2	2	2	3	3	2	2	3	2.8	3.2
student3	4	2	2	0	4	4	3.2	4	4.8	6.2

As the Table 4 and Fig. 4 present, the group consist of the students with different characteristics is worthwhile for each student. Students with high communication skills benefits most from that cooperation. A student who has great ease of learning, but has no interest and no communication skills, during group work acquire only little new knowledge.

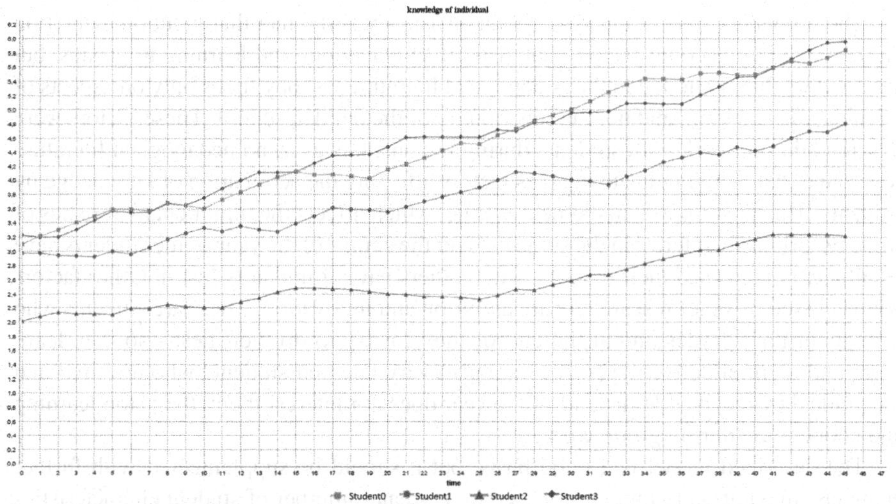

Fig. 4. Increase of knowledge during learning in group of 4. Students with different characteristics.

5 Conclusions

The model described earlier well reflected a specific group of students, its prediction of knowledge growth coincided with the teacher's observations. Real students and agents with similar characteristics achieved a similar increase in knowledge. Based on the given parameters, it was possible to predict which composition of the group of students would work best.

An attempt to apply the model to the same group of people but at a different time of the school year did not bring satisfactory results. The Table 5 shows the model simulation results and the data observed by the teacher. The initial knowledge level observed by the teacher (KBT) and the initial knowledge level determined by the model (KBS) are still similar, however, the increase of knowledge after working in a group (KAT, KAS3) differs significantly.

Table 5. Results of the simulation and new observations of the students. The group consist of the students with similar, high ease of learn and interest level.

	E	G	I	L	C	KBT	KBS	KAT	KAS2	KAS3
student0	3	1	4	4	5	4	4.2	6	7.7	9.4
student1	3	1	3	3	2	3	3.4	7	6.3	7.5
student2	2	1	2	3	3	2	2	4	5.2	6
student3	5	1	3	0	3	5	4.6	5	2.7	3.2

The probable cause of the model's inconsistency is the fact that its implementation did not take into account factors that also affect behaviour and learning in groups, but are not directly mentioned in the pedagogical literature, as they focus only on aspects of learning and teaching, and not the functioning of the child at school. These factors were observed during work with students during lessons, however, no pedagogical literature was found that would indicate them as factors affecting the acquisition of knowledge by students. The most important element is time, which affects the minor characteristics of students, primarily interest in the subject. Over the course of the year, some students have significantly increased their interest, while others have completely lost it. Other factors not discussed by other researchers are ambition and motivation. There are students who care about their grades and at the end of the year try to do their best - so they learn more and more effectively, yet there are also very talented students who are tired and the grade they received at the end of the year does not interest them, they stop learning and cooperating during group work.

The described model is a good basis, but it should be supplemented with further elements. In addition to taking into account a greater number of student characteristics (ambition and motivation), the variability of other characteristics over time will be taken into account in future research. Additionally, we will consider adding another type of agent - a teacher who will have an active part in the first (omitted here) phase of learning - the Initial Phase.

The outlined model can also serve as a solid foundation for a more general model that will allow to present the overall process of learning and knowledge spreading among group members.

References

1. Burke, A.: Group work: how to use groups effectively. J. Effect. Teach. V **11**(2), 87–95 (2011)
2. Berliner, D.C., Rosenshine, B.: The acquisition of knowledge in the classroom. In: Schooling and the Acquisition of Knowledge, pp. 375–396. Routledge (2017)
3. Balaji, P.G., Srinivasan, D.: An introduction to multi-agent systems. In: Srinivasan, D., Jain, L.C. (eds.) Innovations in Multi-agent Systems and Applications-1. SCI, vol. 310, pp. 1–27. Springer, Heidelberg (2010). https://doi.org/10.1007/978-3-642-14435-6_1
4. Wedrychowicz, B., Maleszka, M., Nguyen, V.S.: Agent based model of elementary school group learning. In: Szczerbicki, E., Wojtkiewicz, K., Nguyen, S.V., Pietranik, M., Krótkiewicz, M. (eds.) ACIIDS 2022. CCIS, vol. 1716, pp. 697–710. Springer, Singapore (2022). https://doi.org/10.1007/978-981-19-8234-7_54
5. Sivan, A., Leung, R.W., Woon, C.C., Kember, D.: An implementation of active learning and its effect on the quality of student learning. Innov. Educ. Train. Int. **37**(4), 381–389 (2000)
6. Prince, M.J.: Does active learning work? A review of the research. J. Eng. Educ. **93**(3), 223–231 (2004)
7. Bonwell, C.C., Eison, J.A.: Active learning: creating excitement in the classroom. 1991 ASHE-ERIC higher education reports. ERIC Clearinghouse on Higher Education, The George Washington University, One Dupont Circle, Suite 630, Washington, DC 20036-1183 (1991)
8. Slavin, R.: Cooperative Learning: Theory, Research and Practice. Allyn and Bacon, Boston (1990)
9. Shuell, T.J.: Phases of meaningful learning. Rev. Educ. Res. **60**(4), 531–547 (1990)

10. Carino, P.: Power and authority in peer tutoring. In: The Center will Hold: Critical Perspectives on Writing Center Scholarship, pp. 96–113 (2003)
11. Ehly, S.W., Larsen, S.C.: Peer tutoring to individualize instruction. Elementary Sch. J. **76**(8), 475–480 (1976)
12. Topping, K.J.: The effectiveness of peer tutoring in further and higher education: a typology and review of the literature. High. Educ. **32**(3), 321–345 (1996)
13. Schaffer, H.R.: Psychologia dziecka. Wydawnictwo Naukowe PWN, Warszawa (2009)
14. Dolata, R.: Czy segregacja uczniow ze wzgledu na uprzednie osiagniecia szkolne zwieksza efektywnosc nauczania mierzona metoda EWD?. In: XIV Konferencja Diagnostyki, Opole (2008)
15. Luttmer, E.: Four Models of Knowledge Diffusion and Growth. Federal Reserve Bank of Minneapolis (2015)
16. Lizcano-Dallos, A.R., Vargas-Daza, M., Barbosa-Chacón, J.W.: Collaborative learning and technologies in higher education. Characteristics, advantages and disadvantages for its implementation. In: EDULEARN19 Proceedings, pp. 7713–7719. IATED (2019)

Deep Learning Techniques

Deep Reinforcement Learning for Jointly Resource Allocation and Trajectory Planning in UAV-Assisted Networks

Arwa Mahmoud Jwaifel(✉) and Tien Van Do

Department of Networked Systems and Services, Faculty of Electrical Engineering and Informatics, Budapest University of Technology and Economics (BME), Budapest, Hungary
jwaifel@hit.bme.hu

Abstract. Unmanned aerial vehicles (UAVs) have diverse applications in various fields, including the deployment of drones in 5G mobile networks and upcoming 6G and beyond. In UAV wireless networks, where the UAV is equipped with an eNB or gNB, it is critical to position it optimally to serve the maximum number of users located in high-capacity areas. Furthermore, the high mobility of users leads to greater network dynamics, making it challenging to predict channel link states. This study examines the use of Proximal Policy Optimization (PPO) to optimize the joint UAV position and radio spectrum resource allocation to meet the users' quality-of-service (QoS) requirements.

Keywords: 5G · 6G · Unmanned aerial vehicle (UAV) · resource allocation optimization · deep reinforcement learning (DRL) · Proximal Policy Optimization (PPO) · Deep Reinforcement Learning (DQN)

1 Introduction

The beauty of Unmanned Aerial Vehicles (UAVs), which includes drones, have recently attracted lots of researcher's attention in the industrial fields due to their ability to operate and monitor activities from remote locations; moreover, UAVs are well known for their portability, lightweight, low cost and flying without a pilot. UAV features make it suitable to be integrated into the fifth-generation (5G) and the networks beyond 6G wireless networks, where UAV can be deployed as aerial base stations into what is called the UAV-assisted [1,2]. Such situations include quick service recovery after a natural disaster and offloading base stations or the Next Generation Node B (gNBs) at hotspots in case of failure or malfunction of the ground base station or the gNB. In addition, UAV can be used to enhance network coverage and performance, where the location of the UAV can be controlled and dynamically changed to optimize the network performance according to the users' needs and their mobility model. Such scenarios are represented in Fig. 1.

N. T. Nguyen et al. (Eds.): ICCCI 2023, LNAI 14162, pp. 71–83, 2023.
https://doi.org/10.1007/978-3-031-41456-5_6

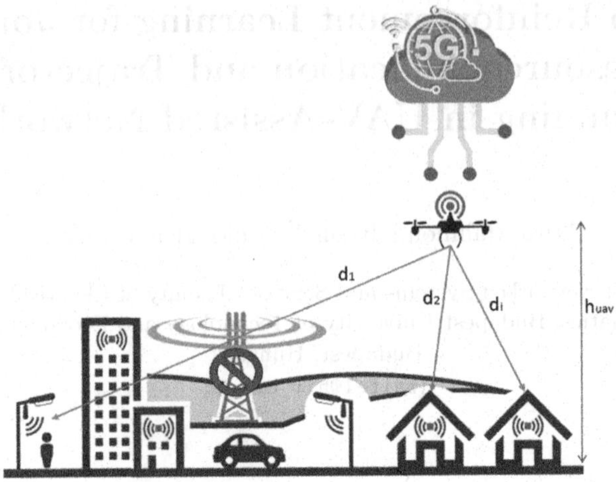

Fig. 1. UAV emergency model.

A UAV-assisted application was investigated in terms of performance analysis, resource allocation, UAV placement and position optimization, channel modeling, and information security as in [3,4] and [5]. UAV-assisted wireless communications have three main types; the first type is called UAV-carried Evolved Node B (eNB) or gNB, where the UAV acts as an aerial base station and is used to extend the network coverage [6,7] and [8]. The second type is called UAV relaying, where the UAVs are used as aerial relays to provide a wireless connection for users that cannot communicate with each other directly [9,10]. Finally, the third type is identified as a UAV-assisted Internet-of-Things (IoT) network, where UAVs assist the IoT network in collecting/disseminating data from/to its nodes or charging its nodes [11] and [12].

However, due to the UAV's limitations, only some applications use UAVs in the existing systems. The fundamental limitation is the battery life of the UAV, which is affected by the high power consumption dissipated in the hovering, horizontal, and vertical movements of the drone. Besides the battery life, the position of the UAV is also a significant concern in implementing real systems.

One of the significant applications of using the UAV in the communication system is during emergencies (such as floods or earthquakes, ... etc.) while the infrastructure is partially or totally unavailable, and the need to provide mobile service to the users is highly required. In these situations, the UAV can perform this task and provide mobile services to the user equipment (UE's) while granting the required quality-of-service (QoS). The main challenge for using the UAV-assisted network is to find the optimal position of the UAV in the cell area before getting a dead battery. Which is very complicated and challenging to determine, and the traditional optimization methods of artificial intelligence (AI) cannot solve those complicated optimization problems.

In order to address those two concerns, Reinforcement learning (RL) algorithms are applied, especially deep reinforcement learning, which has been proven to outperform the existing traditional algorithm. In this work, we introduced a different deep RL algorithm to solve the UAV-assisted joint position and radio resource allocation optimization problem. The main target is to find the optimal position of the UAV that is dynamically changed concerning the UE's required QoS and consider the UAV battery energy level in each time step, in addition to the required energy to get back to the start point.

Our main contribution in this study is presented as follows. We developed a method that collaboratively optimizes communication resource allocation and position for the UAV based on reinforcement learning, where the position and radio resource allocation joint optimization problem is formulated to obtain the maximum cumulative discounted reward. For the non-convexity nature of the optimization problem, we designed and applied different deep reinforcement learning algorithms for the UAV to solve the joint optimization issue, then we compared these algorithms' performance to solve the proposed problem; these algorithms are Proximal Policy Optimization (PPO) and Deep Reinforcement Learning (DQN).

Section 2 reviews the related literature on optimizing the position and resource allocation in UAV-assisted networks. Also, we review the reinforcement learning application in such optimization problems for UAV-assisted wireless networks. System model and problem formulation are illustrated in Sect. 3, and simulation and results are presented in Sect. 4. The conclusion is discussed in Sect. 5.

2 Related Work

The design of UAV position for improving various communication performance metrics has gained significant attention, as shown in various studies such as in [13], which focused on optimizing the spectrum efficiency and energy efficiency of a UAV-enabled mobile relaying system by adjusting the UAV's flying speed, position, and time allocation. [14] aimed to optimize the global minimum average throughput through optimized UAV trajectories and OFDMA (orthogonal frequency-division multiple access) resource allocation. [15] explored the UAV-enabled wireless communication system with multiple UAVs and aimed to increase the minimum user throughput by optimizing communication scheduling, power allocation, and UAV trajectories. In [16], UAVs served as flying Base Stations (BSs) for vehicular networks, delivering data from vehicular sources to destination nodes. The authors determined the optimal UAV position and radio resource allocation by combining Linear Programming and successive convex approximation methods.

Despite the deployment optimization of UAVs, machine learning (ML) algorithms have been introduced to optimize different QoS network requirements. The reinforcement RL and deep learning (DL) received the foremost researchers' focus in this field. Such researches as in [17], where the authors proposed UAV autonomous indoor navigation and target detection approach based on a Q-learning algorithm. While in [18], the authors proposed multi-agent reinforcement learning to optimize the resource allocation of the multi-UAV networks, and the algorithm is designed to maximize the systems' long-term reward. The authors of [19] have considered RL algorithms to optimize UAV's position to maximize sensor network data collection under QoS constraints. Moreover, in [20], the researchers adopted deep learning RL based to dynamically allocate radio resources in heterogeneous networks.

Based on the related literature review, a limited number of researchers are solving the UAV position's joint optimization problem and the UE's resource allocation. Motivated by that, we applied the deep RL algorithms to solve this optimization problem.

3 An RL-Based Approach

We considered a multi-rotor UAV with total energy E_{max} that flying at a fixed altitude of h_{max} from a base point denoted by $s_0 = (x_0, y_0)$. The UAV has an onboard gNB that will serve K subscribers within a specific area. At the beginning (τ_i) of time slot i, the gNB decides the assignment of Resource Blocks (RB) for each customer according to specific criteria; in our study, we adopt the customer's QoS requirements, and the channel quality, where the gNB can measure the channel quality of each user's device and allocate the RB's based on a minimum requirement to maintain the network performance. We assume that the gNB receives the CQI values. ($CQI(i) = [CQI_{1,i}, CQI_{2,i}, \ldots, CQI_{k,i}]$) of $k = \{1, ..., K\}$ user equipment (UEs) at time instance τ_i where $i = 0, \ldots$, which is in accordance with the time-slot operation of the gNB, so $\tau_{i+1} - \tau_i = \Delta$. At each time step $\tau_i = a \times i \times \Delta$, the UAV decides to continue flying or get back to the base point while monitoring the battery level. For this problem, we apply Reinforcement learning (RL) for flight control as follows:

- At each time step τ_i, the state $s_i = [(x_i, y_i, h_{max}, E_i), [CQI_{k,i}]] \quad \forall\, k \in [0, K]$ consists of UAV position, which can be denoted by the coordinates (x_i, y_i, h_{max}) and the UAV battery energy level, in addition to the received CQI values, form the UE's $CQI_{k,i} \forall k \in [1, K]$, and the UAV battery level E_i.
- We assume that the altitude of the UAV is fixed in this study, which can lead to the possible actions: backward, forward, left, right, and hovering in the same location and returning to the base point. The action space is $\mathcal{A} == \{L, R, FW, BW, HO, RE\}$.
- The reward function $r_i = \sum_{k=1}^{K} U_{k,i}$ is defined as the total number of served UE's in each time step, where the binary variable $U_k \in \{0, 1\}, \forall k$, which is asserted if the UAV succeeded in serving the kth UE, and allocated the required resources to guarantee the minimum throughput required to provide coverage for the cell in emergencies. Otherwise, U_k is set to 0. In this study, we adopt the max CQI scheduling allocation of the UE's, where the UE's with the highest values of CQI are allocated while there are available resource blocks in the radio frame.

The energy consumption of the UAV consists of mainly two parts: one that is required to provide the onboard gNB with its energy to operate, and the other is the propulsion energy of the UAV so that it can fly around. The UAV will decide to get back to the base point by monitoring its battery energy level (E_i) at each time step τ_i, and compare it with the energy required to fly back to the start point $s_0 = (x_0, y_0)$ from its position point ($E_{i+1,r}$). The UAV battery energy constraints is assumed to be:

$$E_i > E_{i,r} \text{ AND } E_{i+1} > E_{i+1,r}. \tag{1}$$

4 Simulation and Analysis

4.1 Models Used in Simulation

User Mobility. User mobility modeled in this research is based on the Gauss-Markov Mobility Model [21]. Where the Mobile nodes (UE's) are located in random locations within the cell area, these nodes will set their speed as for the kth UE the speed is denoted as ($V_{i,k}$) and its direction denoted as ($D_{i,k}$) for each specific step (i). At every step i, the current position of the kth UE coordinates $(x_{k,i}, y_{k,i})$ depends on the previous location $(x_{k,i-1}, y_{k,i-1})$, previous speed $V_{k,i-1}$ and previous direction $D_{k,i-1}$, assuming the directions values can be set to $\in [0, 90, 180, 270]$, to follow the proposed grid world model of the network cell. The kth UE position at the ith step, is expressed as

$$\begin{aligned} X_{k,i} &= X_{k,i-1} + V_{k,i-1} \cos D_{k,i-1}, \\ Y_{k,i} &= Y_{k,i-1} + V_{k,i-1} \sin D_{k,i-1}. \end{aligned} \tag{2}$$

Parameters $V_{k,i-1}$ and $D_{k,i-1}$ are chosen from a random Gaussian distribution with a mean equal to 0 and a standard deviation equal to 1.

RB Scheduling Algorithm. In our study, we adopt the best-CQI scheduling algorithm to allocate RB to the UE, where the gNB Scheduler allocates the RBs to the UE's that reported the highest CQI during Transmission Time Interval (TTI), where the higher CQI value means a better channel condition.

Energy Consumption Model for Multi-rotor UAV. In this study, we considered rotary-wing UAV, the UAV has four brushless motors which are powered by the carried battery, and they rotate at the same constant speed ω_{rotor}. The UAV will fly to a specific position and hover or continue flying to the next position. We follow the forces model in [22] to derive the energy consumption for both UAV motion phases. The propulsion power of the UAV is essential to support the UAV's hovering and moving activities either the vertical movement, where in our study, we assumed the UAV height is constant; thus, we will not consider this movement phase, the other movement type is the horizontal movement from one position to another in the cell grid.

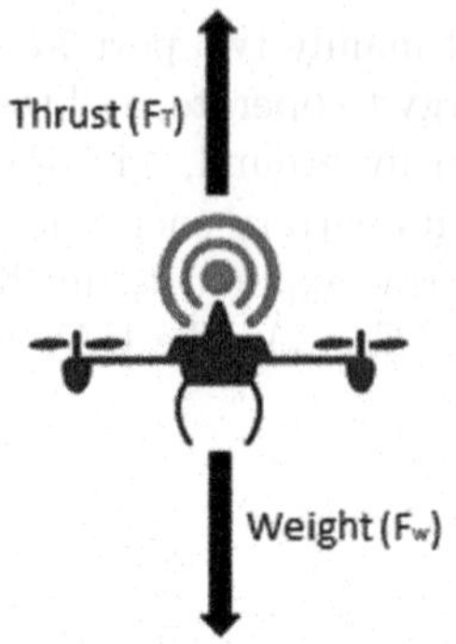

Fig. 2. UAV hovering state forces.

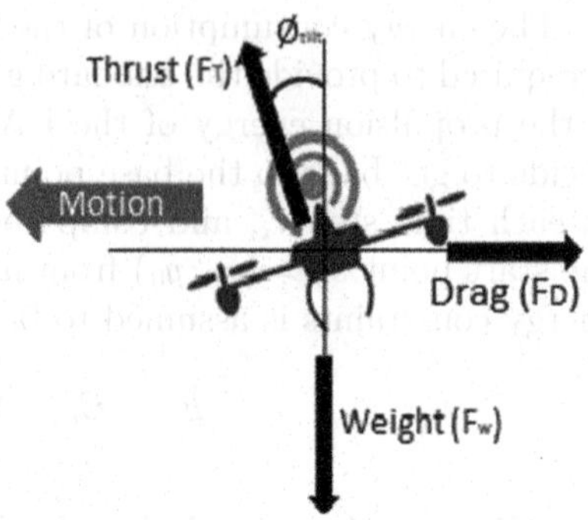

Fig. 3. UAV forward state forces.

Hovering is one of the motion activities of the drone, where the thrust of the rotor is used to equilibrate the gravity effect completely; Fig. 2 represents the hovering phase forces. Thrust is denoted by:

$$F_T = \frac{1}{2}\rho N_{rotor} A_{uav} V_{uav} \omega_{rotor}, \tag{3}$$

where ρ is the air density and equals to (1.225 kg/m^2), the rotor propeller area is A_{uav} and is equal to $A_{uav} = \pi r_{uav}^2$ where r_{uav} is the propeller radius. Finally, the number of UAV rotors is represented by the variable N_{rotor}. The V_{UAV} is the resultant velocity of the drone, and the hovering phase is equal to the motor speed, which is denoted by ω_{rotor} and can also be defined as the induced velocity of the rotor blades.

In the hovering phase, the thrust of the drone motors must equal the gravitational force ($m_{tot} \times g$), where the value of $V_{uav} = \sqrt{2m_{tot} \times g/(\rho A_{uav} N_{rotor})}$. Accordingly, in time step duration Δ where the power is equal to $P_{hov} = F_T V_{uav}$, with $V = 0$, the energy that the battery must supply is only that to defy the weight force, and considering the UAV motor efficiency η_{mot} and the propeller efficiency η_{pro} is defined as

$$E_{hov} = \sqrt{\frac{2(m_{tot} \times g)^3}{\rho A_{uav} N_{rotor}}} \times \frac{1}{\eta_{mot}\eta_{pro}} \times \Delta. \tag{4}$$

where m_{tot} is the total mass in Kg and equals to the sum of UAV mass (m_{uav}), the payload (the carried gNB) (m_{pld}) and the battery (m_b), i.e. $m_{tot} = m_{uav} + m_b + m_{pld}$. The earth gravitational force g and equals to (9.81 $\approx$ 10 m/s^s). Finally, η_{mot} is the efficiency of the UAV motor.

The UAV horizontal movement is considered the most challenging drone motion to estimate; where according to Newton's 1st low where the drone required to generate motors thrust force (F_T) that is equal and opposite to the total sum of forces consists of drag force (F_D) due to the drone speed and the weight force ($F_W = m_{tot} \times g$) due to the total weight of the drone and it is cargo (battery and carried gNB). All horizontal movement forces are shown in Fig. 3. The vertical forces under the equilibrium condition are mathematically represented by

$$F_T \times \cos\phi_{tilt} = m_{tot} \times g. \tag{5}$$

Applying Newton's 1st law to find the UAV velocity required to maintain the required conditions, the forces are denoted by

$$F_D = F_W \times \tan\phi_{tilt} = \frac{1}{2} C_D \rho A_{uav}^{eff} V_{UAV}^2, \tag{6}$$

where C_D represents the drag coefficient, and A_{uav}^{eff} represents the vertical projected area of the UAV and can be evaluated as $A_{uav}^{eff} = A_{uav}^{side} \sin(90 - \phi_{tilt}) + A_{uav}^{top} \sin\phi_{tilt}$, where A_{uav}^{side} and A_{uav}^{top} represents the side and top surface of the UAV, which can be approximated as $A_{uav}^{eff} = A_{uav}^{top} \sin\phi_{tilt}$. To evaluate the UAV energy consumed in the horizontal movement of the drone with constant speed, and using Eqs. 5 and 6, the power formula denoted by $P_{hor} = F_T V_{uav}$ is presented as

$$E_{hor} = \sqrt{\frac{2(m_{tot} \times g)^3}{C_D \rho A_{uav}^{eff} N_{rotor}} \times \frac{\sin\phi_{tilt}}{\cos^3\phi_{tilt}}} \times \frac{1}{\eta_{mot}\eta_{pro}} \times \Delta, \tag{7}$$

where η_{mot} and η_{pro} are the efficiency of the motor and the propeller, respectively. The UAV properties and parameters values used in the simulation are represented in Table 1, in addition to the UAV battery specifications, which represent the battery model installed with DJI Matrice 600 Pro drone models [23]. At a given trajectory (x_i, y_i, h_{max}), the remaining energy of the UAV can be expressed as

$$E_i = E_{max} - \sum_{i=0}^{i} E_i. \tag{8}$$

Energy Model of gNB. Path loss is modeled as the probability model that consists mainly of two components, i.e., LoS and NLoS. LoS connection probability between the receiver and transmitter is an essential factor and can be formulated as [24]

$$p_{\text{LoS},k}(i) = \frac{1}{1 + a_{LOS} \cdot \exp\left(-b_{LOS}\left(\phi_k(i) - a_{LOS}\right)\right)}, \tag{9}$$

where a_{LOS} and b_{LOS} are environmental constants, and $\phi_k(i)$ is the elevation angle in degree, and it depends on the UAV height as well as the distance between the UAV and user k, the elevation angle can be evaluated from $\phi_k = -\frac{180}{\pi} \sin^{-1}(\frac{h(i)}{d_k(i)})$. Furthermore, $h(i)$ is the UAV height, and $d_k(i)$ is the distance between the UAV and the kth UE and defined as

$$d_k(i) = \sqrt{h^2(i) + (x(i) - x_k(i))^2 + (y(i) - y_k(i))^2}. \tag{10}$$

Table 1. UAV energy model parameters simulation values.

UAV and motor parameters		
Notations	Physical definition	Simulation value
m_{uav}	UAV Weight (6×TB48S batteries)	10 kg
ρ	Air density in kg/m^3	1.225
C_D	Drag coefficient	0.044
r_{uav}	Propeller radius in meter [m]	0.1905
A_{uav}^{top}	UAV top area [m^2]	0.3
V_{uav}	Max UAV speed	18 m/s
N_{rotor}	Number of rotors	6
ϕ_{tilt}	Tilt Angle values	25°
$N_{battery}$	Number of batteries	6
η_{mot}	Motor efficiency	0.8
η_{pro}	Propeller system efficiency	0.8
UAV battery model parameters		
Parameter		Simulation value
Battery model		TB48S
Battery type		LiPo 6S
Weight		680 g
Capacity (Q)		5700 mAh
Voltage		22.8 V
Energy		129.96 Wh
eNB model parameters [26]		
Parameter		Simulation value
LTE Mode		TDD
Frequency Bands		400 Mhz: (400–430) Mhz
		600 Mhz: (566–626) Mhz, (606–678) Mhz
		1.4 Ghz: (1447–1467) Mhz
		1.8 Ghz: (1785–1805) Mhz
Channel Bandwidth		5/10/15/20 MHz
Max Output Power		15 W
Power Supply		48V DC or 220 V AC
Power Consumption		150 W
MIMO		2 × 2
Dimensions		330 * 260 * 110 mm
Weight		5.5 kg
Users		200

The probability of having NLoS communication between the UAV and k^{th} UE is denoted by:

$$p_{\text{NLoS},k}(i) = 1 - p_{\text{LoS},k}(i). \quad (11)$$

Hence, the mean path loss model (in dB) we adopt the following equation from [24]

$$L_{\text{k}}(h, d_k, i)\,(\text{dB}) = L_{\text{LoS},k}(i) \times p_{\text{LoS},k}(i) + L_{\text{NLoS},k}(i) \times p_{\text{NLoS},k}(i), \quad (12)$$

where, $L_{\text{LoS},k}(i)$ and $L_{\text{NLoS},k}(i)$ are the path loss for LoS and NLoS communication links and denoted by

$$L_{\text{LoS},k}(i) = 10 \times \alpha_{pl} \log\left(\frac{4\pi f_c d_k(i)}{c}\right) + \delta_{\text{LoS}}, \tag{13}$$

$$L_{\text{NLoS},k}(i) = 10 \times \alpha_{pl} \log\left(\frac{4\pi f_c d_k(i)}{c}\right) + \delta_{\text{NLoS}}, \tag{14}$$

where α_{pl} is the path loss exponent and its environment-dependent variable, both of the δ_{LoS} and δ_{NLoS} are the mean losses due to LoS and NLoS communication links, $c = 3 \times 10^8$ the speed of light and f_c is the network operating frequency.

With $\gamma_k(i)$ represents the Signal-to-Noise Ratio (SNR) of the kth UE at the ith step, while assuming $P_{r,k}(i)$ is the received signal power at the kth UE, the SNR is defined as

$$\gamma_k(i) = \frac{P_{r,k}(i)}{\sigma^2}. \tag{15}$$

The SNR can be rewritten in terms of the path loss and transmitted UAV power as

$$\gamma_k(i) = \frac{P_k(i) \times L_k(i)}{\sigma^2}, \tag{16}$$

where $P_k(i)$ is the transmitted power from the UAV to the kth UE at the ith step.

The 5G NR maximum data rate of the kth UE can be evaluated in Mbps using the formula defined in [25], and expressed as:

$$R_k(i) = 10^{-6} \cdot \sum_{j=1}^{J} \left(\Omega j, k \cdot M_{j,k} \cdot \zeta_{j,k} \cdot C_{R,\max} \cdot \frac{N_{j,k}^{RB}(i) \cdot 12}{T_s^{\mu}} \cdot (1 - OH_{j,k}) \right), \tag{17}$$

where J represents the number of aggregated component carriers, $(\Omega_{j,k})$ is the maximum number of layers, and $(M_{j,k})$ is the modulation order. In contrast, $(\zeta_{j,k})$ is a scaling factor that has values of (1, 0.8, 0.75, and 0.4). The code rate is denoted by $(C_{R,\max})$, and is can have the values in Tables 5.1.3.1-1, 5.1.3.1-2 and 5.1.3.1-3 in 3gpp.38.214 with a maximum value of (948/1024). The numerology μ can have the values of $[0, 1, 2, 3, 4]$ which responds to the subcarrier spacing (SCS) of 15 kHz, 30 kHz, 60 kHz, 120 kHz and 240 kHz. The variable T_s^{μ} represents the average OFDM symbol duration for certain μ and can be evaluated as $(T_s^{\mu} = \frac{10^3}{14 \times 2^{\mu}})$. The $N_{j,k}^{RB}(i)$ is the number of allocated RBs to the kth UE at the ith step. Finally, $OH_{j,k}$ denotes the overhead and can have the values of (0.14, 0.18, 0.08, and 0.10).

Moreover, the data rate can have another formula to be evaluated according to [25], as

$$R_k(i) = 10^{-3} \cdot \sum_{j=1}^{J} TBS_{j,k}(i) \times 2^{\mu}, \tag{18}$$

where $TBS_{j,k}$ is the total maximum number of DL-SCH transport block bits received within a 1ms TTI for the kth UE and j^{th} carrier.

4.2 Simulation Results

In our case study, we considered one UAV that flies at a maximum altitude of $h_{max} = 200$ m over grid area size (1500×1500), The simulation parameters listed in Table 1 and the network setting listed in Table 2. In each episode, there are two scenarios for the UE's mobility. One scenario is considering 20 number of UE which are generated and distributed randomly in the cell area while assuming random walk mobility model to be the mobility model for the UE within the cell, moreover, the second scenario considered placing four UE's and fix their positions at the corners of the cell.

Table 2. Parameters for simulation.

Parameter	Value
Bandwidth	10 MHz
Transmitted power	23 dBm
Frequency	2 GHz
Noise power	−174 dBm
Path loss threshold	−220 dBm
MIMO	2×2

The deep RL algorithms PPO and DQN models were constructed and trained on a random proposed environment where the UAV carries the eNB and flies around the cell to provide mobile services to the maximum number of UE's. The battery capacity of the UAV was initialized with a value E_{max}. The first scenario where the mobility of the UE's is considered, we illustrate the comparison results for applying PPO and DQN RL algorithms then tuned them with different learning rates (lr) values: $[0.01, 0.001, 0.0001]$.

The accumulative rewards for each iteration of the training is illustrated in Fig. 4, in this training results the PPO which was tuned wit learning rate 0.001 has the better performance than the other to solve the optimization problem. The other scenario in which we placed four UE's corners of the cell, Fig. 5 illustrates the accumulative rewards achieved in each training iteration using both model (PPO and DQN) which are in addition tuned with different learning rates (lr) $[0.01, 0.001, 0.0001]$. Comparing the performance of the RL algorithms showed that the PPO agent which tuned with $lr = 0.01$ or $lr = 0.001$ proves a superior performance than the others.

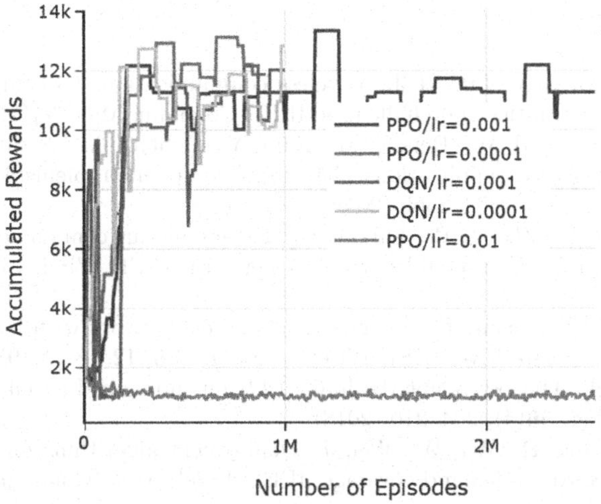

Fig. 4. Max reward per episode - 20 UE with random walk mobility model.

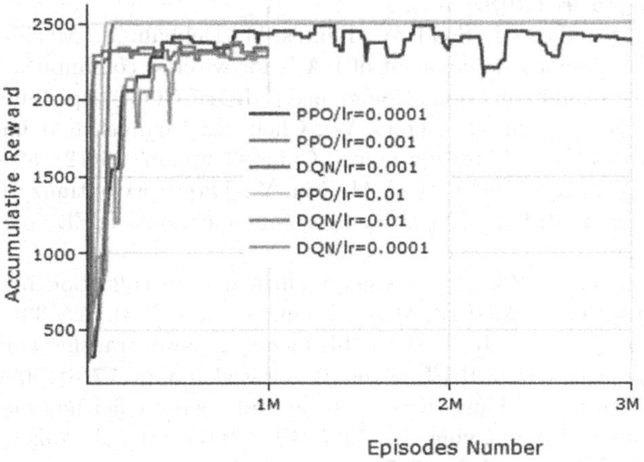

Fig. 5. Max reward per episode - 4 UE places at cell corners.

5 Conclusion

In this paper, we developed a framework for UAV autonomous navigation in urban environments that takes into account trajectory and resource allocation and the battery limitation of the UAV while taking into account the UE mobility within the environment. We deploy the RL PPO-based algorithm, which allows the UAV to navigate in continuous 2D environments using discrete actions, where the model was trained to navigate in a random environment. Then evaluated, the PPO and DQN algorithms while tuning the agents with different learning rate values, and then compared the results accordingly.

References

1. Zeng, Y., Zhang, R., Lim, T.J.: Wireless communications with unmanned aerial vehicles: opportunities and challenges. IEEE Commun. Mag. **54**(5), 36–42 (2016)
2. Mozaffari, M., Saad, W., Bennis, M., Nam, Y., Debbah, M.: A tutorial on UAVs for wireless networks: applications, challenges, and open problems. IEEE Commun. Surv. Tutor. **21**(3), 2334–2360 (2019)
3. Wu, Q., Liu, L., Zhang, R.: Fundamental trade-offs in communication and trajectory design for UAV-enabled wireless network. IEEE Wirel. Commun. **26**(1), 36–44 (2019)
4. Wu, Q., Mei, W., Zhang, R.: Safeguarding wireless network with UAVs: a physical layer security perspective. IEEE Wirel. Commun. **26**, 12–18 (2019)
5. Lin, X., et al.: The sky is not the limit: LTE for unmanned aerial vehicles. IEEE Commun. Mag. **56**(4), 204–210 (2018)
6. Zhao, H., Wang, H., Wu, W., Wei, J.: Deployment algorithms for UAV airborne networks toward on-demand coverage. IEEE J. Sel. Areas Commun. **36**(9), 2015–2031 (2018)
7. Sharma, N., Magarini, M., Jayakody, D.N.K., Sharma, V., Li, J.: On-demand ultra-dense cloud drone networks: opportunities, challenges and benefits. IEEE Commun. Mag. **56**(8), 85–91 (2018)
8. Zhang, Q., Mozaffari, M., Saad, W., Bennis, M., Debbah, M.: Machine learning for predictive on-demand deployment of UAVs for wireless communications. In: 2018 IEEE Global Communications Conference (GLOBECOM), pp. 1–6 (2018)
9. Chen, X., Hu, X., Zhu, Q., Zhong, W., Chen, B.: Channel modeling and performance analysis for UAV relay systems. China Commun. **15**(12), 89–97 (2018)
10. Zhang, G., Yan, H., Zeng, Y., Cui, M., Liu, Y.: Trajectory optimization and power allocation for multi-hop UAV relaying communications. IEEE Access **6**, 48566–48576 (2018)
11. Zhan, C., Zeng, Y., Zhang, R.: Energy-efficient data collection in UAV enabled wireless sensor network. IEEE Wirel. Commun. Lett. **7**(3), 328–331 (2018)
12. Xu, J., Zeng, Y., Zhang, R.: UAV-enabled wireless power transfer: trajectory design and energy optimization. IEEE Trans. Wireless Commun. **17**(8), 5092–5106 (2018)
13. Zhang, J., Zeng, Y., Zhang, R.: Spectrum and energy efficiency maximization in UAV-enabled mobile relaying. In: 2017 IEEE International Conference on Communications (ICC), pp. 1–6 (2017)
14. Qingqing, W., Zhang, R.: Common throughput maximization in UAV-enabled OFDMA systems with delay consideration. IEEE Trans. Commun. **66**(12), 6614–6627 (2018)
15. Yu, X., Xiao, L., Yang, D., Qingqing, W., Cuthbert, L.: Throughput maximization in multi-UAV enabled communication systems with difference consideration. IEEE Access **6**, 55291–55301 (2018)
16. Samir, M., Chraiti, M., Assi, C., Ghrayeb, A.: Joint optimization of UAV trajectory and radio resource allocation for drive-thru vehicular networks. In: 2019 IEEE Wireless Communications and Networking Conference (WCNC), pp. 1–6 (2019)
17. Guerra, A., Guidi, F., Dardari, D., Djurić, P.M.: Reinforcement learning for UAV autonomous navigation, mapping and target detection. In: 2020 IEEE/ION Position, Location and Navigation Symposium (PLANS), pp. 1004–1013 (2020)
18. Cui, J., Liu, Y., Nallanathan, A.: Multi-agent reinforcement learning-based resource allocation for UAV networks. IEEE Trans. Wireless Commun. **19**(2), 729–743 (2020)

19. Cui, J., Ding, Z., Deng, Y., Nallanathan, A., Hanzo, L.: Adaptive UAV-trajectory optimization under quality of service constraints: a model-free solution. IEEE Access **8**, 112253–112265 (2020)
20. Tang, F., Zhou, Y., Kato, N.: Deep reinforcement learning for dynamic uplink/downlink resource allocation in high mobility 5G HetNet. IEEE J. Sel. Areas Commun. **38**(12), 2773–2782 (2020)
21. Camp, T., Boleng, J., Davies, V.: A survey of mobility models for ad hoc network research. Wirel. Commun. Mob. Comput. **2**(5), 483–502 (2002)
22. Valavanis, K.P., Vachtsevanos, G.J.: Handbook of Unmanned Aerial Vehicles. Springer, Dordrecht (2014). https://doi.org/10.1007/978-90-481-9707-1
23. DJI matrice 600 prospecs. https://www.dji.com/hr/matrice600-pro/info#specs. Accessed 20 Mar 2023
24. Al-Hourani, A., Kandeepan, S., Lardner, S.: Optimal lap altitude for maximum coverage. IEEE Wirel. Commun. Lett. **3**(6), 569–572 (2014)
25. 3GPP. 5G, NR, User Equipment (UE) radio access capabilities. 3GPP TS, 15.3.0 edition (2018)
26. IWAVE airborne 4G LTE base station. https://www.iwavecomms.com/. Accessed 20 Mar 2023

DNGAE: Deep Neighborhood Graph Autoencoder for Robust Blind Hyperspectral Unmixing

Refka Hanachi[1(✉)], Akrem Sellami[2], Imed Riadh Farah[1,3], and Mauro Dalla Mura[4]

[1] RIADI Laboratory, ENSI, University of Manouba, 2010 Manouba, Tunisia
refka.hanachi@ensi.u-manouba.tn, riadh.farah@ensi.rnu.tn

[2] CRIStAL Laboratory, University of Lille, Sciences et technologies, Bâtiment Esprit, 59655 Villeneuve-d'Ascq, France
akrem.sellami@univ-lille.fr

[3] ITI Department, IMT Atlantique, 655 Avenue du Technopôle, 29280 Plouzané, France

[4] Grenoble INP, GIPSA-Lab Univ. Grenoble Alpes, CNRS, 38000 Grenoble, France
mauro.dalla-mura@gipsa-lab.grenoble-inp.fr

Abstract. Recently, Deep Learning (DL)-based unmixing techniques have gained popularity owing to the robust learning of Deep Neural Networks (DNNs). In particular, the Autoencoder (AE) model, as a baseline network for unmixing, performs well in Hyperspectral Unmixing (HU) by automatically learning a new representation and recovering original data. However, patch-wise AE based architecture, which incorporates both spectral and spatial information through convolutional filters may blur the abundance maps due to the fixed kernel shape of the used window size. To cope with the above issue, we propose in this paper a novel methodology based on graph DL called DNGAE. Unlike the pixel-wise or patch-wise Convolutional AE (CAE), our proposed method incorporates the complementary spatial information based on graph spectral similarity. A neighborhood graph based on band correlations is firstly constructed. Then, our method attempts to aggregate similar spectra from the neighboring pixels of a target pixel. Consequently, this leads to better quality of both extracted endmembers and abundances. Extensive experiments performed on two real HSI benchmarks confirm the effectiveness of our proposed method compared to other DL models.

Keywords: Spectral unmixing · Neighborhood graph · Representation learning · Graph Autoencoder

1 Introduction

Due to the relatively low spatial resolution of hyperspectral sensors and the intricate distribution of materials, mixed pixels, which frequently contain multiple

N. T. Nguyen et al. (Eds.): ICCCI 2023, LNAI 14162, pp. 84–96, 2023.
https://doi.org/10.1007/978-3-031-41456-5_7

spectral signatures, will inevitably cause high-level Hyperspectral Image (HSI) data processing to perform less efficiently. Therefore, Hyperspectral Unmixing (HU) has become a major preprocessing technique for HSI analysis. It aims to separate each pixel's spectra into a collection of spectral signatures called *endmembers* and estimate their proportions in the mixed pixel known as *the abundance.* Based on various mixing techniques, unmixing models fall into two categories: linear and nonlinear HU. According to the Linear Mixture Model (LMM), the pixel spectrum is supposed to be a linear combination of the spectral components, while the NonLinear Mixture Model (NLMM) holds when there are multiple scattering effects caused by the presence of different materials. Following with the majority of the earlier works, we focus in this paper, more on LMM HU. Thus, it can be divided into geometrical, statistical or sparse regression approaches. The geometrical approach can also be classified into two types: pure pixel-based, and minimum volume-based methods. The first technique assumes that each endmember has at least one pure pixel. Additionally, the most representative algorithms include Pixel Purity Index (PPI) [1], N-FINDR [2], and Vertex Component Analysis (VCA) [3], whereas Minimum Volume Simplex Analysis (MVSA) [4], which is being suggested for the processing of highly mixed HSI data, is a typical illustration of the second technique. Furthermore, statistical methods have also led to favorable results in which the HU problem is formulated as a statistical inference problem using bayesian techniques [5]. Lastly, sparse regression methods were among the first semi-supervised methods proposed [6]. They assume that the observed signatures can be expressed as linear combinations of several previously known pure spectral signatures.

Recently, Deep Learning (DL) based unmixing techniques have gained popularity owing to the robust learning of Deep Neural Networks (DNNs). Hence, various deep networks have been proposed to solve the HU task. These methods are mainly based on Autoencoder (AE) [7] and its variants. In this regard, the HU problem is referred to as *blind unmixing* since the endmembers and corresponding abundances are estimated from the HSI at the same time. Basically, AE receives the spectrum of mixed pixels as input and maps it via an encoder network into a latent representation that corresponds to the abundance coefficients. The decoder then reconstructs the input reflectance spectra using a linear layer from which endmembers are estimated based on its weights. In [8], a Stacked of NonNegative Sparse AE (SNSA) was proposed. By applying the Abundance Sum to one Constraint (ASC) for abundances and a linear decoder with nonnegative weights, such AEs satisfy the LMM. Similarly, in [9], a NN model with Spectral Information Divergence Objective (SIDAE) was built. It uses the Spectral Information Divergence (SID) measure instead of the conventional Mean Square Error (MSE) objective function. In addition, in order to provide better discriminative representations, an EndNet model based on a two-staged AE network was proposed in [10]. It included additional layers and replaced the inner-product operator with a Spectral Angular Mapper (SAM). Moreover, authors in [11] developed a new Deep AE Network (DAEN) to learn spectral signatures and perform blind source separation using both the Stacked

AE (SAE) and Variational AE (VAE) models. Also, an untied Denoising AE with Sparsity (uDAS) [12] was proposed. It employs a sparsity, and denoising constraints on both the encoder and decoder, respectively. Although the benefits of including spatial information for HU have been confirmed in the literature, it is worth noting that all of the aforementioned AE-based techniques are strictly spectral in which the spatial information is ignored. In this regard, numerous works have been proposed based on cube-wise methods to improve the estimation accuracy of endmembers, showing their high performance since they adhere to the concept of endmember bundles. However, due to the fixed patches' lack of sufficient structure for the convolutions to perform well, it may decrease the accuracy of abundance estimation and result in blurred effects. Therefore, how to provide high-quality unmixing while learning the spectro-spatial data from HSI is the main concern of our approach.

In this article, we propose a novel methodology for HU based on graph DL that copes with the problem of fixed patches and allows to incorporate the complementary spatial information based on graph spectral similarity.

The remainder of this paper is structured as follows. Section 2 discusses recent related works. Section 3 presents the key phases of our proposed approach based on GAE model. Section 4 validates the proposed unmixing approach with experiments on two real HSI benchmarks. Section 5 concludes our article and discusses the future directions.

2 Related Works

Many spectro-spatial DL approaches have been explored to improve the estimation accuracy of both abundances and endmembers. For instance, in [13], the method employs multitask learning via a number of AEs operating on image patches in order to simultaneously unmix a neighborhood of pixels. Meanwhile, Convolutional NN (CNN) models have also enabled a great perspective into HU through convolution operations, yielding state-of-the-art performance. According to [14], authors have demonstrated that cube-wise CNN performs better than pixel-wise CNN. Likewise, 2-D Convolutional AE (CAE) has been used successfully in several works [15], since it uses spatial filtering to extract features, thereby directly leveraging the spatial structure of the HSI. Unmixing using deep image prior (UnDIP) model was successfully designed in [16] that utilizes endmembers extracted by a simplex volume maximization (SiVM) technique. Very recently, a CyCU-Net model was developed in [17] by learning two cascaded AEs in an end-to-end fashion.

Furthermore, based on prior research, we can conclude that DL models have demonstrated their high performance in enhancing HU by utilizing efficient spectral and spatial features. Unfortunately, a number of problems relying on the use of spatial features between adjacent pixels have been raised. Essentially mentioned the specified fixed kernel shape of a spatial neighborhood surrounding each mixed pixel to extract features as illustrated in Fig. 1, which blurs the abundance maps and affects the estimation of endmembers. Therefore, this will

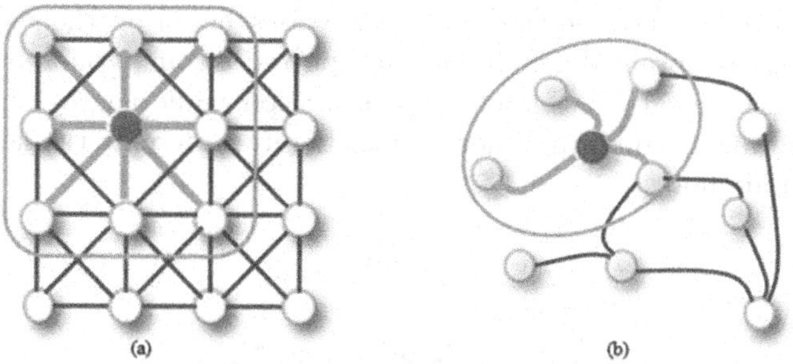

Fig. 1. Comparaison of convolution operation. (a) Euclidean space (CNN). (b) Non-euclidean space (Graph) [18].

result in poor performance as cube-wise models neglect the topological local information between neighboring pixels, and the structural information within HSI. Moreover, an assumption can be made that connected mixed pixels share the same material based on their band correlations. Thus, how can a unified model simultaneously incorporate the structural-spectral HSI connections constitute the main key research of our proposed method. To this end, several graph-based methods have been developed. In particular, GraphAE (GAE) [19] has marked an increasing potential that is able to effectively extract high-level features by taking the weighted average of a node's neighborhood information. Relevant to that, we propose in this paper, a novel method based on graph DL for blind unmixing called DNGAE. It is the first graph deep unmixing network that attempts to consider the spectral signature and spectral similarity of pixels (spatial neighborhood information) as a graph. The contribution of the proposed approach is given below:

- Unlike the pixel-wise or cube-wise CAE based methods, our proposed DNGAE solves the fixed window size issue by incorporating the complementary spatial information based on graph spectral similarity. Based on band correlations, a neighborhood graph through euclidean distance is constructed and adjacent pixels are selected via a fixed neighborhood threshold.
- By coupling the spectral signature and spatial neighborhood based graph, our proposed method enhances the unmixing performances since it attempts to aggregate the information from the neighboring pixels of a target pixel yielding a richer node representations according to their relevance. Therefore, this leads to better quality of both extracted endmembers and abundances.

3 Proposed Method

Let's denote $\mathbf{X} \in \mathbb{R}^{N \times B}$, the original HSI data where N is the number of pixels and B denotes the number of spectral signatures. To fully exploit the complementary spatial information, a neighborhood graph is constructed. The aim here is to integrate the pixels' neighboring connections based on their spectral signature. Then, the obtained graph will be inputted to our proposed end-to-end GAE that learns locally the latent representation while aggregating for each pixel, the relevant neighboring information. Figure 2 presents the key phases of our proposed method.

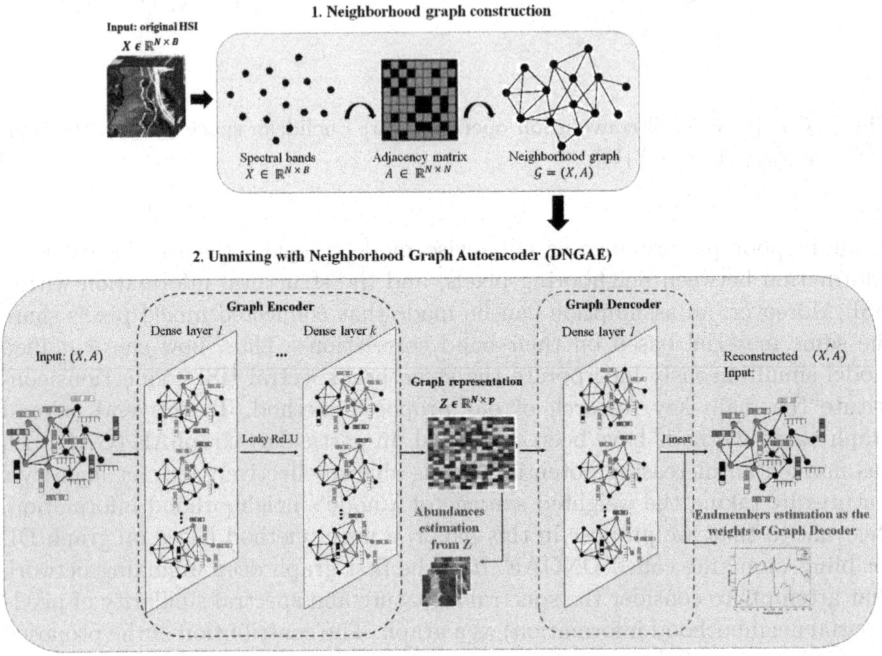

Fig. 2. General overview of the proposed unmixing graph deep learning approach.

3.1 Neighborhood Graph Construction

In order to take advantage of the spectro-spatial information of the HSI and to enhance the unmixing performance, we propose to construct a neighborhood graph $\mathcal{G} = (\mathcal{V}, \mathcal{E})$, where $\mathcal{V} = \{v_1, ..., v_N\}$ are pixels (nodes), $\mathcal{E}$ represent the edge sets. Each vertex v_i is associated with a continuous spectrum of size B. Each edge $e_{i,j} = (v_i, v_j) \in \mathcal{E}$ has an associated weight $\mathcal{W} \in \mathbb{R}^{N \times N}$. Moreover, an edge $e_{i,j}$ is defined between two nodes v_i and v_j based on a similarity criterion. Formally, the weight $w_{i,j}$ for the edge $e_{i,j}$ is computed as follows:

$$w_{i,j} = \exp(\frac{-dist(x_i, x_j)}{2\sigma^2}) \quad (1)$$

where σ is the kernel bandwidth to compute $\mathcal{W}$, $dist(v_i, v_j) = \|v_i - v_j\|_2$ is the euclidean distance, and v_i, v_j are the spectral signatures. To take the closest

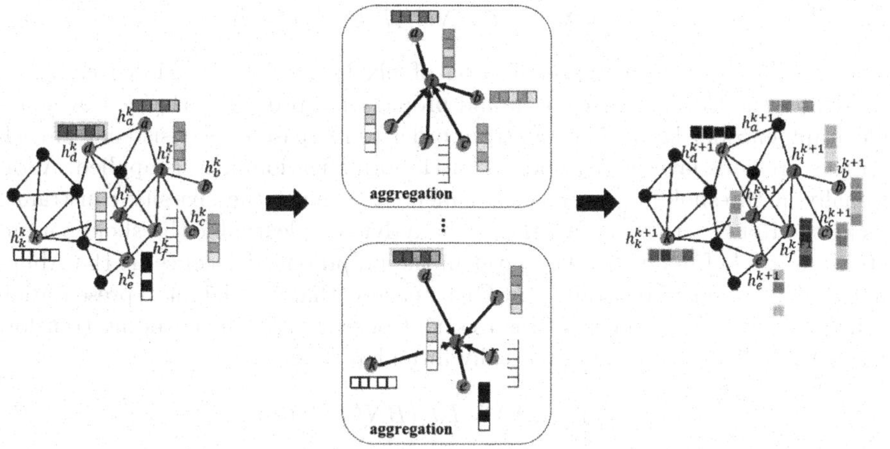

Fig. 3. Single graph encoder layer based-feature aggregation. Arrows specify the direction of feature propagation.

neighbors to v_i, we adjusted the neighborhood size k on the basis of a clearly defined threshold s. Then, the adjacency matrix $\mathbf{A}$ based on $\mathcal{W}$ is generated as follows:

$$\mathbf{A}(v, e_i) = \begin{cases} 1, & \text{if } w_{i,j} < s \\ 0, & \text{otherwise} \end{cases} \tag{2}$$

3.2 Deep Unmixing Using DNGAE

Once we have constructed our neighborhood graph $\mathcal{G}$, we propose to build the DNGAE model to solve the HU task. The main goal is to perform a set of aggregation functions that learn a new representation from a node's local neighbors information, as opposed to training a simple feature vector for each node. Therefore, our model receives $(\mathbf{X}, \mathbf{A})$ as input, where $\mathbf{X}$ denotes the spectral feature matrix and $\mathbf{A}$ represents the structural spatial connectivity. Moreover, it includes a nonlinear dense graph encoder and a linear graph decoder.

The graph encoder is built to be a stacked encoder layers. By taking the graph structure, each graph layer attempts to aggregate information from a target pixel's nearby pixels to project the units of the input layer B into the number of endmembers r. Formally, at each layer k, each target node $i \in \mathcal{V}$ aggregates the representations of the nodes in its local neighborhood $\{h_j^{k-1}, \forall j \in \mathcal{N}(i)\}$ into a single vector $h_{\mathcal{N}(i)}^{k-1}$. For the aggregate function, we opt for the mean aggregator fusion method μ. Therefore, the average value of the target node i and its neighbor node is spliced, followed by the weight parameter (W^k), and finally the nonlinear transformation is performed. Hence, the aggregation function is given below:

$$h_{\mathcal{N}(i)}^{k-1} \leftarrow \mu(\{h_j^{k-1}, \forall j \in \mathcal{N}(i)\}) \tag{3}$$

$$h_i^k = \sigma(\mathbf{W}^k. \quad CONCAT(h_i^{k-1}, h_{\mathcal{N}(i)}^k)) \tag{4}$$

where h_i^k is the feature representation of pixel i at k layer. Moreover, Fig. 3 illustrates the feature aggregation and propagation process performed by a single graph encoder layer. Thereafter, in order to increase the consistency of each batch's previous layer activations, a batch normalization layer is applied. Additionally, a thresholding layer is implemented to meet the sparsity constraints using the ReLU activation function θ and a dynamic learnable threshold parameter $\alpha \in \mathbb{R}^{r\times 1}$. Finally, the last layer in the graph encoder concerns the Abundance Sum to-one Constraint (ASC) to ensure that the latent representation generated by previous layers sums to one. Consequently, the encoding transformation for HU can be mathematically formulated as:

$$g_\theta(A, X) = L\theta_\alpha(BN(h^{(k)})) \tag{5}$$

where L is the activation function. In this regard, the abundance coefficients are estimated from the latent representation.

For the graph decoder, the aim is to reconstruct the input node representations by considering the representations of their neighbors. Unlike the graph encoder, the graph decoder does not specify the same number of layers. It has only one dense layer performed on all B units with a linear activation function. Moreover, the reconstruction can be written as:

$$f_\theta(A, Z) = Wg_\phi(A, X) \tag{6}$$

Therefore, endmembers are estimated from the weight matrix $W \in \mathbb{R}^{Bxr}$.

For the loss function, rather than MSE, our DNGAE model is trained using the Spectral-Angle-Distance (SAD) to mainly cope with the influences of spectral variability and accelerate the overall model's convergence. Therefore, it can be formulated as follows:

$$\mathcal{L} = \frac{1}{N}\sum_i^N cos^{-1}(\frac{x_i\hat{x}_i}{||x_i||_2||\hat{x}_i||_2}) \tag{7}$$

4 Experimental Results

4.1 HSI Data Description

- Jasper Ridge: it is frequently used to represent a subimage from a larger image. It is made up of 100 × 100 pixels that were captured at 198 spectral bands with wavelengths between 380 and 2500 nm. The four endmembers are: "Road," "Soil," "Water," and "Tree".
- Samson: it consists of 95 × 95 pixels captured at 156 bands with wavelengths ranging from 401 to 889 nm. The three reference endmembers are represented by "Soil," "Tree", and "Water".

Figure 4 presents the applied two HSI datasets.

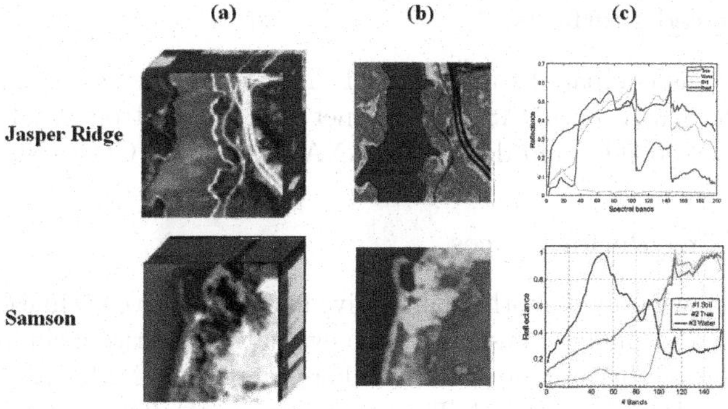

Fig. 4. HSI datasets. (a) RGB image, (b) GT: abundances, and (c) GT: endmembers.

4.2 Hyperparameters Selection

In deep unmixing models, the settings for the hyperparameters typically have a significant impact on the results that can be greatly enhanced by selecting appropriate hyperparameter values. For the two HSI benchmarks, our proposed DNGAE was built as dense multi-layer neural networks using basically three hidden layers in the graph encoder network: $[B, 9 \times r, 6 \times r, 3 \times r, r, B]$. Moreover, for the construction of our neighborhood graph, we set the neighborhood size $k \in [1, ..., 10]$ in accordance with $s = [0.1, ..., 1.0]$. It's worth noting that increasing the neighborhood size can introduce unnecessary sharing of information between pixels. Indeed, getting too big s can also trigger all pixels to have the same representation. Therefore, after several tests, $s = 0.5$ was used for both HSI data. Table 1 summarizes all the hyperparameters used in the experiments.

Table 1. Hyperparameters of DNGAE for the two HSI data used in the experiments.

Hyperparameters	Jasper Ridge	Samson
s	0.5	0.5
LeakyReLU	0.02	0.1
GaussianDropout	0.0045	0.0045
Kernel constraint	NonNeg()	NonNeg()
Optimizer	Adam	Adam
Learning rate	10^{-3}	3×10^{-4}
Epoch	60	40
Batch size	11	5

4.3 Compared Methods

Our method was compared to various DL methods, either being spectral such as SIDAE [9], SNSA [8], uDAS [12], Endnet [10], or spectro-spatial like MTAE [13], fully CNN encoder and decoder (CNNAE) [15], and CyCU-Net [17].

4.4 Unmixing Performances

In this section, we provide both quantitative and qualitative evaluations. For the quantitative performance assessment, two evaluation metrics including SAD for the estimation of the extracted endmembers, and Root-MSE (RMSE) for the extracted abundances were used. They are mathematically expressed as follows:

$$SAD = arccoss(\frac{< r_i, \hat{r}_i >}{||r_i||.||\hat{r}_i||}) \tag{8}$$

$$RMSE = \sqrt{\frac{1}{R}\sum_{j=1}^{1} ||S_j - \hat{S}_j||^2} \tag{9}$$

r is the reference endmember, $\hat{r}$ is the extracted endmember, S, and $\hat{S}$ denote the abundance ground truth, and the estimated one respectively.

Jasper Ridge Dataset: Both quantitative results based on RMSE and SAD are reported in Table 2 and 3 respectively. Based on RMSE evaluation metric, we can interpret that our proposed method presents competitive results compared to other methods with a value equal to 0.0976. Additionally, it shows considerable improvements for three out of four classes namely "Tree", "Water", and "Road" with a value equal to 0.0681, 0.0722, and 0.1208 respectively. For the rest "Soil" class, the uDAS slightly excels our method with a difference of 0.0002. Moreover, CyCU-Net has the second best average performance with a value equal to 0.1160 as well as for the two "Tree", and "Water" endmembers.

For the SAD values, similarly, our DNGAE outperforms other DL based methods with a value equal to 0.1587. For three out of four endmembers, our method presents competitive results of 0.0900, 0.0800, and 0.1270 for "Tree", "Soil", and "Road" endmembers respectively. For the "Water" estimation, SNSA was successfully able to achieve the best performance with a value equal to 0.1263. Furthermore, Fig. 5 shows a qualitative visualisation of the estimated abundances. This again confirms that our DNGAE method provides a relatively accurate performance mainly for the estimation of the "Road" endmember which is known to be the hardest one, since other DL based methods made confusion with the "Soil" material.

Samson Dataset: Tables 4 and 5 quantitatively report both individual and the average scores based on RMSE and SAD evaluation metrics respectively. Hence, it can be clearly observed that our DNGAE model achieves superior results for the estimation of abundances for all three materials with a value equal to 0.0775. Moreover, as for the Jasper Ridge data, CyCU-Net still ranks second

Table 2. RMSE unmixing performances (CNNAE, MTAE, CyCU-Net, SIDAE, Endnet, uDAS, SNSA, and DNGAE): Jasper Ridge HSI. Best performances are in bold. Second performances are underlined.

Class	DL-based methods							
	CNNAE	MTAE	CyCU-Net	SIDAE	Endnet	uDAS	SNSA	DNGAE
Tree	0.1990	0.1236	0.0920	0.5054	0.2861	0.1440	0.2901	**0.0681**
Water	0.1830	0.2456	0.1010	0.7583	0.5116	0.1990	0.3679	**0.0722**
Soil	0.2490	0.1798	0.1480	0.6773	0.4462	**0.1290**	0.4236	0.1292
Road	0.3080	0.1603	0.1260	0.1892	0.5536	0.1210	0.2897	**0.1208**
Average	0.2460	0.1773	0.1160	0.5326	0.4493	0.1480	0.3428	**0.0976**

Table 3. SAD unmixing performances (CNNAE, MTAE, CyCU-Net, SIDAE, Endnet, uDAS, SNSA, and DNGAE): Jasper Ridge HSI. Best performances are in bold. Second performances are underlined.

Class	DL-based methods							
	CNNAE	MTAE	CyCU-Net	SIDAE	Endnet	uDAS	SNSA	DNGAE
Tree	0.2203	0.1336	0.1685	0.3256	0.1548	0.1511	0.3279	**0.0900**
Water	0.1642	0.2356	0.2495	0.2897	0.2287	0.1742	**0.1263**	0.3380
Soil	0.1497	0.1410	0.1964	0.3698	0.2895	0.1939	0.2181	**0.0800**
Road	1.2258	0.1369	0.2871	0.4087	0.2106	0.1797	0.2009	**0.1270**
Average	0.4400	0.1615	0.2253	0.3484	0.2209	0.1747	0.2183	**0.1587**

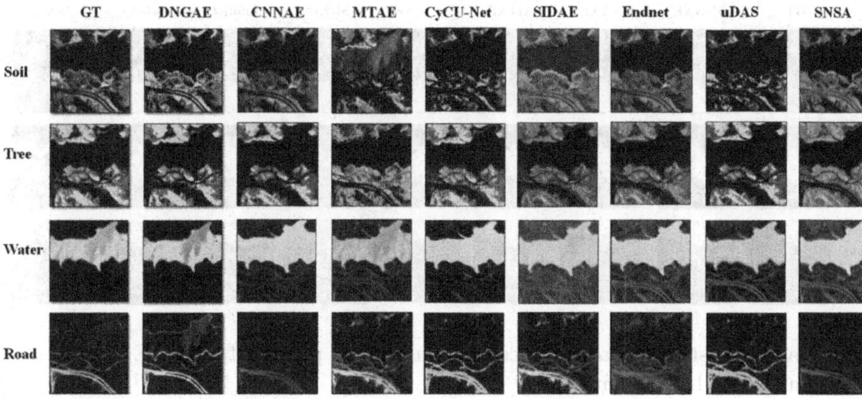

Fig. 5. Jasper Ridge: estimated abundance maps using our proposed DNGAE method and other compared DL based methods.

with a value equal to 0.1760. Whereas, SIDAE, uDAS, and SNSA are at the bottom of ranking with the worst results.

For the SAD results, MTAE model exceeds our DNGAE method and ranks first with a value equal to 0.1204. With a minor difference, our method was able to complete the overall second performance 0.1923, as well as for the estimation of "Tree" endmember 0.1190. For the "Water" material, as it can be seen, our

Table 4. RMSE unmixing performances (CNNAE, MTAE, CyCU-Net, SIDAE, Endnet, uDAS, SNSA, and DNGAE): Samson HSI. Best performances are in bold. Second performances are underlined.

Class	DL-based methods							
	CNNAE	MTAE	CyCU-Net	SIDAE	Endnet	uDAS	SNSA	DNGAE
Tree	<u>0.1720</u>	0.1963	0.1900	0.46628	0.2037	0.255	0.3670	**0.0904**
Water	0.2020	0.3078	0.1570	0.5342	<u>0.1438</u>	0.4110	0.4112	**0.0737**
Soil	0.1980	0.2385	0.1820	<u>0.1725</u>	0.2420	0.2600	0.3464	**0.0684**
Average	0.1910	0.2475	<u>0.1760</u>	0.3909	0.1965	0.3090	0.3756	**0.0775**

Table 5. SAD unmixing performances (CNNAE, MTAE, CyCU-Net, SIDAE, Endnet, uDAS, SNSA, and DNGAE): Samson HSI. Best performances are in bold. Second performances are underlined.

Class	DL-based methods							
	CNNAE	MTAE	CyCU-Net	SIDAE	Endnet	uDAS	SNSA	DNGAE
Tree	0.1965	0.1598	0.1875	0.3269	0.4687	0.1536	**0.0750**	<u>0.1190</u>
Water	0.2847	**0.1026**	0.2518	0.2810	0.3269	<u>0.1974</u>	0.2844	0.2930
Soil	0.3005	**0.0997**	<u>0.1644</u>	0.3364	0.3396	0.2708	0.2493	0.1650
Average	0.2605	**0.1204**	0.2012	0.3147	0.3773	0.2072	0.2029	<u>0.1923</u>

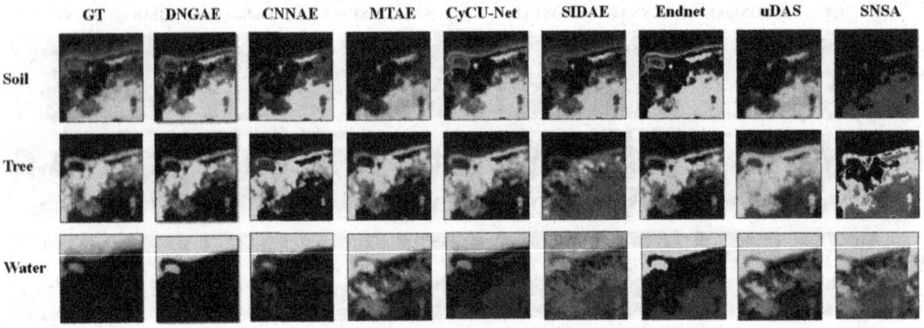

Fig. 6. Samson: estimated abundance maps using our proposed DNGAE method and other compared DL based methods.

method presents the second worst value followed by the Endnet model. Overall, we can conclude that an effect brought on by numerous light reflections and varying lighting conditions might result in an incorrect extraction of the appropriate endmember. Furthermore, it is worth noting that a bad SAD value does not always imply bad abundance maps which is the case with our method in estimating the different abundances as shown in Fig. 6. Accordingly, the abundance of "Water" is more intense and consistent than the one obtained using the MTAE method. For the rest techniques, SIDAE still shows poor estimation. Fur-

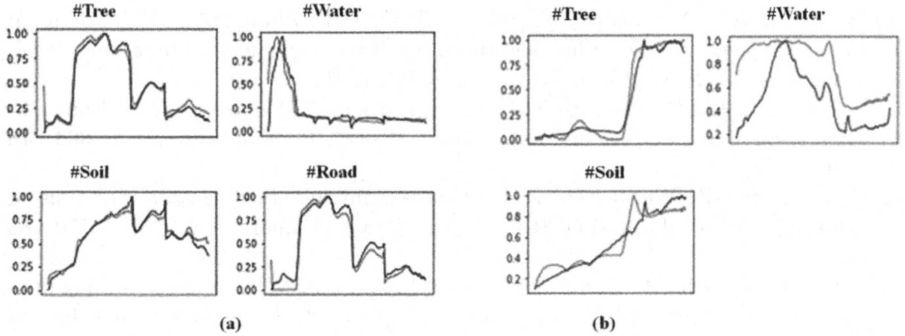

Fig. 7. Extracted endmembers (red) and corresponding GT (black) using our proposed DNGAE method. (a) Jasper Ridge, (b) Samson. (Color figure online)

thermore, Fig. 7 shows the extracted endmembers using our proposed DNGAE method compared to GT for both HSI datasets.

5 Conclusion

In this article, we developed a novel methodology for blind unmixing based on graph DL model. Specifically, a neighborhood graph is constructed based on an euclidean distance that considers spectral and spatial connectivity information. Then, according to the graph specificity, our method aggregates for each target pixel, its neighboring pixels information to yield a new richer representation space from which the quality of the abundance maps is enhanced. Furthermore, our experimental results demonstrate the effectiveness of our proposed method compared to other cube-wise spectro-spatial DL models. As future directions, since the construction of the adjacency matrix in standard graph DL often entails substantial computing costs, we intend to improve our model to learn richer representation from large HSI data. Moreover, other auxiliary geometric spatial information such as Gabor Filter, Morphological Profiles, etc. can be incorporated.

References

1. Gu, J., Wu, Z., Li, Y., Chen, Y., Wei, Z., Wang, W.: Parallel optimization of pixel purity index algorithm for hyperspectral unmixing based on spark. In: Third International Conference on Advanced Cloud and Big Data, Yangzhou, China, pp. 159–166 (2015)
2. Ayma Quirita, V.A., da Costa, G.A.O.P., Beltrán, C.: A distributed N-FINDR cloud computing-based solution for endmembers extraction on large-scale hyperspectral remote sensing data. Remote Sens. **14**(9) (2022)
3. Alves, J.M.R., Nascimento, J.M.P., Plaza, A., Sanchez, S., Bioucas-Dias, J.M., Silva, V.: Vertex component analysis GPU-based implementation for hyperspectral unmixing. In: 4th Workshop on Hyperspectral Image and Signal Processing: Evolution in Remote Sensing (WHISPERS), Shanghai, China, pp. 1–4 (2012)

4. Li, J., Agathos, A., Zaharie, D., Bioucas-Dias, J.M., Plaza, A., Li, X.: Minimum volume simplex analysis: a fast algorithm for linear hyperspectral unmixing. IEEE Trans. Geosci. Remote Sens. **53**(9), 5067–5082 (2015)
5. Nascimento, J.M.P., Bioucas-Dias, J.M.: Hyperspectral unmixing based on mixtures of dirichlet components. IEEE Trans. Geosci. Remote Sens. **50**(3), 863–878 (2012)
6. Tang, W., Shi, Z., Wu, Y., Zhang, C.: Sparse unmixing of hyperspectral data using spectral a priori information. IEEE Trans. Geosci. Remote Sens. **53**(2), 770–783 (2015)
7. Ayed, M., Hanachi, R., Sellami, A., Farah, I.R., Mura, M.D.: A deep learning approach based on morphological profiles for Hyperspectral Image unmixing. In: 6th International Conference on Advanced Technologies for Signal and Image Processing (ATSIP), Sfax, Tunisia, pp. 1–6 (2022)
8. Su, Y., Marinoni, A., Li, J., Plaza, A., Gamba, P.: Nonnegative sparse autoencoder for robust endmember extraction from remotely sensed hyperspectral images. In: IEEE International Geoscience and Remote Sensing Symposium (IGARSS), Fort Worth, TX, USA, pp. 205–208 (2017)
9. Palsson, F., Sigurdsson, J., Sveinsson, J.R., Ulfarsson, M.O.: Neural network hyperspectral unmixing with spectral information divergence objective. In: IEEE International Geoscience and Remote Sensing Symposium (IGARSS), Fort Worth, TX, USA, pp. 755–758 (2017)
10. Ozkan, S., Kaya, B., Akar, G.B.: EndNet: sparse AutoEncoder network for endmember extraction and hyperspectral unmixing. IEEE Trans. Geosci. Remote Sens. **57**(1), 482–496 (2019)
11. Su, Y., Li, J., Plaza, A., Marinoni, A., Gamba, P., Chakravortty, S.: DAEN: deep autoencoder networks for hyperspectral unmixing. IEEE Trans. Geosci. Remote Sens. **57**(7), 4309–4321 (2019)
12. Qu, Y., Qi, H.: uDAS: an untied denoising autoencoder with sparsity for spectral unmixing. IEEE Trans. Geosci. Remote Sens. **57**(3), 1698–1712 (2019)
13. Palsson, B., Sveinsson, J.R., Ulfarsson, M.O.: Spectral-spatial hyperspectral unmixing using multitask learning. IEEE Access **7**, 148861–148872 (2019)
14. Zhang, X., Sun, Y., Zhang, J., Wu, P., Jiao, L.: Hyperspectral unmixing via deep convolutional neural networks. IEEE Geosci. Remote Sens. Lett. **15**(11), 1755–1759 (2018)
15. Palsson, B., Ulfarsson, M.O., Sveinsson, J.R.: Convolutional autoencoder for spectral-spatial hyperspectral unmixing. IEEE Trans. Geosci. Remote Sens. **59**(1), 535–549 (2019)
16. Rasti, B., Koirala, B., Scheunders, P., Ghamisi, P.: UnDIP: hyperspectral unmixing using deep image prior. IEEE Trans. Geosci. Remote Sens. **60**, 1–15 (2022)
17. Gao, L., Han, Z., Hong, D., Zhang, B., Chanussot, J.: CyCU-Net: cycle-consistency unmixing network by learning cascaded autoencoders. IEEE Trans. Geosci. Remote Sens. **60**, 1–14 (2022)
18. Wu, Z., Pan, S., Chen, F., Long, G., Zhang, C., Yu, P.S.: A comprehensive survey on graph neural networks. IEEE Trans. Neural Netw. Learn. Syst. **32**(1), 4–24 (2021)
19. Kipf, T., Welling, M.: Variational Graph Auto-Encoders. arXiv (2016)

Unlocking the Potential of Deep Learning and Filter Gabor for Facial Emotion Recognition

Chawki Barhoumi[1,2(✉)] and Yassine Ben Ayed[2]

[1] National School of Electronics and Telecommunications of Sfax, Sfax, Tunisia
chawki.barhoumi@enetcom.u-sfax.tn

[2] Multimedia, InfoRmation systems and Advanced Computing Laboratory, Sfax, Tunisia
yassine.benayed@isims.usf.tn

Abstract. Automated Facial Emotion Recognition (FER) is a crucial challenge in the field of computer vision, and researchers have proposed numerous methods to enhance the accuracy and efficiency of facial expression identification. Several techniques such as analyzing brain signals (EEG), speech, skin responses, facial expressions, body gestures, and other similar procedures have been used to address this challenge. In this work, we propose a novel approach to detect basic facial expressions using a combination of Gabor filter and Convolution Neural Network (CNN) with Long Short Term Memory (LSTM). Feature extraction and The architecture of the deep learning model, including the number of layers, regularization, normalization, and other factors, plays a vital role in distinguishing one work from another. We tested and validated our proposed approach on the Cohn-Kanad (CK+) database. Our facial expression recognition system achieved an average accuracy of 100%. We further validate our system using different evaluation metrics and compare its accuracy with other works recently published with the same data.

Keywords: Facial Emotion Recognition · Convolution Neural Network · Gabor Filter · Textural Features · Long-Short Term Memory

1 Introduction

The ability to recognize human emotional expressions has become increasingly important for interactions between humans and machines. In recent years, various sectors, such as assisted medicine, distance learning, interactive games, public safety, security monitoring, social robots, and the entertainment industry, have utilized this technology [4,19]. Emotions in human-computer interaction (HCI) are typically spontaneous and not easily identifiable as discrete emotions; they are often weakly expressed, mixed, and difficult to distinguish from each

N. T. Nguyen et al. (Eds.): ICCCI 2023, LNAI 14162, pp. 97–110, 2023.
https://doi.org/10.1007/978-3-031-41456-5_8

other. In the literature, emotional statements are generally categorized as positive or negative, depending on the emotions expressed by an individual [21]. Additionally, studies show that facial expressions that are acted out tend to be more accurate than natural emotions, as actors tend to exaggerate their expressions of emotion [22]. The classification of the fundamental emotions is depicted in the Fig. 1. The valence represents the effect of positivity and negativity on the emotions, whereas the arousal represents the intensity of calmness or excitement in the emotions.

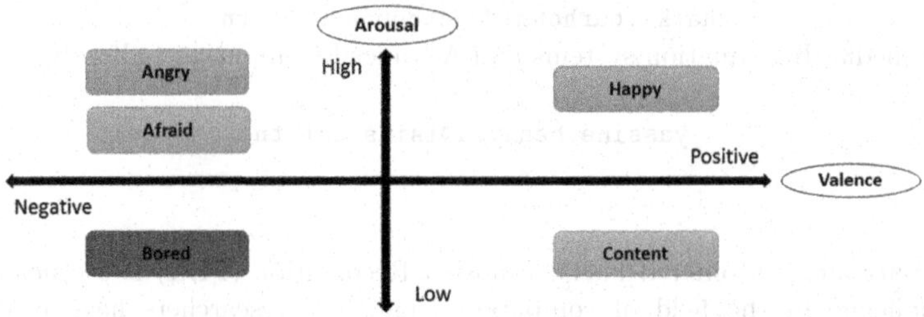

Fig. 1. A two dimensional basic emotional space.

There are various methods to detect human emotional states, including ElectroEncephaloGraphy (EEG) signals, facial expressions, body gestures and postures, speech analysis, and sound analysis [16]. Among these methods, facial expression recognition is the most natural and effective technique to implement using deep learning algorithms. In recent years, advanced machine learning and deep learning algorithms such as Support Vector Machine (SVM), Artificial Neural Network (ANN), and Hidden Markov Model (HMM) have been utilized to detect emotions from facial expressions [24]. Moreover, Convolutional Neural Networks (CNN) and Recurrent Neural Networks (RNN) models have been developed and utilized for recognizing emotions [12]. Despite recent improvements in facial emotion recognition, the accuracy of computer vision-based systems still needs enhancement. To achieve better accuracy in human facial emotion recognition, specific feature extraction techniques such as Local Binary Pattern (LBP), Histogram of Oriented Gradients (HOG), and Gabor Wavelet are widely used to describe textural features of expressions [9].

The aim of this project is to develop an emotion recognition system that accurately detects facial expressions. To achieve this, we will use a textural feature extraction method called Gabor filter, and an advanced hybrid deep learning technique that combines Convolutional Neural Networks (CNN) and Long Short-Term Memory (LSTM) models for emotion classification. We will provide more details on this technique later in our study. In the final stage of our research, we plan to test the developed system to evaluate its performance and ensure its accuracy. The main contributions of this paper are as follows:

1. An effective method for extracting textural information from images is applied to the image dataset.

2. An efficient hybrid deep learning-based facial emotion recognition model is proposed.
3. The deep learning model and textural features method proposed in this paper are tested using a baseline dataset in experiments.

The remainder of the research paper is organised as follows: we consider the first section as related work. The extraction of textural features, the classification method, and the evaluation are presented in the second section. The next section is devoted to the analysis of our experimental examinations. Finally, we conclude our study in the last section.

2 Related Works

In this section, we provide a concise yet comprehensive overview of the literature pertaining to the prevailing machine and deep learning methods, as well as the image processing techniques that are commonly employed in this domain.

Rahul Ravi et al. [18] conducted a study to compare the accuracy of two widely used facial expression recognition techniques: Local Binary Pattern (LBP) and Convolutional Neural Networks (CNN). LBP was used solely for feature extraction, and the Support Vector Machine (SVM) classifier was used to classify the features extracted from LBP. The study used three datasets (CK+, JAFFE, and YALE FACE) for testing and training, with 70% of the data utilized for training and 30% for testing. The results showed that CNN outperformed all other methods, achieving a recognition rate of 97.32% on the CK+ dataset and 31.82% on the YALE FACE dataset, which was the least accurate.

M. Kalpana Chowdary's [3] study utilized deep learning models including Resnet 50, VGG 19, Inception V3, and Mobile Net to classify seven different emotions from the CK+ database, namely anger, contempt, disgust, fear, happiness, sadness, and surprise. The study conducted an experiment on the CK+ database to evaluate and compare the performance of each model. Additionally, the database images underwent pre-processing, where Resnet50, vgg19, and MobileNet models were resized to 224*224, and Inception V3 was resized to 299*299. The VGG19 model achieved 96% accuracy, Resnet50 achieved 97.7% accuracy, Inception V3 achieved 98.5% accuracy, and MobileNet achieved 94.20% accuracy. Notably, MobileNet outperformed the other three pre-trained networks in terms of accuracy.

An approach to facial emotion recognition using data augmentation and deep learning techniques was proposed by [17]. The system consists of four components: Firstly, a face detection algorithm was applied to the input image in the initial component. In the second component, a convolutional neural network (CNN) architecture was proposed to classify facial expressions based on more distinctive and discriminant features. In the third component, data augmentation techniques were used to enhance the CNN model's performance by enriching its learning parameters. Finally, in the fourth component, a trade-off between data augmentation and deep learning features was made for the CNN model. The proposed system was tested on three benchmark datasets, KDEF (seven expression classes), GENKI-4k (two expression classes), and CK+ (seven expression classes). Extensive experimental results showed that the proposed system achieved recognition rates of 83.43%, 94.67%, and 97.69% with the KDEF, GENKI-4K, and CK+ databases, respectively. Overall, [17]'s proposed an effective facial emotion recognition system that combines deep learning and data augmentation techniques to enhance the recognition accuracy of facial expressions. The proposed system's performance was validated using multiple benchmark datasets, demonstrating its potential for real-world applications.

Dharma Karan Reddy Gaddam et al. [8] employed a deep or convolutional neural network to detect human facial emotions. They utilized ResNet 50 to classify the seven different categories of emotions in the FER2013 dataset: anger, disgust, fear, happiness, sadness, surprise, and neutral. The proposed neural network attained a test accuracy of 55.6%. The system was further tested with a static image rather than a real-time video, and the results suggest that the system accurately predicts the emotions portrayed in the static image.

In their research, Xiaoning Zhu et al. [25] developed a novel approach for expression recognition using a combination of the Swin Transformer, a hierarchical transformer, and a CNN model. The proposed network architecture integrates both the Transformer and CNN models, allowing for more effective and efficient recognition of facial expressions. To evaluate the effectiveness of their method, the authors conducted experiments on various publicly available expression datasets, such as FERPlus, CK+, AffectNet-8, and RAF-DB. After the learning phase, their proposed system achieved impressive accuracy rates of 87.4%, 98.2%, 60.7%, and 87% respectively, on these datasets. These results demonstrate the potential of the combined Transformer and CNN model for improving expression recognition tasks, and provide insights for future research in this field.

3 Proposed Work

Gabor filters can be used for feature extraction in deep learning by incorporating them as the initial layers of a convolutional neural network (CNN). This involves convolving the input images with a Gabor filter bank to obtain a set of filtered images or feature maps. The resulting feature maps are then downsampled and concatenated to produce a feature map that captures both the spatial and frequency information of the input image. Also, Convolutional Neural Network (CNN) has strong feature extraction capabilities. It is used to extract features from the hyperspectral image.

Figure 2 shows the different components of a facial expression recognition system based on Gabor filters and deep learning techniques, as suggested in this article.

3.1 Dataset

The CK+ dataset is a commonly used benchmark dataset for facial expression recognition research. It consists of 981 image in total from 123 subjects, where

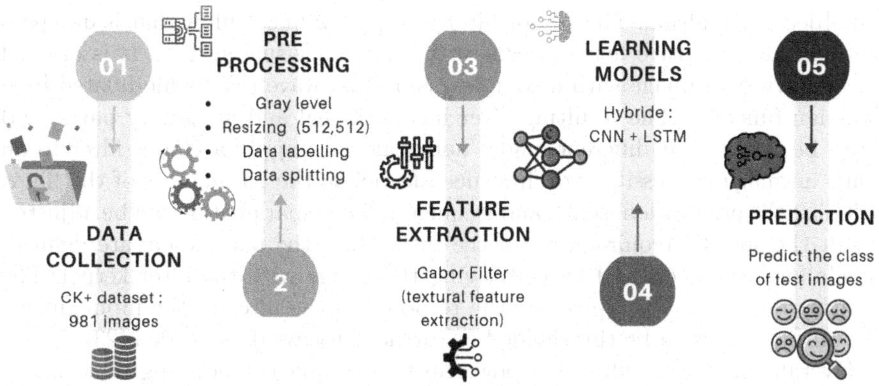

Fig. 2. Proposed system

each sequence displays one of seven facial expressions: angry, contempt, disgust, fearful, happy, sad, and surprised. The images were captured under laboratory conditions and the expressions were elicited using a method called the Facial Action Coding System (FACS). Each sequence starts with a neutral expression, followed by the target expression and ends with the neutral expression again. The images are in grayscale and have a resolution of 640 × 490 pixels. The CK+ dataset is widely used for evaluating and comparing different facial expression recognition methods [5]. The Table 1 shows the number of samples in each emotion category.

Table 1. CK+ representation

Emotions	Happy	Angry	Surprised	Disgust	Fearful	Contempt	Sad	***Total***
Samples number	207	135	249	177	75	54	84	***981***

3.2 Preprocessing

In this important first stage:

- All images in the CK+ dataset are converted to grey levels.
- Following that, we resize them from $(48 * 48)$ to $(512 * 512)$.
- We also label the data, which consists of giving a class of emotion for each image in the dataset.
- Finally, we split the data into 75% for training and 25% for testing.

3.3 Gabor Filter

The Gabor filter is a commonly used filter in image processing that can be used for various tasks, such as feature extraction, edge detection, texture analysis, and object recognition. The Gabor filter is a type of linear filter that is designed to mimic the receptive fields of cells in the human visual system. It is created by convolving an image with a complex sinusoidal wave that is modulated by a Gaussian function. The resulting filter has both real and imaginary parts, and it can be oriented at different angles and scales. To apply a Gabor filter to an image in image processing, you first need to define the parameters of the filter, including the orientation, scale, and frequency. These parameters can be adjusted to suit the specific requirements of the task. Once the parameters are defined, the Gabor filter is created by convolving the image with the filter kernel. The resulting output image represents the response of the filter to the input image. The output can then be thresholded or further processed as needed [23].

Overall, the Gabor filter is a powerful tool in image processing that can be used to extract meaningful features from images and improve the performance of many computer vision tasks. The equation for a 2D Gabor filter in the spatial domain is [1]:

$$G(x, y) = \exp\left(-\frac{(x'^2 + y'^2)}{2\sigma^2}\right) \cdot \cos(2\pi f x' + \phi) \quad (1)$$

$$x' = x \cdot \cos(\theta) + y \cdot \sin(\theta) \quad (2)$$

$$y' = -x \cdot \sin(\theta) + y \cdot \cos(\theta) \quad (3)$$

where: x' and y' are the coordinates of the pixel being filtered. σ is the standard deviation of the Gaussian envelope. f is the frequency of the sinusoidal carrier. ϕ is the phase offset.

Algorithm 1. Gabor Kernel Creation and Image Filtering

function CREATEGABORKERNEL(shape, σ, θ, frequency, γ)
    kernel ← cv2.getGaborKernel(shape, σ, θ, frequency, γ)
    kernel ← kernel/np.max(kernel)
    return kernel
img_data_list ← [] ▷ empty list
input_img ← cv2.imread(img)
input_img ← cv2.cvtColor(input_img, cv2.COLOR_BGR2GRAY)
input_img_resize ← cv2.resize(input_img, (512, 512))
kernel ← CreateGaborKernel((512, 512), $\sigma = 2.0, \theta = \frac{\pi}{4}$, frequency $= 0.18, \gamma = 2.0$)
filtered_img ← cv2.filter2D(input_img_resize, cv2.CV_8UC3, kernel)
img_data_list.append(filtered_img)

In our work, we choose the following values for the hyperparameters of the Gabor filter method (Table 2):

- Sigma (σ): We chose a sigma value of 2.0 for the Gabor filters to control the spatial extent or the spread of the Gaussian envelope.
- Theta (θ): We set the theta value to $\frac{\pi}{4}$, which corresponds to an orientation of 45°.

- Frequency: We select a frequency of 0.18 for the Gabor filters to capture a range of spatial frequencies in the facial images.
- Gamma (γ): The gamma value is set to 2.0, representing an aspect ratio of (2:1) (Fig. 3).

Table 2. Description of Hyperparameters

Hyperparameters	Sigma (σ)	Theta (θ)	Frequence	Gamma (γ)
Value	2.0	$\frac{\pi}{4}$	0.18	2.0

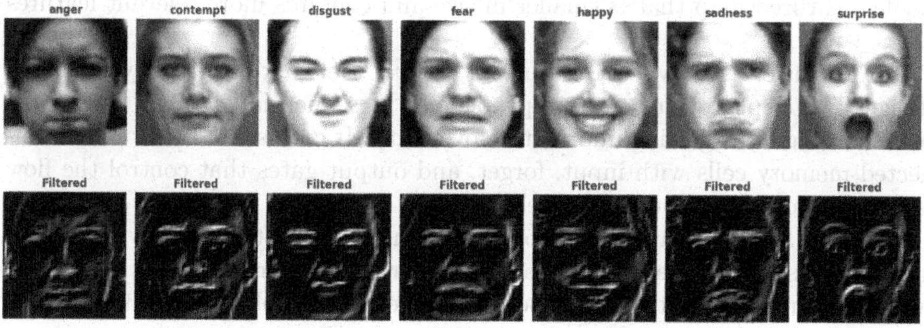

Fig. 3. Result of applying the Gabor filter method on the CK+ dataset

3.4 Hybrid (CNN-LSTM) Model

Particularly, this portion of our work is crucial. The structure of image data is composed of two complementary components: the sequential aspect that designates the actual numerical values of the pixels, and the temporal aspect that describes the distribution of the content over time. Thus, to create a model that considers both aspects, we decided to build a hybrid model that combines CNN and LSTM. CNN is an effective technique for extracting the best features due to its various layers of convolutions, max pooling, and other techniques. On the other hand, LSTM is a recurrent network that focuses on the temporal aspect. As depicted in Fig. 4, the proposed model is split into three parts: the input part, which consists of the pre-processed images from the dataset; the convolution part; and finally, the LSTM and classification part. Four blocks of convolution layers make up the convolution component. A max pooling layer comes after each convolution layer. In the first block, the convolution layer is implemented using 32 $\times$ 5 $\times$ 5 filters (or kernels) and a stride (step) size of 1. Additionally, the 2 $\times$ 2 kernel size max pooling layer is adopted. For the last three blocks, we use identical values, but we multiply the number of filters by two each time. After flattening the data from the final max pooling layer, we enhance our model with a block made up of two equal-sized LSTM layers (256 units). The dense layer with 512 neurons is then added using the Relu activation algorithm. Finally, we implement a dropout layer with a rate of 0.5 before the output layer that employs softmax as the activation function.

The most important operation on CNN is the convolution layer; it takes longer than other transactions. The main role of the convolution layer is to extract the best and most important features from the input image. The filters or kernels (small squares of size, for example, 3×3, 5×5, 7×7) are slid on the image to compute the scalar product and generate the "features map", also called the "activation map" or "convoluted features" [15].

The pooling layer aims to make the feature map's characteristics more compactby reducing the feature map's spatial dimension. This operation produces a pooled featured map that is smaller in size and contains more relevant features [2].

LSTM layer is a type of Recurrent Neural Network (RNN) layer that is designed to capture long-term dependencies in sequential data by selectively remembering or forgetting information over time. It consists of a set of interconnected memory cells with input, forget, and output gates that control the flow of information in and out of the cell [10].

Softmax is an activation function that we have used after the fully connected layer to classify the generated feature vector into different classes [16]. This function converts a vector of numbers into a vector of probabilities. It is defined as follows:

$$\sigma(\overrightarrow{z}_i) = \frac{e^{x_i}}{\sum_{j=1}^{k} e^{x_j}} \tag{4}$$

The softmax function is represented by σ. $\overrightarrow{z}$ represent the input vector, e^{x_i} exponential function for the input vector; K is the number of classes; and e^{x_j} is exponential function for the output vector.

4 Experiment Results

In our experiments, we generate and execute our implementation using Python and Google Collaboration on a Personal Computer (PC) 64-bit system with an Intel Pentium 4 quad-core processor and 4 GB of RAM.

4.1 Evaluation Metrics

To evaluate the proposed FER system. we use some widely evaluation metrics of FER which are : precision, recall, accuracy, and F1-score [11]. The precision is defined as :

$$Precision = \frac{TP}{(TP + FP)} \tag{5}$$

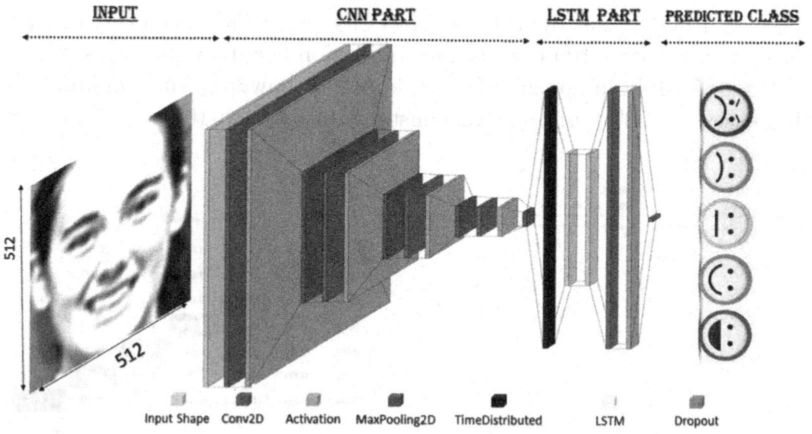

Fig. 4. Hybrid CNN + LSTM approach

And the recall is defined as :

$$Recall = \frac{TP}{(TP + FN)} \quad (6)$$

where TP is the number of true positives in the dataset, FN is the number of false negatives, and FP is the number of false positives. The F1-score is the harmonic mean of these two indicators (recall and precision), both of which must be high [6]. It is defined as:

$$F1 - score = \frac{2 * recall * precision}{recall + precision} \quad (7)$$

The accuracy is defined as the ratio of true outcomes (both true positive and true negative) to the total number of cases examined [7]. It is defined by :

$$Accuracy = \frac{TP + TN}{Total \quad population} \quad (8)$$

We also use the confusion matrix as an evaluation metric to properly evaluate our model. The confusion matrix, as the name implies, produces an output matrix that describes the model's overall performance.

4.2 Results and Discussions

Our proposed CNN + LSTM model was trained using a batch size of 64 and over the course of 100 epochs. The progression of the accuracy (on the training set) and the validation accuracy (on the validation set), as illustrated in Figur 5a, both increase with very close values to reach a value of 100% for the accuracy and validation accuracy. Similarly, for the loss function, the training and validation values decrease in a balanced manner to $4.6949e^{-06}$ and $3.3468e^{-04}$

respectively. Finally, the hybrid model (CNN + LSTM) achieves an average accuracy of 100% after 100 epochs.The validation accuracy increases from 78% in epoch 1 to 99.49% in epoch 30. From epoch 31 onwards, the validation accuracy increases to 100% and remains constant until epoch 100.

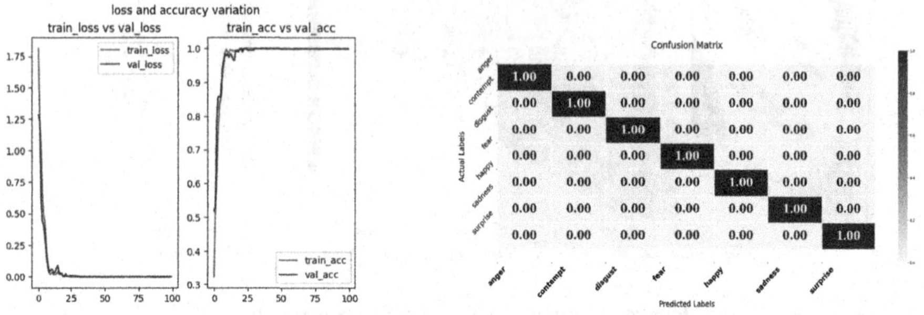

(a) Model Behavior (b) Confution Matrix

Fig. 5. Model behavior during training phase and confusion matrix

Table 3. Performance of our proposed model using the evaluation metrics precision, recall, and F1-score

Emotions	Anger	Contempt	Disgust	Fear	Happy	Sad	Surprise
Precision	1.00	100	1.00	1.00	1.00	100	1.00
Recall	100	1.00	100	1.00	1.00	1.00	100
F1-score	100	100	100	1.00	1.00	100	100

The confusion matrix is a critical evaluation metric that indicates the accuracy of the various emotion categories to be classified. Figure 5b depicts the various precision values by category. As a result, if there is confusion in category classification, we can easily detect the confused categories using this evaluation metric. We can see that all of the emotion categories are correctly predicted with an accuracy of 100%. Table 3 displays the precision, recall, and F1-score results. We notice that the values observed are adequate. a good precision and recall value, and F1-score values of 100%, which appears to be ideal. as we present in Fig. 6, all prediction for the testing set are correct. which we encourage to validate the proposed model.

4.3 Comparison to Other Methods

In order to confirm the effectiveness of our approach, the average recognition accuracy is compared to other approaches for FER methods in the following Table (Table 4):

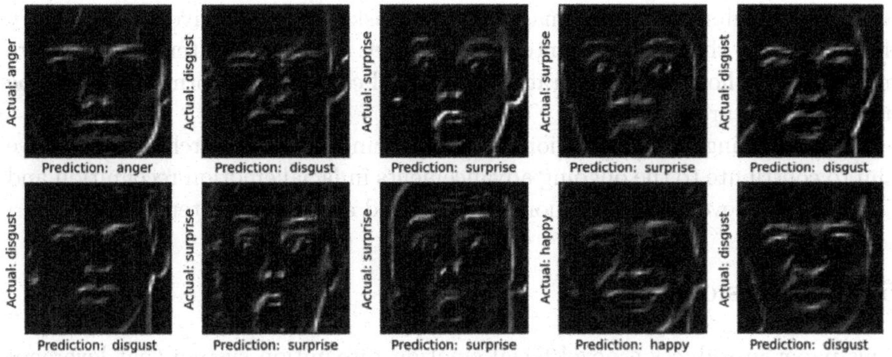

Fig. 6. Model prediction performance

Table 4. Shows the comparison between different approaches and our approach with the CK+ database.

Methods	Accuracy(%)	Reference	Year
DWT CNN	96.46	[9]	2019
LBP CNN	97.32	[18]	2020
CNN and GA-SVM-Based	97.59	[13]	2020
Resnet 50	97.7	[3]	2021
VGG19	96	[3]	2021
CNN	97.69	[20]	2022
LBP CNN	79.5	[14]	2022
LTP CNN	89.2	[14]	2022
CLBP CNN	91	[14]	2022
LBP LSTM	98.43	[17]	2022
PCA +Gabor Filter	94.20	[1]	2022
Transformer and CNN	98.2	[25]	2023
Proposed approach	**100**	#	#

In this study, we propose a facial emotion recognition system utilizing deep learning and Gabor filters, with experiments conducted on the CK+ dataset. While our approach achieved promising results, it is essential to acknowledge and discuss its limitations. One limitation of our approach is the reliance on the CK+ dataset, which, although widely used in the field, may have certain constraints. The dataset comprises a relatively small number of subjects, limiting the diversity and variability of facial expressions captured. Consequently, the generalization of our model to unseen datasets or real-world scenarios could be affected.

Furthermore, our approach assumes that Gabor filters effectively capture relevant facial features for emotion recognition. While Gabor filters have shown promising results in various image analysis tasks, their effectiveness may vary depending on the specific context or dataset. Exploring alternative feature extraction methods or incorporating additional contextual information could be avenues for future research.

By addressing these limitations and suggesting future research directions, we aim to contribute to the ongoing advancements in facial emotion recognition and facilitate the development of more effective and applicable systems.

5 Conclusion

This paper introduces a novel facial emotion recognition system that leverages textural features extracted using the Gabor filter operator and a hybrid CNN-LSTM model for learning. We preprocess all images in the CK+ database by converting them to grayscale, resizing them, and categorizing them. We then apply the Gabor filter operator to extract the features, which are used as input to the CNN-LSTM model.

Our proposed method outperforms traditional machine learning methods due to the effectiveness of the extracted filter characteristics with the Gabor filter in terms of edge visibility and image texture. Additionally, CNN and LSTM are widely used in image recognition and consistently demonstrate excellent results. Our proposed approach achieve an average accuracy of 100%. Specifying special characteristics such as textural features has been shown to significantly increase accuracy, not only in our study but also in several others.

We used only the image modality to build our model, but it can also be extended to multimodal data, such as speech and sound. We suggest that deeper architectures that have the potential to produce successful results, such as transfer learning, should be explored in future research.

References

1. Boughida, A., Kouahla, M.N., Lafifi, Y.: A novel approach for facial expression recognition based on Gabor filters and genetic algorithm. Evol. Syst. **13**(2), 331–345 (2022)
2. Canal, F.Z., et al.: A survey on facial emotion recognition techniques: a state-of-the-art literature review. Inf. Sci. **582**, 593–617 (2022)
3. Chowdary, M.K., Nguyen, T.N., Hemanth, D.J.: Deep learning-based facial emotion recognition for human–computer interaction applications. Neural Comput. Appl. 1–18 (2021)
4. Dang, L.T., Cooper, E.W., Kamei, K.: Development of facial expression recognition for training video customer service representatives. In: 2014 IEEE International Conference on Fuzzy Systems (FUZZ-IEEE), pp. 1297–1303. IEEE (2014)
5. Dhall, A., Goecke, R., Lucey, S., Gedeon, T., et al.: Collecting large, richly annotated facial-expression databases from movies. IEEE Multimedia **19**(3), 34 (2012)
6. Ding, X., Chu, W.S., De la Torre, F., Cohn, J.F., Wang, Q.: Facial action unit event detection by cascade of tasks. In: Proceedings of the IEEE International Conference on Computer Vision. pp. 2400–2407 (2013)

7. Fabian Benitez-Quiroz, C., Srinivasan, R., Martinez, A.M.: Emotionet: An accurate, real-time algorithm for the automatic annotation of a million facial expressions in the wild. In: Proceedings of the IEEE Conference on Computer Vision and Pattern Recognition, pp. 5562–5570 (2016)
8. Gaddam, D.K.R., Ansari, M.D., Vuppala, S., Gunjan, V.K., Sati, M.M.: Human facial emotion detection using deep learning. In: Kumar, A., Senatore, S., Gunjan, V.K. (eds.) ICDSMLA 2020. LNEE, vol. 783, pp. 1417–1427. Springer, Singapore (2022). https://doi.org/10.1007/978-981-16-3690-5_136
9. Ilyas, B.R., Mohammed, B., Khaled, M., Ahmed, A.T., Ihsen, A.: Facial expression recognition based on dwt feature for deep CNN. In: 2019 6th International Conference on Control, Decision and Information Technologies (CoDIT), pp. 344–348. IEEE (2019)
10. Jo, A.H., Kwak, K.C.: Speech emotion recognition based on two-stream deep learning model using Korean audio information. Appl. Sci. **13**(4), 2167 (2023)
11. Ko, B.C.: A brief review of facial emotion recognition based on visual information. Sensors **18**(2), 401 (2018)
12. Li, T.H.S., Kuo, P.H., Tsai, T.N., Luan, P.C.: CNN and LSTM based facial expression analysis model for a humanoid robot. IEEE Access **7**, 93998–94011 (2019)
13. Liu, X., Cheng, X., Lee, K.: GA-SVM-based facial emotion recognition using facial geometric features. IEEE Sens. J. **21**(10), 11532–11542 (2020)
14. Mukhopadhyay, M., Dey, A., Kahali, S.: A deep-learning-based facial expression recognition method using textural features. Neural Comput. Appl. **35**, 1–16 (2022)
15. Mukhopadhyay, M., Dey, A., Kahali, S.: A deep-learning-based facial expression recognition method using textural features. Neural Comput. Appl. **35**(9), 6499–6514 (2023)
16. Mukhopadhyay, M., Dey, A., Shaw, R.N., Ghosh, A.: Facial emotion recognition based on textural pattern and convolutional neural network. In: 2021 IEEE 4th International Conference on Computing, Power and Communication Technologies, pp. 1–6. IEEE (2021)
17. Pandit, D., Jadhav, S.: 2d face emotion recognition and prediction using labelled selective transfer machine and CNN transfer learning techniques for unbalanced datasets. Int. J. Intell. Syst. Appl. Eng. **10**(4), 269–277 (2022)
18. Ravi, R., Yadhukrishna, S., et al.: A face expression recognition using CNN & LBP. In: 2020 Fourth International Conference on Computing Methodologies and Communication, pp. 684–689. IEEE (2020)
19. Suk, M., Prabhakaran, B.: Real-time facial expression recognition on smartphones. In: 2015 IEEE Winter Conference on Applications of Computer Vision, pp. 1054–1059. IEEE (2015)
20. Umer, S., Rout, R.K., Pero, C., Nappi, M.: Facial expression recognition with tradeoffs between data augmentation and deep learning features. J. Ambient. Intell. Humaniz. Comput. **13**(2), 721–735 (2022)
21. Ververidis, D., Kotropoulos, C.: A state of the art review on emotional speech databases. In: Proceedings of 1st Richmedia Conference, pp. 109–119. Citeseer (2003)
22. Vyas, G., Dutta, M.K., Riha, K., Prinosil, J., et al.: An automatic emotion recognizer using mfccs and hidden Markov models. In: 2015 7th International Congress on Ultra Modern Telecommunications and Control Systems and Workshops, pp. 320–324. IEEE (2015)
23. Zadeh, M.M.T., Imani, M., Majidi, B.: Fast facial emotion recognition using convolutional neural networks and Gabor filters. In: 2019 5th Conference on Knowledge Based Engineering and Innovation, pp. 577–581. IEEE (2019)

24. Zhang, Y., Ji, Q.: Active and dynamic information fusion for facial expression understanding from image sequences. IEEE Trans. Pattern Anal. Mach. Intell. **27**(5), 699–714 (2005)
25. Zhu, X., Li, Z., Sun, J.: Expression recognition method combining convolutional features and transformer. Math. Found. Comput. **6**(2), 203–217 (2023)

Graph Convolution Collaborative Filtering with Dense Embeddings

Trung-Nam Bui Huynh, Anh-Tuc Tran, and Ngoc-Thao Nguyen(✉)

Faculty of Information Technology, University of Science, Vietnam National University Ho Chi Minh City, Ho Chi Minh City, Vietnam
{bhtnam19,tatuc19}@clc.fitus.edu.vn, nnthao@fitus.edu.vn

Abstract. Recommender systems have been a vital part of many e-commerce and online services. These systems support profound user personalization by mining the semantic interactions between users and items in the database, thereby increasing customer satisfaction and revenue. Furthermore, collaborative filtering research has significantly advanced in recent years with the compelling expressiveness of graph-based neural networks. In this paper, we introduce a novel collaborative filtering approach that represents users and items as graph embeddings and effectively exploits the knowledge from these embeddings. First, the feature vectors for users and items are refined with multiple embedding propagation layers. We then use many dense layers to get extra information as much as possible, main purpose is to support embedding vectors in the propagation process and allow our model to better learning of the user-item interaction, making a noticeable difference in performance from prior works. Finally, we combine them before mapping to a predicted score. The proposed method has been empirically proven superior to the baselines and competitive with modern approaches on public benchmarks.

Keywords: Recommender system · Graph convolutional network (GCN) · Neural graph collaborative filtering (NGCF)

1 Introduction

In the incredible development of information in many domains, such as shopping, music services, social networking platforms, etc., data has become an essential part of the primary goal of making our lives more and more convenient and comfortable. For that reason, recommender systems were born and used to tell customers if an e-commerce shop sells what they want or are interested in the information boom.

A commonly well-known and fundamental method for the recommender system is Collaborative Filtering(CF), which uses an ID to represent a user or item. The score of user and item pairs will be operated on each pair of IDs. Typically,

T.-N. Bui Huynh, A.-T. Tran—These authors contributed equally to this work.

N. T. Nguyen et al. (Eds.): ICCCI 2023, LNAI 14162, pp. 111–124, 2023.
https://doi.org/10.1007/978-3-031-41456-5_9

models will make an inner product between the user and item embedding vector to get the score of a product based on the customer. After that, several research studies have been conducted based on the CF method, and researchers found that the historical interaction of users on items can be used to improve the performance of models. SVD++ [9] is one excellent example of using historical interaction to enhance the quality of models. But this would not be complete if we forget the outstanding methods in the recommendation task, and it is the method using Graph convolutional networks (GCN [8]). The GCN-based method will update embeddings using high-order propagation to get as much information as possible to improve the model's quality.

Neural graph collaborative filtering (NGCF) [14] is one of the state-of-the-art methods for using GCN [8] on recommendations. NGCF applies two GCN operations at each layer: embedding will be propagated using convolutional neighbourhood aggregation and the embedding will be projected to other spaces using a non-linear transformation of the neural network. Despite the excellent result of NGCF, we argue that the structure of NGCF is more complex and inconvenient for the recommender system. As we know, GCN is applied to many domains having more information, such as computer vision, but in recommender systems, especially in implicit feedback, we get very little information. Therefore, fully applying GCN in the recommender system may bring many problems.

In this paper, we will first perform some experiments and evaluation the NGCF [14] on why we do not need to apply entire operations of GCN [8] into NGCF. Then, inspired by neural networks, which achieve many incredible goals in extracting and getting information, we improve NGCF by adjusting embedding propagation and using dense layers to get more information from surrounding nodes. Thereby improving the quality of the model. To summarize, the contributions of this paper are three-folded:

- Experiments and evaluations are conducted on the problems when applying entire operations of GCN [8] on NGCF [14].
- We propose the enhancing model DenseGCF to improve the problem above and use dense layers to get promising results.
- The model will be conducted experiments on three large datasets and compared with other existing approaches.

2 Related Work

2.1 Collaborative Filtering

CF has been a suitable method to be applied easily for many types of learning ranging from simple matrix factorization (MF) [10] to neural recommendation models(NCF) [7] or GCN [8] for decades. It is sufficient to capture similar users and/or items without any specific large knowledge domain and gives extra serendipity in careful computations.

2.2 Model-Based CF Method

Model-based CF approaches serve the need to define a model for user-item interactions where it parameterizes users and items into vectorized representations and reconstructs interaction data to explain those interactions.

Several efforts have been made and continue to make progress in the field under various methods and hypotheses. For example, simple MF [10] uses the IDs of users and items for mapping their representation into embedding space and using dot-product for interaction prediction. From that point, many side features, such as item content [2], social relations [13], are incorporated to improve model performance. However, as MF models are extremely hard to add side information into vector embeddings, it is more straightforward for Deep Neural Network to enhance over MF models by its flexible input layer. Additionally, the dot product is not the only option for score prediction. For recommender systems, we would like to capture as much information as possible from these latent representations. The growth of deep learning models shows their ability to handle these tasks efficiently and accurately. For instance, NeuMF [7] applies these non-linearities of neural networks to capture the more complex relationship between users and items.

2.3 Graph-Based CF Method

This approach exploits the graph structure of relationships formed by interactions between users and items. GC-MC [1] proposes a graph auto-encoder framework for link predictions in recommendations. Hop-Rec [17] introduces a combined MF [10], and GCN [8] framework that performs random walks on graph structure to enrich interaction data, capture high-order information, and optimize the pairwise relationship between positive and negative multi-order items, whose results convince those high-order connectivities in the user-item interactions are helpful for implicit feedback recommendations. NGCF [14] claims to explicitly encode collaborative signals as user-item high-order connectivity into the embedding process by propagation embeddings on the user-item graph structure. DGCF [15] digs more into user intents by involving the graph disentangling module to construct disentangled representations.

Expensive computation is one of the critical challenges when dealing with graph recommendation. In 2018, PinSage [18] introduced a Web-Scale Recommender System that applies to data with billions of items and millions of users by using random work and graph convolution to generate vector embedding representation. LightGCN [6] points out that only neighbourhood aggregation is essential for collaborative filtering. RGCF [11] eliminates all non-linear latent layers, layer aggregation, and product of user-item to decrease redundant information and better recommend performance. Low-pass Collaborative Filter Network [19] introduced in 2017 uses a 2D low-pass graph filter(LCF) to eliminate noises in observed data and assemble an origin graph convolution that lessens the cost and the model's complexity with the prospect of applying for larger graphs.

3 Preliminaries

We first introduce a few concepts of our baseline model, NGCF [14], a state-of-the-art GCN [8] model for implicit feedback user-item recommendation. We then give our explanations for the hypothesis of our upcoming work.

3.1 Summary of Neural Graph Collaborative Filtering

In NGCF [14], the model leverages these implicit data to learn for user-item vectorized representation as learnable embeddings. These embedding vectors then pass through k layers propagation to refine embedding vectors using message-passing architecture as defined in GNNs [4,16] on the user-item graph as follows:

$$e_u^{(k+1)} = \sigma\left(W_1 e_u^{(k)} + \sum_{i \in \mathcal{N}_u} \frac{1}{\sqrt{|\mathcal{N}_u||\mathcal{N}_i|}}(W_1 e_i^{(k)} + W_2(e_i^{(k)} \odot e_u^{(k)}))\right) \quad (1)$$

where $e_u^{(k+1)}$ is user u representations (similar to item i) after $k+1$ layers of embedding propagation, and obviously, $e_u^{(k)}$ and $e_i^{(k)}$ denote the node embeddings of user u and item i after k steps, W_1, W_2 are trainable transformation matrices, σ is the nonlinear activation function and finally, $\mathcal{N}_u$ and $\mathcal{N}_i$ are the surrounding nodes of user u and item i respectively, $\frac{1}{\sqrt{|\mathcal{N}_u||\mathcal{N}_i|}}$ denotes the graph Laplacian norm to normalize the node embedding vectors from previous layers.

3.2 Evaluation of the NGCF [14] Model

GCN [8] has performed its characteristics and power in many tasks, or more specifically, the application of GCN to the recommender system has shown outstanding results and significant improvements in the qualities of some research in recent years. From the view of the recommender system, it makes perfect sense to apply GCN to the recommender system because it helps to build and update a node based on its neighbourhood nodes. It means that we can update the embedding of a user (similar to the item) by using products that the user purchased or interacted with in history, thereby enhancing the accuracy of the node's embedding. However, a problem has arisen in the process of using GCN in the recommender system: the embedding vectors of users (or items) in the recommender system are really sparse or poor in data. As we all know, the sparsity problem has existed for a long time in recommendation tasks, and it still has a considerable influence on many models using the GCN model now, especially the NGCF [14] model. This problem makes no sense to use transformation matrices or non-linear activations on embeddings in NGCF. This is because the embeddings themselves are very poor in data or nearly the same with zero vector (we find a few valuable properties in embeddings). And obviously, it is extremely meaningless if we project zero vectors into another space using transformation matrices or activation functions like the way we do in other tasks in GCN.

Besides, by updating the embedding vectors in GCN [8] from the surrounding nodes, the graph structure will become smoother and smoother, and the embeddings will become more and more similar to others and similar to zero vector. With n-hop layers, it is pretty sure that if n is large enough, the graph structure will become over-smooth. There have many proofs of over-smooth, such as a linear residual graph convolutional network approach [3], the author has demonstrated the over-smooth process and why most GCNs in recommender systems have at most three layers. This phenomenon harms the performance of the model. In addition, the redundancy of transformation matrices and non-linear activation makes the model more complex, and the training time of the model also increases significantly. Even adding a transformation matrix and a non-linear activation function to NGCF [14] reduces the performance dramatically. We conducted experiments with the same dataset of NGCF (detail in table 2) to demonstrate the issue in the following table (Table 1):

Table 1. Performance of original and adjusted NGCF version.

	Gowalla		Amazon-book		Yelp2018	
	Recall	nDCG	Recall	nDCG	Recall	nDCG
NGCF [14]	0.155	0.226	0.032	0.061	0.054	0.103
NGCF-ta	0.161	0.236	0.038	0.067	0.056	0.109
%Improve	3.90%	4.42%	11.80%	6.30%	3.70%	5.80%

NGCF [14] is the standard model from the author's code[1], and NGCF-ta is the NGCF model that removes all transformation matrices and non-linear activation functions. To make a fair comparison, we keep all the parameter settings (hyper-parameters, learning rate, dropout ratio,...) as standard code and perform them on the same datasets in the author's paper. From the table, the model's performance has increased remarkably on three datasets by removing the transformation matrices and non-linear activation functions. The most significant change is recall value which increased by 11.8% in the amazon-book dataset, a considerable number for little change in the original NGCF version.

In summary, transformation matrices and non-linear activation functions are redundant and meaningless parts in the NGCF [14] model. It not only increases the complexity but also decreases the model's accuracy. Transformation matrices and non-linear activation functions can be more effective in tasks with more extensive and diverse data but not in this case.

4 Proposed Method

In Sect. 3, we discussed how fully applying GCN [8] operations in recommender systems, especially NGCF [14], will bring unexpected results and decrease model

[1] NGCF: https://github.com/xiangwang1223/neural_graph_collaborative_filtering.git.

performance as well as increase complexity. Inspired by transformation matrices, we created a highly competitive model while retaining most of the necessary parts of the standard version of the NGCF called DenseGCF (as illustrated in Fig. 1). The DenseGCF model has two modules for updating embeddings and finally sums all embedding outputs over the graph to get the result.

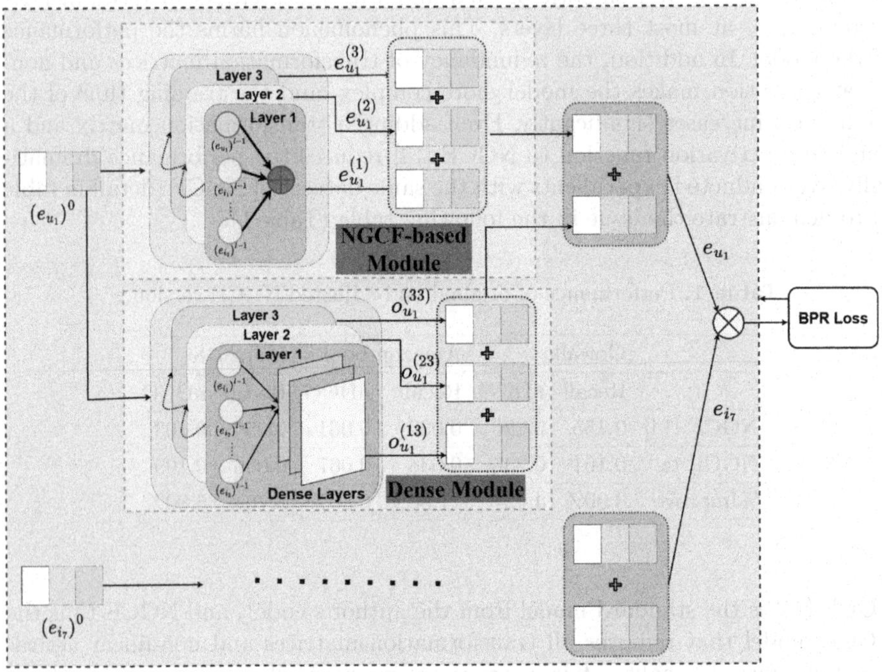

Fig. 1. Illustration of our DenseGCF model, which has two modules, the first module is the adjusted propagation rule of NGCF [14], and the second module is three dense layers that we use to get as much information as possible; the model also integrates high-order propagation that will output many embeddings and finally, we sum all of it together to achieve the complete presentations.

4.1 NGCF-Based Module

In the DenseGCF Model, we did not entirely modify the convolution operation of NGCF [14] to aggregate as in previous research that tries to improve NGCF (RGCF [11] and LightGCN [6]). Although the original model of NGCF used transformation matrices and non-linear activation functions, the result of the model at that time was very excellent and quickly became a state-of-the-art model. Therefore, these propagation rules are still precious to use, so what we need to do is to remove the transformation matrices and activation functions of

Eq. 1. However, a problem happens when we remove the transformation matrices, which is the contribution of the node itself and the surrounding nodes are equal. The information of the self-connection node and the information from its interaction should have different contribution levels. Therefore, we add alpha coefficient at the self-connection of the convolution operation to control the balance between the node itself and its neighbour. The final convolution operation is:

$$e_u^{(k+1)} = \left(\alpha e_u^{(k)} + \sum_{i \epsilon \mathcal{N}_u} \frac{1}{\sqrt{|\mathcal{N}_u||\mathcal{N}_i|}} (e_i^{(k)} + (e_i^{(k)} \odot e_u^{(k)})) \right) \tag{2}$$

To have a holistic view, we can represent it as propagation in matrix form because in reality, all operations are implemented on matrix operations as follow:

$$E^{(k+1)} = \left((\mathcal{L} + \alpha I) E^{(k)} + \mathcal{L} E^{(k)} \odot E^{(k)} \right) \tag{3}$$

where $E^{(k+1)}$ are presentation of user and item after $k+1$ steps of embedding propagation, $\mathcal{L} = D^{-0.5} A D^{-0.5}$, D is the diagonal degree matrix and A is the adjacency matrix.

4.2 Dense Module

During the propagation of the NGCF-based module, using many operations on surrounding nodes is not effective enough in updating the embedding of the current node without parameters, like using aggregation operations in RGCF [11] and LightGCN [6] model. These operations make the attributes of surrounding nodes affect the embedding of the current node under consideration. However, the model will be missing the learning part (models do not have any parameters). But if we use transformation matrices to try to enhance the performance, transformation matrices will cause problems as mentioned in Sect. 3. Therefore, we decide to create a second module named the Dense module to assist the propagation process in improving the performance of the DenseGCF model. Moreover, the way we apply transformation matrices to the second module is independent of the NGCF-base module, avoiding the sparsity problem completely while using the transformation matrices to update the embedding of the current node.

We use dense layers to learn essential properties or features of embeddings, thereby improving the model's performance by using the Dense module as extra information of the NGCF-based module. Furthermore, using dense layers helps DenseGCF to change the final presentations of nodes in a way that model can determine and update the embedding vectors effectively. At each layer in high-order propagation of DenseGCF, we use both the NGCF-based module and Dense Module to get the embeddings and then combine them. For more details, at layer $(k+1)$ of DenseGCF's high-order propagation, we get the embeddings from the NGCF-based module by using the Eq. 2, and at the same time, we also generate the embeddings in the Dense module by using the dense layers. In general, the output of the previous layer is also an input of the next layer in the

Dense module as follows:

$$i_u^{(k+1)(n+1)} = o_u^{(k+1)n} = W_n i_u^{(k+1)n} + b_n \tag{4}$$

where $o_u^{(k+1)n}$ is the output embedding at layer n, it is also an input embedding $i_u^{(k+1)(n+1)}$ at layer $n+1$ in dense layers, $i_u^{(k+1)n}$ denotes the input embedding at layer n of dense layers. We have transformation matrix W_n and bias b_n at layer n of dense layers. After the embedding goes through many layers in the Dense module, the last output embedding will have the same size as the output embedding size in the NGCF-based module. To have an input of the first dense layer, we need to have aggregation of neighbourhood nodes of user u as follows:

$$i_u^{(k+1)1} = \sum_{i \epsilon \mathcal{N}_u} \frac{1}{\sqrt{|\mathcal{N}_u||\mathcal{N}_i|}} e_i^k \tag{5}$$

where $i_u^{(k+1)1}$ is the input of user u at the first layer of dense layers, $e_i^{(k)}$ is surrounding nodes of user u and obviously, it comes from layer k of DenseGCF.

The embedding vectors from the Dense module will enhance the performance of the NGCF-based module as well as the quality of the model. Using transformation matrices in the Dense module not only affects the NGCF-based module but also improves the quality of the DenseGCF's performance by learning the embedding features of neighbouring nodes. The extra information learned from surrounding nodes is very worth the model quality.

4.3 Model Prediction

Two modules of DenseGCF impact each other and lead to an increase in the performance of the model. If we make the final embedding by concatenating the representations at every layer, redundant data may happen. We also can not use the last embedding as a final embedding because we will be unable to use all information from the NGCF-based module as well as the Dense module appropriately. Therefore, we sum up all embeddings from both modules. As a result, the favourite properties of users become stronger and stronger while the unrelated feature of items will become less critical. Final embedding for user u will be formatted as follows:

$$e_u^* = e_u^{(0)} + e_u^{(1)} + ... + e_u^{(K)} + o_u^{0N} + o_u^{1N} + ... + o_u^{KN} \tag{6}$$

where e_u^* is the final representation of user u, K and N are the last layer of high-order propagation and dense layers, respectively (after propagation, we will have two sets of embeddings $\{e_u^{(0)}, e_u^{(1)}, ..e_u^{(K)}\}$ and $\{o_u^{0N}, o_u^{1N}, ...o_u^{KN}\}$ corresponding to NGCF-based module and Dense module). Finally, we use the inner product to get a score of users and items:

$$\hat{y}_{DenseGCF}(u, i) = e_u^{*T} e_i^* \tag{7}$$

5 Experiments

5.1 Experimental Settings

Datasets. We conduct the experiments on the following three benchmarks: Gowalla, Amazon-book[2] and Yelp2018[3]. These are publicly accessible datasets that considerably differ in size and density, as shown in Table 2.

- **Gowalla**: This is a dataset of check-in history in which each item is a location shared by users.
- **Amazon-Book**: The dataset contains product reviews and metadata from the online purchase service Amazon.
- **Yelp2018**: It is a part of the Yelp challenge in 2018, in which business locations like restaurants or bars are viewed as items.

We follow the 10-cores procedure suggested in [5] to preprocess the data so that only users and items with at least ten interactions are retained.

Table 2. Statistics of three benchmarks.

Datasets	#Users	#Items	#Interactions	Density
Gowalla	29,858	40,981	1,027,370	0.00084
Yelp2018	31,668	38,048	1,561,406	0.00130
Amazon-book	52,643	91,599	2,984,108	0.00062

Training Configuration. All the implementations are in Python and Tensorflow. We choose an embedding size of 64 for all layers and a batch size of 1024. Our DenseGCF model is controlled by the BPR [12] loss function with a learning rate of 0.00001 and Adam optimizer. This strategy empirically attains the best performance in our resource-limited situation compared to other settings.

Evaluation Metrics. We adopt two standard evaluation protocols, Recall and Normalized discounted cumulative gain (Ndcg), to evaluate the methods participating in the experiments. For any ranking list, Recall measures its coverage while Ndcg takes position significance into account. We set a cut-off value of k = 20 for both metrics, i.e., Recall@20 and Ndcg@20, to consider the top 20 items.

[2] Gowalla and Amazon-book datasets: https://github.com/xiangwang1223/neural_graph_collaborative_filtering.

[3] Yelp2018: https://github.com/hfutmars/RGCF.

5.2 Baselines

We demonstrate the effectiveness of DenseGCF by comparing it with the following methods:

- **SVD++** [9] is a widely known extension of Singular Value Decomposition (SVD) for recommender systems. It is an integrated model that leverages the advantages of both neighbourhood and latent factor approaches to model user preferences.
- **NeuMF** [7] pioneers using a combination of multi-layer perceptron (MLP) and generalized matrix factorization (GMF), creating a flexible model for non-linear personalized ranking.
- **HOP-Rec** [17] introduces a hybrid model that performs factorization and random walks on the user-item graph.
- **GC-MC** [1] constructs users and items based on message-passing GNNs architecture [4,16] through graph convolution layers and produces new ratings as labelled links by forwarding these to a bilinear decoder.
- **NGCF** [14] learns embedding representations by propagating these vectors through exploiting k-hop neighbours made up of GNN's message-passing architecture [4,16].
- **LightGCN** [6] suggests eliminating several unnecessary details on the vanilla NGCF [14]. Thus, it attains better performance than NGCF in computational expense and recommendation quality.
- **RGCF** [11] redesigned the GCN-based Collaborative Filtering model by pointing out redundancies in prior representations. This simplification improves the capture of high-order connectivities.

5.3 Performance Comparison

Comparison results show in Table 3, based on recall@20 and ndcg@20.Overall, DenseGCF is better than non-graph and conventional methods like SVD++ [9], NeuMF [7], and early graph-based methods such as HOP-Rec [17] and GC-MC [1].

NGCF [14] is a state-of-the-art GCN-based method, baseline for LightGCN [6], RGCF [11] and our model. It leverages high-order connectivity in the user-item graph for the implicit recommendation. Compared to conventional techniques, its performance created a new baseline for the recommender system based on GCN [8] and performs reasonably well in all three datasets. Our NGCF-based module uses only essentials in NGCF architecture and eliminates non-effective activations and weights. DenseGCF dense module helps the model learn faster and achieve much better results than NGCF. Thus, Our DenseGCF improves on the original NGCF on all three datasets with remarkable results.

We conducted experiments on all models many times to make the comparison as fair as possible, and the results are almost not significantly different from the results in Table 2. Our model does not always perform the best among those baselines but is always in the top 2 best models, whose result competes

Table 3. Performance comparison on Recall@20 and Ndcg@20. Numbers in bold are the best metric values recorded, while those underlined are the second-best ones.

Method	Gowalla		Yelp2018		Amazon-book	
	Recall	Ndcg	Recall	Ndcg	Recall	Ndcg
SVD++ [9]	0.1439	0.2198	0.0507	0.0975	0.0332	0.0607
NeuMF [7]	0.1326	0.1985	0.0449	0.0886	0.0253	0.0535
HOP-Rec [17]	0.1399	0.2128	0.0524	0.0989	0.0309	0.0606
GC-MC [1]	0.1395	0.1960	0.0462	0.0922	0.0288	0.0551
NGCF [14]	0.1553	0.2264	0.0541	0.1031	0.0326	0.0610
LighGCN [6]	**0.1830**	0.1554	<u>0.0649</u>	0.0530	0.0411	0.0315
RGCF [11]	0.1761	<u>0.2398</u>	**0.0676**	<u>0.1210</u>	**0.0448**	**0.0790**
DenseGCF	<u>0.1768</u>	**0.2436**	0.0622	**0.1230**	<u>0.0425</u>	<u>0.0723</u>

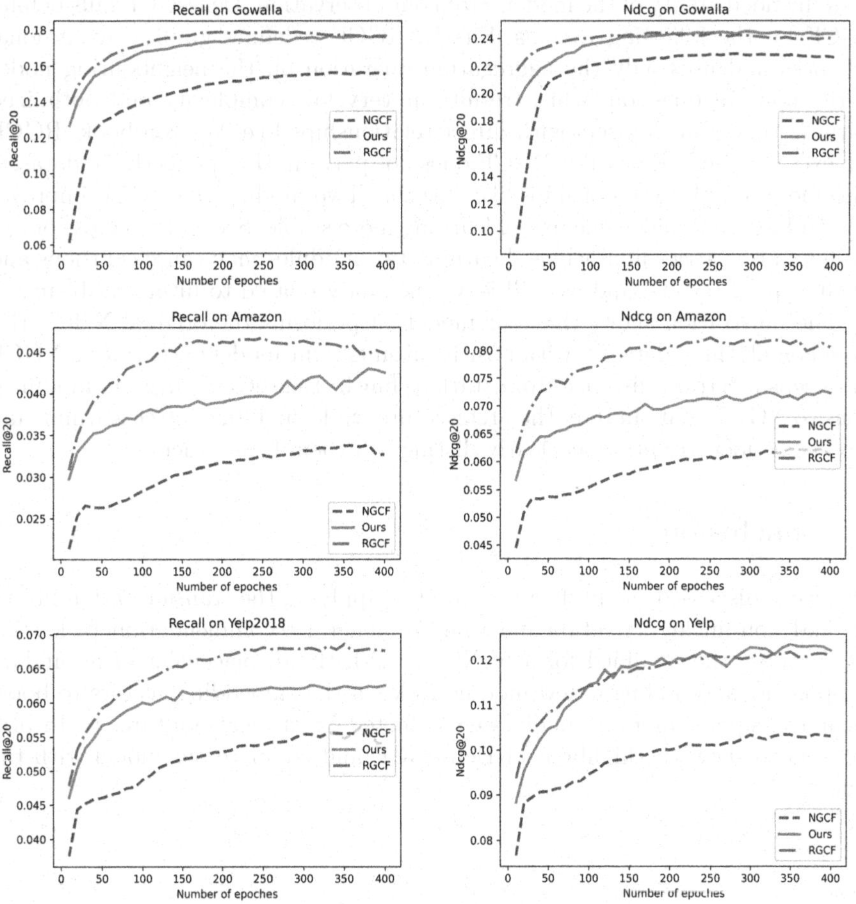

Fig. 2. Result on Gowalla, Amazon-book and Yelp2018 dataset

against the best model. To be more illustrated, we conducted the experiments and plotted the results on three datasets of the baseline NGCF [14] and the two best models: RGCF [11] and DenseGCF, in Fig. 2.

Although our model is lower than LightGCN [6] at the recall@20 measure, the offset on ndcg@20 is much larger than the LightGCN model. Specifically, our model shows a more significant improvement in recommending relevant items in Gowalla (0.0882-56.75%), Yelp2018(0.07-132%) and Amazon-book(0.0408-130%). However, LightGCN is only better in terms of recommender accuracy in the recall@20 measure in Gowalla(0.0062-3.5%) and Yelp2018 (0.0027-4.34%), and lower than our model in the Amazon-book dataset.

DenseGCF consistently achieved the most state-of-the-art results in ngcd@20 on all three datasets compared to other state-of-the-art models. Specifically, in ndcg@20, our model's performance exceeds the most robust baseline in Gowalla (0.0038-1.58%) and Yelp2018 (0.002-1.65%); despite falling behind RGCF in the Amazon-book dataset, in general, the results are satisfactory, ensuring the recommended ability of the model. From our observation, DenseGCF falls behind RGCF for the following reasons. Firstly, RGCF redefines graph convolutional networks and uses only the aggregation operation on the neighbouring nodes of the node in question, which results in very low complexity and optimized learning time. For datasets with direct relationships like Amazon-book, RGCF achieves superior results, but RGCF does not perform that perfectly on datasets with more complex relationships like Gowalla. Two-module DenseGCF improves this problem and makes the model learning more stable. Secondly, the use of two modules also carries limitations. Learning two modules may cause collisions and produce poor results, and we will leave the study related to future problems.

The illustration shows that our model outperforms the original NGCF [14] model on all three datasets with positive results. Our model outperforms NGCF and keeps a certain distance from start to finish. DenseGCF suggests modifications to NGCF that simplify the architecture while enabling better learning and producing good results that clearly distinguish them from others.

6 Conclusion

This work discussed the problems related to applying the transformation matrices and non-linear activation functions in general recommendation tasks. We also propose the modified form of NGCF with the displacement of redundant components and adding a new module to learn the embedding vectors to boost the model's performance. Finally, we conducted experiments on three real-world datasets to show the highlight of DenseGCF and compare our model with the others.

References

1. Berg, R.V.D., Kipf, T.N., Welling, M.: Graph convolutional matrix completion. arXiv preprint arXiv:1706.02263 (2017)
2. Chen, J., Zhang, H., He, X., Nie, L., Liu, W., Chua, T.S.: Attentive collaborative filtering: multimedia recommendation with item-and component-level attention. In: Proceedings of the 40th International ACM SIGIR Conference on Research and Development in Information Retrieval, pp. 335–344 (2017)
3. Chen, L., Wu, L., Hong, R., Zhang, K., Wang, M.: Revisiting graph based collaborative filtering: a linear residual graph convolutional network approach. In: Proceedings of the AAAI Conference on Artificial Intelligence, vol. 34, pp. 27–34 (2020)
4. Hamilton, W., Ying, Z., Leskovec, J.: Inductive representation learning on large graphs. In: Advances in Neural Information Processing Systems, vol. 30 (2017)
5. He, R., McAuley, J.: Vbpr: visual bayesian personalized ranking from implicit feedback. In: Proceedings of the AAAI Conference on Artificial Intelligence, vol. 30 (2016)
6. He, X., Deng, K., Wang, X., Li, Y., Zhang, Y., Wang, M.: Lightgcn: Simplifying and powering graph convolution network for recommendation. In: Proceedings of the 43rd International ACM SIGIR Conference on Research and Development in Information Retrieval, pp. 639–648 (2020)
7. He, X., Liao, L., Zhang, H., Nie, L., Hu, X., Chua, T.S.: Neural collaborative filtering. In: Proceedings of the 26th International Conference on World Wide Web, pp. 173–182 (2017)
8. Kipf, T.N., Welling, M.: Semi-supervised classification with graph convolutional networks. arXiv preprint arXiv:1609.02907 (2016)
9. Koren, Y.: Factorization meets the neighborhood: a multifaceted collaborative filtering model. In: Proceedings of the 14th ACM SIGKDD International Conference on Knowledge Discovery and Data Mining, pp. 426–434 (2008)
10. Koren, Y., Bell, R., Volinsky, C.: Matrix factorization techniques for recommender systems. Computer **42**(8), 30–37 (2009)
11. Liu, K., Xue, F., Hong, R.: RGCF: refined graph convolution collaborative filtering with concise and expressive embedding. Intell. Data Anal. **26**(2), 427–445 (2022)
12. Rendle, S., Freudenthaler, C., Gantner, Z., Schmidt-Thieme, L.: BPR: Bayesian personalized ranking from implicit feedback. arXiv preprint arXiv:1205.2618 (2012)
13. Wang, X., He, X., Nie, L., Chua, T.S.: Item silk road: recommending items from information domains to social users. In: Proceedings of the 40th International ACM SIGIR Conference on Research and Development in Information Retrieval, pp. 185–194 (2017)
14. Wang, X., He, X., Wang, M., Feng, F., Chua, T.S.: Neural graph collaborative filtering. In: Proceedings of the 42nd International ACM SIGIR Conference on Research and Development in Information Retrieval, pp. 165–174 (2019)
15. Wang, X., Jin, H., Zhang, A., He, X., Xu, T., Chua, T.S.: Disentangled graph collaborative filtering. In: Proceedings of the 43rd International ACM SIGIR Conference on Research and Development in Information Retrieval, pp. 1001–1010 (2020)
16. Xu, K., Li, C., Tian, Y., Sonobe, T., Kawarabayashi, K.i., Jegelka, S.: Representation learning on graphs with jumping knowledge networks. In: International Conference on Machine Learning, pp. 5453–5462. PMLR (2018)

17. Yang, J.H., Chen, C.M., Wang, C.J., Tsai, M.F.: Hop-rec: high-order proximity for implicit recommendation. In: Proceedings of the 12th ACM Conference on Recommender Systems, pp. 140–144 (2018)
18. Ying, R., He, R., Chen, K., Eksombatchai, P., Hamilton, W.L., Leskovec, J.: Graph convolutional neural networks for web-scale recommender systems. In: Proceedings of the 24th ACM SIGKDD International Conference on Knowledge Discovery & Data Mining, pp. 974–983 (2018)
19. Yu, W., Qin, Z.: Graph convolutional network for recommendation with low-pass collaborative filters. In: International Conference on Machine Learning, pp. 10936–10945. PMLR (2020)

Automatic Quantization of Convolutional Neural Networks Based on Enhanced Bare-Bones Particle Swarm Optimization for Chest X-Ray Image Classification

Jihene Tmamna[1(✉)], Emna Ben Ayed[1,2], and Mounir Ben Ayed[1,3]

[1] Research Groups in Intelligent Machines, National Engineering School of Sfax (ENIS), University of Sfax, Sfax, Tunisia
jihen.tmamna@enis.tn, {emna.benayed.b,mounir.benayed}@ieee.org

[2] Industry 4.0 Research Lab, Polytech-Sfax (IPSAS), Avenue 5 August, 3002 Sfax Rue Said Aboubaker, Tunisia

[3] Computer Sciences and Communication Department, Faculty of Sciences of Sfax, University of Sfax, Sfax, Tunisia

Abstract. Deep convolutional neural networks (CNNs) have achieved high accuracy in classifying chest X-ray images to diagnose lung diseases, including COVID-19. However, their large number of parameters makes them impractical for deployment on limited-resource devices. To address this issue, we propose a neural network quantization (NNQ) method that reduces the complexity of CNNs for X-ray image classification, while maintaining their original accuracy. Our method, called mixed-precision quantization (MPQ), aims to quantize the layers with different bit widths to achieve good results. To find the optimal bit-width of each layer, we propose an enhanced bare-bones particle swarm optimization algorithm called EBPSOQuantizer. Our experiments on the COVID-19 X-ray dataset with different CNN architectures demonstrate the effectiveness of our method.

Keywords: Convolutional neural network · Network quantization · Bare-bones Particle swarm optimization · Chest X-ray

1 Introduction

The modern healthcare system mainly relies on medical imaging. Therefore, the use of advanced medical imaging devices, such as magnetic resonance imaging (MRI), computed tomography (CT), and X-ray imaging, has become crucial for the diagnosis of disease. Recently, deep convolutional neural networks have played an important role in the healthcare industry [1–4]. They have achieved

Supported by Tunisian Ministry of Higher Education and Scientific Research under the grant agreement number LR11ES48.

N. T. Nguyen et al. (Eds.): ICCCI 2023, LNAI 14162, pp. 125–137, 2023.
https://doi.org/10.1007/978-3-031-41456-5_10

notable success in medical image classification, including chest X-ray image classification to diagnose lung illnesses like COVID-19. According to the literature, there are several CNN architectures adopted to classify normal, pneumonia, and COVID-19 cases from chest X-ray images. Unfortunately, deploying these deep architectures on limited-resource devices like IoT devices is challenging and cannot be done directly [5,6].

To address this problem, several studies have focused on model compression using the neural network quantization (NNQ) technique. NNQ [7] usually aims at converting the full-precision network parameters (32-bit floating point weights and activation) into lower-bit values (for example, 5-bit and 2-bit).

Various NNQ methods have been proposed to enhance the performance of low-precision networks. Some of the existing methods [8–13] aim to quantize the different layers using the same bit width. However, these methods usually cause significant accuracy loss because CNN's layers have different sensitivities to quantization [14]. To maximize network performance, considerable research has focused on mixed-precision quantization (MPQ) [15–17]. MPQ aims to quantize different layers using different bit widths. Due to the fact that neural architecture search (NAS) is widely adopted to find optimal solutions without domain experts, many kinds of NAS algorithms have been adopted for solving MPQ problems. These algorithms include the evolutionary algorithm [18], reinforcement learning [19], and the differential method [20,21]. However, the search space for MPQ problems grows exponentially as CNN's layer number rises. Thus, these methods require high computational costs and usually evolve too slowly to yield good MPQ results. In addition, they can fall into a locally optimal solution due to the lack of theoretical guidance.

In response to the above issues, we propose a new MPQ method to automatically search for the optimal quantization policy with less computational cost. We exploit the Bare-bones Particle Swarm Optimization (BPSO) to achieve mixed precision quantization. However, BPSO suffers from some drawbacks. Specifically, it is vulnerable to falling into the local optimum trap [22]. Motivated by this, we propose an enhanced BPSO called EBPSOQuantizer to deal with the MPQ problem.

The main contributions of this paper are as follows:

1) Develop a novel MPQ method that searches for the optimal bit width for each layer with low computational cost.
2) Formulate the MPQ problem as a constrained optimization model to guide and speed up the search process.
3) Propose an enhanced BPSO called EBPSOQuantizer, as an optimizer to solve the MPQ problem. The proposed EBPSOQuantizer is based on a new update mechanism and a checking process to overcome the limitations of the traditional BPSO and improve its performance. EBPSOQuantizer incorporates a constraint handling method to handle the constrained optimization problem.
4) We illustrate the EBPSOQuantizer's performance for the classification of normal, pneumonia, and COVID-19 cases from the chest X-ray images.

The remainder of this paper is organized as follows: Sect. 2 presents the related works. Section 3 presents the proposed method. Section 4 presents the experiments and the obtained results. Section 5 gives the conclusions.

2 Related Work

Over the last decade, deep convolutional neural networks have been widely used to solve several healthcare problems, including the identification of breast cancer, the detection of brain tumors using MRI pictures, and the classification of lung illnesses using X-ray images. Therefore, deepening the CNN architecture has become a popular trend for dealing with complex classification problems and improving accuracy. However, deploying these deep architectures on limited-resource devices is challenging and cannot be done directly.

To reduce the CNN complexity, several researchers have proposed to quantize the parameters of the CNN to enhance hardware efficiency. Therefore, the CNN model can be used effectively on resource-constrained devices. In this section, we will present previous work on NNQ.

The existing NNQ methods can be divided into two categories: fixed precision quantization (FPQ) and mixed precision quantization (MPQ).

Generally, FPQ [8–13] aims to quantize the parameters using the same number of bits across all layers. For example, 6 bits are allocated for parameters in all layers. However, this strategy may not be optimal [23]. In fact, the layers have different structures and effects on accuracy [14], so they should be treated differently.

To overcome the problem of FPQ, researchers have suggested using MPQ which aims to quantize parameters with a different number of bits across different layers [24,25]. Recently, many MPQ methods have been proposed. Depending on the existing literature, we will divide the MPQ into two categories: the heuristic method and the search-based method.

The heuristic method, such as [17,23,26–28], focuses on finding the bit-width of each layer based on their sensitivity to the accuracy. However, although effective in practice, these methods may have some limits. Since they are sensitive to the criteria used to evaluate the layer sensitivity, they are more likely to result in sub-optimal performance. In addition, they still required domain expertise for bit-width allocation.

Actually, search-based methods, including our work, aim to adopt optimization methods to automatically search for the quantization policy. Wang et al. [19] exploited reinforcement learning to determine the bit-width with hardware feedback. [20] and [21] introduced constraint factors to the loss function and proposed a differentiable method to search for the quantization policy. Nevertheless, they can make the training process computationally expensive and require more time to converge, particularly for deep CNN models on large datasets. Furthermore, [18] used the evolutionary algorithm with limited data to search for the quantization policy, which can lead to a sub-optimal solution.

Overall, given its inherent difficulties, MPQ is still an open problem. In this paper, we propose a novel method to solve it. Specifically, we formulate the MPQ as a constrained optimization problem. Then, we propose an enhanced BPSO to solve it with few computational costs.

3 Preliminaries

This section introduces the basic concept of neural network quantization and particle swarm optimization (PSO).

3.1 Neural Network Quantization

NNQ aims to convert the parameters from 32-bit precision to low-bit values to reduce memory and computational costs. The quantization function used to quantize the parameters is usually defined as [10]:

$$X = \prod\nolimits_{Q(\beta,b)} clamp(X, \beta) \tag{1}$$

where X is the input value, which can be a weight or an activation. $Q(\beta, b)$ is the quantization levels. $clamp(X, \beta)$ is the clamp function that truncates the input 32bits weight and activation to the range $[-\beta, \beta]$ and $[0, \beta]$ respectively. $\prod(.)$ is the projection function used to project each clipped element X into $Q(\beta, b)$.

3.2 Bare-Bones Particle Swarm Optimization

Bare-bones particle swarm optimization (BPSO) [29] is a simple version of particle swarm optimization In the BPSO each particle represents a solution to the optimization problem. At each iteration, each ith particle can be updated as follows:

$$x_i^{t+1} = \begin{cases} G(0.5(Pb_i^t + Gb^t), |Pb_i^t - Gb^t|), & rand < 0.5 \\ Pb_i^t, & otherwise \end{cases} \tag{2}$$

where G(y, z) is a Gaussian distribution with mean y and variance z. Pb_i denotes the best personal solution found by itself $Pb_i = (Pb_{i1}, Pb_{i2}, ..., Pb_{iD})$. Gb denotes the global solution founded by the swarm $Gb = (Gb_1, Gb_2, ..., Gb_D)$.

4 Proposed Method

The goal of this section is to present the proposed method. First, we formulate the MPQ problem as an integer-constrained optimization. Then, we detail our proposed BPSO.

4.1 Integer Optimization Model

Given a pre-trained CNN model M that contains L layers with full-precision (32-bit) parameters, we present the structure of the quantized model M' as $M' = (bit_1, bit_2, ..., bit_L)$, where bit_i is the bit number of the ith layer. The goal is to find the optimal quantization policy (optimal bit-width for each layer) while maximizing the network's accuracy under certain constraints.

Furthermore, we adopt the integer coding to represent a solution to the problem with the following expression:

$$X = (bit_1, bit_2, ..., bit_L), bit_i \in s \tag{3}$$

where s is the bit-width candidate vector s = {1, 2, 3, 4, 5, 6, 7, 8, 16, 32}, $bit_i = \alpha$ indicates that the ith layer's bit width has been reduced to α. Based on this, we formulate the MPQ problem as a constrained integer optimization problem under some given constraints. The objective function can be formulated as follows:

$$\begin{aligned} \max \quad & accuracy(M') \\ \text{s.t.} \quad & C(M') \geq C_{target} \end{aligned} \tag{4}$$

where C() evaluates the computational resources required, and C_{target} is the target given constraint adopted as average operation bit width to evaluate bit-wise operation computational complexity.

The average operation bit width function is formulated as follows:

$$Avrg(M') = \left[\frac{\sum_{j=1}^{L} n^j m^j OP(j)}{\sum_{j=1}^{L} OP(j)} \right]^{\frac{1}{2}} \tag{5}$$

Where OP(j) is the number of float point operations in the jth layer. n^j and m^j denote the bit width of weight and activation for the jth layer.

4.2 BPSO Algorithm

To search for an optimal quantized network, we propose an enhanced BPSO, called EBPSOQuantizer, to solve the integer optimization problem mentioned above. It consists of the standard BPSO plus main improvements adapted to perform CNN quantization.

The main proposed improvements are personal Pb and Gb updating strategy, updating each particle, checking process, and local search process, which will be detailed in the next sections.

Pb and Gb Updating. Since the MPQ problem is a constrained optimization problem, we propose to combine Deb's constraint handling method [30] with the BPSO. In this paper, Deb's rules are adopted to update *Pb* and *Gb*. Given the fitness value and resource constraint of the current position X_i and Pb_i, the algorithm will determine if X_i can replace Pb_i or not. This algorithm is also adopted to update the *Gb* by comparing the feasibility of Pb_i and *Gb*. This strategy may enhance the search process by guiding the population toward feasible regions.

Updating Each Particle. The continuous BPSO updating rules no longer apply because the position of each particle is an integer vector. For this reason, we adopt the updating rule used in [31] as follows:

$$x_{ij} = \begin{cases} \lceil \frac{Pb_{ij}+Gb_{ij}}{2} \rceil + \lceil G(0,1)|Pb_{ij} + Gb_{ij}| \rceil, & ifrand > 0.5 \\ Pb_{ij}, & otherwise \end{cases} \tag{6}$$

Checking Process. During the search process, it is possible to reevaluate the same position vector because no method can guarantee that the new position will not be the same as those which have already been evaluated. To overcome this issue, we introduce a checking process to check the similarity between the new positions and the previously evaluated ones. If there is a similarity, the evaluation of this particle's position is skipped, else the particle is evaluated.

Local Search Process. During the search process, each particle's position is updated based on *Gb* and its best position *Pb*. However, BPSO may fall into the local solution if the *Pb* solution is far from optimal. To this end, we introduce a local search process to enhance the *Pb* values, thereby improving global search performance. The main concept of the local search process is as follows: first, randomly select W bits to be changed to another value in the search space. Next, Deb's rules are adopted to determine the best solution from both the *Pb* and new solution $NewPb$. Therefore, if $NewPb$ is better than the current *Pb*, then the local search process will update *Pb* to $NewPb$.

5 Experiments

In this section, we conduct experiments to demonstrate the effectiveness of our proposed method on the chest X-ray and CIFAR-10 datasets. First, the experimental implementations are detailed. Then, the experimental results are presented.

5.1 Experimental Implementation

In this section, we present the quantization and the fine-tuning details.

Quantization Details. During the quantization, each layer's weights are linearly quantized into m bits using the following function:

$$Q(W^i) = round(clamp(W^i/\alpha^i, -1, 1)(2^{m-1} - 1))h^i \tag{7}$$

Where clamp(.,-1,1) is used to truncate the values into [-1,1], h^i is the scaling factor defined as $h^i = \alpha^i/(2^{m-1} - 1)$, α^i is a learned parameter. As for activations, since the activation of the ReLU layers, convolutional layers, or batch normalization layers are non-negative, we truncate the values into [0,1] and we quantize the values as follows:

$$Q(A^i) = round(clamp(A^i/\alpha^i, 0, 1)(2^n - 1))h^i \tag{8}$$

n is the bit number, the scaling factor h^i defined as $h^i = \alpha^i/(2^n - 1)$. For the bit width candidate vector s, we select the values around the target average operation bit-width. For example, if the target average operation bit-width is 3, the bit-width candidate vector is s = {2,3,4}. If the target operation average bit-width is 4, the bit-width candidate vector is s = {2,3,4,5}. Since The first convolutional layer and the last fully connected layer are critical, we quantize them to 8-bit following conventional quantization methods.

Fine-Tuning Details. To fine-tune the quantized network, we use stochastic gradient descent (SGD) with a momentum of 0.9. On the chest X-ray dataset, the quantized model is fine-tuned for 60 epochs with a learning rate of 0.001 divided by 10 every 20 epochs. On CIFAR-10, we fine-tune the quantized network for 180 epochs with a 0.01 learning rate divided by 10 very 60 epochs. During the search process, we fine-tune each particle for 2 epochs to recover accuracy before calculating its fitness.

5.2 Results

In experimental results, we evaluated BSOPQuantizer in terms of accuracy, average operation bit width (Avrg), and compression ratio. The compression ratio is defined as follows:

$$comp = \frac{32}{avg_{bit}(M')} \tag{9}$$

where $avg_{bit}()$ is the average weight bit width which can be defined as follows:

$$avg_{bit}(M') = \frac{\sum_{j=1}^{L} n^j nbr(j)}{\sum_{j=1}^{L} nbr(j)} \tag{10}$$

where nbr(j) is the number of parameters in the jth layer and n^j is the bit width of weight for the jth layer.

Result on Chest X-ray Dataset. In this section, we focus on searching the quantized model of VGG-16 and ResNet-18 on the chest X-ray dataset. The chest X-ray dataset used in this paper is taken from Kaggle. We used 6902 images, among these COVID-19 (2313 images), Pneumonia (2313 images), and Normal (2313 images). We randomly selected images with proportions of 80% and 20% to split the datasets into the train set and the test set. Figure 1 presents some images from the X-ray dataset from each class. The experimental results are presented in Table 1. For average 4-bit quantization, our method achieves the

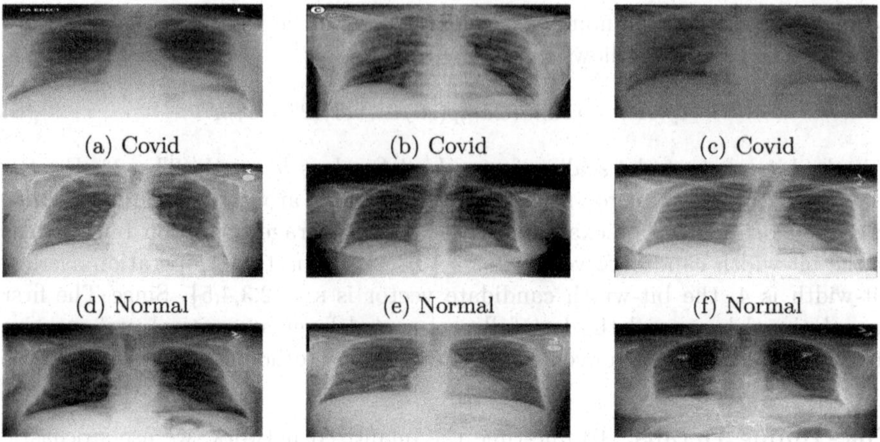

(a) Covid (b) Covid (c) Covid

(d) Normal (e) Normal (f) Normal

(g) Pneumonia (h) Pneumonia (i) Pneumonia

Fig. 1. Some images in the X-ray dataset from each class

Table 1. Quantization results of VGG-16 and ResNet-18 over chest X-ray dataset

Model	W-bits	A-bits	Accuracy %	compression ratio	*Avrg*
ResNet-18 original	32	32	97,6	1	32
EBPSOQuantizer	Mixed	Mixed	97.94	7.9	3.99
VGG16 original	32	32	95.94	1	32
EBPSOQuantizer	Mixed	Mixed	96.1	8.86	4.09

best accuracies, which are better than their full-precision models. For ResNet-18, We achieve a 7.9x compression ratio for weights while improving the accuracy by 0.34%.

Result on CIFAR-10 Dataset. In this section, we demonstrate the effectiveness of EBPSOQuantizer on the CIFAR-10 dataset.CIFAR-10 has 10K test images and 50k train images. Figure 2 presents some images from the CIFAR-10 dataset. We adopt ResNet-20, ResNet-56, ResNet-110, and VGG-16.

From Table 2, we can observe that our MPQ policies achieve better accuracy than the full-precision model. For VGG-16, for average 3, our EBPSOQuantizer has reached 0.29% accuracy improvement with an 11.74x compression ratio for weights. For ResNet-20, we achieve a 10.87x compression ratio for weights while improving the accuracy by 0.34% for an average operation bit of 3. In the case of ResNet-56, for 4-average bit operations, EBPSOQuantizer achieves 0.44% accuracy improvement with an 8.3x compression ratio for weights. For ResNet-110, EBPSOQuantizer improves the accuracy by 0.3% for 4-average bit operation.

These results demonstrate the effectiveness of EBPSOQuantizer in quantizing the CNN models, which enables their deployment on limited-resource devices.

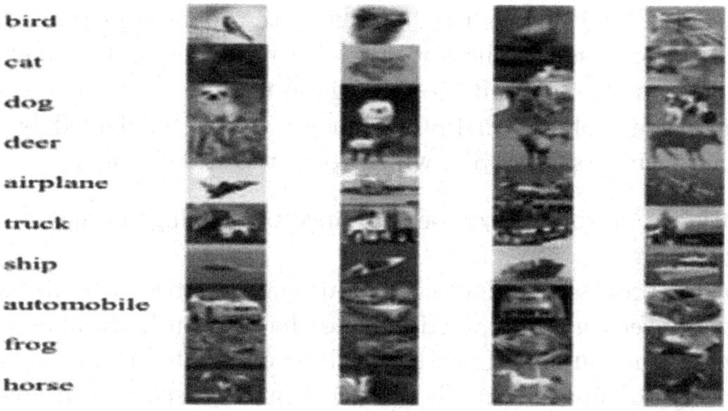

Fig. 2. Some images in the CIFAR-10 dataset from each class

Table 2. Quantization results of VGG-16, ResNet-20, ResNet-56, ResNet-110 over CIFAR-10

Model	W-bits	A-bits	Accuracy %	compression ratio	*Avrg*
ResNet-20 original	32	32	91,96	1	32
EBPSOQuantizer	M	M	92.3	10.87	3.01
EBPSOQuantizer	M	M	92.89	9.10	4.02
VGG16	32	32	93.02	1	32
EBPSOQuantizer	Mixed	Mixed	93.31	11.74	3.03
EBPSOQuantizer	Mixed	Mixed	93.55	8.86	4.09
ResNet-56 original	32	32	93,26	1	32
EBPSOQuantizer	Mixed	Mixed	93.5	10.68	3.08
EBPSOQuantizer	Mixed	Mixed	93.72	8.3	4.03
Resnet-110 original	32	32	93.50	1	32
EBPSOQuantizer	Mixed	Mixed	93.68	10.88	3.07
EBPSOQuantizer	Mixed	Mixed	93.8	8.26	4.07

6 Discussion

The experimental results in Sect. 5.2 demonstrated that EBPSOQunatizer can compress the network with improvement in accuracy. As presented in Table 3, we compare the results of our method with those of Dorefa [8], PACT [9], APoT [10], Lq-nets [32], BP-NAS [20], LLT [33], CLR-RNF [1]. The evaluation is limited to the ResNet-20 model on the CIFAR-10 dataset in order to present a fair comparison by copying the results from each method's corresponding paper.

When comparing our results with FPQ such as Dorefa [8], PACT [9], APoT [10], Lq-nets [32], LLT [33], our proposed method obtains higher compression ratios with better accuracy. For example, our method increases the accuracy by 0.34% for an average of 3 bits. Similarly, when comparing our results with the ones obtained by MPQ such as BP-NAS [20], the proposed method still obtains better quantization results. These results clearly demonstrate the effectiveness of the EBPSOQunatizer's ability to yield good results.

The effectiveness of the EBPSOQunatizer can be explained by the three proposed improvements to BPSO, which consist of the use of:

- Deb's rules to improve search performance by guiding the search process to a feasible region.
- The checking process to reduce computational resources. It aims to check the similarity between updated particles and the previously evaluated ones. The evaluation of these updated particles will be eliminated if there is an overlap.
- LSP strategy to enhance the *Pb*, resulting in increased swarm diversity and, as a result, improved search performance.

Table 3. Comparison of EBPSOQuantizer with state-of-the-art quantization method on ResNet-20 on CIFAR10

Method	W-bit	A-bit	accuracy %	Compression ratio	Avrg
Dorefa [8]	3	3	89.90	10.67	3.00
PACT [9]	3	3	91.10	10.67	3.00
APoT [10]	3	3	92.2	10.67	3.00
Lq-nets [32]	3	3	91.6	10.67	3.00
LLT [33]	3	3	92.17	10.67	3.00
BP-NAS [20]	Mixed	Mixed	92.12	10.74	3.30
EBPSOQuantizer	Mixed	Mixed	92.3	10.87	3.01
Dorefa [8]	4	4	90.50	8.00	4.00
PACT [9]	4	4	91.30	8.00	4.00
APoT [10]	4	4	92.3	8.00	4.00
LLT [33]	4	4	92.71	8.00	4.00
EBPSOQuantizer	Mixed	Mixed	92.89	9.10	4.02

7 Conclusion

In this article, a new MPQ method is proposed in which the bit widths of weights and activations of each layer are automatically found without requiring any domain experts. We propose an enhanced BPSO that can search the quantization policy under some constraints such as average operation bit width. In the searching process, the new update mechanism, checking process and the incorporation of a constrained handling method make the proposed BPSO more efficient in solving the MPQ problem. Extensive experiments demonstrated that our proposed EBPSOQuantizer achieves effective results on chest X-ray image classification using VGG-16, and ResNet-18.

In future work, we will focus on combining our proposed method with other compression techniques like pruning to more efficiently reduce the storage and computation requirements of the CNN models.

References

1. Zhang, X., Yao, L., Wang, X., Monaghan, J., Mcalpine, D., Zhang, Y.: A survey on deep learning based brain computer interface: recent advances and new frontiers, arXiv preprint arXiv:1905.04149 66 (2019)
2. Asiri, N., Hussain, M., Al Adel, F., Alzaidi, N.: Deep learning based computer-aided diagnosis systems for diabetic retinopathy: a survey. Artif. Intell. Med **99**, 101701 (2019)
3. Litjens, G.: A survey on deep learning in medical image analysis. Med. Image Anal. **42**, 60–88 (2017)
4. Midani, W., Ouarda, W., Ayed, M.B.: Deeparr: an investigative tool for arrhythmia detection using a contextual deep neural network from electrocardiograms (ecg) signals. Biomed. Signal Process. Control **85**, 104954 (2023)
5. Tmamna, J., Ayed, E.B., Ayed, M.B., Deep learning for internet of things in fog computing: survey and open issues. In: 5th International Conference on Advanced Technologies for Signal and Image Processing (ATSIP), vol. 2020, pp. 1–6. IEEE (2020)
6. Tmamna, J., Ayed, E.B., Ayed, M.B.: Neural network pruning based on improved constrained particle swarm optimization. In: Mantoro, T., Lee, M., Ayu, M.A., Wong, K.W., Hidayanto, A.N. (eds.) ICONIP 2021. CCIS, vol. 1517, pp. 315–322. Springer, Cham (2021). https://doi.org/10.1007/978-3-030-92310-5_37
7. Lee, J., Yu, M., Kwon, Y., Kim, T.: Quantune: post-training quantization of convolutional neural networks using extreme gradient boosting for fast deployment. Futur. Gener. Comput. Syst. **132**, 124–135 (2022)
8. Zhou, S., Wu, Y., Ni, Z., Zhou, X., Wen, H., Zou, Y.: Dorefa-net: Training low bitwidth convolutional neural networks with low bitwidth gradients, arXiv preprint arXiv:1606.06160 (2016)
9. Choi, J., Wang, Z., Venkataramani, S., Chuang, P.I.-J., Srinivasan, V., Gopalakrishnan, K.: Pact: parameterized clipping activation for quantized neural networks, arXiv preprint arXiv:1805.06085 (2018)
10. Li, Y., Dong, X., Wang, W.: Additive powers-of-two quantization: an efficient non-uniform discretization for neural networks, arXiv preprint arXiv:1909.13144 (2019)
11. Oh, S., Sim, H., Lee, S., Lee, J.: Automated log-scale quantization for low-cost deep neural networks. In: Proceedings of the IEEE/CVF Conference on Computer Vision and Pattern Recognition, pp. 742–751 (2021)
12. Kryzhanovskiy, V., Balitskiy, G., Kozyrskiy, N., Zuruev, A.: Qpp: real-time quantization parameter prediction for deep neural networks. In: Proceedings of the IEEE/CVF Conference on Computer Vision and Pattern Recognition, pp. 10684–10692 (2021)
13. Sun, Q., Ren, Y., Jiao, L., Li, X., Shang, F., Liu, F.: MWQ: multiscale wavelet quantized neural networks, arXiv preprint arXiv:2103.05363 (2021)
14. Cai, Y., Yao, Z., Dong, Z., Gholami, A., Mahoney, M.W., Keutzer, K.: ZeroQ: a novel zero shot quantization framework. In: Proceedings of the IEEE/CVF Conference on Computer Vision and Pattern Recognition, pp. 13169–13178 (2020)

15. Bablani, D., Mckinstry, J.L., Esser, S.K., Appuswamy, R., Modha, D.S.: Efficient and effective methods for mixed precision neural network quantization for faster, energy-efficient inference, arXiv preprint arXiv:2301.13330 (2023)
16. Yao, Z., et al.: Hawq-v3: dyadic neural network quantization. In: International Conference on Machine Learningpp. 11875–11886. PMLR (2021)
17. Chen, W., Wang, P., Cheng, J.: Towards mixed-precision quantization of neural networks via constrained optimization. In: Proceedings of the IEEE/CVF International Conference on Computer Vision, pp. 5350–5359 (2021)
18. Yuan, Y., Chen, C., Hu, X., Peng, S.: EvoQ: mixed precision quantization of DNNs via sensitivity guided evolutionary search. In: 2020 International Joint Conference on Neural Networks (IJCNN), pp. 1–8. IEEE (2020)
19. Wang, K., Liu, Z., Lin, Y., Lin, J., Han, S.: HAQ: hardware-aware automated quantization with mixed precision. In: Proceedings of the IEEE/CVF Conference on Computer Vision and Pattern Recognition, pp. 8612–8620 (2019)
20. Yu, H., Han, Q., Li, J., Shi, J., Cheng, G., Fan, B.: Search what you want: barrier panelty NAS for mixed precision quantization. In: Vedaldi, A., Bischof, H., Brox, T., Frahm, J.-M. (eds.) ECCV 2020. LNCS, vol. 12354, pp. 1–16. Springer, Cham (2020). https://doi.org/10.1007/978-3-030-58545-7_1
21. Sun, Q., Li, X., Jiao, L., Ren, Y., Shang, F., Liu, F.: Fast and effective: a novel sequential single-path search for mixed-precision-quantized networks. IEEE Trans. Cybern. (2022)
22. Ghamisi, P., Benediktsson, J.A.: Feature selection based on hybridization of genetic algorithm and particle swarm optimization. IEEE Geosci. Remote Sens. Lett. **12**(2), 309–313 (2014)
23. Tang, C., et al.: Mixed-precision neural network quantization via learned layer-wise importance. In: Avidan, S., Brostow, G., Cissé, M., Farinella, G.M., Hassner, T. (eds.) ECCV 2022. LNCS, vol. 13671, pp. 259–275. Springer, Cham (2022). https://doi.org/10.1007/978-3-031-20083-0_16
24. Uhlich, S., et al.: Mixed precision DNNs: All you need is a good parametrization, arXiv preprint arXiv:1905.11452 (2019)
25. Cai, Z., Vasconcelos, N.: Rethinking differentiable search for mixed-precision neural networks. In: Proceedings of the IEEE/CVF Conference on Computer Vision and Pattern Recognition, pp. 2349–2358 (2020)
26. Dong, Z., Yao, Z., Arfeen, D., Gholami, A., Mahoney, M.W., Keutzer, K.: Hawq-v2: Hessian aware trace-weighted quantization of neural networks. Adv. Neural. Inf. Process. Syst. **33**, 18518–18529 (2020)
27. Liu, H., Elkerdawy, S., Ray, N., Elhoushi, M.: Layer importance estimation with imprinting for neural network quantization. In: Proceedings of the IEEE/CVF Conference on Computer Vision and Pattern Recognition, pp. 2408–2417 (2021)
28. Tsuji, S., Yamada, F., Kawaguchi, H., Inoue, A., Sakai, Y.: Greedy search algorithm for partial quantization of convolutional neural networks inspired by submodular optimization, Neural Comput. Appl. 1–11 (2022)
29. Kennedy, J.: Bare bones particle swarms. In: Proceedings of the 2003 IEEE Swarm Intelligence Symposium. SIS 2003 (Cat. No. 03EX706), pp. 80–87. IEEE (2003)
30. Deb, K.: An efficient constraint handling method for genetic algorithms. Comput. Methods Appl. Mech. Eng. **186**(2–4), 311–338 (2000)
31. Song, X.-F., Zhang, Y., Gong, D.-W., Gao, X.-Z.: A fast hybrid feature selection based on correlation-guided clustering and particle swarm optimization for high-dimensional data. IEEE Trans. Cybern. **52**(9), 9573–9586 (2021)

32. Zhang, D., Yang, J., Ye, D., Hua, G.: LQ-Nets: learned quantization for highly accurate and compact deep neural networks. In: Proceedings of the European conference on computer vision (ECCV), pp. 365–382 (2018)
33. Wang, L., Dong, X., Wang, Y., Liu, L., An, W., Guo, Y.: Learnable lookup table for neural network quantization. In: Proceedings of the IEEE/CVF Conference on Computer Vision and Pattern Recognition, pp. 12423–12433 (2022)

A Convolutional Autoencoder Approach for Weakly Supervised Anomaly Video Detection

Phan Nguyen Duc Hieu and Phan Duy Hung(✉)

FPT University, Hanoi, Vietnam
hieupndhe153303@fpt.edu.vn, hungpd2@fe.edu.vn

Abstract. Weakly-supervised video anomaly detection uses video-level labels to avoid annotating all frames or segments in the training video. This problem is typically considered as a multiple instance learning problem, the training process aims to learn how to score both abnormal segments and normal segments, and the score of abnormal segments is higher than the score of normal segments. The features are extracted from videos before the training or testing process. Although many models have been proposed and obtained good results, improving the performance of the problem remains a challenge. This study proposes a convolutional autoencoder based approach to reconstruct features, with an assumption that the reconstructed features contain important information early bound to the objective of normal or abnormal video classification (minimizing the cost function). The work is validated on the ShanghaiTech Campus dataset and has produced results that outperform state-of-the-art methods.

Keywords: Anomaly Video Detection · Convolutional Autoencoder · Multiple Instance Learning

1 Introduction

In recent years, surveillance cameras are installed everywhere. Along with that, there is a need for intelligent systems that can detect abnormal events such as theft, accident, violence, etc. To avoid the time-consuming labeling of each frame in the video, video-level annotations were chosen to solve the problem. The unsupervised model uses only normal video for training, based on the assumption that the model can distinguish between normal and abnormal video due to the difference between them [1–3]. However, in reality, there are many different types of normal events that cannot be covered by the training dataset, leading to a very high false alarm rate. Effective methods were weakly supervised using both normal and abnormal video during training [4–7].

Unsupervised methods typically treat this problem as a one-class classification problem, where only normal video is used as training data. Ravanbakhsh et al. [1] used the GANs [8] architecture to learn how to reconstruct frames in normal video. If the model produces poor reconstruction results, it shows that those frames are highly likely to be abnormal. Some methods detect objects in the video before processing, in addition to adding some branches in the architecture so that the model can learn more tasks through

N. T. Nguyen et al. (Eds.): ICCCI 2023, LNAI 14162, pp. 138–150, 2023.
https://doi.org/10.1007/978-3-031-41456-5_11

the training process [9, 10]. Georgescu et al. [10] introduced a method of using pseudo-abnormal images during training as an adversarial learning method, ensuring that the model will not have the ability to reconstruct abnormal images. In reality, normal events in the training dataset do not contain all of the normal events, and some abnormal events are just slightly different from the normal events. Thus, the model is overfitting on the training dataset because of the lack of abnormal video.

Weakly supervised methods are used to avoid overfitting problems of unsupervised methods, by using both normal and abnormal video during the training process. However, the major challenges of weakly supervised anomaly detection are abnormal video containing normal snippets and some abnormal snippets are just slightly different from the normal events, which cause high bias. To solve the above problems, Sultani et al. [4] introduced a method that uses multiple instance learning (MIL). The MIL methods [4, 11] divide each video into multiple segments, then score the anomaly of each segment. The anomaly score of the abnormal videos will be evaluated based on the segments that have the highest anomaly score. But this approach still has disadvantages, segments in the normal video may have a higher anomaly score than actual abnormal segments in the abnormal video.

Tian et al. [6] introduced the robust temporal feature magnitude learning method, called RTFM, which defines loss functions with a mechanism that ensures the anomaly score of the normal segment will be less than the anomaly score of the abnormal segment. RTFM uses a multiscale temporal network to learn feature magnitudes of video segments, abnormal segments tend to have high magnitude, and vice versa, normal segments tend to have low magnitude. However, this model relies heavily on extracted features, so it needs an efficient feature extraction model. Deshpande et al. [7] presented an approach to use the VideoSwin [12] feature, with a proposed attention architecture and proved that the VideoSwin feature works effectively. But the VideoSwin feature is extracted from pre-trained models, which use the Kinetic 400 [13], Kinetic 600 [14], or Something-Something v2 [15] datasets. These datasets do not contain videos that are related to anomaly videos. Moreover, the abnormal segments in the training data of weakly supervised anomaly video detection are very few, causing the lack of inductive bias and the lack of important information.

In summary, previous studies have offered various approaches to detect video anomalies, but improving performance remains a challenge. The current best-performing methods all use pre-extracted features (VideoSwin features) as input data through some pre-trained models. However, the purpose of the original features is to identify actions, they lack information to distinguish an abnormal video from a normal video. This is an important point to make improvements to the model.

We add a proposed convolutional autoencoder network after the VideoSwin feature layer. The result of feature recovery according to the objective of anomaly video detection by the convolutional autoencoder network will be added to the feature vector for the next training process. The improved model gives a result that outperforms state-of-the-art methods on the ShanghaiTech Campus dataset.

2 Video Feature Extraction

Using a backbone with a pre-trained model has long dominated visual modeling in computer vision. The convolutional-based backbones were used widely, with various models [16–20]. In particular, the video processing problem often uses two popular features: I3D [19] and C3D [20]. These two types of backbone have shown their effectiveness in many cases. However, after the transformer model was announced, computer vision problems began to apply this architecture, typically through the introduction of ViTs [21]. These transformer-based backbones exhibit superior results over the convolutional-based approach. The downside of the original transformer-based models is the uneven size of the photos or videos. If input and output can be padded to have the same vector size in natural language processing, then in computer vision, padding or cropping images can lead to data distortion and greatly affect the performance of the model. Liu et al. [22] announced the Swin Transformer model to solve this problem, by 1) Proposing hierarchical transformer architecture. 2) Use self-attention on a local area instead of the entire image. 3) Use shifted windows, to create connections between local self-attention areas. 4) Capable of outputting many different scales, suitable for a variety of computer vision problems.

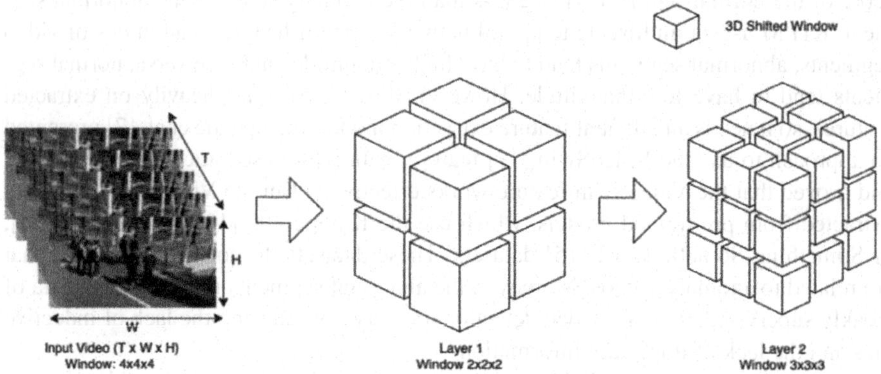

Fig. 1. The architecture of video swin transformer

Liu et al. [12] presented Video Swin Transformer (Fig. 1), this model applied Swin Transformer architecture for video understanding problems. Instead of using 2D shifted windows, Video Swin Transformer uses 3D shifted windows to cover temporal dimensions.

Video Swin Transformer has proven its effectiveness over other backbone models (shown in Table 1). Thus, we use the Video Swin Transformer backbone model to extract features for anomaly video detection problems.

Table 1. Video Swin Transformer models (Swin-T, Swin-L) and other models results

Model	Evaluation Dataset	Accuracy (Top-1)	FLOPs
I3D [19]	Kinetics-400	72.1	75
ViT-B-VTN [23]	Kinetics-400	78.6	4218
ViViT-L/16x2 320 [24]	Kinetics-400	81.3	3992
Swin-T	Kinetics-400	78.8	88
Swin-L (384↑)	Kinetics-400	84.9	2107

3 Proposed Method

Our proposed approach uses video-level annotation for the training process. We consider weakly-supervised anomaly video detection as a multiple instance learning (MIL) problem, which divides each video into a fixed number of segments. We assume that all segments of the normal videos are normal segments, and each abnormal video has at least one abnormal segment. Firstly, we extract the VideoSwin feature from raw videos, then our proposed approach is performed by two stages as given in Fig. 2. Inprite by [25], stage 1 is a convolutional autoencoder-based backbone, which is used to extract and reconstruct the feature. It contains three main parts: the encoder, the decoder, and the self-attention module. Stage 2 is the RTFM module, which is used to score the anomaly magnitude of segments.

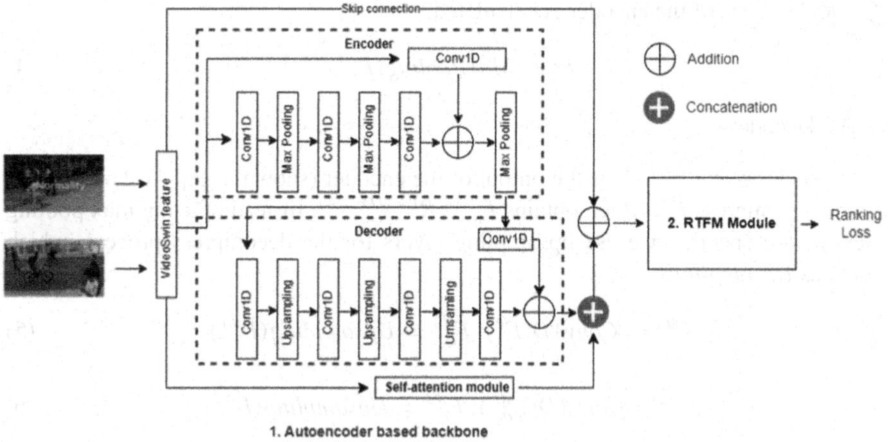

Fig. 2. The architecture of the proposed method

3.1 Convolutional Autoencoder Based Backbone

A. The Encoder

The Encoder aims to compress the VideoSwin features. Given a set of the VideoSwin features, which has T snippets, each has dimension D: $F \in R^{T \times D}$. To compress F, we use multiple convolutional 1×1 layers, which are denoted as $Conv1$D. Each convolutional 1×1 layer is followed by a max pooling 1×1 layer, which is denoted as MaxPooling. After training multiple times, the max pooling 1×1 layer with *kernel size* $= 3$ and *padding* $= 2$ showed the best efficiency. These layers compress feature as below:

Firstly, we apply the $Conv1$D and *MaxPooling* to reduce information of F to $F_o^{c1} \in R^{T \times (D/2-1)}$: $F^{c1} = Conv1D(F); F_o^{c1} = MaxPooling(F^{c1})$. After that $F_o^{c1} \in R^{T \times (D/2-1)}$ is compressed to $F_o^{c2} \in R^{T \times (D/4-1)}$:

$$F^{c2} = Conv1D\left(F_o^{c1}\right); F_o^{c2} = MaxPooling\left(F^{c2}\right) \tag{1}$$

Then a convolutional 1×1 is applied:

$$F^{c3} = Conv1D(F_o^{c2}) \ where \ F^{c3} \in R^{T \times (D/4-1)} \tag{2}$$

Before obtaining the final output of the encoder, we keep the information from the VideoSwin features by making a connection between F and F^{c3} as:

$$F_e^c = Conv1D(F) \ where \ F_e^c \in R^{T \times (D/4-1)}; F_e^{c3} = F_e^c + F^{c3} \tag{3}$$

Reduce information of F_e^{c3} by a max pooling 1×1 layer, the compressed feature $F_o^e \in R^{T \times (D/8-1)}$ of the encoder is calculated:

$$F_o^e = MaxPooling(F_e^{c3}) \tag{4}$$

B. The Decoder

Given $F_o^e \in R^{T \times (D/8-1)}$ is the output of the encoder (shown in Eq. 4). The decoder aims to decompress F_o^e, which obtains $F_o^d \in R^{T \times (D \times 3/4)}$. Instead of using max pooling layers as the encoder, we use upsampling layers for the decompress process, which denote as *Upsampling*:

$$F^{d1} = Conv1D(F_o^e); F_o^{d1} = Upsampling(F^{d1}) \tag{5}$$

$$F^{d2} = Conv1D(F_o^{d1}); F_o^{d2} = Upsampling(F^{d2}) \tag{6}$$

$$F^{d3} = Conv1D(F_o^{d2}); F_o^{d3} = Upsampling(F^{d3}) \tag{7}$$

$$F^{d4} = Conv1D(F_o^{d3}) \tag{8}$$

where $F^{d1} \in R^{T \times (D/8-1)}$; $F_o^{d1}, F^{d2} \in R^{T \times (D/4-1)}$; $F_o^{d2}, F^{d3} \in R^{T \times (D/2-1)}$; $F_o^{d3}, F^{d4} \in R^{T \times (D \times 3/4)}$.

To avoid losing important information from compressed features, a connection between F_o^e and F^{d4} is performed by the convolutional 1 × 1 layer:

$$F_c^d = Conv1D(F_o^e) \ where \ F_c^d \in R^{T\times(D\times3/4)} \tag{9}$$

The output of the decoder F_o^d is calculated by adding F_c^d and F^{d4}:

$$F_o^d = F_c^d + F^{d4} \tag{10}$$

C. The self-attention module

In [6], to achieve the global dependence between video snippets, Tian et al. used a self-attention mechanism that works on the time dimension and has the ability to capture global context modeling, as below:

Use a convolutional 1 × 1 layer to reduce dimension of $F \in R^{T\times D}$ to $F_o^t \in R^{T\times D/4}$: $F_o^t = Conv1D(F)$. Then three 1 × 1 convolutional layers are applied to produce $F^{t1}, F^{t2}, F^{t3} \in R^{T\times D/4}$, as in $F^{ti} = Conv1D(F_o^t)$ for $i \in \{1, 2, 3\}$. The attention map is built with: $M = F^{t1}(F^{t2})^T$. Thus, F^{t4} is produced:

$$F^{t4} = Conv1D(MF^{t3}) \tag{11}$$

The output F^{tsa} of self-attention module is obtained by adding a skip connection: $F^{tsa} = F^{t4} + F_o^t$. The final output $F_a \in R^{T\times D}$ of the autoencoder based backbone is the concatenation of output from self-attention module F^{tsa} and output from the decoder F_o^d (shown in Eq. 10), then adding a skip connection with the origin VideoSwin feature F:

$$F_a = (F_o^d, F^{tsa}) + F \tag{12}$$

3.2 The RTFM Module

Our proposed approach uses robust temporal feature magnitude learning (RTFM), which is introduced by Tian et al. [6]. The feature magnitude is pre-computed in the autoencoder based backbone. RTFM model aims to differentiate between abnormal and normal snippets based on feature magnitude, with the assumption that abnormal snippets have a higher mean magnitude than normal snippets.

Given X^+ as normal videos and X^- as abnormal video, X^+ contains normal snippets (x^+), X^- contains abnormal snippets (x^-). Let $\|x\|$ denotes the feature magnitude of those snippets. The model learns to maximize the difference between l2 norm of top k snippets in the normal bag and the abnormal bag, where k is the number of abnormal snippets in the abnormal video. Given $\delta_{score}(X^+, X^-)$ denotes the value of this difference. The training process maximize $\delta_{score}(X^+, X^-)$ during backpropagation by an optimized loss function:

$$\begin{aligned} l_s(X^+, X^-) = max(0, m - mean(topK(\|X^+\|)) \\ + mean(topK(\|X^-\|))) \end{aligned} \tag{13}$$

where m is a predefined margin.

The model uses a classifier to classify whether a video is abnormal or not. Thus we use binary cross-entropy-based loss during backpropagation. Let x denote the mean of topK feature in video: $x = mean(topK(\|X^+\|))$, y denotes the actual label of video, in which y = 1 means abnormal video and y = 0 means normal video. The loss function of the snippets classifier is performed as:

$$l_f = -ylog(x) + (1-y)log(1-x) \tag{14}$$

To enforce similarity score for neighboring snippets, the temporal smoothness is defined as:

$$s_l = \sum_{t=1}^{T}(x_t - x_{t-1})^2 \tag{15}$$

While the sparsity regularization is defined to impose a prior that abnormal events are rare in each abnormal video:

$$s_p = \sum_{t=1}^{T}|x_t| \tag{16}$$

The final loss function is obtained by adding those terms (Eqs. 13, 14, 15, and 16):

$$l_{final} = \lambda_1 l_s(X^+, X^-) + \lambda_2 l_f + \lambda_3 s_l + \lambda_4 s_p \tag{17}$$

where λ_i for i in {1, 2, 3, 4} are the respective learning rate of each term.

4 Experiment

4.1 Dataset Description

This research uses the ShanghaiTech Campus dataset [26] to evaluate performance. It's a medium-scale dataset with videos from street surveillance cameras. This dataset contains 437 videos in 13 different background scenes, including 307 normal videos and 130 anomaly videos. The abnormal events in ShanghaiTech include bullying, traffic violation, robbing, etc. (Fig. 3).

The original structure of this dataset is mainly used as a benchmark for anomaly detection task that assumes the availability of normal training data. Zhong et al. [27] restructure this dataset by selecting a subset of videos, then the training set and test set both cover 13 scenes. The new structure is typically used for weakly supervised anomaly video detection. This paper uses the same method as used by Zhong et al. [27], Tian et al. [6], and Deshpande et al. [7].

Fig. 3. The normal events (left) and abnormal events (right) in different scenes

4.2 Evaluation Method

The paper uses an AUC score to evaluate the performance of the proposed approach, similar to previous papers [20, 28, 29]. AUC stands for the area under the receiver operating characteristic (ROC) curve. The ROC curve plots the true positive rate (TPR) versus the false positive rate (FPR) at different classification thresholds, where:

$$TPR = \frac{True\ Positive}{True\ Positive + False\ Negative}$$

$$FPR = \frac{False\ Positive}{False\ Positive + True\ Negative}$$

The AUC score with a maximum value of 1 means the model can separate two classes perfectly, and an AUC score with a minimum value of 0 means the model has no ability to separate two classes.

4.3 Implementation Detail

In Eq. 13 set up the hyperparameter m = 100 and k = 3 as [6]. The three fully connected layers in the RTFM module have 512, 128, and 1 node respectively, each of them followed by the activation function ReLU with a dropout rate of 0.7. The VideoSwin feature is obtained from the pre-trained VideoSwin transformer model on the Kinetics dataset, which follows by the setting of Kapil et al. [7]. We trained our model on a Tesla T4 15.36 Gb Memory GPU with CUDA version 12.0.

Table 2. Hyper-parameters

Hyper-parameter	Value
Learning rate	0.001
Training batch size	60
Number epochs	2000
Optimization function	Adam
Adam weight decay	0.005

We trained our model for 2000 epochs, with a batch size of 60, a learning rate of 0.001, and using the Adam optimizer with a weight decay of 0.005 (as shown in Table 2). Each mini-batch contains 32 normal and abnormal videos, which are selected randomly. The benchmark setup for the dataset is the same as Deshpande et al. [7], Zhong et al. [27], and Tian et al. [6] for a fair comparison.

4.4 Result Analysis

We calculate and display the results of the feature magnitude of some video samples as shown in Fig. 4. The results show that our model produces a higher feature magnitude of the abnormal segments than the RTFM model. But the feature magnitude of the normal segments is still the same, even lower than the RTFM's one. As we described above, the abnormal segments should have a high feature magnitude, and vice versa, the normal segments tend to have a low feature magnitude. This means that our model has shown better performance in distinguishing the difference between abnormal segments and normal segments compared to the RTFM model.

Based on the obtained feature magnitude, the segments with the top high value of feature magnitude are chosen. Then the abnormal probabilities of those segments are used to evaluate the anomaly score of the whole video (Fig. 5).

The final results were evaluated on the ShanghaiTech Campus dataset and have shown impressive performance compared to current state-of-the-art methods (Table 3). Therefore, the proposed model of adding an autoencoder network proved to be important in reconstructing the VideoSwin feature while adding more information about anomalous events during training.

Figure 6 visually presents our results using the ROC curve. We achieved an impressive AUC score, which was across the border of 0.98, and higher than RTFM by around 1%.

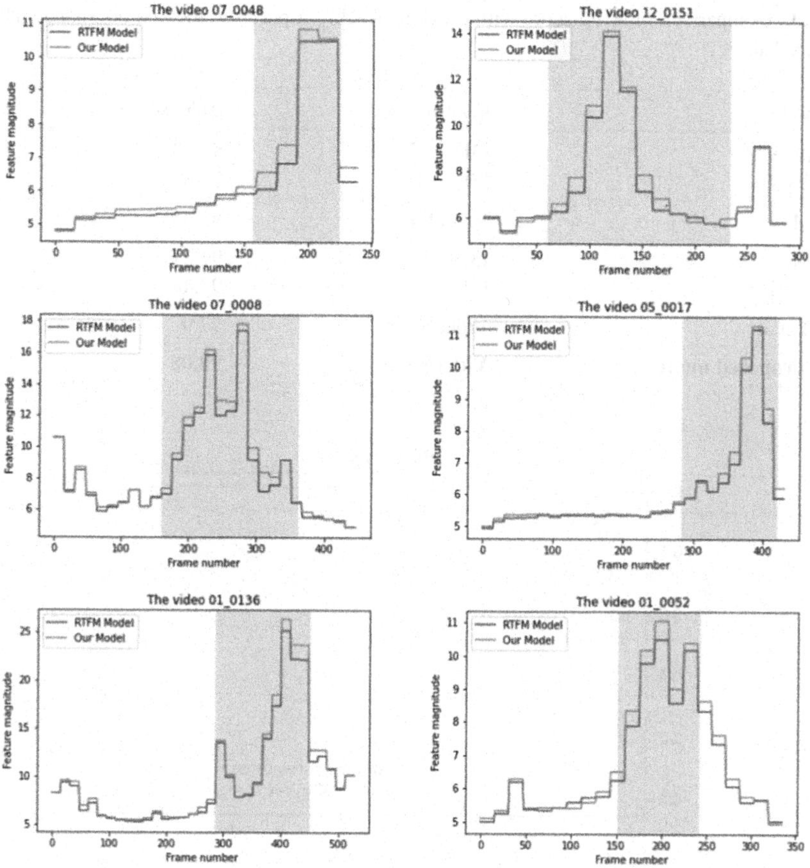

Fig. 4. The feature magnitude of all frames on abnormal videos. The pink area indicates the abnormal frames (Color figure online)

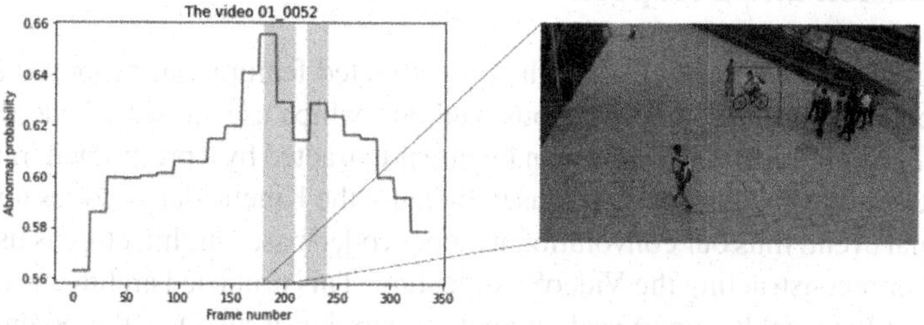

Fig. 5. An example of our prediction on abnormal video. The yellow areas indicate the chosen segments. (Color figure online)

Table 3. Comparison of AUC-score with previous weakly supervised method on ShanghaiTech campus dataset

Method	Feature	AUC-score
Sultani et al.	I3D	85.33
MIST [30]	I3D	94.83
RTFM	VideoSwin	95.45
RTFM	I3D	97.21
S3R [31]	I3D	97.48
Kapil et al.	VideoSwin	97.9
Our proposed model	**VideoSwin**	**98.08**

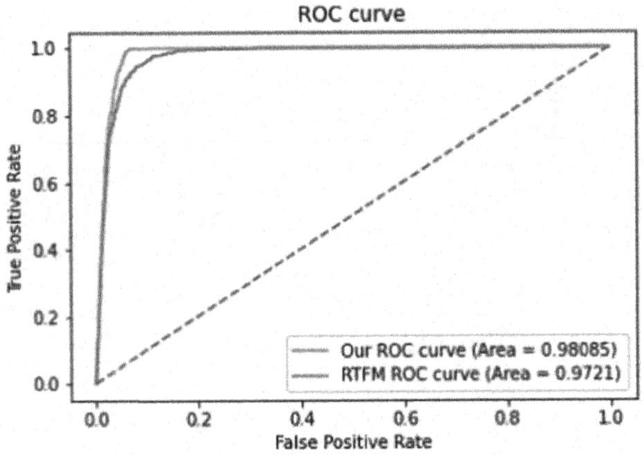

Fig. 6. The ROC curve comparison

5 Conclusion and Perspectives

By solving the disadvantage of using the pre-extracted feature, our proposed approach shows a better performance than previous methods, which use the same VideoSwin feature and RTFM module. The VideoSwin feature is extracted by a pre-trained transformer model that is trained by the Kinetic dataset. Because the Kinetic dataset does not contain the abnormal event, thus our convolutional autoencoder-based architecture is used as the backbone for reconstructing the VideoSwin feature. This proposed architecture may not only be used for weakly-supervised anomaly video, but it also has the potential to be used as a backbone module for other problems which use the pre-extracted features. In the future, to enhance performance in weakly-supervised anomaly video problems, some approaches can be performed to select exactly the number of abnormal segments in the abnormal video, which can achieve the highest performance based on RTFM's theory. The work is also a good reference for image pattern recognition problems [32–36].

References

1. Ravanbakhsh, M., Nabi, M., Sangineto, E., Marcenaro, L., Regazzoni, C., Sebe, N.: Abnormal event detection in videos using generative adversarial nets. arXiv:1708.09644 (2017)
2. Hasan, M., Choi, J., Neumann, J.K.A., Davis, L.S.: Learning temporal regularity in video sequences. arXiv:1604.04574 (2016)
3. Smeureanu, S., Ionescu, R.T., Popescu, M., Alexe, B.: Deep appearance features for abnormal behavior detection in video. In: Battiato, S., Gallo, G., Schettini, R., Stanco, F. (eds.) ICIAP 2017. LNCS, vol. 10485, pp. 779–789. Springer, Cham (2017). https://doi.org/10.1007/978-3-319-68548-9_70
4. Sultani, W., Chen, C., Shah, M.: Real-world Anomaly detection in surveillance videos. arXiv: 1801.04264 (2018)
5. Degardin, B.: Weakly and partially supervised learning frameworks for anomaly detection (2020). https://doi.org/10.13140/RG.2.2.30613.65769
6. Tian, Y., Pang, G., Chen, Y., Singh, R., Verjans, J.W., Carneiro, G.: Weakly-supervised video anomaly detection with robust temporal feature magnitude learning. arXiv:2101.10030 (2021)
7. Deshpande, K., Punn, N.S., Sonbhadra, S.K., Agarwal, S.: Anomaly detection in surveillance videos using transformer based attention model. arXiv:2206.01524 (2022)
8. Goodfellow, I., et al.: Generative adversarial networks. Adv. Neural Inf. Process. Syst. **27**, 3 (2014). https://doi.org/10.1145/3422622
9. Georgescu, M., Barbalau, A., Ionescu, R.T., Khan, F.S., Popescu, M., Shah, M.: Anomaly detection in video via self-supervised and multi-task learning. arXiv:2011.07491 (2020)
10. Georgescu, M., Ionescu, R.T., Khan, F.S., Popescu, M., Shah, M.: A background-agnostic framework with adversarial training for abnormal event detection in video. arXiv:2021. 3074805 (2020)
11. Wu, P., et al.: Not only look, but also listen: learning multimodal violence detection under weak supervision. arXiv:2007.04687 (2020)
12. Liu, Z., et al.: Video Swin Transformer. arXiv:2106.13230 (2021)
13. Kay, W., et al.: The kinetics human action video dataset. arXiv:1705.06950 (2017)
14. Carreira, J., Noland, E., Hillier, C., Zisserman, A.: A short note about kinetics-600. arXiv: 1808.01340 (2018)
15. Goyal, R., et al.: The "Something Something" video database for learning and evaluating visual common sense. In: IEEE International Conference on Computer Vision (ICCV), Venice, Italy, pp. 5843–5851 (2017). https://doi.org/10.1109/ICCV.2017.622
16. Miech, A., Alayrac, J., Smaira, L., Laptev, I., Sivic, J., Zisserman, A.: End-to-end learning of visual representations from uncurated instructional videos. ArXiv. /abs/1912.06430 (2019)
17. Miech, A., Zhukov, D., Alayrac, J., Tapaswi, M., Laptev, I., Sivic, J.: HowTo100M: learning a text-video embedding by watching hundred million narrated video clips. ArXiv. /abs/1906.03327 (2019)
18. Tran, D., Wang, H., Torresani, L., Ray, J., LeCun, Y., Paluri, M.: A closer look at spatiotemporal convolutions for action recognition. ArXiv. /abs/1711.11248 (2017)
19. Carreira, J., Zisserman, A.: Quo Vadis, action recognition? A new model and the kinetics dataset. ArXiv. /abs/1705.07750 (2017)
20. Tran, D., Bourdev, L., Fergus, R., Torresani, L., Paluri, M.: Learning spatiotemporal features with 3D convolutional networks. arXiv:1412.0767 (2014)
21. Dosovitskiy, A., et al.: An image is worth 16×16 words: transformers for image recognition at scale. ArXiv. /abs/2010.11929 (2020)
22. Liu, Z., et al.: Swin transformer: hierarchical vision transformer using shifted windows. ArXiv. /abs/2103.14030 (2021)

23. Neimark, D., Bar, O., Zohar, M., Asselmann, D.: Video transformer network. ArXiv. /abs/2102.00719 (2021)
24. Arnab, A., Dehghani, M., Heigold, G., Sun, C., Lučić, M., Schmid, C.: ViViT: a video vision transformer. ArXiv. /abs/2103.15691 (2021)
25. Michelucci, U.: An introduction to autoencoders. arXiv:2201.03898 (2022)
26. Liu, W., Luo, W., Lian, D., Gao, S.: Future frame prediction for anomaly detection – a new baseline. arXiv:1712.09867 (2017)
27. Zhong, J., Li, N., Kong, W., Liu, S., Li, T.H., Li, G.: Graph convolutional label noise cleaner: train a plug-and-play action classifier for anomaly detection. arXiv:1903.07256 (2019)
28. Wan, B., Fang, Y., Xia, X., Mei, J.: Weakly supervised video anomaly detection via center-guided discriminative learning. In: Proceeding of the IEEE International Conference on Multimedia and Expo (ICME), London, United Kingdom, pp. 1–6 (2020). https://doi.org/10.1109/ICME46284.2020.9102722
29. Zhang, J., Qing, L., Miao, J.: Temporal convolutional network with complementary inner bag loss for weakly supervised anomaly detection. In: Proceeding of the IEEE International Conference on Image Processing (ICIP), Taipei, Taiwan, pp. 4030–4034 (2019). https://doi.org/10.1109/ICIP.2019.8803657
30. Feng, J., Hong, F., Zheng, W.: MIST: multiple instance self-training framework for video anomaly detection. arXiv:2104.01633 (2021)
31. Wu, J.-C., Hsieh, H.-Y., Chen, D.-J., Fuh, C.-S., Liu, T.-L.: Self-supervised sparse representation for video anomaly detection. In: Avidan, S., Brostow, G., Cissé, M., Farinella, G.M., Hassner, T. (eds.) ECCV 2022. LNCS, vol. 13673, pp. 729–745. Springer, Heidelberg (2022). https://doi.org/10.1007/978-3-031-19778-9_42
32. Hung, P.D., Kien, N.N.: SSD-MobileNet implementation for classifying fish species. In: Vasant, P., Zelinka, I., Weber, G.W. (eds.) ICO 2019. AISC, vol. 1072, pp. 399–408. Springer, Cham (2020). https://doi.org/10.1007/978-3-030-33585-4_40
33. Hung, P.D., Su, N.T., Diep, V.T.: Surface classification of damaged concrete using deep convolutional neural network. Pattern Recognit. Image Anal. **29**, 676–687 (2019)
34. Hung, P.D., Su, N.T.: Unsafe construction behavior classification using deep convolutional neural network. Pattern Recognit. Image Anal. **31**, 271–284 (2021)
35. Duy, L.D., Hung, P.D.: Adaptive graph attention network in person re-identification. Pattern Recognit. Image Anal. **32**, 384–392 (2022)
36. Su, N.T., Hung, P.D., Vinh, B.T., Diep, V.T.: Rice leaf disease classification using deep learning and target for mobile devices. In: Al-Emran, M., Al-Sharafi, M.A., Al-Kabi, M.N., Shaalan, K. (eds.) ICETIS 2021. LNNS, vol. 299, pp. 136–148. Springer, Cham (2022). https://doi.org/10.1007/978-3-030-82616-1_13

Sparsity-Invariant Convolution for Forecasting Irregularly Sampled Time Series

Krisztian Buza[1,2(✉)]

[1] Artificial Intelligence Laboratory, Institute Jozef Stefan, Ljubljana, Slovenia
buza@biointelligence.hu

[2] BioIntelligence Group, Department of Mathematics-Informatics, Sapientia Hungarian University of Transylvania, Targu Mures, Romania

Abstract. Time series forecasting techniques range from ARIMA over exponential smoothing to neural approaches, such as convolutional neural networks. However, most of them were designed to work with regularly sampled and complete time series, i.e., time series which can be represented as a sequence of numbers *without* missing values. In contrast, we consider the task of forecasting *irregularly* sampled time series in this paper. We argue that, compared with "usual" convolution, sparsity-invariant convolution is better suited for the case of irregularly sampled time series, therefore, we propose to use neural networks with sparsity-invariant convolution. We perform experiments on 30 publicly-available real-world time series datasets and show that sparsity-invariant convolution significantly improves the performance of convolutional neural networks in case of forecasting irregularly sampled time series. In order to support reproduction, independent validation and follow-up works, we made our implementation (software code) publicly available at https://github.com/kr7/timeseriesforecast-siconv.

Keywords: time series forecasting · convolutional neural network · sparsity-invariant convolution

1 Introduction

Due to its prominent applications in medicine [9], retail [15], finance [10] and other domains [4], time series forecasting has been a key area of research. Time series forecasting techniques range from the well-known autoregressive models [2] over exponential smoothing [8] to approaches based on deep learning [12,19]. Among the numerous methods, a prominent family of methods include forecast techniques based on convolutional neural networks (CNNs) [1,16].

In ideal cases, under the assumption that a reliable sensor is installed, measurements are made continuously or periodically with constant time between subsequent observations. In such cases, time series can be represented as sequences of numbers without missing values. However, in real-world applications, sensors

N. T. Nguyen et al. (Eds.): ICCCI 2023, LNAI 14162, pp. 151–162, 2023.
https://doi.org/10.1007/978-3-031-41456-5_12

are not fully reliable due to various reasons ranging from the capacity of the battery over weather conditions to hardware failures and signal transmission issues. In other cases (e.g. measuring the blood pressure at the family doctor), the measurements are done semi-regularly, thus the time between consecutive observations varies. Consequently, many real-world time series, for example in healthcare [22], finance [17] and meteorology [14], are irregularly sampled.

The vast majority of conventional time series forecasting techniques, including methods based on deep learning, consider time series as sequences of numbers *without* missing values. This corresponds to the assumption that the time series are regularly sampled and complete. Lim and Zohren [12] point out that "deep neural networks typically require time series to be discretised at regular intervals, making it difficult to forecast datasets where observations can be missing or arrive at random intervals." They also note that the domain of irregularly sampled time series is understudied.

In this paper we propose to use convolutional neural networks (CNNs) with sparsity-invariant convolution for forecasting irregularly sampled time series. In experiments on 30 publicly available real-world datasets from various domains, we show that CNNs with sparsity invariant convolution outperform "usual" CNNs, both in terms of mean squared error and mean average error, when it comes to forecasting irregularly sampled time series.

The reminder of the paper is organized as follows. In Sect. 2, we provide a short discussion of related works. We describe our approach in Sect. 3, followed by the experimental evaluation is Sect. 4. Finally, we conclude in Sect. 5.

2 Related Work

Convolutional neural networks have been widely used for classification and forecasting of time series, see e.g. [1,3,6]. Works that are most closely related to ours fall into two categories: (i) methods based on convolutional neural networks for time series forecasting and (ii) approaches based on sparsity-invariant convolution.

As for the works in the former category, we refer to the recent surveys of Lim et al. [12], Sezer et al. [17] and Torres et al. [19] and we point out that our approach is orthogonal to such works in the sense that one could replace convolutional layers in any convolutional network by sparsity-invariant convolution if the data (or its hidden representation, i.e., the input of a convolutional layer within the network) is sparse.

Regarding the works on sparsity-invariant convolution, we note that the operation of sparsity-invariant convolution has originally been introduced in the depth completion (a.k.a. 3D reconstruction) community [20] where a few pixels of an image are associated with distance information, thus the distance information corresponds to sparse data [23]. While various models with sparsity-invariant convolution have been shown to outperform their counterparts with "usual" convolution, see e.g. [13], to the best of our knowledge, ours is the first work that studies sparsity-invariant convolution in the domain of time series.

3 Our Approach

We begin this section with a formal definition of our task followed by the description of sparsity-invariant convolution in the context of time series.

3.1 Problem Formulation

Given an observed time series $x = (x_1, \ldots, x_l)$ of length l, we aim at predicting its subsequent h values $y = (x_{l+1}, \ldots, x_{l+h})$. We say that h is the forecast horizon and y is the target. Furthermore, we assume that a dataset D is given which contains n time series with the corresponding target:

$$D = \{(x^{(i)}, y^{(i)})_{i=1}^{n}\}. \tag{1}$$

We use D to train neural networks for the aforementioned prediction task. We say that $x^{(i)}$ is the input of the neural network.

In our experiments, we assume that an independent dataset D^* is given which can be used to evaluate the predictions of our model. Similarly to D, dataset D^* contains pairs of input and target time series. D^* is called the test set.

The above sequence $x_1, \ldots, x_l$ corresponds to a regularly sampled time series. To account for the fact that time series may be irregularly sampled, we allow for missing values in the aforementioned time series, i.e., each x_i within $x = (x_1, \ldots, x_l)$ is either a real number or a symbol indicating that the value is missing. We assume that time series are represented at a relatively high resolution so that all the actual observations may be mapped to one of the symbols in the sequence $x_1, \ldots, x_l$, while most symbols of the sequence denote missing values. In real-world applications, the ratio of missing values may be as high as 90% or even more [5].

3.2 SiConv: Sparsity-Invariant Convolution

Considering convolutional neural networks working with data containing missing values, it may be useful to encode the missing values by zeros because in this case the multiplication of a missing value (i.e., a zero) by the corresponding weight results in zero and therefore the missing values are ignored in the weighted sum calculated by the convolutional layer, which is an intuitive behaviour. Furthermore, treating missing values as zeros is also inline with dropout, a widely-used regularisation for deep neural networks [18]. For these reasons, we follow the wide-spread convention of denoting missing values by zeros [13,20].

The intuition behind sparsity-invariant convolution [20] is to normalize the output of the convolutional layer according to the number of its non-missing inputs. As we focus on time series forecasting in this paper, we describe sparsity-invariant convolution, denoted as SiConv for simplicity, in the context of time series. Denoting the input of SiConv as $x^{in} = (x_1^{in}, \ldots, x_l^{in})$, the size of the convolutional filter as s, the output $x^{out} = (x_1^{out}, \ldots, x_{l-s+1}^{out})$ of SiConv can be calculated as follows:

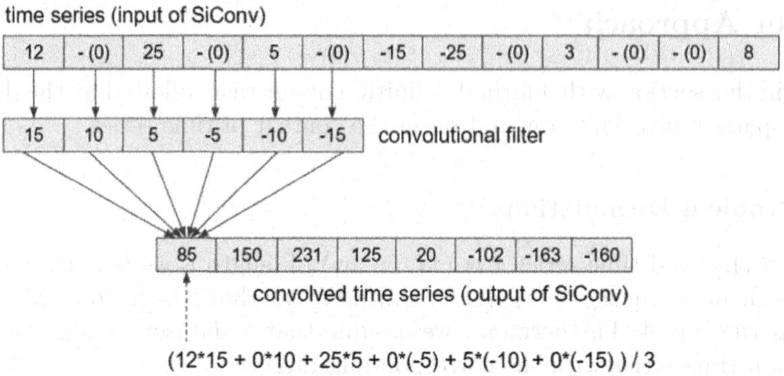

Fig. 1. Illustration of sparsity-invariant convolution (SiConv). The input and output time series of SiConv are shown in the top and bottom, respectively. The convolutional filter in the center is expected to detect a decreasing trend. Compared to "usual" convolution, the difference is that the output values are divided by the number of non-missing input values.

$$x_i^{out} = \begin{cases} \frac{b+\sum_{j=0}^{s} w_j x_{i+j}^{in}}{z_i} & \text{if } z_i \neq 0 \\ 0 & \text{otherwise} \end{cases}, \tag{2}$$

where

$$z_i = \sum_{j=0}^{s} \mathcal{I}(x_{i+j}^{in} \neq 0), \tag{3}$$

while b and w_j denote the bias and weights of the convolutional filter; $\mathcal{I}$ is an indicator function that returns 1 if its argument is true, otherwise it returns zero, therefore z_i is the number of the non-zero (i.e., non-missing) inputs of SiConv within the i-th convolutional window. SiConv is illustrated in Fig. 1.

We note that in case if there are no missing values in the input of SiConv, SiConv is equivalent to "usual" convolution up to the scaling factor $z_i = s$. On the other hand, for those segments of the time series, where all the inputs of SiConv are missing values (zeros) within the convolutional window, the output of SiConv is zero which denotes a missing value according to our encoding. For these reasons, we may use SiConv not only in the first convolutional layer, but in subsequent convolutional layers as well, especially in case of highly sparse input. In such cases, each convolutional layer with SiConv decreases the ratio of missing values in the hidden representation.

Representing irregularly sampled time series at a relatively high resolution results in sequences containing lot of missing values. In such cases, SiConv is more suited than "usual" convolution by its design. Therefore, we propose to use SiConv in neural networks for forecasting irregularly sampled time series.

4 Experimental Evaluation

The goal of our experiments is to examine the effect of SiConv on the forecast performance.

4.1 Experimental Settings

Datasets. We performed experiments on 30 real-world time series datasets from various domains. These datasets are publicly available in *The UEA & UCR Time Series Classification Repository.*[1] The datasets used in our experiments are listed in the first column on Table 1 and Table 2. For all the datasets, we considered a forecast horizon of $h = 16$. We trained the models to predict the last h values of the time series based on its previous values.

Baselines. In order to assess the contribution of SiConv, in all our experiments, we trained three versions of the same convolutional neural network: (i) with SiConv, (ii) with "usual" convolution and (iii) with "usual" convolution and linear interpolation of the missing values.

Experimental Protocol. We performed experiments according to the 10-fold cross-validation protocol. That is: we initially partition the data into 10 splits.[2] Out of them, 9 splits are used as training data, while the remaining one is used as test data. The process is repeated 10-times: in each round of the cross-validation, a different split plays the role of the test set.

Evaluation Metrics. We evaluated the predicted time series both in terms of mean squared error (MSE) and mean absolute error (MAE). MSE and MAE were calculated as follows:

$$MSE = \sum_{(x,y)\in D^*} \sum_{\substack{y_i \in y, \\ y_i \neq 0}} \frac{(\hat{y}_i - y_i)^2}{N} \tag{4}$$

$$MAE = \sum_{(x,y)\in D^*} \sum_{\substack{y_i \in y, \\ y_i \neq 0}} \frac{|\hat{y}_i - y_i|}{N} \tag{5}$$

where D^* denotes the test dataset, x is an instance of the test set and y is the corresponding target (roughly speaking: x contain the "past" values of the

[1] https://www.timeseriesclassification.com.

[2] In our case, each *time series dataset* contains several *time series*. For example, the ECG5000 dataset contains in total 5000 time series, and each of these 5000 time series have a length of 140. In order to avoid data leakage [7], when partitioning data, an entire time series is assigned to one of the splits. For each time series belonging to the test split, we aim to predict its last h values. The segment we aim to predict is *unknown* to the model.

Table 1. Mean squared error (averaged over 10 folds) ± its standard deviation in case of our approach (SiCNN) and the baselines (CNN, linCNN) at a sparsity level of $SL = 80\%$. Lower values indicate better performance. For each dataset, the best approach is underlined. For SiCNN, we provide two symbols in the form of ○/○ which denote whether the difference between CNN and linCNN is statistically significant (●) or not (○) according to paired t-test at significance level of $p = 0.01$.

Dataset	CNN	linCNN	SiCNN
Adiac	0.0220 ± 0.0036	0.1347 ± 0.0400	0.0224 ± 0.0034 ○/●
ArrowHead	0.0397 ± 0.0122	0.3289 ± 0.1052	0.0376 ± 0.0092 ○/●
BeetleFly	0.4711 ± 0.2805	0.4872 ± 0.2996	0.4671 ± 0.2687 ○/○
BirdChicken	0.3893 ± 0.2224	0.6731 ± 0.2880	0.3480 ± 0.1709 ○/●
BME	0.0699 ± 0.0209	0.0586 ± 0.0163	0.0735 ± 0.0202 ○/○
CincECGTorso	0.0750 ± 0.0231	0.0612 ± 0.0195	0.0702 ± 0.0204 ○/○
DiatomSizeReduction	0.0133 ± 0.0040	0.7714 ± 0.1710	0.0144 ± 0.0050 ○/●
ECG200	0.2918 ± 0.1194	0.2980 ± 0.1414	0.2780 ± 0.1069 ○/○
ECG5000	0.7821 ± 0.0671	1.9665 ± 0.1601	0.6645 ± 0.0414 ●/●
ECGFiveDays	0.0371 ± 0.0054	0.0661 ± 0.0075	0.0305 ± 0.0039 ●/●
FacesUCR	1.7111 ± 0.1581	1.7151 ± 0.1620	1.6909 ± 0.1076 ○/○
FiftyWords	0.1670 ± 0.0447	0.2988 ± 0.0684	0.1664 ± 0.0466 ○/●
GunPoint	0.0675 ± 0.0381	0.3287 ± 0.1501	0.0763 ± 0.0387 ○/●
Haptics	1.5011 ± 0.5241	20.124 ± 8.8588	1.3942 ± 0.5036 ○/●
InlineSkate	0.1426 ± 0.0631	0.3934 ± 0.1382	0.1504 ± 0.0705 ○/●
Lightning2	0.1598 ± 0.0837	0.3014 ± 0.0898	0.1511 ± 0.0703 ○/●
Lightning7	0.4505 ± 0.2166	0.5815 ± 0.3696	0.4549 ± 0.2800 ○/●
Mallat	0.0187 ± 0.0012	0.7913 ± 0.8176	0.0183 ± 0.0016 ○/○
MedicalImages	0.1324 ± 0.0403	0.1565 ± 0.0638	0.1240 ± 0.0410 ○/○
MoteStrain	0.7120 ± 0.0916	0.9816 ± 0.1341	0.6299 ± 0.0957 ●/●
OSULeaf	0.3063 ± 0.0724	0.6940 ± 0.1614	0.2786 ± 0.0627 ●/●
Phoneme	2.6407 ± 0.2944	2.5916 ± 0.5279	2.3227 ± 0.3087 ●/○
Plane	0.0932 ± 0.0435	0.3603 ± 0.1098	0.0896 ± 0.0479 ○/●
PowerCons	1.6712 ± 0.3403	2.4377 ± 0.7643	1.5449 ± 0.3347 ○/●
Symbols	0.1063 ± 0.0161	0.6541 ± 0.0592	0.0819 ± 0.0138 ●/●
SwedishLeaf	0.1392 ± 0.0166	0.2674 ± 0.0670	0.1278 ± 0.0195 ○/●
Trace	0.0113 ± 0.0027	0.3073 ± 0.0526	0.0085 ± 0.0023 ●/●
TwoLeadECG	0.0441 ± 0.0059	0.1507 ± 0.0292	0.0336 ± 0.0041 ●/●
WordSynonyms	0.6195 ± 0.0467	0.7266 ± 0.0846	0.4990 ± 0.0565 ●/●
Worms	0.8910 ± 0.2081	1.3738 ± 0.4375	0.9053 ± 0.1951 ○/●

Table 2. Mean absolute error (averaged over 10 folds) ± its standard deviation in case of our approach (SiCNN) and the baselines (CNN, linCNN) at a sparsity level of $SL = 80\%$. Lower values indicate better performance. For each dataset, the best approach is underlined. For SiCNN, we provide two symbols in the form of ∘/∘ which denote whether the difference between CNN and linCNN is statistically significant (•) or not (∘) according to paired t-test at significance level of $p = 0.01$.

Dataset	CNN	linCNN	SiCNN
Adiac	0.1107 ± 0.0094	0.2780 ± 0.0335	0.1124 ± 0.0073 ∘/•
ArrowHead	0.1438 ± 0.0222	0.4636 ± 0.1077	0.1430 ± 0.0178 ∘/•
BeetleFly	0.5735 ± 0.1761	0.5923 ± 0.1956	0.5652 ± 0.1853 ∘/∘
BirdChicken	0.4880 ± 0.1510	0.6739 ± 0.1666	0.4825 ± 0.1222 ∘/•
BME	0.1636 ± 0.0257	0.1631 ± 0.0194	0.1696 ± 0.0259 ∘/∘
CincECGTorso	0.1697 ± 0.0292	0.1716 ± 0.0205	0.1625 ± 0.0262 ∘/∘
DiatomSizeReduction	0.0865 ± 0.0069	0.8229 ± 0.1091	0.0902 ± 0.0097 ∘/•
ECG200	0.3903 ± 0.0642	0.3676 ± 0.0650	0.3691 ± 0.0589 ∘/∘
ECG5000	0.6298 ± 0.0270	1.0300 ± 0.0351	0.5746 ± 0.0183 •/•
ECGFiveDays	0.1461 ± 0.0111	0.2101 ± 0.0176	0.1326 ± 0.0090 •/•
FacesUCR	0.9919 ± 0.0399	1.0092 ± 0.0325	0.9893 ± 0.0221 ∘/∘
FiftyWords	0.2911 ± 0.0283	0.4238 ± 0.0563	0.2898 ± 0.0253 ∘/•
GunPoint	0.1772 ± 0.0396	0.4871 ± 0.1294	0.1860 ± 0.0345 ∘/•
Haptics	0.7583 ± 0.0634	3.2173 ± 0.8438	0.7309 ± 0.0630 ∘/•
InlineSkate	0.2500 ± 0.0328	0.4578 ± 0.1057	0.2574 ± 0.0432 ∘/•
Lightning2	0.2796 ± 0.0486	0.4604 ± 0.0716	0.2828 ± 0.0456 ∘/•
Lightning7	0.4437 ± 0.0935	0.5169 ± 0.1302	0.4418 ± 0.1008 ∘/•
Mallat	0.1068 ± 0.0034	0.7263 ± 0.3777	0.1061 ± 0.0043 ∘/•
MedicalImages	0.2402 ± 0.0214	0.2701 ± 0.0357	0.2340 ± 0.0176 ∘/•
MoteStrain	0.6083 ± 0.0314	0.7850 ± 0.0620	0.5651 ± 0.0331 •/•
OSULeaf	0.4249 ± 0.0572	0.6612 ± 0.0809	0.4140 ± 0.0491 ∘/•
Phoneme	1.1828 ± 0.0501	1.1544 ± 0.1294	1.0860 ± 0.0557 •/∘
Plane	0.2075 ± 0.0380	0.4073 ± 0.0633	0.2064 ± 0.0355 ∘/•
PowerCons	0.9842 ± 0.0896	1.1170 ± 0.2191	0.9371 ± 0.0848 ∘/∘
SwedishLeaf	0.2832 ± 0.0178	0.3940 ± 0.0537	0.2722 ± 0.0185 ∘/•
Symbols	0.2508 ± 0.0159	0.7049 ± 0.0399	0.2160 ± 0.0150 •/•
Trace	0.0842 ± 0.0110	0.5317 ± 0.0519	0.0743 ± 0.0116 ∘/•
TwoLeadECG	0.1631 ± 0.0082	0.3100 ± 0.0334	0.1426 ± 0.0075 •/•
WordSynonyms	0.5762 ± 0.0210	0.6537 ± 0.0505	0.5127 ± 0.0278 •/•
Worms	0.7596 ± 0.0846	0.9599 ± 0.1548	0.7687 ± 0.0805 ∘/•

time series, and y contains its "future" values), y_i is one of the values to be forecast (we assume that missing values are denoted by zeros) and $\hat{y}_i$ is the corresponding prediction of the model. N is the number of non-missing values in the test dataset:

$$N = \sum_{(x,y)\in D^*} \sum_{y_i \in y} \mathcal{I}(y_i \neq 0) \tag{6}$$

Both MSE and MAE were calculated in each of the 10 folds of the cross-validation. We report the average and standard deviation of MSE and MAE in Table 1 and Table 2.

We used paired t-test at significance level (p-value) of 0.01 in order to assess whether the observed differences between our approach SiCNN and its competitors, CNN and linCNN are statistically significant or not.

Implementation. We implemented our neural networks in Python using the PyTorch framework. In order to support reproduction and follow-up works, we made our implementation publicly available in a github repository.[3] Our code can be executed in Google Collaboratory[4].

4.2 Experiments on Datasets from Various Domains

In order to assess the contribution of SiConv relative to "usual" convolution in various domains, first, we consider a simple convolutional network containing a single convolutional layer with 25 filters, followed by a max pooling layer with window size of 2, and a fully connected layer with 100 units. We set the size of convolutional filters to 9. The number of units in the output layer corresponds to the forecast horizon, as each unit is expected to predict one of the numeric values of the target time series. We trained the networks for 1000 epochs. We used mean squared error loss and the Adam optimizer [11] with a batch size of 16. As mentioned previously, we varied the type of convolutional layer, therefore the variants of this simple convolutional neural network are denoted as SiCNN, CNN and linCNN with SiConv, "usual" convolution and "usual" convolution combined with linear interpolation of missing values, respectively.

As the time series of the aforementioned datasets do not contain missing values, we randomly selected 80% of the values of each time series and replaced them by missing values. This is meant by sparsity level $SL = 80\%$ in the caption of Table 1 and Table 2.

As one can see in Table 1 and Table 2, in the majority of the examined cases, SiCNN outperforms it counterparts with "usual" convolution. Moreover, in many cases SiCNN is statistically significantly better than CNN and linCNN. In particular, SiCNN significantly outperforms linCNN on 22 datasets in terms of MSE, and on 23 datasets in terms of MAE. Furthermore, SiCNN is significantly better than CNN on 9 and 7 datasets in terms of MSE and MAE, respectively. On the

[3] https://github.com/kr7/timeseriesforecast-siconv.
[4] https://colab.research.google.com/.

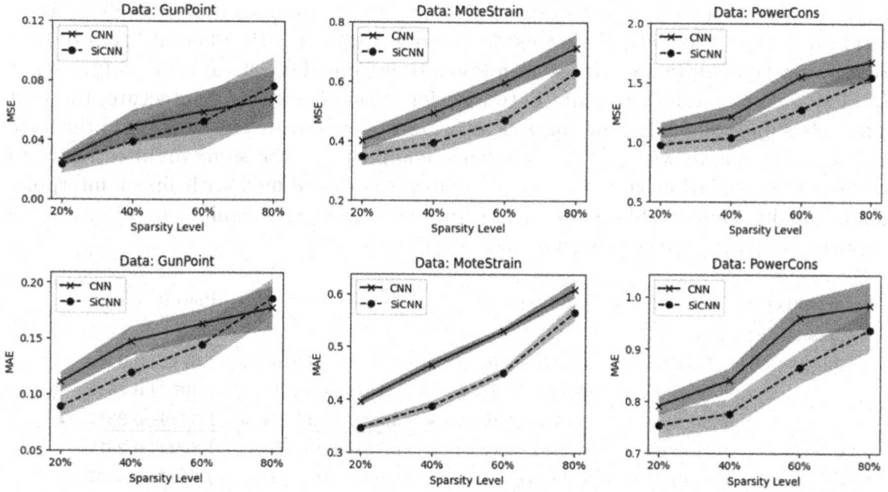

Fig. 2. MSE and MAE of our approach (SiCNN) and the baseline (CNN) as function of sparsity level. The width of the colored area corresponds to the standard deviation of MSE and MAE.

other hand, in those few cases when CNN or linCNN outperform SiCNN, the difference is not significant statistically.

It is interesting to note that CNN with linear interpolation of missing values worked worse that CNN without such an interpolation. This may be attributed to the fact that the actual trend between two observations is not linear and once the interpolation is performed, the network is not able to distinguish between true values and interpolated values.

4.3 The Effect of Sparsity Level

Next, we examine the performance of the simple convolutional network from the previous section in case of various levels of sparsity. For simplicity, we consider three datasets: GunPoint, MoteStrain and PowerCons. As one can see in Fig. 2, we observed similar trends in case of all the three datasets. In particular, with increasing level of sparsity, both the error of our approach (SiCNN) and that of the baseline (CNN) grows which is expected because it is inherently more difficult to predict future values of a time series in case if more of its values are missing. However, we point out that our approach, SiCNN, consistently outperforms CNN for all the examined levels of sparsity both in terms of MSE and MAE, except for the GunPoint dataset at sparsity level of 80%.

4.4 Experiments with Deep Convolutional Networks

After considering various neural networks, such as multi-layer perceptions, multi-scale convolutional neural networks and residual networks, as well as other time

Table 3. Mean squared error and mean absolute error (averaged over 10 folds) ± their standard deviation in case of various neural architectures with different types of convolution on the GunPoint, MoteStrain and PowerCons datasets at a sparsity level of $SL = 80\%$. Lower values indicate better performance. For each architecture, the best approach is underlined. For our approach (SiConv), we provide two symbols in the form of ∘/∘ which denote whether the difference compared to the same architecture with (i) "usual" convolution and (ii) "usual" convolution combined with linear interpolation of missing values (abbreviated as "+lin.") is statistically significant (•) or not (∘) according to paired t-test at significance level of $p = 0.01$.

Architecture	Convolution	GunPoint	MoteStrain	PowerCons
Mean Squared Error				
simple CNN	"usual"	0.0675±0.0381	0.7120±0.0916	1.6712±0.3403
	"usual"+lin	0.3287±0.1501	0.9816±0.1341	2.4377±0.7643
	SiConv	0.0763±0.0387∘/•	0.6299±0.0957•/•	1.5449±0.3347∘/•
ResNet	"usual"	0.2741±0.0872	0.7546±0.1289	1.3002±0.2679
	"usual"+lin	0.5516±0.1041	0.9328±0.1650	2.1404±0.4537
	SiConv	0.0866±0.0434•/•	0.6724±0.1357•/•	1.1735±0.2438∘/•
FCN	"usual"	0.1135±0.0351	0.6053±0.1393	1.2299±0.2153
	"usual"+lin	0.2567±0.0672	0.7628±0.1670	1.6392±0.4356
	SiConv	0.0509±0.0361•/•	0.5901±0.1363•/•	1.1687±0.2438•/•
Mean Absolute Error				
simple CNN	"usual"	0.1772±0.0396	0.6083±0.0314	0.9842±0.0896
	"usual"+lin	0.4871±0.1294	0.7850±0.0620	1.1170±0.2191
	SiConv	0.1860±0.0345∘/•	0.5651±0.0331•/•	0.9371±0.0848∘/∘
ResNet	"usual"	0.4038±0.0603	0.5945±0.0231	0.9035±0.0657
	"usual"+lin	0.6040±0.0590	0.6941±0.0415	1.0675±0.1257
	SiConv	0.1961±0.0347•/•	0.5409±0.0252•/•	0.8460±0.0617•/•
FCN	"usual"	0.2491±0.0289	0.5444±0.0369	0.8809±0.0555
	"usual"+lin	0.4066±0.0553	0.6487±0.0498	0.9200±0.1046
	SiConv	0.1218±0.0310•/•	0.5355±0.0362•/•	0.8470±0.0649•/•

series classifiers, namely: "time series based on a bag-of features", elastic ensemble, 1-nearest neighbor bag-of-SFA-symbols in vector space, shapelet ensemble, flat-COTE (COTE) and 1-nearest neighbor with dynamic time warping, Wang et al. [21] found that their "fully convolutional network" (FCN) "achieves premium performance", i.e., FCN outperforms all the aforementioned models. According to their observations, the difference between FCN and its competitors were statistically significant, expect for the second-best model, a residual network, denoted as ResNet. Therefore we decided to experiment with deep neural networks based on these FCN and ResNet architectures.

As the aforementioned networks were designed for time series classification, we had to adapt them for time series forecasting. In particular, both in case of FCN and ResNet, we removed the final global average pooling layer and replaced it by a fully connected layer in which the number of units corresponds to the forecast horizon, as each unit is expected to predict one of the numeric values of the target time series, just like in case of the simple convolutional networks considered in Sect. 4.2.

Table 3 shows the performance of deep neural networks on the GunPoint, MoteStrain and PowerCons datasets in case of a sparsity level of $SL = 80\%$. As one can see, using SiConv instead of "usual" convolution improves performance both in case of ResNet and FCN.

5 Conclusion and Outlook

This paper focused on forecasting irregularly sampled time series with convolutional neural networks. We proposed to use sparsity-invariant convolution for this task. We performed experiments on 30 real-world time series datasets from various domains with a simple convolutional neural network. Additionally, we examined the effect of sparsity on the prediction error. We also experimented with a more advanced neural architecture, called "fully convolutional network" and a variant of ResNet that had been found to be particularly promising in case of time series previously. Our results show that convolutional neural networks with sparsity-invariant convolution systematically outperform their counterparts with "usual" convolution.

We point out that sparsity-invariant convolution may be used in any convolutional neural network instead of "usual" convolution which makes this operation attractive for many applications. In order to support reproduction of our results as well as follow-up works, we published our implementation (software codes) at https://github.com/kr7/timeseriesforecast-siconv.

Acknowledgement. This work was supported by the European Union through GraphMassivizer EU HE project under grant agreement No 101093202.

References

1. Borovykh, A., Bohte, S., Oosterlee, C.W.: Dilated convolutional neural networks for time series forecasting. J. Comput. Finan. Forthcoming (2018)
2. Box, G.E., Jenkins, G.M., Reinsel, G.C., Ljung, G.M.: Time Series Analysis: Forecasting and Control. Wiley, Hoboken (2015)
3. Buza, K., Antal, M.: Convolutional neural networks with dynamic convolution for time series classification. In: Wojtkiewicz, K., Treur, J., Pimenidis, E., Maleszka, M. (eds.) ICCCI 2021. CCIS, vol. 1463, pp. 304–312. Springer, Cham (2021). https://doi.org/10.1007/978-3-030-88113-9_24
4. Chatfield, C.: Time-Series Forecasting. Chapman and Hall/CRC, Boca Raton (2000)
5. Che, Z., Purushotham, S., Cho, K., Sontag, D., Liu, Y.: Recurrent neural networks for multivariate time series with missing values. Sci. Rep. **8**(1), 6085 (2018)
6. Chen, Y., Kang, Y., Chen, Y., Wang, Z.: Probabilistic forecasting with temporal convolutional neural network. Neurocomputing **399**, 491–501 (2020)
7. David, Z.: Information leakage in financial machine learning research. Algorithmic Finan. **8**(1–2), 1–4 (2019)

8. Gardner, E.S., Jr.: Exponential smoothing: the state of the art-part ii. Int. J. Forecast. **22**(4), 637–666 (2006)
9. Kaushik, S., et al.: Ai in healthcare: time-series forecasting using statistical, neural, and ensemble architectures. Front. Big Data **3**, 4 (2020)
10. Kim, K.j.: Financial time series forecasting using support vector machines. Neurocomputing **55**(1–2), 307–319 (2003)
11. Kingma, D.P., Ba, J.: Adam: A method for stochastic optimization. arXiv preprint arXiv:1412.6980 (2014)
12. Lim, B., Zohren, S.: Time series forecasting with deep learning: a survey. Phil. Trans. R. Soc. A **379**(2194), 20200209 (2021)
13. Ramesh, A.N., Giovanneschi, F., González-Huici, M.A.: SIUNet: sparsity invariant u-net for edge-aware depth completion. In: Proceedings of the IEEE/CVF Winter Conference on Applications of Computer Vision, pp. 5818–5827 (2023)
14. Ravuri, S., et al.: Skilful precipitation nowcasting using deep generative models of radar. Nature **597**(7878), 672–677 (2021)
15. Seeger, M.W., Salinas, D., Flunkert, V.: Bayesian intermittent demand forecasting for large inventories. In: Advances in Neural Information Processing Systems, vol. 29 (2016)
16. Sen, R., Yu, H.F., Dhillon, I.S.: Think globally, act locally: a deep neural network approach to high-dimensional time series forecasting. In: Advances in Neural Information Processing Systems, vol. 32 (2019)
17. Sezer, O.B., Gudelek, M.U., Ozbayoglu, A.M.: Financial time series forecasting with deep learning: a systematic literature review: 2005–2019. Appl. Soft Comput. **90**, 106181 (2020)
18. Srivastava, N., Hinton, G., Krizhevsky, A., Sutskever, I., Salakhutdinov, R.: Dropout: a simple way to prevent neural networks from overfitting. J. Mach. Learn. Res. **15**(1), 1929–1958 (2014)
19. Torres, J.F., Hadjout, D., Sebaa, A., Martínez-Álvarez, F., Troncoso, A.: Deep learning for time series forecasting: a survey. Big Data **9**(1), 3–21 (2021)
20. Uhrig, J., Schneider, N., Schneider, L., Franke, U., Brox, T., Geiger, A.: Sparsity invariant CNNs. In: 2017 International Conference on 3D Vision (3DV), pp. 11–20. IEEE (2017)
21. Wang, Z., Yan, W., Oates, T.: Time series classification from scratch with deep neural networks: A strong baseline. In: 2017 International Joint Conference on Neural Networks (IJCNN), pp. 1578–1585. IEEE (2017)
22. Yadav, P., Steinbach, M., Kumar, V., Simon, G.: Mining electronic health records (EHRs) a survey. ACM Comput. Surv. (CSUR) **50**(6), 1–40 (2018)
23. Yan, L., Liu, K., Belyaev, E.: Revisiting sparsity invariant convolution: a network for image guided depth completion. IEEE Access **8**, 126323–126332 (2020)

Efficient Sparse Networks from Watts-Strogatz Network Priors

Tamás Traub(✉), Mohamad Nashouqu, and László Gulyás

Department of Artificial Intelligence, Institute for Industry-Academy Innovation, Faculty of Informatics, ELTE Eötvös Loránd University, Budapest, Hungary
{c0whdd,fj64me,lgulyas}@inf.elte.hu

Abstract. This paper studies the accuracy and the structural properties of sparse neural networks (SNNs) generated by weight pruning and by using Watts-Strogatz network priors. The study involves Multi-Layer Perceptron (MLP) and Long-Short Term Memory (LSTM) architectures, trained on the MNIST dataset. The paper replicates and extends previous work, showing that networks generated by appropriately selected WS priors guarantee high-quality results, and that these networks outperform pruned networks in terms of accuracy. In addition, observations are made with regard to the structural change induced by network pruning and its implications for accuracy. The findings of this study provide important insights for creating lighter models with lower computational needs, which can achieve results comparable to more complex models.

Keywords: Sparse Neural Networks · Network Science · Deep Learning · Graph Theory

1 Introduction

Artificial neural networks (ANNs) are popular and successful machine learning models. They are able to solve complex problems, but often result in high computational demand. Therefore, creating lighter models with lower computational needs is desirable. Especially, if they can achieve results comparable to more complex models. Most ANNs have layers, every node being connected to every node in the next layer and receiving connections from the previous layer. Since the model's parameters are mainly assigned to the edges, eliminating some of the connections can lead to a lighter model. Interestingly, the human brain, that originally inspired the creation of ANNs, has a sparse connection structure [14].

Network pruning is a technique to reduce the size of a neural network by removing unnecessary or redundant connections or neurons. The goal of network pruning is to simplify the neural network while preserving its performance. As a result, the network may become faster and more robust. In certain cases, it can even achieve better accuracy [17]. There are several types of network pruning techniques, such as weight pruning which involves removing the connections with the smallest weights from the network. This technique is based on the

N. T. Nguyen et al. (Eds.): ICCCI 2023, LNAI 14162, pp. 163–175, 2023.
https://doi.org/10.1007/978-3-031-41456-5_13

idea that small weights have little effect on the overall output of the network. Alternatively, neuron pruning removes entire neurons from the network. Neurons that are not important for the network's output can be removed without significantly affecting the network's performance [2]. On the other hand, filter pruning removes entire convolutional filters that do not contribute much to the network's output [1]. Pruning can be performed during, before, and after training. The best performances were achieved by conducting the pruning after the initial training, and then retraining the pruned network. Since this method has two training steps its process is longer than the other two, but those can not achieve such performance.

There are other methods to create sparse neural networks without requiring two training steps. Mocanu et al. used Erdős-Rényi random graphs, but only for MLPs and convolutional neural networks [12]. Liu et al. created sparse networks inspired by Network Science for both MLP and RNN networks [10,11]. Stier et al. took inspiration from Network Science, too [18]. They start from classes of sparse networks known from Network Science, with known structural properties, and use them as 'priors' to construct artificial neural networks [17]. They trained networks from Watts-Strogatz (WS) and Barabási-Albert (BA) graphs [3,21] as priors and studied the correlation between graph properties and accuracy.

This paper replicates and extends the work of Stier et al [17,18], by comparing the accuracy and structural properties of sparse neural networks generated from WS priors to the properties of networks yielded by pruning. Using both Multi-Layer Perceptron (MLP) and Long-Short Term Memory (LSTM) architectures [8,15], the ANNs are trained on the MNIST dataset. Based on an extended analysis of the correlations between the networks' validation accuracy and various network structural properties, a class of networks is identified that guarantees high quality results.

2 Background

Two kinds of sparse ANNs are studied in this paper:

Multi-Layer Perceptrons (MLP) are feedforward neural networks consisting of at least three layers of nodes: an input layer, one or more hidden layers, and an output layer. The nodes are connected to the nodes in the subsequent layer and receive incoming links from the nodes of the previous one. Nodes in the hidden and output layers compute a weighted sum of their inputs, apply an activation function to the result, and pass the output along its outgoing edges. Sparse ANN's have the aim to be as accurate as possible (as accurate as full networks or better), and have lesser computational demand. Since the computational demand is hard to compare with previous work, because the hardware used is different, we will focus on the number of parameters (weights, links) as a proxy for both memory and wallclock performance.

Long-Short Term Memory (LSTM) Networks are a type of recurrent neural networks designed to learn long-term dependencies in sequential data by selectively, remembering or forgetting information. LSTMs use memory cells and three types of gates: input, output, and forget gates, which are controlled by activation functions. LSTMs are advantageous in tasks where long-term dependencies are important, and are widely used in various applications.

2.1 Network Pruning

The first pruning algorithms appeared in 1988. Optimal Brain Damage [5] and Optimal Brain Surgeon [7] both use the Hessian of the loss function to reduce the connections. Skeletonization [13] tries to pinpoint and eliminate irrelevant units of the network. Thodberg [19] proposed pruning to improve generalization. Some of the most popular pruning methods are magnitude class blinded and magnitude layer wise pruning. Magnitude class blinded pruning prunes the given percentage of weights which have the smallest magnitude in the network. Magnitude layer wise pruning prunes the smallest given percentage of weights in the given layer, so the pruning is not affected by other layers in this case. Random pruning prunes the weights completely randomly and usually serves as a benchmark to other approaches. Recently, pruning the network before training was also proposed, like SNIP [9] and GraSP [20], but these could not outperform magnitude-based pruning.

2.2 Using Network Priors to Generate Sparse ANNs

The method proposed by Stier et al. creates sparse neural networks from networks studied in Network Science [18]. These networks are constructed from empirical observations of real systems, or are generated by stochastic algorithms designed to model real-world networks. Generally, these networks are *very sparse*, thus are ideal candidates as priors to inform the structure of sparse artificial neural networks. The network priors can be arbitrary graphs that are often undirected and may contain cycles. On the other hand, in ANNs nodes are organised into layers. Therefore, the network priors need to be transformed into a directed acyclic graph (DAG). This is done by the method of [16] with some modifications which are changing the isolated nodes (nodes do not have edges to the next layer) to be in the last layer of the hidden layers. The generated DAG is the structure of the hidden layers then we add the first and last layer to match our dataset input data and output classes.

Generating LSTM Networks from Network Priors. In case of LSTM networks, the algorithm that constructs ANNs from network priors must be augmented by an additional step. This is necessary, as in case of these networks, the internal structure of each node is complex, having a number of connections in itself. Following [17], we turn every layer of the transformed DAG into a separate LSTM network of one layer with their hidden size matching the number of nodes in the DAG layer. The outputs of these LSTMs correspond to their hidden size.

Importantly, however, the nodes are connected to each other, not to the layers. Therefore, for every node in a layer, except in the case of the input layer, we check from which layer its input is coming from. Then we feed the whole output of that layer to the node and zero out everything except the output of the node, where its edge is coming from (in the DAG). So, the input size of a layer LSTM is the sum of those layer's sizes that contain a node which is connected to one of the given layer's nodes. If layer A has several outgoing edges into the layer B then those are counted separately. The addition of a final, output layer of perceptrons after the main ANN is preserved, as seen in the generic case. We believe that our WS graph to LSTM transformation is different to Stier's because we achieved better accuracies with our method.

Watts-Strogatz Networks. In this paper we work with Watts- Strogatz (WS) network priors. The WS model generates random undirected graphs that are 'small-worlds', i.e., they have short average path lengths and high clustering (or transitivity) [21]. Many real life biological and social networks have these same properties. Average path length measures the typical separation between two nodes of the network, clustering coefficient (transitivity) measures the cliquishness of a typical neighbourhood. Watts-Strogatz (WS) networks have three parameters. N is the number of nodes, k is the number of edges per nodes and p is the rewiring probability. First, the graph is initialized as a regular ring lattice, where each node connected to their k closest neighbours. Then every edge is randomly rewired with probability p. Consequently, with $p = 0$, we acquire the initial ring lattice, but with $p = 1$ the graph becomes completely random. For small p values (i.e., $p \in [0.001, 0.1]$) the average path length is low and transitivity is high.

3 Methods and Data

We studied the workings of ANNs generated by WS priors and pruning, for both MLPs and LSTMs. First, we created regular, fully connected networks and analyzed their accuracy with regard to pruning. Then, we generated a dataset of WS priors with various parameters and studied the resulting sparse neural networks and their accuracies. Based on this knowledge, we turned to compare the properties of sparse neural networks generated from WS priors to those of sparse networks obtained by pruning. (Pruned networks were not retrained after sparsification.) We designed two different methods for the comparisons.

3.1 Sparse Networks from Pruning

The original MLP network before pruning had 6 layers with the following node counts: (89, 44, 22, 11, 4, 80). The original LSTM network had 3 layers and 16 nodes in every layer. The size of the LSTMs' first layer was fixed to 16 in all our experiments. This is due to the big edge number differences the networks had with different input layer sizes. The first layer was not relevant for our experiments, because we did not sparsify its incoming edges. Therefore, networks with bigger edge number in the first layer could gain an unfair advantage. We repeated all our experiments several times and took their averages as a result. We had 4 different prunings for the LSTMS and MLPs too. All of the prunings done by us were magnitude based. For MLPs, we pruned the weights in the first layer (IH), the weights between the input and the output layer (HH), the weights of the output layer (HO) layer wise. For the LSTMs, we prune the input-to-hidden (IH) edges, the hidden-to-hidden (HH) edges and both of them at the same time (IH, HH), layerwise in every layer. For both network types, the fourth was a blinded pruning (FULL) where the edges with the smallest magnitude were pruned regardless of their layer. Note that with MLPs IH means the literal first layer's weights, meanwhile with LSTMs it is the input of every single layer. For MLPs HH means every weight except the input and output ones, while for LSTMs HH edges connect nodes in the same layer.

3.2 Matching Full Networks and WS Priors

We present two different approaches to match ANNs from network priors to a (FULL) ANN with a specific structure. Such matching is necessary to make the comparisons fair.

- **Method A:** Our first approach matches the number of layers. We begin by generating a number of WS graphs with a number of nodes (N) then we filter these graphs to get those that have the same number of layers (L). Next, we construct a fully connected network with (L) layers and (N) nodes that is pruned using the classical method. The number of nodes in each layer are determined by observing the number of nodes per layer in the filtered WS networks and taking their average.
- **Method B:** In our other approach we fix the number of nodes (N) and the size of the first layer, but the number of layers (L) is not fixed. Both the WS graphs and the fully connected networks are generated with these constraints.

Parameters. We have three types of parameters, WS graph parameters, training parameters, pruning parameters, and The WS graph parameters in the case of MLP are $N = 250$, $k = 2$, $p = [0.7,0.8]$ for both Methods A and B, while for LSTM: $N = 48$, $k = 2$, $p = [1.0]$ for method A, and $N = 48$, $k = [2,4]$, $p = [0.7,0.8,0.9,1.0]$ for Method B. We trained MLPs for 30 epochs, and the LSTMs for 50 epochs on the MNIST dataset, with a learning rate of 0.001 and 0.01 respectively. We used the Adam optimizer in both cases. The fully connected MLP network structure was (89, 44, 22, 11, 4, 80), and we conducted full network pruning from 0% to 100% with a step size of 5%. For the LSTM, the fully connected network structure was (15, 9, 6, 4, 2, 12), and we pruned this network from 0% to 100% with a step size of 10%. To keep the comparisons fair in the case of LSTM, we only pruned the weights between the layers (IH), regardless of their layer.

3.3 Our Experiment

We performed an extensive set of experiments, creating a large pool of sparse neural networks for both the MLP and LSTM architectures. In particular, we created matching pairs of full (i.e., non-sparse) ANNs and sparse networks from WS priors, using both Method A and Method B, for all parameter combinations (see Sect. 3.2). These networks were trained on the MNIST dataset [6].

As a next step, we pruned the full networks using various methods and pruning percentages. Each network was pruned using both a layerwise magnitude pruning, as well as, a class-blinded (FULL) pruning. In addition to applying these methods to all edges in the network, we also experimented with limiting them to input-to-hidden, hidden-to-hidden or, in case of the MLP architecture, to hidden-to-output links. The pruning percentage was varied between 0 and 100% with a stepsize of 5% for the MLP and a step size of 10% for the LSTM.

4 Results

4.1 Accuracy Comparison of Networks from Pruning vs Priors

We first compare the accuracies of the various sparse networks. In particular, in Fig. 1, we compare the accuracy of sparse networks from WS priors to that of networks obtained via various levels of pruning, as a function of the number of edges (i.e., weights or trainable parameters). The key observation is that the level of accuracy obtained from using WS priors matches that of the full (i.e., non-sparse) network even at a significantly lower number of edges. The number of edges, where WS prior based networks perform well, may correspond to regions where the performance of pruned network degrades significantly. This depends on the specific pruning approach used. Another observation from Fig. 1 is that the accuracies of sparse networks from WS priors are very stable. They do not show any significant dependence on the actual number of parameters (edges).

4.2 Structure of Sparse Networks

We also studied the structure of the sparse neural networks obtained via various methods. In order to quantify the structural differences we measured network statistics from Network Science, like eccentricity and various node and edge centralities [4]. The structure of WS priors depends on their generating parameters and it is well understood [21]. Since most of the structure is transferred to the sparse networks generated from these priors, once the generating parameters were fixed (see Sect. 3.2) the structure was also more or less decided upon. These expectations were confirmed by our measurements (not shown here).

Figures 2 and 3 show a summary of the measured networks statistics in case of pruned networks, for the MLP and LSTM architectures, respectively. Both figures contain a table of plots. The rows correspond to, from the top down, degree centrality, eccentricity, closeness centrality, and node and edge betweenness centrality [4]. Since all these network statistics assign a value to each node

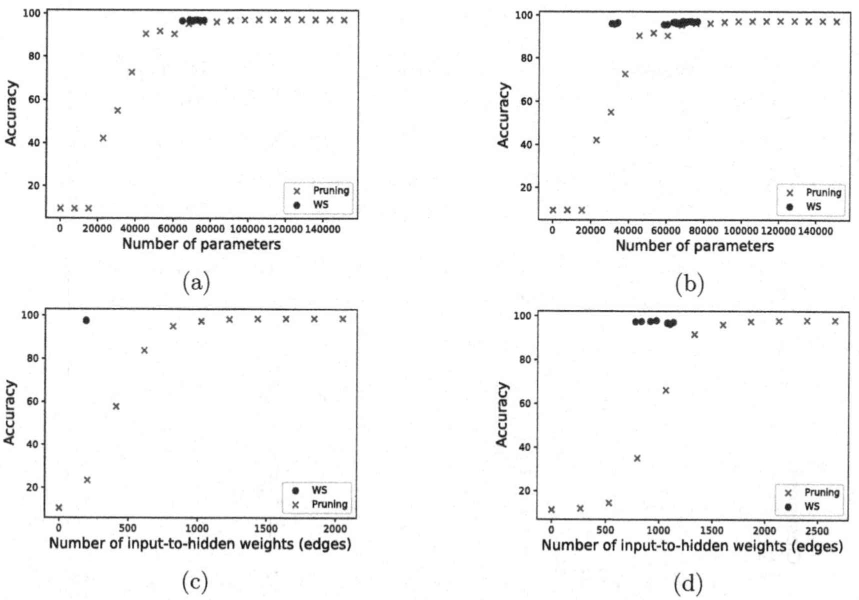

Fig. 1. Accuracy as a function of the number of parameters (weights) for both MLP and LSTM networks. The two plots at the top are for MLP. Plot (a) when the number of nodes is fixed, while (b) when the number of layers is fixed. The two plots at the bottom are for LSTM. Plot (c) when the number of nodes is fixed, while (d) when the number of layers is fixed. The red markers are for fully connected layers pruned between 0 and 100% with a step-size of 5% for the MLP and a step-size of 10% for the LSTM. The blue dots are for networks taken from WS graphs. For the MLPs, in both cases, we only used $k=2$ to create the graphs but the number of parameters differ. This is because the WS prior created the MLPs with a fixed number of hidden-to-hidden weights but we did not fix the number of nodes in the input and output layer. This resulted in different number of input-to-hidden and hidden-to-output parameters. (Color figure online)

(or edge), the network structure is described by their distributions. Therefore, the three columns of the figures depict the mean, the variance, and the maximum, respectively, of the values of the given network statistics. Each panel in the table plots the value of the measure in question as a function of the pruning percentage used, for all the pruning methods used.

The first observation to be made about Figs. 2 and 3 is that the changes in network structure are qualitatively similar, independent of the architecture used (MLP and LSTM, respectively), for all network statistics. There are differences with regard to the behavior of some of the pruning methods, but the interpretation of those methods also varies somewhat for the two architectures. In particular, degree centrality shows a monotonous decay with growing pruning percentage, which is linear in terms of the mean, shows a slight sub-linear tendency for the variance, and is superlinear for the maximum. This is similar

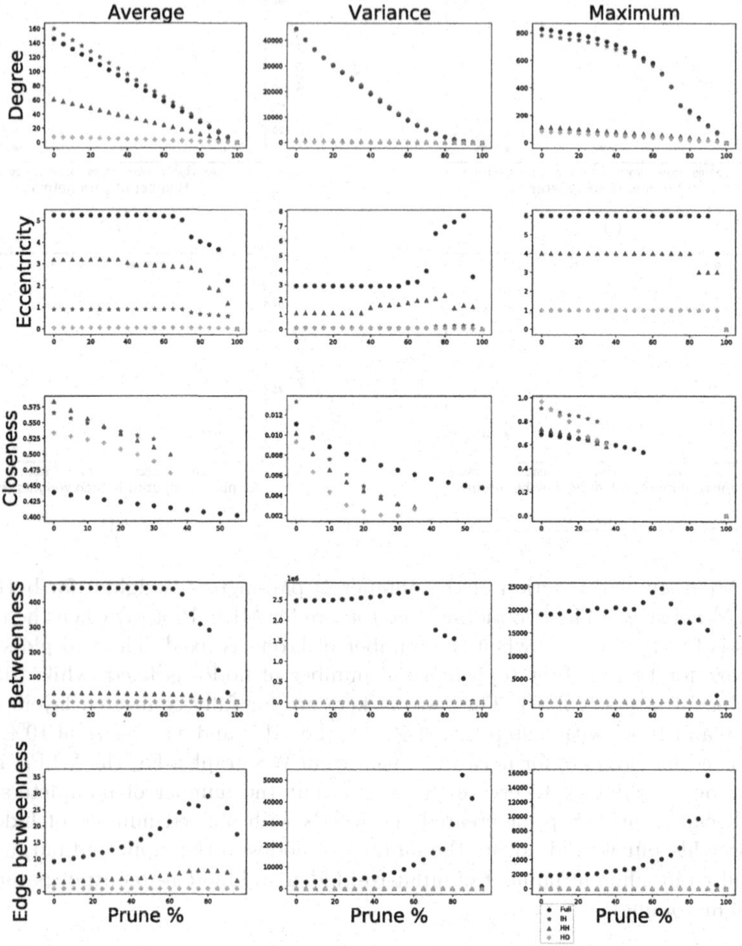

Fig. 2. Network statistics for 20 Multi-Layer Perceptron (MLP) obtained through pruning the fully connected network (89, 44, 22, 11, 4, 80). The pruning process generated 20 pruned models with a range of 0 to 100 pruned networks in increments of 0.05. These models were trained on the MNIST dataset with a learning rate of 0.001 and Adam optimizer for 30 epochs. The first column of the image represents the average values of Degree, Eccentricity, Closeness, Betweenness, and Edge betweenness of the pruned models plotted against the pruning percentage. The second column displays the variance of these same network statistics as a function of the pruning percentage. The third column shows the maximum values of Degree, Eccentricity, Closeness, Betweenness, and Edge betweenness of the pruned models as a function of pruning percentage. The blue dots when we prune the full model. The green marker is when we prune the hidden layers, the red marker is when we prune the input-to-hidden layer only, and the yellow marker is when we prune the hidden-to-output layer only. (Color figure online)

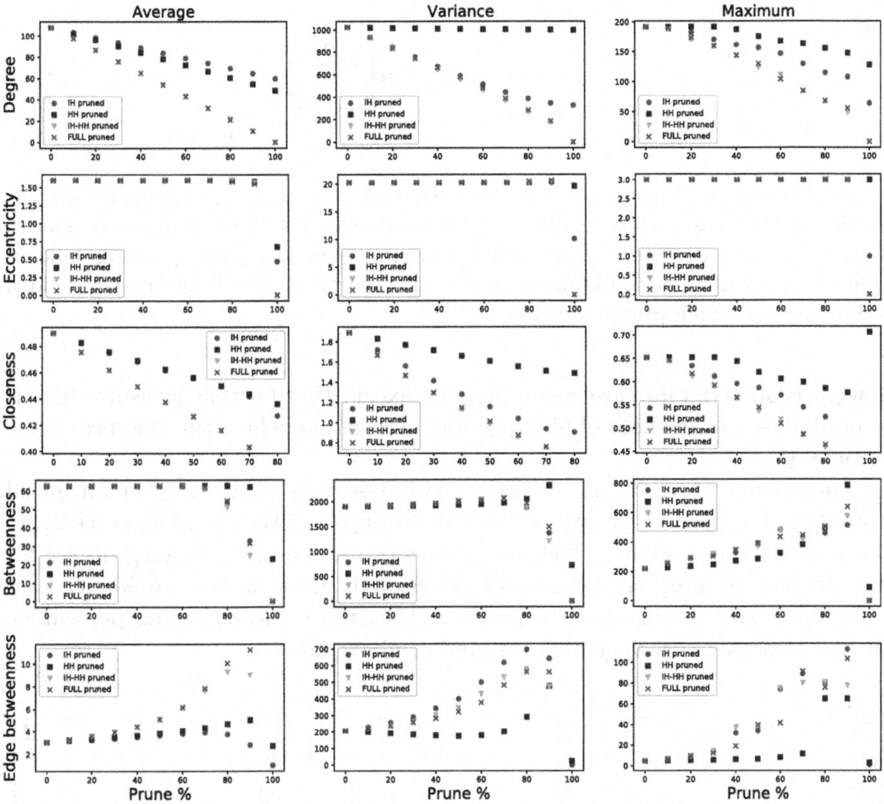

Fig. 3. Network properties compared to the pruning percentage of an LSTM network. All of the plots, except the edge betweenness ones, contain the original graph and its different pruned versions from 10 to 100 percent pruning with a step size of 10 percent. Four pruning methods are shown in the figure: layerwise input-to-hidden (IH), layerwise hidden-to-hidden (IH), both IH and HH at the same time (IH HH), and a layer and edge type blinded pruning (FULL). For the edge betweenness IH HH and FULL prunings the 100% pruned versions are not shown because they result in an empty network. By increasing the pruning percentage the accuracy starts to decrease. Our results suggest that, except for eccentricity, most network properties show a clear dependency on the pruning percentage. In many cases, the dependency is linear, but we also observe non-linearities. In particular, both the average and variance of node betweenness are stable up until a threshold, but then collapses. The average of edge betweenness first shows a non-linear increase and then collapses.

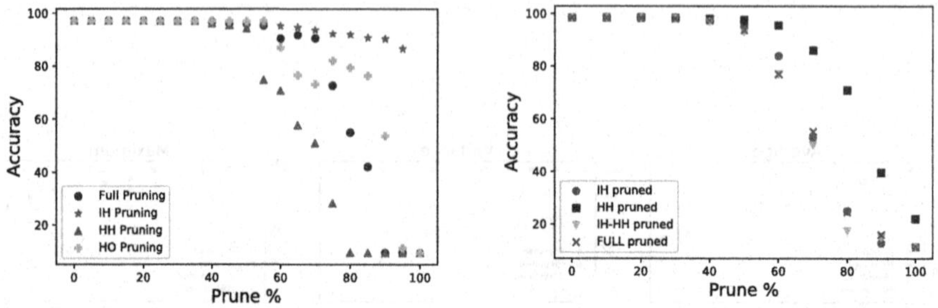

Fig. 4. Accuracy of pruned networks as a function of pruning percentage on the left side is the MLP case, while LSTM is on the right side. The different markers refer to the different pruning policies. These are full pruning, input-to-hidden pruning, hidden-to-hidden pruning, hidden-to-output pruning for the MLPs and both input-to-hidden and hidden-to-hidden pruning for the LSTMs.

to what is observed for closeness centrality, except that for that measure there is a cutoff above a threshold of high pruning percentage, where the closeness value becomes 0.

The other three network statistics exhibit several regimes. After an initial stability at low percentages, their value grows until a critical pruning percentage, above which they collapse. These observations are true to a varying degree for the different pruning strategies and the growth phase is less pronounced for eccentricity and average node centrality. Also, the critical pruning percentage for LSTM networks is very high (around or above 90%).

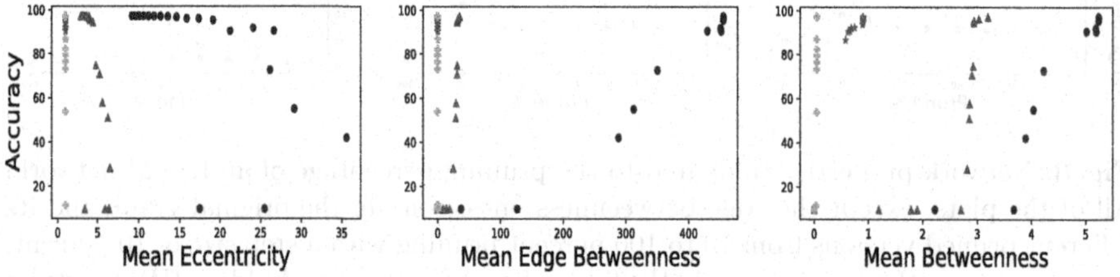

Fig. 5. Accuracy of 21 Multi-Layer Perceptron (MLP) obtained using classical pruning using 4 pruning policies as a function of mean edge betweenness, betweenness, and eccentricity. The pruning from 0 to 1 with 0.05 step. The blue dots mark the full pruning, the green triangles show the hidden-to-hidden pruning, the red stars mark input-to-hidden pruning, and the yellow diamonds indicate when the hidden-to-output pruning was done. (Color figure online)

4.3 Dependence of Accuracy on the Structure of Pruned Networks

The two panels of Fig. 4 show the accuracy of pruned networks as a function of pruning percentage for the MLP and LSTM architectures, respectively. The plots include the accuracies obtained using the various pruning strategies. The main observation is that the accuracy of pruned networks is maintained at a high level, close to that of the original, full (i.e., non-sparse) network until a threshold of pruning percentage is reached. Above this critical threshold, the accuracy drops dramatically.

In the previous section, we have observed a critical threshold in pruning percentage, there with respect to various network statistics. To check the relationship of critical pruning percentages with respect to accuracy and the various network statistics, the three-three panels of Fig. 5 and Fig. 6 plot the accuracy of pruned networks versus mean eccentricity, edge betweenness, and node betweenness centrality, respectively. The plots show this dependence for all the various pruning strategies studied. The plots confirm the expectation about the correspondence of the two kind of thresholds. In case of IH and HO pruning, accuracy is about independent of network structure. However, in case of HH and Full pruning, there are two accuracy regimes, depending on the network structure, with a transition in between them. Accuracy grows as a function of mean eccentricity and mean node betweenness, while it drops with increasing mean edge betweenness. The transition is very sharp (c.f., a phase transition) in case of HH pruning.

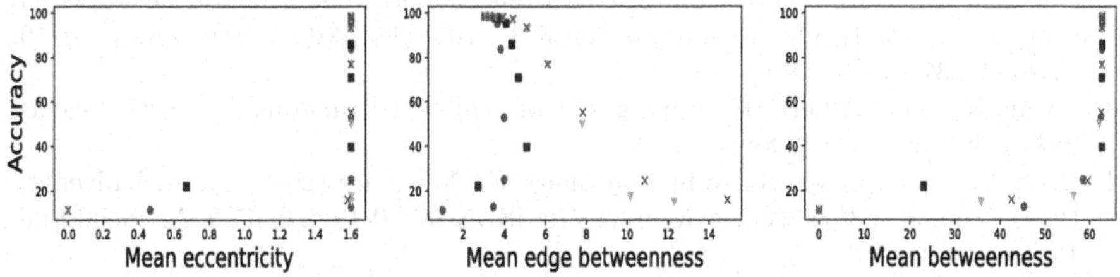

Fig. 6. Accuracy of LSTM networks obtained using classical pruning using 4 pruning policies as a function of mean edge betweenness, betweenness, and eccentricity. The pruning from 0 to 100% with 10% step. Green circles mark the input-to-hidden pruning, blue squares the hidden-to-hidden pruning, yellow triangles mark when both input-to-hidden and hidden-to-hidden pruning was done and red crosses mark the full pruning. (Color figure online)

5 Conclusions

This paper studied sparse networks generated by network pruning and from Watts-Strogatz network priors. It compared the accuracy and structural properties of these sparse networks in case of both Multi-Layer Perceptron (MLP) and Long-Short Term Memory (LSTM) architectures trained on the MNIST dataset. A class of sparse networks generated from WS priors were identified that guarantee high accuracy results. These networks outperform sparse networks from pruning with the same number of parameters. They also consistently exhibit high levels of accuracies.

We also studied the correlation between the accuracy and the structure of the SNNs using network statistics. We found a connection between the eccentricity, node betweenness and edge betweenness of the sparse network and the resulting accuracy, in case of SNNs obtained via pruning. Similar relationships could not be found in case of SNNs from WS priors, given the stable high-accuracy behavior of these networks.

Future works will include testing the approach on other, more complex datasets (e.g., CIFAR-10, CIFAR-100). Other network classes will also be explored as network priors. Barabási-Albert graphs were already tested, but failed to yield satisfying results since the resulting layers contained too few nodes. Determining the properties of ideal network priors will also be subject to future works.

References

1. Anwar, S., Hwang, K., Sung, W.: Structured pruning of deep convolutional neural networks. ACM J. Emerg. Technol. Comput. Syst. **13**(3), (2017). https://doi.org/10.1145/3005348. ISSN 1550–4832
2. Augasta, M., Kathirvalavakumar, T.: Pruning algorithms of neural networks - a comparative study. Open Comput. Sci. **3**(3), 105–115 (2013). https://doi.org/10.2478/s13537-013-0109-x
3. Barabási, A.L., Albert, R.: Emergence of scaling in random networks. Science **286**(5439), 509–512 (2008)
4. Brede,M.: Networks-an introduction. mark EJ Newman. (2010, oxford University Press.) $65.38, £35.96 (hardcover), p. 772. ISBN-978-0-19-920665-0. Artificial Life, 18: 241–242 (2012)
5. LeCun, Y., Denker, J., Solla, S.: Optimal brain damage. In: Advances in Neural Information Processing Systems, pp. 598–605 (1990)
6. Deng, L.: The mnist database of handwritten digit images for machine learning research. IEEE Signal Process. Mag. **29**(6), 141–142 (2012)
7. Hassibi, B., Stork, D., et al.: Second order derivatives for network pruning: optimal brain surgeon. In: IEEE International Conference on Neural Networks, pp. 293–299. IEEE (1993)
8. Hochreiter, S., Schmidhuber, J.: Long short-term memory. Neural Comput. **9**, 1735–1780 (1997). https://doi.org/10.1162/neco.1997.9.8.1735
9. Lee, N., Ajanthan, T., Torr, P.H.: Snip: single-shot network pruning based on connection sensitivity. In: International Conference on Learning Representations (2019)
10. Liu, S., Ni'mah, I., Menkovski, V., Mocanu, D.C., Pechenizkiy, M.: Efficient and effective training of sparse recurrent neural networks. Neural Comput. Appl. **33**(15), 9625–9636 (2021). https://doi.org/10.1007/s00521-021-05727-y. ISSN 1433–3058
11. Liu, S., Mocanu, D.C., Matavalam, A.R.R., Pei, Y., Pechenizkiy, M.: Sparse evolutionary deep learning with over one million artificial neurons on commodity hardware. Neural Comput. Appl. **33**(7), 2589–2604 (2020). https://doi.org/10.1007/s00521-020-05136-7

12. Mocanu, D.C., Mocanu, E., Stone, P., Nguyen, P.H., Gibescu, M., Liotta, A.: Scalable training of artificial neural networks with adaptive sparse connectivity inspired by network science. Nature Commun. **9**(1), 2383 (2018). https://doi.org/10.1038/s41467-018-04316-3. ISSN 2041-1723
13. Mozer, M.C., Smolensky, P.: Skeletonization: a technique for trimming the fat from a network via relevance assessment. In: Advances in Neural Information Processing Systems, pp. 107–115 (1989)
14. Hagmann, P., Cammoun, L., Gigandet, X., et al.: Mapping the structural core of human cerebral cortex. PLoS Biol. **6**(7), e159 (2008)
15. Popescu, M.C., Balas, V.E., Perescu-Popescu, L., Mastorakis, N.: Multilayer perceptron and neural networks. WSEAS Trans. Circ. Syst. **8**, 579–588 (2009)
16. Stier, J.: Correlation analysis between the robustness of sparse neural networks and their random hidden structural priors. [On the electrodynamics of moving bodies]. Elsevier B.V. **322**(10), 891–921 (2021). https://arxiv.org/abs/2107.06158
17. Stier, J., Darji, H., Granitzer, M.: Experiments on properties of hidden structures of sparse neural networks. In: Nicosia, G., et al. (eds.) LOD 2021. Lecture Notes in Computer Science, vol. 13164, pp. 380–394. Springer, Cham (2022). https://doi.org/10.1007/978-3-030-95470-3_29
18. Stier, J., Granitzer, M.: Structural analysis of sparse neural networks. Procedia Comput. Sci. **159**, 107–116 (2019)
19. Hans Henrik Thodberg: Improving generalization of neural networks through pruning. Int. J. Neural Syst. **01**(04), 317–326 (1991)
20. Wang, C., Zhang, G., Grosse, R.: Picking winning tickets before training by preserving gradient flow. In: International Conference on Learning Representations (2020)
21. Watts, D.J., Strogatz, S.H.: Collective dynamics of 'small-world' networks. Nature **393**(6684), 440–442 (1998). https://doi.org/10.1038/30918.https://doi.org/10.1038/30918. ISSN 1476-4687

Natural Language Processing

Exploring the Role of Monolingual Data in Cross-Attention Pre-training for Neural Machine Translation

Khang Pham[1,2], Long Nguyen[1,2(✉)], and Dien Dinh[1,2]

[1] Faculty of Information Technology, University of Science, Ho Chi Minh City, Vietnam
nhblong@fit.hcmus.edu.vn
[2] Vietnam National University, Ho Chi Minh City, Vietnam

Abstract. Recent advancements in large pre-trained language models have revolutionized the field of natural language processing (NLP). Despite the impressive results achieved in various NLP tasks, their effectiveness in neural machine translation (NMT) remains limited. The main challenge lies in the mismatch between the pre-training objectives of the language model and the translation task, where the language modeling task focuses on reconstructing the language without considering its semantic interaction with other languages. This results in cross-attention weights being randomly initialized and learned from scratch during NMT training. To overcome this issue, one approach is to utilize joint monolingual corpora to pre-train the cross-attention weights, improving the semantic interaction between the source and target languages. In this paper, we perform extensive experiments to analyze the impact of monolingual data on this pre-training approach and demonstrate its effectiveness in enhancing the NMT performance.

Keywords: Natural Language Processing · Neural Machine Translation · Pre-training · Cross-attention · Monolingual data

1 Introduction

Pre-training techniques along with large language models [5,10,13,16,20,21] have created a huge boost in almost all NLP tasks, leading to continuous new state-of-the-art results on many benchmarks. Despite their proven transferability, however, how to effectively leverage pre-trained language models into NMT remains a challenge, as there exist many discrepancies between the pretraining and finetuning stage [26]. Specifically, the language models cannot capture the necessary interaction between the source and target languages, thus degrading the quality of the transferred contextual knowledge.

To overcome this challenge, Lewis et al. introduced the BART [13] model, which pre-trains the whole sequence-to-sequence model. Through its denoising autoencoder-based pre-training, BART can effectively leverage monolingual

N. T. Nguyen et al. (Eds.): ICCCI 2023, LNAI 14162, pp. 179–190, 2023.
https://doi.org/10.1007/978-3-031-41456-5_14

data to improve the performance of sequence-to-sequence models in NLP tasks, including machine translation. Song et al. [24] proposed another idea to pre-train the entire sequence-to-sequence model using masked language modeling (MLM) [10]. However, simply using denoising autoencoder and MLM objectives in the pre-training phase means they cannot directly learn the cross-lingual mapping between the source and target languages.

Another research direction investigated by many studies [8,13,24,26], pre-training an autoencoder with a two-step procedure: pre-training an encoder and a decoder independently with large-scale monolingual corpora, then fine-tune the connected model on a parallel dataset or in an unsupervised manner [1,2,7]. While this method improved the performance of the NMT model in many settings, Ren et al. [22] claimed that the impact of such an approach on the decoding phase of the fine-tuned model is subtle. They argued that using a separated pre-training technique without any additional cross-lingual information resulted in a lack of semantic interface between the pre-trained encoder and decoder. Therefore, in an attempt to tackle this problem, Ren et al. propose a new method named SemFace [22], which uses a language-independent space to connect the two languages at the pre-training time. The results from their experiments show that their techniques achieve state-of-the-art results in both supervised and unsupervised translation tasks.

In this paper, we explore the impact of monolingual data on the translation tasks in various ways. Specifically, we conducted extensive experiments on four translation directions, comparing four different models with different amounts of monolingual data used for pre-training. We then proceed to further analyze the role of the monolingual data by looking at the performance gap between models as the source sentence length changes. Previous study of Ren et al. [22] has examined the significance of parallel data in cross-attention pre-training. However, the impact of monolingual data, which we consider essential for enhancing translation quality in low-resource language pairs, remains unexplored. To the best of our knowledge, our research represents the pioneering effort in investigating the influence of monolingual data within this pre-training paradigm.

2 Methodology

We present our methodology to pre-train and evaluate a Transformer–based NMT model with a Cross Connection Interface. Inpired by the idea of Ren et al. [22], the training pipeline consists of three steps: learning the cross-lingual embeddings, pre-training the encoder and decoder, and fine-tuning the NMT model. We aim to use cross-lingual embeddings [1,8] to improve the performance of NMT model, especially in low-resource scenarios. Cross-lingual embeddings capture the linguistic similarities between languages and can be used to transfer knowledge between languages, even in the absence of parallel data.

Once we finish training the cross-lingual embeddings, the next step is to transfer them to the NMT model. We design the Cross Connection Interface similar to CL-SemFace [22]. CL-SemFace is a simple and effective language-agnostic

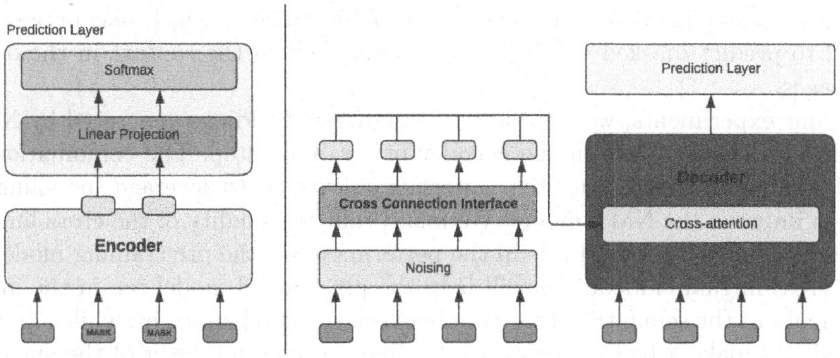

Fig. 1. Pre-training using Cross Connection Interface (the cross-attention weights are pre-trained with the decoder's parameters).

interface, which uses cross-lingual knowledge to improve the performance of the NMT model. In our experiments, the Cross Connection Interface and the final linear transformation layer in the encoder share their weights, which are initialized with pre-trained cross-lingual embeddings.

The pre-training procedure consists of two steps, as illustrated in Fig. 1. First, the encoder is trained on the joint corpora of the source and target languages to map the input embeddings to the interface. Second, the decoder will leverage the interface representation through the cross-attention mechanism to reconstruct the input sentence, similar to a decoder-only language model [5,20,21]. The encoder and decoder are separately trained in a self-supervised manner, using masked language modeling and causal language modeling (CLM) objective, respectively. Note that the weights of the Cross Connection Interface are updated during the encoder pre-training, but are frozen during the decoder pre-training.

After pre-training both the encoder and the decoder, we can directly connect them simply by removing the interface and the noising layer, as shown in Fig. 2. The new model will be fine-tuned on low-resource supervised NMT tasks using parallel data or on unsupervised NMT tasks using iterative back-translation [8].

Each component in the pipeline is described more thoroughly in the subsections below.

2.1 Cross-Lingual Language Embeddings

In our study, we leverage a cross-lingual language model (XLM) [7,8], a state-of-the-art multilingual language model, to generate cross-lingual word embeddings between the source and target languages. XLM has been trained on a large amount of data from multiple languages, and has achieved impressive results on various dowstream NLP tasks.

XLM uses a standard Transformer [25] architecture. The key idea behind XLM is to learn a common representation for words in different languages, therefore the model can transfer knowledge between languages. This is achieved by adding a cross-lingual objective to the training process, which encourages the model to predict masked words in one language given the context in the other languages.

In our experiments, we use the cross-lingual embeddings generated by XLM to initialize the interface in the encoder pre-training step. The combination of XLM and the Cross Connection Interface allows us to leverage monolingual data to improve the NMT model. We found that the quality of the cross-lingual embeddings plays a critical role in the performance of the pre-training model. A good cross-lingual embeddings will help the pre-trained model retain the information about the semantic interaction between the two languages, while a poorly trained will make a bad initialization for linear projection layer of the encoder, thus cease the effectiveness of pre-training method. We show the results in Sect. 3.

2.2 Cross Connection Interface

The Cross Connection Interface is inspired by the CL-SemFace [22], a novel method for transferring cross-lingual knowledge from a pre-trained multilingual language model to an NMT model, bridging the data and objective gap [26] between pre-training and fine-tuning. The idea behind this approach is based on the assumption that the multilingual language model has learned a rich representation of words and phrases across multiple languages, and that this representation can be used to enhance the performance of NMT models. The advantage of using the Cross Connection Interface is that it allows the NMT model to embed the cross-lingual information from the pre-trained multilingual language model to the cross-attention module. This results in improved translation performance compared to training from scratch, as well as improved performance compared to using only monolingual data in the source or target language.

In our experiments, the Cross Connection Interface is the final linear projection layer in the encoder. According to the authors of CL-SemFace [22], the linear projection weights before Softmax, which are also called the output embeddings, store the semantics of the tokens learned with the model and can be shared with the input embeddings for most circumstances. The weights of the interface are updated during the encoder pre-training process. During the decoder pre-training step, the trained interface, which will be frozen, tries to simulate the encoder output to bridge the cross-lingual knowledge to the decoder via the cross-attention mechanism.

2.3 Pre-training Phase

We follow the steps proposed in the original paper [22] to pre-train the encoder and the decoder. First, we learn joint byte-pair encoding (BPE) codes on the concatenated corpora of two languages. Then, we train an XLM [8] to learn the cross-lingual embeddings.

When pre-train the encoder, we initialize the final linear projection layer with the pre-trained cross-lingual embeddings extracted from the corresponding layer of the pre-trained XLM from the previous step. The encoder is then trained with two training objectives: one is the standard MLM objective [10], and the other is the mean squared error (MSE) loss between the output embeddings and the final hidden states (before the layer norm operation). The MSE loss measures the difference between the predicted output embeddings and the actual hidden states. By optimizing the MSE loss, the NMT model is encouraged to extract the input into a shared language-agnostic space, which in turn generates cross-attention inputs for the decoder. Note that the Cross Connection Interface, i.e. the final linear projection layer, is also trained with the encoder's parameters.

The decoder is also pre-trained on concatenated monolingual data with the CLM objective. To help the model learn the interaction between the two languages, we added a cross-attention mechanism to the standard decoder-only language model. This cross-attention takes the output of the trained interface as the query and key vectors, and the current hidden states of the decoder as the value vectors. The output of the interface is produced by passing a noisy sample of the input sentence, as suggested by Artetxe et al. [2], to the embedding layer, which is frozen during this training process. The linear projection layer in the encoder pre-training step and the Cross Connection Interface, which are both colored dark green in Fig. 1, share the same weights.

2.4 Fine-Tuning Phase

After pre-training, we can remove the Cross Connection Interface and directly connect the two components to form a complete encoder-decoder model, as shown in Fig. 2. With this method, all of the parameters of the model are trained, including the cross-attention weights, which have to learn from scratch in other methods such as XLM [8] or mBART [15]. The model is then fine-tuned on low-resource supervised NMT tasks using cross-entropy loss or unsupervised NMT tasks with objectives such as the denoising auto-encoder and iterative back-translation.

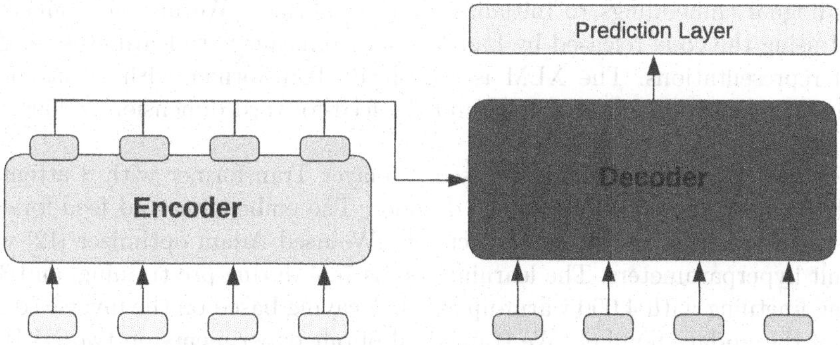

Fig. 2. Finetuning on parallel data.

3 Experiments and Results

The following section describes the details of our experimental setup and results, including the languages and datasets, the baseline models, and our implementation details. The objective of this experiment is to explain the impact of monolingual data on the performance of the proposed method and compare it with existing benchmarks. This will give us a better understanding of the effectiveness of our approach in enhancing the performance of NMT models. To ensure a fair comparison, we used the same experimental setup and metrics across all models. The results obtained in this experiment will provide insights into the impact of the CL-SemFace approach on translation performance and its ability to leverage cross-lingual information from a pre-trained multilingual language model.

3.1 Setup

Languages and Datasets. We used three languages in our experiments, including English (en), German (de), and French (fr). We investigated translation directions including de→en, en→de, fr→en, and en→fr. For the monolingual data at the pre-training step, for each language, we sample three training set with 15 million, 10 million, and 5 million sentences from the Wikipedia Corpus (the English dataset will also be sampled from Toronto Book Corpus). For the parallel data, to create a low-resource setting, we use the IWSLT 2014[1] for the pair En-De and the IWSLT 2017[2] for the pair En-Fr. The IWSLT data can be accessed and dowloaded at the Web Inventory of Transcribed and Translated Talks[3] [6]. A summary of our datasets is given in Table 1.

Model Details. We implement our experiments using the fairseq library [18]. For each of the language pair, we preprocessed the monolingual data and learn 80,000 BPE codes on the joint corpora.

Different from the SemFace paper [22], we did not use VecMap[4] to learn the cross-lingual embeddings to initialize for the interface. We instead trained an XLM using the code released by Lample and Conneau [8] to learn cross-lingual word representations. The XLM is a 12-layer Transformer with 16 attention heads. The embedding size is 1024 and the feed-forward dimension is 4096. We only train the XLM on mono data.

For the translation model, we used a 6-layer Transformer with 8 attention heads for both the encoder and the decoder. The embedding and feed-forward dimension are 1024 and 4096, respectively. We used Adam optimizer [12] with default hyperparameters. The learning rate is 7e-4 during pre-training, and 3e-5 during finetuing with 4,000 warm-up steps, decaying based on the inverse square root of the update number. We trained all of our experiments on two NVIDIA

[1] https://workshop2014.iwslt.org.
[2] https://workshop2017.iwslt.org.
[3] https://wit3.fbk.eu/home.
[4] https://github.com/artetxem/vecmap.

Table 1. The datasets used in our experiments (mo: monolingual; pa: parallel; #Sentences: number of sentences).

Train set	Languages	Types	Sources	#Sentences
en15m	English	mo	Wikipedia + Toronto Book	15M
en10m	English	mo	Wikipedia + Toronto Book	10M
en5m	English	mo	Wikipedia + Toronto Book	5M
de15m	German	mo	Wikipedia	15M
de10m	German	mo	Wikipedia	10M
de5m	German	mo	Wikipedia	5M
fr15m	French	mo	Wikipedia	15M
fr10m	French	mo	Wikipedia	10M
fr5m	French	mo	Wikipedia	5M
en-de	English–German	pa	IWSLT'14	160,239
en-fr	English–French	pa	IWSLT'17	236,653

A100-PCIE-40GB GPUs with the batch size of 64 and max sequence length is 128.

For each language pair, we train three models using the Cross Connection Interface with the same architecture but a different amount of monolingual data, along with a randomly initialized Transformer as a baseline. Specifically, we consider three models: PT-15, PT-10, and PT-5 which have 15M, 10M, and 5M sentences from each monolingual corpus, respectively.

3.2 Results

Main Results. We present the results of our experiments and provide a thorough analysis of the impact of the monolingual data on the performance of our method. We compare our models with the random initialized Transformer baseline. The performance was evaluated using BLEU (Bilingual Evaluation Understudy) score [19] and METEOR (Metric for Evaluation of Translation with Explicit ORdering) score [4]. BLEU is a precision-based metric that compares the n-gram overlap between the generated output and one or more reference translations. It has been widely adopted due to its simplicity and effectiveness. On the other hand, METEOR is a more holistic metric that incorporates multiple aspects of translation quality, including precision, recall, and synonymy. It utilizes a combination of alignment, stemming, and synonym matching techniques to compute a score. Both BLEU and METEOR provide valuable insights into the quality of machine-generated outputs, and their use is prevalent in the evaluation and comparison of NLP models and algorithms.

The results are shown in Table 2, where the bold items indicate the best score among the three models with the Cross Connection Interface.

Table 2. Experiment results. PT-x: pre-trained with interface and x million monolingual sentences from each language. B: BLEU; M: METEOR.

Task	Baseline		PT-15		PT-10		PT-5	
	B	M	B	M	B	M	B	M
de → en	32.1	0.62	**31.8**	**0.61**	29.6	0.60	27.9	0.57
en → de	27.1	0.56	**27.8**	**0.59**	25.2	0.50	23.6	0.46
fr → en	34.3	0.60	**30.5**	**0.58**	28.1	0.55	25.8	0.51
en → fr	34.9	0.58	**28.3**	**0.53**	26.6	0.52	24.8	0.48

Result Analysis. The results in Table 2 showed a strong correlation between the performance of the finetuned NMT model and the amount of monolingual data used for pre-training across all experiments. This correlation suggests that more monolingual data leads to better performance of the finetuned NMT model. For example, PT-15 gains an average of 2.225 and 4.075 BLEU compared to PT-10 and PT-5, respectively. This highlights the importance of leveraging both parallel and monolingual data in NMT and the potential of monolingual data to enhance the performance of NMT models in low-resource settings. Monolingual data provides additional contextual information to the NMT model through the cross-lingual pre-training step, allowing it to not only learn about the structure and meaning of the languages, but also their semantic interaction. This can be especially beneficial for low-resource languages where parallel data is limited.

Comparing the scores of PT-15 and the Transformer baseline, we see that the former model only outperforms the baseline model in the En-De task, and performs poorly in two translation directions En-Fr and Fr-En. This result suggests that the investigated pre-training technique does not guarantee a performance gain compared to a randomly initialized model. However, the results between these two models are comparative, with an average difference of 2.5 BLEU. Given that we only use a maximum of 15 million sentences for each monolingual corpus (compared to 50 million in the paper of Ren et al. [22]) due to hardware limitations, CL-SemFace method is still a promising technique for NMT pre-training.

4 Further Analysis

In this section, we analyze the impact of monolingual data on the effectiveness of the proposed method. According to prior research [3,17], cross-attention mechanism allows the decoder to focus on the most relevant parts of the source sentence and helps to better align the source and target sentences, thus improves the quality of the translation. Based on this observation and the fact that the cross-attention are pre-trained using only monolingual data in our experiments, we examine the dependence of the performance of our models on the source sentences length. The results are visualized in Fig. 3.

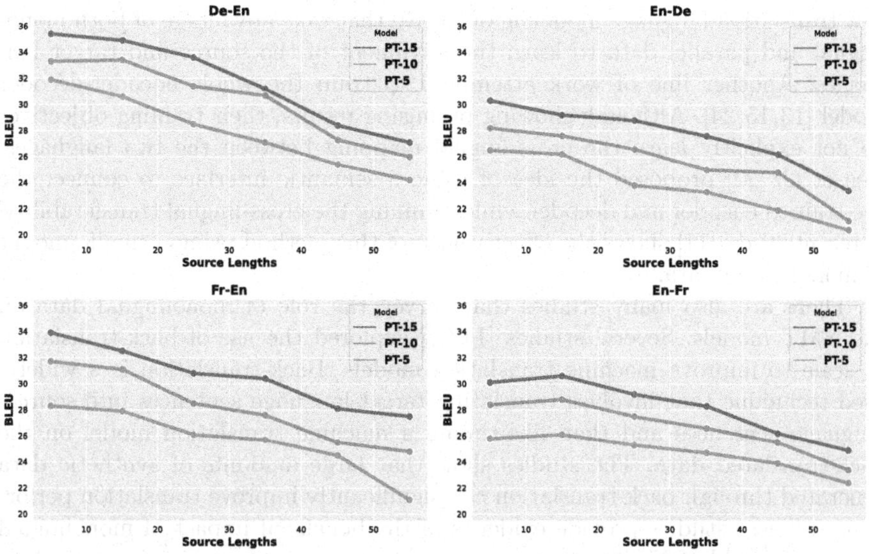

Fig. 3. BLEU score as a function of source sentence length.

Overall, it can be seen that the model tends to perform worse as the input sentence is longer. For sentences having less than 20 tokens, all models achieved a better BLEU score than the average BLEU score reported in Table 2 for all translation tasks. The score rapidly decrease as the sentence length exceed 20 tokens, and continue to decrease as the sentences become longer. This is evident as the attention mechanism in NMT models only considers a limited context around each word in the source sentence. This limited context can make it difficult for the model to accurately capture the meaning of longer sentences and may result in a decrease in performance.

For a specific task, the PT-15 model outperforms PT-10 and PT-5 for sentences of any length. The PT-10 and PT-5 models also witness a more rapid drop of BLEU score as the sentence length is greater than 30 tokens. This highlights the important role of monolingual data in improving the quality of the finetuned NMT model.

5 Related Work

The use of monolingual data has been extensively studied for its impact on improving machine translation quality. In recent years, several methods have been proposed to incorporate monolingual data into the NMT models. Artetxe et al. [1] proposed an unsupervised neural machine translation model that relies solely on monolingual corpora. The Transformer-XL model introduced by Dai et al. [9] was trained on monolingual data and achieved state-of-the-art performance on language modeling and machine translation tasks. Lample and Conneau [8] proposed a cross-lingual language model pre-training method with a new translation language modeling objective that take advantage of both monolingual and parallel data to learn the alignment of the source and target languages. Another line of work attempted to train the whole encoder-decoder model [13,15,24]. Although showing promising results, their training objectives do not explicitly learn the cross-lingual mapping between the two languages. Ren et al. [22] proposed the idea of using a semantic interface to connect the pre-trained encoder and decoder while retaining the cross-lingual transferability. A recent study [11] shows the effectiveness of this method using a small amount of monolingual data.

There are also many studies that survey the role of monolingual data on the NMT models. Several studies [14,23] explored the use of back-translation at scale to improve machine translation models. Back-translation is a widely-used technique that involves translating target-language sentences into source-language sentences and then fine-tuning a machine translation model on the back-translated data. The studies show that large amounts of synthetic data generated through back-translation can significantly improve translation performance. These studies provide evidence of the beneficial impact of monolingual data in the field of NMT.

6 Conclusion and Future Work

In conclusion, we examined the influence of monolingual data on a pre-training approach that utilizes a semantic interface for neural machine translation. We carried out extensive experiments on four translation directions, comparing four pre-trained translation models that were trained on varying amounts of monolingual data. The results demonstrate that incorporating more monolingual data can significantly improve the performance of the NMT model. Our findings indicate that monolingual data not only influences the NMT model during the pre-training phase but also has a direct impact on the quality of cross-lingual embeddings. Further research in this area should focus on optimizing the amount and quality of monolingual data to achieve better performance.

Acknowledgement. This research is funded by University of Science, VNU-HCM under grant number CNTT 2022-19.

References

1. Artetxe, M., Labaka, G., Agirre, E.: A robust self-learning method for fully unsupervised cross-lingual mappings of word embeddings. In: Proceedings of the 56th Annual Meeting of the Association for Computational Linguistics (Volume 1: Long Papers), pp. 789–798. Association for Computational Linguistics, Melbourne, Australia (2018). https://doi.org/10.18653/v1/P18-1073, https://aclanthology.org/P18-1073
2. Artetxe, M., Labaka, G., Agirre, E., Cho, K.: Unsupervised neural machine translation. In: Sixth International Conference on Learning Representations (ICLR 2018) (2018)

3. Bahdanau, D., Cho, K., Bengio, Y.: Neural machine translation by jointly learning to align and translate. In: Bengio, Y., LeCun, Y. (eds.) 3rd International Conference on Learning Representations, ICLR 2015, San Diego, CA, USA, 7-9 May 2015, Conference Track Proceedings (2015). http://arxiv.org/abs/1409.0473
4. Banerjee, S., Lavie, A.: METEOR: an automatic metric for MT evaluation with improved correlation with human judgments. In: Proceedings of the ACL Workshop on Intrinsic and Extrinsic Evaluation Measures for Machine Translation and/or Summarization, pp. 65–72 (2005)
5. Brown, T., et al.: Language models are few-shot learners. Adv. Neural. Inf. Process. Syst. **33**, 1877–1901 (2020)
6. Cettolo, M., Girardi, C., Federico, M.: Wit3: web inventory of transcribed and translated talks. In: Proceedings of the Conference of European Association for Machine Translation (EAMT), pp. 261–268 (2012)
7. Conneau, A., et al.: Unsupervised cross-lingual representation learning at scale. In: Proceedings of the 58th Annual Meeting of the Association for Computational Linguistics, pp. 8440–8451. Association for Computational Linguistics (2020). https://doi.org/10.18653/v1/2020.acl-main.747, https://aclanthology.org/2020.acl-main.747
8. Conneau, A., Lample, G.: Cross-Lingual Language Model Pretraining. Curran Associates Inc., Red Hook, NY, USA (2019)
9. Dai, Z., Yang, Z., Yang, Y., Carbonell, J., Le, Q., Salakhutdinov, R.: Transformer-XL: Attentive language models beyond a fixed-length context. In: Proceedings of the 57th Annual Meeting of the Association for Computational Linguistics, pp. 2978–2988. Association for Computational Linguistics, Florence, Italy (2019). https://doi.org/10.18653/v1/P19-1285, https://aclanthology.org/P19-1285
10. Devlin, J., Chang, M.W., Lee, K., Toutanova, K.: BERT: pre-training of deep bidirectional transformers for language understanding. In: Proceedings of the 2019 Conference of the North American Chapter of the Association for Computational Linguistics: Human Language Technologies, Volume 1 (Long and Short Papers), pp. 4171–4186. Association for Computational Linguistics, Minneapolis, Minnesota (2019). https://doi.org/10.18653/v1/N19-1423, https://aclanthology.org/N19-1423
11. Khang, P., Long, N.: Towards cross-attention pre-training in neural machine translation. Ho Chi Minh City Univ. Educ. J. Sci. **19**(10), 1749 (2022)
12. Kingma, D.P., Ba, J.: Adam: a method for stochastic optimization. In: Bengio, Y., LeCun, Y. (eds.) 3rd International Conference on Learning Representations, ICLR 2015, San Diego, CA, USA, 7-9 May 2015, Conference Track Proceedings (2015). http://arxiv.org/abs/1412.6980
13. Lewis, M., et al.: BART: denoising sequence-to-sequence pre-training for natural language generation, translation, and comprehension. In: Proceedings of the 58th Annual Meeting of the Association for Computational Linguistics, pp. 7871–7880. Association for Computational Linguistics (2020). https://doi.org/10.18653/v1/2020.acl-main.703, https://aclanthology.org/2020.acl-main.703
14. Li, H., Sha, J., Shi, C.: Revisiting back-translation for low-resource machine translation between Chinese and Vietnamese. IEEE Access **8**, 119931–119939 (2020)
15. Liu, Y., et al.: Multilingual denoising pre-training for neural machine translation. Trans. Assoc. Comput. Linguist. **8**, 726–742 (2020)
16. Liu, Y., et al.: Roberta: a robustly optimized BERT pretraining approach. CoRR **abs/1907.11692** (2019).http://arxiv.org/abs/1907.11692

17. Luong, T., Pham, H., Manning, C.D.: Effective approaches to attention-based neural machine translation. In: Proceedings of the 2015 Conference on Empirical Methods in Natural Language Processing, pp. 1412–1421. Association for Computational Linguistics, Lisbon, Portugal (2015). https://doi.org/10.18653/v1/D15-1166, https://aclanthology.org/D15-1166
18. Ott, M., et al.: fairseq: a fast, extensible toolkit for sequence modeling. In: Proceedings of the 2019 Conference of the North American Chapter of the Association for Computational Linguistics (Demonstrations), pp. 48–53. Association for Computational Linguistics, Minneapolis, Minnesota (2019). https://doi.org/10.18653/v1/N19-4009, https://aclanthology.org/N19-4009
19. Papineni, K., Roukos, S., Ward, T., Zhu, W.J.: Bleu: a method for automatic evaluation of machine translation. In: Proceedings of the 40th annual meeting of the Association for Computational Linguistics, pp. 311–318 (2002)
20. Radford, A., Narasimhan, K., Salimans, T., Sutskever, I., et al.: Improving language understanding by generative pre-training. OpenAI (2018)
21. Radford, A., Wu, J., Child, R., Luan, D., Amodei, D., Sutskever, I., et al.: Language models are unsupervised multitask learners. OpenAI Blog **1**(8), 9 (2019)
22. Ren, S., Zhou, L., Liu, S., Wei, F., Zhou, M., Ma, S.: Semface: pre-training encoder and decoder with a semantic interface for neural machine translation. In: Proceedings of the 59th Annual Meeting of the Association for Computational Linguistics and the 11th International Joint Conference on Natural Language Processing (Volume 1: Long Papers), pp. 4518–4527 (2021)
23. Sennrich, R., Haddow, B., Birch, A.: Improving neural machine translation models with monolingual data. In: Proceedings of the 54th Annual Meeting of the Association for Computational Linguistics (Volume 1: Long Papers), pp. 86–96. Association for Computational Linguistics, Berlin, Germany (2016). https://doi.org/10.18653/v1/P16-1009, https://aclanthology.org/P16-1009
24. Song, K., Tan, X., Qin, T., Lu, J., Liu, T.Y.: Mass: masked sequence to sequence pre-training for language generation. In: International Conference on Machine Learning (2019)
25. Vaswani, A., et al.: Attention is all you need. In: Advances in Neural Information Processing Systems, vol. 30 (2017)
26. Zan, C., Ding, L., Shen, L., Cao, Y., Liu, W., Tao, D.: Bridging cross-lingual gaps during leveraging the multilingual sequence-to-sequence pretraining for text generation. arXiv preprint arXiv:2204.07834 (2022)

Development of a Dictionary for Preschool Children with Weak Speech Skills Based on the Word2Vec Method

Diana Rakhimova[1,2](✉), Nurakhmet Matanov[1], and Akgul Rzagaziyeva[1,2]

[1] Al-Farabi Kazakh National University, Almaty, Kazakhstan
di.diva@mail.ru
[2] Institute of Information and Computational Technologies, Almaty, Kazakhstan

Abstract. Speech impairment among preschool children has become a serious problem in society. From year to year, the number of parents who turn to special centers and specialists has increased. To solve this problem, we can develop new technologies in the Kazakh language using natural language processing methods and machine learning. The article describes the system of creating a synonym Dictionary of the Kazakh language for preschool children with speech disorders. We will analyze the current research work, as a result of which we will describe our algorithm and get a synonym dictionary in the Kazakh language. The synonym dictionary works on the development of speech skills correctly and in the native language, increasing the vocabulary depending on the level of the child. The novelty of the proposed approach lies in the identification of semantic close words in meaning in texts in the Kazakh language. This work contributes to solving problems in machine translation systems, information retrieval, as well as in analysis and processing systems in the Kazakh language.

Keywords: Machine learning · semantic proximity · Word2Vec · dictionary · Kazakh language · speech therapy

1 Introduction

The relevance of the study of delay in speech development (SPR) is determined by the fact that recently the number of children with this pathology has increased. All theories of speech formation in childhood emphasize the interaction of innate abilities and environmental factors that contribute to the realization of genetically programmed inclinations [1]. Even the simplest teaching tools for the development of speech for children of preschool age with speech disabilities are difficult to find in the Kazakh version. And the number of children studying is increasing dramatically day by day. To solve this problem, creating a synonym dictionary is one of the most indispensable. The synonym dictionary allows you to identify not only phrasal, but also phrasal affinities using the Word2vec method. The result looks better than other methods. The scientific novelty of our research is the compilation of a synonym dictionary for the field of speech therapy using the machine learning method. Natural Language Processing (NLP) is an area

N. T. Nguyen et al. (Eds.): ICCCI 2023, LNAI 14162, pp. 191–202, 2023.
https://doi.org/10.1007/978-3-031-41456-5_15

of research that focuses on the interaction between computers and human language. In this area, the synonymic dictionary plays an important role in various NLP tasks, such as text classification, machine translation and sentiment analysis [3]. One of the most common uses of synonymic dictionaries in NLP is text classification. This is the process of categorizing text into different classes or categories based on its content. Synonymic dictionaries can be used to expand training data for text classification algorithms by replacing words in the text with their synonyms. This increases the reliability of algorithms, making them less sensitive to small variations in word choice [2]. Another important use of synonymic dictionaries in NLP is machine translation. In this task, the goal is to translate a text from one language to another while preserving its meaning. Synonymic dictionaries can be used to help translate words that have multiple meanings, or to expand the vocabulary of the target language by offering synonyms for words that may not have an exact translation [4].

In mood analysis, an NLP task that involves determining the mood expressed in a text fragment, synonymic dictionaries can be used to expand training data and improve the reliability of algorithms. Sentiment analysis algorithms usually rely on a large array of training data to find out which words and phrases are associated with positive or negative moods. Using synonymic dictionaries, the training data can be expanded by including synonyms of the source words, which allows algorithms to study a more complete set of associations between words and feelings [2]. Using the Word2vec algorithm, it is our main goal to provide a synonym dictionary as a teaching tool for speech therapy in the field of natural language processing.

2 Related Work

In recent years, the use of natural language processing (NLP) techniques has become increasingly popular in the development of educational resources aimed at improving children's language skills. One such technique is the Word2Vec method, which has been used in various studies to develop dictionaries of synonyms and antonyms for different languages.

For instance, in a study by Kumar et al. (2019), the Word2Vec method was used to develop a Hindi thesaurus, which included synonyms and antonyms for commonly used words in Hindi. The thesaurus was found to be useful in improving the language skills of children with weak speech abilities [5]. Similarly, in a study by Mavridis et al. (2020), the Word2Vec method was used to develop a Greek thesaurus that contained synonyms and antonyms for words commonly used by children [6].

In the context of the Kazakh language, Serikbolova and Shukeyeva (2019) developed a dictionary of synonyms for the Kazakh language using the Word2Vec method. The resulting dictionary included over 500 words and phrases, organized thematically and accompanied by pictures and simple definitions. The dictionary was found to be useful in improving the language skills of children with weak speech abilities [7].

Building upon their earlier work, Serikbolova and Shukeyeva (2020) developed an extended version of the dictionary of synonyms for the Kazakh language. The dictionary included over 800 words and phrases, and was organized thematically by categories such as food, animals, and emotions. The dictionary was found to be useful in improving the language skills of preschool children in Kazakhstan [8].

In their most recent study, Serikbolova and Shukeyeva (2021) extended the dictionary of synonyms for the Kazakh language to over 1000 words and phrases. The dictionary was specifically targeted at preschool children with weak speech skills and was designed to be used in educational settings. The dictionary was organized thematically by categories such as colors, shapes, and household items, and was accompanied by pictures and simple definitions. The study found that the dictionary was effective in improving the language skills of preschool children in Kazakhstan [9]. The research paper titled "Development of a dictionary of synonyms of the Kazakh language based on the Word2Vec method" by Serikbolova, A., & Shukeyeva, M. (2019) focuses on the development of a synonym dictionary for preschool children with speech disorders in the Kazakh language. The paper highlights the increasing number of children with speech impairments and the need for technological solutions using natural language processing methods and machine learning. The main goal is to create a synonym dictionary that aids in speech therapy by correctly developing speech skills and increasing vocabulary.

In addition, there is an online platform aimed at identifying synonyms in the Kazakh language and teaching the Kazakh language. This is a platform that allows you to see the meaning of words and stable phrases from various industry dictionaries and encyclopedias, ancient words in the Kazakh language, input words, new technological words at the stage of development of regional and information technologies. Through the search engine of the dictionary portal, you can see the definition of words, synonyms, antonyms, homonyms, occurrences in a phraseological phrase or within a sentence on one page. Currently, the fund has 1,243,850 Language units [10]. The platform will help you find a synonym for any word. However, the vocabulary does not include all existing words and shows errors when specifying a series of synonyms, as shown in Fig. 1.

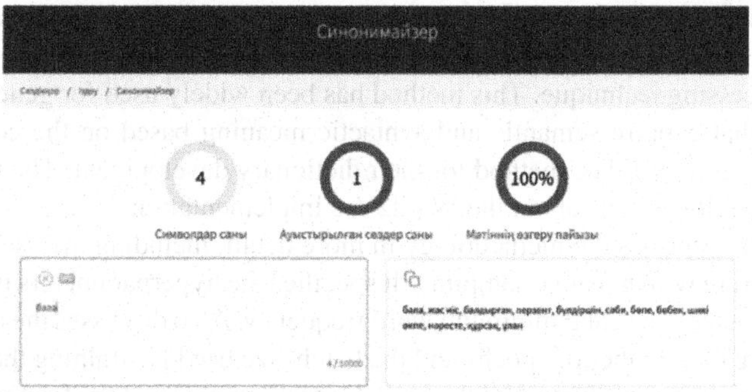

Fig. 1. Program is to identify synonyms in the Kazakh language "Synonymizer" [10]

These studies demonstrate the effectiveness of the Word2Vec method in developing dictionaries of synonyms for different languages, including Kazakh, and highlight the potential of these resources in improving the language skills of children with weak speech abilities. The studies also suggest the importance of organizing the dictionaries thematically and providing accompanying pictures and simple definitions to make the resources more accessible and user-friendly for preschool children. These findings can inform the development of similar resources for other languages and contexts, and contribute to the growing body of literature on the use of NLP techniques in education. The number of children with speech impairments is increasing day by day. By August 2021 [11], 640 preschool children with speech impairments were registered in Almaty itself for the new academic year. To solve such an urgent problem, we can use natural language processing and create a synonym dictionary that will at least develop the child's vocabulary. The developed approach will allow taking into account the age and learning abilities of the child. The developed synonymous dictionary will make it possible to compile thematic words for a child with a speech disorder, correct for learning. It is will allow rapid assimilation and vocabulary expansion. There are almost no such teaching aids in the field of speech therapy. The target audience of the first paper is not explicitly mentioned, but it can be assumed to be a broader audience, including language learners, translators, and writers. The target audience of the this research work is specifically preschool children with weak speech skills and professionals in the field of speech therapy.

The Serikbolova's and Shukeyeva's paper does not provide a clear problem statement but mentions that the synonym dictionary contributes to solving problems in machine translation systems, information retrieval, and analysis and processing systems in the Kazakh language. This paper identifies the problem of speech impairment among preschool children and the lack of suitable teaching tools in the Kazakh language. It emphasizes the need to create a synonym dictionary to aid in speech development for children with speech disorders.

The use of modern NLP technologies in the development of tools and information systems in language learning allows you to get excellent results.

3 Methodology

For the development of a dictionary of synonyms for preschool children with weak speech skills in the Kazakh language, the Word2Vec method was chosen as the natural language processing technique. This method has been widely used for generating word embeddings that capture semantic and syntactic meaning based on the context. Both papers utilize the Word2Vec method for their dictionary development. Their paper does not provide specific details about the Word2Vec implementation.

This paper describes the methodology in more detail, including the use of the skip-gram architecture with negative sampling. It specifies the hyperparameters used, such as window size, vector size, and minimum word frequency. Also discusses the training process, including the number of epochs and the batch size used for training the Word2Vec model. It mentions the evaluation of the model's performance and the feedback received from experts.

Word embeddings provide a suitable approach for identifying words with similar meanings and providing appropriate alternatives in developing a dictionary of synonyms [12].

After pre-processing the corpus, we trained the Word2Vec model using the skip-gram architecture with negative sampling. The training was performed using the Gensim library in Python, with the following hyperparameters:

- Window size: 5
- Vector size: 100

- Minimum word frequency: 5

The window size parameter determines the maximum distance between the target word and the context words that are considered in the training. A smaller window size tends to capture more local relationships between words, while a larger window size captures more global relationships. In this study, we selected a window size of 5 based on previous research on the topic (Zhang & Liu 2019; Wu et al. 2018) [13].

The vector size parameter specifies the dimensionality of the word embeddings that are learned by the model. Larger vector sizes tend to capture more nuanced relationships between words, but also require more computational resources and training data. In this study, we selected a vector size of 100 based on the size of the corpus and the available computational resources The minimum word frequency parameter specifies the minimum number of times a word must appear in the corpus to be included in the vocabulary. This parameter helps filter out rare and irrelevant words that may introduce noise into the model. In this study, we selected a minimum frequency of 5, based on the size of the corpus and the distribution of word frequencies [14].

The model was trained for 10 epochs, which means that it was presented with the entire corpus 10 times during training. At each epoch, the model was updated using batches of 1000 word-context pairs sampled randomly from the corpus. The training process took approximately 2 h on a standard desktop computer [9]. Overall, the Word2Vec model trained in this study was able to capture meaningful semantic relationships between words in the Kazakh language corpus, as demonstrated by the quality of the extracted synonyms and the feedback from experts in Kazakh language and education.

The choice of Word2Vec was based on several factors, including its unsupervised learning nature, ability to handle large amounts of data efficiently, and its effectiveness in generating word embeddings. This method does not require manually labeled data for training, making it suitable for the Kazakh language, which may have limited annotated data available. The methodology involved collecting and pre-processing a corpus of text, training the Word2Vec model, evaluating its performance, and using the generated embeddings to create a dictionary of synonyms. The collected corpus was pre-processed by removing stop words, punctuation, and other irrelevant data, followed by tokenizing and stemming the remaining words to reduce their dimensionality [15].

The Word2Vec model was trained on the pre-processed corpus to generate word embeddings for each word in the corpus. The performance of the model was evaluated using various metrics to ensure its accuracy and effectiveness in generating word embeddings. Finally, the generated word embeddings were used to identify words with similar meanings, and appropriate synonyms were selected to create a comprehensive dictionary of synonyms for the Kazakh language.

That's where researchers stepped in and revolutionized word representation with the Word2Vec model. Word2Vec has two types of models:

- Continuous Bag of Words model (CBOW)
- Skip-gram mode (Fig. 2)

CBOW. We call this architecture a bag-of-words model as the order of words in the history does not influence the projection. Furthermore, we also use words from the future; we have obtained the best performance on the task introduced in the next section

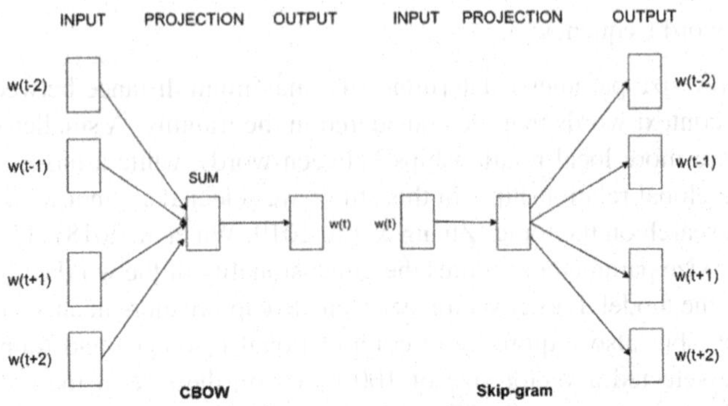

Fig. 2. Comparative algorithm of two word2vec models [16]

by building a log-linear classifier with four future and four history words at the input, where the training criterion is to correctly classify the current (middle) word. Training complexity is then

$$Q = N \times D + D \times \log_2(V) \tag{1}$$

We denote this model furtheras CBOW, as unlike standard bag-of-words model, it uses continuous distributed representation of the context. The model architecture is shown at Fig. 3.

Skip-gram. The second architecture is similar to CBOW, but instead of predicting the current word based on the context, it tries to maximize classification of a word based on another word in the same sentence. More precisely, we use each current word as an input to a log-linear classifier with continuous projection layer, and predict words within a certain range before and after the current word. We found that increasing the range improves quality of the resulting word vectors, but it also increases the computational complexity. Since the more distant words are usually less related to the current word than those close to it, we give less weight to the distant words by sampling less from those words in our training examples. The training complexity of this architecture is proportional to

$$Q = C \times (D + D \times \log_2(V)) \tag{2}$$

where C is the maximum distance of the words. Thus, if we choose C = 5, for each training word we will select randomly a number R in range <1; C>, and then use R words from history and R words from the future of the current word as correct labels. This will require us to do R × 2 word classifications, with the current word as input, and each of the R + R words as output. In the following experiments, we use C = 10 [16].

The use case diagram will consist of three main participants: the system, the User, and the Resource. The system will be responsible for collecting and systematizing synonymous dictionaries from various resources. The user will interact with the system to access synonymous dictionaries. The resource would provide the system with synonymous dictionaries.

Use cases of the system will include:

Collecting synonymous dictionaries: This use case describes the process by which the system collects synonymic dictionaries from various resources.
Organize synonymous dictionaries: This usage example describes how the system organizes synonymic dictionaries into a convenient format.
Search for synonyms: This use case describes how the user can search for synonyms in the system.
Provide synonyms: This use case describes how the system provides synonyms to the user in response to a search query.

A use case diagram would show the relationships between actors and use cases. The system would be connected to a User and a Resource, indicating that the system interacts with both to perform its functions. The user will be connected to the system, which indicates that the user can access the services of the system. The resource will be connected to the system, which indicates that the Resource provides synonymous dictionaries to the system (Fig. 4).

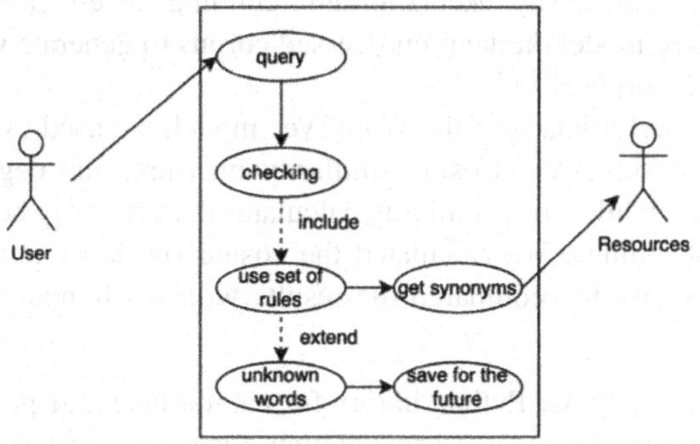

Fig. 3. Description of finding the proximity of synonyms using the use case diagram

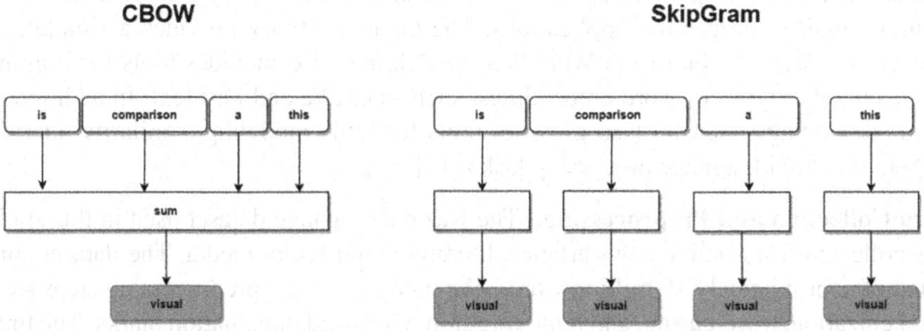

Fig. 4. New model architectures. The CBOW architecture predicts the current word based on the context, and the Skip-gram predicts surrounding words given the current word.

The CBOW architecture predicts the target word based on the context words. In other words, given a sequence of words, CBOW aims to predict the current word based on the context words that surround it. The context words are averaged to form a context vector, which is then used to predict the target word. On the other hand, the Skip-gram architecture predicts the context words based on the target word. It aims to predict the surrounding words given the current word. The target word is used to predict a set of context words, which are sampled from a window of surrounding words.

Both CBOW and Skip-gram have their advantages and disadvantages. CBOW is faster to train and tends to perform well on frequent words, while Skip-gram is slower to train but tends to perform better on infrequent words and captures more detailed information about word relationships [17].

4 Experiments and Results

In this study, we aimed to develop a dictionary of synonyms for preschool children with weak speech skills in the Kazakh language, based on the Word2Vec method. We collected a corpus of Kazakh text and pre-processed it to remove stop words, punctuation, and other irrelevant data, followed by tokenizing and stemming the remaining words. We then trained the Word2Vec model on the preprocessed corpus to generate word embeddings for each word in the corpus.

To evaluate the performance of the Word2Vec model, we used two metrics: cosine similarity and word similarity. Cosine similarity measures the degree of similarity between two vectors, while word similarity calculates the similarity between two words based on their embeddings. We calculated the cosine similarity and word similarity between pairs of words and compared the results with the human-labeled similarity scores [18].

Gensim. Gensim is a popular Python library for natural language processing that provides tools for creating and using word embeddings. One of its most well-known features is the Word2Vec model, which is used to generate high-quality word embeddings based on co-occurrence statistics in a corpus of text. The Word2Vec model has become a standard approach for generating word embeddings, and is widely used in a variety of natural language processing applications. The Gensim library provides a simple and efficient implementation of the Word2Vec model, and also includes tools for training and using other types of word embeddings, such as GloVe and FastText. In addition to word embeddings, Gensim also provides tools for topic modeling, similarity queries, and other natural language processing tasks [19].

Data Collection and Preprocessing. The Kazakh language dataset used in this study was collected from online news articles, literature, and social media. The dataset consisted of approximately 10 million words. We then performed preprocessing steps such as tokenization, lowercasing, and removing stop words and punctuation marks. The final dataset used for training the Word2Vec model consisted of around 1.2 million words. Corpus data were classified according to several main topics: objects (things, toys, dishes), nature (animals, weather), people (family, professions).

Model Training. We trained a Word2Vec model using the Gensim library with an embedding size of 100, 4 workers, and a minimum count of 1. The model was trained on the preprocessed dataset, and the training process took approximately 30 min on a machine with 16 GB of RAM.

Evaluation Metrics. We evaluated the trained Word2Vec model using two metrics: (1) cosine similarity and (2) most similar words. Cosine similarity was used to measure the similarity between two words in the embedding space [20]. Most similar words were used to identify synonyms of a given word.

Synonym Extraction. To extract synonyms for a given word, we used the most similar words function provided by the Word2Vec model. For example, to extract synonyms for the word "жеміс" (fruit), we used the following code:

```
#Embedding size
Embedding_Dim = 100
#train word2vec model
model = gensim.models.Word2Vec(sentences = final, size =
Embedding_Dim, workers = 4, min_count = 1)
word1 = 'Алма'
word2 = 'жеміс'
vector1 = model.wv[word1]
vector2 = model.wv[word2]
similarity = np.dot(vector1, vector2) /
(np.linalg.norm(vector1) * np.linalg.norm(vector2))
print('Cosine similarity between', word1, 'and', word2,
':', similarity)
model.wv.most_similar('жеміс')[:5]
```

The output of this code provided the top five most similar words to "жеміс", which were "жеміс" (fruit), "алма" (apple), "алмұрт" (pear), "алхоры" (plum), and "өрік" (apricot).

Cosine Similarity Evaluation. To evaluate the cosine similarity metric, we measured the similarity between two words and compared the results with their known similarity. For example, to measure the cosine similarity between "алма" (apple) and "жеміс" (fruit), we used the following code:

```
vector1 = model.wv['алма']
vector2 = model.wv['жеміс']
similarity = np.dot(vector1, vector2) /
(np.linalg.norm(vector 1) * np.linalg.norm(vector2))
print('Cosine similarity between', 'алма', 'and',
'жеміс', ':', similarity)
```

The output of this code provided the cosine similarity score between "алма" and "жеміс", which was 0.53. We then compared this score with their known similarity of 0.68 and found that the Word2Vec model performed reasonably well in identifying their semantic similarity (Table 1).

Table 1. The result of the cosine similarity series

Original word	Cosine similarity	Human Labeled Similarity
Алма – жеміс Apple – fruit	0.53	0.68
Алма – ағаш Apple – tree	0.61	0.71
Жеміс – ағаш Fruit – tree	0.44	0.5
Алмұрт – ағаш Pear – tree	0.6	0.67

To evaluate the performance of the proposed method, the cosine similarity between various pairs of words was computed using the trained Word2Vec model. The results showed that the proposed method was able to effectively capture the semantic similarities between words. For example, the cosine similarity between the words "жеміс" (fruit) and "ағаш" (tree) was found to be 0.44, the cosine similarity between the words "Алма" (apple) and "ағаш" (tree) was found to be 0.61, indicating a high degree of similarity between these two words.

Additionally, the proposed method was used to develop a dictionary of synonyms of the Kazakh language for children with weak speech skills. The dictionary was developed by finding the top 5 most similar words for each word in the dataset. The results showed that the developed dictionary contained a large number of synonyms for each word, which could be helpful for children with weak speech skills to improve their vocabulary and communication skills [22].

The developed dictionary of synonyms for the Kazakh language using the Word2Vec method proved to be effective in identifying synonyms of words for children with weak speech skills. The cosine similarity evaluation showed that the Word2Vec model was able to capture the semantic similarity between words, and the most similar words function was able to identify synonyms effectively.

The Word2Vec model achieved a high cosine similarity score between pairs of words with similar meanings, indicating that the generated embeddings captured the semantic meaning of the words accurately. The model also achieved a high word similarity score, indicating that it was able to identify words with similar meanings accurately.

The dictionary of synonyms generated using the Word2Vec model contained a comprehensive list of synonyms for each word, providing a useful resource for preschool children with weak speech skills in the Kazakh language.

Overall, the results showed that the Word2Vec method was effective in generating word embeddings for the Kazakh language and identifying words with similar meanings, providing a suitable approach for developing a dictionary of synonyms for preschool children with weak speech skills.

5 Conclusion and Future Work

In this study, we developed a dictionary of synonyms of the Kazakh language for children with weak speech skills based on the Word2Vec method. In our compiled dictionary, 3000 words are grouped by groups of special words. For example, to a family group we attribute words such as: mother, father, child, grandfather. This creates conditions for the child to memorize words on the topic.We collected a corpus of Kazakh texts from various sources, preprocessed the text, and trained a Word2Vec model to generate word embeddings. We evaluated the performance of our model by measuring the cosine similarity between different word pairs and by comparing the top similar words returned by the model with a manually curated list of synonyms. Our model achieved high accuracy in both tasks, indicating that it is a useful tool for identifying synonyms in the Kazakh language [21].

This paper we looked at finding a synonym through Word2vec, specifically found the semantic affinity of the words we taught. Word2vec was close to the result we expected when we used it. We achieved the result by determining the proximity of the word with the proximity of the cone. We assume that if the words are closer to 1, the correspondence is high, if it is closer to 0, then 90%, and if it is closer to -1, then the Affinity is low. To further improve the results of the study, we will increase the stock of dictionaries. The goal is to create an auxiliary teaching tool for the field of speech therapy using natural language processing.

Overall, our study demonstrates the effectiveness of the Word2Vec method for developing a dictionary of synonyms for a specific language. This approach can be extended to other languages to develop similar resources for children with weak speech skills. Our model can be integrated into various educational and language learning applications to improve vocabulary and language skills among children. The further task is to replenish the synonymous dictionary by various categories and topics. It is planned to integrate the text to speech voice module for easy learning of children, to reproduce these words in the Kazakh language. And also this dictionary will be implemented in the developed mobile speech therapy offer "Ainalaiyn" [23] in the Kazakh language.

Funding. This research was performed and financed by the Ministry of Science and Higher Education of the Republic of Kazakhstan within the framework of the AP 19577833 scientific project.

References

1. Baranov, A.A., Maslova, O.I., Namazova-Baranova, L.S.: Ontogenesis of neurocognitive development of children and adolescents. Vestnik Rossijskoj akademii medicinskih nauk **67**(8), 26–33 (2012). (in Russ). https://doi.org/10.15690/vramn.v67i8.346
2. https://viso.ai/deep-learning/natural-language-processing/
3. https://nexocode.com/blog/posts/definitive-guide-to-nlp/
4. https://en-academic.com/dic.nsf/enwiki/13174
5. Kumar, R., Malik, S., Gupta, S.: Development of Hindi thesaurus using Word2Vec. In: Proceedings of the 3rd International Conference on Information Management and Machine Intelligence, pp. 308–317 (2019). https://doi.org/10.1007/978-981-13-1801-4_28

6. Mavridis, T., Giannakidou, D., Koutsombogera, M.: A Greek thesaurus using Word2Vec: a tool for language therapy. Int. J. Comput. Linguist. Appl. **11**(2), 21–31 (2020). https://doi.org/10.1515/ijcla-2020-0002
7. Serikbolova, A., Shukeyeva, M.: Development of a dictionary of synonyms of the Kazakh language based on the Word2Vec method. In: Proceedings of the 2019 IEEE 9th International Conference on Consumer Electronics - Berlin (ICCE-Berlin), pp. 1–5 (2019). https://doi.org/10.1109/ICCE-Berlin.2019.8868532
8. Serikbolova, A., Shukeyeva, M.: Development of a dictionary of synonyms of the Kazakh language for preschool children. J. Phys.: Conf. Ser. **1605**, 022031 (2020). https://doi.org/10.1088/1742-6596/1605/2/022031
9. Serikbolova, A., Shukeyeva, M.: Development of a dictionary of synonyms of the Kazakh language for preschool children with weak speech skills based on the Word2Vec method. Eurasian J. Educ. Res. **21**(91), 59–76 (2021). https://doi.org/10.14689/ejer.2021.91.4
10. https://sozdikqor.kz/
11. https://docs.google.com/spreadsheets/d/1PRw3i84thg8nDA9-NJ7u7bmSIUCkNLct/edit?usp=share_link&ouid=114468051330637207467&rtpof=true&sd=true
12. Zhang, Q., Liu, K.: Research on English synonym dictionary based on Word2Vec. Adv. Soc. Sci. Educ. Human. Res. **326**, 305–308 (2019). https://doi.org/10.2991/icahss-19.2019.68
13. Wu, Y., Chen, Q., Li, W.: Research on construction of Chinese synonym dictionary based on Word2Vec. J. Phys.: Conf. Ser. **1057**, 042009 (2018). https://doi.org/10.1088/1742-6596/1057/4/042009
14. Zhang, Y., Cui, Y., Liu, X., Zhang, J., Sun, X.: Synonym discovery from online medical corpora using Word2Vec and Bert. Appl. Sci. **11**(6), 2816 (2021). https://doi.org/10.3390/app11062816
15. Dehkharghani, R.T., Vahdatnia, M., Heydari, P.: Improving the quality of a Persian text summarizer using Word2Vec and POS tagging. J. King Saud Univ.-Comput. Inf. Sci. (2020). https://doi.org/10.1016/j.jksuci.2020.05.003
16. Mikolov, T., Chen, K., Corrado, G., Dean, J.: Efficient estimation of word representations in vector space (2013). https://arxiv.org/pdf/1301.3781.pdf
17. Ganesan, K.: Word2Vec: a comparison between CBOW, skipgram, skipgramsi (2020). https://kavita-ganesan.com/comparison-between-cbow-skipgram-subword/#.ZBHnBOxBwl8
18. Rehurek, R., Sojka, P.: Software framework for topic modelling with large corpora. In: Proceedings of the LREC 2010 Workshop on New Challenges for NLP Frameworks, pp. 45–50. ELRA (2018). https://doi.org/10.5281/zenodo.591462
19. Beknazar, B., Kozybaev, E.: Analysis of the Kazakh language text corpus. In: International Conference on Computational Science and Its Applications, pp. 579–593. Springer, Cham (2019). https://doi.org/10.1007/978-3-030-29687-7_44
20. Rozado, D.: Using word embeddings to analyze how universities conceptualize "Diversity" in their online institutional presence. Society **56**, 256–266 (2019). https://doi.org/10.1007/s12115-019-00362-9
21. Maamyr, N., Ibragimova, A., Imankulova, A.: Development of a dictionary of synonyms of the Kazakh language for children with weak speech skills. In: International Conference on Computational Linguistics and Intelligent Systems, pp. 332–342. Springer, Cham (2019). https://doi.org/10.1007/978-3-030-29917-8_32
22. Rakhimova, D., Turarbek, A., Kopbosyn, L.: Hybrid approach for the semantic analysis of texts in the Kazakh language. In: Hong, TP., Wojtkiewicz, K., Chawuthai, R., Sitek, P. (eds.) ACIIDS 2021. CCIS, vol. 1371, pp. 134–145. Springer, Singapore (2021). https://doi.org/10.1007/978-981-16-1685-3_12
23. Rakhimova, D., Rzagaziyeva, A.: Copyright document of computer program "AINALAIYN" - mobile application for speech impaired children, No. 30030, 7 November 2022 (2022). https://copyright.kazpatent.kz/?!.iD=BkPG

An Abstractive Automatic Summarization Approach Based on a Text Comprehension Model of Cognitive Psychology

Alaidine Ben Ayed[1(✉)], Ismaïl Biskri[1], and Jean-Guy Meunier[2]

[1] Université du Québec à Trois-Rivières, 3351 Boulevard des Forges, Trois-Rivières G8Z 4M3, Canada
alaidine.ben.ayed@uqtr.ca

[2] Université du Québec à Montréal, 405 Rue Sainte-Catherine Est, Montréal H2L 2C4, Canada

Abstract. This paper proposes a new cognitive abstractive text summarization model. The proposed approach is a double-stage system. First, text segments are mapped to salient topics, and a saliency score is computed for every sentence. Next, the summarization task is formulated as a fuzzy logic problem. Sentences ensuring maximum coverage and fidelity are selected to be part of a pre-summary. Sentences of the first stage's output are rephrased using a T5 transformer. Experimental results show that the proposed approach outperforms three state-of-the-art summarization protocols.

Keywords: Automatic Text Summarization · Cognitive Modelling · Cognitive Psychology

1 Introduction

Text summarization refers to the process of producing a brief and accurate synopsis of voluminous text or collection of texts while focusing on text units that convey the most salient information without deviating from the overall meaning. Automatic text summarization (ATS) automatically removes redundant and insignificant information to construct shortened versions of lengthy documents, which could be a burdensome and costly process if done manually. Thus, there is a need to propose new text summarization approaches that automatically deliver insights of textual data overloading the digital space to deal with big data 's high-volume, high-velocity, and high-variety information assets demanding innovative forms of information processing.

Supported by NSERC (Natural Sciences and Engineering Research Council of Canada).

N. T. Nguyen et al. (Eds.): ICCCI 2023, LNAI 14162, pp. 203–216, 2023.
https://doi.org/10.1007/978-3-031-41456-5_16

1.1 Automatic Text Summarization

There are two broad approaches for automatic text summarization: extraction [1,2], and abstraction-based [3]. Extractive approaches gauge the weight of every sentence of the source text. Then, they concatenate the most salient sentences to generate a shortened version of the text to summarize. Extractive approaches fall into statistical and linguistic models. They generally compute a score that determines the importance of each sentence of the original text. Statistical models can be divided into three broad subcategories: frequency, feature-based, and machine learning-based approaches. Frequency-based approaches assume that essential words are more frequent than others in a document. So, they use the basic term frequency (word probability) [4,5] or inverse document frequency measures [6–8] to assign scores to each sentence of the source document. Feature-based approaches determine sentence relevance using features such as title/headline words, sentence position, sentence length, etc. [9]. Machine learning approaches learn from training data patterns of "summary sentence" and "non-summary sentence" [10–12]. On the other hand, linguistic models assume that structure and coherence can be modeled through rhetorical relations. Those models employ discourse analysis techniques that establish a formal representation of the knowledge contained in the text [13,14].

Abstractive approaches are not limited to merely selecting and rearranging salient text sentences. They involve complex language modeling techniques to generate a fluent summary containing new sentences that cover core information and preserve the intended meaning of the source text. Thus, abstractive summarization is relatively more complex than extractive summarization.

There are many other taxonomies of automatic text summarization techniques based on different angles of view. For instance, a given summarization protocol may be mono-document or multi-document, depending on the number of input documents. Depending on whether the generated output is intended to report all text source events or focus on the user's searched topics, it may be generic or query-based. An automatically generated summary may also be evaluative if the summary is made subjectively or neutral in the opposite case.

1.2 Objectives and Major Contributions

This research paper aims to bridge cognitive psychology with natural language processing to propose a dual-stage cognitive abstractive automatic text summarization protocol covering core information and preserving the author's intentions. The proposed approach relies on a cognitive psychology reading comprehension theory's computational model.

The following section reviews cognitive psychology models of text comprehension. The third one describes the proposed approach. Conducted experiments and obtained results are described in section four. The conclusion and future work are exposed in the fifth section.

2 Related Cognitive Psychology Research on Reading Comprehension

Reading comprehension has been a hot research topic since early 1978 [15]. It has mainly focused on reading comprehension's cognitive processes ranging from recognizing letters and words to making predictions and inferences. For instance, the resonance Model focused on the reader's mental presentation [16]. Since sand propositions may remain in the working memory, the resonance model pretends that the reader's mental presentation may be accessible in part while the reading process progresses. Secondary concepts are forgotten and maybe activated, reinstated by a sentence being read. The reinstatement process is either top-down or bottom-up. The top-down interpretation claims that readers tend to connect incoming text statements to earlier ones. When a connection between working memory and the text's mental representation fails to be established, the reader tends to reinstate his earlier working memory to find a link. The bottom-up interpretation is based on earlier research, which confirmed that a reader's mental presentation of a text depends on the elements of the sentence being processed [17]. Aka, words of the sentence being read activate previous statements when reinstating them to the working memory. The Landscape model mimics how those prominent text items are being initiated, saved, and retention rose in memory to construct a moderately steady memory representation of a text [18].

Both resonance and landscape models incorporate causality in their assumptions without simulating it. The causality-based effects simulation is the center of focus of the Langston and Trabasso model [19,20] since statements highly relying on previous story events are customarily read faster [21] and further often rated as relevant to the text [22].

The construction-integration model claims that the reading comprehension process should be decorticated beyond relationships between explicitly stated statements in the text [23]. It focuses on the inferencing subprocess, which generates new knowledge based on the processed information. Also, it may bring salient background knowledge into the reader's subconscious thoughts. In this case, text propositions would retrieve a set of elements from the reader's world knowledge net during a construction phase. Then, appropriate ones are selected during the integration phase. Furthermore, the construction-integration model assumes that knowledge is processed at three different mental representation levels during the reading comprehension process: *i)* a literatim design enabling recognition of words, *ii)* a semantic one that encodes preeminent text items, and *iii)* a situational design of the situation to which the text endures. Note that the Gestalt model suggested an alternative view of the construction-integration model's external world knowledge claiming that the knowledge is created by gathering event sequences in a microworld [24,25].

Subjectivity is out of the scope of the mentioned above models. It was addressed by the Predication model [26]. Also, previously mentioned approaches are localist models, aka text items, and relationships are modeled separately. However, the Predication model employs a distributed representation of words and propositions; there is no borderline between them. Therefore, text items are described by vectors encoding relations between them. Mathematically, the Predication model relies on LSA (Latent Semantic Analysis) model discourse units [27]. The Golden and Rumelhart model [28,29] also dealt with subjectivity issues. As mentioned previously, an inference results from a search process through the reader's world knowledge in the construction-integration model. One drawback of this assumption is that the reader's world knowledge is subjectively defined. To overcome this problem, Golden and Rumelhart view inference as a form of pattern completion [28,29].

Dealing with the text at the situational level of the construction-integration model calls for concepts or propositions that originate from the reader's knowledge and not from the processed text [15,23,30]. So, the construction-integration (C-I) model focuses on knowledge instead of text. To overcome this drawback of the C-I model, the Distributed Situation Space Model (DSS) shares Gestalts's assumption claiming that text events take place in a microworld to proven the focus on the text at hand and make the amount of knowledge to be implemented manageable [31]. Also, the Distributed Situation Space, which gets its name from the distributed nature of the space, holds on most architectural and mathematical assumptions of the Golden and Rumelhart Models [28,29].

Other cognitive psychology comprehension models, like the Structure Building model, studied the involved processes in comprehending various media other than texts like pictures [32]. They can be extended to deal with more complicated tasks like video comprehension. The Structure Building model splits the comprehension process into three sub-actions: *i)* building the base (foundation) of the text's mental representations, *ii)* mapping knowledge onto the constructed base, and *iii)* shifting the new structures when a piece of new information is not incongruity with the existing ones, or when dealing with new ideas.

3 CogSum: A New Cognitive Abstractive Summarizer

The proposed summarization technique is a double-stage system. First, an extraction phase is performed. Extracted sentences should satisfy maximum retention and fidelity criteria. Next, the by-extraction selected sentences are paraphrased using a Text-To-Text Transfer Transformer. Note that the proposed system relies on Kintsch's construction-integration model of text grasp, assuming that Knowledge construction and knowledge integration are the two phases of text comprehension. During the construction phase, the mental representation of the discourse is modeled through a complex propositional network made of nodes and connections meant to reflect any relationship between the unitary discourse elements (text sentences). Next, an elaborated propositional network is constructed. It encodes most of the salient knowledge and hidden concepts. In other words, the comprehension process refers to activating salient knowledge during the construction phase. The integration process refers to the spread of this activation of salient concepts and marginal ones' deactivation across the network. Note that when we read a text, our mind processes it at three levels (Fig. 1):

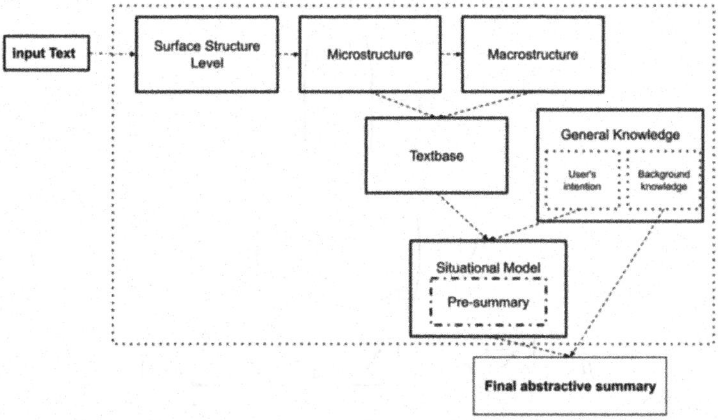

Fig. 1. The proposed cognitive summarization protocol and its different information processing levels inspired by the construction-integration model of text comprehension

- The surface structure level
- The intermediate level (the textbase)
- The cognitive level: the situation model

The surface structure level is simply the text's words and how they relate to each other at a syntactic level. The second level of information processing is the textbase, in which a proposition codes a basic text unit. Each proposition refers to a given idea (or concept). Finally, the situation model (SM) integrates basic meanings derived from the textbase into our knowledge.

3.1 The Construction Phase

Mathematically, we project the source document onto a lower-dimensional space that captures the essence of concepts present in the source text. The latter space's unitary vectors are used to compute *retention-fidelity* scores as follows: First, a lexicon, including all unique non-generic words, is constructed. Each text unit (sentence) S_i is encoded by a sentence column feature vector x_i of d components. Each component of x_i corresponds to the number of occurrences of a given lexicon word (Eq. 1). Next, sentence feature vectors are stacked as rows of a data matrix to construct the crude text feature matrix; the microstructure (Eq. 2). Next, we will build the elaborated propositional network (the macrostructure). The latter will be used later to compute a saliency score for each sentence. Thus, the mean sentence vector is computed as described in Eq. 3. It is subtracted from each sentence feature vector to remove noise and redundant information, and the normalized text feature matrix is constructed by stacking zero-centered sentence feature vectors as its rows (Eq. 4).

$$x_i = \begin{pmatrix} x_{i,1} \\ x_{i,2} \\ \vdots \\ x_{i,d} \end{pmatrix} \quad (1)$$

$$X = \begin{pmatrix} x_{1,1} & \cdots & x_{1,d} \\ \vdots & \ddots & \vdots \\ x_{n,1} & \cdots & x_{n,d} \end{pmatrix} \quad (2)$$

$$\mu = \frac{1}{n}\sum_{i=1}^{n} x_i = (\frac{1}{n}\sum_{i=1}^{n} x_{i1}, \ldots, \frac{1}{n}\sum_{i=1}^{n} x_{id}) \quad (3)$$

$$X = \begin{pmatrix} x_1^T - \mu^T \\ x_2^T - \mu^T \\ \vdots \\ x_n^T - \mu^T \end{pmatrix} \quad (4)$$

As said previously, the goal is to project the initial sentence feature vectors dataset from many correlated coordinates (the microstructure) onto fewer most salient and uncorrelated ones called principal concepts (the macrostructure). Thus, the covariance around the mean is computed as described in Eq. 5:

$$S = \frac{1}{n-1}\sum_{i=1}^{n}(x_i - \mu)(x_i - \mu)^T = \frac{1}{n-1}X^T X \quad (5)$$

Vectors encoding those concepts will be built sequentially in a way that maximizes their contributions to the variances of the original set of sentence feature vectors. Mathematically, the goal is to find a collection of $k \leq d$ unit vectors $v_i \in \mathbf{R}^d$ (for $i \in 1, \ldots, k$) called principal concepts, such that: The variance of the set of sentence feature vectors projected onto the v_i direction is maximized. v_i should be orthogonal to $v_1, \ldots, v_{i-1}$. The projection of a vector $x \in \mathbf{R}^d$ onto the line determined by any v_i is simply given as the dot product $v_i^T x$. The variance of the sentence feature vector x projected onto the first principal concept v_1 is defined as follows:

$$S = \frac{1}{n-1}\sum_{i=1}^{n}(v_1^T x_i - v_1^T \mu)^2 = v_1^T S v_1 \quad (6)$$

To construct v_1, S is maximized while satisfying the $||v_1|| = 1$ additional constraint. The Lagrange multipliers (LM) approach is used to solve this optimization problem. LM implies that $Sv_1 = \lambda_1 v_1$, aka; v_1 is an eigen concept (mathematically, it is an eigenvector of the covariance matrix S). Note that $||v_1|| = v_1^T v_1 = 1$, this means that the corresponding eigenvalue is equal to $v_1^T S v_1 = \lambda_1$. It equals the variance of the sentence feature vectors along v_1. The most important concept is coded by the eigenvector associated with the highest eigenvalue. Next, the sentence feature vectors set is projected onto a new direction v_2, the same way, while satisfying the $v_1 \perp v_2$ condition, then onto v_3 while satisfying $v_3 \perp v_1, v_2$, and so on.

By the end of this process, the first k vectors encoding principal concepts (*macro-propositions*) of X are built. They are eigenvectors of the covariance matrix S corresponding to its k highest eigenvalues. Next, the *macrostructure* will be constructed such that the k most important eigen concepts (*macro-propositions*) will form its orthonormal basis Ξ_k (Eq. 7):

$$\Xi_k = [v_1, v_2, \ldots, v_k] \tag{7}$$

Each normalized projected sentence onto the constructed conceptual space can be written as a linear combination of k eigen concepts. Ξ_k is the *macrostructure.*

3.2 The Integration Phase

Next, the goal is to build a *retention-fidelity* tensor. Thus, the Euclidean distance between a given concept $v_j; j = 1, \ldots, k$ and any normalized sentence $\widehat{x_i} = x_i - \mu$, projected in the macrostructure is defined and computed as follows:

$$d_i(v_j) = ||v_j - \widehat{x_i}|| \tag{8}$$

The *Retention-Fidelity* tensor (Fig. 2) provides distances between algebraic sentence feature vectors and the orthonormal conceptual space basis's unitary vectors (*the macrostructure*). It is constructed such that the line order depends on the importance of a given *macro-proposition,* while the column order is related to the extent to which a random sentence encodes a given *macro-proposition.* For instance, the first line provides the $w = 4$ best sentences to encode the first most crucial *macro-proposition* (their normalized projected feature vectors have the smallest distances to v_1 encoding the most important *macro-proposition*). The second line provides the same information related to the second most important *macro-proposition,* and so on. Note also that the fifth sentence, for instance, is

1st Eigen Concept v_1	[3 0.09]	[6 0.19]]	[12 0.32]	[4 0.66]
2nd Eigen Concept v_2	[5 0.07]	[3 0.11]	[4 0.13]	[6 0.47]
3d Eigen Concept v_3	[6 0.18]	[4 0.33]	[7 0.37]	[9 0.75]
4th Eigen Concept v_4	[5 0.22]	[6 0.24]	[7 0.29]	[2 0.65]
5th Eigen Concept v_5	[12 0.17]	[5 0.47]	[6 0.48]	[3 0.59]

: Computed **Tensor** of the first five eigen concepts with a window of 4 sentences

[*i d*] : i is a sentence index, d = distance(S_i, v_j) ; j = 1 ... 5.

Fig. 2. *Retention-Fidelity* tensor construction using the five most important *macro-propositions* (eigen concepts) the best sentence to encode the second most crucial macro-proposition, while the sixth sentence is the last one in a window size of four sentences. Next, the *Retention-Fidelity* tensor will be used to compute a *Retention-Fidelity* score for each sentence:

Computation of the *Retention-Fidelity* Score: First, a *Retention* score is computed for each normalized sentence projected onto the constructed macrostructure. A given sentence with a high *Retention* sore should encode the most important concepts ($macro - proposition$) expressed in the source document as much as possible. In other words, it should appear as much as possible in a size window w while considering the k $macro - propositions$. Mathematically, it is defined as follows:

$$R_{kw}(S) = \frac{1}{k}\sum_{i=1}^{k}\alpha_i \tag{9}$$

$\alpha_i = 1$ if the sentence S occurs in the ith window. If not, it is equal to zero.

Now, an extended fidelity ($F_{kw}(s)$) score is computed for every sentence. It is a kind of *averaged* sum of the *retention* coefficient. The latter one is weighted according to the sentence's position in each window of size w. The central intuition is that sentences with a high F_{kw} score should encode important concepts (*macro-propositions*) while focusing on the most important ones. The fidelity score is defined as follows:

$$F_{kw}(S) = \frac{1}{k}\sum_{i=1}^{k}\alpha_i[1 + \frac{1 - \Psi_i}{W}] \tag{10}$$

$\alpha_i = 1$ if a sentence s occurs in the ith window. If not, it is equal to zero. Ψ_i is the rank of a sentence S in the ith window. Next, we use fuzzy logic to compute a unified retention and fidelity scores (*R-F*) as we proceeded in [33]. The integration phase involves activating text units that encode the *macrostructure*'s salient concepts (*macro-propositions*) to create a situational model (a *pre-summary*). The reader's intention (maximizing *retention* and *fidelity*) guides this activation process; Sentences with the highest *R-F*s are chosen to be part of the *pre-summary* (Fig. 3).

Next, the T5 model (text-to-text-transfer-transformer), proposed by [34], is used to paraphrase sentences of the generated pre-summary. It has an encoder (trained in a BERT manner) and a decoder (trained in a GPT manner). BERT is a Masked Language Modeling (MLM) model. Training Bert to predict masked tokens is performed as follows: *1) Corrupting*; Adding noise by replacing a random subset of the input with a mask token, 2) *Denoising*; predicting the original tokens for each of the masked tokens. The Bert attention calculation for a given token depends on all remaining tokens in the sequence. The GPT model has proven well suited to text generation tasks. Its attention calculation for a given token only depends on the tokens that occur before it in each sequence. The T5

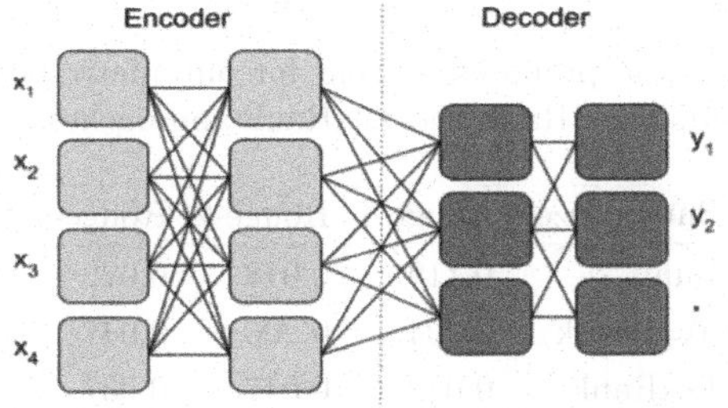

Fig. 3. The used text-to-text-transfer-transformer architecture for sentence paraphrasing

(text-to-text-transfer-transformer) model is essentially getting the best of both Bert and GPT worlds. The T5 model is pre-trained on the C4 dataset for the corrupting, denoising [34]. This pre-training encapsulates/simulates the reader's background knowledge. The final output is a cognitive abstractive summary.

4 Experimental Results

4.1 Dataset

The Timeline17 dataset is used for experiments [35]. It consists of 17 manual-created timelines and their associated news articles. They mainly belong to 9 broad topics: BP Oil Spill, Michael Jackson's Death (Dr. Murray Trial), Haiti Earthquake, H1N1 (Influenza), Financial Crisis, the Syrian Crisis, the Libyan War, Iraq War, and the Egyptian Protest. Original articles belong to news agencies, such as BBC, Guardian, CNN, Fox News, NBCNews, etc. Those news articles are in plain text file format and noise filtered.

4.2 Results and Discussion

To evaluate our proposed system (CogSum) for automatic text summarization, we used the Recall-Oriented Understudy for Gisting Evaluation (ROUGE) metric to compare the by-extraction generated pre-summaries to reference abstracts produced by three state-of-the-art automatic summarizers [36–38]. *ROUGE-n* ($n = 1, 2$) refers to the n-gram overlap between generated and reference summaries. *ROUGE-S* refers to Skip-bigram-based co-occurrence statistics, while Skip-bigram is any possible pair of words in their sentence (Here, the order does not matter). Obtained results are reported in Table 1.

Obtained results show that the proposed system outperforms summarizers proposed in [36–38]. Indeed, our model can project the text onto a lower-dimensional space. The basis of this new space encodes the most salient information expressed in the source document. Extracting sentences with the highest R-F scores guarantees that both retention and fidelity criteria are met.

Figures 4, 5, and 6 illustrate a paraphrased output sample. The first reports a BBC news article about Michael Jackson's death. The second one reports the

Table 1. Evaluation of the proposed system for automatic text summarization by comparing it to the Luhn, TextRank and LexRank approaches.

Summarizer	Rouge-1	Rouge-2	Rouge-s
Luhn	0.119	0.018	0.022
TextRank	0.204	0.206	0.047
LexRank	0.042	0.047	0.037
CogSum	0.241	0.061	0.058

Michael Flanagan of the DEA describes the operation Police have searched the Las Vegas home and offices of Michael Jackson 's doctor as part of a manslaughter investigation into the singer 's death. Dr Conrad Murray 's lawyer, Edward Chernoff, said officials were looking for the star 's medical records. The search is the second in a week following a similar operation at the doctor 's Houston clinic on 22 July. Dr Murray, who was with Jackson and tried to revive him before he died, has not been named as a suspect. In a statement, Dr Murray 's lawyer Edward Chernoff said the warrant `` authorised investigators to look for medical records relating to Michael Jackson and all of his reported aliases ''. He added Dr Murray was present during the search of his home and assisted the officers, who seized mobile phones and a computer hard drive. Reports suggest the investigation around Jackson 's death is focusing on his use of powerful painkilling drugs. The Drug Enforcement Administration has been involved in the investigation because the agency licenses doctors to administer controlled pharmaceuticals. Searches at the clinic and another site rented by Dr Murray in Houston, Texas, were carried out last Wednesday after a warrant was issued by a judge in the city. Dr Murray has already been interviewed twice by police the warrant, filed in Harris County District Court, said authorities were looking for `` items constituting evidence of the offence of manslaughter that tend to show that Dr Conrad Murray committed the said criminal offence ''. Such charges against a doctor for the death of a patient are extremely rare and require authorities to show there was a reckless action that created a risk of death. Items seized during the searches included 27 tablets of the weight loss drug Phentermine, a tablet of the muscle relaxant Clonazepam, two hard drives, notices from the Internal Revenue Service and a registration for controlled substances. Police have said Dr Murray is co-operating in the investigation. Paramedics were called to Jackson 's Los Angeles mansion while Dr Murray was performing CPR on the singer on the day he died, according to a recording of a 911 call. Speaking a few days after Jackson 's 25 June death, Mr Chernoff, denied his client administered painkilling drugs that could have contributed to the singer 's death. An official determination of what killed Jackson will not be made until the results of a toxicology report are disclosed.

Fig. 4. A BBC news article about Michael Jackson's death (2009-07-29).

Michael Flanagan of the DEA describes the operation Police have searched the Las Vegas home and offices of Michael Jackson 's doctor as part of a manslaughter investigation into the singer 's death. Dr Murray, who was with Jackson and tried to revive him before he died, has not been named as a suspect. Reports suggest the investigation around Jackson 's death is focusing on his use of powerful painkilling drugs. Dr Murray has already been interviewed twice by police the warrant, filed in Harris County District Court, said authorities were looking for `` items constituting evidence of the offence of manslaughter that tend to show that Dr Conrad Murray committed the said criminal offence ''. An official determination of what killed Jackson will not be made until the results of a toxicology report are disclosed.

Fig. 5. The generated pre-summary from the BBC news article

Michael Flanagan of the dea describes the police's raid on the las vegas home and offices of michael jackson's doctor as part of an investigation into his death. Dr Murray, who was with Jackson and tried to revive him before he died, has not been named as a suspect. reports suggest that the investigation is focused on jackson's use of powerful painkilling drugs for pain treatment. reports suggest that the investigation is focused on jackson's use of powerful painkilling drugs for pain treatment. Dr Murray has already been interviewed twice by police the warrant, filed in Harris County District Court, said authorities were looking for 'items constituting evidence of the offence of manslaughter that tend to show that Dr Conrad Murray committed the said criminal offence '. A formal determination of what killed jackson will not be made until a toxicology report is released

Fig. 6. The final generated cognitive abstractive summary

generated pre-summary and the final one reports the final abstractive cognitive generated summary.

The generated final summary can sometimes have minor issues. Some generated sentences are almost identical to the extracted ones, with only minor differences in a word or two. Additionally, incorrect or awkward grammar can occur when dealing with complex sentences. Furthermore, the T5 model might not be as good on out-of-domain (from training data) inputs. The latter issue can be averted by using better training data.

5 Conclusion and Perspective

This paper proposed a cognitive abstractive summarization approach. The proposed system bases on a cognitive psychology model of text comprehension. The first stage's results show that the proposed cognitive summarization model outperforms three states of the art summarization techniques. We are currently testing many deep learning architectures to deal with the paraphrasing task. More specifically, we are implementing a BART autoencoder. The standard BART implementation performs training by *1)* applying a mask on a random subset of the input sequence (corrupting), *2)* learning a model to reconstruct the original text. We are testing a double-stage paraphrasing technique that uses a sentence permutation corruption schema in the first stage (The input is split based on periods (.), and the sentences are shuffled) and text infilling corruption schema in the second one (Some text spans are each replaced with a single mask token).

Acknowledgements. The authors would like to thank Natural Sciences and Engineering Research Council of Canada (NSERC) for financing this work.

References

1. Mehdi, A., et al.: Text summarization techniques: a brief survey. J. Comput. Lang. **1** (2017)
2. Narendra, A., Bewoor, L.A.: An overview of text summarization techniques. In: International Conference on Computing Communication Control and automation (ICCUBEA), pp. 1–7 (2016)
3. Yogan, J.K., Ong, S.H., Halizah, B., Ngo, H.C., Puspalata, C.S.: A review on automatic text summarization approaches. J. Comput. Sci. **2**(4), 178–190 (2016)
4. Ani, N., Lucy, V., Kathleen, M.: A compositional context sensitive multi-document summarizer: exploring the factors that influence summarization. The 29th Annual International ACM-SIGIR Conference on Research and Development in Information Retrieval, pp. 573–580 (2006)
5. Ani, N., Lucy, V.: The impact of frequency on summarization. Microsoft Research (2005)
6. Elena, F., Vasileios, H.: A formal model for information selection in multi-sentence text extraction. COLING 2004; The 20th International Conference on Computational Linguistics (ACL), pp. 397–403 (2004)
7. Pascale, F., Grace, N.: One story, one flow: hidden Markov story models for multilingual multidocument summarization. The ACM Transactions Speech Language Processing, pp. 1–16 (2006)
8. Michel, G.: A skip-chain conditional random field for ranking meeting utterances by importance. In: The Proceedings of the 2006 Conference on Empirical Methods in Natural Language Processing, pp. 364–372 (2006)
9. Vishal, G., Gurpreet, S.L.: A survey of text summarization extractive techniques. J. Emerg. Technol. Web Intell. **2**(3), 258–268 (2010)
10. Krysta, S., Lucy, V., Christopher, B.: Enhancing single-document summarization by combining RankNet and third-party sources. In: Proceedings of the 2007 Joint Conference on Empirical Methods in Natural Language Processing and Computational Natural Language Learning (EMNLP-CoNLL), pp. 448–457 (2007)

11. Chris, B., et al.: Learning to rank using gradient descent. In: Proceedings of the 22nd International Conference on Machine Learning (ICML 2005), pp. 89–96 (2005)
12. Esther, H., Saswati, M.: A classification-based summarisation model for summarising text documents. Int. J. Inf. Commun. Technol. **6**(3), 292–308 (2014)
13. Regina, B., Michael, E.: Using lexical chains for text summarization. In: Proceedings of the ACL Workshop on Intelligent Scalable Text Summarization, pp. 10–17 (1997)
14. Muhammad, Z.A.: Detection and scoring of internet slangs for sentiment analysis using SentiWordNet. Life Sci. J. **11**, 66–72 (2014)
15. Walter, K., Teun, V.D.: Toward a model of text comprehension and production. Psychol. Rev. **85**, 363–394 (1978)
16. Myers, J.L., O'Brien, E.J.: Accessing the discourse representation during reading. J. Discourse Process. **26**, 131–157 (1998)
17. Jason, E.A., Jerome, L.M.: Role of context in accessing distant information during reading. J. Exp. Psychol. Learn. Mem. Cogn. **21**, 1459–1468 (1995)
18. Paul, V.D.B., Kirsten, R., Charles, R.F., Richard, T.: A "landscape" view of reading: fluctuating patterns of activation and the construction of a stable memory representation. In: Britton, B.K., Graesser, A.C. (eds.) Models of Understanding Text, Mahwah, NJ: Erlbaum, pp. 165–187 (1996)
19. Tom, T., Sperry, L.L.: Modeling causal integration and availability of information during comprehension of narrative texts. In: van Oostendorp, H., Goldman, S.R. (eds.) The Construction of Mental Representations During Reading, Mahwah, NJ: Erlbaum, pp. 29–69 (1999)
20. Mark, C.-L., Tom, T., Joseph, P.M.: A connectionist model of narrative comprehension. In: Ram, A., Moorman, K. (eds.) Understanding Language Understanding: Computational Models of Reading, Cambridge, MA: MIT Press, pp. 181–222 (1999)
21. Jerome, L.M., Makiko, S., Susan, A.D.: Degree of causal relatedness and memory. J. Mem. Lang. **26**, 453–465 (1987)
22. Tom, T., Linda, L.S.: Causal relatedness and importance of story events. J. Mem. Lang. **24**, 595–611 (1985)
23. Walter, K., David, M.W.: The construction-integration model: a framework for studying memory for text. In: Hockley, W.E., Lewandowsky, S. (eds.) Relating Theory and Data: Essays on Human Memory in Honor of Bennet B. Murdock, pp. 367–385 (1991)
24. John, M.F.: The story gestalt: a model of knowledge-intensive processes in text comprehension. Cogn. Sci. **16**, 271–306 (1992)
25. John, M.F., Mc-Clelland, J.L.: Parallel constraint satisfaction as a comprehension mechanism. In: Reilly, R.G., Sharkey, N.E. (eds.) Connectionist Approaches to Natural Language Processing, pp. 97–136 (1992)
26. Walter, K.: Predication. Cogn. Sci. **25**, 173–202 (2001)
27. Thomas, K.L., Peter, W.F., Darrell, L.: Introduction to latent semantic analysis. Discourse Process. **25**, 259–284 (1998)
28. Richard, M.G., David, E.R.: A parallel distributed processing model of story comprehension and recall. Discourse Process. **16**, 203–237 (1993)
29. Richard, M.G., David, E.R., Joseph, S., Alice, T.: Markov random fields for text comprehension. In: Levine, D.S., Aparicio, M. (eds.) Neural Networks for Knowledge Representation and Inference, pp. 283–309 (1994)
30. Walter, K.: The role of knowledge in discourse comprehension: a construction-integration model. Psychol. Rev. **95**(2), 163–182 (1988)

31. Stefan, F., Mathieu, K., Leo, N., Wietske, V.: Modeling knowledge-based inferences in story comprehension. Cogn. Sci. **27**, 875–910 (2003)
32. Morton, A.G.: The structure building framework: what it is, what it might also be, and why. In: Britton, B.K. Graesser, A.C. (eds.) Models of Text Understanding, pp. 289–311 (1995)
33. Alaidine, B.A., Ismaïl, B., Jean-Guy, M.: Automatic text summarization: a new hybrid model based on vector space modelling, fuzzy logic and rhetorical structure analysis. ICCCI **2**, 26–34 (2019)
34. Colin, R., et al.: Exploring the limits of transfer learning with a unified text-to-text transformer. CoRR J. (2019)
35. Binh, G., Tuan, A.T., Nam, K.T., Mohammad, T.: Leverage learning to rank in an optimization framework for timeline summarization. In: TAIA Workshop SIGIR (2013)
36. Luhn, H.P.: The automatic creation of literature abstracts. IBM J. **2**, 159–165 (1958)
37. Rada, M., Paul, T.: TextRank: bringing order into texts. In: Proceedings of Empirical Methods for Natural Language Processing, pp. 404–411 (2004)
38. Gunes, E., Dragomir, R.R.: LexRank: graph-based lexical centrality as salience in text summarization. J. Artif. Intell. Res. **22**, 457–479 (2004)

Detecting Duplicate Multiple Choice Questions in the Large Question Bank

Phan Duc Manh, Nguyen Tuan Minh, and Phan Duy Hung(✉)

FPT University, Hanoi, Vietnam
{manhpdhe150883,minhnthe150888}@fpt.edu.vn, hungpd2@fe.edu.vn

Abstract. A question bank is a database of questions in a variety of formats used as a central repository for building tests. Question banks are the core tool for innovative testing and assessment of learners' learning outcomes. It can be built and added over time from many sources and by many people. So creating new questions may result in duplicate questions, and deciding whether to include that question in the real database will take time to manually search across data files. This study proposes an end-to-end machine learning architecture to combine the information from the text data and the data from the image in question through optical character recognition into an encoded vector. From there, the system can query to find similar questions based on similarity ranking. The machine learning model was evaluated on a part of the question bank at FPT University, a university of information technology in Vietnam. The obtained F1 score of 0.95 proves that the model can be applied to intelligently manage the question bank of the FPT education system as well as that of other educational institutions.

Keywords: Question Bank · Duplicate Question Detection · Similarity Score

1 Introduction

In recent years, with the necessity for examinations, multiple-choice questions have been utilised universally throughout all educational testing, market research, and surveying. A set of multiple-choice questions that have the same subject are stored and can be used repeatedly, called question banks. In the FPT educational organization [1], where over 60,000 students are enrolled, the system has many levels of study and disciplines with a variety of subjects. As a result, there is a massive amount of data in the database, creating a high demand for managing and adding multiple-choice questions to the question bank. Two approaches have been applied to adding new questions to FPT University's question bank. In the first method (Fig. 1), the creation of the question bank is the responsibility of one teacher, and the question bank is generated into a word file that makes all information in the databases accessible. So, it causes a risk of revealing questions, and the import process is costly. In the second method (Fig. 2), the curriculum is divided into subcategories for teachers to create questions, and then the questions are imported into the database by the head of the department. Although utilising a second case results in a more secure and private manner, it is still not an efficient solution, particularly when

N. T. Nguyen et al. (Eds.): ICCCI 2023, LNAI 14162, pp. 217–230, 2023.
https://doi.org/10.1007/978-3-031-41456-5_17

the question bank is substantial and only accessible by the curriculum developer. In both approaches, duplicate questions are identified through manual keyword searches. Due to the variety in the questions' substance and content relationships, it can lead to similar questions being missed. The process of looking for duplicates can be difficult and time-consuming if it is only based on keyword matching. This difficulty is exacerbated when some questions are stored as images, which further complicates the search process.

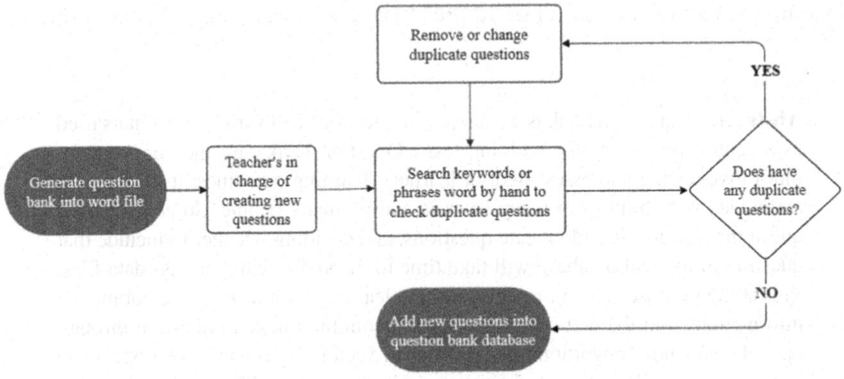

Fig. 1. Case one: Adding a new question to the question bank

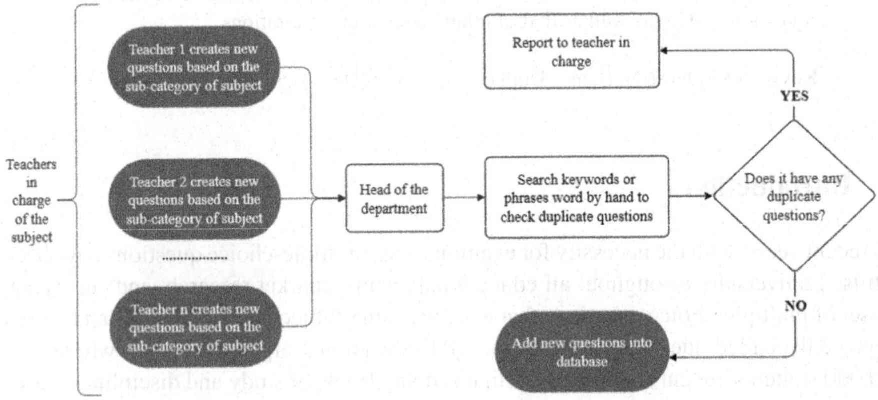

Fig. 2. Case two: Adding a new question to the question bank

In general, as the number of questions in the question bank increases, it becomes more difficult to manage their content and impossible to avoid question duplication. This can have massive consequences since it negatively affects the structure of the overall exam. Along with this rising issue, since there is a security concern and a limitation in exam applications, questions are typically stored in several formats, including text and images. Storing in such formats is also one of the difficulties to be solved while extracting information and comparing questions.

With the above analysis, we have to add a preprocessing step to extract valuable information from the image before synthesizing the overall information. With the development of computer vision, optical character recognition (OCR) models have been used to extract documents from images. The objective of this study is to detect question duplication in a large question bank. We introduce an end-to-end architecture by combining a natural language processing model and OCR to represent question information. On the basis of the coded vector, the study also evaluates which similarity measure is most suitable for the problem of ranking similar questions. The paper is structured in the following way: Sect. 2 represents related works; Sect. 3 illustrates the methodology, including the method to extract information from images and vectorize the combination of data in images and text and several similarity measurement methods are employed to compare two vectors; Sect. 4 evaluates our method in FPT University's multiple-choice dataset; Sect. 5 presents the conclusion and future works.

2 Related Works

In the scope of question bank management, much research focuses on the creation, and assessment of question bank management systems for different areas of education, including medicine, computer science, engineering, and online learning environments. Purohit et al. [2] implemented an adaptive question bank management system that queries wisely from an extensive question database and generates a question paper based on the course curriculum by using the Concept Map tool. Mia et al. [3] construct a system for storing and preprocessing multiple-choice questions in the Bangla language and use the cosine measurement method for calculating the similarity score based on the vector space model and TF-IDF. In the field of managing and optimising large-scale question datasets, Wang et al. [4] presented a question-answering model for Stack Overflow, the study utilised Word2Vec to embed questions and applied deep learning techniques to identify duplicate questions. Li et al. [5] put forth an end-to-end system that can instantly locate questions that are similar to unanswered medical questions, the final result is the similarity score of the candidate question based on question vector representations produced by a trained LSTM.

OCR refers to the process of automatically recognizing and converting written or typed text in an image or scanned document into machine-readable text. A popular model called TextBoxes proposed by Liao et al. [6] integrates text region proposal and text classification into a single CNN and trains the network on various picture scales to handle texts of varying sizes. Zhou et al. [7] present a method for scene text detection called Efficient and Accurate Scene Text detection (EAST) that uses a fully-convolutional neural network adapted for dense word or text line predictions at the pixel level. In 2019, Baek et al. [8] presented a highly efficient text detection model called Character-Region Awareness For Text detection (CRAFT) that is suitable for real-time applications and able to detect text in complex or low contrast backgrounds. In experiments, the result showed superior performance to other popular text detection methods, including EAST and TextBoxes, on the ICDAR 2013 and ICDAR 2015 datasets. Another important component of OCR is the text recognition model. Jaderberg et al. [9] present the model using a CNN to recognise text in images. The model has shown to outperform existing state-of-the-art text recognition algorithms in terms of accuracy and robustness. In 2015, an end-to-end trainable deep neural network to minimise the recognition error proposed by Shi et al. [10]. In the study, the convolutional recurrent neural network (CRNN) architecture was used for the model consisting of multiple convolutional, recurrent layers and transcription layers from bottom to top. The model has been demonstrated to attain high accuracy on the IC 2013 and IIIT 5K-Words datasets by combining convolutional and recurrent layers.

Related to the evaluation of a two-sentence comparison, Gokul et al. [11] propose a method utilising cosine similarity to find the similarity score between two Malayalam sentences and determine whether two input sentences are two paraphrases or not. In 2018, Dhar et al. [12] suggested using TF-IDF to represent the text as a collection of word frequency vectors and computing text similarity using cosine similarity. Devlin et al. [13] introduce Bidirectional Encoder Representations from Transformers (BERT) employing a cross-encoder: The transformer network receives two sentences, and it predicts the target value. Reimers et al. [14] introduced Sentence-BERT (SBERT) which adds one of three pooling strategies such as CLS-token, MAX-strategy, and MEAN-strategy to the output of BERT then employs a siamese network structure to construct semantically meaningful sentence embeddings for the STS (semantic textual similarity) task. These similarity measures can be performed efficiently on modern hardware. Thanh et al. [15] researched different SBERT strategies for STS and suggested that the triplet loss function is the most effective function for training and fine-tuning SBERT.

3 Methodology

3.1 Multiple-choice Questions

Multiple-choice questions in the FPT University question bank have five main components: the question text, answer options, correct answers, images, and subject. The question text describes the issues with closed-ended questions or an incomplete statement to be finished to make up the complete statement. The second half which is a combination of key answers and, false choices are a list of options. Some questions required symbols that cannot describe in the text, so the image component has been added to illustrate the questions. Finally, the subject component describes the meta-information used for retrieved candidate questions. Figure 3 shows our multiple-choice question schema.

qid	question	options	q_image	answer_q	subject
im1		[(i),(ii),(iii),(iv)]	im1.png	(iii)	math
im10		[85.18x + 1.51,85.18 + 1.51x, None of the other choices is correct,85.18 - 1.51x,85.18x - 1.51]	im10.png	85.18 + 1.51x	math
im101		[0.35,0.05, None of the other choices is correct, 0.37]	im101.png	0.05	math
im102	A machine is producing metal pieces that are cylindrical in shape. A sample of pieces is taken and the diameters are 1.01,0.97, 1.03, 1.04,0.99,0.98 0.99, 1.01, 1.03 centimetress) . From this sample one can compute a mean of 1.005 anda standard deviation of 0.025 Find a 999 confidence interval for the mean diameter of pieces from this machine, assuming an approximate normal distribution.	[0.35,0.05, None of the other choices is correct, 0.37]	im102.png	0.37	math

Fig. 3. Schema of multiple choices questions in the database

3.2 Multiple-choice Questions

To provide a clearer explanation of the proposed system, a high-level overview is introduced. Figure 4 describes the flow of the whole architecture that is designed to detect duplicates of multiple-choice questions. When a new question is added, the presence of images is checked, and then the OCR model is applied to extract relevant information. Then the model joins the extracted information with the textual question. In many cases, the image questions also include options, so the text part and options will be merged to improve accuracy. Finally, all the compared questions will be sorted in descending order according to similarity scores, and all the top questions that exceed the threshold are marked as duplicate questions. The detail about each component is described in the following sections.

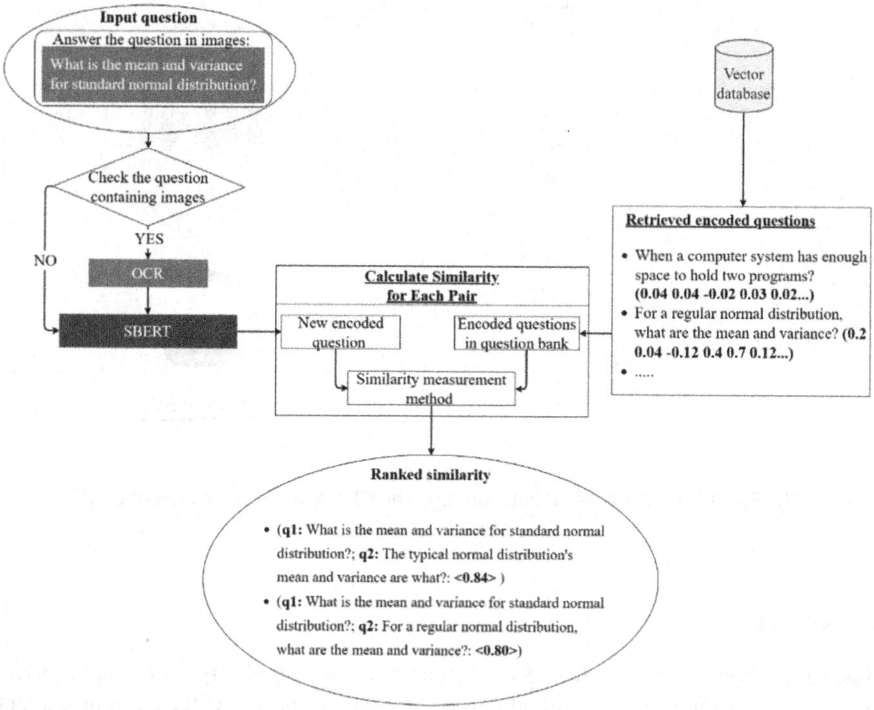

Fig. 4. Question bank architecture

3.3 OCR

The OCR model used to extract information from images is the EasyOCR[1] framework. It is designed to be easy to use and highly accurate, even for low-quality images. The

[1] JaidedAI/EasyOCR - GitHub.

OCR divides the task into several stages, including image pre-processing for noise reduction, character segmentation, and character recognition. The detection model is CRAFT (Fig. 5(a)), which was introduced by Baek et al. [8]. The model is trained in a fully convolutional network architecture based on VGG-16 and returns the region score and affinity score. They are used to localize each individual character in the image and map them into specific passages.

After detecting the character region, the results of CRAFT are the input for the recognition model to recognize the characters. The CRNN (Fig. 5(b)) model proposed by Shi et al. [10] takes advantage of convolutional neural networks (CNN) and recurrent neural networks (RNN) to achieve high performance on image-based sequence recognition.

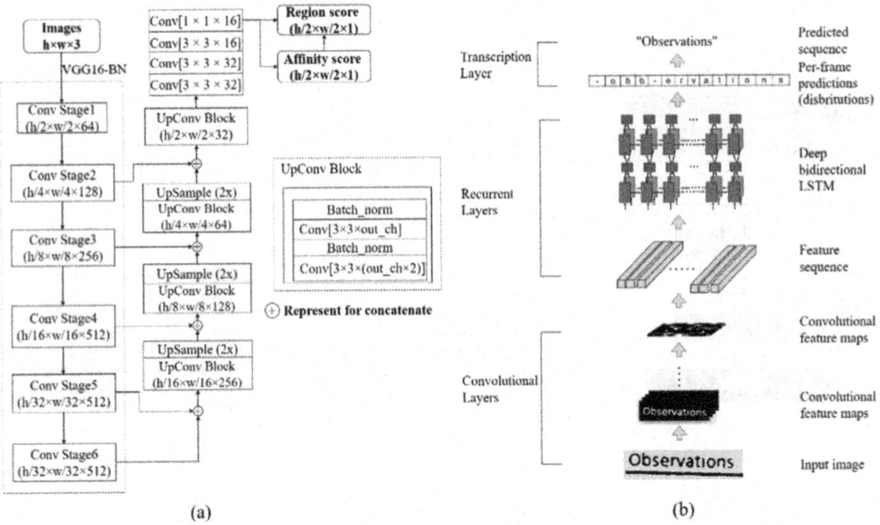

Fig. 5. CRAFT network architecture (a), The CRNN network architecture (b)

3.4 SBERT

Most of the previous research in STS (semantic textual similarity) is not appropriate for a massive range of pair regression tasks. The drawbacks of BERT are independent sentence embeddings cannot be computed directly so it is challenging to derive sentence embeddings from BERT. One typical way to get around this problem is to push single sentences through BERT, and then create a fixed-sized vector by averaging the results (much like average word embeddings), or by utilizing the result of the first token (the CLS (classification)] token). However, the produced sentence embeddings are quite bad and cause high computational costs and time-consuming search time. To bypass this issue, we used SBERT, which adds a pooling layer to the BERT model's output to create fixed-sized sentence embeddings. Three pooling layers can be used as CLS-token, computing the mean of all output vectors (MEAN-strategy) and computing a max of the output vectors (MAX-strategy). To construct semantically relevant phrase embeddings and to update the weights, a siamese network is applied to fine-tuned in SBERT. There are several loss functions for fine-tuned SBERT that can be used, and this study focuses on three loss functions: triplet loss, cross-entropy loss, and multiple negative loss functions. The approach is efficient in terms of search time while preserving the accuracy of BERT on STS tasks [15].

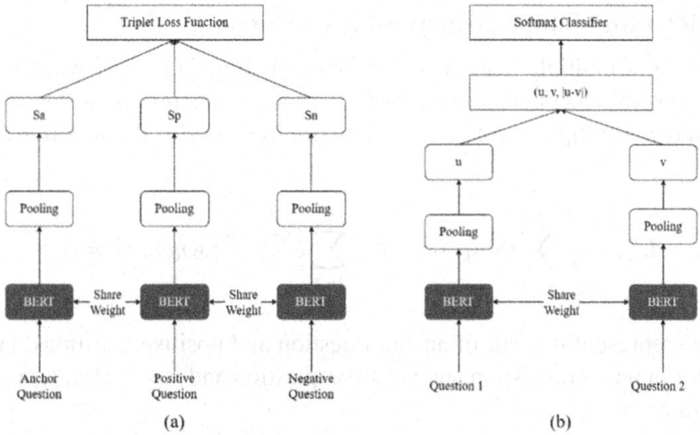

Fig. 6. SBERT with triplet loss function (a), cross-entropy loss function (b)

3.4.1 SBERT with Triplet Loss Function

The triplet loss function in SBERT (Fig. 6(a)) employs the anchor question, the positive question, and the negative question. The triplet loss function tries to reduce the distance of the anchor question with positive question embedding and increase the distance with negative question embedding simultaneously. The desired embedding is obtained when the distance of the anchor-positive gets longer than the anchor-negative equals a margin m. The loss function can be defined:

$$L = \sum_{i=1}^{N} max(||s_a - s_p|| - ||s_a - s_n|| + m, 0)$$

with s_a, s_p, s_n is the sentence embeddings for anchor, positive, and negative questions respectively; $||\ldots||$ represent the distance metric; margin m ensures that s_p is closer to s_a than s_n.

3.4.2 SBERT with Cross-Entropy Loss Function

The cross-entropy loss function is applied by adding a softmax layer and a cross-entropy loss to learn weight and directly predict a label. The structure of SBERT with cross-entropy loss function is shown in Fig. 6(b). This function is followed where N is the number of pair questions, y_i and $\widehat{y_i}$ are true and predicted values.

$$L = -\frac{1}{N}\sum_{i=1}^{N}(y_i log(\widehat{y_i}) + (1 - y_i) log(1 - \widehat{y_i}))$$

3.4.3 SBERT with Multiple Negatives Loss Function

SBERT utilising a multiple negatives loss function (Fig. 7) is used when the training set only has positive pairs. The function focuses on balancing the distance of a positive question over multiple negative questions simultaneously. The loss function can be defined as

$$L = -\frac{1}{K}\sum_{i=1}^{K}[S(x_i, y_i) - log\sum_{j=1}^{K} e^{S(x_i, y_j)}]\ where\ (i \neq j)$$

where (x_i, y_i) represent the pair of anchor question and positive questions, (x_i, y_j) represent the pair of anchor question and negative question and $i \neq j$. $S(x_i, y_i)$ is a distance of two questions.

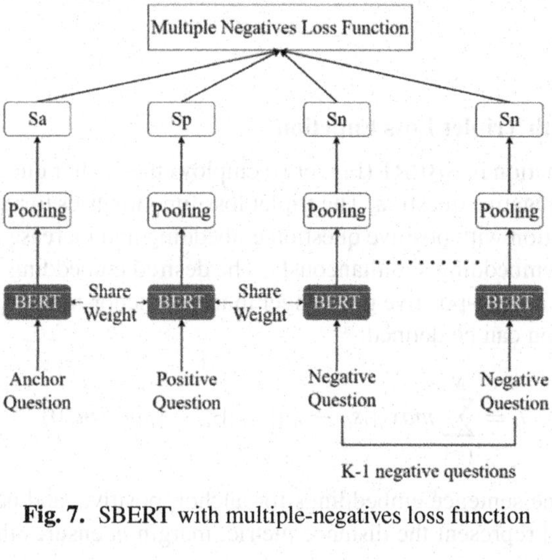

Fig. 7. SBERT with multiple-negatives loss function

3.5 Similarity Measurement Method

We utilise similarity measurement methods to determine the similarity score between each vector representation output of SBERT and each encoded question from the database. Three proposed methods are cosine-similarity, Euclid distance, and Spearman rank correlation coefficient.

3.5.1 Cosine-Similarity

Cosine similarity is a metric for calculate the similarity of two non-zero vectors specified in an inner product space. In other words, it is the dot product of the vectors divided by the product of their lengths. Cosine similarity is the cosine of the angle between two vectors and the result is constrained to the range [0, 1]. Where $\vec{A}$ and $\vec{B}$ are two sentence embeddings vector for multiple-choice question A and B respectively. The formula of cosine-similarity can be defined as

$$sim(\vec{A}, \vec{B}) = cos(\theta) = \frac{A.B}{||A||.||B||} = \frac{\sum_{i=1}^{n} A_i B_i}{\sqrt{\sum_{i=1}^{n} A_i^2}\sqrt{\sum_{i=1}^{n} B_i^2}}$$

3.5.2 Euclid Distance

Euclidean distance is the square root of the sum of squared differences between corresponding elements of the two vectors. In a multidimensional space, the closer two-word vectors are to one another, the more probable it is that their meanings are similar.

$$sim(\vec{A}, \vec{B}) = d(\vec{A}, \vec{B}) = \sqrt{\sum_{i=1}^{n} (A_i - B_i)^2}$$

3.5.3 Spearman's Rank Correlation Coefficient

The Spearman's rank correlation coefficient is a nonparametric measurement method of the correlation between two variables. The value is constrained in the range of [−1, 1] the closer a value is to 1, the more similar two variables are. The formula for computing similarity score between vectors $\vec{A}$ and $\vec{B}$ is:

$$sim\left(\vec{A}, \vec{B}\right) = \rho = 1 - \frac{6\sum_{i=1}^{n}(A_i - B_i)^2}{n(n^2 - 1)}$$

where A_i, B_i is the value of two sentence embedding vectors $\vec{A}$ and $\vec{B}$.

3.6 Evaluation Metric

The F1 score is a machine learning assessment statistic that focuses on a model's performance inside each class rather than its overall performance to evaluate a model's predictive ability. F1 score based on four components which are true positives (TP) - the number of samples correctly predicted as "positive", false positives (FP) - the number of samples wrongly predicted as "positive", true negatives (TN) - the number of samples correctly predicted as "negative", false negatives (FN) - the number of samples wrongly predicted as "negative".

$$F1\ score = \frac{TP}{TP + \frac{1}{2}(FP + FN)}$$

F1 score is useful when the classes are imbalanced. Especially in finding duplicate question cases, when the number of samples duplicates class is significantly smaller than non-duplicates.

4 Implementation and Evaluation

4.1 Implement

Machine learning is implemented in PyTorch. The experiments were conducted on a GPU Nvidia Tesla T4 15 Gb GPU. The encoding model uses two pre-trained sentence transformations models SBERT[2]. The all-mpnet-base-v2 model is trained on a 1 billion sentence pairs dataset with a sequence length limited to 128 tokens, batch size of 1024, and learning rate of 2e−5 with 100,000 steps. The multi-qa-mpnet-base-dot-v1 model is concatenated from total 215 million question-answer pairs dataset to trained and fine-tuned. We fine-tuned SBERT for detecting duplicate multiple-choice questions on our datasets with multiple-negative loss function, 5 epochs, and batch size of 8. The fine-tuned SBERT was compared with other models with different similarity measurement methods. For deciding whether the pair multiple choices are duplicated or not, we set a threshold after calculating the similarity score. If the score crosses the threshold the pair is considered a duplicate.

4.2 Dataset

We collected data from 1242 multiple-choice questions based on the FPT university question bank, the datasets including two types: English which indicates the questions referring to studying skills, common situations in university; Math implies that the problems are probability and statistics, function definitions, etc. The number of English questions and Math questions are 682 and 560 respectively. Table 1 shows the general information of the data statistics. 398 Math questions are in the form of an image or a combination of text and images where the images represent figures, functions, and special characters. Figure 8 shows an illustration of a few multiple-choice questions from the dataset.

Table 1. Data statistic

Information	Value
Corpus size	312811
Vocabulary size	10306
Average length of question	252

To better understand the question domain, we use nltk (Natural Language Toolkit) to display word frequency that appears commonly in the dataset. Tables 2 and 3 represent the top 5 common words for each question type. In the English type, the domain of words is mostly based on the request for candidates to choose an option when answering the multiple-choice questions, while the domain in the Math type represents the words in the probability and statistics fields.

[2] Pretrained Models-Sentence-Transformers documentation.

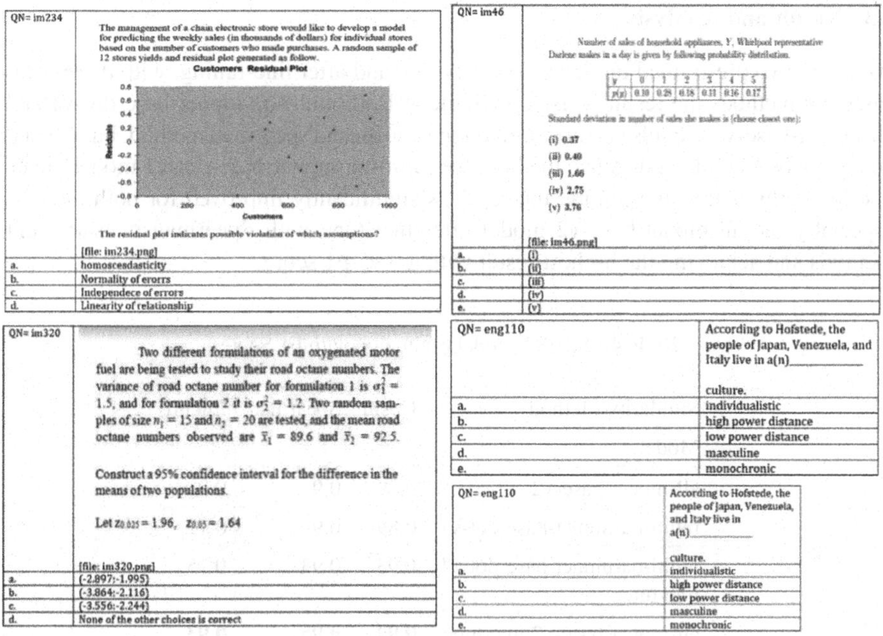

Fig. 8. Examples of the Mcqs in the database

Table 2. Word frequency for English questions types

Word	Value
group	244
following	143
members	132
check	107
option	99

Table 3. Word frequency for Math questions types

Word	Value
probability	216
random	193
none	187
distribution	180
mean	176

4.3 Result and Analysis

We apply two pre-trained models SBERT before and after fine-tuning, with three measurement methods the result is listed in Table 4. Both multi-qa-mpnet-base-dot-v1 and all-mpnet-base-v2 models perform well on the cousin and spearman method, but when it comes to the Euclidean distance method, the multi-qa-mpnet-base-dot-v1 model yields poorly results. After fine-tuning, the result is significantly improved for both models, especially the all-mpnet-base-v2 model after fine tune with Spearman measurement methods and achieving the highest result with a 0.95 F1 score.

Table 4. SBERT model evaluation with F1 Score

Similarity Method Model	Cosin	Spearman	Euclid
all-mpnet-base-v2	0.89	0.9	0.9
multi-qa-mpnet-base-dot-v1	0.89	0.9	0.12
multi-qa-mpnet-base-dot-v1 fine-tune	0.93	0.93	0.15
all-mpnet-base-v2 fine-tune	**0.94**	**0.95**	**0.93**

5 Conclusion and Future Works

This study uses and fine-tunes an end-to-end machine learning architecture that represents questions in text or image form as a vector. The model takes advantage of OCR to extract information from images and vectorize the combination of data in images and text using SBERT. Various similarity measures were examined on the collected dataset, and in the end, the Spearman measure was the best with an F1 score of 0.95. The obtained results show that the proposed method can effectively support question bank management, making the process of adding more questions more efficient by reducing the rate of duplicate multiple-choice questions.

Currently, the constructed test bank only covers a small portion of the questions, which are written only in English. In future work, we aim to tackle the problem of question duplication on an actual question bank of FPT University with different languages such as Vietnamese, Chinese, and Japanese. The work is also a good reference for natural language processing and data mining problems [16–20].

Acknowledgements. This work is part of the DHFPT/2023/01 project funded by the FPT University, Hanoi, Vietnam.

References

1. FPT Education. Accessed https://fpt.com.vn/en/business/education
2. Purohit, V.K., et al.: Design of adaptive question bank development and management system. In: 2nd IEEE International Conference on Parallel, Distributed and Grid Computing, Solan, India, pp. 256–261 (2012)
3. Mia, M.R., Latiful Hoque, A.S.M.: Question bank similarity searching system (QB3S) using NLP and information retrieval technique. In: 1st International Conference on Advances in Science, Engineering and Robotics Technology (ICASERT), Dhaka, Bangladesh, pp. 1–7 (2019)
4. Wang, L., Zhang, L., Jiang, J.: Duplicate question detection with deep learning in stack overflow. IEEE Access **8**, 25964–25975 (2020)
5. Li, Y., et al.: Finding similar medical questions from question answering websites. arXiv: 1810.05983 (2018)
6. Liao, M., Shi, B., Bai, X., Wang, X., Liu, W.: TextBoxes: a fast text detector with a single deep neural network. arXiv:1611.06779 (2016)
7. Zhou, X., et al.: EAST: an efficient and accurate scene text detector. In: IEEE Conference on Computer Vision and Pattern Recognition (CVPR), Honolulu, HI, USA, pp. 2642–2651 (2017)
8. Baek, Y., Lee, B., Han, D., Yun, S., Lee, H.: Character region awareness for text detection. In: IEEE/CVF Conference on Computer Vision and Pattern Recognition (CVPR), Long Beach, CA, USA, pp. 9357–9366 (2019)
9. Jaderberg, M., Simonyan, K., Vedaldi, A., Zisserman, A.: Reading text in the wild with convolutional neural networks. arXiv:1412.1842 (2014)
10. Shi, B., Bai, X., Yao, C.: An end-to-end trainable neural network for image-based sequence recognition and its application to scene text recognition. arXiv:1507.05717 (2015)
11. Gokul, P.P., Akhil, B.K., Shiva, K.K.M.: Sentence similarity detection in Malayalam language using cosine similarity. In: 2017 2nd IEEE International Conference on Recent Trends in Electronics, Information & Communication Technology (RTEICT), Bangalore, India, pp. 221–225 (2017)
12. Dhar, A., Dash, N.S., Roy, K.: Application of TF-IDF feature for categorizing documents of online Bangla web text corpus. In: Bhateja, V., Coello Coello, C., Satapathy, S., Pattnaik, P. (eds.) Intelligent Engineering Informatics. AISC, vol. 695, pp. 51–59. Springer, Singapore (2018). https://doi.org/10.1007/978-981-10-7566-7_6
13. Devlin, J., Chang, M.W., Lee, K., Toutanova, K.: BERT: pre-training of deep bidirectional transformers for language understanding. arXiv:1810.04805 (2018)
14. Reimers, N., Gurevych, I.: Sentence-BERT: sentence embeddings using Siamese BERT-networks. arXiv:1908.10084 (2019)
15. Thanh, T.N., Nha, N.K., Hieu, N.K., Anh, N.K., Khoat, T.Q.: Utilizing SBERT for finding similar questions in community question answering. In: 13th International Conference on Knowledge and Systems Engineering (KSE), Bangkok, Thailand, 2021, pp. 1–6 (2021)
16. Hung, P.D., Loan, B.T.: Automatic Vietnamese passport recognition on Android phones. In: Dang, T.K., Küng, J., Takizawa, M., Chung, T.M. (eds.) FDSE 2020. CCIS, vol. 1306, pp. 476–485. Springer, Singapore (2020). https://doi.org/10.1007/978-981-33-4370-2_36
17. Duy, H.A., Hung, P.D.: Kernel analysis for handwritten digit recognition using support vector machine on MNIST dataset. In: Yang, X.S., Sherratt, S., Dey, N., Joshi, A. (eds.) Proceedings of Seventh International Congress on Information and Communication Technology. LNNS, vol. 465, pp. 131–142. Springer, Singapore (2023). https://doi.org/10.1007/978-981-19-2397-5_13

18. Hung, P.D., Giang, T.M., Nam, L.H.: Vietnamese speech command recognition using recurrent neural networks. (IJACSA) Int. J. Adv. Comput. Sci. Appl. **10**(7), 194–201 (2019)
19. Giang, T.M., Hung, P.D.: Relation classification based on Vietnamese Covid-19 information using BERT model with typed entity markers. In: Dang, T.K., Küng, J., Chung, T.M., Takizawa, M. (eds.) FDSE 2021. CCIS, vol. 1500, pp. 460–468. Springer, Singapore (2021). https://doi.org/10.1007/978-981-16-8062-5_33
20. Tram, N.N., Hung, P.D.: Analysing hot Facebook users posts' sentiment using deep learning. In: Hassanien, A.E., Bhattacharyya, S., Chakrabati, S., Bhattacharya, A., Dutta, S. (eds.) Emerging Technologies in Data Mining and Information Security. AISC, vol. 1300, pp. 561–569. Springer, Singapore (2021). https://doi.org/10.1007/978-981-33-4367-2_53

A Context-Aware Approach for Improving Dialog Act Detection in a Multilingual Conversational Platform

Hai-Yen Vu[1] and Phuong Le-Hong[1,2](✉)

[1] FPT Technology Research Institute, FPT University, Hanoi, Vietnam
yenvh2@fpt.com.vn
[2] Vietnam National University, Hanoi, Vietnam
phuonglh@vnu.edu.vn

Abstract. This paper proposes a method to exploit and integrate dialogue context information into two neural models for dialogue act detection, including recurrent networks and transformers networks. The proposed models are evaluated on two standard benchmark datasets for English and Vietnamese. Extensive experimental results show that our method achieves a significant better performance in comparison to baseline results. Our proposed method has been deployed as a core component of a commercial conversational platform, effectively serving millions of clients in multiple markets.

1 Introduction

There have been important advances in the research of task-oriented dialogue systems in recent years which are attributed to two reasons. On the one hand, this is due to the public availability of large dialogue datasets like DSTC2 [1], MultiWOZ [2], CrossWOZ [3]. The most notable corpus is MultiWOZ, a large-scale multi-domain dataset that consists of crowd-sourced human-to-human dialogues. On the other hand, this is because of the prosperity of strong neural architectures for task-oriented dialogue models such as sequence-to-sequence [4], user modeling [5], transfer learning [6], few-shot learning with pretrained auto-regressive models [7], schema-driven prompting using large language models [8].

In a pipelined task-oriented dialogue system, there are different components which are chained together including natural language understanding (NLU), dialogue state tracking (DST), dialogue policy learning (DPL), and natural language generation (NLG). This paper concerns with the NLU component. In this task, the system takes an utterance as input and outputs the corresponding semantic representation, namely, a dialogue act. The task can be divided into two subtasks: intent/act detection and slot tagging which identifies the value of a slot. The dialogue act detection is the most crucial component in task-oriented dialog systems, not only for immediately following components but also for later ones. The DST component takes as input user dialogue act and encodes user

N. T. Nguyen et al. (Eds.): ICCCI 2023, LNAI 14162, pp. 231–242, 2023.
https://doi.org/10.1007/978-3-031-41456-5_18

goals into the predefined system state. The NLG component converts a dialog act represented in a semantic form into a response in natural language.

In this paper, we make the following main contributions:

- We present and compare two neural models for dialogue act detection. The proposed models make use of different sentence encoders, including recurrent neural network and the transformers network.
- We propose a method to exploit and integrate dialogue context information into the models. Extensive experiments demonstrate that context-aware neural models give better accuracy than those without context.
- In addition to English, we perform evaluation on a task-oriented corpus in Vietnamese and also obtain significant improvement. Our findings are potentially valid for many languages. This method has been deployed in a core NLU component of the commercial FPT. AI[1] conversational platform, effectively serving millions API requests of chatbots and voicebots in international markets, across multiple industry sectors, notably in banking, finance, securities and insurance.

The remainder of this paper is structured as follows. Section 2 describes the different neural network models in use and our proposed method. Section 3 presents experimental results on two datasets. Finally, we provide concluding remarks and discuss future work in Sect. 4.

2 Methods

We use two deep learning models in this work including recurrent neural networks and transformers. In this section, we first briefly present the two foundation models and then describe our approach which is built upon them.

2.1 Recurrent Neural Networks and LSTM

Recurrent Neural Network (RNNs) process input sequence of arbitrarily length via the recursive application of a transition function on *a hidden state vector*. More precisely, it takes as input a list of input vectors $x_1, x_2, \ldots, x_n$ together with an initial state vector s_0, and returns a list of state vectors $s_1, s_2, \ldots, s_n$ as well as a list of output vectors $y_0, y_1, \ldots, y_n$. Mathematically, we have a recursively defined function $f(\cdot)$ that takes as input a state vector s_{t-1} and an input vector x_t and produces a new state vector s_t. An additional function $g(\cdot)$ is used to map a state vector s_t to an output vector y_t. That is $s_t = f(s_{t-1}, x_t)$ and $y_t = g(s_t)$. The functions f, g are the same across the sequence positions. The parameter vector θ is also shared across all time steps. Figure 1 shows the graphical representation of an RNN.

The common transition function f used in RNNs is an affine transformation followed by a point-wise non-linearity such as the hyperbolic tangent function:

$$s_t = \tanh\left(W x_t + U s_{t-1} + b\right).$$

[1] https://fpt.ai/.

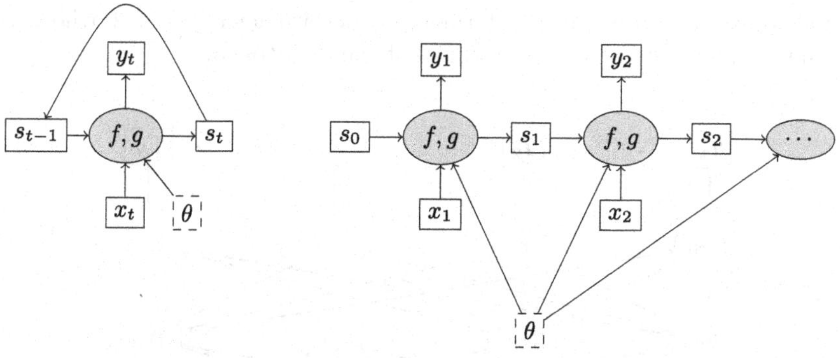

Fig. 1. Graphical representation of an RNN. The left figure shows the recursive definition. The right figure shows the unrolled version. The parameter vector θ is shared across all time steps.

However, this transition function has a problem in that it may make the gradient vector grow or decay exponentially over long sequence during training [9]. Long Short-Term Memory (LSTM) network is a special type of RNNs which was designed to overcome the exploding or vanishing gradients problem of simple RNNs. The main idea of LSTMs is that they maintain *a memory cell* that is able to preserve state over a long period of time. While there are numerous variants of LSTMs, in this work, we use the version as in [10].

The LSTM unit at the t-th word consists of a collection of multi-dimensional vectors, including an input gate i_t, a forget gate f_t, an output gate o_t, a memory cell c_t, and a hidden state s_t. The unit takes as input a d-dimensional input vector x_t, the previous hidden state s_{t-1}, the previous memory cell c_{t-1}, and calculates the new vectors using the following six equations:

$$\begin{aligned} i_t &= \sigma\left(W^i x_t + U^i s_{t-1} + b^i\right); & u_t &= \tanh\left(W^u x_t + U^u s_{t-1} + b^u\right) \\ f_t &= \sigma\left(W^f x_t + U^f s_{t-1} + b^f\right); & c_t &= i_t \odot u_t + f_t \odot c_{t-1} \\ o_t &= \sigma\left(W^o x_t + U^o s_{t-1} + b^o\right); & s_t &= o_t \odot \tanh(c_t) \end{aligned}$$

where σ denotes the logistic sigmoid function, the dot product $\odot$ denotes the element-wise multiplication of vectors, W and U are weight matrices and b are bias vectors. The LSTM unit at t-th word receives the corresponding word embedding as input vector x_t.

2.2 Transformers and BERT

Transformers models [11] dispense entirely with recurrence mechanisms and rely solely on the *attention mechanism*, which significantly decreases training time.

Introduced in late 2018, BERT [12] stands for Bidirectional Encoder Representation from Transformers, which is designed to pretrain deep bidirectional language representations by jointly training on both left and right contexts of a given word in all layers of the model. The core of BERT's model architecture is a multi-layer bidirectional transformer encoder as shown in Fig. 2, where Trm are transformers and E_k are embeddings of the k-th token.

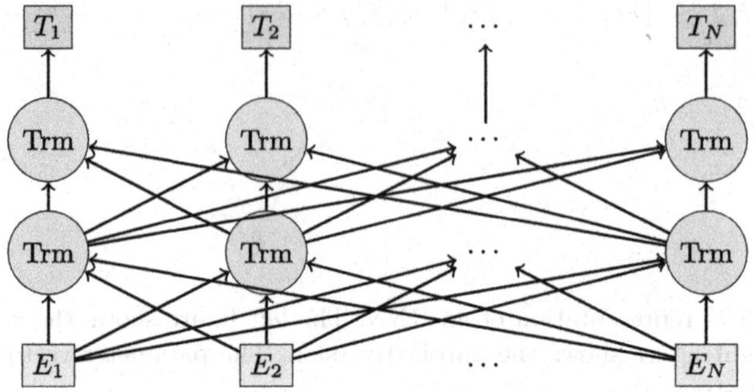

Fig. 2. BERT architecture with multiple transformer blocks [12]

Each transformer block consists of two sub-layers, a multi-head self-attention mechanism followed by a simple position-wise fully-connected feed-forward network. Residual connections exist around each of the two sub-layers, and dropout, following after each sub-layer, provides layer normalization.

In essence, the multi-head attention layer in the transformer architecture encodes a value V according to the attention weights from query Q to key K. If $\mathcal{G}_f$ is a position-wise feed-forward network, then the transformer $\mathcal{F}(Q, K, V)$ computes an output as follows

$$O = V + \mathcal{G}_f(\texttt{MultiHead}(Q, K, V)),$$

where Q, K, V, O are matrices of size $N \times o$. The attention mechanism is performed in parallel for each token in the sentence to obtain their updated features in one shot. This parallel computation offers a plus point for transformers over recurrent network models.

A BERT encoder can use different word segmentation algorithms, including byte-pair encoding – a subtoken segmentation method that encodes rare and unknown tokens as sequences of subtoken units [13]. In this work we use token representation for the BERT model and leave the subtoken representation for future work.

2.3 Context-Aware Dialogue Act Detection

In this subsection, we first present the baseline model and then propose improved versions where dialogue context information is incorporated. The first model uses a bidirectional multilayer LSTM as utterance encoder. The last hidden state of the top LSTM layer is then fed into a single-layer feed-forward neural network and the last softmax layer to perform act classification, as shown in Fig. 3.

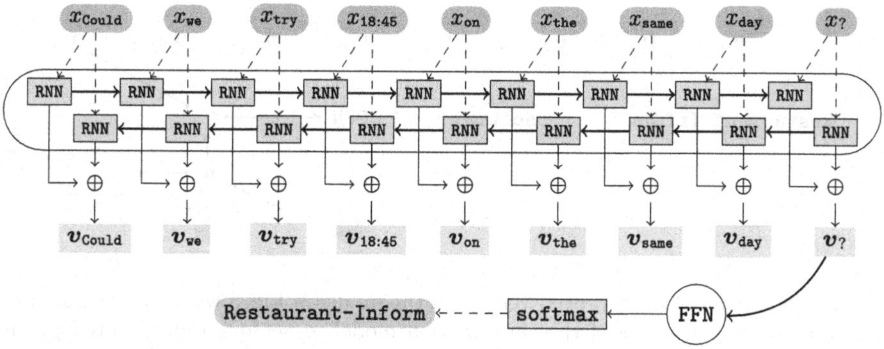

Fig. 3. Illustration of the baseline model. The embeddings x_i of the tokens in an utterance are learned by a multilayer bidirectional LSTM. The last output of the LSTM is fed into a feed-forward network (FFN) before passing through a softmax layer to perform multiway classification.

The second model that we experiment with in this work is similar to the baseline model but the LSTM encoder is replaced with the BERT encoder. Pre-trained language models, especially BERT-based models, have helped produce improvements for a variety of tasks. However, in this work, we train the BERT model from scratch on the same training set without using any pretrained BERT models. We opt for this choice in order to compare models fairly in a pure supervised learning approach. Experiments with the fine-tuning and transfer-learning approach is left for future work.

Both of two models above treat each utterance independently. This observation inspires us to come up with a research question: "Can dialogue history help improve dialogue act prediction?". The third model aims to answer this question. We define the dialogue context at the t-th utterance of a dialogue to be the set of all dialogue acts known up to time $t-1$. For instance, the dialogue context at the fifth utterance of the example dialogue shown in Table 1 is the set {Hotel-Inform, Hotel-Request, Booking-Inform}. Intuitively, this context may provide valuable information to help predict the fifth dialogue acts of {Booking-Inform, Hotel-Inform} better.

Figure 4 illustrates the improved model. The colored vectors at the lower right of the figure represent multihot act vectors which are added together into vector $\boldsymbol{w}$. Two contextualized vectors $\boldsymbol{v}$ and $\boldsymbol{w}$ are then concatenated before being passed to the FFN for act classification.

3 Experimental Results

3.1 Datasets

In this work, we conduct experiments on two dialogue datasets. The first dataset is MultiWOZ. Multi-Domain Wizard-of-Oz dataset (MultiWOZ) is a

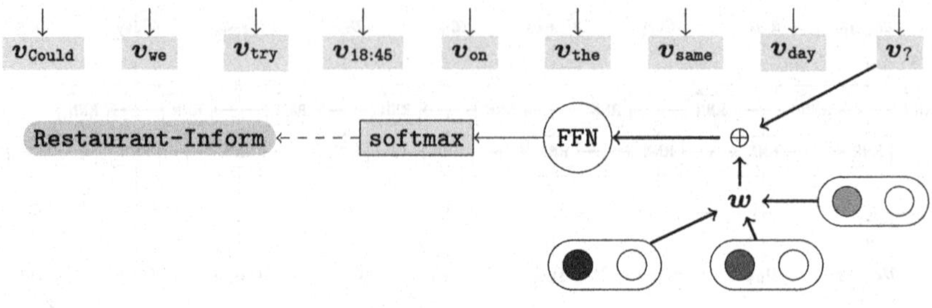

Fig. 4. Illustration of an improved version of the model in Fig. 3 where act vectors are integrated as core features of the classification model. $\boldsymbol{v}$ vectors are generated by an encoder (either LSTM or BERT) as shown in Fig. 3 while $\boldsymbol{w}$ if a bag-of-act multihot vector. The corresponding $\boldsymbol{v}$ and $\boldsymbol{w}$ vectors are then concatenated.

fully-labeled collection of human-human written conversations spanning over 7 domains. At a size of 10,437 dialogues, it is at least one order of magnitude larger than all previous annotated task-oriented corpora. The original version of the dataset was introduced in 2018 [2,14]. A newer, corrected versions were introduced later in 2019 [15]. The newest, corrected version of the dataset was introduced in 2020 [16]. It is this latest version that we use in our experiments. There are 3,406 single-domain dialogues that include booking if the domain allows for that and 7,032 multi-domain dialogues consisting of at least 2 up to 5 domains. The corpus was randomly split into a train, test and development set. The test and development sets contain 1,000 examples each. Table 1 shows a complete dialogue in the development set. There are 113,552 and 14,748 and 14,744 utterances in the training, development and test set, respectively.

The second dataset is also a multi-domain task-oriented dialogue corpus, which is the first dialogue corpus towards building automated conversations in e-commerce. The corpus is fully labeled with rich information on dialogue structure and contextual information. It contains 1,910 dialogues, with a total of more than 18,000 turns in four domains: ProductInfo, OrderInfo, Shipping and Chatchit [17]. This dataset is split randomly into a training, development and test set with the ratio 80%, 10% and 10% respectively.

3.2 Experimental Settings

All models are initialized with random token vectors rather than reference pre-trained word vectors. This allows to establish results in a pure supervised learning setting rather than a semi-supervised or transfer learning setting. The models are all trained by the Adam optimizer [18] with a learning rate of 5×10^{-4}. We use the cross-entropy loss function for multiway classification as usual. Given a score distribution output of the softmax layer, top two labels with highest scores are selected. All models are trained in 50 epochs.

We first evaluate the performance of the LSTM model with respect to the token embedding size varying in the set $\{16, 32, 64\}$, with recurrent size varying in the set $\{32, 64, 128, 256, 512\}$, and with one, two or three recurrent layers. This experiment allows investigation of the effect of these hyperparameters on the performance of the LSTM encoder. Each model is trained repeatedly five times with different randomly initialized parameters, and their scores are averaged.

In the experiments with the BERT models, we vary the number of transformer blocks (or layers) and the number of self-attention heads in the set $\{2, 4, 8\}$, the hidden size in the set $\{16, 32, 64\}$[2]. The intermediate size (i.e., feed-forward size) is either 32 or 64. These varied hyperparameters allow us to evaluate the scalability of the models, i.e. how their performance changes as they are made to have more parameters or layers. As in recurrent models, each BERT model is trained repeatedly five times with different randomly initialized parameters, and their averaged scores are reported. We observed that training a BERT model requires significantly more time than that of recurrent models.

All the models presented in this work are implemented by ourselves in the Scala programming language. We use the BigDL library[3] as the deep learning framework. These libraries provide an end-to-end pipeline for applying AI models and high-level machine learning workflow for automating machine learning tasks. Furthermore, we can quickly code inline with Apache Spark code for distributed training and inference, easily scale out on multiple commodity servers, without relying on expensive GPU devices. Our code and detailed experimental results are publicly available in a GitHub repository.[4]

3.3 Evaluation Metrics

Since each utterance can have multiple acts or intents, we need to use a multilabel classification metrics. Because the labels are not mutually exclusive, the predictions and true labels are now vectors of label sets, rather than vectors of labels. Multilabel metrics, therefore, extend the fundamental ideas of precision, recall, etc. to operations on sets. For example, a true positive for a given class now occurs when that class exists in the predicted set and it exists in the true label set, for a specific data point.

We define the label set as $\mathcal{L} = \{\ell_1, \ell_2, \dots, \ell_M\}$. There are N utterances, each utterance i has the correct label set L_i and a prediction set P_i, for all $i = 1, 2, \dots, N$. Note that the set all unique labels is given by $\mathcal{L} = \cup_{i=1}^{N} L_i$. We use the following evaluation metrics:

[2] Note that in transformers-based models, the hidden size must be a multiple of the number of self attention heads.

[3] https://github.com/intel-analytics/BigDL.

[4] https://github.com/phuonglh/vlp/, under the `woz` module.

Table 1. An example dialogue in the MultiWOZ dataset with annotated dialogue acts in multiple domains. There are 20 turns, user utterances are in italic font.

Turn	Utterance	Acts
0	*While in Cambridge I need a hotel that has free parking and free wifi.*	[Hotel-Inform]
1	There are 29 hotels that meet your needs. Would you like to narrow your search by area and/or price range?	[Hotel-Inform, Hotel-Request]
2	*Yes, please. I need a cheap hotel in the city centre.*	[Hotel-Inform]
3	The Alexander Bed and Breakfast and the El Shaddai both fit your specifications. Would you like me to book either of those?	[Booking-Inform, Hotel-Inform]
4	*Alexander Bed and Breakfast sounds nice. What kind of hotel is it?*	[Hotel-Inform]
5	Alexander bed and breakfast is a guesthouse, it has a 4 star rating. Would you like me to book you a room?	[Booking-Inform, Hotel-Inform]
6	*No, but I would like the address, please.*	[Hotel-Request]
7	The Alexander Bed & Breakfast is located at 56 saint barnabas road. Can I help you with something else today?	[Hotel-Inform, general-reqmore]
8	*I also need an international restaurant in the same price range as the hotel.*	[Restaurant-Inform]
9	I have an African restaurant and some European restaurants located in the city centre. Any preferences?	[Restaurant-Inform, Restaurant-Select]
10	*Do you have a restaurant that serves international food, that's in the cheap range?*	[Restaurant-Inform]
11	Alright, I have one location for that: The Missing sock. Would you like me to make you reservations here?	[Booking-Inform, Restaurant-Inform]
12	*Can you book a table for 6 people at 19:45 this Wednesday*	[Restaurant-Inform]
13	I am sorry, they cannot accommodate six in that time slot. Would you like to try a different time?	[Booking-NoBook, Booking-Request]
14	*Could we try 18:45 on the same day?*	[Restaurant-Inform]
15	Booking was successful for 18:45. The table will be reserved for 15 min. Reference number is: 5D209RMX.	[Booking-Book]
16	*Great, that's all need for now, you've been very helpful!*	[general-thank]
17	Is there anything else I can help you with today?	[general-reqmore]
18	*No, that's it. Goodbye!*	[general-bye]
19	Thank you for contacting the Cambridge TownInfo centre today!	[general-bye]

$$\text{Accuracy} = \frac{1}{N}\sum_{i=1}^{N} \frac{|P_i \cap L_i|}{|P_i| + |L_i| - |P_i \cap L_i|}$$

$$\text{F1 Measure} = \frac{1}{N}\sum_{i=1}^{N} 2\frac{|P_i \cap L_i|}{|P_i| \cdot |L_i|}$$

$$\text{Micro F1 Measure} = 2\frac{\sum_{i=1}^{N} |P_i \cap L_i|}{2\sum_{i=1}^{N} |P_i \cap L_i| + \sum_{i=1}^{N} |L_i \setminus P_i| + \sum_{i=1}^{N} |P_i \setminus L_i|}$$

These metrics are provided by the Apache Spark machine learning library, which are readily available for our evaluation.[5]

[5] https://spark.apache.org/docs/latest/mllib-evaluation-metrics.html.

Table 2. Performance of the single layer LSTM model with respect to the token embedding size (e) and the encoder size (r – the number of hidden units of the LSTM) on the development set of MultiWOZ

e	r	Accuracy	F1	Micro F1
16	32	0.7508	0.8004	0.7842
16	64	0.7655	0.8139	0.7998
16	128	0.7770	0.8228	0.8095
32	32	0.7529	0.8028	0.7878
32	64	0.7717	0.8174	0.8030
32	128	0.7811	0.8261	0.8125
64	32	0.7670	0.8149	0.8008
64	64	0.7805	0.8260	0.8122
64	128	**0.7848**	**0.8293**	**0.8162**

3.4 Results

In the first set of experiments, we conduct experiments of the LSTM model on the MultiWOZ dataset. We first fix a single recurrent layer and observe the effect of two hyperparameters, i.e., token embedding size and encoder size to the performance. Table 2 shows the scores on the development set.

We observe that the scores improve when the embedding and encoder sizes increase. The best F1 score is 82.93% with $e = 64$ and $r = 128$. We also observe the same tendency when using two or three LSTM layers. In particular, with two or three recurrent layers, the best F1 score is 83.08%, the best micro F1 score is 81.80; both are obtained by using $e = 64$ and $r = 128$. Using these best hyperparameters, on the test set the LSTM model achieves the scores of 78.46%, 83.03%, and 81.64% of accuracy, F1 score and micro F1 score, respectively.

In the second set of experiments, we run the BERT model on this corpus. The number of transformer blocks is varied in the set $\{2, 4, 8\}$, the number of self-attention heads is also varied in the set $\{2, 4, 8\}$, the hidden size in the set $\{16, 32, 64\}$, and the intermediate size (i.e., feed-forward size) in the set $\{32, 64\}$. Table 3 shows a portion of experimental results on the development set. The best development scores are obtained with 8 attention heads, 4 transformer blocks, a hidden size of 32 and an intermediate size of 32. Using these best hyperparameters, on the test set the BERT model achieves the scores of 79.15%, 83.70% and 82.38% of accuracy, F1 score and micro F1 score, respectively. These scores are about 0.7% of absolute points better than the LSTM models.

In the third set of experiments, we run LSTM and BERT models on the Vietnamese corpus. For the LSTM models, the best scores on the development set are obtained when $e = 64, r = 256$ and a single recurrent layer. At these chosen hyperparameters, the test accuracy, F1 score and micro F1 score is 52.77%, 61.26% and 58.92%, respectively. For the BERT models, the best test scores are 60.61%, 67.45% and 64.22% respectively. The performance gap between the

Table 3. Performance of the BERT model on the development set of the MultiWOZ dataset. h is the number of attention heads, k is the hidden size, b is the number of transformer blocks, and f is the intermediate size (aka feed-forward size)

h	k	b	f	Accuracy	F1	Micro F1
8	16	4	32	0.7721	0.8203	0.8061
8	16	4	64	0.7746	0.8223	0.8086
8	32	4	32	**0.7909**	**0.8358**	**0.8231**
2	16	8	32	0.7735	0.8219	0.8085
2	16	8	64	0.7751	0.8237	0.8103
4	16	8	32	0.7745	0.8235	0.8106
4	16	8	64	0.7740	0.8227	0.8092
8	16	8	32	0.7793	0.8266	0.8134
8	16	8	64	0.7785	0.8255	0.8124

LSTM and BERT models are about 7%, much larger than those on the English corpus. It seems that the Vietnamese dialogue dataset is more difficult than the English dataset – the best obtained scores are much lower.

Finally, in the fourth set of experiments, we run the improved version of LSTM and BERT models on the two corpus using their best hyperparameters optimized on their development sets. With dialogue context information integrated, the improved models outperform significantly their baseline versions. The average score improvement is about 0.56% of absolute F1 points on the English dataset and about 0.88% of absolute F1 points on the Vietnamese dataset.[6]

In summary, the following table shows the summarized test F1 scores of the proposed models on two datasets. The plus sign indicates the improved model where dialogue context information is integrated:

Model	English	Vietnamese
	F1 (%)	F1 (%)
LSTM	83.03	61.26
LSTM+	**83.58**	**62.23**
BERT	83.70	67.45
BERT+	**84.24**	**68.32**

These empirical results confirm our research question that the global dialogue context information helps improve dialogue act prediction.

[6] Detailed experimental results and code are available on the GitHub repository.

4 Conclusion

In this work, we have presented a method to integrate dialogue context information into two neural models for improving dialogue act detection. Extensive experiments demonstrate that context-aware models achieve significantly better performance on two standard task-oriented dialogue benchmarks for English and Vietnamese. Our findings are potentially valid for many languages. Our method has been deployed in the core NLU component of FPT. AI, a leading commercial conversational platform, effectively serving millions of monthly requests in chatbot and voicebot applications. The platform provides chatbot and voicebot services across multiple industry sectors, notably in banking, finance, securities and insurance. It served about 180 million API requests in 2022, not including requests deployed for on-premise contracts.

We proposed a simple bag-of-act method in this work where the order of previous acts is not taken into account. An alternative way is to use a sequence-of-act method where the order of acts are kept and their representation can be learned by a sequence model. We believe that such a more complex treatment of dialogue act context may improve upon the current method. This line of research is left for a follow up work. Finally, it is not our purpose in this work to outperform the state-of-the-art performance of dialogue act detection method but to test our scientific hypothesis on the usefulness of dialogue act history. For this reason, we choose a purely supervised learning method and not opt for the most performant method like fine-tuning pretrained models. Integration of rich dialogue context information into pretrained large language models is another interesting line of research that we aim for in future work.

References

1. Henderson, M., Thomson, B., Williams, J.D.: The second dialog state tracking challenge. In: Proceedings of the 15th Annual Meeting of the Special Interest Group on Discourse and Dialogue (SIGDIAL), pp. 263–272. Philadelphia, PA, U.S.A.: Association for Computational Linguistics (2014)
2. Budzianowski, P., et al.: MultiWOZ - a large-scale multi-domain wizard-of-Oz dataset for task-oriented dialogue modelling. In: Proceedings of the 2018 Conference on Empirical Methods in Natural Language Processing (EMNLP) (2018)
3. Zhu, Q., Huang, K., Zhang, Z., Zhu, X., Huang, M.: CrossWOZ: a large-scale Chinese cross-domain task-oriented dialogue dataset. Trans. Assoc. Comput. Linguist. **8**, 281–295 (2020)
4. Lei, W., Jin, X., Kan, M.Y., Ren, Z., He, X., Yin, D.: Sequicity: Simplifying task-oriented dialogue systems with single sequence-to-sequence architectures. In: Proceedings of the 56th Annual Meeting of the Association for Computational Linguistics, vol. 1 (Long Papers), pp. 1437–1447. Melbourne, Australia: Association for Computational Linguistics (2018)
5. Gür, I., Hakkani-Tür, D., Tür, G., Shah, P.: User modeling for task oriented dialogues. In: *2018 IEEE Spoken Language Technology Workshop (SLT)*, pp. 900–906 (2018)

6. Lin, Z., Madotto, A., Winata, G.I., Fung, P.: MinTL: minimalist transfer learning for task-oriented dialogue systems. In: Proceedings of the 2020 Conference on Empirical Methods in Natural Language Processing (EMNLP), pp. 3391–3405. Association for Computational Linguistics (2020)
7. Peng, B., et al.: Few-shot natural language generation for task-oriented dialog. In: Findings of the Association for Computational Linguistics: EMNLP 2020, pp. 172–182. Association for Computational Linguistics (2020)
8. Lee, C.-H., Cheng, H., Ostendorf, M.: Dialogue state tracking with a language model using schema-driven prompting. In: Proceedings of the 2021 Conference on Empirical Methods in Natural Language Processing. pp. 4937–4949. Online and Punta Cana, Dominican Republic: Association for Computational Linguistics (2021)
9. Pascanu, R., Mikolov, T., Bengio, Y.: On the difficulty of training recurrent neural networks. In: Proceedings of ICML, Atlanta, Georgia, USA (2013)
10. Graves, A.: Generating sequences with recurrent neural networks (2013). arXiv preprint arXiv:1308.0850
11. Vaswani, A., et al.: Attention is all you need. In: Guyon, I., et al. (eds.) Advances in Neural Information Processing Systems, vol. 30. Curran Associates Inc (2017)
12. Devlin, J., Chang, M.-W., Lee, K., Toutanova, K.: BERT: pre-training of deep bidirectional transformers for language understanding. In: Proceedings of NAACL, Minnesota, USA, 2019, pp. 1–16 (2019)
13. Sennrich, R., Haddow, B., Birch, A.: Neural machine translation of rare words with subword units. In: Proceedings of the 54th Annual Meeting of the Association for Computational Linguistics, Berlin, Germany, 2016, pp. 1715–1725 (2016)
14. Ramadan, O., Budzianowski, P., Gasic, M.: Large-scale multi-domain belief tracking with knowledge sharing. In: Proceedings of the 56th Annual Meeting of the Association for Computational Linguistics, vol. 2, pp. 432–437 (2018)
15. Eric, M., et al.: MultiWOZ 2.1: multi-domain dialogue state corrections and state tracking baselines. arXiv preprint arXiv:1907.01669 (2019)
16. Zang, X., Rastogi, A., Sunkara, S., Gupta, R., Zhang, J., Chen, J.: MultiWOZ 2.2: a dialogue dataset with additional annotation corrections and state tracking baselines. In: Proceedings of the 2nd Workshop on Natural Language Processing for Conversational AI, ACL 2020, pp. 109–117 (2020)
17. Luong, C.T., Le-Hong, P., Tran, T.O.: A rich task-oriented dialogue corpus in Vietnamese. Lang. Res. Eval. 1–20 (2022)
18. Kingma, D.P., Ba, J.: Adam: a method for stochastic optimization. In: Bengio, Y., LeCun, Y. (eds.) Proceedings of the 3rd International Conference on Learning Representations, ICLR 2015, pp. 1–15. San Diego, CA, USA (2015)

Data Mining and Machine Learning

Efficient Association Rules Minimization Using a Double-Stage Quine-McCluskey-Based Approach

Lidia Bedhouche, Mohamed Amir Koalal, Alaidine Ben Ayed, and Ismaïl Biskri(✉)

Université du Québec à Trois-Rivières, Trois-Rivières, Canada
{Bedhouche,Koalal,Benayed,Biskri}@uqtr.ca

Abstract. Association rules are used to identify relationships between variables in large datasets. They help us explain obtained results in a transaction database by uncovering associations between items. One major limitation of association rules is the combinatorial explosion that occurs when the number of constructed rules is enormous. Several state-of-the-art techniques try to define a given threshold to overcome this issue; Rules with scores below previously established thresholds are deleted. Nevertheless, those threshold-based strategies have often implied the loss of salient association rules, which have yet to be scored higher than the established threshold because their context of extraction is not recurrent. Ditto, thresholds are usually established in a quasi-arbitrary way.

This paper proposes a novel Quine-McCluskey-based double-stage approach that effectively reduces the number of association rules. The Quine-McCluskey technique is widely used in simplifying Boolean logic expressions. First, the number of initial association rules is reduced through the Quine-McCluskey technique. Next, we optimize the salient information loss rate. Conducted experiments show that the proposed approach significantly reduces the number of rules while keeping salient information.

Keywords: Data mining · Association rules minimization · Quine-McCluskey approach

1 Introduction

The computing power available on computers nowadays and the massive increase in data volumes urged the emergence of data mining techniques to ensure better decision-making. Data mining has remarkably evolved thanks to artificial intelligence and big-data developments. Wherever there is data, data mining is applicable. Indeed, all transactions generate data in different formats (text, images, etc.). Professionals use data mining techniques to automatically identify and extract the most crucial information and analyze it later.

Association rules, first introduced by Agrawal et al. in 1933 [2], are a subset of information retrieval techniques. They are usually used to study and analyze databases

N. T. Nguyen et al. (Eds.): ICCCI 2023, LNAI 14162, pp. 245–255, 2023.
https://doi.org/10.1007/978-3-031-41456-5_19

to discover relationships between elements often used together. The use of association rules allows extracting the essential information with an explicability effect that provides the information in a more accessible format while avoiding the black box effect of abstract representation and increasing data volume. Nevertheless, this method can generate a large number of association rules, some of which are redundant and irrelevant [1]. The evaluation of association rule extraction algorithms is mainly based on optimality, execution time, completeness, and memory consumption. The main challenge for those algorithms is to reduce the number of association rules while maintaining valuable and essential ones.

In this work, we propose a novel double-stage approach that effectively reduces the number of association rules. The proposed technique uses a minimization of Boolean functions technique, namely the Quine-McCluskey (QM) method [13, 14, 16]. The latter can be applied to any data type and only requires binarized data. Moreover, no parameters or metrics are required from the user. Our experiments show that the proposed approach significantly reduces the number of rules while keeping the most salient information.

The rest of this paper is broken down as follows: the second section describes related work on association rules. The third one details the QM-based association rules reduction. The fourth section reports and discusses experimental results and the fifth section puts forth conclusions.

2 Related Work

2.1 Association Rules

Association rules are a data mining technique used to discover patterns in large data sets by examining the relationships between different data elements. These patterns can be used to predict future outcomes and other predictions about specific subsets of the data, such as which customers are likely to buy a particular product.

An association rule is usually presented in the form (If-Then) where:

A(Antecedent) → B(Consequent) [3]. The antecedent presents the triggering event whose outcome is the consequent and $\sum(A, B) \geq 1$ [4]. If we take the example of customers buying items A, B, and also item C, the corresponding association rule takes the following form: A, B → C. Association rules are extracted from transactions and can have several applications in different domains. Each transaction is a piece of data collected in raw form. Depending on the context, each piece of data consists of elements called items, which can be actions, texts, images, sounds, etc.

Let the transaction $T = \{t1, t2, \ldots, ti, \ldots, tn\}$. The elements $ti \in T$ are the items of the transaction T. An item is an element of a transaction. The association rule mining process aims to reveal hidden relationships between different objects. There is no particular method to target the items to be considered, but there are measures to target the items to be ignored, like Support, Trust, and Lift.

The data is usually presented in a table that groups all the transactions, each one identified with a TID (Transaction Identifier) as shown in the following table (Table 1):

To extract an association rule, we first need to identify the frequent items, which are items that, according to a threshold established by the user, appear with a particular

Table 1. An example of transactions.

TID	Transactions
1	*A, B, C*
2	*A, D*
3	*E, D*
4	*A, B, D*
5	*A, B, F, D, C*
6	*B, C, F*

frequency. A rule must have at least two elements: an antecedent and a consequent, i.e., at least two items. Therefore, the next step is to look for item-sets. The latter comprises frequent items that appear together in the database. Like frequent items, item-sets must also be frequent according to the threshold given by the user.

The item-set is given by: $I = \{A, B, C, D, E, F\}$, which is more generally represented by: $I = \{i1, i2, ..., in\}$. Therefore, *Transaction1* in our table is $T1 = \{A, B, C\}$. All the item-sets are elements of I. An item set contains at least two elements, and any empty set or set containing only one item is not considered an item set. An item set is said to be frequent, if and only if: Support $\geq$ minSup. minSup is the minimum support predefined by the user.

An A $\rightarrow$ B rule is considered a quality rule according to many measures, such as Support, Confidence, and Lift. The number of generated rules and their relevance depend on the measures and the minimum thresholds initially set. The support represents the frequency of an item, an item-set, or a given rule in the database and is given by the number of transactions where A and B co-occur compared to the number of transactions. The support of a given rule is defined as described in Eq. 1 [5]:

$$Sup(\mathrm{A} \rightarrow \mathrm{B}) = NH(\mathrm{A} \cup \mathrm{B})/TNT \quad (1)$$

$NH(\mathrm{A} \cup \mathrm{B})$ and *TNT* in Eq. 1 are respectively the *Number of Hits of* (A ∪ B) and the *Total Number of Transactions*.

The Support for a given item A is given as follows:

$$Sup(\mathrm{A}) = NH(\mathrm{A})/TNT \quad (2)$$

The support of an item-set is given as follows:

$$Sup(\mathrm{A}, \mathrm{B}) = NH(\mathrm{A} \cup \mathrm{B})/\mathrm{TNT} \quad (3)$$

If we take the example of the rule $\{F, C \rightarrow B\}$, the support of this rule is:

$$Sup(\mathrm{F}, \mathrm{C} \rightarrow \mathrm{B}) = NH(\mathrm{F}, \mathrm{C} \cup \mathrm{B})/TNT = 2/6 = 33\% \quad (4)$$

NH and *TNT* in Eqs. 2, 3, and 4 are the same as in Eq. 1.

The confidence of an association rule represents the frequency of an item in the database. In other words, it represents the conditional relative frequency of B given A, i.e., the probability that B will be purchased if A is also purchased [5]:

$$Conf\,(\mathrm{A} \to \mathrm{B}) = Sup(\mathrm{A} \cup \mathrm{B})/Sup(\mathrm{A}) \quad (5)$$

The Confidence of the rule: $\{F, C \to B\}$ is:

$$Conf\,(\mathrm{F, C} \to \mathrm{B}) = Sup((\mathrm{F, C} \to \mathrm{B}) \cup \mathrm{B})/Sup(\mathrm{F, C}) \quad (6)$$

For the below example; *Sup*((F, C → B) ∪ B) = 2/6 and *Sup*(F, C) = 2/6. So, *Conf*(F, C → B) = 1.

The lift of an association rule stands for the relationship between the confidence of a rule and the expected confidence, so it is the ratio between the confidence of the rule ($A \to B$) and its consequent (B) [5]:

$$Lift(\mathrm{A} \to \mathrm{B}) = Conf\,(\mathrm{A} \to \mathrm{B})/Sup(\mathrm{B}) \quad (7)$$

Therefore, the Lift of the rule: {F, C → B} is:

$$Lift(\mathrm{F, C} \to \mathrm{B}) = Conf\,(\mathrm{F, C} \to \mathrm{B})/\mathrm{Sup(B)} = 1/(4/6) = 1.5 \quad (8)$$

Many extraction approaches of association rules have been proposed since the early thirteenth. The most standard ones are the FP-Growth [2, 7] and the Apriori algorithm [6]. The previously proposed association rules approaches are greedy regarding memory/processor consumption and execution time. These algorithms can generate many redundant and irrelevant rules.

- Data preparation: First, the data is preprocessed. Only relevant data for the coming two steps is kept.
- The search for frequent items: The goal is to find the most recurrent items. This step is costly in terms of execution time, mainly when we deal with a large amount of data.
- Association rules generation: The last step consists in finding rules with $support \geq minSup$, $Confidence \geq minConf$ and $Lift \geq minLift$ where *minSup*, *minConf*, and *minLift* are set by the user and represent the minimum values that a rule must satisfy for it to be accepted.

To further understand the third step, which aims to generate a set of association rules, we give the following example using the Apriori algorithm (Fig. 1):

Let $E = \{A, B, C, D\}$ be a set of elements and $T = \{T1, T2, T3, T4, T5\}$ a set of transactions. We represent the elements and the transactions as follows:

By applying the Apriori algorithm to the transactions in Table 2, we obtain the following results: Notice that the confidence scores for rules R1 and R5 are computed, respectively, as follows: *Conf*(R1) = *Sup*(B, C, E)/Sup(B, C) = 2/3 = 66.66% and *Conf*(R5) = *Sup*(B, C, E)/Supp(E) = 2/4 = 50% (Table 3).

As we can see, the algorithm generates many association rules (like all algorithms related to support and trust), or several rules can be redundant and irrelevant, occupying a huge memory space, especially when we have a large dataset, which makes the execution time very long.

```
Input : a minimum support and a transaction dataset.
Output: generation of frequent item sets.
  1. Mi=Ø, i = 0;
  2. C1= all 1-Item sets of the data set
  3. 1=all frequent item sets of the data set
     While ( Mi is non-empty)
  1. Ci+1= Candidate-gen(Li);
  2. Fi+1=all frequent item sets of Ci+1;
  3. i++;
  4. Return U Mi;
     End
```

Fig. 1. Apriori algorithm.

Table 2. The representation of transactions.

TID	Transactions
t1	*A, B, C*
t2	*A, C, D*
t3	*B, C, D*
t4	*A, D, E*
t5	*B, C, E*

Table 3. Extracted association rules.

Rule name	Mathematical formalism	Confidence	result
R1	$\{B, C\} \rightarrow (\{B, C, E\} - \{B, C\})$	66.66%	Retained
R2	$\{B, E\} \rightarrow (\{B, C, E\} - \{B, E\})$	66.66%	Retained
R3	$\{C, E\} \rightarrow (\{B, C, E\} - \{C, E\})$	66.66%	Retained
R4	$\{B\} \rightarrow (\{B, C, E\} - \{B\})$	66.66%	Retained
R5	$\{C\} \rightarrow (\{B, C, E\} - \{C\})$	50%	Rejected
R6	$\{E\} \rightarrow (\{B, C, E\} - \{E\})$	50%	Rejected

2.2 The QM Approach

The QM method is widely used for the minimization of Boolean functions. It allows us to determine the minimal form of the functions in a deterministic way. The method was developed by [13, 14] and extended by [15]. It starts with a unique presence/absence combination in the truth table. The method minimizes pairs of product combinations whose variables appear only once in the True or False form (Example: $xy'z(101)$), called minterms, which must have a different bit [8].

QM uses three annotations: '1', representing the true value, '0' for false, and '-' for ignored variables. The main objective is to find the non-combinable elements that represent the prime implicants. If we consider the following expression: E = W X′Y Z′ + W XY′Z′ + W XY′Z (in binary: E = 1010 + 1100 + 1101), W X′YZ′ cannot be combined with any other term of the expression E. Finally, the method looks for the essential prime implicants. A prime implicant is essential if it contains a minterm that is not included in any other prime implicant [9].

Some association rules may share the same consequents or antecedents. Example: abc → D, ab → D, ac → D. Since the rules share the same consequent D, their antecedents can be rewritten in Boolean algebra: abc + abc′ + ab′c where (′) represents negation. Thus, we have our antecedents in minterms abc → D, abc′ → D, ab′c → D.

QM phases are:

1. The switch from the canonical form to the binary form.
2. The classification and comparison of the terms according to their weights (the number of 1's), i.e., comparison of the terms of the group 'i' with the terms of the group 'i + 1'. Each different bit is replaced by a '-'.
3. The search for the prime implicants (the non-combined terms)
4. The search for the essential prime implicants.

3 Methodology

3.1 System Architecture

The proposed approach works according to the following steps:

1. The system receives a set "E" of association rules as input.
2. The number of association rules is reduced by applying QM to obtain a new "E" set.
3. The system uses the set "E" as a knowledge base to classify a set of test data T and records the results. It then uses set "E′" as a knowledge base to classify the same test data set T and records the new results. The two results are compared to deduce whether a loss of important information has occurred (Fig. 2).

3.2 Our Method for Applying the QM on Association Rules

Before using a Boolean function minimization method, such as the QM method, on association rules, we need to define a relationship between the binary form and the association rules. This relationship is a gap between the form of the association rules and the binary form. Since the input to QM is in boolean form, we take inspiration from negative association rules [10], where the negation of an element represents its absence. Example: AB′ → C is equal to A → C since B′ represents the absence of B. Now we have a relationship between the form of the association rules and the Boolean form. Once the rules are in Boolean form, we write them in the binary form where negation represents 0. We now have our second relationship between the binary form and the Boolean form. Next, we minimize the rules with the same consequents together, and the rules with the same antecedents are minimized together to keep the meaning of the rules. Finally, we

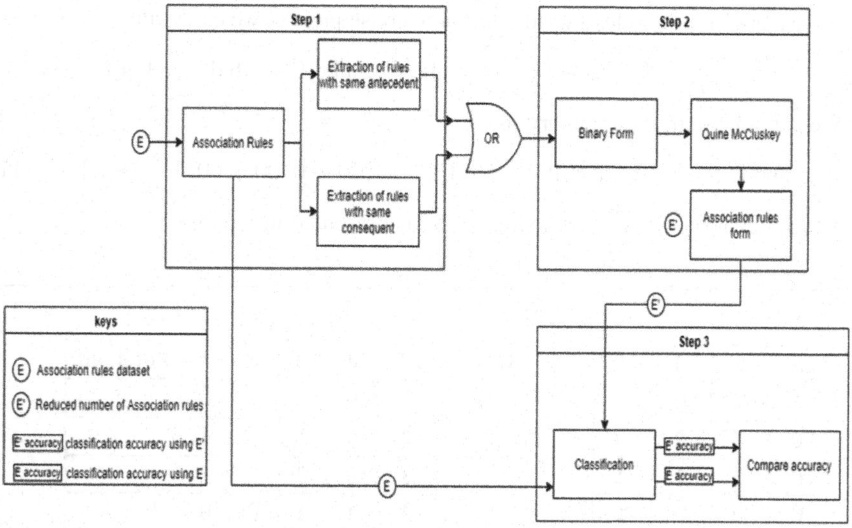

Fig. 2. System architecture.

will have to return to the form of the association rules. We can change the form of a rule as needed in any direction without losing it, e.g., ab → d, ab → d, ef → h, ef → hg. For this purpose, we have four functions for changing the presentation of association rules, namely: *ARtoNAR* for switching association rules to negative association rules. *NARtoBinary*, for the passage of negative association rules to the binary form. Finally, respectively *NARtoAR* and *BinaryToNar* do the opposite operations. All functions apply to rules with the same antecedent or consequent. The element in common between the rules (consequent or antecedent) is not affected by the previous functions, as shown in the following examples:

Function for switching from Association rules to negative Association rules;

$$ARtoNAR([\text{abc}, \text{ac}]) = \left[\text{abc}, \text{ab}' \rightarrow \text{c}\right] \quad \text{(S2)}$$

Function to switch from negative association rules to binary;

$$NARtoBinary\left(\left[\text{ab} \rightarrow \text{c}, \text{ab}' \rightarrow \text{c}\right]\right) = [11, 10] \rightarrow \text{c}$$

Function for switching from binary to negative association rules;

$$BinarytoNAR([11, 10] \rightarrow \text{c}) = \left[\text{ab} \rightarrow \text{c}, \text{ab}' \rightarrow \text{c}\right]$$

Function of switching from negative to Method of association rules;

$$NARtoAR\left(\left[\text{ab} \rightarrow \text{c}, \text{ab}' \rightarrow \text{c}\right]\right) = [\text{ab} \rightarrow \text{c}, \text{a} \rightarrow \text{c}]$$

By using our approach to change the form of association rules, it is possible to minimize the rules as if they were Boolean terms. As an example of minimization, consider the rules below:

$$\text{ab} \rightarrow \text{m}, \text{ab} \rightarrow \text{mn}, \text{ab} \rightarrow \text{e}, \text{b} \rightarrow \text{e}, \text{df} \rightarrow \text{e}, \text{f} \rightarrow \text{e}. \quad (9)$$

If we start with the rules sharing the same consequent e, we can write:

$$S1 = ab + b + df + f = S2 = abd'f' + a'bd'f' + a'b'df + a'b'd'f \quad (10)$$

We can now write S2 in binary form:

$$abd'f' + a'bd'f' + a'b'df + a'b'd'f] \Rightarrow [1100 + 0100 + 0011 + 0001] \quad (11)$$

The application of the QM method on S2 is presented in Fig. 3.

a	b	d	f
1	1	0	0
0	1	0	0
0	0	1	1
0	0	0	1

Group	TID	a	b	d	f	Retained
1	1	0	1	0	0	
	2	0	1	0	1	
2	3	0	0	1	1	
	4	1	1	0	0	

Group	TID	a	b	d	f	Retained
3	1,3	-	1	0	0	#
	2,4	0	0	-	1	#

TID	1	2	3	4
1,3	1		1	
2,4		1		1

Fig. 3. Application of the QM method on S2.

The result $S' = -100 + 00 - 1$. We can rewrite the result in the form of negative association rules as follows:

$$[-100 + 00 - 1] \Rightarrow [bd'f' + a'b'f] \quad (12)$$

Finally, we can rewrite as association rules: b → e, f → e.
We can, also apply the same process on the rules sharing the same antecedent ab:

$$ab \rightarrow m, ab \rightarrow mn, ab \rightarrow e \quad (13)$$

We obtain:

$$S1 = m + mn + e = S2 = mn'e' + mne' + m'n'e \quad (14)$$

The result of the QM on S2 will be $me' + m'n'e$. We can furthermore rewrite it as: ab → m, ab → e.

3.3 Redundancy Elimination After System Reduction

After reducing the number of rules, the knowledge base may be overwhelmed with redundant rules. For example: $\{ab \to F, a \to F\}$ would infer $a \to F$, the latter induces $a \to F$ (*i*). Symmetrically, $ac \to F$, $a \to F$ would infer $a \to F$. The latter induces $a \to F$ (*ii*). Rules (*i*) and (*ii*) are redundant. Next, only one representative rule ($a \to F$) is kept for each duplicate set of rules.

4 Experimental Results

Processing data with classic data reduction techniques usually results in salient information loss. To validate the proposed system, especially its resilience to information loss, we use E', a set of association rules obtained by reducing E (an initial set of rules) in a common classification task F. Furthermore, we compare obtained results in both scenarios (before and after association rules reduction). The intuition behind this validation approach is that if the performance of the classifications (accuracy rate) decreases, we admit that important information has been lost. Otherwise, we can admit that the association-rules reduction process was successfully performed without salient information loss.

Table 4. A sample of association rules extracted from articles in [11].

Class	Antecedent	Consequent
Medical	مرض، ممرضة، طبيب	الربو
Politics	الدستور، الحكومة	الدولة
Culture	الحضارة، الأدب	التعليم، التنوع

An Arabic news articles dataset named SANAD (Single-Label Arabic News Articles Dataset for Automatic Text Categorization) [11, 12] is experimented to assess the proposed approach's performance. SANAD includes 190.000 Arabic news articles belonging to seven categories: Culture, Finance, Medical, Politics, Religion, Sports, and Tech. All the news articles were collected from three popular news websites: AlKhaleej, AlArabiya, and Akhbarona. Table 4 illustrates a sample of extracted association rules from news articles belonging to the Medical, Sport, and Culture categories.

The results illustrated in Table 5 show that we could significantly reduce the number of rules from 1749 to 615. The achieved reduction rate is 64.8%. A strong point of our approach is the no need to set an empirical threshold. Moreover, the classification accuracy rate remains approximately the same for most classes after the association-rules reduction process. Even there are some scenarios where the precision rate was remarkably improved. It is the case for the culture class. The average classification accuracy rate is improved from 88% to 90%. This improvement in system accuracy can be explained by the fact that our approach improves the quality of our crud data by getting rid of redundant information.

Table 5. Classification precision and number of association rules before and after the application of our QM-based association rules reduction.

Class	Classification precision		Number of association rules	
	Before QM	After QM	Before QM	After QM
Culture	66%	73%	193	33
Finance	93%	90%	242	85
Medical	96%	93%	168	86
Religion	90%	68%	132	44
Sport	96%	93%	492	164
Politics	90%	86%	120	44
Technology	96%	93%	402	159
Average	88%	90%	1749	615

5 Conclusion

Association rules have widely demonstrated their usefulness in different domains, such as detecting influential users in social networks [16], interpreting failure risk assessment in continuous production processes [17], etc. Indeed, its formalism of antecedent(s)/consequent(s) is easy to understand for humans. Also, it can be processed by machines. Several researchers have introduced association rules-based information extraction techniques. In this work, we have addressed this problem while trying to keep the most salient information. We used a technique of Boolean function minimization, namely the QM method. In order to use the QM method, we had to determine new annotations, allowing us to keep the readability of the association rules and to allow the minimization of the rules. If the QM method has as input a boolean function, then our rules had to transform this form. We were inspired by negative association rules, where the negation "'" of a variable means its absence. We had to figure out how to express the association rules in a binary format. We annotated absence by 0 and presence by 1. For minimization, we considered the dash "-" to say that the element is ignored, as it has no direct effect on the result. Conducted experiments showed that the proposed method could significantly reduce the number of association rules without any information loss. Quite the opposite, the overall precision rate of classification was improved by 2% due to eliminating unnecessary, redundant information.

Acknowledgements. The authors would like to thank Natural Sciences and Engineering Research Council of Canada for financing this work.

References

1. Ashrafi, M.Z., Taniar, D., Smith, K.: Redundant association rules reduction techniques. Int. J. Bus. Intell. Data Min. **2**, 29–63 (2007)

2. Agrawal, R., Srikant, R.: Fast algorithms for mining association rules. In: Proceedings of the 20th International Conference on Very Large Data Bases, VLDB, pp. 487–499. Citeseer (1994)
3. Zaki, M.: Generating non-redundant association rules. In: Proceedings of the Sixth ACM SIGKDD International Conference on Knowledge Discovery and Data Mining, pp. 34–43 (2000)
4. Turčínek, P., Turčínková, J.: Exploring consumer behavior: use of association rules. Acta Universitatis Agriculturae et Silviculturae Mendelianae Brunensis **63**, 1031–1042 (2015)
5. Lin, W.-Y., Tseng, M.-C., Su, J.-H.: A confidence-lift support specification for interesting associations mining. In: Chen, MS., Yu, P.S., Liu, B. (eds.) PAKDD 2002. LNCS, vol. 2336, pp. 148–158. Springer, Heidelberg (2002). https://doi.org/10.1007/3-540-47887-6_14
6. Han, J., Pei, J., Kamber, M.: Data mining: concepts and techniques. Elsevier (2011)
7. Zeng, Y., Yin, S., Liu, J., Zhang, M.: Research of improved FPGrowth algorithm in association rules mining. Sci. Program. **2015**, 6 (2015)
8. Staneva, L.A.: Minimising using the method of Quine-McCluskey with generalised nets. In: 29th Annual Conference of the European Association for Education in Electrical and Information Engineering (EAEEIE), pp. 1–3. IEEE (2019)
9. Majumder, A., Chowdhury, B., Mondai, A.J., Jain, K.: Investigation on Quine McCluskey method: a decimal manipulation based novel approach for the minimization of Boolean function. In: International Conference on Electronic Design, Computer Networks Automated Verification (EDCAV), pp. 18–22. IEEE (2015)
10. Dong, X., Hao, F., Zhao, L., Xu, T.: An efficient method for pruning redundant negative and positive association rules. Neurocomputing **393**, 245–258 (2020)
11. SANAD. https://data.mendeley.com/datasets/57zpx667y9/2
12. El Bazzi, M.S., Zaki, T., Mammass, D., Ennaji, A.: Automatic indexing of Arabic texts: state of the art. Electron. J. Inf. Technol. **9**, 1–2 (2016)
13. Quine, W.V.: The problem of simplifying truth functions. Am. Math. Mon. **59**(8), 521–531 (1952)
14. Quine, W.V.: A way to simplify truth functions. Am. Math. Mon. **62**(9), 627–631 (1955)
15. McCluskey Jr., E.J.: Minimization of boolean functions. Bell Syst. Tech. J. **35**(6), 1417–1444 (1956)
16. Agouti, T.: Graph-based modeling using association rule mining to detect influential users in social networks. Expert Syst. Appl. **202**, 117436 (2022)
17. Pohlmeyer, F., Kins, R., Cloppenburg, F., Gries, T.: Interpretable failure risk assessment for continuous production processes based on association rule mining. Adv. Ind. Manuf. Eng. **5**, 100095 (2022)

Complexity-Based Code Embeddings

Rares Folea(✉), Radu Iacob, Emil Slusanschi, and Traian Rebedea

University Politehnica of Bucharest, Bucharest, Romania
rares.folea@stud.acs.upb.ro

Abstract. This paper presents a generic method for transforming the source code of various algorithms to numerical embeddings, by dynamically analysing the behaviour of computer programs against different inputs and by tailoring multiple generic complexity functions for the analysed metrics. The used algorithms embeddings are based on r-Complexity [7]. Using the proposed code embeddings, we present an implementation of the XGBoost algorithm that achieves an average 90% F1-score on a multi-label dataset with 11 classes, built using real-world code snippets submitted for programming competitions on the Codeforces platform.

Keywords: algorithm classification · code embeddings · complexity · tree-based classification

1 Introduction

Algorithmic classification is an important problem in Computer Science, which aims to identify the programming techniques and specific algorithms referenced in a code snippet. Solving this task requires a deep understanding of code semantics which may provide insights for many further applications, such as the detection of code vulnerabilities or the design of automatic code generation assistants.

While most of the recent community work is focused on the static code analysis, we focus on **dynamic** analysis[1], by analysing the actual execution part to assert how the algorithm behaves. Thus, we aim to investigate how the resource usage (e.g. CPU time, memory) evolves in relation to the input size. We hypothesize that these metrics, along with more advanced architectural aspects (e.g. branch and cache misses), can be used to distinguish between different types of algorithmic approaches.

In our study, we have investigated the applicability of our approach for classifying solutions to competitive programming challenges, written in C++. Thus, we report encouraging results using decision tree models, random forest classifiers

[1] We define dynamic analysis as the process of developing a computer software evaluation based on data acquired from experiments conducted out on a real computing system by executing programs against a range of different inputs.

N. T. Nguyen et al. (Eds.): ICCCI 2023, LNAI 14162, pp. 256–269, 2023.
https://doi.org/10.1007/978-3-031-41456-5_20

and XGBoost [5] for deriving algorithmic labels from dynamic code embeddings, generated using our method.

This paper is structured as follows. In Sect. 2 we report on related approaches from existing literature. Afterwards, in Sect. 3 we describe our approach for creating dynamic code embeddings. In Sect. 4 we present a general overview of the system architecture. In Sect. 5 we provide experimental details behind the creation of a novel comprehensive dataset that we used for evaluation. Next, in Sect. 6 we present the results achieved using several machine learning solutions. Finally, in Sect. 7 we conclude with a final perspective on the applicability of our solution.

2 Related Work

A critical step before applying a machine learning model to analyze data is how to choose a meaningful input representation. In this section we explore several representative approaches for creating distributed program embeddings.

Firstly, researchers have investigated techniques borrowed from the field of natural language processing, which rely on the distributional properties of individual words (e.g. Word2Vec [10]. These approaches seek to capture the statistical co-occurrence patterns of different lexical features. These features may be derived using different segmentation strategies from the textual representation of source code [3,12] or from the representation pertaining to different compilation stages (e.g. LLVM-IR [2], Java bytecode [9], assembly [11]) or bytecode [16].

Another option is to train neural architectures to encode graph representations of code, such as the AST [1] or the CFG [2]. The advantage of this approach is that it can explicitly model semantic relationships between distant program elements.

An alternative perspective can be attained from dynamic analysis of the program runtime behaviour. One such approach is to monitor execution traces, which capture the state of variables during different moments of execution [13–15]. A different direction is to collect and analyze the interactions with the operation system, such as system calls to create, open or modify files [6]. Notably, this approach may not be suitable to distinguish between programs which perform minimal interactions with the operating system.

Static code representations entail direct access to the program source code. On the other hand, dynamic code representations discussed above leverage specific knowledge about target program semantics and rely heavily on the number and diversity of program executions. In contrast, the solution discussed in this paper requires no prior assumptions about the program structure. As such, it relies only on collected statistics about runtime behaviour, as seen through the lens of a profiling tool.

3 Converting an Algorithm to an Embedding

As shown in [7], r-Complexity is a revised complexity model, that offers better complexity feedback for similar programs than the classic Bachmann-Landau notations. Let $f : \mathbb{N} \longrightarrow \mathbb{R}$ denote the function describing an algorithm computational complexity. We define the set of all complexity calculus $\mathcal{F} = \{f : \mathbb{N} \longrightarrow \mathbb{R}\}$ Also, we will consider an arbitrary complexity function $g \in \mathcal{F}$.

The **Big *r*-Theta** class is defined as a set of mathematical functions similar in magnitude with $g(n)$ in the study of asymptotic behavior. A set-based description of this group can be expressed as:

$$\Theta_r(g(n)) = \{f \in \mathcal{F} \mid \forall c_1, c_2 \in \mathbb{R}_+^* \ s.t. c_1 < r < c_2, \exists n_0 \in \mathbb{N}^* \\ s.t. \ \ c_1 \cdot g(n) \le f(n) \le c_2 \cdot g(n) \ , \ \forall n \ge n_0\}$$

The big **r-Theta** notation proves to be useful also in creating Dynamic code embeddings. The idea behind these embeddings is simple: try to automatically provide estimations, for various metrics, the r-Theta class for the analyzed algorithm (usually with unknown Bachmann-Landau Complexity).

A generic solution (generalization of [4]) to provide a good automatic estimation of the r-Complexity class is to try fit a regressor described by:

$$f(n) = \sum_{t=1}^{y} \sum_{k=1}^{x} c_k \cdot n^{p_k} \cdot log_{l_k}^{j_k}(n) \cdot e_t^n \cdot$$

In this research, we will attempt to fit a simplified version of the generic expression as a Big r-Theta function, described generic by one of the following function:

$$\begin{cases} r \cdot log_2^p log_2(n) + X \\ r \cdot log_2^p(n) + X \\ r \cdot p^n + X, p < 1 \\ r \cdot n^p + X \\ r \cdot p^n + X, p > 1 \\ r \cdot \Gamma(n) + X \end{cases} .$$

The search space for regressor functions is not feasible to be exhaustively searched during for automatic computation, as there are infinitely many regressors that can be analyzed. To overcome this problem, our approach is to avoid performing the continuous space search, but obtain similar results only by sampling a number of highly relevant configurations, that are relevant for algorithms in general. This way, we can discretize the search space, and the functions we decided to search towards are:

$$\begin{cases} r \cdot log_2^p log_2(n) + X, p \in \{0, 1, 2, 3\} \\ r \cdot log_2^p(n) + X, p \in \{0, 1, 2, ..., 10\} \\ r \cdot p^n + X, p < 1, p \in \{0.1, 0.2, ..., 0.9\} \\ r \cdot n^p + X, p \in \{1, 1.3, 1.5, 1.7, 2, 2.5, 2.7, 3, 3.5, 4, 4.5, 5, 5.5, 6, 7, 8, 9, 10\} \\ r \cdot p^n + X, p > 1, p \in \{1.5, 2, 2.5, 3, 3.5, 4, 5\} \\ r \cdot \Gamma(n) + X \end{cases} .$$

Each fitting of a Big r-Theta on a metric has as result a quadruple:

(FEATURE_TYPE, FEATURE_CONFIG, INTERCEPT, R-VAL)

where:

1. FEATURE_TYPE has one of the following values[2]:
   (a) LOGLOG_POLYNOMIAL,
   (b) LOG_POLYNOMIAL,
   (c) FRACTIONAL_POWER,
   (d) POLYNOMIAL,
   (e) POWER,
   (f) FACTORIAL,
2. FEATURE_CONFIG is defined[3] by a value $n \in \mathbb{R}_+$, such that the generic Big r-Theta respects the above FEATURE_TYPE.
3. INTERCEPT is the expected value of the complexity function when the input size is null.
4. R-VAL is the value of r, such that the defined g complexity class includes f, which is the real complexity function of the algorithm: $f \in \Theta_r(g(n))$

Even if the model is generic and works for any arbitrary metric, in order to use it, we are required to instantiate the model with tangible metrics, with respect to the input size. We analyze an algorithm by all the associated r-Complexities, bundled as one code-embedding. Using the native Linux perf profiler, we obtained and used the following metrics to compute our code embeddings. The set of these metrics covers both hardware events: ***branch-misses*** (number of branch missed predictions), ***branches*** (number of branches instructions executed), ***cycles*** (number of executed cycles), ***instructions*** (number of executed instruction), ***stalled-cycles-frontend*** (number of "wasted" CPU cycles where the frontend[4] did not feed the backend with micro-operations.), as well as software events, ***context-switches*** (number of procedures of storing the state of the process/thread, at suspension time), ***CPU-migrations*** (number of times a process/thread has been scheduled on a different CPU), ***page-faults*** (number of events when the virtual memory was not mapped to the physical memory), ***task-clock*** (stores the clock count specific to the task that ran).

In computing the embedding, we require no knowledge about the structure of the analyzed algorithm. However, the resulting embedding is dependent on the architecture it has been generated against. Typically, metrics vary from architecture to architecture. The general complexity class of the algorithm may not change, thus making the FEATURE_TYPE and FEATURE_CONFIG parameters likely

[2] The model is generic and other values can be used as well, yet these are the most relevant values that we have used in our research.

[3] In our research, we have searched only a small discrete set of values for n, described earlier in this section.

[4] Frontend refers here to the part of the hardware responsible for fetching and decoding instructions.

to remain the same on multiple computing architectures. The sample embeddings in this paper have been obtained when running on a 3rd Generation Intel Core processor (3.10 GHz), i5-3210M (2.5 GHz, 3MB L3 cache, 2 cores). On the other hand, given another algorithm, with a different complexity, the previously mentioned parameters are susceptible to changes.

4 System Architecture

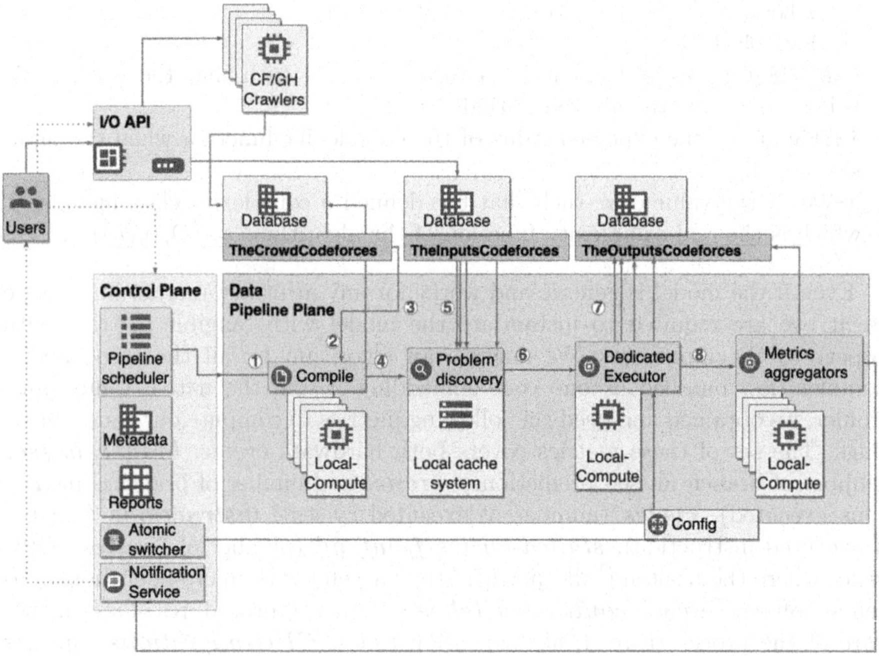

Fig. 1. An overview of our data acquisition system, capable of generating a set of metrics from the binaries.

The *system* we proposed to analyse the solutions to the problems contained in the dataset presented above is complex. It can be seen as two distinct entities: **the data acquisition subsystem** (Fig. 1) and the **embeddings subsystem** (Fig. 2). The key steps involved in running the pipeline is illustrated by the labels in Fig. 1. The Control Plane initiates the data pipeline in **1**, by providing the required arguments. Step **2** fetches all the matching solutions, to all problems, from TheCrawlCodeforces (the solutions dataset). It compiles the sources and store the results back in the database, as indicated in **3**. Next, in **4**, the data is passed, in form of a compiled executable, to the discovery service. Next, the

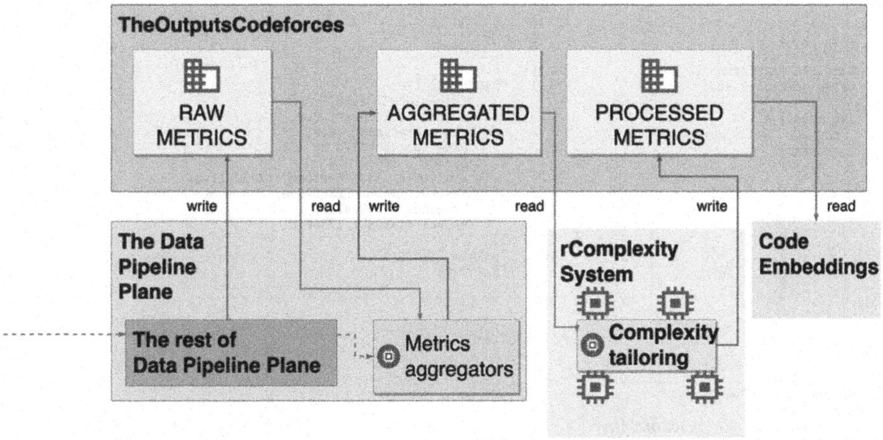

Fig. 2. An overview of our data embedding system that converts the raw metrics into code embeddings, and how it interacts with other parts of the systems.

synthetic inputs from TheInputsCodeforces[5] (input dataset) are being fetched, in **5**. Once this is complete, in step in **6**, the pipeline goes into a schedule state, where the execution on a dedicated executors is being prepared. In our research, to avoid variations in data due to difference in hardware, we have only used one executor, but this may have serious implication on the scalability. Once tasks have been scheduled and completed, the resulting profiling data is stored to the TheOutputsCodeforces (profiling dataset) in in **7**. At the end of the pipeline, metrics obtained from profiling are being aggregated in **8** and the pipeline is marked as succeeded.

After raw metrics with profiling data are being generated, the data embedding system (Fig. 2) aggregates them so that the complexity mapping can be applied. The embeddings system is responsible of building code embeddings from the available data provided by the Data Acquisition System. It is responsible of computing at scale dynamic code-embeddings based on r-Complexity with respect to the various metrics analyzed against the input dimensions.

Because the resulting embedding is somewhat dependent to the underlying architecture it has been profiled against, for best result, we evaluated all the solutions from our dataset on the same architecture. This doesn't make our solution architecture-dependent however, as we can re-process our metrics by launching the pipelines on any given architecture. It's also possible that similar are obtained even without performing this step when computing embeddings on new architecture, assuming that the two architectures are from the same family and have similar performances, or if there is a mapping function estimate regarding performance difference for the analyzed metrics.

[5] TheInputsCodeforces is a public dataset: https://github.com/raresraf/TheInputsCodeforces.

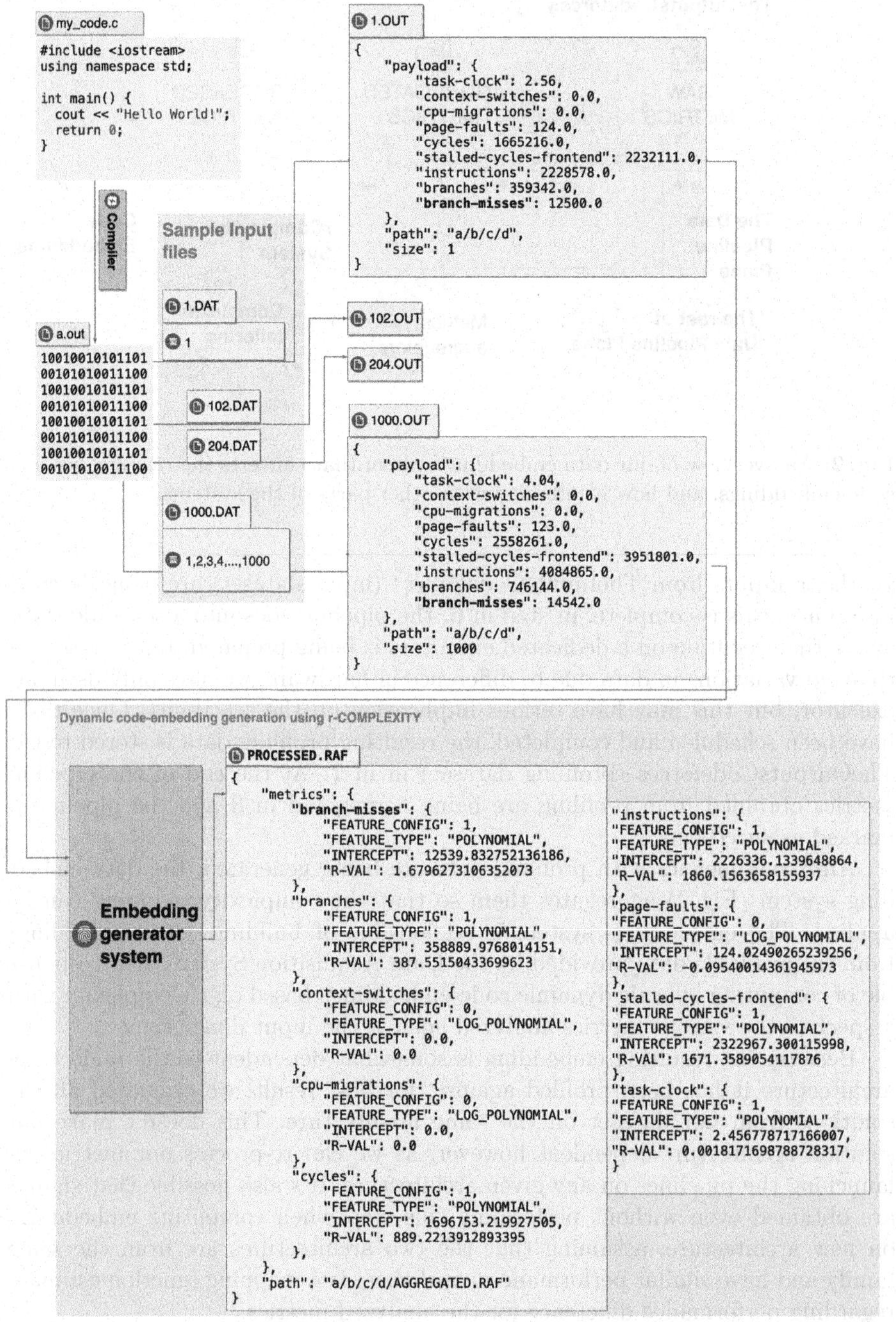

Fig. 3. An in-depth view on the process of generating a code-embedding for a given algorithm, based on r-Complexity code-embeddings, using this system.

5 Dataset

In this research, we built a automatic system that searches for open-source implementations for Codeforces technical challenges. We use the AlgoLabel [8] dataset in order to obtain the mapping between problems and algorithm labels.

In order to achieve dynamic measurements out of which we can create the dynamic code embeddings, synthetic test inputs are required for each individual problem. The generation of such inputs is performed manually and usually requires some degree of reasoning, around choosing an appropriate dimension and input space for the problem, so that the samples will be relevant in computing the complexity. For instance, consider a problem, for which the number of required processing cycles to compute for the input x is described by the function c:

$$c(x) = \begin{cases} 10, & x = 10000 \\ 1, & x = 20000 \\ 100 \cdot x^2, & \text{otherwise} \end{cases}$$

For this problem, sampling the algorithm for any input is relevant in computing the associated r-Complexity, except of the results of analysing inputs $x = 10000$ and $x = 20000$, which are outliers. In practice, these outliers exists, and usually correspond to particular cases, when solving a difficult problem is trivial; for example, the problem of determining whether a number is prime or not is trivial for all even numbers, but has a non-constant complexity for arbitrary odd numbers. Hence, in order to provide relevant estimates of the r-Complexity functions for a given problem, the step of creating synthetic inputs requires some degree of judgement, to ensure that the inputs are representative for the difficulty of the problem.

This generation can be toilsome for a large dataset. In our research, we picked 50 problems, based on the number of available sources. For every problem, we evaluate each compiled binary against a set of 50 inputs. The trade-off here is the following: the more support points, the better the estimate for the complexity function becomes, but this comes at the cost of slowing down the pipeline. We validate empirically that this number of inputs may provide sufficient data points for inferring the program complexity.

Then, while executing the binaries on the previously generated inputs, the pipeline measures several statistics. These measurements are stored, obtaining the profiling files for each execution. Consequently, there are over one million such files in the resulting dataset (referenced as TheOutputsCodeforces dataset).

Next we create an embedding, using the techniques described in Sect. 3. Thus, each program is represented *as a* 36-*long vector*, built using approximations of the r-Theta complexity against the inputs, for each individual metric. We depict this process in Fig. 3.

6 Results

At this stage, we approach the classification problem of solution labelling with standard machine learning approaches. We study two scenarios: classifying each problem in a binary form, such as distributing each solution into belongs to category X or not, and performing multi-label classification, aiming to find all the classes a solution belongs to.

Three methods yield the best results: **decision tree classifier**, **random forest classifier** and **XGBoost**. We analyze the performance of two models based on multiple metrics: **accuracy**, **precision**, **recall** and **f1-score** on 5949 inputs, using a 66/34 split for the training/testing dataset. For all the analyzed methods, we perform the same split, simulating a similar training environment for all analyzed models.

In this research, several custom neural networks and deep neural networks, as well as convolutional networks, were trained, on the same datasets, but the overall performance was rather unsatisfactory. We could not maximise the performance of either to be close to the performance of a simple decision tree classifier. Going forward, we present the results of tree-based classifiers.

All models have been implemented in Python and published open-source[6]. We use pandas to operate datasets, sklearn to compute metrics and for ensemble models, xgboost library for an efficient implementation of XGBoost trees and tensorflow for experimenting with neural networks.

6.1 Binary Classification

We perform binary classification for math/non-math problems. The dataset is unbalanced, with 4937 problems not being labeled as math and 1012 for problems that were classified as math-related. The aim was to keep the ratio from the original dataset in both testing and training dataset. The testing evaluation results are captured in **Table** 1.

The accuracy is similar for both methods: **96%** for the decision tree classifier and **97%** for the random forest classifier. Overall, only the recall is smaller for the random forest classifier, while all the other metrics, including the f1-score is slightly higher for this classifier.

A visualisation of the decision tree model is available in Fig. 4. High-quality renderings are available[7].

6.2 Multi-label Classification

For Multi-Label Classification, XGBoost yield the best results. In a similar setup, we benchmark the performances of a XGBoost classifier against the problem of algorithm classification. In our research, this method exhibits the best performance, in terms of *precision*, *recall* and *F1-score* for the analyzed scenarios. Detailed results are provided in **Table** 2.

[6] https://www.github.com/raresraf/AlgoRAF.

[7] https://www.github.com/raresraf/AlgoRAF/tree/master/viz.

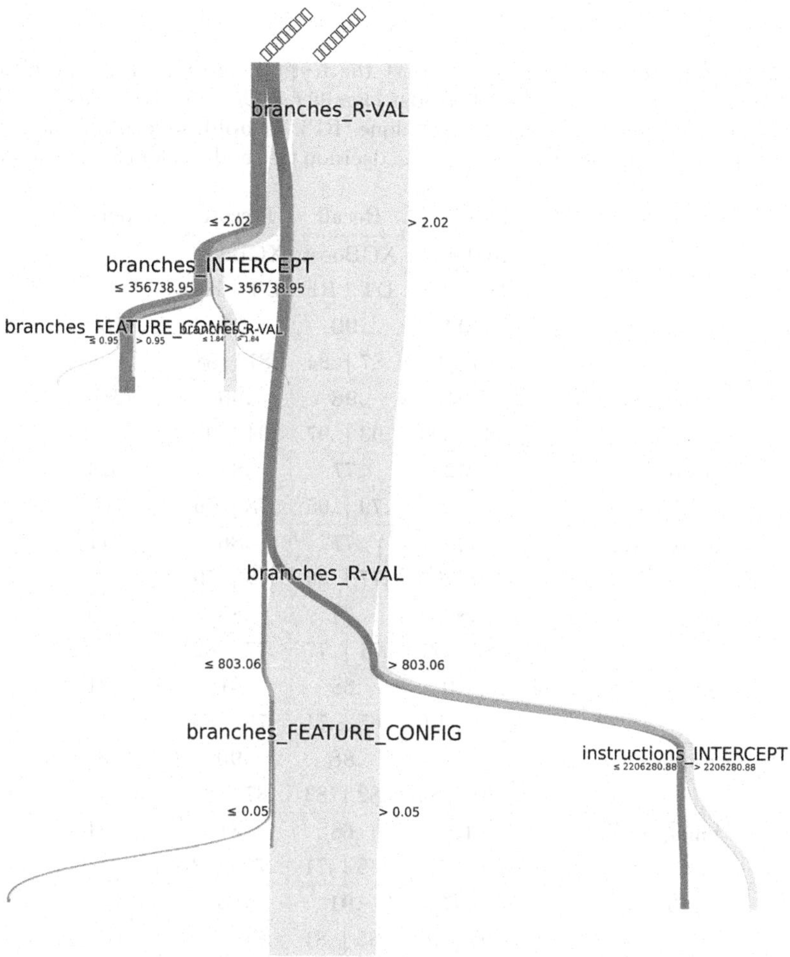

Fig. 4. The decision tree classifier that has achieved over 96% accuracy on the task of labelling algorithmic challenges with the math/non-math label against our testing dataset, while trained on dataset we prepared, with open-source Codeforces submissions. The figure contains the tree plotted with a maximum depth of three. The total depth of our decision trees was between twelve and sixteen. Purple are branches that evaluate to math class, while in yellow are plotted branches that evaluate to non-math class. (Color figure online)

Table 1. The metrics obtained for the **decision tree classifier** (DT) and **random forest classifier** (RF) evaluation against testing dataset.

Metric Class	precision (DT | RF)	recall (DT | RF)	f1-score (DT | RF)	support
non-math	**.98** | .97	.98 | **.99**	**.98** | **.98**	1663
math	.89 | **.96**	**.87** | .83	.88 | **.89**	301

Table 2. A classification report ran against the testing dataset, for the problem of algorithm classification, using the **XGBoost** classifier, a Decision Tree Classifier (DT) and using the random forest classifier technique (RF). In **bold**, we capture the results that are better than the previous two models, decision tree and random forest classifiers.

Class	Precision	Recall	F-score	Support
	XGBoost DT | RF	XGBoost DT | RF	XGBoost DT | RF	
strings	**.94** .86 | .93	**.90** .87 | .84	**.92** .87 | .88	756
implementation	.94 .95 | .93	**.98** .93 | .97	**.96** .94 | .95	1387
greedy	**.92** .78 | .91	.77 .79 | .65	**.84** .78 | .76	523
brute force	.98 .79 | 1.0	.77 .77 | .66	**.86** .78 | .79	311
dp	**.87** .83 | .87	.74 .71 | .77	.80 .77 | .82	35
divide and conquer	**1.0** .91 | 1.0	.68 .65 | .71	.81 .75 | .83	31
graphs	.91 .92 | .84	**.88** .82 | .83	**.90** .87 | .84	83
binary search	**1.0** .91 | 1.0	.68 .65 | .71	.81 .75 | .83	31
math	**.97** .91 | .95	**.91** .85 | .81	**.94** .88 | .88	301
sortings	.95 .66 | .96	.61 .66 | .42	**.74** .66 | .58	176
shortest paths	.91 .92 | .84	**.88** .82 | .83	**.90** .87 | .84	83
micro avg	**.94** .87 | .93	**.88** .85 | .82	**.91** .86 | .87	3717
macro avg	**.94** .86 | .93	**.80** .77 | .74	**.86** .81 | .82	3717
weighted avg	**.94** .87 | .93	**.88** .85 | .82	**.91** .86 | .86	3717
samples avg	**.94** .89 | .91	**.91** .88 | .86	**.91** .88 | .87	3717

The model scores really well in the precision of identifying a problem belonging to the class. Slightly worse, the recall is diminished, especially for classes where the number of support entries is low, such as *divide and conquer* or *binary search*. It's interesting that the model does match all the 30+ entries in the testing dataset where these two techniques are used, yet, a recall of just above two thirds is recorded. However, for large sets, such as strings or math classes, the model scores very high in both precision and recall, with sustained results of over 90%.

Our experiments also included the use of decision trees in junction with *r-Complexity* embeddings, as well as random forests classifiers. Overall, the results obtaining this ensemble model are better than by using a single, simple, decision tree classifier, for almost all classes and all analyzed metrics. Between these two methods, it seems that the Random Forest Classifier is optimized for higher precision, with a slightly lower recall score. Just like XGBoost, the model does match all the entries for the *divide and conquer* and *binary search*, and even obtains a higher recall score for these two classes than the XGBoost classifier. However, the average of recall is 4% smaller.

7 Conclusions and Further Research

In this paper we present a way of building code embeddings based on Complexity related measurements and use these telemetry as insights for the problem of algorithm classification. The method showcased for transforming the source code to numerical embeddings is a helpful solution when needing to analyze the behaviour of algorithms. Using these embeddings that are based on r-Complexity [7], we achieve high accuracy classification even when using simple decision tree-based classifiers for the problem of labelling of competitive programming challenges.

This shows the potential of this embedding method, for building a more general understanding of the source code. The greater goal of our research is to build a generic model of mapping an algorithm to a code embedding (based on the r-Complexity code embeddings technique), that can later be used for more competitive and advanced programming challenges. We believe that these embeddings covers a good amount of information about the code, and can be used to further analysis, such as: *plagiarism detection, software optimisations and classification* or *malware detection*. Tailoring the collected metrics for a certain algorithm can help reach this goal, by introducing other more relevant metrics for solving a certain task.

Further work on the development of the TheInputsCodeforces database, in order to support more generators, that would produce more synthetic inputs. This might enhance the generality of our dataset and is likely to make our models more relevant to a wider set of problems.

References

1. Alon, U., Zilberstein, M., Levy, O., Yahav, E.: code2vec: learning distributed representations of code. Proc. ACM Program. Lang. **3**(POPL), 1–29 (2019)
2. Ben-Nun, T., Jakobovits, A.S., Hoefler, T.: Neural code comprehension: a learnable representation of code semantics. In: Proceedings of the 32nd International Conference on Neural Information Processing Systems. pp. 3589–3601. NIPS2 018, Curran Associates Inc., Red Hook, NY, USA (2018)
3. Buratti, L., et al.: Exploring software naturalness through neural language models. CoRR abs/2006.12641 (2020). https://arxiv.org/abs/2006.12641
4. Calotoiu, A.: Automatic empirical performance modeling of parallel programs (2018)
5. Chen, T., Guestrin, C.: XGBoost: a scalable tree boosting system. In: Proceedings of the 22nd ACM SIGKDD International Conference on Knowledge Discovery and Data Mining, pp. 785–794 (2016)
6. Chistyakov, A., Lobacheva, E., Kuznetsov, A., Romanenko, A.: Semantic embeddings for program behavior patterns. CoRR abs/1804.03635 (2018). http://arxiv.org/abs/1804.03635
7. Folea, R., Slusanschi, E.I.: A new metric for evaluating the performance and complexity of computer programs: a new approach to the traditional ways of measuring the complexity of algorithms and estimating running times. In: 2021 23rd International Conference on Control Systems and Computer Science (CSCS), pp. 157–164. IEEE (2021)
8. Iacob, R.C.A., Monea, V.C., Rădulescu, D., Ceapă, A.F., Rebedea, T., Trăusan-Matu, S.: Algolabel: a large dataset for multi-label classification of algorithmic challenges. Mathematics **8**(11), 1995 (2020)
9. Koc, U., Saadatpanah, P., Foster, J.S., Porter, A.A.: Learning a classifier for false positive error reports emitted by static code analysis tools. In: Proceedings of the 1st ACM SIGPLAN International Workshop on Machine Learning and Programming Languages, pp. 35–42 (2017)
10. Mikolov, T., Grave, E., Bojanowski, P., Puhrsch, C., Joulin, A.: Advances in pre-training distributed word representations. In: Proceedings of the Eleventh International Conference on Language Resources and Evaluation (LREC 2018). European Language Resources Association (ELRA), Miyazaki, Japan (2018). https://aclanthology.org/L18-1008
11. Redmond, K., Luo, L., Zeng, Q.: A cross-architecture instruction embedding model for natural language processing-inspired binary code analysis. CoRR abs/1812.09652 (2018). http://arxiv.org/abs/1812.09652
12. Svyatkovskiy, A., Lee, S., Hadjitofi, A., Riechert, M., Franco, J.V., Allamanis, M.: Fast and memory-efficient neural code completion. In: 2021 IEEE/ACM 18th International Conference on Mining Software Repositories (MSR), pp. 329–340. IEEE (2021)
13. Wang, K.: Learning scalable and precise representation of program semantics. CoRR abs/1905.05251 (2019). http://arxiv.org/abs/1905.05251
14. Wang, K., Singh, R., Su, Z.: Dynamic neural program embeddings for program repair. In: 6th International Conference on Learning Representations, ICLR 2018, Vancouver, BC, Canada, April 30 - May 3, 2018, Conference Track Proceedings. OpenReview.net (2018). https://openreview.net/forum?id=BJuWrGW0Z
15. Wang, K., Su, Z.: Blended, precise semantic program embeddings. In: Proceedings of the 41st ACM SIGPLAN Conference on Programming Language Design and

Implementation, pp. 121–134. PLDI 2020, Association for Computing Machinery, New York, NY, USA (2020). https://doi.org/10.1145/3385412.3385999

16. Yousefi-Azar, M., Hamey, L., Varadharajan, V., Chen, S.: Learning latent byte-level feature representation for malware detection. In: Cheng, L., Leung, A.C.S., Ozawa, S. (eds.) ICONIP 2018. LNCS, vol. 11304, pp. 568–578. Springer, Cham (2018). https://doi.org/10.1007/978-3-030-04212-7_50

Differentially Private Copulas, DAG and Hybrid Methods: A Comprehensive Data Utility Study

Andrea Galloni[1(✉)] and Imre Lendák[1,2]

[1] Faculty of Informatics, Department of Data Science and Engineering, ELTE – Eötvös Loránd University, Budapest, Hungary
andrea.galloni@inf.elte.hu, lendak@uns.ac.rs

[2] Faculty of Technical Sciences, University of Novi Sad, Novi Sad, Serbia

Abstract. Differentially Private (DP) synthetic data generation (SDG) algorithms take as input a dataset containing private, confidential information and produce synthetic data with comparable statistical characteristics. The significance of such techniques is rising due to the growing awareness of the extent of data collection and usage in organizational contexts, as well as the implementation of new stricter data privacy regulations. Given the growing academic interest in DP SDG techniques, our study intends to perform a comparative evaluation of the statistical similarities and utility (in terms of machine learning performances) of a specific set of related algorithms in the realistic context of credit-risk and banking. The study compares PrivBayes, Copula-Shirley, and DPCopula algorithms and their variants using a proposed evaluation framework across three different datasets. The purpose of this study is to perform a thorough assessment of the score and to investigate the impact of different values of the privacy budget (ϵ) on the quality and usability of synthetic data generated by each method. As a result, we highlight and examine the deficiencies and capabilities of each algorithm in relation to the features' properties of the original data.

Keywords: Synthetic Data Generation · Differential Privacy · Evaluation Metrics · Copula Functions · Bayesian Networks

1 Introduction

The overall Differentially Private (DP) Synthetic Data Generation (SDG) task given a private dataset D_p composed by n_p records and m features: $D_p \subset X_1 \times X_2 \times \cdots \times X_m$ of n_p records and m features is to generate a synthetic dataset D_s which keeps attributes types and their number $X_1, X_2, \cdots, X_m$ as D_p. The goal is to generate a new synthetic dataset D_s such that it resembles the statistics and subsequently the utility of D_p while guaranteeing privacy of its records implementing Differential Privacy as introduced in [10] and refined in

N. T. Nguyen et al. (Eds.): ICCCI 2023, LNAI 14162, pp. 270–281, 2023.
https://doi.org/10.1007/978-3-031-41456-5_21

[11]. In this context, the generation of synthetic data serves as a common practice to address privacy concerns and adhere to regulations, enabling researchers to employ a substitute for sensitive data. Consequently, synthetic data must meet qualitative and quantitative criteria to sufficiently support scientists in conducting Exploratory Data Analysis (EDA) and subsequently training Machine Learning (ML) models, while ensuring comparable outcomes to those obtained using the original dataset. A quality algorithm should provide as output data that is qualitatively good enough to keep similar performances when used to train a machine learning models if compared to the original dataset.

This study focuses on the comparison of a specific set of interrelated generative methods that adhere to the principles and characteristics of Differential Privacy. The selection of these algorithms is guided by specific criteria to ensure both a fair and rigorous evaluation of individual methods as well as a comprehensive comparison across the group. To facilitate this comparison, we employ a novel and comprehensive evaluation metric for synthetic data generation, as recently introduced in [12] as to date it represents the most advanced and complete evaluation methodology accepted by the scientific community.

2 Related Work

Differential Privacy is a mathematical framework widely used and well recognized by the academic community [9,11]. A differentially private algorithm - given its sensitivity to the input - is mathematically guaranteed to inject a specific amount of noise [10] making sure to quantify the privacy of each of the records provided as input given a predefined privacy budget ϵ.

For what concerns classical machine learning generative techniques a conspicuous number of differentially private SDG algorithms were developed. Privelet+ [21] making use of wavelet transforms. In PSD (Private Spatial Decomposition) [6] and [24] authors use Tree-based models to model the distributions of a spacial datasets. Filter Priority [7]; P-HP method [2]; PrivateERM [22]; PrivGene [25]; PrivBayes [23] utilizing Bayesian Networks DPCopula [16] focusing on Gaussian Copula functions as learning model or an improved and parallelized approach using Copula Functions as well in [3] and only recently in [13] authors utilize DP Vine Copula models.

The main issue we do aim to tackle is that in literature authors used different evaluation metrics for estimating the quality of synthetic data and consequentially compare an algorithm to another and often these results are not considering the type of usage of generated data if not queries. In [23] authors use *α-way marginals* namely evaluating counting queries on subsets of attributes. In [5] authors evaluate their work by measuring the distance of each marginal for each attribute between the learned noisy marginals and the original marginals. In [20] authors used multiple classifiers fed with synthetic data, where each classifier predicts a specific attribute, here the metric used is Accuracy, Recall and F1 Score compared with different DP SDG algorithms: [22] and [25] which also uses clustering. While [16] authors evaluate the quality of the synthetic data generated by DPCopula answering random range-count queries and compare results against other methods such as [7] and [2].

Finally the aim of our work is to cover the lack of comprehensiveness of two proposed evaluation frameworks available to date: DPBench [14] which uses only counting queries and [1] using attributes ranges, counts and macro-statistics such as Pearson correlation. Furthermore wo do aim to compare a specific family of algorithms Copula Based, *DAG* (Directed Acyclic Graph) Based and Hybrid version of them.

Our evaluation framework G_ϵ introduced in [12] aims to cover the gap considering three main factors used to compute the quality of output data as a composition of several indicators:

1. *privacy guarantee* (ϵ);
2. the *macro-statistics* between attributes: significant correlation among attributes X_i should be preserved:
3. *data utility* in terms of machine learning performances: similar classification performances.

3 Generative Algorithms Selection

For a matter of focus and in order to perform reasonable comparison between algorithms we've picked a specific set of methods which share properties making them belong to the same set. The selection of the privacy algorithms have been carried based on the following principles.

1. **Differential Privacy:** the generative algorithm must include end-to-end differential privacy with mathematical proof of it.
2. **Tabular Data:** the generative algorithm must be designed to ingest and generate heterogeneous tabular data.
3. **Publication Relevance:** the algorithm must be published in a top conference or journal specialized in data generation and/or privacy.
4. **Code:** authors must have published at least pseudo-code of their implementation or the source-code must be publicly available.
5. **Model:** the algorithm must make use of marginal probabilities and correlation matrix or represent attributes dependence as Directed Acyclic Graphs (DAG).

Table 1. Properties of each algorithm.

Algorithm	Marginal	Corr. Matrix	DAG Dependence
NPGauss	✓	✓	X
Gauss	✓	✓	X
Copula-Shirley	✓	✓	✓
DPBayes	✓	X	✓

We select algorithms that represent data distributions using marginal histograms and/or correlation matrices (which form the basis for copula functions) and/or Directed Acyclic Graphs (DAG) of marginal histograms to model attributes dependence. Specifically, the algorithms considered in our evaluation include *NPGauss* and *Gauss*, which utilize marginal distributions and correlation matrices (Gaussian Copulae). Copula Shirley incorporates marginal histograms, correlation matrices and a tree structure (DAG). Lastly, PrivBayes employs marginal histograms and a DAG to model attributes dependence. Table 1 provides a summary of the key characteristics of each algorithm.

3.1 PrivBayes

PrivBayes [23] is a differential privacy method for disclosing high-dimensional data. It creates a Bayesian Network (namely a DAG) N from a dataset D, which serves as a model of the correlations between attributes in D, and an approximation of the distributions in D using a set P of low-dimensional marginals. Then, PrivBayes introduces noise into each marginal in P to ensure differential privacy and uses the noisy marginals and the Bayesian network to construct an approximation of the data distribution in D. Finally, PrivBayes takes samples from the approximate distribution to create a synthetic dataset. By injecting noise into the low-dimensional marginals in P instead of the high-dimensional dataset D, PrivBayes overcomes the well-known curse of dimensionality issue. PrivBayes uses both low-dimensional marginal probabilities and DAG dependence by nature.

3.2 DPCopula and Gaussian

DPCopula [16] is a collection of techniques for generating differentially private synthetic data using Copula functions for multi-dimensional data. The method works by computing a differentially private copula function from which synthetic data can be sampled. Copula functions are used to describe the dependence between multivariate random vectors and enable the construction of the multivariate joint distribution using one-dimensional marginal distributions. The authors propose two methods for estimating the parameters of the copula functions with differential privacy: maximum likelihood estimation and Kendall's τ correlation estimation (**NPGauss**). Additionally, the authors provide an improved version of the algorithm that aggregates low-cardinality attributes to overcome the degradation performances on those (**Gauss**) through dataset partitioning.

3.3 Copula-Schirley (Vine)

A vine copula is a family of copulas used to model dependencies between variables in high-dimensional data. The term "vine" is used to describe the tree-like structure used to represent the dependence structure between the variables in the copula. This structure is typically represented as a directed acyclic graph (DAG), with nodes representing variables and edges representing the direction of dependence between them. COPULA-SHIRLEY, presented in [13], is a differentially private approach for synthesizing data using vine copulas with differential privacy training. COPULA-SHIRLEY is an interpretable model that can be applied to heterogeneous types of data while maintaining utility. To overcome the curse of dimensionality, COPULA-SHIRLEY uses a set of bi-variate copulas interconnected by a tree-like structure (DAG) to model dependencies. Each node in the DAG represents a bi-variate copula, and the edges between the nodes represent the direction of the dependence between the variables similarly to Bayesian Networks.

4 Evaluation Framework

Within this context, the evaluation framework is similar to the one introduced in [12], but it includes more data utility metrics and machine learning models. The evaluation framework is a combined metric that considers privacy guarantee, macro-statistics, and data utility:

$$G_\epsilon = \alpha\mu(D_s, D_p) + \beta\delta(D_s, D_p) \tag{1}$$

where α and β are weights that the scientist defines to determine the importance of the two metrics, and ϵ represents the privacy budget value fed into the algorithms as any DP algorithm requires.

4.1 Macro Statistics

The proposed macro-statistics measure μ is computed using ϕ_k introduced in [4], as it represents a practical correlation coefficient for heterogeneous datasets where m denotes the number of attributes of the dataset.

$$\mu(D_s, D_p) = \frac{\|\phi_k(D_s) - \phi_k(D_p)\|_2}{m(m-1)/2} \tag{2}$$

In Eq. 2 we do compute the L_2 norm of the difference of the correlation matrices ϕ_k computed on both private and synthetic datasets divided by the number of elements of an upper triangular matrix (having dimension $m \times m$) due to the symmetric nature of ϕ_k.

4.2 Data Utility

The data utility measure δ is calculated as

$$\delta(D_s, D_p) = \frac{1}{mKL}\sum_{i=1}^{m}\sum_{k=1}^{K}\sum_{l=1}^{L} \|acc^l(M^k_{X_i,D_s}) - acc^l(M^k_{X_i,D_p})\|_2 \tag{3}$$

where as described more in depth in [12] m is the number of Machine Learning Tasks (one per attribute in [12]), K is the number of different Machine Learning Models and L is the total number of different Accuracy Scores which can be any metric used to evaluate machine learning tasks. It is important to note that M can be any machine learning task which is compatible with the nature of the target attribute in question.

5 Experimental Setup and Results

We consider four datasets with different characteristics, record sizes, and attribute types, all related to credit and financial status. The *Default of Credit Card Clients* (Default Credit) [15] dataset mostly consists of numerical attributes. The *Adults Census* (Adults) [19] and *Credit Approval* (CRX) [18] datasets are mostly composed of categorical attributes, but differ in their sizes as shown in Table 2. The *Financial Services* (Fin Services) [17] dataset is also related to finance, but is distinct from the other three datasets in terms of its characteristics. Most of these datasets include a classification label. The first three datasets can be found in the UCI machine learning repository [8] while *Financial Services* comes from OTP Bank which is lacking classification labels.

We have used the following settings: $K = 3$ (*SVC, Logistic Regression and Decision Trees*) and $L = 3$ in Eq. (3), $\alpha = 1$ and $\beta = 1$ in Eq. (1). In this context in the data utility metric δ the parameter $m = 1$ and it refers to the specific target class of the dataset in question. While the values of the privacy budget ϵ (parameter of the SDG algorithms) the following values have been selected: (0.05, 0.1, 0.2, 0.4, 0.8, 1.6).

All the classifiers' hyper-parameters are the default ones as we used *Scikit-Learn 0.24.2*. All the algorithms have been run using a computer equipped with an Intel *CPU i7-7500U@2.70GHz* and *16GB RAM DDR4*. All the ML tasks have been deployed using Python's *3.5.10 Scikit-Learn 0.22.2* and the average score of three runs have been accounted for each accuracy metric: Accuracy, Recall and F1 Score. The values of degree of PrivBayes network has been fixed to 2.

5.1 G Score

Taking into account the overall score G_ϵ it is observable that the overall behavior at varying of ϵ it's consistent to all the methods. This behavior most probably is due to the fact that the tested methods belong to the same set of algorithms - sharing at least partially the same theoretical foundations. This factor not only validates our results but also enforces previous findings regarding this family of algorithms.

In general it is possible to observe that no algorithm clearly dominates as in Figs. 1 and 2. But COPULA-SHIRLEY (Vine) and DPCopula Hybrid (Gauss) tend to have similar results both on curve shape/convergence and score values, this is confirmed by both members of Eq. (1).

The overall G_ϵ score for varying ϵ can be observed in Figs. 1 and 2. While for the ML performances the data utility term δ in Eq. 3 over different values of ϵ can be observed in Figs. 3 and 4. At higher values of ϵ both methods show to perform more reliably than the PrivBayes or NPGauss as they do converge more steadily than the others.

On the other end PrivBayes and NPGauss look similar on their convergence but for the Adults dataset. Further research lead us to the conclusion that Copula Gauss in general tends to miss-generate low cardinality attribute values and in our experimental setting the Adults dataset is the dataset with the most of those.

It is worth to note that all of the algorithms had their worst performances on the same dataset, namely the Default Credit, this dataset has mostly only numerical attributes except for the target class. This outcome had been imputed to the fact that correlations among attributes are not linear and most of the models used to validate the data utility can't really capture non-linear relations between features, furthermore also the correlation coefficient used for macro-statistics reduces to Pearson's correlation (linear correlation) when evaluating two numerical features.

Table 2. Properties of each dataset.

Data Set	Categorical	Numerical	N. Attributes	N. Records	N. Classes
Default Credit	1	23	24	30000	2
Adults	9	5	14	32561	2
CRX	10	5	15	653	2
Fin Services	3	11	14	4122	0

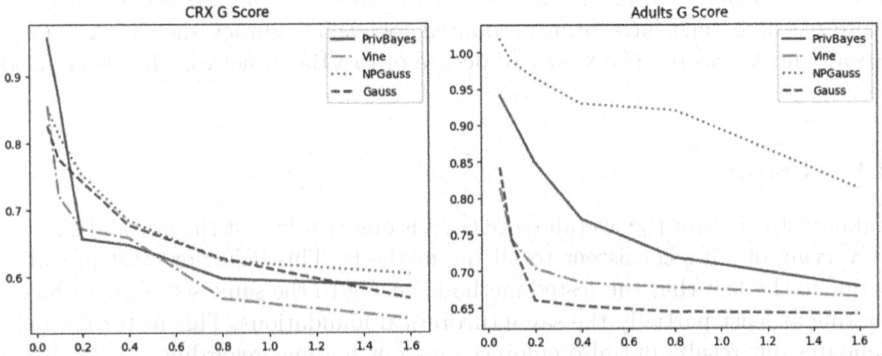

Fig. 1. Values of G_ϵ over the four algorithms deployed on CRX and Adults datasets (a lower value G_ϵ is better as it means that the synthetic dataset is similar to the original private one). The x axes represent values of ϵ while the y axes represent G_ϵ.

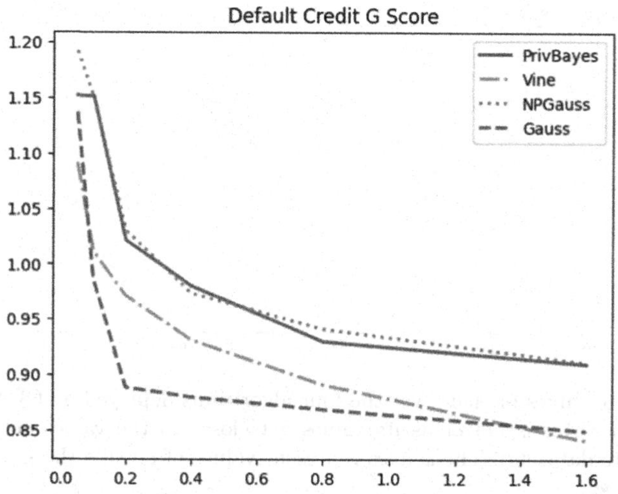

Fig. 2. Values of G_ϵ over Default Credit dataset (a lower value G_ϵ is better as it means that the synthetic dataset is similar to the original one). The x axis represents values of ϵ while the y axis represents G_ϵ.

5.2 Accuracy Metrics

Regarding δ, it is noticeable that the behavior of all methods is quite similar when varying ϵ. At higher values of ϵ, all methods perform more reliably, as the average of the three accuracy metrics used visibly increases (Figs. 3 and 4). Once again, PrivBayes and NPGauss look similar, but their convergence regarding this metric is different, with PrivBayes resulting in the best performing method and NPGauss being the worst. Further analysis led us to the conclusion that Copula Gauss tends to misgenerate low cardinality attributes in general, and this might occur when binning continuous variables into too small bins.

All of the algorithms had their worst performances on the same dataset, namely the Default Credit. This dataset mostly contains numerical attributes except for the target class. This outcome had been attributed to the fact that correlations among attributes are not linear, and most of the models used to validate the data utility cannot capture non-linear relations between features.

5.3 Macro-Statistics

Along this study we've recognized that the overall preservation of macro-statistics term μ for different values of ϵ it's fundamental both for practicing *Exploratory Data Analysis* (EDA) and eventually for *Machine Learning* (ML) performances and benchmarks. As expected we've observed that in terms of macro-statistics defined in Eq. (2) as the value of ϵ decreases correlations get weaker and weaker.

At the same time given a fixed value of ϵ (which defines a lower-bound of privacy thus a lower-bound of noise injection but not necessarily an upper-bound)

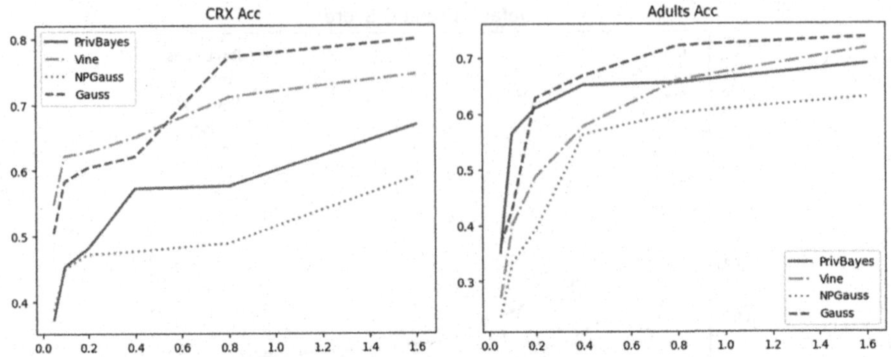

Fig. 3. Average values of Acc_ϵ over the four algorithms deployed on CRX and Adults datasets (higher *Acc* is better as its values get closer to the values achieved on the original private datasets). The x axes represent values of ϵ while the y axes represent the average Acc_ϵ.

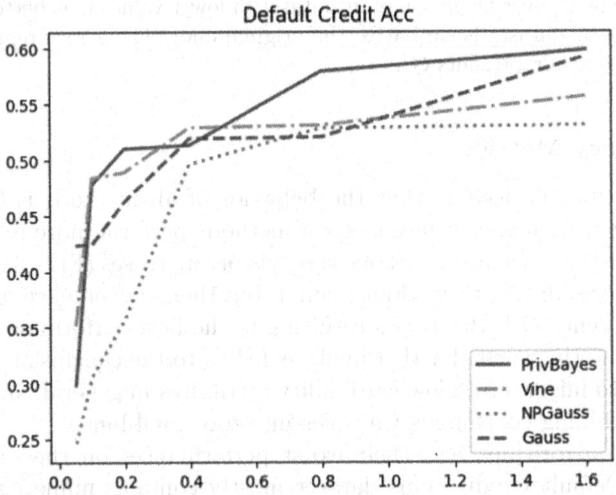

Fig. 4. Average values of Acc_ϵ over Default Credit dataset (higher *Acc* is better as its values get closer to the values achieved on the original private datasets). The x axes represent values of ϵ while the y axes represent the average Acc_ϵ.

each algorithm can behave differently depending on its design and thus to its internal representation of the attributes distributions/relations possibly leading to a different magnitude of the sampling error Fig. 5 gives an illustration of this outcome. In Fig. 5 it is possible to observe the four correlation matrices (NPGauss has been omitted because the results are very similar to PrivBayes). It is possible to note that for the same dataset (Default Credit) the pairwise values of ϕ_k appear to be more unstable as we look clockwise from the ground truth onward Vine tends to slightly weaken all the main correlations but it's still possible to observe the main structure of the matrix (though some "new stronger" correlations seem to be created). Gauss Copula maintain an overall weaker structure with several new correlations. While PrivBayes preserves mainly the correlations of the categorical attributes. This latter behavior might be due to the splitting of continuous values performed by PrivBayes as per its design.

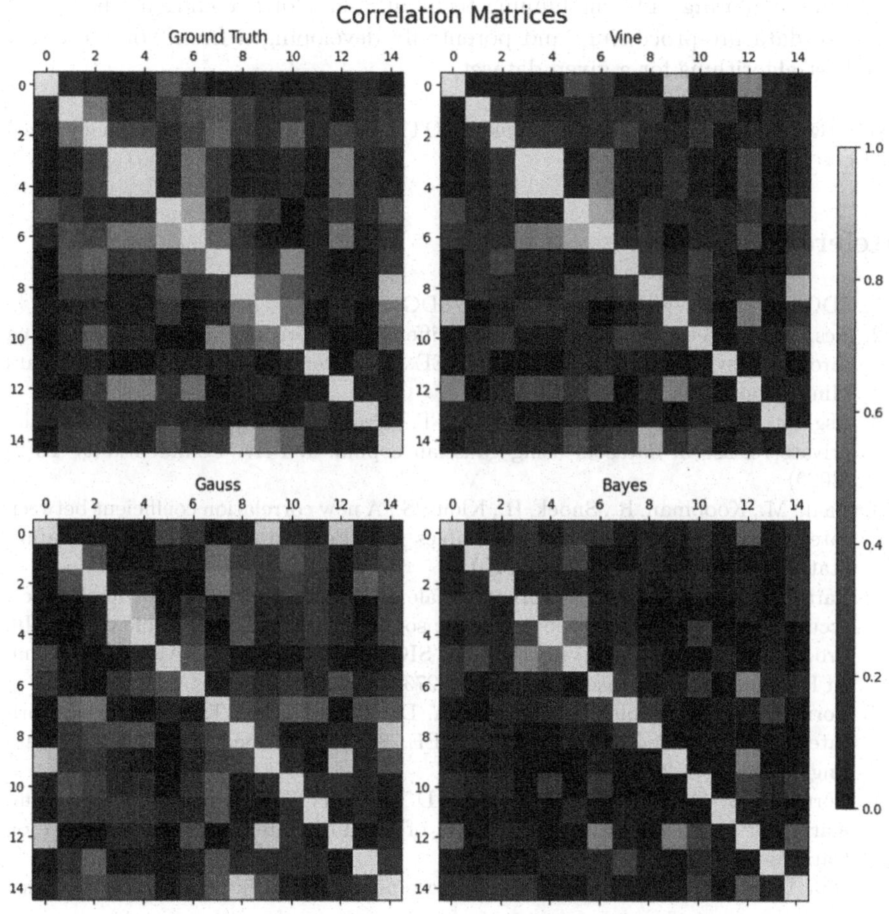

Fig. 5. Correlation matrices over Fin Services dataset given a fixed value of $\epsilon = 0.8$, x and y axes are the attributes while the values of ϕ_k between each attribute are represented by the colored cells of the matrix.

6 Conclusions and Future Work

We have performed an empirical evaluation study on DP SDG. Specifically, we have performed a benchmark of differentially-private synthetic data generation

(DP SDG) algorithms for tabular data with heterogeneous attributes in the field of finance and credit. We evaluated a specific set of algorithms that are related, and found that their overall performances confirm this. Our evaluation considered their utility in terms of machine learning and macro-statistics, such as pairwise correlations in a balanced setup. However, we found that on numeric data, these algorithms tend to be weak or require further pre-processing to improve their performances. Our research raises important questions for future research, including exploring different binning techniques and/or encoding methods as a form of data pre-processing, and potentially developing a framework to select the best algorithms for a given dataset.

Acknowledgments. We are thankful to OTP Bank for sharing their anonymized data.

References

1. SDGym. https://github.com/sdv-dev/SDGym
2. Acs, G., Castelluccia, C., Chen, R.: Differentially private histogram publishing through lossy compression. In: 2012 IEEE 12th International Conference on Data Mining, pp. 1–10. IEEE (2012)
3. Asghar, H.J., Ding, M., Rakotoarivelo, T., Mrabet, S., Kaafar, D.: Differentially private release of datasets using gaussian copula. J. Priv. Confidentiality **10**(2) (2020)
4. Baak, M., Koopman, R., Snoek, H., Klous, S.: A new correlation coefficient between categorical, ordinal and interval variables with Pearson characteristics. Comput. Stat. Data Anal. **152**, 107043 (2020)
5. Barak, B., Chaudhuri, K., Dwork, C., Kale, S., McSherry, F., Talwar, K.: Privacy, accuracy, and consistency too: a holistic solution to contingency table release. In: Proceedings of the Twenty-Sixth ACM SIGMOD-SIGACT-SIGART Symposium on Principles of Database Systems, pp. 273–282 (2007)
6. Cormode, G., Procopiuc, C., Srivastava, D., Shen, E., Yu, T.: Differentially private spatial decompositions. In: 2012 IEEE 28th International Conference on Data Engineering, pp. 20–31. IEEE (2012)
7. Cormode, G., Procopiuc, C., Srivastava, D., Tran, T.T.: Differentially private summaries for sparse data. In: Proceedings of the 15th International Conference on Database Theory, pp. 299–311 (2012)
8. Dua, D., Graff, C.: UCI machine learning repository (2017). http://archive.ics.uci.edu/ml
9. Dwork, C.: Differential privacy. In: Bugliesi, M., Preneel, B., Sassone, V., Wegener, I. (eds.) ICALP 2006. LNCS, vol. 4052, pp. 1–12. Springer, Heidelberg (2006). https://doi.org/10.1007/11787006_1
10. Dwork, C., McSherry, F., Nissim, K., Smith, A.: Calibrating noise to sensitivity in private data analysis. In: Halevi, S., Rabin, T. (eds.) TCC 2006. LNCS, vol. 3876, pp. 265–284. Springer, Heidelberg (2006). https://doi.org/10.1007/11681878_14
11. Dwork, C., Roth, A., et al.: The algorithmic foundations of differential privacy. Found. Trends Theor. Comput. Sci. **9**(3–4), 211–407 (2014)
12. Galloni, A., Lendák, I., Horváth, T.: A novel evaluation metric for synthetic data generation. In: Analide, C., Novais, P., Camacho, D., Yin, H. (eds.) IDEAL 2020.

LNCS, vol. 12490, pp. 25–34. Springer, Cham (2020). https://doi.org/10.1007/978-3-030-62365-4_3
13. Gambs, S., Ladouceur, F., Laurent, A., Roy-Gaumond, A.: Growing synthetic data through differentially-private vine copulas. Proc. Priv. Enhancing Technol. **2021**(3), 122–141 (2021)
14. Hay, M., Machanavajjhala, A., Miklau, G., Chen, Y., Zhang, D.: Principled evaluation of differentially private algorithms using DPBench. In: Proceedings of the 2016 International Conference on Management of Data, pp. 139–154 (2016)
15. Yeh, I.-C.: Default of credit card clients data. https://archive.ics.uci.edu/ml/datasets/default+of+credit+card+clients. Accessed 31 Mar 2023
16. Li, H., Xiong, L., Jiang, X.: Differentially private synthesization of multi-dimensional data using copula functions. In: Advances in Database Technology: Proceedings. International Conference on Extending Database Technology, vol. 2014, p. 475. NIH Public Access (2014)
17. OTP Bank: Financial Services, Proprietary Data Set
18. Quinlan: Credit approval data set. https://archive.ics.uci.edu/ml/datasets/Credit+Approval. Accessed 31 Mar 2023
19. Kohavi, R., Becker, B.: Adult data set. https://archive.ics.uci.edu/ml/datasets/adult. Accessed 31 Mar 2023
20. Tsybakov, A.B.: Introduction to Nonparametric Estimation. Springer, Cham (2008)
21. Xiao, X., Wang, G., Gehrke, J.: Differential privacy via wavelet transforms. IEEE Trans. Knowl. Data Eng. **23**(8), 1200–1214 (2010)
22. Zhang, J., Zheng, K., Mou, W., Wang, L.: Efficient private ERM for smooth objectives. In: Proceedings of the 26th International Joint Conference on Artificial Intelligence, IJCAI 2017, pp. 3922–3928. AAAI Press (2017)
23. Zhang, J., Cormode, G., Procopiuc, C.M., Srivastava, D., Xiao, X.: Privbayes: private data release via Bayesian networks. ACM Trans. Database Syst. (TODS) **42**(4), 1–41 (2017)
24. Zhang, J., Xiao, X., Xie, X.: PrivTree: a differentially private algorithm for hierarchical decompositions. In: Proceedings of the 2016 International Conference on Management of Data, pp. 155–170 (2016)
25. Zhang, J., Xiao, X., Yang, Y., Zhang, Z., Winslett, M.: PrivGene: differentially private model fitting using genetic algorithms. In: Proceedings of the 2013 ACM SIGMOD International Conference on Management of Data, pp. 665–676 (2013)

Analysing Android Apps Classification and Categories Validation by Using Latent Dirichlet Allocation

Elena Flondor[1(✉)] and Marc Frincu[2]

[1] Faculty of Mathematics and Computer Science, West University of Timisoara, bv. Vasile Parvan, Timisoara, Romania
elena.flondor97@e-uvt.ro

[2] School of Science and Technology, Nottingham Trent University, Cliftom Campus, Nottingham, UK
marc.frincu@ntu.ac.uk

Abstract. A key step in publishing on Google Play Store (GPS) is the manual selection of the app category. The category is highly relevant for users when searching for a suitable app. To prevent misclassification, existing work focused on automating the apps' categories identification through different learning methods. However, most existing approaches do not consider a validation of the categories. This research proposes Latent Dirichlet Allocation (LDA) for categories' validation and for identification of similar apps. LDA can provide human-understandable topics (mixture of words) and it can help in discovering Android apps' categories based on their descriptions. For diversity, the most popular 5,940 apps in US and Romania were considered. LDA performance is evaluated under different scenarios defined by data set processing methods. The evaluation relies on the user's defined categories from GPS. LDA topics are labeled with categories' names based on these and by applying cosine similarity and human interpretation. Results show a model with a corpus containing various parts of speech (i.e., nouns, adjectives, verbs) and improved with phrases can achieve a precision of 0.69. Moreover, the analysis hints there might exist discrepancies between the GPS guideline regarding the categories' content and their actual content, but further studies are required.

Keywords: Unsupervised Machine Learning · Topic Modeling · Latent Dirichlet Allocation · Classification · Topic Labeling · Android Applications

1 Introduction

In the last decade, the arrival and continuous development of the smartphones changed our lives significantly. Developers of Android [2] applications are constantly sharing their products in this ever-growing market. Google Play Store

N. T. Nguyen et al. (Eds.): ICCCI 2023, LNAI 14162, pp. 282–297, 2023.
https://doi.org/10.1007/978-3-031-41456-5_22

(GPS) [1] is one of the primary sources of distribution for Android device users. On publishing on this market, besides other information, developers choose the category for their applications. It should reflect the utility of their applications and can be selected from a predefined list [24].

Current focus of existing work is on developing automated methods for categorizing Android applications. Researchers applied Supervised to Unsupervised Machine Learning methods and used Topic Modeling and other Natural Language Processing (NLP) techniques for feature extraction from application descriptions for instance (see Sect. 2). Nevertheless, the validation of the correspondence between what categories contain and what specialty markets recommend as being suitable for their content is not considered.

In this work, *we concentrate our attention to automatize the process of grouping applications with similar behaviors to prevent wrong categorization.* We consider Topic Modeling on applications' descriptions, specifically Latent Dirichlet Allocation (LDA) [6], to solve this problem. Due to its capacity in content resuming and in automatically determining the cluster of words (further called *topics*) based on a collection of applications descriptions, we can analyze if the content of the categories corresponds to content examples proposed by Google Play Store [24]. In summary, we highlight our key contributions as follows:

- We propose an automatic method for Android applications categorization using LDA and processing applications' public descriptions and titles;
- We conduct experiments on the process of building the dictionary corpus of LDA. Our study shows that LDA achieves better results with a dictionary corpus rich in parts of speech and improved with phrases (Sect. 3.2);
- We adopt an approach of labeling topics generated by LDA based on categories' content suggested by Google Play Store. Our results hint at the existence of discrepancies between the proposed content and the actual content of the categories.

The rest of the paper is structured as follows: Sect. 2 discusses several relevant works applying LDA; Sect. 3 discusses the applied NLP techniques, LDA and several methods of evaluation; in Sect. 4 the experiments and results discussed and the quality of the discovered clusters will be analysed; Sect. 5 summarizes the results and outlines future work.

2 Literature Survey

This section provides an overview of NLP (Sect. 2.1) techniques usually used to prepare document corpus for further topic modeling analysis; and discusses applications of LDA (Sect. 2.2).

2.1 Natural Language Processing

NLP is a widely used Machine Learning branch that provides multiple techniques [4] that can be used depending on the task and data involved. A various range of NLP techniques have been extensively applied to prepare data for Topic Modeling techniques. In [17] is mentioned the usage of stop words removal and stemming techniques to process the description of the applications. For mobile app reviews labeling, lowering, tokenization, stop words removal, punctuation removal, and parts of speech tagging are implied [22]. In other work, which supposes topic labeling of new documents tokenization and stop words removal are combined with n-gram splitting [3]. In [7], besides other common NLP techniques, the dictionary corpus is improved by the usage of bi-grams.

In our work, the steps we decided to apply in the data processing phase were chosen to help LDA to discover hidden relations between the words and for a better exploration of the descriptions structures [21]. Compared to previous works, we apply a wider range of NLP techniques.

2.2 Latent Dirichlet Allocation

LDA was mentioned for the first time by Blei et al. in the Journal of Machine Learning Research [6]. They took into account the problem of modeling text corpora and proposed an algorithm capable to discover brief descriptions for the components of a given document corpus through Unsupervised Learning. It uses statistical methods to learn the underlying structure of the data and is often used in NLP applications.

As our work is made in the context of mobile applications, some of the contributions in this domain brought by LDA consist in obtaining good results for labeling mobile applications users' reviews [22]. LDA document topic matrix was implied in detection of misclassified Android applications published on Google Play Store [16]. In [26] the researchers use it for applications' categorization based on native code. In [20] the authors extracted topic vectors for a K-Means clustering using LDA. Garg et al. [10] applied LDA on apps descriptions to validate whether an application has the behavior defined by its description. In the same direction, Ma et al. [17] used, LDA for processing applications descriptions. Furthermore, LDA was used to study the grayware level of an application [5].

In contrast to the above-discussed work focused on Android, the objective of our work follows to observe which is the real performance of the LDA in applications clustering without any help from other Machine Learning methods previously used in the mentioned studies. Moreover, we base our study on data extracted from public information, avoiding any time or memory expensive costs implied by static or dynamic analysis [26]. On the other hand, we label the generated topics in a validation process of the categories' content.

3 Methodology

In the context of the current research work, we studied the performance and the help that LDA algorithm can bring in the problem of categorization of Android applications based only on data present in Android market stores. The entire framework of the process is represented in Fig. 1. The process is based on [25]

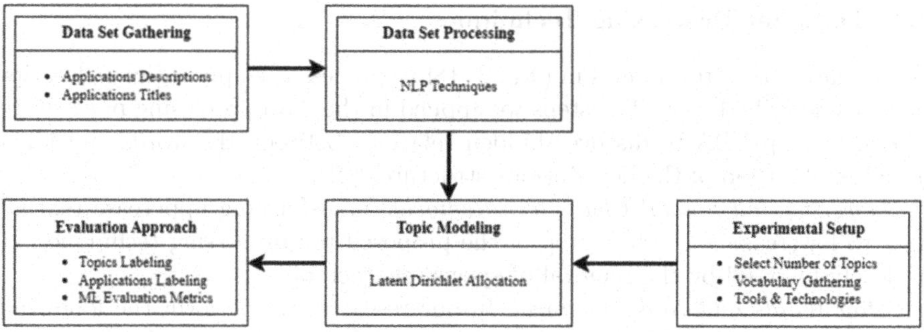

Fig. 1. Research framework.

which we adapted to our study by adding multiple techniques of data processing (Sect. 3.2) and by changing the process of topics labeling.

The first step consists of **Data Set Gathering** (Sect. 3.1) and choosing relevant information for the topic modeling approach. The second step is given by **Data Set Processing** (Sect. 3.2) phase through *NLP Techniques*. The third step represents applying *Latent Dirichlet Allocation*, which was chosen as **Topic Modeling** technique (Sect. 3.3). The **Experimental Setup** (Sect. 3.4), consists in taking important decisions regarding the *number of topics* to be generated, the approach applied in case of *vocabulary gathering*, respectively regarding the *tools and technologies* used. **Evaluation Approach** (Sect. 3.5) describes the *topics labeling* process and how we choose the best performance of LDA.

3.1 Data Set Gathering

The data set used contains Android applications published on Google Play Store. The market provides for the Android developers 32 categories and 17 subcategories of games. For each category, is briefly exemplified its content and the types of categories that a developer or a typical user can find on the market [24]. To ensure variation in our data set, it contains the **top free** and **top grossing** applications in Romania and in the United States from the beginning of December 2022, summing up a total of **5,940 Android applications**[1]. For each one, we considered descriptions and titles. In the case of applications included in Romanian tops, we considered English versions of the descriptions and titles.

The main reason to build the data set based on the most popular Android applications is due to the fact that the popularity of the applications can represent a validation for the category of an application. If a user searches for an application type and he/she finds it, uses it, and reviews it, the application must be in the proper category and should reflect the content of the category. Secondly, such a data set can help us in validating if our approach can understand natural language and the variety of expressions of different app descriptions.

[1] https://www.kaggle.com/datasets/elenaflondor/most-popular-applications-from-google-play-store.

3.2 Data Set Processing Techniques

We applied classic techniques in (NLP) [18] to process the applications' descriptions, as described next. The steps we applied in the data processing phase were chosen to help LDA to discover hidden relations between the words and for a better exploration of the descriptions structures [21].

Lowering and Special Characters Removal. Transforming uppercase textual data to lowercase is the first step in the proposed pre-processing techniques. It is closely followed by the removal of special characters.

Stop Words and Noise Removal. In our research, we perform the following steps to preserve the most relevant words in applications' descriptions:

- *Stop words*, *URLs* and *emojis* are removed. They can increase the computational time and can prevent LDA from focusing on the most relevant information.
- We performed statistics based on unique occurrences of the remaining words and discovered words not reflecting the applications' behavior (*noise words*). They were removed because most of them are present in the descriptions to *promote* and *popularize* different activities related to the developer's work or to encourage the users to share among different social platforms the corresponding application (Fig. 2). Examples of noise words (lowercase) and the unique number of descriptions in which they occur: android - 1336, facebook - 970, google - 884, twitter - 423, instagram - 418, youtube - 253, etc.
- Moreover, *the most used words* are removed based on scenario rules (Sect. 4).

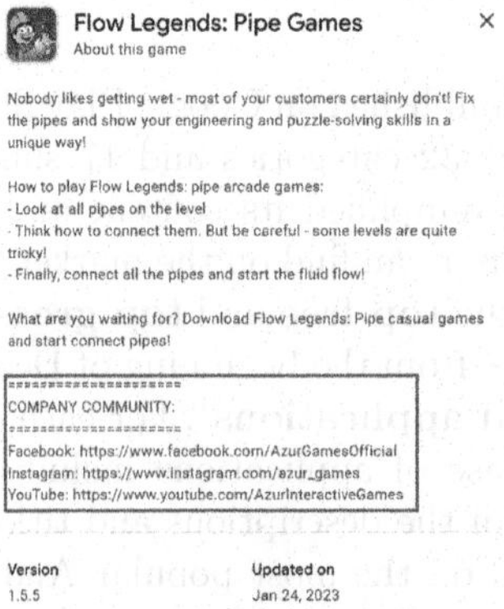

Fig. 2. Application description containing noise words [9].

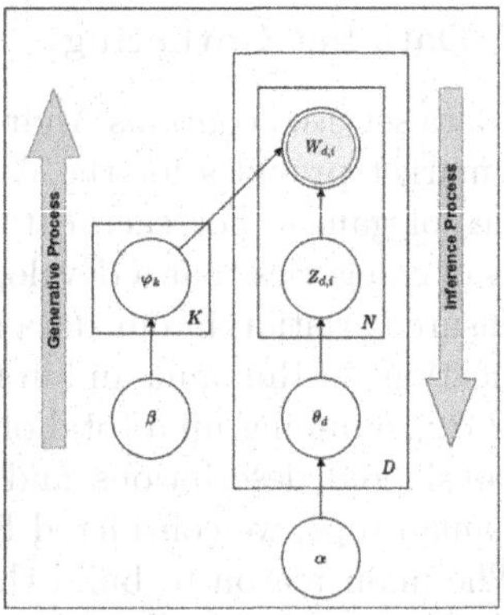

Fig. 3. Graphical representation of Latent Dirichlet Allocation.

Tokenization. Each description was transformed into smaller units term by removing white spaces.

Part of Speech Tagging and Selection. Depending on scenarios, we labeled each word based on its part of speech (e.g., NN - noun, JJR - adjective comparative, JJS - adjective superlative, etc.).

Lemmatization. Normalizing the textual data through lemmatization made it possible to identify the root of any given word. In this way, words with similar roots (lemmas), but different inflections or derivatives of meaning can be associated and viewed as one element.

Phrases Creation. We improved our dictionary corpus in several scenarios, by using the approach proposed by Mikolov et al. [19]. Having a tokenized text, a model is trained to identify co-occurring word pairs that frequently appear together. These co-occurring word pairs are then combined into multi-word phrases, which are represented as a single token in subsequent processing. We considered phrases of length 2, called *bi-grams*. Examples of used bi-grams and their number of occurrences: *real_time* (1205), *game_play* (576), *real_money* (535), *social_medium* (498), *play_game* (460), *weather_forecast* (459), *phone_number* (367), *photo_editor* (354), *video_chat* (338), *blood_pressure* (337).

3.3 Topic Modeling with Latent Dirichlet Allocation

LDA [6] came as an improvement for Probabilistic Latent Semantic Indexing (PLSI) [14], by dealing with its overfitting and achieving better results. Its principal scope is to discover the latent variable in a text document which is represented by the document topic. The output of the method is represented by a topic-keyword matrix. Each discovered topic can be defined by analysis and comprehension of the logical relations between the words with a higher probability. In this research, LDA presumes that each description corresponding to a specific Android application, represents a combination of an ensemble of topic probabilities, and each topic is presumed to be a combination of a fundamental set of words. Figure 3 describes the algorithm. The generative process for topic modeling of the LDA has been adapted from [15] and can be resumed as follows:

Phase 1 - Select $\theta_d \sim Dir(\alpha), d \in \{1, ..., D\}$ and $Dir(\alpha)$ is a Dirichlet distribution with $\alpha < 1$
Phase 2 - Select $\varphi_k \sim Dir(\beta), k \in \{1, ..., K\}$
Phase 3 - Given d, i indices for a word position, $d \in \{1, ..., D\}$ and $i \in \{1, ..., N_d\}$, for each word:
select a topic $Z_{d,i} \sim Multinomial(\theta_d)$
select a word $W_{d,i} \sim Multinomial(\varphi_{Z_{d,i}})$, where $Multinomial(x)$ refers to Multinomial distribution of x.

With respect to content of the data set we use, the modeling notations can be defined as follows: D - number of Android applications descriptions; N_d - number of words in a description; K - number of topics to be determined; α - parameter of the previous Dirichlet regarding the topic distribution per-description; β - parameter of the previous Dirichlet regarding the word distribution per-topic;

θ_d - distribution of the topic corresponding to the description d; φ_k - distribution of the words for a given topic k; $Z_{d,i}$ - topic for the ith word in the description d; $W_{d,i}$ - the ith word in the description d.

3.4 Experimental Setup

The performance of LDA was evaluated by generating a fixed number of 33 topics: one topic for each category of applications. We force the algorithm to validate via topics the description of the applications and the categories' content guideline proposed by GPS. Finally, they ought to correspond. All applications from *Game* categories were labeled under one category because they refer to applications designed for entertainment or educational purposes and have elements of gameplay or game mechanics.

Table 1. Criteria of forming vocabularies in proposed scenarios.

Scenario	PoS Criteria		Bi-grams Criteria	Remove Most Used Words Criteria	
	All PoS	NN & ADJ		50%	20%
S1	X		X	X	
S2		X	X	X	
S3	X		X		X
S4		X	X		X
S5	X			X	
S6		X		X	
S7	X				X
S8		X			X

Cf. Table 1, eight scenarios based on different methods of dictionary corpus generation were analyzed. We chose three main criteria for generating it: (1) we considered using either nouns and adjectives (NN & ADJ), either all parts of speech (PoS) [15]; (2) we were wondering if in our study, a dictionary corpus improved with bi-grams can help LDA in achieving better results [7]; (3) we studied if the presence of the most used words influences the results: we removed either 50%, either 20% of the most used words. Table 1 defines each scenario depending on the criteria for forming the vocabulary. Each present criteria in a given scenario is marked with an **X**.

The experiments are implemented using Python programming language under Windows 10. For example: *pos_tag* from *NLTK 3.4.2* library was used to identify the part of speech of each word and *WordNetLemmatizer* from *nltk.stem* was used for lemmatization. Regarding LDA, it was considered the algorithm implementation from *Gensim 3.7.2* library [11] and the value of hyper-parameters α and β were chosen the same as in the Griffiths's research:

$\frac{50}{number\_of\_topics}$ and 0.1 [13]. From *Gensim*, we also used *Phrases* [12] to compute bi-grams.

3.5 Evaluation Approach

To evaluate LDA regarding its performance in grouping Android applications with similar functionality, our approach is based on topic labeling [3]. The process of topics labeling consists in predicting suitable topics for each Android application category based on the recommendations guideline of GPS [24]. We predict the topic for each stated category using what LDA learned from the applications' descriptions. We observed that in each scenario, several topics were labeled with multiple categories (Fig. 4a). As a consequence, there remained unlabeled topics (Fig. 4b). To determine which scenario offers a better classification of the applications, it was decided *to force the labeling process for the unlabeled topics.* For this we applied two techniques: **cosine similarity** [23] - the label/labels for the most similar topic was assigned to the unlabeled one; respectively through **human interpretation** [8] - the unlabeled topics received a suitable category. To avoid labeling a single topic with multiple categories, for human interpretation we selected the most relevant category name.

The capacity of LDA to categorize applications (Table 2), was measured through: $F1 - Score = 2 \times \frac{Precision \times Recall}{Precision + Recall}$, $Precision = \frac{TP}{TP+FP}$, respectively $Recall = \frac{TP}{TP+FN}$. We define: TP - True positive as being the number of the applications for which the initial category label corresponds to the label of assigned topic; TN - True negative as being the number of applications correctly excluded from unsuitable topics; FP - False positive as being defined as the number of applications wrongly assigned to a labeled topic; FN - False negative as being the number of applications wrongly excluded from suitable topics.

Besides the results obtained for applications categorization, for our experiments we consider: (1) the relation between multiple categories assigned to a single topic; (2) how similar are labels decided through cosine similarity and human interpretation; (3) the number of uniquely labeled topics - should be maximized; (4) and the number of unlabeled topics - should be minimized.

4 Experiments and Results

In this section we compare and analyze our results (Sect. 4.1); the word topics and their relation with the categories labels in the best scenario (Sect. 4.2).

4.1 Comparative Analysis of the Scenarios Results

During the labeling process, multiple situations occurred: 2, or even 3, 4, or 5 categories were assigned to each topic (Fig. 5), but between 7 and 18 were uniquely assigned to one topic (Fig. 4a). Nevertheless, in each scenario there remained topics without a category assigned (Fig. 4b). A poor list of examples or a poor definition of a category might cause these cases (e.g, *Comics* category – *Comic players, comic titles* – might not be associated very well with any topic).

Cf. Fig. 4, scenario S5 manages to uniquely assign the highest number of topics and it obtains the smallest number of unlabeled topics. However, it did not perform the best in applications' categorization. It has one topic labeled with three categories and five topics labeled with two categories (Fig. 5): *Health and Fitness*, with *Medical* and with *Parenting*; *News and Magazines* with *Personalization*; *Auto and Vehicles* with *Finance*; *Libraries and Demo* with *Tools*; *Books and Reference* with *Comics*; *Food and Drink* with *Shopping*; *Maps and Navigation* with *Travel and Local.* Compared to S1 (Table 2), these mistakes seem to have a higher impact. As mentioned previously (Sect. 3.5), relations between the categories assigned to the same topics are important. Similarly, we notice many differences between topic labels assigned through cosine similarity and human interpretation (Table 3), compared to S1 (Sect. 4.2).

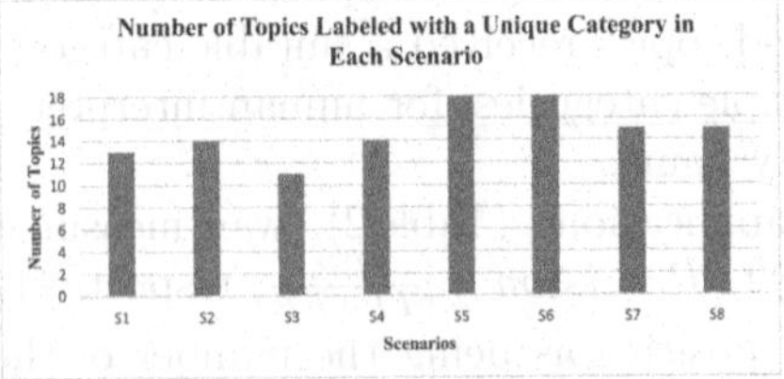

(a) Number of topics labeled with a unique category in each scenario.

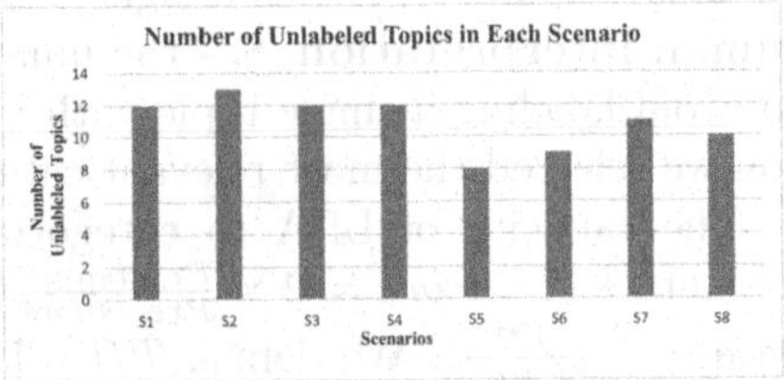

(b) Number of unlabeled topics in each scenario.

Fig. 4. Results of labeling process in each scenario: number of topics labeled with a unique category (4a), respectively number of unlabeled topics in each scenario (4b).

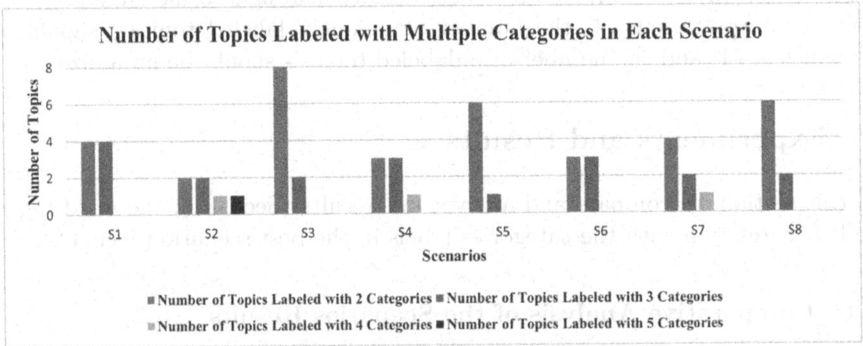

Fig. 5. Number of topics labeled with multiple categories.

Table 2. Table containing the values of evaluation metrics for each scenario. The values of best overall performance (S1) are written in bold.

Scenario		S1	S2	S3	S4	S5	S6	S7	S8
Similarity Method	Evaluation Metric								
Cosine Similarity	Precision	**0.692**	0.626	0.688	0.585	0.636	0.596	0.668	0.620
	Recall	**0.521**	0.502	0.414	0.427	0.432	0.463	0.433	0.397
	F1-Score	**0.550**	0.515	0.431	0.448	0.464	0.477	0.461	0.425
Human Interpretation	Precision	**0.685**	0.621	0.663	0.626	0.654	0.615	0.663	0.596
	Recall	**0.563**	0.532	0.511	0.484	0.513	0.479	0.531	0.486
	F1-Score	**0.579**	0.541	0.526	0.512	0.535	0.500	0.543	0.501

Table 3. Scenario S5: cosine similarity and human interpretation category names assigned to unlabeled topics, and words in topics.

Cosine Similarity Label	Human Interpretation Label	Words in Topics
Game	Game	game, drive, race, simulator, city, park, real, car, truck, realistic
Entertainment	Health & Fitness	watch, select, digital, please, face, support, display, available, heart, wear
Lifestyle	Events	right, want, make, even, experience, ever, come, never, find, back
Weather	Business	business, price, search, sell, market, notification, real, receive, alert, stock
Game	Game	game, slot, casino, play, earn, reward, real, money, coin, bonus
Social	Tools	service, download, privacy, update, user, link, status, mobile, allow, require
Game	Game	world, battle, build, fight, hero, character, adventure, power, unique, become
Lifestyle	Education	question, test, find, answer, know, help, quiz, school, problem, type

By further analyzing the results (Table 2), we observe that the best overall performance is obtained in the case of S1 scenario. In several scenarios precision is higher in the case of *cosine similarity* compared with the value obtained when *human interpretation* was applied (S3, S8), or vice-versa (S4, S5, S6). This indicates that the decisions in topics labeling of the two methods are not similar. We obtained a *precision* value of approximately 0.69 for both methods in the case of S1 scenario, which indicates coherence and similarity in topics labeling and helps us in choosing this scenario as having the best performance. Also, it proves better results for *recall* and *f1-score*.

The assignment on the same topic of 5 categories in S2 scenario caught our attention. The S2 model decides to put together the following categories: *Art and Design, Books and Reference, Business, Comics, and Communication*, which are different in scope and utility. Several scenarios put together categories such: *Entertainment, Medical, News and Magazines* (S3), *Lifestyle, Medical, Parenting, Social* (S4), *Art and Design, Books and Reference, Communication* (S6), *Entertainment, News and Magazines, Sports* (S7), *Education, Personalization* (S8). It can be observed how different should be these categories even from the market recommendations [24], and we are aware of the fact that there are other similar assignations. Simultaneously, we observed that some topics are labeled with categories that can be considered related in a slightly manner: *Photography* and *Video Players and Editors* (S3); *Maps and Navigation* and *Travel and Local* (S4, S5, S7, S8).

4.2 Analysis of the Best Model

We previously claimed that the criteria applied in scenario S1, for building the dictionary corpus, achieved the best overall results compared to other proposed scenarios. In the following paragraphs, we analyze the content of the generated topics and if they can be indeed associated with Android applications categories. We discuss the relations between the categories assigned to a single topic. Moreover, we argue the decision of forcing the labeling process of the unlabeled topics.

Words and phrases that can be considered keywords of each topic were discovered (Tables 5 and 6). In the given context, including bi-grams in the dictionary corpus proved to improve the identification of similar applications. In topics generated in scenario S1, LDA helped in discovering important key phrases: *real_time*, *weather_forecast*, *phone_number*, etc. Other key phrases included in top the 20 most important words are: *photo_editor* (topic 11), *credit_card* (topic 14), *text_message* (topic 16), *home_screen* and *high_quality* (topic 18).

Simple keywords can be easily observed on a succinct human interpretation and several correlations can be made: topic 1 - Weather, through words such as: *weather*, *forecast*, etc. and *weather_forecast* and *real_time*; topic 5 - Sports: *team*, *live*, *sport*, etc; topics 16 and 28 - Communication, respectively Dating; words in topic 26 - Maps and Navigation; *topic 32 - Game*, etc.

Table 4. Categories assigned to topics after LDA prediction performed on categories descriptions and examples in the case of S1 scenario.

Topics ID	Categories	Topics ID	Categories	Topics ID	Categories
0	Music & Audio, Video Players & Editors	11	Art & Design, Beauty, Photography	22	Food & Drink
1	Weather	12	House & Home	26	Auto & Vehicles, Maps & Navigation, Travel & Local
2	Productivity	13	Education	27	Entertainment, Medical, News & Magazines
4	Books & Reference, Comics	14	Finance	28	Dating, Events, Social
5	Sports	16	Communication	29	Libraries & Demo, Tools
6	Shopping	18	Personalization	31	Health & Fitness, Parenting
10	Lifestyle	21	Business	32	Game

In the process of topics labeling, there were 13 topics uniquely labeled with one category. Four topics had 3 categories assigned, and 4 topics had 2 categories assigned Table 4. In several cases, these assignations might suggest that the categories are somehow related: *Music and Audio* with *Video Players and Editors*; *Art and Design* with *Photography*; *Auto and Vehicles*, with *Maps and Navigation*, and with *Travel and Local.* On the other hand, several assignations might suggest that there exist discrepancies between the way of exemplification of the categories' content and the assignation of the applications in those categories: *Parenting* with *Fitness and Medical*; *Books and Reference* with *Comics*; *Entertainment* with *Medical* and with *News and Magazines.* Poorer descriptions and succinct examples of what should categories include, can confuse and provoke unwanted misclassifications of the Android applications on the markets.

Several topics have no label assigned (Table 6), though, based on human interpretation, several unlabeled topics seemed to correspond to specific categories (*Topic 3 - Tools*, *Topics 8 and 25 - Game*, *Topic 9 - Education*, etc.). This is the reason for forcing the labeling process. Table 7 describes which are the similar topics discovered using cosine similarity and the categories chosen through human interpretation.

Table 5. Words with highest weights in labeled topics.

Topic 0	Topic 1	Topic 2	Topic 4
video, music, song, audio, sound, record, download, voice, player, play	weather, real_time, alert, location, information, forecast, hour, data, weather_forecast, day	list, note, share, event, calendar, schedule, keep, group, task, easy	story, read, book, love, favorite, girl, popular, reading, enjoy, anime
Topic 5	**Topic 6**	**Topic 10**	**Topic 11**
team, live, match, player, sport, score, world, league, football, soccer	order, product, store, find, item, shop, offer, deal, delivery, fashion	help, guide, plan, home, tip, exercise, tour, well, work, body	photo, color, picture, face, draw, filter, image, sticker, edit, effect
Topic 12	**Topic 13**	**Topic 14**	**Topic 16**
search, price, find, history, vehicle, speed, use, tool, check, information	learn, kid, child, language, baby, help, game, parent, course, english	account, business, payment, card, money, service, manage, customer, bank, company	phone, call, message, number, contact, clean, send, text, phone_number, notification
Topic 18	**Topic 21**	**Topic 22**	**Topic 26**
screen, theme, wallpaper, background, cool, best, customize, skin, custom, icon	file, scan, email, document, share, scanner, easily, page, text, support	recipe, food, train, cook, make, become, restaurant, time, meal, ingredient	drive, map, travel, location, park, place, route, navigation, trip, city
Topic 27	**Topic 28**	**Topic 29**	**Topic 31**
news, watch, content, show, favorite, stream, live, channel, access, movie	chat, date, people, friend, find, single, meet, profile, community, match	device, control, smart, support, connect, home, camera, light, button, use	track, tracker, health, help, care, sleep, doctor, medical, step, activity
Topic 32			
game, battle, race, fight, real, simulator, hero, skill, mode, challenge			

Table 6. Words with highest weights in unlabeled topics.

Topic 3	Topic 7	Topic 8
data, device, access, internet, secure, website, security, private, network, protect	create, design, make, room, style, home, name, different, party, house	game, play, card, slot, player, friend, coin, casino, bonus, classic
Topic 9	**Topic 15**	**Topic 17**
question, test, want, know, find, first, star, need, answer, official	reward, make, earn, every, point, cash, start, time, money, extra	world, build, character, adventure, explore, unique, collect, animal, island, magic
Topic 19	**Topic 20**	**Topic 23**
include, mobile, available, experience, full, charge, access, best, download, million	system, service, require, setting, permission, allow, upgrade, experience, support, download	time, information, please, use, display, version, change, problem, select, show
Topic 24	**Topic 25**	**Topic 30**
subscription, privacy, purchase, user, access, trial, month, time, plan, play	game, word, level, play, puzzle, challenge, match, relax, brain, tile	right, even, want, best, take, good, every, make, bring, never

Table 7. Topic IDs assigned to unlabeled topics through cosine similarity and the category name assigned to topics based on human interpretation.

Unlabeled Topic ID	Cosine Similarity Topic ID	Human Interpreted Category
3	29	Tools
7	11	Art & Design
8	32	Game
9	13	Education
15	22	Finance
17	5	Game
19	27	Entertainment
20	29	Tools
23	1	Weather
24	10	Lifestyle
25	32	Game
30	10	Lifestyle

5 Conclusion and Future Work

This paper discussed the performance of Latent Dirichlet Allocation (LDA) in the context of the identification of groups of Android applications with similar functionalities revealed through their descriptions published on GPS. The process has been done by applying suitable NLP techniques to the data set information (Sect. 3.2). The experimental setup was based on eight scenarios presenting differences in the process of dictionary corpus generation. Labeling the generated topics was a challenge; it implied using the public examples and recommendations made by the GPS for the content of the categories. The challenge came in the case of the unlabeled topics, for which cosine similarity and human interpretation were used to force the labeling process.

According to our results, LDA can achieve good results in applications' classification if the dictionary corpus is improved with phrases and contains multiple types of parts of speech. Our results showed that removing the words present in more than 50% of the documents helps more than reducing words occurring in more than 20%. Overall, the values obtained for precision, recall, and f1-score, 0.69 (0.68 - for human interpretation), 0.52 (0.56 - for human interpretation), and respectively 0.55 (0.58 - for human interpretation) show S1 achieves better results and stability in its prediction decision compared with the rest of the studied scenarios. It obtained the best results not only due to the fact that it had the highest values for evaluation metrics, but because the cosine similarity assigned labels were similar to the labels chosen with human interpretation. We consider the results show promising results for LDA to categorize Android applications. Moreover, we found that the association of multiple categories, with high differences regarding to the utility of the applications, to a single topic, insinuates discrepancies between the applications' descriptions and categories' content recommendations made by GPS. They suggest that an improvement with clearer information in both content recommendations and applications' descriptions, might increase the performance of the LDA.

For future work, a separate evaluation of each criterion used to form the dictionary corpus might be necessary to observe which criteria helped more to achieve the results. In addition, it remains to include information extracted from applications' archive - static analysis, and applications' run time behavior - dynamic analysis, and to observe if there is an improvement of the performance in LDA. Lastly, we will study if an improvement in content categories recommendations might help in better categorization of the Android apps.

References

1. Google play store. https://play.google.com/store. Accessed 14 Feb 2023
2. Android. Software (2008). https://source.android.com/. Accessed 14 Feb 2023
3. Adhitama, R., Kusumaningrum, R., Gernowo, R.: Topic labeling towards news document collection based on latent Dirichlet allocation and ontology. In: 2017 1st International Conference on Informatics and Computational Sciences (ICICoS), pp. 247–252 (2017). https://doi.org/10.1109/ICICOS.2017.8276370
4. Alam, S.: Applying natural language processing for detecting malicious patterns in Android applications. Forensic Sci. Int.: Digit. Invest. 301270 (2021). https://doi.org/10.1016/j.fsidi.2021.301270
5. Andow, B., Nadkarni, A., Bassett, B., Enck, W., Xie, T.: A study of grayware on google play. In: 2016 IEEE Security and Privacy Workshops (SPW), pp. 224–233 (2016). https://doi.org/10.1109/SPW.2016.40
6. Blei, D.M., Ng, A.Y., Jordan, M.I.: Latent Dirichlet allocation. J. Mach. Learn. Res. 993–1022 (2003)
7. Bunyamin, H., Sulistiani, L.: Automatic topic clustering using latent Dirichlet allocation with skip-gram model on final project abstracts. In: 2017 21st International Computer Science and Engineering Conference (ICSEC), pp. 1–5 (2017). https://doi.org/10.1109/ICSEC.2017.8443795
8. Chang, J., Boyd-Graber, J., Gerrish, S., Wang, C., Blei, D.M.: Reading tea leaves: how humans interpret topic models. In: Proceedings of the 22nd International Conference on Neural Information Processing Systems, NIPS 2009, pp. 288–296. Curran Associates Inc., Red Hook (2009)
9. Games CA: Flow legends: Pipe games. Android Application (2021). https://play.google.com/store/apps/details?id=com.vladk.pipemasters. Accessed 14 Feb 2023
10. Garg, M., Monga, A., Bhatt, P., Arora, A.: Android app behaviour classification using topic modeling techniques and outlier detection using app permissions. In: 2016 Fourth International Conference on Parallel, Distributed and Grid Computing (PDGC), pp. 500–506 (2016). https://doi.org/10.1109/PDGC.2016.7913246
11. Gensim: Parallelized latent Dirichlet allocation. Technology. https://radimrehurek.com/gensim/models/ldamulticore.html. Accessed 14 Feb 2023
12. Gensim: Phrases. https://radimrehurek.com/gensim/models/phrases.html. Accessed 14 Feb 2023
13. Griffiths, T.L., Steyvers, M.: Finding scientific topics. Proc. Natl. Acad. Sci. **101**(Suppl_1), 5228–5235 (2004). https://doi.org/10.1073/pnas.0307752101
14. Hofmann, T.: Unsupervised learning by probabilistic latent semantic analysis, pp. 177–196 (2001). https://doi.org/10.1023/A:1007617005950

15. Joung, J., Kim, H.: Automated keyword filtering in LDA for identifying product attributes from online reviews. J. Mech. Des. **143** (2020). https://doi.org/10.1115/1.4048960
16. Priya Kalaivani, K., Arulanand, N.: Mobile app categorization based on app descriptions and API calls. Int. J. Aquatic Sci. **12**(2), 3718–3728 (2021). http://www.journal-aquaticscience.com/article_135795.html
17. Ma, S., Wang, S., Lo, D., Deng, R.H., Sun, C.: Active semi-supervised approach for checking app behavior against its description. In: 2015 IEEE 39th Annual Computer Software and Applications Conference, vol. 2, pp. 179–184 (2015). https://doi.org/10.1109/COMPSAC.2015.93
18. Manning, C.D., Schütze, H.: Foundations of Statistical Natural Language Processing. MIT Press, Cambridge (1999)
19. Mikolov, T., Sutskever, I., Chen, K., Corrado, G., Dean, J.: Distributed representations of words and phrases and their compositionality (2013). https://doi.org/10.48550/ARXIV.1310.4546
20. Mokarizadeh, S., Rahman, M., Matskin, M.: Mining and analysis of apps in Google Play, pp. 527–535 (2013)
21. Pollock, L., Vijay-Shanker, K., Hill, E., Sridhara, G., Shepherd, D.: Natural language-based software analyses and tools for software maintenance. In: De Lucia, A., Ferrucci, F. (eds.) ISSSE 2009-2011. LNCS, vol. 7171, pp. 94–125. Springer, Heidelberg (2013). https://doi.org/10.1007/978-3-642-36054-1_4
22. Puspaningrum, A., Siahaan, D., Fatichah, C.: Mobile app review labeling using LDA similarity and term frequency-inverse cluster frequency (TF-ICF). In: 2018 10th International Conference on Information Technology and Electrical Engineering (ICITEE), pp. 365–370 (2018). https://doi.org/10.1109/ICITEED.2018.8534785
23. Salton, G., Wong, A., Yang, C.S.: A vector space model for automatic indexing. Commun. ACM **18**(11), 613–620 (1975). https://doi.org/10.1145/361219.361220
24. Store, G.P.: Choose a category and tags for your app or game. https://support.google.com/googleplay/android-developer/answer/9859673?hl=en. Accessed 14 Feb 2023
25. Suadaa, L.H., Purwarianti, A.: Combination of latent Dirichlet allocation (LDA) and term frequency-inverse cluster frequency (TFxICF) in Indonesian text clustering with labeling. In: 2016 4th International Conference on Information and Communication Technology (ICoICT), pp. 1–6 (2016). https://doi.org/10.1109/ICoICT.2016.7571885
26. Yang, C.Z., Tu, M.H.: Yang, C.Z. Tu, M.H.: LACTA: An enhanced automatic software categorization on the native code of Android applications. In: Proceedings of the International Multiconference of Engineers and Computer Scientists (IMECS), vol. 1, pp. 1–5 (2012)

Staircase Recognition Based on Possibilistic Feature Quality Assessment Method

Mouna Medhioub[1,2](✉), Sonda Ammar Bouhamed[1,2], Imen Khanfir Kallel[3,5], Nabil Derbel[3], and Olfa Kanoun[4]

[1] National School of Electronics and Telecommunications of Sfax, University of Sfax, Sfax, Tunisia
mouna.medhioub28@gmail.com

[2] Digital Research Center of Sfax (CRNS), Laboratory of Signals, systeMs, aRtificial Intelligence, neTworkS(SM@RTS), University of Sfax, Sfax, Tunisia

[3] National School of Engineers of Sfax, University of Sfax, CEM Laboratory, Sfax, Tunisia

[4] Measurement and Sensor Technology, Chemnitz University of Technology, Chemnitz, Germany

[5] (iTi), IMT-Atlantique, Technopôle Brest, Brest, France

Abstract. In the decision-making systems, sensors data are often affected by diversity types of imperfections which significantly reduce system performance. Thus, data quality assessment has become a primordial step in data learning process. In this work, feature quality assessment approach is used to select only useful and reliable information from those depth data in order to improve the performances of the staircase recognition system for the visually impaired. Possibility theory is utilized as a tool to deal with imperfect data and to represent knowledge. The developed feature quality assessment method is composed of two main steps. In the first step, the extracted features are classified in different quality levels. In the second step, an optimal feature subset is determined to discriminate between ascending and descending stairs. The proposed approach has experimentally shown to be very valuable with depth data, acquired from an ultrasonic sensor and a LiDAR sensor. The performance of the proposed approach has evaluated based on the classification accuracy which reached 94.7% using the ultrasonic sensor dataset and 92.42% using the laser rangefinder dataset.

Keywords: Feature quality · Possibility theory · Staircase classification · Depth sensors · Feature complementarity · Decision making

1 Introduction

In the decision-making systems, input data are often influenced by several imperfection sources. In fact, with the abundance of imperfection sources during experiment, data is generally affected by different types of imperfection, especially

N. T. Nguyen et al. (Eds.): ICCCI 2023, LNAI 14162, pp. 298–310, 2023.
https://doi.org/10.1007/978-3-031-41456-5_23

when the research become practical. This work resolves the stair detection and recognition system for visually impaired in order to improve their quality of life. Therefore, to ensure the system efficiency as well as system performances, it is significant to clarify the degree of validity of data to achieve a good understanding of knowledge. In this context, several researches, in literature, have long focused on analyzing input data during data processing.

Feature selection is one of the key steps in data processing whose objective is selecting appropriate features among a set of input variables such as [1–3]. In this context, numerous feature selection methods are proposed to be efficient to classify features according to relative conditions. In the literature, several of them are developed to deliver diverse degrees of relevance for features, such as in [4], where two degrees of relevancy have been defined: strong and weak. Strong relevant feature is defined as a feature that cannot be changed by another one. However, weak relevant feature is the feature that can be replaced by another even if it has useful information. In [5], authors have proposed a feature selection method to classify them using the separation degree and the representative aspect. Authors in [6] have proposed a new feature selection algorithm to evaluate feature relevance, redundancy and complementarity. Feature quality assessment is a widely known subject to inspect information in feature level. In [7], authors have proposed four new measures of feature quality to be used for dynamic feature selection. To enhance detection accuracy, in [8], a new depth quality-inspired feature manipulation (DQFM) process has been proposed.

Several feature selection methods take advantage of feature classification to generate an optimal feature subset to describe perfectly and effectively the target. An optimal feature subset is defined linked to the search context. For example, Fisher Score [9] is a feature selection algorithm aim to select an optimal feature subset. Linear Forward Selection (LFS) has been used to find the smaller feature subset, as in [10], to increases the system accuracy.

Feature relationships survey are very important when there is synergism between some features. Therefore, it is important to take advantage of feature complementarity to define an optimal feature subset. In [11], a filter-based feature selection criterion has been proposed which relies on feature complementarity for searching an optimal subset. In [12] a new feature selection method with redundancy-complementariness dispersion has been proposed. A novel multi-label feature selection algorithm based on label distribution and feature complementarity [13] has estimated the feature complementarity based on neighborhood mutual information without discretization. In [14], a new heuristic feature-selection (FS) algorithm has been developed integrated the three key FS components: relevance, redundancy, and complementarity. The feature complementarity has been quantified using partial correlation coefficients.

The extraction of an optimal feature subset is accurately linked to feature quality. The question is to make a specific definition of an optimal feature subset according to the search context. In this work, the main contribution is the identification of an optimal feature subset, which reported by feature quality measurement. Several works in the literature classify the extracted features into only two subsets, when in this work features are classified into three feature subsets. The developed method aims not only to select useful features, but to define an optimal feature subset. The feature quality assessment method is applied in the possibilistic framework, which make it a specific scenario. In order to achieve an accurate description of the scene, imperfections are taken into account in the staircase recognition process. For that, a reasoning mechanism in uncertain context is developed to have more faithful results. The possibility theory is applied to model data affected by the different imperfection types and to deal with epistemic uncertainty. Therefore, our challenge by the feature quality assessment in the possibilistic framework is to select only useful information based on two steps. In the first step, a new possibilistic data quality assessment approach of depth data is developed for stair detection and classification recognition for the visually impaired. Two types of sensors are used for data collection: an ultrasonic sensor and LiDAR sensor. For feature classification, three levels of feature quality are defined according to relevancy of the feature. In the second step, feature complementarity is applied to have an optimal feature subset. There, the idea is the calculation of feature complementarity through mutual information.

The rest of this paper is organized as follows. Section 2 provides an introduction to the basic concept of staircase recognition process. Section 3 introduces the feature quality estimation technique by describing the different evaluation criteria. The next section, at first, gives the experimental settings and the descriptions of acquired databases. Then, the experimental results are showed as a second part. Finally, the last section concludes this paper.

2 Basic Concept of Staircase Recognition Process

In this section, the basic concept of staircase recognition, shown in Fig. 1, is introduced. This concept aims to classify stairs into one of the considered classes, namely ascending stair, noted (C_1), and descending stair, noted (C_2). The proposed decision-making system is constructed with different steps in concordance with the intended objective. The staircase recognition system is based on depth signal observed by two types of sensors, which are the ultrasonic sensors and the LiDAR sensor. The basic concept of stair recognition process is based on five main steps: (1) Laboratory experience has been done to collect data using the both depth sensors for scene perception. (2) Pre-processing to multiscale

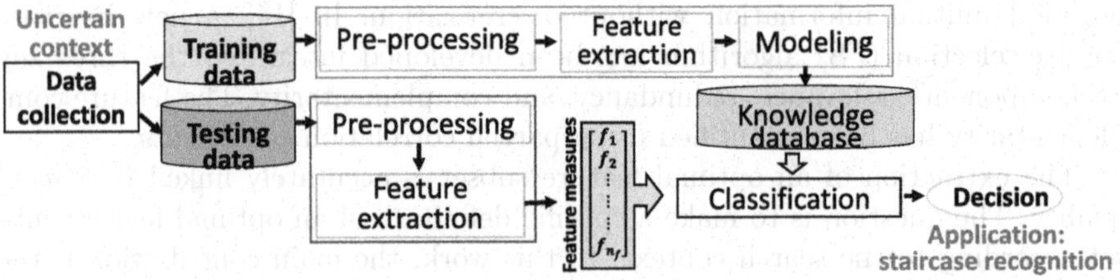

Fig. 1. Basic concept of staircase recognition process, where n_f is a total number of the extracted features.

signal representations and filtering data. (3) Statistical and spectral features are extracted to building another representation of the signal magnitude and frequency. (4) The possibility distribution is used to model imperfect data. (5) Classification of the sample in one of the two stair classes. The decision-making is performed to fulfil a recognition rate.

2.1 Data Collection

The collected data are constructed from two sources: an ultrasonic and a LiDAR sensors. Data collected from ultrasonic sensor is of two types, analog and pulse width signals, likewise data collected from LiDAR sensor is also of two types: distance and pulse width signals. For each sensor, $N_S = 100$ samples are captures and each sample is constructed with 80 measurements for each class.

2.2 Pre-processing: Multi-scale Signal Representation and Filtering

In data representation step, both time and frequency domains are opted in this work. In time domain, the two types of depth signals, whether the signals obtained by the ultrasonic sensor or those obtained using the LiDAR sensor, allow the representation and discrimination between stair classes. In frequency domain, two signal representations are considered, spectrum representation and Power Spectral Density (PSD) representation adopt the repetitive aspect of the signal. In this phase, data filtering is an important operation to reduce this noise. In this work, a window filter is used on the spectrum.

2.3 Feature Extraction and Fusion

In this step, as shown in Fig. 2, several statistical and spectral features [15] are extracted from time and frequency representations of sensor data. Each sensor, ultrasonic and LiDAR, is presented by two sources: source 1 and source 2. For the ultrasonic sensor, source 1 represents analog signals and source 2 represents pulse width signals. For LiDAR sensor, source 1 represents distance signals and source 2 represents pulse width signals. The feature vector of source 1 is denoted by $F_1 = \{f_1, f_2, ..., f_{N1}\}$, with $N1$ is a total number of the extracted features from source 1. The feature vector of source 2 is denoted by $F_2 = \{f_1, f_2, .., f_{N2}\}$, with $N2$ is a total number of the extracted features from source 2. Finally, the two feature vectors, F_1 and F_2, are fused to obtain only one feature vector denoted by $F = \{F_1, F_2\}$ using a concatenation fusion function. Consequently, each sensor data is presented by n_f features, where $n_f = N1 + N2 = 80$.

2.4 Possibilistic Modeling of Uncertain Feature Measurements

In the literature, numerous uncertainty theories have been applied in the case where data is affected by different imperfection forms. Uncertainty theories aim to model imperfect data and also take into consideration these imperfections in

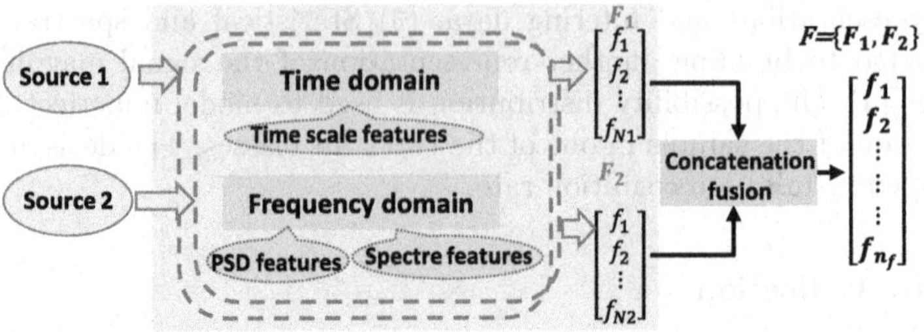

Fig. 2. Feature extraction set from time and frequency domains of each source, for the ultrasonic sensor: analog signals and pulse width signals (source 1 and source 2), and for LiDAR sensor: distance signals and pulse width signals (source 1 and source 2).

model construction. Among these theories, we cite theory of evidence [16], fuzzy set theory [17], probability theory [18] and possibility theory [19]. The choice of the suitable theory to model the available information depends on the nature of the imperfection that taints it, which promotes the selection of a particular theory for the benefit of others. In this work, the possibility theory seems an appropriate tool because the available data is affected by different imperfection types, especially by epistemic uncertainty that can not be modeled with law of probability. In fact, the probability theory is more adequate to model random uncertainty [20].

A specific attention is made in this paper to the possibility theory which proposes simple and natural representation of imperfect data. This theory offers simple and understandable models for uncertain, imprecise, incomplete knowledge and even for ambiguity information [20].

This theory used the possibility distribution, denoted by π, to model the data. In the literature, there have been numerous proposed methods to construct possibility distribution. Probability-possibility transformation based on Sison-Glaz simultaneous confidence intervals [21] is the more appropriate technique for this work, since a small sample size is available. The possibility distribution estimation process consists in the construction of an histogram, constructed with K classes, from the normalized feature measurements. Then, probability distributions are estimated based on the constructed histogram. Lastly, using the simultaneous confidence intervals, the possibility distribution is inferred for each feature for the two classes as shown in Fig. 3.

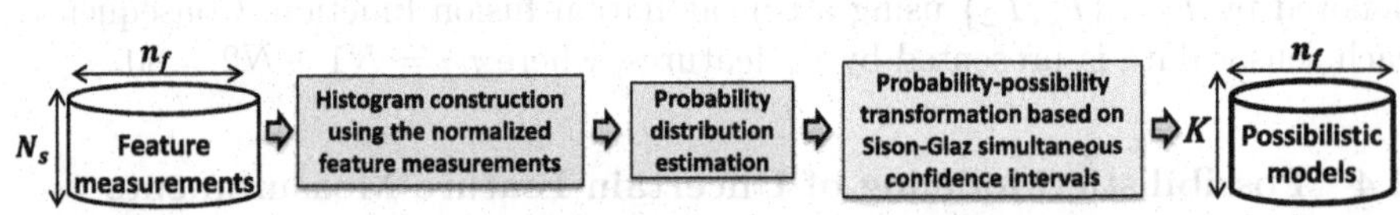

Fig. 3. Construction of possibility models, where n_f is a total number of extracted features, N_S is a total number of samples and K is the number of classes of the histogram.

2.5 Classification

The concept of the classification process aims to classify each testing sample into one of the two considered classes. The idea is to match testing samples with the constructed possibilistic models obtained in the training step. The maximum possibility criterion is used as classification criterion. As previously mentioned, the main objective of this work is to improve the decision-making system. For that, a possibilistic feature quality estimation method is applied to extract useful information based on feature quality investigation. Useful information extraction step is employed after modeling step as shown in Fig. 4. In the next section, the proposed feature quality assessment approach is described and detailed.

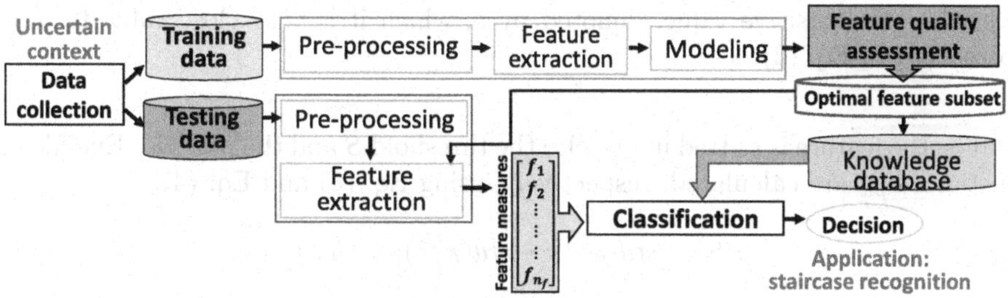

Fig. 4. Basic concept of staircase recognition process integrating feature quality assessment, where N is the number of features in the optimal feature subset.

3 Feature Quality Assessment Method

The feature quality assessment method is often relying on two main steps to extract useful information. The first step consists of classify the extracted features into three quality levels, namely good, medium and bad feature quality. The second step consists of evaluate the synergy between features to determine an optimal feature subset to be used in the classification system. The feature quality assessment process is independent to the number of features. In the follows, these two steps are described and detailed.

3.1 Feature Classification Based on Feature Quality

The feature classification based on feature-quality is developed in accordance with the capability of feature to discriminate between classes. The classification strategy is often relying on two concepts: pairwise Euclidean and deviation distances. The deviation distance is used to observes the separability between two possibilistic distributions and the pairwise Euclidean distance is applied to examine the spacing of the two possibilistic distributions in Euclidean space. Figure 5 represents feature quality classification procedure between the two classes relative to the feature: $f_k^{C_1}$ and $f_k^{C_2}$, where $k = 1..n_f$. Features are classified into three quality sets: Q_1, Q_2 and Q_3 while Q_1 defines the high quality feature set, Q_2 defines the medium quality feature set and Q_3 defines the weak quality feature set. The constructed possibilistic models, using the feature measurements, are used as the inputs to the feature quality assessment process. First, the deviation distance d between two possibilistic distribution $\pi_{f_k}^{C_1}$ and $\pi_{f_k}^{C_2}$ is calculated using Eq. (1):

$$d = \frac{1}{\|\pi_{f_k}^{C_1}, \pi_{f_k}^{C_2}\|} \sqrt{\sum_{t=1}^{K} (\pi_{f_k}^{C_1}(t) - \pi_{f_k}^{C_2}(t))^2} \qquad (1)$$

Then, the first Axiom 1 aims to testing if the calculated deviation distance is less than the positive value, denoted by ε, which it is very close value to 0 as presented in Eq. (2):

$$d < \varepsilon \qquad (2)$$

If it is, the feature is putted in Q_3, else the threshold S and the pairwise Euclidean distance d_{pw} are calculated, respectively, using Eq. (3) and Eq. (4):

$$S = [std(\pi_{f_k}^{C_1}) + std(\pi_{f_k}^{C_2})] \times Coef \qquad (3)$$

$$d_{pw} = \left| \pi_{f_k}^{C_1} - \pi_{f_k}^{C_2} \right| \qquad (4)$$

where std is the standard deviation and $Coef$ is a coefficient in $]0,1[$ given by the expert.The set of the intersection points are determined using Eq. (5):

$$\pi_{pt} / \pi_{pt} \in \{\pi_{f_k}^{C_1} \cap \pi_{f_k}^{C_2}\} \qquad (5)$$

Equation (5) presents the solution of the equation $d_{pw} = 0$. The second Axiom 2 consists of verify if the deviation distance is greater than the threshold S, Eq. (6):

$$d > S \qquad (6)$$

If it is verified, the search continues passing to the next conditions. Let S_L and S_U two possibilistic thresholds. If $\pi_{pt} < S_L$, so the $f_k \in Q_1$, else if $S_L \leq \pi_{pt} \leq S_U$ so the $f_k \in Q_2$, else the $f_k \in Q_3$.

3.2 Feature Complementarity for Optimal Feature Subset

Feature complementarity is used to study the synergy between features and also to determine an optimal feature subset. Initially, the optimal feature subset is constructed only by all features belonging in Q_1. Then, the optimal feature subset can incorporates some features of Q_2 which present a high complementarity score with features of Q_1. Indeed, the complementarity is estimated between each feature in the high quality set Q_1 with all features in the medium quality set Q_2. The feature complementarity is defined using the formula of complementarity

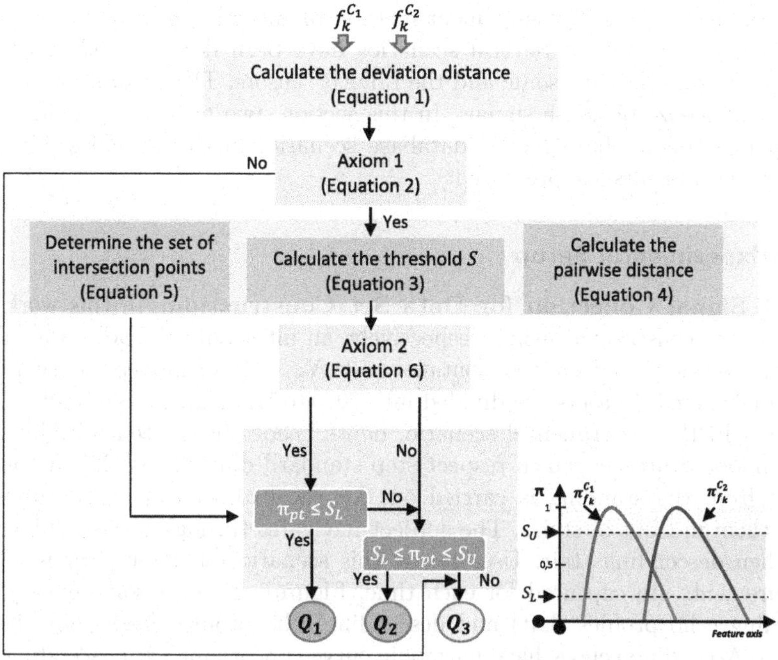

Fig. 5. Feature quality classification procedure between the two classes: $f_k^{C_1}$ and $f_k^{C_2}$, where C_1 presents ascending stair, C_2 presents descending stair and $k = 1..n_f$, Q_1 is the strong feature quality set, Q_2 is the medium feature quality set and Q_3 is the weak feature quality set

score proposed in [6]. Let $f_k \in Q_1$ and $f_{k'} \in Q_2$, two complementarity scores are calculated based on Eq. (7) and Eq. (8):

$$S_1 = Comp(f_k, f_{k'}, C_1) \tag{7}$$

$$S_2 = Comp(f_k, f_{k'}, C_2) \tag{8}$$

In the case where S_1 and S_2 are positives (or at most one of them is equal to 0) the feature $f_{k'}$ is added to the optimal feature subset. In the case where Q_1 or Q_2 is empty, the optimal feature subset receipts the no empty feature set, but if the both sets are empty, so the extracted features neither able to present nor to discriminate between the classes. In such condition, it is better to extract other features or adjust the used thresholds (S_U and S_L).

4 Experimental Results

Experiments are conducted to evaluate the efficiency of, on the one hand, the proposed approach for stair recognition using the depth signals and, on the other hand, the feature quality assessment method mainly in performance improving of the proposed system. Several scenarios have been done to collect the two databases using the ultrasonic and the LiDAR sensors. These databases contain small sample size of depth signals. In this section, two parts are provided. The first part presents the acquired database scenario. In the second section, the experimental results are presented.

4.1 Experimental Setup

Depth Signal Collection for Data Set Construction: In this work, two datasets are constructed using, respectively, an ultrasonic sensor and a LiDAR sensor. Each acquired dataset contains only $N_S = 100$ samples for each class. The constructed datasets are divided into 70% to train the system and 30% for the test. In the experimental scenario, depth echoes have been initially taken from indoor staircases which respect step standard dimensions [22]. A rotation of 30° from the standing is carried out for the two sensors by the user and make them in front of stairs. The subject navigates through an ascending stair and then descending stair. User renew this scenario for several times and 80 measurements are captured for each time. Figure 6 presents some examples of ascending echo profiles (left) and descending echo profiles (right) for the two sensors. Ascending echoes have harmonic curve concordant with ascending stair steps. For the two sensors, Echo 1 of ascending stairs presents a peak in the signal when a step is detected. Otherwise, it is referred as a step depth. In the same manner, for the descending case, Echo 1 reproduces the same descending stair aspect by presenting a descending peak when a descending step is exposed. According to the visualization and the analysis of the different collected echoes, it is noticed that for some echoes, imperfections are present. The presence of imperfections has a direct effect in the signal aspect. This is plainly observed in Echo 2 for ascending and descending stairs which recall the previous phenomenon only in certain regions. Consequently, the raw sensor data quality is degraded by residual signals like noise effect during experiments and even by missing values in certain case. For that reason, a window filter is applied in the pre-treatment step to reduce this noise.

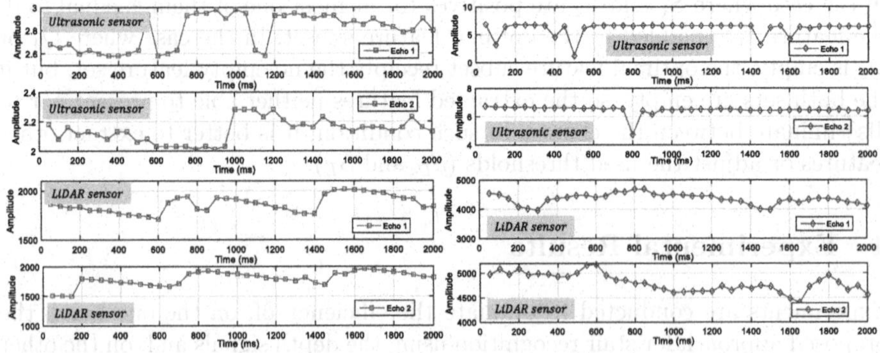

Fig. 6. Echoes profiles for ascending stairs (left) and for descending stairs (right).

Feature Extraction: Time and frequency domain representations are used to extract, 80 features considering sensor data. For more detail about the list of all extracted features, see work in [15].

Possibilistic Modeling: The transformation of feature measures to possibilistic model requires an intermediate step. In this work, the probability-possibility transformation based on Sison-Glaz simultaneous confidence intervals [21] is used to model uncertain data. Figure 7 gives illustrative examples of possibility distribution models of the two classes C_1 and C_2. The first feature (Fig. 7(a)), achieves moderate and suitable possibilistic models for the two classes, as well as the good discrimination between the two possibilistic distributions. However, the second feature (Fig. 7(b)), even though the moderate representation of models, it presents a non-discriminate feature.

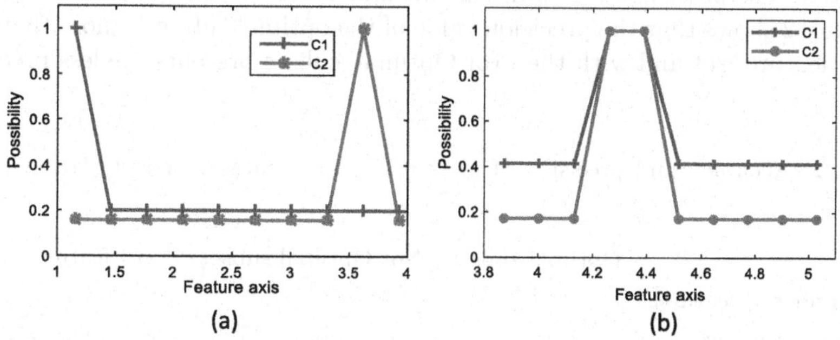

Fig. 7. Illustrative example of features with different quality degree: (a) a good quality feature, (b) a weak quality feature, C_1: ascending class and C_2: descending class

Method Implementation Details: After various empirical tests, the parameters of feature quality classification algorithm are setting up. Table 1 summarizes the inputs parameters values.

Table 1. Inputs parameters values for feature quality assessment algorithm

	Range	Ultrasonic sensor	LiDAR sensor
$Coef$	$]0,1[$	0.1	0.1
S_L	$[0,S_U[$	0.25	0.1
S_U	$]S_L,1]$	0.7	0.5

4.2 Performance Results of Stair Recognition System Using Depth Data

In this section, the basic concept of staircase recognition process performance is evaluated with the two sensors. To evaluate the proposed approach, the two acquired datasets (Ultrasonic and LiDAR sensors) are used separately. Two evaluation metrics are used: accuracy (Eq. (9)) and precision rates (Eq. (10)):

$$Accuracy\ (\%) = \frac{TP + TN}{TP + FP + TN + FN} \times\ 100 \tag{9}$$

$$Precision = \frac{TP}{TP + FP} \tag{10}$$

where TP is the true positive, FN is the false positive, TN is the true negative and FN is the false negative.

The obtained system performances are detailed with Table 2 and Fig. 8. Table 2 provides the accuracy and the precision values of ultrasonic sensor dataset and LiDAR sensor dataset. For the ultrasonic sensor dataset, the accuracy is reached 94.70% using 45 features. For LiDAR sensor dataset, the accuracy is reached 92.42% using 62 features. In addition to the detection accuracy of the algorithm, the precision is also important indicators of the algorithm.

Table 2 shows that the precision value of the optimal subset is more than it is for all features set and with the 'Not Optimal' subset presents the less precision value.

Table 2. Accuracy and precision of ultrasonic sensor dataset and of LiDAR sensor dataset.

	Optimal subset	Not Optimal subset	All features
Number of features	45 | 62	35 | 18	80 | 80
Accuracy	94.7% | 92.42%	71.9% | 48.15%	84.73% | 82.46%
Precision	0.9480 | 0.9342%	0.7385 | 0.4803%	0.8508 | 0.8346%

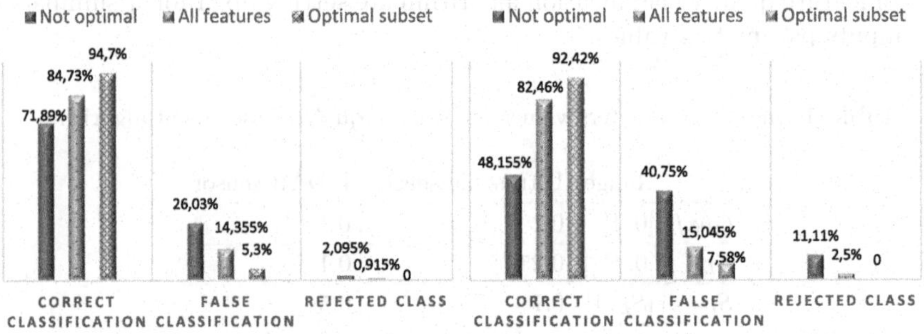

Fig. 8. Data quality investigation results on ultrasonic sensor (left) dataset and on LiDAR (right) sensor dataset.

Figure 8 compares the performances of the proposed system for staircase recognition obtained after and before the use of feature quality investigation approach. Each criterion is calculated when the proposed system uses the correct classification, the false classification and the rejected classes as comparison criterion. Each criterion is calculated when the proposed system uses the optimal feature subset, all features and even for not optimal subset.

Using the two databases, it is perceived that the highest accuracy is achieved when the optimal feature subset is used. Moreover, the inclusion of the optimal subset in all features allows having recognition rates better than recognition rates obtained using only 'Not Optimal' subset.

Using the optimal subset, the recognition accuracy is increased by 9.97% and 9.96% over recognition rate when all feature subset is considered by the system based, respectively, on the ultrasonic sensor and the LiDAR sensor. We can note, also, an improvement in the recognition accuracy of 22.8% and 44.27% over recognition rate when the system uses the 'Not Optimal' subset to present, respectively, the data collected using the ultrasonic sensor and Lidar sensor. When 'No class' is predicted, the recognition accuracy of the optimal subset produces the value '0' which highlight the usefulness of the appropriate possibilistic models.

5 Conclusion

In this paper, the purpose is to classify staircases, ascending and descending, using ultrasonic and 1D LiDAR sensors as scene perception tools. A conception-based stair classification has been developed. After data collection and filtering, a feature extraction and fusing step has been achieved. Then, possibilistic distributions are inferred for each stair class using the extracted features. using the generated possibilistic models, a feature quality assessment method has been used to achieve a good selection of an optimal feature subset. In all the conducted experiments using the both datasets, performed classification accuracy have been obtained for staircase classification. In fact, the performance results showed that the stair classification accuracy can be improved to 94.7% and 92.42% while using, respectively, ultrasonic and LiDAR sensors. As future work, we propose to merge data, obtained from the two depth sensors considered in this work, in order to improve the staircase classification system performances.

Acknowledgements. The authors wish to acknowledge the contribution of Measurement and Sensor Technology (MST) laboratory in TU-Chemnitz-Germany.

References

1. Wan, J., Chen, H., Yuan, Z., Li, T., Yang, X., Sang, B.B.: A novel hybrid feature selection method considering feature interaction in neighborhood rough set. Knowl.-Based Syst. **227**, 107167 (2021)
2. Sun, L., Yin, T., Ding, W., Qian, Y., Xu, J.: Multilabel feature selection using ML-ReliefF and neighborhood mutual information for multilabel neighborhood decision systems. Inf. Sci. **537**, 401–424 (2020)

3. Dai, J., Chen, J., Liu, Y., Hu, H.: Novel multi-label feature selection via label symmetric uncertainty correlation learning and feature redundancy evaluation. Knowl.-Based Syst. **207**, 106342 (2020)
4. Kohavi, R., John, G.H.: Wrappers for feature subset selection. Artif. Intell. **97**(1–2), 273–324 (1997)
5. Ammar Bouhamed, S., Khanfir Kallel, I., Sellami Masmoudi, D., Solaiman, B.: Feature selection in possibilistic modeling. Pattern Recogn. **48**(11), 3627–3640 (2015)
6. Li, C., Luo, X., Qi, Y., Gao, Z., Lin, X.: A new feature selection algorithm based on relevance, redundancy and complementarity. Comput. Biol. Med. **119**, 103667 (2020)
7. Naqvi, S.S., Browne, W.N., Hollitt, C.: Feature quality-based dynamic feature selection for improving salient object detection. IEEE Trans. Image Process. **25**(9), 4298–4313 (2016)
8. Zhang, W., Ji, G.-P., Wang, Z., Fu, K., Zhao, Q.: Depth quality-inspired feature manipulation for efficient RGB-D salient object detection (2021)
9. Gu, Q., Li, Z., Han, J.: Generalized fisher score for feature selection. arXiv preprint arXiv:1202.3725 (2012)
10. Gutlein, M., Frank, E., Hall, M., Karwath, A.: Large-scale attribute selection using wrappers. In: 2009 IEEE Symposium on Computational Intelligence and Data Mining, pp. 332–339. IEEE (2009)
11. Singha, S., Shenoy, P.P.: An adaptive heuristic for feature selection based on complementarity. Mach. Learn. **107**(12), 2027–2071 (2018)
12. Chen, Z., et al.: Feature selection with redundancy-complementariness dispersion. Knowl.-Based Syst. **89**, 203–217 (2015)
13. Qian, W., Long, X., Wang, Y., Xie, Y.: Multi-label feature selection based on label distribution and feature complementarity. Appl. Soft Comput. **90**, 106167 (2020)
14. Tsanas, A.: Relevance, redundancy, and complementarity trade-off (RRCT): a principled, generic, robust feature-selection tool. Patterns **3**(5), 100471 (2022)
15. Medhioub, M., Kallel, I.K., Bouhamed, S.A., Derbel, N., Solaiman, B., Kanoun, O.: Electronic embedded system for stair recognition based on possibilistic modeling of ultrasonic signal. IEEE Sens. J. **21**(5), 5787–5797 (2021)
16. Shafer, G.: A Mathematical Theory of Evidence, vol. 42. Princeton University Press, Princeton (1976)
17. Zadeh, L.: Fuzzy sets. Inform. Control **8**, 338–353 (1965)
18. Sandri, S.: La combinaison de l'information incertaine et ses aspects algorithmiques. Ph.D. thesis, Toulouse (1991)
19. Zadeh, L.A.: Fuzzy sets as a basis for a theory of possibility. Fuzzy Sets Syst. **100**, 9–34 (1999)
20. Kallel, I.K.: Mécanismes de raisonnement possibiliste pour l'aide à la décision et l'interprétation de scènes. Ph.D. thesis, Ecole Nationale des Ingénieurs de Sfax, Université de Sfax (2019)
21. Sison, C.P., Glaz, J.: Simultaneous confidence intervals and sample size determination for multinomial proportions. J. Am. Stat. Assoc. **90**(429), 366–369 (1995)
22. Friedman, D.: Ideal stair rise run specifications (2021)

Social Networks and Intelligent Systems

Toward Effective Link Prediction Based on Local Information in Organizational Social Networks

Paweł Szyman and Dariusz Barbucha(✉)

Department of Information Systems, Gdynia Maritime University, Morska 83, 81-225 Gdynia, Poland
p.szyman@wznj.umg.edu.pl, d.barbucha@umg.edu.pl

Abstract. An important branch of a social network analysis is the identification of missing links and the prediction of future connections in the networks. The problem, known as the link prediction problem, has attracted the attention of many researchers, who have proposed different methods to solve it. In this paper, a few similarity-based methods based on the number of common neighbors as local information have been considered in order to estimate the possibility of the presence of a link between two nodes in the network. An extensive computational experiment has been carried out where ten similarity measures have been compared using the organizational social network of a public organization as a dataset. The experimental results allowed us to select the methods with the highest prediction quality as good predictors of future connections in networks, referring to organizational relationships.

Keywords: Social networks · Link prediction · Similarity · Organizational network analysis · E-mail communication

1 Introduction

Social networks are getting lots of attention of researchers last years, partly as a result of the increased use of social media platforms. Among the topics in this area, the problem of identifying the existence of new relationships or yet unknown interactions between pairs of entities based on their properties and the currently observed links [18] (known as link prediction (LP)) seems to be one of the most important.

Taking into account the rapid growth of social network theory and applications, the problem of LP has found a large number of applications in different areas. A few examples of the variety of applications that can benefit from predicting non-existing links analyzed by different researchers are: finding possible interactions between pairs of proteins in a protein-protein interaction network [16], detecting malicious users in the network [14], recommending new friends or collaborators with similar interests [21], predicting the evolution in dynamic networks [34], and predicting tendencies spread across society [19].

Although there are a lot of applications of the LP problem to networks referring to different social structures, to the authors' best knowledge, there are few

N. T. Nguyen et al. (Eds.): ICCCI 2023, LNAI 14162, pp. 313–325, 2023.
https://doi.org/10.1007/978-3-031-41456-5_24

applications of this problem referring to organizational social networks. For the purpose of the study, an organizational social network (OSN) is meant as a network, where nodes represent people or units of the organization, and edges between nodes represent relations between employees (formal or informal) or information flow between these people or units. Depending on the source and form of information used in its construction, OSN may have different forms. It may refer to formal relations between employees, which stem, for example, from the position of each person in an organization, but it may also refer to informal relations between them based, for example, on trust or confidence. Solving the LP problem in OSN allows us to get the knowledge which people in an organization are likely to connect. It could be leveraged to make introductions and get collaborations moving faster [9] or to attempt the reconstruction of project teams where new employees could be considered to join the team.

The aim of the paper is to experimentally verify to what extent, if any, the similarity-based methods may support the process of predicting potential new (non-existing yet) connections between employees in OSN. In the paper, the authors want to find an answer to the question of which similarity measures may be considered as good predictors of these future connections. The experiment has been carried out on the organizational network of a middle-sized public organization located in Poland. The structure of the network is based on digital communication (electronic mail) between employees. The paper continues the authors' research on email-based organizational (institutional) social networks. Previous authors' papers in this area have focused on identifying the most important actors in the network [3] and detecting potential communities in it [30].

The paper is divided into five sections. The rest of the paper has the following structure. Section 2 presents a formal definition of the LP problem and describes groups of methods used to solve it. Section 3 presents a review of similarity-based approaches based on different similarity measures. Section 4 focuses on a computational experiment that has been carried out to solve the LP problem in OSN with different methods based on local information. It presents the goal of the experiment, the dataset constructed and used in the experiment, settings, evaluation metrics used, dedicated algorithms for solving the LP problem, and experimental results and analysis. Finally, Sect. 5 concludes the paper and presents directions for future work.

2 Link Prediction in Social Networks

2.1 Problem Formulation

Let $G = (V, E)$ be an undirected network, without multiple links and self-connections, where $V = \{1, 2, 3, \ldots, n\}$ is the set of n ($n = |V|$) vertices (or nodes) and $E \subset V \times V$ is a set of edges (or links) indicating the relationships between nodes. If there exists a link between two nodes i and j ($i, j \in V$), it is denoted by (i, j) ($(i, j) \in E$), and the nodes are considered as neighbors.

Let $\Gamma(i)$ be the set of all neighbors of node i, i.e., $\Gamma(i) = \{j|(i,j) \in E\}$. The size of $\Gamma(i)$ represents the degree of node i and is denoted as $deg(i)$ ($deg(i) = |\Gamma(i)|$). Additionally, let $A = [a(i,j)]_{n \times n}$ be an adjacency matrix of G, where each element $a(i,j) = 1$ if vertices i and j are neighbors, otherwise $a(i,j) = 0$ ($a(i,j) \in A$). It is easy to see, that in terms of the adjacency matrix A of the network G, $deg(i) = \sum_j a(i,j)$.

Let U denote the universal set containing all $n(n-1)/2$ possible links. The set of non-existing links E^N is, therefore, $E^N = U - E$. Assuming that some links that are missing may appear in the future in the set E^N, finding such links is the aim of the *link prediction.* More formally, one can say that link prediction is a process of predicting future connections between pairs of unconnected links based on existing connections, Its goal is to estimate the probability of existence (or formation in the future) of each of the non-existing links in the network.

2.2 Methods

Different methods have been proposed by researchers over the last years for the LP problem. A few existing surveys include different taxonomies for techniques proposed last years [5,20,23] and [15]. Following one of the most representative review of the state-of-the-art LP approaches based on analysis of 60 papers from different sources such as IEEExplore, ScienceDirect, ACM, Springer and Google Scholar (period: 2012–2020) by Daud et al. [5], the approaches can be divided into four groups according to the prediction strategy, the technique used, and complexity of the approaches. They include: similarity, probabilistic, algorithmic, and hybrid approaches.

The first group of approaches (*similarity* approaches) belongs to a conventional and commonly used LP group of methods. As a fundamental step, for each pair of unconnected nodes, the similarity scores between them are computed based on selected LP measures (graph-based, content-based, or both). A link between a pair of nodes with higher similarity is assumed to be established in the future. As it was reported [5], similarity approaches can be further divided into three groups based on local [11], global [24] and quasi-local indexes [26].

The second group (*probabilistic* approaches) focuses on solving the problem of LP by building a statistical probability model that fits with the network structure. The model computes a mathematical statistic to produce a probability value for each pair of nodes in the graph. Then, the probability values are classified according to the hypothesis, where the higher the probability value of the node pairs, the higher the possibility of link formation between the node pairs. Recent probabilistic models proposed by different researchers include: Probability Tensor Factorization model [8], Probability Latent Variable model [32], Markov model [6] and Link Label Modeling [13].

Algorithmic approaches allow researchers to perform calculations, data processing, and automated prediction tasks in a process that follows certain rules and problem-solving operations. Contrary to the similarity and probabilistic approaches, the algorithmic approaches often employ extra information from the network and consider other factors that affect link formation. For instance, algorithmic methods may use network structural information, community structure information, or users' behavior patterns. Algorithmic approaches fall into three categories namely, Metaheuristic [4], Matrix Factorization [31], and Machine Learning [24].

Finally, *hybrid* approaches are combinations of one or more methods, attached to a framework or model. It is expected that they provide a better performance result to predict future links than each method used separately. An example of a hybrid approach is a combination of a similarity approach with an algorithmic approach [7].

3 Similarity-Based Approaches to the LP Problem

The key solution to tackle the problem of link prediction with similarity-based methods is how to measure the similarity between the nodes in a network with higher accuracy. Several methods have been suggested to determine the similarity score between nodes to estimate their proximity in the network. These methods essentially differ on what they use to estimate the similarity score between two nodes, which is then used to compute the likelihood of each non-existing link. The section presents representative examples of methods based on local information (they have been used in the experiment) that focus only on the properties of the first-order neighborhoods of a given pair of vertices $i, j \in V$.

Common Neighbors Index. Common Neighbors Index (CNI) [25] is one of the most frequently used methods for predicting links, mainly due to its simplicity. It defines the similarity score of two nodes as a number of their common neighbors. It assumes that two users are more likely to collaborate in the future if they have collaborated with the same group of people in the past. Different studies have confirmed this hypothesis by observing a correlation between the number of shared neighbors between pairs of nodes and the probability of being linked [25] (see Eq. (1)).

$$CNI(i,j) = |\Gamma(i) \cap \Gamma(j)| \tag{1}$$

Jaccard Index. Jaccard Index (JAI) was proposed by P. Jaccard [12] to compare the similarity and diversity of sample sets. It measures the ratio between the intersection (the number of common neighbors between each pair of nodes) and the union of the neighborhoods of two vertices (see Eq. (2)).

$$JAI(i,j) = \frac{|\Gamma(i) \cap \Gamma(j)|}{|\Gamma(j) \cup \Gamma(j)|} \tag{2}$$

Salton Index. Salton Index (SCI) [28], also known as the cosine similarity, is closely related to the JAI. It measures the cosine of the angle between columns of the adjacency matrix, corresponding to two given vertices (see Eq. (3)).

$$SCI(i,j) = \frac{|\Gamma(i) \cap \Gamma(j)|}{\sqrt{deg(i)deg(j)}} \tag{3}$$

Sörensen Index. Sörensen Index (SDI), also known as the Dice index, was developed by the botanist T. Sörensen [29] to compare the similarity between different ecological community data samples. It is a variation of the SCI and it measures the relative size of an intersection of two neighbors' sets (see Eq. (4)).

$$SDI(i,j) = \frac{2|\Gamma(i) \cap \Gamma(j)|}{(deg(i) + deg(j))} \tag{4}$$

Hub Promoted Index. Hub Promoted Index (HPI) was proposed by Ravasz et al. [27] as a result of studying modularity in metabolic networks. It measures the ratio of the number of common neighbors to the minimum degree of two given nodes. This measure assigns higher scores to links adjacent to high-degree nodes (hubs), as the denominator depends only on the lower degree. Using this similarity index, the link formation between hub nodes is avoided and the link formation between low-degree nodes and hubs is promoted (see Eq. (5)).

$$HPI(i,j) = \frac{|\Gamma(i) \cap \Gamma(j)|}{\min\{deg(i), deg(j)\}} \tag{5}$$

Hub Depressed Index. Hub Depressed Index (HDI) [27] is similar to the HPI, but opposite to it, the nodes with higher degrees determine the denominator, making the similarity between the hub and other nodes lower. It means that HDI promotes link formation between hubs and between low-degree nodes, but not between hubs and low-degree nodes (see Eq. (6)).

$$HDI(i,j) = \frac{|\Gamma(i) \cap \Gamma(j)|}{\max\{deg(i), deg(j)\}} \tag{6}$$

Preferential Attachment Index. Preferential Attachment Index (PAI) is a direct result of the well known Barabasi-Albert complex network formation model [2]. They built a theoretical model based on the observation that the probability of link formation between two nodes increases as the degree of these nodes does. Hence, PAI assumes that the likelihood of link formation is determined by the degree of two nodes. It means that the nodes that currently have a greater number of relations tend to create more links in the future. Following the intuition behind the preferential attachment model, that nodes with a high degree are more attractive to connect to, we may expect that links are more likely to be incident on nodes with a high degree (see Eq. (7)).

$$PAI(i,j) = deg(i)deg(j) \tag{7}$$

Adamic-Adar Index. Adamic-Adar Index (AAI) [1] is also related to the JAI. It extends the idea of counting common neighbors by introducing weights inversely proportional to their degrees. The common neighbors that have a smaller number of neighbors have greater significance than the high-degree neighbors (see Eq. (8)).

$$AAI(i,j) = \sum_{k \in \Gamma(i) \cap \Gamma(j)} \frac{1}{log(deg(k))} \tag{8}$$

Resource Allocation Index. Resource Allocation Index (RAI) is motivated by the resource allocation process that takes place in complex networks [33] and is strongly related to the CNI and the AAI. It models the transmission of units of resources between two unconnected nodes through neighborhood nodes. Each neighborhood node gets a unit of resource from a node i and equally distributes it to its neighbors. The amount of resources obtained by node j can be considered as the similarity between both nodes (see Eq. (9)).

$$RAI(i,j) = \sum_{k \in \Gamma(i) \cap \Gamma(j)} \frac{1}{|deg(k)|} \tag{9}$$

Leicht-Holme-Newman Index. Leicht-Holme-Newman Index (LHNI) [17] is a variant of CNI based on the intersection of two sets of neighbors of i and j ($i, j \in V$) (see Eq. (10)).

$$LHNI(i,j) = \frac{|\Gamma(i) \cap \Gamma(j)|}{deg(i)deg(j)} \tag{10}$$

4 Predicting Links in the Organizational Social Network - Computational Experiment

4.1 Goal of the Experiment

The goal of the experiment was to check to what extent, if any, the similarity-based methods using local information may support the process of predicting potential new (non-existing) connections between vertices in OSN. It is expected that the results of the experiment will allow us to select the best similarity measures to use in the process of predicting changes (especially new connections between employees) in OSN.

4.2 Dataset

The experiment has been carried out on OSN referring to a middle-sized public organization located in Poland where the structure of the network reflects the scheme of digital communication (electronic mail) between employees within the organization. The process of building the network has been organized as a sequence of steps, including the selection of the observation period and investigated departments of the organization, the extraction and collection of data from organization's email server logs referring to the selected period and departments, and building a graph model.

For the purpose of the experiment, it has been decided to select a single department with the number of employees equal to 91 (out of the 380 employed in the whole organization), for which the data referring to digital communications between persons employed in this department have been extracted from the organization's email server logs from Jan to Jun 2020 (6 months). The number of messages exchanged between the employees identified within the whole organization was equal to 251129, and the number of internal messages exchanged between the employees of the selected department was equal to 10364. In the process of building the network, employees were represented by vertices, and communication between employees was represented by edges connecting respective vertices. It has been assumed that an edge between two vertices exists if two persons represented by these vertices exchanged at least a single message within the observed period without considering the roles of the employees (sender or receiver). For the sake of personal data security, each email address was anonymized by assigning it an individual number from 1 to 91.

Hence, the OSN created from the above data consists of 91 nodes and 448 edges. The density of the network is 0.1094, and the average degree of the node is 9.846154.

4.3 Experimental Settings

It has been assumed that the LP problem can be treated as a binary classification task [10], and that the evaluation of this task can be represented as a confusion matrix (CM) [22]. In fact, the CM is used to compare the binary predicted labels against the actual class labels, as shown in Table 1. The matrix identifies: True Positives (*TP*) - correctly predicted existing links, True Negatives (*TN*) - correctly predicted not-existing links, False Positives (*FP*) - not-existing links but predicted by the algorithm, and False Negatives (*FN*) - links available but no links have been predicted by the algorithm.

Table 1. Confusion matrix

Predicted	Actual	
	Link	No Link
Link	True Positive (TP)	False Positive (FP)
No Link	False Negative (FN)	True Negative (TN)

Commonly established settings used in LP experiments have been adopted. The observed links E in the network G has been randomly divided into two parts: the training set E^T (treated as known information) and the test (or probe) set E^P used for testing. No information in E^P is allowed to be used for prediction. Clearly, $E^T \cup E^P = E$ and $E^T \cap E^P = \emptyset$. In the experiment, we randomly select 90% of edges from E as E^T and the remaining 10% of edges as E^P. The process has been repeated 10 times independently, and the average results were recorded.

Ten methods have been used for comparison using the following similarity measures: Common Neighbors Index, Jaccard Index, Salton Index, Sörensen Index, Hub Promoted Index, Hub Depressed Index, Preferential Attachment Index, Adamic-Adar Index, Resource Allocation Index, and Leicht-Holme-Newman Index.

4.4 Evaluation Metrics

As commonly used in many LP algorithms, four comprehensive evaluation metrics have been used to compare the similarity-based methods investigated in the experiment: *Accuracy*, *Recall*, *Precision*, and *Area Under the receiver operating characteristic Curve (AUC)*.

Classification *accuracy* is a metric that summarizes the performance of a classification model as the number of correct predictions divided by the total number of predictions made for a dataset: $Accuracy = (TP+TN)/(TP+TN+FP+FN)$.

The second metric, *Recall* is a metric that summarizes the performance of a classification model as the number of positive class predictions made out of all positive examples in the dataset: $Recall = TP/(TP+FN)$.

Precision quantifies the number of positive class predictions that actually belong to the positive class: $Precision = TP/(TP+FP)$.

The fourth metric used in the experiment to assess the accuracy of the methods - AUC is computed by picking an edge from E^P and an edge from the set of non-observed edges E^N, and calculating the similarity score between the pair of nodes connected to each of the edges. This process is repeated n times, and AUC is calculated as $AUC = (n_1 + 0.5n_2)/n$, where n_1 is the number of times when the similarity score of the nodes connected by the edge picked from the set E^P is higher than the similarity score of the nodes connected by the edge picked from the set E^N, and n_2 is the number of times when the two similarity scores are equal. Every pair of links in E^P and E^N has been compared in the experiment. The value of AUC is between $[0, 1]$, where a higher value of AUC means higher accuracy of the method.

4.5 Dedicated Algorithms for Solving the LP Problem in OSN

Dedicated algorithms have been used to solve the LP problem in considered OSN. It has been decided to use `R` software package [35]. Although `R` is a general purpose analytics tool used for statistical calculations and visualization of research results, it is supported by different packages. Taking into account the purpose of the paper, the following packages have been used in the experiment: `iGraph` [36] - dedicated generally to the social network analysis, `linkprediction` [37] which implements most of the existing vertex similarity measures that can be used to predict links in networks, including methods presented in Sect. 3, and `caret` [38] which includes a set of functions that support the process of creating predictive models, including the confusion matrix.

Using the main function of the `linkprediction` package, which is *proxfun()*, similarity scores have been calculated for each pair of vertices, no matter if they are connected or not. For this purpose, the ten measures of similarity presented earlier were used. The similarity value was obtained for all possible connections, i.e., 8281 pairs of links.

In order to calculate the *Accuracy*, *Recall*, and *Precision*, the confusion matrices have been created using all similarity measures. For this purpose, the previously mentioned `caret` package was used. An important element of this part of the experiment was determining how to define a predicted network. For all similarity measures, it was specified that a link can be expected if the similarity value exceeds approximately 30% of the entire range of a given measure. For example, in Jaccard's similarity measure, the lowest observed value was 0.0256 and the highest was 0.5714. It was assumed that the threshold at which we would consider that the link may appear in the future was 0.18. Then, using the `caret` package, two networks, actual and predicted, were compared with each other. From the obtained values of TP, TN, FP and FN, the remaining measures were calculated.

In order to calculate the value of AUC, the obtained similarity values were divided into two sets: a set of linked pairs of nodes and a set of unlinked pairs of nodes. From the first set, 10% of linked pairs of links were randomly selected, and then their values of similarity measures were compared with the similarity measures of all non-existing pairs of links within the same measure. This process was performed 10 times, and the average AUC results have been saved.

4.6 Experimental Results and Analysis

The results of the experiment are presented in Fig. 1 and Table 2. Figure 1 presents a set of confusion matrices calculated for the investigated OSN using ten similarity measures. Table 2 illustrates the performance of the different link prediction methods for the investigated network as measured by four evaluation metrics: *Accuracy*, *Recall*, *Precision* and AUC. The three best results in each column of the Table 2 are highlighted in bold, and additionally, the best ones are underlined.

Taking the goal of the experiment into account an analysis of the results of the computational experiment presented in the Table 2 allows one to make a few interesting findings. Looking at the first column with *Accuracy* values, the best quality of prediction is observed for JAI (0.8783) but two other methods belonging to the group of the top-3 best performers (RAI with accuracy equal to 0.8570 and LHNI with accuracy equal to 0.8561) have accuracy values very a)

CNI		Actual	
		Link	No Link
Predicted	Link	384	852
	No Link	512	6533

b)

JAI		Actual	
		Link	No Link
Predicted	Link	254	366
	No Link	642	7019

c)

SCI		Actual	
		Link	No Link
Predicted	Link	510	1216
	No Link	386	6169

d)

SDI		Actual	
		Link	No Link
Predicted	Link	490	1195
	No Link	406	6190

e)

HPI		Actual	
		Link	No Link
Predicted	Link	396	848
	No Link	500	6537

f)

HDI		Actual	
		Link	No Link
Predicted	Link	548	1498
	No Link	348	5887

g)

PAI		Actual	
		Link	No Link
Predicted	Link	386	2454
	No Link	510	4937

h)

AAI		Actual	
		Link	No Link
Predicted	Link	388	884
	No Link	508	6501

i)

RAI		Actual	
		Link	No Link
Predicted	Link	342	624
	No Link	554	6761

j)

LHNI		Actual	
		Link	No Link
Predicted	Link	332	628
	No Link	564	6757

Fig. 1. Confusion matrices calculated for investigated OSN with using different similarity measures: a) Common Neighbors Index, b) Jaccard Index, c) Salton Index, d) Sörensen Index, e) Hub Promoted Index, f) Hub Depressed Index, g) Preferential Attachment Index, h) Adamic-Adar Index, i) Resource Allocation Index, and j) Leicht-Holme-Newman Index

Table 2. Average prediction accuracy measured by *Accuracy*, *Recall*, *Precision* and *AUC* for investigated OSN

Similarity measure	Accuracy	Recall	Precision	AUC
Common Neighbor Index (CNI)	0.8353	0.4286	0.3107	0.8058
Jaccard Index (JAI)	**0.8783**	0.2835	**0.4097**	0.7993
Salton Index (SCI)	0.8067	**0.5692**	0.2955	0.7993
Sörensen Index (SDI)	0.8065	**0.5469**	0.2908	**0.8130**
Hub Promoted Index (HPI)	0.8372	0.4420	0.3183	0.8036
Hub Depressed Index (HDI)	0.7771	**0.6116**	0.2678	**0.8130**
Preferential Attachment Index (PAI)	0.6421	0.4308	0.1359	0.6180
Adamic-Adar Index (AAI)	0.8319	0.4330	0.3050	**0.8075**
Resource Allocation Index (RAI)	**0.8570**	0.3817	**0.3540**	0.7668
Leicht-Holme-Newman Index (LHNI)	**0.8561**	0.3705	**0.3458**	0.7474

close to the best one presented by JAI. By analysis of the *Recall* values, one can see that HDI works best (its recall value is equal to 0.6116), but within the top-3 best performers, we can also find SCI (0.5692) and SDI (0.5469). Looking at the *Precision* values, similarly to *Accuracy*, JAI, RAI, and LHNI are the top rankers, with precision values equal to 0.4097, 0.3540, and 0.3458, respectively. And, in terms of *AUC*, the best performance is observed for SDI and HDI (both with an AUC value of 0.8130). They perform better than all other local information-based methods; however, the differences between their AUC values and the AUC values of other methods are not significant.

Looking at the obtained results from the perspective of the goal of the experiment, which was to select the best similarity measure to accurately predict non-existing links in OSN, there is no clear answer to the question: what measure is the best for investigating OSN? One can observe that the Jaccard Index (JAI) outperforms the existing methods in terms of two measures (*Accuracy* and *Precision*), and the Hub Depressed Index (HDI) in terms of two other measures (*Recall* and *AUC*). These observations could suggest to consider them for further analysis of OSN. It is also worth noticing that RAI and LHNI (in terms of *Accuracy* and *Precision*) as well as SDI (in terms of *Recall* and *AUC*) also present very good behavior.

On the other hand, we can also observe that in terms of three out of four evaluation metrics, the worst performance has definitely been presented by the Preferential Attachment Index (PAI). Its accuracy, precision, and AUC values (equal to 0.6423, 0.1359, and 0.6180, respectively) are the worst in each column and worse than the best ones by 26.9%, 66.8%, and 24.0%, respectively. Taking into account the fourth metric (*Recall*), the worst performance is observed for the Jaccard Index (JAI). Its recall value of 0.2835 is worse than the best one by 53,6%.

5 Conclusions

The problem of link prediction in social networks has been considered in the paper. The main contribution of the paper was to experimentally verify to what extent, if any, the similarity-based methods using different similarity measures may support the process of predicting potential new (non-existing yet) connections between employees in the organizational social network. Several similarity measures based on local information have been analyzed. The extensive computational experiment allowed one to suggest the similarity measures that can be used as good predictors in the process of link prediction of the organizational social network based on email communication.

The natural way of extending the research presented in this paper is to focus on LP methods that use not only local information (the neighborhood of a given pair of vertices) but also global information coming from the properties of the whole graph. Future work will also aim at considering the LP problem in a time-evolving social network. Verifying if the edges detected by a LP algorithm as potential connections at some stage will appear at later stages in the investigated networks will be one of the challenging tasks of the future work.

References

1. Adamic, L., Adar, E.: Friends and neighbors on the web. Soc. Netw. **25**, 211–230 (2001)
2. Barabasi, A.-L., Albert, R.: Emergence of scaling in random networks. Science **286**(5439), 509–512 (1999)
3. Barbucha, D., Szyman, P.: Identifying key actors in organizational social network based on e-mail communication. In: Wojtkiewicz, K., Treur, J., Pimenidis, E., Maleszka, M. (eds.) ICCCI 2021. CCIS, vol. 1463, pp. 3–14. Springer, Cham (2021). https://doi.org/10.1007/978-3-030-88113-9_1
4. Bliss, C.A., Frank, M.R., Danforth, C.M., Dodds, P.S.: An evolutionary algorithm approach to link prediction in dynamic social networks. J. Comput. Sci. **5**(5), 750–764 (2014)
5. Daud, N.N., Hamid, S.H.A., Saadoon, M., Sahran, F., Anuar, N.B.: Applications of link prediction in social networks: a review. J. Netw. Comput. Appl. **166**, 102716 (2020)
6. Das, S., Das, S.K.: A probabilistic link prediction model in time-varying social networks. In: 2017 IEEE International Conference on Communications (ICC), pp. 1–6. IEEE (2017)
7. Deylami, H.A., Asadpour, M.: Link prediction in social networks using hierarchical community detection. In: 2015 7th Conference on Information and Knowledge Technology (IKT), pp. 1–5. IEEE (2015)
8. Gao, S., Denoyer, L., Gallinari, P.: Probabilistic latent tensor factorization model for link pattern prediction in multi-relational networks (2012). http://arxiv.org/abs/1204.2588
9. Golbeck, J.: Analyzing the Social Web. Elsevier (2013)
10. Hasan, M.A., Chaoji, V., Salem, S., Zaki, M.: Link prediction using supervised learning. In: Proceedings of SDM 2006 Workshop on Link Analysis, Counterterrorism and Security (2006)
11. Hou, L., Liu, K.: Common neighbour structure and similarity intensity in complex networks. Phys. Lett. **381**(39), 3377–3383 (2017)
12. Jaccard, P.: The distribution of the flora in the alpine zone. New Phytol. **11**(2), 37–50 (1912)
13. Javari, A., Qiu, H., Barzegaran, E., Jalili, M., Chang, K.C.-C.: Statistical Link Label Modeling for Sign Prediction: Smoothing Sparsity by Joining Local and Global Information (2018). http://arxiv.org/abs/1802.06265
14. Kagan, D., Elovici, Y., Fire, M.: Generic anomalous vertices detection utilizing a link prediction algorithm. Soc. Netw. Anal. Min. **8**(1), 27 (2018)
15. Kumar, A., Singh, S.S., Singh, K., Biswas, B.: Link prediction techniques, applications, and performance: a survey. Phys. A **553**, 124289 (2020)
16. Lei, C., Ruan, J.: A novel link prediction algorithm for reconstructing protein-protein interaction networks by topological similarity. Bioinformatics **29**(3), 355–364 (2012)
17. Leicht, E.A., Holme, P., Newman, M.E.J.: Vertex similarity in networks. Phys. Rev. E **73**(2), 026120 (2006)
18. Liben-Nowell, D., Kleinberg, J.: The link-prediction problem for social networks. J. Am. Soc. Inf. Sci. **58**, 1019–1031 (2007)
19. Lu, X., Szymanski, B.: Predicting viral news events in online media. In: Proceedings of the 2017 IEEE International Parallel and Distributed Processing Symposium Workshops (IPDPSW), pp. 1447–1456. IEEE (2017)

20. Lü, L., Zhoua, T.: Link prediction in complex networks: a survey. Physica A **390**(6), 1150–1170 (2011)
21. Ma, C., Zhou, T., Zhang, H.-F.: Playing the role of weak clique property in link prediction: a friend recommendation model. Sci. Rep. **6**, 1–12 (2016)
22. Manning, C.D., Raghavan, P., Schütze, H.: Introduction to Information Retrieval. Cambridge University Press, New York (2008)
23. Martinez, V., Berzal, F., Cubero, J.-C.: A survey of link prediction in complex networks. ACM Comput. Surv. **49**(4), 1–33 (2016)
24. Muniz, C.P., Goldschmidt, R., Choren, R.: Combining contextual, temporal and topological information for unsupervised link prediction in social networks. Knowl.-Based Syst. **156**, 129–137 (2018)
25. Newman, M.E.J.: Clustering and preferential attachment in growing networks. Phys. Rev. E **64**(2), 025102 (2001)
26. Ozcan, A., Oguducu, S.G.: Temporal link prediction using time series of quasi-local node similarity measures. In: Proceedings of the 2016 15th IEEE International Conference on Machine Learning and Applications (ICMLA), pp. 381–386. IEEE (2016)
27. Ravasz, E., Somera, A.L., Mongru, D.A., Oltvai, Z.N., Barabasi, A.-L.: Hierarchical organization of modularity in metabolic networks. Science **297**(5586), 1551–1555 (2002)
28. Salton, G., McGill, M.J.: Introduction to Modern Information Retrieval. McGraw-Hill Inc, New York (1986)
29. Sörensen, T.: A method of establishing groups of equal amplitude in plant sociology based on similarity of species content and its application to analyses of the vegetation on Danish commons. Biologiske Skrifter **5**, 1–34 (1948)
30. Szyman, P., Barbucha, D.: Impact of similarity measure on the quality of communities detected in social network by hierarchical clustering. In: Nguyen, N.T., Manolopoulos, Y., Chbeir, R., Kozierkiewicz, A., Trawinski, B. (eds.) ICCCI 2022. LNCS, vol. 13501, pp. 29–42. Springer, Cham (2022). https://doi.org/10.1007/978-3-031-16014-1_3
31. Wu, Z., Chen, Y.: Link prediction using matrix factorization with bagging. In: Proceedings of the IEEE/ACIS 15th International Conference on Computer and Information Science (ICIS) (2016)
32. Yang, Q., Dong, E., Xie, Z.: Link prediction via nonnegative matrix factorization enhanced by blocks information. In: Proceedings of the 2014 10th International Conference on Natural Computation (ICNC), pp. 823–827. IEEE (2014)
33. Zhou, T., Lu, L., Zhang, Y.-C.: Predicting missing links via local information. Eur. Phys. J. B **71**(4), 623–630 (2009)
34. Zhu, L., Guo, D., Yin, J., Steeg, G.V., Galstyan, A.: Scalable temporal latent space inference for link prediction in dynamic social networks. IEEE Trans. Knowl. Data Eng. **28**, 2765–2777 (2016)
35. R software package. https://www.r-project.org/
36. R iGraph. https://cran.r-project.org/web/packages/igraph/
37. R linkprediction. https://cran.r-project.org/web/packages/linkprediction
38. R caret. https://cran.r-project.org/web/packages/caret/

A New Topic Modeling Method for Tweets Comparison

Jose Fabio Ribeiro Bezerra[1], Marcin Pietranik[1], Thanh Thuy Nguyen[2], and Adrianna Kozierkiewicz[1](✉)

[1] Faculty of Information and Communication Technology, Department of Applied Informatics, Wrocław University of Science and Technology, Wyb. Wyspiańskiego 27, 50-370 Wrocław, Poland
{josefabio.ribeirobezerra,marcin.pietranik, adrianna.kozierkiewicz}@pwr.edu.pl

[2] University of Engineering and Technology, Vietnam National University, Hanoi, Vietnam

Abstract. Fake news detection is a real problem, especially in social media. The untruth news dispreads very quickly and brings huge damage. This paper is devoted to proposing a topic modeling method that allows for comparing tweets, which is one of the stages of fake news detection. Our method, named Content Weighted Topic (CWT), is based on applying WordNet. Experiments showed that our method is better than the well-known Latent Dirichlet Allocation (LDA) algorithm regarding topic coherence measure. Our CWT method assigns topics for tweets that are more consistent than topics assigned by the LDA algorithm.

Keywords: topic modeling · fake news detection · tweet comparison · news

1 Introduction

Information overloads us. When we wake up, we check our mobile phones for the following e-mail. We listen to the latest trends on our favorite podcasts while reading the covers of the magazines next to our bus stop on our way to the university. We arrive at the cafeteria surrounded by the music coming from the loudspeakers and the occasional news announcement from its broadcasting. Still, we receive so much of it that it becomes natural to make it imperceptible. Handling it in our daily routines eventually leads to neglecting to verify the quality of the information that reaches us. As such, a significant problem that has become noticeable over the past few years is spreading misinformation and fake news. Access to reliable information becomes a challenge that surmounts every individual effort from processing it, as much as we have it plentiful.

The most common way to identify fake news is through content moderators' analysis of the text and its context. This process is slow and inefficient; therefore, the original message can reach millions worldwide before it is verified. Thus, there is a need to develop an automated solution that will make it possible to speed up the process and increase the effectiveness of fake news detection.

N. T. Nguyen et al. (Eds.): ICCCI 2023, LNAI 14162, pp. 326–336, 2023.
https://doi.org/10.1007/978-3-031-41456-5_25

In our work, we will focus on information published as tweets. We claim that it is possible to develop an automated method of recognizing fake tweets, which, like a human expert, can assess the credibility of information based on its content and context. We have developed a fake news model consisting of two layers: social and topic. The social layer reflects the tweet's author and his relationship with other community members, whereas the topic layer represents a set of categories or keywords the tweet fits. This part of the fake news model is essential for comparing two or more tweets. The general idea of the multilayer fake news detection model is presented in Fig. 1.

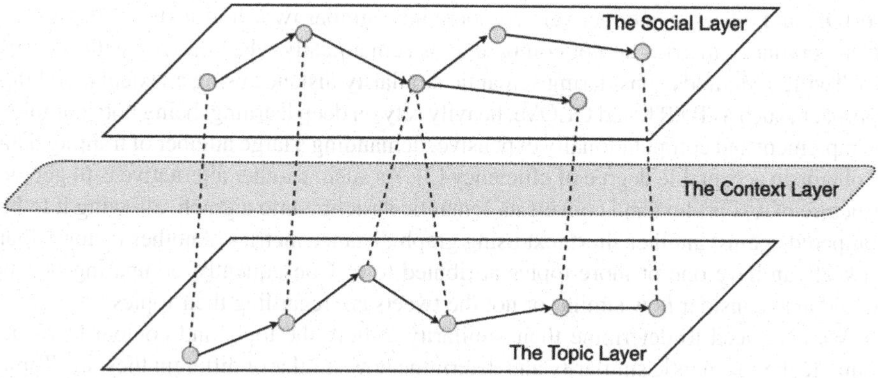

Fig. 1. The general idea for a multilayer fake news detection model

The main goal of this paper is to propose a new topic modeling method for tweet comparison, herein named Content Weighted Topic (CWT). The contributions of this paper are twofold: (1) developing a new method for topic modeling by applying WordNet called CWT (Context Weighted Topic), (2) experimental comparison of the proposed CWT method with the Latent Dirichlet Allocation (LDA) algorithm based on topic coherence measure [1].

To better illustrate the goal, let us consider two different tweets [2]:

1. "I will DONATE $100 for EVERY pass I catch next season to whatever Boston Marathon Relief Fund there is. And $200 for any dropped pass."
2. "For every retweet, I will donate 2 to the Boston marathon tragedy! RIP".

Twitter users retweeted both messages more than 17000 times, and although they appear plausible, the truth is that the second one is fake. Their initial analysis would allow judging which one should be rejected. The method proposed in this article for the first tweet determines the following topic sequence: *"fund, finance, pay, regular payment, payment, cost, be, metal, chemical element, substance, part, relation, abstract entity, entity,"* and for the second one: *"marathon, task, work, activity, human activity, event, psychological feature, abstract entity, entity."* As we can see, although both messages seem similar at first glance, the keywords/categories they belong to differ significantly. Therefore, comparing these two messages and their topics can help detect that the first is real and the second is fake, which is the main aim of this paper.

The paper is structured as follows. The next section describes related works. Section 3 contains the most important definitions and notations used to describe the developed method in Sect. 4. We describe the results of the experiments in Sect. 5. Finally, we present the conclusions in the last section.

2 Related Work

Tweets are user-generated, unstructured short texts with one or more topics. String similarity metrics, such as Jaccard similarity, Jaro-Wrinkler distance, Tanimoto coefficient, TF-IDF, and others, can effectively compare how similar two short texts are. However, string similarity metrics do not compare texts semantically when dealing with sources like Twitter. Methods considering semantic similarity distance using a lexical matching approach, such as BERT, and GLOVe, heavily rely on deep learning, being both complex to implement and computationally expensive, demanding a large number of training data to obtain an acceptable degree of efficiency [3]. As such, another alternative is to get the structure of a short text and convert its semantic structure into a graph, allowing it to be compared against another short text using graph distance metrics. Another factor is that a tweet can have one or more topics attributed to it. Consequently, comparing tweets should also consider how similar or not the tweets are regarding their topics.

We also need to determine their similarity at both the topic and content levels to compute their semantic similarity and determine how similar or different they are. Topic modeling approaches such as LDA (Latent Dirichlet Allocation) and GDSMM (Gibbs Sampling Dirichlet Multinomial Mixture) are either unsuitable for short texts (in the case of LDA) or underperforming (in the case of GSDMM). LDA is a probability-based Bayesian hierarchical generative model for collecting discrete data because words and topics in a document are interchangeable; documents are considered to contain probabilistic distributions of terms as topics [4]. A later variant of LDA [5] that includes Gibbs-based sampling has been used more frequently as part of models. Though LDA is primarily used for topic modeling for long-text documents (as opposed to short-text documents containing 50 or fewer words), some authors have utilized it for performing tweet clustering over a predefined set of topics; an example is [6] which uses LDA to cluster Twitter posts in the Indonesian language into four topics (Economics, Military, Sports, Technology) and compare how similar they are by calculating their matrix similarity over the obtained corpus from the LDA algorithm. Nevertheless, the authors had to manually select the topics for producing the results in this study. Although this manual selection of topics is a standard practice when dealing with LDA-based topic modeling approaches, it might not be suitable for processing Twitter data.

The attempt from [7] to incorporate an external source of knowledge using Wordnet by introducing the concept of probabilities of word senses instead of words proved unsuccessful when comparing its accuracy measure against the classic LDA model. One of the reasons for its shortcomings is that the authors utilized the first sense of the word and, more importantly, did not consider the role of the ontological relations between synsets and words and between words themselves, causing their model to underperform. [8] described the BDM model, which utilizes bi-terms as a base of modeling topics in the same way as LDA; the authors, however, inferred that, for short-text similarity and topic modeling, an external source of knowledge could be relevant for producing superior results when such a source is available.

In conclusion, to the best of our knowledge, there are no effective methods for modeling topics for short text messages. Thus, in our work, we will try topic modeling for tweets free of the mentioned above defects. We will show that using an external source such as WordNet is adequate for topic modeling tasks.

3 Basic Notions

We represent the set of tweets as $\tilde{\boldsymbol{T}}$ and the set of alphabet words as $\tilde{\boldsymbol{W}}$. The content $\boldsymbol{t} = <\boldsymbol{content}>$ represents each tweet $\boldsymbol{t} \in \tilde{\boldsymbol{T}}$, where $\boldsymbol{content} \in 2^{\tilde{\boldsymbol{W}}}$ is built from the words $\boldsymbol{w} \in \tilde{\boldsymbol{W}}$. Additionally, we define an auxiliary function ***tokenize*** with signature $\boldsymbol{tokenize}: \boldsymbol{t} \rightarrow \boldsymbol{2}^{\tilde{\boldsymbol{W}}}$. $\boldsymbol{H}$ is the set of relations where $\boldsymbol{h}$ is a relation between words and $\boldsymbol{h} \subseteq \tilde{\boldsymbol{W}} \times \tilde{\boldsymbol{W}}$.

For experimental purposes, we use the Topic Coherence measure, which evaluates how consistent the topic is against the documents it labels [2]. This metric is used for measuring the quality of topics assigned to a document by evaluating the coherence between topics and their respective assigned documents through co-occurrence frequency analysis of words from the topics into the documents. Topic Coherence is calculated in the following way:

$$C\left(top, W^{(top)}\right) = \sum_{m=2}^{M} \sum_{l=1}^{m-1} log \frac{f\left(w_m^{(top)}, w_l^{(top)}\right) + 1}{f(w_l^{(top)})}. \quad (1)$$

where:

- $f(w_l^{(top)})$ is the document frequency of word $w_l^{(top)}$,
- $f\left(w_m^{(top)}, w_l^{(top)}\right)$ is the co-document frequency of words $w_m^{(top)}$ and $w_l^{(top)}$,
- $W^{(top)} = (w_1^{(top)}, \ldots, w_M^{(top)})$ is a list of the M mt probable words in the topic *top*.

4 Proposed Modeling Method

The Context Weighted Topic model is based on finding a graph $\boldsymbol{G}$ represented as a set of triples of the form $<\boldsymbol{w}, \boldsymbol{r}, \boldsymbol{g}>$ where $\boldsymbol{w} \in \tilde{\boldsymbol{W}}, \boldsymbol{r}$ is a hypernym relation (a set of pairs of the given word $\boldsymbol{w}$ and its hypernyms taken from the external lexical knowledge base), and $\boldsymbol{g}$ is the weight of word $\boldsymbol{w}$ determined by the function $\boldsymbol{freq}(\boldsymbol{w})$ representing the frequency of a specified word within an external corpus (e.g., the British National Corpus for the English language). We also define the auxiliary function $\boldsymbol{hypernymOf}(\boldsymbol{w}) = \{\boldsymbol{y} \in \tilde{\boldsymbol{W}} | <\boldsymbol{w}, \boldsymbol{y}> \in \boldsymbol{r}\}$. As such, the proposed research problem is that, given the set of words resulting from applying ***tokenize*** function to a tweet $\boldsymbol{t}$, obtain the paths of hypernyms with the highest total weight possible as for every word $\boldsymbol{w}$ in a tweet $\boldsymbol{t}$ there will be one or more paths.

4.1 Algorithm

Figure 2 illustrates the general steps for the algorithm. The main idea of the CWT algorithm depends on the tokenization of tweets and the creation of hypernym chains. Next, a weighted hypernym graph is created, and the path with the highest total weighted through node similarity distance is determined. The core topic and topic sequence are created based on the chosen path.

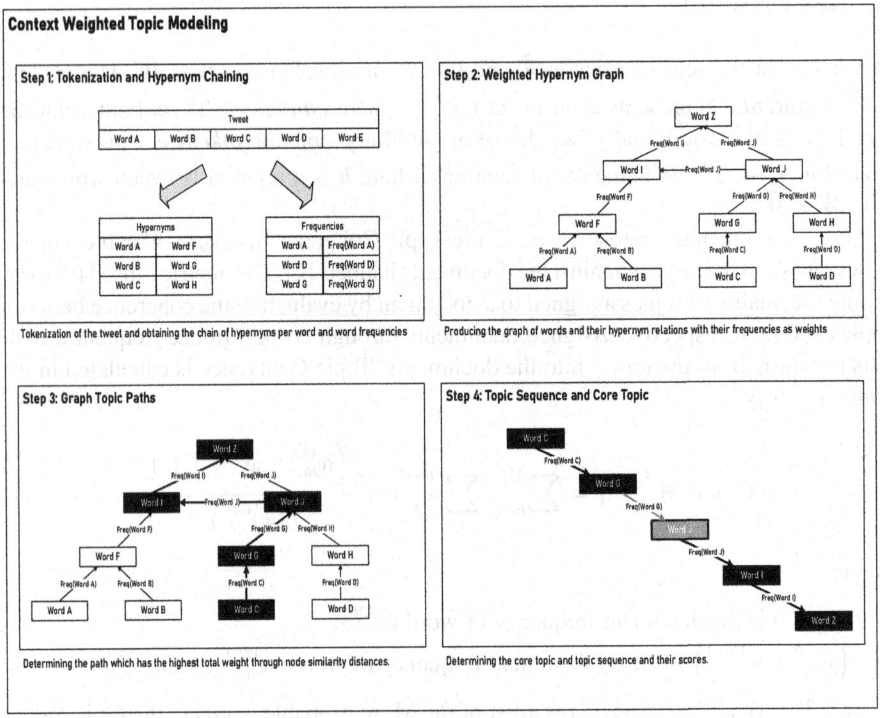

Fig. 2. Illustrating the steps for the CWT (Context Weighted Topic) algorithm.

Below is the CWT procedure presented in detail.

The proposed CTW method takes as an input a single tweet denoted as *t*. Its output contains four elements:

- *Topic sequence*: a sequence of words obtained by traversing the path between two words from the hypernym graph.
- *Topic sequence score*: the sum of individual word weights from the topic sequence.
- *Core topic*: the central node of the path obtained from the topic sequence.
- *Core topic score*: the sum of the weight of all the outgoing edges from the core topic.

Below we present four main steps of the CTW procedure, illustrated in Fig. 2.

Step 1: Tokenization and Hypernym Chaining

1. For every word $w \in tokenize(t)$

1.1 Create the auxiliary variables u and n where $n = 0$ and u is an empty string.
1.2 Assign to $u_n = hypernymOf(w)$
1.3 Assign to $f_n = freq(w)$
1.4 Append to graph G the word w, their hypernym u_n and frequency f as $s_n = <w, u_n, f_n>$.

Step 2: Weighted Hypernym Graph

2. While $u_{n-1} <> u_n$
2.1 Increment $n+ = 1$
2.2 Assign $u_n = hypernymOf(u_{n-1})$
2.3 Assign to $f_n = freq(u_n)$
2.4 Append to graph G the word u_{n-1}, their hypernym u_n and frequency f_n

Step 3: Graph Topic Paths

3. For every node $w \in G$ where $w \in tokenize(t)$
3.1 Create the auxiliary variable j where j is an empty string
3.2 Create the auxiliary variable k where $k = 0$
3.3 Obtain the highest value of the outgoing edge from the current node
3.4 For every edge matching the highest value
3.4.1 Append the node w label in j as $j = j + \text{``,''} + w$ and edge weight r as $k = k + r$
3.4.2 Mark the node as traversed
3.4.3 Traverse to the next node and go to step 3.4.1
3.4.4 If no more nodes are to traverse, output all paths and their total weights.

Step 4: Topic Sequence and Core Topic

4. From all paths and weights from step 3.4.4
4.1 Obtain the topic sequence by selecting the path with the maximum total weight.
4.2 Obtain the sequence core topic by selecting the node within the path located in the middle of the path
4.2.1 The topic sequence score is the total weight value of the selected path.
4.2.2 The core topic sequence score is the value of the outbound edge in the node in the middle of the selected path.

Optionally, in Step 4.1, adding a constant coefficient in the computed weight is interesting in favor of nouns in detriment of adjectives, as they carry a higher semantic quantity of information than other types of words. Also, please note in Step 4.2 that in many situations, there are multiple topic sequences with precisely the same score; we recommend selecting the path with the lowest amount of topics, as they carry a higher individual semantic value than a similar path with more words and the same core topic sequence score value).

Example 1. Figure 3 presents the example of a weighted hypernym graph determined by the CTW algorithm for the tweet: *For every retweet, I will donate 2 to the Boston marathon tragedy! RIP* The core topic sequence is the path with the maximum total weight. Based on our algorithm, we obtain the following topic sequence: *marathon, task, work, activity, human activity, event, psychological feature, abstract entity, entity* (marked in black bold in Fig. 3). The sequence core topic is the node within the path with the highest edge weight: *human activity* (marked in gray in Fig. 3).

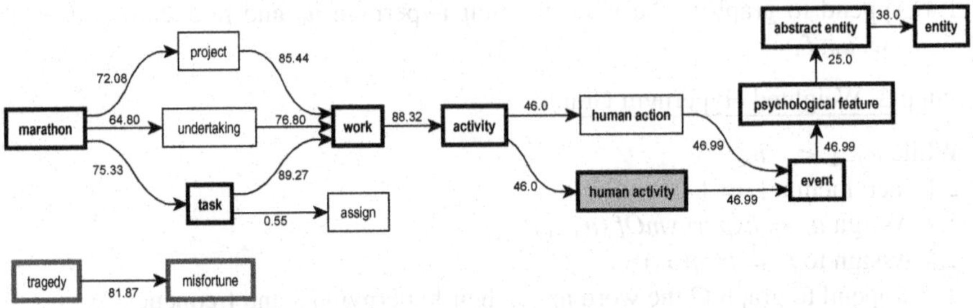

Fig. 3. Identifying the topic sequence and core topic of a tweet using CWT

Example 2. Figure 4 presents an illustrative drawing of the weighted hypernym graphs determined by the CTW algorithm for two tweets:

TWEET 1: *I will DONATE $100 for EVERY pass I catch next season to whatever Boston Marathon Relief Fund there is. And $200 for any dropped pass.*
TWEET 2: *For every retweet, I will donate 2 to the Boston marathon tragedy! RIP*

As mentioned in Introduction Section, the first tweet is real, and the second is fake. Figure 1 illustrates the difference obtained through the processing via the CWT method. This illustration resonates with the findings from McCornack et al. [3], stating that there is significantly more information in deceptive content.

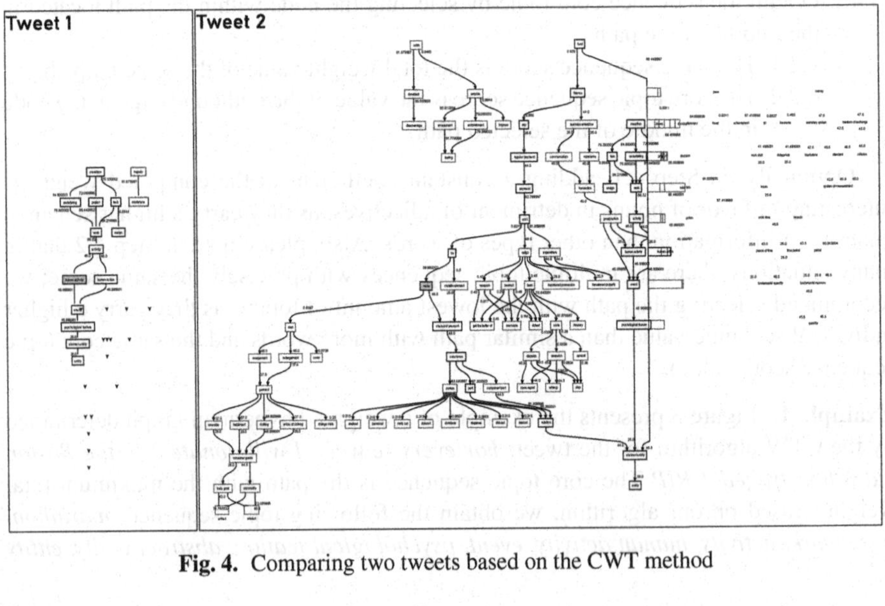

Fig. 4. Comparing two tweets based on the CWT method

5 Experimental Results

The authors have experimentally verified the method proposed in Sect. 4. For this purpose, we selected the Twitter News Dataset [9] developed by Kalyanam, Quezada, Poblete & Lanckriet [10], which contains 43256261 Twitter posts, representing a series of news events captured from Twitter between 01/08/2013 and 30/06/2014, each event having or more tweets assigned to it, originally containing references to 5234 events (referred henceforth as baseline topics). The original dataset contains a list of tweet identifiers and their respective news events. In more detail, the authors of the original dataset first selected a set of verified accounts from news outlets published on Twitter and collected their news events headlines hourly. They manually selected the keywords for further search on the Twitter API to obtain their respective set of matching tweets for these keywords. Once the authors collected the hourly batch of tweets, they preprocessed the data to reduce noisy and irrelevant tweets. The authors validated the data through pairwise keyword checks for the consistency of tweet groups.

Despite being outdated, to the best of the author's knowledge, this was the only validated news dataset that included keywords representing the topics of a given tweet, hence its selection as our primary data source. After 2016, Twitter launched a new policy to prevent data privacy issues related to disclosing its user's data. The author's new dataset (which we can call the dry dataset, in opposition to the hydrated dataset with complete Twitter data) only makes the *tweet_id* (the primary identifier of a tweet) and its related keywords available.

As such, we queried Twitter API using a hydration mechanism (on which we provide the tweet identifier and recover the original tweet data when available) and retrieved the respective tweet data. We utilized the Twitter API, ran over the first 5% of the total dataset tweet identifiers, and collected a total of 218252 tweets; after cleaning up the retrieved tweets to remove empty or tweets with error messages and excluding all the tweets, not in the English language, we got the final count of 145272 valid tweets (representing 66,56% of the amount of the retrieved tweets), assigned to 221 events (representing 4,22% of the total amount of events in the dataset). Because the identifier for specific tweets might have changed over the years, the authors could not match some tweets with the event they originally were sourced from, and we have filtered those out, resulting in a final count of 137090 tweets. We used the resulting dataset as our source for our experiments, to which we applied our model and compared the results with LDA.

Additionally, the source dataset has associated topics in addition to tweet id and tweet text. The topic coherence score is also computed based on these topics. The obtained results serve as a baseline (control) to validate if the CWT method improves the quality or delivers acceptable results compared to the baseline.

We have computed five scores: one for the baseline records (from the topics assigned to the tweets from the original dataset), one for the CWT method (where we appended the calculated topic sequences to the original tweet), and three for LDA (100, 200, 300 topics respectively). It is essential to mention that LDA requires a priori knowledge of the number of topics to be computed; hence we adopted this range of topics to measure eventual improvements compared to the baseline and against our CWT method.

The median (and standard deviation) for baseline topic coherence score was $-1251564.970 \pm 5931386.964$; for the CWT method, $-370420.926 \pm 2453845.256$; for

LDA, we have obtained –4531882.280 ± 7045759.144 (100 Topics, labeled henceforth T100), –3237760.898 ± 7325127.135 (200 Topics, labeled henceforth T200), and –3226926.257 ± 7440704.806 (300 Topics, labeled henceforth T300), as seen in Fig. 5.

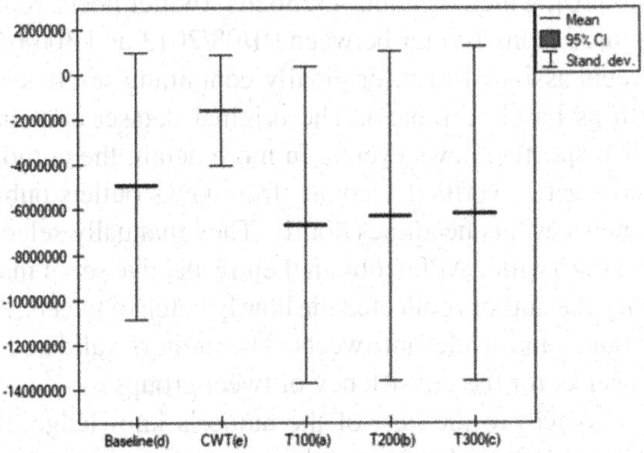

Fig. 5. Median and standard deviation for the measured Topic Coherence Scores (LDA T100 (a), LDA T200 (b), LDA T300 (c), baseline (d), CWT (e)).

The non-parametric test of Kruskal-Wallis ANOVA (Analysis of Variance) with Dunn post-hoc, with its results (see Table 1, Table 2, and Table 3) has specific sensitivity for the data utilized in this experiment, considering that it is not normally distributed, as evidenced by a Kolgomorov-Smirnov Test (which, when testing for the Baseline data, and considering an alpha of 0.5 and a population size of 137090, resulted in a maximum difference of 0.202865627 over the expected value of 0.003673128, thus rejecting the standard distribution hypothesis). The results of Dunn's post-hoc tests demonstrated a significant difference between the topic coherence scores of all samples (p-value 0.000001 is smaller than the assumed significance level equal to 0.05). Data analysis in Tables 1, 2 and 3 showed that the highest topic coherence score was obtained using the developed CWT method. This confirms the usefulness of the developed method, confirms the usefulness of the developed method, in particular in the task of modeling topics for tweets.

Table 1. Dunn Post-Hoc (Mean Result Distributed)

MRD	Baseline	CWT	T100	T200	T300
Baseline		123492.192815	93408.187979	73676.028372	66399.715067
CWT	123492.192815		216900.380794	197168.221187	189891.907882
T100	93408.187979	216900.380794		19732.159607	27008.472912
T200	73676.028372	197168.221187	19732.159607		7276.313305
T300	66399.715067	189891.907882	27008.472912	7276.313305	

Table 2. Dunn Post-Hoc (Statistic)

Statistic	Baseline	CWT	T100	T200	T300
Baseline	–	163.399815	123.593891	97.485105	87.857385
CWT	163.399815	–	286.993706	260.88492	251.2572
T100	123.593891	286.993706	–	26.108786	35.736506
T200	97.485105	260.88492	26.108786	–	9.62772
T300	87.857385	251.2572	35.736506	9.62772	-

Table 3. Descriptive Statistics Summary

Group	Baseline	CWT	T100	T200	T300
Sample size	137090	137090	137090	137090	137090
Median	–1251564.970	–370420.925	–4531882.280	–3237760.898	–3226926.257
Lower quartile	–12350885.500	-1660169.048	–10461766.394	-9821293.747	-9585486.888
Upper quartile	–152291.170	–115726.752	–1194595.472	–1082909.207	–986673.894

6 Conclusions

The topic modeling task is one of the most challenging tasks in natural language processing. There is much research on this concept. The interest will only grow because of the increasing amount of textual data on the internet and because of problems related to it, like information retrieval or fake news detection problem.

This work proposed an original method of modeling topics for tweets based on WordNet. Experimental verification allowed us to conclude that the CTW method is better than the existing methods in the context of topic coherence measure. So far, no effective methods have been for modeling topics for short messages such as tweets. Usually, the coherence score will increase with the increase in the number of topics. Therefore, the LDA method worked better for long texts. Our work fills this gap. In addition, compared to the LDA method, the CTW method does not require the number of topics to be specified in advance.

Our future works will focus on developing a method that distinguishes real from fake news. For this task, both the news content and the context should be considered. Our preliminary research has shown that the statement's context is critical in detecting fake news. Therefore various types of additional information, such as: who is the author of the news, whether it is an original message or reposted, what is the topic of the statement, and many others, will be used to develop the method.

References

1. Mimno, D., Wallach, H., Talley, E., Leenders, M., McCallum, A.: Optimizing semantic coherence in topic models. In: Proceedings of the 2011 Conference on Empirical Methods in Natural Language Processing (2011)
2. Gupta, A., Lamba, H., Kumaraguru, P.: 1.00 per RT #BostonMarathon #PrayForBoston: analyzing fake content on Twitter. In: 2013 APWG eCrime Researchers Summit (2013)
3. McCornack, S.A., Morrison, K., Paik, J.E., Wisner, A.M., Zhu, X.: Information manipulation theory 2. J. Lang. Soc. Psychol. **33**, 348–377 (2014)
4. Zhou, X., Zafarani, R.: A survey of fake news. ACM Comput. Surv. **53**, 1–40 (2020)
5. Nguyen, H.T., Duong, P.H., Cambria, E.: Learning short-text semantic similarity with word embeddings and external knowledge sources. Knowl.-Based Syst. **182**, 104842 (2019)
6. Blei, D.M., Ng, A.Y., Jordan, M.I.: Latent Dirichlet allocation. In: Proceedings of the 14th International Conference on Neural Information Processing Systems: Natural and Synthetic, Cambridge (2001)
7. Stoyanova, L., Wallace, W.: Topic Modelling, Sentiment Analysis and Classification of Short-form Text, p. 159 (2019)
8. Negara, E.S., Triadi, D., Andryani, R.: Topic modelling Twitter data with latent Dirichlet allocation method. In: 2019 International Conference on Electrical Engineering and Computer Science (ICECOS) (2019)
9. Ferrugento, A., Oliveira, H.G., Alves, A., Rodrigues, F.: Can topic modelling benefit from word sense information? In: Proceedings of the Tenth International Conference on Language Resources and Evaluation (LREC 2016), Portoro, Slovenia (2016)
10. Yang, S., Huang, G., Ofoghi, B., Yearwood, J.: Short text similarity measurement using context-aware weighted biterms. Concurr. Comput.: Pract. Exp. **34** (2020)
11. Quezada, M.: Jkalyana@Ucsd.Edu, Bpoblete@Dcc.Uchile.Cl and Gert@Ece.Ucsd.Edu, Twitter News Dataset, figshare (2016)
12. Kalyanam, J., Quezada, M., Poblete, B., Lanckriet, G.: Prediction and characterization of high-activity events in social media triggered by real-world news. PLoS ONE **11**, e0166694 (2016)

Measuring Gender: A Machine Learning Approach to Social Media Demographics and Author Profiling

Erik-Robert Kovacs(✉), Liviu-Adrian Cotfas, and Camelia Delcea

Department of Economic Informatics and Cybernetics, Bucharest University of Economic Studies, 010552 Bucharest, Romania

{erik.kovacs,camelia.delcea}@csie.ase.ro, liviu.cotfas@ase.ro

Abstract. Social media has become a preeminent medium of communication during the early 21st century, facilitating dialogue between the political sphere, businesses, scientific experts, and everyday people. Researchers in the social sciences are focusing their attention on social media as a central site of social discourse, but such approaches are hampered by the lack of demographic data that could help them connect phenomena originating in social media spaces to their larger social context. Computational social science methods which use machine learning and deep learning natural language processing (NLP) tools for the task of author profiling (AP) can serve as an essential complement to such research. One of the major demographic categories of interest concerning social media is the gender distribution of users. We propose an ensemble of multiple machine learning classifiers able to distinguish whether a user is anonymous with an F1 score of 90.24%, then predict the gender of the user based on their name, obtaining an F1 score of 89.22%. We apply the classification pipeline to a set of approximately 44,000,000 posts related to COVID-19 extracted from the social media platform Twitter, comparing our results to a benchmark classifier trained on the PAN18 Author Profiling dataset, showing the validity of the proposed approach. An n-gram analysis on the text of the tweets to further compare the two methods has been performed.

Keywords: author profiling · gender identification · ensemble methods · social media analysis · COVID-19

1 Introduction

The present economic and social environment is characterized by a series of unexpected events having a major impact on the lives of people across the world [1, 2]. In this context, social media has become a meeting ground where people connect in real time, sharing ideas and information regarding the events that alter their daily lives [3, 4]. At the same time, social media has become an ideal data source that can be explored by both researchers and policy makers when trying to better understand the issues, fears and information needs of society. In the process of addressing these issues, knowing the

N. T. Nguyen et al. (Eds.): ICCCI 2023, LNAI 14162, pp. 337–349, 2023.
https://doi.org/10.1007/978-3-031-41456-5_26

audience is an important step for devising adequate policy [5]. Among the demographic characteristics of the users posting in social media, gender plays an important role since events can affect women and men differently [6, 7].

The specific problem we aim to solve with our contribution is the lack of information regarding the underlying demographics of text data sampled from social media sources. This lack of insight has widely been cited as an intrinsic issue with computational social science research [8–10]. An estimation of the actual underlying demographics would be valuable as it would allow an evaluation of how representative the sample is. Additionally it would allow a very granular approach to computational social science that could generate deeper insights into the many factors that correlate with certain opinions, such as the opposition towards vaccination [9, 11]. The development of a comprehensive demographic classification methodology, associated with the availability of appropriate training data, would push the field towards becoming a valuable complement to traditional methods such as surveys, with the advantage of being able to leverage a vastly superior number of data points.

As a result, the aim of our contribution is to suggest an improved method for estimating the gender distribution of a sample of online texts gathered from the microblogging platform Twitter using computational tools. We use publicly available datasets to train a series of classifiers for two sub-problems: the identification of a given name as opposed to a surname or other English word, and the identification of the gender of that given name. We obtain the best results using random forest (RF) classifiers for both sub-problems. We compare our approach to a baseline inspired by the PAN18 Author Profiling task [12] using the text component of the provided dataset. We validate our approach on domain data gathered by Banda et al. [13] during the COVID-19 pandemic, obtaining a gender distribution that matches the true estimated distribution of Twitter users [14]. Additionally, we extract and compare the top n-grams for each gender for the purpose of analyzing if there are meaningful differences among genders in the discourse related to the COVID-19 pandemic. We release the composite dataset used for the given name identification sub-problem for further research use.

The paper is structured as follows: Sect. 2 provides a brief literature review which supports the need for the current study, while Sect. 3 describes the data and methods used in the current approach. Section 4 analyzes the performance of the gender identification approach, with a focus on the results obtained on the selected COVID-19 dataset. The paper ends with concluding remarks and further research directions.

2 Related Work

Natural language processing (NLP) uses computational tools for operating on inputs in natural language. The field has evolved tremendously during the past few years, seeing the introduction of the Transformer neural network architecture [15] and the development of large transfer learning models such as BERT [16].

At the same time, there has been increased interest from fields associated with the social sciences in using these computational tools to analyze various aspects related to public opinion [1, 5, 9, 17]. The challenge with these approaches is that in most of the studies, demographics information is missing, the analysis being conducted on the entire dataset, without considering any differences that could exist in terms of gender, age, or ethnicity [18]. Thus, it is difficult to connect any findings back to the social context in which the social media discourses studied arose in the first place.

The NLP task that is concerned with extracting such information from text data is known as author profiling (AP) [19]. It aims to identify details about the user such as gender, age, native language, etc. [19–21]. An important subtask of AP is gender identification. This can be defined formally as the task of finding tuple $<a,g>$ given any sample of text x_i, where a is the author and g is the gender, $g \in \{female, male\}$. We have identified two main approaches to gender identification: intrinsic gender identification, when x_i is one document out of a corpus X of annotated documents $<x_i, g_i>$, and metadata-based gender identification, when the document x_i is a piece of information concerning the author, such as their name, occupation, place of employment, preferred pronouns, etc.

Approaches to gender identification can be grouped from a technical standpoint into dictionary-based [22], classical machine learning [19], and deep learning [21]. A comprehensive review that compares the results achieved on the PAN18 Author Profiling dataset[1] by the approaches described in 23 papers focusing on gender detection is included in [12]. Out of these, the best accuracy (82.21%) has been achieved by Daneshvar and Inkpen [23], where the authors used a Support Vector Machine classifier with a combination of different n-grams as features.

The gender identification method we propose is a metadata-based one, as by using the Twitter API it is possible to retrieve the public name field of any tweet's author. Inferring a person's gender from their name is possible because most European names are inherently gendered. It is important to note that this is not applicable to all languages and cultural contexts; for instance, not all Mandarin Chinese names can be assigned a gender [24]. Thus, great care must be taken to avoid using the name-based approach when dealing with non-European contexts and languages. In such cases, domain knowledge should be used to determine how well the approach fits local naming customs.

3 Data and Methods

3.1 Domain and Training Data

The domain data on which we aimed to validate our approach is the Large-Scale COVID-19 Twitter Chatter Dataset made available by Banda et al. [13]. This dataset contains 1.2 billion tweets related to COVID-19, collected between January 2020 and June 2021, presented in the form of a list of tweet IDs that can be used to retrieve each individual tweet from the Twitter API [13].

Due to issues of scale, we have further reduced the number of tweets by restricting the timeframe to the period between January 2021 and March 2021.We retrieved the name of the user who posted each tweet for gender identification. Our curated domain data contained 44,248,682 tweets from 6,999,706 distinct users. One of the difficulties with using the user's name to identify their gender is that on Twitter, the name field is free text; as such, it can also contain non-name related tokens, such as titles, job-related

[1] https://pan.webis.de/data.html.

information, political affiliation, preferred pronouns, etc. in addition to allowing the user to simply use a pseudonym. Nevertheless, after cleaning up the date and removing special characters, we have observed that many of the most common unigrams ranked by term frequency appear to be personal names (see Table 1.), lending credence to the fact that many users prefer to use actual human names instead of other signifiers. At the same time, the incidence of given names decreases when bigrams and trigrams are considered, with email addresses ("gmail com"), pandemic-related ("wear mask") and political messages ("black lives matter", "president elect") becoming more common.

Table 1. Top-10 n-grams ranked by term frequency found in the name field.

Type	N-grams
Unigrams	dr (41718), david (32122), john (31899), michael (26795), chris (24236), james (22820), kumar (21670), singh (20656), paul (20322), mark (18835)
Bigrams	gmail com (2895), wear mask (2079), stan account (2055), president elect (1962), lives matter (1845), black lives (1816), kinda ia (1816), yoongi day (1418), semi ia (1163), de la (1139)
Trigrams	black lives matter (1631), name cannot blank (577), wear damn mask (210), hu tao haver (192), sb ikalawang yugto (186), de la cruz (151), happy yoongi day (123), bts paved way (108), de la torre (102), certified lover boy (100)

The data appears to contain the name information, simply requiring special pre-processing. Pre-trained named-entity recognition (NER) models can be used to identify given name – surname tuples, but as the name order used on Twitter might be variable or interspersed with tokens such as "dr" or "mr", these might not generalize well to arbitrary data and might skew the resulting distribution in ways we cannot easily explain, account or compensate for. Thus, we propose a novel, machine learning approach to given name identification, in which we evaluate each token individually and classify it as a given name or not.

Because to the best of our knowledge this exact technique has not been applied in the literature, we know of no publicly available dataset relevant to this task. Nevertheless, the n-gram analysis from Table 1 suggests the presence of at least four categories of signifiers in the field: given names ("david", "john", "michael"), surnames ("singh", "de la *x*"), other English words ("dr", "name", "cannot"), and non-English words ("hu tao haver", "sb ikalawang yugto"). As such, a dataset containing these classes of tokens can be constructed from other publicly available datasets and annotated automatically.

For this purpose, we have merged three separate datasets: for given names, we used the Gender by Name Data Set available in the University of California Irvine Machine Learning Repository, containing 147,270 personal names and the associated biological sex of the persons bearing those names, dating from between 1880 and 2019 and gathered from the US, the UK, Canada, and Australia [25]. For surnames, we used the Wiktionary Names Appendix Scraped Surnames Dataset containing 45,136 surnames from persons across the world, gathered from Wiktionary[2]. Finally, for arbitrary English words, we used the 1/3 million most frequent words corpus [26][3], containing the top 333,331 words used in the English language ranked by term frequency. Because certain tokens were present in more than one dataset, we removed all duplicates. The merged dataset, consisting of 476,089 tokens, can be accessed at: https://github.com/erkovacs/measuring-gender-a-machine-learning-approach-social-media-demographics-author-profiling-data. For the gender identification problem, we have used the Gender by Name Data Set individually.

3.2 Preprocessing and Tokenization

We have substituted all special characters from the data with their English phonetic transcriptions using the software package unidecode[4]. In addition, we substituted all punctuation with the character "*" and lowercased all the tokens in the dataset. We applied this same preprocessing to tokens in all categories, and for both sub-problems.

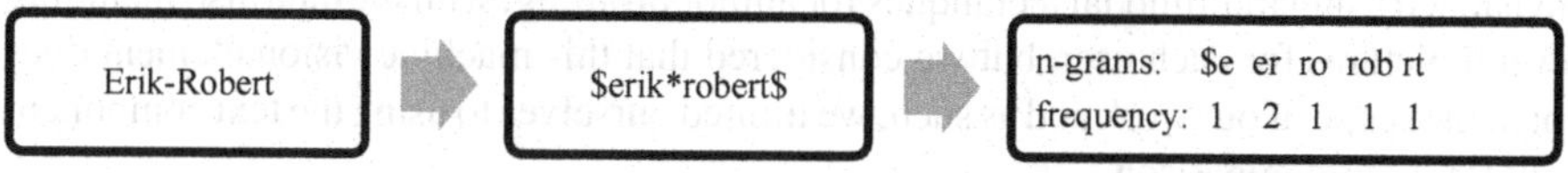

Fig. 1. Data representation steps with a toy feature set consisting of bigrams and trigrams.

For feature representation, we have used a character-level tokenization scheme based on the one proposed by Malmasi and Dras [27]. This tokenization scheme can capture sub-word structures that encode gender information at the level of names using a compact alphabet composed of unigram, bigram and trigram features with the addition of special tokens "*" mentioned above and "$", marking the beginning or end of a string [27]. After building this feature set and transforming the data, we used the most representative 2048 features to build a document-term matrix for each token, as shown in Fig. 1.

3.3 Ensemble Classifier

The final ensemble pipeline we propose consists of two classifiers and decision points (Fig. 2.). The first one is the given name identification step, which takes a list of tokens for each author and classifies each token as a given name or surname/other word. Binary classification is sufficient for our purposes in this case because we are only interested in whether the token is a given name or not. The tokens that are classified as given names are kept in the list; all other tokens are removed.

Users with zero tokens identified are labelled as "anonymous" and will not be evaluated for their gender during the next step. For the remaining users, each given name

[2] https://github.com/solvenium/names-dataset.
[3] https://norvig.com/ngrams/.
[4] https://pypi.org/project/unidecode/.

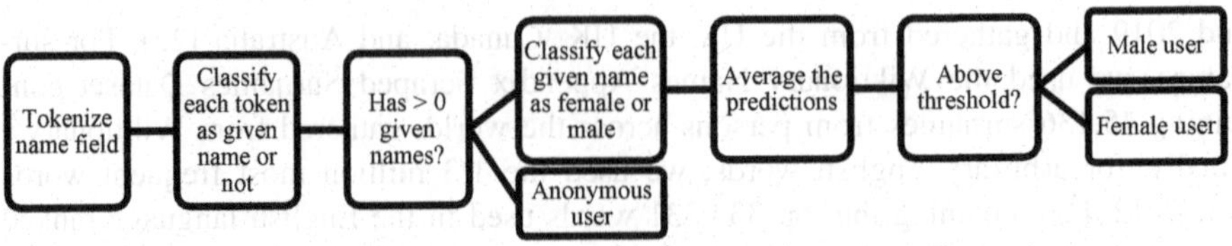

Fig. 2. Illustration of the ensemble method steps and decision points.

identified in the previous step is identified as *female* or *male* and the predictions averaged over the number of tokens. For simplicity the decision threshold was set at 0.5.

3.4 Benchmarking

In order to compare our metadata-based approach to an intrinsic gender identification approach, we have decided to use the English text component of the PAN18 Author Profiling dataset [12], containing 4,900 users annotated as *female* or *male* and 100 tweets from each user. We have chosen this dataset because of its proximity to our own application and because it has also been collected from Twitter. The original task envisioned using multimodal techniques for author profiling, with the data also including several pictures for each user, but we considered that this machine vision element does not fit the scope of our work and as such, we limited ourselves to using the text component only for a fair comparison.

We fine-tuned a BERT [16] classifier on the full English part of the dataset for 10 epochs, with a maximum sentence length of 16 tokens (the average sentence length being 20.45 tokens), and a learning rate of 55e–6, chosen by running several training cycles with different learning rates we have experimented with in the past [9]. To match our approach from Sect. 3.3, we merged the train and the test data made available by the organizers and performed 5-fold cross validation. The model obtained an F1 score of 79.40% and an accuracy of 79.38%, an above-average performance considering the results reported by Rangel et al. [12]. We then removed all duplicate tweets, being left with 12,432,935 unique tweets, and used the model trained on the PAN18 AP dataset to predict the gender of the user for each of these.

4 Results

4.1 Classifier Evaluation

We have trained multiple classifiers, using both classical machine learning and deep learning, for each of the two sub-problems: random forest (RF), support vector machine (SVM), multinomial naïve Bayes (NB), a feedforward neural network (FFN), a recurrent neural network (RNN), and a long short-term memory network (LSTM). We compared the classifiers using the F1 score (Eq. 3), computed as the harmonic mean between precision (Eq. 1) and recall (Eq. 2). All values given are mean values obtained over 5-fold cross-validation.

$$recall = \frac{TP}{TP + FN} \tag{1}$$

$$precision = \frac{TP}{TP + FP} \tag{2}$$

$$F_1 = 2 \cdot \frac{precision \cdot recall}{precision + recall} \tag{3}$$

For the given name identification sub-problem, we have obtained the best results using the RF classifier with n-gram counts as features (see Table 2). Despite experimenting with different architectures and hyperparameter tuning, the deep learning models have not been able to surpass the performance of some of the classical machine learning algorithms. This highlights the continued relevance of these models, especially if well-fitting feature sets can be found. It is worth mentioning that these models are much faster to train than their deep learning counterparts and have much more modest hardware requirements.

Table 2. Classifiers performance in the case of the given name identification sub-problem.

Classifier	Vectorization	Precision	Recall	F_1-score	Accuracy
RF	TF	86.47%	81.27%	**90.24%**	90.27%
SVM	TF-IDF	81.27%	75.76%	86.91%	87.09%
NB	TF	74.00%	77.87%	84.78%	84.69%
FFN	TF	82.56%	78.35%	80.35%	88.25%
RNN	TF	81.40%	76.01%	78.59%	87.20%
LSTM	TF	80.73%	73.70%	77.05%	86.39%

For the gender identification sub-problem, it is also the RF classifier with n-gram count features that obtained the best results (see Table 3). The same underperformance in the case of the deep learning models can be seen here as well. It is likely that the selected feature set [27] is not well-suited to these models.

In comparison to a purely dictionary-based approach, we expect this classifier to capture sub-word structures common to given names, allowing it to generalize better to new data. To test this hypothesis, we have gathered a list of 70 fictional character names from the online computer game World of Warcraft[5]. This game takes place in a medieval fantasy setting and as such most characters have invented names that reflect their in-game culture and ethnicity. Nevertheless, most of these names contain the same sub-word structures as real-life names, allowing the classifier to obtain an 84.29% accuracy. A sample of the predictions, both accurate and inaccurate, can be seen in Table 4.

In both cases it should be noted that all classifiers had good performance, lending credence to the hypotheses that human given names are sufficiently morphologically distinct from other English words to be easily learnable by the classifiers, and that gender information is encoded at the level of the form of given names.

[5] https://wowwiki-archive.fandom.com/wiki/Major_characters.

Table 3. Performance of the classifiers in the case of the gender identification sub-problem.

Classifier	Vectorization	Class	Recall	F_1-score	Balanced accuracy
RF	TF	*female*	91.66%	**89.22%**	88.44%
		male	85.23%		
SVM	TF-IDF	*female*	89.53%	87.07%	86.27%
		male	83.02%		
NB	TF	*female*	85.47%	83.81%	83.18%
		male	80.88%		
FFN	TF	*female*	88.52%	82.43%	85.96%
		male	83.40%		
LSTM	TF	*female*	88.64%	81.61%	85.28%
		male	81.93%		
RNN	TF	*female*	88.81%	80.73%	84.52%
		male	80.24%		

Table 4. Examples of predictions on fantasy names.

Name	Actual gender	Predicted gender
Sen'jin	male	male
Chen Stormstout	male	male
Sylvanas Windrunner	female	female
Uther the Lightbringer	male	male
Daelin Proudmoore	male	female
Velen	male	female
Ysera	female	male
Varian Wrynn	male	female

4.2 Discussion

By applying the best performing classifier to the COVID-19 domain data, described in Sect. 3.1, the predicted distribution of the users by gender is as follows: 30.76% are anonymous users, 33.71% have been classified as female, and 35.53% have been predicted as male (Fig. 3).

When excluding anonymous users, the predicted distribution (48.69% female, 51.31% male) is very close to the empirically-observed distribution (43.60% female, 56.40% male) [14]. The distribution obtained by the benchmark model is 49.58% female and 50.42% male, which is also very close. Note however that the benchmark model cannot distinguish anonymous users at all.

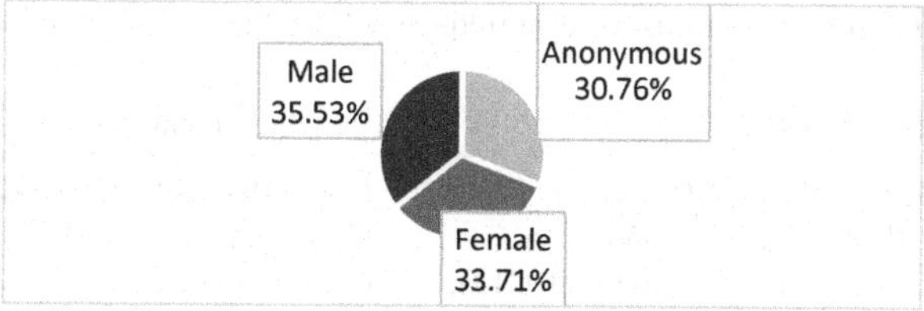

Fig. 3. The distribution of users by gender.

It is noteworthy that among the anonymous users, Black Lives Matter-related messages and COVID-19-related messages appear to have been preeminently featured in their names (see Table 5).

Table 5. Top 10 n-grams by term frequency from the name field of users marked as anonymous

Type	N-grams
Unigrams	mr (8923), com (7944), dr (7814), news (7416), health (5258), black (4956), de (4567), el (4538), blm (4495), big (4056)
Bigrams	gmail com (2013), black lives (1652), lives matter (1629), wear mask (1205), commissions open (461), high school (439), mental health (369), public health (324), blm acab (314), yahoo com (314)
Trigrams	black lives matter (1437), wear damn mask (205), black lives still (119), lives still matter (118), boop bop beep (63), grammy nominated bts (60), please wear mask (51), wear fucking mask (49), trans lives matter (47), new year new (46)

At the same time, the n-gram analysis performed on both the predictions produced by our pipeline and the benchmark model reveals that our approach has significantly more female names in the top 15 n-grams (except for "mike") than the benchmark model, which actually has many male names (see Table 6). The same phenomenon, albeit less pronounced, can be seen at the level of the users predicted as male. This issue in the case of the benchmark classifier can be caused by the fact that its predictions take only the text into account, and as such many users who are of a given gender but have an anonymous Twitter presence have been included, resulting in an incorrect correlation. It is also possible that the model simply did not generalize well from the PAN18 dataset to the domain data. Limitations such as these show that the two approaches can be used either independently or as complements, depending on the aims of the research and the available data.

Furthermore, an analysis of the top-20 n-grams has been performed on the tweets for which the author has been classified as male or female. In the case of unigrams and bigrams it has been observed that the top-20 n-grams are highly specific to the topic of the dataset, namely the the COVID-19 pandemic (e.g., "'covid", "vaccine", "coronavirus", "pandemic", "death", "covid vaccine", "covid pandemic", "covid vaccination", "wear mask", "get covid", etc.), with the same n-grams being present in the tweets written by both female and male authors.

Table 6. Top 15 n-grams by term frequency from the name field of users.

Gender	Ensemble classifier	Benchmark classifier
Female	dr (21325), mike (18218), sarah (17390), maria (11622), mary (11558), lisa (11521), laura (11172), taylor (10213), michelle (9108), kelly (8949), karen (8809), jennifer (8636), emily (8598), anna (8527), marie (8501)	news (193919), com (64199), dr (59689), john (39664), health (39660), david (34122), michael (27250), patch (26813), covid (25038), world (24087), james (23164), md (22733), paul (21763), mark (21532), iweller (20243)
Male	david (30317), john (29899), michael (25146), chris (22962), james (20781), kumar (20030), paul (18929), mark (17932), alex (16357), dr (16266), singh (14323), daniel (14191), andrew (14002), matt (13706), joe (12831)	news (222578), bot (83877), corona (72025), update (70978), corona update (70011), update bot (70011), corona update bot (70011), dr (55677), com (47832), david (43410), john (42967), covid (32276), michael (31729), health (27166), james (26695)

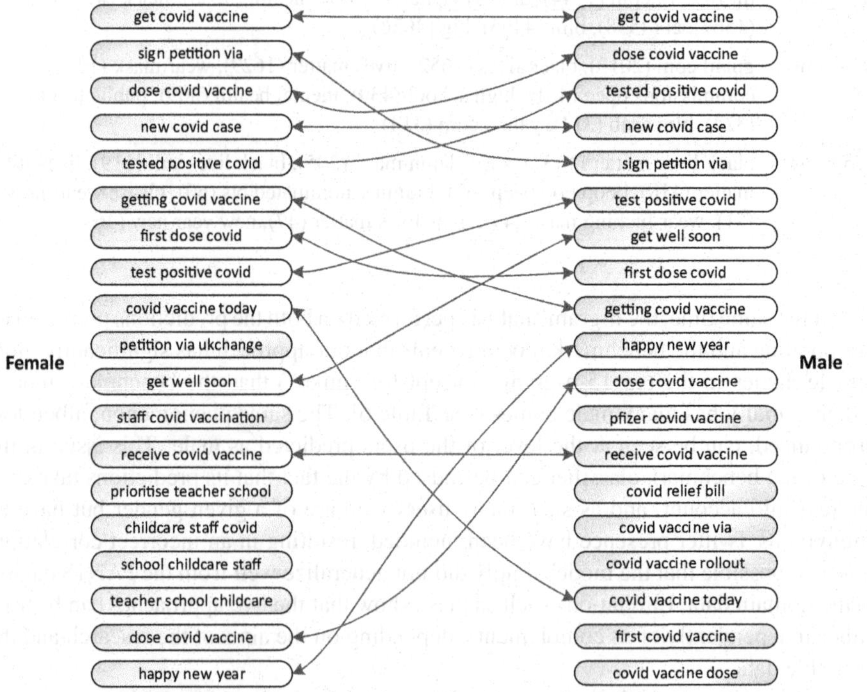

Fig. 4. Top 20 trigrams by TF-IDF score from the text of the tweets.

A significant difference between female and male written tweets becomes visible in the case of the top-20 trigrams. Thus, while the first nine trigrams are common in the discourse of both genders, as they pertain to general topics related to COVID-19 (e.g., "get covid vaccine", "new covid case", "tested positive covid", etc.), for the rest, differences can be noted among genders. While female authors focused their speech on encouraging the signing of a petition (e.g., "petition via ukchange", "petition via change") and expressed concern regarding the safety of children (e.g., "prioritise teacher school", "teacher school childcare", "school childcare staff", "childcare staff covid", "staff covid vaccination"), the discourse of male authors revolves around relief funds (e.g., "covid relief bill") and the vaccination process (e.g., "pfizer covid vaccine", "covid vaccine via", "covid vaccine rollout", "first covid vaccine", "covid vaccine dose", "rollout covid vaccine"). The common trigrams are depicted in grey in Fig. 4, while the ones that are specific to female and male authors are represented with red and blue respectively.

On the other hand, if the same n-grams analysis is performed on the tweets for which the gender of the authors has been determined using the benchmark classifier, no significant differences can be distinguished.

5 Conclusion

Correctly identifying the differences in gender discourse can be of the utmost importance in shaping the right information campaigns. The present approach is most relevant in situations where more details are available regarding the authors, such as the text of their tweets or profile photos, as a complementary analysis tool, where it can be incorporated as an important component of a multimodal gender detection approach that also considers the traditional or stylistic text features extracted from the tweets, as well as the results of the profile photos analysis.

One of the limitations of the study is that it, by necessity, does not consider the full complexity of gender within society. Our approach is also unable to detect instances of gender deception, or the use of pseudonyms that do in fact conform to standards of human given names. The approach also does not distinguish between anonymous users and organizational users, which state the name of a company, product, or institution as their name. Finally, as our reference benchmark does not leverage its full potential because we have omitted using the machine vision element; it is possible that its performance could be improved by complementing it with image-based data (though the authors report mixed results from such attempts [12]). These issues can be solved in the future by extending or modifying our approach.

Funding. This study was co-financed by The Bucharest University of Economic Studies during the PhD program.

References

1. Öztürk, N., Ayvaz, S.: Sentiment analysis on Twitter: a text mining approach to the Syrian refugee crisis. Telemat. Inform. **35**(1), 136–147 (2018). https://doi.org/10.1016/j.tele.2017.10.006

2. Ruz, G.A., Henríquez, P.A., Mascareño, A.: Sentiment analysis of Twitter data during critical events through Bayesian networks classifiers. Future Gener. Comput. Syst. **106**, 92–104 (2020). https://doi.org/10.1016/j.future.2020.01.005
3. D'Andrea, E., Ducange, P., Bechini, A., Renda, A., Marcelloni, F.: Monitoring the public opinion about the vaccination topic from tweets analysis. Expert Syst. Appl. **116**, 209–226 (2019). https://doi.org/10.1016/j.eswa.2018.09.009
4. Kullar, R., Goff, D.A., Gauthier, T.P., Smith, T.C.: To tweet or not to tweet—A review of the viral power of twitter for infectious diseases. Curr. Infect. Dis. Rep. **22**(6) (2020). Art. no. 14. https://doi.org/10.1007/s11908-020-00723-0
5. Cristescu, M.P., Nerisanu, R.A., Mara, D.A., Oprea, S.-V.: Using market news sentiment analysis for stock market prediction. Mathematics **10**(22), 4255 (2022). https://doi.org/10.3390/math10224255
6. Flor, L.S., et al.: Quantifying the effects of the COVID-19 pandemic on gender equality on health, social, and economic indicators: a comprehensive review of data from March, 2020, to September, 2021. Lancet **399**(10344), 2381–2397 (Jun.2022). https://doi.org/10.1016/S0140-6736(22)00008-3
7. Vloo, A., et al.: Gender differences in the mental health impact of the COVID-19 lockdown: longitudinal evidence from the Netherlands. SSM - Popul. Health **15**, 100878 (2021). https://doi.org/10.1016/j.ssmph.2021.100878
8. Cascini, F., et al.: Social media and attitudes towards a COVID-19 vaccination: a systematic review of the literature. eClinicalMedicine **48**, 101454 (2022). https://doi.org/10.1016/j.eclinm.2022.101454
9. Kovacs, E.-R., Cotfas, L.-A., Delcea, C.: COVID-19 vaccination opinions in education-related tweets. In: Bilgin, M.H. Danis, H., Demir, E. (eds.) Eurasian Business and Economics Perspectives. EBES, vol. 24, pp. 21–41. Springer, Cham (2022). https://doi.org/10.1007/978-3-031-15531-4_2
10. Cotfas, L.-A., Delcea, C., Roxin, I., Ioanăş, C., Gherai, D.S., Tajariol, F.: The longest month: analyzing COVID-19 vaccination opinions dynamics from tweets in the month following the first vaccine announcement. IEEE Access **9**, 33203–33223 (2021). https://doi.org/10.1109/ACCESS.2021.3059821
11. Cotfas, L.-A., Delcea, C., Gherai, R.: COVID-19 vaccine hesitancy in the month following the start of the vaccination process. Int. J. Environ. Res. Public Health 18(19) (2021). Art. no. 19. https://doi.org/10.3390/ijerph181910438
12. Rangel, F., Rosso, P., Montes-y-Gómez, M., Potthast, M., Stein, B.: Overview of the 6th Author Profiling Task at PAN 2018: Multimodal Gender Identification in Twitter
13. Banda, J.M., et al.: A large-scale COVID-19 Twitter chatter dataset for open scientific research—An international collaboration. Epidemiologia **2**(3) (2021). Art. no. 3. https://doi.org/10.3390/epidemiologia2030024
14. Global Twitter user distribution by gender 2022. Statista. https://www.statista.com/statistics/828092/distribution-of-users-on-twitter-worldwide-gender/. Accessed 16 Dec 2022
15. Vaswani, A., et al.: Attention is all you need. In: Guyon, I., et al. (eds.) Advances in Neural Information Processing Systems. Curran Associates, Inc. (2017). https://proceedings.neurips.cc/paper/2017/file/3f5ee243547dee91fbd053c1c4a845aa-Paper.pdf
16. Devlin, J., Chang, M.-W., Lee, K., Toutanova, K.: BERT: pre-training of deep bidirectional transformers for language understanding. In: Proceedings of the 2019 Conference of the North American Chapter of the Association for Computational Linguistics: Human Language Technologies, Volume 1 (Long and Short Papers), pp. 4171–4186. Association for Computational Linguistics, Minneapolis, June 2019. https://doi.org/10.18653/v1/N19-1423
17. Cotfas, L.-A., Delcea, C., Gherai, R., Roxin, I.: Unmasking people's opinions behind mask-wearing during COVID-19 pandemic—A Twitter stance analysis. Symmetry **13**(11), 1995 (2021). https://doi.org/10.3390/sym13111995

18. (Zack) Hayat, T., Lesser, O., Samuel-Azran, T.: Gendered discourse patterns on online social networks: a social network analysis perspective. Comput. Hum. Behav. **77**, 132–139 (2017). https://doi.org/10.1016/j.chb.2017.08.041
19. Sezerer, E., Polatbilek, O., Tekir, S.: A Turkish dataset for gender identification of Twitter users. In: Proceedings of the 13th Linguistic Annotation Workshop, pp. 203–207. Association for Computational Linguistics, Florence, August 2019. https://doi.org/10.18653/v1/W19-4023
20. Soler, J., Wanner, L.: A semi-supervised approach for gender identification. In: Proceedings of the Tenth International Conference on Language Resources and Evaluation (LREC 2016), pp. 1282–1287. European Language Resources Association (ELRA), Portorož, May 2016. Accessed 12 Dec 2022. https://aclanthology.org/L16-1204
21. Ouni, S., Fkih, F., Omri, M.N.: Bots and gender detection on Twitter using stylistic features. In: Bădică, C., Treur, J., Benslimane, D., Hnatkowska, B., Krótkiewicz, M. (eds.) ICCCI 2022. CCIS, vol. 1653, pp. 650–660. Springer, Cham (2022). https://doi.org/10.1007/978-3-031-16210-7_53
22. Bartl, M., Leavy, S.: Inferring gender: a scalable methodology for gender detection with online lexical databases. In: Proceedings of the Second Workshop on Language Technology for Equality, Diversity and Inclusion, pp. 47–58. Association for Computational Linguistics, Dublin, May 2022. https://doi.org/10.18653/v1/2022.ltedi-1.7
23. Daneshvar, S., Inkpen, D.: Gender identification in Twitter using N-grams and LSA. In: Proceedings of the Ninth International Conference of the CLEF Association (CLEF 2018). CEUR-WS (2018)
24. van de Weijer, J., Ren, G., van de Weijer, J., Wei, W., Wang, Y.: Gender identification in Chinese names. Lingua **234**, 102759 (2020). https://doi.org/10.1016/j.lingua.2019.102759
25. Rao, A.: UCI Machine Learning Repository. University of California, Irvine, School of Information and Computer Sciences (2017). http://archive.ics.uci.edu/ml
26. Norvig, P.: Natural language corpus data. In: Beautiful Data, pp. 219–242. O'Reilly Media (2009)
27. Malmasi, S.: A data-driven approach to studying given names and their gender and ethnicity associations. In: Proceedings of the Australasian Language Technology Association Workshop 2014, Melbourne, Australia, pp. 145–149, November 2014. Accessed 12 Dec 2022. https://aclanthology.org/U14-1021

Crisis Detection by Social and Remote Sensing Fusion: A Selective Attention Approach

Marwen Bouabid[1(✉)] and Mohamed Farah[2]

[1] Univ. Manouba, ENSI, RIADI LR99ES26,
University Campus Manouba, 2010 Manouba, Tunisia
marwen.bouabid@ensi-uma.tn

[2] Univ. Manouba, ISAMM, University Campus Manouba, 2010 Manouba, Tunisia
mohamed.farah@riadi.rnu.tn

Abstract. Deep learning has revolutionized event detection in social media and remote sensing, allowing for more precise and efficient analysis of immense amounts of data to unveil hidden patterns and insights. Moreover, Merging both data sources has proven efficient despite the absence of multi-sensed datasets. In today's data-driven globe, it is becoming increasingly critical to process and explore heterogeneous data and to design models handling such data. This paper proposes a new multi-sensed fusion approach that leverages satellite images and tweets as input. We combined two open datasets to obtain a multi-sensed dataset concerning the 2017 hurricane Harvey. We extracted features from satellite imagery using Resnet34 and generated embeddings from tweets using Bert. We fused the embeddings and the features using a selective attention module incorporating cross and self-attention. Our module can filter misleading features from weak modalities on a sample-by-sample basis. We demonstrate that our approach surpasses unimodal models based on tweets or satellite imagery. We compared our results to a few baselines associated with hurricane Harvey and proved that our model surpasses them in accuracy, precision, recall, and F1 measure.

Keywords: Remote Sensing · Social media · disaster detection · Selective Attention · Deep Learning · Resnet · BERT · CNN · Data Fusion

1 Introduction

Social bookmarking websites are bursting with various data, with a continuous stream of events, updates, and news being transmitted and recorded. This tremendous amount of data has made it possible to detect, monitor, and examine real-world events and trends in near real-time. With the increasing number of individuals using social media platforms to convey their incidents, reflections, and observations, it has become a vital tool for monitoring the pulse of humanity. Similarly, satellite data has evolved into a valuable data source, providing a bird's eye view of various occurrences, such as natural catastrophes and environmental shifts.

N. T. Nguyen et al. (Eds.): ICCCI 2023, LNAI 14162, pp. 350–362, 2023.
https://doi.org/10.1007/978-3-031-41456-5_27

Combining these two data sources can provide a complete picture of complex crises and help detect and respond to events more effectively. However, several challenges are associated with integrating social and remote sensing data. Data quality and accuracy are among the most significant challenges, as social media data is often unverified and subject to errors, biases, and manipulation. Remote sensing has limitations, such as cloud cover, availability, and low temporal and spectral resolution. There is also a necessity to ensure that data is adequately integrated, analyzed, and interpreted. Despite these challenges, integrating social and remote sensing data has enormous potential for driving positive change and improving our understanding of the world. Deep learning models can handle various inputs, including social media posts and satellite images. However, their fusion techniques still need to be improved. This is partly due to the complexity of combining and processing two different forms of data, each with its unique properties and challenges. Furthermore, there is a need for large and diverse datasets that can support the training of such models and for efficient approaches that can handle the high dimensional input space.

Despite these challenges, researchers are actively developing models to process social media posts and satellite imagery effectively. This can significantly improve various applications, such as social and remote sensing disaster response, and urban planning. Prior approaches that tackle the detection of crisis events have focused on a single data type or combined the outputs of multiple data source models. Whether text or satellite images, each source has its limitations, and their fusion still needs to be improved in terms of the developed techniques and the used approaches. To handle these problems, we present a framework to detect crisis events by fusion of satellite imagery and tweets text. In particular, we offer a method to automatically label satellite images, tweets, and images-tweets pairs. Given an image-text pair, we create a feature map and successfully generate word embeddings for images and text, respectively. We present a selective-attention mechanism based on self-attention and cross-attention to combine data from the two modalities. Our approach differs from the previous classification techniques in how it fuses information. We introduce a novel, multi-sensed framework for classifying multisource data for crisis detection. Our model outperforms strong unimodal baselines.

2 Related Works

Over the past years, researchers investigated the association between social bookmarking websites and remote sensing, revealing the potential of linking these data sources to acquire a more comprehensive understanding of various phenomena and crisis events. Such a combination enables overcoming both methods limits and highlights the importance of merging multiple data sources for crisis event detection; Kashif et al. have introduced Jord. This system collects social media data about natural disasters and links it with remotely sensed data. The author also illustrated the importance of using local language queries for the accuracy of the results [8]. Furthermore, Bischke et al. introduced a scalable satellite imagery contextual enrichment system with multimedia content from social media [3]. Pittaras et al. introduced GeoSensor, a novel, open-source system that improves change detection over satellite images with event content from social media [13]. Avvenuti et al. introduced CrisMap [2] a crisis mapping system, that incorporates damage detection and geoparsing. Their main goal was to create maps estimating the crisis impact in its early phases, distinguishing areas severely struck, and acquiring a grander situational awareness.

Combining social media and remote sensing has been involved in studying environmental and natural resource management. Qi et al. examines the integration of remote sensing and social media data for urban observation [14]. It presents a framework for combining these two data types to enhance understanding of urban phenomena such as land use, transportation, and social activities. Huang et al. presents a near real-time flood-mapping technique by incorporating social media and post-event satellite imagery [7]. The presented approach uses deep learning techniques to examine social media data and merges it with satellite imagery to quickly recognize flood extent and severity for catastrophe response and management. Yang et al. describes the use of remote sensing and social media data for observing ecological conditions in Sanya City, China [18]. The study presents a framework that integrates remote sensing data with social media information to assess the status of environmental change, including vegetation and water quality. Many recent works study image-text fusion [9,11,15]. Thangavel et al. present a method for accurately detecting fire under challenging conditions using satellite images. Which involves generating alerts and enabling immediate actions [16]. The paper addresses the detection of the Australian wildfire that occurred in December 2019. Convolutional neural networks (CNNs) were developed, trained, and used for that purpose. Various hardware accelerators were assessed for the implementation. Li et al. propose a cross-band 2-D self-attention Network (CBANet) for end-to-end hyperspectral images HSI change detection [10]. Our work builds upon the existing body of research on crisis detection by integrating social and remote sensing data. While previous studies have focused on using remote sensing data or social media data separately, and while the existing fusion techniques are based on feature-level fusion and decision-level fusion our approach uses a multi-modal deep learning architecture for fusion to enhance the accuracy of crisis detection.

3 Methodology

In this paper, we present an architecture for binary classification problems that take as input satellite image-tweet pairs, as illustrated in Fig. 1, using RESNET34 [6] and BERT [5] as deep models. Our methodology consists of 2 parts: the first part is about extracting feature maps from the image, and extracting embeddings from the text. The second part incorporates a selective attention approach to fuse satellite images features and text embeddings. We describe each part in the sub-sections that follows.

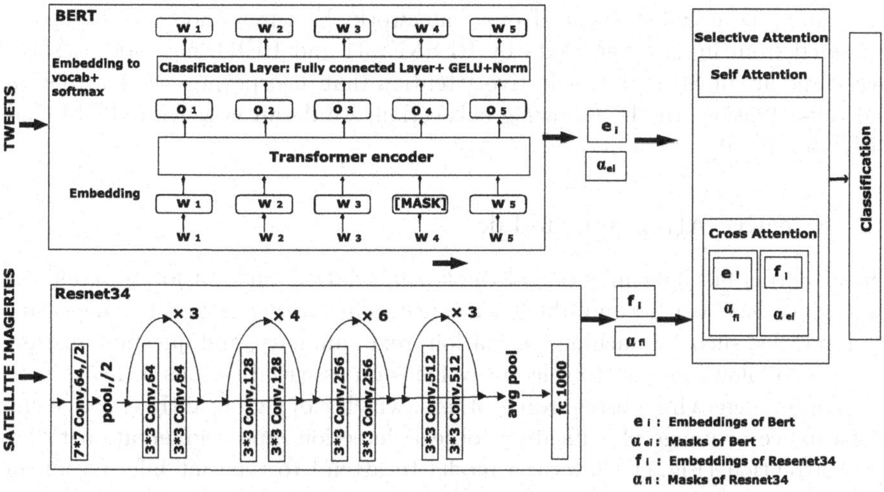

Fig. 1. Fusion Architecture RESNET34 and BERT Language Model

3.1 Feature Map and Embedding Extraction

A critical step in our work is extracting satellite imagery features using convolutional neural networks (CNN) and generating tweet embeddings using language models. In our architecture, we choose RESNET34 [6], which was introduced to solve the problem of the vanishing gradient by introducing the concept of residual blocks. This network employs a technique called skip connections, that connects the activation of a layer to further layers by cutting some layers in between, which forms a residual block. Resnets are made by stacking these residual blocks together. The extraction of feature maps from satellite images is expressed by the following equation, so that for each satellite image s_i, we have:

$$f_i = \boldsymbol{RESNET34(s_i)} \tag{1}$$

where s_i is the input satellite image, $s_i \in R^{Df}$ is the vectorized form of a deep feature map in the RESNEt34 with dimension $Df = W \times H \times C$, where W, H, C are the feature map's width, height, and number of channels, respectively.

As for the language model, we have chosen BERT [5] to extract the embeddings of tweets. BERT is known to achieve state-of-the-art results for text classification on various natural language processing tasks by leveraging close and next-sentence prediction tasks as weakly-supervised pre-training. Therefore, we use it as our core model for extracting tweet embeddings. The extraction of word embedding is expressed by the following equation, so that for each tweet t_i, we have:

$$e_i = \boldsymbol{BERT(t_i)} \tag{2}$$

where t_i is a sequence of word-piece tokens and $t_i \in R^{768}$ the sentence embedding. Similar to the BERT paper [5], we take the embedding associated with [CLS] to represent the whole sentence.

Figure 1 is an illustration of our framework. Features and embedding are extracted from images and texts by RESNET34 and BERT networks, respectively, and are integrated by selective attention that incorporates cross-attention and self-attention. In the following subsection, we detail how RESNET34 and BERT are fused.

3.2 Selective Attention Module

The attention mechanism is one of the key innovations in transformer architecture, which has been accountable for its success in various natural language processing tasks, such as machine translation, text summary, and question answering. It also allows models to selectively focus on essential regions or features in a satellite image while disregarding others, which can significantly enhance the performance of image classification, object detection, and segmentation tasks. Cross-attention (Fig. 1) allows the model to attend to relevant information in one sequence while making predictions for another. This is particularly useful in tasks where the relationship between the two sequences is essential, such as machine translation. The model should attend to relevant parts of the source sentence while translating to the target language. In comparison, self-attention calculates attention scores between each element in a single sequence and all other elements in the same sequence. Self-attention is used to model relationships within a single sequence, while cross-attention allows the model to attend to relationships between two different sequences. In conclusion, cross-attention allows the model to attend to elements in one sequence while making predictions for another sequence, making it well-suited for tasks involving multiple input data.

To Fuse the features we obtain from satellite images f_i (RESNET34) and the sentence embedding e_i (BERT), we apply a cross-attention mechanism. Text-vision tasks are very vulnerable to noise. Modalities may contain non-informative or misleading information, especially in the case of social media posts such as tweets. Therefore negative information transfer can occur. Our framework deals with this issue by blocking one modality over another case by case.

In other words, we use a combination of cross-attention and self-attention layers in our selective-attention module. In this module, each modality can block the features of the other modality based on its input usefulness using the cross-attention layer. Partially blocked features from both modalities are fed into a self-attention layer to determine which knowledge should be forwarded to the next layer.

The self-attention layer exploits a fully-connected layer to project the satellite image feature map into a fixed dimensionality K (we use $K = 100$) and similarly project the sentence embedding so that:

$$\tilde{f}_i = \boldsymbol{F}\left(\boldsymbol{W}_f^T f_i + \boldsymbol{b}_f\right), \tilde{e}_i = \boldsymbol{F}\left(\boldsymbol{W}_e^T e_i + \boldsymbol{b}_e\right) \tag{3}$$

where F represents an activation function such as ReLU (used in our experiments) and both $\tilde{f}_i$ and $\tilde{e}_i$ are of dimension $K = 100$.

In the case of misleading information in one modality, without an attention mechanism (such as co-attention [17]), the resulting $\tilde{f}_i$ and $\tilde{e}_i$ cannot be easily combined without hurting performance. Here, we propose an attention mechanism called cross-attention, which differs from standard co-attention mechanisms: the attention mask α_{f_i} for the satellite image is entirely dependent on the tweet embedding e_i. In contrast, the attention masks α_{e_i} for the tweet are entirely dependent on the satellite image embedding f_i. Mathematically, this can be expressed as follows:

$$\alpha_{f_i} = \sigma\left(W_f^{\prime T} e_i + b_f^{\prime}\right), \alpha_{e_i} = \sigma\left(W_e^{\prime T} f_i + b_e^{\prime}\right), \tag{4}$$

where σ is the Sigmoid function.

After we have the attention masks $\alpha_{f_i}, \alpha_{e_i}$ for satellite image and tweet, respectively, we can augment the projected image and text embeddings $\tilde{f}_i, \tilde{e}_i$ with $\alpha_{f_i} \cdot \tilde{f}_i$ and $\alpha_{e_i} \cdot \tilde{e}_i$ before performing concatenation.

The last step of this module takes the concatenated embedding, which jointly represents the satellite image and tweet tuple and feeds it into the two-layer fully-connected networks. We add self-attention in the fully-connected networks and use the standard softmax cross-entropy loss for the classification.

4 Experiment Results

This paper targets a binary classification problem. We performed three experiments. The first experiment used BERT for tweet classification, the second used RESNET34 for satellite imagery classification, and the third addressed their fusion. The fusion classification problem is formulated as follows: we have as input $(s_1, t_1), \ldots, (s_i, t_i), \ldots, (s_n, t_n)$, where n is the number of training tuples and the i-th tuple consists of both image s_i and text t_i. The respective labels for s_i and t_i are also given in training data. We aim to predict the correct class for any unseen (s, t) pair.

Satellite images and text from tweets in our dataset were annotated independently. Each tweet labelled as informative is associated with a satellite image labelled with damage. Each tweet labelled as not-informative is associated with a satellite image labelled with no damage. Given the different evaluation conditions, we conduct three evaluations with the same settings. The dataset is divided into three main parts test, validation and training. To counter over-fitting, a recurrent issue of deep learning, we also adopt data augmentation in the training set. This can effectively expand the number of training examples to assure adequate generalization and better validation and test accuracy (Note that we do not conduct data augmentation in the validation and test sets). Furthermore, we also employ 50% dropout in the fully connected layer. Dropout effectively prevents over-fitting, specifically in neural networks with many neurons. The technique prevents neurons from memorizing too much training data by dropping out randomly picked neurons and their connections during training. These actions fight over-fitting effectively and greatly enhance the validation accuracy. We use pre-trained RESNET34 and BERT as our image and text backbone networks and fine-tune them separately. We do not freeze the pre-trained weights and train all the backbone networks layers. We use the standard SGD optimizer. We start with the base learning rate of 2×10^{-3} with a $10\times$ reduction when the validation loss is saturated. We used a batch size of 32 for RESNET34 and BERT tuning, and we used a batch size of 16 while doing the fusion. In all the practical experiments, we select hyperparameters with cross-validation on the accuracy of the validation set.

4.1 Dataset

There are very few crisis datasets, and CrisisMMD is the best of our knowledge for social media disaster events [1]. It consists of annotated social media image-tweet pairs where images and tweets are independently labelled. The dataset was collected using event-specific keywords and hashtags during seven natural disasters in 2017: Hurricane Irma, Hurricane Harvey, Hurricane Maria, the Mexico earthquake, the California wildfires, the Iraq-Iran earthquakes, and the Sri Lanka floods. We were only interested in the tweets about Hurricane Harvey for this paper. So we filtered the data in the crisisMMD dataset. We also targeted the first task, Informative vs Not Informative: whether a given tweet text or image is helpful for humanitarian aid purposes, defined as assisting people in need. The training dataset contains 3286 tweets, the validation dataset contains 582 tweets, and the test dataset contains 569 tweets. As for satellite images, we downloaded a dataset from the IEEE Dataport associated with [4]. The dataset contains satellite images that are labelled with damage and no damage. The images are also marked with the geo-coordinates. We combined both datasets as a geosocial dataset for our experiments. Figure 2 shows four samples of satellite images associated with class Damage and Fig. 3 shows four images related to class No damage. For tweet normalization, we remove double spaces and lowercase all characters. In addition, we replace any hyperlink in the tweet with the sentinel word "I ink". When cleaning tweets for BERT classification, replacing hyperlinks with the sentinel word "I ink" is done to prevent the model from overfitting on URLs and to reduce the vocabulary size. Hyperlinks in tweets can often be unique and specific to a given tweet. The presence of many different URLs in the dataset can lead to a large vocabulary size, making the model slower and harder to train. Additionally, URLs are not typically relevant to the classification task and can cause the model to overfit specific URLs rather than learn generalizable patterns in the text. This can lead to better generalization and faster training times.

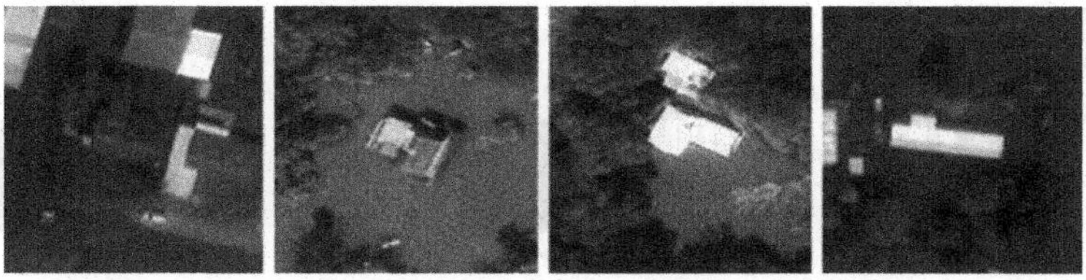

Fig. 2. Satellites Images Samples of Class Damage Hurricane Harvey

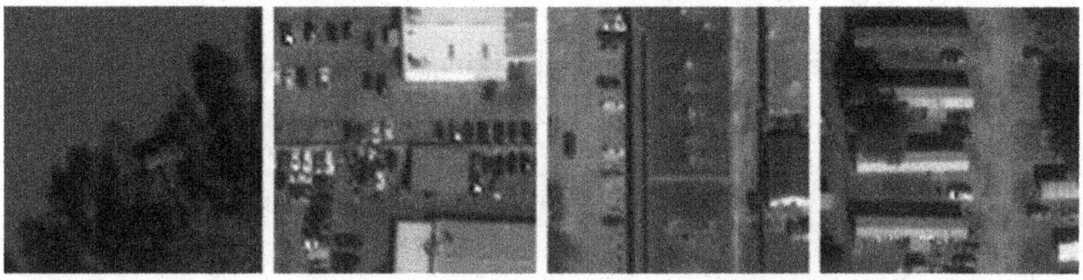

Fig. 3. Satellites Images Samples of Class No damage Hurricane Harvey

4.2 Baselines

We compare our method against several state-of-the-art text and image classification methods. There are several categories of baseline methods we compare against, but we had to search for works that addressed the same event and used the same data, which reduced the number of baselines. In the first category, we compare to the RESNET34 and BERT, the most commonly used classification networks for images and texts, respectively. We use Wikipedia pre-trained BERT and pre-trained RESNET on ImageNet and fine-tune them on the training sets.

The second baseline method category includes several proposed classification techniques in [4]. The paper performed different classifications on the satellite images of hurricane Harvey. We also compare to [12], which conducted classification on tweets related to hurricane Harvey on the same task.

4.3 Evaluation Metrics

We evaluate the models in this paper using classification accuracy, F1-score, precision and recall. Note that while the number of samples from different categories often significantly varies in a crisis, it is essential to detect all of them. F1-score take both false positives and false negatives into account, and therefore, along with accuracy as an intuitive measure, are proper evaluation metrics for our datasets.

4.4 Results and Discussion

In this section, we present the findings of our study and provide a comprehensive analysis and interpretation of the results. We evaluated the performance

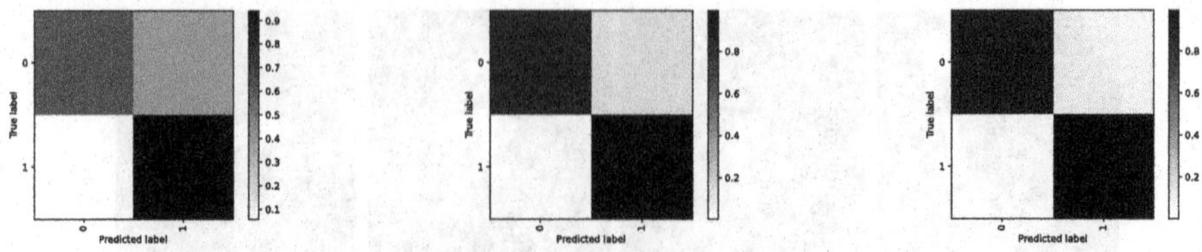

(a) BERT (b) RESNET34 (c) Fusion

Fig. 4. Confusion Matrix of the three Models

Table 1. Models and base lines performance

Model	Accuracy	F1 Score	Precision	Recall
	satellites images classification			
CNN	94.69	95.75	–	–
CNN + DA + DO	96.44	96.74	–	–
CNN + DA + DO (Adam)	97.29	97.23	–	–
RESNET34	96.47	97.78	96.09	99.55
	tweets classification			
CNN	72.07	72	73	72
ANN	71.39	71	72	71
CNN + ANN [12]	75.9	76	76	76
BERT	86.97	91.86	89.70	94.14
	classification by fusion			
Fusion	**98.23**	**98.88**	**98.01**	**99.77**

of different models for classification tasks, specifically RESNET34, BERT, and our selective attention model. We compared these models with baselines and analyzed their accuracy, F1 score, precision, and recall metrics. Additionally, we examined their training progress using accuracy and loss graphs and explored the confusion matrices to gain insights into their performance. RESNET34 fine-tuning performed well compared to baselines, and providing additional data for training are expected to contribute to further improvement. The CNN + Data augmentation + Dropout (Adam) model has higher accuracy and lower F1 scores. However, it is essential to note that the model demonstrated superior accuracy since it was trained on the entire dataset, while we only used 3286 images from that dataset in our implementation. Moreover, RESNET34 performed better at balancing precision and recall, which is essential when dealing with imbalanced class distributions. Figure 4(b) display the confusion matrix of RESNET34.

On the other hand, BERT tuning generated impressive results as well. It outperformed the baselines for tweet classification. Figure 6 shows the accuracy and loss during the training. Figure 4(a) depicts the confusion matrix of BERT. When reaching 100 epochs, the model's performance remains the same on the

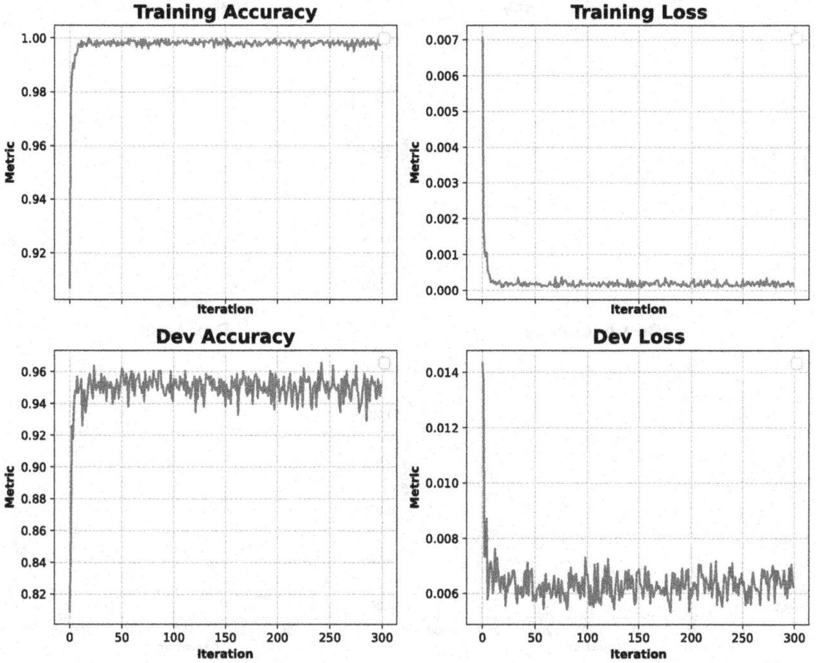

Fig. 5. Metrics For RESNET34 Tuning

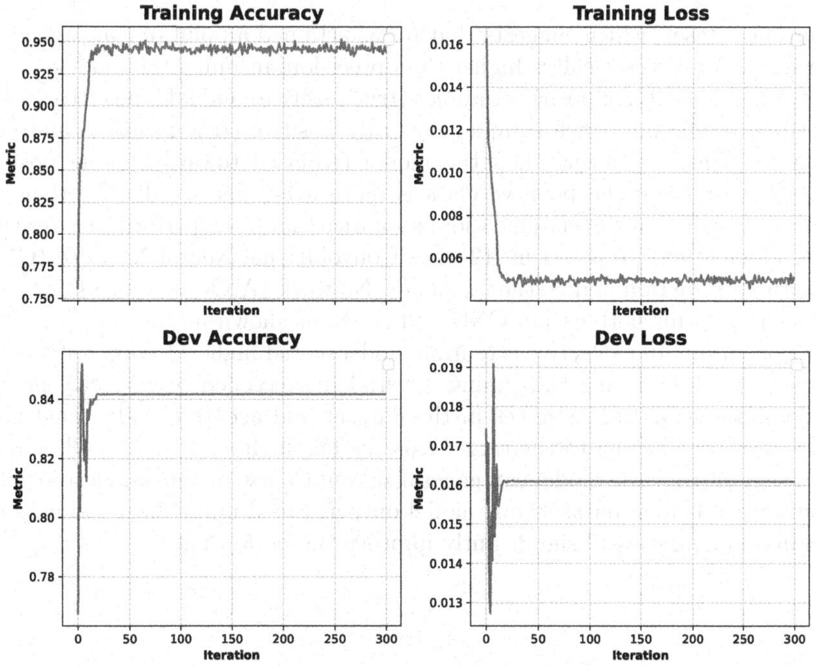

Fig. 6. Metrics For Bert Tuning

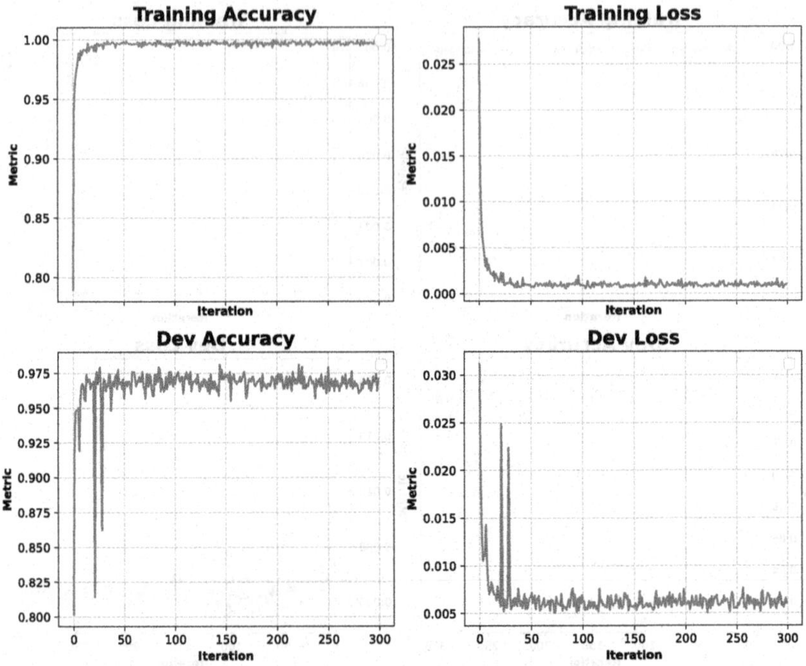

Fig. 7. Metrics For Selective Attention Model

validation dataset, which suggests that it has attained a point of convergence or saturation. We notice recall is higher than precision, meaning the model is more successful at identifying positive samples (true positives and false negatives) than accurately predicting which samples are truly positive (true positives and false positives). This can occur when the model is biased toward making positive predictions or when the positive class is more accessible to identify than the negative class. For tweets classification, we notice that CNN performs better than ANN. The method proposed in [12] uses Convolutional Neural Network (CNN) for feature extraction and Artificial Neural Network (ANN) as a classifier. This approach performs better than CNN and ANN, as shown in Table 1.

In conclusion, our selective attention model scored higher. Figure 7 shows the accuracy and loss during the tuning. Overall it succeeded to correctly predict the class labels for the instances in the dataset and accurately identified most of the cases that belong to the target classes. The high accuracy, recall, and F1 scores suggest that the model can generalize well to new instances. Despite that, we only used a small dataset, our model outperformed unimodal baselines, and providing more data will significantly improve the performance.

5 Conclusions and Future Work

This paper presented a framework for fusing satellite images and tweets as textual input. We applied a selective attention module that can filter non-informative or misleading information from modalities and only combine the valuable information. We evaluate this approach on hurricane Harvey crisis tasks involving social media text posts, and satellite imagery. We show that our approach outperforms image-only and text-only methods, which have been the field's mainstay. For future work, we plan to test how our approach generalizes to other crisis detection problems, such as earthquake detection in social media posts, and experiment with different image and text feature extractors. Given that the corpus we created is the only geo-social sensor dataset available for this task and is limited in size, we also aim to construct a more extensive set, which is a significant effort.

References

1. Alam, F., Ofli, F., Imran, M.: CrisisMMD: multimodal Twitter datasets from natural disasters. In: Proceedings of the International AAAI Conference on Web and Social Media, vol. 12 (2018)
2. Avvenuti, M., Cresci, S., Del Vigna, F., Fagni, T., Tesconi, M.: CrisMap: a big data crisis mapping system based on damage detection and geoparsing. Inf. Syst. Front. **20**(5), 993–1011 (2018)
3. Bischke, B., Bhardwaj, P., Gautam, A., Helber, P., Borth, D., Dengel, A.: Detection of flooding events in social multimedia and satellite imagery using deep neural networks. In: MediaEval (2017)
4. Cao, Q.D., Choe, Y.: Building damage annotation on post-hurricane satellite imagery based on convolutional neural networks. Nat. Hazards **103**(3), 3357–3376 (2020)
5. Devlin, J., Chang, M.W., Lee, K., Toutanova, K.: BERT: pre-training of deep bidirectional transformers for language understanding. arXiv preprint arXiv:1810.04805 (2018)
6. He, K., Zhang, X., Ren, S., Sun, J.: Deep residual learning for image recognition. In: Proceedings of the IEEE Conference on Computer Vision and Pattern Recognition, pp. 770–778 (2016)
7. Huang, X., Wang, C., Li, Z.: A near real-time flood-mapping approach by integrating social media and post-event satellite imagery. Ann. GIS **24**(2), 113–123 (2018)
8. Kashif, A., Pogorelov, K., Riegler, M., Conci, N., Halvorsen, P.: Social media and satellites. Multimed. Tools Appl. **78**(3), 2837–2875 (2019)
9. Li, L.H., Yatskar, M., Yin, D., Hsieh, C.J., Chang, K.W.: VisualBERT: a simple and performant baseline for vision and language. arXiv preprint arXiv:1908.03557 (2019)
10. Li, Y., et al.: CBANet: an end-to-end cross band 2-D attention network for hyperspectral change detection in remote sensing. IEEE Trans. Geosci. Remote Sens. (2023)
11. Lu, J., Batra, D., Parikh, D., Lee, S.: VilBERT: pretraining task-agnostic visiolinguistic representations for vision-and-language tasks. In: Advances in Neural Information Processing Systems, vol. 32 (2019)

12. Madichetty, S., Sridevi, M.: Detecting informative tweets during disaster using deep neural networks. In: 2019 11th International Conference on Communication Systems & Networks (COMSNETS), pp. 709–713. IEEE (2019)
13. Pittaras, N., et al.: Geosensor: semantifying change and event detection over big data. In: Proceedings of the 34th ACM/SIGAPP Symposium on Applied Computing, pp. 2259–2266. ACM (2019)
14. Qi, L., Li, J., Wang, Y., Gao, X.: Urban observation: integration of remote sensing and social media data. IEEE J. Sel. Top. Appl. Earth Obs. Remote Sens. **12**(11), 4252–4264 (2019)
15. Tan, H., Bansal, M.: LXMERT: learning cross-modality encoder representations from transformers. arXiv preprint arXiv:1908.07490 (2019)
16. Thangavel, K., et al.: Autonomous satellite wildfire detection using hyperspectral imagery and neural networks: a case study on Australian wildfire. Remote Sens. **15**(3), 720 (2023)
17. Vaswani, A., et al.: Attention is all you need. In: Advances in Neural Information Processing Systems, vol. 30 (2017)
18. Yang, T., et al.: Monitoring ecological conditions by remote sensing and social media data—Sanya city (China) as case study. Remote Sens. **14**(12), 2824 (2022)

Educational Videos Recommendation System Based on Topic Modeling

Manar Joundy Hazar[1,2(✉)], Alaa Abid Muslam Abid Ali[1,2], Salah Zrigui[3], Mohsen Maraoui[1], Mohamed Mabrouk[1], and Mounir Zrigui[1]

[1] University of Monastir (RLANTIS), 5019 Monastir, Tunisia
manar.joundy@qu.edu.iq, alaa.abidmuslam@qu.edu.iq, mounir.zrigui@fsm.rnu.tn

[2] University of Al-Qadisiyah, Qadisiyah, Iraq

[3] DATAMOVE - Data Aware Large Scale Computing, LIG, Grenoble, France

Abstract. Video recommendation systems in e-learning platforms are a specific type of recommendation system that use algorithms to suggest educational videos to students based on their interests and preferences. Student's written feedback or reviews can provide more detailed about the educational video, including its strengths and weaknesses. In this paper, we build education video recommender system based on learners' reviews. We use LDA topic model on textual data extracted from educational videos to train language modle as an input to supervised CNN model. Additionally, we used latent factor modle on extracts the educational videos' features and learner preference from learners' historical data as an output CNN model. In Our proposed technique, we hybrid user ratings and reviews to tackle sparsity and cold start problem in recommender system. Our recommender use user review to suggest a new recommended videos, but in case there is no review (empty cell in matrix factorization) or unclear comment then we will take user rating on that educational video. We work on real-world big and heterogynous dataset from coursera. Result shows that new production rating from learners reviews can be used to make good new recommended videos to student that not previously seen and reduce cold start and sparsity problem affects.

Keywords: Recommendation systems · LDA · reviews · educational video

1 Introduction

E-learning uses the Internet or other digital content for learning and teaching activities, which takes full advantage of modern education technology to provide a new communication mechanism and resource-rich learning environment to achieve a new way of education [1]. In an e-learning platform, a video recommendation system can analyze data such as the videos that a student has

N. T. Nguyen et al. (Eds.): ICCCI 2023, LNAI 14162, pp. 363–376, 2023.
https://doi.org/10.1007/978-3-031-41456-5_28

previously watched, the amount of time they spent watching each video, and their performance on quizzes and assessments related to the video. Based on this data, the system can suggest videos that are similar to ones the student has already watched or that are related to topics that the student has shown an interest in [2,3]. This can be achieve by analyzing the student's progress in the course and identifying areas where they may be struggling, then suggesting videos that cover the topics they need to review [4]. Recommendation systems based on user reviews are similar to those based on user ratings, but instead of rating an item on a scale, users are asked to provide written feedback or reviews about the item [5]. These reviews can provide more detailed information about the item, including its strengths and weaknesses, and can also include additional information like usage scenarios or personal anecdotes [6,7]. A recommendation system based on user reviews can use natural language processing (NLP) techniques to analyze the text in the reviews and extract meaningful information about the item. This information can then be used to make recommendations to other users. The main advantage of User reviews recommendation systems is the wealth of information that can be gained from user reviews, and that the reviews can provide more context about the item. But this type of system can be more complex to implement because of the unstructured nature of the data, and there was a need for a preprocessing step to extract features from the reviews, then it can be used to train the model. This type of systems can also be applied in various fields like e-commerce, online music and video platforms, and e-learning platforms to recommend courses, videos, or articles to users based on the feedback or reviews of other users [8–10]. The paper organized as Sect. 2 is a related work, in Sect. 3 we explain the proposed approach, Sect. 4 describe a realword data set that we used it in this work, experiments and results presented in Sect. 5 and Sect. 6 is a rating hybridization of our model.

2 Related Work

Based on the importance of studies related to the topic of the current research, the researcher obtained many past studies related to a subject of a study. and they were dealt with according to the goal, method, sample, procedures and the most prominent results. Then clarifying what distinguished the current study from previous studies, and to facilitate the benefit of what the researcher obtained. Fraihat and Shambour, 2015 [11] semantic recommendation algorithm research. Using the algorithm of Semantic Recommendation System framework to supply personalized e-learning. The dataset type was inter- and additive semantic relationship between LOS and the needs of learners. There are two important implications of the proposed system. First, the proposed system can help learners find the appropriate LOS to successfully complete the learning process. Secondly, the suggested system can help the instructor or course designer suggest materials that can be used to improve the course curriculum. The future research will concentrate on verifying an accomplishment and fineness of recommendations of the Indicative recommendation algorithm, and fulfillment the submitted scope on a prototype of the recommendation method. Choudrey, 2021 [12] quantitative and qualitative research method on AWS. Try a prototype recommendation system, relied on "AWS Recognition". Movie trailer recommendations and recommendation ratings, in this thesis are based on vector uniformity calculations using several formularizations. Experiments conducted in the thesis showed that the fineness of the recommendations was mixed due to limitations in the movie trailer collection and also due to the truth that in many conditions rating movies based merely on visual data can be misleading.

3 Proposed Approach

We proposed a recommender system based on the educational videos' content and learner reviews to satisfy what students actually need to learn. Our model builds on a combined content-based recommendation system and convolutional neural network (CNN) that runs on three levels, as illustrated in Fig. 1. Level one in Fig. 1 on the left line is an input of a CNN training model. We used a language model of educational videos after proposing steps for source videos. Where the right line is an output of the CNN training model, we use the latent factor model (LFM) for learners' historical data. Learners' reviews of educational videos were used as training data for LFM. At this level, we made a preprocessing step to formulate the CNN model's input and output data. Level two is a training level at which all CNN parameters will be trained by the input and output data. Level 3 is the recommendation level. At this level, a new educational video will be recommended.

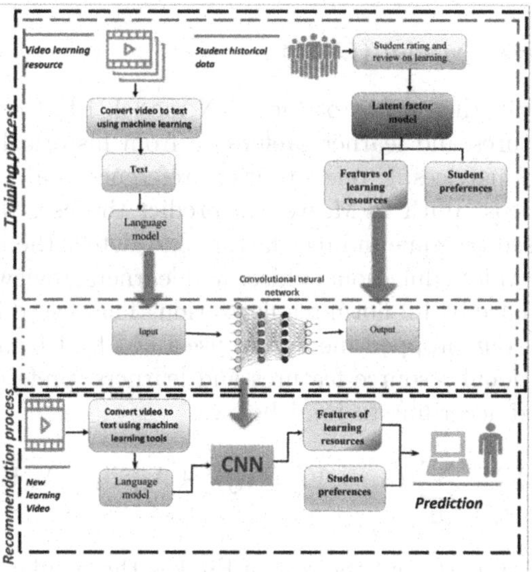

Fig. 1. Proposed Educational video recommendation system

3.1 Preprocessing

The first step was extracting audio from educational videos [13]; second, we exploited Google's API to extract textual data from audio, keeping track of the original contents. This transformation was done automatically by speech-to-text operation. API borrowed from Google had an audio length limitation, which was a challenge for our model, so we fixed it with our source code, breaking down long audio sequences into small junk. Then, we combined text from all junk belonging to the same source video. This process keeps the original content of the source video stable.

3.2 Language Model

As we mentioned, the input of the CNN model is a language model. Here, we use topic modelling to justify the input of CNN. When recommending suitable online learning videos to students, each video has given content. LDA mostly used for topic modelling to extract the subject and semantic structure that the video covers. Because LDA enables us to acquire a topic from each educational video, we can use its output as a feature vector for educational videos to configure items according to a content-based recommendation system. After we convert the source video to its textual data, each video represented by a document. A document contains latent topics. Every single topic represented by a probabilistic distribution of words. LDA assists with extracting topics related to that document; it scans the document and discovers the statistics of the words, then represents those words as a probability of topics [14].

3.3 Latent Factor Model (LFM)

LFM used to justify the output of the CNN model. LFM extracts the educational videos' features and learner preference from historical data; these data represented in two matrices: U refers to user preference, and V refers to features of educational videos. With LFM, we can predict the user rating on any educational video based on some indirect factors and detect the learners' interests. Figure 2 shows LFM for educational videos and learners' reviews. Tradition LFM reduces solution space by L2-norm regularization. That cased in over-smoothing problem. Thus, in our propped model, we use LFM by L1-norm regularization to indicate educational resource features and learners' preferences. Matrix factorization modified according to Eq. 1 below.

$$j(U,V) = \sum_{ij}(U_{i*.} - V_{*j} - r_{ij})^2 + \lambda_1|U|_1 + \lambda_2|V|_{1,2}2 \qquad (1)$$

j(U,V) is the fidelity part, and the rest of Eq. 1 is the regularization part.
U: It is a matrix of relations between learners and latent factors.
V: It is a matrix of relations between educational videos and latent factors.
rij: It is a rating given by learner i on educational video j.

λ_1,λ_2: are the regularization parameters to balance the fidelity and regularization parts.

As we mentioned previously, we applied these computations on non-empty cells in the matrix To minimize the non-convex function in the equation, cross-validation and a grid search were used to optimize parameters. A cross-validation procedure runs for the proposed recommendation algorithm, and then the LAD model captures the mathematical framework.

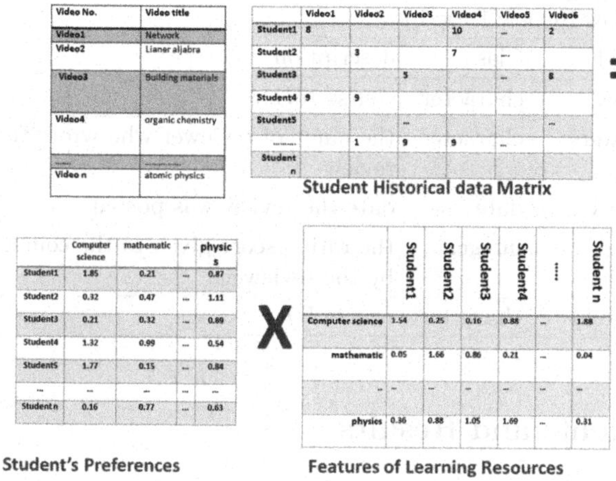

Fig. 2. Process of the Latent factor model (LFM)

4 Dataset

We worked on from Coursera platform [15]; the data size was 1.45 million comments and reviews written by learners on educational videos. The data are describe in Table 1. For testing purposes, we reduced the data size and selected three courses from the dataset. Those three courses contain 178 educational videos, 198856 learners' comments, and the same number of learner ratings from 1 to 5 stars on source videos. The three courses used can be accessed via the Coursera platform as follows:

1. machine-learning course from Stanford University
   URL: https://www.coursera.org/learn/machine-learning
2. python-data from University of Michigan
   URL: https://www.coursera.org/learn/python-data
3. e-learning from University of Illinois at Urbana-Champaign
   URL: https://www.coursera.org/learn/elearning

These courses have been chosen for many reasons, such as the courses' experts, authority and quality of spoken English.

Table 1. Disruption of dataset

Course Description		
Variable	Class	Description
Name	Character	Course Name
Institution	Character	Reviewer Name
course_url	Character	Course URL
course_id	Character	Course ID
Student Review Description		
variable	Class	description
reviews	character	course review
reviewers	character	the name of reviewer who wrote the review
date$_r$eviews	date	date the review was posted
rating	integer	the rating score given to the course by the reviewer
course_id	character	course ID

5 Experiments and Results

5.1 Originality Source Data Evaluation

In this experiment, we try to prove that our source input data preprocessing preserves information originality and accuracy. Therefore, we calculate the distance (similarity) between textual data after the conversion process and the original transcript text provided by Coursera below every educational video in the dataset. We apply two strategies of similarity. First, we use the Python and Cython-written natural language processing module SpaCy library. Researchers in [16] demonstrated that the SpaCy library is significantly faster than many other libraries. Then, we have included cosine similarity because it is a simple, reliable similarity metric used with the TF/IDF weighting scheme [7].

For more experiment interpretation, Table 2 shows a small sample of videos. Since the size of dataset is big, only a very small sample can be displayed here for documentation purposes, which is used for result display and discussion. In Fig. 3, we use the same small sample as Table 2 to explain and present the results because the dataset is too large to exhibit here. Figure 3 illustrates the great similarity between the two texts; some brief especially non-mathematical videos has a similarity 100%. Therefore, we can observe the following:

1. In all 10 shown educational videos, spacy is a built-in module in the version of Python that we used to create our model. There is no information loss throughout the computation process, and as a result, spacy provides higher similarity than cosine.

Table 2. Details about small sample of educational videos from dataset

Video ID	Title	Length (min.)	Size (MB)	Course ID
Vd. 1	Manipulating Lists	9:13	12.6	Python-ata
Vd. 2	Processing Files	11:42	40.0	Python-ata
Vd. 3	Counting with Dictionaries	11:52	14.7	Python-ata
Vd. 4	Tuples	17	20.0	Python-ata
Vd. 5	Active Knowledge Making, Part 2C: Memory Work in Learning	5:13	8.67	e-learning
Vd. 6	Recursive Feedback, Part 4B: Summative Assessment vs Formative Assessment	10:38	16.2	e-learning
Vd. 7	Metacognition, Part 6B: Metacognition in e-Learning Ecologies	11:40	17	e-learning
Vd. 8	Applications of Machine Learning	4:28	9.51	Machine-learning
Vd. 9	Gradient Descent for Multiple Linear Regression	7:45	7.23	Machine-learning
Vd. 10	Logistic Regression	9:48	8.60	Machine-learning

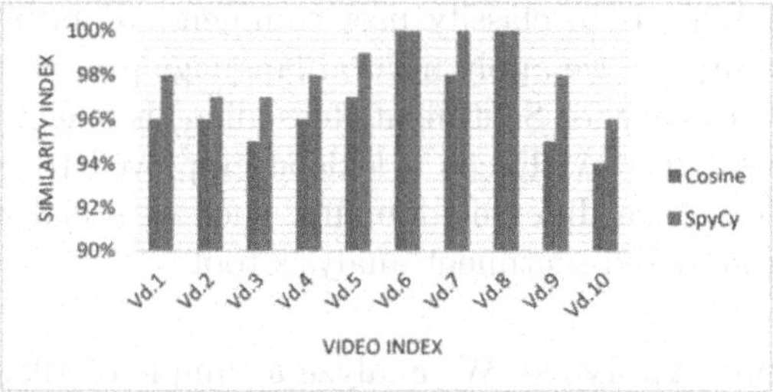

Fig. 3. Similarity measurement.

2. videos performed more similarly than others in both metrics, fully driven by the video's content. Where there is a lot of arithmetic in the videos, it cannot be convert to text 100% of the time since, for instance, symbols may be translated into words or formulas translated into sentences.

Since all evaluated videos had an index of similarity greater than 95%, the overall result appears satisfactory.

5.2 Leaner Historical Data Preparing

User historical ratings are a common basic input source for a recommendation system. These data are numerical, which seems restricted in expressing user opinions and interests. Therefore, free text written by the user will be good data to extract his/her preference to build an accurate RS [17]. This is why we build our educational video recommendation system based on learners' reviews through sentiment analysis of their opinion to extract preferences from all information in written text comments on learning resources to match their learning needs. In this study, we develop our learner comment-based RS model for a variety of reasons [18] that are briefly discussed in the following items:

1. We can use learners' comments and reviews to deal with sparsity issues, where text comments offer helpful information in the absence of a rating that can be used to predict a rating.
2. review text is a good choice to fix cold-start problems by providing all necessary information about new items or new users.
3. Learners' reviews are the best choice for dense data problems, causing it to deliver more features to make an accurate recommendation system performance by guaranteeing high-quality ratings in case of conflict between ratings and comments of the same user on the same source; for example, user x rates item y 5 stars incorrectly, and the same user x on the same item y writes a very negative comment.
4. User reviews powered in fine-grained sentiment can help in extracting more features about a single item that will be very flexible to personalized use/item models.

We use sentiment analysis to classify user comments as positive, natural, and negative. For this purpose, we apply natural language processing tools. VADER (Valence Aware Dictionary for Sentiment Reasoning) is one of the most suitable sentiment analyzers [19]. VADER is a lexicon employed to make a sentiment analysis of textual data in different domains, such as social media, education, and news. It is a rule-based sentiment analysis tool.

Review Sentiment Analysis. We analyze a sample of 198,856 negative and positive learners' reviews on 178 educational videos from three different courses. This sample is handpick from the bigger real-world dataset of 1.45 million reviews on 622 courses presented by the Coursera online platform. The NLP toolkit of sentiment analyzer VADER is use to classify and score the reviews based on English adjectives in learner comments [20]. Additionally, VADER's lexicon allows qualitative analysis that can strongly detect all characteristics and proprieties of text review that influence how strongly the text's sentiment is perceive. Then we have five syntactical and grammatical heuristics that can modify and change the intensity of review sentiments. The five heuristics listed are as follows:

1. Exclamation point (!) punctuation, which keeps semantic orientation stable but increases the intensity score. For example, the learner comment "this course is good!!" will be a more intense comment than "this course is good".
2. Full capitalization, or ALL CAPS, which also keeps semantic orientation stable and will highlight the sentiment of the relevant term. That increases the intensity score of the sentiment. For example, "this course is GOOD" will be more intense than the comment "this course is good".
3. Adverb degree. Some words intensify the sentiment intensity or reduce intensity. For example, the comment "this course is extremely good" will be more intense than "this course is good".

4. "But" conjunction, which affects shifting sentiment scoring; the text that comes after "but" will be the main learner opinion. In this case, the comment contained a mixed sentiment, such as "lecture is great, but need more explanation", and the second part of the comment identified the sentiment polarity.
5. Most words can influence sentiment polarity, and flipped text scoring is a negation "not". For example, consider the comment "This course is not good".

5.3 Rating Prediction

Sentiment polarity was employed to rate the learner's comment. The text review already had been classified by the VADER lexicon as positive, negative, or natural. To detect the polarity sentiment in an individual review, a compound value was used. We used (1) as a threshold of compound value to classify learners' comments where:

- If the compound value > 0.001, then the sentiment was positive, and polarity $= 1$.
- If the compound value > -0.001 and < 0.001, then the sentiment was natural, and polarity $= 0$.
- If the compound value < -0.001, then the sentiment was negative, and polarity $= -1$

VADER lexicon scores are between $+4$ and -4, where $+4$ is a very positive sentiment and -4 is a very negative sentiment. In our proposed framework, we put polarity between $+1$ and -1. For normalization and comparative purposes, as shown in Fig. 4 we need to formulate scoring fraction values between $+1$ and -1 to integer numbers from 1 to 5. This value will represent a new rating protected from text-review sentiment analysis.

```
if vader_compound_score >= -1 and vader_compound_score < -0.5:
    Return 1
  elif vader_compound_score >= -0.5 and vader_compound_score < -0.05:
    Return 2
  elif vader_compound_score >= -0.05 and vader_compound_score <= 0.05:
    Return 3
  elif vader_compound_score > 0.05 and vader_compound_score < 0.5:
    Return 4
  else:
    Return 5
```

Fig. 4. Vader compound value formulation.

6 Rating Hybridization

Cold starts are among the most challenging aspects of any recommender system. Hence, in our proposed model, we try to solve it or at least reduce its effects on recommender system performance. We use a hybrid approach incorporating users' historical data: rating and text review data. From text review data, we predict a new matrix rating. As previously mentioned, we analyzed learners' reviews by sentiment lexicon to predict the user's new matrix rating. However, not all users will comment on educational videos, which means if a user rates an educational video, they are not necessarily giving feedback; they may have provided a blank or non-readable comment that yields nothing or a wrong rating prediction. Thus, we will have empty cells in the new predicted matrix. In the original matrix, we also have empty cells and maybe the wrong rating value. For this reason, we make a hybrid matrix factorization of the original and predicted ratings in case one of these reasons happen. In the new prediction rating, we will substitute it with the original rating in an equivalent cell in the hybrid matrix; otherwise, we will keep using the new rating. In Table 3 we present different samples of the source datasets pre-described in Sect. 4. Samples were selected to clarify the deference and accuracy between the original and predicted ratings. We carefully chose rating pairs with a high deference rating in the resulting matrix. In examining Table 3, we see four different cases of rating degradation between the user and new predicted ratings that are fixed in the new proposed model.

6.1 Discussion

Table 3 displays a different sample of a new rating prediction made by a proposed model and shows the users' original ratings of the learning resource. The results in table and user ratings and comments clearly explain that users' text reviews gave the recommender system greater efficiency and accuracy than rating. Additionally, we combined the users' ratings and reviews to get a filtered matrix factorization, directly influencing features extracting educational videos and learners' preferences, thus improving the recommender system. Table 3 contains four cases in which the proposed model presented a positive rating prediction over the original user rating:

- Case 1: The user wrote a positive review but gave a low rating. A new predicted rating will have a high rate according to the learner's opinion in the text comment. For example, see rows 2, 6, 7 and 13 in Table 3.
- Case 2: The user wrote a negative review but gave a high rating. The new predicted rating will be low according to the learner's opinion in the text comment. For example, row 3 in Table 3.
- Case 3: The user review and rating matched, regardless if positive or negative. A new predicted rating will be exactly equal to the original rating. For example, rows 1, 5, 11, 12, 14 and 15 in Table 3.
- Case 4: The user wrote a positive or negative review, and the rating was almost equivalent to the given opinion. The new predicted rating will be slightly different from the original rating but more expressive about the user's opinion because the sentiment analysis of the review takes into account all the information in the text review. For example, rows 4, 8, 9, 10 and 16 in Table 3.

Table 3. Sample of rating prediction from users' reviews using sentiment analysis

Review -id	Text-reviews	Reviewer name	Review date	User rating	course_id	Predicted rating
1.	One of the best courses i studied in Coursera	Baccouche M S	25-Feb-19	5	machine -learning	5
2.	good	SRUTHI P N	4-Jun-20	1	machine -learning	4
3.	A bit boring!	Abu M R	15-May-20	4	machine -learning	2
4.	great course	onkar p	3-Apr-18	4	machine -learning	5
5.	Excellent...!	RAHUL S	16-May-19	5	machine -learning	5
6.	Nice	Rupak K p	10-Apr-20	1	python-data	4
7.	best course	rajyagurusaisri k	3-May-20	2	python-data	5
8.	Good Lectures	Himanshu V	12-Sep-20	3	python-data	4
9.	Great Course for starting!	Mahmud M	23-Jul-18	4	python-data	5
10.	very good course actually!	Dipu	26-Sep-16	4	python-data	5
11	It's good learning course	Yogesh u	2-Aug-20	4	python-data	4
12	I really loved it.	Szabolcs S	12-Mar-20	5	python-data	5
13.	Dr. Chuck is amazing. I'm too dumb to code.	Puja G	1-May-20	2	python-data	4
14.	Interesting overview.	Dorottya B	30-May-18	4	e-learning	4
15	I'd love to learn such topics in future as well.	Manisha o	29-Jul-20	5	e-learning	5
16	Excellent start for passionate educators ? those who want to make a difference in education systems.	By Nida A	1-Jun-20	4	e-learning	5

As we can notice in Cases 1 and 2, a big conflict exists between the original and predicted ratings possibly caused by different reasons like a wrong rating if the user clicked on the wrong number. On the other hand, it could happen if the user was in a hurry to click the rating stars. From the presented results, we can show the degradation between the original users' ratings and the new predicted ratings, especially in cases 1, 2 and 4, so we measure the distance similarity between the user rating matrix and the predicted rating matrix. That explains why using user data reviews will help to build a good learning RS more than using numerical rating data. Cosine similarity and TF/DF are used for similarity calculations [21]. These calculations are made for all source datasets, which already contain different text reviews that vary in text length, size and type of content. In Fig. 5, we show a similar result for samples from each of the four cases.

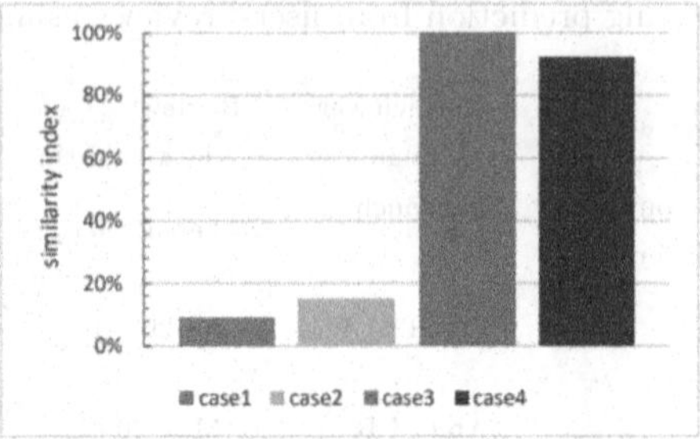

Fig. 5. Similarity distance between original user rating and predicted rating in four case of new rating.

In contrast, the similarity in the overall dataset was 98%, which means there is an incompatibility between learners' ratings and preferences reflected in the text reviews. This proves the difference can transform what is recommend or not recommend to the user. In other words, this changes the behavior of the recommender model.

Conclusion

Recommendation system is one of the important aspects of a machine learning system. The importance of this system in e-learning environment increase day by day. Similarly, machine learning and data mining techniques were combined with traditional recommendation strategies to improve the personalization factor of target recommendation. We used a hybrid of both types of historical user data (rating and comment) in the presented model to reduce cold-start and sparsity problem effects. We used a real-world dataset to train and test the proposed model (70% training and 30% testing). This data came from the Coursera platform. Results showed that using online user reviews is more accurate than using numerical user ratings, which yields a high-performing recommendation system. In the short-term future work, we will use a transformer instead of a CNN.

References

1. Hazar, M.J., Toman, Z.H., Toman, S.H.: Automated scoring for essay questions in E-learning. J. Phys.: Conf. Ser. **1294**(4) (2019). https://doi.org/10.1088/1742-6596/1294/4/042014
2. Li, L.Y.: Effect of prior knowledge on attitudes, behavior, and learning performance in video lecture viewing. Int. J. Hum. Comput. Interact. **35**(4–5), 415–426 (2018). https://doi.org/10.1080/10447318.2018.1543086
3. Ali, A.A.M.A., Mabrouk, M., Zrigui, M.: A review: blockchain technology applications in the field of higher education. J. Hunan Univ. Nat. Sci. **49**(10), 88–99 (2022). https://doi.org/10.55463/ISSN.1674-2974.49.10.10

4. Legrand, A., Trystram, D., Zrigui, S.: Adapting batch scheduling to workload characteristics: what can we expect from online learning? In 2019 IEEE International Parallel and Distributed Processing Symposium (IPDPS), pp. 686–695. IEEE (2019)
5. Chen, L., Chen, G., Wang, F.: Recommender systems based on user reviews: the state of the art. User Model. User-adapt. Interact. **25**(2), 99–154 (2015). https://doi.org/10.1007/S11257-015-9155-5/TABLES/4
6. Jaballi, S., Zrigui, S., Sghaier, M.A., Berchech, D., Zrigui, M.: Sentiment analysis of Tunisian users on social networks: overcoming the challenge of multilingual comments in the Tunisian dialect. In: Nguyen, N.T., Manolopoulos, Y., Chbeir, R., Kozierkiewicz, A., Trawiński, B. (eds.) ICCCI 2022. LNCS (LNAI and LNB), vol. 13501, pp. 176–192. Springer, CHam (2022). https://doi.org/10.1007/978-3-031-16014-1_15
7. Mahmoud, A., Zrigui, M.: Semantic similarity analysis for corpus development and paraphrase detection in Arabic. Int. Arab J. Inf. Technol. **18**(1), 1–7 (2021). https://doi.org/10.34028/iajit/18/1/1
8. Gomathi, R.M., Ajitha, P., Krishna, G.H.S., Pranay, I.H.: Restaurant recommendation system for user preference and services based on rating and amenities. In: ICCIDS 2019–2nd International Conference on Computational Intelligence in Data Science Processing (2019). https://doi.org/10.1109/ICCIDS.2019.8862048
9. Musto, C., de Gemmis, M., Lops, P., Semeraro, G.: Generating post hoc review-based natural language justifications for recommender systems. User Model. User-Adapt. Interact. **31**(3), 629–673 (2021). https://doi.org/10.1007/S11257-020-09270-8/TABLES/19
10. Sghaier, M.A., Zrigui, M.: Sentiment analysis for Arabic E-commerce websites. In: 2016 International Conference on Engineering MIS (ICEMIS), pp. 1–7 (2016). https://doi.org/10.1109/ICEMIS.2016.7745323
11. Fraihat, S., Shambour, Q.: A framework of semantic recommender system for e-learning (2015). ammanu.edu.jo, https://www.ammanu.edu.jo/english/pdf/StaffResearch/IT/923/00. Accessed 12 Feb 2023. Paper-A Framework of Semantic Recommender System for elearning.pdf
12. Choudrey, S.: Video recommendation through machine learning in Amazon web services (2021). http://urn.kb.se/resolve?urn=urn:nbn:se:kth:diva-303010. Accessed 12 Feb 2023
13. Slimi, A., Hamroun, M., Zrigui, M., Nicolas, H.: Emotion recognition from speech using spectrograms and shallow neural networks. In: Proceedings of the 18th International Conference on Advances in Mobile Computing & Multimedia, pp. 35–39 (2020)
14. Ayadi, R., Maraoui, M., Zrigui, M.: Latent topic model for indexing Arabic documents. Int. J. Inf. Retrieval Res. (IJIRR) **4**(2), 57–72 (2014). https://doi.org/10.4018/IJIRR.2014040104, https://services.igi-global.com/resolvedoi/resolve.aspx?doi=10.4018/ijirr.2014040104
15. Hazar, M.J., Zrigui, M., Maraoui, M.: Learner comments-based recommendation system. Procedia Comput. Sci. **207**, 2000–2012 (2022). https://doi.org/10.1016/J.PROCS.2022.09.259
16. Treude, C., Sicard, M., Klocke, M., Robillard, M.: TaskNav: task-based navigation of software documentation. Proc. - Int. Conf. Softw. Eng. **2**, 649–652 (2015). https://doi.org/10.1109/ICSE.2015.214
17. Bsir, B., Zrigui, M.: Bidirectional LSTM for author gender identification. In: Nguyen, N.T., Pimenidis, E., Khan, Z., Trawiński, B. (eds.) ICCCI 2018. LNCS

(LNAI), vol. 11055, pp. 393–402. Springer, Cham (2018). https://doi.org/10.1007/978-3-319-98443-8_36
18. Zhang, Y., Liu, R., Li, A.D.: A novel approach to recommender system based on aspect-level sentiment analysis (2016). atlantis-press.com, https://www.atlantis-press.com/proceedings/nceece-15/25847127. Accessed 21 June 2022
19. Hutto, C.J., Gilbert, E.: VADER: a parsimonious rule-based model for sentiment analysis of social media text (2014). http://sentic.net/. Accessed 21 June 2022
20. Maraoui, M., Antoniadis, G., Zrigui, M.: CALL System for Arabic based on natural language processing tools. In: IICAI, pp. 2249–2258 (2009)
21. Ayadi, R., Maraoui, M., Zrigui, M.: Intertextual distance for Arabic texts classification. In: 2009 International Conference for Internet Technology and Secured Transactions (ICITST), pp. 1–6. IEEE (2009)

Cybersecurity, Blockchain Technology and Internet of Things

A Two-Hop Neighborhood Based Berserk Detection Algorithm for Probabilistic Model of Consensus in Distributed Ledger Systems

Deepanjan Mitra[1(✉)], Agostino Cortesi[2], and Nabendu Chaki[1]

[1] University of Calcutta, Kolkata, India
deepanjanm@acm.org, nabendu@ieee.org
http://cucse.org/nc/

[2] Ca' Foscari University, Venice, Italy
cortesi@unive.it
http://www.unive.it/persone/cortesi

Abstract. Emerging distributed ledger technologies are often not based on Proof of Work (PoW) or Proof of Stake (PoS) consensus protocols. The lightweight protocols, based on the voter model, are typically used for handling contention. However, such protocols are fraught with a particular type of Byzantine adversary known as Berserk adversaries who intend to break the consensus. The existing method of Berserk detection involves the exchange of signatures. This in turn requires key servers, subject to a single point of failure. This paper investigates a new method of Berserk detection. Unlike most of the existing deterministic detection methodologies, the proposed method does not use signatures for the detection of Berserk behavior. The proposed solution is based on two-hop neighborhood opinion information gathering and detects Berserk nodes with some degree of certitude. We also try to ensure that the proposed approach detects most of the Berserk nodes and at the same time keeps the number of false detections marginal.

Keywords: Distributed Ledger Technology · Consensus · Byzantine Adversary · Berserk adversary · Adversary Detection

1 Introduction

Consensus protocols are integral to any Distributed Ledger Technology (DLT). Blockchain-based technologies like Bitcoin [1] and Ethereum [2] use Proof of Work (PoW) -based consensus protocols [3]. However, PoW-based schemes are computation-intensive because they involve checking over many nonce values to find the right solution to the cryptographic puzzle. Other consensus schemes like Proof of Stake (PoS) result in a tendency for DLTs to be more centralized in comparison to PoW-based schemes. Thus, these consensus schemes become

N. T. Nguyen et al. (Eds.): ICCCI 2023, LNAI 14162, pp. 379–391, 2023.
https://doi.org/10.1007/978-3-031-41456-5_29

a limitation for DLTs with respect to the scalability and throughput [5,6]. The unresolved concerns of scalability on an architectural level create difficulties in adopting Blockchain in practical applications. Decentralized consensus protocols of low computational complexity were proposed to overcome these limitations. The Fast Probabilistic Consensus (FPC) protocol is a protocol that is based on the idea of probabilistic consensus. Based on the voter model of consensus [7], it takes a series of initial Boolean values as input and outputs a final value. In FPC, nodes query other nodes about their current opinion of the ledger. Then they adjust their own opinion over the course of several rounds. However, these protocols are fraught with Byzantine adversaries that prove lethal to the achievement of consensus.

This paper addresses the problem of a special type of Byzantine adversary known as Berserk and proposes a novel mechanism for the detection of these adversaries. The key idea is to gather information from the two-hop neighborhood of each node with the hope that some discrepancy occurs that allows identifying the suspected nodes. Unlike the existing approach [19], where nodes ask for signatures on detecting discrepancies, the proposed detection method does not employ the validation of proofs. An extensive experimental evaluation provides evidence of the effectiveness of this probabilistic approach.

The rest of the paper is structured as follows: In Sect. 2, we discuss briefly the background and the published work that technically relates to FPC and Berserk adversary. In Sect. 3, we describe the proposed detection method along with an illustration. In Sect. 4, we run our algorithm and test the performance of the proposed approach against one of the closest existing methods [19]. Section 5 is the conclusion of this paper, where we summarize our findings and state the future scope of our work.

2 Related Work

There is a wide range of work on consensus protocols [8–11] for distributed systems. However, Byzantine adversaries are a major threat to consensus schemes. The Byzantine adversary traces its roots to the well-known game theoretic problem known as the Byzantine generals problem [12]. The problem requires the actors of a system to agree on a particular strategy in the absence of any trusted centralized entity. But the system contains some unreliable actors. These adversaries are hidden among other nodes in a network and try to prevent the honest nodes from reaching a consensus. They may adopt various strategies including fake messaging, forging messages, and two-faced behavior. These attacks are a serious security issue for consensus mechanisms and DLTs at large where they can also create inconsistency. A number of works [13–16] have been proposed to make consensus schemes Byzantine fault-tolerant. This paper focuses on a particular type of Byzantine behavior known as Berserk. Popov and Buchanan introduced the notion of Berserk adversary in [17]. The Berserks prevent the network nodes from arriving at a consensus by employing the maximum variance strategy. Using this strategy, the adversary tries to subdivide the honest nodes into two equally sized groups of different opinions while maximizing the variance of eta values, where eta is the mean of the opinions of the honest nodes. An agreement failure is a serious attack on distributed ledger technology, and proofs in [18] show how the system is vulnerable to attacks by Berserk nodes. Popov et al. in [19] introduced a method to detect Berserk adversaries where an honest node asks a queried node for the list of opinions that it had received during the previous round of consensus. Such a list of opinions is referred to as the *v-list*. It contains the identity of the queried node and the opinion that it has given. The algorithm works as follows. Suppose, a node n received k votes, submitted by nodes n_1, ..., n_k, in the previous round. When a node n_x asks its neighboring node n_y for a *v-list*, then n_y sends the opinions given by nodes n_1, ..., n_k accompanied by the identities but without their signatures. Node n_x then compares the v-list submitted by n_y with the *v-lists* received from other nodes. If any discrepancy in opinion for a node n_s is detected, then node n_x holds the node n_s in suspicion and asks the node n_y to send the associated signature so that the malicious behavior can be proved. If the verification of the signature is satisfactory, then node n_x deems node n_s as Berserk and informs its one-hop neighboring nodes about it. The existing method of Berserk detection in [19] involves nodes asking for signatures when a discrepancy in opinion is detected. Suppose node n_x finds a discrepancy in opinion against node n_B on comparing the *v-list* of nodes n_p and n_q. The nodes n_p and n_q need to send node n_x the signature of the message that it had obtained from n_B. This requires nodes to exchange keys with their neighbors during the initial stage like neighbor discovery and node registration. Key servers play an important role in public-key cryptography. In public-key cryptography, an individual is able to generate a key pair, where one of the keys is kept private while the other is distributed publicly. The key servers are, however, not robust, being subjected to a single point of failure. Distributed key generation schemes were proposed to overcome this limitation. However, those are rarely used as they come with some limitations [20]. First, most distributed key generation schemes have a very high reliance on synchronous communication which makes them impractical for DLTs. Second, though there has been quite a research on Asynchronous Distributed Key generation (ADKG), however, they incur large communication complexity. For instance, Kogias et al. in [21] proposed an ADKG method that provides optimal resilience against Byzantine adversaries in the asynchronous model. However, it incurs a high communication complexity of $O(kn^4)$. A similar observation is true for the ADKG proposed by Das et al. in [22]. Third, consensus algorithms find major applications in wireless sensor networks for distributed detection, task-allocation [23], rendezvous problem, and sensor data fusion [24,25]. In sensor networks, the cost of signing a message is a limitation. Due to the resource-constraint nature of sensor motes, there is a need to regulate the cost of computations, included in the digital signature. The Consensus algorithms like PoS [4] in Blockchain also incur a major cost [26] in terms of bandwidth, space, and computational resources needed for signature verification. Moreover, the exchange of signatures for expressing an opinion is a shortcoming, as far as message size is concerned [27]. Keeping in mind these challenges, we proposed to develop an algorithm to detect Berserk adversaries without the need for an exchange of signatures. We also make our objective to ensure that the developed algorithm should be able to detect almost all the Berserk adversaries while keeping the number of false detection as marginal as possible.

3 A New Berserk Detection Algorithm

3.1 Abbreviations and Annotations of Terms

Before thoroughly describing the algorithm, let us first introduce some terminologies used and their definitions in Table 1.

The Berserk detection method is undertaken after every round of the consensus process. The preconditions to the Berserk detection algorithm 1 are

1. v-list(n) is initialized with the opinions received from quorum(n) in that round of consensus, $\forall n \in$N.
2. ORANGEset(n) $= \emptyset, \forall n \in$N.
3. opinionList$_n(p) = \emptyset, \forall n \in$N.
4. whpBerserk(n) $= \emptyset, \forall n \in$N.

3.2 Method

The central idea is to gather information from the two-hop neighborhood of node n with the hope that there will be some other nodes like n that might have received opinions from a suspected node. Instead of asking for signatures as proof, a node n_x temporarily holds nodes n_1, n_2, and n_s in suspicion. This is because we cannot be sure if node n_s is really Berserk or that n_s is honest but nodes n_1 and n_2 are doing some foul play by tinkering with opinions given by n_s. Thus to be more sure about these suspicious nodes, node n_x tries looking into the two-hop neighborhood to gather information about them.

The proposed method is described in Algorithm 1. The Algorithm 1 has been explained using a small example. Let us consider the following network as shown in Fig. 1 and try to understand the problem from the perspective of node 1. It is assumed that node 2 is in the quorum of node 1 while node 9 is not. Node 2 is Berserk and sends different opinions in response to queries of its one-hop neighbors as shown in Fig. 1a. Node 1 and node 9 receive opinions '1' and '0' respectively from node 2. When node 1 asks for v-lists (*VL*) from its one-hop neighbors, it learns that node 9 has received an opinion of '0' from node 2. In such a case, the opinion from node 2 appears contradictory. Thus, node 1 holds both node 2 and node 9 in suspicion, (marked in orange colour) and adds them to its *ORANGEset* as shown in Fig. 1n. Node 1 then tries to gather information from its one-hop neighbors about the nodes in its ORANGEset. The one-hop neighbors of node 1 further forward this query to their neighbors. Accordingly, node 1 learns that node 7, node 8, node 10, and node 11 have received an opinion of '0' from node 9. Since the majority of opinions, in this case, are the same, node 1 keeps node 9 out of suspicion as shown in Fig. 1c. However, for ORANGE

Table 1. Annotations of terms used in the algorithm

Term	Meaning
N	Total set of nodes. Each node $n_i \in$ N is identified by a node identity i, where i $\in Z^+$
neighborsID(n)	$\{n_i \mid n_i$ is a one-hop neighbor of node $n\}$
opinion$_{n_i}$	The opinion given by node n_i regarding the object of consensus. It is a binary variable that can assume a value of either 0 or 1
v-list(n)	The v-list of a node n, contains a record of the opinions given by its one-hop neighbors in a particular round of the consensus. Mathematically, v-list(n) = $\{(i, opinion) \mid n_i \in neighborsID(n), opinion \in \{0, 1\}\}$
Discrepancy_condition(n_d, v-list(n), v-list(n_i), v-list(n_j))	True iff $\exists(k, opinion_{n_k}) \in v\text{-}list(n_i) \wedge (l, opinion_{n_l}) \in v\text{-}list(n_j) \vee (m, opinion_{n_m}) \in v\text{-}list(n) \mid k = l = m = d \wedge opinion_{n_k} \neq opinion_{n_l} \vee opinion_{n_k} \neq opinion_{n_m} \vee opinion_{n_l} \neq opinion_{n_m} \vee opinion_{n_m} \neq opinion_{n_k}$
ORANGEset(n)	Set containing suspected one-hop neighbor identities of a node n, in a round of the consensus process. ORANGEset(n) = $\{n_d \mid \exists n_i, n_j$, Discrepancy($n_d$, v-list(n), v-list($n_i$),v-list($n_j$)) = True$\}$
quorum(n)	The set of one-hop neighbors that are queried by a node n in a round of the consensus process
2hVL	A message sent by a node to its one-hop neighbors after forming a non-empty ORANGEset. This message contains the ORANGEset and has a hop count of two
opinionList$_n(p)$	An accumulation of opinions about node p in ORANGEset(n). opinionList$_n(p)$ = $\{$(i, x)$\mid i \in Z^+$, $x \in \{0, 1\}$; where x is the opinion received by node n_i from node $p\}$
whpBerserk(n)	The set of nodes concluded with high probability as Berserk, by node n $\{n_i \mid$node n concludes node n_i as Berserk with high probability$\}$

Algorithm 1 Two-hop neighbor-based Berserk detection algorithm

```
for each node n ∈ N do
    Randomly choose two nodes n1 & n2 from neighborsID(n).
    Request v-list(n1) & v-list(n2) from nodes n1 & n2 respectively.
    for each node nd| Discrepancy_condition(nd, v-list(n), v-list(n1), v-list(n2)) = True do
        ORANGEset(n) = ORANGEset(n) ∪ {nd}
    end for
    if ORANGEset(n) ≠ ∅ then
        for each node p ∈ ORANGEset(n) do
            if p ∈ neighborsID(n) then
                Send 2hVL to nodes ni ∈ neighborsID(n) − ORANGEset(n)
            end if
        end for
    end if
    for each node n1 ∈ neighborsID(n), receiving 2hVL, do
        for each node p ∈ ORANGEset(n) ∩ quorum(n1) do
            Node n1 forwards the opinion it received from node p to node n.
        end for
        Node n1 forwards the 2hVL message to nodes ni ∈ neighborsID(n1)
    end for
    for each node n2 ∈ neighborsID(n1), receiving 2hVL, do
        for each node p ∈ ORANGEset(n) ∩ quorum(n2) do
            Node n2 forwards the opinion it received from p to node n1.
            Node n1 further forwards it to node n.
        end for
    end for
    for each node p ∈ ORANGEset(n) do
        opinionList_n(p) ← opinions received from two-hop neighbors
        if ∀x ∈ opinionList_n(p), x=0 ∨ x=1 and node p ∈ quorum(n) then
            if x ∈ opinionList_n(p) ≠ opinion, ∃(p, opinion) ∈ v-list(n) then
                whpBerserk(n) = whpBerserk(n) ∪ {p}
            end if
        else if opinionList_n(p) contains neither a majority of 0s nor of 1s then
            whpBerserk(n) = whpBerserk(n) ∪ {p}
        end if
    end for
end for
```

node 2, node 1 receives opinion information '0' from node 11 and node 31, while opinion information '1' is received from node 3 and node 30. In this case, the majority of two-hop opinion information is not the same. So, node 1 deems node 2 as Berserk (marked in red in Fig. 1e) and adds node 2 to its whpBerserk set. The same process is performed by every honest node in the network. This is a minimal example. However, for evaluation purposes, graphs with a large number of nodes and neighbors have been considered as discussed in the next section.

Assuming that the average number of one-hop neighbors of a node in the network is 'm' and the average size of the ORANGEset per node is 'd', the average number of messages exchanged per node is $d \times (2 + (m - d) \times m)$ which is $O(d \times m^2)$.

4 Evaluation

In this section, the results obtained from the evaluation of the Algorithm 1 have been presented. The experimental setting and the network model considered in this work have been described, followed by the experimental results.

4.1 Experimental Setting

The Algorithm 1 was evaluated using a Go-Lang based simulation[1] and run on Intel dual-core 2.00 GHz processor with 8 G.B. RAM. Several runs of the experiment were conducted on random networks generated using the Watts-Strogatz model [28]. The Watts-Strogatz model is a random graph generation model that produces graphs with small-world properties, including short average path lengths and high clustering. The objective of setting up the experiment is to validate if the proposed method effectively detects Berserk nodes without using a signature for the verification of the malicious behavior.

4.2 Results

The results of the experiments conducted were taken as an average over several runs of the experiment and over several random graphs. The false positive rate (*FPR*), and false negative rate (*FNR*) were then recorded for a proportion of Berserk adversaries (q) varied from 3% to 10%. The threshold has been taken to be 80% for the experimental results in Fig. 2. This means, for the opinions collected from the two-hop neighborhood, it is checked if 80% of the opinions are the same. The *FPR* and *FNR* have been defined in Eqs. 1 and 2 respectively where *FP* denotes the number of false positives and *FN* is the number of false negatives.

$$FPR = \frac{FP}{Total\ number\ of\ honest\ nodes} \times 100\% \quad (1)$$

$$FNR = \frac{FN}{Total\ number\ of\ Berserk\ nodes} \times 100\% \quad (2)$$

An experiment was conducted to observe how the number of false positives and false negatives vary with different values of the threshold. Figure 3 shows the results, where along the x-axis we see the threshold being varied from 100% down to 60%. The different colors in the legend denote the varying proportion of

[1] https://github.com/DeepanjanMitra/NewBerserkDetectionMethod.git refer to this repository to find the simulation and data used for evaluation.

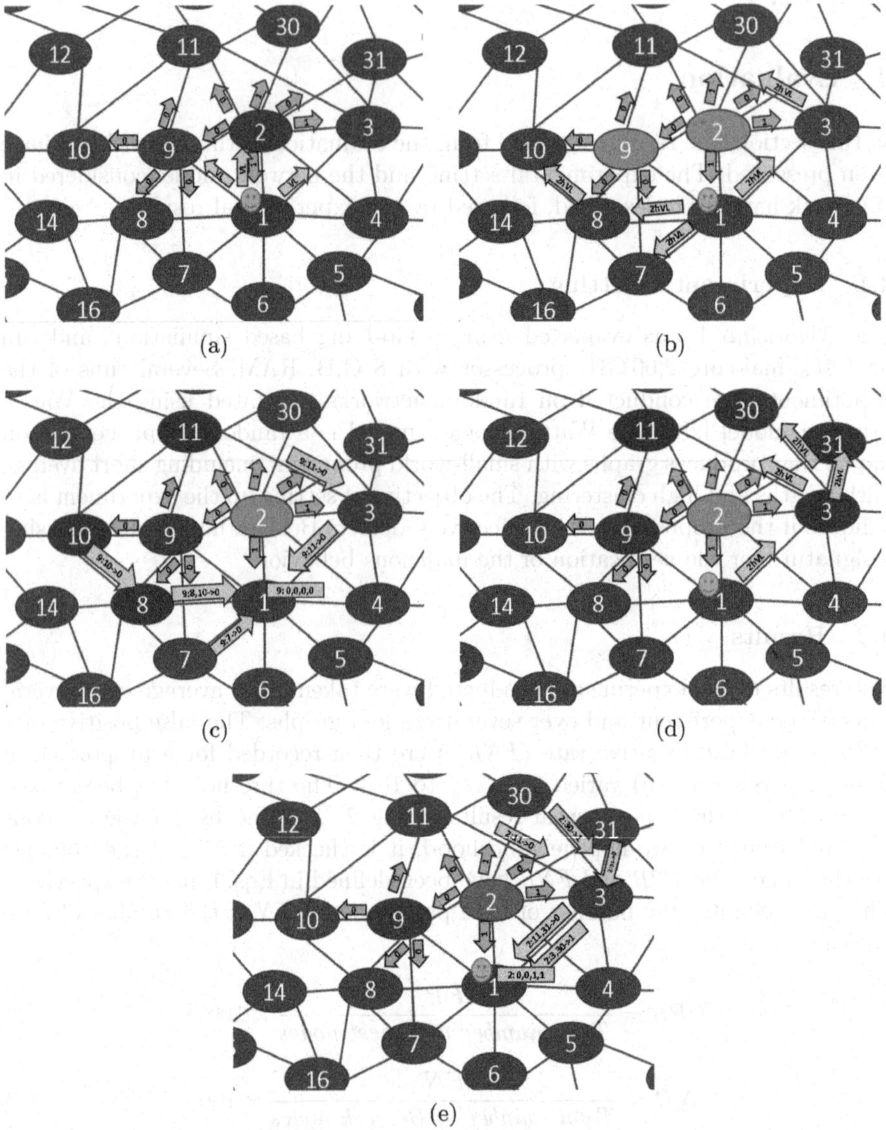

Fig. 1. (a) to (e) illustrates with a small network how a node detects Berserk adversaries following the approach in Algorithm 1

Berserks. The false positives are a matter of great concern. This is because it is important to ensure that no honest node should be detected as a Berserk adversary. Thus, a prime objective is to achieve a minimal number of false positives and at the same time, the number of false negatives should be small, ensuring that a large number of Berserks indeed get detected. As seen from the plots in Fig. 3, if the threshold is kept from seventy to eighty percent. The number of false positives is appreciably low and at the same time, the number of false negatives is under control for almost all values of 'q'.

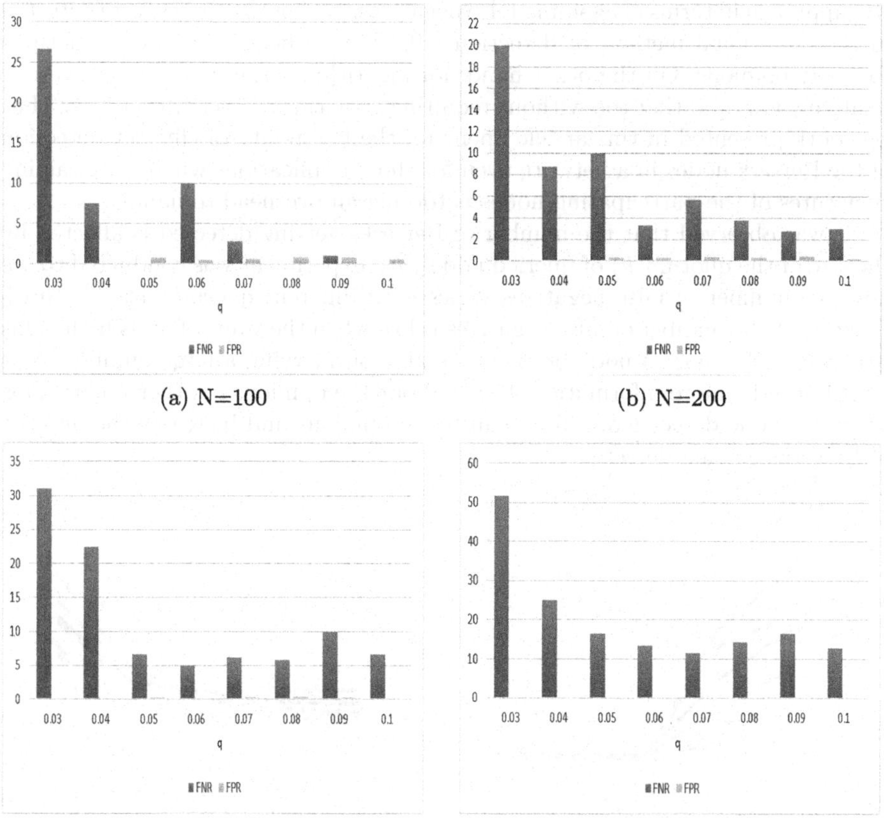

(a) N=100 (b) N=200

(c) N=300 (d) N=400

Fig. 2. (a), (b), (c) and (d) show the experimental results obtained by running the Algorithm 1 on random networks of one hundred, two hundred, three hundred and four hundred number of nodes (N) with the proportion of Berserks(q) being varied from 3% to 10% in each case.

4.3 Discussion

The proposed algorithm uses a probabilistic way of detecting Berserks where it tries to form a high-certitude conclusion about a maliciously behaving node by collecting information from the two-hop neighborhood. A comparison of the false positives rate and false negative rate for the proposed Algorithm 1 as compared to the algorithm in [19] has been presented in Fig. 4. The experiments were run for a number of random networks of nodes, and the proportion of Berserks(q) has been varied from 3% to 10% of nodes in each case. It is evident that the proposed Algorithm 1 gives better performance as compared with the existing [19] approach in terms of avoiding false negatives. No false positives were detected in the traditional method of detection [19]. This is because it uses signatures to verify opinions. On the other hand, for algorithm 1 the false positive rate is relatively low, and that too without requiring signatures to verify opinions. Thus the work presented in this article opens up the possibility of efficient detection of the Berserk nodes in a network even for those applications where maintaining signatures of the participating nodes is too big an overhead to handle.

It was observed that the number of Berserks getting detected is affected by the size of the quorum(k) of queried nodes. An experiment was conducted to see how the number of false negatives varies with different quorum sizes. Figure 5 shows that the number of false negatives is low when the value of 'k' is high. This is because, the more a node becomes capable of querying a large number of its neighbors, the more information it gets about the opinions of other nodes. This helps the node detect more discrepancies in opinions and increases the number of Berserks getting detected.

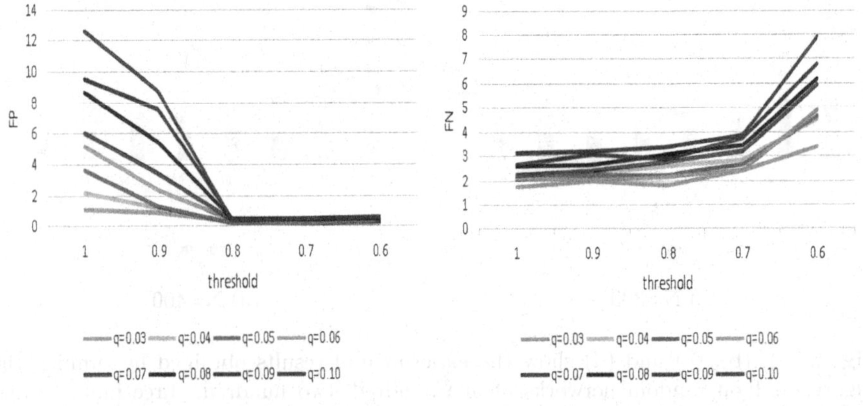

(a) False Positives (b) False Negatives

Fig. 3. (a) and (b) show the experimental results obtained by running the Algorithm 1 on random networks with the threshold being varied from 100% down to 60% in each case.

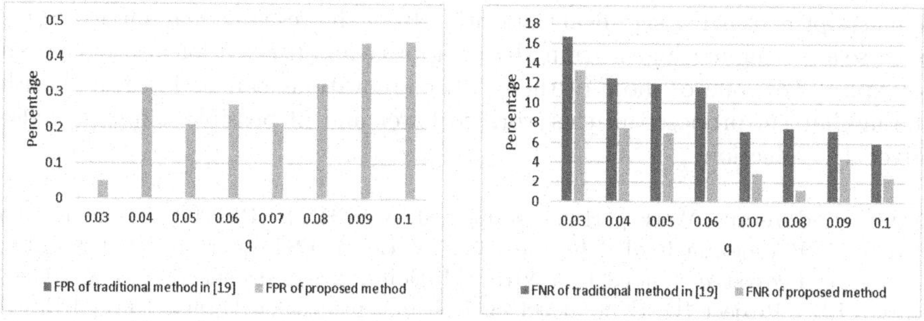

(a) False Positives (b) False Negatives

Fig. 4. (a) and (b) show the comparison in the false positive rate and false negative rate for the proposed Algorithm 1 and the existing method in [19].

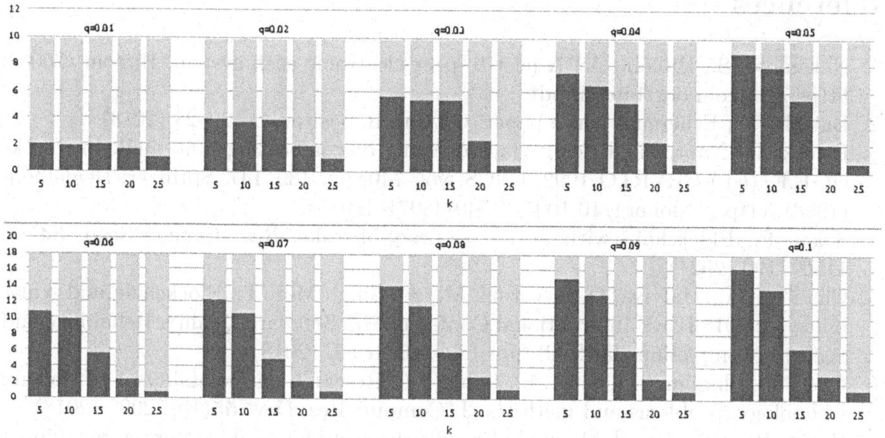

Fig. 5. Experimental results for Algorithm 1 on a random network of two hundred nodes with different proportions of Berserk adversaries - quorum-size(k) is varied between 5 to 25 in each case.

5 Conclusions

In this work, we developed a new approach to detect Byzantine adversaries exhibiting Berserk behavior in FPC. We have shown how the proposed method works by collecting information from the two-hop neighborhoods about the suspicious nodes. Finally, we ran a series of simulations that tested our approach's ability to detect the Berserk adversaries. In particular, it was important to make sure that honest nodes should not ideally be detected as Berserks.

Compared to the existing adversary detection methods like in [19], our proposed approach detects adversaries only with some probability of certitude and does not require signatures. The average number of honest nodes detected as Berserks was found to be appreciably low. The problem handled in the manuscript is drawing significant attention from the research community. Some of these are using machine learning-based approaches. It is left for future research to explore how one or more of these other innovations can be integrated with the mechanism proposed in this work to lower and, if possible, eliminate false adversary detection.

Acknowledgment. Work partially supported by SERICS (PE00000014) under the PNRR MUR program funded by the EU - NGEU, iNEST-Interconnected NordEst Innovation Ecosystem funded by PNRR (Mission 4.2, Investment 49 1.5) NextGeneration EU - Project ID: ECS 00000043, Research project on Formal Method Based Security Evaluation funded by M/s Keysight Technologies, USA and Research project on Connected Smart Health Services for Rural India under the cluster IoT Research funded by DST, Government of India.

References

1. Nakamoto, S., Bitcoin, A.: A peer-to-peer electronic cash system. Bitcoin (2008). https://bitcoin.org/bitcoin.pdf
2. Buterin, V.: Ethereum white paper. GitHub Repository **1**, 22–23 (2013)
3. Dwork, C., Naor, M.: Pricing via processing or combatting junk mail. In: Brickell, E.F. (ed.) CRYPTO 1992. LNCS, vol. 740, pp. 139–147. Springer, Heidelberg (1993). https://doi.org/10.1007/3-540-48071-4_10
4. Saleh, F.: Blockchain without waste: proof-of-stake. Rev. Financ. Stud. **34**(3), 1156–1190 (2021)
5. Chauhan, A., Malviya, O.P., Verma, M., der Singh Mor, T.: Blockchain and scalability. In: 2018 IEEE International Conference on Software Quality, Reliability and Security Companion (QRS-C), pp. 122–128. IEEE (2018)
6. Chen, P., Zhiqiang, L., Zhen, L., Long, Yu.: Research on scalability of blockchain technology: problems and methods. J. Comput. Res. Dev. **55**(10), 2099 (2018)
7. Holley, R.A., Liggett, T.M., et al.: Ergodic theorems for weakly inter- acting infinite systems and the voter model. Ann. Probab. **3**(4), 643–663 (1975)
8. Bracha, G.: Asynchronous Byzantine agreement protocols. Inf. Comput. **75**(2), 130–143 (1987)
9. Feldman, P., Micali, S.: An optimal probabilistic algorithm for synchronous Byzantine agreement. In: Ausiello, G., Dezani-Ciancaglini, M., Della Rocca, S.R. (eds.) ICALP 1989. LNCS, vol. 372, pp. 341–378. Springer, Heidelberg (1989). https://doi.org/10.1007/BFb0035770
10. Mitra, D., Cortesi, A., Chaki, N.: ALEA: an anonymous leader election algorithm for synchronous distributed systems. In: Choraś, M., Choraś, R.S., Kurzyński, M., Trajdos, P., Pejaś, J., Hyla, T. (eds.) CORES/IP&C/ACS -2021. LNNS, vol. 255, pp. 46–58. Springer, Cham (2022). https://doi.org/10.1007/978-3-030-81523-3_5
11. Friedman, R., Mostefaoui, A., Raynal, M.: Simple and efficient oracle-based consensus protocols for asynchronous Byzantine systems. IEEE Trans. Dependable Secure Comput. **2**(1), 46–56 (2005)
12. Lamport, L., Shostak, R., Pease, M.: The Byzantine generals problem. ACM Trans. Program. Lang. Syst. **4**(3), 382–401 (1982). https://doi.org/10.1145/357172.357176
13. Marano, S., Matta, V., Tong, L.: Distributed detection in the presence of Byzantine attacks. IEEE Trans. Signal Process. **57**(1), 16–29 (2008)

14. Ayday, E., Fekri, F.: An iterative algorithm for trust management and adversary detection for delay-tolerant networks. IEEE Trans. Mob. Comput. **11**(9), 1514–1531 (2011)
15. Dong, Y., et al.: Secure distributed on-device learning networks with byzantine adversaries. IEEE Netw. **33**(6), 180–187 (2019)
16. Kailkhura, B., et al.: Distributed Bayesian detection in the presence of Byzantine data. IEEE Trans. Signal Process. **63**(19), 5250–5263 (2015)
17. Popov, Serguei, Buchanan, William J.: FPC-BI: fast probabilistic consensus within Byzantine infrastructures. J. Parallel Distrib. Comput. **147**, 77–86 (2021). https://doi.org/10.1016/j.jpdc.2020.09.002. ISSN 0743-7315
18. Capossele, A., Müller, S., Penzkofer, A.: Robustness and efficiency of voting consensus protocols within byzantine infrastructures. Blockchain Res. Appl. **2**(1), 100007 (2021). https://doi.org/10.1016/j.bcra.2021.100007. ISSN 2096-7209
19. Popov, S., et al.: The coordicide, pp. 1–30 (2020)
20. Gennaro, R., Jarecki, S., Krawczyk, H., Rabin, T.: Secure distributed key generation for discrete-log based cryptosystems. In: Stern, J. (ed.) EUROCRYPT 1999. LNCS, vol. 1592, pp. 295–310. Springer, Heidelberg (1999). https://doi.org/10.1007/3-540-48910-x_21
21. Kokoris Kogias, E., Malkhi, D., Spiegelman, A.: Asynchronous distributed key generation for computationally-secure randomness, consensus, and threshold signatures. In: Proceedings of the 2020 ACM SIGSAC Conference on Computer and Communications Security (CCS 2020), pp. 1751–1767. ACM, New York (2020). https://doi.org/10.1145/3372297.3423364
22. Das, S., Yurek, T., Xiang, Z., Miller, A., Kokoris-Kogias, L., Ren, L.: Practical asynchronous distributed key generation. In: 2022 IEEE Symposium on Security and Privacy (SP), San Francisco, CA, USA, pp. 2518–2534 (2022). https://doi.org/10.1109/SP46214.2022.9833584
23. Mahato, P., Saha, S., Chayan, S., Shaghil, M.: Consensus-based, fast and energy-efficient multi-robot task allocation. Robot. Auton. Syst. **159**, 104270 (2023). https://doi.org/10.1016/j.robot.2022.104270. ISSN 0921-8890
24. Olfati-Saber, R., Shamma, J.S.: Consensus filters for sensor networks and distributed sensor fusion. In: Proceedings of the 44th IEEE Conference on Decision and Control. IEEE (2005)
25. Bonomi, S., Del Pozzo, A., Potop-Butucaru, M., Tixeuil, S.: Approximate agreement under mobile Byzantine faults. Theor. Comput. Sci. **758**, 17–29 (2019)
26. Gorbunov, S., Wee, H.: Digital signatures for consensus. Cryptology ePrint Archive (2019)
27. Tseng, Y.-M., Jan, J.-K., Chien, H.-Y.: Digital signature with message recovery using self-certified public keys and its variants. Appl. Math. Comput. **136**(2–3), 203–214 (2003)
28. Watts, D.J., Strogatz, S.H.: Collective dynamics of 'small-world' networks. Nature **393**(6684), 440–442 (1998)

Trust Assessment on Data Stream Imputation in IoT Environments

Tao Peng[1], Sana Sellami[1(✉)], Omar Boucelma[1], and Richard Chbeir[2]

[1] Aix Marseille Univ, CNRS, LIS, Marseille, France
{tao.peng,sana.sellami,omar.boucelma}@univ-amu.fr
[2] Univ Pau & Pays Adour, E2S-UPPA, LIUPPA, EA3000, Anglet, France
richard.chbeir@univ-pau.fr

Abstract. In the era of internet of Things, stream data emitted by sensors may rise quality issues such as incompleteness caused mainly by sensors failure or transmission problems. It is therefore necessary to recover missing data because missing values can impact decision making. Within this landscape, trust on data imputation is a key issue for helping stakeholders involved in such process. In this paper, we address the problem related to the trustworthiness on imputed data streams in IoT environments. We propose here a method called CSIV (Confidence Score for Imputed Values) to assess trust by assigning a confidence score to imputed data. CSIV considers both trust score of non-missing values and neighboring sensors. We have evaluated CSIV on real datasets using accuracy and trustworthiness as evaluation metrics. Experiments show that CSIV is able to assign correctly a trust score to the imputed values.

Keywords: Internet of Things · Stream data · Imputation · Trust

1 Introduction

Since the advent of IoT, access to sensor data has become commonplace in many fields: environmental monitoring, road traffic monitoring, or e-health to cite a few.

Data emitted by sensors at real time are aggregated as data streams than may be ingested by different IoT applications or services. However, those streams may rise quality issues such as inaccuracy or incompleteness, due to issues such as sensor failure or network issues and leading to loss of precision and difficulties in a decision making process.

Missing value repairing can be performed in adopting different strategies such as [15]: 1) Delete incomplete observations; 2) Manual repair; 3) Substitute by a constant/last-observation/mean; and 4) Estimate the most probable value. The first three strategies are not suitable for IoT data streams. The last strategy, also called imputation, does not need human intervention and is much more efficient than manual ones. Data imputation estimates the most probable value by using

N. T. Nguyen et al. (Eds.): ICCCI 2023, LNAI 14162, pp. 392–404, 2023.
https://doi.org/10.1007/978-3-031-41456-5_30

as much information as possible from the gathered observations to repair missing values [15].

In this paper, we address the problem of assessing trustworthiness on imputed data streams in IoT environments. Most of the data imputation works [5,8] are based on the assumption that data imputation can be evaluated according to the difference between the reference values and the simulated missing ones. However, in the real scenarios, data is unavailable. Here, we propose a method called CSIV, standing for Confidence Score for Imputed Values, to assess trust by assigning a confidence score to imputed data, which extends our previous work on data trust assessment [12]. We adopt the same definition provided in [1] stating the *"Data Trustworthiness in IoT Networks is the subjective probability that data observed by a user is consistent with the data at the source"*, and consequently define imputed data trustworthiness as the subjective probability that imputed data is close to the expected value. CSIV is based on: (1) trust score of non-missing data, and (2) trustworthy neighboring sensors. Experiments conducted on real datasets demonstrate the efficiency of CSIV while assessing imputed data accuracy, hence ensuring trustworthiness of the values being imputed.

This paper is organized as follows. We present a literature review in Sect. 2 and describe our approach in Sect. 3. Section 4 presents the experiments and validation setting. Finally, Sect. 5 concludes the paper and pin down several future directions.

2 Related Works

In this section, we review related works on data Trustworthiness and the evaluation of imputation accuracy.

The work described in [9] proposed a cyclic trust computation framework for data streams: (a) the more trusted data reported by the sensor, the higher is the (provider's) reputation; (b) data trust depends on all of data similarity, provenance similarity and sensor reputation. This approach is based on the hypothesis that the sensor data is independent of one another and follows the same Gaussian Distribution $N\left(\mu, \sigma^2\right)$. However, data streams are non-stationary which means that they do not have the same distribution and are time-dependent.

Other recent works [1,4,10] suppose that the residual ($r_{f,t} = \hat{d}_{f,t} - d_{f,t}$), where $\hat{d}_{f,t}$ is the estimated value and $d_{f,t}$ is the emitted value by a sensor f, follows a Gaussian Distribution. If the prediction is not biased, then the expected value μ is close to zero. A prediction is trustworthy if the residual is within the confidence interval of 95% (i.e. $[\mu \pm 1.98 * \delta]$, where δ is the standard deviation). In [1,10], a trust score ($s_{f,t}$ in the Eq. 1), is proposed. Cumulative Distribution function takes the residual as input and outputs a trust score: if this score exceeds a threshold, the received data is trusted. However, confidence interval and trust score $s_{f,t}$ can not be applied to assess trust on missing values because they are based on the hypothesis that missing values are simulated and then available, which is not the case in real scenarios.

$$s_{f,t} = \begin{cases} \frac{2}{\sigma\sqrt{2\pi}} \int_{-\infty}^{r_{f,t}} EXP\left(-\frac{(x-\mu)^2}{2\sigma^2}\right) \mathrm{d}x, \text{si } r_{f,t} < \mu \\ \frac{2}{\sigma\sqrt{2\pi}} \int_{r_{f,t}}^{+\infty} EXP\left(-\frac{(x-\mu)^2}{2\sigma^2}\right) \mathrm{d}x, \text{si } r_{f,t} \geq \mu \end{cases} \tag{1}$$

According to [6], evaluation methods for imputed values can be classified into two groups: indirect and direct. Indirect methods consist in: 1) training a classifier with the set of imputed data, 2) using a classifier on a set of test data without missing values, and 3) using accuracy of better classifier to assess the accuracy of imputation. However, indirect methods can not be done in real time because they need to access to all imputed data. Direct methods are based on the difference between imputed and missing values. They can be applied on the simulated missing values, but in real scenario missing values are often unavailable [14]. In [5,8], the authors proposed imputation methods on data streams and used direct method based on the root mean squared error $RMSE_{SMV}$ (Eq. 2) to evaluate the accuracy of imputed simulated missing values (SMV).

$$RMSE_{SMV} = \sqrt{\frac{1}{|SMV|} \sum_{d_{f,t} \in SMV} \left(\hat{d}_{f,t} - d_{f,t}\right)^2} \tag{2}$$

In [2], the authors used RMSE of the sliding window (w) (Eq. 3) to assess the accuracy of the regression model in data streams. Equation 3 takes into account accuracy changes due to the non stationary data but assumes that $d_{f,t}$ exists which is not always true since it is a missing value.

$$RMSE_t = \sqrt{\frac{1}{w} \sum_{i=t-w}^{t} \left(\hat{d}_{f,t} - d_{f,t}\right)^2} \tag{3}$$

In a nutshell, most of the evaluation methods in data streams are applied in the case of simulated data and consider the difference between the estimated value and the simulated one to determine the accuracy of the prediction. In our work, we take advantage of the spatial and temporal characteristics of data streams withing an IoT and assess trust of imputed data based on the confidence score of non-missing values and the trustworthiness of neighboring sensors.

3 CSIV Method

In this section, we describe our method CSIV (Confidence Scores of Imputed Values) for assessing trustworthiness in imputed values. Notations used in the followng subsections are detailed in Table 1.

3.1 Method Description

As shown in Fig. 1, CSIV consists of three steps: 1) trust assessment of data, 2) trust evaluation of sensors, and 3) trust assessment of imputed data. Due to

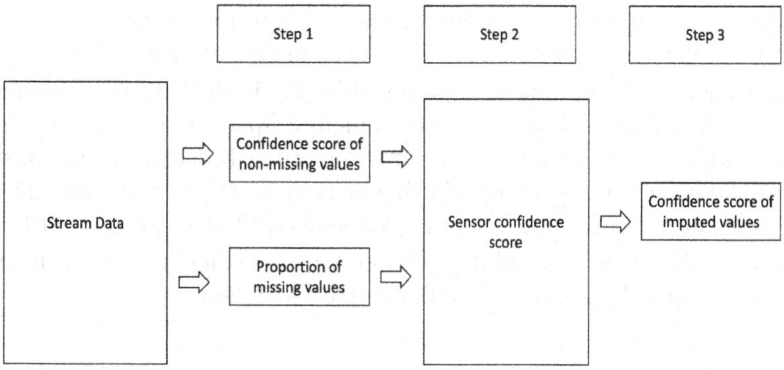

Fig. 1. CSIV method processes

the non-stationary data, the accuracy of imputed values can change over time [5] which leads to a concept drift. In view of the concept drift and in order to represent the trust score at one point, a sliding window is used for the next steps.

Phase 1: Data Trustworthiness: For each sensor $f \in F$ at time t, if $d_{f,t}$ is not a missing value, we calculate a trust score of $d_{f,t}$ according to Eq. 1. If the error is low, then $d_{f,t}$ will have a higher trust score. Indeed, the more the errors are higher, the low will be the trust score. Also, we determine, for each sensor $f \in F$ in the sliding window, the proportion of missing values in order to evaluate its trust score.

Phase 2: Sensors Trustworthiness: For each sensor $f \in F$ at time t, we consider that the more trusted data reported by the sensor, the higher is the (provider's) reputation in a sliding window (i.e., $[t-w, t]$) [3]. Moreover, if the sensor rarely generates missing values in the sliding window, then its trust score will be higher at time t [7].

Phase 3: Imputed values Trustworthiness: Given an imputed value $\hat{d}_{f,t}$, $\{f\} \bigcup K_f$ is the set of relevant sensors. The trust score of imputed value $\hat{d}_{f,t}$ is determined based on the trust score $\Re_{f,t} = \{sc_{f',t} \mid f' \in K_f\} \bigcup \{sc_{f,t}\}$ of relevant sensors which generate trustworthy data. For each imputed value, if the trust score of relevant sensors is higher, then the trust score of imputed value will be higher.

3.2 Algorithm

Algorithm 1 illustrates the pseudo-code description of CSIV. At time t, for all the sensors $f \in K$ (Algorithm 1 lines 2, 3), the trust score of a sensor $sc_{f,t}$ is determined by $sc_{f,t} \leftarrow (\frac{1}{w}\sum_{i=t-w}^{t-1} s_{f,i}) * (1 - RatioMV_{f,t})$. $(\frac{1}{w}\sum_{i=t-w}^{t-1} s_{f,i})$ is the average trust scores of the sensor values f in the sliding window w at time t. If $d_{f,t}$ is a missing value, the residual, being the difference between the predicted value $\hat{d}_{f,t}$ and the real value $d_{f,t}$, is denoted $r_{f,t} = \hat{d}_{f,t} - d_{f,t}$ (line 7). Assuming that the residual follows a Gaussian Distribution (Expected value μ and standard deviation δ), the trust score $s_{f,t}$ of $d_{f,t}$ is calculated at line 8. For all sensors $f \in K$ at time t, if $d_{f,t}$ is a missing value, then $\hat{d}_{f,t}$ is the estimated value by an imputation algorithm such as ISTM (Incremental Space-Time-based model) [11] which provides an estimation for the missing value based on nearly historical data and the observations of neighboring sensors of the default one. The trust score of relevant sensors (line 10) of $d_{f,t}$ depends on the trust score of f and its neighbors K_f. The trust sore of $\hat{d}_{f,t}$ (denoted $\hat{s}_{f,t}$) is calculated by a function G that takes as input $\Re_{f,t}$ (line 11) and is defined as follows:

Table 1. CSIV algorithm notations

Notation	Explanation
F	is a set of sensors
f	is a sensor, $f \in K$
K_f	is the neighbors set of f where $K_f \in F$
$d_{f,t}$	is the real value generated by a sensor f at time t
$\hat{d}_{f,t}$	is the predicted value of $d_{f,t}$
$r_{f,t}$	is the error which is the difference between the predicted value and the real value
μ	is the expected value of $r_{f,t}$
δ	is the standard deviation of $r_{f,t}$
$s_{f,t}$	is the trust score of $d_{f,t}$
$\hat{s}_{f,t}$	is the trust score of $\hat{d}_{f,t}$
$sc_{f,t}$	is the trust score of a sensor f at time t
w	is the length of a sliding window
$RatioMV_{f,t}$	is the proportion of missing values in the sliding window
	for a sensor f at time t
$f \bigcup K_f$	are the relevant sensors of $\hat{d}_{f,t}$
$\Re_{f,t}$	$= \{sc_{f',t} \mid f' \in K_f\} \bigcup \{sc_{f,t}\}$, are trust scores of relevant sensors of $\hat{d}_{f,t}$
CSIV	is the proposed method
G	is a function that takes as input $\Re_{f,t}$ ad gives as output the trust score of $\hat{d}_{f,t}$ (denoted $\hat{s}_{f,t}$).
$G_{avg}(\Re_{f,t})$	$= average(\Re_{f,t})$.
$G_{min}(\Re_{f,t})$	$= \min(\Re_{f,t})$.
$CSIV_{min}$	is CSIV , where G is G_{min}
$CSIV_{avg}$	is CSIV , where G is G_{avg}

- $G_{min}(\Re_{f,t}) = \min(\Re_{f,t})$ which means that the trust score of the imputed value is equal to the minimum trust score values of the relevant sensors.
- $G_{avg}(\Re_{f,t}) = average(\Re_{f,t})$ which is the average of $\Re_{f,t}$.

Algorithm 1 Trust Assessment on imputed values

Require: F: set of sensors
$d_{f,t}$: a value emitted by a sensor f at time t;
$\hat{d}_{f,t}$: the estimation of $d_{f,t}$
K_f: a neighbor set on a sensor $f \in F$.
$N(\mu, \sigma^2)$: Gaussian Distribution of $\hat{d}_{f,t} - d_{f,t}$
w: the length of sliding window
$RatioMV_{f,t}$: the proportion of missing values in the sliding window with a width of w foe each sensor f at time t

Ensure: $\hat{s}_{f,t}$: Trust score estimation for imputed values

```
1: for For t = n, n+1, .... do
2:     for each sensor f ∈ F do
3:         sc_{f,t} ← ((1/w) Σ_{i=t-w}^{t-1} s_{f,i}) * (1 − RatioMV_{f,t})
4:     end for
5:     for each sensor f ∈ F do
6:         if d_{f,t} is a non missing value then
7:             r_{f,t} ← d̂_{f,t} − d_{f,t}
8:             s_{f,t} = (see equation below)
9:         else
10:            ℜ_{f,t} ← {sc_{f',t} | f' ∈ K_f} ∪ {sc_{f,t}}
11:            ŝ_{f,t} ← G(ℜ_{f,t})
12:            s_{f,t} ← ŝ_{f,t}
13:        end if
14:    end for
15: end for
```

$$s_{f,t} = \begin{cases} \frac{2}{\sigma\sqrt{2\pi}} \int_{-\infty}^{r_{f,t}} EXP\left(-\frac{(x-\mu)^2}{2\sigma^2}\right) \mathrm{d}x, \text{si } r_{f,t} < \mu \\ \frac{2}{\sigma\sqrt{2\pi}} \int_{r_{f,t}}^{+\infty} EXP\left(-\frac{(x-\mu)^2}{2\sigma^2}\right) \mathrm{d}x, \text{si } r_{f,t} \geq \mu \end{cases}$$

4 Experiments

We present here the experiments that have been conducted on two real-world datasets in order to assess the accuracy of CSIV and trustworthiness of imputed data. Also, it is worthy to note that the experiments have been conducted using a MAC mini 2014, Core i5 chip, 8GB RAM, with Python 3.7.

4.1 Description of the Datasets

Our experiments are performed on two datasets: CityPulse[1] and Appliances energy prediction Data Set from UCI Machine Learning Repository [2].

[1] http://www.ict-citypulse.eu/.
[2] https://archive.ics.uci.edu/ml/datasets/Appliances+energy+prediction.

- CityPulse dataset covers seven different domains: Road Traffic, Parking, Pollution, Weather, Cultural, Social and Library Events Data of Aarhus, Denmark and Brasov, Romania for years 2014 and 2015. Among all these parts, Road Traffic Data is of greatest importance and represents data about travel information of Aarhus (Danmark) during the following periods: "2/2014–6/2014", "8/2014–9/2014", "10/2014–11/2014", "07/2015–10/2015". There is a total of 449 monitors (assuming that one sensor was installed in one area). The volume of the data in format CSV is 747.2 MB. Traffic Data is collected by many sensors installed on the road. Every 5 min, each sensor will send a bunch of information (one line of table Traffic Data) to a central computer center. Every 5 min, the center receives 29,940 Bytes (0.029 MB). All the sensors located within 1 km are considered as neighbors. There are on average 21 neighbors per sensor. The minimum value is 5 and the maximum value is 68.
- AEP data consists of the following attributes: energy assumption, humidity and temperature. Data is averaged for 10 min period and gathered during 4.5 months (from 11/01/2016 to 05/27/2016) resulting in a total 12 MB CSV file with 19735 instances. One humidity sensor and one temperature sensor are installed in each room and outside the building (18 sensors in total and all of them are regarded as neighbors).

Real Missing Value: For CityPulse data, the total missing value rate is close to 9%. The dataset AEP does not have missing values.

Simulated Missing Value (SMV): We simulate some values randomly (Missing completely at random or MCAR) for datasets: we randomly select a percentage of data (5%, 10%, 15%, 20%, 25%, 30%) according to the discrete uniform distribution and mark them as Simulated Missing Values (SMV). Thanks to SMV and its ground truth, we can measure the effectiveness of the reparation. The percentage rate of simulated missing values is borrowed from work [13] where the percentage of missing value or simulated missing value vary from 5% to 30%. There are both real missing values and simulated missing value in our test data.

Figure 2 shows CityPulse data distribution (SMV in red and original one in blue) for 10 sensors over a period of 5 h.

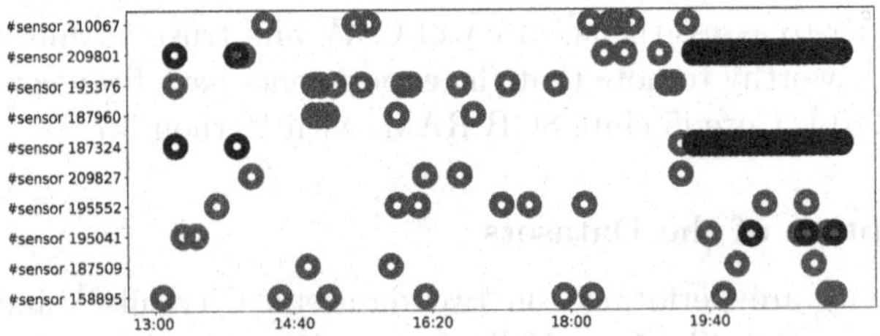

Fig. 2. 5% of SMV (red circle) and real missing value (blue circle) in CityPluse (Color figure online)

Figure 3 shows the distribution of the error of non missing values in AEP and CityPulse. We note that the residual does not follow a Gaussian Distribution. After Kolmogorov-Smirnov test (KS test), all the PValue are higher than 0.05.

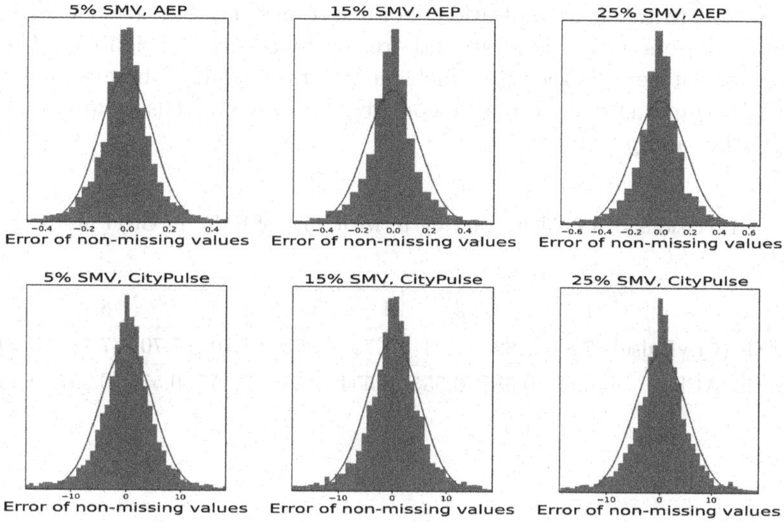

Fig. 3. Error distribution of the estimation of non-missing values, ISTM

4.2 Evaluation Metrics

For evaluation purposes, we used *Accuracy* and *trustworthiness* metrics:

- Prediction **Accuracy** is evaluated in terms of the root mean squared error (RMSE) of all variables (Eq. 4).

$$RMSE = \sqrt{\frac{1}{|SMV|} \sum_{d_{f',t'} \in SMV} \left(\hat{d}_{f',t'} - d_{f',t'}\right)^2} \quad (4)$$

- Trust **Assessment:** To measure trustworthiness in a predicted value, we use Confidence Score as defined in Eq. 5.

$$RMSE_{trust} = \sqrt{\frac{1}{|SMV|} \sum_{d_{f',t'} \in SMV} (\hat{s}_{f',t'} - s_{f',t'})^2} \quad (5)$$

4.3 Configurations

In order to evaluate the trustworthiness of predicted values, we use ISTM [11] model which is an Incremental Spatio-Temporal regression method for repairing missing values in IoT data streams. The configuration of ISTM is as follows: 30% of instances are taken for initiation. For CityPulse dataset, given one sensor, neighbors' sensors within 1 km around are considered as its neighbors. The size of reference dataset g is set to 6 which represents the value where the precision of ISTM becomes stable (Table 2). For AEP dataset, all sensors are neighbors to each other and $g = 4$.

Table 2. Precisions of ISTM by varying g, with 25% of SMV in CityPulse and AEP datasets

g	1	2	3	4	5	6	7	8	9
RMSE (CityPulse)	7.84	7.82	7.74	7.72	7.73	7.70	7.70	7.71	7.70
RMSE (AEP)	0.62	0.558	0.555	0.554	0.556	0.557	0.556	0.557	0.556

4.4 Results

In this section, we highlight the obtained results along the line of two metrics: accuracy and trustworthiness.

Table 3. RMSE with different sliding window length (w), AEP

MV (%)	5	10	15	20	25	5	10	15	20	25
	$CSIV_{min}$	$CSIV_{min}$	$CSIV_{min}$	$CSIV_{min}$	$CSIV_{min}$	$CSIV_{avg}$	$CSIV_{avg}$	$CSIV_{avg}$	$CSIV_{avg}$	$CSIV_{avg}$
w =5	0.28	0.32	0.37	0.4	0.45	0.09	0.09	0.09	0.11	0.12
w =10	0.22	0.25	0.29	0.32	0.37	0.08	0.09	0.09	0.11	0.12
w =30	0.16	0.18	0.21	0.24	0.27	0.09	0.09	0.1	0.11	0.13
w =60	0.15	0.16	0.18	0.21	0.23	0.09	0.09	0.1	0.12	0.13
w =90	0.14	0.15	0.17	0.2	0.22	0.09	0.09	0.1	0.12	0.13
w =120	0.13	0.15	0.17	0.19	0.22	0.09	0.1	0.1	0.12	0.14
w =150	0.13	0.15	0.17	0.19	0.21	0.1	0.1	0.11	0.12	0.14
w =180	0.13	0.15	0.16	0.18	0.21	0.1	0.1	0.11	0.12	0.14
w =200	0.13	0.15	0.17	0.19	0.21	0.1	0.1	0.11	0.13	0.14
w optimal	120	90	180	180	150	10	10	10	10	10
RMSE optimal	0.13	0.15	0.16	0.18	0.21	0.08	0.09	0.09	0.11	0.12

Sliding Window Analysis: We evaluated the accuracy of $CSIV_{avg}$ and $CSIV_{min}$ by varying sliding window size. The results (Tables 3 and 4) show that: 1) For $CSIV_{avg}$, the best length value of window is 10 and RMSE tends to increase when the length of window increases, and 2) For $CSIV_{min}$, the optimum value of sliding window is between 90 and 180 and RMSE varies slightly when the length of window increases.

Table 4. RMSE with different sliding window length (w), CityPulse

MV (%)	5	10	15	20	25	5	10	15	20	25
	$CSIV_{min}$	$CSIV_{min}$	$CSIV_{min}$	$CSIV_{min}$	$CSIV_{min}$	$CSIV_{avg}$	$CSIV_{avg}$	$CSIV_{avg}$	$CSIV_{avg}$	$CSIV_{avg}$
w =5	0.3	0.34	0.38	0.42	0.45	0.09	0.1	0.11	0.12	0.14
w =10	0.25	0.28	0.31	0.35	0.38	0.09	0.1	0.11	0.12	0.14
w =30	0.21	0.23	0.26	0.28	0.31	0.1	0.1	0.12	0.13	0.15
w =60	0.2	0.22	0.24	0.26	0.29	0.1	0.11	0.12	0.13	0.15
w =90	0.19	0.21	0.23	0.25	0.28	0.1	0.11	0.12	0.14	0.16
w =120	0.18	0.2	0.22	0.24	0.27	0.1	0.11	0.12	0.14	0.16
w =150	0.17	0.19	0.2	0.24	0.26	0.1	0.11	0.12	0.14	0.16
w =180	0.17	0.19	0.21	0.23	0.26	0.1	0.11	0.12	0.14	0.16
w =200	0.17	0.19	0.2	0.23	0.26	0.1	0.11	0.12	0.14	0.16
w optimal	150	150	150	180	150	10	15	10	10	10
RMSE optimal	0.17	0.19	0.2	0.23	0.26	0.09	0.1	0.11	0.12	0.14

Impact of SMV: We analyzed the impact of SMV on the accuracy of trust scores. Figure 4(a) and Fig. 4(b) show that the RMSE of $CSIV_{min}$ and $CSIV_{avg}$ is higher when the proportion of SMV increases. In addition, we note that the accuracy of $CSIV_{avg}$ is better than $CSIV_{min}$ for both dataset. Indeed, the lower the RMSE value of $CSIV_{avg}/CSIV_{min}$, the more accurately their trust scores are estimated. Moreover, $CSIV_{min}$ underestimates trust score in comparison to $CSIV_{avg}$.

Trust Score of Sensors: Trust score of a sensor relies on the trustworthiness of his neighbors and the accuracy of the non missing values. Figure 5 illustrates the trust score of a sensor 158895 and its neighbors over a two days period. We can note that the trust score of sensors is positively correlated to the accuracy of predicted values and ISTM is able to ensure continuous accurate in the streaming data because it is updated incrementally. Moreover, when the proportion of missing values increases (this is the case of CityPulse data which have original missing data), the trust score of the sensor is close to 0.

Trustworthiness Evaluation: We assess trustworthiness (according to Eq. 5) of $CSIV_{avg}$ and $CSIV_{min}$. Figure 6(a) and Fig. 6(b) show that the scores of $CSIV_{avg}$ (red curve), when the ratio of missing values is equal to 15%, are closer to the expected values (black curve) than $CSIV_{min}$ (green curve). This can be explained by the fact that $CSIV_{avg}$ combines trust scores of several sensors. Then, according to $CSIV_{avg}$, CSIV is able to assign correctly a trust score to the imputed values.

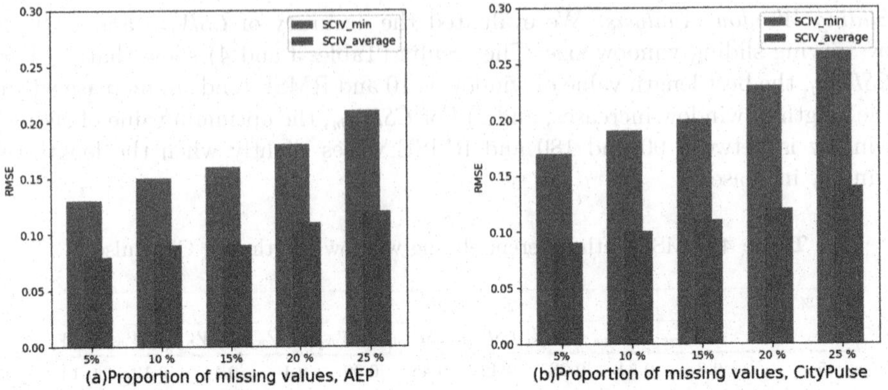

Fig. 4. RMSE of confidence score with varying proportions of missing data (sliding window lengths are optimized), ISTM.

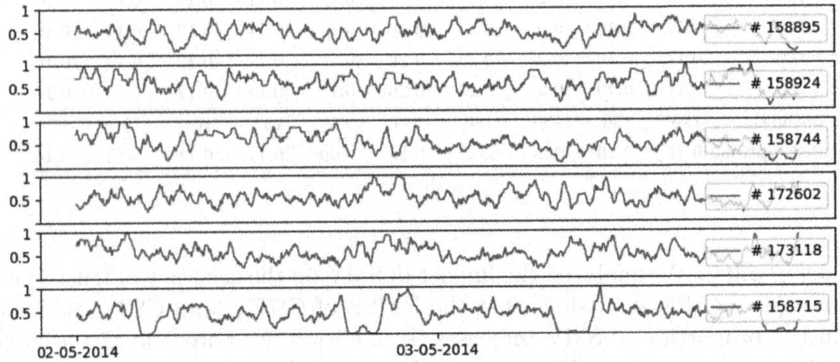

Fig. 5. Trust score of sensor 158895 and his neighbors over a two day period, CityPulse, 15% SMV, w = 10, ISTM.

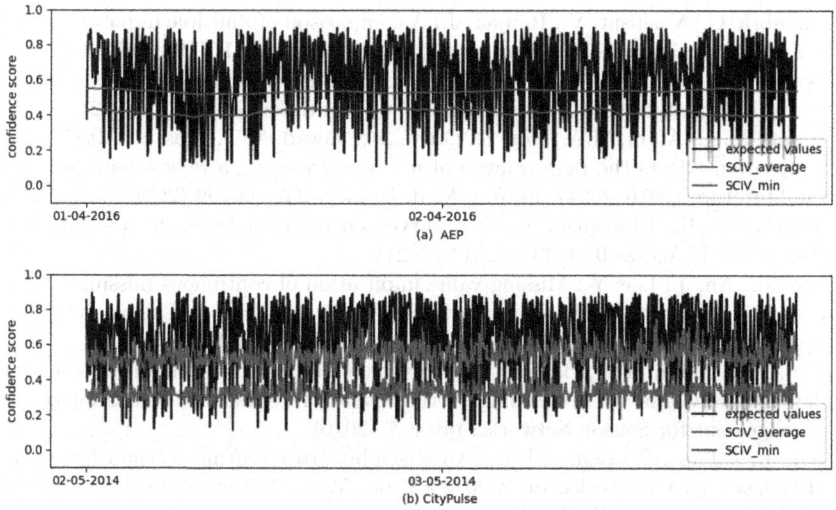

Fig. 6. Trust score of imputed values (15% SMV) of G_{min} and G_{avg} over a two day period, ISTM (Color figure online)

5 Conclusion and Future Work

In this paper, we described CSIV, a method that assigns a Confidence Score to Imputed Values.

For validation purposes, we conducted several experiments with imputation model on real datasets using *accuracy* and *trustworthiness* as evaluation metrics.

For the future, we intend to optimize the confidence score by taking into account only sensors which produce small proportion of missing data in order to avoid the risk of underestimation. Moreover, we aim to apply our method on other imputation methods such as deep learning models in order to be able to explain the imputation of missing values within a dataset [16].

References

1. Adams, S., Beling, P.A., Greenspan, S., Velez-Rojas, M., Mankovski, S.: Model-based trust assessment for internet of things networks. In: 2018 17th IEEE International Conference On Trust, Security And Privacy In Computing And Communications/12th IEEE International Conference On Big Data Science And Engineering (TrustCom/BigDataSE), pp. 1838–1843. IEEE (2018)
2. Barddal, J.P.: Vertical and horizontal partitioning in data stream regression ensembles. In: 2019 International Joint Conference on Neural Networks (IJCNN), pp. 1–8. IEEE (2019)
3. Bertino, E.: Data trustworthiness—approaches and research challenges. In: Garcia-Alfaro, J., Herrera-Joancomartí, J., Lupu, E., Posegga, J., Aldini, A., Martinelli, F., Suri, N. (eds.) DPM/QASA/SETOP -2014. LNCS, vol. 8872, pp. 17–25. Springer, Cham (2015). https://doi.org/10.1007/978-3-319-17016-9_2

4. Chhabra, G., Vashisht, V., Ranjan, J.: A comparison of multiple imputation methods for data with missing values. Indian J. Sci. Technol. **10**(19), 1–7 (2017)
5. Dong, W., Gao, S., Yang, X., Yu, H.: An exploration of online missing value imputation in non-stationary data stream. SN Comput. Sci. **2**(2), 1–11 (2021)
6. Hasan, M.K., Alam, M.A., Roy, S., Dutta, A., Jawad, M.T., Das, S.: Missing value imputation affects the performance of machine learning: a review and analysis of the literature (2010–2021). Inform. Med. Unlock. **27**, 100799 (2021)
7. Junior, F.M.R., Kamienski, C.A.: A survey on trustworthiness for the internet of things. IEEE Access **9**, 42493–42514 (2021)
8. Lee, M., An, J., Lee, Y.: Missing-value imputation of continuous missing based on deep imputation network using correlations among multiple IoT data streams in a smart space. IEICE Trans. Inf. Syst. **102**(2), 289–298 (2019)
9. Lim, H.S., Moon, Y.S., Bertino, E.: Provenance-based trustworthiness assessment in sensor networks. In: Proceedings of the Seventh International Workshop on Data Management for Sensor Networks, pp. 2–7 (2010)
10. Liu, J., Adams, S., Beling, P.A.: An ensemble trust scoring method for internet of things sensor networks. In: 2020 IEEE 6th World Forum on Internet of Things (WF-IoT), pp. 1–6. IEEE (2020)
11. Peng, T., Sellami, S., Boucelma, O.: IoT data imputation with incremental multiple linear regression. Open J. Internet Things **5**(1), 69–79 (2019)
12. Peng, T., Sellami, S., Boucelma, O.: Trust assessment on streaming data: a real time predictive approach. In: Lemaire, V., Malinowski, S., Bagnall, A., Guyet, T., Tavenard, R., Ifrim, G. (eds.) AALTD 2020. LNCS (LNAI), vol. 12588, pp. 204–219. Springer, Cham (2020). https://doi.org/10.1007/978-3-030-65742-0_14
13. Puiu, D., et al.: CityPulse: large scale data analytics framework for smart cities. IEEE Access **4**, 1086–1108 (2016)
14. Ramirez-Gallego, S., Krawczyk, B., Garcia, S., Wozniak, M., Herrera, F.: A survey on data preprocessing for data stream mining: current status and future directions. Neurocomputing **239**, 39–57 (2017)
15. Somasundaram, R., Nedunchezhian, R.: Evaluation of three simple imputation methods for enhancing preprocessing of data with missing values. Int. J. Comput. Appl. **21**(10), 14–19 (2011)
16. Vu, M.A., et al.: Conditional expectation for missing data imputation. CoRR abs/2302.00911 (2023)

Optimizing Merkle Tree Structure for Blockchain Transactions by a DC Programming Approach

Thi Tuyet Trinh Nguyen[1](✉), Hoai An Le Thi[1,2], and Xuan Vinh Doan[3]

[1] Département IA, LGIPM, Université de Lorraine, 57000 Metz, France
{thi-tuyet-trinh.nguyen,hoai-an.le-thi}@univ-lorraine.fr
[2] Institut Universitaire de France (IUF), Paris, France
[3] Warwick Business School, University of Warwick, Coventry CV4 7AL, UK
Xuan.Doan@wbs.ac.uk

Abstract. Merkle tree is a fundamental part of blockchain technology, especially in Ethereum cryptocurrency system. The balance of the accounts involved in each transaction is stored on the leaf nodes and must be updated in the State Merkle tree. In this paper, we take advantage of typical transaction characteristics for better constructing the Merkle tree to improve blockchain network performance. It consists of identifying a tree structure with the minimum number of hash values required to update the account data associated with each transaction based on the distribution of all transactions. The proposed optimization model is a combinatorial problem with quadratic functions and binary variables. By using the binary character of variables and penalty techniques, we provide a conventional DC (Difference of Convex functions) program that is efficiently solvable by the DCA (DC Algorithm). Additionally, we suggest an effective recursive DCA-based method for building a Merkle tree for a great amount of blockchain accounts. Numerical experiments on several datasets illustrate the efficiency of our approaches.

Keywords: Merkle tree · blockchain transactions · DC Programming · DCA · binary quadratic programming

1 Introduction

In recent years, blockchain technology has attracted considerable interest as a decentralized, secure ledger with no central authority. It first gained popularity as the technology behind Bitcoin [10], an innovative cryptocurrency, and has subsequently been expanded to include electronic voting, supply chain communications, and medical informatics [1,3,4]. It is impossible to change a block without also modifying all subsequent blocks, as each block after the original (genesis) block carries the result of a cryptographic hash function computed on the content of the previous block.

N. T. Nguyen et al. (Eds.): ICCCI 2023, LNAI 14162, pp. 405–417, 2023.
https://doi.org/10.1007/978-3-031-41456-5_31

The Merkle tree is a well-known tool in cryptography, first suggested by Ralph Merkle [7], which enables efficiently verifying the validation of a data element in a set without revealing the entire set. In a Merkle tree, every node has a hash value. For the leaves, this label is the hash of a data item, and for every non-leaf node, this label is the hash of the concatenation of the labels of its children. The hash value ensures the integrity and immutability of the transaction which is used as the input of hash function. In order to verify that some data is included in a Merkle tree, each node needs to obtain a label R for the root of the tree, called the Merkle root, from a trusted source. A Merkle proof for the containment of some data x, which corresponds to a leaf in the tree, consists of the sibling path of the leaf and includes the labels for the siblings of the nodes in a path from the leaf to the root.

Merkle trees are critical components of blockchain technology, as they enable the secure verification of transactions. The State Merkle tree in Ethereum, the second-largest blockchain network, contains the current balance and other relevant data for each account. Each block in the chain is associated with the Merkle root computed for the network state following the execution of the block transactions. The block approval process includes verifying the validity of transactions and their impact on the state. For instance, a payment requires a minimum value of the payer's balance, and when successful, it implies a change in the balance of the two involved accounts. Indeed, the data from two accounts and the corresponding nodes on the Merkle tree needs to be recalculated.

In actuality, the distribution of accounts involved in transactions is not uniform. The majority of accounts transfer value to a small number of other accounts, while a minority of accounts are linked to several others. Similarly, when a transaction is seen as a collection of accessible addresses, a small number of unique transactions account for a significant share of the transactions. The transaction frequency is characterized by a few transactions being repeated several times, whereas the majority of transactions occur just once. Furthermore, as frequently used accounts move closer to the root of the State tree due to overlapping paths, fewer tree nodes must be read and updated.

Different heuristic-based approaches can be used to build Merkle hash tree for a specific transaction distribution that were proposed in [8,9,16]. The algorithms differ in several aspects, including (i) the codeword lengths they generate (fixed or variable length), and (ii) the data they rely on, such as the complete distribution of transactions or only the distribution of accounts. The first random algorithm allocates for all n accounts fixed-length codewords of the minimal possible length of $\lceil \log_2(n) \rceil$ bits [16]. Therefore, every account is presented at the same tree height. The second approach, which is based on the Huffman-Merkle Hash Tree (HuffMHT), considers the account distribution inferred by the transaction distribution input [9]. Based on the probability of each account, the method assigns variable-length codewords as Huffman codes. In [8], the authors proposed the design of codes for account's information organized as Merkle trees in blockchain networks to reduce the number of the required hash values used in proofs for data membership. They attempt to modify the Huffman algorithm to consider the distribution of transactions rather than just accounts. However, they have not constructed a mathematical optimization model for this transaction encoding problem. Additionally, their algorithms are primarily based on logical/heuristic arguments.

Our Contributions. In this work, we propose an optimization model for constructing the Merkle tree based on the transaction distribution in Ethereum system. The objective is to minimize the number of changed hash values in the Merkle tree required for updating the information of accounts involved in each transaction. To our knowledge, this is the first work introducing an optimization model that constructs the Merkle tree based on the transaction distribution. The proposed optimization model is a combinatorial problem with quadratic objective function and binary variables. Consequently, it is very challenging to handle such kinds of programs by standard methods where the source of difficulty comes from the nonconvexity of the objective and the binary nature of the solutions. By using the binary character of variables and exact penalty techniques [14], the problem can be reformulated as a DC program, where the DCA is at our disposal as an efficient algorithm in DC programming. For a large number of accounts, the DCA is unable to solve the problem because the dimension of the optimal variable increases exponentially with the number of accounts. Moreover, we propose a recursive DCA-based approach for solving the problem of building a Merkle tree for blockchain transactions in cases where the number of accounts is significant.

The rest of the paper is organized as follows. Section 2 gives an overall description of the Merkle tree in Ethereum. The optimization model for the problem of constructing the Merkle tree in Ethereum system is developed in Sect. 3, while Sect. 4 presents the solution method based on DC programming and DCA. The implementation of the algorithm for solving the problem and numerical experiments are presented in Sect. 5. Finally, some conclusions are provided in Sect. 6.

2 Merkle Tree in Ethereum System

A Merkle tree is illustrated in Fig. 1. It is computed for eight data items $x_0 - x_7$ (shown as leaf nodes). Internal nodes are associated with hash values computed hierarchically including the Merkle root R. The amount of data needed to update an item, which corresponds to a leaf in the tree, is the number of hash values for the sibling nodes in a path from this assigned leaf node to the root. This can show that the known Merkle root R is computed from a set of data elements with x among them without disclosing the Merkle tree's whole values. To demonstrate the presence of x_2, it is sufficient to give simply three values (shown in red in the figure): (i) h_3 (ii) $h_{0-1} = H(h_0\|h_1)$ (iii) $h_{4-7} = H(H(h_4\|h_5)\|H(h_6\|h_7))$, where for $i \in [0,7]$, h_i denotes the hash H values of x_i, $X\|Y$ denotes result of concatenating data items X and Y in that order. With these three values and x_2, the root value R can be computed as $R = H(H(h_{0-1}\|H(H(x_2)\|h_3))\|h_{4-7})$.

In Ethereum system, the State Merkle tree is a key-value map in which the account addresses are the keys and values include the balance and potentially

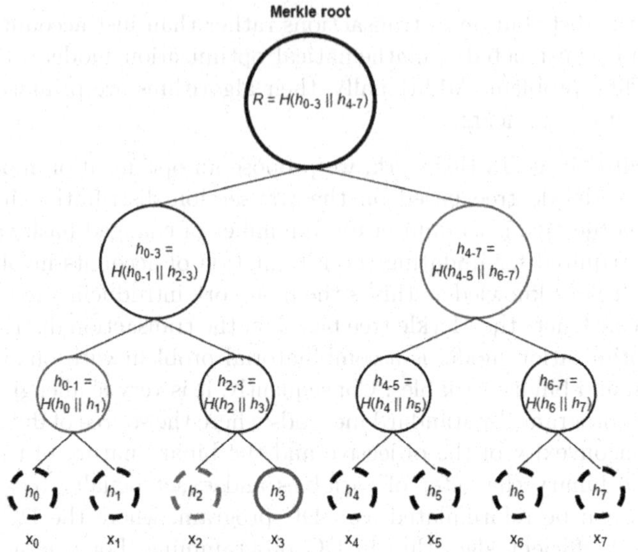

Fig. 1. Illustration of a Merkle tree of 8 items. Merkle proof of item x_2 (with a dashed blue leaf) includes nodes h_3, h_{0-1}, and h_{4-7} (in solid red) [8].

code or storage assigned for the account. Additionally, when the state of a transaction is modified as a consequence of its execution, all nodes on the paths from the modified accounts to the root are adjusted. When frequently used accounts move closer in the state tree due to their overlapping paths to the root, fewer tree portions must be read and updated. For example, account x_1 transfers 0.01 Ethereum (ETH) to account x_2. The data of two accounts, especially the balance assigned to two leaf nodes on the Merkle tree has to be updated. The siblings paths for x_1 (with h_0, h_{2-3}, and h_{4-7}) and x_2 (with h_3, h_{0-1}, and h_{4-7}) share the node h_{4-7} in the example from Fig. 1. As a result, just $2 * 3 - 1 = 5$ values on the tree are required to update the Merkle tree. The position of the nodes in the tree has an impact on possible savings. Because the nodes along their paths do not overlap, there are no savings when the data of x_2 and x_5 are modified.

3 Optimization Model for the Problem of Constructing Merkle Tree in Blockchain Based System

3.1 Problem Definition

According to research, the distribution of accounts engaging in transactions is not consistent, and its bias can be expressed in two major properties. In fact, the majority of accounts only transfer value to a small number of other accounts, whereas a small number of accounts are linked to a large number of others. As seen with Ethereum [2], these highly connected nodes, which are frequently exchanges or mining pool accounts, are significantly influencing the structure of the network. Similarly, if a transaction is defined as its collection of accessible addresses, a small number of unique transactions account for a substantial fraction of transactions. A subsequent research [15] found comparable findings for other blockchain networks. The duration of the measurement interval influences both distributions. Therefore, we take use of common transaction features to better organize Merkle trees and propose an optimization approach to solve this problem. Assume that a transaction has two distinct accounts, as in the common case of payment transactions. We investigate an optimization model for constructing Merkle trees associated with the transaction distribution. The objective is to minimize the number of hash values required for account information modification in each transaction.

3.2 The Optimization Model

Based on the above problem description, we propose an optimization model in this subsection. Given $A = \{1, 2, ..., n\}$ is the set of accounts and (TX, D) is the transaction distribution included the frequency of a transaction between two accounts. A full binary tree can be represented as an ordered set $\mathbb{T} = \{2^l + m$: there exists a node at the m-th horizontal position of level l on the tree, $0 \leq l \leq h, 0 \leq m \leq 2^l - 1, l, m \in \mathbb{N}\}$, where h is the height of tree, $T = |\mathbb{T}|$.

Let z_{it} be binary variables defined by $z_{it} = 1$ if an account $i \in A$ is added into node t of the Merkle tree, $z_{it} = 0$ otherwise, $\forall i = \overline{1,n}, t = \overline{1,T}, T = 2^n - 1$. Since every account is appended at only one node of the tree, $\sum_{t=1}^{T} z_{it} = 1, \forall i = \overline{1,n}$. The Merkle tree is a full binary tree in which every node has 0 or 2 children. If $z_{it} = 1$ then $z_{jt'} = 0, i = \overline{1,n}, j = \overline{1,n}$, for all t' belongs to the path from the node t to the root (index of the root is 1). Let $P(t)$, which is defined by Algorithm 1, be the set of all nodes on the path from the node t to the root.

Algorithm 1. Algorithm of finding all nodes on the path from the node t to the root

```
Initialization: P(t) = [], t ∈ T.
while t > 1 do
    t' = [t/2].
    P(t).append(t').
    t = t'.
end while
```

The computability of a node in the tree is defined as follows: A node t is computable if and only if there exists a node t in the Merkle tree or both children of node t is computable. We define a binary variable c_t by $c_t = 1$ if there is a node t in the tree, $c_t = 0$ otherwise. Therefore, the following constraints ensure the computability of a node in the tree $\sum_{i=1}^{n} z_{it} \leq c_t, t = \overline{1,T}, (c_{2t} + c_{2t+1}) - 1 \leq c_t, t = \overline{1,T}, c_t \leq \sum_{i=1}^{n} z_{it} + \frac{1}{2}(c_{2t} + c_{2t+1}), t = \overline{1,T}$.

On the other hand, there exists node t on the tree, so the sibling node of t is also one node of this tree because the Merkle tree is a full binary tree. If $z_{it} = 1$

then $c_{s(t)} = 1$, where $s(t)$ is denoted as the sibling node of node t. Therefore, we obtain the constraint as $\sum_{i=1}^{n} z_{it} \leq c_{s(t)}$, where $s(t) = t - 1$ if t is odd, $s(t) = t+1$ otherwise. The objective of the problem is to minimize the total cost for the transaction verification between two accounts. If two accounts are added into two leaf nodes in the Merkle tree as $\sum_{i=1}^{n} z_{it} = 1$ and $\sum_{j=1}^{n} z_{js} = 1, \forall t = \overline{1,T}, s = \overline{1,T}$, we can define the cost of validating a transaction between accounts i and j that is assigned to node t and s, respectively, as a value C_{ts}. The total cost for a transaction distribution D over n accounts is defined as $\sum_{t=1}^{T} \sum_{s=1}^{T} C_{ts}\bar{q}_{ts}$, where $\bar{q}_{ts}$ is the frequency of a transaction that involves two accounts i and j that are assigned to node t and s on the tree, $\bar{q}_{ts} = \sum_{i=1}^{n} \sum_{j=1}^{n} q_{ij} z_{it} z_{js}$. Finally, our optimization problem takes the following form:

$$\min \sum_{t=1}^{T} \sum_{s=1}^{T} C_{ts} \sum_{i=1}^{n} \sum_{j=1}^{n} q_{ij} z_{it} z_{js} \tag{1}$$

$$\text{subject to} \sum_{t=1}^{T} z_{it} = 1, \forall i = \overline{1,n}, \tag{2}$$

$$\sum_{i=1}^{n} z_{it} + \sum_{j=1}^{n} z_{jt'} \leq 1, t = \overline{1,T}, t' \in P(t) \tag{3}$$

$$\sum_{i=1}^{n} z_{it} \leq c_t, t = \overline{1,T}, \tag{4}$$

$$(c_{2t} + c_{2t+1}) - 1 \leq c_t, t = \overline{1,T}, \tag{5}$$

$$c_t \leq \sum_{i=1}^{n} z_{it} + \frac{1}{2}(c_{2t} + c_{2t+1}), t = \overline{1,T}, \tag{6}$$

$$\sum_{i=1}^{n} z_{it} \leq c_{s(t)}, t = \overline{1,T}, \tag{7}$$

$$z_{it} \in \{0,1\}, c_t \in \{0,1\}, \forall i = \overline{1,n}, t = \overline{1,T}. \tag{8}$$

It is observed that (1) is an optimization problem with binary variables and quadratic objective. Let

$$K = \{(z,c) : \sum_{t=1}^{T} z_{it} = 1, \sum_{i=1}^{n} z_{it} + \sum_{j=1}^{n} z_{jt'} \leq 1, \sum_{i=1}^{n} z_{it} \leq c_t, (c_{2t} + c_{2t+1}) - 1 \leq c_t,$$
$$c_t \leq \sum_{i=1}^{n} z_{it} + \frac{1}{2}(c_{2t} + c_{2t+1}), \sum_{i=1}^{n} z_{it} \leq c_{s(t)}, z_{it} \in [0,1], c_t \in [0,1], i = \overline{1,n}, t = \overline{1,T},$$
$$t' \in P(t)\}.$$

Problem (1) can be rewritten as follows

$$\min\left\{\sum_{t=1}^{T}\sum_{s=1}^{T} C_{ts}\sum_{i=1}^{n}\sum_{j=1}^{n} q_{ij}z_{it}z_{js} : (z,c) \in K, z \in \{0,1\}^{n\times T}, c \in \{0,1\}^{T}\right\}. \quad (9)$$

4 Solving the Merkle Tree Designing Problem by DCA

DC programming and DCA, which constitute the backbone of nonconvex programming and global optimization, were introduced by Pham Dinh Tao in 1985 and have been extensively developed since 1994 by Le Thi Hoai An and Pham Dinh Tao ([5,6,11–13] and references therein). DCA has been effectively applied to numerous nonconvex/nonsmooth programs due to its flexibility, robustness, and adaptability to the problem's specific structure. In [14], a continuous approach based on the DC programming and DCA was proposed to solve binary quadratic programs and this method is also available to solve the problem (9).

Then (9) can be rewritten as

$$\min\left\{z^T Q z : (z,c) \in K, z \in \{0,1\}^{n\times T}, c \in \{0,1\}^{T}\right\}, \quad (10)$$

where Q is a matrix $((n\times T)\times(n\times T))$. According to [14], the problem (10) and the following problem are equivalent:

$$\min\left\{\rho z^T e - z^T(\rho I - Q)z : (z,c) \in K, z \in \{0,1\}^{n\times T}, c \in \{0,1\}^{T}\right\}, \quad (11)$$

where $e \in \mathbb{R}^{n\times T}$ is the vector of ones, I is the identity matrix of order $n \times T$ and $\rho \geq \lambda(Q)$, the largest eigenvalue of matrix Q.

The concave quadratic function

$$p(z,c) := \sum_{i=1}^{n}\sum_{t=1}^{T} z_{it}(1-z_{it}) + \sum_{t=1}^{T} c_t(1-c_t) = z^T[e-z] + c^T[e-c],$$

can be used as exact penalty function for (11). Then (11) can be rewritten as

$$\min\left\{\rho z^T e - z^T(\rho I - Q)z : (z,c) \in K, p(z,c) \leq 0\right\}. \quad (12)$$

There exists $\bar{\tau}$ such that the problem (12) and the following penalized problem are equivalent for all $\tau \geq \bar{\tau}$:

$$\min\left\{(\rho+\tau)z^T e + \tau c^T e - (z^T(\rho I - Q)z + \tau z^T z + \tau c^T c) : (z,c) \in K\right\}. \quad (13)$$

The following DC formulation of (13) seems to be natural:

$$\min\{f(z,c) = g(z,c) - h(z,c) : (z,c) \in \mathbb{R}^{n\times T} \times \mathbb{R}^{T}\}, \quad (14)$$

where $g(z,c) := (\rho+\tau)z^T e + \tau c^T e + \chi_K(z,c)$, $h(z,c) := z^T(\rho I - Q)z + \tau z^T z + \tau c^T c$, are clearly convex functions.

Applying the general DCA scheme to (14) amounts to computing two sequences $\{(z^l, c^l)\}$ and $\{(y^l, b^l)\}$ in the way that $(y^l, b^l) \in \partial h(z^l, c^l)$. Since $(y^l, b^l) \in \partial h(z^l, c^l)$ is equivalent to

$$y^l = 2(\rho + \tau - Q)z^l, \tag{15}$$

$$b^l = 2\tau c^l, \tag{16}$$

following is a description of the algorithm.

Algorithm 2. DCA for solving the problem (14)

Initialization: Let $(z^0, c^0) \in [0,1]^{n \times T} \times [0,1]^T$ be a guess, set $l := 0, \epsilon > 0, \rho > 0, \tau_l > 0, \theta > 0$.

repeat

Compute $(y^l, b^l) \in \partial h(z^l, c^l)$ via (15) and (16).

Solve the following linear program to obtain (z^{l+1}, c^{l+1})

$$\min \{(\rho + \tau_l) z^T e + \tau_l c^T e - \langle z, y^l \rangle - \langle c, b^l \rangle : (z, c) \in K\}. \tag{17}$$

if $p(z^{l+1}, c^{l+1}) > 0$ **then**

$\tau_{l+1} \leftarrow \tau_l + \theta.$

end if

$l = l + 1.$

until $\|(z,c)^{l+1} - (z,c)^l\| \leq \epsilon$

The convergence properties of Algorithm 2 are stated as follows [14].

Theorem 1. *For $\rho \geq \lambda(Q)$, the largest eigenvalue of matrix Q, there hold*

(i) Exists τ^* such that: if $\tau_l > \tau^*$ and (z^l, c^l) is binary, then (z^s, c^s) remains binary for all $s \geq l$.

(ii) If at iteration l, $\tau_l > \tau^*$ and (z^l, c^l) is binary, then the algorithm 2 has a finite convergence: the sequence $\{(z^s, c^s)\}$ has a subsequence that converges to a DC critical point of $f = g - h$ after a finite number of iterations.

It is noted that $T = 2^n - 1$ is exponential large with the number of accounts n. In fact, for a period of 1 h, the number of active accounts ranges between 5160 − 31182 with an average of 18270 [8]. Consequently, it makes the dimensions of optimization variables too enormous which is not available to be solved by Algorithm 2. Therefore, we propose a recursive DCA-based approach for solving the problem of designing Merkle tree structures for blockchain transactions with a large number of accounts.

The primary objective of this strategy (illustrated in Fig. 2) is to divide the huge number of accounts into a subgroup of m members (m should be small, for instance $m = 6, 7, 8, 9, 10$). Then, we apply DCA scheme to construct the Merkle tree for each subgroup based on the specific transaction distribution. Gather m subtrees sequentially into a set and calculate the correlation coefficients of transaction frequency between the accounts in each bunch of m subtrees. The correlation coefficient is defined as $\sum_{tx=\{a_i,a_j\}\in TX} q_{ij}$ where q_{ij} is the frequency of a transaction between each pair of accounts a_i and a_j in two subtrees. Then it is continued to apply the DCA scheme to build a Merkle tree for the above set of m Merkle trees (the root value represents each group). The above process repeats until the Merkle tree is built for all n accounts. The number of iterations to construct a Merkle tree for a group of n accounts is $\lceil log_m(n)\rceil$. Note that the construction of Merkle trees for subgroups can be done in parallel. The size of matrix Q in the Algorithm 2 is $(m\times T)\times(m\times T)=(m\times 2^m)\times(m\times 2^m)$, where m is the size of subgroup. The detailed algorithm is described in Algorithm 3.

Algorithm 3. An optimization approach for solving the problem of constructing Merkle tree for blockchain transactions

Input: Transaction distribution (TX, D); Accounts $A=\{1,2,...,n\}$. The size of subgroup m.
Output: Merkle tree for n accounts.
Divide n accounts into each subgroup including m members (the last subgroup can have a smaller number of members than m).
Apply DCA scheme (Algorithm 2) to construct the Merkle tree for each $\lceil \frac{n}{m}\rceil$ subgroup based on (TX, D).
loop = 1.
repeat
  Gather m subtrees sequentially into a set and calculate the correlation coefficients of transaction frequency between the accounts in each $\lceil \frac{n}{m^{loop+1}}\rceil$ set of m subtrees.
  Apply DCA scheme (Algorithm 2) to build a Merkle tree for the above set of m subtrees.
  loop = loop +1.
until loop $\leq \lceil log_m(n)\rceil$
return Merkle tree for n accounts.

5 Numerical Experiments

5.1 Experiment Setting

We used Ethereum transaction data from August 28, 2022 00:00:00 to August 29, 2022 00:00:00. We refer to lengths of 1 min, 5 min, 10 min, 20 min, 30 min, 6 h, 12 h, and 1 day to collect the transactions. We implement Algorithm 3 to construct Merkle tree for Ethereum transactions involved a large number of accounts.

The optimization approach was implemented in the Matlab R2019b, other algorithms were implemented in the Python 3.8, and performed on a PC Intel Xeon Gold 5118 CPU with two processors (2.30 GHz and 2.29 GHz) of 128 GB RAM. CPLEX 12.9 was used for solving linear programs. We stop the DCA scheme with the tolerance $\epsilon = 10^{-5}$. Concerning the parameter τ, as τ_0 is hard to compute, we take a quite large value τ_0 at the beginning and use an adaptive procedure for updating τ during our scheme. In practice, it is difficult to

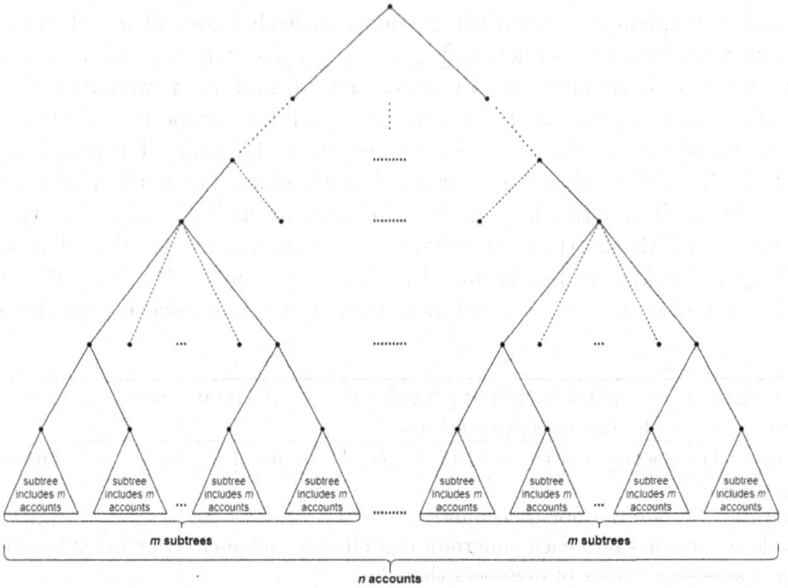

Fig. 2. Construct Merkle tree for blockchain transactions using Algorithm 3.

determine the efficient size of the subgroup because it depends on the specific datasets. For these experimental datasets, a good choice could be $m = 7$.

5.2 Comparative Algorithms

We will compare our optimization approach with some heuristic-based schemes that were proposed in [8,9,16]. In [16], accounts are sorted randomly in the Merkle tree, for instance based on the order of their associated addresses. Therefore, every account is presented at the same tree height. The first approach assigns fixed-length codewords of the shortest possible length of $\lceil \log_2(n) \rceil$ bits to each of n accounts. This method arbitrarily assigns codewords to accounts.

The second method, based on the Huffman-Merkle Hash Tree (HuffMHT), takes into consideration the account distribution deduced from the input transaction distribution [9]. The approach assigns variable-length codewords as Huffman codes based on the probability of each account. Shorter codewords are given to accounts that take part in more transactions in order to minimize the average codeword length based on account distribution.

In [8], the authors proposed the design of codes for data organized as Merkle trees in blockchain networks to reduce the number of the required hash values used in proofs for data membership. They tend to assign long common prefixes to pairs of accounts with frequent joint transactions, in addition to assigning short codewords to common accounts. The authors determined the upper bounds for the optimal communication cost $OPT(D)$ for a given distribution D. The optimal communication cost for a transaction distribution D defined over n accounts satisfies $OPT(D) \leq 2 \times \lceil \log_2(n) \rceil$.

5.3 Comparative Results

We compare the performance of our optimization approach DCA_Merkle_tree (Algorithm 3) with the existing algorithms (Random_tree [16], Huffman_tree [9], Pairs-first Huffman_tree [8]) in terms of the following two criteria: the communication cost (bits) and the running time (seconds). The number of variables and constraints in Algorithm 3 are defined as $\frac{m}{m-1}(m^{\lceil \log_m n \rceil} - 1)(m+1)(2^m - 1)$ and $\frac{m}{m-1}(m^{\lceil \log_m n \rceil} - 1)(3 \times (2^m - 1) + m)$ respectively, where n is the number of accounts and m is the chosen size of the subgroup (Table 1).

Table 1. Comparative results in different numbers of accounts and numbers of transactions (no of trans, in short).

No of accounts	No of trans	No of variables	No of constraints	Algorithm	Cost (bits)	Running time (s)
1305	1002	2,844,800	1,086,400	DCA_Merkle_tree	**18.14**	9.2
				Random_tree	19.60	**0.2**
				Huffman_tree	20.75	0.7
				Pairs-first Huffman_tree	19.47	1.7
5998	5245	19,920,712	7,607,516	DCA_Merkle_tree	**22.02**	37.4
				Random_tree	23.76	**1.3**
				Huffman_tree	23.31	14.6
				Pairs-first Huffman_tree	23.22	40.9
73106	74656	139,452,096	53,255,328	DCA_Merkle_tree	**26.15**	498.4
				Random_tree	28.68	**76.9**
				Huffman_tree	27.73	1080.9
				Pairs-first Huffman_tree	26.64	4650.2
78750	77654	139,452,096	53,255,328	DCA_Merkle_tree	**25.24**	487.3
				Random_tree	29.19	**84.7**
				Huffman_tree	27.88	1127.1
				Pairs-first Huffman_tree	26.98	5164.2
81371	80653	139,452,096	53,255,328	DCA_Merkle_tree	**25.86**	583.9
				Random_tree	28.97	**91.7**
				Huffman_tree	27.53	1266.3
				Pairs-first Huffman_tree	26.47	4534.6
137546	180435	976,171,784	372,790,012	DCA_Merkle_tree	**28.42**	940.3
				Random_tree	32.40	**299.3**
				Huffman_tree	31.37	5140.7
				Pairs-first Huffman_tree	30.09	20478.2
227977	329067	976,171,784	372,790,012	DCA_Merkle_tree	**29.64**	2024.6
				Random_tree	33.70	**791.6**
				Huffman_tree	32.12	15654.6
				Pairs-first Huffman_tree	30.94	65227.5
445407	662847	976,171,784	372,790,012	DCA_Merkle_tree	**31.33**	3419.8
				Random_tree	35.66	**2921.5**
				Huffman_tree	34.12	34561.3
				Pairs-first Huffman_tree	33.90	151374.9

Comments on numerical results:

- In terms of communication cost, our approach DCA_Merkle_tree results the lowest cost than the existing methods to construct a Merkle tree. In all cases, our method provides a lower average cost than the Random algorithm, Huffman algorithm, and Pairs-first Huffman method by 10.5%, 8.1%, and 5%, respectively.
- In terms of execution time, the Random algorithm is much faster than our technique when the number of accounts is not large $n = 1305, 5998$. For a significant number of users, the ratio of gains in terms of running time between the Random algorithm and our approach is approximately 4 times. Nevertheless, our method is on average 5 and 21 times faster than the Huffman algorithm and Pairs-first Huffman method for medium-sized and large-sized instances, respectively.

Overall, our optimization approach provides a competitive trade-off between communication cost and running time than other algorithms for constructing a Merkle tree based on the transaction distribution of accounts in the Ethereum system.

6 Conclusion

We have proposed an optimization model for constructing the Merkle tree in Ethereum transaction system. In our knowledge, this is the first mathematical model for solving this Merkle tree structure problem based on the transaction distribution. The suggested optimization problem has binary variables and an objective function that is quadratic. It is first equivalently formulated as a concave quadratic program. By using recent results on exact penalty techniques in DC programming, the problem can be reformulated as a DC program. We then applied an efficient DCA for solving this problem. Furthermore, we suggested the more effective DCA-based approach for building a Merkle tree from a large number of blockchain accounts. Our method separates accounts into small subgroups and recursively builds the Merkle tree for all accounts using the DCA scheme. Numerical experiments have been conducted in order to confirm the benefits of our suggested model and the corresponding DCA. In future work, we will investigate the choice of the subgroup size in the recursive DCA-based method and enhance the performance of the DCA scheme.

References

1. Bodkhe, U., et al.: Blockchain for industry 4.0: a comprehensive review. IEEE Access **8**, 79764–79800 (2020)
2. Chen, T., Li, Z., Zhu, Y., Chen, J., Luo, X., Lui, J.C.S., Lin, X., Zhang, X.: Understanding Ethereum via graph analysis. ACM Trans. Internet Technol. (TOIT) **20**(2), 1–32 (2020)

3. Gao, W., Hatcher, W.G., Yu, W.: A survey of blockchain: techniques, applications, and challenges. In: 2018 27th International Conference on Computer Communication and Networks (ICCCN), pp. 1–11. IEEE (2018)
4. Kshetri, N., Voas, J.: Blockchain-enabled E-voting. IEEE Softw. **35**(4), 95–99 (2018)
5. Le Thi, H.A., Pham Dinh, T.: The DC (difference of convex functions) programming and DCA revisited with DC models of real world nonconvex optimization problems. Ann. Oper. Res. **133**(1–4), 23–46 (2005)
6. Le Thi, H.A., Pham Dinh, T.: DC programming and DCA: thirty years of developments. Math Program Spec. Issue: DC Program. - Theory Algorithms Appl. **169**(1), 5–68 (2018)
7. Merkle, R.C.: A digital signature based on a conventional encryption function. In: Pomerance, C. (ed.) CRYPTO 1987. LNCS, vol. 293, pp. 369–378. Springer, Heidelberg (1988). https://doi.org/10.1007/3-540-48184-2_32
8. Mizrahi, A., Koren, N., Rottenstreich, O.: Optimizing Merkle proof size for blockchain transactions. In: 2021 International Conference on COMmunication Systems & NETworkS (COMSNETS), pp. 299–307. IEEE (2021)
9. Muñoz, J.L., Forné, J., Esparza, O., Rey, M.: Efficient certificate revocation system implementation: Huffman Merkle hash tree (HuffMHT). In: Katsikas, S., López, J., Pernul, G. (eds.) TrustBus 2005. LNCS, vol. 3592, pp. 119–127. Springer, Heidelberg (2005). https://doi.org/10.1007/11537878_13
10. Nakamoto, S.: A peer-to-peer electronic cash system (2008). https://bitcoin.org/bitcoin.pdf
11. Pham Dinh, T., Le Thi, H.A.: Convex analysis approach to DC programming: theory, algorithms and applications. Acta Math. Vietnam **22**(1), 289–355 (1997)
12. Pham Dinh, T., Le Thi, H.A.: A DC optimization algorithm for solving the trust-region subproblem. SIAM J. Optim. **8**(2), 476–505 (1998)
13. Pham Dinh, T., Le Thi, H.A.: Recent advances in DC programming and DCA. Trans. Comput. Intell. XIII 1–37 (2014)
14. Pham Dinh, T., Nguyen, C.N., Le Thi, H.A.: An efficient combined DCA and B&B using DC/SDP relaxation for globally solving binary quadratic programs. J. Glob. Optim. **48**(4), 595–632 (2010)
15. Somin, S., Gordon, G., Altshuler, Y.: Social signals in the Ethereum trading network. arXiv preprint arXiv:1805.12097 (2018)
16. Wood, G., et al.: Ethereum: a secure decentralised generalised transaction ledger. Ethereum Proj. Yellow Pap. **151**, 1–32 (2014)

Wearable Tag for Indoor Localization in the Context of Ambient Assisted Living

Mariana Jacob Rodrigues[1,2](✉), Octavian Postolache[1,2](✉), and Francisco Cercas[1,2]

[1] Iscte–Instituto Universitário de Lisboa, Av. das Forças Armadas, 1649-026 Lisbon, Portugal
mariana_jacob@iscte-iul.pt, opostolache@lx.it.pt

[2] Instituto de Telecomunicações, Av. Rovisco Pais, 1, 1049-001 Lisbon, Portugal

Abstract. The ageing population and the increasing demand for personalized and efficient healthcare have led to the implementation of assistive technologies to provide healthcare in home environments. Ambient assisted living (AAL) is an important research area that addresses this need. The accurate localization of individuals within indoor environments and recognition of their daily life activities is a crucial aspect of AAL, where machine learning (ML) algorithms have been widely explored for this purpose. In this paper, we present the development of a wearable sensor node for real-time indoor localization, and the implementation of machine learning algorithms for human activity recognition in the context of AAL. A wearable Tag and four fixed anchors characterized by ultra-wide band technology (UWB) for real-time indoor localization and an inertial measurement unit (IMU) for 3D acceleration acquisition associated with motor activity classification are described and evaluated in this paper. The proposed approach has the potential to improve the provision of personalized interventions and support for elderly or people with chronic diseases using smart sensors and technologies that follow an Internet of Things (IoT) architecture.

Keywords: Ambient Assisted Living (AAL) · Machine Learning (ML) · Indoor Localization · Ultra-Wide Band (UWB) · Internet of Things (IoT) · Activity Recognition

1 Introduction

In this ageing world, it has become increasingly necessary to implement assistive technologies to provide health care for the population in their home environment. In this context, ambient assisted living is an important research area that has been growing to respond to the growth of an increasingly elderly population and the demand for personalised and efficient healthcare [1]. One of the main aspects and challenges of AAL is the accurate localization of individuals within indoor environments and the recognition of their daily life activities. This is a crucial aspect of such assistive technologies since it allows the monitoring of their health conditions by detecting behavior patterns associated with the accomplishment of certain daily activities. Artificial intelligence and its machine

N. T. Nguyen et al. (Eds.): ICCCI 2023, LNAI 14162, pp. 418–430, 2023.
https://doi.org/10.1007/978-3-031-41456-5_32

learning algorithms have been extensively explored in the field of human activity recognition by analyzing real-time location data in indoor environments and human body acceleration and rotation patterns. When it comes to indoor localization, several technologies have been proposed in the literature. These methods can be mechanical-based, acoustic-based, light-based or use radio-frequency transmissions [2]. The Ultra-Wide Band (UWB) technology, that falls under the radio-frequency methods, has been widely used for indoor localization applications thanks to its high-precision and accuracy [3–5]. Compared to other localization methods, such as Wi-Fi or Bluetooth beacons, UWB stands out for its high accuracy of up to 10 cm, which makes it ideal for tracking a very precise location of individuals and objects within an indoor environment. UWB is less susceptible to interference from other radio frequency transmissions when comparing with other technologies, and it effectively passes through walls, equipment, and other obstacles [3].

The recognition of the most common human activities, such as walking, sitting, going upstairs or downstairs and lying, and its fusion with the indoor location information allows a better and more precise estimation of movements and behavior of the individuals within the AAL environment. This recognition can be based on the analysis of acceleration and rotation patterns of the human body, by means of inertial sensors. Supervised ML algorithms are used to estimate these activities based on the 3-axis acceleration signals, and several studies have been reporting very good results on classifying these activities and analyzing human posture by using these methods [6–9].

In this paper, we present the development of a wearable sensor that includes real-time indoor localization and machine learning for human activity recognition in the context of AAL. The development of the wearable sensor node based on Ultra-wide band technology (UWB) for real-time indoor localization and an inertial measurement unit (IMU) for activity classification will be described and evaluated in this paper.

The paper is organized as follows: Sect. 2 presents a detailed description of the system; Sect. 3 addresses the materials and methods used for this study; Sect. 4 presents and discusses the obtained results and, finally, Sect. 5 summarizes the conclusions.

2 System Description

In this section, a description of the hardware and software components of the developed system is presented. The proposed system follows the standard architecture of an Internet of Things (IoT) framework. It is divided into 4 layers: (1) the device layer, formed by the wearable sensor node, (2) the edge computing layer, with a gateway node that collects and processes information from the sensor node, (3) a cloud service and (4) the application layer, with a graphical user interface. A general architecture of the system is depicted in Fig. 1.

The device layer integrates an indoor positioning system based on UWB tags and anchors, an inertial measurement unit (IMU) and a microcontroller, as demonstrated in Fig. 2.

The wearable node is based on the ESP32-S2 microcontroller, which is a versatile system-on-chip (SoC) designed for embedded applications. It presents Wi-Fi (IEEE 802.11) wireless connectivity, a single-core 32-bit CPU with 240 MHz clock frequency,

12-bit resolution ADCs, and an ultra-low power (ULP) co-processor, giving more processing power and lower energy consumption when compared to the previous ESP boards.

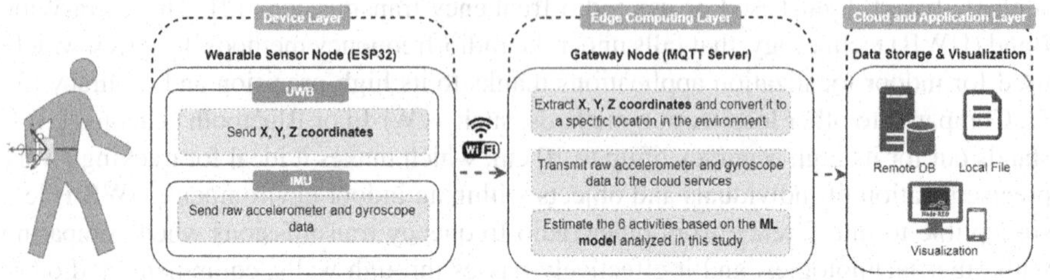

Fig. 1. General architecture of the IoT system and designated tasks

Regarding the edge computing layer, the Raspberry Pi 4 Model B, 8 GB RAM, was selected to serve as the gateway/aggregator node. This new Raspberry model features much better performance levels when compared to its predecessor, with a much faster CPU speed and better performance levels thanks to its Quad core Cortex-A72 (ARM v8) 64-bit SoC with 1.5 GHz clock frequency. These specifications are an advantage as additional processing power is going to be required for the future integration of the generated ML models in this system. This computing platform functions as an MQTT server, and it is responsible for collecting and processing the data that come from the wireless sensor node. After processing the data, the information is sent and stored in a remote database if there is an internet connection via Wi-Fi. Simultaneously, the data is stored locally on the microSD card. The Node-RED visual programming tool was used to configure the MQTT connections in the gateway node. In addition to establishing these connections, Node-RED was also used to perform other operations on the data received from the MQTT broker, such as data processing and transformation.

Fig. 2. Wearable sensor node composed of an UWB tag, IMU and ESP32 microcontroller

The indoor positioning information was obtained using the wearable tag and anchors based on the Pozyx® UWB system [10]. A single UWB tag was considered for this experiment, along with four UWB anchors placed in fixed locations, to serve as reference points for the tags and the positioning algorithm. All anchors were situated at the corners of the room where this experiment took place, at 2.46 m from the floor, and in line of sight of the tag and each other, as depicted in Fig. 3.

Each UWB transmitted at a pulse rate frequency of 64 MHz and had an update rate of 850 kbits/s.

The wearable UWB tag was connected to the ESP32-S2 via I^2C. The microcontroller collected all information regarding the X, Y and Z tag coordinates measured by the tag and sent it via Wi-Fi and MQTT protocol to the gateway node in real-time, at a sample frequency of 24 samples/s.

As for the IMU, responsible for detecting the 6 activities performed by the users, the MPU9250 was considered. This device integrates triple-axis MEMS accelerometer and gyroscope and was connected via I^2C. X, Y and Z-axis accelerometer and gyroscope data up to 6 decimal places are sent to the gateway node via MQTT together with the positioning coordinates, at a sample frequency of 24 samples/s.

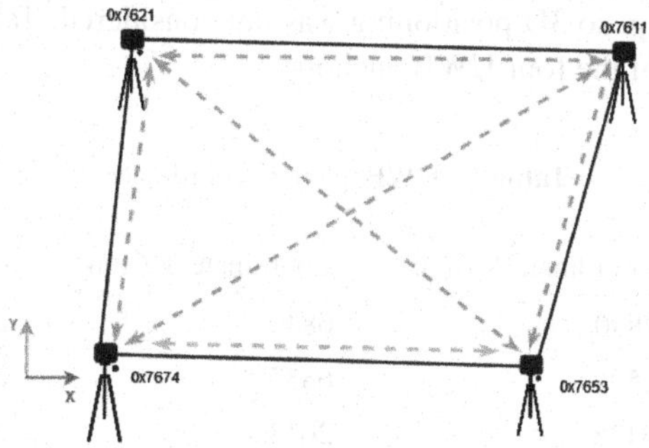

Fig. 3. Positioning of the four UWB anchors and their line of sight (green: good transmission quality; yellow: medium transmission quality) (Color figure online)

3 Methods

3.1 Experimental Procedure and Participants

This study was aimed to estimate indoor positioning based on UWB technology, as well as to estimate the type of activity performed by the individual using the wearable sensor node. The first topic included the positioning of the person in the experimental room in the various regions. The first validation of the positioning given by the UWB system was done by viewing the real-time position of the tag in the web application of the Pozyx® system. The second topic that addressed activity estimation using the accelerometer and gyroscope data was based on the execution of the 6 most common activities performed daily: sitting, standing, walking, climbing stairs, walking downstairs and lying down. In this phase, the participant was asked to perform the above-mentioned activities for approximately 25 s.

The study included 28 participants aged between 22 and 55 years old. All participants provided informed consent before enrolling in the experiment. The purpose and procedures involved in this study were given before their participation. All participants reported being in good health and had no locomotor problems. The wearable sensor node was placed at the lower back region of the participant's body, since it is close to the center of mass and is therefore a good location to capture the movements of the entire body. Moreover, the lower back is a relatively stable and fixed region that is less likely to move independently of the rest of the body during physical activities. This helps reduce the risk of measurement errors that could arise from movements of the wearable sensor unit itself.

3.2 Data Analysis

Indoor Positioning

The UWB anchors were calibrated automatically with the autocalibration method offered by the Pozyx® system. The only parameter manually introduced was the anchor height, which was the same for all four anchors. In this study, we do not pretend to measure the height of the UWB tag, so 3D positioning was not considered. Table 1 presents the X, Y and Z coordinates of the four UWB anchors.

Table 1. UWB anchors coordinates

UWB Anchor ID	Coordinate X (mm)	Coordinate Y (mm)	Coordinate Z (mm)
0x7611	7890	6840	2460
0x7621	650	6837	2460
0x7653	6475	2013	2460
0x7674	−477	2456	2460

The positioning coordinates measured by the UWB tag and collected by the ESP32 were transmitted to the gateway node. For this study, the environment where this experiment took place was sub-divided into different areas to simulate the common room-divisions of a house with different furniture, as it is presented in Fig. 4. An association was made between the coordinates of each area with a specific division of the house. Furthermore, the coordinates for specific areas of each room were also configured, such as the sofa area in the living room, the different desks in an office, among others, as shown in Fig. 4.

This was implemented with a JavaScript function in the Node-RED development tool.

Activity Classification Based on Machine Learning

The different types of movements performed while doing the previously mentioned activities are characterized by different motion patterns of the x-axis, y-axis and z-axis

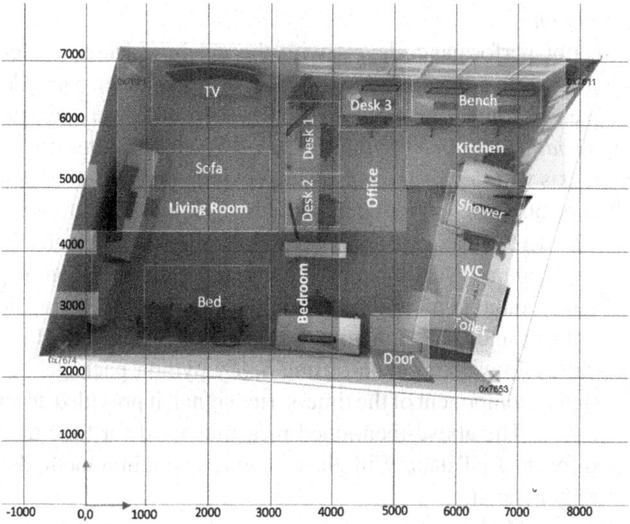

Fig. 4. Floor plan displaying the room divisions and the X and Y coordinates grid

of the accelerometer and gyroscope. The analysis of the acceleration and rotation patterns of these axis allow to easily distinguish between different types of movements. Walking has a very distinctive periodic pattern in the z-axis and larger movements in the x-axis and y-axis when compared to sitting or standing activities. Climbing stairs, for instance, has a similar pattern to walking, but can be distinguished by a more accentuated vertical component in the z-axis.

The produced dataset has a total of 85923 instances and 6 features: acceleration in the x-axis, y-axis and z-axis, and angular velocity in the x-axis, y-axis and z-axis. The number of samples collected by each participant for all activities are presented in Fig. 5. For all ML models, 20% of the data was used for testing, and 80% was used for training.

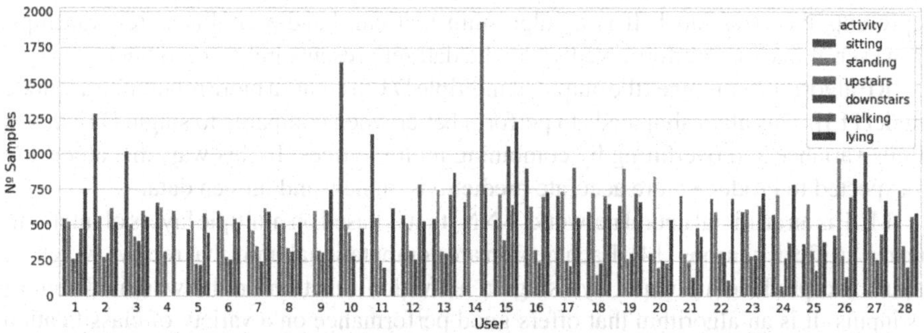

Fig. 5. Number of samples collected from each participant for all six activities

Feature Extraction

To achieve better performance levels with the machine learning algorithms, new informative features were generated based in raw accelerometer data. Common time-domain and frequency-domain features used in the literature were selected [6, 7], and calculated using *pandas* and *NumPy* python libraries. These attributes were calculated for each acceleration axis within 5 s segments, which correspond to 120 samples, and using a sliding window of 50 samples. Regarding the time-domain, the following statistical measures were considered: mean value, standard deviation, average absolute deviation, minimum value, maximum value, median, median absolute deviation, negative values count, positive values count, number of values above mean, number of peaks, skewness, kurtosis, energy entropy and signal magnitude area. For the frequency-domain, the Fast-Fourier Transform (FFT) was calculated using *SciPy* python package. As this method retrieves the frequency component of the time-series signal, it provided an additional way for analysing the data. The above-mentioned measures used for time-domain analysis were also applied for the FFT data. With these feature extraction methods, a total of 90 new features were generated.

Machine Learning Models

After performing the feature extraction, ML classification algorithms were applied to make predictions about the type of activity performed by the participants. The used algorithms were Support Vector Machines (SVM), Decision Trees (DT), Random Forest (RF) and Multilayer Perceptron (MLP). *Scikit-learn* machine learning library for Python was used for this purpose. These algorithms were selected based on their ability to learn from complex data patterns. In addition, these are extensively studied algorithms that have demonstrated reaching high levels of accuracy in human activity recognition applications.

The SVM is an algorithm that is based on the separation of data points by finding a hyperplane that maximizes the margin between the target classes. It is effective in high-dimensional spaces and robust to overfitting [11].

The DT is a non-parametric algorithm that builds a hierarchical tree structure of decision rules and their possible outcomes [12]. Each internal node represents a decision based on a feature, each branch denotes the result from that decision and each leaf node represents the class label. It is an algorithm that can handle nonlinear relationships. However, it may not perform well when the dataset presents imbalanced data.

RF algorithm combines the output of multiple DT to create a more robust and accurate model [13]. This algorithm tends to perform better when compared to single DT since it limits variance and overfitting by combining multiple trees. In this way, this algorithm is expected to produce more accurate predictions on new and unseen data.

MLP is an artificial neural network (ANN) that is based on multiple layers of interconnected artificial neurons [14]. Each neuron are computational units that receive weighted inputs and produce an output by using an activation function on the weighted sum of its inputs. It is an algorithm that offers good performance on a variety of classification problems and can easily learn the non-linear relationships between features.

To ensure the optimal performance of the machine learning algorithms, their hyperparameters were fine-tuned. We used grid search cross-validation (CV) to systematically explore different combinations of hyperparameters and identify the best performing set for each algorithm [15]. The optimal hyperparameters for each ML model are shown in Table 2.

Table 2. Hyperparameters selection of the ML models

Classifiers	Hyperparameter	Type	Selected value
SVM	*C*	Continuous	10
	kernel	Categorical	rbf
RF	*criterion*	Categorical	entropy
	max_depth	Discrete	8
	n_estimators	Discrete	300
	max_features	Continuous	sqrt
DT	*criterion*	Categorical	gini
	max_depth	Discrete	9
	max_features	Continuous	auto
MLP	*activation*	Categorical	tanh
	alpha	Continuous	0.05
	learning_rate	Categorical	adaptive
	solver	Categorical	adam

Additionally, we explored the use of the Long Short-Term Memory (LSTM) algorithm [16], to predict the 6 activities based on the raw accelerometer and gyroscope data, without performing any of the traditional feature engineering process for human activity recognition. This comes with the thought that this approach may bring some limitations such as the possibility of information loss during feature extraction, and the lack of adaptability to new data. The LSTM is being considered to overcome these limitations by automatically learning the features from the raw sensor data. This algorithm is a type of Recurrent Neural Network (RNN) that can process entire sequences of data and learn long-term dependencies. It introduces the concept of memory cells that can store information for longer periods. The information stored in these cells are controlled by a gating unit which, based on an activation function, will determine which information should be kept or discarded from the cell [16].

This algorithm is considered suitable for time-series data and sequential modeling and can learn the nonlinear relationships between features, which makes it useful for recognizing temporal sequences of activities over time. This approach excludes the need for feature engineering and may result in better performance than conventional techniques. The hyperparameters for this LSTM model were tuned to find the best performance results and are listed in Table 3.

Table 3. Hyperparameters for the LSTM model

Hyperparameter	Value
Input time steps	50
Input feature dimension	6
Batch size	1024
Learning Rate	0.002
Optimization Algorithm	Adam ($\beta_1 = 0.9, \beta_2 = 0.999$)
Epochs	100
Nodes in LSTM output layer	128
Nodes in the Fully Connected layer	64
Nodes in the softmax layer	6

4 Results and Discussion

In this study, we addressed the development of a wearable tag for indoor positioning characterized by UWB technology. The accuracy of the used UWB system is considered to be highly precise, reaching an accuracy of up to 10 cm in a typical indoor environment [10]. The collection of X, Y and Z coordinates from the UWB tag and its association to specific locations in the environment showed no margin of error since this is entirely dependent on the adjustments of the X and Y limits of each room divisions programmed in the gateway node. Figure 6 displays the graphical user interface developed for this system, which aims to provide real-time tracking and monitoring of the wearable tag using the measured X and Y coordinates. One of the primary objectives of the graphical user interface was to display an estimation of the tag's location in real-time, allowing for dynamic monitoring of the person's movements.

Moreover, we investigated the use of accelerometer and gyroscope data to classify six different types of activities – sitting, standing, walking, climbing stairs, walking downstairs and laying. New features were generated using time-domain and frequency-domain analysis of the raw accelerometer data and various machine learning algorithms were applied to the classification task.

To optimize the machine learning models, their hyper-parameters were fine-tuned via grid search cross-validation. By doing so, we managed to improve the accuracy of the models and to minimize overfitting.

The Random Forest algorithm achieved the highest accuracy of 93.9%, followed by Decision Trees with an accuracy of 86.2%, Multilayer Perceptron with an accuracy of 81.5%, and SVM with an accuracy of 71.2% (Table 4).

Furthermore, we applied LSTM to the raw accelerometer and gyroscope signals without any additional feature engineering. LSTM achieved an accuracy of 92.6%, which is comparable to the best performing machine learning algorithms previously tested.

The LSTM training session's progress over the iterations is presented in Fig. 7. a). A decreasing trend in the validation and train loss and an increasing trend in accuracy

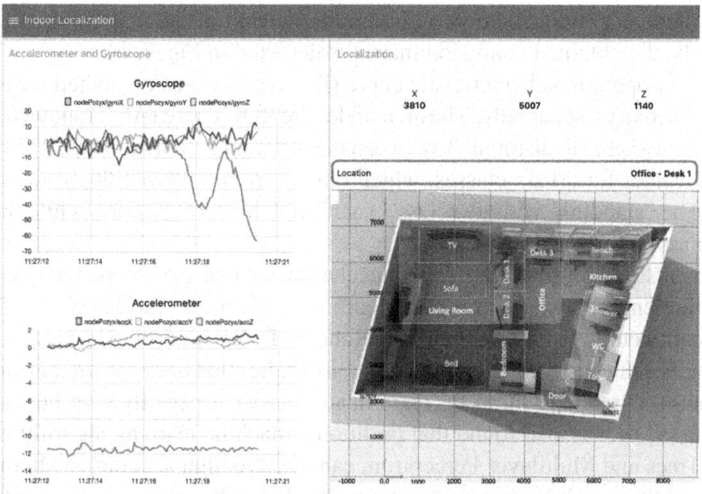

Fig. 6. Graphical user interface for the indoor localization system. Real-time accelerometer and gyroscope data, UWB coordinates, and the room's divisions are displayed.

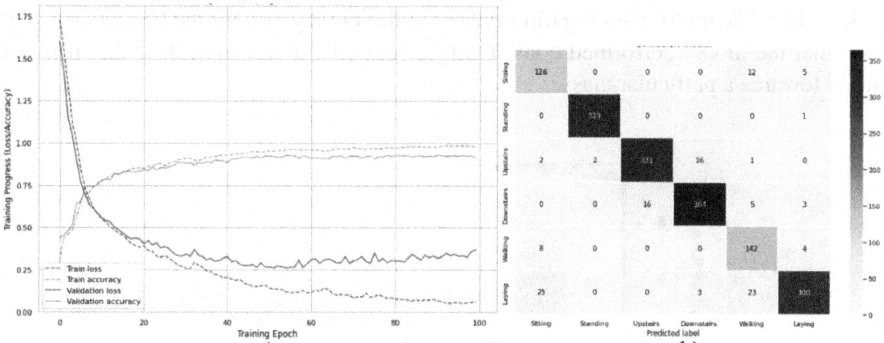

a) b)

Fig. 7. a) Logarithmic loss of the LSTM algorithm over the epochs; b) Confusion matrix

Table 4. Accuracy, precision, recall and F1-score values obtained for the four algorithms

Evaluation Metric	RF	DT	SVM	MLP
Accuracy	0.939	0.862	0.712	0.815
Precision	0.938	0.865	0.757	0.817
Recall	0.938	0.863	0.713	0.816
F1 Score	0.938	0.862	0.724	0.815

over the course of training, shows a good improvement of the model over the epochs. Additionally, the obtained confusion matrix is depicted in Fig. 7. b).

A receiver operating characteristic curve (ROC) curve was computed for each class (i.e. type of activity), separately. The area under the ROC curve (AUC) showed how well the classifier was able to distinguish between the different activities. The LSTM achieved high AUC values for all six classes, which ranged from 0.98 to 1.00, as demonstrated in Fig. 8. The "standing" activity (class 1) achieved the perfect score, while the "lying" activity (class 5) achieved 0.98.

Our results demonstrate that using accelerometer and gyroscope data with appropriate feature engineering and machine learning algorithms, various types of physical activities can accurately be classified. The Random Forest algorithm had the best performance results, which is consistent with previous studies that have shown this model to be a robust and accurate algorithm for classification tasks, especially with human activity recognition [9]. It was also found that traditional machine learning algorithms, such as Decision Trees and Multilayer Perceptron, can achieve high accuracy with appropriate feature extraction and hyperparameter tuning. SVM, on the other hand, did not perform as well as expected, which may be due to the imbalanced nature of the dataset. Furthermore, the study shows that LSTM can achieve very good accuracy without the need of any additional feature engineering. This is an important finding as it suggests that LSTM can be used as an alternative approach when feature engineering is not feasible or desirable. The multi-class logarithmic loss and accuracy plot for the LSTM also suggests that the model performed consistently across all classes, indicating that it is not biased towards a particular class.

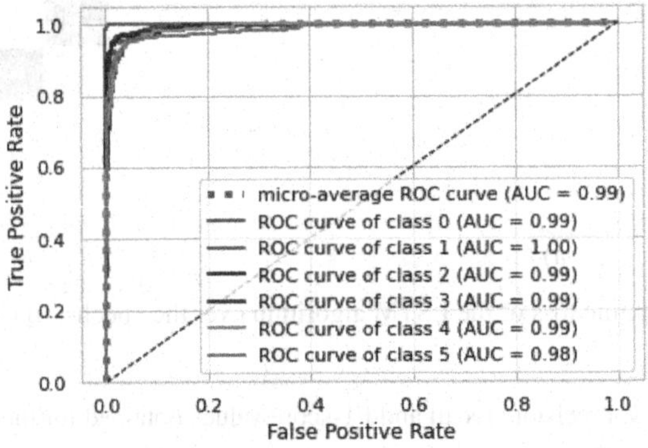

Fig. 8. ROC curve and AUC values for each class using the LSTM algorithm

5 Conclusions

This paper presents the development of a wearable sensor that integrates UWB technology for real-time indoor localization and an IMU for human activity recognition in the context of AAL. The accuracy of the UWB positioning, and the association of its measured X-Y coordinates to specific locations in the indoor environment showed to be highly accurate. A graphical user interface was implemented to provide real-time tracking and monitoring of the wearable tag positions. In addition, 3D acceleration and rotation data of the human body were obtained for 28 participants to estimate six different types of common human activities, such as sitting, standing, walking, climbing stairs, walking downstairs, and lying. Various machine learning algorithms were used in this classification task. Feature extraction methods based on time-domain and frequency-domain were applied to the raw acceleration data for improving the ML models performance. The RF algorithm achieved the highest accuracy of 93.9%, followed by DT, MLP and SVM. Furthermore, the LSTM algorithm, having input raw accelerometer and gyroscope signals without considering additional feature engineering, achieved a very good accuracy of 92.6%. Future work involves the identification of anomalous behavior that may be indicative of health problems, unusual activity levels, irregular movements, or the occurrence of other potentially harmful accidents, including fall detection.

References

1. Cicirelli, G., Marani, R., Petitti, A., Milella, A., D'Orazio, T.: Ambient assisted living: a review of technologies, methodologies and future perspectives for healthy aging of population. Sensors **21**(10), 3549 (2021). https://doi.org/10.3390/s21103549
2. Jacob Rodrigues, M., Postolache, O., Cercas, F.: Physiological and behavior monitoring systems for smart healthcare environments: a review. Sensors **20**(8), 2186 (2020). https://doi.org/10.3390/s20082186
3. Alarifi, A., et al.: Ultra wideband indoor positioning technologies: analysis and recent advances. Sensors **16**(5), 707 (2016). https://doi.org/10.3390/s16050707
4. Zhang, H., Zhang, Z., Gao, N., Xiao, Y., Meng, Z., Li, Z.: Cost-effective wearable indoor localization and motion analysis via the integration of UWB and IMU. Sensors **20**(2), 344 (2020). https://doi.org/10.3390/s20020344
5. Obeidat, H., Shuaieb, W., Obeidat, O., Abd-Alhameed, R.: A review of indoor localization techniques and wireless technologies. Wirel. Pers. Commun. **119**(1), 289–327 (2021). https://doi.org/10.1007/s11277-021-08209-5
6. Avci, A., Bosch, S., Marin-Perianu, M., Marin-Perianu, R., Havinga, P.: Activity recognition using inertial sensing for healthcare, wellbeing and sports applications: a survey. In: 23th International Conference on Architecture of Computing Systems 2010, pp. 1–10, February 2010
7. Steven Eyobu, O., Han, D.: Feature representation and data augmentation for human activity classification based on wearable IMU sensor data using a deep LSTM neural network. Sensors **18**(9), 2892 (2018). https://doi.org/10.3390/s18092892
8. Sinha, V.K., Patro, K.K., Pławiak, P., Prakash, A.J.: Smartphone-based human sitting behaviors recognition using inertial sensor. Sensors **21**(19), 6652 (2021). https://doi.org/10.3390/s21196652
9. Leone, A., Rescio, G., Caroppo, A., Siciliano, P., Manni, A.: Human postures recognition by accelerometer sensor and ML architecture integrated in embedded platforms: benchmarking and performance evaluation. Sensors **23**(2), 1039 (2023). https://doi.org/10.3390/s23021039
10. Pozyx|Multi Technology RTLS - Indoor & Outdoor. https://www.pozyx.io/. Accessed 12 Mar 2023
11. Porcello, J.C.: Designing and implementing SVMs for high-dimensional knowledge discovery using FPGAs. In: 2019 IEEE Aerospace Conference, Big Sky, MT, USA, pp. 1–8, March 2019. https://doi.org/10.1109/AERO.2019.8741916

12. Song, Y., Lu, Y.: Decision tree methods: applications for classification and prediction. Shanghai Arch. Psychiatry **27**(2), 130–135 (2015). https://doi.org/10.11919/j.issn.1002-0829.215044
13. Breiman, L.: Random forests. Mach. Learn. **45**(1), 5–32 (2001). https://doi.org/10.1023/A:1010933404324
14. Murtagh, F.: Multilayer perceptrons for classification and regression. Neurocomputing **2**(5), 183–197 (1991). https://doi.org/10.1016/0925-2312(91)90023-5
15. 3.2. Tuning the hyper-parameters of an estimator. scikit-learn. https://scikit-learn.org/stable/modules/grid_search.html. Accessed 14 Mar 2023
16. Sak, H., Senior, A., Beaufays, F.: Long short-term memory based recurrent neural network architectures for large vocabulary speech recognition (2014). https://doi.org/10.48550/ARXIV.1402.1128

Hyperledger Blockchain-Enabled Cold Chain Application for Flower Logistics

Pin-Jung Tang[1], Chien-wen Shen[1], Phung Phi Tran[2(✉)], and Yin-Shi Lin[1]

[1] Department of Business Administration, National Central University, Taoyuan City, Taiwan
[2] Faculty of Business Administration, Ton Duc Thang University, Ho Chi Minh City, Vietnam
tranthiphiphung@tdtu.edu.vn

Abstract. Flower logistics usually encounter difficulties like disrupted temperature control, inadequate packaging or damaged goods, contamination issues, damaged products, massive document exchanges, and many other cold chain challenges. To tackle these difficulties, we developed a blockchain application based on Hyperledger technologies for the flower cold chain. The Fabric under the Hyperledger was used as the underlying architecture of the blockchain network, and then the application scenarios and business processes of the blockchain were constructed by the Hyperledger Composer. Cold chain partners can have a holistic view of transactions through the Composer and retrieve detailed information by querying specific shipments or transactions. The specification of Hyperledger smart contracts can also avoid tampering with data during cold chain shipments and the temperature data can be monitored in real-time via sensors. In addition, smart contracts created by Hyperledger can offer automated functionality and availability of validated data. The developed application can increase trust, security, transparency, and the traceability of flower logistics transactions.

Keywords: Blockchain · Cold Chain · Flower Supply Chain · Orchid · Hyperledger

1 Introduction

Flowers logistics requires a cold chain system that keeps the items at the right temperature along the supply chain until they reach the consumers because flowers are per-perishable goods with an age-dependent demand rate that could easily result in physical decay [1]. However, cold chain systems can lead to fresh flower waste if the management of perishable goods is inadequate or the storage conditions could be more efficacious [2]. Challenges for an efficient cold chain include the diverse temperature range requirements with different flower categories [3] or regulation differences among countries [4]. For instance, the Ethiopian flower export industry must improve its infrastructure and logistics coordination among post-harvest cold chain facilities to adapt to the high standards of the EU market [5]. To overcome the international trade disputes over US market access, cold chain technologies have been placed in the US and Colombian cut flower commodity chains [6]. Cold chain storage infrastructure needs further

N. T. Nguyen et al. (Eds.): ICCCI 2023, LNAI 14162, pp. 431–443, 2023.
https://doi.org/10.1007/978-3-031-41456-5_33

improvement for the Kenyan flower industry and the East African suppliers, producers, and exporters to secure easy-damaged flowers adequately [7]. In the Iranian flower industry, lack of technology, such as cold chain innovation, is one of the significant barriers affecting international flower supply chain management [8]. Lack of temperature norms, inadequate infrastructure, out-of-date technology, and professional shortages are the cold chain issues faced in Taiwan [9]. Maintaining the temperature of perishable products within the correct range at all stages of the cold chain is an essential issue for flower logistics. As such, ensuring the integrity of the cold chain for temperature-sensitive flower products entail additional requirements for proper packing, temperature assurance, and monitoring. Applying blockchain technology may tackle some of the difficulties mentioned above because it can streamline complicated processes across the supply chain [10]. Distributed ledger and smart contracts in blockchain can provide enhanced transparency, visibility, governance, security, and audibility in the cold chain [11]. Transactions in blockchain are safer, more transparent, traceable, and more efficient in the cold chain [12, 13]. Collaborations between supply chain members can be increased, and the waste of supply chain documents can be reduced with the applications of blockchain smart contracts [14], where the execution of a smart contract occurs after deploying it [15]. For example, Maersk and IBM have formed a joint venture to develop a global blockchain-based system for digitizing trade procedures and tracking shipments end-to-end [16]. In the flowers industry, blockchain technology could be used to enable each party along the supply chain [17], including producers, processors, and distributors, to provide traceability information about their specific role and for each batch, such as dates, locations, farm buildings, distribution channels, and potential treatments [18].

As far as our current understanding extends, there exists no prior literature exploring the utilization of blockchain technology in the context of cold chain management, with a particular emphasis on the flower cold chain. This research aims to propose two research questions as follows

1. How to use blockchain ideas to solve cold chain supply chain issues?
2. What is the feasibility of implementing a cold chain system for fresh flowers, utilizing the technical features of blockchain technology such as Hyperledger?

A blockchain application was developed utilizing Hyperledger technology to facilitate the cold chain logistics of flowers. A subsequent section of this work presents an analysis of Orchid Logistics as a case study to exemplify its practicality. The orchid holds significant importance in the cut flower industry due to its aesthetic appeal, prolonged durability, high yield, suitable flowering period, and ease of packaging and transportation. Furthermore, it is noteworthy that orchids constitute approximately 10% of the worldwide trade in fresh-cut flowers and a substantial proportion of the global floriculture trade, encompassing both cut flowers and potted plants [19]. According to the literature, the implementation of a well-managed cold chain during supply chain shipments can potentially extend the vase life of orchid flowers [20]. The utilization of blockchain technology in flower logistics has the capacity to provide a secure and transparent system throughout the entirety of the global supply chain. This has the potential to eliminate instances of fraud and errors, improve the management of the supply chain, decrease expenses, minimize waste, and reduce the amount of time required for lead times [21]. Hyperledger, which is an umbrella project under the Linux Foundation, is considered the largest alliance blockchain platform globally within the realm of blockchain technology research [17, 22, 23].

The present investigation employed the Fabric technology within the Hyperledger framework as the foundational infrastructure for the blockchain network. Subsequently, the Hyperledger Composer was utilized to establish the use cases and commercial procedures of the blockchain. The present state can be observed via the Composer, while comprehensive or elaborate details can be obtained by executing targeted queries on individual blocks or transactions. The cold chain application that has been developed with Hyperledger technology facilitates the secure sharing of information among flower logistics stakeholders, including buyers, producers, and sellers. Furthermore, Hyperledger smart contracts have the potential to provide automated functionality and accessibility to verified data. According to reference [24], the implementation of blockchain technology in the flower supply chain can result in expedited and more lucid transactions for all relevant parties. In addition, monitoring the storage temperatures of flower products throughout the cold chain can prevent expensive recalls and ensure the safety of shipments [22].

2 Flower Cold Chain Problem and BlockChain Applicability

The problems in cold chain logistics have been discussed extensively. For example, Aung (2014) discussed temperature control in a cold chain as the most critical aspect in extending the practical shelf life of produce and preserving perishable items from quality loss and wastage [25]. Tsai, K.M (2019) researched the effect of ambient temperature exposure to determine how refrigerated items' quality and safety are controlled in sustainable cold chains [26]. Temperature humidness management is critical for perishable products to stay fresh and non-deteriorating [27]. Negi (2017) identified that the primary reason for the logistics and supply chain losses and wastage in the agricultural products of fruits and vegetables is the shortage of cold storage [28]. In the U.S., it is estimated that nearly 40% of food waste happens during distribution, amounting to $165 billion per year, primarily due to insufficient refrigeration [29]. Monitoring products subjected to intermittent and brief temperature interruptions along the cold chain is vital. Automation and intelligent handling of fresh produce distribution become critical considering the central problem of high produce waste and low transit efficiency [30]. However, research about cold chain applications in flower logistics is still rare. A framework based on the global value chain and global commodity chain analysis was proposed to examine the problems of the South African floriculture business [31]. To evaluate the applicability of blockchain for flower logistics, we adopted the criteria suggested by the National Institute of Standards and Technology (NIST) for blockchain technology [21]. The reasons why flower logistics is suitable for blockchain applications is shown in Table 1.

3 Hyperledger Framework

For the advancement of cross-industry blockchain technologies, Hyperledger is an open-source collaborative initiative [22]. Studies showed that Hyperledger exhibited better transactions per second compared to the Ethereum private network because of different

Table 1. Reasons to adopt blockchain in flower logistics based on the NIST framework

Features	Explanation
Many participants	There are 13 different roles for participants involved in the preparation process, export process, and payment
Distributed participants	Participants belong to different organizations, and many different organizations must write information
Want or need for lack of trusted third party	In the flower supply chain business scenario involves a lot of units, it is not appropriate to find a participant to save files, and there is no suitable or trustworthy data storage
Workflow is transactional	Each transaction requires an identification code to ensure that the transaction is trusted
A need for a globally scarce digital identifier	The order of the customs clearance process, each checkpoint in the entire transaction process needs to be verified and ordered login
A need for a decentralized naming service or ordered registry	Every organization must have access control. For example, the industry cannot simply view the information of government units
A need for a cryptographically secure system of ownership	In this scenario, manual verification of data is often required, or it is often necessary to communicate with other organizations to obtain data
A need to eliminate manual efforts of reconciliation and dispute resolutions	In cold chain logistics, the temperature of the moment will be the quality of the flower. When the problem occurs, monitoring can be processed immediately
A need for full provenance of digital assets to be shared among participants	Each time the transaction process and data storage can query the history when the process is out of the way

consensus algorithms [32, 33]. Hyperledger is a non-currency project for industrial applications. It means there is no Hyperledger coin in circulation, as the project has no intention of hosting its cryptocurrencies, such as Ethereum or Bitcoin. By utilizing non-currency, an organization might circumvent several political difficulties associated with maintaining a globally uniform currency [34]. Enterprises can decide where the nodes should be and do not need public miners to sustain them. Hyperledger, as a permission blockchain, has different characteristics, like a channel for upgraded data security and confidentiality. Based on enterprises' specific requirements, a modular design approach enables Hyperledger to plug and play different elements in the stack [35].

In our development, Hyperledger Fabric was used as the underlying architecture of the blockchain network. The Hyperledger Composer constructed the application scenarios and business processes of the blockchain. We used Ubuntu 18.04 LTS (Bionic Beaver) to build the environment system of Hyperledger Fabric. We installed the software needed to build the Fabric in the environment, such as Go, Java, or Node.js. Hyperledger Fabric, the platform on which applications are built, enables plug-and-play components such as consensus and membership services. The Hyperledger Fabric ledger comprises smart contracts dubbed "chain code" that comprise the system's application logic and govern transactions [36]. A chain code function allows one to read and return assets, build and change assets and save them in the local ledger database.

After the changes are locally persistent on a node, they are present to the network "endorsement" and deposited into the blockchain after being accepted by the other organizations [35]. The Fabric network comprises different entities, nodes, sorting service nodes, and clients of different organizations. Hyperledger Fabric also offers various pluggable options, such as ledger data being stored in various formats, exchanging consensus mechanisms in and out, and supporting different MSPs [37]. Then the Composer network was installed in the Fabric network. Hyperledger Composer is a tool for implementing a Fabric blockchain network that makes it easier to build a blockchain network. Composer is a higher-level abstraction of Fabric, which can significantly reduce the code written, make it easy to construct a commercial network and quickly write a simple, smart contract and deploy it to the internal blockchain network. It is easier to manage the identity of a network participant. In a significant development environment, only a few core users update the ledger code (such as Fabric). Most users will access the blockchain in Composer and perform daily actions to access and update the blockchain. The composer features an easy-to-use graphical interface for managing all of its components and a REST server that connects the blockchain to third-party apps. Composer for Hyperledger Fabric enables using the existing Hyperledger Fabric blockchain infrastructure [38, 39]. Figure 1 shows the Hyperledger implementation framework used in this study, based on the transaction processing flow for the Hyperledger Fabric and Hyperledger Composer [40].

Based on the abstraction of installing the chain code onto the Fabric, the business network is a model of all the data in the blockchain, including all the objects, functions, transactions, and identities related to one another and kept in the ledger. The business network has four main resource types: participants, assets, transactions, and events. Participants have a specific role in the business network and can own assets and submit transactions. Participants have unique identifiers (such as IDs) and other attributes. Attributes can be mandatory or optional, depending on the integrity of the data. An asset is a property a participant can own (tangible or intangible). Like a participant, an asset must also have a unique set of identifiers and include defined attributes. In addition, assets may be transferred to other participants. A transaction is a mechanism for interaction between participants and assets.

Participants can submit transactions to change one or more attributes of an asset or create or delete assets. The transaction handler function issues an event to indicate something has happened to the external system. Any application or existing system can submit and receive events in the future. The composer has a custom modeling language that makes it easier to define a business network. It is divided into four definition files, namely model (.cto), transaction logic (.js), access control (.acl), and query (.qry). After the file is defined, merge and export a bna file, as shown in Fig. 1. The commercial network (bna archive) is packaged. It can be deployed to run on a specific number of fabric nodes, using the Composer CLI interface to generate domain models for the.bna archives or to trigger transaction logic defined by the.bna archive.

4 Hyperledger Application for Orchid Logistics

To illustrate the applicability of Hyperledger-enabled blockchain for flower logistics, the application scenario of the Taiwan orchid companies exporting Orchid to the United States was considered. According to the Taiwan Bureau of Animal and Plant Health Inspection Service, Taiwan orchids exported to the United States in the early stage can only be exported as bare roots. However, the lack of medium protection during transportation is highly vulnerable to damage. After arriving in the United States, it is necessary to re-enter the media for Phalaenopsis Orchid. It can only be sold to the market for several months. Orchid qual would seriously deteriorate with cargo consolidation because there is no particular-sized chilled facility for flowers in Taiwan's airport and different temperature requirements in nature. So, it is crucial to upgrade the cold-chain cargo handling facilities and techniques to solve this problem in international shipping [41]. Blockchain gives an opportunity to radically transform by providing a standard architecture to address problems due to its characteristics of transparency, integrity, immutability, security, and reducing transaction costs [42]. Since Taiwan's first exporter of orchids to the United States is Taida Horticultural Co., Ltd., this study assumes that the manufacturer exports orchids to the California area importer Allstate Floral, Inc as a case scenario. After the exporter packages, the shipment is submitted to the "goods shipment" transaction to update the goods. The smart contract defined in the transaction broadcasts the event simultaneously. It lets the relevant participants know that the goods have been packed and can be picked up. Once the exporter has shipped, the exporter will mark the shipment status in the letter of credit. The land transporter picks up the goods from the location notified by the exporter and submits a "goods pick-up" transaction to update the goods. The smart contract of the transaction will simultaneously broadcast the event to let the relevant participants know that the goods have been picked up and are being loaded for shipment.

The shipping company loads the goods onto the container ship and submits a "cargo delivery" transaction to update the goods. The smart contract broadcasts the event simultaneously, letting the relevant participants know that the goods have been loaded onto the container ship. In shipping, picking up, and transporting the above package, the IoT sensor in the container updates the reading on the blockchain by transmitting data. Temperature Readings are the temperature sensor applying a reading by submitting a "temperature reading" transaction that transmits data updates as the container is shipped to the destination. Humidity Readings mean the humidity sensor submits a reading through the Humidity Reading transaction, which transmits data updates as the container is shipped to the destination. GPS Readings are introduced by GPS Sensors that submit readings via a "GPS Readings" transaction that transmits data updates as the container is shipped to its destination. During transport, if the temperature sensor or humidity sensor detects a violation of the temperature and humidity in the contract during transportation, the Temperature Threshold Event and the Humidity Threshold Event will be broadcast to the relevant parties to know. When the container ship arrives at the destination, the event "The goods have been shipped to the port" will be broadcast to the relevant participants. The "received goods" event will be broadcast to the relevant participants when the importer receives the goods. In the credit-like blockchain network, the importer will review the received goods, check whether the received goods meet the letter of credit requirements, and submit the receipt of the goods after the review. The building steps for the Hyperledger Fabric network are shown in Fig. 2.

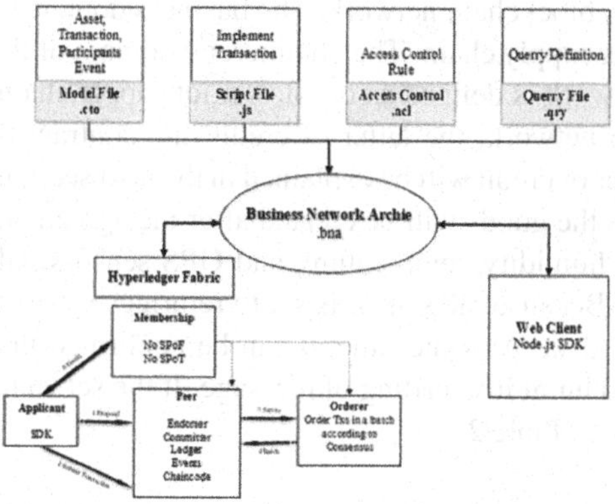

Fig. 1. Hyperledger implementation framework

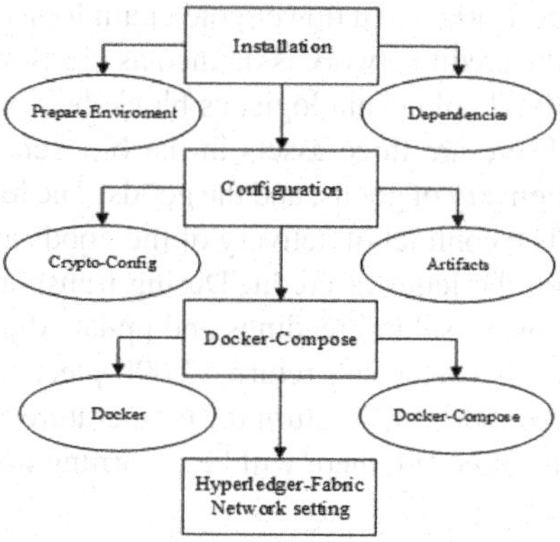

Fig. 2. Hyperledger Fabric network process

Ubuntu 18.04 LTS was used to build the environment system of Hyperledger Fabric, and the software needed was installed to build the fabric in the environment (Node.js, npm, Docker, Docker Compose, Python). Once the Composer is set up, we install the primary Hyperledger Fabric environment deployment blockchain. Then the blockchain network used Docker to package essential components of the blockchain to call these essential components when opening the network, such as MSP's Fabric-ca, Kafka, and Zookeeper, to achieve consensus. Docker is a lightweight virtual machine. Because of the variety of programs involved in the blockchain environment, the program will have compatibility problems. Therefore, this study uses Docker to make different programs compatible in the same environment. After the final download is complete, then clone to https://github.com/hyperledger/fabric-samples.git to download the binary files and Docker images required by the Hyperledger Fabric, and finally execute./startFabric.sh to generate the version 1.2 fabric networks. Next, we confirm the configuration of the four Dockers, CA Node, Orderer Node, Peer Node, and Couchdb (Database). The current blockchain network core is already in operation (Fig. 3).

Next, we execute ./createPeerAdminCard.sh to generate the PeerAdminCard, which includes the information of the fabric network and the information required by the node administrator (Peer Admin). It is the identity certificate of the node administrator. The composer will use PeerAdminCard. It is connected to the fabric. In addition, we execute a

NO	CONTAINER ID	IMAGE	COMMAND	PORTS	NAMES
1	33568f4762dc	hyperledger/fabric-peer:1.2.1	"peer node start"	0.0.0.0:7051->7051/tcp, 0.0.0.0:7053->7053/tcp	peer0.org1.example.com
2	451f36f8695e	hyperledger/fabric-ca:1.2.1	"sh -c 'fabric-ca-se..."	0.0.0.0:7054->7054/tcp	ca.org1.example.com
3	5adf629b5ada	hyperledger/fabric-couchdb:0.4.10	"tini -- /docker-ent..."	4369/tcp, 9100/tcp, 0.0.0.0:5984->5984/tcp	couchdb
4	3cc32f96fd28	hyperledger/fabric-orderer:1.2.1	"orderer"	0.0.0.0:7050->7050/tcp	orderer.example.com

Fig. 3. Docker example in the orchid blockchain

hyper ledger-composer: business network to generate the flower supply chain network for this study. The study is divided into two commercial networks, a credit-like blockchain network, and a flower cold chain logistics blockchain network. The business domain of the credit network is defined as org.flower.supply.chain. The commercial domain of the floral cold chain logistics blockchain network is defined as org.flower.iot.supply.chain. There are three assets in the blockchain network, the letter of credit, the contract of delivery of goods, and the goods. The letter of credit will be explained in the next section. The contract of delivery of the goods and the goods will be created after the agreement on the letter of credit. During transport, humidity, temperature, and GPS sensors will always submit readings and update data. Because the sensor is set to return every 30 s, each sensor will return 72,000 pieces of data. At same time, it can be confirmed that JavaScript will return the temperature and humidity reading of message. If the set value is exceeded, there will be a warning notice (Table 2).

Table 2. An example of how a sensor submits reading code

Sensor	Reading
Temperature sensor	"$class": "org.flower.iot.supply.chain.TemperatureReading", "centigrade": 18, "shipment": "resource:org.flower.iot.supply.chain.Shipment#SHIP_001"
Humidity sensor	"$class": "org.flower.iot.supply.chain.HumidityReading", "percent": 85, "shipment": "resource:org.flower.iot.supply.chain.Shipment#SHIP_001"
GPS sensor	"$class": "org.flower.iot.supply.chain.GpsReading", "readingTime": "120000", "readingDate": "20190619", "latitude": "35.1915", "latitudeDir": "N", "longitude": "164.2110", "longitudeDir": "E", "shipment": "resource:org.flower.iot.supply.chain.Shipment#SHIP_001"

At this point, the status of the goods is in transit. All temperature, humidity, and GPS readings are recorded in the asset and recorded as shown in Fig. 4.

In the event that the temperature measurement surpasses the minimum or maximum range stipulated in the contract, the exporter's remuneration will be reduced, and the

Compliance Status will indicate OUT_OF_COMPLIANCE. The present investigation posits that the temperature sensor exhibits two instances of data that fall outside the expected range, specifically 21° and 17°, along with two degrees of humidity, measuring 91% and 92%, respectively. The summary of each reading will be presented and exhibited within the SHIP_001 Shipment Asset Registry.

Upon arrival at the destination, the relevant participants are notified through the broadcasting of the Shipment In Port Event. Upon receipt of the goods by the importer, the ShipmentReceived transaction is initiated in accordance with the contractual parameters, thereby activating the contract pertaining to the goods identified as SHIP_001 and designated for the importer under the reference CON_001. The ShipmentReceived transaction will subsequently disseminate an activity notification to the pertinent participants. The entity responsible for receiving the goods is the importer.

The dataset will present the minimum and maximum wet temperature measurements, and the corresponding penalty will be determined in a proportional manner. The present investigation stipulates that a fine of 1 cent per degree shall be imposed if the temperature surpasses (falls below) a certain threshold, while a fine of 1 cent shall be levied for every percentage point by which the humidity exceeds (falls short of) a predetermined level. The ultimate step involves the computation of the penalties imposed on the importer and the corresponding payment that the exporter is entitled to receive, which amounts to 115,509,24.99 cents, as illustrated in Fig. 5.

Fig. 4. Temperature, humidity, GPS sensor transmission data screen

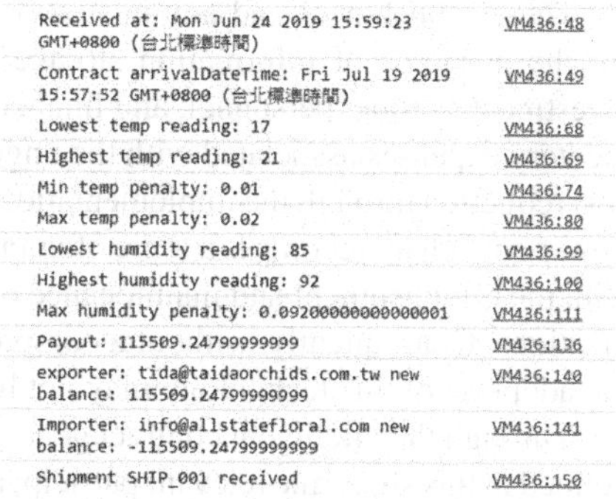

Fig. 5. Penalty calculation screen

We continue to access the management interface to retrieve comprehensive transaction records, encompassing transaction timing, transaction occurrences, submitters, and detailed record particulars. Upon reaching this stage, the importer initiates the "Receive Product" transaction within the credit network, and the Morgan Chase traveler is notified of the importer's receipt of the goods through the dissemination of information across the blockchain network. Subsequent to verifying the merchandise in accordance with the provisions of the letter of credit, the agent affirms the absence of any issues by executing the "ReadyForPayment" transaction on the blockchain network. As per the communication disseminated by the blockchain network, the Bank of Taiwan has been apprised of the readiness of the letter of credit for disbursement. The code presented below demonstrates that upon verifying the successful transfer of funds by the importer, the submission of the "Close" transaction results in the closure of the letter of credit and the subsequent remittance of funds to the exporter.

5 Discussions and Conclusions

There exists a need for greater emphasis on the utilization of blockchain technology in the management of cold chains for flowers. This research investigated the potential applications of blockchain technology within the flower cold chain, with the aim of enhancing its supply chain management and overcoming the primary challenges that currently exist.

Efficient supply chain management is closely linked to the cold chain of fresh-cut flowers. In order to effectively integrate blockchain technology into this system, it is imperative to establish a suitable method for storing flower data and facilitating information exchange between various systems involved in the blockchain application [43]. It is recommended that international standardization bodies establish multiple authenticated and certified standards. The established criteria can prove to be advantageous in assessing the dimensions, data characteristics, and structure of the data transmitted within blockchain implementations. The aforementioned criteria serve the purpose of not only examining disseminated data but also functioning as a preventative safety measure [44].

The establishment and administration of a conventional flower cold chain system for the purposes of information storage and data exchange necessitate a substantial investment of time, personnel, and financial resources. Furthermore, there exist supplementary expenses associated with the ongoing updating of the system. The potential for cost reduction through the implementation of a blockchain system in the management of flower cold chain records is a topic of interest. However, the precise expenses associated with the establishment and maintenance of such a system remain unclear to many organizations. Consequently, without a comprehensive understanding of the costs involved, the adoption of this technology may not be feasible [43].

Through the intelligent contract generated by the transaction logic of the blockchain defined in this study, the relevant participants of the flower logistics process can be monitored and quickly notified. The content of the contract definition cannot be easily changed after mutual consent so that the conflict in the transaction is reduced [45]. Any problems in the transaction process can also be handled promptly. In summary, blockchain technology is a feasible and effective solution for flower cold chain logistics because transactions in blockchain operations are safer, more transparent, traceable, and efficient. In addition, there is cooperation between members of the cold chain supply chain, and the relationship between the members of the cold chain supply chain can ensure that customers can thoroughly check the flow of goods in the entire cold chain supply chain. Moreover, the contract in this study cannot change the tracking data once the input temperature and humidity tracking data are on the blockchain ledger. Other roles in the blockchain can also track shipping locations, delivery status, and progress. This way, the blockchain can generate trust between the cold chain supply chains, eliminating intermediaries, increasing efficiency, and reducing costs. Future research directions may center on examining the potential collaboration and interplay among diverse blockchain-based fresh-cut flower cold chains. Interoperability and cooperation are salient concerns. Moreover, data exchange among various segments of the flower cold chain could potentially streamline customer service.

Acknowledgments. This research was funded by National Science and Technology Council, grant number MOST 111-2410-H-008-015. We are very grateful to the Associate Editor and four anonymous referees for their valuable feedback and comments that helped improve the content of the paper.

References

1. Gupta, Y., Sundararaghavan, P., Ahmed, M.U.: Ordering policies for items with seasonal demand. Int. J. Phys. Distrib. Logist. Manag. **33**(6), 500–518 (2003)
2. Gwanpua, S.G.: The FRISBEE tool, a software for optimizing the trade-off between food quality, energy use, and global warming impact of cold chains. J. Food Eng. **148**, 2–12 (2015)
3. Mercier, S., Villeneuve, S., Mondor, M., Uysal, I.: Time–temperature management along the food cold chain: a review of recent developments. Compr. Rev. Food Sci. Food Saf. **16**(4), 647–667 (2017)
4. FAO: Globalization of food systems in developing countries: impact on food security and nutrition (2004). http://www.fao.org/3/a-y5736e.pdf. Accessed 10 Nov 2004
5. Gebreeyesus, M., Sonobe, T.: Global value chains and market formation process in emerging export activity: evidence from Ethiopian flower industry. J. Dev. Stud. **48**(3), 335–348 (2012)
6. Patel-Campillo, A.: Rival commodity chains: agency and regulation in the US and Colombian cut flower agro-industries. Rev. Int. Polit. Econ. **17**(1), 75–102 (2010)
7. Rikken, M.: The global competitiveness of the Kenyan flower industry. In: Fifth Video Conference on the Global Competitiveness of the Flower Industry in Eastern Africa (2011)
8. Riasi, A.: Barriers to international supply chain management in Iranian flower industry. Manag. Sci. Lett. **5**(4), 363–368 (2015)
9. Zhao, Y.X.: Discussion on countermeasures of Chinese agricultural product cold-chain logistics. J. Harbin Univ. Commer.: Soc. Sci. **2** (2010)
10. Casino, F., Dasaklis, T.K., Patsakis, C.: A systematic literature review of blockchain-based applications: current status, classification and open issues. Telemat. Inform. **36**, 55–81 (2019)
11. Lawton, G.: 10 blockchain problems supply chains need to look out for (2019). https://searcherp.techtarget.com/feature/10-blockchain-problems-supply-chains-need-to-look-out-for. Accessed 15 Apr 2019
12. Aste, T., Tasca, P., Di Matteo, T.: Blockchain technologies: the foreseeable impact on society and industry. Computer **50**(9), 18–28 (2017)
13. Kshetri, N.: Blockchain's roles in meeting key supply chain management objectives. Int. J. Inf. Manag. **39**, 80–89 (2018)
14. Queiroz, M.M., Wamba, S.F.: Blockchain adoption challenges in supply chain: an empirical investigation of the main drivers in India and the USA. Int. J. Inf. Manag. **46**, 70–82 (2019)
15. Zheng, Z., et al.: An overview on smart contracts: challenges, advances and platforms. Future Gener. Comput. Syst. **105**, 475–491 (2020)
16. White, M.: A global trade platform using blockchain technology aimed at improving the cost of transportation, lack of visibility and inefficiencies with paper-based processes (2018). https://www.ibm.com/blogs/blockchain/2018/01/digitizing-global-trade-maersk-ibm/. Accessed 16 Jan 2018

17. Wang, K., Xie, W., Wu, W., Pei, J., Zhou, Q.: Blockchain-enabled IoT platform for end-to-end supply chain risk management. J. Blockchain Res. **1**(1), 1–17 (2022)
18. IBM: Maersk and IBM Unveil First Industry-Wide Cross-Border Supply Chain Solution on Blockchain (2017). https://www-03.ibm.com/press/us/en/pressrelease/51712.wss. Accessed 16 Jan 2017
19. Degruyter: Global Orchid Industry (2019). https://www.degruyter.com/down-loadpdf/books/9783110426403/9783110426403.2/9783110426403.2.pdf. Accessed 29 Jan 2015
20. Floriculture, Cold Chain Management in Cut Flowers (2019). http://www.florinews.com/index.php/past-featured-articles/40-past-featured-articles/201-cold-chain-management-in-cut-flowers. Accessed 30 Dec 2019
21. Yaga, D., Mell, P., Roby, N., Scarfone, K.: Blockchain technology overview. arXiv preprint arXiv:1906.11078 (2019)
22. IBM: What is the benefit of blockchain technology? (2020). https://www.ibm.com/topics/benefits-of-blockchain. Accessed 01 Jan 2020
23. Elrom, E., Elrom, E.: Hyperledger. The Blockchain Developer: A Practical Guide for Designing, Implementing, Publishing, Testing, and Securing Distributed Blockchain-Based Projects, pp. 299–348 (2019)
24. Chamira, R.: Streamlining the Cold Supply Chain with a Blockchain Powered Solution (2020). https://blockchain.oodles.io/blog/supply-chain-management-blockchain/. Accessed 10 Dec 2020
25. Aung, M.M., Chang, Y.S.: Temperature management for the quality assurance of a perishable food supply chain. Food Control **40**, 198–207 (2014)
26. Tsai, K.-M., Lin, K.-S.: Studying the effect of ambient temperature exposure on refrigerated food quality and safety for sustainable food cold chains. In: Liu, X. (ed.) Environmental Sustainability in Asian Logistics and Supply Chains, pp. 135–151. Springer, Singapore (2019). https://doi.org/10.1007/978-981-13-0451-4_8
27. Shukla, M., Jharkharia, S.: Agri-fresh produce supply chain management: a state-of-the-art literature review. Int. J. Oper. Prod. Manag. **33**(2), 114–158 (2013)
28. Negi, S., Anand, N.: Post-harvest losses and wastage in Indian fresh agro supply chain industry: a challenge. IUP J. Supply Chain Manag. **14**(2) (2017)
29. Gunders, D.: Wasted: How America Is Losing Up to 40 Percent of Its Food from Farm to Fork to Landfill (2017). https://www.nrdc.org/resources/wasted-how-america-losing-40-percent-its-food-farm-fork-landfill. Accessed 16 Aug 2017
30. De Carvalho, P.R., Naoum-Sawaya, J., Elhedhli, S.: Blockchain-enabled supply chains: an application in fresh-cut flowers. Appl. Math. Model. **110**, 841–858 (2022)
31. Matthee, M., Naudé, W., Viviers, W.: Challenges for the floriculture industry in a developing country: a South African perspective. Dev. South. Afr. **23**(4), 511–528 (2006)
32. Mingxiao, D.: A review on consensus algorithm of blockchain. In: 2017 IEEE International Conference on Systems, Man, and Cybernetics (SMC). IEEE Conference (2017)
33. Pongnumkul, S., Siripanpornchana, C., Thajchayapong, S.: Performance analysis of private blockchain platforms in varying workloads. In: 2017 26th International Conference on Computer Communication and Networks (ICCCN). IEEE Conference (2017)
34. Behlendorf, B., Belur, J., Kumar, S.: Peering through the kaleidoscope: variation and validity in data collection on terrorist attacks. Stud. Confl. Terror. **39**(7–8), 641–667 (2016)
35. Verhoelen, J.: Implementation of a blockchain application with Hyperledger Fabric and Composer (2018). https://blog.codecentric.de/en/2018/04/blockchain-application-fabric-com-poser/. Accessed 17 Apr 2018
36. Androulaki, E.: Hyperledger fabric: a distributed operating system for permissioned blockchains. In: Proceedings of the Thirteenth EuroSys Conference. ACM Conference (2018)

37. Thakkar, P., Nathan, S., Viswanathan, B.: Performance benchmarking and optimizing hyperledger fabric blockchain platform. In: 2018 IEEE 26th International Symposium on Modeling, Analysis, and Simulation of Computer and Telecommunication Systems (MASCOTS). IEEE Conference (2018)
38. Costa, P.M.L: Supply Chain Management with Blockchain Technologies (2018). https://repositorio-aberto.up.pt/bitstream/10216/114335/2/278462.pdf
39. Dhillon, V., Metcalf, D., Hooper, M.: The Hyperledger project. In: Dhillon, V., Metcalf, D., Hooper, M. (eds.) Blockchain Enabled Applications, pp. 139–149. Springer, Berkeley (2017). https://doi.org/10.1007/978-1-4842-3081-7_10
40. Gaur, N.: Hands-On Blockchain with Hyperledger: Building Decentralized Applications with Hyperledger Fabric and Composer edn. Pack Publishing Ltd. (2018)
41. Comuzzi, M., Grefen, P., Meroni, G.: Blockchain for Business: IT Principles into Practice. Taylor & Francis (2023)
42. ChainDigit: Is Hyperledger a good fit for Enterprises? (2019). https://chaindigit.com/why-hyperledger%3F. Accessed 02 Jan 2019
43. Urbano, O., et al.: Cost-effective implementation of a temperature traceability system based on smart RFID Tags and IoT services. Sensors **20**(4), 1163 (2020). https://doi.org/10.3390/s20041163
44. Raj, J.S., Bashar, A., Ramson, S.J.: Innovative Data Communication Technologies and Applications. Springer, Singapore (2022). https://doi.org/10.1007/978-981-16-7167-8
45. Siyal, A.A., Junejo, A.Z., Zawish, M., Ahmed, K., Khalil, A., Soursou, G: Applications of blockchain technology in medicine and healthcare: challenges and future perspectives. Cryptography **3**(1), 3 (2019). https://doi.org/10.3390/cryptography3010003

A Fully Decentralized Privacy-Enabled Federated Learning System

Andras Ferenczi(✉) and Costin Bădică

Faculty of Automatics, Computers and Electronics, University of Craiova, Craiova, Romania
ferenczi.andras.h5f@student.ucv.ro, costin.badica@edu.ucv.ro

Abstract. This paper looks into the field of blockchain-based federated learning, an area that's been studied a lot but is often too abstract for real-world use. Most solutions stay inside academic discussions, and there's a lack of practical, usable options. Our work introduces a new system that uses blockchain for federated learning in a straightforward, real-world way. Our system includes novel features such as an innovative anti-plagiarism mechanism and a unique consensus method for validating training results. We explain our methods, main results, and what our work could mean for the future in the paper. Our study could help make blockchain-based federated learning more useful by changing how data is shared and learned, all while keeping privacy and decentralization. This could drive more work into creating usable solutions in this field.

Keywords: Federated Learning · Privacy · Decentralized · Blockchain

1 Introduction

Machine Learning (ML) models, such as regression, support-vector machines and neural networks, are trained using an optimization algorithm, for example stochastic gradient descent search (SGD). The model is trained with sample data and the more data is available, the better the training results are.

Often, the training needs geographically or demographically dispersed data that is not readily available. Even when available, a host of privacy and security concerns may prevent collection and usage of the data for training purposes in a centralized fashion. The training of complex models also requires massive computing resources and/or storage.

Decentralized ledger technologies, specifically blockchain, have enabled the crowdsourcing of tasks. This study focuses on a collaborative approach to train a central model using local data, while ensuring data privacy, training quality and integrity even in presence of participants that behaves in an unexpected, malicious way and do conform to the protocol's requirements (a.k.a. Byzantine participants).

Our paper is structured as follows. Section 2 briefly touches on Federated Learning (FL) concepts aggregation methods and Security and Privacy concepts that we will be leveraging later. In Sect. 3 we briefly state the primary problems faced with our approach and we elaborate on our unique method and implementation. In Sect. 4 we present

N. T. Nguyen et al. (Eds.): ICCCI 2023, LNAI 14162, pp. 444–456, 2023.
https://doi.org/10.1007/978-3-031-41456-5_34

our experimental results and provide some benchmarks on simulating the system on a local computer. Finally, in Sect. 6 we conclude our findings and elaborate on future research plans.

2 Literature Review

2.1 Federated Learning

Advances in ML algorithms facilitated decentralization in this domain as well.

Federated Averaging. In 2016, Google researches published a first version of paper [10] featuring a "practical method for the FL using deep networks based on iterative model averaging". The concrete use case is for using the local and sensitive data on mobile devices (e.g. text messages and images) to train a model locally and then to upload the updated-weights to a data center where all the updates are aggregated. A practical example is predicting the next word to be typed in a messaging communication on a mobile device. The process repeats after the updated model is sent out to registered mobile devices.

Training a neural network assumes the minimization of a (usually non-convex) function $f : \mathbb{R}^d \to [0, +\infty)$ defined as $f = \frac{1}{n}\sum_{i=1}^{n} f_i(w)$ such that w are the network weights, d is the dimension of the weight vector, n is the number of samples and $f_i(w) = \ell(x_i, y_i; w)$. Here ℓ denotes the loss on prediction (x_i, y_i) for w.

The sample dataset is denoted by P and it is distributed across K devices with $n_k = |P_k|$ representing the size of dataset on device $k \in 1 \ldots K$. In this case, the equation that defines f becomes: $f(w) = \sum_{k=1}^{K} \frac{n_k}{n} F_k(w)$ where $F_k(w) = \frac{1}{n_k}\sum_{i \in P_k} f_i(w)$. If the training data distribution were uniform for each P_k, the mean of the distribution would be $\mathbb{E}_{P_k}[F_k(w)] = f(w)$. This is, unfortunately, not the case as in general we have non-IID samples at hand.

The Federated Stochastic Gradient Descent – FederatedSGD a.k.a. $FedAVG$ – works by selecting a fraction $0 \le C \le 1$ of all clients. For $C = 1$ we have a non-stochastic gradient descent. In this case, each client performs one epoch of training on its local data and the server updates the global model by subtracting the weighed average of the gradients from the current weights. Clients perform multiple iterations locally before the central server computes the global model for the next epoch. This approach is called FederatedAveraging (or $FedAvg$). The latter approach reduces significantly the number of communications rounds, and, as the authors conclude, the trained model has high performance.

Krum and Multi-krum. A novel and efficient aggregation rule for Byzantine-resilient distributed ML is provided in [1], showing its effectiveness through experiments. The Krum rule has important applications in distributed ML in various domains where Byzantine failures can occur.

The paper [1] states that in the presence of Byzantine workers, the FederatedAveraging aggregation is challenging as the malicious updates can significantly degrade the performance of the model. FederatedAveraging by assuming linear combinations of worker updates, cannot tolerate even a single Byzantine worker, as the malicious worker can force the parameter server to choose an arbitrary vector. Therefore, a non-linear aggregation rule called Krum is proposed which selects the vector closest to its $n - f$ neighbors, where n is the total number of workers and f is the number of Byzantine workers. The Krum rule satisfies a resilience property, which guarantees that the vector output chosen by the parameter server has statistical moments bounded above by a homogeneous polynomial in the moments of a correct estimator of the gradient. Krum and its variant, Multi-Krum are proven to be resilient to various attacks by Byzantine workers, including those that send the opposite vector multiplied by a large factor and those that send random vectors drawn from a Gaussian distribution.

2.2 Security and Privacy

Plagiarism and inference attacks are a major concern around FL. Publicly trained models can be copied by "lazy" participants for quick gain. Locally trained models can leak information, and depending the use case, it can be sensitive private data such as coming from patients in a health care use case.

Pedersen Commitment. Commitment schemes [11] allow one to commit to a secret and sharing it later, if at all. An example is a hash: $commitment = SHA256(secret)$, where $SHA256$ is the 256-bit cryptographic hash, or a one-way digest, of the *secret*. The issue with this scheme is that secrets can be brute-forced, especially if the *secret* is short.

A more secure version of this scheme would be:

$$commitment = SHA256(secret \oplus blinding\_factor)$$

where *blinding_factor* is used to hinder brute-force attacks. Committer would eventually have to share both the *secret* and the *blinding_factor* for validation and the same method would be used to verify the *commitment*.

One issue with this scheme is that it is not secure under collision and preimage resistance. This concern is addressed by Pedersen's commitment scheme [11], that, in the author's own words, is "a non-interactive verifiable (b, n)-threshold scheme which is at least as efficient as earlier proposals."

Pedersen's commitment scheme [11] states that given generators g and h (elements of group G_q) with $log_g h$ unknown, a committer chooses a secret $s \in \mathbb{Z}_q$ and a random integer $t \in \mathbb{Z}_q$, then computes and shares the following commitment envelope:

$$E(s, t) = g^s h^t$$

The committer discloses at a later point s and t such that the verifier can validate that $E(s, t)$ returns the same result. It is easy to show that a commitment $E(s', t') == E(s, t)$ can only be opened if one knows $log_g h$. For this reason, it is important to have the values of g and h chosen using a coin-flipping method, given the decentralized nature of our application. We will delve into the specifics of the decentralized method to be used, Perfectly Decentralized Lottery-Style Non-Malleable Commitment, by Collins [2], in a separate publication. Some of the properties of Pedersen commitment are that it is binding, i.e. the content cannot be altered, and it is hiding, as the message doesn't leak. Unlike the $Sha256$-based method, Pedersen commitment is preimage resistant. For any chosen s, as long as t is randomly uniformly distributed, so is $E(s,t)$.

Pedersen commitments are additively homomorphic, meaning one can create a commitment of the sum of the committed values:

$$E(s_1, t_1) + E(s_2, t_2) = E(s_1 + s_2, t_1 + t_2)$$

This is important for us, as it will be shown in what follows. In our application we will use an Elliptic Curve implementation of the commitment. Given an elliptic curve, $E \ mod \ q$ and two generators G and H, it is assumed that there is no known integer x, such as $G = xH$. The commitment will be calculated as:

$$E(s,t) = sG + tH$$

Differential Privacy. Protection of individuals privacy is increasingly gaining focus, especially as Big Data makes its way into people's everyday life. Legislation, such as General Data Protection Regulation (GDPR), aims at enforcing it. A practical solution to the problem is Differential Privacy (DP) proposed by Dwork et al. [5]. A database is represented as a vector of size n from domain D of the form $\{0,1\}^d$ or $\mathbb{R}^d$. The Hamming distance $d_H(\cdot,\cdot)$ over D^n is defined as the number of entries in which two databases differ. We define a transcript t as a single query function and response.

A mechanism is ϵ-indistinguishable if for all pairs $x, x' \in D^n$ which differ in only one entry, for all adversaries A, and for all transcripts t:

$$|ln(\frac{Pr(\mathcal{T}_{\mathcal{A}}(x) = t)}{Pr(\mathcal{T}_{\mathcal{A}}(x') = t)})| \leq \epsilon$$

Here $Pr(\cdot)$ is the probability function and $\mathcal{T}_{\mathcal{A}}$ represents the transcript of the adversary A. The idea is to build sufficient randomness into $\mathcal{T}_{\mathcal{A}}$ so that it does not reveal which of x or x' was the input. The ϵ represents the privacy parameter. It can be tuned and ideally it must be greater than 1.

The *Laplace mechanism*. A *mechanism* is defined as a function that implements differential privacy. For a function $f : D \rightarrow \mathbb{R}$ over a database D, the mechanism $\mathcal{T}$ ensures ϵ-indistinguishable differential privacy, if [5]:

$$M(D) = f(D) + Lap(\frac{\Delta f}{\epsilon})$$

where Δf is the sensitivity of f and $Lap(b)$ is the Laplace distribution with center 0 and scale b.

Differential privacy can be applied in different ways in the ML process [13]: at the input layer as part of pre-processing of training dataset, in the hidden layer by using the Differentially Private Stochastic Gradient Descent (dpSGD) consisting of addition of carefully calibrated random noise to the gradients during training, or output layer where it becomes an optimization (loss minimization) problem.

2.3 Prior Art

Wang et al. [12] perform a comprehensive survey for Blockchain-Based Federated Learning (BCFL). The paper covers various architectures. In the Coupled Blockchain-based Federated Learning model (FuC-BCFL), federated learning (FL) clients also act as blockchain nodes. In case of Flexibly Coupled Blockchain-based Federated Learning model (FlC-BCFL), the blockchain and FL system exist in distinct networks. The clients are responsible for local data collection and training, while blockchain miners verify local model updates.

The paper covers existing verification methods. The PoV (Proof of Verifying) [7] consensus works by preparing a testing dataset in advance and setting an accuracy threshold. The testing dataset, which is provided by the task publisher is prepared on the blockchain. Miners then use this dataset to verify the uploaded updates and only apply the ones meeting certain threshold. The method proposed in [8] is similar, but is performed by a consortium of miners. The solution proposed in [3] proposes randomly selected consortium members to vote whether the updates are reliable or not, and the smart contract to decide based on vote counts. Finally, [9] leverages cumulative reputations of the trainers to assess the quality of their updates.

There isn't much variation in terms of how aggregation is implemented in SOTA aside from the selection of participants in this phase. For privacy Multi-Party Computation and Differential Privacy is used in most cases.

3 Methodology

We proceed to introducing our own proposal for a plagiarism-proof, privacy-enabled, decentralized federated learning system. An implementation is available [6] and it is based on a generic framework built for such experimentation [4]. The participants in this system are: The *Sponsor*, that provides model and the cryptocurrency that serves as incentive, the *Trainers* (50+) that perform the training and assess the trustfulness of their peers by providing a ranking using a novel decentralized Multi-Krum algorithm. 1. They then load the weights from the locally trained model into decentralized storage represented by Inter Planetary File System (IPFS), and the *Aggregators* that perform the aggregation.

We use a simple feed forward neural network model built using Keras for a multi-class classification hand-written character recognition with the MNIST split up in a non-IID fashion.

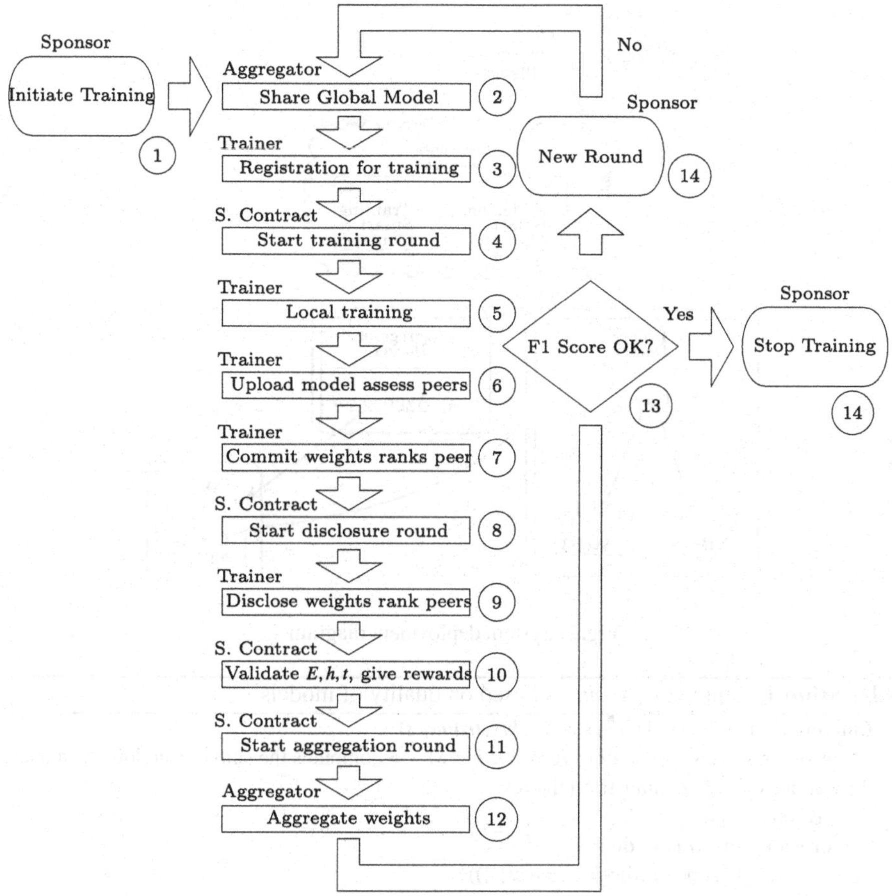

Fig. 1. High-level flow diagram of the training steps. Sponsor decides after each round whether to continue the training, based on the quality of the model (F1 score).

A complete implementation for the solution is a distributed architecture, consisting of separate processes running in docker containers running on the same host (Fig. 2). The *Trainers* have a public/private key pair each and awarded sufficient cryptocurrency (e.g., MATIC, Ξ) to pay the network fees for their submissions. They are granted access to host's shared volume to gain access to the training/test data as well as to the Solidity Application Binary Interface (ABI) so that they can interact with the contract using the web3 Python library. The address of the contract is passed via the *docker-container* script to the *Trainer* and the *Aggregator*. A pre-configured number of Ethereum dockerized clients perform mining with Proof of Authority (PoA) consensus on a private Ethereum network. A local IPFS network accessible by clients serves as the decentralized storage for the global and the local weights. The communication between the participating processes is facilitated by a docker network.

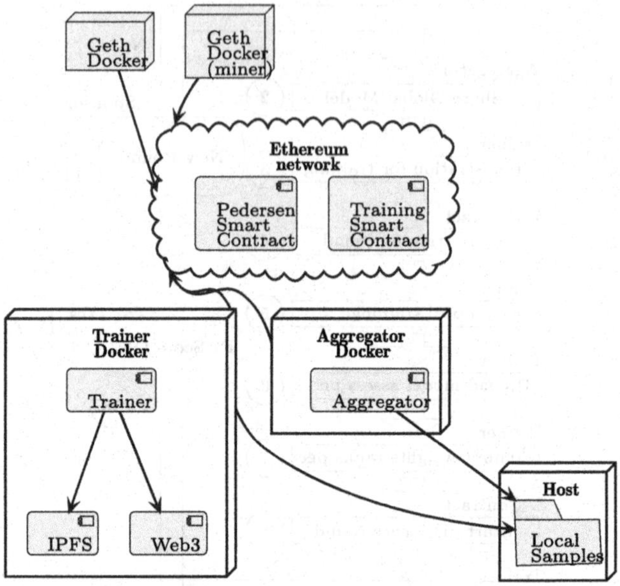

Fig. 2. System deployment diagram

Algorithm 1. Ranking of *Trainers* based on quality of models

---

function SELECTHONESTTRAINERS(*weights*, *trainers*)
    trainers, *scores* ← SCORE(*weights*, *trainers*)   ▷ computes the sum of Euclidian distances for weights of each *Trainer* from the rest
    medians ← []
    for each *t* **in** *trainers* **do**
        medians.append(MEDIAN(*scores*[*t*]))
    end for
    $f \leftarrow$ LEN(*trainers*)//3 − 1
    honest_trainers ← ARGSORT(*medians*)
    remove the last *f* **elements from** *honest_trainers*
    return *honest_trainers*
end function

Figure 3 shows the sequence of events after the local training has started (step 4 in Fig. 1):

1. *Trainer* calls *Training Contract* () function to get the IPFS addresses of its peers' submissions for prior round
2. *Trainer* invokes IPFS component to get the peers' weights by passing the addresses obtained from prior step.
3. *Trainer* runs Algorithm 1 to identify the trusted peers.
4. *Trainer* calls *TC* function to get the IPFS location of the global weights produced by the *Aggregator(s)* for the prior round
5. *Trainer* invokes IPFS component to download the global weights from IPFS

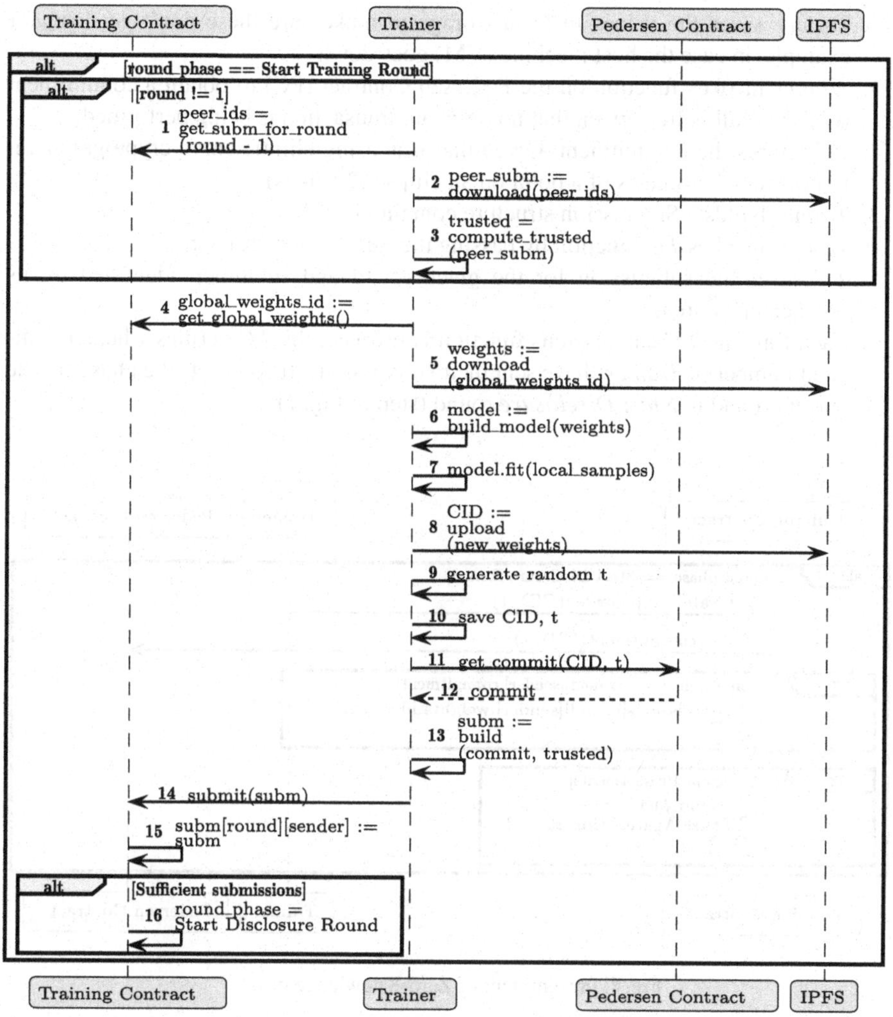

Fig. 3. Updates from *Trainers*

6. *Trainer* builds the model using TensorFlow by loading the global weights obtained at prior step.
7. *Trainer* trains the model using the local samples using differentially private Stochastic Gradient Descent (dpSGD) on the local data (to preserve privacy) for a number of iterations (e.g. 3)
8. *Trainer* invokes IPFS component to load the newly trained weights into decentralized storage. The IPFS component returns the address of the weights. This is not information the *Trainer* wants to share, or else it risks being plagiarized.
9. *Trainer* generates a random value to be used for the Pedersen commitment

10. *Trainer* saves the values in local storage to make sure these don't get lost, for example, in case the host machine (VM) goes down
11. *Trainer* invokes function on the Pedersen Contract (PC) to obtain a commitment (C). This call is free, given that no on-chain transaction is being performed.
12. *TC* returns the commitment. Given that it is using elliptic curve cryptography, it returns the coordinates of a point on an ellipse (2 values)
13. *Trainer* builds a Submission structure containing C
14. *Trainer* invokes *TC* function by passing the Submission structure
15. *TC* saves the submission for the given round and submitter, identified by its blockchain address
16. Each time the *TC* submissions function is invoked, the *TC* verifies whether sufficient number of *Trainers* have sent their submissions. If so, it sets the phase for the current round to *Start Disclosure* round (step 8, Fig. 1).

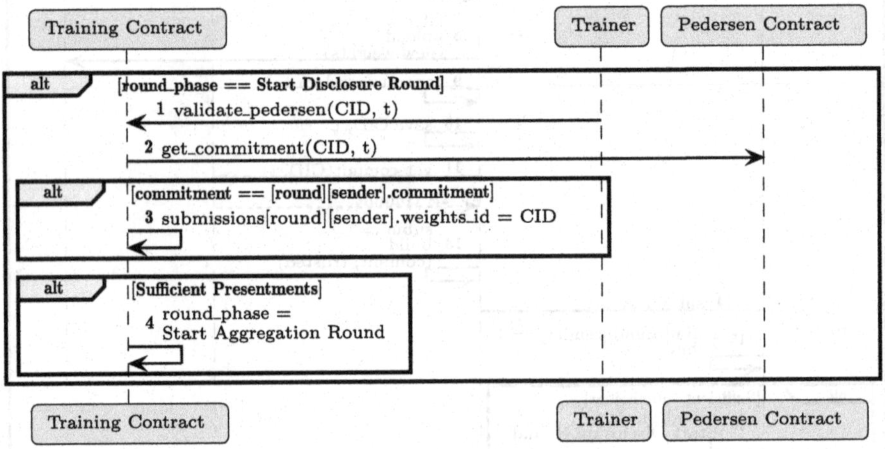

Fig. 4. Presentment of Zero-Knowledge proof

Interaction shown in Fig. 4 starts when *TC* initiates the *Start Disclosure* round (step 8, Fig. 1). In this phase, the eligible *Trainers* are expected to disclose the IPFS location of their weights obtained by training the global model locally. This approach will prevent plagiarism. Adversarial Trainers can copy models from prior rounds but not the current one, and this round can only submit the commitment to their current trained model.

1. To be considered in the current round, *Trainer* needs to disclose the IPFS location (*CID*, or Content Identifier) of its weights along with the blinding factor, *t*. For this, it invokes the *validate_pedersen* on *TC* with those 2 values.
2. *TC* invokes the same function on the Pedersen Contract (PC) to get the commitment based on the *CID* and *t*.

3. *TC* compares the generated commitment (point on the Elliptic Curve) with the one originally submitted by this *Trainer*. If the values are identical, it assigns the *CID* (*weight_id*) to the submission. Else, the it remains blank and hence the *Trainer* will not be considered for this round.
4. Each time a *Trainer* submits a presentment, *TC* checks whether it has received a minimum number of responses within a pre-agreed upon set time (number of blocks). Since the SC is stateful, it keeps track of sequence of phases. If prior round was for the local updates, it sets the next phase for global aggregation. The *Trainers* that did not submit their presentments on time will be left out from the remaining part of the training, and hence will not qualify for monetary reward.

4 Results

Our experiment consisted of 2 parts. First, we had to verify that the global model would converge even in the presence of Byzantine participants. For this, we tracked the performance of the training using our approach and separately using the well-known FedAvg solution. We gradually increased the percent of byzantine participants from 0 to 40% using 50 *Trainers* and 1 *Aggregator*. Figures 6 and 7 show the outcome of a simulated training with 30% byzantine trainers that perform label flipping. The results empirically indicate the fact that this particular training with the MNIST dataset can be completed in a decentralized fashion. The second test was an end-to-end stress test 5 of the entire system on a single desktop computer, including the Miners, Trainers, Aggregators, and the Owner. We could only ramp up to maximum 15 Trainers and the results are captured in. We managed to run a complete training session with multiple rounds. This experiment gives us an idea of what the system resource utilization would be to run such a network. Considering that a node hosting a Trainer may only need to run 2 dockers (the Trainer and the Miner) the systems resource utilization was sufficiently low to potentially run it even on a Raspberry Pi. Our conclusion is that not only did we conceive but also have successfully built a complete decentralized privacy-enabled BCFL system.

5 Discussion

To validate that the model convergence, we used 50 *Trainers* out of which 15 (30 %) were byzantine. We used a single *Aggregator*, although in "real life" we could employ multiple of them to eliminate the need for trust. In that case, besides computing the FedAvg on the updates that were selected by the *TC* based on Trainer rankings, Aggregators would rank their own peers using the same Algorithm 1 based on weights Euclidean distances. Unlike is the case for Trainer updates, the Aggregator-provided global model weights should be very close and any outliers would be an indication of adversarial update. Alternately, the *Sponsor* could also play the role of an *Aggregator*. These were randomly flipping the labels in their trainings. The results of the experiments can be seen in Figs. 6 and 7. The training was successful using our method, but fared poorly using the regular FedAvg method.

Our aim was to prove that the method works with at least one type of AI model training, as defining a generalized solution is likely a very difficult challenge. One would need to experiment with specific models to decide on the solution's feasibility.

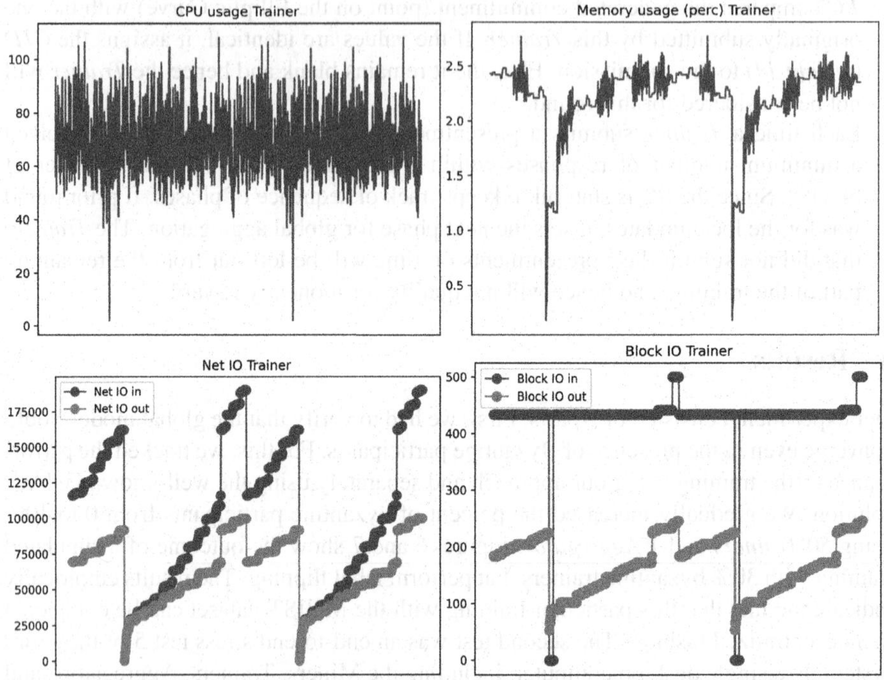

Fig. 5. Metrics collected for a stress-test run of the system on a single computer with 15 Trainers: CPU usage with no set quota for docker, Memory percent out of 32 GB, Network IO (in KiB) and Block IO (in KB), respectively.

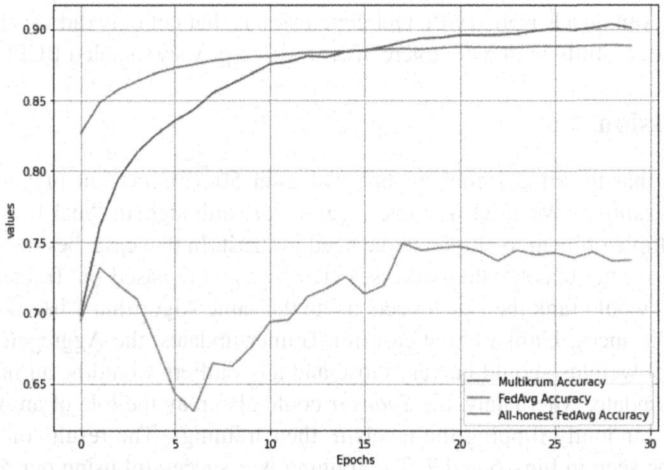

Fig. 6. Accuracy of various aggregation methods for 100 *Trainers* with 30 % byzantine ones that perform a Label Flip attack. The curve representing a regular FedAVG approach with all-honest *Trainers* is also presented.

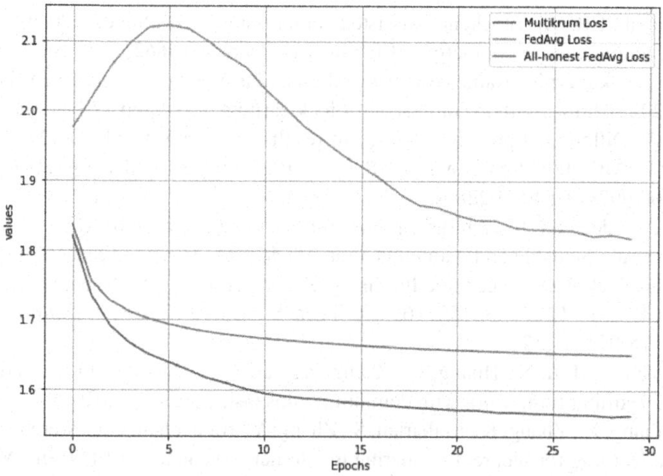

Fig. 7. Loss of various aggregation methods for 100 *Trainers* with 30 % byzantine ones that perform a Label Flip attack. The curve representing a regular FedAVG approach with all-honest *Trainers* is also presented.

6 Conclusion

This paper presents the first practical end-to-end solution for blockchain-based Federated Learning, addressing adversarial behavior such as plagiarism, non IID data, and privacy concerns. To the best of our knowledge, there is no prior art describing a practical system that would address all these issues simultaneously. We provide empirical evidence for the feasibility of our proposed solution.

We acknowledge the potential limitations of our proposal. The success of the training can be impacted by the characteristics of the local samples and the model used. The solution is, nevertheless, more robust than the SOTA we encountered in our research and our experiments go beyond pure theoretical discussions.

In the future, we plan to explore alternative solutions to address privacy concerns, such as Zero-Knowledge Proofs, Homomorphic Encryption, or Multi-Party Computation. We are excited to see our proposed solution being implemented in real-world scenarios.

References

1. Blanchard, P., El Mhamdi, E.M., Guerraoui, R., Stainer, J.: Machine learning with adversaries: Byzantine tolerant gradient descent. In: Guyon, I., et al. (eds.) Advances in Neural Information Processing Systems, vol. 30. Curran Associates, Inc. (2017). https://proceedings.neurips.cc/paper_files/paper/2017/file/f4b9ec30ad9f68f89b29639786cb62ef-Paper.pdf
2. Collins, D.R.: Perfectly decentralized lottery-style non-malleable commitment. In: Advances in Cryptology-CRYPTO 2018: 38th Annual International Cryptology Conference, pp. 245–274. Springer, Heidelberg (2018)

3. Cui, L., et al.: CREAT: blockchain-assisted compression algorithm of federated learning for content caching in edge computing. IEEE Internet Things J. **4662**(c), 1 (2020)
4. Dias, H.: BlockLearning framework master thesis. Master's thesis, Eindhoven Technical University (2023). https://github.com/hacdias/blocklearning. Accessed 17 Jan 2023
5. Dwork, C.: Differential privacy: a survey of results. In: Agrawal, M., Du, D., Duan, Z., Li, A. (eds.) TAMC 2008. LNCS, vol. 4978, pp. 1–19. Springer, Heidelberg (2008). https://doi.org/10.1007/978-3-540-79228-4_1
6. Ferenczi, A.: decfed (2023). https://github.com/andrasfe/decfed-eth. Accessed 17 Jan 2023
7. Kang, J., et al.: Scalable and communication-efficient decentralized federated edge learning with multi-blockchain framework. In: Zheng, Z., Dai, H.N., Fu, X., Chen, B. (eds.) BlockSys 2020. CCIS, vol. 1267, pp. 152–165. Springer, Singapore (2020). https://doi.org/10.1007/978-981-15-9213-3_12
8. Li, Y., Chen, C., Liu, N., Huang, H., Zheng, Z., Yan, Q.: A blockchain-based decentralized federated learning framework with committee consensus, pp. 1–7 (2020)
9. Lu, Y., Huang, X., Zhang, K., Maharjan, S., Zhang, Y.: Blockchain empowered asynchronous federated learning for secure data sharing in internet of vehicles. IEEE Trans. Veh. Technol. **69**(4), 4298–4311 (2020)
10. McMahan, H.B., Moore, E., Ramage, D., Hampson, S., y Arcas, B.A.: Communication-efficient learning of deep networks from decentralized data (2023). https://doi.org/10.48550/arxiv.1602.05629
11. Pedersen, T.P.: Non-interactive and information-theoretic secure verifiable secret sharing. In: Feigenbaum, J. (ed.) CRYPTO 1991. LNCS, vol. 576, pp. 129–140. Springer, Heidelberg (1992). https://doi.org/10.1007/3-540-46766-1_9
12. Wang, Z., Hu, Q.: Blockchain-based federated learning: a comprehensive survey (2021)
13. Zhao, J., Chen, Y., Zhang, W.: Differential privacy preservation in deep learning: challenges, opportunities and solutions. IEEE Access **7**, 48901–48911 (2019). https://doi.org/10.1109/ACCESS.2019.2909559

Cooperative Strategies for Decision Making and Optimization

Two-Dimensional Pheromone in Ant Colony Optimization

Grażyna Starzec[1], Mateusz Starzec[1], Sanghamitra Bandyopadhyay[2], Ujjwal Maulik[3], Leszek Rutkowski[1,4], Marek Kisiel-Dorohinicki[1], and Aleksander Byrski[1](✉)

[1] AGH University of Science and Technology, Krakow, Poland
{gstarzec,rutkowski,doroh,olekb}@agh.edu.pl
[2] Indian Statistical Institute, Kolkata, India
[3] Department of Computer Science and Engineering, Jadavpur University, Kolkata, India
ujjwal.maulik@jadavpuruniversity.in
[4] Systems Research Institute, Polish Academy of Sciences, Warsaw, Poland

Abstract. Ant Colony Optimization (ACO) is an acclaimed method for solving combinatorial problems proposed by Marco Dorigo in 1992 and has since been enhanced and hybridized many times. This paper proposes a novel modification of the algorithm, based on the introduction of a two-dimensional pheromone into a single-criteria ACO. The complex structure of the pheromone is supposed to increase ants' awareness when choosing the next edge of the graph, helping them achieve better results than in the original algorithm. The proposed modification is general and thus can be applied to any ACO-type algorithm. We show the results based on a representative instance of TSPLIB and discuss them in order to support our claims regarding the efficiency and efficacy of the proposed approach.

Keywords: ant-colony optimization · metaheuristics · two-dimensional pheromone

1 Introduction

Many efficient optimization algorithms are based on some kind of learning process (e.g., pheromone deposition in Ant Colony Optimization (ACO) or direction change towards the current best global solution in Particle Swarm Optimization). Modern research related to optimization algorithms (especially in the field

This research was funded in part by Polish National Science Centre, Grant no. 2021/41/N/ST6/01776 (GS). For the purpose of Open Access, the author has applied a CC-BY public copyright license to any Author Accepted Manuscript (AAM) version arising from this submission. This research received partial support from the funds assigned to AGH University of Science and Technology by the Polish Ministry of Education and Science (AB, MKD). This research was supported by the PLGrid infrastructure.

N. T. Nguyen et al. (Eds.): ICCCI 2023, LNAI 14162, pp. 459–471, 2023.
https://doi.org/10.1007/978-3-031-41456-5_35

of evolutionary algorithms) usually focuses on elitist approaches. In particular, the most popular variants of ACO learn only from the most generated feasible solutions, and the information collected is stored in a very simple structure [1,6,7,13].

The aim of our research was to extend the Ant Colony Optimization algorithm to extract knowledge from more than only the top candidate solutions, store it in a more comprehensive form than the standard pheromone table, and, presumably, improve optimization results. Our previous research [11,12] showed that allowing more solutions to improve pheromone trails improves the quality of the final results. However, the classic pheromone model is too simple to properly encode and interpret information from all feasible solutions, thus, we want to extend its structure to make it more meaningful. Using such an approach, the algorithm is able to make better use of computational effort dedicated to preparing feasible solutions and also to gain more information from negative examples. We believe that this kind of approach would increase the diversity of the search, allowing better solutions to be found in shorter time than the reference algorithms.

Multi-dimensional pheromone is an idea already present in the literature, see, e.g. [9,10], however these works are very closely related to the discussed applications (e.g. Vehicle Routing Problem when the authors actually save the local optimization outcomes, very valuable for undertaking the decisions when looking for global solution) and our idea is to propose general algorithms aimed at solving global and multi-criteria optimization problems with ACO.

This research stems from our works on metaheuristics summarized in [2] from the substantial point of view and in [8] from the technical point of view. Further sections of this paper focus on related work regarding Ant Colony Optimization, description of the idea of two-dimensional pheromone in ACO and discussion of the experimental evaluation of this idea followed by the conclusions and future work.

2 Ant Colony Optimization

The first version of ACO was introduced by Marco Dorigo [4] to solve the Traveling Salesman Problem (TSP). The algorithm was inspired by the behavior of natural ant colonies and the way they share their knowledge. ACO as a metaheuristic algorithm was described a few years later by Dorigo and Caro [5].

The single-objective ACO meta-heuristic algorithm expects the optimization problem to be specified as a graph consisting of a finite set of components (vertices) connected by edges with assigned cost. A valid solution is a path that respects the restrictions posed and meets the requirements defined by the problem. The cost of a solution is defined as a function of all the costs of all the connections that make up the path. The optimal solution is the valid path with a minimum cost.

The optimization process is based on a population of ants (agents). They iteratively traverse the graph creating candidate solutions. In each iteration, each ant starts from an initial vertex, which can be selected randomly, as in TSP or can be specified by the problem, as in VRP. A probabilistic decision rule (see Eq. 1) is a basis for the ant's decision regarding selection of the next vertex. The rule takes into account the heuristic attractiveness value and the values of pheromone trails left on the edges by previous generations of ants. The heuristic attractiveness (also referenced as desirability) is a function that describes the chances (based on optimization objectives) that the edge will be part of a high-quality solution. For example, in the case of TSP it can be defined as an inverted length of the edge. The pheromone trails indicate how often previous solutions contain specific edges.

The probability of moving from the vertex i to the vertex j of the ant k in iteration t is based on $\tau_{ij}(t)$ the intensity of the trail of pheromones at the edge and $\eta_{ij}(t)$ the heuristic attractiveness of the edge. The parameters α and β control the relative importance of the trail versus heuristic information. The value is relative to the values in all other possible moves A_k.

The probabilistic decision rule is defined as follows:

$$p_{ij}^k(t) = \begin{cases} \frac{\tau_{ij}^{\alpha}(t)\,\eta_{ij}^{\beta}(t)}{\sum_{l \in A_k} \tau_{il}^{\alpha}(t)\,\eta_{il}^{\beta}(t)} & \text{if } j \in A_k \\ 0 & \text{otherwise} \end{cases} \tag{1}$$

The tour ends when a complete feasible solution is found.

Based on the constructed paths, the ants update the pheromone trails. In the classic Ant System (AS) version, the update is performed at the end of each single iteration, controlled by parameters $\rho \in [0, 1)$ – a pheromone persistence coefficient, and m – the number of ants, according to the following formula:

$$\tau_{ij}(t+1) = \rho\tau_{ij}(t) + \sum_{k=1}^{m} \Delta\tau_{ij}^k \tag{2}$$

The value of pheromone update for each ant, with the cost of the solution L_k and a constant Q, is defined as follows:

$$\Delta\tau_{ij}^k = \begin{cases} \frac{Q}{L_k} & \text{if } k\text{-th ant uses edge } (i,j) \\ 0 & \text{otherwise} \end{cases} \tag{3}$$

where, in the case of TSP, the cost of the tour is simply the length of the route and Q often equals 1.

Since the first version of the ACO algorithm, multiple variations have been proposed to further improve its effectiveness and performance. One type of such a variation is based on introducing modifications to the original sequential algorithm but without introducing parallelism or distribution. Elitist Ant System (EAS, [7]) modifies Eq. 2, allowing only some ants with the best solutions to update pheromone trails. The rank-based Ant System (ASRank, [1]) is similar to EAS but weights the update left by the specific solution by its rank, so that the best solution modifies the trail most, while the second best modifies it slightly less, etc. Max-Min Ant System (MMAS, [13]) introduced the idea of minimum and maximum bounds of the pheromone trail value that are regularly enforced after performing standard pheromone modifications based on solutions found and evaporation. Ant Colony System (ACS, [6]) proposed two modifications: sometimes allowing an ant to choose the best option available as the next step instead of following the probability formula – Eq. 1 and the so-called local update, that is, decreasing the pheromone value, similar to standard evaporation, right after choosing a specific edge when creating a solution.

The most popular variants of ACO tend to reduce the importance of many solutions produced by the ants in each iteration, or even completely ignore most of them. In this way, they force the ants to focus on the most promising solutions. Although such an approach is natural, it wastes a lot of computational effort. In fact, it does not extract any knowledge from the rest of the proposed solutions [11].

3 Two-Dimensional Pheromone for Ant Colony Optimization

Despite multiple popular versions of the ACO algorithm, none of them aims at achieving effective knowledge extraction from all feasible solutions. One of the most popular variants of ACO — the Max-Min Ant System [13] – uses only one solution (iteration or global best) to update pheromones. In a colony with 25 ants, this approach discards 96% of the collected data. The experimental results of our previous research showed that larger colonies and more solutions used for the pheromone update improve the final results [11].

To collect more complex information about the feasible solutions created so far, we propose a two-dimensional pheromone structure. Each edge in the graph representing the problem will be connected not with a single value of the pheromone trail strength, but with multiple values representing pheromones left by various feasible solutions. This modification requires novel strategies for the three main components of the ACO algorithm: handling the solutions in the repository, updating the two-dimensional pheromones, and interpreting them during the solution construction.

We actually plan to apply the two-dimensional pheromone for solving multicriteria problems; however, now we would like to apply this idea to increasing the efficiency and efficacy of the single-criteria ACO. Therefore, we introduce many values for the pheromone deposited on the particular edge, and the idea for updating those values closely connects them with a certain order of the solutions produced by the ants. The path with lower cost will be marked closer to the "top" value in the pheromone, and worse paths will be marked "lower". Therefore, we may include information about not only the best solutions found by ants, but also a wider range of them. Thus, the ant choosing its next step may have much more information than the ant perceiving only the best solution (or actually the solutions gathered in the form of pheromone marking); see Fig. 1.

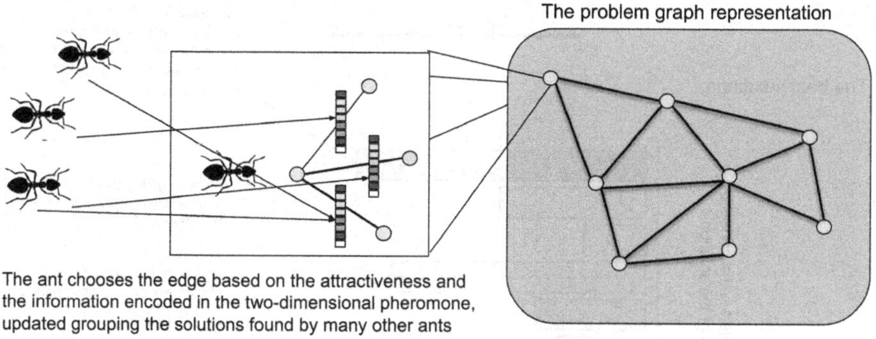

Fig. 1. Idea of functioning of ACO using 2D pheromone. The ants have more information than in the previous versions of ACO to use, i.e. vector of pheromones instead of a single value.

3.1 Depositing the Pheromone

In the standard approach (let us call it a one-dimensional pheromone), each edge is associated with a single pheromone value that represents how often this edge was used by the solutions found so far by the colony (usually taking into account only the top solutions). Its value is usually modified by two mechanisms:

- After each iteration, it decreases by some percentage (*extinction*) (the so-called pheromone evaporation or extinction),
- if the edge is part of the solution selected for the pheromone update, it increases by some particular value (*increment*).

In the two-dimensional pheromone, each edge is instead associated with a set of *twoDimPheromoneSize* values instead of just a single value. Therefore, we have to adjust the above mechanisms to this condition. For this, we need to have a context to evaluate a specific solution with respect to others. Therefore, multiple solutions (possibly all generated by the specific iteration) are passed to the pheromone update procedure and divided into groups based on their evaluation, and each group updates a single value in the two-dimensional pheromone (see Fig. 2).

Grouping is done in one of two ways (update types):

- PartFromEvaluation (PFE) — the cost range covered by the solutions is divided into *twoDimPheromoneSize* equal subranges and each solution is assigned to the *i*-th subrange according to its cost,
- PartFromIndex (PFI) — the solutions are sorted and divided equally into *twoDimPheromoneSize* groups of equal (or almost equal) sizes.

Once the solutions are divided into groups assigned to one of the values of the two-dimensional pheromone, each group updates their part of the pheromone. The value of *increment* (the algorithm parameter) is divided by the size of the

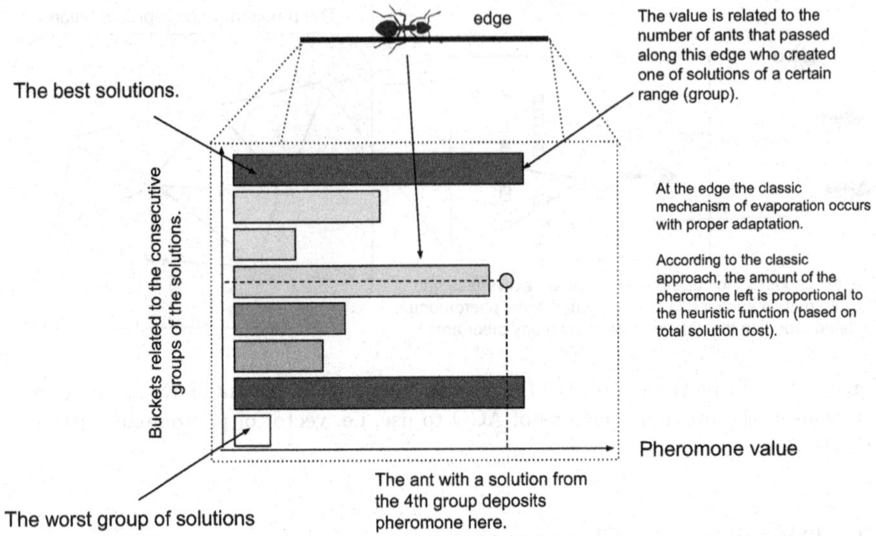
edge
The value is related to the number of ants that passed along this edge who created one of solutions of a certain range (group).
The best solutions.
Buckets related to the consecutive groups of the solutions.
At the edge the classic mechanism of evaporation occurs with proper adaptation.
According to the classic approach, the amount of the pheromone left is proportional to the heuristic function (based on total solution cost).
Pheromone value
The ant with a solution from the 4th group deposits pheromone here.
The worst group of solutions

Fig. 2. Structure of the 2D pheromone.

group and the result value is added to the current pheromone value for each solution of the group that contains this edge.

The pheromone extinction is simply applied to all pheromone values for each edge in the same way as for the one-dimensional pheromone.

3.2 Interpreting the Pheromone Information

For a one-dimensional pheromone, the value for the specific edge is inserted directly into the formula 1. In the case of two-dimensional pheromones, we have a set of values instead. The simplest way to bring that to the standard ACO version is to combine these multiple values associated with the specific edge to a single value in some way and put that into the aforementioned formula as if it were the value of a one-dimensional pheromone.

We propose three versions (interpretation types) of reducing multiple values of the pheromone to a single one:

- ExponentialRandom (ER) – from the available values, we choose a single one in such a way that the value updated by the best solutions is taken 50% of the time, the second value is chosen 25% of the time, the next one is taken half as often, and so on,
- WeightedCombination (WC) – the final value is calculated as the weighted product of the values where the first value is assigned the weight of 0.5, the second one – 0.25 and so on (the last two ones are assigned the same weight so that the weights sum up to 1,
- PairingCombination (PC) – this method pairs up the values from the outside towards the center (assuming that *twoDimPheromoneSize* is even). For each

pair, we consider the first one as "positive" (updated by better solutions) and the second one as "negative" (updated by worse solutions), calculate their average and difference, multiply the difference by the decreasing index of the pair (so that the difference is reinforced the most for the extreme pair, i.e., the first and last value of the pheromone, and the least for the "middle pair") and add the average to that. Finally, we compute the average of such values calculated for the pairs. Since this method does not ensure that the ultimate value is within reasonable limits, we ensure that it does not exceed $maxValue$ and the current minimum value of the pheromone ($maxPhValue * (1 - extinction)^{iterationsSoFar}$).

4 Experimental Evaluation

In order to evaluate the proposed modifications to the ant colony optimization Algorithm, a new testing framework has been developed, and a series of experiments have been conducted using it.

4.1 Testing Framework

The testing framework developed for the purpose of this research was created from scratch and is written in Scala. It is designed to represent the algorithm as an extensible model that contains interchangeable components. With that we aim to support not only running various (including new, experimental) versions of the Ant Colony Optimization algorithm but also solving different types of optimization problem.

For now, the framework supports a standard ACO version as described earlier in the document (called *Basic*) and the new version that uses the proposed two-dimensional pheromone in a few variants, in lieu of the usual "one-dimensional" pheromone. As of now, it is possible to solve TSP, MTSP and CVRP optimization problems, and the research presented here is focused on TSP based on popular benchmarks available from the TSPLIB database. For the sake of clarity, the framework does not apply any local optimizations (e.g. 2-opt) to the created solutions yet.

The framework allows for setting the following common parameters:

- $repeat$ – the number of repeated runs for each specific configuration,
- $iterationsNums$ — the number of iterations of the algorithm,
- $minPhValue$ — the minimum value of the pheromone,
- $maxPhValue$ — imposed maximum value of the pheromone,
- $antsNum$ — the number of ants in the colony,
- α — pheromone power in the probabilistic decision rule,
- β — heuristic value power in the probabilistic decision rule,
- $pheromoneType$ — $Basic$ or $TwoDim$ – choice between the standard "one-dimensional" and the experimental two-dimensional pheromone,
- $increment$ — the value used for the pheromone update increment,

- *extinction* — pheromone extinction fraction,
- *updateNum* — the number of the best solutions passed to the pheromone update procedure (with -1 meaning all the solutions from the iteration).

When *pheromoneType* is set to *TwoDim*, there are a few more parameters that can be set:

- *twoDimensionalPheromoneSize* – the number of values associated with a single edge,
- *interpretationType* – *ExponentialRandom*, *WeightedCombination*, or *PairingCombination* – choice among variants of the two-dimensional pheromone interpretation
- *updateType* – *PartFromEvaluation* or *PartFromIndex* – choice between variants of the two-dimensional pheromone update type.

It is possible to define a set of values for each of the parameters and run each combination of those possibilities.

4.2 Experimental Results

In order to evaluate the potential of our proposed modification of the ACO algorithm, we have conducted a wide range of experiments with various combinations of algorithm parameters for a single optimization problem – namely *Berlin*52 from *TSPLIB*.

In Figs. 3 and 4, we can see the results grouped by the number of ants in the colony for the types of pheromones *Basic* and *TwoDim*, respectively. They show an important difference between these two types. Since the pheromone does not influence the algorithm much at the beginning, we can see that they both start similarly, giving better results for more ants (better exploration, better chance of finding a better solution). However, in the case of *Basic*, it ends up giving worse final results for larger colonies, which might be interpreted as a faster fall into some local minimum. On the other hand, in the case of *TwoDim*, the results are consistently better for larger colonies for all iterations from the beginning to the very end. It might be interpreted as a sign of more effective knowledge extraction from solutions proposed by the ants. It is also worth noting that even for 20 ants, the average for two-dimensional pheromone is better than *Basic*.

Looking closer at the results generated for various combinations of parameters, we have concluded which values of some basic parameters seem to work best, that is, 100 ants, both α and β set to 3.0, and pheromones *increment* and *extinction* set to 0.05. In Fig. 5 we show average results for some selected combinations of *twoDimPheromoneSize* and *interpretationType* from among the runs with the basic parameters set as mentioned above. As we can see, we get the best results for 20 and *ExponentialRandom* and the worst results for 20 and *PairingCombination* which also shows very poor convergence.

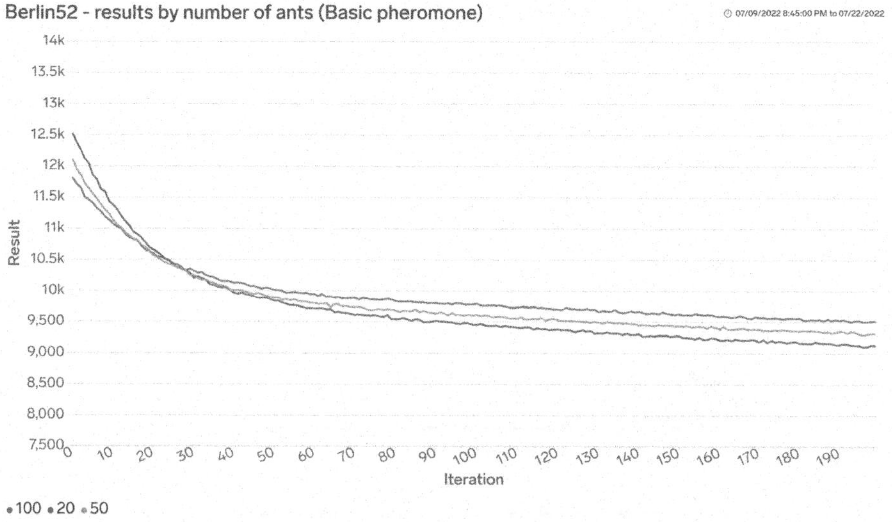

Fig. 3. Average results for various number of ants - algorithm with basic pheromones.

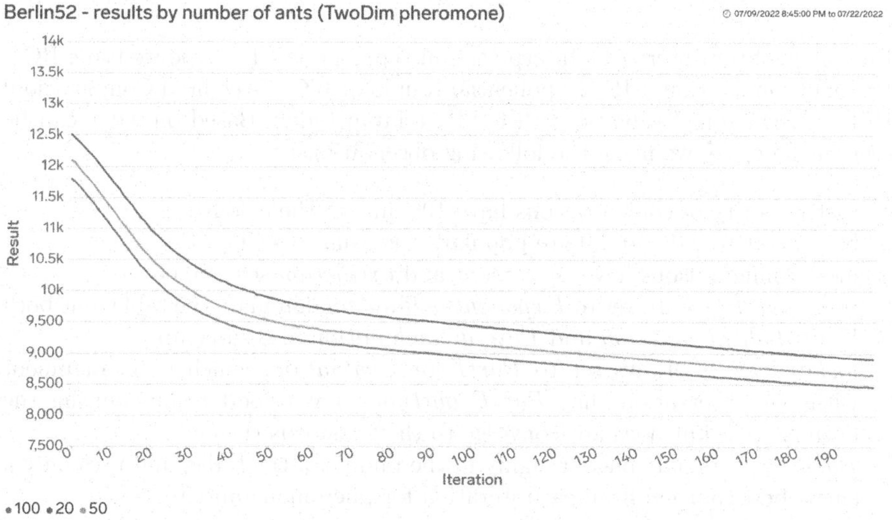

Fig. 4. Average results for various number of ants - algorithm with two dimensional pheromones.

In Table 1 we list the top configurations based on the results achieved in the last iteration. Each line of the table contains the score for the specific configuration that was calculated as an average from 20 repeats. The abbreviations of the parameter names and values have the following meanings: Inc. – increment; Ext. – extinction; UN – update solution number; TDS – Two-Dimensional

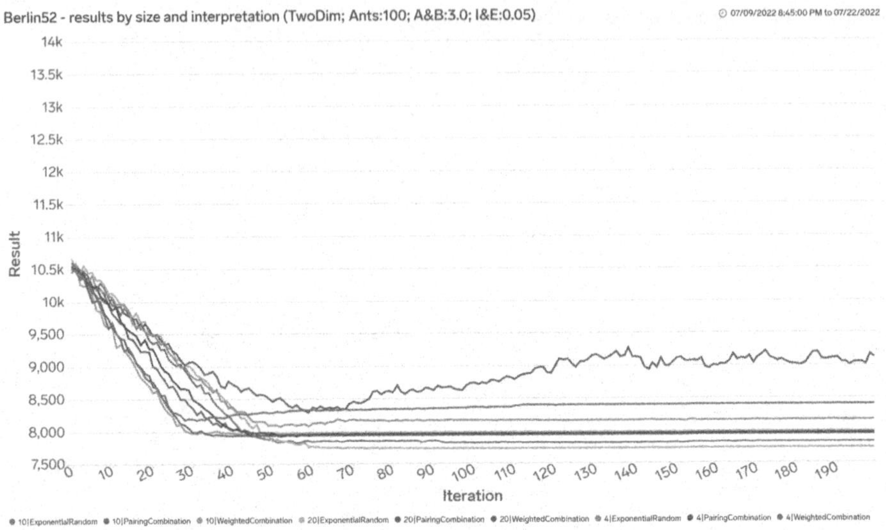

Fig. 5. Average results for various combinations of size and interpretation methods of two dimensional pheromones.

Pheromone Size; InterpT. – Interpretation type; UpdateT. – update type; PC – Pairing Combination; ER – Exponential Random; WC – Weighted Combination; PFE – Part From Evaluation; PFI – Part From Index. Based on what can be seen in the table, we make the following observations:

- vast majority of configurations have 100 ants in the colony,
- both α set to 2.0 and 3.0 are popular, β is usually set to 3.0,
- most configurations have *increment* and *extinction* set to 0.05,
- *interpretationType* set to *ExponentialRandom* dominate the table, but both *WeightedCombination* and *PairedCombination* also show up,
- *updateType* is always set to *PartFromEvaluation*, which is in alignment with our observation that *PartFromIndex* gives good results during the optimization but does not converge to them towards the end,
- *Basic* appears only once, roughly in the middle of the table, and uses only a single best solution from each iteration for pheromone update.

Table 1. Average last iteration results from 20 repeats (*berlin52*)

Ants	α	β	Pheromone	Inc.	Ext.	UN	TDS	InterpT.	UpdateT.	Avg. score
100	2	3	TwoDim	0.05	0.05	50	20	ER	PFE	7641.93
100	3	3	TwoDim	0.05	0.05	50	20	ER	PFE	7656.87
100	2	3	TwoDim	0.05	0.05	50	4	ER	PFE	7699.16
100	3	2	TwoDim	0.05	0.05	50	20	ER	PFE	7702.64
50	2	3	TwoDim	0.1	0.1	25	20	ER	PFE	7705.11
100	2	2	TwoDim	0.05	0.05	50	10	ER	PFE	7711.96
100	3	3	TwoDim	0.1	0.1	50	20	ER	PFE	7715.82
100	2	2	TwoDim	0.05	0.05	50	20	ER	PFE	7719.61
100	3	3	TwoDim	0.05	0.05	50	10	ER	PFE	7719.61
100	2	3	TwoDim	0.05	0.05	50	4	PC	PFE	7734.02
50	3	3	TwoDim	0.05	0.05	25	20	ER	PFE	7740.89
100	2	3	TwoDim	0.05	0.05	-1	20	PC	PFE	7742.79
100	2	2	TwoDim	0.05	0.05	50	4	ER	PFE	7743.03
100	2	2	TwoDim	0.05	0.05	-1	10	ER	PFE	7746.44
100	2	3	TwoDim	0.05	0.05	50	20	WC	PFE	7746.84
100	**2**	**3**	**Basic**	**0.05**	**0.05**	**1**	-	-	-	**7747.77**
100	2	3	TwoDim	0.05	0.05	-1	20	ER	PFE	7748.98
100	2	3	TwoDim	0.1	0.1	-1	20	ER	PFE	7750.97
100	3	3	TwoDim	0.01	0.01	50	10	WC	PFE	7754.45
100	3	3	TwoDim	0.1	0.1	50	10	ER	PFE	7755.76
100	2	2	TwoDim	0.1	0.1	50	4	ER	PFE	7758.33
50	2	3	TwoDim	0.05	0.05	25	20	ER	PFE	7768.05
100	3	3	TwoDim	0.05	0.05	50	4	ER	PFE	7768.28
100	3	3	TwoDim	0.01	0.01	-1	20	PC	PFE	7768.36
100	3	3	TwoDim	0.01	0.01	50	20	WC	PFE	7770.58
100	3	3	TwoDim	0.01	0.01	50	4	PC	PFE	7777.40
50	3	3	TwoDim	0.01	0.01	25	20	WC	PFE	7781.24
100	2	3	TwoDim	0.1	0.1	50	10	ER	PFE	7785.18

5 Conclusion

In this article we have shown how the introduction of a new pheromone structure (2D pheromone) affects the efficiency and efficacy of ACO applied to solving one of the popular TSP benchmarks. Even though the original algorithm uses all created solutions to update the pheromone, its later modifications reduce that to only top solutions, sometimes only to a single one, and because of that achieve better results. However, our work proves that using more or all solutions is more effective, provided that the information that can be collected from such variety of solutions is encoded in a more advanced structure than just a single value per edge.

The results presented demonstrate that the proposed pheromone makes the algorithm significantly better than its predecessor utilizing the original pheromone structure. We focused in this paper on one of the most popular benchmarks; however, we are planning to publish an extended version of this paper (abridged because of lack of space) in the near future, covering more benchmark functions.

We believe that utilizing a wider range of solutions (not only the best ones) increases the diversity of the search and helps in reaching better solutions earlier. We already developed a method for measuring the diversity of ACO [3,14], however we will apply this method in future to the newly developed algorithms. Moreover, in the future, we will apply 2D pheromone for solving not only single but also multi-criteria optimization problems, encoding e.g. different levels of Pareto front in our 2D pheromone structure, tackling more benchmark and real-life problems. Even though our idea stems from the existing ones cited in this paper, we aim at working-out a general algorithm aimed at solving global and multi-criteria optimization problems with ACO, while the cited papers focus on the applications.

References

1. Bullnheimer, B., Hartl, R., Strauß, C.: A new rank based version of the ant system: a computational study. In: WorkingPaper 1, SFB Adaptive Information Systems and Modelling in Economics and Management Science, WU Vienna University of Economics and Business (1997)
2. Byrski, A., Kisiel-Dorohinicki, M.: Evolutionary Multi-Agent Systems. SCI, vol. 680. Springer, Cham (2017). https://doi.org/10.1007/978-3-319-51388-1
3. Byrski, A., et al.: Population diversity in ant-inspired optimization algorithms. Comput. Sci. **22**(3), 297–320 (2021). https://doi.org/10.7494/csci.2021.22.3.4301
4. Dorigo, M.: Optimization, learning and natural algorithms. Ph. D. Thesis, Politecnico di Milano (1992)
5. Dorigo, M., Di Caro, G.: Ant colony optimization: a new meta-heuristic. In: Proceedings of the 1999 Congress on Evolutionary Computation-CEC99 (Cat. No. 99TH8406), vol. 2, pp. 1470–1477. IEEE (1999)
6. Dorigo, M., Gambardella, L.M.: Ant colony system: a cooperative learning approach to the traveling salesman problem. IEEE Trans. Evol. Comput. **1**(1), 53–66 (1997)
7. Dorigo, M., Maniezzo, V., Colorni, A.: Ant system: optimization by a colony of cooperating agents. IEEE Trans. Syst. Man Cybern. Part B (Cybernetics) **26**(1), 29–41 (1996)
8. Faber, L., Pietak, K., Byrski, A., Kisiel-Dorohinicki, M.: Agent-based simulation in AgE framework. In: Byrski, A., Oplatková, Z., Carvalho, M., Kisiel-Dorohinicki, M. (eds.) Advances in Intelligent Modelling and Simulation - Simulation Tools and Applications. Studies in Computational Intelligence, vol. 416, pp. 55–83. Springer, Cham (2012). https://doi.org/10.1007/978-3-642-28888-3_3

9. Guo, N., Qian, B., Na, J., Hu, R., Mao, J.L.: A three-dimensional ant colony optimization algorithm for multi-compartment vehicle routing problem considering carbon emissions. Appl. Soft Comput. **127**, 109326 (2022). https://doi.org/10.1016/j.asoc.2022.109326, https://www.sciencedirect.com/science/article/pii/S1568494622005014
10. Li, Y., Soleimani, H., Zohal, M.: An improved ant colony optimization algorithm for the multi-depot green vehicle routing problem with multiple objectives. J. Clean. Prod. **227**, 1161–1172 (2019). https://doi.org/10.1016/j.jclepro.2019.03.185, https://www.sciencedirect.com/science/article/pii/S0959652619308790
11. Starzec, M., Starzec, G., Byrski, A., Turek, W.: Distributed ant colony optimization based on actor model. Parallel Comput. **90**, 102573 (2019)
12. Starzec, M., Starzec, G., Byrski, A., Turek, W., Pietak, K.: Desynchronization in distributed ant colony optimization in HPC environment. Futur. Gener. Comput. Syst. **109**, 125–133 (2020)
13. Stützle, T., Hoos, H.H.: Max-min ant system. Futur. Gener. Comput. Syst. **16**(8), 889–914 (2000)
14. Świderska, E., et al.: Measuring diversity of socio-cognitively inspired ACO search. In: Squillero, G., Burelli, P. (eds.) EvoApplications 2016. LNCS, Part I, vol. 9597, pp. 393–408. Springer, Cham (2016). https://doi.org/10.1007/978-3-319-31204-0_26

Analysis of Different Reinsertion Strategies in Steady State Genetic Algorithm

Márk Domonkos(✉), Majd Koshakji, Ali Youssef, Issa Kalloumah, Modar Alshamali, and János Botzheim

Department of Artificial Intelligence Faculty of Informatics, Eötvös Loránd University, Pázmány P. Sétány 1/A, Budapest 1117, Hungary
{domonkos,botzheim}@inf.elte.hu, majd@koshakji.net

Abstract. Usually, it is uncommon to think about the reinsertion of generated offspring in evolutionary computing as a property of the algorithm that can be changed and optimized for a problem. This way reinsertion strategies are mostly overlooked properties of such algorithms. In this paper, we would like to introduce some novel versions and analyze their effectiveness. For this, a test was conducted where ten altered reinsertion strategies (including three commonly used strategies as reference and seven new strategies we came up with) were tested with a Steady State Genetic Algorithm. We tested the strategies with two kinds of population and on five different (three continuous and two discrete) benchmark functions and problems. The results show that there are strategies that work particularly badly, while others work with similar effectiveness. Also, it turns out that the number of the individuals and the nature of the problem can change the relative effectiveness of the strategies previously categorized in the effective group.

Keywords: SSGA · Reinsertion strategies · Evolutionary algorithms

1 Introduction

Evolutionary algorithms are methods that have become popular tools for solving problems such as optimization, search, design, etc. These algorithms are simulating evolution in different ways while pursuing solutions to the problem they are meant to solve. Such problem can be the optimal path of a mobile robot or a bipedal robot's controlling neural network's structure, where the algorithm's performance is crucial in finding a sufficiently good solution. When using such an algorithm, the optimal solution is not guaranteed, but by optimizing the algorithm a balance between computational cost and the quality of the result can be achieved. One of the historical basic forms of these algorithms is the Genetic Algorithm (GA) that was developed in the US by John Holland and his students [5,6]. Genetic Algorithms can deliver a good, and fast enough solution for some of the most difficult problems which could otherwise take a very long time to be solved [17].

N. T. Nguyen et al. (Eds.): ICCCI 2023, LNAI 14162, pp. 472–483, 2023.
https://doi.org/10.1007/978-3-031-41456-5_36

Steady-State Genetic Algorithm (SSGA) is an altered version of GA developed by Gilbert Syswerda where the main difference of the algorithm is that, in contrast to Holland's GA, the SSGA changes only a small portion of individuals during the establishment of the next generation [16]. It also differs from simple GAs in the reinsertion method used (instead of replacing parents, it reinserts the best from the parent-child pool, resulting in a constant population size) [1].

In [15] authors investigated four metaheuristics for a permutation flow-shop problem, with a weighted squared tardiness objective function in which all four methods (including SSGA) performed well. As the title of the paper says, in [3] the authors were combining a new optimization approach, the Sine Cosine Algorithm, with SSGA. They tested the proposed algorithms on two different engineering problems and found that it has a better performance.

In the next section (Sect. 2) we introduce the main focus of this research, namely the usage of reinsertion strategies. In Sect. 3 we present our solutions used, and after that, in Sect. 4 we present the experiment conducted and its results on the benchmarks. Finally, in Sect. 5 we conclude our findings.

2 Problem Statement

The main motivation of this paper comes from the question: Is the reinsertion strategy used in a GA a property that can be the subject of the algorithmic optimization process when searching for the best method for a problem? Does the relative efficiency to other applied strategies varies on different problems? As we mentioned, the main question with which this paper is concerned is the following: Is it possible to somehow improve the algorithms only by modifying the method of the algorithm's reinsertion strategy? Also, it is on the focus that what kind of conclusions can be made about the presented strategies (similar functioning in certain test cases, etc.).

By a reinsertion strategy, we mean only the process of the insertion of newly generated individuals (offspring) into the population of the next generation. This definition of ours means that we are not including the process of generating new individuals (selection, crossover, mutation). We focus only on the reinsertion part of the individuals.

To answer the questions above, in this paper we tested multiple modified versions of SSGA with different reinsertion strategies, then analyzed the results on multiple benchmarks. Next, in Sect. 3, we present our methodology, which is applied in the experiment.

3 Methodology

To measure the effectiveness of each reinsertion strategy we tested all of the reinsertion strategies on all benchmark functions and problems described below in 5 dimensional space on two configurations described in Table 1.

Table 1. Configurations during the experiment.

	Population Size	Generations	Number of runs
Config1	20	100000	30
Config2	100	100000	10

3.1 Unchanged Parameters of SSGA During the Experiment

We used the roulette wheel selection method, to select parents. The roulette wheel is constructed based on the relative fitness of all individuals, where the area occupied by each individual on the wheel is proportional to their relative fitness, and since the individuals with better fitness value will occupy a larger area on the chart, the probability of selecting them will be higher [9,11].

We used single-point crossover. This is a simple and widely used method, where a randomly selected point in the individual is selected and the genes are exchanged between them with respect to their relative position to the selected point [8].

For mutation, we used two methods. We used simple bit-flip mutation on the discrete problems (Knapsack problem and Multidimensional Knapsack problem) [2]. When using bit-flip mutation a random gene is selected in the individual whose binary value will be flipped [12]. For continuous problems, we use the random deviation mutation, where a random value is given to a gene with a Gaussian distribution [4].

3.2 Reinsertion Strategies Used

- **Replace Worst:** Worst individuals are replaced by newly generated offspring.
- **Replace Best:** Best individuals are replaced by newly generated offspring.
- **Replace Parents:** Replacement of the selected parents by their offspring.
- **Replace Parents With Probability:** The replacement of selected parents by their offspring is controlled by probability.
- **Replace Random:** Random individuals are replaced by the offspring.
- **Random:** Offspring are added to the population, then the population is shuffled and finally the last individuals are removed.
- **Positive Fitness:** The fitness value of an individual is proportional to the probability of selecting its replacement (similar logic to roulette wheel selection).
- **Negative Fitness:** The fitness value of an individual is inversely proportional to the selection probability of its replacement (similar logic to roulette wheel selection).
- **Positive Fitness times Random:** Randomly selected scaling factors are used on the fitness of the individuals. Then the two worst are deleted.
- **Negative Fitness times Random:** Randomly selected scaling factors are used on the reciprocal of fitness of the individuals. Then the two worst are deleted.

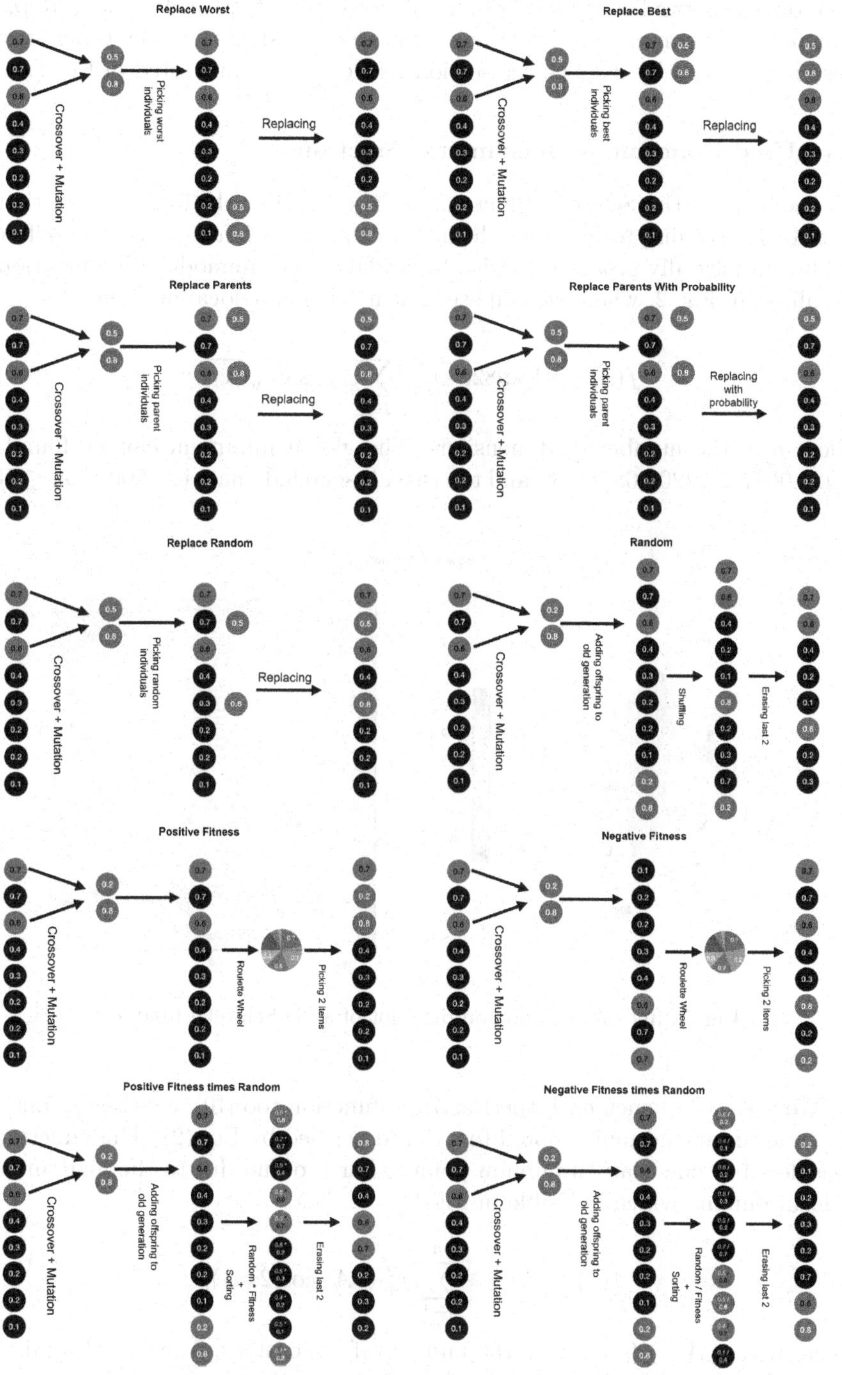

Fig. 1. Visualization of the used strategies.

From the above list, we used the 'Replace Worst', 'Replace Parents', 'Replace Random' as commonly used strategies for reference strategies, the other strategies are proposed by us. The reinsertion strategies are illustrated in Fig. 1.

3.3 Used Continuous Benchmark Functions

We used one of the Schwefel functions for the benchmark [14]. The function is described according to Eq. (1), which is a continuous function, that is differentiable and partially separable. It is also scalable and unimodal. The function is visualized in Fig. 2, where we can see that it has many local minima.

$$f(x) = 418.9829 \cdot n - \sum_{i=1}^{n} x_i \cdot \sin(\sqrt{|x_i|}) \tag{1}$$

where n is the number of dimensions. The global minimum can be found at $f(420.9687, ..., 420.9687) = 0$, and the (usual) search domain is $-500 \leq x_i \leq 500$.

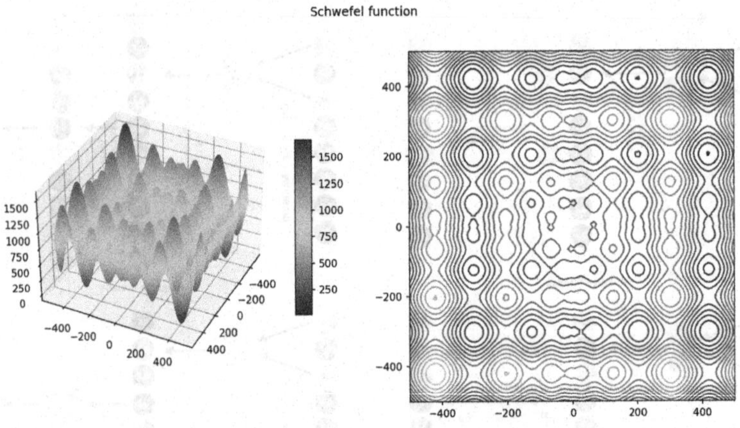

Fig. 2. 3D surface and contour plot of a 2D Schwefel function

We used as a benchmark the Rastrigin function too [10], which is a continuous, non-linear and multi-modal function described by Eq. (2). This function is considered as one that's minimum point is hard to find due to the high amount of local minima which is visible in Fig. 3.

$$f(x) = A \cdot n + \sum_{i=1}^{n} [x_i^2 - A \cdot \cos(2\pi x_i)] \tag{2}$$

where we set $A = 10$ and n is the number of dimensions. The global minimum can be found at $f(0, ..., 0) = 0$ and the search domain of the function is defined as $-5.12 \leq x_i \leq 5.12$.

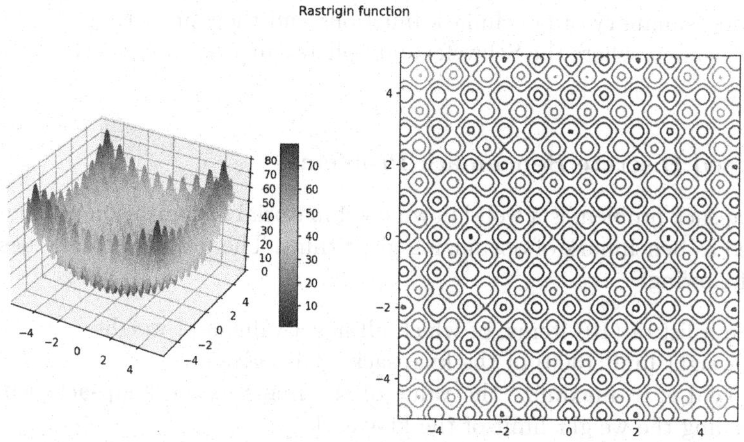

Fig. 3. 3D surface and contour plot of a 2D Rastrigin function

We also used the Sphere function [13] to test the strategies. This function is also a continuous convex function described by Eq. (3) and can be seen in Fig. 4.

$$f(x) = \sum_{i=1}^{n} x_i^2 \tag{3}$$

where n is the number of dimensions. The global minimum can be found at $f(0, ..., 0) = 0$ and its search domain is $-\infty \leq x_i \leq \infty$.

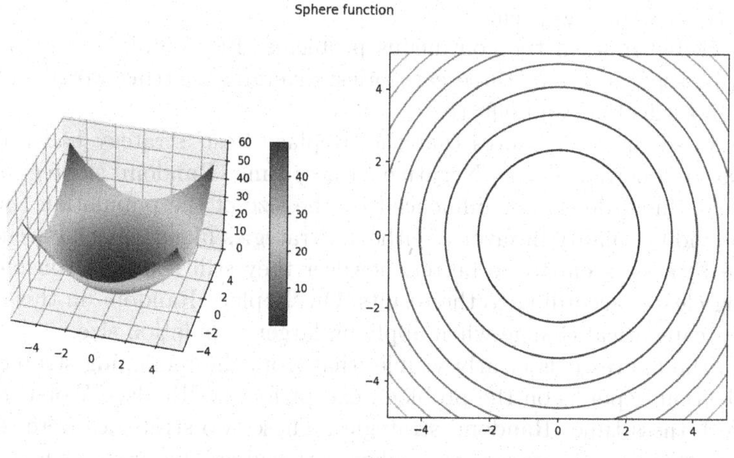

Fig. 4. 3D surface and contour plot of a 2D Sphere function

A good summary of benchmark functions and their properties can be found in the [7] survey, where the Schwefel and Sphere functions are mentioned in more detail.

3.4 Used Discrete Benchmark Problems

The knapsack problem is a well-known combinatorial optimization problem, usually used as benchmark of optimizing algorithms. The problem can be described as the following:

- Given a list of (10) items, of which all has a value and weight.
- The weight limit (300) of the knapsack is also given.
- The goal is to maximize the value of the items in the knapsack, while not exceeding the weight limit of the knapsack.

We used this as a discrete problem in our tests. We also used the multidimensional version of the knapsack problem (MKP), where the above-mentioned rules are extended in one dimension (i.e.: all items have volume as well and the knapsack has an extra volume limitation). The number of items from which the selection was made was 28 this time.

In the following, in Sect. 4 we present the results of the experiment.

4 Results

The results of the experiment can be seen in Figs. 5, 6, 7, and 8. The figures mentioned demonstrate the errors of the best individuals, and this is done by taking the average of the squared errors of the best individuals of the runs. Also, the y axis is on the $\log_{10}$ scale.

It is visible that on the continuous problems (Fig. 5 and Fig. 6) the methods can be separated into three categories: diverging (getting worst and worst results), not-effective, and effective.

We can see in both figures that the 'Replace Best' strategy had the worst performance followed by the 'Negative Fitness times Random' strategy. Also it seems that this order is not influenced by the size of the population (quantity is not providing quality in favor of either). Strategies like 'Replace Parents' and 'Positive Fitness' seem to be better, however they still could be considered as diverging clearly according to the results. On 'Replace Random' in this case we can see a categorical change when applying larger population size.

From the figures it is clearly visible, that from the remaining strategies the categorization depends on the problem, except for the 'Replace Worst' and the 'Positive Fitness times Random' strategies. These two strategies were reaching similar performance on average even when performing inferior to other strategies (in the case of Schwefel's function).

An interesting thing to note is the clear difference in performance between 'Replace Parents' and 'Replace Parents With Probability'. Adding the randomness can be seen to increase performance dramatically compared to always replacing the parents, as 'Replace Parents With Probability' is convergent, and performs very well especially on the Schwefel function, while 'Replace Parents' is divergent and is among the three worst performing strategies in all benchmarks.

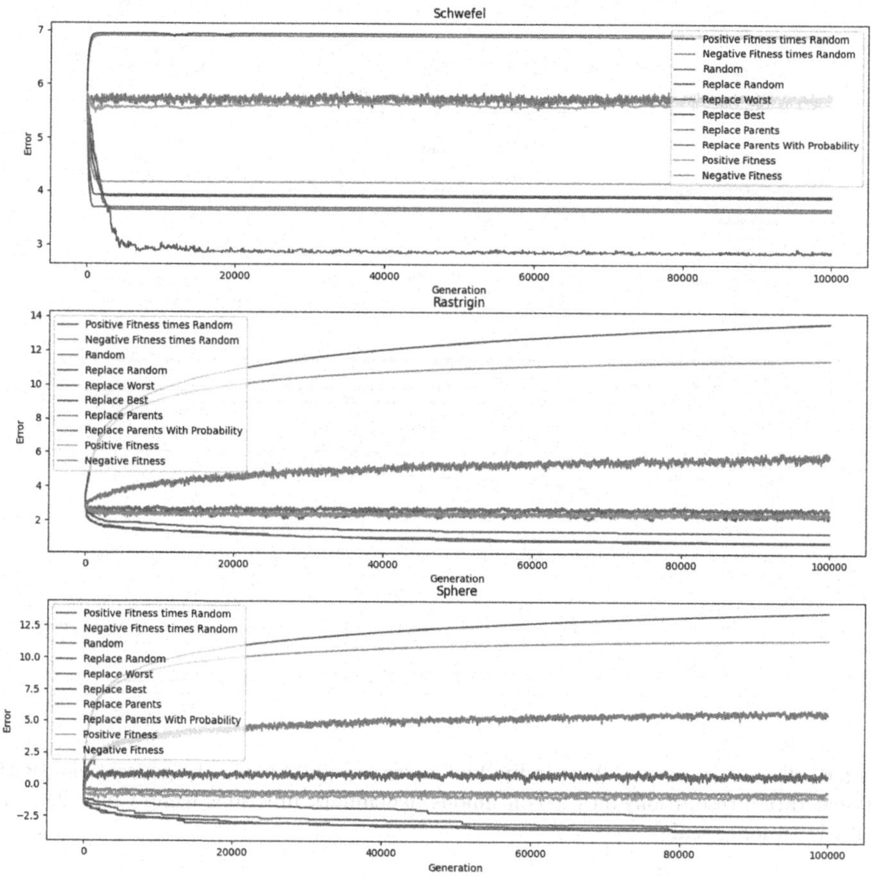

Fig. 5. Plot of the average best individual's error's square along the generations (with 10 generation resolution) on the continuous benchmark functions using Config1. (The error is on $\log_{10}$ scale)

When analyzing the result on the discrete problems (Fig. 7 and Fig. 8), it is visible that the Knapsack problem (which is considered an easy problem) was relatively fast solved by all strategies (that's why the algorithm stops before the maximum number of generations and the average cannot be calculated for the rest of the whole run) except for the 'Negative Fitness times Random'. On the harder MKP, a similar picture emerges as on the continuous problems. 'Negative Fitness times Random', 'Replace Best', 'Replace Parents' can be considered as divergent strategies. 'Random', 'Replace Parents With Probability' can be

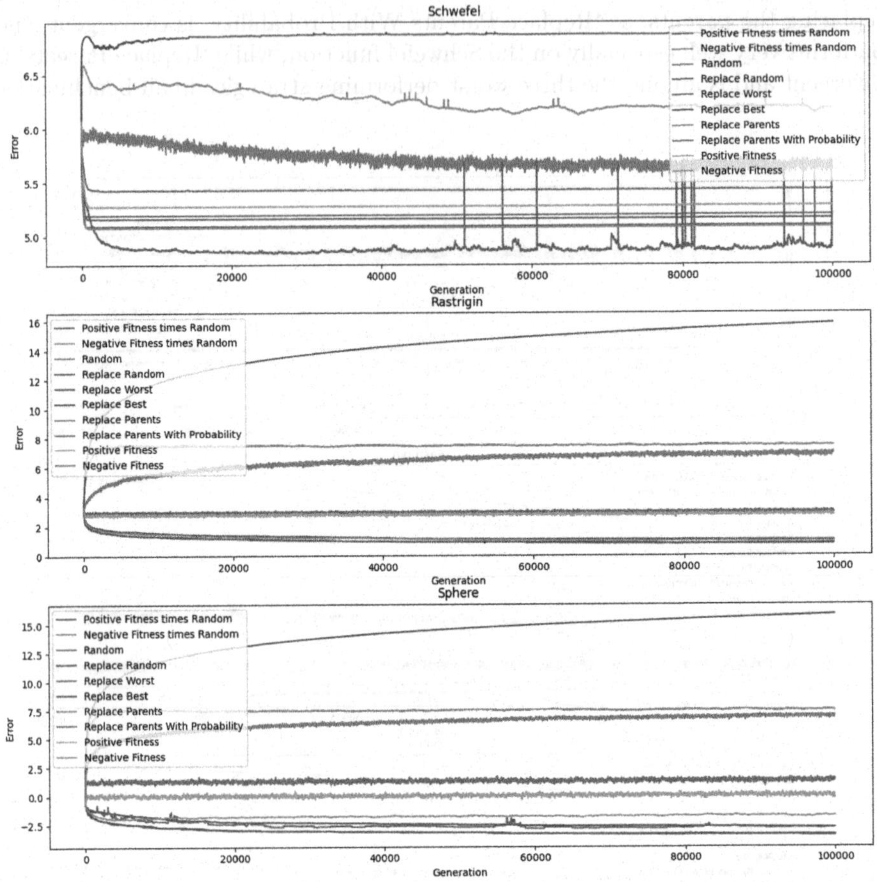

Fig. 6. Plot of the average best individual's error's square along the generations (with 10 generation resolution) on the continuous benchmark functions using Config2. (The error is on $\log_{10}$ scale)

considered as not-effective, while the others are showing some convergence to a solution. It is also worth mentioning that on the easy Knapsack problem the 'Replace Best' and the 'Replace Parents' strategies have an oscillation in the calculated error, before finally finding the good solution. This can be considered as pure luck in the oscillation between better and worst solutions.

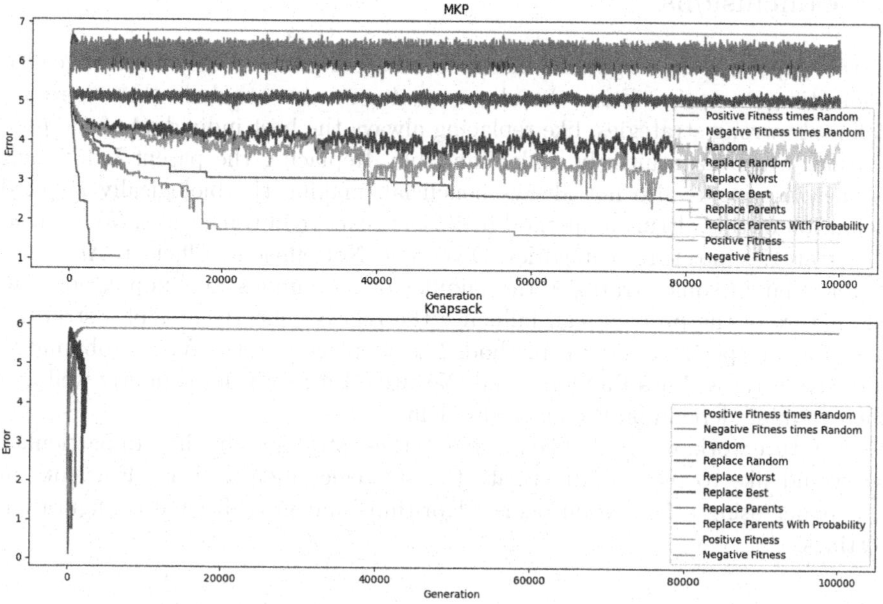

Fig. 7. Plot of the average best individual's error's square along the generations on the discrete benchmark problems. Config1 is used. (The error is on $\log_{10}$ scale)

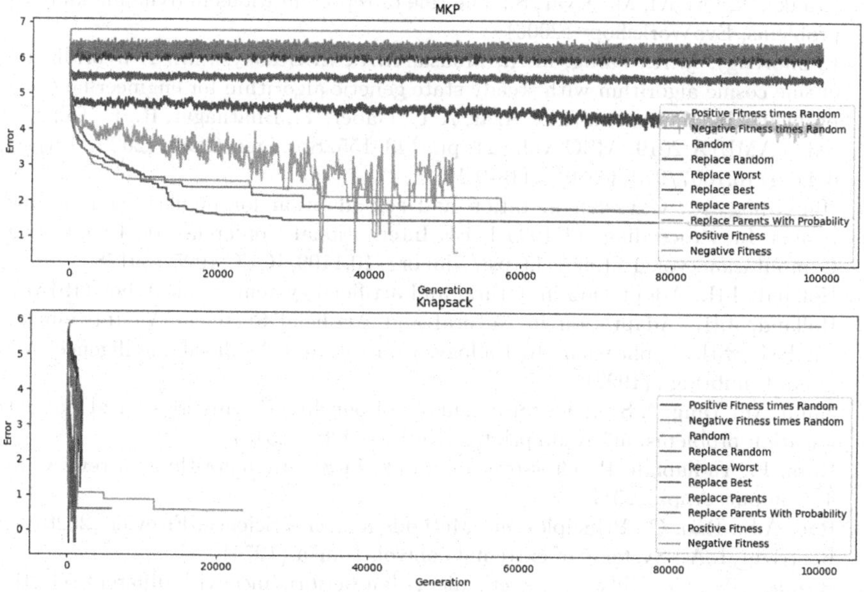

Fig. 8. Plot of the average best individual's error's square along the generations on the discrete benchmark problems. Config2 is used. (The error is on $\log_{10}$ scale)

5 Conclusions

In this paper, we investigated a mostly overlooked part of GAs, which we called reinsertion strategies. From the above results we can conclude that there are definitely wrong strategies, like replacing always the best individual of the population, which is intuitively understandable. Replacing the parent individuals of the offspring is also not always beneficial, making the biologically inspired definition of this altruistic method inefficient, except in some cases. We divided the strategies into three categories: Divergent, Not-efficient, Efficient. Also, it is visible that in some strategies the number of individuals in a population and the nature of the problem can influence the relative effectiveness of a strategy. This way, in specific cases our methods like 'Replace Parents With Probability', 'Positive Fitness times Random', and 'Negative Fitness' work similarly well and their ranking depend on the given problem.

In future work, we would like to explore these strategies further. In particular, we would like to further investigate the strategies identified as "Efficient" in this paper using other evolutionary algorithms and in additional configuration settings.

References

1. Agapie, A., Wright, A.H.: Theoretical analysis of steady state genetic algorithms. Appl. Math. **59**(5), 509–525 (2014)
2. Branke, J., Orbayı, M., Uyar, S.: The role of representations in dynamic knapsack problems. EvoWorkshops (2006)
3. El-Shorbagy, M.A., Farag, M.A., Mousa, A.A., El-Desoky, I.M.: A hybridization of sine cosine algorithm with steady state genetic algorithm for engineering design problems. In: Hassanien, A.E., Azar, A.T., Gaber, T., Bhatnagar, R., F. Tolba, M. (eds.) AMLTA 2019. AISC, vol. 921, pp. 143–155. Springer, Cham (2020). https://doi.org/10.1007/978-3-030-14118-9_15
4. Hinterding, R.: Gaussian mutation and self-adaption for numeric genetic algorithms. In: Proceedings of 1995 IEEE International Conference on Evolutionary Computation, vol. 1 (1995). https://doi.org/10.1109/ICEC.1995.489178
5. Holland, J.H.: Adaptation in natural and artificial systems. Ann Arbor (1975)
6. Holland, J.H.: Adaptation in Natural and Artificial Systems: An Introductory Analysis with Applications to Biology, Control, and Artificial Intelligence. MIT press, Cambridge (1992)
7. Jamil, M., Yang, X.S.: A literature survey of benchmark functions for global optimization problems. arXiv preprint arXiv:1308.4008 (2013)
8. Kora, P., Yadlapalli, P.: Crossover operators in genetic algorithms: a review. Int. J. Comput. Appl. (2017)
9. Rao, A.S., Rao, C.: Principles and Methods for Data Science. Elsevier (2020)
10. Rastrigin, L.A.: Systems of extremal control. Nauka (1974)
11. Razali, N.M., Geraghty, J.: Genetic algorithm performance with different selection strategies in solving TSP. In: Proceedings of the World Congress on Engineering 2011, vol. II (2011)

12. Rifki, O., Ono, H.: A survey of computational approaches to portfolio optimization by genetic algorithms. In: 18th International Conference Computing in Economics and Finance. Society for Computational Economics (2012)
13. Schumer, M., Steiglitz, K.: Adaptive step size random search. IEEE Trans. Autom. Control **13**(3), 270–276 (1968)
14. Schwefel, H.P.: Numerical Optimization of Computer Models. Wiley, Hoboken (1981)
15. Silva, A.F., Valente, J.M., Schaller, J.E.: Metaheuristics for the permutation flowshop problem with a weighted quadratic tardiness objective. Comput. Oper. Res. **140**, 105691 (2022). https://doi.org/10.1016/j.cor.2021.105691, https://www.sciencedirect.com/science/article/pii/S0305054821003865
16. Syswerda, G.: A study of reproduction in generational and steady-state genetic algorithms. In: Foundations of Genetic Algorithms, vol. 1, pp. 94–101. Elsevier (1991)
17. Vose, M.D.: The Simple Genetic Algorithm. Foundations and Theory, Massachusetts Institute of Technology (1999)

Traffic Optimization by Local Bacterial Memetic Algorithm

Szilárd Kovács(✉), Zoltán Barta, and János Botzheim

Eötvös Loránd University, Pázmány P. sétány 1/A, Budapest 1117, Hungary
{kovacsszilard,dguqkf,botzheim}@inf.elte.hu

Abstract. Transport is an essential part of our lives. Optimizing transport provides significant economic and life quality improvements. Real-time traffic optimization is possible with the help of a fast communication network and decentralized sensing in smart cities. There are several analytical and simulation-based methods for traffic optimization. Analytical solutions usually look at more straightforward cases, while simulations can also consider the behavior of individual drivers. This article focuses on optimization methods and provides efficient traffic control based on simulations. The optimization goal is to find the proper sequence and timings of traffic light signals to ensure maximum throughput. In the article only the waiting time is selected as optimization criterion, but with knowledge of the vehicle stock (fuel type, fuel consumption, start-stop settings, number of passengers, etc.) it can be easily expanded to multi-objective optimization.

In the literature, there are many optimization solutions, but all have some disadvantages mainly the scalability and the connectivity. Bacterial evolutionary algorithm and hill climbing algorithm are proposed in this paper with special area operators for the traffic optimization task. The developed memetic optimization algorithm can be efficiently scaled to optimize the traffic of even large cities. The method is efficient and well parallelized for real-time optimization use. For this study, a part of the city is examined in a SUMO simulation environment. The simulation result shows that our scalable memetic algorithm outperforms the currently applied methods by 35–45%.

Keywords: traffic control · memetic algorithm · scalable optimization · smart city · evolutionary computing

1 Introduction

Traffic optimization is complex, it has many important segments, like statistical data collection, real-time data collection, driver and vehicle behavior, and the optimization algorithm. In this paper, we only focus on the optimization algorithms and add a brief introduction about the other segments for better understanding. There is no doubt about the importance of data collection and traffic identification. Semet et al. collected traffic statistical data to calibrate

N. T. Nguyen et al. (Eds.): ICCCI 2023, LNAI 14162, pp. 484–496, 2023.
https://doi.org/10.1007/978-3-031-41456-5_37

a simulation model with a memetic algorithm and used a genetic algorithm to optimize the traffic flow [23]. A genetic algorithm achieved significantly better results than an expert. Collecting statistical data will improve traffic control and play an essential role in developing new road networks. There are many ways to use statistics to install a new road network [24]. The traffic is changing rapidly, and traffic control needs to be adapted to this dynamic system. The traffic is not fully observable, but good estimations can be created. The observation and estimation of the current state of traffic become the initial condition for short-term prediction. Monitoring can be performed using connected vehicles (CVs) and external sensors. Smart camera-based systems for intersection control provide an excellent decentralized capability and enable efficient management [25]. Complete observation of all intersections is not an efficient method and in the predicted future, it is not required for CVs. Another critical part of traffic management is communication. The 5G network offers significant optimization opportunities [20]. Ning et al. developed a hierarchical reinforcement learning-based model and caching model for managing the Internet of Vehicles. The system has been optimized based on the limitations of the 5G network and the processing capacity [17]. Sachenko et al. examined the system signal flow, including sensors, embedded devices, and a cloud server built with LabView and ThingSpeak [4]. One of the most popular topics is CVs and their integration into traditional non-connected cars. Coordinating CVs and conventional vehicles is a vital task. Karimi et al. examined highway merging options in different scenarios for connected and conventional vehicles [11]. A detailed traffic simulation uses different models for people's behavior in certain traffic situations. People's behavior is difficult to describe, so several models have been developed to manage traffic better. A good example is a driver behavior model in work zones [13]. Model identification and calibration are often used to examine specific areas [10]. The importance of drivers' behavior models decreases with the spreading of CVs. Every car is predicted to be a CV in a future smart city. Effective adaptive traffic control can only be implemented for CV. Jamal et al. studied in the real test environment the CVs and adaptive control at an intersection [12]. Wu et al. tested the Speed Guidance model using a simulated environment for CV. The model helps CV to approach the intersection at a more optimal speed. The method's effectiveness was examined according to the CV prevalence rate and traffic density. The Speed Guidance model has been optimized for the intersection signal control scheme [27]. In the future, traffic optimization will also include route planning. Nguyen and Jung have optimized the paths of the CVs using a multi-source, multi-destination ant colony algorithm. Selective (colored) pheromones were used from sensors for the information on road load. Only ants with the same destination pick the same pheromone. A negotiation mechanism was developed for the CV in signal control-free intersections [16].

The paper focuses on the optimization algorithms and does not further investigate the sensors, the CV communication, the data collection, the driver behaviors, and the route planning. These parameters can be used as initial and behavior conditions for the simulation. The paper aims to provide a more efficient scalable simulation-based optimization solution for traffic control. Thereby, Sect. 2 only focuses on different simulation software and optimization methods.

2 Related Literature

There are many possible optimization criteria in transport. Dealing with disparate aspects is a complex task [22]. Al-Turki et al. examined effective traffic control based on time delay, the number of stops, fuel consumption, and emission with the non-dominated sorting genetic algorithm II (NSGAII) in a simulated dual intersection from the real world [3]. In most cases, traffic control aims to ensure the highest possible throughput and delay minimization. The number of passengers is usually not considered the highest possible throughout, although it is crucial. Novačko et al. examined public transport prioritization in Zagreb by simulation. A weighting with an estimated number of passengers was introduced between zero and maximum prioritization. The new weighting strategy has helped optimize traffic based on simulation [18]. There are many metadata, like fuel type, fuel consumption, start-stop settings, number of passengers, and many more to realistically optimize. Knowing the distribution of the listed metadata is not necessarily enough, the route of the specific vehicle should also be considered. Based on the listed reasons we chose only the throughput maximization without the number of passengers. The most used simulation environments are SUMO and VISSIM from PTV Group. SUMO is one of the most famous free traffic simulation software. It allows intermodal traffic systems including different vehicles, public transport, and pedestrians. SUMO has a wealthy number of supporting tools that handle tasks such as route finding, visualization, network import, and emission calculation. SUMO can be enhanced with custom models and provides various APIs to remotely control the simulation [2]. Next to SUMO, another famous traffic simulation software is VISSIM from PTV Group. PTV Group similarly has many software and add-on applications related to traffic. The software group is one of the most popular in real-world applications. There are other good simulation options like AnyLogic, NVIDIA Omniverse, and Aimsun that can be used.

We differentiate two optimization categories: simulation-based optimization and analytical solutions. We chose a simulation environment for the optimization, connecting to the digital twin concept, because it has many advantages like flexibility, easy visualization, and opportunity for scenario analysis. Due to the strong interconnectedness of road networks, evolutionary algorithms have become widespread for fast traffic control optimization. Genetic algorithms are the most common, but differential evolution methods and local derivative-free methods are also used [6]. Hill climbing is the most common derivate-free local search or traffic optimization. Evolutionary-based methods like GA often have quick initial convergence but slow down quickly. They are well-parallelized and applied efficiently for fast and long-term convergence. Genetic algorithms can be boosted with machine learning solutions [14]. Local search methods usually have slower initial convergence in large search spaces but improve continuously to the nearest local optimum. To overcome the disadvantages of the two approaches memetic algorithms have been developed by combining them. Memetic algorithms are not spread in the field of traffic control. There are some not dynamically scalable, not classically memetic algorithms that use static locational operators for sub-dimensional search [9,21].

Reinforcement Learning (RL) is the other promising solution for traffic optimization. It performs excellently in a homogeneous environment where all intersections have the same property [1,8]. The main problem with the RL method is the scalability in an inhomogeneous environment because the general rule for every scenario and the communication between different intersections is complex. RL methods are not used with real traffic yet, but they can be viable in the future.

In addition to simulation-based optimization methods, analytical methods become more manageable with the spread of CVs. Mahyar et al. developed an analytical solution for CV and intersections' optimal synchronous control. They worked with a probability distribution and used a specific layout during the elaboration. Their results can be further generalized [5]. Wang et al. developed a new multi-intersection phase representation of traffic control. This representation can flexibly work from one-to-many intersections [26].

In summary, the current traffic optimization methods are not efficiently scalable or not considering the strong interconnectivity of the traffic system. In Sect. 3, we present the Bacterial Evolutionary Algorithm (BEA) specified for traffic optimization. With the special location-based operator, its use, and the structure of the BEA, we want to provide answers to the listed weaknesses.

3 Memetic Traffic Optimization

One of the most efficient memetic algorithms is the Bacterial Memetic Algorithm (BMA) [7]. The BMA uses a local search embedded in the bacterial evolutionary algorithm (BEA) [15]. BEA includes bacterial mutation and a gene transfer operation. BMA was implemented with unique local parameters for traffic control optimization. The local parameter refers to the hierarchical location-based mutation and local search. Hill-Climbing (HC) was used as a gradient-based local search. Figure 1 shows an overview of the algorithm.

Unlike in the general BMA, we used local, area-specific operators. The area-specific operators ensured that the influence of bacterial mutation and gene transfer could be continuously varied from one intersection to the entire study area. Figure 2 shows an example of a change in the area of influence.

Four mutation strategies were used in the mutation phase, and applied to: some of the worst areas, the worst crossing, a random area, or unrelated random crosses were mutated. In the mutation phases, a local search was performed on the genes associated with the area. The local search was performed on the timings of the control sequence. Different strategies have also been added for the gene transfer: replacing the worst area control with the best of the total population for that area, replacing one of the worst areas with one of the bests, randomly

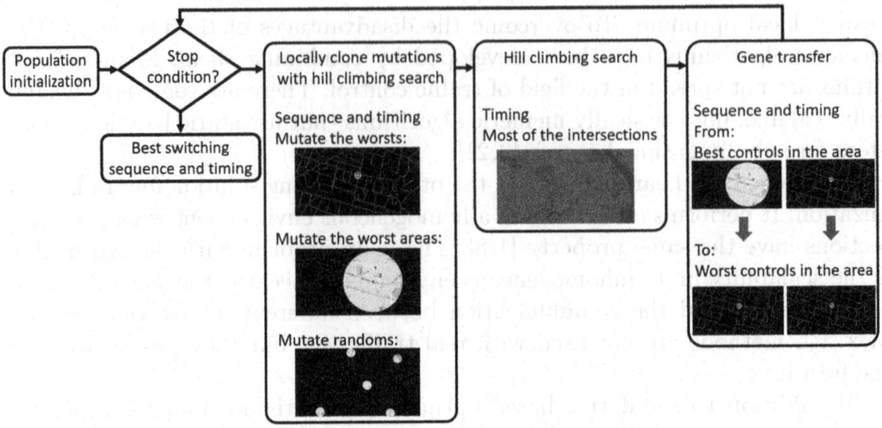

Fig. 1. BMA with local operators and Hill climbing as local search.

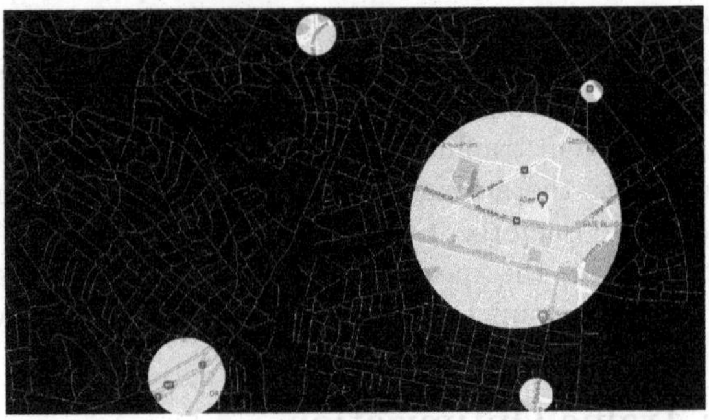

Fig. 2. Illustration of different areas of influence and the parallel optimization capabilities using Google map and the topological skeleton of the road network.

transferring an area from a better individual to a worse individual, or random intersection controls of better individuals replace a worse individual's control strategy. Figure 2 also shows that the applied operators allow the formation of complex regions, that are independent and connected areas for simultaneous optimization. Each variable size area is evaluated separately and may change simultaneously during the bacterial mutation, the gene transfer, and the local search phase.

In addition to the introduced area-specific operators, the evaluation was also area-specific. Area-specific processing significantly increases the manageability of the control optimization. The parameters encoding and the optimization overview are presented in Fig. 3. The individuals contained the list of intersections with the switching sequence, the timings, and the total waiting times. In Fig. 3 at "List of switching state" 'r' refers to "red" and 'g' refers to "green".

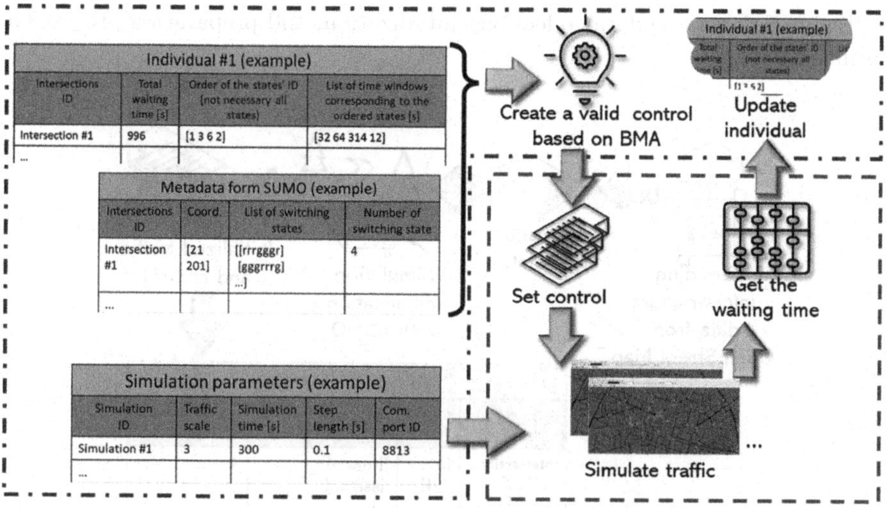

Fig. 3. Simulation overview.

4 Experiment

A SUMO traffic simulation program was used for the experiments. Real-time route planning and lane change models were not part of the study. The experiments were based on the road network of the 11th district of Budapest, shown in Fig. 4. The simulation included 1055 crossings and 1636 roads, the number of controlled intersections was 69. The exact transport network was extracted from OpenStreetMap [19]. The data is freely available under the Open Database License.

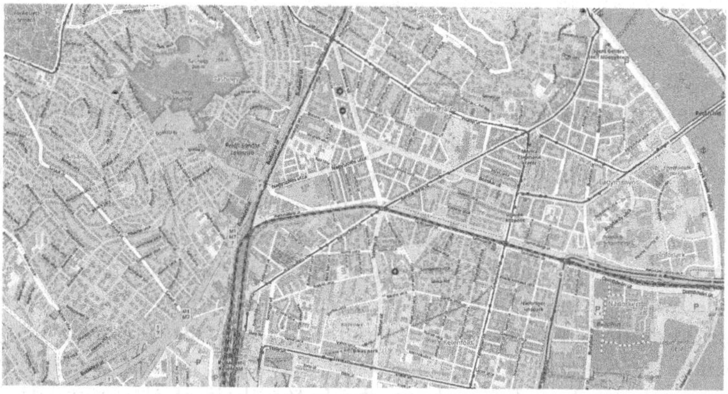

Fig. 4. The Open Street Map view of the 11th district of Budapest.

Figure 5 shows the data collection, initialization, and preparation process for optimization.

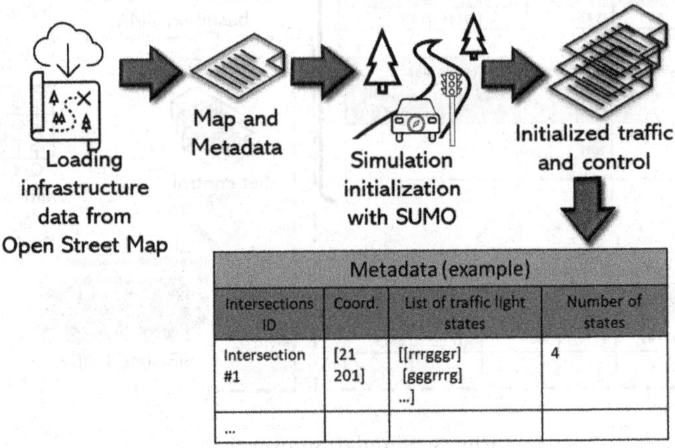

Fig. 5. Data collection and pre-processing for the optimization.

4.1 Experiment Description

The starting point for optimization was the traditional fixed-time sequential traffic light control. The duration of each phase was initialized randomly. This has been extended to variable time and sequence control. The number of vehicles was set by the traffic scaling option. It increased quasi-linearly during the simulation time, based on the file containing the default generated route. The vehicles traveled on random routes. Two types of control were compared: circular and adaptive. In the circular case, the traffic light phases repeat a short sequence. In the adaptive case, the result is not necessarily a repetitive switching sequence depending on the traffic condition.

Eight test cases were examined based on the traffic scale, the simulation time, and the control types combination described in Table 1.

As we introduced in Sect. 1 and in Sect. 2 the Genetic Algorithm and the Hill Climbing are the methods that are used in the real world so we chose them as the baseline. A population size of 24 was used for all algorithms. Table 2 contains the parameters for the algorithms. For each algorithm, the number of parallel evaluations was maximized by the size of the population, so in the case of Hill Climbing, 24 random neighbors were examined. In the case of BMA, only the best 8 individuals were mutated in the bacterial mutation, during the gene transfer, random genes were transferred from the better half of the population to all individuals, thus expanding the number of evaluations to 24. The total number of evaluations was 24×50 in all cases. In the Local BMA, the influence radius of the intersections was randomly chosen in each iteration. In the bacterial mutation,

Table 1. Tests for the comparison.

Test cases	Time [min.]	Traffic scale	Number of Vehicles	Control
Test 1	2	1	147	Cyclic
Test 2	2	2	289	Cyclic
Test 3	4	1	291	Cyclic
Test 4	4	2	576	Cyclic
Test 5	4	2	576	Adaptive
Test 6	4	3	811	Adaptive
Test 7	6	2	801	Adaptive
Test 8	6	3	1204	Adaptive

random areas were selected with a 30% chance, worst areas were chosen with a 50% chance, and random intersections were chosen with a 20% chance. In gene transfer, the worst-performing areas were examined with a 30% chance replaced with the best-performing areas of the entire population, with a 50% chance replaced with random from the best-performing half of the population, and a 20% chance of unrelated crossings being transferred from the better half of the population to the worst.

Table 2. Parameters of each algorithm.

Algorithm and Parameter	Value
Bacterial Memetic Algorithm	
Number of clones	3
Number of mutated genes	10
Number of local searches	3
Number of genes for local searches	75%
Number of transferred genes	10
Genetic Algorithm	
Crossover probability	100%
Number of mutated genes	10
Selection type	Elitist
Hill Climbing	
Random reset	
Decreasing step size	from 5 to 1
Neighbor selection maximized	24
Neighbor selection	random

4.2 Experimental Results

First, the results of the first 4 tests are presented. 25 replicates were conducted of each test with uniform initialization. In each case, BMA gave the best final result, as shown in Table 3. Both in Table 3 and 4 the mean values and the 95% confidence radius (in round brackets) are presented for the 25 replicates of the total waiting time in seconds.

Table 3. Mean values and the 95% confidence radius (in round brackets) of the total waiting time for the 25 replicates in seconds for cyclic tests.

Tests	BMA	GA	HC
Test 1	1512 (85)	2038 (104)	3090 (142)
Test 2	2445 (109)	3560 (183)	4503 (210)
Test 3	5753 (288)	8047 (442)	9962 (426)
Test 4	10639 (470)	14503 (783)	17089 (736)

From Fig. 6, 7, 8 and 9, the optimization process can be seen for every 24 evaluations. The HC algorithm primarily shows the complexity of the task since the entire transport network is connected. A good initial decision may turn into a wrong one later in the other part of the network. BMA takes the lead every time after roughly the 20th batch evaluation. The local search could only work with low efficiency due to resource constraints. In the future, we will examine other local search methods and supplemental methods to improve efficiency. The initial lag from the standard methods in this field is caused by greater elitism. In the future, we plan to investigate a method combined with an initial genetic algorithm.

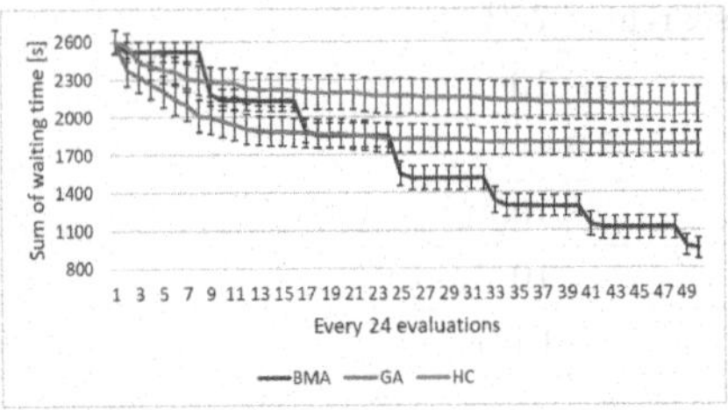

Fig. 6. Results on Test 1.

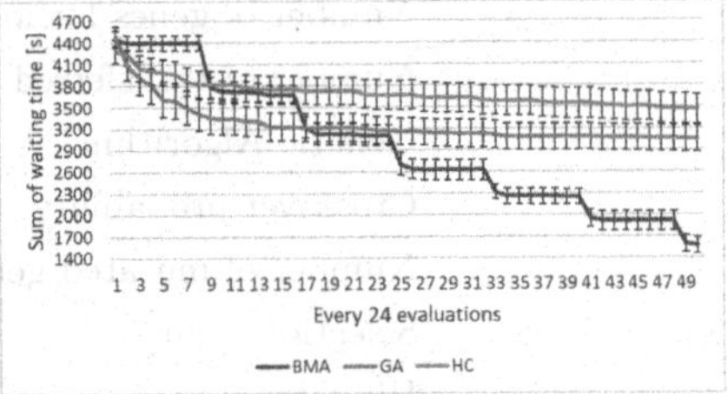

Fig. 7. Results on Test 2.

Table 4 and Figs. 10, 11, 12 and 13 show the results for the case of adaptive cycle controls. In the adaptive tests, only BMA and GA were compared, since the switching order is more important in this case. Tests 4 and 5 show the difference between the adaptive and traditional switching sequences. Contrary

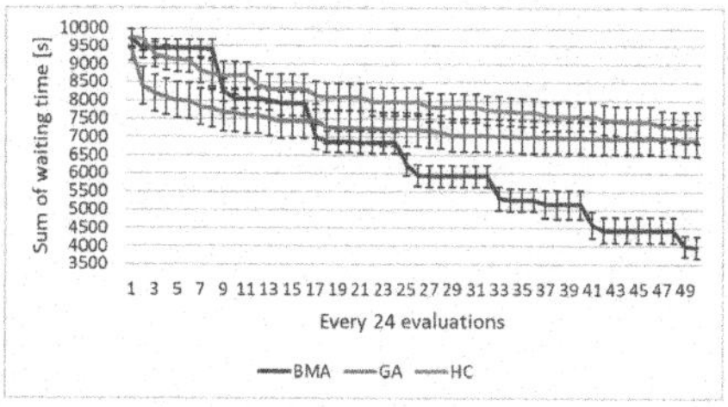

Fig. 8. Results on Test 3.

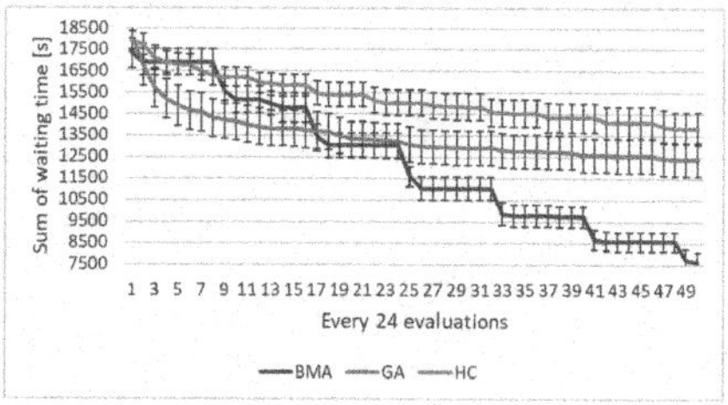

Fig. 9. Results on Test 4.

to our preliminary expectations, in the case of a few iterations, the variable series did not prove to be beneficial. More switching options increased the dimension of the search in real-time, not enough time is available to utilize the larger search space. In terms of algorithm comparison, we can see similar results as in the first 4 tests, in addition, the bacterial algorithm can work more efficiently in larger spaces by dividing the entire search space in the bacterial mutation phase.

Table 4. Mean values and the 95% confidence radius (in round brackets) of the total waiting time for the 25 replicates in seconds for adaptive tests.

Tests	BMA	GA
Test 5	11443 (842)	19720 (716)
Test 6	15626 (865)	27660 (785)
Test 7	22591 (1112)	36679 (1331)
Test 8	30210 (1881)	52256 (1294)

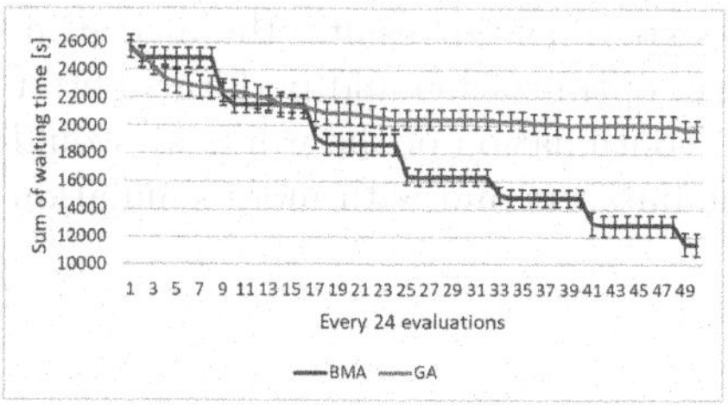

Fig. 10. Results on Test 5.

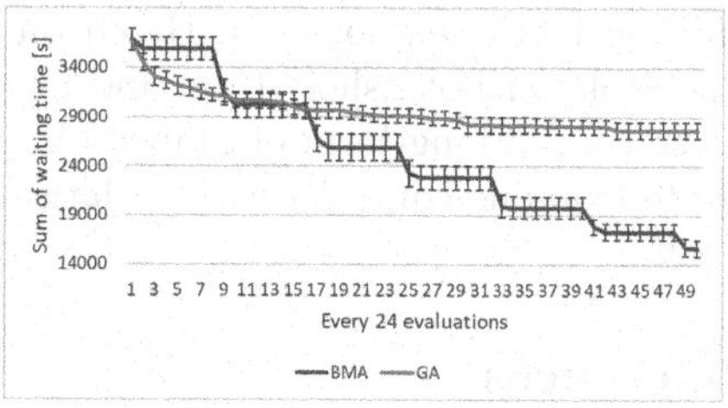

Fig. 11. Results on Test 6.

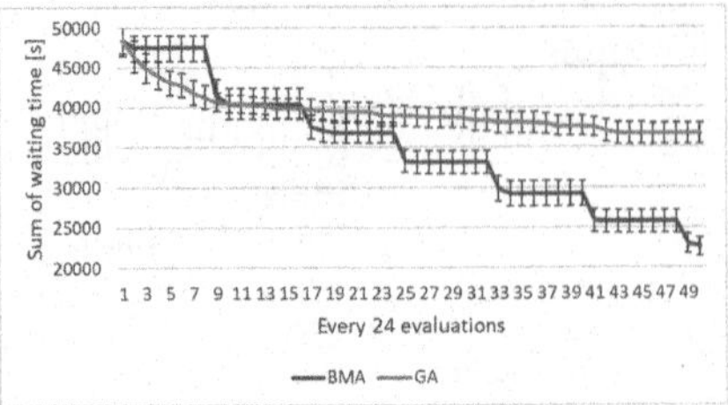

Fig. 12. Results on Test 7.

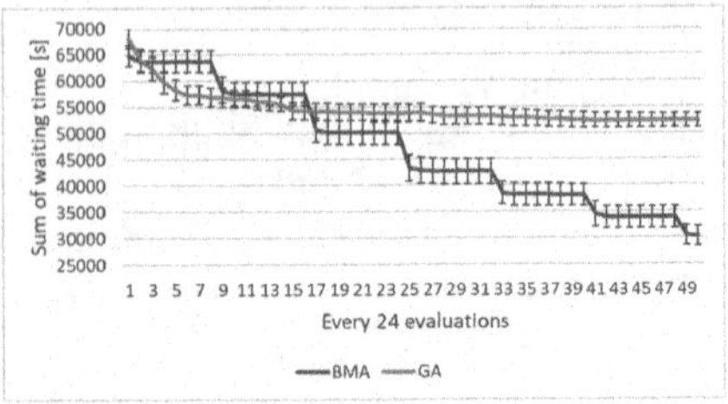

Fig. 13. Results on Test 8.

4.3 Discussion

A good traffic simulation takes a significant time even with good software. A batch simulation could take around 5...15% of the real-time in a common computer and 1...5% in a server computer with the same setting. The modified scalable BMA provided a 35–45% improvement in all test scenarios after 50 parallel evaluations and took the lead after around 18 batch evaluations.

5 Conclusion and Further Work

Traffic simulation is evolving and the required simulation time will decrease in the future. The faster simulations will provide time for more complex optimizations. This article investigated the applied optimization methods in the field of traffic optimization. A new efficiently scalable optimization was developed based on BMA. The proposed flexible area-based BMA can efficiently optimize large areas by scheduled subdivisions. Subareas can vary from one intersection to the entire area. The subareas sizes adjustment was our strategy, so a better compromise was formed between local and global search. Contrary to the literature, the algorithm can be considered a memetic algorithm not only based on location but also subject to a gradient-based method. A further advantage is prioritizing the locations within the population, which helps to perform a focused search in addition to the exploration. Based on the experimental results, the algorithm is suitable for both short-term and long-term optimization and performs better in the case of long-term optimization. As a continuation of the work, we would like to examine control with real large-scale datasets and with more simulation detail.

References

1. Toward a thousand lights: Decentralized deep reinforcement learning for large-scale traffic signal control
2. Acosta, A.F., Espinosa, J.E., Espinosa, J.: TraCI4Matlab: enabling the integration of the SUMO road traffic simulator and Matlab® through a software re-engineering process. In: Behrisch, M., Weber, M. (eds.) Modeling Mobility with Open Data. LNM, pp. 155–170. Springer, Cham (2015). https://doi.org/10.1007/978-3-319-15024-6_9

3. Al-Turki, M., Jamal, A., Al-Ahmadi, H.M., Al-Sughaiyer, M.A., Zahid, M.: On the potential impacts of smart traffic control for delay, fuel energy consumption, and emissions: an NSGA-II-Based optimization case study from Dhahran, Saudi Arabia. Sustainability **12**(18) (2020). https://doi.org/10.3390/su12187394, https://www.mdpi.com/2071-1050/12/18/7394
4. Albini, A., Mester, G., Iantovics, L.B.: Unified aspect search algorithm. Interdisc. Description Complex Syst. INDECS **17**, 20–25 (2019). https://doi.org/10.7906/indecs.17.1.4
5. Amirgholy, M., Nourinejad, M., Gao, H.O.: Optimal traffic control at smart intersections: Automated network fundamental diagram. Transp. Res. Part B Methodol. **137**, 2–18 (2020). https://doi.org/10.1016/j.trb.2019.10.001, https://www.sciencedirect.com/science/article/pii/S0191261519302449, advances in Network Macroscopic Fundamental Diagram (NMFD) Research
6. Astarita, V., Giofré, V.P., Festa, D.C., Guido, G., Vitale, A.: Floating car data adaptive traffic signals: a description of the first real-time experiment with "connected" vehicles. Electronics **9**(1), 114 (2020). https://doi.org/10.3390/electronics9010114, https://www.mdpi.com/2079-9292/9/1/114
7. Botzheim, J., Cabrita, C.K.L., Ruano, A.: Fuzzy rule extraction by bacterial memetic algorithms. J. Intell. Syst. **24**(3), 312–339 (2009). https://doi.org/10.1002/int.20338
8. Busch, J., Latzko, V., Reisslein, M., Fitzek, F.: Optimised traffic light management through reinforcement learning: traffic state agnostic agent vs. holistic agent with current V2I traffic state knowledge. IEEE Open J. Intell. Transp. Syst. **1**, 201–216 (2020). https://doi.org/10.1109/OJITS.2020.3027518
9. Gao, K., Zhang, Y., Sadollah, A., Su, R.: Optimizing urban traffic light scheduling problem using harmony search with ensemble of local search. Appl. Soft Comput. **48**, 359–372 (2016). https://doi.org/10.1016/j.asoc.2016.07.029
10. Jamal, A., Rahman, M.T., Al-Ahmadi, H.M., Ullah, I., Zahid, M.: Intelligent intersection control for delay optimization: using meta-heuristic search algorithms. Sustainability **12**(5), 1896 (2020). https://doi.org/10.3390/su12051896, https://www.mdpi.com/2071-1050/12/5/1896
11. Karimi, M., Roncoli, C., Alecsandru, C., Papageorgiou, M.: Cooperative merging control via trajectory optimization in mixed vehicular traffic. Transp. Res. Part C Emerg. Technol. **116**, 102663 (2020). https://doi.org/10.1016/j.trc.2020.102663, https://www.sciencedirect.com/science/article/pii/S0968090X20305787
12. Kasac, J., Milic, V., Stepanic, J., Mester, G.: A computational approach to parameter identification of spatially distributed nonlinear systems with unknown initial conditions. In: 2014 IEEE Symposium on Robotic Intelligence in Informationally Structured Space (RiiSS), pp. 1–7 (2014). https://doi.org/10.1109/RIISS.2014.7009170
13. Mahmood, B., Kianfar, J.: Driver behavior models for heavy vehicles and passenger cars at a work zone. Sustainability **11**(21) 6007 (2019). https://doi.org/10.3390/su11216007, https://www.mdpi.com/2071-1050/11/21/6007
14. Mao, T., Mihăiţă, A.S., Chen, F., Vu, H.L.: Boosted genetic algorithm using machine learning for traffic control optimization. IEEE Trans. Intell. Transp. Syst. **23**(7), 7112–7141 (2022). https://doi.org/10.1109/TITS.2021.3066958
15. Nawa, N., Furuhashi, T.: Fuzzy system parameters discovery by bacterial evolutionary algorithm. IEEE Trans. Fuzzy Syst. **7**(5), 608–616 (1999). https://doi.org/10.1109/91.797983

16. Nguyen, T.H., Jung, J.J.: Ant colony optimization-based traffic routing with intersection negotiation for connected vehicles. Appl. Soft Comput. **112**, 107828 (2021). https://doi.org/10.1016/j.asoc.2021.107828, https://www.sciencedirect.com/science/article/pii/S1568494621007493
17. Ning, Z., et al.: Joint computing and caching in 5G-envisioned internet of vehicles: a deep reinforcement learning-based traffic control system. IEEE Trans. Intell. Transp. Syst. **22**(8), 5201–5212 (2021). https://doi.org/10.1109/TITS.2020.2970276
18. Novačko, L., Babojelić, K., Dedić, L., Rožić, T.: Simulation-based public transport priority tailored to passenger conflict flows: a case study of the city of Zagreb. Appl. Sci. **11**(11), 4820 (2021). https://doi.org/10.3390/app11114820, https://www.mdpi.com/2076-3417/11/11/4820
19. OpenStreetMap contributors: Planet dump retrieved from (2017). https://planet.osm.org, https://www.openstreetmap.org
20. Pisarov, J., Mester, G.: Ipsi tar July 2020 - the impact of 5G technology on life in the 21st century **16**, 11–14 (2020)
21. Sabar, N.R., Le Minh Kieu, E.C., Tsubota, T., de Almeida, P.E.M.: A memetic algorithm for real world multi-intersection traffic signal optimisation problems. Eng. Appl. Artif. Intell. **63**, 45–53 (2017). https://doi.org/10.1016/j.engappai.2017.04.021
22. Sachenko, A., Osolinskyi, O., Bykovyy, P., Dobrowolski, M., Kochan, V.: Development of the flexible traffic control system using the LabView and ThingSpeak. In: 2020 IEEE 11th International Conference on Dependable Systems, Services and Technologies (DESSERT), pp. 326–330 (2020). https://doi.org/10.1109/DESSERT50317.2020.9125036
23. Semet, Y., Berthelot, B., Glais, T., Isbérie, C., Varest, A.: Expert competitive traffic light optimization with evolutionary algorithms. In: International Conference on Vehicle Technology and Intelligent Transport Systems (2019)
24. Skabardonis, A.: Chapter 11 - traffic management strategies for urban networks: smart city mobility technologies. In: Deakin, E. (ed.) Transportation, Land Use, and Environmental Planning, pp. 207–216. Elsevier (2020). https://doi.org/10.1016/B978-0-12-815167-9.00011-6, https://www.sciencedirect.com/science/article/pii/B9780128151679000116
25. Tchuitcheu, W.C., Bobda, C., Pantho, M.J.H.: Internet of smart-cameras for traffic lights optimization in smart cities. Internet Things **11**, 100207 (2020). https://doi.org/10.1016/j.iot.2020.100207, https://www.sciencedirect.com/science/article/pii/S2542660520300433
26. Wang, P., Li, P., Chowdhury, F., Zhang, L., Zhou, X.: A mixed integer programming formulation and scalable solution algorithms for traffic control coordination across multiple intersections based on vehicle space-time trajectories. Transp. Res. Part B Methodol. **134**, 266–304 (2020). https://doi.org/10.1016/j.trb.2020.01.006, https://www.sciencedirect.com/science/article/pii/S0191261519303844
27. Wu, W., Huang, L., Du, R.: Simultaneous optimization of vehicle arrival time and signal timings within a connected vehicle environment. Sensors **20**(1), 191 (2020). https://doi.org/10.3390/s20010191, https://www.mdpi.com/1424-8220/20/1/191

Optimizing Fire Control Monitoring System in Smart Cities

Mahdi Jemmali[1,2,3](✉), Loai Kayed B. Melhim[4], Wadii Boulila[5,6], and Mafawez T. Alharbi[7]

[1] Department of Computer Science and Information, College of Science at Zulfi, Majmaah University, Al-Majmaah 11952, Saudi Arabia

[2] MARS Laboratory, University of Sousse, Sousse, Tunisia

[3] Department of Computer Science, Higher Institute of Computer Science and Mathematics, Monastir University, 5000 Monastir, Tunisia
mah_jem_2004@yahoo.fr

[4] Department of Health Information Management and Technology, College of Applied Medical Sciences, University of Hafr Al Batin, Hafr Al Batin 39524, Saudi Arabia

[5] Robotics and Internet-of-Things Laboratory, Prince Sultan University, Riyadh 12435, Saudi Arabia

[6] RIADI Laboratory, National School of Computer Sciences, University of Manouba, Manouba, Tunisia

[7] Unit of Scientific Research, Applied College, Qassim University, Buraydah 51452, Saudi Arabia

Abstract. Fires are a constant threat to human lives and property because their appearance and location are unexpected, and their spread can inflict major damage and loss of life. Data from various monitoring systems are utilized to prevent, detect, and respond to fires to lessen this hazard. Drone-based surveillance systems with complex algorithms are especially effective for covering broad, difficult-to-reach areas and providing crucial data to authorities. In this paper, we present a set of developed algorithms that have been created to enhance the effectiveness of drone-based monitoring systems in detecting and recognizing fire indicators in cities. These algorithms enable continuous monitoring by maximizing drone flying times and minimizing the total time needed to complete all assigned monitoring tasks within a specified time frame. The monitoring system's efficacy and dependability may be increased by increasing the number of assigned tasks, resulting in greater assistance for firefighting teams. We conducted practical experiments on 480 different instances to show how the proposed algorithms may minimize the maximum time necessary to complete all monitoring tasks assigned to available drones at the drone launch center. The best algorithm was PLT, with a success rate of 68.1%, when compared to other algorithms, an average gap of 0.003, and an average running time of 0.073 s.

Keywords: Drone · Fire detection · Optimization · Internet of Things (IoT) · Smart cities

N. T. Nguyen et al. (Eds.): ICCCI 2023, LNAI 14162, pp. 497–509, 2023.
https://doi.org/10.1007/978-3-031-41456-5_38

1 Introduction

Smart cities employ various monitoring tools to gather data from different sources. This data is then processed by artificial intelligence-based programs to support decision-makers in making informed decisions [16,27], ensuring sustainable resource management while maintaining the quality of life for urban residents [6].

Fires are one of the most significant crises that human civilization faces, as recent years have witnessed waves of fires in various parts of the world, including urban and rural areas, and even uninhabited areas like forests [9]. Dealing with fires becomes more complicated when their causes are complex and when we cannot predict their spread, especially in a forest or residential communities. Therefore, local authorities strive to provide the best means of fighting fires to prevent their emergence, control them and prevent their spread. The effectiveness of firefighting methods is greatly enhanced when appropriate data is provided on time, increasing their efficiency and contributing significantly to reducing losses and minimizing the time required to fight fires.

In this paper, as shown in Fig. 1, an artificial intelligence-based approach, using a set of algorithms is presented. This part of the monitoring system leverages the capabilities of artificial intelligence to extract relevant data from multimedia processing tools used by the monitoring system, avoiding redundancy and irrelevant data. The proposed approach aims to enhance the monitoring system in smart cities by leveraging drone technologies to provide relevant data to assist relevant authorities in making quick and informed decisions.

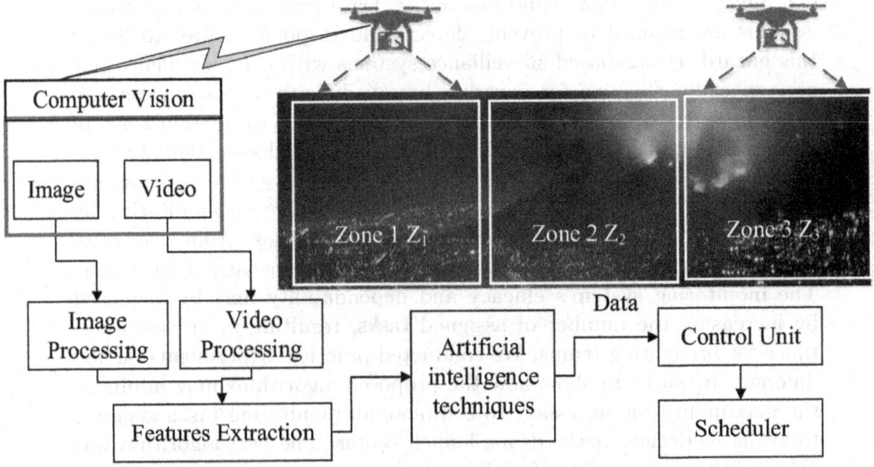

Fig. 1. General overview about the role of artificial intelligence and multimedia processing tools to extract monitoring data

The amount and quality of the data provided by drones depend on the drones' flying time over the monitored areas. To increase captured data and improve its quality it is necessary to maximize drones' flying time as much as possible. Therefore, the presented algorithms in this research aim to increase drones' total flying time over the monitored areas by maximizing the number of assigned tasks in a specified period. The proposed algorithms minimize the total maximum time required to finish all the assigned tasks within that time slot, which results in more available time to carry out additional tasks during that period, as shown in Example 1.

Figure 2 provides a general overview of the district monitoring system in smart cities. The monitoring system collects appropriate data from various sources and sends it to the control unit, which uses decision support systems to process the received data and provide the information to local authorities. Based on this information, local authorities issue necessary instructions to the firefighting teams, who then fight the fires according to the directions received from the local authorities. The firefighting unit provides reports on the fires that were dealt with and the current status of each fire incident. Local authorities use these reports to update the data of the control unit, which then adjusts the information it provides about the general condition of the monitored area. The control unit prepares the tasks required to achieve the desired monitoring based on the current situation of each area and the reports received from the local authorities or the fire brigades. These tasks are then sent to the organizer, which coordinates the operation of the drones, allocates tasks to each drone based on advanced algorithms, and ensures permanent monitoring, which provides the concerned authorities with the required data to ensure the stability of the monitored areas, update the current status of each area, or end firefighting operations.

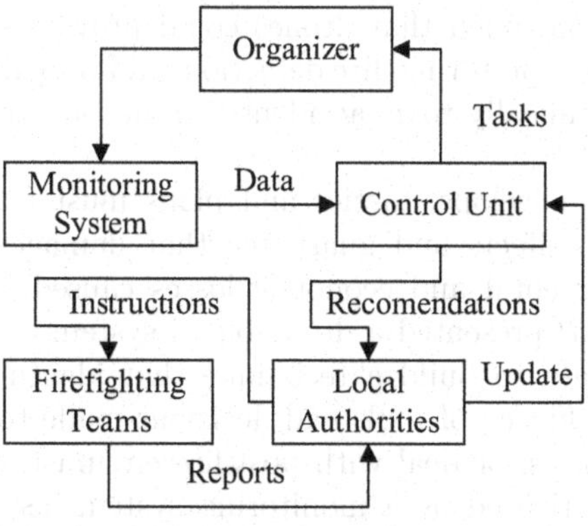

Fig. 2. Overview of the district monitoring system in smart cities

This research proposed a new mathematical model related to utilizing drone technologies for surveillance tasks in the event of a fire in a city. The proposed model minimizes the total completion time of all assigned tasks to save some time for the authorities. This valuable time can be decisive in determining the fate of the firefighting operations. Besides that, this work presented a simple city monitoring system composed of five components: a monitoring system, a control unit, local authorities, firefighting teams, and the organizer.

Figure 2 in the context clearly shows how captured data is used to support authorities in issuing the required instructions while receiving field reports from the firefighting teams, which boast the firefighting operations. Also, it presented a mathematical formulation of the studied problem related to the drone-based system in case of fire. The model is implemented, tested, and validated. The proposed algorithms were developed based on probabilistic and iterative methods. Moreover, several probabilities were selected to measure the performance of the *PLT* algorithm. Also, benchmark instances were generated and used to measure the performance of the proposed algorithms compared to other algorithms based on three indicators to point to the best-performing algorithm.

The rest of this work is detailed as follows: Previous studies are detailed in Sect. 2, while Sect. 3 presents the description of the presented problem. The developed algorithms are explored in Sect. 4. Section 5 discusses the results derived from the experimental part performed on the developed algorithms. The conclusion part will be presented in Sect. 6.

2 Literature Review

Many researchers have discussed the importance of using drones to deal with the emergence of various disasters within a city or a wildfire, especially fires. The authors in [31] evaluated the use of drones in disaster management by focusing on the drone's operational and tactical applications through time-scaled segregation of the disaster's state applications. The presented research focuses on five disaster types. The authors concluded that drones could provide surveillance, location selection, atmospheric monitoring, fire detection, and post-fire monitoring. In the case of nuclear or chemically toxic accidents, drones are the proper supporting tools.

However, if a fire develops, tactics and plans must be devised and implemented to reduce its effects and guarantee that damages are minimized. To decrease the environmental and economic losses caused by underground coal fires, the authors in [7] presented a drone-based system outfitted with gas sensors to collect gas data to build a technique that identifies coal rank by gas ratio. To ensure the efficacy of tools and decisions made to detect the presence of flames, deal with fires, or deal with post-fire circumstances, the capabilities of drones must be activated as a monitoring system, as addressed in several research articles. For example, in the model presented by [33], drones were used for air surveillance, monitoring, and fire detection. The gathered information is forwarded to the appropriate authorities.

The authors' objective in [25] was to improve firefighting performance. The authors introduced Zerologic, a fire monitoring system that employs drones with machine learning capabilities. The described system locates hotspots using cameras and image processing technologies. The presented approach, according to the authors, might pinpoint hotspots that are impossible for ground personnel to access or discover. This technology can be utilized to assist ground firefighting personnel.

Employing drones as supporting tools has also been discussed in several types of research. For example, collecting data on areas exposed to disasters to build spatial maps of the affected spots without using GPS and relying only on the data extracted from videos documented by drones is the goal of the research presented by [29]. The notion of deploying trucks outfitted with drones to monitor forests was addressed by [28], with the drone acting as the monitoring agent and the vehicle serving as the route ground agent. Other researchers examined the potential of employing drone-based systems as fire extinguishers, such as the study presented by [1], in which the authors looked for a plastic alternative to design a drone that would be utilized as a firefighting instrument to extinguish forest fires. The suggested drone is thermally insulated and designed to withstand severe temperatures. Recently, the fire fighting problem is treated in [5,30].

Load balancing is explored in several study disciplines across the literature. Several algorithms are proposed in the field of health care to obtain an equitable distribution of the number of people in the vehicle to different parking [15,22] and in the field of regional development, as the authors in [2,11–14]. Furthermore, in the industrial area, the creators of [3,4] offered new algorithms and compared them to prove which algorithm was the best. In contrast, the authors of [18] proposed numerous strategies for the equitable allocation of a given quantity of files to various storage infrastructures. Finally, many methods in the network sector were provided in [19].

To complete the efforts expended in this field, as well as the participation of researchers for their belief in the importance of humans, we developed a set of algorithms that can maximize the minimum completion time required by the used drones in any monitoring system to complete all given tasks regarding the adapted monitoring systems. The suggested algorithms will be developed based on many heuristics offered by [8,17,21,23,24,26]. Such methods might be designed to aid relevant authorities in determining the scope of the catastrophe and calculating the degree of the resultant damage with as little human interaction as feasible and as quickly as possible.

3 Process and Problem Presentation

The suggested solution attempts to maximize the value of the drone-based surveillance system. Drones are a tremendous resource that should be utilized to their full potential. The monitoring system in the proposed method is dependent on the presence of drones in the air for as long as possible, and this is where the proposed approach comes into play, which is based on scheduling the entrusted tasks to drones in a way that minimizes the maximum total finishing time, allowing drones to handle more tasks in the same amount of time, increasing surveillance time and the captured monitoring data. Minimizing the gap between the flying times of different drones ensures the presence of drones at any time over the monitored areas, which leads to continuous monitoring that obtains the necessary data to inform the competent authorities of any fire's appearance. Obtained data can be used to treat fires as soon as possible. In the proposed system, the monitored area is divided into a set of zones, where the zone's monitoring tasks are assigned to each drone. Drones are launched from the drone launching center to perform many monitoring tasks within a limited time, as specified by the capabilities and technical specifications of the used drones. Figure 3 shows an overview of the drone controlling system.

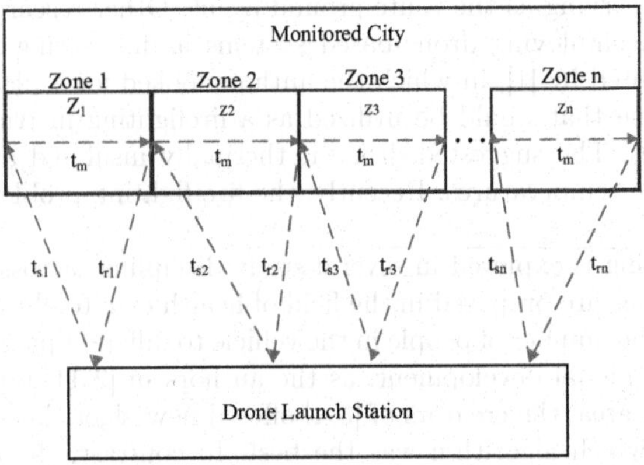

Fig. 3. Overview of the drone controlling system

4 Mathematical Modeling

The studied problem is described as follows. Drones are grouped at the drones launch center, which is identified as DLC, while each drone will be identified from Dr_j $\forall j=\{1, \cdots, nd\}$ and nd represents the total number of drones at DLC. The monitored extent is partitioned into equal zones. Each zone is denoted by Z_i $\forall i=\{1, \cdots, nz\}$, the total number of resulted zones is known as nz. Inside the launch center, the distance between the launching points of each drone is negligible and assumed to be equal to zero. The flying time from any point within the drone launch center to any zone Z_i is known as going time and is denoted by t_{Z_i}, while the flying time from any zone Z_i in the city back to any point in the drone's launch center is known as the returning time, in this context the going time and the returning time is identical. The required time to finish the assigned monitoring tasks in any zone Z_i is denoted by ts_i.

Proposition 1. *The required time to move from any point at the drone launch center and complete the assigned monitoring task, then return to the drones launch center is* $t_i = 2 \times t_{Z_i} + ts_i$ $\forall i=\{1,\cdots,nz\}$.

The cumulative time after finishing the assigned monitoring task in zone i by any drone is denoted by C_i. The calculation of C_i will be as follows $C_i = C_k + t_i,\ \forall i = \{1, \cdots, nz\}$.

Where k is the last zone that was visited by the given drone. If zone i is the first zone visited by the given drone, then $C_i = t_i$. The time required by all drones to finish all the assigned tasks is known as the completion and will be denoted by T_c is calculated as follows $T_c = \max_{1 \leq i \leq nz} C_i$. The objective of this research is to schedule the assigned monitoring tasks in the zones of interest within the smart city to minimize the maximum completion time T_c.

Example 1. Suppose that the observed extent of a smart city is divided into seven zones, which will be visited by two drones to perform monitoring tasks. The total time to finish the monitoring task for each zone are $\{30, 40, 60, 10, 20, 15, 50\}$. To solve this example, adopt two schedules, schedule 1 and schedule 2, to assign drones to the different zones. For schedule 1, the completion time T_c is equal to 125. However, for schedule 2, the completion time T_c is equal to 130. Therefore, the result obtained by schedule 1 is better than the result obtained by schedule 2.

5 Proposed Algorithms

A set of four algorithms is proposed to solve the presented problem. The first algorithm is based on the dispatching rules approach. Indeed, we apply two method types to arrange t_i, and we schedule the defined drones for the visited zones. The best solution will be selected. The second algorithm is based on choosing the longest t_i value, and after scheduling the $nz - 1$ zones, we assign the selected zone. For the third algorithm, use the same method as the second one, but instead of selecting the longest t_i, we select the smallest one. The latest algorithm is based on the randomized method. Indeed, the probabilistic procedure is applied to select between the two longest t_i values.

5.1 Longest-Smallest Time Algorithm (*LST*)

This algorithm is based on the dispatching rule. The first step in this algorithm is to arrange the t_i values according to the non-increasing order. Then, assign the zone of interest to the most available drone. After that, the obtained completion time is denoted by T_c^1. The second step is to arrange the t_i values according to the non-decreasing order. Then, schedule the zone of interest for the most available drone. The obtained completion time is denoted by T_c^2. The minimum value between T_c^1 and T_c^2 is returned. To summarize, $T_c = \min(T_c^1, T_c^2)$.

5.2 Longest-Smallest Time Excluding the Longest-Area Time Algorithm (*LELT*)

This algorithm is based on the following: First, search for the zone that has the longest t_i, this zone is denoted by Z^L, then apply the *LST* algorithm on the remaining $nz - 1$ zones. Finally, assign the zone Z^L to the most available drone.

5.3 Longest-Smallest Time Excluding the Smallest-Area Time Algorithm (*LEST*)

This algorithm is based on the following: First, search for the zone that has the smallest t_i. This zone is denoted by Z^S. After that, apply the LST algorithm to the remaining $nz - 1$ zones. Finally, assign the zone Z^S to the most available drone.

5.4 Probabilistic Longest-Area Time Algorithm (*PLT*)

This algorithm is built as follows: Firstly, we select the two zones that have the longest t_i values among these two zones, and we select the one that is scheduled for the most available drone. This selection is based on probabilistic choices. Indeed, we fix a probability θ. The choice of the first zone that has the longest t_i is applied with probability θ. However, the second zone that has the largest t_i is applied with probability $1 - \theta$. We will continue the scheduling until all zones are scheduled.

6 Results and Discussion

In this research, the developed algorithms are implemented using C++. The used machine has a Windows 10 operating system with a Core i5 6200 CPU @ 2.30 GHz 2.40 GHz and a RAM of 8.00 GB. This research will choose two classes to be tested. The selected classes have a different way of generating t_i. The uniform distribution $U(60, 150)$ is the first class to be chosen, while the uniform distribution $U(20, 100)$ is the second chosen class. The uniform distribution is used in several works [10,20,32]. The selected total number of zones nz and the selected total number of drones nd are shown in Table 1.

Table 1. Number of areas and drones' distribution

nz	nd
10,20	2,3,5
30,50,100	2,3,5,10
200,250	10,15,20

In this context, ten instances were generated for each class and each nz and nd fixed value. Table 1 shows the number of the total generated instances $(2 \times 3 + 3 \times 4 + 2 \times 3) \times 10 \times 2 = 480$. To measure the performance of the developed algorithms, the following indicators will be tested.

- $\hat{T}$ the best T_c the value returned after all algorithms are executed.
- T the T_c the returned value when executing the studied heuristic.

- $G = \frac{T-\hat{T}}{\hat{T}}$.
- Prg the percentage of instances when $T{=}\hat{T}$ is reached.
- $Time$ the average running time of the algorithm. The time is calculated in seconds. We are denoted by "-" if the time is less than 0.001 s.

Table 2. Overview of all algorithms in Prg and $Time$

	LST	$LELT$	$LEST$	PLT
Prg	51.9%	0.0%	55.4%	68.1%
G	0.005	0.052	0.004	0.003
$Time$	-	-	-	0.073

The overall results of the developed algorithms are shown in Table 2. The best algorithm is PLT as it has a percentage of 68.1 % of cases, an average gap of 0.003, and an average running time of 0.073 s. While, the algorithm $IELT$ is the worst with a percentage result of 0.0%, an average gap of 0.052, and an average running time of less than 0.001s. The average gap G and $Time$ performance values when changing the number of zones nz are shown in Table 3. The given results showed that increasing the number of zones nz does not affect the performance of the developed algorithms, even with large nz values. Moreover, the given results show that as nz increases, the performance of the developed algorithms increases in most of the tested cases, except for the average running time of the PLT algorithm. The average gap values of PLT algorithm reach zero when nz= 20, while the LST and $LEST$ algorithms reach zero average gaps when nz=$\{200, 250\}$.

Table 3. The performance in G and $Time$ for all algorithms when the number of zones changed

nz	LST		$LELT$		$LEST$		PLT	
	G	$Time$	G	$Time$	G	$Time$	G	$Time$
10	0.018	-	0.111	-	0.009	-	0.017	0.008
20	0.012	-	0.068	-	0.012	-	0.000	0.012
30	0.003	-	0.066	-	0.003	-	0.002	0.020
50	0.003	-	0.041	-	0.003	-	0.001	0.032
100	0.002	-	0.023	-	0.001	-	0.001	0.066
200	0.000	-	0.037	-	0.000	-	0.002	0.182
250	0.000	-	0.030	-	0.000	-	0.001	0.226

Figure 4 illustrates the average gap variation for LST and $LELT$ algorithms as the pair (nz, nd) changes. This figure shows that the $LELT$ curve is always above the *LST* curve. Figure 5 illustrates the average gap variation for *LEST* and *PLT* algorithms as the pair (nz, nd) changes. This figure shows that the *PLT* curve has a remarkable peak of 0.45 when the pair $(nz, nd) = (10, 5)$

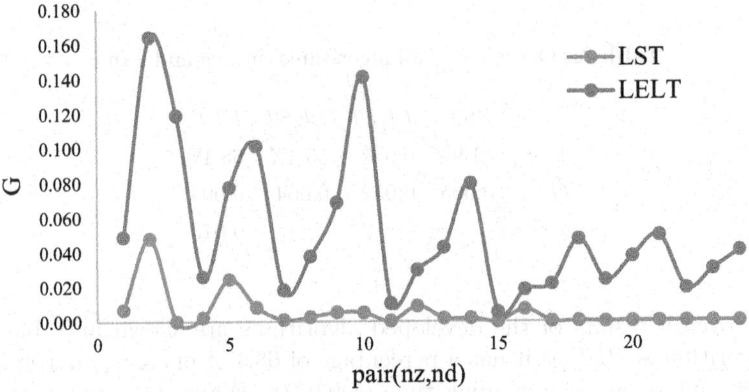

Fig. 4. The average gap variation for *LST* and *LELT* algorithms the pair(nz, nd) changes

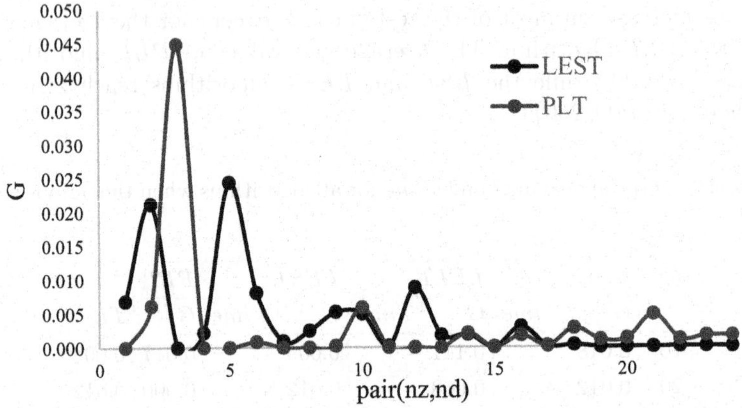

Fig. 5. The average gap variation for *LEST* and *PLT* algorithms the pair(nz, nd) changes

The average gap G and $Time$ performance values when changing the number of drones nd are shown in Table 4. The given results showed that increasing the number of drones nd has a direct effect on the performance measurements of the developed algorithms. Moreover, the given results show that as nz increases, the performance of the developed algorithms increases in most of the tested cases, except for the average running time of the *PLT* algorithm. The average gap values of *PLT* algorithm reach zero when *nd*= 2, while the *LST* and *LEST* algorithms reach zero average gaps when *nd*= 15.

Table 4. The performance in *G* and *Time* for all algorithms when the number of drones changed

nd	*LST*		*LELT*		*LEST*		*PLT*	
	G	*Time*	*G*	*Time*	*G*	*Time*	*G*	*Time*
2	0.002	-	0.022	-	0.002	-	0.000	0.025
3	0.018	-	0.065	-	0.012	-	0.002	0.025
5	0.003	-	0.071	-	0.003	-	0.009	0.028
10	0.001	-	0.062	-	0.001	-	0.003	0.103
15	0.000	-	0.034	-	0.000	-	0.001	0.204
20	0.000	-	0.045	-	0.000	-	0.003	0.224

The average gap *G* and *Time* performance values of all the developed algorithms for classes 1 and 2 are shown in Table 5. The average gap values of the *PLT* algorithm for classes 1 and 2 are 0.003, which indicates a stable behavior of the developed algorithm when different classes are used. Besides, all algorithms showed similar performance behavior for the two used classes. The average running time of the *LST*, *LEST*, and *LEST* algorithms was below 0.001s for the two used cases. Based on the results shown in Table 5, the *PLT* algorithm has the best performance, and the *LELT* algorithm has the worst performance, based on *G* and *Time* calculations for the two used cases.

Table 5. The performance in *G* and *Time* for all algorithms and classes

class	*LST*		*LELT*		*LEST*		*PLT*	
	G	*Time*	*G*	*Time*	*G*	*Time*	*G*	*Time*
1	0.005	-	0.063	-	0.004	-	0.003	0.074
2	0.005	-	0.042	-	0.003	-	0.003	0.073

7 Conclusion and Future Works

Early notice and intervention are two effective ways to minimize the impact of fires. As a result, employing drones for city surveillance and fire detection has grown in importance. The algorithms suggested in this study seek to improve response time and reduce the consequences of fires by minimizing the maximum total time necessary to complete various tasks within a specific time window for a smart city monitoring system. The algorithms were developed, implemented, and tested in 480 different instances. Practical experiments yielded favorable results, confirming the algorithms' potential to improve monitoring functions and enhance the system by providing additional data and recommendations. Three major guidelines will guide future efforts on this subject. The first is to employ the presented algorithms as initial solutions in various metaheuristics to solve the problem more efficiently. The second step is to use a branch-and-bound technique to get an exact solution. Finally, the third direction is to hunt for a good, practical solution using machine learning techniques.

References

1. Alappatt, T.B., Ajith, S.S., Jose, J., Augustine, J., Sankar, V., George, J.M.: Design and analysis of fire fighting drone. In: Sengodan, T., Murugappan, M., Misra, S. (eds.) Advances in Electrical and Computer Technologies. LNEE, vol. 711, pp. 1015–1033. Springer, Singapore (2021). https://doi.org/10.1007/978-981-15-9019-1_85
2. Alharbi, M., Jemmali, M.: Algorithms for investment project distribution on regions. Comput. Intell. Neurosci. **2020** (2020)
3. Alquhayz, H., Jemmali, M.: Max-min processors scheduling. Inf. Technol. Control **50**(1), 5–12 (2021)
4. Alquhayz, H., Jemmali, M., Otoom, M.M.: Dispatching-rule variants algorithms for used spaces of storage supports. Discrete Dyn. Nat. Soc. **2020** (2020)
5. Chaoxia, C., Shang, W., Zhang, F., Cong, S.: Weakly aligned multimodal flame detection for fire-fighting robots. IEEE Trans. Ind. Inform. (2022)
6. Corchado, J.M., Pinto-Santos, F., Aghmou, O., Trabelsi, S.: Intelligent development of smart cities: deepint.net case studies. In: Corchado, J.M., Trabelsi, S. (eds.) SSCTIC 2021. LNNS, vol. 253, pp. 211–225. Springer, Cham (2022). https://doi.org/10.1007/978-3-030-78901-5_19
7. Dunnington, L., Nakagawa, M.: Fast and safe gas detection from underground coal fire by drone fly over. Environ. Pollut. **229**, 139–145 (2017)
8. al Fayez, F., Melhim, L.K.B., Jemmali, M.: Heuristics to optimize the reading of railway sensors data. In: 2019 6th International Conference on Control, Decision and Information Technologies (CoDIT), pp. 1676–1681. IEEE (2019)
9. Gomez Isaza, D.F., Cramp, R.L., Franklin, C.E.: Fire and rain: a systematic review of the impacts of wildfire and associated runoff on aquatic fauna. Glob. Change Biol. **28**(8), 2578–2595 (2022)
10. Hmida, A.B., Jemmali, M.: Near-optimal solutions for mold constraints on two parallel machines. Stud. Inform. Control **31**(1), 71–78 (2022)
11. Jemmali, M.: Approximate solutions for the projects revenues assignment problem. Commun. Math. Appl. **10**(3), 653 (2019)
12. Jemmali, M.: Budgets balancing algorithms for the projects assignment. Int. J. Adv. Comput. Sci. Appl. **10**(11) (2019)
13. Jemmali, M.: An optimal solution for the budgets assignment problem. RAIRO-Oper. Res. **55**(2), 873–897 (2021)
14. Jemmali, M.: Projects distribution algorithms for regional development. ADCAIJ. Adv. Distrib. Comput. Artif. Intell. J. **10**(3), 293–305 (2021)
15. Jemmali, M.: Intelligent algorithms and complex system for a smart parking for vaccine delivery center of COVID-19. Complex Intell. Syst. **8**(1), 597–609 (2022)
16. Jemmali, M., Alharbi, M., Melhim, L.K.B.: Intelligent decision-making algorithm for supplier evaluation based on multi-criteria preferences. In: 2018 1st International Conference on Computer Applications & Information Security (ICCAIS), pp. 1–5. IEEE (2018)

17. Jemmali, M., Alourani, A.: Mathematical model bounds for maximizing the minimum completion time problem. J. Appl. Math. Comput. Mech. **20**(4), 43–50 (2021)
18. Jemmali, M., Alquhayz, H.: Equity data distribution algorithms on identical routers. In: Khanna, A., Gupta, D., Bhattacharyya, S., Snasel, V., Platos, J., Hassanien, A.E. (eds.) International Conference on Innovative Computing and Communications. AISC, vol. 1059, pp. 297–305. Springer, Singapore (2020). https://doi.org/10.1007/978-981-15-0324-5_26
19. Jemmali, M., Bashir, A.K., Boulila, W., Melhim, L.K.B., Jhaveri, R.H., Ahmad, J.: An efficient optimization of battery-drone-based transportation systems for monitoring solar power plant. IEEE Trans. Intell. Transp. Syst. (2022)
20. Jemmali, M., Ben Hmida, A.: Quick dispatching-rules-based solution for the two parallel machines problem under mold constraints. Flex. Serv. Manuf. J. 1–26 (2023)
21. Jemmali, M., Melhim, L.K.B., Al Fayez, F.: Real time read-frequency optimization for railway monitoring system. RAIRO-Oper. Res. **56**(4), 2721–2749 (2022)
22. Jemmali, M., Melhim, L.K.B., Alharbi, M.T., Bajahzar, A., Omri, M.N.: Smart-parking management algorithms in smart city. Sci. Rep. **12**(1), 1–15 (2022)
23. Jemmali, M., Melhim, L.K.B., Alourani, A., Alam, M.M.: Equity distribution of quality evaluation reports to doctors in health care organizations. PeerJ Comput. Sci. **8**, e819 (2022)
24. Jemmali, M., Otoom, M.M., al Fayez, F.: Max-min probabilistic algorithms for parallel machines. In: Proceedings of the 2020 International Conference on Industrial Engineering and Industrial Management, pp. 19–24 (2020)
25. Marind, G., Nevriansyah, E., Putra, Z.Y., Febyola, C., Pratama, R.F., et al.: Drone hunter and fire use fire extinguisher ball-based image processing and machine learning methods. ARITMETIKA **1**(01), 10–17 (2022)
26. Melhim, L.K.B.: Health care optimization by maximizing the air-ambulance operation time. IJCSNS **22**(2), 357 (2022)
27. Melhim, L.K.B., Jemmali, M., Alharbi, M.: Intelligent real-time intervention system applied in smart city. In: 2018 21st Saudi Computer Society National Computer Conference (NCC), pp. 1–5. IEEE (2018)
28. Momeni, M., Soleimani, H., Shahparvari, S., Afshar-Nadjafi, B.: Coordinated routing system for fire detection by patrolling trucks with drones. Int. J. Disaster Risk Reduction **73**, 102859 (2022)
29. Nath, N.D., Cheng, C.S., Behzadan, A.H.: Drone mapping of damage information in GPS-denied disaster sites. Adv. Eng. Inform. **51**, 101450 (2022)
30. Panahi, F.H., Panahi, F.H., Ohtsuki, T.: An intelligent path planning mechanism for firefighting in wireless sensor and actor networks. IEEE Internet Things J. (2023)
31. Restas, A., et al.: Drone applications for supporting disaster management. World J. Eng. Technol. **3**(03), 316 (2015)
32. Sarhan, A., Jemmali, M.: Novel intelligent architecture and approximate solution for future networks. PLoS ONE **18**(3), e0278183 (2023)
33. Singh, V.P., et al.: RtC drone: implementation of intelligent autonomous patrolling using round the clock drone. Turkish J. Comput. Math. Educ. (TURCOMAT) **12**(13), 582–590 (2021)

Computational Intelligence for Digital Content Understanding

Desertification Detection in Satellite Images Using Siamese Variational Autoencoder with Transfer Learning

Farah Chouikhi[1,2](✉), Ali Ben Abbes[1], and Imed Riadh Farah[1]

[1] RIADI Laboratory, National School of Computer Science, 2010 Manouba, Tunisia
chouikhi.farah@gmail.com

[2] LESOR, Institute of Arid Regions, 4119 Medenine, Tunisia

Abstract. This paper proposes a deep transfer learning (TL) model based on Siamese Variational Autoencoder (SVAE) for change detection (CD) in satellite imagery using limited labeled data. The proposed approach has two steps: pre-training the SVAE in the source scene and fine-tuning it for deploying in the target scene for desertification detection. The model was tested using Landsat images from 2001 to 2020 from two study areas in Tunisia's arid regions. The results were compared with the Siamese Convolutional Neural Network (SCNN) model. Results showed that SVAE outperformed in all metrics with an accuracy of 93%.

Keywords: Transfer learning · Siamese Variational Autoencoder · classification · desertification detection · feature extraction

1 Introduction

The feature extraction step in the classification process allows for the improvement of deep learning (DL) model performance in several fields [1–3]. In fact, Convolutional Neural Networks (CNNs) have been efficiently employed to solve computer vision problems in a variety of fields, including image and text recognition, environment, and medical [4–6]. Nevertheless, the performance of the algorithms depends on the datasets used. Furthermore, CNNs have shown low performance in classification tasks due to the high similarity and non-dispersity of the input data. Recently, with these challenges, Variational AutoEncoder (VAE) have demonstrated their good performance in classification tasks as they are based on distribution-free assumptions and nonlinear approximations [7–9].

However, the periodicity of the input data reduces its efficiency and makes it unable to ensure the spatiotemporal consistency of the extracted features [10]. Moreover, traditional DL models, such as CNNs and VAEs, cannot capture temporal information and have limited capability to extract temporal features. To overcome this limitation, the Siamese structure, which is one of the best approaches for CD in bi-temporal images, can resolve this issue. Siamese networks were first utilized for signature verification and subsequently applied in

N. T. Nguyen et al. (Eds.): ICCCI 2023, LNAI 14162, pp. 513–525, 2023.
https://doi.org/10.1007/978-3-031-41456-5_39

feature matching, particularly between bi-temporal images [11,12] for CD. The CD process consists of identifying the differences between bi-temporal images of the same geographic location undergoing anthropic and climatic factors.

Exploring the generalization of Siamese DL models is a key challenge. Discussing its TL capabilities is one of the most popular analyses [13,14]. The TL aims at gaining knowledge by solving a problem and applying it to another related problem. The use of TL in practice is to apply knowledge from one context with several labeled data to another situation with limited labels. In application, TL consists of re-using the weight values of the trained model with source data, while applying a fine-tuning approach to provide a model adapted to the target data [15]. By employing the pre-trained model source as the target scene adapter instead of starting from scratch, the fine-tuning technique reinforces learning and considerably reduces the model overfitting [16].

The contributions of the present work are presented below:

- Proposing a new method for bi-temporal image classification based on SVAE, in order to extract relevant temporal features.
- Using a TL strategy to transfer the pre-trained SVAE from the source to the target scene.
- Evaluating the introduced method w.r.t. SCNN, in two study areas, using bi-temporal multispectral Landsat images.

The rest of this manuscript is organized as follows: related works are described in Sect. 2. The developed method, the background of the SVAE, and the TL strategy used in this study are presented in Sect. 3. Section 4 depicts the experimental settings, implementation details, and applied evaluation metrics. The obtained results are provided and discussed in Sect. 5, while Sect. 6 concludes the paper and offers some future perspectives.

2 Related Work

Recently, numerous studies have focused on using Siamese structures with bi-temporal images to enhance feature extraction-based classification models for CD. For example, [17] designed a Siamese global learning (Siam-GL) framework for high spatial resolution (HSR) remote sensing images. The Siamese structure has been used to improve the feature extraction of bi-temporal HSR images. Researchers have concluded that the Siam-GL framework outperformed advanced semantic CD methods as it provided more pixel data and ensured high-precision classification. Moreover, [10] presented a semi-supervised technique that relied on a Variational Autoencoder (VAE) with the Siamese structure to detect changes in Synthetic Aperture Radar (SAR) images. This method concatenated the extracted features of bi-temporal images in a single latent space vector to extract the pixel change characteristics. Furthermore, [18] proposed a CD framework based on a Siamese CNN. In this method, Sentinel-2 multispectral pair images were encoded via a Siamese network to extract a new data representation. Then, the extracted bi-temporal representations were combined to produce an urban CD map. The designed network was trained in a fully supervised manner and showed excellent test performance.

The performance of a DL model can be enhanced by applying TL strategies, particularly for convolutional neural network (CNN) models based on Siamese structures. Some research works have relied on Siamese CNNs and TL to improve performance. For instance, [19] proposed a DL-based CD framework with a TL strategy to apply a learned source CD model in a target domain. The framework includes pre-training and fine-tuning steps and utilizes image differences in the target domain to improve the CD network. The results showed that the method outperforms state-of-the-art CD techniques and effectively transfers the concept of change from the source domain to the target domain. In another study, [20] presented a face recognition platform based on TL in a Siamese network made up of two identical CNNs. The Siamese network extracts features from input images and determine if they belong to the same person. The results revealed that the accuracy of the proposed model (95.62%) is better than state-of-the-art face recognition methods. [21] also designed a transformer-based Siamese network architecture (ChangeFormer) for CD using co-registered remote sensing images. The proposed network outperformed existing ones by enhancing CD performance. Additionally, [22] suggested a Siamese network trained using labeled imagery data of the same land scene acquired by Sentinel-2 at different times to detect changes in land cover in bi-temporal images. The trained network was transferred to a new unlabeled scene using a fine-tuned TL strategy, and pseudo-change labels were estimated in an unsupervised manner. The experiments conducted in Cupertino and Las Vegas showed that the proposed strategy performed better than standard Siamese networks trained in a supervised or unsupervised manner.

3 Method

We consider two bi-temporal image scenes with two different pixel grids that have different spatial locations: X_s as the source and X_t as the target. We also take into account the matrices C_s and C_t, which contain information about the truth classes available for pixels in the scenes X_s and X_t, respectively. Note that the size of C_t is always smaller than that of C_s. The SVAE method classifies the detected changes in a supervised manner in two steps. In the first step, a Siamese network is trained using a supervised classification task, depending on the type of CD method for the bi-temporal image source scene X_s and ground truth C_s. In the second step, the trained SVAE is deployed to the bi-temporal image target scene X_t and the labeled data of C_t is used with a fine-tuning approach. The schema of the proposed methodology is illustrated in Fig. 1.

3.1 Variational Autoencoder Background

The VAE is made up of two components [23], as indicated in Fig. 2. The first one called the encoder, is a clustering part that projects data input X into a latent

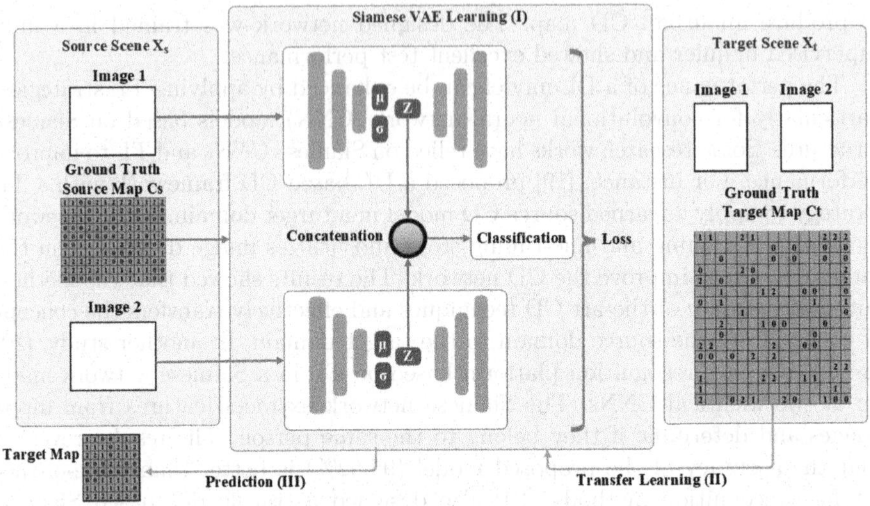

Fig. 1. Flowchart of the proposed method: (I) The SVAE was used to extract the latent spaces from the source scene of bi-temporal images. These latent spaces are then concatenated to create a feature vector, which is used as input for the classifier trained on ground truth data. (II) A TL strategy was employed to improve the performance of the trained SVAE on the bi-temporal target images. (III) The classification map of the target scene was predicted using the transferred SVAE.

space Z according to a Gaussian probability P(Z|X), with a regularization trick provided by a vector of means u and a vector of standard deviations σ. However, the second component, named the decoder part, generates the original data X as X' from the latent space Z according to a probability distribution Q(X|Z).

The VAE model can be presented by the expressions:

$$\begin{cases} u = f(X) \\ \sigma = (X) \\ X' = g(Z) \\ Z = u \oplus \sigma \otimes \epsilon \\ \epsilon \sim N(0, I) \\ Z \sim N(u, \sigma^2) \end{cases} \tag{1}$$

where u is the vector of means, σ denotes the vector of the standard deviations, and ϵ designates a small constant equal to the value of the reduced normal distribution $N(0, I)$, Z corresponds to the latent space, X refers to the input image and X' is the reconstructed image. The encoder is f, while the decoder is g. The VAE model aims to minimize the loss function L by optimizing the two functions: f (encoder) and g (decoder). L comprises the regularization loss (KL), which is the kullback-Leibler divergence loss, and reconstruction loss (RL). the

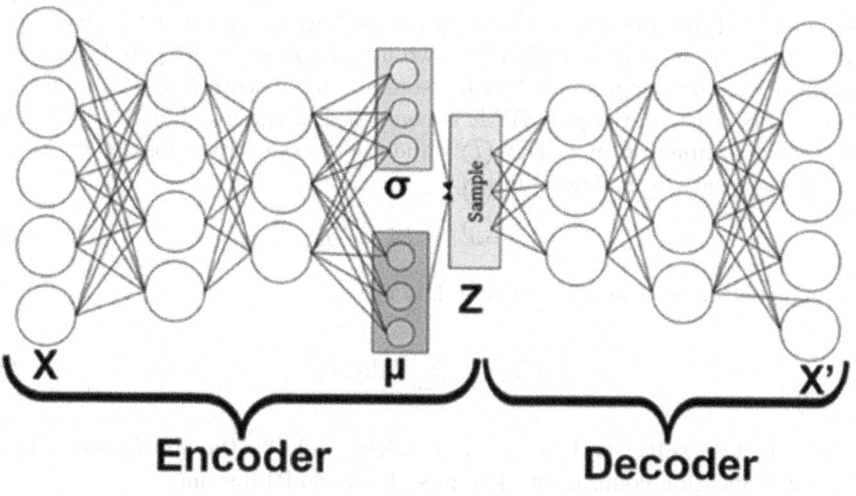

Fig. 2. Variational Autoencode model.

loss function L can be presented as explained in [23] as:

$$L = RL + KL \tag{2}$$

The explanation for the reconstruction loss RL as explained in [23] and [10] is:

$$RL = 1/2|X - X'|^2 \tag{3}$$

The explanation for the kullback-Leibler divergence loss KL as explained in [23] and [10] is:

$$\begin{aligned} KL = DKL(q(X)||p(Z)) = DKL(N(u, \sigma^2)||N(0, I)) \\ = \frac{1}{2}\sum_{1}^{n}(1 + \log(\sigma^2) - \mu^2 - \sigma^2) \end{aligned} \tag{4}$$

And by incorporating (Eq. 3) and (Eq. 4) into (Eq. 2), our model's loss function L becomes:

$$L = 1/2|X - X'|^2 + \frac{1}{2}\sum_{1}^{n}(1 + \log(\sigma^2) - \mu^2 - \sigma^2) \tag{5}$$

The term n represents the hidden space dimension n=dim(Z).

3.2 Siamese Variational Autoencoder Background

A Siamese network is an architecture containing two parallel neural networks having identical configurations with identical parameters and shared weights.

The suggested architecture is made up of two VAEs connected by a vector of features created by concatenating the two latent spaces of the pair VAE and a classification component trained with a source ground truth map (C_s). The loss function LS of the developed SVAE is composed of the loss function of VAE_1 ($L1$), the loss function of VAE_2 ($L2$) and the cross-entropy loss (CE) of the classification part as explained in [10].

$$LS = L1 + L2 + CE \tag{6}$$

The explanation for the cross-entropy loss CE is:

$$CE = -\sum_{i=1}^{c} T_i \log Y_i \tag{7}$$

where Y is the result, c is the number of classes, and C is the ground truth input to the classification component. The loss of our model becomes.

$$LS = 1/2|X_1 - X'_1|^2 + 1/2|X_2 - X'_2|^2 + \frac{1}{2}\sum_{1}^{n}(1 + \log(\sigma_1^2) - u_1^2 - \sigma_1^2) + \frac{1}{2}\sum_{1}^{n}(1 + \log(\sigma_2^2) - u_2^2 - \sigma_2^2) - \sum_{i=1}^{c} T_i \log Y_i \tag{8}$$

3.3 Transfer Learning

We consider a source domain D_s consisting of the source scene X_s, containing the ground truth C_s, and the target domain D_t made up of the target scene X_t containing the ground truth C_t and the unknown knowledge to be learned. The knowledge learned in the source domain can be transferred to the target domain through TL. TL applies the knowledge in D_s to help learn the knowledge in D_t. In this study, the condition $D_s \neq D_t$ and C_t are always smaller, compared to C_s. In the learning process, the classification knowledge of the source scene X_s is employed to detect the classification of the target scene X_t. Besides, TL is used to address the classification issue by utilizing the fine-tuning technique that can be divided into freezing and retraining, as explained in [24,25] and shown in Fig. 3. Firstly, feature extraction and classification are applied using a pre-trained SVAE on the source scene. Then, the target SVAE model is initialized with the saved weights of the source model which is the freezing part. Finally, the ground truth of the target scene is used to retrain the target model and predict the classification map.

4 Experimental Evaluation

Recently, computer vision techniques have been widely used in environmental monitoring because of significant improvements in machine learning algorithms

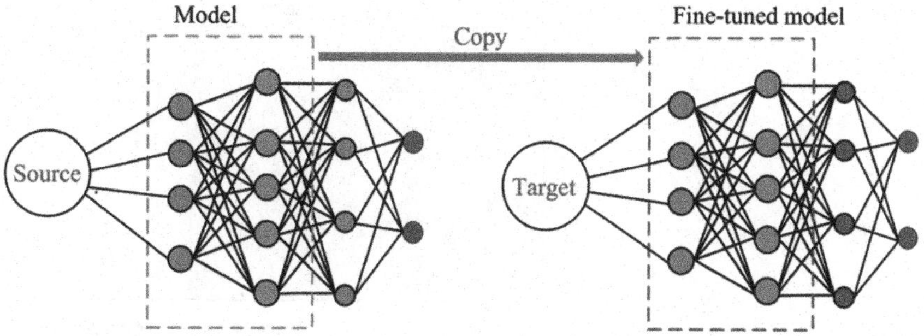

Fig. 3. TL with model fine-tuning adapted [24]

and the increasing availability of free remote sensing data with moderate spatial and temporal resolution. Enhancing the ability of DL models to monitor the spatial and temporal distribution of desertification is highly recommended to improve efforts to combat desertification and ensure ecosystem security. In this work, the introduced SVAE method, with a TL strategy, is applied to detect desertification risk in two study areas.

4.1 Study Area and Dataset

Each of the considered scenes is composed of three bands of the Landsat visible spectrum (RGB) and the normalized difference vegetation index (NDVI). To calculate NDVI, the reflectance of the red (R) and near-infrared (NIR) channels, which are measured in the visible band, are used. The formula for calculating NDVI is written below.

$$NDVI = \frac{NIR - R}{NIR + R} \quad (9)$$

Bi-temporal Landsat images were acquired from Menzel Habib in Gabes as the source scene, and from Jeffara in Medenine as the target scene, located in the southern region of Tunisia using the Google Earth Engine platform[1]. Figure 4 illustrates the two study areas. Each pair of images was acquired in 2001 and 2004, with a spatial resolution of 30 m. The desertification risk information of both scenes is utilized to verify the accuracy of the produced method.

4.2 Implementation Details

The proposed method was implemented using Keras. The categorical cross-entropy loss was used as the loss function for the classification, while stochastic gradient descent (Adam) was employed as the optimizer. The batch size was set to 256 and the number of the training data in the source scene was more than 520 000 and about 100 000 in the target scene. The introduced model was applied to train 100 epochs. The learning rate was set to 0.01 and the latent space dimension was equal to 24, as demonstrated in Table 1.

[1] https://code.earthengine.google.com/.

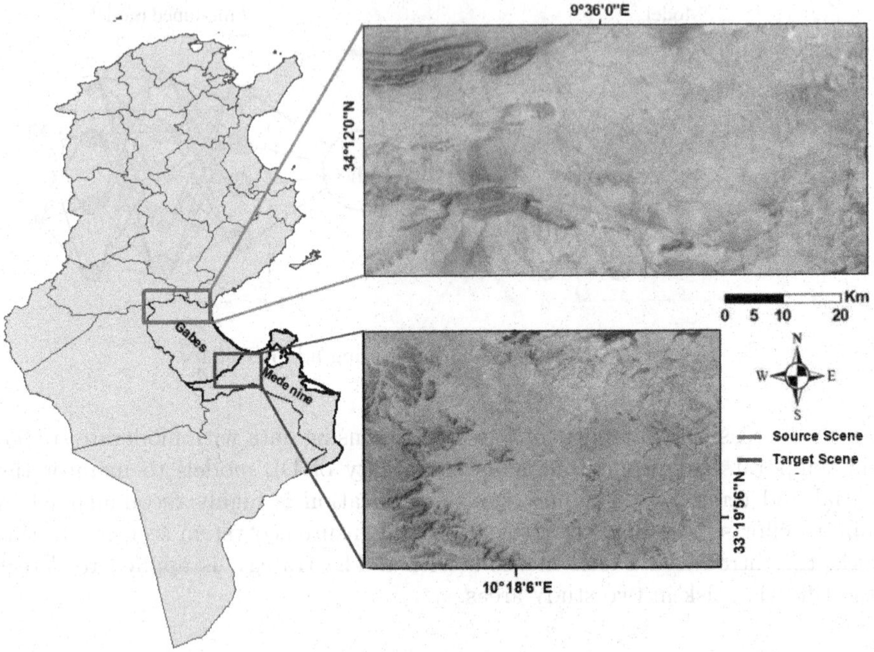

Fig. 4. Study Areas: Source and Target Scenes.

Table 1. Specifics of the grid search considered by each method. The ideal setting for each hyper-parameter is indicated with a bold font.

Method	Searching Range of Hyperparameters
SVAE	learning rate: [0.001, **0.01**, 0.1], latent space dim [2,4,8,16,**24**,32], batch size [64,128,**256**,512,1024], epoch [100,500,**1000**,2000]
SCNN	learning rate: [0.001, **0.01**, 0.1], hidden space dim [2,4,8,16,**24**,32], batch size [64,128,**256**,512,1024], epoch [100,500,**1000**,2000]

4.3 Evaluation Metrics

Desertification detection results were compared with the reference data per pixel to assess quantitatively the efficacy of the developed method in terms of *Accuracy*, recall (R), precision (P) and $F1-score$. The classification Accuracy was obtained by dividing the total number of correct predictions by the total number of predictions. However, recall measured the number of positive class predictions made out of all positive examples, as demonstrated in Eq. 10.

$$R = \frac{TP}{TP + FN} \tag{10}$$

where true-positive (TP) and true-negative (TN) denote the correct number of changed and unchanged correctly detected pixels. In fact, false-positive (FP) and false-negative (FN) denote the number of the changed and unchanged incorrectly detected pixels, respectively. On the other hand, precision quantifies the number of positive class predictions, as revealed in Eq. 11.

$$P = \frac{TP}{TP + FP} \tag{11}$$

The $F1 - score$ is a comprehensive evaluation index expressed by the average harmonic value of precision and recall, as illustrated in Eq. 12.

$$F1 - score = \frac{2 * Precision * Recall}{Precision + Recall} \tag{12}$$

Generally, a method is considered more efficient if it provides higher accuracy, precision, recall, and $F1 - score$.

5 Results and Discussion

5.1 Comparative Method Evaluation

An SCNN framework was developed in parallel with the SVAE framework based on CNN containing layers similar to the encoder part of the VAE.

The SVAE was compared to SCNN, with and without the application of the TL strategy, to demonstrate its better efficiency. In the conducted experiments, the same number of training samples was used. More than 520000 labeled pixels from the source scene (divided and around 100000 labeled pixels were extracted from the target scene to make up the ground truth data. The dataset is then partitioned, with 70% of the data allocated as training data and the remaining 30% as validation data in both scenes. Table 2 displays the outcomes of the SVAE and SCNN applications on the ground truth data in source and target scenes. The obtained results show that the two methods (SVAE and SCNN) perform well in desertification detection, the standard deviations were stable and only varied within a small range. More precisely, the SVAE provided the best Accuracy, Recall, Precision, and $F1 - score$ in source and target scenes. It also ensured better feature extraction thanks to 1) the normal distribution (Gaussian) of the latent space by the VAE, and 2) the spatial consistency conservation of the extracted features by the Siamese structure.

Table 2. Quantitative results on the source and the target scene.

Model	Accuracy	Precision	Recall	$F1-score$
SVAE Source	**97,43**	**97,42**	**96,86**	**97,39**
SCNN Source	96,02	95,38	95,50	95,78
SVAE Target with TL	**93.42**	**91,19**	**91,31**	**91,44**
SCNN target with TL	91.80	88,43	88,82	89,71
SVAE Target without TL	92.34	90,15	89,90	90,62
SCNN target without TL	90,11	88,14	88,83	88,90

5.2 Desertification Detection Outcomes

The distribution of desertification (Fig. 5) along the two study areas during the period 2001–2004 shows that the whole territory presents a relative risk of land degradation with very high agricultural pressure and overgrazing. In fact, the most important agricultural activity is mainly based on rainfed olive cultivation, which consists mainly of clearing areas of spontaneous plants, thus degrading the ecosystem. On the other hand, the areas with low agricultural pressure may have a low to high risk, given their combination with pastoral and forestry activities, and/or the very low availability of resources in the case of mountain slopes [26]. Human pressure, combined with unfavorable climatic conditions, has intensified the risk of desertification. Indeed, the climate of the two study areas is characterized by hot, dry summers that last from May to August. Rainfall is very irregular with a measured annual average of about 170 mm and reaching minimum values of 14 mm during dry years [27]. Desertification in the source scene could be detected more effectively using the SVAE framework. By fine-tuning the trained SVAE in the source scene by the target scene data, the model can learn more efficiently to detect desertification and improve the accuracy and reliability of the desertification detection process.

5.3 The Advantages and Limitations

In two dry areas of southern Tunisia, the Siamese DL model, and TL strategy were used to create a desertification risk map with a high spatial and temporal resolution from bi-temporal Landsat images. The obtained findings demonstrate that the developed method was efficiently employed to detect the land surface change and monitor desertification. Obviously, TL was more sophisticated than a single method SVAE or SCNN and it showed higher performance in the target scene with less ground truth data. It is also clear that, in the target scene, the accuracy of both Siamese methods was less than 94%, depending on the quantity and quality of the labeled data. These results may impede the identification of desertified areas and alter the outcomes of desertification monitoring. To produce more reliable results, In future studies, the labeled data in the target scene should be improved in quantity and quality. The Siamese structure is complex

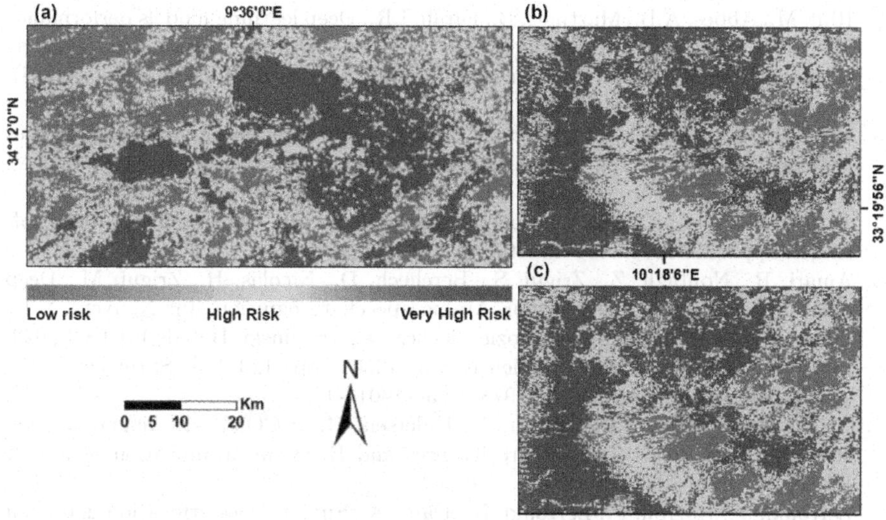

Fig. 5. Desertification detection outcomes: (a): SVAE prediction in source Scene, (b): SVAE prediction in Target Scene with TL and (c): SVAE prediction in Target Scene without TL

and requires a significant amount of high-quality data for training. This can make implementation, maintenance, and parameterization challenging.

6 Conclusion and Outlook

In this paper, we have proposed a classification method based on SVAE and TL for CD using bi-temporal Landsat images. It is based on a Siamese network trained on a labeled source scene, which is then fine-tuned on a bi-temporal image of the target scene with less labeled data. The method was tested on two datasets of Landsat bi-temporal images collected in Tunisia's southern regions and was found to be more efficient than SCNN in terms of CD and desertification classification. Future research perspectives include investigating the appropriate classification in the target scene using an active learning approach and testing the method with more input data with high quality to improve the quality of the desertification detection in the target scene.

Acknowledgments. We want to thank the Institute of Arid Regions of Medenine, Tunisia, LESOR (Laboratory of Economics and Rural Societies), for providing the ground truth data.

References

1. Xiong, Y., Zuo, R.: Robust feature extraction for geochemical anomaly recognition using a stacked convolutional denoising autoencoder. Math. Geosci. **54**(3), 623–644 (2022)

2. Rhif, M., Abbes, A.B., Martinez, B., Farah, I.R.: Deep learning models performance for NDVI time series prediction: a case study on northwest Tunisia. In: Mediterranean and Middle-East Geoscience and Remote Sensing Symposium (M2GARSS), pp. 9–12. IEEE, Tunisia (2020)
3. Ferchichi, A., Abbes, A.B., Barra, V., Farah, I.R.: Forecasting vegetation indices from spatio-temporal remotely sensed data using deep learning-based approaches: a systematic literature review. Ecol. Inf. **68**, 101552 (2022)
4. Alzubaidi, L., et al.: Review of deep learning: concepts, CNN architectures, challenges, applications, future directions. J. Big Data **8**(1), 1–74 (2021)
5. Amari, R., Noubigh, Z., Zrigui, S., Berchech, D., Nicolas, H., Zrigui, M.: Deep convolutional neural network for Arabic speech recognition. In: Nguyen, N.T., Manolopoulos, Y., Chbeir, R., Kozierkiewicz, A., Trawinski, B. (eds.) ICCCI 2022. Lecture Notes in Computer Science, vol. 13501, pp. 120–134. Springer, Cham (2022). https://doi.org/10.1007/978-3-031-16014-1_11
6. Aslan, M.F., Sabanci, K., Durdu, A., Unlersen, M.F.: COVID-19 diagnosis using state-of-the-art CNN architecture features and Bayesian optimization. Comput. Biol. Med. **142**, 105244 (2022)
7. Zerrouki, Y., Harrou, F., Zerrouki, N., Dairi, A., Sun, Y.: Desertification detection using an improved variational autoencoder-based approach through ETM-landsat satellite data. IEEE J. Select. Top. Appl. Earth Observations Remote Sens. **14**, 202–213 (2020)
8. Ran, X., Xu, M., Mei, L., Xu, Q., Liu, Q.: Detecting out-of-distribution samples via variational auto-encoder with reliable uncertainty estimation. Neural Netw. **145**, 199–208 (2022)
9. Farah, C., Manel, R., Abbes, A.B., Farah, I.R.: Desertification detection based on landsat time-series images and variational auto-encoder: application in Jeffera, Tunisia. In: IEEE International Geoscience and Remote Sensing Symposium, pp. 3688–3691. IEEE, Malaysia (2022)
10. Zhao, G., Peng, Y.: Semisupervised SAR image change detection based on a siamese variational autoencoder. Inf. Process. Manage. **59**(1), 102726 (2022)
11. Ghosh, S., Ghosh, S., Kumar, P., Scheme, E., Roy, P.P.: A novel spatio-temporal siamese network for 3d signature recognition. Pattern Recognit. Lett. **144**, 13–20 (2021)
12. Zhang, K.: Content-based image retrieval with a convolutional siamese neural network: distinguishing lung cancer and tuberculosis in CT images. Comput. Biol. Med. **140**, 105096 (2022)
13. Krishnamurthy, S., Srinivasan, K., Qaisar, S.M., Vincent, P.M.D.R., Chang, C.: Evaluating deep neural network architectures with transfer learning for pneumonitis diagnosis. Comput. Math. Methods Med. **2021**, 1–12 (2021)
14. Baker, N.A., Zengeler, N., Handmann, U.: A transfer learning evaluation of deep neural networks for image classification. Mach. Learn. Knowl. Extr. **4**(1), 22–41 (2022)
15. Raffel, C., et al.: Exploring the limits of transfer learning with a unified text-to-text transformer. Mach. Learn. **21**(140), 1–67 (2020)
16. Cao, H., Xie, X., Shi, J., Jiang, G., Wang, Y.: Siamese network-based transfer learning model to predict geogenic contaminated groundwaters. Environ. Sci. Technol. **56**(15), 11071–11079 (2022)
17. Zhu, Q., et al.: Land-use/land-cover change detection based on a siamese global learning framework for high spatial resolution remote sensing imagery. ISPRS J. Photogrammetry Remote Sens. **184**, 63–78 (2022)

18. Daudt, R.C., Le Saux, B., Boulch, A., Gousseau, Y.: Urban change detection for multispectral earth observation using convolutional neural networks. In: International Geoscience and Remote Sensing Symposium, pp. 2115–2118. IEEE, Spain (2018)
19. Yang, M., Jiao, L., Liu, F., Hou, B., Yang, S.: Transferred deep learning-based change detection in remote sensing images. IEEE Trans. Geosci. Remote Sens. **57**(9), 6960–6973 (2019)
20. Heidari, M., Fouladi-Ghaleh, K.: Using siamese networks with transfer learning for face recognition on small-samples datasets. In: International Conference on Machine Vision and Image Processing (MVIP), pp. 1–4. IEEE, Iran (2020)
21. Bandara, W.G.C., Patel, V.M.: A transformer-based siamese network for change detection. In: International Geoscience and Remote Sensing Symposium, pp. 207–210. IEEE, Malaysia (2022)
22. Andresini, G., Appice, A., Dell'Olio, D., Malerba, D.: Siamese networks with transfer learning for change detection in sentinel-2 images. In: Bandini, S., Gasparini, F., Mascardi, V., Palmonari, M., Vizzari, G. (eds.) AIxIA 2021. Lecture Notes in Computer Science, vol. 13196, pp. 478–489. Springer, Cham (2022). https://doi.org/10.1007/978-3-031-08421-8_33
23. Kingma, D.P., Welling, M.: Auto-encoding variational Bayes. arXiv preprint arXiv: 1312.6114 (2013)
24. Wang, W., et al.: Anomaly detection of industrial control systems based on transfer learning. Tsinghua Sci. Technol. **26**(6), 821–832 (2021)
25. Philip, K., Dominik, S., Barbara, H.: Novel transfer learning schemes based on Siamese networks and synthetic data. Neural Comput. Appl. **35**(11), 8423–8436 (2023)
26. Loireau, M., et al.: Système d'information sur l'environnement á l'échelle locale (Siel) pour évaluer le risque de désertification: situations comparées circumsahariennes (réseau Roselt). Sci. changements planétaires/Sécheresse **18**(4), 328–335 (2007)
27. Van Delden, H., et al.: User driven application and adaptation of an existing policy support system to a new region. In: 4th International Congress on Environmental Modelling and Software, Barcelona-Spain (2008)

Speaker Identification Enhancement Using Emotional Features

Jihed Jabnoun[1(✉)], Ahmed Zrigui[2], Anwer Slimi[1], Fabien Ringeval[3], Didier Schwab[3], and Mounir Zrigui[1]

[1] Research Laboratory in Algebra, Numbers Theory and Intelligent Systems, University of Monastir, Monastir, Tunisia
jihed.jabnoun@gmail.com, Mounir.zrigui@fsm.rnu.tn

[2] LaBRI Laboratory, University of Bordeaux, Nouvelle-Aquitaine, France

[3] Université Grenoble Alpes, CNRS Grenoble, Grenoble, France
fabien.ringeval@imag.fr, didier.schwab@univ-grenoble-alpes.fr

Abstract. Speaker recognition is a broad field that encompasses many different tasks related to identifying speakers in audio recordings. Two specific sub-tasks that are often studied are speaker segmentation and speaker identification. These tasks typically involve analyzing acoustic features of the audio to determine who is speaking. However, one limitation of traditional speaker identification methods is that they can struggle when dealing with emotional conversations, as the acoustic features can change due to the emotions being expressed. To address this limitation, focuses on studying the effect of emotion on speaker identification by combining features of both the emotions and speakers. This approach has shown to improve identification accuracy, increasing it from 72% using speaker features alone to 75% when both emotion and speaker features are used.

Keywords: SR · Speaker Segmentation · Triplet Loss · Emotion Recognition · CNN · Bi-LSTM

1 Introduction

Speech is the primary means of communication between humans. It is a complex set of signals containing mixed types of information; including linguistic and acoustic information. In other words, from a signal we can extract both verbal and non-verbal information, and they are both generic in nature but also specific to each individual (reflecting their idiosyncrasies) [21,31]. For humans, it's only natural to extract that kind of information unconsciously, just by hearing someone talking, we can tell if they are male or female, local or foreigner, happy or sad, etc.

What differentiates between speakers is the differences in the acoustic properties of the speech signal. In addition, there are differences related to the inherited vocal tract and the spoken accent of each speaker. Speaker recognition takes

N. T. Nguyen et al. (Eds.): ICCCI 2023, LNAI 14162, pp. 526–539, 2023.
https://doi.org/10.1007/978-3-031-41456-5_40

these differences into consideration and uses them to distinguish between different speakers [30].

Speaker Recognition (SR) is the task of automatically recognizing someone based on specific features present in the speech signal [7,8]. It has been widely deployed in various fields; including voice access control systems, indexing or labeling speakers in recorded conversations or dialogues, surveillance, and criminal and forensic investigations involving recorded voice samples [3,13,15]. In order to accurately identifying someone based on the acoustic features, several factors should be taken into consideration, such as the environment, the background noise, including the emotional state of the speaker [23,24].

In this paper, we will begin by providing a comprehensive overview of the most successful methods used in Voice Activity Detection, Speaker Segmentation, Speaker Embedding, and Speaker Identification (classification). Following that, we will introduce a novel approach aimed at improving the accuracy of speaker identification by incorporating emotional features.

2 Related Works

SR is a large topic that embraces many speaker-specific tasks. These tasks can be classified into two different groups: simple and compound. The simple branches of speaker recognition are autonomous tasks, while the compound branches utilize one or more of the simple manifestations, often with additional techniques. The simple branches of speaker recognition include speaker verification, speaker identification, and speaker classification. Speaker verification involves confirming the identity of a claimed speaker, speaker identification aims to determine the identity of an unknown speaker, and speaker classification focuses on categorizing speakers into predefined classes. On the other hand, the compound branches of speaker recognition include speaker segmentation, speech detection, and speaker tracking. These tasks, when combined, form a speaker diarization system. Speaker segmentation is the process of separating speech segments based on individual speakers, speech detection focuses on identifying regions of speech within an audio signal, and speaker tracking aims to track speaker changes or movements over time. For this work, our main focus will be on voice activity detection, speaker segmentation, speaker embedding, and speaker identification.

2.1 Voice Activity Detection (VAD)

VAD, also known as speech detection, aims to detect the presence or absence of speech and differentiates speech from non-speech sections in an audio recording. In the literature, several VAD algorithms have been developed based on different principles. These algorithms detect sudden changes in energy, spectral, or cepstral distances to meet various requirements in terms of features and compromises among latency, sensitivity, accuracy, and computational cost [27]. The general approach used is maximum-likelihood classification with Gaussian mixture models (GMMs) trained on labeled training data. However, different classification models can also be employed, such as multistate HMMs.

Thilo et al. [19] proposed an HMM-based speech/non-speech model for voice activity detection using normalized mean (log) energy features extracted from 20 min of conversational speech in a four-speaker meeting, consisting of three males and one female. The conducted experiments demonstrated an average equal error rate of 18.0%. Gregory et al. [9] conducted a comparison between several models for VAD and proposed an RNN-based Speech Activity Detection method. The experiments were performed on the AMI dataset using MFCC features. The best results in terms of Equal Error Rate (EER) were achieved using a Basic RNN with a rate of 16.13% and LSTM with a rate of 15.25%.

2.2 Change Point Detection/Speaker Segmentation

Speaker change point detection aims to locate time points or frames in an audio stream that correspond to a transition from one speaker to another, or from noise to speech. Ajmera et al. [2] Proposed a BIC Revisited approach for Speaker Change Detection varying the parameter λ values, The best results were obtained with ($\lambda = 6$ or 7). The experiments were conducted using the HUB-4 1997 dataset and MFCCs as features achieving a 68.0% F-measure. Mori et al. [18] introduced a Vector Quantization (VQ) approach for speaker segmentation and compared it with other commonly used methods such as GLR, BIC, and GMM. The experiments utilized the NHK (Japan Broadcasting Corporation) dataset, and the proposed VQ method achieved the highest F-measure of 89.3%. In more recent research, Bredin et al. [4] developed a Bidirectional Long Short-Term Memory Networks (BLSTM) model for Speaker Change Detection in Broadcast TV. The model was tested on the ETAPE TV subset and outperformed the existing state-of-the-art methods, achieving a score of 93.6%.

2.3 Speakers Embedding

Speaker embedding is a simple but effective methodology to represent the speaker's identity as a vector of fixed size, regardless of the length of the utterance. Two main approaches are used for speaker embedding, namely, identity vectors(i-vectors) and d-vectors. I-vectors encode both speaker and channel variability in a lower-dimensional space by decreasing the high-dimensional feature vector to a low-dimensional one, while preserving most of the pertinent information. A more effective approach is to use trained deep neural networks (DNNs) to predict a speaker's identity from given acoustic features. DNNs use hidden layers to extract a fixed-length vector representative of the speaker's features from each frame by averaging all activations of a selected hidden layer in an utterance [16]; those embeddings of fixed length are called d-vectors. This approach works for unseen speakers, which solves the first problem of the i-vector. Gregory et al. [20] carried a comparison between i-vector with (PLDA) + agglomerative hierarchical clustering (AHC) and d-vector with (BLSTM) DNN using NIST SRE '04, '05, '06, and '08, subset. The evaluation metric they used was DER, so they evaluated the speaker embedding as part of a speaker diarization system, and the best result was given by d-vector 23.42%. Wang et al. [28] carried a comparison between i-vector and d-vector as part of a diarization system with different clustering algorithms and d-vector with Spectral clustering gave the best result with an overall DER of 12.48%.

2.4 Speaker Identification (Classification)

Speaker identification is the task of identifying who is speaking in an audio signal. So, the objective is to match an input voice sample called a test sample with the available voice samples that are pre-enrolled in the system, where the speaker of a test utterance is called the target speaker. For that, we can consider the identification task as a multi-class classification. Several papers have made significant contributions to the field of speaker identification. Snyder et al. [25] introduced x-vectors, which are robust DNN embeddings used for large-scale speaker recognition. Zhang et al. [26] further enhanced speaker embedding learning with triplet loss and attention mechanisms in DNNs, improving the discriminative power of speaker embeddings.

3 Proposed Method

In order to study the effect of emotion on speaker identification accuracy, we proposed a compound speaker recognition model as shown in Fig. 1 consists of, VAD to eliminate background noise and the non-speech areas using **WebRTC**, Speaker segmentation to obtain homogeneous audio segments using **BiLSTM** followed by speaker embedding to extract the features representing speakers and emotions characteristics from those speech segments using a **Triplet Loss Function**. Finally, we used **Keras functional API** for classifying speakers and emotions joined together.

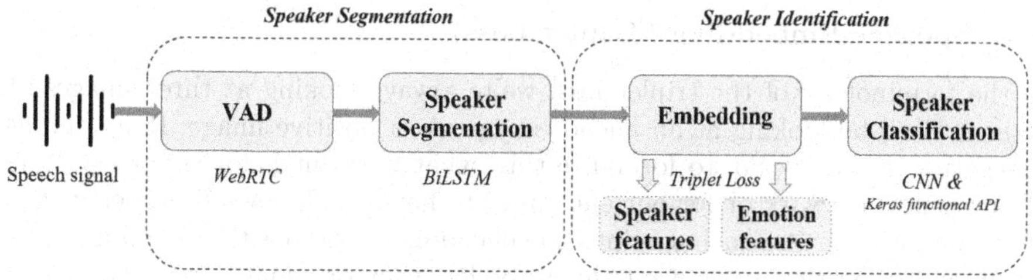

Fig. 1. Proposed method architecture.

3.1 Voice Activity Detection (WEBRTC VAD)

For this part, we used a free and open-source framework called WebRTC developed by Google that provides web browsers and mobile applications with real-time communication (RTC) via application programming interfaces (APIs). WebRTC uses two Gaussian functions, one for speech, and one for non-Speech, in order to cluster PLP acoustic features. The Perceptual Linear Prediction PLP models human speech based on the concept of psychophysics of hearing [12,29].

3.2 Change Point Detection or Speaker Segmentation (BiLSTM)

Speaker segmentation or change detection aims to identify in terms of milliseconds where the speaker's change point is, and use those points as boundaries to divide the speech into segments. For this part, we used a BiLSTM network [22]. In traditional neural networks like CNN, all inputs and outputs are independent of each other, CNN can be used to predict the identity of a speaker in a segment that belongs to one speaker but can't deal with sequential data. Bidirectional Long Short-Term Memory (Bi-LSTM) is a recurrent neural network (RNN). RNN is a type of neural network that we use to develop speech recognition and natural language processing models [5,10,11,17]. Our speaker segmentation model addresses' speaker change detection as a binary sequence labeling task using two Bidirectional Long Short-Term Memory recurrent neural networks (Bi-LSTM). Each of them is followed by a Dropout layer that randomly sets input units to 0 with a frequency of rate at each step during training time, which helps prevent overfitting. At last, we placed three Time Distributed layers that help in detecting intentions behind chronological inputs. When a Time Distributed Layer is applied, it helps to obtain the flattened output separately for each time step and prevent unwanted intervention between different time steps. Also, TimeDistributedDense layer is widely used in one-to-many and many-to-many architectures, as their outputs should have the same function for every time step.

3.3 Speaker Embedding (Triplet Loss)

In the terminology of the triplet loss, we're always looking at three images at a time. We'll be looking at an anchor image, A, a positive image, P, as well as a negative image, N. So, to formalize this, what we want is for the parameters of our neural network or for our encodings to have the following property. The encoding between the anchor minus the encoding of the positive example to be small, and in particular we want this to be less than or equal to the distance or the squared norm between the encoding of the anchor and the encoding of the negative.

$$l(A,P,N) = max(\|f(A) - f(P)\|^2 - \|f(A) - f(N)\|^2 + \alpha, 0) \qquad (1)$$

This is how we define the loss on a single triplet. And the overall cost function for our neural network can be sum over a training set of these individual losses on different Triplets:

$$J = \sum_{i=0}^{n} L(A^{(i)}, P^{(i)}, N^{(i)}) \tag{2}$$

Now coming to the general architecture Fig. 2, the idea is to have three identical neural networks with the same architecture and shared weights where the last layer of the Network has to learn a D-dimensional vector representation. The Anchor, Positive and Negative images, each are passed through a respective network and with the shared architecture during backpropagation the weight vectors are updated. The main objective of using triplet loss is to extract 256-vector representatives of the speaker's features and emotion's features.

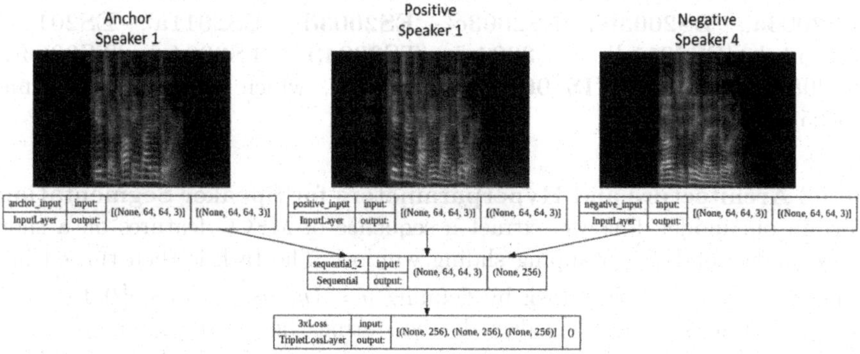

Fig. 2. Triplet loss model architecture.

3.4 Speaker Classification (Sequential/Functional Keras API)

Now that we've extracted the embedded vectors of both speakers and emotions, we've got two new datasets. At first, we're going to use the speaker embedded features to train a CNN model for a speaker classification part [1,14]. The architecture of the first CNN model is shown in Fig. 4a.

As for the second model, we used a Keras functional API with two inputs and one output. The advantage of Functional API is their ability to handle models with non-linear topology, multiple inputs or outputs and even shared layers. Another advantage of the Functional API is their ability to manipulate models that use shared layers. Shared layers are layer graphs that are reused repeatedly in the same model, they learn features that correspond to multiple paths in the layer graph. They allow data to be shared between different input branches and make it possible to train a model with fewer data. As we mentioned above, the second model has two inputs, one for the emotion's embeddings and the other for the speaker embeddings. It's a functional API with two identical brunches, as shown in Fig. 4b.

4 Experiments and Results

4.1 Speaker Segmentation

As we've already mentioned, change point detection is the task of segmenting a speech based on the transition from a speaker to another.

About DataSet. In order to test our change point detection model, we used a subset of the Augmented Multi-party Interaction (AMI) [6]. The AMI dataset contains 375 meeting records divided into four parts (a, b, c, d), that's a total of 1500 audio files. The length of utterances in the dataset fluctuates between 20 and 90 min. For our experiments we used a subset that contain only four meeting records (16 utterances), Namely {**'ES2003a'**, **'ES2003b'**, **'ES2003c'**, **'ES2003d'**, **'ES2011a'**, **'ES2011b'**, **'ES2011c'**, **'ES2011d'**, **'TS3004a'**, **'TS3004b'**, **'TS3004c'**, **'TS3004d'**, **'IS1008a'**, **'IS1008b'**, **'IS1008c'**, **'IS1008d'**}, which is about 483.63 min (8.0605 H).

Model Architecture and Hyperparameters for Speaker Segmentation. To train our model, first we extract a sequence of MFCC features on a short (a few milliseconds) overlapping sliding window. The task is then turned into a binary sequence labeling task by defining $y = (y_1, y_2, ..., y_T) \in \{0,1\}^T$ such that $y_i = 1$ if there is a speaker change during the ith frame, or $y_i = 0$ if there is none. The architecture of our network is made up of two Bi-LSTM layers and a multilayer layer's perceptron (MLP) whose weights are shared over the sequence. The Bi-LSTMs enable the processing of the sequences in both forward and backward ways, using past and future contexts. The outputs of both backward and forward LSTMs are appended together and passed to the next layer. The shared MLP consists of three fully connected feedforward layers, with a Tanh activation function for the 2 first layers and a sigmoid function for the last one, enabling the network to output a score between 0 and 1.

Results Interpretation. After 50 epochs of training Fig. 3, the accuracy of our model on test data reaches 98.54237% and less than 0.1% for the loss.

4.2 Effect of Emotions on Speaker Identification

About DataSet. Ryerson Audio-Visual Database of Emotional Speech and Song (RAVDESS) This version of RAVDESS includes 1440 files: 60 utterances for each actor by 24 actors, that's a total of 1440. RAVDESS contains 24 professional actors, including 12 males and 12 females, performing in a neutral North American accent in two lexically similar sentences. The vocal emotions include expressions of **joy**, **calm**, **anger**, **sadness**, **surprise**, **disgust**, and **fear**. Each expression is performed at two emotional intensity levels (normal, strong), with an extra neutral expression.

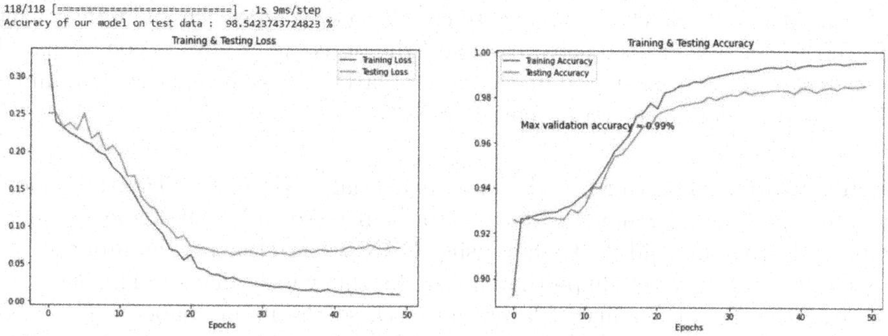

Fig. 3. Training and testing plot for change point detection.

Embedding Extraction. Our network consists of a batch input layer and a deep CNN followed by L2 normalization, which results in the emotions embedding and the same for the speaker embedding. This is followed by the triplet loss during training. To train our model we used LIBROSA library to extract Log Mel Spectrogram images from our audio dataset with the size of (46, 46), each image has two labels: Speaker ID and Speaker emotion. At first, we created pairs of images based on the speaker ID labels. So, for each image in the dataset, we assigned a positive example from the same class and a negative example from a different class randomly. And the same thing we did for the Speaker emotion labels. The Triplet Loss minimizes the distance between an anchor and a positive, both of which belong to the same class, and maximizes the distance between the anchor and a negative of a different class. At first the data is randomly distributed, after 1000 iterations we have 24 clusters of 256-embedding vectors for speaker ID and 7 clusters for speaker emotions.

4.3 Speaker Classification

After extracting the embedding vectors, we conducted several experiments with different architectures and input shapes in order to get the best results.

First Model. The first model in Fig. 4a is a sequential CNN model for speaker identification. For this model we reshaped the 256-embedding vector into a 16×16 matrix, so the input shape is (None, 16, 16, 1). The first dimension represents the batch size, which is None in this case. When using CNN with 2D layers, the input shape is always a 4D array of shape (batch_size, height, width, depth). After 50 epochs of training, the first model reached an accuracy of 72%.

Second Model. The second model in Fig. 4b is a Keras functional API model with two inputs for speaker ID vectors and emotion vectors. It has the same input shape as the first model (None, 16, 16, 1). The structure of this model is like two identical branches concatenated at the end. Where each input of speaker ID and emotion is treated separately and the outcome of both is concatenated at the end, passed to a shared linear stack of layers. After 50 epochs of training, the second model reached an accuracy of 73%.

Third Model. The third model is a sequential CNN model. For this model we used the original 256-embedding vector as it is, so the input shape is (None, 256, 1). Earlier we said that when using CNN with 2D layers the input shape is always a 4D array of shape (batch_size, height, width, depth). This time we changed the dimensionality of layers into 1D, so the input shape is just a 3D array of shape (batch_size, embedding_legth, depth). After 50 epochs of training, the third model reached an accuracy of 72% same as the first model.

Fourth Model. For the last model, we have a Keras functional API model with two inputs for speaker ID vectors and emotion vectors. This time the input shape is (None, 256, 1). Both inputs are concatenated at the first layer, and used to train the rest of the shared linear stack of layers. After 50 epochs of training, the fourth model reached an accuracy of 75%.

4.4 Discussion

In this section we're going to discuss the results that we get from all the conducted experiments for the speaker classification and for that, to make things easier, we summarized all the classification reports in Table 1.

Table 1. classification report summary for the proposed models.

Model	Metric	Precision	Recall	F1-score
First model (Sequential 2D-CNN)	Accuracy	–	–	0.72
	Macro avg	0.73	0.72	0.70
	Weighted avg	0.75	0.72	0.71
Second model (Keras functionalAPI)	Accuracy	–	–	0.72
	Macro avg	0.78	0.73	0.73
	Weighted avg	0.78	0.73	0.72
Third model (Sequential 1D-CNN)	Accuracy	–	–	0.72
	Macro avg	0.77	0.72	0.71
	Weighted avg	0.79	0.72	0.71
Fourth model (Keras functional API)	Accuracy	–	–	0.75
	Macro avg	0.81	0.75	0.74
	Weighted avg	0.82	0.75	0.75

The goal of those experiments is to study the effect of emotion on speaker identification. In the first model we applied a simple classification task for speaker

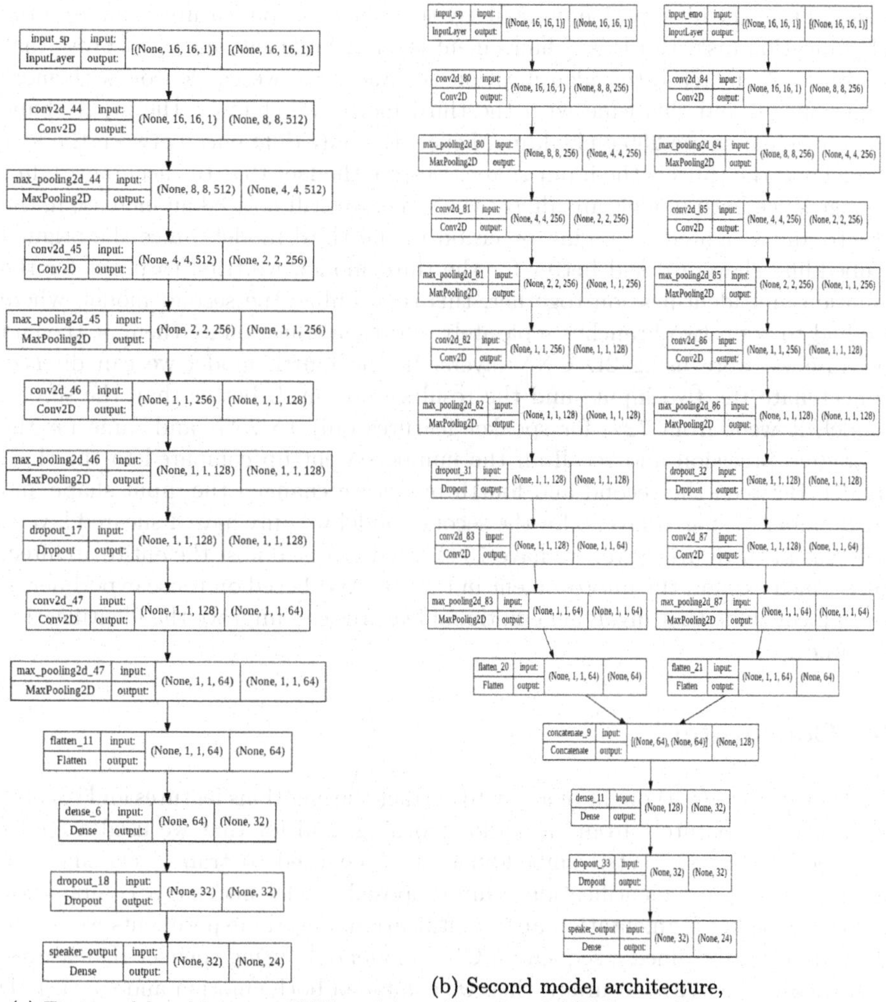

(a) First model architecture, CNN model for speaker identification with input shape (None,16,16,1).

(b) Second model architecture, Functional API for speaker identification with two inputs of shape (None,16,16,1).

Fig. 4. (a) First model architecture, CNN model for speaker identification with input shape (None, 16, 16, 1). (b) Second model architecture, Functional API for speaker identification with two inputs of shape (None, 16, 16, 1).

identification, as a result we got a micro-averaging, accuracy of 72% on test data. For the second model when we added the emotion embedding to the training process the accuracy went from 72% to 73% even the macro-averaging precision advanced by 0.05% from 73% to 87% and same for the weighted-averaging precision. From the observation, we can say that the emotion features enhanced the identification task. But this enhancement is still insufficient and can't prove that emotion can increase the identification accuracy. So, we carried on with more experiments, and this time with the third model we changed the input shape to its original shape 256-embedding, hence, the only difference between the first model and the third is the input shape. Despite the fact that the accuracy didn't change since both models are almost the same, we still noticed an increase in the macro and weighted averaging precision in the third model. Since the original embedding shape worked better for the third model, we tried to use it for the emotion and identification together, this time unlike the second model, where we had to train two branches separately and then concatenate them at the end because we were using 2D CNN layers. In the fourth model we can directly concatenate the two inputs and the results were much better than the second model, it went from 72% for speaker features only to 75%, and same for the averaging precision and recall all the numbers went up compared to the third model. Between the second and fourth model we changed the input shape and the number of shared layers, for the second model we only have 4 sheared layers, whereas in the fourth layer we have 15 sheared layers almost the entire architecture which explain the improvement in results. And based on those experiments, we can conclude that involving emotional features can improve the identification accuracy.

5 Conclusion

In this research, we thought of a way to extract the emotions features and speaker ID features separately from an audio recording, and for that we used a triplet loss model. The extracted embeddings are then used to train a classification model for speaker identification. Our proposed model became a combination between speaker segmentation and identification. Several experiments were conducted, first we trained a sequential CNN model only using speaker ID features, and we obtained 72% accuracy, then we combined both emotion and speaker ID features using Keras functional API, the accuracy went up to 75%. Adding the emotions features means giving the model more information about the speaker, which helps increase the identification accuracy. The aim of our research was to look into the relation between emotions and speaker identification, but compared to the state of the art the identification accuracy is considered low due to of the lack of data that we used to train our classification model since we're only using RAVDESS dataset. We considered concatenating some other datasets together that contain utterances from speakers with different emotions, but the accuracy was even lower owing to the fact that those datasets are recorded in different environments and with different equipment. The only way to overcome this problem is to record our own samples with the same equipment and under the same conditions, which consume a lot of time and effort. We also can try models other than triplet loss to extract more advanced features than log Mel spectrograms.

References

1. Abd Allah, M.A.H., Haffar, N., Zrigui, M.: Contribution to the methods of indexing Arabic textual documents to improve the performance of IRS. In: 2022 International Conference on INnovations in Intelligent SysTems and Applications (INISTA), pp. 1–6. IEEE (2022)
2. Ajmera, J., McCowan, I., Bourlard, H.: BIC revisited for speaker change detection. Technical report IDIAP-RR02-39, IDIAP, Martigny, Switzerland (2002)
3. Amari, R., Noubigh, Z., Zrigui, S., Berchech, D., Nicolas, H., Zrigui, M.: Deep convolutional neural network for Arabic speech recognition. In: Nguyen, N.T., Manolopoulos, Y., Chbeir, R., Kozierkiewicz, A., Trawiński, B. (eds.) ICCCI 2022. LNAI, vol. 13501, pp. 120–134. Springer, Cham (2022). https://doi.org/10.1007/978-3-031-16014-1_11
4. Bredin, H., Barras, C., et al.: Speaker change detection in broadcast TV using bidirectional long short-term memory networks. In: Interspeech 2017. ISCA (2017)
5. Bsir, B., Zrigui, M.: Enhancing deep learning gender identification with gated recurrent units architecture in social text. Computación y Sistemas **22**(3), 757–766 (2018)
6. Carletta, J.: Announcing the AMI meeting corpus. ELRA Newslett. **11**(1), 3–5 (2006)
7. Furui, S.: Recent advances in speaker recognition. Pattern Recogn. Lett. **18**(9), 859–872 (1997)
8. Furui, S.: Digital Speech Processing, Synthesis, and Recognition. CRC Press, Boca Raton (2018)
9. Gelly, G., Gauvain, J.L.: Optimization of RNN-based speech activity detection. IEEE/ACM Trans. Audio Speech Lang. Process. **26**(3), 646–656 (2017)
10. Haffar, N., Ayadi, R., Hkiri, E., Zrigui, M.: Temporal ordering of events via deep neural networks. In: Lladós, J., Lopresti, D., Uchida, S. (eds.) ICDAR 2021. LNCS, vol. 12822, pp. 762–777. Springer, Cham (2021). https://doi.org/10.1007/978-3-030-86331-9_49
11. Haffar, N., Hkiri, E., Zrigui, M.: Using bidirectional LSTM and shortest dependency path for classifying Arabic temporal relations. Procedia Comput. Sci. **176**, 370–379 (2020)
12. Hermansky, H.: Perceptual linear predictive (PLP) analysis of speech. J. Acoust. Soc. Am. **87**(4), 1738–1752 (1990)
13. Jaballi, S., Zrigui, S., Sghaier, M.A., Berchech, D., Zrigui, M.: Sentiment analysis of Tunisian users on social networks: overcoming the challenge of multilingual comments in the Tunisian dialect. In: Nguyen, N.T., Manolopoulos, Y., Chbeir, R., Kozierkiewicz, A., Trawiński, B. (eds.) ICCCI 2022. LNAI, vol. 13501, pp. 176–192. Springer, Cham (2022). https://doi.org/10.1007/978-3-031-16014-1_15
14. Jabnoun, J., Haffar, N., Zrigui, A., Nsir, S., Nicolas, H., Trigui, A.: An image retrieval system using deep learning to extract high-level features. In: Bădică, C., Treur, J., Benslimane, D., Hnatkowska, B., Krótkiewicz, M. (eds.) ICCCI 2022. CCIS, vol. 1653, pp. 167–179. Springer, Cham (2022). https://doi.org/10.1007/978-3-031-16210-7_13

15. Legrand, A., Trystram, D., Zrigui, S.: Adapting batch scheduling to workload characteristics: what can we expect from online learning? In: 2019 IEEE International Parallel and Distributed Processing Symposium (IPDPS), pp. 686–695. IEEE (2019)
16. Mahmoud, A., Zrigui, M.: Deep neural network models for paraphrased text classification in the Arabic language. In: Métais, E., Meziane, F., Vadera, S., Sugumaran, V., Saraee, M. (eds.) NLDB 2019. LNCS, vol. 11608, pp. 3–16. Springer, Cham (2019). https://doi.org/10.1007/978-3-030-23281-8_1
17. Maraoui, M., Antoniadis, G., Zrigui, M.: CALL system for Arabic based on natural language processing tools. In: IICAI, pp. 2249–2258 (2009)
18. Mori, K., Nakagawa, S.: Speaker change detection and speaker clustering using VQ distortion for broadcast news speech recognition. In: 2001 IEEE International Conference on Acoustics, Speech, and Signal Processing. Proceedings (Cat. No. 01CH37221), vol. 1, pp. 413–416. IEEE (2001)
19. Pfau, T., Ellis, D.P., Stolcke, A.: Multispeaker speech activity detection for the ICSI meeting recorder. In: IEEE Workshop on Automatic Speech Recognition and Understanding 2001, ASRU 2001, pp. 107–110. IEEE (2001)
20. Sell, G., et al.: Diarization is hard: some experiences and lessons learned for the JHU team in the inaugural DIHARD challenge. In: Interspeech, pp. 2808–2812 (2018)
21. Sghaier, M.A., Zrigui, M.: Sentiment analysis for Arabic e-commerce websites. In: 2016 International Conference on Engineering & MIS (ICEMIS), pp. 1–7. IEEE (2016)
22. Sharfuddin, A.A., Tihami, M.N., Islam, M.S.: A deep recurrent neural network with BiLSTM model for sentiment classification. In: 2018 International Conference on Bangla Speech and Language Processing (ICBSLP), pp. 1–4. IEEE (2018)
23. Slimi, A., Hafar, N., Zrigui, M., Nicolas, H.: Multiple models fusion for multi-label classification in speech emotion recognition systems. Procedia Comput. Sci. **207**, 2875–2882 (2022)
24. Slimi, A., Hamroun, M., Zrigui, M., Nicolas, H.: Emotion recognition from speech using spectrograms and shallow neural networks. In: Proceedings of the 18th International Conference on Advances in Mobile Computing & Multimedia, pp. 35–39 (2020)
25. Snyder, D., Garcia-Romero, D., Sell, G., Povey, D., Khudanpur, S.: X-Vectors: robust DNN embeddings for speaker recognition. In: 2018 IEEE International Conference on Acoustics, Speech and Signal Processing (ICASSP), pp. 5329–5333. IEEE (2018)
26. Tang, Y., Ding, G., Huang, J., He, X., Zhou, B.: Deep speaker embedding learning with multi-level pooling for text-independent speaker verification. In: ICASSP 2019–2019 IEEE International Conference on Acoustics, Speech and Signal Processing (ICASSP), pp. 6116–6120. IEEE (2019)
27. Tranter, S.E., Reynolds, D.A.: An overview of automatic speaker diarization systems. IEEE Trans. Audio Speech Lang. Process. **14**(5), 1557–1565 (2006)
28. Wang, Q., Downey, C., Wan, L., Mansfield, P.A., Moreno, I.L.: Speaker diarization with LSTM. In: 2018 IEEE International Conference on Acoustics, Speech and Signal Processing (ICASSP), pp. 5239–5243. IEEE (2018)
29. Xie, L., Liu, Z.Q.: A comparative study of audio features for audio-to-visual conversion in MPEG-4 compliant facial animation. In: 2006 International Conference on Machine Learning and Cybernetics, pp. 4359–4364. IEEE (2006)

30. Zhonghua, F., Rongchun, Z.: An overview of modeling technology of speaker recognition. In: International Conference on Neural Networks and Signal Processing 2003. Proceedings of the 2003, vol. 2, pp. 887–891. IEEE (2003)
31. Zouaghi, A., Zrigui, M., Antoniadis, G.: Compréhension automatique de la parole arabe spontanée. Traitement Automatique des Langues **49**(1), 141–166 (2008)

Classification of Punches in Olympic Boxing Using Static RGB Cameras

Piotr Stefański(✉), Tomasz Jach, and Jan Kozak

Department of Machine Learning, University of Economics in Katowice, 1 Maja, 40-287 Katowice, Poland
{piotr.stefanski,tomasz.jach,jan.kozak}@ue.katowice.pl

Abstract. Cameras in sports continuously track athletes, recognize their activities, and monitor performance. This capability is ensured by sophisticated computer vision systems with machine learning algorithms and massive computation power. Combat sports are rather challenging because punches happen rather quickly. This paper provides comprehensive research on approaches to measuring the performance of athletes in combat sports. We use RGB cameras to measure athletes' activity from a distance without interfering with their equipment, in contrast to the approach which uses wearable sensors. The aim of this paper is to provide a solution to classify punches in Olympic boxing based on static RGB cameras opposite the boxing ring. The proposed solution classifies three types of punches and the best classifier obtained sequentially 94%, 84%, and 81% of the F1 score for them. Finally, we measured the impact of the data augmentation process on classification performance and provide future works.

Keywords: Punch classification · Combat sports analysis · Computer vision

1 Introduction

In the current world, a massive amount of cameras were installed and produce an enormous amount of data. The main challenge is to understand recording scenes, which is nearly impossible without automatic solutions. In order to make sense of data, extracting valuable information is necessary [2,9,37].

Cameras are also crucial in sports, widely used in football [26], tennis [31], and other popular sports [5,14,30]. Using them, live broadcasts can be transmitted to a remote audience and automatically analyze by computer vision systems. Those sophisticated systems provide additional excitement to the audience by tracking players and drawing a virtual footprint on the pitch. They also help camera operators by automatically detecting interesting areas in the pitch (e.g. place where the action is happening) and focusing the camera on them [33].

N. T. Nguyen et al. (Eds.): ICCCI 2023, LNAI 14162, pp. 540–551, 2023.
https://doi.org/10.1007/978-3-031-41456-5_41

Using machine learning methods in the domain of combat sports is also growing in popularity [18,19,24]. Current approaches to measuring boxers' performance could be divided into two groups. One of them, based on cameras, could be called "non-invasive" because it doesn't interfere with boxers' equipment [4,16,17,34]. The second one could be called "invasive" which uses wearable sensors and devices to monitor boxers' performance, which is more hazardous to players' health because of a possible injury [12,35,36,39]. Furthermore, it is currently forbidden in Olympic boxing to alter boxers' outfits [17].

The aim of this paper is to propose a solution to classify punches in Olympic boxing using computer vision algorithms. We decided to use a "non-invasive" approach with RGB cameras. To do this we needed to record and label necessary footage on real boxing bouts. To train classifiers, we used the well-known CNN architecture of neural networks, to one of them we added a data augmentation step and compared obtained performance metrics. Thereby we contribute a new approach to classify punches in Olympic boxing using RGB cameras.

The remainder of the article is organized as follows. Section 1 contains the introduction to the topic of this article. Section 2 contains a description of the current state of the science. Section 3 presents the authors' proposed approach and the data collection and labelling process. Section 4 contains the results of experiments with the evaluation of trained classifiers to punch classification. In the last Sect. 5 we summarise the paper along with ideas for further works.

2 Related Works

Object detecting and object tracking are among the most important topics in computer vision [25,38,40]. In industry, systems automatically monitor employee behaviour and personal protective equipment to improve health and safety during work [21,25,42]. There are also applications that monitor the quality of produced items [3,11]. It is widely used in traffic [6,15], public areas (like railway stations) [6,7], construction industry [23,25], or sports [32]. Object tracking provides wide possibilities to study the behaviour of detected objects in many different areas of our life, like fall prevention in hospitals [22], assault detection in public spaces [6], or analyzing the motion of players in the pitch [33].

In many sports, cameras are used by sophisticated computer vision systems which may provide additional valuable information about a recorded scene. Therefore, dozens of cameras in stadiums were installed and automatically track athletes and analyze their movement to further analysis [33]. Such data has a wide range of stakeholders such as referees, sports commentators, or remote audiences. Also coaches widely use that data to analyze the performance of the entire team or individual athlete [8,20,43].

In combat sports, two approaches have emerged to analyze boxers' performance which can be divided by the type of devices they use to analyze boxers'. One of them uses wearable devices like textile sensors [39], sensors incorporated into boxers' equipment (boxing gloves and head guards) [12,36] or sensor on the boxers' back [36]. The second approach doesn't interfere with boxers' equipment using RGB-D overhead camera [4,16,17], or static RGB camera opposite the boxing ring [34], thereby not exposing the boxer to health risks.

During the work with stakeholders, we rejected the idea of using wearable sensors which is prohibited by boxing regulations [17]. To measure boxers' performance from a distance we can use cameras. The camera over the ring (used by [4,16,17]) records cleaner data without the audience and obfuscation between boxers than the camera opposite the boxing ring. However, not all boxing rings were prepared for installation devices over them, on the ring where we collected the data (See Sect. 3.1) also. Therefore we decided to use static RGB cameras like on [34] where authors created the system for tracking boxers' gloves.

Machine learning is commonly used to solve classification problems. There are a lot of algorithms to work with, like Random Forest or Support Vector Machines (SVM) used by authors [17] to classify punches from depth data. Also [5] used Convolutional Neural Network (CNN) to classify actions in sports based on images. CNN is one of the most popular deep neural networks which consists of multiple layers including a convolutional layer, a non-linearity layer, a pooling layer, and a fully connected layer. CNN is being successfully used in machine learning problems like image classification or Natural Language Processing (NLP) [1]. Therefore we decided to use CNN to classify punches from images.

3 Methodology

The main goal of this paper is to propose a solution to classify punches in Olympic boxing. We decided to use RGB cameras around the boxing ring to capture the scene. Due to the lack of such data, it was necessary to prepare our own data set. Section 3.1 describes the process of collecting data on the selected competition. To prepare recorded footage for classification, each frame was treated individually by a licensed boxing referee. This labour-intensive process is described in Sect. 3.2. For classification, the CNN model was used, additionally, a data augmentation preprocessing step was added in order to diversify the data set and prevent overfitting [13,41].

3.1 Data Collection

In dynamic sports analysis problems, it is hard to find good, stable, and valuable data sets. This is even more difficult for combat sports, especially for footage recorded on genuine competition, verified and labeled by experts. Therefore we need to record, collect and label data on our own. The necessary footage of the boxing fights was recorded in Poland at the Silesian league for juniors, cadets, and seniors. For this purpose four GoPro Hero8 cameras with power banks and 128 GB memory cards were used. The cameras were mounted behind each corner on 1.8 m tripods and recorded video in full HD resolution at 50 fps rate. In the end, we collected nearly 500 GB of footage [28,29].

3.2 Data Labeling

The labelling process is one of the most challenging problems because of the amount of data. Boxing fights is a very dynamic sport and punches happen pretty fast, therefore precision in recording and labelling is critical. Four hours of recording at a 50 fps rate with four cameras give about three million frames to label. To reduce the amount of data we provided clash detecting solution to filter moments from footage where boxers stand far apart without any chance for punches [28,29]. Clash detecting works well and reduces about 70% of footage given to the labelling process. The reduced footage was loaded into a CVAT[1] labelling tool and labelled by a licensed boxing referee. So far referee labelled footage from two cameras. The referee marks each detected punch and assigns it to one of three classes of punch (head, corpus, block). Examples of marked punches and his class are presented in Fig. 1.

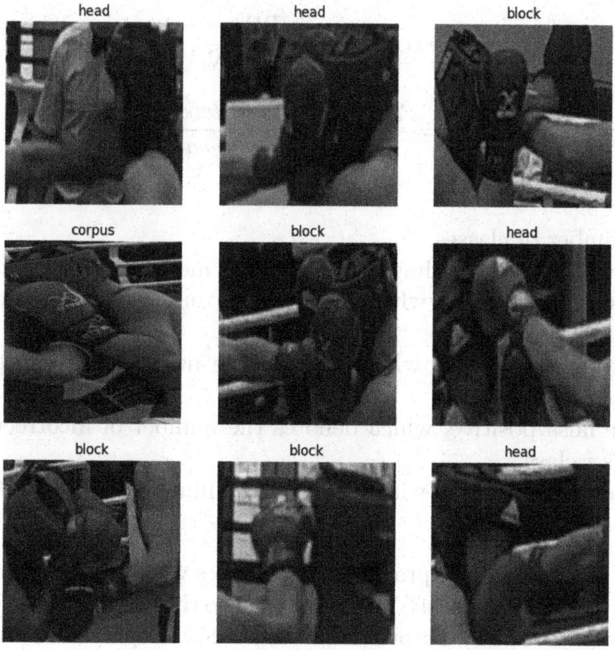

Fig. 1. Samples of labelled punches

3.3 Classification

In order to classify punches we decided to use the Convolutional Neural Network (CNN) which is the popular structure of deep neural networks, commonly used

[1] https://github.com/opencv/cvat.

in image classification problems. A trained neural network is designed to detect three classes of punches:

1. Head - hit punch to the opponent's head.
2. Corpus - hit punch to the opponent's corpus.
3. Block - punch to the opponent's gloves.

Classification performance is presented on Sect. 4 and evaluated by following metrics: accuracy (Eq. (1)), precision (Eq. (2)), recall (Eq. (3)) and F1 score (Eq. (4)) [10,27].

$$accuracy = \frac{\sum_{i=1}^{k} \frac{FP_i+FN_i}{TP_i+TN_i+FP_i+FN_i}}{k}, \tag{1}$$

$$precision_i = \frac{TP_i}{TP_i + FP_i}, \tag{2}$$

$$recall_i = \frac{TP_i}{TP_i + FN_i}, \tag{3}$$

$$F1_i = \frac{2 \cdot Precision_i \cdot Recall_i}{Precision_i + Recall_i}, \tag{4}$$

where:

- k is the number of classes.
- i is a generic class, depending on which class metric is calculated for.
- TP_i is the true positive, which denotes the number of correctly classified punches as i class.
- TN_i is the true negative, which denotes the number of correctly classified punches as not i class.
- FP_i is the false positive, which denotes the number of incorrectly classified punches as i class.
- FN_i is the false negative, which denotes the number of incorrectly classified punches as not i class.

The data labeling process provided 5115 images with punches categorized into three classes; 3575 (roughly 70%) were assigned to the "Head" class; 458 (roughly 9%) were assigned to the "Corpus" class and 1082 (roughly 21%) were assigned to the "Block" class. To diversify the data set and prevent overfitting [13,41], a data augmentation process was applied. This technique applies random, but realistic transformations in each processed image:

1. Random flip - operation to randomly flips images.
2. Random rotation - operation to randomly rotates images.
3. Random zoom - operation to randomly zooms images.
4. Random contrast - operation to randomly adjusts contrast on images.

Figure 2 presents several image transformations from the data augmentation process.

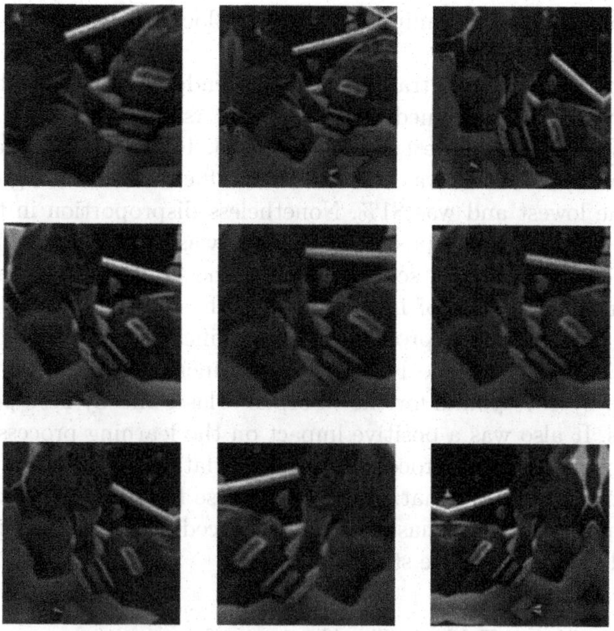

Fig. 2. Data augmentation transformations

4 Experiments

The results of experiments were obtained on a computer with Intel Core i9-11900K @ 3.50 GHz 16-core processor, 64 GB of RAM, and an Nvidia Geforce GTX 1080Ti graphic card, on the Ubuntu operation system.

During our experiments, we trained two classifiers based on neural networks and CNN architecture. First based on data set straight from the labelling process, without any transformations. The second one was based on the same data set but additionally has preprocessing step with data augmentation. The step with image transformations was proposed in order to diversify the data set and prevent overfitting problems, details of transformations were described in Sect. 3. Both networks on the input layer obtain images on 180 × 180 resolution with a color channel, in addition, classifiers were trained with Adam optimizer and cross-entropy loss function.

Classifiers were evaluated by four metrics which were described in Sect. 3.3. Table 1 and Table 2 contain values of Precision, Recall and F1 score metrics for each class. Meanwhile, Fig. 3 and Fig. 4 present the learning process with training and validating values of accuracy and loss function.

The first classifier obtain 82% of accuracy and achieved the best Precision (85%), Recall (92%), and F1 (88%) for the "Head" class. Even though the "Block" class was more examples than the "Corpus" class it was the most difficult to classify, his Precision was 69%, and Recall was 55%. The "Corpus" class has more than half fewer examples than the "Block" class and obtains 81% of Precision and 68% of Recall.

The second classifier was trained on the extended data set by the data augmentation process and obtained 90% accuracy. As with the first classifier, the "Head" class achieved the best Precision (93%), Recall (94%), and F1 (94%). Classification "Block" class was still the most difficult, considering the F1 score which was the lowest and was 81%. Nonetheless disproportion in the F1 score metric between classes "Corpus" and "Block" was reduced by 10% points. A significant increase in the F1 score metric for the "Block" class was caused by an increase in the Precision of 12% points and the Recall of 26% points.

The data augmentation process was a significant impact on classification performance. Considering the F1 score it was increased by 6% points for the "Head" class, by 10% points for the "Corpus" class, and by 20% points for the "Block" class. It also was a positive impact on the learning process, Fig. 3 contains charts of the learning process without the data augmentation process, and Fig. 4 contains charts after that. Comparing these figures it could be concluded that the data augmentation has effectively reduced the overfitting problem and the second classifier was more stable.

Table 1. Classification performance

Class	Precision	Recall	F1
Head	**0.85**	**0.92**	**0.88**
Corpus	0.81	0.68	0.74
Block	0.69	0.55	0.61

Table 2. Classification performance with data augmentation

Class	Precision	Recall	F1
Head	**0.93**	**0.94**	**0.94**
Corpus	0.90	0.78	0.84
Block	0.81	0.81	0.81

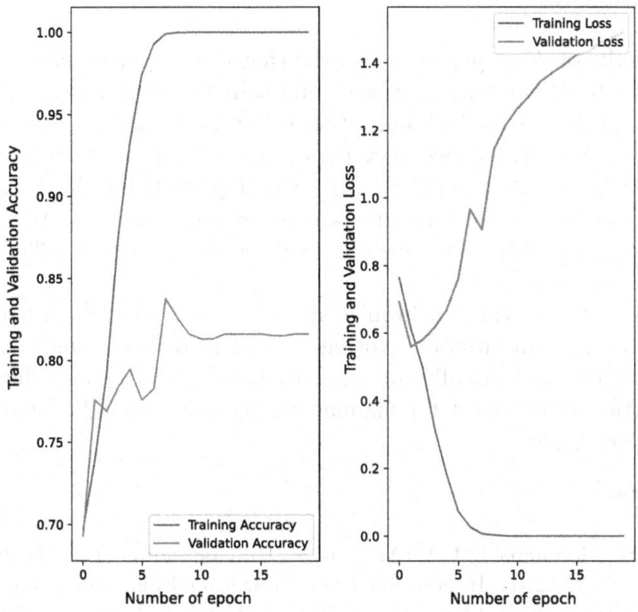

Fig. 3. Learning process

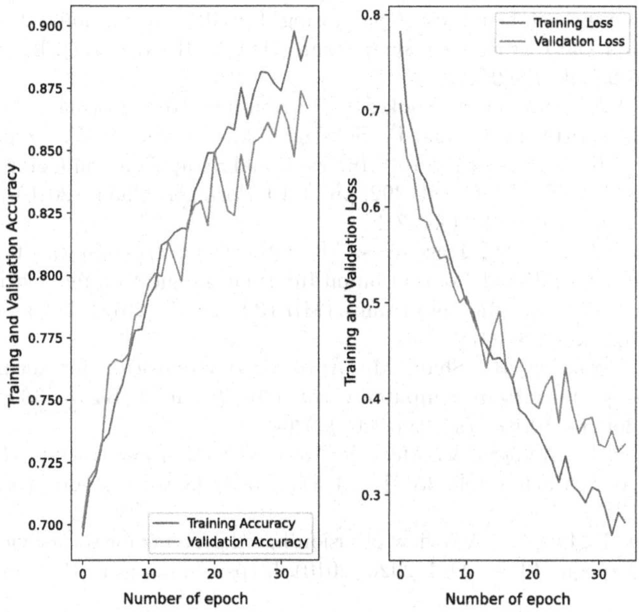

Fig. 4. Learning process

5 Conclusions

Obtained results of the experiments proved that the proposed solution to classify punches using RGB cameras is possible and achieves high-performance metrics. To do so the authors collected and labeled their own data set with real boxing bouts. In the experiments, two classifiers were trained and tested on the CNN architecture of the neural network. Also, the impact of the data augmentation process on classification performance was measured. Classifiers predicted three classes of punches and the best one obtained sequentially 94%, 84%, and 81% of the F1 score for them.

In the future, we will synchronize recorded and labeled data between all cameras to prepare an ensemble voting system in order to improve classification performance. Additionally, we want to automatically label the rest of the recorded footage and pass it for manual verification to finally build large data set with boxing fights.

References

1. Albawi, S., Mohammed, T.A., Al-Zawi, S.: Understanding of a convolutional neural network. In: 2017 International Conference on Engineering and Technology (ICET). IEEE (2017). https://doi.org/10.1109/icengtechnol.2017.8308186
2. Barnich, O., Droogenbroeck, M.V.: ViBe: a universal background subtraction algorithm for video sequences. IEEE Trans. Image Process. **20**(6), 1709–1724 (2011). https://doi.org/10.1109/tip.2010.2101613
3. Baygin, M., Karakose, M., Sarimaden, A., Erhan, A.: Machine vision based defect detection approach using image processing. In: 2017 International Artificial Intelligence and Data Processing Symposium (IDAP). IEEE (2017). https://doi.org/10.1109/idap.2017.8090292
4. Behendi, S.K., Morgan, S., Fookes, C.B.: Non-invasive performance measurement in combat sports. In: Chung, P., Soltoggio, A., Dawson, C.W., Meng, Q., Pain, M. (eds.) Proceedings of the 10th International Symposium on Computer Science in Sports (ISCSS). AISC, vol. 392, pp. 3–10. Springer, Cham (2016). https://doi.org/10.1007/978-3-319-24560-7_1
5. Buric, M., Pobar, M., Ivasic-Kos, M.: Object detection in sports videos. In: 2018 41st International Convention on Information and Communication Technology, Electronics and Microelectronics (MIPRO). IEEE (2018). https://doi.org/10.23919/mipro.2018.8400189
6. Chen, C., Surette, R., Shah, M.: Automated monitoring for security camera networks: promise from computer vision labs. Secur. J. **34**(3), 389–409 (2020). https://doi.org/10.1057/s41284-020-00230-w
7. Comaniciu, D., Ramesh, V., Meer, P.: Kernel-based object tracking. IEEE Trans. Pattern Anal. Mach. Intell. **25**(5), 564–577 (2003). https://doi.org/10.1109/tpami.2003.1195991
8. D'Orazio, T., Leo, M.: A review of vision-based systems for soccer video analysis. Pattern Recogn. **43**(8), 2911–2926 (2010). https://doi.org/10.1016/j.patcog.2010.03.009
9. Garcia-Garcia, B., Bouwmans, T., Silva, A.J.R.: Background subtraction in real applications: challenges, current models and future directions. Comput. Sci. Rev. **35**, 100204 (2020). https://doi.org/10.1016/j.cosrev.2019.100204

10. Grandini, M., Bagli, E., Visani, G.: Metrics for multi-class classification: an overview (2020). https://doi.org/10.48550/ARXIV.2008.05756
11. Elbehiery, H., Hefnawy, A., Elewa, M.: Surface defects detection for ceramic tiles using image processing and morphological techniques (2007). https://doi.org/10.5281/ZENODO.1084534
12. Hahn, A., et al.: Development of an automated scoring system for amateur boxing. Procedia Eng. **2**(2), 3095–3101 (2010). https://doi.org/10.1016/j.proeng.2010.04.117
13. Hinton, G.E., Srivastava, N., Krizhevsky, A., Sutskever, I., Salakhutdinov, R.R.: Improving neural networks by preventing co-adaptation of feature detectors (2012). https://doi.org/10.48550/ARXIV.1207.0580
14. Jeffries, C.T.: Sports analytics with computer vision (2018). https://openworks.wooster.edu/independentstudy/8103/
15. Jia, W., et al.: Real-time automatic helmet detection of motorcyclists in urban traffic using improved YOLOv5 detector. IET Image Process. **15**(14), 3623–3637 (2021). https://doi.org/10.1049/ipr2.12295
16. Kasiri, S., Fookes, C., Sridharan, S., Morgan, S.: Fine-grained action recognition of boxing punches from depth imagery. Comput. Vis. Image Underst. **159**, 143–153 (2017). https://doi.org/10.1016/j.cviu.2017.04.007
17. Kasiri-Bidhendi, S., Fookes, C., Morgan, S., Martin, D.T., Sridharan, S.: Combat sports analytics: boxing punch classification using overhead depthimagery. In: 2015 IEEE International Conference on Image Processing (ICIP). IEEE (2015). https://doi.org/10.1109/icip.2015.7351667
18. Kato, S., Yamagiwa, S.: Predicting successful throwing technique in judo from factors of kumite posture based on a machine-learning approach. Computation **10**(10), 175 (2022). https://doi.org/10.3390/computation10100175
19. Khasanshin, I.: Application of an artificial neural network to automate the measurement of kinematic characteristics of punches in boxing. Appl. Sci. **11**(3), 1223 (2021). https://doi.org/10.3390/app11031223
20. Li, H., Tang, J., Wu, S., Zhang, Y., Lin, S.: Automatic detection and analysis of player action in moving background sports video sequences. IEEE Trans. Circ. Syst. Video Technol. **20**(3), 351–364 (2010). https://doi.org/10.1109/tcsvt.2009.2035833
21. Li, J., et al.: Safety helmet wearing detection based on image processing and machine learning. In: 2017 Ninth International Conference on Advanced Computational Intelligence (ICACI). IEEE (2017). https://doi.org/10.1109/icaci.2017.7974509
22. Ni, B., Nguyen, C.D., Moulin, P.: RGBD-camera based get-up event detection for hospital fall prevention. In: 2012 IEEE International Conference on Acoustics, Speech and Signal Processing (ICASSP). IEEE (2012). https://doi.org/10.1109/icassp.2012.6287947
23. Paneru, S., Jeelani, I.: Computer vision applications in construction: current state, opportunities & challenges. Autom. Constr. **132**, 103940 (2021). https://doi.org/10.1016/j.autcon.2021.103940
24. Quinn, E., Corcoran, N.: Automation of computer vision applications for real-time combat sports video analysis. In: European Conference on the Impact of Artificial Intelligence and Robotics, vol. 4, no. 1, pp. 162–171 (2022). https://doi.org/10.34190/eciair.4.1.930
25. Seo, J., Han, S., Lee, S., Kim, H.: Computer vision techniques for construction safety and health monitoring. Adv. Eng. Inform. **29**(2), 239–251 (2015). https://doi.org/10.1016/j.aei.2015.02.001

26. Setterwall, D.: Computerised video analysis of football - technical and commercial possibilities for football coaching. Unpublished Masters Thesis, Stockholms Universitet (2003)
27. Sokolova, M., Lapalme, G.: A systematic analysis of performance measures for classification tasks. Inf. Process. Manag. **45**(4), 427–437 (2009). https://doi.org/10.1016/j.ipm.2009.03.002
28. Stefański, P., Kozak, J., Jach, T.: The problem of detecting boxers in the boxing ring. In: Szczerbicki, E., Wojtkiewicz, K., Nguyen, S.V., Pietranik, M., Krótkiewicz, M. (eds.) ACIIDS 2022. CCIS, vol. 1716, pp. 592–603. Springer, Cham (2022). https://doi.org/10.1007/978-981-19-8234-7_46
29. Stefański, P.: Detecting clashes in boxing. In: Proceedings of the 3rd Polish Conference on Artificial Intelligence, Gdynia, Poland, 25–27 April 2022, pp. 29–32 (2022). https://wydawnictwo.umg.edu.pl/pp-rai2022/pdfs/06_pp-rai-2022-026.pdf
30. Stein, M., et al.: Bring it to the pitch: combining video and movement data to enhance team sport analysis. IEEE Trans. Vis. Comput. Graph. **24**(1), 13–22 (2018). https://doi.org/10.1109/tvcg.2017.2745181
31. Sudhir, G., Lee, J., Jain, A.: Automatic classification of tennis video for high-level content-based retrieval. In: Proceedings 1998 IEEE International Workshop on Content-Based Access of Image and Video Database. IEEE Computer Society (1998). https://doi.org/10.1109/caivd.1998.646036
32. Thomas, G.: Real-time camera tracking using sports pitch markings. J. Real-Time Image Process. **2**(2–3), 117–132 (2007). https://doi.org/10.1007/s11554-007-0041-1
33. Thomas, G., Gade, R., Moeslund, T.B., Carr, P., Hilton, A.: Computer vision for sports: current applications and research topics. Comput. Vis. Image Underst. **159**, 3–18 (2017). https://doi.org/10.1016/j.cviu.2017.04.011
34. Wattanamongkhol, N., Kumhom, P., Chamnongthai, K.: A method of glove tracking for amateur boxing refereeing. In: IEEE International Symposium on Communications and Information Technology 2005, ISCIT 2005. IEEE (2006). https://doi.org/10.1109/iscit.2005.1566786
35. Worsey, M., Espinosa, H., Shepherd, J., Thiel, D.: Inertial sensors for performance analysis in combat sports: a systematic review. Sports **7**(1), 28 (2019). https://doi.org/10.3390/sports7010028
36. Worsey, M.T.O., Espinosa, H.G., Shepherd, J.B., Thiel, D.V.: An evaluation of wearable inertial sensor configuration and supervised machine learning models for automatic punch classification in boxing. IoT **1**(2), 360–381 (2020). https://doi.org/10.3390/iot1020021
37. Wu, Y.J., Tsai, C.M., Shih, F.: Improving leaf classification rate via background removal and ROI extraction. J. Image Graph. **4**(2), 93–98 (2016). https://doi.org/10.18178/joig.4.2.93-98
38. Wu, Y., Lim, J., Yang, M.H.: Object tracking benchmark. IEEE Trans. Pattern Anal. Mach. Intell. **37**(9), 1834–1848 (2015). https://doi.org/10.1109/tpami.2014.2388226
39. Ye, X., et al.: All-textile sensors for boxing punch force and velocity detection. Nano Energy **97**, 107114 (2022). https://doi.org/10.1016/j.nanoen.2022.107114
40. Yilmaz, A., Javed, O., Shah, M.: Object tracking. ACM Comput. Surv. **38**(4), 13 (2006). https://doi.org/10.1145/1177352.1177355
41. Zhong, Z., Zheng, L., Kang, G., Li, S., Yang, Y.: Random erasing data augmentation. In: Proceedings of the AAAI Conference on Artificial Intelligence, vol. 34, no. 07, pp. 13001–13008 (2020). https://doi.org/10.1609/aaai.v34i07.7000

42. Zhou, F., Zhao, H., Nie, Z.: Safety helmet detection based on YOLOv5. In: 2021 IEEE International Conference on Power Electronics, Computer Applications (ICPECA). IEEE (2021). https://doi.org/10.1109/icpeca51329.2021.9362711
43. Zhu, G., et al.: Event tactic analysis based on broadcast sports video. IEEE Trans. Multimedia **11**(1), 49–67 (2009). https://doi.org/10.1109/tmm.2008.2008918

Learning Human Postures Using Lab-Depth HOG Descriptors

Safa Mefteh[1(✉)], Mohamed-Bécha Kaâniche[1], Riadh Ksantini[2], and Adel Bouhoula[3]

[1] Innov'COM Lab/Digital Security Lab, Higher School of Communication of Tunis (SUP'COM), University of Carthage, Ariana, Tunisia
{safa.mefteh,medbecha.kaaniche}@supcom.tn

[2] Department of Computer Science, College of IT, University of Bahrain, Zallaq, Kingdom of Bahrain
rksantini@uob.edu.bh

[3] Department of Next-Generation Computing, College of Graduate Studies Arabian, Gulf University, Manama, Kingdom of Bahrain
a.bouhoula@agu.edu.bh

Abstract. Human Posture Recognition is gaining increasing attention in the field of computer vision due to its promising applications in the areas of health care, human-computer interaction, and surveillance systems. This paper presents a novel method for human posture recognition by combining both color and depth images and feeding the resulting information into the vision transformer (ViT) model. We want to take advantage of integrating the Lab-D HOG descriptor [18] into the ViT architecture [8]. First, we compute the multispectral Lab-D edge detector by opting for the maximum eigenvalue of the multiplication of the jacobian matrix by its transpose. Second, we select the multispectral corner points by picking the minimum of the eigenvalues of the multispectral Harris matrix. Third, for each selected corner point, we compute a Lab-D HOG descriptor. Last, we feed the extracted Lab-D HOG descriptors into the transformer encoder/decoder by implementing two different strategies. Results show that we outperform state-of-the-art methods.

Keywords: Multispectral Lab-D corner detector (MCD) · Multispectral Lab-D HOG descriptor · Human posture recognition · Vision Transformer (ViT) · Multispectral Lab-D edge detector

1 Introduction

Human posture recognition is a critical and challenging research field especially for human gesture recognition and human action recognition [21]. In fact, human posture recognition methods must deal with several constraints such as 2D image noise, depth image noise, complex background, occlusion and the ratio of pixels per person. There are three main categories of approaches for human posture

N. T. Nguyen et al. (Eds.): ICCCI 2023, LNAI 14162, pp. 552–564, 2023.
https://doi.org/10.1007/978-3-031-41456-5_42

recognition: (1) Methods based on using wearable sensors [4,10,13], (2) methods based on analyzing joint information acquired from RGB-D cameras [2,6,7] and (3) methods based on analyzing video sequences [3,21,29]. For the first category, subjects are using different physical sensors such as wearing accelerometers and pressure sensors. However, wearing such devices make persons feel uncomfortable. As for methods based on joint detection that locate the positions of joints in the body such as elbows, knees, shoulders, and hips, they are sensitive to occlusions which affects dramatically the human action recognition rate [9]. However, video sequence processing methods offer several key benefits over methods based on analyzing joint information and methods based on using wearable sensors. Firstly, video analysis provides a more complete and nuanced view of human posture and movements, capturing not only the position and orientation of joints, but also the shape and behavior of the entire body. This allows for a more comprehensive analysis of posture patterns. Secondly, video analysis is typically easier to perform and more accessible, as it does not require specialized equipment or technical expertise to use. In most approaches, salient features are extracted in order to reduce the high dimensionality of images without losing their information. Several methods have captured the attention of researchers in the last decades. These approaches can be split into three subcategories: (a) approaches based on traditional computer vision methods [14,22], (b) approaches based on deep learning methods [2,28] and (c) hybrid methods [3,12].

In this paper, we propose an approach for human posture recognition based on processing color-depth images by using deep learning algorithms. Inspired by [17], we want to take advantage of the use of the multispectral edge detector by combining both color and depth images in a well-posed way. For that matter, we detect people by implementing the approach proposed by [24]. For each detected person, we compute the edges. After, we select salient multispectral corner features by picking the minimum of the eigenvalues of the multispectral Harris matrix as described in detail in [18]. Next, we compute the multispectral Lab-D HOG descriptor on top of extracted Lab-D corners. Finally, we fed the computed multispectral Lab-D HOG descriptors to the vision Transformer (ViT) [8]. Our method has been validated on an image dataset portraying three human postures: standing, sitting and lying. Results show that the proposed method is more effective and accurate w.r.t. state-of-the-art methods.

Our main contribution is the integration of color-depth images into the ViT architecture. We assume that color images combined with depth images can provide more detailed and accurate information about a person's posture compared to working with the whole image. The additional depth information can help to accurately locate body parts and joints, which can improve the overall performance of a human posture recognition system. Complementarily, the use of RGB images can provide additional information about the person's clothing and surroundings, which can also be useful for posture recognition. Moreover, applying the Lab-D HOG descriptor can represent postures better than simply doing a linear projection which enhances the attention process effectively in the ViT.

The remaining of this paper is structured as follows. First, an overview of related works is presented in Sect. 2. Second, the proposed approach for human posture recognition is detailed in Sect. 3. Third, the conducted experiments and the obtained results are showcased and discussed in Sect. 4. Last, Sect. 5 concludes the paper by summarising our contributions and highlighting some perspectives.

2 Previous Work

In this section, we give an overview of vision-based human posture classification methods. Hereafter, we focus solely on methods based on color and/or depth multispectral posture classifiers. As stated above, we can split human posture classification methods into three main categories: (i) color-based classification, (ii) depth-based classification, and (iii) color-depth-based classification.

A posture can be defined as the position that each person adopts when performing his activities such as walking, sitting, standing, or sleeping. Recognizing postures is considered a crucial step for action or behavior recognition. Through the past years, many researchers have concentrated on implementing algorithms for color images in order to detect postures effectively. Authors in [22] proposed an algorithm that uses human contour samples to obtain human edge deformable templates and a gradient descent method to estimate postures. Liu and Ostadabbas [14] presented a non-invasive in-bed posture monitoring system. They described the posture using a histogram of oriented gradients (HOG) feature descriptors. To determine the posture, they classify these descriptors with a support vector machine (SVM) classifier. In [11], authors developed a human posture recognition solution based on the human shape using a new histogram projecting method. Then, they fed extracted shape descriptors to SVM for the classification step. In addition, in [3], authors proposed a hybrid model for human detection, segmentation, and posture classification. They used Mask R-CNN in order to detect and segment each human subject in the scene. Then, they extracted regional features and then passed a revised Inception-ResNet-V2 model for posture recognition. Similar methods proved to be more efficient [3,12]. However, they are sensitive to some outliers features extracted from people's clothing, illumination, and background interference, and complex environmental conditions.

With increasingly cheaper depth image sensors, posture recognition based on RGB-D images has become an important research focus in the field of human action recognition. Li et al. [12] proposed to detect human posture by using only depth images. First, they used a head model in order to locate the human position. Then, they applied an edge extraction for human detection. Next, the authors extract the HOG features from the original depth image to get the human posture descriptor. Last, they classify these descriptors using the generalized regression neural network. Also, Wang et al. [26] used Kinect camera to acquire their dataset. The human silhouette was extracted using background subtraction and connected component technique based on the depth image. Then, the center of gravity of the human silhouette was extracted. Features such as the ratio of upper to lower body and the distance between the center and the body contour were extracted. Finally, a learning vector quantization (LVQ) neural network was used for action recognition.

Recently, works have exploited deep learning approaches for the human posture recognition task. For instance, Ahmed et al. [1] proposed an approach using the AlexNet model in order to estimate joint positions and joint angles from depth images. Authors trained the model on synthetic depth images. Also, Elforaici et al. [2] proposed to train a convolutional neural network (CNN) either on RGB images or on depth images to recognize static body postures. The authors showed that classifying postures by training their CNN model on depth images gave better results compared to RGB images. However, the depth images lose their mapping quality at distances greater than three meters from the camera. So far, we assume that human posture can be better detected while combining both color and depth information. Among the most recent relevant RGB-D human posture recognition algorithms, Wu et al. [27] recognized the lying posture by combining the color image and its corresponding depth information. First, authors extracted the 2D keypoints from the RGB image. Then, they obtained the 3D movement of humans by combining depth information and coordinate transformation. Finally, they used the OpenPose method to match the 3D information and obtain the 3D posture of the individual. Also, in [5], authors proposed 3D human pose predictions based on RGB-D images. First, they extract 2D pose estimations from RGB images by applying hierarchical parallel and multi-scale residual structures. Then, they estimated a 3D pose from a depth image based on 2D predicted joints and computed patches.

In this paper, we propose an accurate human posture recognition method using an original multispectral Lab-D edge detector. Our main contribution is the integration of color and depth information into a unique meaningful result, without requiring empirical parameters. Hence, we integrate the Lab-D HOG descriptor computed on top of the Lab-D corner points in the ViT architecture. In fact, the utilization of Lab-D HOG descriptors in place of the linear projection step in ViT presents several benefits. According to [18], the Lab-D HOG descriptor provides a more robust and discriminative representation of image features by capturing the local gradient information of the Lab-D edge image, which is invariant to variations in illumination and viewpoint. Additionally, the Lab-D HOG descriptor has a higher computational efficiency, as it can be computed in a fast manner and requires less memory. Furthermore, the Lab-D HOG descriptor is highly scalable and easily adapted for larger images. We have shown that it is quite straightforward and efficient to use such edge information for posture recognition tasks.

3 Proposed Method

In this paper, we investigate the use of both color and depth images for human posture classification by using the ViT model. Inspired by [17], we employ a fusion scheme that uses a Jacobian matrix from paired color and depth images. The color and depth image channels are meant to be complementary, where color images tend to provide color and texture details, while depth images cope better with object occlusion, which comes handful in different complex situations. In order to integrate the Lab-D HOG descriptor into the ViT architecture, we have adopted two different strategies: (1) the first strategy consists of computing the Lab-D HOG on different patches of a single image, and (2) the second strategy considers the whole image as a single patch.

As detailed by Fig. 1, we emphasize the first strategy. First, from a given color-depth video sequence, we detect a person. Second, for each detected person, we compute a multispectral Lab-D edge image by picking the maximum eigenvalue of the jacobian matrix. Third, we split the Lab-D edge image into patches. Fourth, for each patch, we select the multispectral Lab-D corner points based on the Lab-D patch image by getting the minimum eigenvalues of the Harris matrix. Fifth, we compute the Lab-D HOG descriptor on top of selected corner points. Last, we include positional embeddings and we feed the Lab-D HOG descriptor to the transformer encoder.

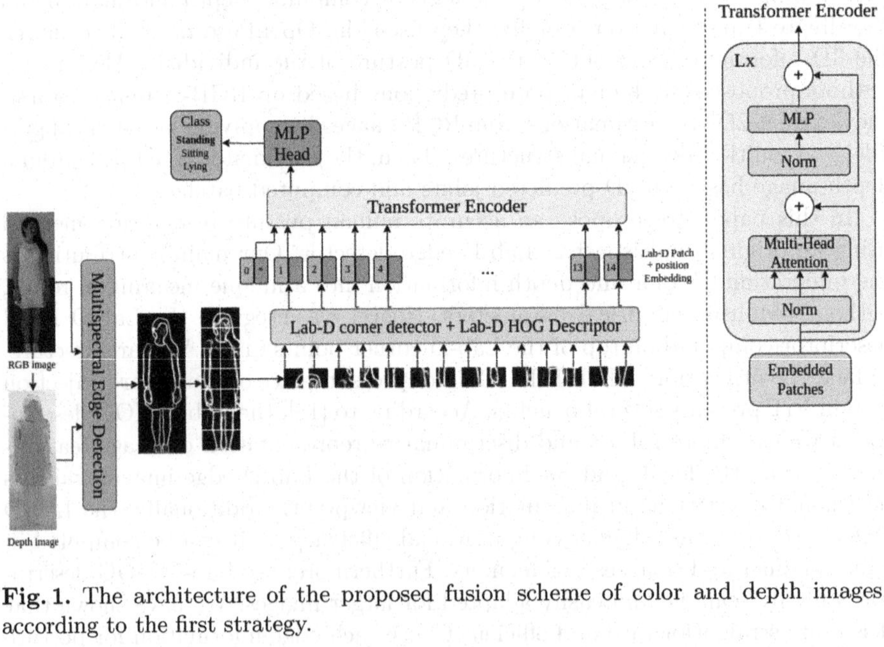

Fig. 1. The architecture of the proposed fusion scheme of color and depth images, according to the first strategy.

For the second strategy, a modification of the attention module is necessary to account for the fact that the whole image is mapped to a single patch [16]. As indicated by the Fig. 2, in the beginning, we acquire Lab-D video sequences. Next, we apply the multispectral edge detection algorithm to extract the edge image. After, we compute the Lab-D HOG descriptor on top of extracted salient

Lab-D corner points from the edge image. Then, we form the final Lab-D HOG descriptor sequence by concatenating the computed descriptors. Late, we feed the result sequence to the transformer encoder.

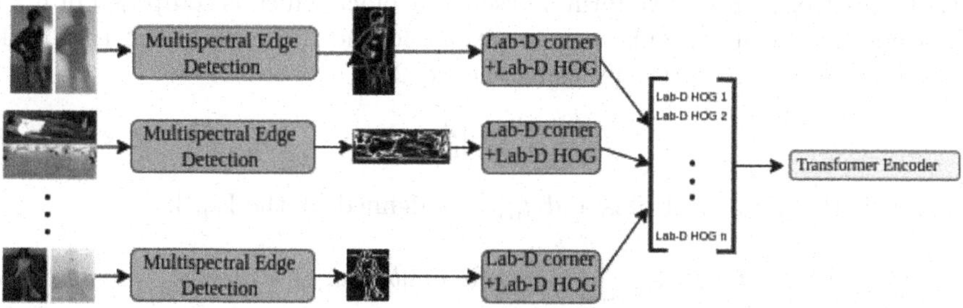

Fig. 2. The main steps according to the second strategy.

3.1 People Detection

Given a video sequence, we apply YOLO (You Only Look Once) [24] object detection method to determine the bounding boxes of people in the scene. This approach achieves a fair compromise between efficiency and accuracy. This step is used to identify different people in the scene by extracting a set of bounding boxes around them. We use these bounding boxes as masks for the following steps.

3.2 The Multispectral Lab-D Edge Detection

The multispectral Lab-D edge image is computed by combining both color and depth images. The key idea is to integrate different information into one meaningful combination, without requiring empirical parameters in order to be quite straightforward and efficient. Firstly, we form a Jacobian matrix J with the first-order gaussian derivative for each channel separately. After that, in order to find the best compromise between all the columns of the proposed Jacobian matrix, we perform a product of this latter and its transpose $J^T J$. At last, we form the Lab-D edge image by picking the maximum eigenvalue of the $J^T J$ matrix. Authors showcase an improvement compared to recent state-of-the-art methods. In fact, the proposed method distinguishes occluded objects even if they have the same color. Also, it takes into account even the small details in an image.

3.3 The Multispectral Lab-D HOG Descriptor

Based on [18], for each detected person, we compute a set of multispectral Lab-D corner points based on the multispectral edge image by using the Eq. 1.

$$W(x,y) = \sum_{u=x-(r/2)}^{x+(r/2)} \sum_{v=y-(r/2)}^{y+(r/2)} (J^T J)(u,v), \tag{1}$$

where W is the corner strength matrix, (x, y) is the coordinate of the center of the patch and r is the size of the side of the image patch. The corner strength is set to the minimum of the eigenvalues of the latter computed matrix.

On top of each detected corner point, we compute the 2D multispectral Lab-D HOG descriptor. First, we form a descriptor block which is composed of $n \times n$ cells where each cell contains $m \times m$ pixels. Second, for each cell in the block, we compute a feature vector by using the Eq. 2.

$$f_{\mathrm{ij}} = [f_{\mathrm{ij}}(\beta)]^T_{\beta \in [1..K]}, \tag{2}$$

where K is the number of bins and $f_{\mathrm{ij}}(\beta)$ is defined by the Eq. 3.

$$f_{\mathrm{ij}}(\beta) = \sum_{(u,v) \in c_{\mathrm{ij}}} edge(u,v)\delta[bin(u,v) - \beta], \tag{3}$$

where bin(u, v) denotes the function that returns the index of the direction bin associated with the pixel (u, v) extracted from the gradient orientation matrix, $\delta[]$ is the Kronecker delta function and edge(u, v) is the gradient magnitude of the pixel (u, v) from the obtained Lab-D edge image. Last, for each block, we obtain a 2D vector descriptor by concatenating the feature vectors of all its cells with a normalization step.

3.4 Human Posture Classification

In order to classify postures, we feed the Lab-D edge images to the Vision Transformer (ViT) model [8].

Vision Transformers and deep learning models are both widely used in computer vision tasks such as image classification, object detection, and segmentation. It has been gaining popularity by outperforming the recent CNN-based methods [8]. Vision Transformers use self-attention mechanisms to process images, which allows them to consider the relationships between all parts of an image at once. This makes them more efficient at handling large images and allows them to be trained with fewer data. Authors in [25] introduce several training strategies that allow ViT to be effective using a smaller dataset. The main architecture of a ViT model is based on the transformer encoder/decoder. It consists of an adapted encoder and a decoder to process images. The encoder is composed of multiple layers of self-attention and feed-forward neural networks for extracting features from the input image, while the decoder is responsible for making predictions based on the extracted features. The vision transformer model also includes position embeddings to help the model understand the spatial relationships between different parts of the image. According to [15], the ViT achieves an impressive speed-accuracy trade-off on image classification compared to convolutional networks.

To take advantage of the ViT model, we apply improvements to the main architecture as illustrated in Figs. 1 and 2. Actually, in the original ViT, a linear projection of flattened patches is applied, before feeding the data to the transformer module. In our method, we feed the Lab-D HOG descriptors to the transformer. The idea behind using the Lab-D HOG descriptor is to join color-depth images into one powerful piece of information. We believe that the computed Lab-D HOG descriptor represents the patch significantly better than simply applying a linear projection.

4 Experimental Evaluation and Results

In this section, in order to tease out the advantage of using the resulting edge information, we compare our results by passing directly RGB images, Depth images, RGB-D and edge images in the ViT model against computing HOG descriptor and Lab-D HOG descriptors on these images. These comparisons are performed on a collected RGB-D dataset.

4.1 Dataset

We have carried out our experiments on a newly built RGB-D Human posture dataset collected from both human activity recognition datasets: RGBD-HuDaAct [19] and RGBD PRECIS dataset [20]. Both datasets contain aligned and synchronized color-depth video streams. The two datasets are challenging because they are captured under different lighting conditions and contain body part occlusions. The RGBD-HuDaAct dataset contains different actions for the task of human posture recognition such as: standing still, sitting, or exchanging the use of left and right hands. In addition, the RGBD PRECIS dataset contains various activities like standing up, sitting down, sitting still, moving hands in front of the body, moving hands close to the body, and falling from the bed. From these different activities, we have collected 712 aligned RGB-D postures: 392 images for standing posture, 208 images for sitting posture, and 112 images for lying posture.

4.2 Experimental Protocol

We have evaluated the accuracy of our approach using two experimental protocols. In the first one, we compared the performance of our proposed algorithm using RGB, depth, RGB-D, and Lab-D images. In the second one, we have shown the superiority of our proposed method when feeding the Lab-D edge information in different ViT strategies. We have used the precision, recall, and F1-score as the validation metrics to evaluate our solution [23].

4.3 Implementation Details

Experiments were conducted on NVIDIA QUADRO RTX GPU with 8 GB RAM. For YOLOv3, we used the PyTorch framework which supports GPU computing. Our custom model ViT was implemented based on [16] method but with some configurations and modifications in order to adapt the model to the Lab-D HOG descriptors. We trained our model on 10 epochs with a mini-batch size equal to 10. As an optimizer, we used Adam with an initial learning rate of 0.0001. For the original ViT, we have fixed the image resolution to 224×224. For the first strategy, the patch size was set to 16×16. For the HOG descriptor, we extracted from each sample in our dataset, a different number of features noted n. Hence, the final local Lab-D HOG descriptor size is equal to $n \times 83$. We have applied Principal Component Analysis (PCA) technique to the obtained descriptors to forward the same input size to the classification step.

4.4 Results

To test the effectiveness of our proposed algorithm, we started by showing the result of applying our Lab-D edge detector on top of acquired color and depth images to compute both the Lab-D corner detector and the Lab-D HOG descriptor. Next, we compare the computed the F1-score of our posture classification approach based on the fusion of the Lab-D HOG descriptor against the original HOG descriptor with the ViT model, computed over different images.

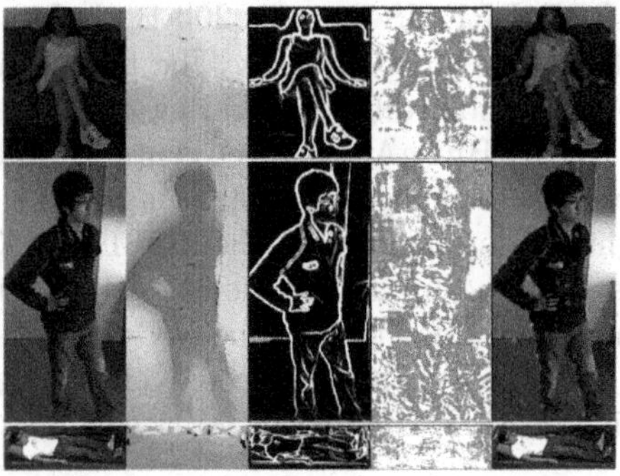

(a) (b) (c) (d) (e)

Fig. 3. Our Lab-D HOG Descriptor Computation process for sitting, standing, and lying postures, on top of our MCD corner detector: (a, b) represent acquired RGB-D images, (c, d) after detecting people, we compute the people edge boundary and its correspondent angle map. Next (e), we extract multispectral corner points for each detected human and associate a 2D multi-spectral Lab-D HOG descriptor to each feature. Last, the prepared descriptors are passed to the transformer encoder.

Figure 3 illustrates the prepared Lab-D corners for later computing the Lab-D HOG descriptors. We show that the detected corner points accurately describe the person's shape.

Table 1. The precision score results of the human posture classification by feeding the Lab-D edge images to the original ViT compared to the modified ViT.

Various	Original-ViT [8]	HOG-ViT (strategy1)	HOG-ViT (strategy2)	LabD-HOG-ViT (strategy 1)	LabD-HOG-ViT (strategy 2)
Depth	30.10%	63.96%	68.35%	68.81%	72.36%
RGB	45.31%	61.63%	62.77%	82.57%	84.72%
RGB-D edge	70.21%	74.95%	75.32%	85.49%	87.90%
Lab-D edge	**84.05%**	**82.73%**	**83.93%**	**94.69%**	**96.20%**

Table 2. The recall score results of the human posture classification by feeding the Lab-D edge images to the original ViT compared to the modified ViT.

Various	Original-ViT [8]	HOG-ViT (strategy1)	HOG-ViT (strategy2)	LabD-HOG-ViT (strategy 1)	LabD-HOG-ViT (strategy 2)
Depth	54.86%	62.32%	66.29%	63.63%	69.39%
RGB	63.19%	62.82%	63.81%	80.17%	83.37%
RGB-D edge	70.14%	74.32%	74.52%	85.13%	88.25%
Lab-D edge	**81.94%**	**78.61%**	**83.93%**	**95.72%**	**95.64%**

Table 3. F1-Score results of the human posture classification by feeding the Lab-D edge images to the original ViT compared to the modified ViT

Various	Original-ViT [8]	HOG-ViT (strategy1)	HOG-ViT (strategy2)	LabD-HOG-ViT (strategy 1)	LabD-HOG-ViT (strategy 2)
Depth	38.87%	73.24%	76.06%	77.62%	80.42%
RGB	52.62%	72.54%	73.94%	81.20%	83.76%
RGB-D edge	68.79%	79.58%	79.58%	88.11%	90.21%
Lab-D edge	**79.84%**	**83.80%**	**85.92%**	**95.77%**	**96.48%**

Tables 1, 2 and 3 overview the average precision, recall and F-Score for each experiment. We can notice a clear improvement obtained by using our Lab-D HOG Descriptor. We showcase the performance of passing the original HOG and Lab-D HOG descriptor to the transformer encoder compared to feeding the Lab-D edge image directly to the ViT.

As we can see, we find better results by integrating the Lab-D edge image in the ViT compared to RGB, depth and RGB-D images. Moreover, as illustrated in Tables 1, 2 and 3, our multispectral HOG descriptor computed over CIE-Lab color space gives better results compared to when it is computed over RGB color space. Also, we show that the fusion between the ViT model and the Lab-D HOG descriptor gives the best outcomes in place of using the original HOG descriptor computed over the Lab-D edge, RGB, depth, or RGB-D images. According to Table 2 and 1, the combination between Lab-D HOG descriptor and ViT has a high sensitivity which means that there are few false negatives. Also, the precision is high and it can be improved.

4.5 Discussion

Our main contribution is to integrate the Lab-D HOG descriptor in the Vision transformer architecture. The use of the Lab-D edge images in the ViT model enhances effectively the human posture classification task compared to depth, RGB and RGB-D images as shown in Tables 1, 2 and 3.

For the original ViT, feeding the Lab-D edge image into the ViT model enhances perfectly the results. This is quite understandable since the fusion between color and depth images into the Lab-D edge image preserves only the important information in the scene. As for replacing the linear projection of flattened patches with the computed HOG descriptors, we have shown better results as illustrated in the above tables. Hence, we clearly consider that our Lab-D HOG descriptor could be a good choice for any classification pre-processing step since it gives the best outcomes (*i.e.* precision, recall and F-score) compared to the original HOG descriptors. We can explain this enhancement by the fact that the use of Lab color space enhances clearly the quality of our descriptor compared to the use of RGB color space. Hence, we assume that selecting the best color space affects the quality of the computed HOG descriptor. Indeed, CIE(l*a*b*) can measure efficiently a small color difference which can be calculated as the Euclidean distance between two color points. Results show that the implementation based on Lab color space outperforms RGB color space in all the proposed configurations.

By training the ViT model on top of the Lab-D HOG descriptors, the training time will be reduced compared to the original ViT which is based on feeding raw images. We underline the fact that using hybrid approaches like Lab-D HOG descriptor combined with ViT leads to an improvement in the classification performance.

Experiments have shown that the second strategy improves the classification task slightly more than the first one. We can explain this by the fact that computing the Lab-D HOG descriptor of the whole image gives us close and more accurate information than computing the Lab-D HOG on small patches of size 16×16. Moreover, detecting corner points on the whole blob gives more salient features than extracting corner points from patches of the blob.

5 Conclusion

A novel Lab-D vision transformer based on the Lab-D HOG descriptor has been proposed for human posture classification. Our main contribution is the straightforward integration of depth information with the channels of the Lab color system into the vision transformer architecture. We have presented two different approaches for integrating the Lab-D descriptor into the vision transformer. Results demonstrate a significant improvement over state-of-the-art methods. We have shown that by combining both Lab-D HOG descriptors with the vision transformer, we achieve on average the highest classification accuracies.

For future work, we plan to develop a solution for human gesture recognition based on the Lab-D vision transformer.

References

1. Abobakr, A., Nahavandi, D., Iskander, J., Hossny, M., Nahavandi, S., Smets, M.: RGB-D human posture analysis for ergonomie studies using deep convolutional neural network. In: 2017 IEEE International Conference on Systems, Man, and Cybernetics (SMC), pp. 2885–2890 (2017)
2. Amine Elforaici, M.E., Chaaraoui, I., Bouachir, W., Ouakrim, Y., Mezghani, N.: Posture recognition using an RGB-D camera: exploring 3D body modeling and deep learning approaches. In: 2018 IEEE Life Sciences Conference (LSC), pp. 69–72 (2018). https://doi.org/10.1109/LSC.2018.8572079
3. Ayre-Storie, A., Zhang, L.: Deep learning-based human posture recognition. In: 2021 International Conference on Machine Learning and Cybernetics (ICMLC), pp. 1–6 (2021). https://doi.org/10.1109/ICMLC54886.2021.9737241
4. Baronti, P., Girolami, M., Mavilia, F., Palumbo, F., Luisetto, G.: On the analysis of human posture for detecting social interactions with wearable devices. In: 2020 IEEE International Conference on Human-Machine Systems (ICHMS), pp. 1–6 (2020). https://doi.org/10.1109/ICHMS49158.2020.9209510
5. Cai, Y., Wang, X., Kong, X.: 3D human pose estimation from RGB+D images with convolutional neural networks. In: Proceedings of the 2nd International Conference on Biomedical Engineering and Bioinformatics, ICBEB 2018, pp. 64–69. Association for Computing Machinery, New York (2018). https://doi.org/10.1145/3278198.3278225
6. Cao, B., Bi, S., Zheng, J., Yang, D.: Human posture recognition using skeleton and depth information. In: 2018 WRC Symposium on Advanced Robotics and Automation (WRC SARA), pp. 275–280 (2018). https://doi.org/10.1109/WRC-SARA.2018.8584233
7. Ding, W., Hu, B., Liu, H., Wang, X., Huang, X.: Human posture recognition based on multiple features and rule learning. Int. J. Mach. Learn. Cybern. **11**, 2529–2540 (2020). https://doi.org/10.1007/s13042-020-01138-y
8. Dosovitskiy, A., et al.: An image is worth 16 × 16 words: transformers for image recognition at scale (2020). https://doi.org/10.48550/ARXIV.2010.11929. https://arxiv.org/abs/2010.11929
9. Giannakos, I., Mathe, E., Spyrou, E., Mylonas, P.: A study on the effect of occlusion in human activity recognition, pp. 473–482 (2021). https://doi.org/10.1145/3453892.3461337
10. Gjoreski, H., Gams, M.: Activity/posture recognition using wearable sensors placed on different body locations. In: Proceedings of Signal and Image Processing and Applications (2011). https://doi.org/10.2316/P.2011.716-067
11. Iazzi, A., Rziza, M., Thami, R.O.H.: Human posture recognition based on projection histogram and Support Vector Machine. In: 2018 9th International Symposium on Signal, Image, Video and Communications (ISIVC), pp. 329–333 (2018). https://doi.org/10.1109/ISIVC.2018.8709235
12. Li, X., Sun, M., Fang, X.: An approach for detecting human posture by using depth image. In: 2016 2nd International Conference on Artificial Intelligence and Industrial Engineering (AIIE 2016), pp. 257–261. Atlantis Press (2016)
13. Li, X., Zhou, Z., Wu, J., Xiong, Y.: Human posture detection method based on wearable devices. J. Healthc. Eng. **2021**, 1–8 (2021). https://doi.org/10.1155/2021/8879061
14. Liu, S., Ostadabbas, S.: A vision-based system for in-bed posture tracking. In: 2017 IEEE International Conference on Computer Vision Workshops (ICCVW), pp. 1373–1382 (2017). https://doi.org/10.1109/ICCVW.2017.163

15. Liu, Z., et al.: Swin transformer: hierarchical vision transformer using shifted windows (2021). https://doi.org/10.48550/ARXIV.2103.14030. https://arxiv.org/abs/2103.14030
16. Malmsten, J., Cengiz, H., Lood, D.: Histogram of oriented gradients in a vision transformer (2022)
17. Mefteh, S., Kaâniche, M.B., Ksantini, R., Bouhoula, A.: A novel multispectral lab-depth based edge detector for color images with occluded objects. In: VISIGRAPP (4: VISAPP), pp. 272–279 (2019)
18. Mefteh, S., Kaâniche, M.B., Ksantini, R., Bouhoula, A.: A novel multispectral corner detector and a new local descriptor: an application to human posture recognition. Multimed. Tools Appl. **82**, 28937–28956 (2023). https://doi.org/10.1007/s11042-023-14788-1
19. Ni, B., Wang, G., Moulin, P.: RGBD-HuDaAct: a color-depth video database for human daily activity recognition. In: Fossati, A., Gall, J., Grabner, H., Ren, X., Konolige, K. (eds.) Consumer Depth Cameras for Computer Vision. ACVPR, pp. 193–208. Springer, London (2013). https://doi.org/10.1007/978-1-4471-4640-7_10
20. Popescu, A.C., Mocanu, I., Cramariuc, B.: PRECIS HAR (2019). https://doi.org/10.21227/mene-ck48
21. Qi, L., Han, Y.: Human motion posture detection algorithm using deep reinforcement learning. Mob. Inf. Syst. **2021**, 1–10 (2021). https://doi.org/10.1155/2021/4023861
22. Ramanan, D., Sminchisescu, C.: Training deformable models for localization, vol. 1, pp. 206–213 (2006). https://doi.org/10.1109/CVPR.2006.315
23. Reddy, B.H., Karthikeyan, P.: Classification of fire and smoke images using decision tree algorithm in comparison with logistic regression to measure accuracy, precision, recall, f-score. In: 2022 14th International Conference on Mathematics, Actuarial Science, Computer Science and Statistics (MACS), pp. 1–5. IEEE (2022)
24. Redmon, J., Divvala, S.K., Girshick, R.B., Farhadi, A.: You only look once: unified, real-time object detection. CoRR abs/1506.02640 (2015). https://arxiv.org/abs/1506.02640
25. Touvron, H., Cord, M., Douze, M., Massa, F., Sablayrolles, A., Jegou, H.: Training data-efficient image transformers & distillation through attention. In: Meila, M., Zhang, T. (eds.) Proceedings of the 38th International Conference on Machine Learning. Proceedings of Machine Learning Research, vol. 139, pp. 10347–10357. PMLR (2021). https://proceedings.mlr.press/v139/touvron21a.html
26. Wang, W.J., Chang, J.W., Haung, S.F., Wang, R.J.: Human posture recognition based on images captured by the kinect sensor. Int. J. Adv. Robot. Syst. **13**(2), 54 (2016). https://doi.org/10.5772/62163
27. Wu, Q., Xu, G., Zhang, S., Li, Y., Wei, F.: Human 3D pose estimation in a lying position by RGB-D images for medical diagnosis and rehabilitation (2020). https://doi.org/10.1109/EMBC44109.2020.9176407
28. Wu, Y., et al.: Rethinking classification and localization for object detection, pp. 10183–10192 (2020). https://doi.org/10.1109/CVPR42600.2020.01020
29. Zhang, J., Wu, C., Wang, Y.: Human fall detection based on body posture spatio-temporal evolution. Sensors **20**(3), 946 (2020). https://doi.org/10.3390/s20030946. https://www.mdpi.com/1424-8220/20/3/946

SemiMemes: A Semi-supervised Learning Approach for Multimodal Memes Analysis

Pham Thai Hoang Tung, Nguyen Tan Viet, Ngo Tien Anh, and Phan Duy Hung(✉)

FPT University, Hanoi, Vietnam
{tungpthhe141564,vietnthe153763,anhnthe141442}@fpt.edu.vn, hungpd2@fe.edu.vn

Abstract. The prevalence of memes on social media has created the need to sentiment analyze their underlying meanings for censoring harmful content. Meme censoring systems by machine learning raise the need for a semi-supervised learning solution to take advantage of the large number of unlabeled memes available on the internet and make the annotation process less challenging. Moreover, the approach needs to utilize multimodal data as memes' meanings usually come from both images and texts. This research proposes a multimodal semi-supervised learning approach that outperforms other multimodal semi-supervised learning and supervised learning state-of-the-art models on two datasets, the Multimedia Automatic Misogyny Identification and Hateful Memes dataset. Building on the insights gained from Contrastive Language-Image Pre-training, which is an effective multimodal learning technique, this research introduces SemiMemes, a novel training method that combines auto-encoder and classification task to make use of the resourceful unlabeled data.

Keywords: Memes analysis · Multimodal learning · Semi-supervised learning

1 Introduction

An "internet meme" or "meme" is a concept, well-known phrase, pattern, or action that is distributed through the internet [1]. The most prevalent type of internet meme is composed of a picture and a brief caption overlaid on top of it, which is what our research primarily concentrates on. In order to comprehend the significance of memes, it is occasionally necessary to grasp the significance of both the image and the text, and then connect them together.

As memes have become more popular, there is a trend of creating memes that are not meant to be funny or amusing, but to express irony or to spread negative content on sensitive topics such as discrimination, race, gender, religion, or politics. Consequently, social media platforms are paying attention to the

N. T. Nguyen et al. (Eds.): ICCCI 2023, LNAI 14162, pp. 565–577, 2023.
https://doi.org/10.1007/978-3-031-41456-5_43

issue of "memes sentiment analysis" to prevent the dissemination of memes that contain harmful content.

In earlier times, harmful content was mainly conveyed through text that could be detected using Natural Language Processing. However, identifying harmful content hidden in memes has become a challenging task. The examples presented in Fig. 1 demonstrate that the "memes sentiment analysis" approach to detect harmful content is complicated as it necessitates understanding and merging the visual and textual aspects of the meme. Even humans require time to comprehend it, so it is even more challenging to teach machines to recognize such content. Additionally, manually labeling data is exhaustive and could be subjective due to labeling participants, leading to disputes and arguments, as each person might interpret the meme's content differently [4,5,19,21,22]. A semi-supervised

a) text: me/my eternal love and affection /my perfect wife. Label: not misogynous.

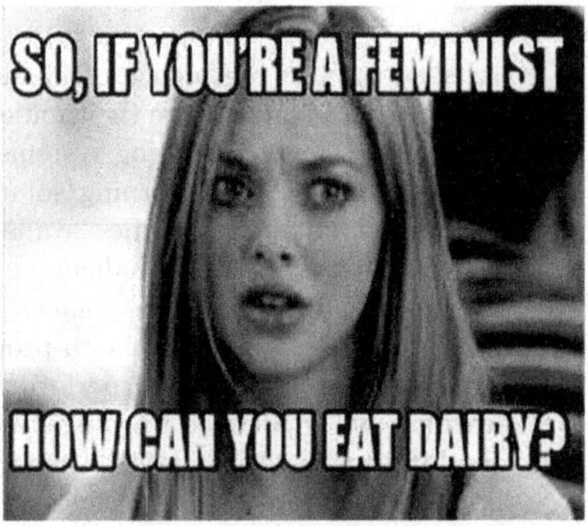

b) text: so, if you're a feminist/ how can you eat dairy? Label: misogynous, stereotype, objectification.

c) text: when your ex ask you /for help. Label: not hateful.

d) text: don't decide the lineage given to you by / your forefathers do what's right, keep it white. Label: hateful.

Fig. 1. Illustrative examples from the Multi-media Automatic Misogyny Identification dataset (a, b) and examples from the Hateful Memes dataset (c, d).

learning approach using multimodal data containing both images and text could help ease the annotation process.

Therefore, our team realizes that the current urgent problem is to solve the issue of "memes sentiment analysis" to detect harmful content in the direction of research of "multimodal semi-supervised learning." By creating a multimodal semi-supervised learning approach, we can outline our contributions as follows:

- Develop a pre-trained model, named Cross Modality Auto Encoder (CROM-AE), based on Contrastive Language-Image Pre-Training (CLIP) features that can be trained on small datasets without labels.
- Create a custom supervised model called RAW-N-COOK that incorporates the extracted features of both CROM-AE and CLIP, hence, utilizing knowledge from unlabeled data for a supervised model.

2 Related Works

Tasks involving multimodal content, consisting of both images and text, typically rely on the success of visual-linguistic pre-train models such as VisualBERT [14] and CLIP [20]. Especially CLIP, based on self-supervised learning, hence, is trained on a large-scale dataset including 300M pairs of image-text from the internet. Thus, it may have learned popular concepts of visual and linguistic features on the internet, including memes. By utilizing CLIP encoders and feature interaction between modalities, in 2022, Kumar and Nanadakumar proposed the Hate-CLIPper architecture [11]. This model achieved the highest performance on the Hateful Memes Challenge dataset, obtaining an ROC-AUC score of 85.80, which surpassed human performance of 82.62 on the same dataset. Previously, the top solutions for Hateful Memes Challenge were based on VisualBERT or its variants [12]. In other meme sentiment analysis competitions [4,21], successful approaches have typically employed supervised learning based on either VisualBERT or CLIP [4,18].

Various studies on semi-supervised learning in multimodal data, such as images, text, and other modalities, have been conducted for different objectives. For example, Hu et al. [9] utilized feature projection on an embedding space and implemented cross-modal retrieval tasks to retrieve either text by image or vice versa. Sunkara et al. [23] utilized a large unlabelled audio and text corpus to pre-train modality encoders and fused the encoder's output to train punctuation prediction in conversational speech. Liang et al. [15] worked on emotion recognition in videos by extracting visual, acoustic, and lexical signals from both labeled and unlabeled videos. Their end-to-end model simultaneously performs an auto-encoder task on the entire data and an emotion classification task on the latent representations of the labeled data's modalities. In the domain of memes, Gunti et al. [6] tried to embed images and words in the same space by training a Siamese network that receives a pair of image-word belonging to a meme. As a result, they make the image embedding of a meme have a semantic meaning driven by word embedding. This way, they demonstrate how valuable unlabeled meme data can be used. Although these studies have different tasks and modalities compared to ours, they have inspired us with possible methods for applying semi-supervised learning on multimodal data.

In relation to our interest in implementing semi-supervised classification for images and text, there was a state-of-the-art (SOTA) study by Yang et al. [25] in 2019. They proposed a method called Comprehensive Semi-Supervised Multimodal Learning (CMML), which utilized unlabeled data to strike a balance between consistency and diversity among modalities through the introduction of diversity and consistency measurements. Diversity measurements were optimized to increase the diversity among modalities' predictions, while consistency measurements were optimized to minimize disagreement among them. CMML achieved competitive results on large-scale multimodal datasets like FLICKR25K [10], IAPR TC-12 [3], NUS-WIDE [2], and MS-COCO [16]. However, it is a difficult method to optimize because the loss function includes multiple supervised losses and regularized unsupervised losses. Additionally, it depends on the vector of multi-label predictions, making it only available for multi-label classification tasks.

3 Methodology

3.1 Overview

In Fig. 2, the initial step involves inputting a pair of (image, text) into the CLIP model's image and text encoders to extract CLIP feature vectors (F_{image}, F_{text}). The process then proceeds in two stages:

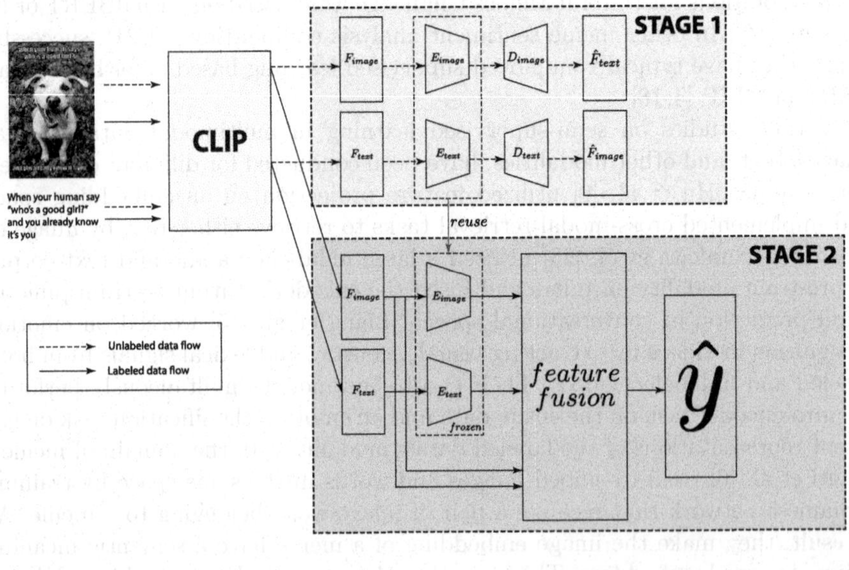

Fig. 2. The overall architecture of our semi-supervised learning approach

Stage 1 - Unsupervised Pre-training: An unsupervised pre-training phase where the Cross Modality Auto Encoder (CROM-AE) is trained. CROM-AE uses one modality's CLIP feature to predict the other modality's CLIP feature, i.e., image feature F_{image} predicts text feature F_{text} and vice versa. This pre-training phase is carried out using only unlabeled data.

Stage 2 - Supervised Fine-tuning: A new model is designed for learning the classification task on labeled data. First, the pre-trained encoders of CROM-AE are frozen to extract new representations from the original CLIP features. Then, both the new representations (cooked features) and the original CLIP features (raw features) are fused to predict the classification target. The resulting model is called the Raw and Cooked Features Classification Model (RAW-N-COOK).

We call our 2-stages method SemiMemes. The following Subsects. 3.2 and 3.3, will discuss the model used in each stage in detail.

3.2 Cross Modality Auto Encoder (CROM-AE) - Stage 1

We define the Cross Modality Auto Encoder (CROM-AE) as a model that uses one modality to reconstruct the other modality. Specifically, there are two CROM-AE models, AE_{image} and AE_{text}, where AE_{image} takes CLIP features F_{image} as input and predicts $\hat{F}_{text}$ as output, and AE_{text} takes F_{text} as input and predicts $\hat{F}_{image}$ as output. Formally, we can represent this as follows:

$$\hat{F}_{text} = AE_{image}(F_{image}) \tag{1}$$

$$\hat{F}_{image} = AE_{text}(F_{text}) \tag{2}$$

Here, F_{image} and F_{text} are the CLIP features of the image and text, respectively, and $\hat{F}_{image}$ and $\hat{F}_{text}$ are the estimations of AE_{text} and AE_{image}, respectively.

In practice, both auto-encoders have the same underlying architecture consisting of *Linear* > *PReLU* > *Linear* where all the linear layers have the same dimensions of 768. We use PReLU [8] instead of the popular ReLU activation function to ensure that the model learns the negative values of the encoder's output. This is helpful in later stage. The encoder linear layer and decoder linear layer of each modality are denoted as E_k and D_k with $k \in image, text$ in Fig. 3.

CROM-AE can be used to capture the underlying distribution of each modality for semi-supervised learning. The latent representations of images are driven by the distribution of the remaining text $p(text)$, which may contain the information of the posterior distribution $p(y|text)$, where y is the supervised classification target and vice versa [17]. We exclude all labeled data when training the CROM-AE models to prevent introducing new bias and variance to the labeled training, validation, and test sets. The two CROM-AE models are trained separately using the Mean-Square-Error loss function.

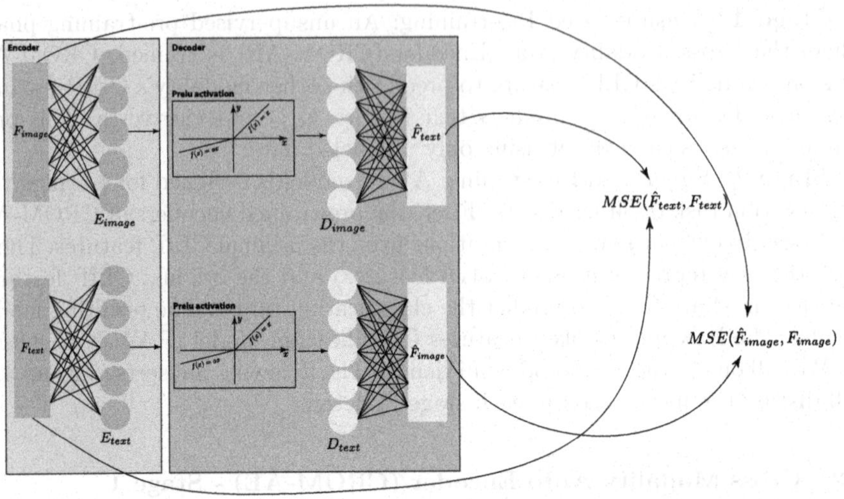

Fig. 3. The pipeline of two CROM-AEs

$$\mathcal{L}_{AE_{image}} = MSE(\hat{F}_{text}, F_{text}) \tag{3}$$

$$\mathcal{L}_{AE_{text}} = MSE(\hat{F}_{image}, F_{image}) \tag{4}$$

3.3 Raw and Cooked Features Classification Model (RAW-N-COOK) - Stage 2

RAW-N-COOK is a classification model that incorporates both learned latent representation from CROM-AE and the original CLIP features as follows. Firstly, we take only the encoder part E_{image}, E_{text} of two pre-trained CROM-AE models and freeze them. Then, both CLIP features F_{image} and F_{text} go through their corresponding CROM-AE encoder E_{image}, E_{text} to obtain latent extracted features Z_{image}, Z_{text}. Then, four vectors: F_{image}, F_{text}, Z_{image}, Z_{text} are projected to four 256-length vectors by a simple sequence of layers: *Linear* > *ReLU* > *Dropout*, then concatenate to obtain a 1024-length vector. The concatenated vector goes through the last *Linear* layer to learn the classification target. The flow is described in Fig. 4.

Our intuition is that Z_{image}, and Z_{text} are informative features because they were learned on a large unlabeled dataset. Therefore, encoders are frozen to keep what CROM-AE learned on unlabeled data. However, both Z_{image} and Z_{text} were driven by different tasks, if we use only Z_{image} and Z_{text} for classification, it is not too powerful. Therefore, we decided to fuse Z_{image} and Z_{text} (cooked features) with the original features outputted from CLIP F_{image}, F_{text} (raw features).

Recall the PReLU discussion in Sect. 3.2, if we use ReLU in the decoder, negative values on Z_{image}, and Z_{text} are not learned by CROM-AE that will become noise in the classification model, which makes the model harder to learn on the classification task. Therefore, in CROM-AE, we choose PReLU.

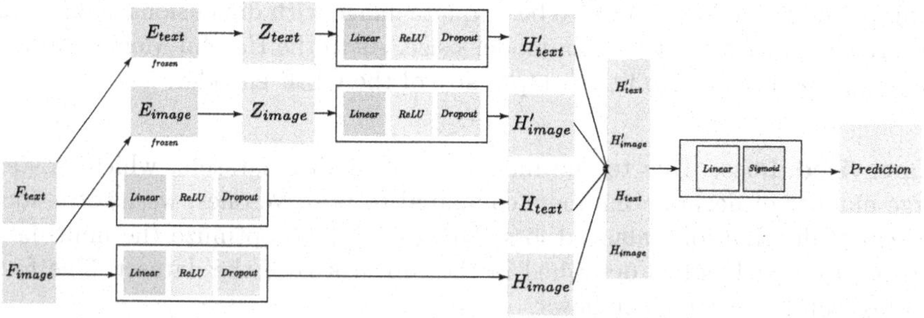

Fig. 4. The architecture of RAW-N-COOK model for classification

4 Experimental Results

4.1 Datasets

Multimedia Automated Misogyny Identification (MAMI) is SemEval-2022 task 5's dataset [4]. It is designed to identify inappropriate memes towards women using both images and texts. The task consists of 2 sub-tasks: sub-task A and sub-task B. Sub-task A is a binary classification problem that aims to classify memes with hateful content into 2 categories: misogyny and not misogyny. Sub-task B involves identifying memes with misogynistic content, which incorporates identifying more fine-grained classes: stereotyping, shame, protest, and violence. This sub-task has 4 binary labels and is formulated as a multi-label classification problem. The MAMI dataset contains 10K memes for training and 1K memes for testing. We further select 2K samples from the training set to use as a validation set, the remaining samples of the training set are divided into labeled training set and unlabeled training set In this study, we focus on sub-task B.

Hateful Memes is in Hateful Memes Challenge [13], constructed by Facebook, which focuses on detecting hate speech in multimodal memes. It is a binary classification task in which the labels of each meme need to be identified as either hateful or not hateful. The entire "seen" set consists of exactly 10K memes, which have been divided into 5%, 10%, and 85% for the development set, test set, and training set, respectively. Additionally, the dataset includes "unseen" sets hidden during most of the challenge evaluation. We do not consider the "unseen" sets in this study.

4.2 Setup

Preprocessing. As being in done [7] for the MAMI dataset, we undertook text preprocessing for SemiMems and CMML-CLIP through the following sequence of actions: elimination of text with mixed-in URLs, removal of non-ASCII characters, conversion of all characters to lowercase, and deletion of punctuation. In addition, we resized the image to be a square image with dimensions of 224×224 to correspond with the pre-train model's size. As to the Hateful Memes dataset, we just resized images to fit the input size of the CLIP encoder.

Supervised Loss. Due to the imbalance of MAMI datasets, which exists a large number of negative numbers compared to positive ones, we use the focal version of distribution balanced loss (DB loss) [24] to optimize the multi-label classification problem as described in the sub-task B of the dataset. The focal DB loss can be written as follows:

$$\mathcal{L}_{DB-focal}(x^k, y^k) = -\frac{1}{C}\sum_{i=0}^{C} \hat{r}_i^k[(1-p_+)^\gamma y_i^k log(p_+) + \frac{1}{\lambda}p_-^\gamma(1-y_i^k)log(1-p_-)] \tag{5}$$

$$p_- = \frac{1}{1+e^{-\lambda(z_i^k-\nu_i)}} \tag{6}$$

$$p_+ = \frac{1}{1+e^{-(z_i^k-\nu_i)}} \tag{7}$$

$$\nu_i = \kappa\hat{b}_i \tag{8}$$

$$\hat{b}_i = -log(\frac{1}{p_i} - 1) \tag{9}$$

where C is the number of classes, $\hat{r}_i^k$ is the re-balanced weight as defined in [24], p_-, p_+ is the negative probability and positive probability, respectively, z_i^k is the logit of model, γ is the focusing parameter, λ is the scale factor that regularizes the loss gradient of negative samples, ν_i is the class-specific bias, $\hat{b}_i$ is the estimated bias variable, κ is the scale factor of $\hat{b}_i$, and p_i is the class prior probability which is equal to $\frac{Number\ sample\ of\ class\ i}{total\ number\ of\ training\ sample}$. We set $\gamma = 2$, $\lambda = 5$, $\kappa = 0.1$ in our implementation.

For the Hateful Memes dataset, we use the traditional BCE loss to optimize the binary classification task.

Experimental Setting and Hyperparameters. To experiment, we randomly create a labeled set and an unlabeled set for training from the original training set. We experiment on 3 scenarios, each of which has the proportion of labeled set equal to 5%, 10%, and 30% of the original dataset. We use Adam optimizer with an initial learning rate of 1e−4 and 0.25 for the initial value of a in PReLU activation. During training, we reduce the learning rate after each epoch by StepLR scheduler with different $\gamma_{scheduler}$ for each scenario as shown in Table 1.

The number of pre-training epochs, fine-tuning epochs and batch size are 200, 200 and 40, respectively. For the Stage 1 on MAMI, we use L2 regularization with 1e−4 weight decay. The model is trained on NVIDIA-RTX 6000.

Baselines. We compare SemiMemes with the following baselines, including SOTA methods of multimodal semi-supervised learning and multimodal supervised learning.

Table 1. Values of $\gamma_{scheduler}$ for each setting.

Dataset	Labeled ratio	$\gamma_{scheduler}$
MAMI	5%	0.93
	10%	0.9
	30%	0.85
Hateful Memes	5%	0.96
	10%	0.96
	30%	0.96

1. Multimodal Semi-supervised
   - **CMML-CLIP**: We find that using only the original CMML model, the performance is significantly low on the MAMI dataset, so we replace CMML's encoder with CLIP encoder for more robust representations.
2. Multimodal supervised learning
   - **TIB-VA** [7]: is the top winner solution in the MAMI competition 2022. The model uses CLIP encoders as backbones and the training follows multitasking objectives for both sub-task A and sub-task B. TIB-VA achieved 1st place on sub-task B.
   - **Hate-CLIPper** [11]: is the current SOTA model on the Hateful Memes dataset. There are 2 types of fusions that Hate-CLIPper proposed, which are align-fusion and cross-fusion. We run the model with cross-fusion and 1 pre-output layer as this configuration achieves the best result on Hateful Memes.

We use the ViT-Large-Patch14 version for the CLIP encoder. We train all other models also in 200 epochs, and use the last checkpoint to evaluate the score on the test set. For supervised models, we just use labeled data in each scenario. For MAMI, we use the weighted F1 score as it is the standard metric used in the competition, for Hateful Memes' evaluation, the area under the receiver operating characteristic curve (AUROC) metric is used.

4.3 Results

MAMI Benchamrk. As can be seen in Table 2, SemiMemes's validation and test scores are all higher than the other 2 models on 3 label settings. In the 5% label setting, SemiMemes achieves 0.693 on the test set which is more than that of CMML-CLIP and TIB-VA, by 0.034 and 0.039, respectively. These performance gaps decrease as the labeled samples increase, to 0.024 for SemiMemes versus CMMLP-CLIP and 0.023 for SemiMemes versus TIB-VA, in the 10% labeled setting. In the 30% labeled setting, the performance gap of SemiMemes with respect to CMMLP-CLIP is 0.017, while the performance gap of SemiMemes with respect to TIB-VA increases to 0.031. This may demonstrate that, with a large number of unlabeled examples, our method can be more advantageous than other SOTA methods.

Table 2. Weighted-average F1-Measure on Validation and Test Set of MAMI dataset.

Models	5 (%)		10 (%)		30 (%)	
	Val	Test	Val	Test	Val	Test
SemiMemes	**0.693**	**0.6782**	**0.7258**	**0.7113**	**0.7520**	**0.7413**
CMML-CLIP	0.6778	0.6438	0.717	0.6878	0.7313	0.7242
TIB-VA	0.68	0.6392	0.6992	0.6886	0.7095	0.7104

Hateful Memes Benchmark. As shown in Table 3, SemiMemes is also capable of achieving higher scores than Hate-CLIPper in all settings. The results of SemiMemes are not very higher than Hate-CLIPper on both development and test sets. Specifically, for the test set, the performance gaps are 0.004, 0.009, and 0.003 for 5%, 10%, and 30% settings, respectively. However, when taking into account the number of parameters in each method, the total parameters of our models, CROM-AE and RAW-N-COOK included, are significantly lower than that of Hate-CLIPper, with about 3.1 million parameters compared to 1.5 billion parameters of Hate-CLIPper. Therefore, SemiMemes can save significant training resources, while still assuring high performance.

Table 3. AUROC on Dev Seen and Test Seen Set of Hateful Memes.

Models	Trainable params	5 (%)		10 (%)		30 (%)	
		Dev	Test	Dev	Test	Dev	Test
SemiMemes	**3.1M**	**0.6897**	**0.7011**	**0.7061**	**0.7281**	**0.7399**	**0.7765**
Hate-CLIPper (cross)	1.5B	0.6652	0.6973	0.6827	0.7196	0.7030	0.7731

5 Conclusion

In conclusion, this research highlights the prevalence of internet memes and the need to sentiment analyze their underlying meanings for censoring harmful content. To achieve this, the proposed multimodal semi-supervised learning approach, SemiMemes, utilizes a combination of CROM-AE and RAW-N-COOK models to leverage the vast amount of unlabeled memes on the internet and mitigate the difficulties of the annotation process. This approach surpasses other state-of-the-art models on two datasets, demonstrating its effectiveness in identifying misogynistic and hateful memes in low-labeled data settings.

References

1. Börzsei, L.K.: Makes a meme instead. The Selected Works of Linda Börzsei, pp. 1–28 (2013)
2. Chua, T.S., Tang, J., Hong, R., Li, H., Luo, Z., Zheng, Y.: NUS-WIDE: a real-world web image database from National University of Singapore. In: Proceedings of the ACM International Conference on Image and Video Retrieval, CIVR 2009. Association for Computing Machinery, New York (2009). https://doi.org/10.1145/1646396.1646452
3. Escalante, H.J., et al.: The segmented and annotated IAPR TC-12 benchmark. Comput. Vis. Image Underst. **114**(4), 419–428 (2010). https://doi.org/10.1016/j.cviu.2009.03.008. Special Issue on Image and Video Retrieval Evaluation
4. Fersini, E., et al.: SemEval-2022 task 5: multimedia automatic misogyny identification. In: Proceedings of the 16th International Workshop on Semantic Evaluation (SemEval-2022), Seattle, United States, pp. 533–549. Association for Computational Linguistics (2022). https://doi.org/10.18653/v1/2022.semeval-1.74
5. Goldberg, A., Zhu, X., Singh, A., Xu, Z., Nowak, R.: Multi-manifold semi-supervised learning. In: van Dyk, D., Welling, M. (eds.) Proceedings of the Twelfth International Conference on Artificial Intelligence and Statistics. Proceedings of Machine Learning Research, Hilton Clearwater Beach Resort, Clearwater Beach, Florida, USA, vol. 5, pp. 169–176. PMLR (2009)
6. Gunti, N., Ramamoorthy, S., Patwa, P., Das, A.: Memotion analysis through the lens of joint embedding (student abstract). In: Proceedings of the AAAI Conference on Artificial Intelligence, vol. 36, no. 11, pp. 12959–12960 (2022). https://doi.org/10.1609/aaai.v36i11.21616
7. Hakimov, S., Cheema, G.S., Ewerth, R.: TIB-VA at SemEval-2022 task 5: a multimodal architecture for the detection and classification of misogynous memes. In: Proceedings of the 16th International Workshop on Semantic Evaluation (SemEval-2022), Seattle, United States, pp. 756–760. Association for Computational Linguistics (2022). https://doi.org/10.18653/v1/2022.semeval-1.105
8. He, K., Zhang, X., Ren, S., Sun, J.: Delving deep into rectifiers: surpassing human-level performance on ImageNet classification. In: Proceedings of the IEEE International Conference on Computer Vision, pp. 1026–1034 (2015)

9. Hu, P., Zhu, H., Peng, X., Lin, J.: Semi-supervised multi-modal learning with balanced spectral decomposition. In: Proceedings of the AAAI Conference on Artificial Intelligence, vol. 34, no. 01, pp. 99–106 (2020). https://doi.org/10.1609/aaai.v34i01.5339
10. Huiskes, M.J., Lew, M.S.: The MIR flickr retrieval evaluation. In: Proceedings of the 1st ACM International Conference on Multimedia Information Retrieval, MIR 2008, pp. 39–43. Association for Computing Machinery, New York (2008). https://doi.org/10.1145/1460096.1460104
11. Karthik Kumar, G., Nandakumar, K.: Hate-CLIPper: multimodal hateful meme classification based on cross-modal interaction of CLIP features (2022). https://doi.org/10.48550/ARXIV.2210.05916. arXiv e-prints arXiv:2210.05916
12. Kiela, D., et al.: The hateful memes challenge: competition report. In: NeurIPS 2020 Competition and Demonstration Track, pp. 344–360. PMLR (2021)
13. Kiela, D., et al.: The hateful memes challenge: detecting hate speech in multimodal memes. In: Larochelle, H., Ranzato, M., Hadsell, R., Balcan, M., Lin, H. (eds.) Advances in Neural Information Processing Systems, vol. 33, pp. 2611–2624. Curran Associates, Inc. (2020)
14. Li, L.H., Yatskar, M., Yin, D., Hsieh, C.J., Chang, K.W.: VisualBERT: a simple and performant baseline for vision and language. arXiv preprint arXiv:1908.03557 (2019)
15. Liang, J., Li, R., Jin, Q.: Semi-supervised multi-modal emotion recognition with cross-modal distribution matching. In: Proceedings of the 28th ACM International Conference on Multimedia, pp. 2852–2861 (2020)
16. Lin, T.Y., et al.: Microsoft COCO: common objects in context. In: Fleet, D., Pajdla, T., Schiele, B., Tuytelaars, T. (eds.) ECCV 2014. LNIP, vol. 8693, pp. 740–755. Springer, Cham (2014). https://doi.org/10.1007/978-3-319-10602-1_48
17. Ouali, Y., Hudelot, C., Tami, M.: An overview of deep semi-supervised learning. arXiv preprint arXiv:2006.05278 (2020)
18. Patwa, P., et al.: Findings of memotion 2: sentiment and emotion analysis of memes. In: Proceedings of De-Factify: Workshop on Multimodal Fact Checking and Hate Speech Detection. CEUR (2022)
19. Pramanick, S., et al.: Detecting harmful memes and their targets. In: Findings of the Association for Computational Linguistics: ACL-IJCNLP 2021, pp. 2783–2796. Association for Computational Linguistics (2021). https://doi.org/10.18653/v1/2021.findings-acl.246
20. Radford, A., et al.: Learning transferable visual models from natural language supervision. In: International Conference on Machine Learning, pp. 8748–8763. PMLR (2021)
21. Ramamoorthy, S., et al.: Memotion 2: dataset on sentiment and emotion analysis of memes. In: Proceedings of De-Factify: Workshop on Multimodal Fact Checking and Hate Speech Detection. CEUR (2022)
22. Sharma, C., et al.: SemEval-2020 task 8: memotion analysis-the visuo-lingual metaphor! In: Proceedings of the Fourteenth Workshop on Semantic Evaluation, pp. 759–773. International Committee for Computational Linguistics, Barcelona (2020). https://doi.org/10.18653/v1/2020.semeval-1.99
23. Sunkara, M., Ronanki, S., Bekal, D., Bodapati, S., Kirchhoff, K.: Multimodal semi-supervised learning framework for punctuation prediction in conversational speech. In: Interspeech 2020 (2020)
24. Wu, T., Huang, Q., Liu, Z., Wang, Yu., Lin, D.: Distribution-balanced loss for multi-label classification in long-tailed datasets. In: Vedaldi, A., Bischof, H., Brox,

T., Frahm, J.-M. (eds.) ECCV 2020. LNCS, vol. 12349, pp. 162–178. Springer, Cham (2020). https://doi.org/10.1007/978-3-030-58548-8_10

25. Yang, Y., Wang, K.T., Zhan, D.C., Xiong, H., Jiang, Y.: Comprehensive semi-supervised multi-modal learning. In: Proceedings of the Twenty-Eighth International Joint Conference on Artificial Intelligence, IJCAI-2019, pp. 4092–4098. International Joint Conferences on Artificial Intelligence Organization (2019). https://doi.org/10.24963/ijcai.2019/568

Extrinsic Calibration Framework for Camera-Lidar Fusion Using Recurrent Residual Network

Massinissa Aouragh[1,2](✉) and László Gulyás[1]

[1] Faculty of Informatics, Department of Artificial Intelligence, ELTE Eötvös Loránd University, Budapest, Hungary
{m2j7au,lgulyas}@inf.elte.hu
[2] Robert Bosch Kft, Budapest, Hungary
massinissa.aouragh@hu.bosch.com

Abstract. Combining the use of 3D LiDAR's and 2D cameras is getting increasingly popular in sensor suits for perception tasks, making them two important sets of sensors for 3D object detection. Fusing the data of these two sensors results in a highly descriptive environment. However, the combination into a single representation is not straightforward due to the difference in signal characteristics and distribution. Thus the robustness of such system is highly dependent on calibration. In case of most methods the image quality is also a predominant condition for performance. This paper proposes a calibration framework in PyTorch for both KITTI and nuScenes. CalibRRNet takes monocular images and 3D depth information as input and outputs a 6 DoF rigid body transformation. Using similar architecture to ResNet18, leveraging the advantage of jumping connection, we add a recurrent network on the last stage to keep track of the previously predicted transformations. Training CalibRRNet is against photometric consistency and point cloud distance. CalibRRNet solves the geometric problem and predicts the extrinsic calibration parameters. The application of the proposed framework is not limited to only pure calibration tasks. It can also be used as a preprocessing module for camera-lidar fusion models to alleviate the need for an accurate calibration to ensure performance. Our experiments results confirm the validity of the proposed approach, with primary improvements observed on translation, but also on rotation.

Keywords: Point cloud · Multiple sensors · camera-lidar calibration

1 Introduction

For driver-less systems, such as autonomous driving cars or robots, the representation and comprehension of the surrounding environment, whether indoors or outdoors, is a crucial task. This highlights the necessity of 3D object detection for the aim of localisation and categorisation. To achieve such tasks, a robust

N. T. Nguyen et al. (Eds.): ICCCI 2023, LNAI 14162, pp. 578–590, 2023.
https://doi.org/10.1007/978-3-031-41456-5_44

perception mechanism or strategy is highly needed. Single sensor detection is not sufficient, perception systems need a variety of sensors to build a consistent model of their surrounding world [4]. Camera and LiDAR have a strong complementary relationship. For example, cameras perceive colour and texture, but their detection range is limited. Moreover their performance degrades in limited lighting or adverse weather conditions. On the other hand, LiDARs are precise with distance information; they work well in limited lighting, but they lack colour information and decrease in performance under heavy rain. Another important factor in the camera-LIDAR fusion, or any sensor framework, is calibration, the guarantor of synergy between the sensors. Without accurate extrinsic parameters, the laser distance measurements cannot be accurately projected onto the camera images, and thus colour pixels in the images cannot be accurately associated with distance information [12]. The process of calibration can be very tedious as for most of the techniques it requires a custom calibration target such as checker boards or spheres. In addition, they are unable to correct for any deviation due to environmental changes or vibrations during live operation [12]. Regarding deviation, there are techniques that provide automatic calibration [14] by detecting mis-calibration, but this makes them vulnerable to accurate initialisation of the calibration parameters. On the other hand, there are also other approaches to the problem of estimating the 6-DoF rigid body transformation between 3D lidar and 2D camera in a target-less environment (i.e. no assumptions about existence of landmarks on the scene) [12]. Leveraging such a capability, a self-calibrated object detection framework is proposed in this paper. The proposed framework calibrates camera and lidar from rgb and depth feature extraction. Using a geometric supervision training the network learns to solve the underlying geometric problem from miscalibration. The rest of the paper is structured as follows. Section 2 discusses related work, including both target-based and targetless classical calibration approaches, along with promising deep neural networks. Section 3 introduces our proposed pipeline, including dataset pre-processing, network architecture, output processing, loss functions and training procedure. Experimental results are discussed in Sect. 4. Finally Sect. 5 concludes the paper.

2 Related Work

LiDAR-Camera Calibration in multi-sensor systems is crucial to enable reliable perception. Therefore the calibration problem has been well-studied and there has been a number of proposed solutions over the past few years. A sensor is characterised by its intrinsic parameters, which are proper to the nature of the sensor and extrinsic parameters that describe the relation of the sensor to its environment or the world. In extrinsic calibration we estimate the rigid body transformation that would describe the position and orientation of the sensor with respect to world coordinates. Such transformation allows association between sensors like projecting a lidar point cloud onto an image from a specific camera. Most calibration approaches fall into two categories: target based or targetless.

Target based methods rely on identifying and matching features from a dedicated calibration target that is visible to both camera and lidar like a checker board [8,23]. Many target based methods were proposed that facilitate the process of target creation [18,22]. Although accurate, these techniques need a dedicated artificial target object and they are labour intensive.

Recent work explores automatic calibration without any preset targets. One of the first work on the automatic calibration [16,17], which proposed to estimate extrinsic calibration parameters by maximising the mutual information between the reflectivity of point clouds and the intensity of images. Other approaches, like [21], use independent motion estimates from the sensors and match them to obtain extrinsic calibration parameters.

Deep neural networks have shown enormous success in computer vision tasks. Even with the success of deep neural networks, only a few approaches based on deep learning have been applied to solve the calibration problem. One of the first deep neural networks for lidar-camera calibration is [20]. It trains the network by regressing to the calibration parameters with large amount of data. However, geometry properties are not learned, even though that would be feasible. Consequently, [12] proposed a network that addresses the underlying geometric problem, leveraging the success of self-supervised learning [15,24]. It approaches the problem by attempting to reduce dense photometric error and point cloud distance error. In [12] they show good results, but they also show problems in estimating translation and the training approach is not in a one go estimation. They first train the network to estimate rotation and then they freeze rotation and iteratively train for translation, which slows down training. In our approach we propose a network that solves the issue of erroneous initial translation and train the network in one go and achieve promising results. Figure 4 shows the predicted red point cloud alignment to green expected point cloud position. The network quickly converges to both rotation and translation with only point cloud loss, photometric loss can be used after some iterations for fine tuning. Our approach leverages the power of recurrent and residual neural networks. This helps solving the sequential transformation problem and vanishing gradients. We also extend the training and validation to the nuScenes data set [6].

3 Methodology

In this section, we present a pipeline based on CalibNet [12] with a pipeline and implementation in PyTorch and adaptation to nuScenes dataset [6]. This pipeline is to be used as a calibration validation for the Transfusion LiDAR-camera 3D object detection [3].

3.1 Architecture

The network is composed of two asymmetric convolution branches, one for RGB images and one for depth map. The RGB branch uses the ResNet-18 feature extraction [10], with frozen pretrained weights to not learn features from scratch. Like in [20] the depth branch uses similar architecture for the RGB, but with half filter output channels. To avoid the problem of vanishing gradients due to the amount of convolutional networks, we use jumping connections or identity connections. Both outputs of the branches are then concatenated along the channel or feature dimension to create one global feature vector.

The concatenated global feature vector is passed through additional convolutional networks (or aggregation network like in [12]) with the exception that we use also residual connections at this stage. Then the output get to be decoupled into two separate convolutional branches: one for rotation and the other for translation. We use recurrent hidden layer for rotation and translation. After every convolutional layer we use BatchNorm [11] and ReLu [1]. Before the fully connected layers (rotation, translation) we apply average pooling and dropout. Before passing the average pooling to the last fully connected layer we concatenate it with a hidden state vector in order to have two parallel branches, i.e., containing output and a hidden state to be used as a recursive input like a recursive neural network (RNN) (see Fig. 2). The final output of the network is a 1×6 vector $\xi = (v, \omega) \in se(3)$, where v is the translation vector, and ω is the rotational velocity vector [12]. The overall system architecture is illustrated in Fig. 1. The system pipeline is composed of three stages. Stage (a) is the place of inference, where the model takes RGB and depth map and estimates $\xi = (v, \omega) \in se(3)$. Exponential map is applied in stage (b) to convert from $se(3)$ to $SE(3)$ resulting in a rotation and translation matrix. In stage (c) of the pipeline a new depth map and a sparse point cloud is generated based on the calculated transformation matrix. The sparse point cloud is used to calculate the point distance loss. The new depth map is used both to calculate the pixel intensity loss and as an iterative input to the network for refinement.

3.2 Output Processing

Before diving in the output processing, we define some notations for the used geometric methods. In this work the geometry focus is on Euclidean space R^3. Over this space we define all the invertible 3×3 matrices that form the general linear group $\mathrm{GL}(3, \mathbb{R})$. The set of proper orthogonal transformations or matrices with determinant $+1$ constitute the special orthogonal group $SO(3) \subset O(3)$, which represents pure rotations only [9].

In order to handle translation 4×4, rigid body transformations need to be formed $\begin{pmatrix} R & t \\ 0 & 1 \end{pmatrix}$. The set of rigid body transformations constitute the ES(3) special Euclidean group. The Lie groups[1] SO(3) and SE(3) have associated Lie algebras[2] so(3) and se(3) represented as vectors in $\mathbb{R}^3$ and $\mathbb{R}^6$ respectively [9].

[1] A Lie group is a group that is a differential manifold, which is a space that locally resembles Euclidean space.

[2] Lie algebras are vector spaces together with an operation called Lie bracket, an alternating bi-linear map.

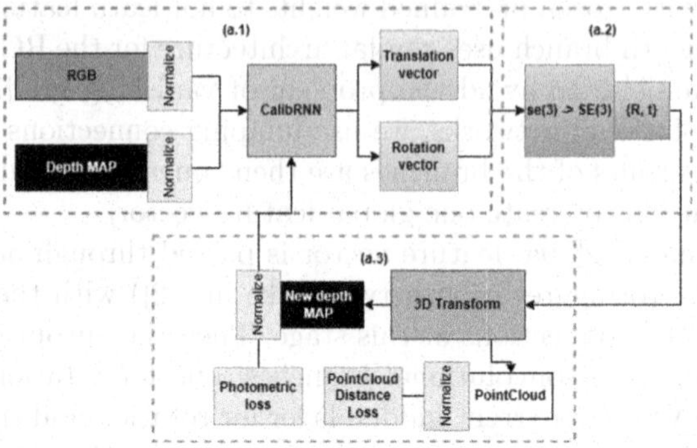

Fig. 1. Overall system model. Stage (1) is the place of inference, where the model takes RGB and depth map and estimates $\xi = (v, \omega) \in se(3)$. Exponential map is applied in stage (2) to convert from $se(3)$ to $SE(3)$ resulting in rotation and translation matrix. In stage (3) of the pipeline a new depth map and a sparse point cloud is generated based on the calculated transformation matrix. The sparse point cloud is used to calculate the point distance loss. The new depth map is used to calculate pixel intensity loss and as an iterative input to the network for refinement.

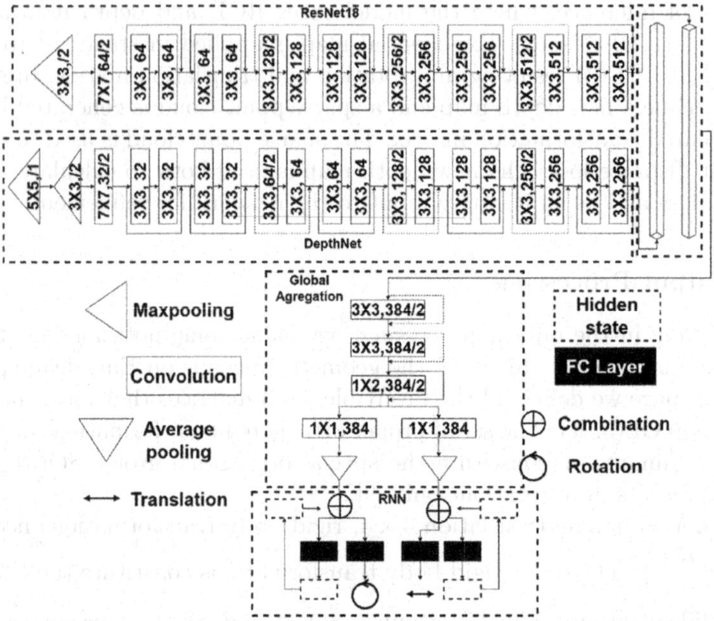

Fig. 2. Calibration Network with residual connections and recurrent hidden states. The network is composed of a pretrained resnet18 branch [10], a depth net like [12,20], and a global aggregation stage like [12]. In our case we modify the global aggregation stage to also use residual connections to avoid vanishing gradients. Last average pooling and a recurrent fully connected layer is added for both rotation and translation.

Using the geometric properties defined in the previous paragraph, we can use exponential map between Lie groups in order to convert translation and the rotational velocity vectors (v, ω) as $u = \begin{pmatrix} v \\ \omega \end{pmatrix}$ from $se(3)$ to $SE(3)$:

$$exp : se(3) \rightarrow SE(3),\ e^u \equiv e^{A(u)} = \begin{pmatrix} e^{\hat{\omega}} & Vv \\ 0 & 1 \end{pmatrix}$$
$$V = I_3 + \frac{1 - cos\theta}{\theta^2}\hat{\omega} + \frac{\theta - sin\theta}{\theta^3}\hat{\omega}^2 \tag{1}$$

While the translation velocity vector can be used directly in Eq. (1), the rotational velocity vector need to be converted to a rotation matrix. Using Rodrigues' rotation formula [2], where: $\theta = \|\omega\|$:

$$e^{\hat{\omega}} = R = I_3 + \frac{\hat{\omega}}{\theta} sin\theta + \frac{\hat{\omega}^2}{\theta^2}(1 - cos\theta) \tag{2}$$

Combining the resulting rotation matrix $R = e^{\hat{\omega}}$ and $t = Vv$ gives the 3D rigid body transformation $T \in SE(3)$: $T = \begin{pmatrix} R & t \\ 0 & 1 \end{pmatrix}$ where $R \in SO(3)$ and $t \in \mathbb{R}^3$. For more details see [5].

3.3 Dataset Pre-processing

We use recordings from KITTI [7] and nuScenes [6]. The sensor setup is different for the two datasets. KITTI has only front view from three different cameras. nuScenes has 360 view from six cameras surrounding the vehicle. Both datasets use one lidar Velodyne.

KITTI Calibration: The coordinate system (CS) is based on a reference camera. In order to transform from lidar CS to a camera of choice, we transform to cam reference CS first then to specific camID and finally project to image plane. In this paper we used the camera marked 'cam_02'.

nuScenes Calibration: Here the CS is based on the ego vehicle body frame. The ego position at a given specific time is given with respect to global world coordinate system map. The map-based localisation algorithm is described in [6]. In order to transform from lidar CS to a camera of choice, we transform to the ego vehicle CS at the same specific time stamp. From that we transform to the global map CS. At this stage we transform back to the ego vehicle CS, with the time stamp that corresponds to a camera time stamp. Finally we transform from the ego position CS to the camera CS, and project to the camera plane. In the nuScenes data set, the rotation is described as a quaternion $q = (q_r, q_x, q_y, q_z)$, which can be converted to R(Q) using 3D+Quat to matrix [5].

Calibration Perturbation: The random transformation (simulating the miscalibration) like in [12,20], is created by samplin (u_x, u_y, u_z) and $(\omega_x, \omega_y, \omega_z)$ randomly from a uniform distribution, in the range of $\pm 10°$ (rotation) and ± 0.2 m (translation) for all axes. In both the KITTI and nuScenes data sets the random transformation is applied before projecting to the camera plane.

3.4 Loss Functions

Similarly to [12] we use two types of loss terms during training:

Photo-Metric Loss: we calculate the depth intensity error within the depth maps as a pixel-wise error between the predicted depth map, the result of applying the predicted transformation to project point cloud, and the target depth map. The error term is defined as:

$$MSE_{photo} = \frac{1}{N}\sum_{1}^{N}(D_{gt} - KT[D_{miscalib}])^2 \tag{3}$$

Equation (3) is a mean squared error between pixel intensity. D_{gt} is the target depth based on the inverse random transformation and $D_{miscalib}$ is the initial miscalibrated depth map. In other terms, we transform the miscalibrated 3D depth information with the predicted transform, then we project them using the camera intrinsic matrix K. For the image comparison we do not use the full size. We apply a convolution to the predicted and expected depth map with a 2×2 pixel average kernel and a stride of 2. This means that the image size will be half of the height and half of the width of the original, and four neighbouring pixels will be averaged.

Point Cloud Distance Loss: Using the 3D input depth information we sample two point clouds. We use the predicted transformation to have the predicted point cloud position and use the inverse random transformation to have the expected point cloud position. We normalise the point clouds: $X = \frac{X}{\|X\|}$. Having the two point clouds, we need a distance metric to measure the error.

In this paper we consider the Chamfer distance. This is the sum of squared distances of the nearest points between the two clouds. We use the implementation used in [19]. The error term is defined as:

$$L_{CD}(S_1, S_2) = \sum_{x \in S_1} \min_{y \in S_2} \|x - y\|_2^2 + \sum_{y \in S_2} \min_{x \in S_1} \|x - y\|_2^2 \tag{4}$$

In order to be applied to dense point clouds, the number of points per point cloud needs to be reduced. Therefore, we sample the point cloud, before calculating the CD term, by taking only point centroid with a size that is a multiple of 1024.

Like in [12] the final loss function consists of a weighted sum of the photometric loss and point cloud distance loss:

$$L_{final} = \alpha(L_{photo}) + \beta(L_{CD}) \tag{5}$$

3.5 Training Procedure

To train the network we use the Adam optimiser [13] with a learning rate of 5e–4 and a momentum of 0.9. We train for a few epochs counting only on chamfer distance loss by setting $\alpha = 0.0$ and $\beta = 1.0$. We introduce the photometric loss when a certain minimum on the chamfer distance loss is reached. We observed that in the initial stage, by using only chamfer distance we could iteratively reduce the distance between the point clouds. Here the problem is more addressed as ICP (iterative closest point) to align two sets of 3D points. By choosing to learn first by reducing the pcd loss, we reach a loss of 0.02 on the first epoch. This leads to a considerable decrease in learning time on both translation and rotation.

For the recursive input passing, we used only two iterations for both residual transforms and recursive hidden states. This was originally introduced due to concerns of memory consumption, but it proved to be enough. For the residual transform we accumulate it with the previous transforms $T = I_4 \times T \times T^{'}$.

During training we project the predicted depth map over the RGB image (see Fig. 3) to visualise the depth to pixel association and to show the evolution of the calibration correction.

Fig. 3. Depth projection on the RGB image over mis-calibration correction steps. It is visible how depth projection improves over the calibration steps. Red rectangles show two misaligned regions of interest. Misalignment is quite visible on (a). From (b) to (d), however, as calibration progresses, the depth-pixels alignment of the region of interest improves. (Color figure online)

We compare the transformation matrices (predicted, ground truth) on rotation and translation. The translation metric is straightforward and defined as:

$$diff_{Tr} = |X_i - X_j| \tag{6}$$

For rotation we need to define a metric that calculates the difference and show the angular distance between the two values. For the rotation metric we use Riemannian geodesic distance defined as:

$$d_R(R_{pred}, R_{gt}) = \frac{1}{\sqrt{2}} \| \log(R_{pred}^{-1} R_{gt}) \|_F \tag{7}$$

where: $\|.\|_F = \sqrt{2} \times length$. For the calculation of the logarithm map in Eq. (7), the Rodrigues' rotation formula ($\log(R)$) is used. We also calculate Yaw, Pitch, Roll difference angles between the predicted and expected rotation. For more details refer to [5].

4 Results and Discussion

In this section we present qualitative and quantitative results on camera-lidar mis-calibration correction on two popular datasets KITTI [7] and Nuscenes [6]. We use the 2011_09_26 recordings on [7] and the v1.0-trainval on [6]. Since we are training against mis-calibrated data with randomly generated rigid body transforms, we can generate an infinite set of training, validation and testing data.

Figure 4 shows the iterative alignment or calibration steps. The green points represent the calibrated sampled point cloud and red points depict the mis-calibrated point cloud. Initially, the red point cloud are randomly rotated and translated to represent a non-calibrated setup. The alignment is shown in the final iteration, which exhibits low distance between the point clouds. In Fig. 4 the alignment was based only on the distance metric (chamfer distance).

Fig. 4. Iterative point cloud alignment based only on Chamfer distance Eq. (4). The ground truth point cloud is green, while the predicted point cloud is red. The red point cloud position is the result of applying the rigid body transformation predicted by our network. Here the training of our network is performed using only the distance metric between the point clouds (Chamfer distance). That is, the calibration problem is rather approached as a point registration task like ICP (iterative closest point). In the final result, the two point clouds are nearly identical to each other.

Figure 6a presents the point cloud loss Eq. (4). The function shows an exponential decrease for 14 epochs. The abscissa depicts the epochs, while the ordinate shows the Chamfer distance between the expected position of the point cloud and the expected position of the transformed point cloud. Exponential decrease reflects the speed of convergence in point cloud alignment.

Over training we calculate different errors for over 30 epochs between the predicted and expected transform (inverse of the random transform). Figure 6b shows the overall loss. Overall loss stands for the photometric loss plus the point cloud loss (see Eq. (5)). On Fig. 6b a sudden decrease in loss can is visible. It is from that point that only point cloud loss (Eq. (4)) was considered. In this situation the use of Eq. (3 and 4) would decrease the error rapidly. However, this loss combination shows stagnation after reaching a certain minimal value. To avoid loss stagnation we consider only point cloud distance.

We see that Eq. (3) helps a lot in estimating rotation, especially roll and yaw angles. However, it fails when it comes to translation. That is where Eq. (4) comes to better estimate the translation.

Figure 6c shows the geodesic distance loss in radians between the predicted and expected transform see Eq. (7). We see the change at 0.1 rad, from using Eq. (5) to only considering Eq. (4), where we notice a continuous improvement. We report a minimum loss of 0.0175 in radians for $\pm 20°$ rotation error.

In the top row of Fig. 5 we present the losses for Yaw, Pitch and Roll angles in degrees. We report an absolute minimum of 0.2043°, 0.2290°, 0.0931° respectively for $\pm 10°$ rotation mis-calibration. The figure shows the exponential decrease for the angles. Compared to 5a and 5c, the Figs. 5b show clearly the effect of the transition from using final loss to only consider point cloud distance.

The bottom row of Fig. 5 shows the absolute error for x, y, z in cm using Eq. (6). We report an absolute minimum error of 1.0590 cm, 0.9319 cm, 1.4131 cm respectively for ± 0.2 m translation mis-calibration. The figures show the decrease of distance along the three axes. More importantly, the effect of the transition from using final loss to only consider point cloud distance is clearly visible.

In order to show the performance of our approach, we compare it with [12,20]. On order to have similar test conditions, we take reported results for calibrating $\pm 10°$ for rotation and 0.2 m for translation to compare with [12] and $\pm 20°$ for rotation and ± 1.5 m for translation to compare with [20]. As shown on Table 1, CalibRRNet achieves lower mean absolute errors than previous works. The main improvement is in the XYZ translation, where we report a mean absolute error of 1.1347 cm compared to 6 cm [20] and 7.82 cm [12]. In rotation we report also relatively low absolute mean errors, especially in Roll angle (0.0931°). Compared with previous approaches, CalibRRnet almost cuts the error values in half. We report Yaw and Pitch angles close to [20]. Overall, in rotation we report an absolute mean error of 0.1754° compared to 0.41° [12] and 0.28° [20].

Table 1. Yaw, Pitch, Roll, and X, Y, Z mean absolute error comparison with [12,20]. Tests were conducted in ways matching those of the earlier approaches. Clearly, CalibRRNet overperforms both Regnet and Calibnet, especially in the translation terms (XYZ), indicating the value added in using full residual connections and a recurrent network.

Approach	*Yaw*°	*Pitch*°	*Roll*°	X cm	Y cm	Z cm
Regnet	0.24	0.25	0.36	7	7	4
Calibnet	**0.15**	0.9	0.18	12.1	3.49	7.87
CalibRRnet	0.2043	**0.2290**	**0.0931**	**1.0590**	**0.9319**	**1.4131**

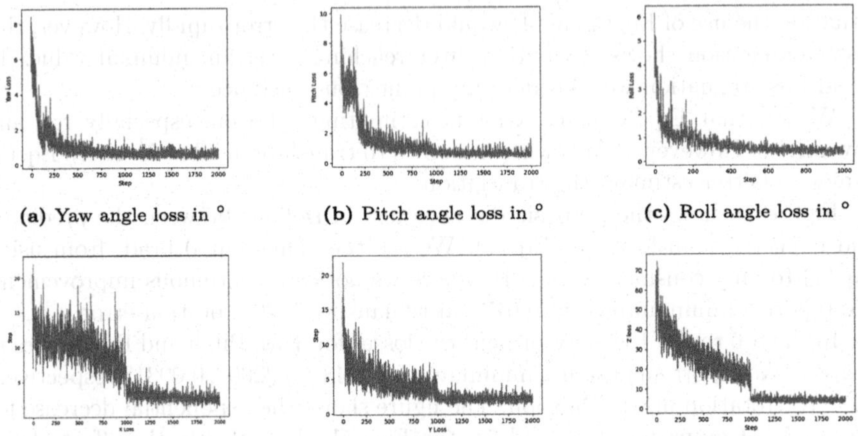

(a) Yaw angle loss in ° **(b)** Pitch angle loss in ° **(c)** Roll angle loss in °

(d) X loss in cm **(e)** Y loss in cm **(f)** Z loss in cm

Fig. 5. D+YPR losses between the predicted and expected 6 DoF rigid body transform. In 5d, 5e and 5f the distance is represented in cm. In 5a, 5b and 5c the angles are represented in degrees. The 6D pose losses show an exponential decrease. More importantly, the figures show the effect of the transition from using the final loss to only considering point cloud distance.

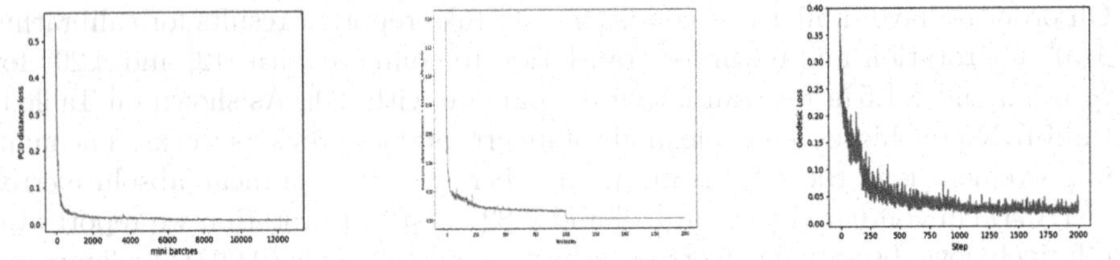

(a) Point cloud distance loss after 14 epochs **(b)** Overall loss (30+ epochs) **(c)** Geodesic distance loss

Fig. 6. Various loss functions. The horizontal axis depicts the epochs, while the vertical one shoes the losses calculated based on the 6 DoF predicted and expected transform. 6a shows point cloud distance after 14 epochs, 6b depicts the final loss for more than 30 epochs and 6c plots the geodesic distance. The ordinate of 6a shows the chamfer distance Eq. (4): the function decreases exponentially showing the convergence in the point cloud registration. The ordinate of 6b shows the overall loss Eq. (5) for over 30 epochs showing transition with a sudden decrease, since in the last training phase we consider only point cloud loss Eq. (4). 6c shows geodesic distance loss in radians Eq. (7).

Our network is able to accurately estimate the calibration, over a wide variety of scenes and over a wide range of initial mis-calibrations. Figure 3 shows some of these results. Even with very high initial errors in all the 6 axes, our network successfully aligns the mis-calibrated depth map to the RGB frame, achieving close to ground truth re-alignment. In each of the cases, the network portrays its efficacy. In Fig. 3 we show the alignment of the depth to the RGB map. The way how our network matches the extracted features from the residual networks is clearly visible in the regions of interests (red rectangles).

5 Conclusion

In this paper we introduced a novel approach for extrinsic calibration based on residual and recurrent deep convolutional neural networks. Compared to existing approaches, our network concept replaces the iterative refinement and the separation of training focus on translation and rotation with recurrent neural networks and extended residual connections through the convolution stages. The network infers directly the 6 DOF rigid body transformation between 3D LIDAR and 2D camera. Our approach does not rely on special targets in the scene, nor on any human intervention. Our method yields a mean calibration error of 1.14 cm for translation and 0.18° for rotation with a magnitude of ±20° in rotation and ±1.5 cm in translation. These results significantly improve on previous calibration networks. Next steps will cover ablation study and result comparison with different deep neural network architectures. Future works will explore the online application of the network in fusion detection frameworks. We intend to leverage the learned underlying geometry to align LIDAR and camera and to create a robust detection framework capable of online calibration and rectification, allowing transition from one representation to another.

References

1. Agarap, A.F.: Deep learning using rectified linear units (relu). CoRR abs/1803.08375 (2018). http://arxiv.org/abs/1803.08375
2. Altafini, C.: The de casteljau algorithm on se(3). In: Isidori, A., Lamnabhi-Lagarrigue, F., Respondek, W. (eds.) Nonlinear Control in the Year 2000, pp. 23–34. Springer, London (2001). https://doi.org/10.1007/BFb0110205
3. Bai, X., et al.: Transfusion: robust lidar-camera fusion for 3d object detection with transformers. In: 2022 IEEE/CVF Conference on Computer Vision and Pattern Recognition (CVPR), pp. 1080–1089 (2022). https://doi.org/10.1109/CVPR52688.2022.00116
4. Banerjee, K., Notz, D., Windelen, J., Gavarraju, S., He, M.: Online camera lidar fusion and object detection on hybrid data for autonomous driving. In: 2018 IEEE Intelligent Vehicles Symposium (IV), pp. 1632–1638 (2018). https://doi.org/10.1109/IVS.2018.8500699
5. Blanco-Claraco, J.L.: A tutorial on **SE**(3) transformation parameterizations and on-manifold optimization. CoRR abs/2103.15980 (2021). http://arxiv.org/abs/2103.15980
6. Caesar, H., et al.: nuscenes: a multimodal dataset for autonomous driving (2019)
7. Geiger, A., Lenz, P., Stiller, C., Urtasun, R.: Vision meets robotics: the kitti dataset. Int. J. Rob. Res. (IJRR) **32**, 1231–1237 (2013)
8. Geiger, A., Moosmann, F., Car, O., Schuster, B.: Automatic camera and range sensor calibration using a single shot. In: Proceedings - IEEE International Conference on Robotics and Automation, pp. 3936–3943 (2012). https://doi.org/10.1109/ICRA.2012.6224570

9. Hall, B.C.: Lie Groups, Lie Algebras, and Representations. GTM, vol. 222. Springer, Cham (2015). https://doi.org/10.1007/978-3-319-13467-3
10. He, K., Zhang, X., Ren, S., Sun, J.: Deep residual learning for image recognition. CoRR abs/1512.03385 (2015). http://arxiv.org/abs/1512.03385
11. Ioffe, S., Szegedy, C.: Batch normalization: accelerating deep network training by reducing internal covariate shift. CoRR abs/1502.03167 (2015). http://arxiv.org/abs/1502.03167
12. Iyer, G., Ram, R.K., Murthy, J.K., Krishna, K.M.: Calibnet: geometrically supervised extrinsic calibration using 3D spatial transformer networks. In: 2018 IEEE/RSJ International Conference on Intelligent Robots and Systems (IROS), pp. 1110–1117 (2018). https://doi.org/10.1109/IROS.2018.8593693
13. Kingma, D., Ba, J.: Adam: a method for stochastic optimization. In: International Conference on Learning Representations (2014)
14. Levinson, J., Thrun, S.: Automatic online calibration of cameras and lasers (2013). https://doi.org/10.15607/RSS.2013.IX.029
15. Li, R., Wang, S., Long, Z., Gu, D.: Undeepvo: monocular visual odometry through unsupervised deep learning. In: 2018 IEEE International Conference on Robotics and Automation (ICRA), pp. 7286–7291 (2018). https://doi.org/10.1109/ICRA.2018.8461251
16. Nieto, J.I., Taylor, Z.: A mutual information approach to automatic calibration of camera and lidar in natural environments (2012)
17. Pandey, G., McBride, J.R., Savarese, S., Eustice, R.M.: Automatic targetless extrinsic calibration of a 3D lidar and camera by maximizing mutual information. In: Proceedings of the Twenty-Sixth AAAI Conference on Artificial Intelligence, AAAI 2012, pp. 2053–2059. AAAI Press (2012)
18. Pusztai, Z., Hajder, L.: Accurate calibration of lidar-camera systems using ordinary boxes. In: 2017 IEEE International Conference on Computer Vision Workshops (ICCVW), pp. 394–402 (2017). https://doi.org/10.1109/ICCVW.2017.53
19. Ravi, N., et al.: Accelerating 3D deep learning with pytorch3d. arXiv:2007.08501 (2020)
20. Schneider, N., Piewak, F., Stiller, C., Franke, U.: Regnet: multimodal sensor registration using deep neural networks. In: 2017 IEEE Intelligent Vehicles Symposium (IV), pp. 1803–1810 (2017). https://doi.org/10.1109/IVS.2017.7995968
21. Taylor, Z., Nieto, J.: Motion-based calibration of multimodal sensor arrays. In: 2015 IEEE International Conference on Robotics and Automation (ICRA), pp. 4843–4850 (2015). https://doi.org/10.1109/ICRA.2015.7139872
22. Tóth, T., Pusztai, Z., Hajder, L.: Automatic lidar-camera calibration of extrinsic parameters using a spherical target. In: 2020 IEEE International Conference on Robotics and Automation (ICRA), pp. 8580–8586 (2020). https://doi.org/10.1109/ICRA40945.2020.9197316
23. Zhang, Q., Pless, R.: Extrinsic calibration of a camera and laser range finder (improves camera calibration), vol. 3, pp. 2301–2306 (2004). https://doi.org/10.1109/IROS.2004.1389752
24. Zhou, T., Brown, M., Snavely, N., Lowe, D.G.: Unsupervised learning of depth and ego-motion from video. CoRR abs/1704.07813 (2017). http://arxiv.org/abs/1704.07813

GAN-Based Data Augmentation and Pseudo-label Refinement for Unsupervised Domain Adaptation Person Re-identification

Anh D. Nguyen[1], Dang H. Pham[1,2], and Hoa N. Nguyen[1(✉)]

[1] VNU University of Engineering and Technology, Hanoi, Vietnam
{19021208,dangph,hoa.nguyen}@vnu.edu.vn
[2] University of Khanh Hoa, Khanh Hoa, Vietnam

Abstract. Person re-identification (re-ID) by using an unsupervised domain adaptation (UDA) approach has drawn considerable attention in contemporary security research. Thus, UDA person re-ID usually employs a model learned from a labeled source domain, adjusted by pseudo-labels, for an unlabeled target domain. However, this method still needs to overcome two main challenges: a significant gap between the source and target domains and the accuracy of pseudo-labels generated by a clustering algorithm. To address these problems, we propose a novel method to improve UDA person re-ID performance by combining GAN-based Data Augmentation and Unsupervised Pseudo-Label Editation methods for training on Target Domain, named DAUET. In particular, we first use a generative adversarial network (GAN) method to bridge the distribution of the source and target domains. Then we propose a supervised learning approach to maximize the benefits of the virtual dataset. Finally, we utilize a pseudo-label refinement to enhance the unsupervised learning process. Extensive experiments on two popular datasets, Market-1501 and DukeMTMC-reID, indicate that our DAUET method can substantially outperform the state-of-the-art performance of the UDA person re-ID.

Keywords: Unsupervised Person Re-Identification · Unsupervised Domain Adaptation · GAN-based Data Augmentation · Pseudo-Label Refinement

1 Introduction

The increased demand for social security has resulted in the installation of numerous cameras in various positions and angles. It results in an influx of requests for solutions to the person re-ID challenge, which seeks to determine the same person from many perspectives in a distributed multi-camera system. Deep Convolutional Neural Network (DCNN) accomplishments in the presentation of visual characteristics have lately inspired academics to investigate new

N. T. Nguyen et al. (Eds.): ICCCI 2023, LNAI 14162, pp. 591–605, 2023.
https://doi.org/10.1007/978-3-031-41456-5_45

person re-ID models based on deep learning [11]. Researchers concentrated on building innovative network structures and practical loss functions based on the supervised learning methodology, considerably enhancing the performance of the model and producing exceptional results. However, these supervised learning approaches are data-driven and require a vast amount of labeled data, which incurs substantial labeling expenses. Moreover, person re-ID models are frequently trained on datasets that do not adequately represent real-world scenarios, such as variations in illumination, weather conditions, camera perspectives, etc. Therefore, poor outcomes are unavoidable when these models are utilized with genuine personal information. To solve these challenges, researchers have concentrated on unsupervised learning methods for person re-ID work for the purpose of training models without the use of labeled datasets.

Most currently person re-ID unsupervised learning approaches have relied on clustering algorithms to produce pseudo-labels that can replace truth labels. They are classified into two main lines: *"Pure Unsupervised Learning"* (USL) and *"Unsupervised Domain Adaptation"* (UDA). In particular, USL is a traditional approach to directly train models on unlabeled sets. However, almost state-of-the-art (SOTA) in this approach, such as pseudo-label refinery [3,18], primarily rely on multi-GPU machines and large batch sizes to reduce label noise when training from scratch. On the other hand, UDA first trains on labeled datasets to learn about human characteristics before learning on the unlabeled set. This process, called "knowledge transformation", improves the reliability of initial pseudo-labels and enhances performance. According to the robust pre-trained model, the initial pseudo-label in early epochs is more reliable and rapidly improves the person re-ID model's performance in learning on the unlabeled domain. Despite UDA's recent progress, its performance gap compared to supervised learning remains significant, falling short of expectations in the research community.

Research Challenges: While researching a novel method, in comparison to earlier works on UDA, we face two main challenges, which are as follows:
(1.) There is a substantial disparity between the source and target domains due to the different surroundings, such as models trained on one domain may perform worse when applied to another. Thus, there are noticeable differences in lighting and background clutter between photos from various datasets.
(2.) The dependence on pseudo-labels assigned by the clustering algorithm is a crucial reason for the poor performance in several person re-ID unsupervised learning methods. These algorithms sometimes generate incorrect labels corresponding to the samples. That results in the fact that several identities allocated the same pseudo-labels, and ones that may be suggested to more than one label in the unlabeled dataset. The learning could become ineffective as a result.

Contribution Highlights: From the challenges above, the primary objective of this work is to overcome the inevitable limitations of the clustering algorithm and find a way to alleviate the gap between the two data domains. Our most important contributions are outlined below:

(1.) We suggest utilizing a GAN method in order to make a virtual dataset that bridges the distribution of two data domains. Then we can utilize this dataset to make the pre-trained model more generalized.
(2.) We propose a supervised learning approach to maximize the benefits of the virtual dataset while minimizing the impact of low-quality samples generated by GAN models.
(3.) We elaborate on a simple pseudo-label refinement mechanism to enhance the unsupervised learning process.
(4.) We carry out numerous experiments on two well-known benchmarks, Market-1501 and DukeMTMC-reID, to evaluate our proposed method's performance. The result demonstrates the practical potential of the research direction. Our method outperforms the performance of some SOTA achievements.

The rest of this work is structured as follows. Section 2 provides some related works in UDA person re-ID. Section 3 introduces our proposed method. In Sect. 4, we present our experiments, evaluate our proposed work, and compare the results with recent publications. Finally, Sect. 5 summarizes the contribution and identifies possible future works.

2 Related Works

2.1 GAN-based Data Augmentation

According to [2], GAN-based data augmentation methods were usually conditionally conducted on some factors: **(1.) Pose**: GAN can produce a target person in new poses under the supervision of 2D poses to augment the dataset. **(2.) Illumination**: Because datasets are often recorded in uniform illumination, GAN can generate human pictures in the style (light) of a target domain. **(3.) Camera style**: GAN is able to transform images obtained by one camera into the style (light, scale, revolution,...) of another camera in order to reduce inter-camera style gaps. **(4.) Background**: GAN was also designed to remove and switch the backdrop of a human picture in order to reduce the background effect on UDA person re-ID. **(5.) Generic structure**: By recoloring gray-scaled human photographs with the color distribution of other images, some GAN models trained disentangled identity representations invariant to structural variables.

Inspired by the achievement in [15], we provide a cross-domain camera style transformation module that takes pictures from the source domain to various cameras in the target domain while explicitly considering camera-level discrepancies. In addition, we employ a powerful method by combining real and fake datasets for supervising the DCNN model.

2.2 Label Noise Refinement Method for Unsupervised Person Re-ID

Handling noisy pseudo-labels in clustering-based algorithms has recently been an appealing research topic. Representative label refinement algorithms include some nearest neighbor search methods [10,18] and additional information assisted pseudo-label refinement methods [3,6,17]. ISE [18] and CGL [10] produce boundary samples using real samples and the surrounding clusters. The network's discriminability is increased by requiring produced samples to be accurately categorized. The part-based pseudo-label refining proposed by PPLR [3] employs additional trustworthy supplementary information to enhance the pseudo-label quality. MMT [6], MEBNet [17] suggest leveraging numerous predictions from auxiliary networks to improve the pseudo-labels and train the network through mutual learning.

In our work, we apply the CGL method [10], which utilizes the relationship of feature vectors to alleviate harms brought on by label noise in training.

3 Proposed Method: DAUET

3.1 Overview

Problem Statement: The objective is to leverage a model $\boldsymbol{\Omega}$ trained on a labeled dataset (source domain) to transfer knowledge and learn new features on an unlabeled dataset (target domain). Specifically, we assume that the labeled dataset is $\mathcal{D}_s = \{x_i^s, y_i^s\}_{i=1}^{\mathcal{N}_s}$, where $(x_i^s,\ y_i^s)$ denote the i-th labeled sample, $\mathcal{N}_s$ denotes the quantity of source-domain samples. Similarly, we also denote $\mathcal{D}_t = \{x_i^t\}_{i=1}^{\mathcal{N}_t}$ as the target domain, where x_i^t and $\mathcal{N}_t$ correspond the i-th unlabeled sample and the length of this dataset. Clearly, the target domain dataset's photos are not attached with identification labels. In light of this, we can formulate the re-ID problem as follows:

$$\boldsymbol{\Omega} = \mathcal{F}_{USL}\left(\mathcal{F}_{SL}(\boldsymbol{\Omega}, \mathcal{D}_s), \mathcal{D}_t\right) \tag{1}$$

Approach Direction: To solve the challenges described in Sect. 1, we approach a novel method with the following ideas: (i) mitigating the significant disparity between the source and target domains by using the GAN-based data augmentation and (ii) applying the unsupervised pseudo-label editation methods for training on the target domain. We call the proposed method DAUET standing for the GAN-based **D**ata **A**ugmentation and **U**nsupervised Pseudo-Label **E**ditation methods for training on **T**arget Domain. The DAUET method is illustrated in Fig. 1 by two stages described in detail as follows.

Stage I: Supervised Training in Source Domain. Because our objective is to transfer the knowledge of the DCNN model trained from the labeled domain to the unlabeled domain, to achieve this, we initially train our model on the labeled source dataset as the *baseline*. Similar to previous works, the baseline model is trained with the cross-entropy loss $\mathcal{L}_{ce}$ and the triplet loss $\mathcal{L}_{tr}$ simultaneously.

Stage II: Unsupervised Training in Target Domain. In the same way as previous works, we utilize DBSCAN [5] for generating pseudo-labels corresponding to each sample. It will group the training image features $\mathcal{F} = \{\mathbf{f}\}_{i=1}^{N}$ into clustered

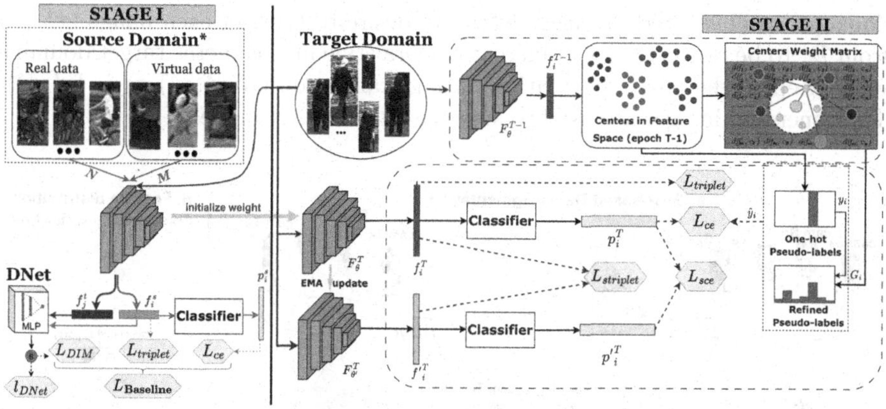

Fig. 1. Overall architecture of our proposed approach - DAUET.

inliers and un-clustered outliers, where the outliers are discarded in the following training epochs. Then, we use these cluster assignments as labels for the samples and train the person re-ID model by a supervised manner, which is similar to stage I. Besides, because of the small number of samples chosen by DBSCAN in early epochs, which easily makes the model become over-fitting, we follow the mean teacher architecture [14] as illustrated in stage II of Fig. 1.

Note that, our method differs from previous UDA person re-ID studies mainly in two aspects:

1. Camera Style Adaption: Inspired by [15], we utilize StarGAN [4] to diminish the distribution disparity of samples between the source and target domains as described in Sect. 3.2. Based on that, we can train robust pre-trained models in stage I.
2. Pseudo-Label Refinement: Instead of directly using pseudo-labels generated by DBSCAN [5], we conduct a score based on the distance relationship among samples and all cluster centers in feature space to refine the pseudo-label. Details of this stage are described in Sect. 3.3.

The combination of these two above stages is coordinated by a mean teacher model to optimize the person re-ID models. This framework is regulated by an overall loss function for the entire training process.

3.2 GAN-Based Training Data Augmentation

Virtual Dataset Generation: Our goal is to address the distribution discrepancy between the target and source domains caused by the different styles of cameras. We consider a camera as an individual domain, resulting in $C+1$ different style-domains for an unlabeled dataset with images collected from C camera views and a labeled dataset. To achieve this, we train an image-image translation generator G by using StarGAN [4] to learn the style mapping among those domains, as illustrated in Fig. 2 (left). We desire to transfer each image (x_i^s, y_i^s) from $\mathcal{D}_s^*$ to be converted to a different camera style in C cameras target domains while keeping the label information during translation $G((x_i^s, y_i^s), c) \rightarrow (x_i^t, y_i^s)$. The generated images are used to supervise the DCNN model.

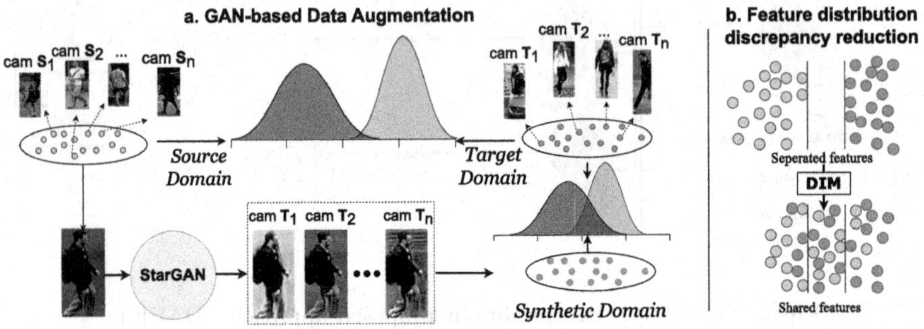

Fig. 2. Two methods improve strong baseline.

Besides, StarGAN uses an auxiliary classifier to improve Generator G, which allows a single discriminator to regulate multiple domains $D : x \rightarrow D_{src}(x), D_{cls}(x)$. The overall objectives to optimize Generator G and Discriminator D are written, respectively, as below:

$$\begin{aligned} \mathcal{L}_D &= -\mathcal{L}_{adv} + \lambda_{cls}\mathcal{L}_{cls}^r \\ \mathcal{L}_G &= \mathcal{L}_{adv} + \lambda_{cls}\mathcal{L}_{cls}^f + \lambda_{rec}\mathcal{L}_{rec} \end{aligned} \tag{2}$$

where λ_{cls} and λ_{rec} are hyperparameters that regulate the relative impact of domain classification and reconstruction losses in comparison to adversarial loss. In our work, we use $\lambda_{cls} = 1$ and $\lambda_{\text{rec}} = 10$.

Training Coarse Deep Re-ID Model: The style-transferred dataset $\mathcal{D}_{st}$ can be used in supervised learning alongside the labeled dataset $\mathcal{D}_s$ because the Generator produces samples with identical labels to the original. However, we notice the noise in the style-transferred dataset, for example, low-quality images as Fig. 3. These images lost almost discriminative characteristics of identities, hence, re-ID model can confuse the model in learning feature representation. To reduce the noise's affect, batches are composed of real images and fake images (style-transferred) with a corresponding ratio N:M. Note that, from now when we refer to the source domain, it means the mixed dataset between the real images and fake images $\mathcal{D}_s^*$.

In addition, we employ the Domain-Invariant Mapping (DIM) method [9] to minimize the feature distribution disparity between the source and target domains at the feature-level. DIM comprises a feature extractor, which is a DCNN model, and a domain classifier called DNet. The feature extractor learns to present domain-invariant features, while the domain classifier ensures the production of discriminative features for person re-ID. This is illustrated in Fig. 2 (right). In training, DNet uses both source and target domain information as input, and produces domain recognition scores in the range [0,1]. The target value of the domain recognition scores is 1 for f_i^s from the source domain $\mathcal{D}_s^*$ while 0 for f_j^t from the target domain $\mathcal{D}_t$. By Mean Square Error, DNet will be optimized by the loss function as follows:

$$l_{DNet} = \frac{1}{N_s}\sum_{i=0}^{N_s}(DNet(f_i^s) - 1)^2 + \frac{1}{N_t}\sum_{j=0}^{N_t}(DNet(f_j^t))^2 \tag{3}$$

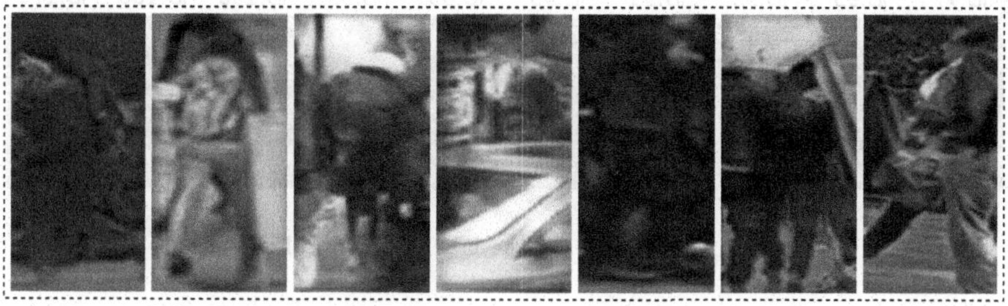

Fig. 3. Low-quality samples generated by StarGAN.

Then, we use DNet to supervise DCNN model Ω with the objective that the model can confuse DNet by extracting features whose domain recognition scores are 0.5 through the DIM loss as follows:

$$\mathcal{L}_{DIM}(\Omega) = \frac{1}{N_s}\sum_{i=0}^{N_s}(DNet(f_i^s) - 0.5)^2 + \frac{1}{N_t}\sum_{j=0}^{N_t}(DNet(f_j^t - 0.5))^2 \tag{4}$$

Now, the final objective loss for supervising the DCNN model is formulated as:

$$\mathcal{L}_{SL} = \mathcal{L}_{ce} + \mathcal{L}_{tr} + \lambda * \mathcal{L}_{DIM} \tag{5}$$

where λ is loss weight. In each iteration, we first train DNet with Eq. 3.

3.3 Pseudo-Label Refinement

Noise labels are one of the unavoidable issues when employing a clustering algorithm to create pseudo-labels. As presented in Fig. 4, when individuals wear the same clothing colors, the clustering algorithm, namely DBSCAN [5], can occasionally be fooled. Then, it makes inconsistent clusters, for instance, the Red cluster consists of four different persons with yellow skirts as well as the problem in the Blue cluster. As a result, samples assigned incorrect labels make a limitation for the model training. Therefore, to reduce side-effect of the noise labels, we will modify the basic one-hot pseudo-label y_i generated by the clustering method through the relationship between samples and all clusters in the feature space:

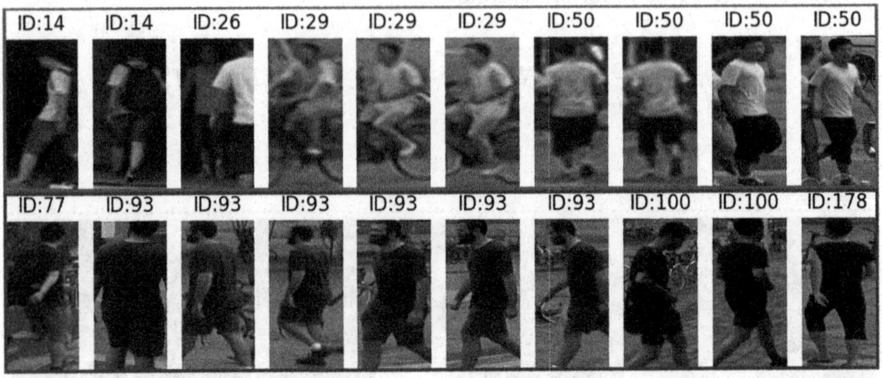

Fig. 4. Example for the label noise problem.

$$\hat{\mathbf{y}}_i = (1 - \alpha)\mathbf{y}_i + \alpha\mathbf{G}_i \tag{6}$$

with $\hat{\mathbf{y}} \in \mathbb{R}^K$ defined as the refined pseudo-label, it is a soft target label (one-soft) instead of the original fixed label (one-hot). Furthermore, $\mathbf{G}_i$ is a score vector indicating a distance relationship between the $i - th$ feature vector and centers of the clusters generated by the DBSCAN. The goals labeling encourages samples to approach not only the initially assigned centroid but their neighbor centroids where their identity information is potentially embedded.

In order to calculate $\mathbf{G_i}$, we built an overall graph of the initial cluster centers and feature vectors. Let the matrix $\mathbf{G}$ represent that diagram, with $G_{i,j} = sigmoid(-d_E(\mathbf{f}_i, \mathbf{m}_j)) \in (0, 0.5)$ is the Euclidean distance score between the feature vector f_i corresponding the *i-th* sample from $\mathcal{D}_t$ extracted from the DCNN model and the cluster center vector m_j corresponding the *j-th* cluster from cluster set $\mathcal{C}$ generated by DBSCAN. With $|.|$ denotes the operation to get the number of elements, m_j can be determined by the formula:

$$m_j = \frac{1}{|S_j|} \sum_{f_i \in S_j} f_i \text{ with } S_j = \{f_i \in \mathcal{C}_j \mid s_i > \sigma\} \tag{7}$$

Here, a confidence subset S_j is selected from the original cluster $\mathcal{C}_j$ according to the threshold σ. σ is Silhouette score [13] to evaluate the correlations between sample and cluster centers. This filtering will alleviate the impact of low-quality images or early background clutter, which may belong to other identities.

3.4 Mean Teacher Architecture

As illustrated in Fig. 1, in stage II, we train two models simultaneously, which assumes a dual role as a teacher $F_{\theta'}$ and a student F_{θ}. The overall goal of this architecture is to train the student model to generate results that are aligned with the teacher model, even when the input data is noisy or corrupted.

In detail, we use Kullback-Leibler divergence loss $\mathcal{L}_{kl}$ and Soft-Triplet loss $\mathcal{L}_{stri}$ to evaluate the disparity of the distribution of predictions between the teacher and the student [14]. As a student, the overall model learns objective is:

$$\begin{aligned} \mathcal{L}_{USL} &= (1 - w_1)\mathcal{L}_{ce}(p_i, \hat{\mathbf{y}}_i) + (1 - w_2)\mathcal{L}_{tr}(f_i, y_i) \\ &+ w_1\mathcal{L}_{kl}(p_i, {p'}_i) + w_2\mathcal{L}_{str}(f_i, {f'}_i) \end{aligned} \tag{8}$$

where p_i, ${p'}_i$, f_i, and f'_i represent the output of the classification class and feature vectors extracted from the student and EMA teacher model. The two weights w_1, w_2, which are adjusted to 0.4 and 0.6, are used to manage learning from the mean teacher and learning new information from the data-batch. Then, the teacher model $F_{\theta'}$ is updated by the *exponential moving average strategy* from the student network as illustrated in Fig. 1. This ensures that the teacher model remains stable even during the training process.

4 Experiments and Evaluation

In order to prove the effectiveness of DAUET, we carry out deep experiments to respond to the following research questions:

- RQ1: Does using style-transferred images and DIM improve the knowledge transformation?
- RQ2: Does the proposed pseudo-label refinement reduce the label noise's impact and enhance the re-ID model's discriminative performance?
- RQ3: What are the optimal hyper-parameters for our proposed method?
- RQ4: Could the DAUET approach outperform the current SOTA methods?

The following sections will describe our experimental results and evaluation.

4.1 Implementation Details

Datasets and Evaluation Metrics. Our experiments are conducted on two well-known person re-ID benchmarks: (1)*Market-1501* [21]: There are 1501 identities with 32,668 images from 6 different cameras. (2.)*DukeMTMC-reID* [12]: There are 1,812 identities with 36,411 images from 8 different cameras. Hereafter, in this work, we use the term "Market" to denote "Market-1501" and "Duke" to denote "DukeMTMC-reID". We set up two adaptation tasks based on Market-to-Duke and Duke-to-Market benchmarks. Following previous works [3,8,18], the evaluation of our approach is measured using mean average precision (mAP) and CMC Rank-1/5/10 (R1/R5/R10) accuracy metrics.

GAN Training Setting. We use the StarGAN [4] architecture with 256×128 resized images as input, Adam optimizer with β_1 is 0.5 and β_2 is 0.999, the batch size of 16, and the learning rate of 3.5×10^{-5}. After GAN training, every source domain image is transformed into C camera target styles. In the "Market-to-Duke" case, for each image in Market, we generate 8 virtual images corresponding to 8 cameras in Duke, and conversely, for each image in Duke, we create 6 new images corresponding to 6 cameras in Market.

Person Re-ID Model Training Setting. For data augmentation, cropping and flipping are used randomly. Each mini-batch particularly is sampled with 16 identities and 8 images randomly, with a batch size of 128. We use triplet loss with a margin value of 0.3, the learning rate of 3.5×10^{-4} in Adam optimizer. The total epoch is 80, and the learning rate is multiplied by 0.1 at the 40th and 70th epochs. The architecture of DNet consists of two full connection layers and an inter-batch normalization layer. Finally, the value of λ in Eq. 5 is set to 0.05, similar to the original paper. For stage II, we train the model in 26 epochs with 400 iters per epoch and use DBSCAN with an epsilon coefficient of 0.6. Random cropping, flipping, and erasing [22] are used for the data augmentation. All our experiments deploy on the server includes one NVIDIA Tesla T4 (16 GB) GPU, 2 x Xeon-Platinum 8160, and 256 GB RAM.

Table 1. Baseline model performance.

Method	Duke → Market				Market → Duke			
	mAP	R1	R5	R10	mAP	R1	R5	R10
Base	26.2	55.3	67.8	75.2	25.8	43.7	57.9	66.2
+GAN	36.2	66.4	81.1	86.1	34.3	57.6	70.3	76.0
+DIM	30.1	60.4	75.1	80.8	28.8	51.1	66.0	71.2
Our base	36.4	68.9	83.2	87.9	35.4	58.2	72.4	77.5

4.2 Ablation Study and Analysis

Analysis of Training Baseline. For question RQ1, we first discuss the effectiveness of our proposal in stage I. Table 1 shows that when we use the supervised baseline models (*Base.*), which are trained by the labeled domain. To test on another domain directly, the performance of these models only reaches 26.2%, 55.3%, 25.8%, and 43.7% on mAP and Rank-1 in the case Duke-to-Market and Market-to-Duke respectively. The table also illustrates the efficacy of the strategy proposed in Sect. 3.2. Specifically, training with the style-transferred dataset improves the baselines by about 10–13% performance while the DIM method also improved it from 26.2%, 55.3% to 30.1% and 60.4% on mAP and rank-1, respectively, in the Duke-to-Market case. Finally, we achieve the best results in

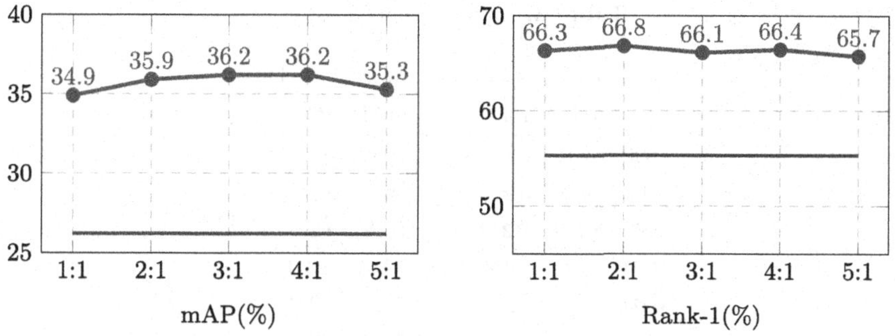

Fig. 5. Evaluation of Market-1501 training mini-batch with different ratio of $N : M$. The blue line shows the baseline while the red line is Baseline+GAN. (Color figure online)

all cases by combining both methods in training models. Our method surpasses them significantly compared to [15,16] in Table 4 with the same target.

Effectiveness of the ratio N:M. The ratio N:M is an essential parameter in training a solid baseline, where N and M denote the ratio between real and fake training samples in a mini-batch. The experimental results are presented in Fig. 5 in varying ratios. Clearly, the best performance is achieved when $N : M = 4 : 1$.

Table 2. Impact Analysis of α.

α	Duke → Market		Market → Duke	
	mAP	R1	mAP	R1
0.0	79.9	90.8	69.8	82.0
0.5	81.5	92.2	69.8	82.0
0.4	82.0	92.4	70.0	81.4
0.3	**82.9**	**92.7**	**70.8**	**83.0**
0.2	81.9	92.1	70.1	81.8
0.1	81.4	92.1	70.0	82.1

Analysis of Coefficient α. We analyze the impact of the coefficient α in Eq. 6 by fixing $\sigma = 0$ and tuning α from 0.1 to 0.5. The results on the two benchmarks in Table 2 show that the model attains the best performance when α is 0.3.

Analysis of Coefficient σ. Through the training model with $\sigma = 0$, we observe that the values of Silhouette scores of samples increase throughout all epochs. We determine the optimal threshold σ by varying in $[0, 0.05]$ with a step of 0.01. The results in Table 3 suggest that the best performance on the Market-to-Duke benchmark is achieved with $\sigma = 0.03$, while the highest performance on

Table 3. Impact Analysis of σ.

σ	Duke → Market		Market → Duke	
	mAP	R1	mAP	R1
0.00	82.9	92.7	70.8	83.0
0.01	82.9	92.8	70.6	82.2
0.02	**82.9**	**92.9**	70.8	82.3
0.03	82.6	92.9	**71.3**	**83.1**
0.04	82.5	92.5	71.2	82.7
0.05	82.7	92.6	70.8	82.6

the Duke-to-Market case is obtained with $\sigma = 0.02$. In addition, we also inspect that if σ is too high, larger than 0.05, some clusters' samples are eliminated when calculating new centroids using Eq. 7, leading to a training crash. Consequently, prior analyses allow answering questions RQ2 and RQ3.

Table 4. Comparison with SOTA methods.

Method	Venue	Duke → Market				Market → Duke			
		mAP	R1	R5	R10	*mAP*	R1	R5	R10
PGPPM [16]	IEEE.TMM22	33.9	63.9	81.1	86.4	17.9	36.3	54.0	61.6
CDCSA [15]	ACM.MM22	34.0	66.8	82.1	87.9	31.4	53.8	67.8	72.2
MMT [6]	ICLR20	71.2	87.7	94.9	96.9	65.1	78.0	88.8	92.5
MEB-Net [17]	ECCV20	76.0	89.9	96.0	97.5	66.1	79.6	88.3	92.2
UNRN [19]	AAAI21	78.1	91.9	96.1	97.8	69.1	82.0	90.7	93.5
GLT [20]	CVPR21	79.5	92.2	96.5	97.8	69.2	82.0	90.2	92.8
RDSBN+MDIF [1]	CVPR21	81.5	92.9	**97.6**	98.4	66.6	80.3	89.1	92.6
SECRET [7]	AAAI22	**83.0**	93.3	–	–	69.2	82.0	–	–
CMFC [15]	ACM.MM22	81.0	**94.0**	97.1	98.3	71.2	**83.2**	**91.6**	94.0
DAUET		82.9	92.9	97.5	**98.6**	**71.3**	83.1	91.5	**94.1**

4.3 Comparison with SOTA Methods

To answer question RQ4, we compare DAUET with recent UDA person re-ID methods in Table 4. Experimental results indicate that DAUET surpasses SOTA methods, achieving 82.9% mAP and 92.9% Rank-1 accuracy on Duke-to-Market, 71.3% mAP, and 83.1% Rank-1 on Market-to-Duke. Compared to current UDA methods such as UNRN [19], GLT [20], and RDSBN+MDIF [1], DAUET achieves higher mAP by 1–2% in both cases. When compared to CMFC [15], which uses StarGAN, DAUET outperforms it by 1.9% and 0.1% on mAP in both scenarios. DAUET also outperforms SECRET [7] by 2.1% and 1.1% on mAP and Rank-1 in Market-to-Duke. Therefore, with its efficient performance on limited hardware, DAUET shows potential for real-world applications.

5 Conclusions

This work identifies two primary challenges in UDA person re-ID: (i) domain-intensive training models and (ii) pseudo-labels supplied by the clustering process. Thus, we propose the DAUET method to address these challenges. We first use StarGAN to bridge the distribution of two data domains brought on by environmental factors. Secondly, we use the fake dataset with supervised learning to build a robust pre-trained model. Lastly, we suggest using the mean instructor architecture and method to improve one-hot labels to enhance UDA task performance. Our experiments on Market-1501 and DukeMTMC-reID datasets prove that the DAUET method outperforms SOTA methods in the UDA person re-ID.

There are still various ways to improve the DAUET method. Indeed, the current GAN method needs to be optimized due to leading to many low-quality samples. Additionally, the pseudo-label refining method assumes that the proportion of inaccurate labels in the pseudo-label collection is relatively low. Thus such a pseudo-label refining method would lose effectiveness if the clustering findings were highly subpar. Therefore, in the near future, we will concentrate on improving and optimizing the DAUET method for perspective works.

References

1. Bai, Z., Wang, Z., Wang, J., Hu, D., Ding, E.: Unsupervised multi-source domain adaptation for person re-identification. In: 2021 IEEE/CVF Conference on Computer Vision and Pattern Recognition (CVPR), pp. 12909–12918 (2021). https://doi.org/10.1109/CVPR46437.2021.01272
2. Chen, H., Wang, Y., Lagadec, B., Dantcheva, A., Bremond, F.: Learning invariance from generated variance for unsupervised person re-identification. IEEE Trans. Pattern Anal. Mach. Intell. 1–15 (2022). https://doi.org/10.1109/TPAMI.2022.3226866
3. Cho, Y., Kim, W.J., Hong, S., Yoon, S.E.: Part-based pseudo label refinement for unsupervised person re-identification. In: 2022 IEEE/CVF Conference on Computer Vision and Pattern Recognition (CVPR), pp. 7298–7308 (2022). https://doi.org/10.1109/CVPR52688.2022.00716
4. Choi, Y., Choi, M., Kim, M., Ha, J.W., Kim, S., Choo, J.: StarGAN: unified generative adversarial networks for multi-domain image-to-image translation. In: 2018 IEEE/CVF Conference on Computer Vision and Pattern Recognition, pp. 8789–8797 (2018). https://doi.org/10.1109/CVPR.2018.00916
5. Deng, D.: DBSCAN clustering algorithm based on density. In: 2020 7th International Forum on Electrical Engineering and Automation (IFEEA), pp. 949–953 (2020). https://doi.org/10.1109/IFEEA51475.2020.00199
6. Ge, Y., Chen, D., Li, H.: Mutual mean-teaching: pseudo label refinery for unsupervised domain adaptation on person re-identification. In: International Conference on Learning Representations (2020). https://openreview.net/forum?id=rJlnOhVYPS
7. He, T., Shen, L., Guo, Y., Ding, G., Guo, Z.: Secret: Self-consistent pseudo label refinement for unsupervised domain adaptive person re-identification, vol. 36, pp. 879–887, June 2022. https://doi.org/10.1609/aaai.v36i1.19970

8. Le, H.V., Nguyen, T.N., Nguyen, H.N., Le, L.: An efficient hybrid webshell detection method for webserver of marine transportation systems. IEEE Trans. Intell. Transp. Syst. **24**(2), 2630–2642 (2023). https://doi.org/10.1109/TITS.2021.3122979
9. Liu, X., Zhang, S.: Domain adaptive person re-identification via coupling optimization. In: Proceedings of the 28th ACM International Conference on Multimedia, pp. 547–555. MM '20, ACM (2020). https://doi.org/10.1145/3394171.3413904
10. Miao, Y., Deng, J., Ding, G., Han, J.: Confidence-guided centroids for unsupervised person re-identification (2022). https://doi.org/10.48550/ARXIV.2211.11921
11. Nguyen, A.D., Nguyen, D.T., Du, H.P., Dao, H.N., Nguyen, H.N.: EnsFace: an ensemble method of deep convolutional neural networks with novel effective loss functions for face recognition. In: The 11th International Symposium on Information and Communication Technology, pp. 231–238. SoICT 2022, ACM (2022). https://doi.org/10.1145/3568562.3568638
12. Ristani, E., Solera, F., Zou, R., Cucchiara, R., Tomasi, C.: Performance measures and a data set for multi-target, multi-camera tracking. In: Hua, G., Jégou, H. (eds.) ECCV 2016. LNCS, vol. 9914, pp. 17–35. Springer, Cham (2016). https://doi.org/10.1007/978-3-319-48881-3_2
13. Shahapure, K.R., Nicholas, C.: Cluster quality analysis using silhouette score. In: 2020 IEEE 7th International Conference on Data Science and Advanced Analytics (DSAA), pp. 747–748 (2020). https://doi.org/10.1109/DSAA49011.2020.00096
14. Tarvainen, A., Valpola, H.: Mean teachers are better role models: weight-averaged consistency targets improve semi-supervised deep learning results. In: Proceedings of the 31st International Conference on Neural Information Processing Systems, pp. 1195–1204 (2017). https://doi.org/10.5555/3294771.3294885
15. Tu, Y.: Domain camera adaptation and collaborative multiple feature clustering for unsupervised person re-id. In: Proceedings of the 3rd International Workshop on Human-Centric Multimedia Analysis, pp. 51–59. ACM (2022). https://doi.org/10.1145/3552458.3556446
16. Yang, F., Zhong, Z., Luo, Z., Lian, S., Li, S.: Leveraging virtual and real person for unsupervised person re-identification. IEEE Trans. Multimed. **22**(9), 2444–2453 (2020). https://doi.org/10.1109/TMM.2019.2957928
17. Zhai, Y., Ye, Q., Lu, S., Jia, M., Ji, R., Tian, Y.: Multiple expert brainstorming for domain adaptive person re-identification. In: Vedaldi, A., Bischof, H., Brox, T., Frahm, J.-M. (eds.) ECCV 2020. LNCS, vol. 12352, pp. 594–611. Springer, Cham (2020). https://doi.org/10.1007/978-3-030-58571-6_35
18. Zhang, X., et al.: Implicit sample extension for unsupervised person re-identification. In: 2022 IEEE/CVF Conference on Computer Vision and Pattern Recognition (CVPR), pp. 7359–7368, June 2022. https://doi.org/10.1109/CVPR52688.2022.00722
19. Zheng, K., Lan, C., Zeng, W., Zhang, Z., Zha, Z.J.: Exploiting sample uncertainty for domain adaptive person re-identification, vol. 35, pp. 3538–3546, May 2021. https://doi.org/10.1609/aaai.v35i4.16468
20. Zheng, K., Liu, W., He, L., Mei, T., Luo, J., Zha, Z.J.: Group-aware label transfer for domain adaptive person re-identification. In: 2021 IEEE/CVF Conference on Computer Vision and Pattern Recognition (CVPR), pp. 5306–5315 (2021). https://doi.org/10.1109/CVPR46437.2021.00527

21. Zheng, L., Shen, L., Tian, L., Wang, S., Wang, J., Tian, Q.: Scalable person re-identification: a benchmark. In: 2015 IEEE International Conference on Computer Vision (ICCV), pp. 1116–1124 (2015). https://doi.org/10.1109/ICCV.2015.133
22. Zhong, Z., Zheng, L., Kang, G., Li, S., Yang, Y.: Random erasing data augmentation. In: Proceedings of the AAAI Conference on Artificial Intelligence, vol. 34, no. 07, pp. 13001–13008 (2020). https://doi.org/10.1609/aaai.v34i07.7000

Intelligent Automated Pancreas Segmentation Using U-Net Model Variants

Wilson Bakasa and Serestina Viriri(✉)

School of Mathematics, Statistics and Computer Science,
University of KwaZulu-Natal, Durban, South Africa
219098448@stu.ukzn.ac.za, viriris@ukzn.ac.za

Abstract. Various algorithms and models can be generated for any given machine-learning problem. Many options are beneficial, but deciding which model to implement in segmentation is critical. Even though we have a variety of performance metrics to evaluate a model, it is not prudent to implement every algorithm for every problem. This will take significant time and effort to decide the best model for the task. As a result, knowing how to choose the best algorithm for a given task is critical. Three models will be trained for the pancreas CT image segmentation task: U-Net, Attention U-Net, and Residual Attention U-Net. The authors examine the factors that can aid in selecting a model that best suits any segmentation task and with specific requirements in this article. We'll do this by considering several factors that can help us narrow our choices. A Model Analyser (MA) and an Intelligent Automation Model implement these factors in the Inference Engine. Understanding these factors will assist the MA in understanding the task that each model can perform, depending on the complexity of a problem, memory requirements, training time, number of features and parameters, training data size, and accuracy or interpretability. Many factors influence which algorithm is used, from the type of problem at hand to the expected output. This guide provides several considerations when determining the best U-Net model for a new dataset. Accuracy and mean IoU are the performance metrics used to evaluate segmentation models.

Keywords: Pancreas · Segmentation · U-Net · Attention U-Net · Residual Attention U-Net · Intelligent Automation Model

1 Introduction

Image segmentation [1] is a computer vision task that divides an image into multiple areas by labelling each pixel. It provides significantly more information about an image than object detection, which draws a bounding box around the detected object, or image classification, which labels the object. Segmentation is useful in real-world applications such as medical imaging segmentation. Image segmentation is classified into two types [2]:

N. T. Nguyen et al. (Eds.): ICCCI 2023, LNAI 14162, pp. 606–618, 2023.
https://doi.org/10.1007/978-3-031-41456-5_46

1. Semantic segmentation: classify each pixel with a label.
2. Instance segmentation: classify each pixel and differentiate each object instance.

U-Net [3] is a semantic segmentation technique developed initially for medical imaging segmentation. It was one of the first deep-learning segmentation models. The U-Net architecture was later modelled into other variants, such as Attention U-Net [4] and Residual Attention U-Net [5].

2 Related Work

Statistical shape models [6], or multi-atlas techniques [7,8] were used in early work on pancreas segmentation from abdominal CT. Atlas approaches, in particular, benefit from implicit shape constraints enforced by manual annotation propagation. Dice similarity coefficients (DSC) for atlas-based frameworks range from 69.6% to 73.9% in public benchmarks such as the TCIA dataset [9]. In [10], a classification-based framework is proposed to alleviate the atlas' reliance on image registration.

Importantly, previous applications of Attention U-Net have only been in medical settings, such as brain tumour segmentation [11], liver CT scan segmentation [12], and gland segmentation [13]. Previously, U-Net was used to successfully segment deforestation in the Amazon Rainforest using Sentinel-2 satellite imagery [14], and this paper aims to investigate the incorporation of an attention mechanism into U-Net to improve upon U-Net.

Several methods for segmenting surgical instruments have recently been proposed. Ozturk et al. [15] presented a network based on Fully Convolutional Networks (FCN) and optic flow to solve surgical instrument occlusion and deformation problems. RASNet [4] used an attention module to draw attention to the target region and improve feature representation. Olivier et al. [16] proposed a novel U-shape network for instrument segmentation and pose estimation simultaneously. Arunkumar et al. [17] used a method that combined the recurrent and convolutional networks to improve segmentation accuracy.

3 Variants of U-Net Model

The variants of the U-Net model that were experimented on in this paper are U-Net, Attention U-Net and Residual Attention U-Net.

3.1 U-Net Model for Image Segmentation:

Although some interesting non-learning algorithms, such as the Otsu method or the Watershed algorithm, have been used for image segmentation, most of today's real-world segmentation problems are solved by training encoder-decoder convolutional neural networks [CNNs]. U-Net is one of the most well-known network architectures. U-net is made up of two parts [18]:

1. encoder - converts an image into an abstract representation of image features by employing a series of convolutional blocks that gradually decrease the height and width of the representation while increasing the number of channels corresponding to image features.
2. decoder decodes an image representation into a binary mask by applying a series of up-convolutions that gradually increase the representation's height and width to the original image's size and decrease the number of channels to the number of classes we are segmenting.

In addition, U-Net implements skip connections that connect corresponding encoder and decoder levels. They allow the model to avoid "losing" features extracted by earlier encoder blocks, which improves segmentation performance [19]. U-Net extends the standard FCN architecture by introducing skip connections, which allow blocks of layers in the contraction phase to send their output directly to blocks in the expansion phase, greatly improving the ability to extract high-level features from images.

3.2 Attention U-Net Model for Image Segmentation

Attention The U-Net architecture [13] is the foundation for U-Net, a fully convolutional network (FCN), a family of neural networks distinguished by an encoder-decoder. These are intended for semantic segmentation, also referred to as pixel-wise classification. The goal of an attention mechanism is to mimic the human ability to direct focus or concentrate on specific stimuli. This is done in the domain of neural networks by learning which parts of the input to focus attention on.

Attention U-Net is created by adding an attention gate to the U-Net skip connection. Rather than concatenating each up-scaled layer in the expansion phase with the corresponding contraction-phase layer, the up-scaled layer is concatenated with the attention mechanism output, which is a function of the pre-up-scaled layer and the aforementioned contraction-phase layer [20].

3.3 Residual Attention U-Net Model for Image Segmentation

The Residual Attention U-Net (RAUNet) employs an encoder-decoder architecture to obtain high-resolution masks. To extract semantic features, the encoder is ResNet34 [5] pre-trained on ImageNet. It contributes to model reduction and faster inference. A new augmented attention module (AAM) is designed in the decoder to fuse multi-level features and capture global context. Furthermore, transposed convolution is used to perform up-sampling to obtain refined edges.

4 Methods and Techniques

To do experiments, the TCIA dataset was used. It was randomly divided into Dataset A and Dataset B. Dataset A was used to train the models, and then Dataset B was used as new data to test for model selection.

4.1 Model Selection Factors

To come up with the decision to select the right model to use for the segmentation of every new data, the MA will look at the following factors:

Number of Features and Parameters: Longer training usually results in better, more accurate model performance. If there is time to let the model train longer, more features and parameters can be specified to interpret [21].

Memory Requirements: Many models can be applied if the entire dataset can be loaded into the computer's RAM. If this is not possible, incremental learning models can be used. Incremental learning is a machine learning method in which input data is continuously used to extend the knowledge of an existing model, designed to adapt to new data without forgetting previous knowledge, eliminating the need to retrain the model [22].

Training Time: The time it takes an algorithm to learn and create a model is called training time. It is, therefore, critical to consider the time required to train the model. It is chosen if a pre-trained model can reduce training time. The long time it takes to train a neural network model is well-known. Some models require different training times depending on the number of CPU cores used [23].

Prediction Time: Prediction time is the time it takes the model to make predictions. Even if an algorithm produces good results, it is useless if it is slow at making predictions. However, It is worth noting that accuracy is more important than prediction time for medical imaging. This is true in situations like cancerous cell segmentation [24].

The Number of Data Points and Features: Algorithms such as neural networks perform well with large amounts of data and many features. However, some models only support a limited number of features. The size of the data and the number of features should be considered when choosing a model [17].

Data Format: Data is frequently derived from a combination of open-source and custom data resources, and as a result, it can be in various formats. Categorical and numerical data formats are the most common. Any given dataset may contain only categorical, numerical, or both data. As a result, a model should be chosen because it was trained using the same data input format [25].

Size of the Training Data: Collecting a large amount of data is usually recommended to obtain reliable results. However, data availability is frequently a constraint. So, if the training data is smaller or the dataset has fewer observations but a greater number of features, a model capable of segmenting such pancreas images must be chosen. If the training data is large enough and the number of observations exceeds the number of features, a matching model must be chosen for the task [17].

Accuracy And/or Interpretability of the Output: A model's accuracy predicts a response value for a given observation close to its true response value. A highly interpretable model means that any individual predictor can be easily associated with the response, whereas flexible models provide higher accuracy at the expense of low interpretability [26].

4.2 Proposed Model

The authors propose an Intelligent Automated segmentation model, Fig. 1, for the pancreas using the variants of the U-Net model, that is, U-Net, Attention U-Net, and the Residual Attention U-Net models. Each model is trained on the same data to determine the best results. The training information is sent to the Model Analyser (MA) [27] for storage to be used as a reference for model selection when a new dataset is made available. The process of decision-making for the model to use when a segmentation task is presented is done in the Inference Engine, which consists of two parts, the MA and the Intelligent Automation Model (IAM).

Inference Engine: An inference engine interprets and evaluates the facts in the MA to provide the best model for the new dataset. Deep learning model experts will be interviewed and observed to gather facts for an MA. This knowledge is then represented as "if-then" rules known as production rules: "If a condition is met, the following inference can be made, or a model selection action can be taken, or data is sent for training a model [28]." In this paper, the inference engine is divided into two parts, the MA, which represents the knowledge base and the IAM, for decision-making and data interpretation.

Model Analyser (MA): A unified interactive framework for investigating segmentation models and applications. It analyses and evaluates a model's behaviour and limitations and its robustness to changes in the dataset. It seeks to improve segmentation accuracy by matching model behaviour to dataset properties and investigating the factors considered when manually selecting a model when we have new pancreas images to segment. When working with segmentation models in deep learning, exploring and analysing alternative possibilities to a model's decision is necessary. During this exploration and analysis, data scientists will ask questions like the ones below [27,29]:

- Which model is best for the dataset given different requirements?;
- How will the model behave if the features of the selected data point are changed and data size changes?;
- Did the model performs well, producing accurate results by considering metrics like IOU and dice coefficient?;

The above questions are asked to determine the robustness of a segmentation model. The MA enables data scientists to answer those questions by automatically selecting models based on the new data segmentation constraints and the capabilities of each model. Each model's performance benchmark on different data constraints is saved for future reference.

Intelligent Automation Model (IAM): Automation is now a well-known technical concept in segmentation, with many organisations automating manual, repeatable tasks to improve efficiency. The intelligent aspect is introduced by emerging technologies such as artificial intelligence and deep learning, which can carry out human actions and act independently by making decisions or interpreting data without direct human intervention. So, Intelligent Automation is the combination of smart technologies and automated processes to improve segmentation process automation [30].

The IAM is presented with new pancreas images to segment, and it has to decide which model, from the trained U-Net variants models, to use to segment the images and update the MA. This decision-making process is done using information from the MA. The MA provides the knowledge base with information on each model and the segmentation constraints used to train the models. If no model is suitable to segment the new pancreas images, then new training is done using the new dataset, and the MA is updated.

A model selected to do the segmentation task is executed. For it to be successful, it must satisfy the condition that its IoU and accuracy are greater than or equal to that of the previous task the model was trained on. If it is less, the IAM is informed to update the MA. If the IAM decides that no model is suitable for the segmentation task, the New dataset is sent to be used for training the models, and all components must be updated on the results.

Proposed Segmentation Intelligent Automated System (IAS): We proposed an IAS for medical imaging focusing on CT pancreas images for the following reasons:

1. **Increased process efficiency -** speed up segmentation processes while ensuring they are completed to a high standard;
2. **Technology Integration -** rather than executing complete individual segmentation tasks in isolation, integrate them with other technologies to achieve intelligent automation;
3. **Release boredom with repetitive tasks -** To be confident that routine segmentation tasks are being carried out fully, effectively, and error-free with intelligent technologies helping to make informed decisions;
4. **Interpret Big Data -** intelligent automation can handle and interpret large amounts of data that would take humans a long time to manage;
5. **Reduced costs -** Tasks are segmented using best-selected models rather than doing trial and error, wasting resources.

Image pre-processing of the pancreas CT images is done, and the U-Net variants models are trained. Validation and testing are done to have the IoU

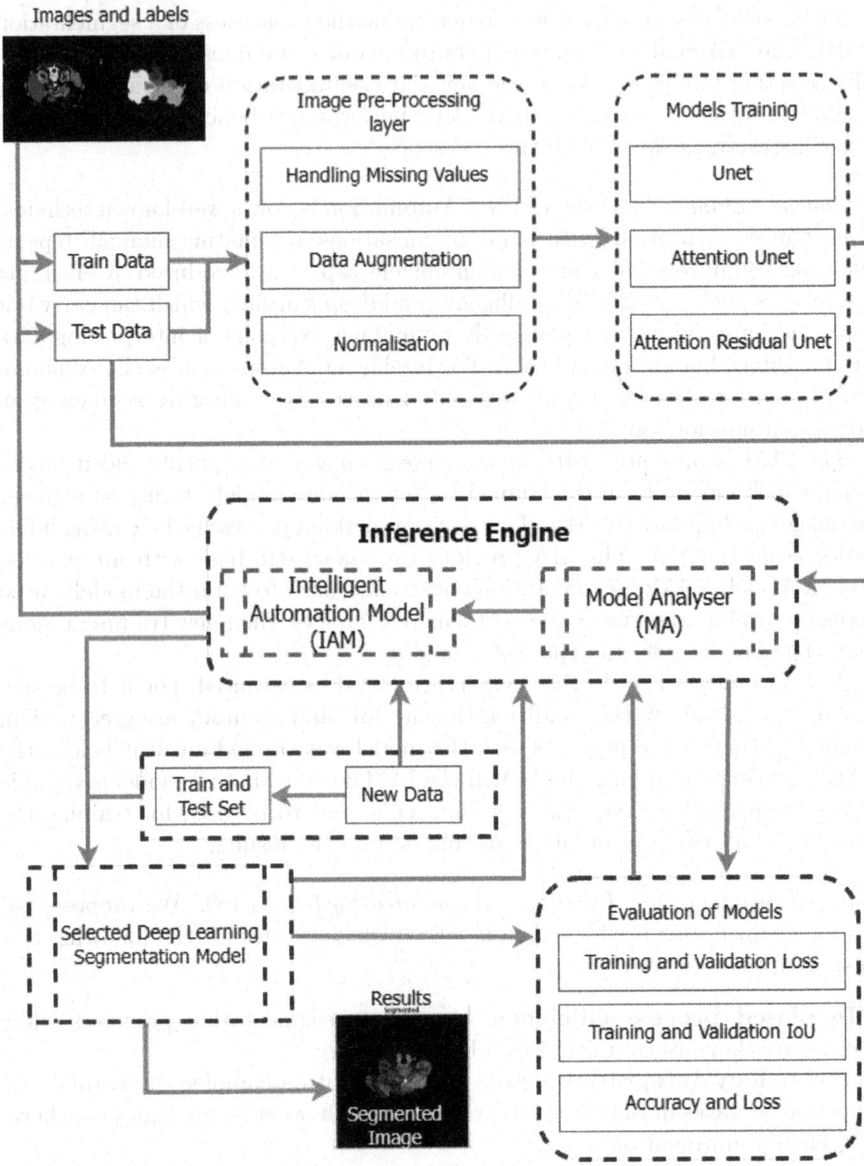

Fig. 1. Proposed Segmentation Intelligent Automated System Architecture

and accuracy. If below a threshold image, pre-processing and retraining are done again in case the images are not well prepared, as it also affects the results. Retraining is necessary in case the model has not learned enough. Training is also done if no model can do the segmentation task given the new dataset. If

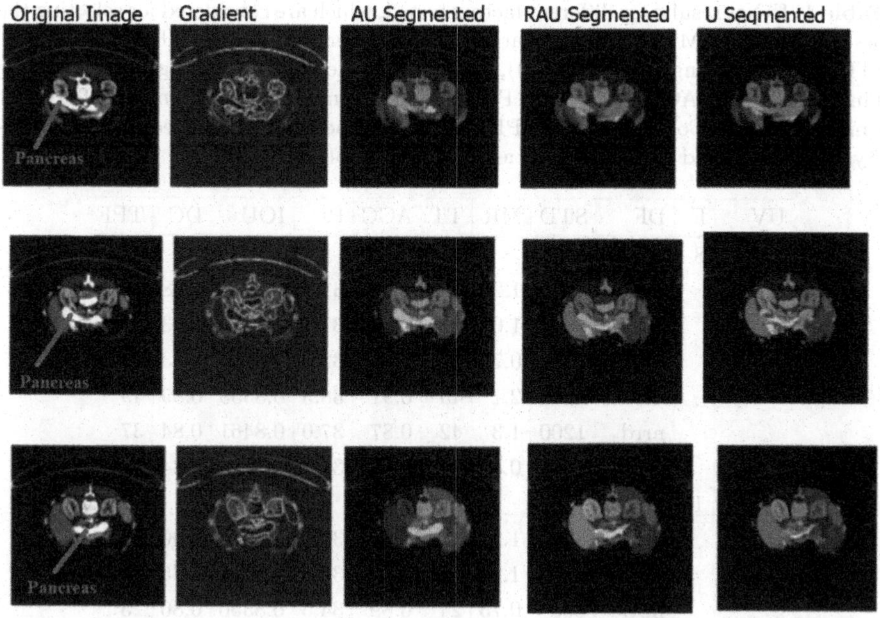

Fig. 2. An illustration of a sample of original images randomly selected from the dataset and segmented using Attention U-Net, Residual Attention U-Net, and the U-Net. The Gradient images show colour intensity changes.

a model is selected to segment the new dataset, the inference engine must be updated on the evaluation matrices and model configurations.

Model Selection. Models are trained, and the MA is updated on the performance of each model given different data constraints provided in the data description or according to the model's analysis. For the Inference Engine to select the model to use on new data, it will follow the following steps:

1. Train and test data is input for image pre-processing;
2. All three models are trained using the same train and test pre-processed images;
3. The results from the training are stored in the MA, which makes a summary of all the parameters;
4. When new data is available, the IAM analyse the data description and retrieves the performance metrics summary from the MA and analyse if the new data has the same requirements;
   - if parameters match to a threshold of 75% and above, the model which produced the best segmentation results is selected to work on the new data
   - If parameters match a threshold of less than 75%, then the data goes for pre-processing and training as completely new data.

Table 1. U-Net results for different factors tested, which are considered for selecting the best model by the MA. UV(U-net Variants), F(number of Features), DF(Data Format), STD(Size of Training Data - images)), MR(Memory Requirements - Gigs), TT(Training Time - seconds), ACC(Accuracy), P(Parameters - millions), IOU(Intersection Over Union), DC(Dice Coefficient, and TPE(Time Per Epoch - seconds). Requires less memory for training and takes less time as compared to other variants.

UV	F	DF	STD	MR	TT	ACC	P	IOU	DC	TPF
U-Net	8									
		dicom	800	1.2	33	0.89	31.4	0.8421	0.88	26
		nrrd	800	1.0	29	0.97	31.1	0.8033	0.83	26
		nifti	800	0.75	19	0.89	32.0	0.8350	0.83	18
		dicom	1200	2.1	45	0.91	38.3	0.8555	0.89	49
		nrrd	1200	1.3	42	0.87	37.0	0.8461	0.84	37
		nifti	1200	0.87	26	0.87	38.2	0.8489	0.84	25
	12									
		dicom	800	1.24	33	0.90	33.3	0.8622	0.90	33
		nrrd	800	1.2	35	0.88	33	0.8231	0.85	34
		nifti	800	0.75	24	0.89	34.5	0.8350	0.86	23
		dicom	1200	2.2	50	0.90	38.3	0.8232	0.90	50
		nrrd	1200	1.25	42	0.89	37.8	0.8461	0.87	42
		nifti	1200	0.89	24	0.90	36.6	0.8589	0.87	32
	16									
		dicom	800	1.4	34	0.84	40.3	0.7321	0.84	37
		nrrd	800	1.4	33	0.84	37.1	0.7432	0.81	38
		nifti	800	0.80	29	0.82	33.9	0.7733	0.84	26
		dicom	1200	2.3	52	0.87	44.3	0.7813	0.83	50
		nrrd	1200	2.0	40	0.89	48.2	0.7347	0.82	46
		nifti	1200	1.1	26	0.80	38.4	0.7588	0.88	38

5 Results and Discussion

This section will discuss some performance metrics the MA will analyse to decide which model best fits the new Data. The models were tested on two different samples set of train and test data [(A(train and test set)] and [B(train and test set)]. Figure 2 shows a sample of some images from the dataset that were segmented using the three variants of the U-Net model. Attention U-Net segmented the images better than the other variants, followed by Residual Attention U-Net. This could also be seen in Tables 1, 2 and 3, where the accuracy, IOU, and dice coefficient of Attention U-Net is always higher than that of the other variants. Results from these tables are the factors that will be stored in the MA and used to determine the best model to segment new data based on these factors. From the results of Table 1, we notice that the U-Net model requires less memory than

Table 2. Attention U-Net results for different factors tested, which are considered for selecting the best model by the MA. UV(U-net Variants), F(number of Features), DF(Data Format), STD(Size of Training Data - images)), MR(Memory Requirements - Gigs), TT(Training Time - seconds), ACC(Accuracy), P(Parameters - millions), IOU(Intersection Over Union), DC(Dice Coefficient, and TPE(Time Per Epoch - seconds). Best when the data size is large, and there are more parameters.

UV	F	DF	STD	MR	TT	ACC	P	IOU	DC	TPF
AU	8									
		dicom	800	2.1	42.3	0.96	31.6	0.8532	0.91	34
		nrrd	800	1.7	37	0.94	31.2	0.8499	0.90	32
		nifti	800	1.7	23	0.94	32.2	0.8343	0.91	23
		dicom	1200	3.2	61	0.98	38.6	0.8675	0.93	56
		nrrd	1200	2.3	48	0.97	37.3	0.8500	0.91	56
		nifti	1200	2.1	38	0.97	38.5	0.8489	0.91	31
	12									
		dicom	800	2.3	48	0.96	31.7	0.8536	0.91	36
		nrrd	800	1.7	37	0.97	31.5	0.8500	0.90	32
		nifti	800	1.9	22	0.94	32.8	0.8366	0.91	21
		dicom	1200	3.1	63	0.98	38.2	0.8657	0.94	53
		nrrd	1200	2.1	43	0.97	37.6	0.8633	0.92	53
		nifti	1200	2.4	37	0.98	38.8	0.8532	0.92	34
	16									
		dicom	800	1.4	35	0.84	32.4	0.8421	0.88	31
		nrrd	800	1.3	31	0.83	33.1	0.8033	0.83	29
		nifti	800	0.79	20	0.83	30.0	0.8350	0.83	24
		dicom	1200	2.2	49	0.90	39.3	0.8555	0.89	48
		nrrd	1200	1.4	46	0.90	37.0	0.8461	0.84	33
		nifti	1200	0.87	28	0.91	36.2	0.8489	0.85	29

other variants and has less training time. Compared to other variants, Attention U-Net Table 2 is good when the data size is large and works well with high data parameters. Residual Attention U-Net, Table 3, proves to work well with more features as indicated by increased accuracy, IOU, and dice coefficient as the number of features increases.

Table 3. Residual Attention U-Net results for different factors tested, which are considered for selecting the best model by the MA. UV(U-net Variants), F(number of Features), DF(Data Format), STD(Size of Training Data - images)), MR(Memory Requirements - Gigs), TT(Training Time - seconds), ACC(Accuracy), P(Parameters - millions), IOU(Intersection Over Union), DC(Dice Coefficient, and TPE(Time Per Epoch - seconds). Proves to be efficient with many features and can work well with all data formats.

UV	F	DF	STD	MR	TT	ACC	P	IOU	DC	TPF
RAU	8									
		dicom	800	2.1	42.3	0.93	31.6	0.8421	0.87	28
		nrrd	800	1.6	36	0.92	31.2	0.8033	0.83	28
		nifti	800	1.7	23	0.91	32.2	0.8350	0.80	20
		dicom	1200	3.2	57	0.92	38.6	0.8555	0.88	48
		nrrd	1200	1.9	48	0.91	37.3	0.8461	0.88	41
		nifti	1200	2.1	36	0.90	38.5	0.8489	0.89	27
	12									
		dicom	800	2.1	42.3	0.95	31.6	0.8531	0.87	31
		nrrd	800	1.6	36	0.93	31.2	0.8124	0.83	33
		nifti	800	1.7	23	0.91	32.2	0.8650	0.80	30
		dicom	1200	3.2	57	0.93	38.6	0.8601	0.88	37
		nrrd	1200	1.9	48	0.94	37.3	0.8441	0.88	37
		nifti	1200	2.1	36	0.92	38.5	0.8420	0.89	26
	16									
		dicom	800	3.1	43	0.96	35.6	0.8531	0.89	34
		nrrd	800	2.0	38	0.95	31.9	0.8424	0.85	40
		nifti	800	1.9	22	0.91	36.2	0.8750	0.85	31
		dicom	1200	3.1	54	0.94	37.9	0.8501	0.89	39
		nrrd	1200	2.1	50	0.94	37.3	0.8641	0.87	36
		nifti	1200	2.3	37	0.95	38.4	0.8620	0.91	29

6 Conclusion

When choosing a model for a deep learning task, performance may appear to be the most obvious metric. However, performance alone will not help you choose the best model for the job. Additional criteria include memory requirements, training and prediction time, interpretability, and data format, which the model must meet. Makes a more confident decision by incorporating a broader range of factors. When choosing the best model for new data from a few options is difficult, the MA can test them on a validation dataset. This provides metrics for the MA to compare each model and make a final decision.

References

1. Minaee, S., Boykov, Y., Porikli, F., Plaza, A., Kehtarnavaz, N., Terzopoulos, D.: Image segmentation using deep learning: a survey. IEEE Trans. Pattern Anal. Mach. Intell. **44**(7), 3523–3542 (2021)
2. Abdul Mueed Hafiz and Ghulam Mohiuddin Bhat: A survey on instance segmentation: state of the art. Int. J. Multimed. Inf. Retr. **9**(3), 171–189 (2020)
3. Le'Clerc Arrastia, J., et al.: Deeply supervised UNet for semantic segmentation to assist dermatopathological assessment of basal cell carcinoma. J. Imaging **7**(4), 71 (2021)
4. Valanarasu, J.M.J., Oza, P., Hacihaliloglu, I., Patel, V.M.: Medical transformer: gated axial-attention for medical image segmentation. In: de Bruijne, M., et al. (eds.) MICCAI 2021. LNCS, vol. 12901, pp. 36–46. Springer, Cham (2021). https://doi.org/10.1007/978-3-030-87193-2_4
5. Li, Z., Zhang, H., Li, Z., Ren, Z.: Residual-attention UNet++: a nested residual-attention u-net for medical image segmentation. Appl. Sci. **12**(14), 7149 (2022)
6. Ambellan, F., Tack, A., Ehlke, M., Zachow, S.: Automated segmentation of knee bone and cartilage combining statistical shape knowledge and convolutional neural networks: data from the osteoarthritis initiative. Med. Image Anal. **52**, 109–118 (2019)
7. Sun, L., Zhang, L., Zhang, D.: Multi-atlas based methods in brain MR image segmentation. Chin. Med. Sci. J. **34**(2), 110–119 (2019)
8. Jiong, W., Tang, X.: Brain segmentation based on multi-atlas and diffeomorphism guided 3D fully convolutional network ensembles. Pattern Recognit. **115**, 107904 (2021)
9. Suman, G., et al.: Quality gaps in public pancreas imaging datasets: implications & challenges for AI applications. Pancreatology **21**(5), 1001–1008 (2021)
10. Qadri, S.F., Shen, L., Ahmad, M., Qadri, S., Zareen, S.S., Khan, S.: OP-convNet: a patch classification-based framework for CT vertebrae segmentation. IEEE Access **9**, 158227–158240 (2021)
11. Islam, M.K., Ali, M.S., Miah, M.S., Rahman, M.M., Alam, M.S., Hossain, M.A.: Brain tumor detection in MR image using superpixels, principal component analysis and template based k-means clustering algorithm. Mach. Learn. Appl. **5**, 100044 (2021)
12. Almotairi, S., Kareem, G., Aouf, M., Almutairi, B., Salem, M.A.M.: Liver tumor segmentation in CT scans using modified SegNet. Sensors **20**(5), 1516 (2020)
13. Zhao, P., Zhang, J., Fang, W., Deng, S.: SCAU-net: spatial-channel attention U-net for gland segmentation. Front. Bioeng. Biotechnol. **8**, 670 (2020)
14. Bragagnolo, L., da Silva, R.V., Grzybowski, J.M.V.: Amazon forest cover change mapping based on semantic segmentation by u-nets. Ecol. Inform. **62**, 101279 (2021)
15. Ozturk, O., Saritürk, B., Seker, D.Z.: Comparison of fully convolutional networks (FCN) and U-Net for road segmentation from high resolution imageries. Int. J. Environ. Geoinform. **7**(3), 272–279 (2020)
16. Olivier, A., et al.: Active learning strategy and hybrid training for infarct segmentation on diffusion MRI with a u-shaped network. J. Med. Imaging **6**(4), 044001 (2019)
17. Arunkumar, N., Mohammed, M.A., Mostafa, S.A., Ibrahim, D.A., Rodrigues, J.J., De Albuquerque, V.H.C.: Fully automatic model-based segmentation and classification approach for MRI brain tumor using artificial neural networks. Concurr. Comput. Pract. Exp. **32**(1), e4962 (2020)

18. Tripathi, M.: Facial image denoising using autoencoder and UNet. Herit. Sustain. Dev. **3**(2), 89–96 (2021)
19. Wang, B., Qiu, S., He, H.: Dual encoding U-Net for retinal vessel segmentation. In: Shen, D., et al. (eds.) MICCAI 2019. LNCS, vol. 11764, pp. 84–92. Springer, Cham (2019). https://doi.org/10.1007/978-3-030-32239-7_10
20. Falk, T., et al.: U-Net: deep learning for cell counting, detection, and morphometry. Nat. Methods **16**(1), 67–70 (2019)
21. Thrane, E., Talbot, C.: An introduction to Bayesian inference in gravitational-wave astronomy: parameter estimation, model selection, and hierarchical models. Publ. Astron. Soc. Aust. **36**, 1–12 (2019)
22. Isensee, F., Jager, P.F., Kohl, S.A., Petersen, J., Maier-Hein, K.H.: Automated design of deep learning methods for biomedical image segmentation. arXiv preprint arXiv:1904.08128 (2019)
23. Hemelings, R., Elen, B., Stalmans, I., Van Keer, K., De Boever, P., Blaschko, M.B.: Artery-vein segmentation in fundus images using a fully convolutional network. Comput. Med. Imaging Graph. **76**, 101636 (2019)
24. Ullah, I., Raza, B., Malik, A.K., Imran, M., Islam, S.U., Kim, S.W.: A churn prediction model using random forest: analysis of machine learning techniques for churn prediction and factor identification in telecom sector. IEEE Access **7**, 60134–60149 (2019)
25. Caicedo, J.C., et al.: Nucleus segmentation across imaging experiments: the 2018 data science bowl. Nat. Methods **16**(12), 1247–1253 (2019)
26. Nam, S., et al.: Introduction to digital pathology and computer-aided pathology. J. Pathol. Transl. Med. **54**(2), 125–134 (2020)
27. Zakarija, I., Škopljanac-Mačina, F., Blašković, B.: Automated simulation and verification of process models discovered by process mining. Automatika: časopis za automatiku, mjerenje, elektroniku, računarstvo i komunikacije **61**(2), 312–324 (2020)
28. Shaban, W.M., Rabie, A.H., Saleh, A.I., Abo-Elsoud, M.A.: Detecting COVID-19 patients based on fuzzy inference engine and deep neural network. Appl. Soft Comput. **99**, 106906 (2021)
29. Oh, S.L., Vicnesh, J., Ciaccio, E.J., Yuvaraj, R., Acharya, U.R.: Deep convolutional neural network model for automated diagnosis of schizophrenia using EEG signals. Appl. Sci. **9**(14), 2870 (2019)
30. Khaparde, A.R., et al.: Differential evolution algorithm with hierarchical fair competition model. Intell. Autom. Soft Comput. **33**(2), 1045–1062 (2022)

Knowledge Engineering and Application for Industry 4.0

Energy and Congestion Awareness Traffic Scheduling in Hybrid Software-Defined Network with Flow Splitting

C. S. Lim, S. C. Tan(✉), A. Imanuel, J. S. L. Teh, and N. Q. Baderulhisham

Faculty of Computing and Informatics (FCI), Multimedia University, Cyberjaya, Malaysia
sctan1@mmu.edu.my

Abstract. Software-Defined Networking (SDN) has received a lot of interest in recent years because of its benefits over network controllability. Nonetheless, the deployment of SDN in legacy networks is likely to take months or years due to funding constraints. Traffic scheduling that involve flow splitting provides the flexibility for traffic flow. It is able to minimize the maximum link capacity of a network and to reduce the traffic congestion in the network. The majority of the studies focus on how to balance the flows coming out of the conventional nodes and how to partition the flows that gather at the SDN nodes so that the maximum link usage of the entire network can be reduced. Energy efficiency of a network are important to save cost and energy. During traffic scheduling, the energy consumption of a traffic flow should be considered. As a result, in hybrid SDN, we offer a heuristic approach for energy and congestion awareness traffic scheduling with flow splitting. We first define the aforementioned issue in an Integer Linear Programming (ILP) model, and then we assess the suggested ILP model and heuristic algorithm in terms of solution quality and processing time. The findings indicate that with polynomial time complexity, our suggested approach retains its overall soundness.

Keywords: Energy-awareness · congestion · hybrid Software Defined Networking

1 Introduction

SDN promotes potential qualities as the next generation communication network architecture [1, 2], although obstacles occur from SDN adoption in legacy networks. Network operators are often concerned with three key aspects of challenges: economic, organizational, and technological. The cost of converting old infrastructure to SDN-enabled equipment is high, making SDN implementation a significant financial burden for network operators. Due to financial constraints, the implementation of SDN is likely to span numerous months or years, particularly for large networks with thousands or more nodes. As a result, during the transition of SDN deployment, hybrid SDN (hSDN) is produced, in which a network comprises of both traditional and SDN-enabled nodes to act as a whole. Furthermore, network stability remains a high need in the hybrid SDN context.

N. T. Nguyen et al. (Eds.): ICCCI 2023, LNAI 14162, pp. 621–633, 2023.
https://doi.org/10.1007/978-3-031-41456-5_47

With the advent of SDN technology, dynamic routing route management for flows becomes feasible. An OpenFlow network [3], the most widely used SDN enabler, is made up of OpenFlow-enabled switches and a central controller. The controller plans routing pathways and subsequently manipulates flow tables in switches using the OpenFlow protocol. The SDN controller may centrally regulate the network state by altering the flow tables that routers maintain [4–8]. Through the use of SDN, network administrators may partition arbitrary flows to outgoing links in a flexible manner. However, SDN has its own set of deployment issues, making comprehensive SDN implementation problematic in the immediate future. Some approaches can be used to route multiple flows to the same destination to separate next hops, resulting in traffic splitting at the network layer. The deployment of SDN in the network provides a straightforward and effective approach to undertake traffic engineering and can significantly increase network performance. The majority of the work is on how to balance the flows coming out of the normal nodes and how to separate the flows that gather at the SDN nodes so that the maximum link usage of the total network may be reduced. Traffic scheduling that involve flow splitting provides the flexibility for traffic flow. It is able to minimize the maximum link capacity of a network and to reduce the traffic congestion in the network. Energy efficiency [9–12] of a network are important to save cost and energy. The energy consumption of a traffic flow should be taken into account during traffic scheduling. Therefore, in this paper, we explore energy and congestion awareness traffic scheduling in hybrid software-defined network with flow splitting. The proposed method provides complete solution to H-SDN in terms of: Traffic congestion by minimizing maximum link utilization with flow splitting and cost optimization by selecting path with low energy consumption.

The remainder of this article is organized as follows. The second portion analyses previous research, and the third section offers the energy and congestion-aware traffic scheduling in hybrid SDN problem formulation in Integer Linear Programming (ILP) model and a heuristic algorithm is provided. Section 4 evaluates and discusses the results of the proposed method with various network sizes. Section 5 brings our paper to a close.

2 Related Works

In this part, we show some recent relevant work. Firstly, [13] A1 detecting congestion on network service, obtain policy associated with the congested network service and causing bandwidth on demand in the network to mitigate the congestion. However, it does not consider congestion issue in MLU in H-SDN by proposing a routing algorithm. In [14], machine learning method is used for the optimal route selection algorithm to solve the quick dynamic routing of different business stream in SDN. It is applicable to SDN and congestion issue is not considered. In [15], Path Computation Element (PCE) is used as a central controller of the SDN network to transition a traditional network to an SDN enabled network and focusing on SDN migration. In [16], open shortest path first (OSPF) routing is used for H-SDN to determine the network topology and send tunneling instructions between 2 non-SDN portion separated by an SDN portion. It does not consider to minimize the MLU in traffic routing. Instead, it uses OSPF purely for determining the network topology in non-SDN and SDN networks. In [17], a centralized control plane device is implemented to select a candidate path for forwarding data traffic in SDN. The work in [18] providing tools to manage the hybrid network for conceptualizing the overall security and functionality requirements of a network and plan how these can be satisfied using a hybrid network parts as appropriate. The tools are to find paths in networks satisfying access-control, capacity, bandwidth and routing policy constraints by utilizing simultaneous multi-threading (SMT) solver. However, it is focusing on legacy policy enforcement of SDN instead of routing.

The work in [19] is using a hybrid routing table which is in the form of hash table for network traffic routing to strike a balance between lookup performance and memory. In [20], Path selection update processes that are optimized for a hybrid network in which many hybrid devices may be used for a certain path may be used. Path updating for load balancing may be affected by whether a packet stream is elastic or inelastic. An approach [21] that using hybrid networking devices along with advanced control algorithm to implement path selection, load balancing, stream splitting/aggregation and packet loss minimization. Link capacity and bandwidth is being considered for path selection. This approach is implemented for hybrid network. In [22], Path selection mechanisms may also entail determining end-to-end path capacity for various pathways. End-to-end route capacity may be determined in part by contention groups associated with shared media. A hybrid network device is implementing an automatic path selection system to modify the previously selected path associated with a packet stream [23]. The path must not be exceeding the medium utilization threshold and the network interface is working. This approach is able to select the best network path, maximize bandwidth and avoid packet drops.

However, many of the contributions are only applicable to SDN. The hybrid SDN also need to be take into consideration because many companies are in the migration stage to SDN. Besides that, the early work also having limitation to minimize the maximum link utilization and energy together in a network, at the same time include the flow splitting in traffic route. The summary of related work as shown in Table 1.

Table 1. Summary of Energy-aware traffic scheduling and routing

Reference	Objective & Contribution	Issue and Challenges
[13]	Detecting network service congestion, obtaining policy related with the congested network service, and creating bandwidth on demand in the network to alleviate congestion	It does not consider congestion issue in MLU in H-SDN by proposing a routing algorithm
[14]	Machine learning method is used for the optimal route selection algorithm to solve the quick dynamic routing of different business stream in SDN	It is not H-SDN and congestion issue is not considered

(continued)

Table 1. (*continued*)

Reference	Objective & Contribution	Issue and Challenges
[15]	Path Computation Element (PCE) is used as a central controller of the SDN network to transition a traditional network to a SDN enabled network	Focusing on SDN migration instead of traffic routing in H-SDN
[16]	A method of open shortest path first (OSPF) routing is used for H-SDN to determine the network topology and send tunneling instructions between 2 non-SDN portion separated by an SDN portion	It does not consider to minimize the MLU in traffic routing. Instead, it uses OSPF purely for determining the network topology in non-SDN and SDN networks
[17]	A centralized control plane device is implemented to select a candidate path for forwarding data traffic	SDN is the focus of the above approach however, H-SDN is excluded
[18]	Providing tools to manage the hybrid network for conceptualizing the overall security and functionality requirements of a network and plan how these can be satisfied using a hybrid network parts as appropriate. The tools are to find paths in networks satisfying access-control, capacity, bandwidth and routing policy constraints by utilizing simultaneous multi-threading (SMT) solver	The above approach is on SDN. However, it is focusing on legacy policy enforcement of SDN instead of routing,
[19]	Using a hybrid routing table which is in the form of hash table for network traffic routing to strike a balance between lookup performance and memory	The approaches are in legacy network instead of H-SDN
[20]	Path selection update processes that are optimized for a hybrid network in which many hybrid devices may be used for a certain path may be used. Path updates for load balancing may be affected by whether a packet stream is elastic or not	

(*continued*)

Table 1. *(continued)*

Reference	Objective & Contribution	Issue and Challenges
[21]	An approach that using hybrid networking devices along with advanced control algorithm to implement path selection, load balancing, stream splitting/aggregation and packet loss minimization. Link capacity and bandwidth is being considered for path selection. This approach is implemented for hybrid network	
[22]	The path selection method may also compute end-to-end path capacity for potential pathways. End-to-end route capacity might be determined in part by contention groups associated with shared media	
[23]	A hybrid network device is implementing an automatic path selection system to modify the previously selected path associated with a packet stream. The path must not be exceeding the medium utilization threshold and the network interface is working. This approach is able to select the best network path, maximize bandwidth and avoid packet drops	

3 Energy and Congestion Awareness Traffic Scheduling in Hybrid Software-Defined Network with Flow Splitting

Taking into account the elements and restrictions mentioned, we provide a hybrid SDN traffic scheduling method in this paper by constructing an energy and congestion awareness traffic scheduling issue in an ILP model. In addition, the developed ILP model intends to improve network performance by reducing energy consumption and congestion during SDN implementation. Several inputs are required, which are mentioned below:

3.1 Model Formulation

All math's formulation/equation: Input notation, Objective functions, constraints.

List of notations:

- E: set of all links
- R *within* V: set of objects R requested by SDN nodes

- O: set of network object (k)
- $S\{O\}$ *within* V: set of nodes store object
- P: set of all path
- $PathWithLink$ $\{P\}$ *within* E: path in term of link
- $Path\{i, j\}$ *within* P: path number
- $C\{E\} \geq 0$: The link's capacity C on the link E must be greater or equal to zero with default value
- $B\{E\} \geq 0$: Background traffic B on the link E must be greater than or equal to zero.
- $d_{\{i,k,s\}}$: Traffic demand $i \in R,\ k \in RR[i],\ S[O]$ must be greater than zero and default 0.
- $enegyfactor\{E\}$: energy factor of link E
- $totaltrafficDemand = \sum_{i,k,j} d(i, k, j)$: Total traffic demand. $i \in R,\ k \in RR[i],\ j \in s[O]$.

List of variables

- $Weight_{\{V,V\}}$: Weight of nodes two dimensional
- $L \in (0, 1)$: maximum link utilization.
- $flowInLink\{E\}$: flow in link E.
- $flowForRequest\{i, k, j, Path\}$: Source destination for the flow in path. $i \in$ R, k in RR[i], j in S{k}, Path[j, i]
- $energy = \sum_{e \in E} flowInLink\{e\}.energyFactor\{e\}$: energy for each link E.

The objective function is to minimize the maximum link utilization by energy and total Traffic demand:

$$\min \quad L + \frac{energy}{totalTrafficDemand} \tag{1}$$

Subjects to the constraints:

$$flowInLink\{e\} + b\{e\} \leq c\{e\} \leq 0 \qquad \forall e \in E \tag{2}$$

Constraint (2) Flow in link plus Background traffic on the link must be less than or equal to the link's capacity.

$$\sum_{i,k,j,p[j,i]} flowForRequest[i, k, j, p] = \sum_{j,k,l} d[j, k, l] \qquad \forall i \in R,\ \ k \in RR[i],\ \ j \in S[k] \tag{3}$$

Constraint (3) Source destination for the flow in path must be equal to total traffic demand. Traffic demand $i \in R,\ k \in RR[i],\ S[O]$ must be greater than zero and default 0.

$$flowForRequest\{i, k, j, p\} \geq 0 \qquad \forall i \in R,\ \ k \in RR[i], j \in S[k],\ \ p \in Path \tag{4}$$

Constraint (4) Source destination for the flow in path must be greater or equal to zero to ensure there is a flow in a path.

$$flowInLink\{e\} = \sum_{i,k,j,p[j,i],e2} flowForRequest\{i, k, j, p\} \quad \forall e \in E \tag{5}$$

Constraint (5) is flow in link E must be equal to source destination for the flow in path.

$$flowInLink\{e\} + b\{e\} \leq L.c\{e\} \quad \forall e \in E \tag{6}$$

Constraint (6) Summation of source destination for the flow in path Background traffic B on the link E less than equal to maximum link utilization multiply the link's capacity C on the link E.

3.2 Heuristic Algorithm

The calculation of an MLU optimized energy and congestion aware traffic scheduling in hybrid SDN with respect to restrictions was shown to be an NP-complete issue [6]. The computation of an optimum traffic scheduling in the solution space is time consuming. For big networks, brute forcing every potential combination is wasteful. As a result, taking into account the limitations described in this part, we suggest a heuristic method for the given NP-complete issue. Figure 1 depicts a flowchart/pseudo-code description of the suggested method.

```
Start
Get user input from data file
Find all possible paths for all nodes
Find the shortest path for each request
Set total energy = 0
FOR each request
    Set fit = true
    FOR each link in shortest path
        IF traffic demand > link capacity
            fit = false
            END for loop
        ENDIF
    END for loop
    IF fit = true
        FOR each link in shortest path
            energy = traffic demand * energy factor
            total energy = total energy + energy
            Link capacity = link capacity – traffic demand
        END for loop
    ELSE
        END for loop
    ENDIF
END for loop
IF fit = true AND total energy < threshold energy
    Print results
Else
    Print no results
ENDIF
```

Fig. 1. The proposed Algorithm

The proposed algorithm searching for the shortest path for each request as shown in line 3 and line 4 in the Fig. 1. If the link capacity unable to support the traffic demand on any link of the shortest path, that path will be eliminated for choosing as the route as shown in line 8 to line 12. Then, the proposed algorithm will find the total energy on each chosen route by summation of the energy in each link as line 15 to line 19. Finally, the route that fulfil the link capacity and threshold energy is selected as best route as in line 24 to line 27. The MLU is calculated according to the target node with highest traffic flow. The path chosen to assign traffic flow are path with lowest energy and the MLU of the path is less than MLU value calculated earlier. If the MLU value for a path is less than or equals to MLU value calculated earlier, split the traffic flow to another path. An assign-remove technique is being used if no path is available for the traffic flow. It will restore the related traffic assigned previously to reduce the MLU value of the current path and assign the new traffic flow. The current path will then be locked to avoid restoring. The details of flowchart of the proposed algorithm as shown in Fig. 2.

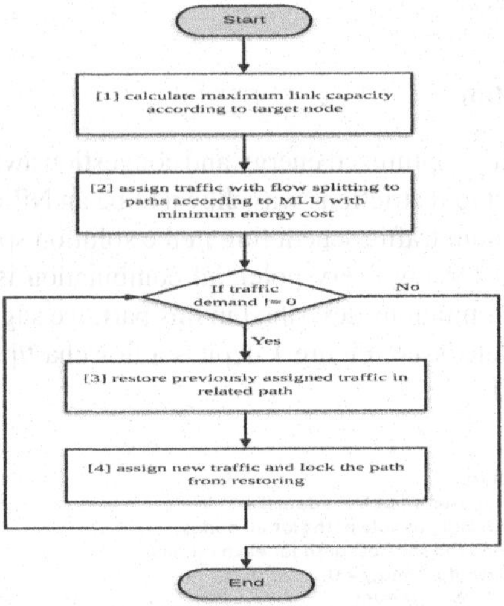

Fig. 2. The flowchart of the proposed algorithm

4 Result and Discussion

In this part, we will exhibit the simulation results and compare the performance of our suggested heuristic method to that of the ILP formulation model. Simulations are conducted on a Dell Poweredge T330 server with 16 GB RAM installed. For ILP formulation model, simulations are coded in AMPL environment with CPLEX solver and the proposed heuristic algorithm is coded in Java version 1.8. In terms of temporal complexity, our suggested technique outperforms the results of the ILP formulation model while preserving overall accuracy. To test our proposed heuristic approach, we ran tests in two different real-world topologies, a 5-node mesh topology in Fig. 3 and a 10-node mesh

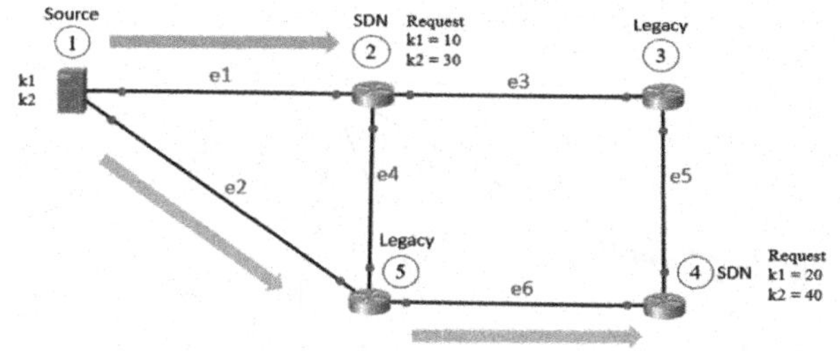

(a) Test Case 1

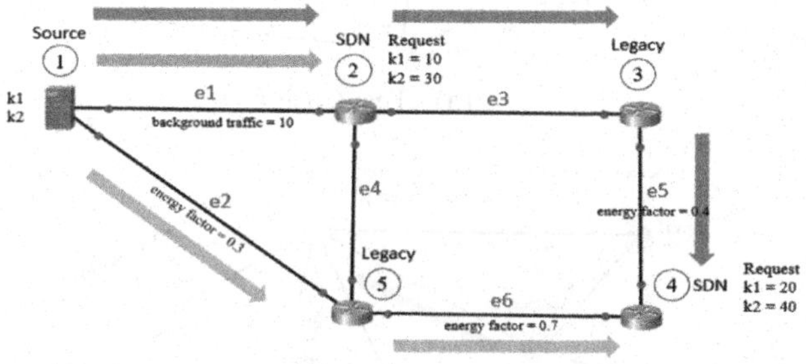

(b) Test Case 2

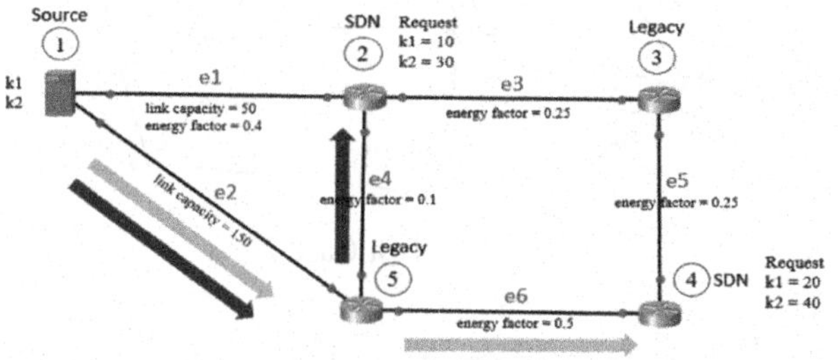

(c) Test Case 3

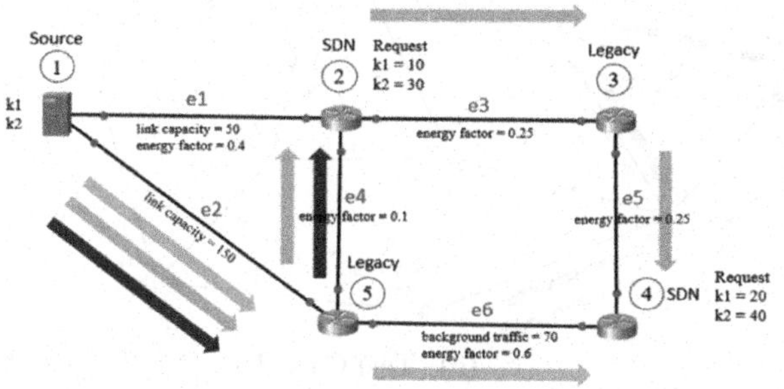

(d) Test Case 4

Fig. 3. Five-nodes Mesh Topology

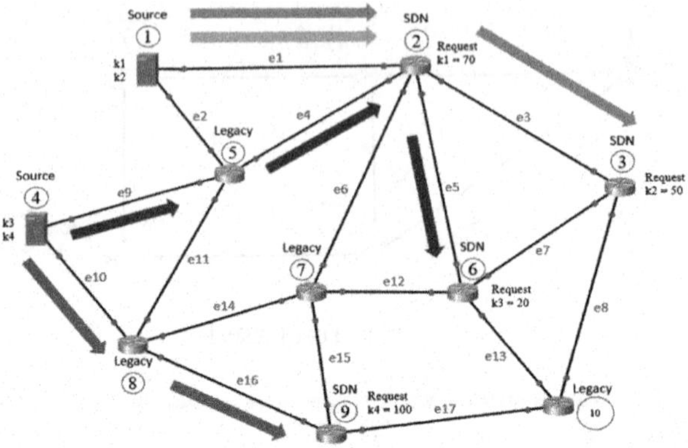

(a) Test Case 1

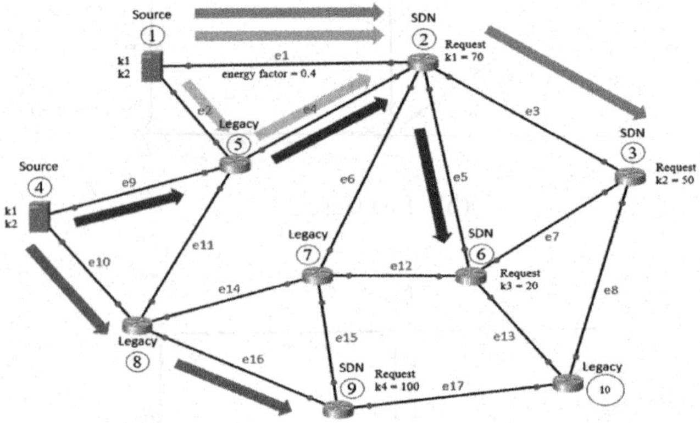

(b) Test Case 2

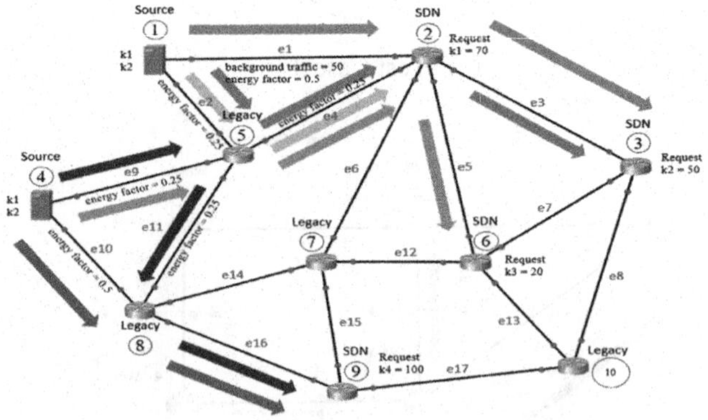

(c) Test Case 3

Fig. 4. 10-nodes Mesh Topology

topology in Fig. 4. Figures 3(a), 3(b), 3(c), and 3(d) illustrate the topology specification for each test scenario, as do Figs. 4(a), 4(b), and 4(d) (c).

To begin, we test the accuracy of our suggested algorithm by comparing its output to the ILP formulation. In Table 2, we show the minimum MLU and energy consumption varies to varies test cases 5-nodes mesh network with different traffic conditions. It is noteworthy to highlight that in the majority of circumstances; our suggested method produces the same results as the ILP formulation.

Table 2. Simulation Result of 5-Nodes Mesh Topology

	MLU		Energy		Computation Time (s)	
	AMPL	Algorithm	AMPL	Algorithm	AMPL	Algorithm
Test Case 1	0.6	0.61	32	32	0.015625	0.004724120
Test Case 2	1	1	58	58	0.015625	0.006216550
Test Case 3	0.66667	0.66667	54	54	0.0171875	0.005461840
Test Case 4	0.85	0.86	60	60	0.015625	0.005744500

In addition to soundness, our suggested Heuristic method has a major advantage over the ILP formulation in terms of time complexity. Time complexity is an important factor in computing because it influences the application of massive network computations such as an ISP network.

As illustrated in Table 2 and Table 3, we compare the average computational time over 10 simulations in 5-nodes mesh and 10-nodes mesh networks between ILP model and the proposed heuristic algorithm. We note that the suggested heuristic approach is substantially quicker than the ILP model across all test cases in both topologies. This raises the level of uncertainty in the ILP model for SDN traffic scheduling computation in big networks. The suggested heuristic approach, on the other hand, stays stable in all instances.

Table 3. Simulation Result of 10-Nodes Mesh Topology

	MLU		Energy		Computation Time (s)	
	AMPL	Algorithm	AMPL	Algorithm	Algorithm	AMPL
Test Case 1	0.6	0.61	86	86	0.0125	0.05344476
Test Case 2	0.5	0.55	110	110	0.0203125	0.05016853
Test Case 3	0.5	0.55	154	154	0.015625	0.05439731

5 Conclusion

We proposed an energy and congestion awareness traffic scheduling heuristic algorithm in hybrid SDN. In particular, our method takes into account critical parameters such as energy consumption and MLU while adopting dependable traffic scheduling in hybrid SDN. We also demonstrated the performance of our suggested heuristic algorithm vs the ILP model in terms of solution quality and processing time. With polynomial time complexity, the suggested heuristic method maintains its overall accuracy. This assures that our suggested technique is applicable in big networks such as an ISP network.

References

1. Kaljic, E., Maric, A., Njemcevic, P., Hadzialic, M.: A survey on data plane flexibility and programmability in software-defined networking. IEEE Access **7**, 47804–47840 (2019)
2. Maity, I., Misra, S., Mandal, C.: SCOPE: cost-efficient QoS-aware switch and controller placement in hybrid SDN. IEEE Syst. J. **16**(3), 4873–4880 (2022)
3. Alsaeedi, M., Mohamad, M.M., Al-Roubaiey, A.A.: Toward adaptive and scalable OpenFlow-SDN flow control: a survey. IEEE Access **7**, 107346–107379 (2019)
4. Bhardwaj, S., Girdhar, A.: Software-defined networking: a traffic engineering approach. In: 2021 IEEE 8th Uttar Pradesh Section International Conference on Electrical, Electronics and Computer Engineering (UPCON), pp. 1–5 (2021)
5. Josbert, N.N., Ping, W., Wei, M., Muthanna, M.S.A., Rafiq, A.: A framework for managing dynamic routing in industrial networks driven by software-defined networking technology. IEEE Access **9**, 74343–74359 (2021)
6. Guo, Y., Wang, Z., Yin, X., Shi, X., Wu, J.: Traffic engineering in hybrid SDN networks with multiple traffic matrices. Comput. Netw. **126**, 187–199 (2017)
7. Lin, C., Wang, K., Deng, G.: A QoS-aware routing in SDN hybrid networks. Proc. Comput. Sci. **110**, 242–249 (2017)
8. Tseng, S.H., Tang, A., Choudhury, G.L., Tse, S.: Routing stability in hybrid software-defined networks. IEEE/ACM Trans. Netw. **27**(2), 790–804 (2019)
9. Awad, M.K., Rafique, Y., M'Hallah, R.A.: Energy-aware routing for software-defined networks with discrete link rates: a benders decomposition-based heuristic approach. Sustain. Comput.: Inform. Syst. **13**, 31–41 (2017)

10. Fernandez-Fernandez, A., Cervello-Pastor, C., Ochoa-Aday, L.: Achieving energy efficiency: an energy-aware approach in SDN. In: 2016 IEEE Global Communications Conference (GLOBECOM) (2016)
11. Tao, J.: Research on SDN-based dynamic management of energy consumption of cloud data center. In: 2021 IEEE 4th Advanced Information Management, Communicates, Electronic and Automation Control Conference (IMCEC), pp. 1266–1270 (2021)
12. Naeem, F., Tariq, M., Poor, H.V.: SDN-enabled energy-efficient routing optimization framework for industrial internet of things. IEEE Trans. Industr. Inf. **17**(8), 5660–5667 (2021)
13. US 20170244606 A1: Systems and Methods for Bandwidth Management in Software Defined Networking controlled multi-layer Networks, 24 August 2017
14. CN109831386A: Optimal route selection algorithm based on machine learning under a kind of SDN, 31 May 2019
15. US 20160359735 A1: Using PCE as SDN controller, 8 Dec 2016
16. US 20170005910 A1: Open shortest path first routing for hybrid networks, 5 Jan 2017
17. US 20160218917 A1: SDN based inter-domain and intra-domain traffic engineering, 28 July 2016
18. US 20170006067 A1: Hybrid SDN/legacy policy enforcement, 5 Jan 2017
19. US 20190140951 A1: Hybrid routing table for routing network traffic, 9 May 2019
20. US 20140269260 A1: Distributed path update in hybrid networks, 18 September 2014
21. US 20130128738 A1: Hybrid networking path selection and load balancing, 23 May 2013
22. 61956164: Distributed path selection in hybrid networks, 4 December 2012
23. US 20120320919 A1: Automatic path selection for hybrid communication networks, 20 December 2012

"Is Proton Good Enough?" - A Performance Comparison Between Gaming on Windows and Linux

Marek Kopel(✉) and Michał Bożek

Faculty of Information and Communication Technology, Wroclaw University of Science and Technology, wybrzeże Wyspiańskiego 27, 50-370 Wroclaw, Poland
marek.kopel@pwr.edu.pl

Abstract. In this paper a performance comparison of Proton - a Linux-based compatibility layer - and native Windows is carried out for the purpose of video gaming. Proton, being a fork project of Wine, is a compatibility layer and just as Wine allows to run Windows software in general on Linux - Proton is specialized to run Windows native games on Linux. Recently Proton gained traction because of being the platform used in Valve gaming console Steam Deck. So the ability to play Windows games is crucial for new owners of this Linux-based console, when their whole game library so far have been played only on Windows. With this study, through a more detailed analysis, we try to answer a general question, for this purpose, "Is Proton good enough?".

Keywords: video game platform · compatibility layer · Proton · Linux · Windows

1 Introduction

Linux Gaming is on the rise with Steam Deck, the new Linux-based handheld gaming computer by Valve, released in early 2022. This means that more and more users every day are being affected by how good of a replacement a Linux-based gaming platform can be for a Windows-based gaming platform, even if most of those users are completely unaware that their device is running Linux, or even what Linux is. The solution named Proton[1] that is utilized by Steam Deck [2] has been available in early-release versions for quite some time and yet a severe lack of information regarding how well this solution holds up on different hardware platforms can be noticed while researching this subject. Since the user base of the Linux operating system is much bigger than just the subset that owns or will own a Steam Deck, a closer look into how well video games native to Windows run on Linux under Proton seems warranted, especially seeing as Proton is in the spotlight now as an integral part of the gaming experience on a device that is a complete product.

[1] https://github.com/ValveSoftware/Proton.

N. T. Nguyen et al. (Eds.): ICCCI 2023, LNAI 14162, pp. 634–646, 2023.
https://doi.org/10.1007/978-3-031-41456-5_48

2 Related Works

Since Proton is a fork project of Wine[2] in a broader sense the problem of running Windows application on Linux has been explored for a long time. In [9] author discuss possibility and performance of MS Office suite applications on Linux. The possibility of porting software to Linux from a Windows-based medical device is investigated in [8]. And from the malware point of view, security implications of running Windows software on a Linux system using Wine is covered in [3].

When talking about the performance of video games it is important to explain what difference does it make for the player. If the smoothness of the experience did not matter, it would be enough for Proton to just run the games, even with worse performance. While for some games this might be the case, in most cases the game performance can directly translate into the player performance and enjoyment. In [1] a direct link between the game's frame rate and the player's performance was found during the study conducted on players of first person shooter games. It was found that not only the player's score increases along with the frame rate displayed on the screen, but also the games were more visually appealing the higher the displayed frame rate was. Similar results can be found in [5], where participants would click the more moving targets in fixed time the higher the frame rate was. Also in [4] authors found that while frame rate did not impact the viewer rate of information assimilation, it did heavily impact the viewer subjective opinion on quality of the video and the enjoyment they got out of the video. While viewing videos is not exactly the same as playing video games, an argument can be made that whatever impact frame rate would have on viewing videos can only be magnified when it comes to video games, as it is an interactive medium. The problem of player enjoyment was also previously explored by authors as one of the aspects depending on player performance in [6,7].

The above examples show that visual performance greatly affects both main aspects of the video game experience: the performance that the player achieves in competitive games, as well as the enjoyment the player can get out of any type of game. Maybe with an exception of games with a static visual presentation, which are only a marginal part of all video games.

3 Experiment Setup

Video game performance testing is a complex subject with many different ways to go about it. In this case, since all that is required is a comparison between two systems, the following research problems have been formulated:

- What is the performance difference in running video games between Windows and Linux (Proton)?
- Is running a video game native to Windows under Proton on Linux a straightforward experience or does it require additional time and/or steps as compared to running it under Windows?

[2] https://www.winehq.org/.

- Does running video games under Proton on Linux introduce technical issues as compared to running them under Windows? If so, what kind of issues can be expected?
- Is resource utilization comparable between the two environments?
- Does Proton provide a good enough video game experience on Linux for it to be used in place of running the games natively on Windows?

3.1 Research Environment

For this research to be conducted, an appropriate research environment is necessary. This environment must allow for tracking and recording of the performance of selected video games. Since each operating system itself could be described as an environment, the complete research environment will consist of two separate software environments deployed on a singular hardware platform which will be configured in the exact same way as to not introduce another testing variable.

The Hardware Platform has been constructed out of the best parts available to the authors at the time of conducting the research for this work. The hardware meets or exceeds all elements of the most popular hardware configuration among all Steam users according to the monthly Steam hardware survey[3] performance-wise. The most popular hardware configuration consists of:

- A CPU with 4 physical cores and clock speeds between 2.3 GHz and 2.7 GHz.
- 16 GB of system RAM.
- An NVIDIA GeForce GTX 1060 GPU with 6 GB of VRAM - a midrange offering from the GeForce 1000 series.
- A monitor with resolution of 1920×1080.

On the other hand, the constructed hardware platform consists of:

- An Intel Core i9 9900k CPU, with a base clock speed of 3.6 GHz and maximum clock speed between 4.7 GHz (3 or more cores under load) and 5.0 GHz (1 or 2 cores under load).
- 16 GB of Kingston Fury Renegade DDR4 system RAM, in configuration of 2 dies of 8 GB with clock speed of 3200 MT/s.
- An NVIDIA GeForce GTX 980 Ti GPU with 6 GB of VRAM - a top of the line GeForce 900 series offering, comparable to an NVIDIA GeForce GTX 1070.
- A monitor with resolution of 1920×1080.

In addition to the performance-deciding components mentioned above, the hardware platform consists of following additional parts:

- Fractal Design Meshify 2 computer case.
- A Z390 AORUS PRO WIFI motherboard.

[3] https://store.steampowered.com/hwsurvey.

- A CPU cooling solution Noctua NH-D14.
- A 750 W power supply Corsair HX750.
- Two identical solid state drives - Samsung SSD 870 EVO 500GB.

The solid state drives mentioned above were purchased new and never used before conducting this research, so as to make sure not to introduce another variable in the form of uneven performance between the two storage mediums.

Linux Distribution Selection might seem like a difficult task, but for a Linux distribution to be eligible for this study, all it technically needed to offer was the support for the steam platform. To support the Steam platform, a distribution needs to be based on Ubuntu and one of the Linux distributions that are geared for gaming that are based on Ubuntu is Pop![4]. Pop!_OS offers preinstalled NVIDIA drivers and promises bloat-free experience by minimizing the amount of Ubuntu packages. The selected distribution offers a straightforward installation process with a high degree of control available to the user, allowing him to manually manage all of the disk partitions through the graphical interface. The NVIDIA drivers featured in the installation image were up to date and after installing Steam the system was more or less ready to play video games.

Software and Firmware Versions can, in some cases, heavily influence the results of any benchmark, so for the sake of a thorough and repeatable study, versions of all software and firmware (other than the games themselves) relevant to performance and data collection which was used during the research have been documented and presented in Table 1. All possible software and firmware was updated to newest available version at the time of testing, with the exception of the motherboard's UEFI BIOS. An attempt was made to update it to the newest version, but every time the update process failed and reverted back to the previously installed version, hence the older version used for testing.

Table 1. Software and firmware versions used in the study.

Piece of software/firmware	Version
Pop!_OS	22.04 LTS (NVIDIA)
Windows 10	21H1 19043.1806
MSI Afterburner	4.6.4
MangoHud	0.6.6-1
Proton	7.0-3
Windows NVIDIA driver	516.59
Linux NVIDIA driver	515.57
Z390 AORUS PRO WIFI UEFI BIOS	F8

[4] https://pop.system76.com.

3.2 Benchmark Data Collection Software

One difficulty that presented itself while designing the research environment was the lack of a benchmark data collection software that would support both the Windows environment and the Linux environment. For the Windows environment selection was relatively easy - MSI Afterburner[5] has been an industry staple for years. It provides a wide range of features, from configuring and overclocking the parameters of the GPU to measuring and recording performance data. On the other hand, selection for the Linux environment proved to be quite difficult - MSI Afterburner is not an open-source solution and has not been ported for Linux. After some research it turned out that an exact equivalent for MSI Afterburner does not exist for Linux, but an open-source solution by the name of MangoHud[6] provides a feature set that is sufficient for nearly all aspects of the planned study, and since the project is open-source the missing functionality could be added by the author. MangoHud, compared to MSI Afterburner, lacks the feature set geared towards configuring hardware parameters. However, similarly to the solution used for Windows it provides the functionality of tracking and recording performance data, which is enough for the scope of this study.

MSI Afterburner features performance and hardware data tracking which can be freely configured through its graphical interface. Many different parameters can be tracked, more than the scope of this study requires. The hardware and performance data recorded through the utility gets saved to a seemingly proprietary data format with an .hml extension. However, after taking a closer look at the recorded data, a standard, comma-separated values (CSV) format can be seen. This kind of format allows for easy analysis of the recorded data through spreadsheet software or using Python with libraries dedicated to computing. MSI Afterburner logs data 10 times per second, making the time between each data point 100ms.

MangoHud - similarly to MSI Afterburner - allows for performance and hardware data tracking. However, the recording feature works slightly different as compared to its counterpart on Windows - the tool enables the user to freely configure what performance metrics out of the ones available are being tracked, but the set of metrics that can be recorded is hardcoded into the application. Thankfully, the solution is open-source, so the missing functionality can be added. Configuration of the tracked metrics can be done through the configuration file in the installation folder, or for a more user-friendly experience an additional open-source tool by the name of GOverlay[7] can be used. GOverlay provides a graphical user interface that allows for the configuration of MangoHud and includes a quick render, which the user can test his settings with. For the sake of this study MangoHud's source code was downloaded and edited with the goal

[5] https://www.msi.com/Landing/afterburner/graphics-cards.
[6] https://github.com/flightlessmango/MangoHud.
[7] https://github.com/benjamimgois/goverlay.

of adding the required functionality of recording all of the performance values that were necessary for this study. The only parameter selected for this study that was missing from the original solution was the CPU frequency. Adding this functionality required fairly little modification, which was possible thank to the solution being open-source. Similarly to data saved by MSI Afterburner, the performance and hardware data collected by MangoHud gets written to a standard CSV format file at the end of the benchmark. Despite using the same format however, different order and convention of writing the metrics can be observed - some of the data uses different units, such as MSI Afterburner tracking system and video RAM as MB compared to MangoHud tracking them as GB, so additional work was required during data analysis to standardize the data. Unlike MSI Afterburner, MangoHud allows data to be logged at very short intervals, down to it being logged every single frame, but to make the data comparable with MSI Afterburner the same time between data points had to be configured - 100 ms.

3.3 Measured Metrics

For the experience to be objectively measured and compared, performance metrics that are going to be tracked and recorded need to be selected. After referencing various sources for the industry standards of measuring video game performance, following metrics to be tracked throughout the gameplay have been selected:

- Average performance measured in frames per second.
- Lowest average performance measured as the average of 1% of slowest frames.
- Lowest momentary dip in performance measured as the average of 0.1% of slowest frames.
- GPU temperature measured in degrees Celsius.
- GPU utilization measured as a percentage.
- GPU frequency measured in megahertz.
- GPU power consumption measured in watts.
- GPU memory utilization in megabytes.
- GPU memory frequency measured in megahertz.
- CPU temperature measured in degrees Celsius.
- CPU utilization measured as a percentage.
- CPU frequency measured in megahertz.
- System memory utilization measured in megabytes.

In addition to the performance metrics above, there are also important aspects that cannot be represented by numerical values - such as encountering technical issues during the gameplay, which is definitely possible as the games are going to be run outside of their native environment. On paper, the game might be running very well, but on closer inspection it turns out that some graphical elements might not be rendered properly or some audio might be missing or played incorrectly. In the most extreme cases some games might crash mid-game or not start at all. For that reason, additional metrics have been selected:

- Occurrence of technical issues related to sound.
- Occurrence of technical issues related to graphics.
- Occurrence of technical issues related to running the game.

3.4 Video Game Selection

To compare how do the video games run under both environments, not only did a number of video games had to be selected for testing, but also an algorithm that would assure a fair testing procedure had to be devised. Video game selection was predicated primarily on two factors: presence of an automated benchmark section in the game and whether authors already owned the game on the Steam platform. An automated benchmark section is the best way of conducting performance testing, as it removes any possible variables in the form of player movement, reaction time, random events and others. It assures that, with exception of small details (like paths of pedestrians or the movement of some physics-based objects), each test will be repeatable and comparable between different runs. Additionally, there is a well-known issue with Proton, that at the time of this study cannot be solved - many solutions that are supposed to prevent cheating interpret the compatibility layer as a possible tampering with the game's code, making a lot of multiplayer games (such as Player Unknown's Battlegrounds) impossible to play. After considering aforementioned factors, 7 following titles with release dates spanning from the year 2011 to the year 2020 have been selected:

- Batman: Arkham City, first released in 2011.
- Grand Theft Auto V, first released in 2013.
- Middle-earth: Shadow of Mordor, first released in 2014.
- Rise of the Tomb Raider, first released in 2015.
- Hitman, first released in 2016.
- Metro Exodus, first released in 2019.
- Mafia II: Definitive Edition, first released in 2010 and remastered in 2020.

For each of the selected games, after careful consideration 4 distinct sets of graphical fidelity settings have been prepared: low, medium, high and very high. These configuration presets have been composed of available configuration options and their levels for each of the games, in a way that is supposed to ensure different levels of performance for each of the presets. In addition to the 4 of the aforementioned presets, in the case of Rise of the Tomb Raider an additional preset has been prepared: one that utilizes DirectX 12 API instead of DirectX 11 API, which is a newer technology and should provide a boost in performance on hardware that supports it, which the GeForce GTX 980 Ti does in full. Benchmarking the same game with two different APIs should present a good insight into how well Proton handles newer technologies.

3.5 The Testing Procedure

Each of the graphical configuration presets was tested for each game by running the built-in benchmark four times consecutively. The first run served as a warm-up run, making sure that all assets are properly loaded into memory, so as not to impact performance by loading them mid-benchmark on the first run and to let hardware temperatures stabilize. For each of the remaining three runs, data was tracked and recorded from the start of the benchmark until the end of the benchmark. To make sure that all configuration has been applied properly when switching to another preset, all games were restarted after applying configuration, and the configuration was verified after starting them up again. If the settings were applied properly, the next step was a warm-up benchmark run.

4 Results

A great amount of data has been collected through the course of this study and presenting all of it here would be impossible. Since the main point was a comparison of how well video games run on Linux as compared to Windows, all of the performance data has been collected, averaged and aggregated in Table 2. Similarly, all of the resource utilization data has been presented in Table 3. The top 3% of data with the highest frame rates has been pruned to eliminate any outliers that would muddle the results - momentary spikes in performance for one or two frames do not really impact player's experience, but they can change how the graphs are scaled, making the overall data harder to interpret. Bottom part of the data has been kept, as momentary dips in performance can heavily impact the gameplay, causing the game to stutter which is especially important in fast-paced titles.

Table 2. Performance data from all benchmarks (for different games, with different quality settings) averaged for all, the lowest 1% and 0.1% of measures taken every 100ms in frames per second (FPS) for operating systems: Windows and Linux

OS	FPS	1% low FPS	0.1% low FPS
Windows	160.37	106.81	100.54
Linux	139.60	89.93	73.27

Table 3. Performance and resource utilization data from all benchmarks (for different games, with different quality settings) averaged for all, the lowest 1% and 0.1% of measures taken every 100ms for operating systems: Windows and Linux

OS	GPU temp [$^{\circ}C$]	GPU usage [%]	GPU clock [MHz]	GPU power [W]	VRAM usage [MB]	VRAM clock [MHz]	CPU temp [$^{\circ}C$]	CPU usage [%]	CPU clock [MHz]	RAM usage [MB]
Windows	73.65	88.25	1333.61	206.96	2713.49	3600.00	62.73	21.05	4676.26	6324.84
Linux	73.04	87.45	1333.75	201.97	3042.72	3600.00	61.67	19.38	3786.60	6166.94

On average, performance on Linux was 13% worse than on Windows, the 1% of the lowest performance dips on Linux was 16% worse than on Windows, and the 0.1% of the lowest performance was 27% worse than on Windows. Considering that Proton is a form of emulation, a 13% difference in overall performance could be considered a success, but a 27% difference when it comes to performance dips is a problem, and not a small one - this means that not only do they occur more often, but also are more severe, and any hitches or freezes lower the gameplay quality much more than lower, but stable performance.

When it comes to resource utilization, many of the measured metrics stay very close between the two systems, with some of them like the GPU clock or temperature being within the margin of error. As it turns out, VRAM frequency is not dynamic - it has a single speed dictated by the GPU BIOS and it cannot be manipulated by overclocking, hence the exact same result between systems. Most interesting however, are the disparities between the systems when it comes to VRAM usage, CPU clock and RAM usage. Starting with the VRAM usage, it can be noted that it is notably higher on Linux, as Proton works by translating one API calls to calls supported by Vulkan and Linux, which means that it has to hold all the elements of both the native API required by the game, as well as the elements needed to translate API calls in the video memory. The difference in performance might also have something to do with how the CPU is utilized on Linux compared to Windows - Windows pushes the CPU clock a fair bit higher than Linux, and with some games depending on the CPU clock quite a bit, this can lead to better performance on Windows. RAM usage was consistently lower on Linux as compared to Windows - while Proton might need additional memory to run a game on Linux, on average the lower memory overhead of Linux as compared to Windows makes up for any memory that is needed by the compatibility layer.

4.1 DirectX 12's Impact on Performance

One of the biggest factors in a game's performance is the API that it uses, and in case of Proton not all APIs are supported equally well. The most popular API today is DirectX 11, but some newer games can utilize DirectX 12, and some require it to run at all. One of the games benchmarked in this study, Rise of the Tomb Raider, can utilize DirectX 12. The 'High' preset has been tested twice - once using DirectX 11, and once using DirectX 12. The performance averages from all of the presets have been presented in Table 4.

To have a closer look at how DirectX 12 has impacted the performance, entire data from averaged benchmark runs for the selected DirectX 11 and DirectX 12 preset has been presented in Fig. 1.

Looking at the comparison diagram, the performance on Windows stays almost the same, while on Linux it plummets to half as soon as DirectX 12 is enabled. While this situation might be different on a newer generation of hardware, not every user has hardware from the newest generation, and on the GeForce GTX 980 Ti Proton offers acceptable performance with DirectX 11 while being on the verge of being unplayable with DirectX 12.

Table 4. Performance data for Rise of the Tomb Raider (with different quality settings) averaged for all, the lowest 1% and 0.1% of measures taken every 100ms in frames per second (FPS) for operating systems: Windows and Linux

quality	OS	FPS	1% low FPS	0.1% low FPS
Low DX11	Windows	176.28	129.40	126.27
	Linux	137.46	66.63	51.96
Medium DX11	Windows	130.89	100.32	100.27
	Linux	116.49	75.02	63.89
High DX11	Windows	93.86	66.10	66.00
	Linux	82.63	51.73	46.94
High DX12	Windows	93.62	65.81	65.70
	Linux	40.58	27.04	23.36
Very high DX11	Windows	59.68	39.68	39.27
	Linux	49.51	24.04	19.52

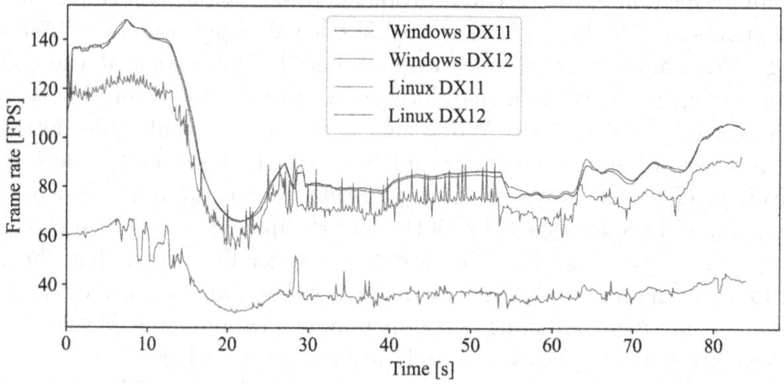

Fig. 1. Comparison of the frame rate over time on both systems, using both DirectX 11 and DirectX 12.

4.2 Technical Difficulties Present When Running Games on Linux

While five of the selected games worked more or less problem-free, Proton still had some problems, and two games were not playable at all. Regarding games that were playable, Rise of the Tomb Raider had technical issues when utilizing DirectX 12, again going back to the poor support that Proton seems to have for it. DirectX 12 in Rise of the Tomb Raider in addition to the poor performance, caused light sources to flash like a strobe light, making the gameplay very uncomfortable, to the point of being impossible at times. In case of Hitman, the game was able to install and start properly, but after a random amount of time it would crash straight to the desktop without as much as an error message. The time before the game crashed was never longer than around two minutes - if the game crashes every hour or more it is possible to overlook the crashes and keep playing the game, but since they happened so often it was not even possible to carry out the tests, let alone enjoy the game as a player. Finally, when it comes to Metro Exodus, the game did not crash, but playing the game was not possible either. After starting the game an introduction video would play, showcasing the game's developers and technologies used. After the video ends, the game goes into a fully 3D rendered menu, which rendered incorrectly in a small box, surrounded by an image from the introduction video. The image surrounding the menu would rapidly flash between a black background and the image, making the gameplay extremely uncomfortable in case if the player forced himself to play the game anyway. Additionally, the game recognized mouse cursor position as if it was still rendered properly, which means that to target an element of the game menu the cursor had to be placed where the element would be placed if the menu was rendered properly, rather than where it was really placed.

5 Discussion

To conclude this study, the research problems posed in the experiment idea can now be answered. The first question was: What is the performance difference in running video games between the two systems? Looking back at the collected data, on average the performance difference in running video games between the two systems was around 13%. While this is not a bad result considering that Proton is a form of emulation, the problem lies in the lower end of performance - the average 1% of the lowest dips in performance was around 16% worse than on Windows, and the average 0.1% of the lowest dips in performance was around 27% worse than on Windows. This last 27% especially means that the games stutter more often on Linux than they do on Windows, and when they do stutter, those stutters are worse, making the gameplay less comfortable. While those are not unacceptable results, they definitely are not great either.

Continuing, the next research problem was formulated as follows: Is running a video game native to Windows under Proton on Linux a straightforward experience or does it require additional time and/or steps as compared to running it under Windows? The answer to this question has two sides. When speaking about the difficulty of running a video game native to Windows on Linux, Proton makes it as easy as enabling the compatibility layer and just pressing play, which is great - no additional configuration or steps required. On the other hand, the second part of this question mentions time, and playing any game using Proton sadly requires additional patience. Every single game needs to compile its shaders first, and the worst offenders can take upwards of forty minutes to complete this process, which can make the game impossible to play if the user does not have that much time - in case the user only has an hour that he can spend playing a game, then spending forty of those sixty minutes waiting for the game to launch is a big downside, even if it needs to happen only once. This means, that until this process gets perfected, Proton suffers another hit.

The next problem was: Does running video games under Proton on Linux introduce technical issues as compared to running them under Windows? If so, what kind of issues can be expected? The answer to this problem is an unfortunate and definitive yes. Two of the seven tested games were unplayable altogether, two other had their performance drop radically compared to playing them on Windows when certain configuration options were enabled, and one of them additionally introduced rendering errors with DirectX 12 enabled, which is required for some newer games. Additionally, many multiplayer games that feature anti-cheat software are unable to launch under Proton due to the anti-cheat software interpreting running under a compatibility layer as a potential threat. All of this means that in this case Proton also does not achieve a passing grade.

The next question was: Is resource utilization comparable between the two environments? The answer to this question is a no, even though Proton and Linux do have a small win here. Overall, RAM utilization was around 2,5% higher on Windows, making Linux and Proton slightly better at utilizing system memory. However, VRAM utilization was around 12% higher on Linux, which is more of a loss than the RAM utilization is a win, especially because in most cases it is quite hard to fill up all of the system memory when playing a game, while filling up video memory is completely possible, and when that happens graphics data has to be moved to system memory or even to a hard drive, which causes a heavy drop in the game's performance.

6 Conclusions

To summarize, overall evaluation of this work research is not in favour of Proton. The ultimate research answer is to the question: "Does Proton provide a good enough alternative to running the games natively on Windows?". The answer to this question is an amalgam of the answers to all previous research problems, and it is not a positive one. If Proton scored some wins in research problems discussed, one could find an argument for using it on Linux in place of a Windows machine. Sadly, taking the results of this study into consideration, Proton in current form is not an answer for the group of users that crave a good gaming experience on Linux.

References

1. Claypool, M., Claypool, K., Damaa, F.: The effects of frame rate and resolution on users playing first person shooter games. In: Multimedia Computing and Networking 2006, vol. 6071, p. 607101. SPIE (2006)
2. Deck, V.S., Dempsey, P.: Theteardown: the gaming specialist has translated its open-hardware platform into a console. Eng. Technol. **17**(4), 1–5 (2022)
3. Duncan, R., Schreuders, Z.C.: Security implications of running windows software on a linux system using wine: a malware analysis study. Journal of Computer Virology and Hacking Techniques **15**, 39–60 (2019)
4. Gulliver, S.R., Ghinea, G.: Changing frame rate, changing satisfaction?[multimedia quality of perception]. In: 2004 IEEE International Conference on Multimedia and Expo (ICME)(IEEE Cat. No. 04TH8763), vol. 1, pp. 177–180. IEEE (2004)

5. Janzen, B.F., Teather, R.J.: Is 60 fps better than 30? The impact of frame rate and latency on moving target selection. In: CHI'14 Extended Abstracts on Human Factors in Computing Systems, pp. 1477–1482 (2014)
6. Kopel, M., Rutkowska, M.: Which gameplay aspects impact the immersion in virtual reality games? In: Wojtkiewicz, K., Treur, J., Pimenidis, E., Maleszka, M. (eds.) ICCCI 2021. CCIS, vol. 1463, pp. 159–171. Springer, Cham (2021). https://doi.org/10.1007/978-3-030-88113-9_13
7. Kopel, M., Stanasiuk, B.: How to handle head collisions in VR. In: Fujita, H., Fournier-Viger, P., Ali, M., Sasaki, J. (eds.) IEA/AIE 2020. LNCS (LNAI), vol. 12144, pp. 626–637. Springer, Cham (2020). https://doi.org/10.1007/978-3-030-55789-8_54
8. Lustbader, S.B.: Feasibility of GNU/Linux as the OS for a PC-based Medical Product. Ph.D. thesis, Massachusetts Institute of Technology (2002)
9. Petersen, R., Petersen, R.: Office applications, email, editors, and databases. Beginning Fedora Desktop: Fedora 28 Edition, pp. 171–210 (2018)

Complete Coverage and Path Planning for Emergency Response by UAVs in Disaster Areas

Krzysztof Trojanowski[1], Artur Mikitiuk[1], Jakub Grzeszczak[1(✉)], and Frédéric Guinand[1,2]

[1] Cardinal Stefan Wyszyński University in Warsaw, Warsaw, Poland
{k.trojanowski,a.mikitiuk,jakub.grzeszczak}@uksw.edu.pl
[2] Normandy University of Le Havre, Le Havre, France
frederic.guinand@univ-lehavre.fr

Abstract. Determining paths for a team of Unmanned Aerial Vehicles (UAVs) that pass over a disaster area for reconnaissance and communication delivery for ground users is a subject of our research. It is assumed that the location of disaster victims is unknown because there is no contact with them. However, we have some statistical information about population density levels in subsequent regions of the area. Thus, to maximize the number of localized victims in the first minutes and hours of the rescue operation, we use information about these regions in the UAVs' path planning and optimization process. We present a heuristic optimization algorithm working with a new model of the disaster area that takes into account population density. We also show the results of path planning simulations for selected regions in Poland.

Keywords: Coverage Path Planning · Unmanned Aerial Vehicles · Terrain Coverage · Heuristic Optimization

1 Introduction

Unexpected natural phenomena like, for example, earthquakes or torrential rains following months of drought bring floods that destroy buildings, dam walls, and other crucial hydrological infrastructure, which cause rivers to overflow further and ruin houses. Many people become homeless, and some of them are injured. Often the location of the victims is unknown, and there is no contact with them because they are, for example, out of the range of the base transceiver stations (BTSs). In this case, Unmanned Aerial Vehicles (UAVs) may provide first reconnaissance and bring directions for the rescue teams. The choice of UAVs is justified because they offer unlimited access to any region where ground communication tracks and roads have been destroyed by, for example, the effects of flood or snowstorm. The first aim of UAVs is to offer at least intermittent communication services to people. Precisely, UAVs may gather information about

N. T. Nguyen et al. (Eds.): ICCCI 2023, LNAI 14162, pp. 647–659, 2023.
https://doi.org/10.1007/978-3-031-41456-5_49

the identification of the victims (we assume that phone numbers or IMEI numbers identify persons), their precise location (GPS coordinates), and their moves when possible. UAVs equipped with Mobile Base Stations (MBSs) form Flying Ad-Hoc Networks (FANET), which can deliver communication among flying nodes and simultaneously for users on the ground. Moreover, FANET may route received messages (e.g., SMS) from victims to the nearest BTS and transfer messages from BTSs to victims when the location of victims is already known.

Application of FANET in the disaster area may define several subproblems to solve. In our research, we optimize UAV paths, maximizing the number of ground users found in the area over time. The first minutes following an accident are crucial in emergency management. The more victims are localized and can report their condition, injuries, or needs in the first minutes or hours, the better. Some people may be injured, and others, like refugees on the rooftops of their homes, may need immediate evacuation due to rivers continuing to swell. Eventually, the UAV path planning procedure has two objectives: to get information about the condition and location of all persons in the disaster area and find out the victims demanding immediate help first. Therefore, we have to use additional information delivered by, for example, the local government to predict the localization of victims in the path-planning process. For example, selected regions, like farmlands or wastelands, have population levels different from villages and cities. Another example is the location of floodplains or flood-prone areas, that is, land areas susceptible to water inundation. We use this additional information to divide the disaster area into regions with different priorities. The priorities reflect chances for the location of victims demanding immediate help and influence the order of visits by UAVs.

In this research, we propose a heuristic optimization algorithm searching for paths for a set of UAVs operating over the disaster area. The number of UAVs is predetermined, as well as the division of the area into regions and their assignment of priorities. In the algorithm, we propose a new representation of the solution and novel perturbation operators adjusted to the model of the problem. The test cases come from Test Case Generator building benchmarks for selected regions in Poland using statistical data about population density. We propose an evaluation function for the coverage paths generated for these test cases. For four test cases, we empirically verify the proposed algorithm's effectiveness.

The paper consists of seven sections. Section 2 presents the model of the disaster area. Section 3 discusses the representation of the set of paths for a team of UAVs, while the evaluation function is described in Sect. 4. Section 5 describes the Local Search approach and problem-specific operators. The experimental part of the research is described in Sect. 6. Finally, Sect. 7 concludes the paper.

2 The Problem Model—A Disaster Area Map

A disaster area is a convex region where ground communication tracks and roads cannot be used, and no BTS signal is available. We aim to localize everyone in this area by contacting their phones via WiFi and exchanging basic information.

Thus, our goal is to build paths for a team of UAVs that explore every location in the area. Due to the unlimited access of UAVs to any place, the disaster area is fully accessible, and every path which satisfies UAV mobility features is acceptable. This problem belongs to the class of Coverage Path Planning (CPP).

For fully accessible uniform rectangle areas, there exist algorithms that generate covering paths of the shape of a single spiral, zigzag, or back-and-forth motion (boustrophedon) [2,3,6]. However, in our case, the disaster area is not uniform but consists of not necessarily convex regions. The division into regions whose union exactly fills the area is not a novel idea. In most approaches to the Coverage Path Planning problem, authors started building the model of the problem with a decomposition of the area into simple, non-overlapping convex regions containing no obstacles [1,5,7–10]. In our case, the regions differ in shape and area and may have different priorities. The priority of a region represents chances for the presence of victims. The priority may originate from the estimated population density in the region but also from other natural disasters circumstances like the epicenter's location and the strength of tremors in the case of quakes or hydrographical conditions in the case of floods. A region represents a terrain where every point has the same priority for UAVs. Its neighbor regions have different priorities. Otherwise, they must unite. We want to localize everyone, but being unconnected is not necessarily equivalent to being a victim. Hence, we aim at complete coverage of the area but follow priorities to find the victims first. For the experimental purpose, we used the Test Case Generator for Problems of Complete Coverage and Path Planning (TCG-CCPP) [4], which divides the area into rectangle regions based on population density statistical data.

The goal for a team of UAVs is to maximize the number of already-found victims over time. TCG-CCPP generates rectangle regions, that is, convex ones. Therefore, we can use existing algorithms to find covering paths for each. Hence, one can simplify the given path-planning problem to a combinatorial one optimizing just the order of visiting convex regions to minimize the length of paths for respective UAVs. Each path considers the overall time of regions' coverage and the time necessary to traverse between them.

When calculating a path's cost, we assume that the location of the region's entry and exit points does not impact the estimated number of found victims over time. Moreover, regions that are neighbors in the path do not have to be adjacent on the map of the area. When the regions are adjacent, UAV traverses directly through any point on a common boundary. Otherwise, UAV follows a straight line between the two closest points of the region boundaries. The cost of such traversal also influences the overall cost of the path.

In the experimental part of the research, we optimize the coverage paths for a team of UAVs. As a test bed, we use cases from TCG-CCPP powered by data on residents in a 1-kilometer grid from the "2021 Population and Housing Census in Poland" published by Statistics Poland[1]. Initially, TCG-CCPP test cases represent grids of size n by n squares with population density estimates from the

[1] Geostatistics Portal, https://geo.stat.gov.pl, the date of access: Dec 28, 2022.

Census. These densities are not discretized; thus, TCG-CCPP discretizes them first. It uses m threshold values to assign squares to $m+1$ population density classes, corresponding to $m+1$ priority levels. The threshold values are adjusted to generate comparable numbers of squares in the classes [4].

Then, neighboring squares with the same priority level unite into regions. Eventually, TCG-CCPP generates the map of the area divided into regions with assigned priority levels. Unfortunately, some of the regions may be non-convex. We regard the region as convex when it has a rectangular shape. Otherwise, the region is concave. Therefore, in the next step, TCG-CCPP splits concave regions into several convex ones, which often can be achieved in several ways. The detailed description of the splitting procedure is in [4]. Finally, we obtain the map where all the regions contributing to the area are convex.

Figure 1 depicts the main stages of building an example test case. The example area consists of 100 squares. In Fig. 1a, their population densities are discretized into four levels represented by shades of gray and level numbers. Figure 1b presents the map of this area where squares are united into regions according to their density levels. Figure 1c shows the final division into regions, where all of them are convex. This example represents only one of several valid divisions. The splitting procedure should consider more problem-specific data to determine a strategy for a particular test instance.

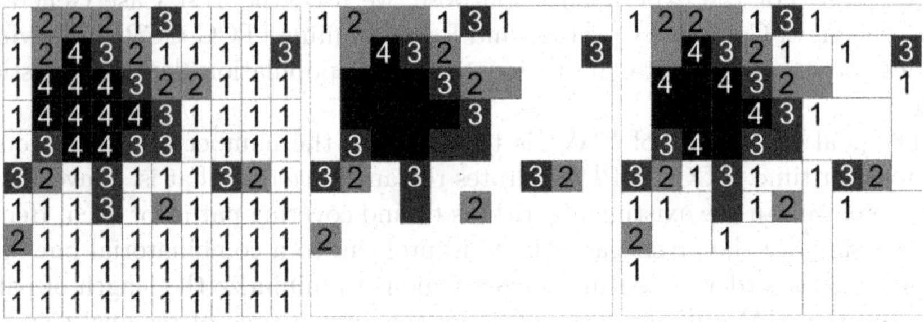

(a) raw squares (b) regions (c) convex regions

Fig. 1. Stages of the area division into convex regions

3 The Problem Solution—UAVs' Paths

We assume that our team of UAVs consists of u vehicles. For the team, a central computational unit is responsible for generating paths visiting every disaster area region at least once and returning to starting points. The input data for the unit consist of a set of convex regions, the number of available UAVs, their mobility features, and starting locations.

The algorithm is run while the rescue team has already been dispatched with a given number of UAVs and is on its way to the operating area. Therefore, our approach doesn't consider the number of UAVs as a parameter to optimize. It just searches for the best possible usage of them.

A UAV's path represents a sequence of regions to cover. A solution contains paths for all UAVs. The sum of the sets of covered regions from UAVs' paths must contain all regions in the area, and every region should appear in exactly one of these sets to avoid redundant workload.

When all the neighboring regions in the sequence are neighbors in the area, that is, they share mutual borders, the execution time of the UAV's path equals the sum of the regions' coverage times. When two consecutive regions in the sequence share no boundary edge, UAV follows the shortest transit path between them, and the time necessary for such traversal is considered when calculating the solution's value. Traversing a region always takes significantly less time than its coverage. Single execution by all UAVs of their path assignments is called "a round". Continuous communication between MBSs over time is guaranteed; thus, managing distances between UAVs is unnecessary.

Regions have two attributes: a surface area and an expected number of victims (ENV) in a region. Hence, ENV for a path equals the sum of ENVs for the regions in this path, whereas ENV in the area equals the sum of ENVs for all regions in this area. A region's coverage time depends on its surface area and UAV's mobility features, whereas traversing time is approximated by the function of the distance to traverse and the UAV's cruising velocity. The UAV's covering and cruising velocities may or may not be the same, but they do not vary over time. We assume that the shortest path between two consecutive regions always represents the traverse path, which means that the region coverage path always ends where the shortest traverse path starts.

Our problem is a variant of the Vehicle Routing Problem (VRP) with a minimum makespan objective with the additional requirement that the customers have assigned weights that impact the order of visiting them. In the VRP, we want to find an optimal set of routes for a set of vehicles to deliver goods to a set of customers. In our case, UAVs are vehicles, and convex regions represent customers. Instead of delivering goods to customers, we want to find prospective victims in the corresponding regions. Our search space is a directed complete graph. The regions are its vertices. In our problem, the route cost is associated with visiting and traversing regions. To make it the VRP, we define the cost of edge XY as the time of visiting region X plus the time of traversing between regions X and Y. This means that XY's cost may differ from YX's. For neighboring regions X and Y, the traversing time is 0.

Since the Vehicle Routing Problem is NP-hard, we need a heuristic solution that can be computed relatively fast—during an emergency, every minute counts. The approach presented in the next section satisfies this requirement.

4 Evaluation of UAVs' Paths

In our research, we maximize the number of disaster victims localized in the first minutes of the UAVs' work and minimize the execution time of the round. When

UAVs start the round, the chart of the number of already localized victims over time starts from zero and grows as time goes on and UAVs execute their paths. Eventually, it reaches the level of the area's ENV when the round is over. The chart for a team is the sum of charts calculated for each UAV.

For path generation and evaluation purposes, we propose the model where we assume that:

1. Both the area's and the regions' side lengths are expressed in terms of one-kilometer base units.
2. The area has the size of $n \times n$ kilometers.
3. When the UAV's path covers the region:
   (a) the number of already localized victims in this region grows linearly over time from zero to the region's ENV,
   (b) the time necessary to cover the entire region equals its area in square kilometers multiplied by a unit coverage time T_{sc}.
4. When the UAV traverses on the way between two regions:
   (a) no victims are localized,
   (b) time necessary to traverse from one point to another equals the length of a straight line connecting these two points divided by UAV's cruise velocity V_{cr}.

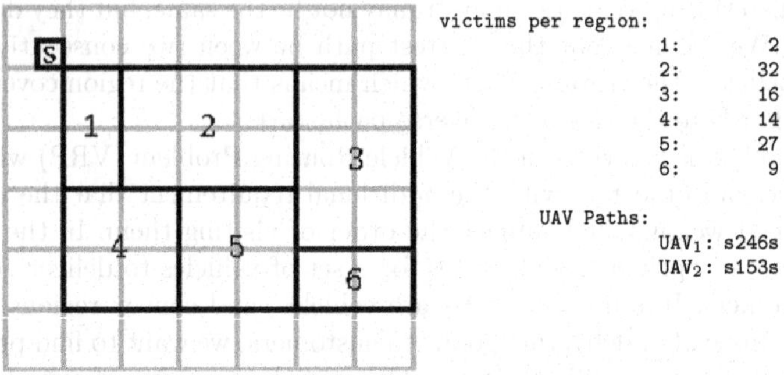

Fig. 2. An example test case and its solution: layout of an area divided into regions (on the left) and paths for two working UAVs having a starting point in the corner of the area (on the right).

Figure 2 depicts an example layout of different convex regions (on the left) together with their ENV (on the right). Additionally, example paths for two UAVs are defined: s246s and s153s. Each UAV begins at the same starting position s and is scheduled to visit and explore a different selection of regions in a particular order before returning to the starting point.

For clarity, this example assumes values of $T_{sc} = 2$ and $V_{cr} = 1$, which differ from the values used in our experiments. Using these values, one can follow a single UAV and plot the changes in the number of already found victims on the suggested paths, as seen in Fig. 3.

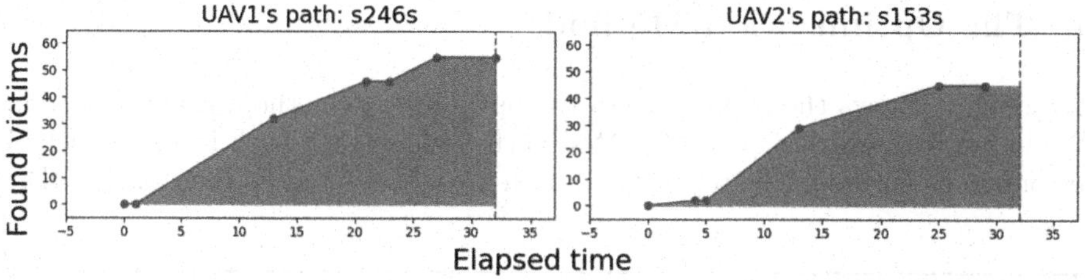

Fig. 3. The number of detected victims over time

Let us analyze the chart for UAV1 in Fig. 3 in detail. This UAV begins its route (s246s) in the starting position and goes to the first region on its path. Region 2 is located one unit of distance away from the starting position, and the cruise velocity $V_{\mathrm{cr}} = 1$. Thus, it takes precisely 1 unit of time to travel. No victims are discovered during that step. Once the UAV reaches Region 2, it begins the search for new victims. It takes $6 * T_{\mathrm{sc}} = 12$ units of time to find all 32 victims. Then UAV moves to the next region on its path, Region 4. This region shares a mutual border with the previous one. Therefore, the search for victims in this region starts immediately after completing the previous region. After $4 * T_{\mathrm{sc}} = 8$ units of time, UAV manages to find all 14 victims and begins its journey towards the final region in its path (Region 6). Traversing takes two units of time. Then, it explores and finds nine new victims throughout $2 * T_{\mathrm{sc}} = 4$ units of time. UAV completes its journey by returning to the starting position after the other five units of time.

For a single UAV, the quality of its path depends on the area under the curve describing the number of victims found over time, called A_{UAV} (the gray areas in charts in Fig. 3). An ideal solution would require all victims to be found at the start of the region's exploration phase, which is an unrealistic scenario. However, we exploit this fact and represent the quality of a path as the ratio between the calculated area A_{UAV} and its bounding rectangle area.

Each path can have a different total time cost. Therefore, we extend the curve describing the number of victims found over time by an idle period for any UAV that finishes its task earlier than the last and has to wait. Eventually, we define a fitness function for the entire solution as follows:

$$f(\mathbf{x}) = \frac{A}{T_{\max} \times v_{\exp}} \text{ where } A = \sum_{i=1}^{u} A_{UAV_i} \quad (1)$$

$\mathbf{x}$ represents a solution, and A_{UAV_i} is an area under the curve of the ENV defined by the i-th UAV's path. $T_{\max}$ represents the round execution time, and $v_{\exp}$ defines the ENV of the entire disaster area.

5 The Optimization Method

Algorithm 1 shows the main steps of the optimization method, a Local Search. A solution $\mathbf{x}$ represents a list of UAVs' paths, where each path is a sequence of regions to be covered. The regions in a path are represented by their unique IDs.

Algorithm 1. Local Search

```
Initialize x ∈ D;
repeat
    S ← modify(x)                  ▷ Step #1: modify x to create neighbors set S
    x' ← best(S)                   ▷ select the best neighbor solution in S
    if f(x') > f(x) then
        x ← x';                    ▷ Step #2: replace the current solution x by x'
until termination condition met
return x
```

In the first step of the main loop, we generate p_{size} candidate solutions in the neighborhood of the current solution. If the best element in this set is better than the current solution, it replaces this solution (Step #2). The steps of generation and selection are repeated until the termination condition, that is, an arbitrary limit of evaluation function calls, is met.

In Step #1, two problem-specific modification operators are applied to generate a set of p_{size} candidate solutions. They represent two types of perturbation: local and global. Each type has two variants. The main steps of all of them are described below:

- local (L)—modifying sequences within a path of a single UAV:
  1. LT: change of the region's location in the path promoting shorter execution time of the path; steps:
     (a) weighted random selection of a path with the weights equal total execution times of the paths (the longer time, the higher weight),
     (b) uniform random selection and removal of one region in the path,
     (c) evaluation of traverse distances for all positions in the path where the removed region could be inserted, including its previous position,
     (d) for the removed region, a weighted random selection of a new position in the path with the weights equal to the reciprocal of one plus the sum of the traverse distances for the positions,
     (e) inserting the region in the selected position.
  2. LD: change of the region's location in the path promoting higher ENV at the beginning of the path; steps:
     (a) weighted random selection of a path with the weights equal to the paths' ENV,
     (b) uniform random selection and removal of one region in the path,

   (c) for all positions in the path where the removed region could be inserted (including its previous position), evaluation of the differences between ENVs of two regions: the one preceding the position and the removed one; then, to have all values positive, all of the resulting differences are increased by the absolute value of the smallest of them plus one,
   (d) inserting the region in the selected position.
- global (G)—swapping elements of two paths within a solution:
  1. GT: swap the regions between two selected paths in the way promoting shorter execution time of both paths; steps:
     (a) weighted random selections of two paths, one with the weights w_{p} equal total execution times of the paths (the longer time, the higher weight), and the other one with the weights $\frac{1}{w_{\mathrm{p}}}$ (the longer time, the lower weight),
     (b) for both selected paths, uniform random selection and removal of one region,
     (c) for both regions, evaluation of traverse distances for all positions in the opposite path,
     (d) for both regions, a weighted random selection of a position in the opposite path with the weights equal to the reciprocal of one plus the sum of the traverse distances calculated in the previous step,
     (e) inserting the regions in the selected positions in the opposite paths.
  2. GD: swap the regions in two paths promoting higher ENV at the beginning of the path; steps:
     (a) two weighted random selections of paths, one with the weights w_{d} equal to the regions' ENV and the other one with the weights $\frac{1}{w_{\mathrm{d}}}$,
     (b) for both selected paths, uniform random selection and removal of one region,
     (c) for both removed regions, for all positions in the opposite path, evaluation of the differences between ENVs of two regions: the one preceding the position and the removed one; then, to have all values positive, all of the resulting differences are increased by the absolute value of the smallest of them plus one,
     (d) for both removed regions, a weighted random selection of a position in the opposite path with the weights equal to the values calculated in the previous step,
     (e) inserting the regions in the selected positions in the opposite paths.

Hence, we obtain four configurations of the operators' pair to apply in the algorithm framework: LT:GT, LD:GT, LT:GD, and LD:GD.

6 Experimental Research

In the experimental part, we verify the efficiency of four variants of Local Search equipped with pairs of operators. Our benchmark comes from TCG-CCPP and consists of four test cases.

6.1 Test Cases and Plan of Experiments

The test cases originate from TCG-CCPP powered by the data published in the Geostatistics Portal by Statistics Poland. The data contain numbers of residents in squares of a 1-kilometer grid. We selected four areas of size 30×30 squares from the data for our experiments. The areas are diversified; they contain primarily urban terrains but with different numbers of residents.

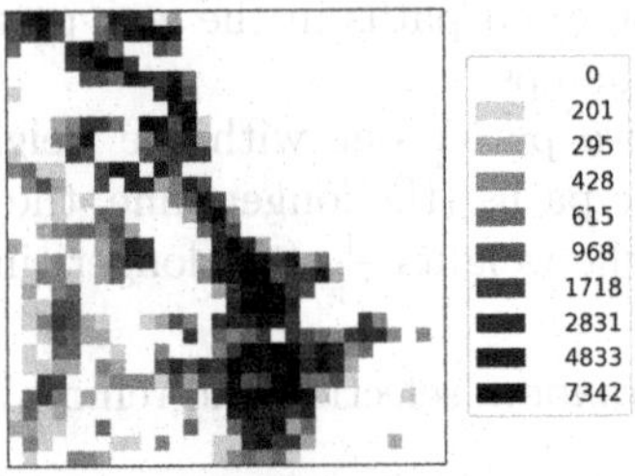

(a) the Gdansk Bay area

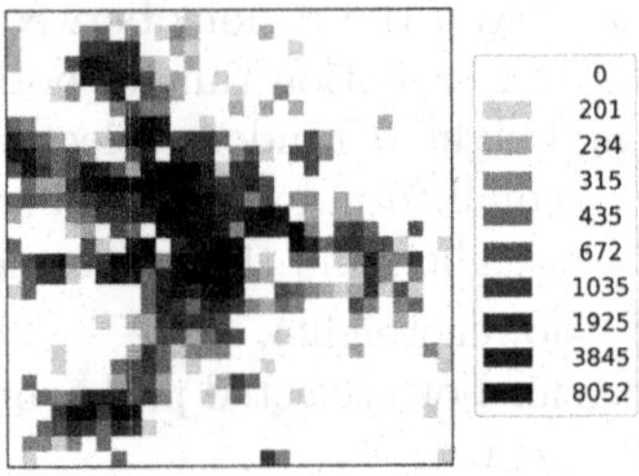

(b) the Lodz area

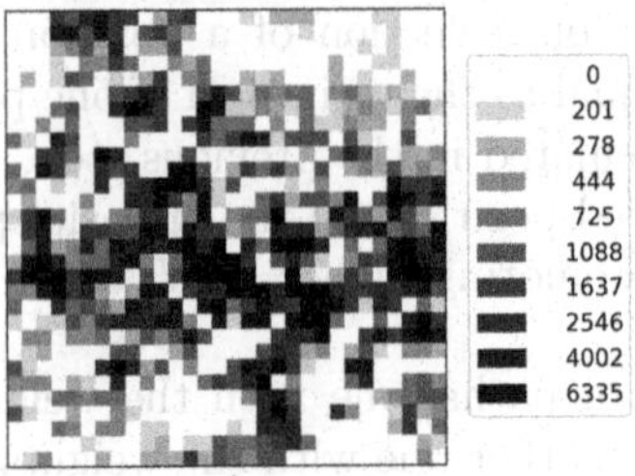

(c) the Gliwice area

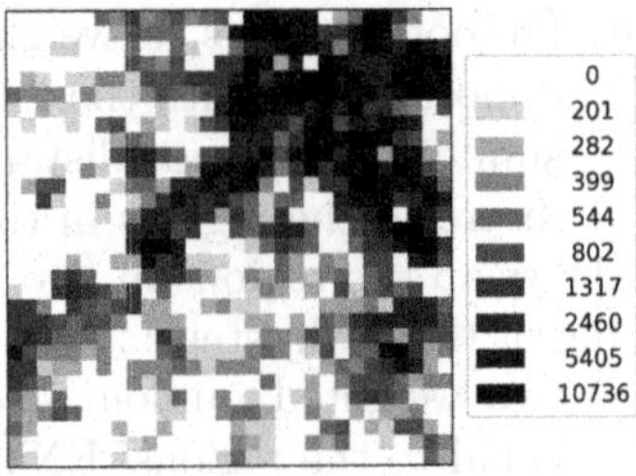

(d) the Warsaw suburbs area

Fig. 4. Four test cases extracted from the data containing results of "2021 Population and Housing Census in Poland" published by Geostatistics Portal

Figure 4 depicts maps of four selected areas obtained from the Census where squares are united into regions according to their population density levels (just like in Fig. 1b). In the areas, population density threshold values defining priority classes vary because we select them to obtain comparable numbers of squares in the priority classes and additionally maximum population densities for the Gdansk Bay area (7342), the Lodz area (8052), the Gliwice area (6335), and the Warsaw suburbs area (10736) differ.

We did four sets of experiments with four variants of Local Search. The following parameters were the same in every case: the number of UAVs $u = 10$, the size of the disaster area's side $n = 30$, the number of threshold values $m = 10$, the unit coverage time $T_{sc} = 10$, the UAV's cruise velocity $V_{cr} = 1$, the total expected number of victims $v_{exp} = 100\%$ of the population in the test area, the number of candidate solutions $p_{size} = 10$ and stopping condition, that is, the maximum number of fitness function calls $max_{nffc} = 100000$. The variants share the steps in the main loop but apply different pairs of modification operators. For every iteration, both used operators can be selected with equal probability.

We repeated the experiment 32 times for every problem instance. We tracked the algorithm runs and recorded all the experiment-related information. Then, we excluded the ones with the best and worst values of $f(\mathbf{x})$ in the last iteration. We calculated and visualized the mean $f(\mathbf{x})$ values for the remaining runs.

6.2 Results of Experiments

Figure 5 depicts the mean $f(\mathbf{x})$ values over iterations for four test cases. For each test case, we show graphs for four variants of the Local Search.

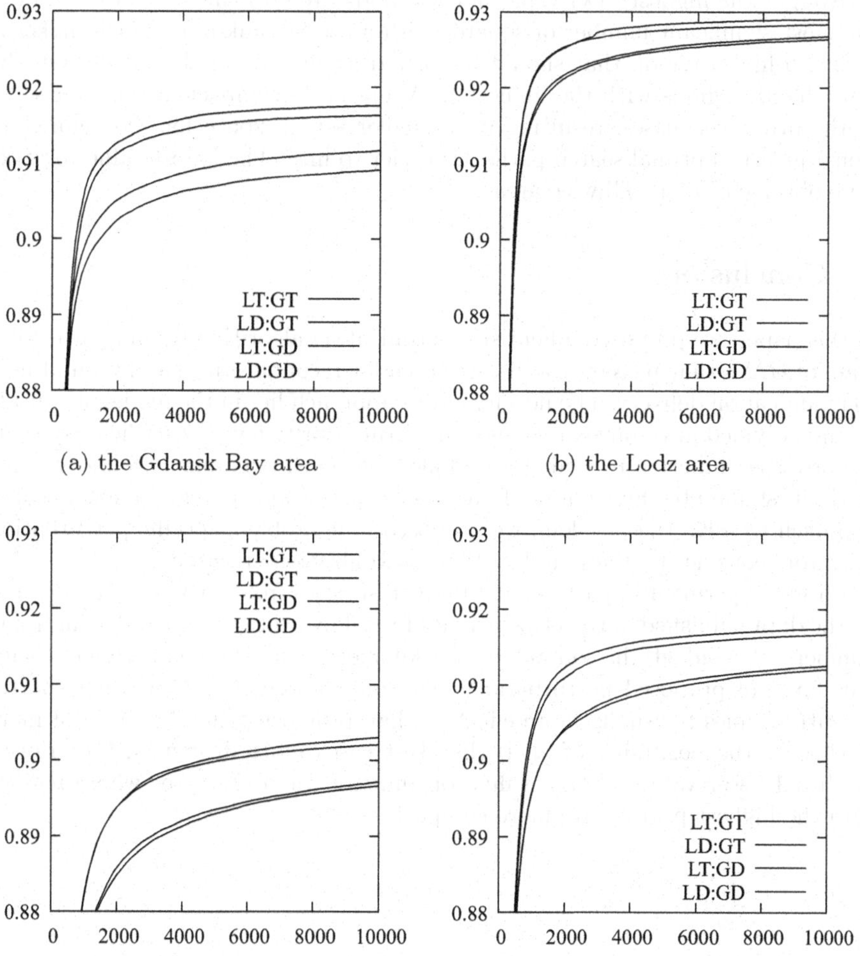

(a) the Gdansk Bay area

(b) the Lodz area

(c) the Gliwice area

(d) the Warsaw suburbs area

Fig. 5. Mean values of $f(\mathbf{x})$ in subsequent iterations for the four test cases

Results show that using a pair of operators LT:GT gives the best results in two out of four cases. In the third test case, the pair LD:GT proved more effective, while in the last test case, the winner was the pair LT:GD. In three out of four test cases, pairs of operators containing GT were more efficient than pairs containing GD, while the differences between results produced by pairs containing GT and the differences between results produced by pairs containing GD were small. However, for the Gdansk Bay area, pairs of operators containing LT give better results than pairs containing LD, while the results given by the best and worst pairs differ more than in the remaining test cases. In three out of four of our test cases, the worst pair of operators was LD:GD. Thus, promoting shorter execution times is usually more effective than promoting the detection of more victims at the beginning of all paths.

We got the highest $f(\mathbf{x})$ values for the Lodz area. In this test case, we have the most significant number of squares with a sector rank of 0, which makes it easier to find a region that should be visited at the end of the search. On the other hand, regions with the highest ENV are more compact in this area than in the other test cases, resulting in a smaller search space for the algorithm. Consequently, optimal search paths are easier to find. The lowest values of $f(\mathbf{x})$ were obtained for the Gliwice area.

7 Conclusions

In this paper, we proposed a heuristic optimization algorithm to find paths for a team of UAVs that pass over a disaster area for reconnaissance and ground-user communication delivery. The novelty of our approach lies in the model of a disaster area divided into convex regions of uniform priority levels. Another novelty is the proposed function to evaluate problem solutions, maximizing found victims in the first minutes and hours of the rescue operation. Using the local search approach to solve the problem, we proposed four problem-specific perturbation operators considering the found victims maximization criterion.

In the experimental part, we used four test cases from TCG-CCPP powered by the data published in the Geostatistics Portal by Statistics Poland, containing numbers of residents in squares of a 1-kilometer grid. Our experiments with four pairs of proposed perturbation operators showed that promoting shorter execution times is usually more effective than promoting the detection of more victims at the beginning of all paths. Test cases more diversified for priority produced lower values of the evaluation function than the cases where regions with the highest priority are more compact.

References

1. Basilico, N., Carpin, S.: Deploying teams of heterogeneous UAVs in cooperative two-level surveillance missions. In: 2015 IEEE/RSJ International Conference on Intelligent Robots and Systems (IROS), pp. 610–615. IEEE, September 2015. https://doi.org/10.1109/iros.2015.7353435
2. Cabreira, T., Brisolara, L., Ferreira Jr., P.R.: Survey on coverage path planning with unmanned aerial vehicles. Drones **3**(1), 4 (2019). https://doi.org/10.3390/drones3010004
3. Galceran, E., Carreras, M.: A survey on coverage path planning for robotics. Robot. Auton. Syst. **61**(12), 1258–1276 (2013). https://doi.org/10.1016/j.robot.2013.09.004
4. Grzeszczak, J., Trojanowski, K., Mikitiuk, A.: Test case generator for problems of complete coverage and path planning for emergency response by UAVs. In: Artificial Intelligence and Soft Computing. Springer International Publishing (2023). (accepted for publication at The 22nd Int. Conference on Artificial Intelligence and Soft Computing, ICAISC 2023)
5. Kapanoglu, M., Alikalfa, M., Ozkan, M., Yazici, A., Parlaktuna, O.: A pattern-based genetic algorithm for multi-robot coverage path planning minimizing completion time. J. Intell. Manuf. **23**(4), 1035–1045 (2010). https://doi.org/10.1007/s10845-010-0404-5
6. Khan, A., Noreen, I., Habib, Z.: On complete coverage path planning algorithms for non-holonomic mobile robots: survey and challenges. J. Inf. Sci. Eng. **33**(1), 101–121 (2017). https://jise.iis.sinica.edu.tw/JISESearch/pages/View/PaperView.jsf?keyId=154_1997
7. Li, L., et al.: Complete coverage problem of multiple robots with different velocities. Int. J. Adv. Robot. Syst. **19**(2), 172988062210916 (2022). https://doi.org/10.1177/17298806221091685
8. Lin, H.Y., Huang, Y.C.: Collaborative complete coverage and path planning for multi-robot exploration. Sensors **21**(11), 3709 (2021). https://doi.org/10.3390/s21113709
9. Nasirian, B., Mehrandezh, M., Janabi-Sharifi, F.: Efficient coverage path planning for mobile disinfecting robots using graph-based representation of environment. Front. Robot. AI **8**(March), 1–19 (2021). https://doi.org/10.3389/frobt.2021.624333
10. Tan, C.S., Mohd-Mokhtar, R., Arshad, M.R.: A comprehensive review of coverage path planning in robotics using classical and heuristic algorithms. IEEE Access **9**, 119310–119342 (2021). https://doi.org/10.1109/access.2021.3108177

Complex Layers of Ranked Prognostic Models

Leon Bobrowski[1,2(✉)]

[1] Faculty of Computer Science, Bialystok University of Technology, Wiejska 45A, Bialystok, Poland
l.bobrowski@pb.edu.pl

[2] Institute of Biocybernetics and Biomedical Engineering, PAS, Warsaw, Poland

Abstract. Complex layers of linear classifiers or prognostic models are designed on the basis of datasets consisting of a small number of multidimensional feature vectors representing individual objects. Elements of a complex layer are designed on the basis of subsets of features selected from a large initial set of features.

Linear prognostic models forming a complex layer can be designed using the ordering of feature vectors in selected pairs of such vectors. The prognostic models have the form of such linear transformations of multidimensional feature vectors into points on a straight line, which maintain the given ordering relationships in pairs of some feature vectors. Linear ordering (ranked) transformations can be designed by minimizing convex and piecewise linear criterion functions.

Keywords: ranked pairs of feature vectors · linear prognostic models · complex layers · convex and piecewise linear criterion functions

1 Introduction

High-dimensional datasets often appear in practical tasks [1]. Such datasets consist of a small number of multidimensional feature vectors. Genetic data sets, among others, have such a structure.

The multidimensionality of feature vectors can cause difficulties in designing good classification or regression models [2]. A large number of features means that the obtained model may have many parameters, which may be associated with the problem of data overfitting [3]. In addition, numerical difficulties may arise in a multidimensional parameter space [4].

According to the complex layer approach, a number of low-dimensional feature subspaces associated with individual layer elements are extracted from the multidimensional feature space [5]. As a result, individual elements of the layer are designed in their own feature subspaces. The principle of maximizing the margins of the L_1 norm is used in the design procedures.

In the presented work, complex layers of ranked prognostic models have been taken into account. The ranked model has the form of a linear transformation of feature vectors into a straight line that best preserves a given order of feature vectors in certain pairs of these vectors.

N. T. Nguyen et al. (Eds.): ICCCI 2023, LNAI 14162, pp. 660–669, 2023.
https://doi.org/10.1007/978-3-031-41456-5_50

The design of ranked prognostic models based on the minimization of convex and piecewise linear functions (*CPL*) is described. This paper proposes and analyzes a new concept of complex layers of ranked prognostic models.

2 Datasets with Ranked Relations

Consider the data set $\boldsymbol{C}$, composed of m feature vectors $\mathbf{x}_j = [x_{j,1}, \ldots, x_{j,n}]^T$ belonging to the n-dimensional feature space $\boldsymbol{F}[n](\mathbf{x}_j \in \boldsymbol{F}[n])$ [1]:

$$\boldsymbol{C} = \{\mathbf{x}_j : j = 1, \ldots, m\} \tag{1}$$

We assume that feature vectors $\mathbf{x}_j$ in the data set $\boldsymbol{C}$ (1) are high-dimensional. This means that the number m of feature vectors $\mathbf{x}_j$ in the data set $\boldsymbol{C}$ (1) is much smaller than the dimension n of these vectors ($m << n$) [5].

The feature vectors $\mathbf{x}_j$ (1) represent m objects O_j in the feature space $\boldsymbol{F}[n]$.

The component $x_{j,i}$ of the feature vector $\mathbf{x}_j = [x_{j,1}, \ldots, x_{j,n}]^T$ is the numerical result of the measurement of the i-th feature X_i of the j-th object O_j. Feature vectors $\mathbf{x}_j$ are often of a mixed type, because they represent different types of measurements ($x_i \in \{0,1\}$) or $x_i \in R$).

Let the symbol "$\prec$" means the ranked relation "*follows*" which may be fulfilled between two feature vectors $\mathbf{x}_j$ and $\mathbf{x}_k$:

$$\mathbf{x}_j \prec \mathbf{x}_k \Leftrightarrow \mathbf{x}_k \textit{ follows } \mathbf{x}_j \tag{2}$$

The relation "$\prec$" between the feature vectors $\mathbf{x}_j$ and $\mathbf{x}_k$ means that the pair $\{\mathbf{x}_j, \mathbf{x}_k\}$ is *ranked*. The ranked relations (2) between particular feature vectors $\mathbf{x}_j$ and $\mathbf{x}_k$ could result from an additional information about objects (patients) O_j and O_k, e.g. the condition of patient O_k is more dangerous (*risky*) than that of patient O_j ($O_j \prec O_k$).

Consider linear transformation of feature vectors $\mathbf{x}_j$ (1) into numbers y_j:

$$(\forall j \in \{1, \ldots, m\}) \quad y_j = \mathbf{w}^T\mathbf{x}_j \tag{3}$$

where $\mathbf{w} = [w_1, \ldots, w_n]^T$ is the vector of parameters (*weights*) $w_i (w_i \in R)$.

The relation "$\prec$" (2) is preserved by the linear transformation (3) if and only if the following implication holds:

$$(\forall (j, k)) \quad \mathbf{x}_j \prec \mathbf{x}_k \Rightarrow y_j(\mathbf{w}) < y_k(\mathbf{w}) \tag{4}$$

The linear transformation (3) is *ranked* if preserves the relations "$\prec$" (2) as precisely as possible [4]. The procedure of the ranked line designing can be based on the concept of positively and negatively oriented *dipoles* $\{\mathbf{x}_j, \mathbf{x}_{j'}\} (j < j')$.

Definition 1: The ranked pair $\{\mathbf{x}_j, \mathbf{x}_{j'}\} (j < j')$ of feature vectors $\mathbf{x}_j$ and $\mathbf{x}_j'$ is a *positively oriented dipole* $\{\mathbf{x}_j, \mathbf{x}_{j'}\}$ $((j, j') \in J^+)$, if and only if $\mathbf{x}_j \prec \mathbf{x}_{j'}$:

$$(\forall (j, j') \in J^+) \quad \mathbf{x}_j \prec \mathbf{x}_{j'} \tag{5}$$

Definition 2: The ranked pair $\{\mathbf{x}_j, \mathbf{x}_{j'}\}$ $(j < j')$ of feature vectors $\mathbf{x}_j$ and $\mathbf{x}_j{}'$ is a *negatively oriented dipole* $\{\mathbf{x}_j, \mathbf{x}_{j'}\}$ $((j, j') \in J^-)$, if and only if $\mathbf{x}_{j'} \prec \mathbf{x}_j$:

$$(\forall\, (j, j') \in J^-)\ \mathbf{x}_{j'} \prec \mathbf{x}_j \tag{6}$$

Definition 3: The line $y(\mathbf{w}) = \mathbf{w}^T\mathbf{x}$ (3) is fully consistent (*ranked*) with the dipoles $\{\mathbf{x}_j, \mathbf{x}_j{}'\}$ orientations (5) and (6) if and only if the following relations are satisfied:

$$\begin{aligned} &(\forall (j, j') \in J^+) \quad y_j(\mathbf{w}) < y_{j'}(\mathbf{w}) \ \textit{and} \\ &(\forall (j, j') \in J^-) \quad y_j(\mathbf{w}) > y_{j'}(\mathbf{w}) \end{aligned} \tag{7}$$

where J^+ and J^- are sets of the index pairs (j, j') of positively and negatively oriented dipoles $\{\mathbf{x}_j, \mathbf{x}_{j'}\}$ $(j < j')$.

If the line $y = \mathbf{w}^T\mathbf{x}$ (3) is fully consistent with the dipoles $\{\mathbf{x}_j, \mathbf{x}_{j'}\}$ orientations, then the below implication holds:

$$(\forall (j, k))\ \ \mathbf{x}_j \prec \mathbf{x}_k \Rightarrow \mathbf{w}^T\mathbf{x}_j < \mathbf{w}^T\mathbf{x}_k \tag{8}$$

If the above implication holds, then the linear transformation $y(\mathbf{w}) = \mathbf{w}^T\mathbf{x}$ preserves all the ranked relations (7).

3 Linear Separability and Ranked Models

Relations (7) mean the following inequalities on the line (3):

$$\begin{aligned} &(\forall (j, j') \in J_k^+) \quad \mathbf{w}^T(\mathbf{x}_{j'} - \mathbf{x}_j) > 0 \\ &(\forall (j, j') \in J_k^-) \quad \mathbf{w}^T(\mathbf{x}_{j'} - \mathbf{x}_j) < 0 \end{aligned} \tag{9}$$

where J_k^+ and J_k^- are sets of the index pairs (j, j') of positively and negatively oriented dipoles $\{\mathbf{x}_j, \mathbf{x}_{j'}\}$ $(j < j')$.

Let us introduce a positive set $\boldsymbol{R}^+$ and a negative set $\boldsymbol{R}^-$ of difference vectors $\mathbf{r}_{j,j'} = \mathbf{x}_{j'} - \mathbf{x}_j$ related to the above inequalities:

$$\begin{aligned} \boldsymbol{R}^+ &= \{\mathbf{r}_{j,j'} = (\mathbf{x}_{j'} - \mathbf{x}_j) : (j, j') \in J^+\} \\ \boldsymbol{R}^- &= \{\mathbf{r}_{j,j'} = (\mathbf{x}_{j'} - \mathbf{x}_j) : (j, j') \in J^-\} \end{aligned} \tag{10}$$

Under certain conditions, the positive differences set $\boldsymbol{R}^+$ and the negative set $\boldsymbol{R}^-$ (10) can be linearly separated by the following hyperplane $H(\mathbf{w})$ which passes through the origin (zero) of the feature space $\boldsymbol{F}[n]$:

$$H(\mathbf{w}) = \{\mathbf{x} : \mathbf{w}^T\mathbf{x} = 0\} \tag{11}$$

Definition 4: The sets $\boldsymbol{R}^{+}$ and $\boldsymbol{R}^{-}$ (10) are linearly separable in the feature space $\boldsymbol{F}[n]$ if and only if the following inequalities are satisfied:

$$(\exists \mathbf{w})\left(\forall \mathbf{r}_{j,j'} \in \boldsymbol{R}^{+}\right) \ \mathbf{w}^{T}\mathbf{r}_{j,j'} \geq 1 \qquad (12)$$
$$\left(\forall \mathbf{r}_{j,j'} \in \boldsymbol{R}^{-}\right) \ \mathbf{w}^{T}\mathbf{r}_{j,j'} \leq -1$$

The following lemma has been proven true [4]:

Lemma 1: The line $y(\mathbf{w}) = \mathbf{w}^{T}\mathbf{x}$ (3) is fully consistent (*ranked*) with dipoles $\{\mathbf{x}_j, \mathbf{x}_{j'}\}$ orientations (*Definition* 3) if and only if the hyperplane $H(\mathbf{w})$ (11) separates (12) the difference sets $\boldsymbol{R}^{+}$ and $\boldsymbol{R}^{-}$ (10).

4 Ranked Criterion Functions $\Phi_k(\mathbf{w})$

Designing the separating hyperplane $H(\mathbf{w})$ (11) could be carried out through the minimisation of the convex and piecewise linear criterion functions $\Phi_k(\mathbf{w})$ similar to the perceptron criterion function [4]. For this purpose, the following positive $\varphi^{+}_{j,j'}(\mathbf{w})$ and negative $\varphi^{-}_{j,j'}(\mathbf{w})$ penalty functions are defined on the elements $\mathbf{r}_{j,j'}$ of the sets $\boldsymbol{R}^{+}_{k}$ and $\boldsymbol{R}^{-}_{k}$ (10):

$$\left(\forall \mathbf{r}_{j,j'} \in \boldsymbol{R}^{+}_{k}\right)$$

$$\varphi^{+}_{j,j'}(\mathbf{w}) = \begin{matrix} 1 - \mathbf{w}^{T}\mathbf{r}_{j,j'} & if\, \mathbf{w}^{T}\mathbf{r}_{j,j'} < 1 \\ 0 & if\ \mathbf{w}^{T}\mathbf{r}_{j,j'} \geq 1 \end{matrix} \qquad (13)$$

and

$$\left(\forall \mathbf{r}_{j,j'} \in \boldsymbol{R}^{-}_{k}\right)$$

$$\varphi^{-}_{j,j'}(\mathbf{w}) = \begin{matrix} 1 + \mathbf{w}^{T}\mathbf{r}_{j,j'} & if\, \mathbf{w}^{T}\mathbf{r}_{j,j'} > -1 \\ 0 & if\ \mathbf{w}^{T}\mathbf{r}_{j,j'} \leq -1 \end{matrix} \qquad (14)$$

The ranked criterion function $\Phi_k(\mathbf{w})$ is defined as the sum of the *CPL* penalty functions $0^{+}_{j.j'}(\mathbf{w})$ (13) and $0^{-}_{j.j'}(\mathbf{w})$ (14) [4]:

$$\Phi_k(\mathbf{w}) = \sum \varphi^{+}_{j,j'}(\mathbf{w}) + \sum \varphi^{-}_{j,j'}(\mathbf{w}) \qquad (15)$$

$\Phi_k(\mathbf{w})$ is the convex and piecewise linear criterion function as the sum of such type of the penalty functions $\#^{+}_{j,j'}(\mathbf{w})$ (13) and $\#^{-}_{j,j'}(\mathbf{w})$ (14). The basis exchange algorithms allow to find efficiently the minimum Φ^{*} of the function $\Phi_k(\mathbf{w})$ (15) [4].

$$\Phi^{*}_{k} = \Phi\left(\mathbf{w}^{*}_{k}\right) = \min_{\mathbf{w}} \Phi_k(\mathbf{w}) \geq 0 \qquad (16)$$

Lemma 2: The minimum value Φ^{*}_{k} (16) of the ranked criterion function $\Phi_k(\mathbf{w})$ (15) is equal to zero if and only if there exists such a vector $\mathbf{w}$ that the ranking points $y_j(\mathbf{w})$ (3) on the line $y(\mathbf{w}) = \mathbf{w}^{T}\mathbf{x}$ is fully consistent (*Definition* 3) with the ranked relations "$\prec$" (4).

The optimal parameter vector $\mathbf{w}_k^*$ (16) constituting the minimum value Φ_k^* of the ranked criterion function $\Phi_k(\mathbf{w})$ (15) determines the ranked line $y = (\mathbf{w}_k^*)^T \mathbf{x}$ (3).

The regularized criterion function $\Psi_k(\mathbf{w})$ is defined as the weighted sum of the ranked criterion function $\Phi_k(\mathbf{w})$ (15) and the absolute values $|w_i|$ of weighs w_i [4]:

$$\Psi_k(\mathbf{w}) = \Phi_k(\mathbf{w}) + \sum_{i \in \{1,\ldots,n\}} |\mathbf{w}_i| \tag{17}$$

where $\mathbf{w} = [w_1, \ldots, w_n]^T$.

The optimal vector $\mathbf{w}_k^*$ is the global minimum $\Psi_k(\mathbf{w}_k^*)$ of the *CPL* criterion function $\Psi_k(\mathbf{w})$ (17) defined on difference vectors $\mathbf{r}_{j,j'} = \mathbf{x}_{j'} - \mathbf{x}_j$ forming the learning sets $\boldsymbol{R}_k^+$ and $\boldsymbol{R}_k^-$ (10);

$$(\exists \mathbf{w}_k^*)(\forall \mathbf{w} \in R^n) \Psi_k(\mathbf{w}) \geq \Psi_k(\mathbf{w}_k^*) = \Psi_k^* \geq 0 \tag{18}$$

The optimal vector $\mathbf{w}_k^*$ constituting the minimum value $\Psi_k(\mathbf{w}_k^*)$ of the criterion function $\Psi_k(\mathbf{w})$ (17) has been used e.g. in the selection of optimal gene subsets by the *relaxed linear separability* (*RLS*) method [6].

5 Designing Complex Layers of Ranked Prognostic Models

Complex layers can be designed on the basis of sets of differences $\boldsymbol{R}^+$ and $\boldsymbol{R}^-$ (10), when the number $m = m^+ + m^-$ of elements $\mathbf{r}_{i,j}'$ of these sets is much smaller than dimension n of the feature space $\boldsymbol{F}[n]$ ($m << n$) [5]. In this problem, a number K of low-dimensional feature subspaces $\boldsymbol{F}_k[n_k]$ ($k = 1,\ldots, K$) are extracted from the multidimensional feature space $\boldsymbol{F}[n]$ ($\boldsymbol{F}_k[n_k] \subset \boldsymbol{F}[n]$) [9]. Feature subspaces $\boldsymbol{F}_k[n_k]$ are associated with individual ranked models (3) in the layer. The extracted feature subspaces $\boldsymbol{F}_k[n_k]$ are disjoint and have dimension n_k not greater than the number m of elements $\mathbf{r}_{j,j'}$ of the sets $\boldsymbol{R}_k{}^+$ and $\boldsymbol{R}_k{}^-$ (10) ($n_k \leq m$) [5].

Feature subspaces $\boldsymbol{F}_k[n_k]$ ($k = 1,\ldots, K$) are extracted from the multidimensional feature space $\boldsymbol{F}[n]$ in a sequential manner by minimizing regularized criterion functions $\Psi_k(\mathbf{w})$ (17). The regularized criterion functions $\Psi_k(\mathbf{w})$ (17) are convex and piecewise linear and can be minimized by the basis exchange algorithm [4].

In the first Step (k = 1) the criterion function $\Psi_1(\mathbf{w})$ (17) is defined on m vectors $\mathbf{r}_{j,j'} = \mathbf{x}_{j'} - \mathbf{x}_j$ (10) determined on the set $F1(n)$ of all n features X_i:

$$F_1(n) = \{X_1, \ldots, X_n\}. \tag{19}$$

The regularized criterion functions $\Psi_1(\mathbf{w})$ (17) is the following sum:

$$\Psi_1(\mathbf{w}) = \Phi_1(\mathbf{w}) + \sum_{i \in \{1,\ldots,p\}} |\mathbf{w}_i| \tag{20}$$

The below theorem can be proved:

Theorem 1: The minimum value $\Phi_1^* = \Phi_1(\mathbf{w}_1^*)$ (16) of the ranked criterion function $\Phi_1(\mathbf{w})$ (15) defined on the sets $\boldsymbol{R}^+$ and $\boldsymbol{R}^-$ (10) is equal to zero if the vectors $\mathbf{r}_{j,j'} = \mathbf{x}_{j'} - \mathbf{x}_j$ forming these sets are linearly independent in the feature space $\boldsymbol{F}[n]$.

If the assumptions of *Theorem* 1 are met, then $\Phi_1(\mathbf{w}_1^*) = 0$, and the task of minimizing the criterion function $\Psi_1(\mathbf{w})$ (20) can be formulated as a search with the constraints for the optimal vertex $\mathbf{w}_1^*$ [4]:

$$\left(\exists \mathbf{w}_1^*\right)\left(\forall \mathbf{w} \in R^n\right) \quad \Sigma_i|w_i| \geq \Sigma_i\left|w_{1,i}^*\right| > 0 \text{ and } \Phi_1\left(\mathbf{w}_1^*\right) = 0 \tag{21}$$

where $\mathbf{w}_1^* = \left[w_{1,1}^*, \ldots, w_{1,n}^*\right]^T$ is the vector of the optimal parameters $w_{1,i}^*$.

The optimal vector (*vertex*) $\mathbf{w}_1^*$ is the global minimum $\Psi_1(\mathbf{w}_1^*)$ of the *CPL* criterion function $\Psi_1(\mathbf{w})$ (17) defined on difference vectors $\mathbf{r}_{j,j'} = \mathbf{x}_{j'} - \mathbf{x}_j$ forming the learning sets $\boldsymbol{R}_1^+$ and $\boldsymbol{R}_1^-$ (10).

It can be shown, that the optimal vertex $\mathbf{w}_1^* = [w_{1,1}^*, \ldots, w_{1,n}^*]^T$ constituting the minimum $\Phi_1(\mathbf{w}_1^*)$ of the criterion function $\Phi_1(\mathbf{w})$ (17) has at least $n - m$ components $w_{1,i}^*$ equal to zero ($w_{1,i}^* = 0$) [6]. Features $\boldsymbol{X}_i$ related to weights $w_{1,i}^*$ equal to zero are neglected []. As a result, the optimal vector $\mathbf{w}_1^*$ is associated with the following subset $R_1^*(n_1)$ of n_1 ($n_1 \leq m$) *active features* X_i with weights $w_{1,i}^*$ different from zero:

$$R_1^*(n_1) = \left\{X_{i(1)}, \ldots, X_{i(n1)}\right\} = \left\{X_i : w_{1,i}^* \neq 0\right\} \tag{22}$$

After this step, the feature set $F_1(n)$ (19) is reduced to $F_2(n - n_1)$ by such n_1 features $X_{i(l)}$, which are active at the first optimal vertex $\mathbf{w}_1^*$ (21):

$$F_2(n - n_1) = F_1(n) \backslash R_1^*(n_1). \tag{23}$$

In the second step ($k = 2$), the criterion function $\Psi_2(w)$ (17) is defined on m vectors $\mathbf{r}_{j,j'} = \mathbf{x}_{j'} - \mathbf{x}_j$ (10) determined on the reduced set $F_2(n - n_1)$ (23) of $n - n_1$ features X_i. The minimization of the criterion function $\Psi_2(w)$ (17) allows to find the optimal vector $w_2^* = [w_{2,1}^*, \ldots, w_{2,n-n1}^*]^T$ and to determine the subset $R_2^*(n_2)$ of $n_2(n_2 \leq m)$ active features X_i with weights $w_{2,i}^*$ different from zero ($w_{2,i}^* \neq 0$).

In the third step ($k = 3$), the criterion function $\Psi_3(w)$ (17) is defined and minimized on m vectors $\mathbf{r}_{j,j'} = \mathbf{x}_{j'} - \mathbf{x}_j$ (10) determined on the reduced set $F_2(n - n_1 - n_2)$ (23) of $n - n_1 - n_2$ features X_i.

The procedure is continued until K optimal vertices $\mathbf{w}_k^*$ (18) and subsets $R_k^*(n_k)$ (22) of active features X_i are determined ($k = 1, \ldots, K$).

6 Margins Based on the L_1 Norm

If the assumption of *Theorem* 1 are met in the k-th step, then $\Phi_k(\mathbf{w}_k^*) = 0$ and the task of minimizing the criterion function $\Psi_k(\mathbf{w})$ (20) can be formulated as the constrained minimization problem (21) [3]:

Find the optimal vertex $\mathbf{w}_k^* = [w_{k,1}^*, \ldots, w_{k,n}^*]^T$ such that $\Phi_k(\mathbf{w}_k^*) = 0$ and:

$$\left(\forall \mathbf{w}_k \in R^n\right) \quad \Sigma_i\left|w_{k,i}\right| \geq \Sigma_i\left|w_{k,i}^*\right| \tag{24}$$

Or

$$(\forall \mathbf{w}_k \in R^n) \quad \|\mathbf{w}_k\|_{L1} \geq \|\mathbf{w}_k^*\|_{L1} \tag{25}$$

where $\|\mathbf{w}_k\|_{L1}$ is the L_1 norm of the k-th vertex $\mathbf{w}_k = [w_{k,1},\ldots, w_{k,n}]^T$ [5].

The optimal vertex w_k^* (25) is the global minimum $\Psi_k(w_k^*)$ of the *CPL* criterion function $\Psi_k(w)$ (17) defined on m difference vectors $\mathbf{r}_{j,j'} = \mathbf{x}_{j'} - \mathbf{x}_j$ determined on the reduced set $F_2(n - n_1 - n_2 - \ldots - n_{k-1})$ (23) of $n - n_1 - n_2 - \ldots - n_{k-1}$ features X_i [5].

The inequalities (25) can be given also in the following form:

$$(\forall \mathbf{w}_k \in R^n) \quad \delta(\mathbf{w}_k^*)_{L1} \geq \delta(\mathbf{w}_k)_{L1} \tag{26}$$

where $\delta(\mathbf{w}_k)_{L1}$ is the margin based on the L_1 norm:

$$\delta(\mathbf{w}_k)_{L1} = 2/\left(\Sigma_i |w_{k,i}|\right) = 2/\|\mathbf{w}_k\|_{L1} \tag{27}$$

The margin $\delta(\mathbf{w}_k)_{L2}$ based on the L_2 (*Euclidean*) norm is used in the *Support Vector Machines* (*SVM*) method [2]:

$$\delta(\mathbf{w}_k)_{L2} = 2/\left(\mathbf{w}_k^T \mathbf{w}_k\right)^{1/2} = 2/\left(\Sigma_i w_{k,i})^2\right)^{1/2} \tag{28}$$

Lemma 3: If $\Phi_k(\mathbf{w}_k^*) = 0$ (16), then the optimal vertex $\mathbf{w}_k^*$ (25) defines such hyperplane $H(\mathbf{w}_k^*) = \{\mathbf{x}: (\mathbf{w}_k^*)^T\mathbf{x} = 0\}$ (11) which separates (12) the difference sets $\boldsymbol{R}^+$ and $\boldsymbol{R}^-$ (10) with the greatest margin $\delta(\mathbf{w}_k^*)_{L1}$ (27).

$$\begin{aligned}
&(\forall \mathbf{r}_{j,j'} \in \boldsymbol{R}^+) \quad \left(\mathbf{w}_k^*/\|\mathbf{w}_k\|_{L1}\right)^T \mathbf{r}_{j,j'} \geq 1/\|\mathbf{w}_k\|_{L1} \\
&(\forall \mathbf{r}_{j,j'} \in \boldsymbol{R}^-) \quad \left(\mathbf{w}_k^*/\|\mathbf{w}_k\|_{L1}\right)^T \mathbf{r}_{j,j'} \geq -1/\|\mathbf{w}_k\|_{L1}
\end{aligned} \tag{29}$$

The designed complex layer consists of K prognostic models $y_j(\mathbf{v}_k^*)$ defined by the reduced optimal vertices $\mathbf{v}_k[n_k] = [v_{k,1}, \ldots, v_{k,nk}]^T$ (25) with n_k non-zero components $v_{k,i}$ ($v_{k,i} \neq 0$):

$$\begin{aligned}
&(\forall k \in \{1, \ldots, K\})(\forall j \in \{1, \ldots, m\}) \\
&y_j(\mathbf{v}_k[n_k]) = \mathbf{v}_k[n_k]^T \mathbf{x}_j[n_k]
\end{aligned} \tag{30}$$

where $\mathbf{x}_j[n_k]$ is the j-th feature vector $\mathbf{x}_j = [x_{j,1}, \ldots, x_{j,n}]^T$ (1) reduced to n_k components $x_{j,i}$ associated with the active features X_i ($X_i \in R_k^*(n_k)$ (22)).

The reduced vector $\mathbf{v}_k[n_k] = [v_{k,1},\ldots, v_{k,nk}]^T$ is obtained from the optimal vertex $\mathbf{w}_k^* = [w_{k,1}^*,\ldots, w_{k,n}^*]^T$ (25) ignoring the components $w_{k,i}^*$ equals zero ($w_{k,i}^* = 0$).

Each prognostic model $y_j(\mathbf{v}_k^*[n_k])$ (30) of the complex layer operates on its own subset $R_k^*(n_k)$ (22) of n_k active features X_i. The subsets $R_k^*(n_k)$ (22) of active features X_i are disjoint:

$$if\ (k' \neq k),\ then\ \left(R_{k'}^*(n_{k'}) \cap R_k^*(n_k) = \varnothing\right) \tag{31}$$

As follows from the described design procedure, the sequence of optimal vertices $\mathbf{w}_1^*, \mathbf{w}_2^*, \ldots, \mathbf{w}_K^*$ calculated for the complex layer is characterized by non-increasing margins $\delta(\mathbf{w}_k)_{L1}$:

$$d(\mathbf{w}_1^*)_{L1} \geq \delta(\mathbf{w}_2^*)_{L1} \geq \ldots \geq \delta(\mathbf{w}_K^*)_{L1} \tag{32}$$

7 Example: Causal Sequence of Liver Diseases

The *Hepar* database contains descriptions of m_k patients O_j associated with the following chronic liver diseases ω_k ($k = 1, \ldots, 7$) [8]:

ω_1 - Non hepatitis patients ($m_1 = 16$ patients Oj)
ω_2 - Hepatitis acuta ($m_2 = 8$)
ω_3 - Hepatitis persistens ($m_3 = 44$)
ω_4 - Hepatitis chronica activa ($m_4 = 95$)
ω_5 - Cirrhosis hepatitis compensate ($m_5 = 38$)
ω_6 - Cirrhosis decompensata ($m_6 = 60$)
ω_7 - Carcinoma hepatis ($m_7 = 11$)

Each patient O_j in this dataset was represented by a feature vector $\mathbf{x}_j = [x_{j,1}, \ldots, x_{j,n}]^T$ based on approximately 200 features X_i ($n \approx 200$). Feature vectors $\mathbf{x}_j$ were divided into learning sets $\boldsymbol{C}k$ of size n_k according to diseases ω_k patients O_j:

$$(\forall k \in \{1, \ldots, 7\}) \quad C_k = \{\mathbf{x}_j(k) : O_j \in \omega_k\} \tag{33}$$

Medical knowledge allows to form a *causal sequence* among liver diseases ω_k:

$$\omega_1 \rightarrow \omega_2 \rightarrow \ldots\ldots \rightarrow \omega_K \tag{34}$$

The symbol "were divided into learning "$\omega_k \rightarrow {}_{k+1}$" in the above sequence means that the disease ω_{k+1} the given patient O_j resulted from the disease ω_k ($k = 1, \ldots, K - 1$). In other words, the disease ω_{k+1} is *more advanced* than ω_k in the process of development of the disease in a given patient.

The ranked prognostic model $y_j(\mathbf{w}^*) = (\mathbf{w}^*)^T\mathbf{x}_j(k)$ (30) was designed on the learning sets $\boldsymbol{C}_k$ (33) according to the following principle (8) (Fig. 1):

$$if\ \ \omega_{\mathbf{k}} \rightarrow \omega_{\mathbf{k}'}\ \ then\ \ \left(\mathbf{w}^*\right)^T \mathbf{x_j}(k) < \left(\mathbf{w}^*\right)^T \mathbf{x_{j'}}(k') \tag{35}$$

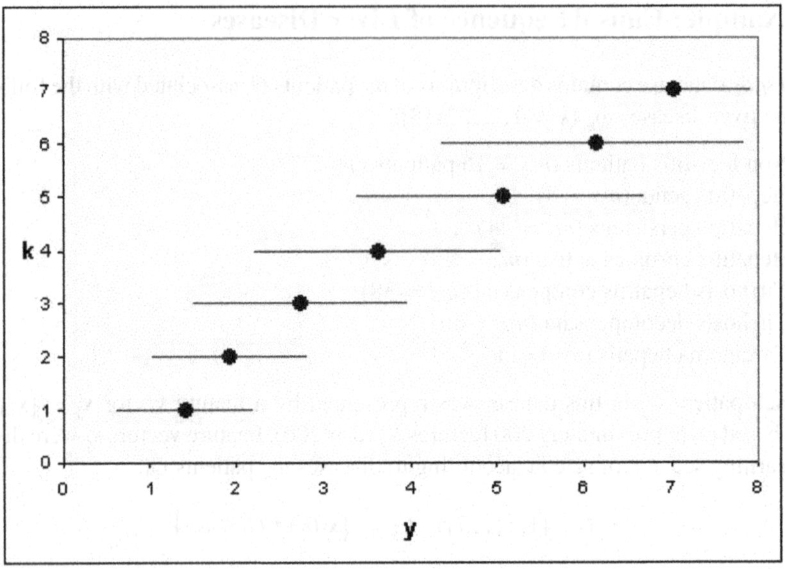

Fig. 1. Graphical representation of the learning sets C_k (33) after ranked transformation $y_j(\mathbf{v}_k^*) = (\mathbf{v}_k^*)^T\mathbf{x}_j(k)$ (30) [8].

8 Concluding Remarks

The ranked prognostic models (30) are obtained from sets of feature vectors $\mathbf{x}_j$ (1) with some additional knowledge in the form of ranked relations "$\lessdot$" (2) in some pairs $\{\mathbf{x}_j, \mathbf{x}_{j'}\}$ of these vectors. The prognostic models have the form of such linear transformations $y_j = \mathbf{w}^T\mathbf{x}_j$ (3) of multidimensional feature vectors $\mathbf{x}_j$ into points y_j on a straight line, which preserve the given a priori rank relations "$\lessdot$" (2) in selected pairs (dipoles) $\{\mathbf{x}_j, \mathbf{x}_{j'}\}$ of feature vectors.

The article considers the design of complex layers of ranked prognostic models (30). The described design is based on linear separability of high dimensional sets $\boldsymbol{R}_k^+$ and $\boldsymbol{R}_k^-$ (10) composed of differences $\mathbf{r}_{j,j'} = \mathbf{x}_{j'} - \mathbf{x}_j$ of oriented dipoles $\{\mathbf{x}j, \mathbf{x}_{j'}\}$ of feature vectors (9).

Prognostic model (30) can be treated as a trend extracted from set of feature vectors $\mathbf{x}_j$ which reflects additional information about patients O_j and O_k, e.g. patient O_k is *more risky* than patient O_j ($O_j \lessdot O_k$). In such a case, the prognostic model (30) can be used as a tool to support medical diagnosis, which allows to assess the condition of new patients O_l represented by new feature vectors $\mathbf{x}_l$ ($\mathbf{x}_l \notin \boldsymbol{C}$ (1)) [4].

The prognostic models $y_j(\mathbf{v}_k^*[n_k])$ (30) operate in the complex layer on their own subsets $R_k^*(n_k)$ (22) of n_k active features X_i [7]. As a consequence, precision and generalization power of the prognosis can be increased by averaging multiple models $y_j(\mathbf{v}_{k'}^*[n_k])$ (30) operating on disjoint subsets $R_{k'}^*(n_{k'})$ (31) of active features X_i. This possibility has recently been confirmed experimentally [9].

Acknowledgments. The presented study was supported by the grant WZ/WI-IIT/3/2023 from the Bialystok University of Technology and funded from the resources for research by the Polish Ministry of Science and Higher Education.

References

1. Duda, O.R., Hart, P.E., Stork, D.G.: Pattern Classification. Wiley, New York (2001)
2. Bishop, C.M.: Pattern Recognition and Machine Learning. Springer, New York (2006)
3. Johnson, R.A., Wichern, D.W.: Applied Multivariate Statistical Analysis. Prentice-Hall Inc., Englewood Cliffs, New York (2002)
4. Bobrowski, L.: Data Exploration and Linear Separability, pp. 1–172. Lambert Academic Publishing (2019)
5. Bobrowski, L.: Complex layers of formal neurons. In: Iliadis, L., Jayne, C., Tefas, A., Pimenidis, E. (eds.) EANN 2022. CCIS, vol. 1600, pp. 81–89. Springer, Cham (2022). https://doi.org/10.1007/978-3-031-08223-8_7
6. Bobrowski, L., Łukaszuk, T.: Relaxed Linear Separability (RLS) Approach to feature (gene) subset selection. In: Xia, X. (eds.) Selected Works in Bioinformatics, pp. 103–118. INTECH (2011)
7. Bobrowski, L.: Computing on vertices in data mining. In: Data Mining, pp. 1–19. Intech Open (2021)
8. Bobrowski, L., Łukaszuk, T., Wasyluk, H.: Ranked modelling of liver diseases sequence. Eur. J. Biomed. Inform. **1**(1) (2007)
9. Bobrowski, L., Zabielski, P.: Classification model with collinear grouping of features. J. Inf. Telecommun. (2022). https://www.tandfonline.com/doi/full/10.1080/24751839.2022.2129133

Configuration of Project Team Members' Competences: A Proactive and Reactive Approach

Jarosław Wikarek and Paweł Sitek(✉)

Kielce University of Technology, Kielce, Poland
{j.wikareksitek,sitek}@tu.kielce.pl

Abstract. To implement IT, business, educational, scientific, etc. projects, it is required to have a team of employees with specific competences. A very important aspect is also to guarantee the availability of these employees during the implementation of individual stages of the project. From the point of view of project management, it is crucial to provide an answer e.g. to the question: *Do the competences of team members guarantee the completion of the project on time*? If constraints related to the absence of team members, costs, limited working time, etc. are additionally considered, then the problem becomes non-trivial. The paper proposes a MILP (Mixed Integer Linear Programming) model for the configuration of project team members, which makes it possible to find answers to many questions related to project management in the context of the project team. The model can be used to make decisions both proactively and reactively. The implementation of the model using mathematical programming and the author's procedure for reducing the size of the modeled problem were also presented.

Keywords: project management · decision support · mathematical programming · staff allocation problem (SAP)

1 Introduction

Certain resources are usually needed to complete any project. Most often these are material resources (machines, tools, materials, etc.), financial resources, human resources, etc. Although project management has a long tradition and rich literature, which resulted in the development of many methodologies, such as Prince 2, PMI, PBOK, etc., modern technological projects require a new look at management issues. This is due to the fact that project team members with high specialist competences play a key role in such projects.

Therefore, now project management has to focus more on project team management than in the past. In particular, it is about selecting a project team whose competence would guarantee the completion of the project on time. In addition, the limited availability of resources must be taken into account. In the case under consideration, this translates into difficulties in acquiring team members with specific competences for the duration of the

N. T. Nguyen et al. (Eds.): ICCCI 2023, LNAI 14162, pp. 670–684, 2023.
https://doi.org/10.1007/978-3-031-41456-5_51

project (market situation) and taking into account the absence of individual members already during the project implementation (pandemic, accidents, etc.).

Our motivation to undertake research in this area was the desire to find answers to key questions such as:

Does a given project team have the right composition and competence to complete the project on time? Will it be possible to implement the project if a member of the project team is absent? What competencies does the project team lack to implement the project?

There may also be questions related to the costs of project implementation by a specific project team. Questions arising in the context of the composition and configuration of the project team can be proactive as well as reactive.

The paper proposes a model for configuration of project team competence, which can be the basis for supporting decisions both proactively and reactively in the context of the project team. In addition, the implementation of the model in the mathematical programming environment was presented and supplemented with the author's procedure for reducing the size of the modeled problem.

2 Background

The considered problem can be described as a significant variant of the Generalized Assignment Problem (GAP) known from the literature. Simply put, the GAP is the problem of assigning a set of tasks to a set of resources (machines, persons, tools, software, etc.) with a minimum total cost. Most often, resources have a limited capacity. The GAP is a well-known, NP-complete combinatorial optimization problem [1]. It has been applied in many real-world problems such as machine loading in manufacturing systems, production planning, job assignment in computer networks, healthcare transportation, timetabling etc. [2, 3]. There are many variants of GAP. In the context of the considered problem, the most interesting GAP variants are Timetabling Problem, Staff Allocation, Student Project Allocation etc. [4–6]. Exact methods, heuristics and metaheuristics (local search and population search-based), and hybrid methods, are used to implement GAPs and their variants [7]. Exact methods provide an optimal solution, while heuristic methods just try to produce a good but most often only feasible solution. Exact methods include, for example, dynamic programming, constraint programming, and mathematical programming. If the considered problem becomes too large for the use of exact methods, i.e., for example, the time to solve it, is unacceptable, then very often heuristics and metaheuristics [8] are used. Metaheuristic methods can be divided into two categories: local search techniques and population search techniques. Local search techniques iteratively use a single candidate solution for improvement. The examples of the local search techniques are Simulated Annealing (SA), Tabu Search (TS) and Great Deluge (GD) [9]. Unlike these, population-based techniques use a population of potential solutions in an iterative search process for further improvements such as fly algorithm, genetic algorithm (GA) and ant colony optimization [10].

What makes our approach different can be considered in two aspects, i.e. modeling and implementation. First of all, when it comes to the modeled problem, unlike the

Timetabling Problem or Staff Allocation Problem, we take into account employee competencies that can be supplemented and modified. In addition, the proposed structure of the model makes it possible to support various decisions regarding the configuration of the project team in proactive and reactive mode. In the implementation aspect, our contribution consists in using the method of pre-solving the modeled problem by introducing a proprietary procedure for reducing the number of decision variables and constraints.

3 Problem Statement and Mathematical Model

A project P is given, which consists of tasks $c \in C$. To perform the task, team members $w \in W$ who have the competencies $k \in K$ are required. Each team member $w \in W$ may have a finite number of competencies $k \in K$. A schedule for the performance of tasks $c \in C$ under the project P is given. Absences/unavailability of team members $u \in U$ are taken into account. In addition, the limitation of team members' working time is taken into account.

For this problem, the following questions (*Q1..Q6*) can be asked (Table 1). These questions are crucial in the context of project team management and consequently affect the management and implementation of the entire project.

Table 1. Description of possible questions asked to model the problem

Question		Description
Q1		*Is the available project team sufficient to perform all tasks within the project (taking into account competences, working time and schedule)?*
If the answer to question Q1 is positive then Q2 and Q3		
Q2		*Which member/members of the project team should perform which task so that the cost of work is as low as possible?*
Q3		*The cost of the implementation of which tasks is greater than the expected profits from their implementation?*
If the answer to question Q1 is negative then Q4 variants /A,B,C/		
Q4	A	*Is it possible to complete all tasks with changes in the working time of team members?*
	B	*What competencies do team members lack to complete the project?*
	C	*How to change the qualifications of team members to complete the project?*
Q5		*Is it possible to complete the project (implement all tasks) with certain states of absence of team members?*
Q6		*How should the qualifications of team members be supplemented so that the project can always be completed in the event of certain absences?*

For the problem presented in this way, a certain meta mathematical model has been developed. It was formulated in the form of a set of constraints (1)..(15) and a set of questions *Q1* to *Q6*. A description of the constraints of the modeled problem is presented in Table 3. In the next step, the questions were also modeled with constraints and, in some cases, objective function (Table 4). Depending on the selection of constraints and the choice or lack thereof of objective function, detailed models were created for individual questions, which took different forms. These were BILP (Binary Integer Linear Programming) or CSP (Constraint Satisfaction Problem) models. In all detailed models, the decision variables were binary. Model parameters, indexes and calculable values are shown in Table 2.

The proposed questions *Q1..Q3* are proactive or reactive. The nature of these questions depends on when they are asked in time. If they are asked before the start of the project, they are proactive, and if they are asked during the project, they are reactive. On the other hand, questions *Q4..Q6* are typical proactive questions. It should be emphasized that the solution of detailed models with proactive questions enables more effective management of the competences and configuration of the project team and makes it more resistant to the occurrence of specific disturbances. In the present case, it concerns disturbances resulting from the absence of team members.

A very interesting feature of the proposed model is the introduction of additional decision variables $Y_{u,c,k}$. These variables do not result directly from the nature of the modeled problem. However, their use is of fundamental importance in the process of finding a solution. Without these variables, a solution could not be found for certain data instances, and an NSF (No Solution Found) situation could arise. Such a situation in the context of the answer to the question did not bring practically any in-depth information about the reasons for the lack of a solution. However, the introduction of these additional variables meant that, firstly, it was always possible to find a solution (the NSF situation did not appear), as well as the values $Q_{u,c}$ of these variables determined which tasks could not be performed and for what reason (the lack of which and how many competences).

$$\sum_{w\in W} s_{u,w} \cdot X_{u,w,c,k} = (1 - Y_{u,c,k}) \cdot g_{c,k} \forall u \in U,\ c \in C,\ k \in K \tag{1}$$

$$X_{u,w,c,k} \le r_{w,k} + J_{w,k} \forall u \in U,\ w \in W, c \in C, k \in K \tag{2}$$

$$b_w \le \sum_{c\in C} (t_c \cdot Z_{u,w,c}) \le f_w \forall u \in U,\ w \in W \tag{3}$$

$$\sum_{k\in K} X_{u,w,c,k} \le con \cdot Z_{u,w,c} \forall u \in U,\ w \in W,\ c \in C \tag{4}$$

$$X_{u,w,c,k} \le 1 - Y_{u,c,k} \forall u \in U,\ w \in W,\ c \in C,\ k \in K \tag{5}$$

$$Z_{u,w,c1} + Z_{u,w,c2} \le 1 \forall u \in U,\ w \in W, c1, c2 \in C \wedge h_{c1,c2} = 1 \tag{6}$$

$$\sum_{w\in W} Z_{u,w,c} \le con \cdot Q_{u,c} \forall u \in U,\ c \in C \tag{7}$$

$$\sum_{w\in W} Z_{u,w,c} \ge Q_{u,c} \forall u \in U,\ c \in C \tag{8}$$

Table 2. Indices, parameters, and decision variables of the model

Symbol	Description
Sets and Indexes	
K	A set of team members competencies
W	A set of team members
C	A set of tasks to be performed
U	A set of absence states
k	Competence index $k \in K$
w	Team member index $w \in W$
c	Task index $c \in C$
u	Absence status index $u \in U$
Parameters	
rw,k	If a team member w has the competency k then $r_{w,k} = 1$, otherwise $r_{w,k} = 0$
mw,k	If team member w can get competency k (e.g. after training) then $m_{w,k} = 1$, otherwise $m_{w,k} = 0$
t_c	Duration of the task c
pc	Profit from the complete task c
dc	How many team members w can perform the task c
ew	Cost of work of the team member w per time unit
b_w	Minimum working time of the team member w
f_w	Maximum working time of the team member w
gc,k	If completing the task c requires the competency k then $g_{c,k} = 1$, otherwise $g_{c,k} = 0$
su,w	If the team member w is available in the state u then $s_{u,w} = 1$, otherwise $s_{u,w} = 0$
hc1,c2	If the schedule assumes the completion of task $c1$, which coincides with the completion of task $c2$ then $h_{c1,c2} = 1$ otherwise $h_{c1,c2} = 0$
con	Arbitrarily large constant
Decision variables	
Xu,w,c,k	If, in the unavailability state u, the team member w using competency k completes task c then $X_{u,w,c,k} = 1$ otherwise $X_{u,w,c,k} = 0$
Zu,w,c	If, in the unavailability state u, the team member w complete the task then c $Z_{u,w,c} = 1$ otherwise $Z_{u,w,c} = 0$
$Y_{u,c,k}$	If the task c cannot be completed due to the impossibility of obtaining competency k in the unavailability state u then $Y_{u,c,k} = 0$ (decision variable introduced only to achieve a solution in each case – so that the NFSF/No Feasible Solution Found situation/state does not appear), otherwise $Y_{u,c,k} = 1$

(continued)

Table 2. (*continued*)

Symbol	Description
$J_{w,k}$	If team member *w* is required to obtain competency *k* to perform all tasks, then $J_{w,k} = 1$, otherwise $J_{w,k} = 0$
$Q_{u,c}$	If in the unavailability state *u* complete the task *c* than $Q_{u,c} = 1$, otherwise $Q_{u,c} = 0$
Calculated parameters	
Cost	The cost of completing tasks
Count_1	The number of uncompleted tasks
Count_2	The number of new competencies that team members need to acquire
Income	Income from completed tasks

$$\sum_{w \in W} Z_{u,w,c} \leq d_c \forall u \in U,\ c \in C \tag{9}$$

$$J_{w,k} \leq m_{w,k} \forall w \in W, k \in K \tag{10}$$

$$\begin{aligned} &X_{u,w,c,k} \in \{0,1\} \forall u \in U,\ w \in W,\ c \in C,\ k \in K; \\ &Z_{u,w,c} \in \{0,1\} \forall u \in U,\ w \in W,\ c \in C; \\ &Y_{u,c,k} \in \{0,1\} \forall u \in U,\ c \in C,\ k \in K; \\ &J_{w,k} \in \{0,1\} \forall w \in W,\ k \in K; \\ &Q_{u,c} \in \{0,1\} \forall u \in U,\ c \in C \end{aligned} \tag{11}$$

$$Count\_1 = \sum_{u \in U} \sum_{c \in C} (1 - Q_{u,c}) \tag{12}$$

$$Count\_2 = \sum_{w \in W} \sum_{k \in K} J_{w,k} \tag{13}$$

$$Cost = \sum_{u \in U} \sum_{w \in W} \sum_{c \in C} t_c \cdot e_w \cdot Z_{u,w,c} \tag{14}$$

$$Income = \sum_{u \in U} \sum_{c \in C} p_c \cdot Q_{u,c} \tag{15}$$

Table 3. Constraints of the modeled problem

Number	Description
1	The constraint forces the setting of the value $Y_{u,c,k} = 1$ in the case of the impossibility of assigning team members to the task *c* due to the lack of competencies of *k*, taking into account the state *u*
2	The constraint specifies that a team member uses only their competencies to perform a task
3	The constraint ensures that the working time of team members is within the specified range
4	The constraint defines the binding of the variables $X_{u,w,c,k}$ and $Z_{u,w,}$
5	The constraint defines the binding of the variables $X_{u,w,c,k}$ and $Y_{u,c,k}$
6	The constraint ensures that a given team member cannot perform two tasks at the same time
7,8	The constraint defines the binding of the variables $Z_{u,w,c}$ and $Q_{u,c}$
9	A constraint specifies that only the allowed number of team members can perform a given task
10	A constraint specifies that a team member can gain competencies in a specific scope available to them
11	The constraint ensures that the variables are binary
12	Calculation of the number of uncompleted tasks
13	Calculation of the number of required competency changes
14	Calculation of the cost of performing tasks by team members
15	Calculation of income from completed tasks

Table 4. Questions - types, ways of modeling, and modes

Question	Problem type	Constrains	Objective	Solution	Mode
Q1	CSP	1..13, Count_1 = 0, Count_2 = 0	—	$X_{u,w,c,k}$	*P/R*
Q2	BILP	1..14, Count_1 = 0, Count_2 = 0	Min (Cost)	$X_{u,w,c,k}$	*P/R*
Q3	BILP	1..15, Count_2 = 0	Max (Income – Cost)	$Q_{u,c}$	*P/R*
Q4a	BILP	1..15, Count_1 = 0, change f_w, d_c	Max (Income – Cost)	$Y_{u,c,k}$	*P*
Q4b	BILP	1..15, Count_2 = 0	Min (Count_1)	$Y_{u,c,k}$	*P*

(*continued*)

Table 4. (*continued*)

Question	Problem type	Constrains	Objective	Solution	Mode
Q4c	BILP	1..15, Count_1 = 0	Max (Income – Cost)	Jw,k	P
Q5	CSP	1..15, Count_1 = 0, Count_2 = 0	—	$X_{u,w,c,k}$	P
Q6	BILP	1..15, Count_1 = 0,	Min(Count_2)	$X_{u,w,c,k}$	P

4 Implementation and Computational Examples

The AMPL (A Mathematical Programming Language) language and the *Gurobi* mathematical programming optimization package (MP solver) were used to implement the model (Sect. 3). AMPL is an algebraic modeling language to describe and solve high-complexity problems for large-scale mathematical computing. The general scheme of the implementation is shown in Fig. 1. Due to the discrete and combinatorial nature, finding an exact solution for larger problems can be problematic in terms of computation time and resource commitment.

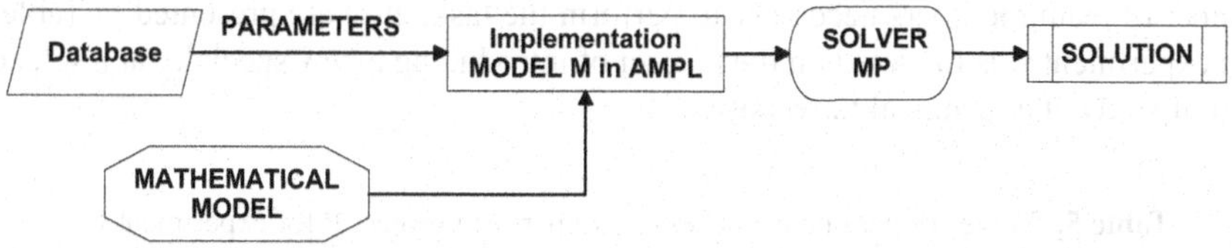

Fig. 1. Method of implementing the modeled problem using the AMPL and the MP solver

Therefore, a certain modification of the method of implementing the modeled problem was proposed, which is shown in Fig. 2. This modification consisted in using the procedure of reducing the size of the modeled problem before solving it. So, it is a kind of presolving procedure. Its application makes it possible to reduce the number of decision variables and reduce the number of constraints and/or simplify them.

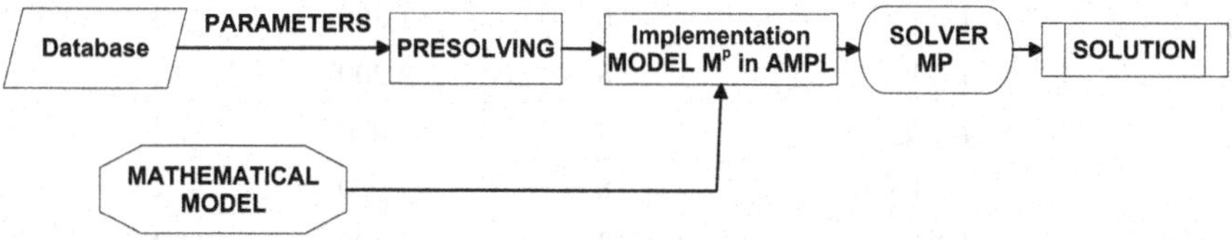

Fig. 2. Modified method of implementing the modeled problem using the AMPL and the MP solver, as well as the proprietary presolving procedure

The M^P model thus reduced is then solved in the same way as the M model by using the MP solver. The procedure algorithm is described in detail in [11]. It is based on the use of the features of the relational/factual problem data record and their appropriate transformation to the matrix format used by MP solvers for MILP, ILP, BILP, etc. models. in the table) then it is filled with zeros in the matrix representation. In the case of our procedure, data matrices [11] are transformed.

After the implementation of the modeled problem, numerous computational experiments were carried out. The experiments were carried out in two stages. The first stage involved solving a small problem manually and using the problem model and its implementation in AMPL and Gurobi. In the second stage, for larger data instances, the effectiveness of the implementation methods shown in Fig. 1 and Fig. 2 was compared.

The First Stage of the Experiments

In the experiment E1, project P is carried out that consists of 12 tasks (c_1.. c_{12}). Figure 3 shows the given schedule for the implementation of tasks within the project (the schedule also includes the time of implementation of each task and the required competences).

The six members of the project team (w_1.. w_6) have been appointed to perform these tasks, who may have four different competencies (k_1.. k_4). The competencies of individual team members are presented in Table 6 (additionally, there is data on the required minimum and maximum working time and the cost of work of each team member per time unit). The required competencies to perform the tasks and additional parameters characterizing the task (task duration, profit for task completion, maximum number of team members necessary to perform the task, etc.) are presented in Table 5. The experiment was modeled on the project of introducing a new specialty at a selected field of study at a technical university.

Table 5. Values of parameters necessary to perform project P for experiment E1

Task for	competencies	tc	pc	d_c
c1	k1	4	1 000	1
c_2	k3	4	1 200	1
c_3	k1, k2	6	2 500	2
c_4	k3	4	1 200	1
c_5	k_1, k_4	6	2 800	1
c6	k_1, k_4	6	3 200	1
c_7	k_3	6	1 800	1
c_8	k_1, k_2	8	2 200	1
c_9	k_2, k_4	4	2 000	1
c_{10}	k_1, k_2, k_4	8	4 000	2
c_{11}	k4	4	1 400	1
c_{12}	k_3	2	1 000	1

As part of the experiment E1, the answer to question Q1 was first sought. Finding the answer to this question is crucial because it determines the next questions. If the

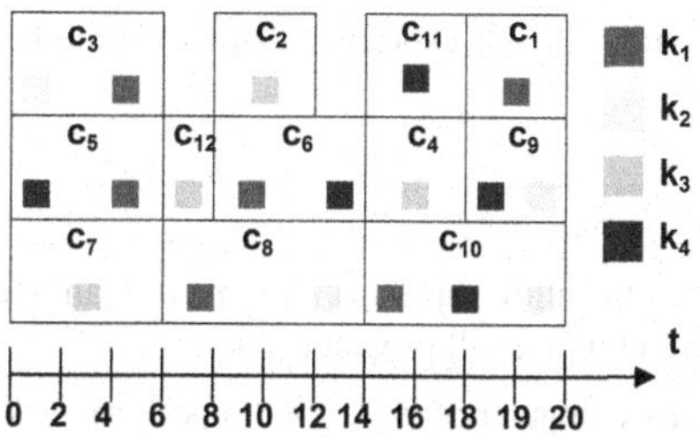

Fig. 3. Project implementation schedule for experiment E1

Table 6. Parameters describing individual members of the project team for experiment E1

Team member	Competencies				Working time		ew
	k_1	k2	k3	k_4	b_w	fw	
w1	1	1	0	0	2	16	30
w_2	1	1	0	1	2	16	30
w_3	0	1	x	0	2	16	50
w_4	1	1	0	x	2	16	60
w_5	1	1	1	0	2	16	90
w6	x	0	1	1	2	16	50

1 - has a given competence
0 - does not have a given competence
x - it is not possible to obtain a given competence

answer to question Q1 is positive, i.e. YES, then we can ask questions Q2, Q3, Q4 and Q6, otherwise we can ask different variants of question Q4. Finding the answer to question Q1 was done in two ways. At first, manually, i.e. directly by the project manager. Unfortunately, after about 30 min, no positive answer could be found, so the answer to question Q1 = No. Then, the mathematical model presented in Sect. 3 was used to find the answer. After about 2 s, the answer Q1 = No was obtained. In the subsequent stages of the research, answers to the remaining questions were sought using the proposed model. The results obtained are presented collectively in Table 7 and, respectively, for questions Q2 and Q5, also in Fig. 4 and Fig. 5, 6.

The Second Stage of the Experiments

The goal of the second stage of the experiments was to assess the effectiveness of the proposed method of implementing the mathematical model using the original presolving procedure (Fig. 2) in relation to the classic way of implementing the language and Solver MP (Fig. 1). Both methods were compared in terms of time finding the answer to the question and the necessary memory resources.

Experiments were carried out for the nine instances (*EII1.. EII9*), which differed in parameters in, *k*, *c,* and thus sizes. Table 8 shows the time to find answers to questions

Table 7. Results obtained during the E1 experiment using the model for individual Q questions

Question	Answer	Objective
Q1	NO	—
Q4A	If we increase the allowable working time of team members by 25%, we will complete all project tasks	21 140
Q4B	There is no k_4 competence to be able to perform task c_{11}	1
Q4C	After team member w_4 obtains k_4 competencies, it is possible to perform all tasks of the project	20 160
Team member w_4 obtained the k_4 competency		
Q1	YES	—
Q2	The answer to this question is shown in Fig. 4	3 140
Q3	It is profitable to complete all the tasks (the profit for the task is always greater than the cost), the solution is the same as for Q2	21 160
Q5		
Missing w_1	YES (the profit from the project will be 20 500, Fig. 5)	—
Missing w_2	NO	—
Missing w_3	YES (the profit from the project will be 21 460, Fig. 6)	—
Missing w_4	NO	—
Missing w_5	NO	—
Missing w_6	NO	—
Q6	To complete all tasks under the project, it is required that the w_3 member obtains the competence of k_3 and a member of the w_6 obtains the competence of k_1	2

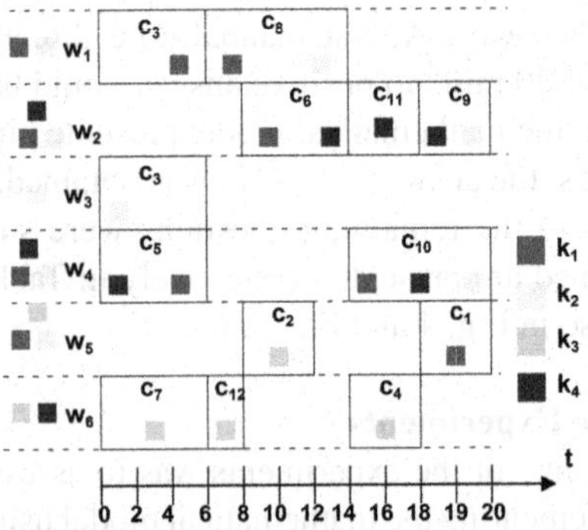

Fig. 4. Optimal allocation of team members to tasks in relation to Cost_1- (Q2)

Q1, Q2, Q3 and the memory necessary for this using the classic implementation of the model M in Fig. 1. However, Table 9 presents the same but when using the presolving

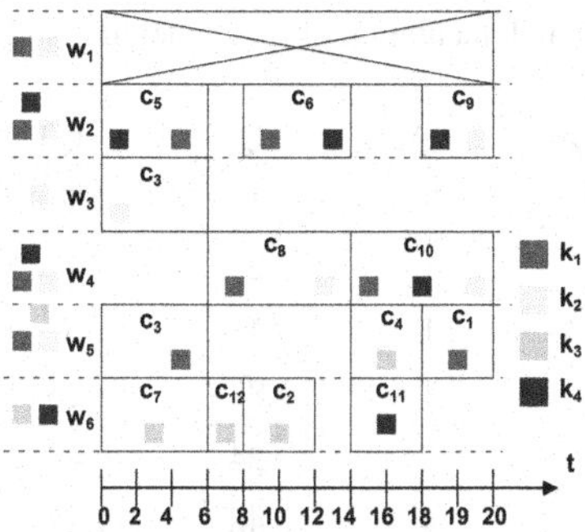

Fig. 5. Assignment of team members to tasks in case no team member w1- (Q5)

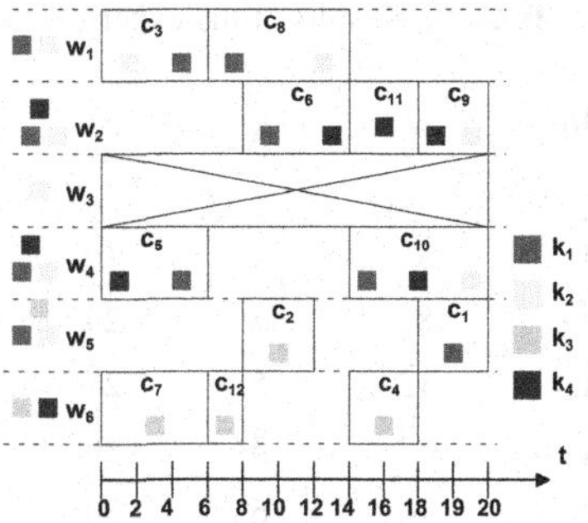

Fig. 6. Assignment of team members to tasks in case no team member w3- (Q5)

procedure when implementing the model M^P (Fig. 2). Analyzing the results obtained, it can be stated that the use of an author's original method with the presolving procedure (Fig. 2) shortened the calculation time to 10 times for more compulsory computational questions Q2 and Q3. What is more, for some other data, the answer to the question Q2 and Q3 was not able to use the method without the procedure of presolving (Fig. 1). As for the committed memory in the calculation process, a reduction between 30% and 40% was obtained depending on the data instance. Graphically, these results for Q1, Q2 and Q3 questions are presented in Fig. 7, 8, 9 10.

Table 8. Results of the experiments using the implementation of the model in Fig. 1

EIIn	w	k	c	Memory	Q1	Q2	Q3
					T	T	T
EII_1	8	4	16	674	3	2	3
EII_2	8	4	24	840	3	12	14
EII_3	12	5	24	1140	6	65	124
EII_4	12	5	36	1570	6	121	323
EII_5	16	6	30	1676	6	324	451
EII_6	16	6	40	2222	7	546	745
EII_7	20	6	40	2509	7	756	834
EII_8	20	6	50	3502	9	900^{**}	900^{**}
EII_9	24	8	60	5602	23	900^{**}	900^{**}

Table 9. Results of the experiments using the implementation of the model in Fig. 2

EIIn	w	k	c	Memory	Q1	Q2	Q3
					T	T	T
EII_1	8	4	16	542	1	2	2
EII_2	8	4	24	640	1	4	6
EII_3	12	5	24	878	1	8	23
EII_4	12	5	36	1021	2	24	47
EII_5	16	6	30	1123	4	48	67
EII_6	16	6	40	1456	4	98	142
EII_7	20	6	40	1645	4	123	194
EII_8	20	6	50	2346	6	246	354
EII_9	24	8	60	3534	8	345	472

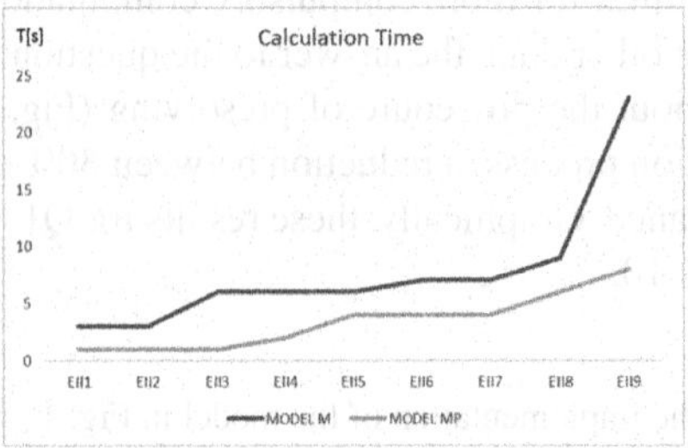

Fig. 7. Calculation times for question Q1 for both approaches.

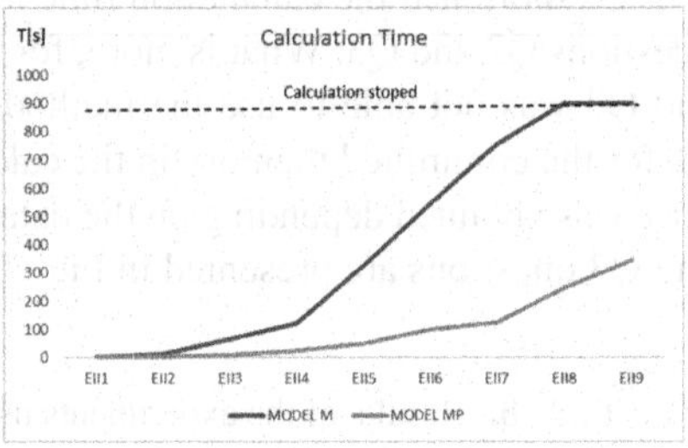

Fig. 8. Calculation times for question Q2 for both approaches.

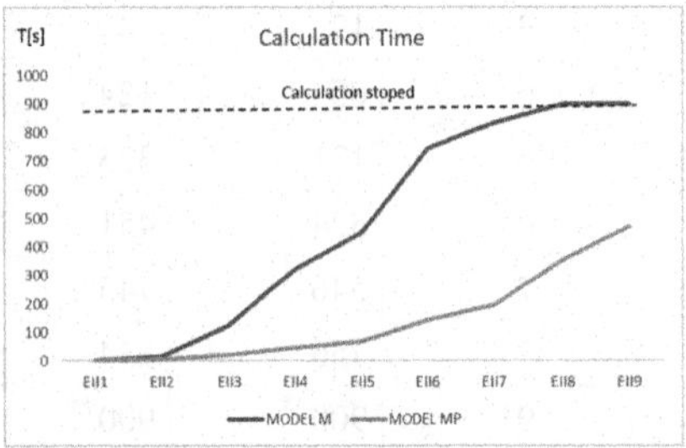

Fig. 9. Calculation times for question Q3 for both approaches.

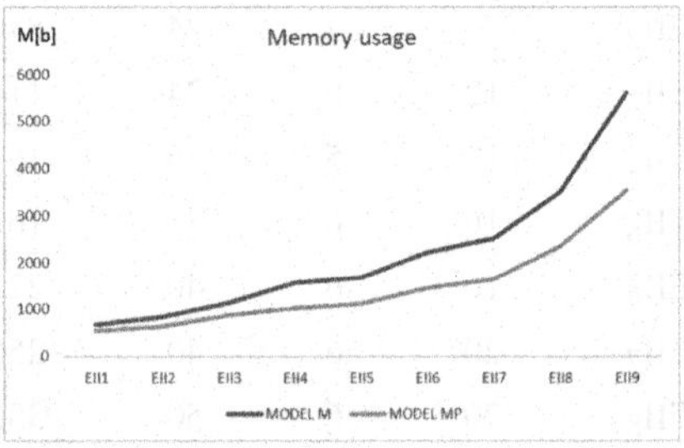

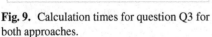

Fig. 10. The degree of resource (memory) utilization for both approaches for Q1, Q2, Q3.

5 Conclusions

The formal model proposed in the paper makes it possible to support a number of decisions in the area of project team management, which facilitates/enables the implementation of the project within a given time and schedule. The uniqueness of the proposed model lies in the fact that the supported decisions have been formulated in the form of answers to questions Q1..Q6, they can be reactive and proactive. In addition, the proposed structure of the model always ensures finding a solution. In the absence of competencies and/or members of the project team, the solution of the model shows what and how much of it is missing.

The most important decisions that can be supported using the proposed model include:

a) *Does your project team guarantee that the project will be completed on time and on schedule?*
b) *Will the absence of the selected team member allow the project to be completed on time and on schedule?*
c) *How to supplement the competencies and composition of the project team to ensure project execution on time and on schedule?*

Due to the nature of the modeled problem, the method of implementing the model is interesting. The paper proposed two ways of implementation. An original method using the developed presolving procedure – this procedure uses a proprietary algorithm for reducing the size of the modeled problem [11] and can be used with any MP solver that works with the AMPL language or uses the MPS format. The effectiveness of the proposed method of implementation was tested in relation to the use of only the MP solver (Gurobi). The obtained results (Fig. 7 to Fig. 10) showed the degree of reduction of computation time and resources involved (memory).

In further works, it is planned to extend the scope of the model with additional questions (concerning short-term absences of individual team members, the need to implement many projects simultaneously by the same team, etc.) and integration with project management systems. It is also envisaged to apply the proposed model to employee teams in the industry, especially in multimodal processes [12], maintenance management [13], and also for it to be applied by teachers [14] in schools and universities, and by medical personnel [15].

References

1. Peres, F., Castelli, M.: Combinatorial optimization problems and metaheuristics: review, challenges, design, and development. Appl. Sci. **11**(14), 6449 (2021). https://doi.org/10.3390/app11146449
2. Floudas, C.A., Pardalos, P.M. (eds.): Encyclopedia of Optimization. https://doi.org/10.1007/978-0-387-74759-0
3. Öncan, T.: A survey of the generalized assignment problem and its applications. INFOR Inf. Syst. Oper. Res. **45**(3), 123–141. Taylor & Francis (2007) https://doi.org/10.3138/infor.45.3.123

4. Mokhtari, M., Vaziri Sarashk, M., Asadpour, M., Saeidi, N., Boyer, O.: TI - Developing a model for the university course timetabling problem: a case study. Hindawi Complex. **2021**, Article ID 9940866, 12 (2021). https://doi.org/10.1155/2021/9940866
5. Krynke, M., Mielczarek, K., Vaško, A.: Analysis of the problem of staff allocation to work stations. Sciendo **1**((1)July 2019), 545–550 (2019). https://doi.org/10.2478/cqpi-2019-0073
6. Mourtzis, D., Siatras, V., Angelopoulos, J., Panopoulos, N.: An intelligent model for workforce allocation taking into consideration the operator skills. Procedia CIRP **97**, 196–201 (2021). https://doi.org/10.1016/j.procir.2020.05.225
7. Nauss, R.M.: Solving the generalized assignment problem: an optimizing and heuristic approach. INFORMS J. Comput. **15**(3), 249–266 (2003). https://doi.org/10.1287/ijoc.15.3.249.16075
8. Gonzalez, T.F.(Ed.): Handbook of Approximation Algorithms and Metaheuristics Methologies and Traditional Applications, vol. 1, New York (2018). :https://doi.org/10.1201/9781351236423
9. Junn, K.Y., Obit, J.H., Alfred, R.: Advanced Science Letters, Volume 23, Number 11, November 2017, pp. 11413–11417(5). American Scientific Publishers (2017). https://doi.org/10.1166/asl.2017.10295
10. Giagkiozis, I., Purshouse, R.C., Fleming, P.J.: An overview of population-based algorithms for multi-objective optimisation. Int. J. Syst. Sci. **46**(9), 1572–1599 (2015). https://doi.org/10.1080/00207721.2013.823526
11. Wikarek, J., Sitek, P.: A new approach to the allocation of multidimensional resources in production processes. Appl. Sci. **12**(14), 6933 (2022). https://doi.org/10.3390/app12146933
12. Bocewicz, G., Nielsen, P., Banaszak, Z.A., Dang, V.Q.: Cyclic steady state refinement: multimodal processes perspective. In: Frick, J., Laugen, B.T. (eds.) Advances in Production Management Systems. Value Networks: Innovation, Technologies, and Management. APMS 2011. IFIP AICT, vol. 384, pp. 18–26. Springer, Berlin, Heidelberg (2012). https://doi.org/10.1007/978-3-642-33980-6_3
13. Antosz, K., Pasko, L., Gola, A.: The use of intelligent systems to support the decision-making process in lean maintenance management. IFAC PapersOnLine **52**(10), 148–153 (2019). https://doi.org/10.1016/j.ifacol.2019.10.005
14. Babaei, H., Karimpour, J., Hadidi, A.: A survey of approaches for university course timetabling problem. Comput. Ind. Eng. **86**, 43–59 (2015). https://doi.org/10.1016/j.cie.2014.11.010
15. Abdalkareem, Z.A., Amir, A., Al-Betar, M.A., et al.: Healthcare scheduling in optimization context: a review. Health Technol. **11**, 445–469 (2021). https://doi.org/10.1007/s12553-021-00547-5

Computational Intelligence in Medical Applications

Teeth Disease Recognition Based on X-ray Images

Mazin S. Mohammed[1,2](✉), Salah Zrigui[1,3], and Mounir Zrigui[1]

[1] Research Laboratory in Algebra, Numbers Theory and Intelligent System (RLANTIS), University of Monastir, 5019 Monstir, Tunisia
mazinsalm@uomosul.edu.iq, Monuir.zrigui@fsm.rnu.tn
[2] University of Al-Mosul, University of the Presidency, Nineveh, Iraq
[3] IRIT, Toulouse, France

Abstract. Teeth caries or lesions have a huge impact on people health. Hence, the early diagnosis of these diseases plays an important role of the healthcare provided by medical professionals. Therefore, researchers have proposed an automatic recognition based on AI methods to help medical examiners to offer the correct decision. However, the automatic identification of dental decay using X-ray images can be considered as an open area and it requires more works and researches, So, we propose in this paper a new dataset of 5 types caries of 1290 dental X-ray images. The collected data is used to extract hand-engineering features to solve the recognition problem using the traditional analysis. Then, we use the deep learning strategies by training a customized CNN from scratch to learn the optimal features of our dataset. Deep learning features have outperformed the traditional ones. Therefore, we use the transfer learning approach to improve the results by retraining without the random initialization. In this direction, we have investigated 10 different types of pre-trained CNNs. We have achieved about 94% of accuracy by modifying VGG19 model to apply the retraining process using the collected images.

Keywords: Teeth disease classification · X-ray images · dental caries recognition · deep learning

1 Introduction

Lately, artificial intelligence (AI), machine learning, and computer vision methods have been used in medical applications [1], medical imaging [2], and even in healthcare crisis or pandemic management [3]. More specifically, machine learning algorithms [4–12] and deep learning techniques [8, 13–16] have been exploited widely to implement different types of applications [17–21]. Researcher developed algorithms to provide disease diagnosis, estimating prognosis, or evolving patient-procedures that provide treatment techniques and strategies. Recently, the huge development of medical science requires accurate and efficient clinical medication [22]. However, clinic treatments require human operators to do the medical procedures manually which demands tedious works, high-quality data, and accurate tests. On the other hand, the judgment decision could be prone

N. T. Nguyen et al. (Eds.): ICCCI 2023, LNAI 14162, pp. 687–699, 2023.
https://doi.org/10.1007/978-3-031-41456-5_52

to mistakes due to many circumstances such as: lack of experience, subjective opinions, Fatigue, and tiredness which medical professional may suffer during long working hours, especially in crisis times [23, 24]. Therefore, researchers have tried to automate these sorts of operations. By integrating the artificial intelligence algorithms with the medical science to come up with hybrid system can offer the ability to provide systematic diagnosis. The decision, of a such system, is based on training of machine learning algorithms to imitate the ability of medical expert humans [25].

Tooth caries, or sometimes it is called dental decay, is a particular disease like any other diseases which influences millions of people in the globe. Tooth decay can be categorized into different types of caries: initial stage disease, medium, or late stage illness which damage the root of individual tooth. The stage of each type depends on the damage of the teeth by the lesion. Late stages of teeth decay can be avoided by early diagnosis which can save not only money, but also effort by obviating difficult treatment procedures [26]. Sometimes, tooth decay can be detected using clinical investigation procedures which depends entirely on the dentist's skills. On the other hand, the radiographs can be used to offer an accurate diagnosis and detect hidden problems. The dental radiography is highly recommended to be used more frequently to detect proximal tooth decay with visual X-ray image [27]. However, the identification of tooth caries can be varied for the same particular case due to the subjectivity. Professional medical observers may give different opinions in term of the existence or the type of caries lesions even for the same X-ray image. The variations of diagnosis decision could be subjected to many factors such as amount of experience, examination period, and environment circumstances [28]. Therefore, dental clinics can take advantage of the machine learning improvement to help in decision-making procedures. Generally, artificial intelligence can support and help dentists to dismiss any human error and offer an optimal diagnosis to increase the provided health care and decrease and stress or pressure on the care providers [29].

Different algorithms and methods have been suggested by researchers to detect and classify medical images to provide accurate diagnoses. Some of these methods presented solutions based on hand-engineering features. While the late works used deep learning strategies. However, teeth caries recognition is very challenging task and it depends on the collected data [30]. Hence, this problem is still an open one and it is broadly unresolved issue, therefore it demands more improvement. So, this paper proposes teeth disease classification based on X-ray images. First, we start our work by collecting real-world X-ray images. The gathering process is done by some local clinics. Then, we use the help of professional dentists to label the collected data. After that, we prepare the data to perform diseases classification by splitting the data into training set and testing set. We extracted both traditional and deep learning features to capture the characteristics of our data. The extracted features, from the training set, are used to train different recognizer models. Finally, we evaluate the performance of the trained models using the testing data. The rest of this paper is organized into five sections. Section 2 discuses some of the pervious works. The data collecting is presented in Sect. 3. Section 4 describes the proposed classification models. The experimented results are shown in Sect. 5, and finally, we conclude our findings in Sect. 6.

2 Literature Review

Researchers have suggested different kinds of methods to solve the problem of the oral diseases. In this section, we survey some of the previous works. The early methods of dental caries recognition were done by extracting handcraft features and then classifying the features by training machine learning techniques. For example, the researchers in [31] trained A stacked auto-encoder neural network to identify teeth caries from the normal ones using X-ray images. The inputs of proposed networks were the raw data of the X-ray images where the network contained three hidden layers and one soft max layer. In [32] 87 dental images of five different diseases were used to present Dental Diagnosis System. The designed system combined three stages of segmentation, classification and decision making. The segmentation was done by semi-supervised fuzzy clustering, then Local Binary Patterns (LBP), Entropy, edge-value and intensity features, Patch Level Feature, Red-Green-Blue, and the Gradient were extracted to perform the classification which was implemented using affinity propagation clustering algorithm. On the other hand, some of the proposed methods used deep learning algorithms, more specifically, the authors in [33] collected 251 X-ray images of three different diseases. Convolutional neural network was trained using the collected images. Additionally, they extracted features by applying the images into VGG16 to improve the results using transfer learning technique. In [34] the authors utilized panoramic X-ray images to classify different dental implant brands by adopting convolutional neural networks (CNN). The CNN network was trained using 8859 implant images of 11 implant systems. In [35] the authors classified X-ray images into decay/no decay classes. They used adaptive approach to modify images brightness. Then, a graph-cut segmentation method was used to isolate the foreground and background of dental X-Ray dataset. After that, they used Alex network to extract features to perform the classification process.

The researchers in [36] gathered 108 images for normal/not normal teeth. They started their methods with Laplacian filter to sharpen the collected images. Then, a window based adaptive thresholding was applied to perform the segmentation. Sixteen statistical features were extracted to capture the texture characteristics of their data. Lastly, a back-propagation neural network with two hidden layers was trained by the extracted features. In [37] the researchers classified four different types of dental diseases by applying filtering, segmentation, features extraction, and classification processes. They extracted size, shape, and density form the segmented images. Finally, Stacked Sparse Auto-Encoder network and Logistic regression Classifier were trained using the extracted features.

The authors in [38] trained faster R-CNN network using 2900 digital dental pictures. They training R-CNN was done in four different subsets of the collected images. Then, these models were compared using statistical analysis to measure the significant of their performance. In [39] the authors collected 16,000 dental X-ray images from 5000 patients. Three CNN networks were used to classify the images into healthy/non-healthy cases. AlexNet, ResNet-18, and ResNet-34 were retrained using the collected data to perform disease classification. The researchers in [40] created a dataset of 800 panoramic X-rays images of four different diseases. The images were labeled manually by an expert doctor by performing the annotation process. Then, the labeled data was increased to 1200 images using data augmentation. Finally, YOLO network was retrained using the gathered dataset to recognize four types of teeth diseases: root canals, cavities, dental crowns, and broken root canals.

3 Data Preparation

The work of our project can be structured into five stages: data collecting, data annotation, data preparation for training, training process, and the assessment of the trained models, these stages are shown in Fig. 1.

The first stage of this work is the data collecting. In this phase, we collect X-ray images of different types of teeth diseases. The gathering of these X-ray images is done by some local clinics with cooperation of professional dentists. The collected data includes 1290 dental X-ray images of five popular classes. Our dataset is gathered from male/female patients of age ranging from 15 to 60 years. The gathered images were acquired anonymously without recording any information such as name, age, or medical condition of the patients.

The Second step of our project is data labeling. Unfortunately, this procedure cannot be done automatically. Some manual laboring is required to achieve the labeling process. Even though, it is tedious work and demands huge effort. Particularly, in our case the manual work cannot be done using ordinary operators. So, the manual annotation of our dataset is inevitable and it should be performed by expert in dentistry field. Therefore, the collected data were examined, under optimal conditions of brightness, contrast, and lighting, by professional dentists and radiologists to interpret and offer an accurate diagnosis. Some of these samples' images are shown in Fig. 2. Additionally, the quality of the collected images is enhanced by applying Gaussian filter to remove the noise and unwanted objects. Furthermore, histogram equalization is used to improve the contrast of images.

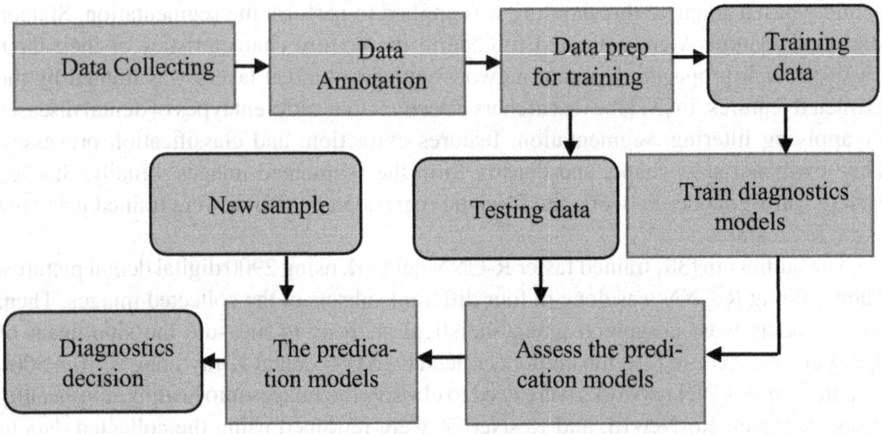

Fig. 1. Block diagram of the proposed system

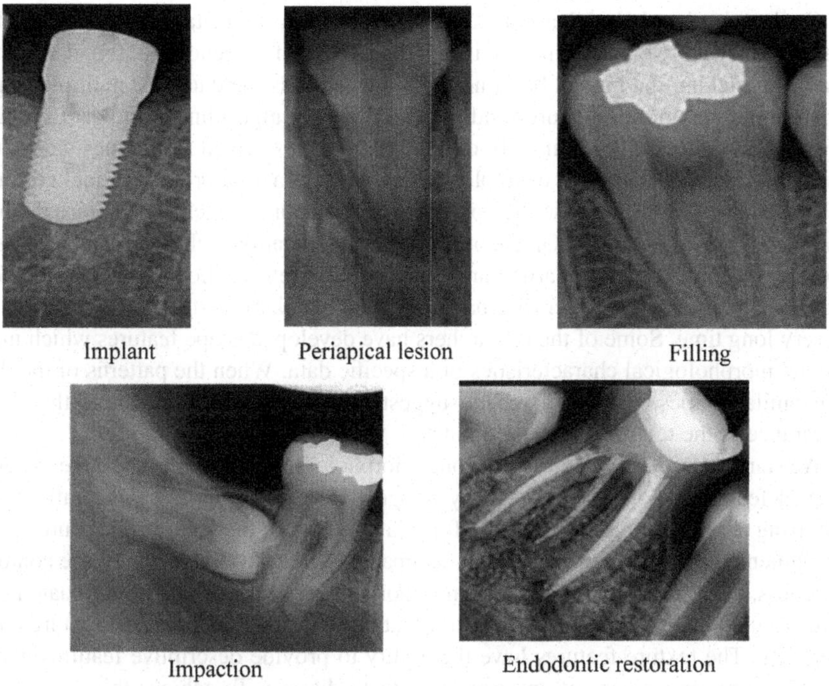

Fig. 2. Image samples of the collected data

4 Diseases Recognition

After we prepare the data, the ultimate goal in this stage is to learn different types of models that can identify various sorts of teeth diseases. In order to carry out the training process, we divide the prepared images into two partitions. The first part of our data is called the training dataset. While the second one is called the testing dataset. The training dataset is about 80% of the entire dataset. This part of the data is used to learn models throughout the training process. The second part of the collected data is used to perform an evaluation measurement to assess the learned model from the training process. The testing dataset is about 20% of our data.

As we mentioned in the literature, carries classification by X-ray images can be done by applying a process of either two stages or one stage. The researchers have spent a large amount of effort to improve the classification and the recognition of different types of diseases based on medical images. Hence The learning mechanism of machine learning models can be implemented in two different techniques. Two-stages technique of object recognition is considered as traditional methods which come from the old school of computer vision strategies. This approach utilizes hand-engineering features to extracts some descriptive features in the first stage. While in the second stage exploits the extracted features to train classification algorithms to perform the identification process.

On the other hand, deep learning techniques can perform the task of classification in one stage instead two stages mechanism. The deep learning schools is founded on the idea of mimicking the human brain neurology to process the data into multiple stages to determine the optimal features and the classification algorithm of the data simultaneously. Two stages algorithms rely on the type of the selected techniques within the first and the second stage. For example, the features extraction process should consider the type of the data and choose the optimal type of features which can capture the best characteristics and attributes. On the other hand, classification technique can be an issue whether if it suitable for the particular data or not. Therefore, choosing the perfect features with the optimal classifier for a particular data is under investigation by researchers for very long time. Some of the researchers have developed shape features which measure the morphological characteristics of a specific data. When the patterns of the data have similar shapes, some researchers suggested texture features to capture the visual appearance of the texture surface attributes.

We start our project by extracting some morphological features to measure the geometrical features of our medical X-ray images. Hence, we apply segmentation process using adaptive thresholding and after that we extract the following features from the segmented contour: perimeter, area, compactness, fractal dimension of the contour, roundness, and the aspect ratio based on minor and major axis. To accommodate more representative features, we extract texture features to capture the surface texture characteristics. The texture features have the ability to provide descriptive features which capture the interior pieces of any particular teeth disease. To achieve this, we extract the intensities level statistics (mean, variance, and entropy), pixels histogram features, GOLC matrix (gray level co-occurrence) features, LBPH descriptors (local binary pattern histogram), SURF (speeded up robust features), HOG (histogram of oriented gradients), and SIFT (scale-invariant feature transform) descriptors.

The extracted features are used to train a classification algorithm to create a predication model. A logistic regression classifier is trained using the extracted features to perform the identification process. After that, the testing data is used to assess the efficiency of the trained model by applying the features from the testing to the predication model to measure the accuracy performance. All the results of these experiments are presented in the result section. The training process of the classifier starts with fitting some parameters (Φ) by minimizing a loss function using gradient descent strategy. Then, the predication of a specific sample for particular class can be calculated according to the following formula:

$$Y(class\,k/x_i) = \frac{e^{\theta k^T} x_i}{1 + \sum_{j=1}^{N-1} e^{\theta j^T} x_i} \tag{1}$$

In order to improve the results accuracy, deep learning strategies are adopted to perform the recognition process. More specifically, convolutional neural networks (CNN) are used to classify the collected images. CNN is a class of pattern-classification network which has the ability to learn from the trained images the optimal features and classifier on the same time. Learn the optimal features using CNN saves time and effort which replace all the traditional methods of finding the right hand-engineering features to implement the classification process. Hence, we partition the deep learning analysis into two stages. In the first one, we train a customized convolutional neural network with random initialization. The trained CNN consists of 19 layers, 4 convolutional layers where each one is followed by a batch normalization layer, a rectified layer (ReLUs), and a pooling layer. Figure 3 shows the information architecture of our CNN network. To achieve the training process, a zero-mean Gaussian distribution is sampled to initialize the parameters of the designed network. Additionally, the biases of the network are initialized with values of ones. Unfortunately, the number of collected images is very small compared to the number of the learnt parameters of the trained CNN. Therefore, the direct training to estimate the network's parameters may suffer from overfitting problem. To overcome the overfitting effect and improve the training process, data-augmentation strategies are utilized to increase our dataset artificially. Different types of data transformations are used to increase the training images by applying scaling, translation, reflection, illumination changes, and rotation.

In the second stage of the learning process of CNN, we try to improve the results by adopting transfer learning techniques. This approach relies on gaining the previous knowledge from a pre-trained model using big data instead of the random initialization of the network's parameters. There are many pre-trained models which can be used as base classifiers instead of training CNNs from the scratch. We select Resnet50 [41] to obtain the learned knowledge. However, we need to modify the selected network to perform the training process using our own dataset. Therefore, we remove the classification layer of Resnet50 (last layer) and we attach our own classification layer to apply fine-tune process to shape the resulted network parameters in a suitable way to learn the best features from our medical images. The classification layer consists of a fully connected layer of 512 nodes followed by a drop-out layer by factor of half to reduce the effect of the over-fitting. After that, we add another fully connected layer of 256 nodes with second drop-out layer followed by soft-max layers with classification layer of 5 output nodes. The designed network is shown in Fig. 4.

Clearly, the results of the deep learning features from the pre-trained models offer a reasonable performance. Therefore, we extend the range of the base classifiers by adopting more pre-trained models to improve the accuracy results. In order to improve the results, we utilize the previous knowledge from the following networks: AlexNet, VGG16, VGG19, GoogleNet, Xception, InceptionV3, InceptionResNetV2, DenseNet201, MobileNetV2, and NASNetLarge. More specifically, similar approach is repeated to perform the fine-tuning process to reshape the trained features by removing the last layer from each individual network and adding our own classification layers which consist of 512 nodes of fully connected layer, drop-out layer, 256 nodes of fully connected layer, drop-out layer, and 5 nodes of soft-max layer. The results section will contain all the results of the conducted experiments.

5 The Experiments Results

In this section, we present the results of all the conducted experiments. The results of our project can be categorized into three parts. First, we apply the traditional methods of caries identification by extracting some well-known/defined features to capture shape and texture characteristics of our X-ray images. After that, the extracted features are

Name	Type	Activations	Learnables	Total Learnab...
imageinput 128x128x1 images with 'zerocenter' normalization	Image Input	128×128×1	-	0
conv_1 64 9x9x1 convolutions with stride [1 1] and padding [0 0 0 0]	Convolution	120×120×64	Weights 9×9×1×64 Bias 1×1×64	5248
batchnorm_1 Batch normalization with 64 channels	Batch Normalization	120×120×64	Offset 1×1×64 Scale 1×1×64	128
relu_1 ReLU	ReLU	120×120×64	-	0
maxpool_1 2x2 max pooling with stride [2 2] and padding [0 0 0 0]	Max Pooling	60×60×64	-	0
conv_2 32 7x7x64 convolutions with stride [1 1] and padding [0 0 0 0]	Convolution	54×54×32	Weights 7×7×64×32 Bias 1×1×32	100384
batchnorm_2 Batch normalization with 32 channels	Batch Normalization	54×54×32	Offset 1×1×32 Scale 1×1×32	64
relu_2 ReLU	ReLU	54×54×32	-	0
maxpool_2 2x2 max pooling with stride [2 2] and padding [0 0 0 0]	Max Pooling	27×27×32	-	0
conv_3 16 5x5x32 convolutions with stride [1 1] and padding [0 0 0 0]	Convolution	23×23×16	Weights 5×5×32×16 Bias 1×1×16	12816
batchnorm_3 Batch normalization with 16 channels	Batch Normalization	23×23×16	Offset 1×1×16 Scale 1×1×16	32
relu_3 ReLU	ReLU	23×23×16	-	0
maxpool_3 2x2 max pooling with stride [2 2] and padding [0 0 0 0]	Max Pooling	11×11×16	-	0
conv_4 10 3x3x16 convolutions with stride [1 1] and padding [0 0 0 0]	Convolution	9×9×10	Weights 3×3×16×10 Bias 1×1×10	1450
batchnorm_4 Batch normalization with 10 channels	Batch Normalization	9×9×10	Offset 1×1×10 Scale 1×1×10	20
relu_4 ReLU	ReLU	9×9×10	-	0
fc 5 fully connected layer	Fully Connected	1×1×5	Weights 5×810 Bias 5×1	4055
softmax softmax	Softmax	1×1×5	-	0
classoutput crossentropyex	Classification Output	-	-	0

Fig. 3. List of the customized CNN layers

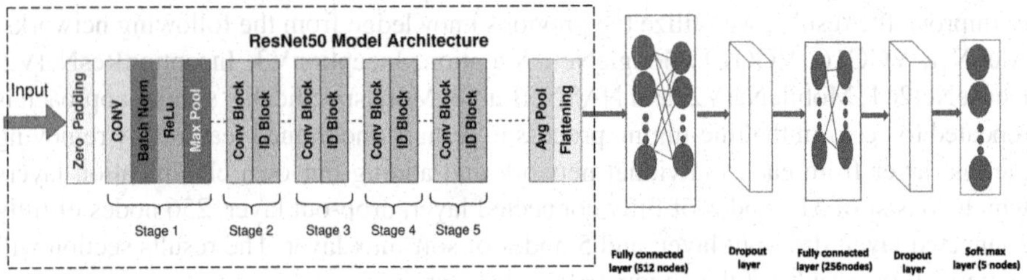

Fig. 4. The architecture network of the proposed CNN

used to train logistic regression classifier to perform the diseases recognition process. The testing dataset is used to evaluate the performance of the trained classifiers. Accuracy, precision, and recall measurements are used as metrics performance to perform the assessment validation comparison analysis. Table 1 shows the results of these experiments. The second part of our project includes deep learning features experiments. We train customized convolutional neural network of 19 layers to learn the best combination of features and classifier simultaneously. The trained CNN achieved about 83% of accuracy which outperformed all the hand-engineering features trials.

Table 1. Accuracy rate of the classification using logistic classifier.

Method	Accuracy	Precision	Recall
Geometrical features, fractal dimension	49.69%	48.93%	48.81%
Histogram descriptive, Pixel level statistics	46.56%	45.93%	45.63%
Gray level co- occurrence matrix, Gabor features	47.55%	48.07%	47.17%
HOG features	52%	51.37%	52.02%
SIFT features	50%	49.96%	49.86%
LBPH features	54.69%	54.19%	53.74%
SURF features	48.76%	49.13%	48.90%
BOW histogram	78.44%	77.89%	77.36%
BOW hitogram, geometrical features, fractal dimension, Histogram descriptive, Pixel level statistics, LBPH features	80.02%	79.92%	79.87%
Customized trained CNN	83.87%	83.79%	83.47%

The deep learning results encourage us to apply the transfer learning technique by adopting Resnet50 network as base model to improve the classification accuracy results. Hence, we modify the selected CNN to implement teeth caries recognition by retraining the modified version of the network using our datasets. By adopting this approach, we achieved almost 92% of accuracy. The previous knowledge of pre-trained model using large dataset offers a reasonable features representation to classify 5 different types teeth diseases.

To improve the results, we applied the same procedure of the transfer learning to 10 different models of previously trained networks using big data. The comparison results of these base models are shown in Table 2. It is worth to mention that all the conducted experiments were carried out using Lenovo laptop with Cor I 7 of 16G RAM. These deep learning models are different in term of architecture shape, mapping connection, number of layers, level of complexity, and number of parameters. The models were trained using a big data of general object recognition problem. Their performance may vary from one to another depending on their characteristics. Additionally, the transfer learning may give a different performance due to the variations of the new task and the data distribution.

By observing table II, the comparison results indicate that the best base network is VGG19 which achieved 94.72% accuracy. Clearly, VGG19 offers the best trained features which capture the optimal characteristics of the collected images. Additionally, we computed the confusion matrix of modified trained VGG19, the result of this matrix is shown in Fig. 5.

Table 2. Accuracy of deep learning networks.

Base network model	Accuracy	Precision	Recall
AlexNet	90.79%	90.27%	92.57%
Resnet50	92.08%	92.10%	91.77%
GoogleNet	93.96%	94.06%	93.88%
VGG16	92.45%	92.36%	92.84%
VGG19	**94.72%**	**94.68%**	**94.78%**
NasNet-Mobile	88.83%	88.21%	88.45%
DenseNet201	94.65%	94.21%	94.43%
MobileNetV2	0.8969	0.8946	0.8972
InceptionResNetV2	93.58%	93.76%	93.68%
Xception	92.11%	91.87%	91.80%
InceptionV3	91.76%	92.26%	91.95%

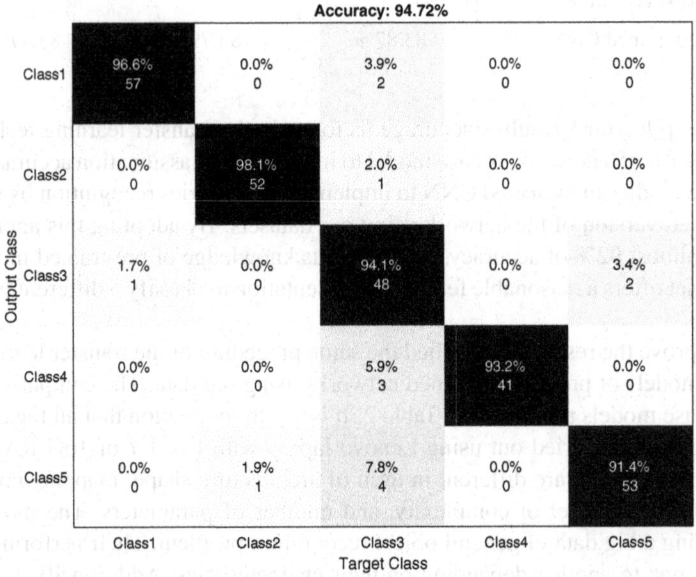

Fig. 5. Confusion matrix of the trained VGG19.

6 Conclusion

In this project, we present a new dataset to provide an accurate diagnosis of 5 types of teeth diseases using X-ray images. The collected images are labeled using professional medical operators. The labeled data is used to train different types of models to perform the recognition. First, we extract hand-designed features to represent shape and texture characteristics. Additionally, we train a CNN of 19 layers to learn the optimal features of our dataset. In the same direction of deep learning strategies, we use the transfer learning approach to train Resnet50 with the previous parameters to obtain the knowledge of the trained model. Furthermore, we modified network architecture of 10 pre-trained models to improve the accuracy of the classification performance. The learnt features from VGG19 offers a classification rate of 94%.

References

1. Magoulas, G.D., Prentza, A.: Machine learning in medical applications. In: Paliouras, G., Karkaletsis, V., Spyropoulos, C.D. (eds.) ACAI 1999. LNCS (LNAI), vol. 2049, pp. 300–307. Springer, Heidelberg (2001). https://doi.org/10.1007/3-540-44673-7_19
2. Erickson, B.J., Korfiatis, P., Akkus, Z., Kline, T.L.: Machine learning for medical imaging. Radiographics **37**(2), 505 (2017)
3. Mohammed, M.R., Daood, A.: Smart surveillance system to monitor the committed violations during the pandemic. Int. J. Comput. Digit. Syst. **11**, 1415–1426 (2021)
4. Maraoui, M., Antoniadis, G., Zrigui, M.: CALL system for Arabic based on natural language processing tools. In: IICAI, pp. 2249–2258 (2009)
5. Legrand, A., Trystram, D., Zrigui, M.: Adapting batch scheduling to workload characteristics: What can we expect from online learning? In: 2019 IEEE International Parallel and Distributed Processing Symposium (IPDPS), pp. 686–695. IEEE (2019)
6. Merhbene, L., Zouaghi, A., Zrigui, M.: A semi-supervised method for Arabic word sense disambiguation using a weighted directed graph. In: Proceedings of the Sixth International Joint Conference on Natural Language Processing, pp. 1027–1031 (2013)
7. Terbeh, N., Zrigui, M.: Vocal pathologies detection and mispronounced phonemes identification: case of Arabic continuous speech. In: Proceedings of the Tenth International Conference on Language Resources and Evaluation (LREC 2016), pp. 2108–2113 (2016)
8. Farhani, N., Terbeh, N., Zrigui, M.: Image to text conversion: state of the art and extended work. In: 2017 IEEE/ACS 14th International Conference on Computer Systems and Applications (AICCSA), pp. 937–943. IEEE (2017)
9. Batita, M.A., Zrigui, M.: Derivational relations in Arabic wordNet. In: Proceedings of the 9th Global WordNet Conference, pp. 136–144 (2018)
10. Terbeh, N., Labidi, M., Zrigui, M.: Automatic speech correction: a step to speech recognition for people with disabilities. In: Fourth International Conference on Information and Communication Technology and Accessibility (ICTA), pp. 1–6. IEEE (2013)
11. Mansouri, S., Charhad, M., Zrigui, M.: Arabic text detection in news video based on line segment detector. Res. Comput. Sci. **132**, 97–106 (2017)
12. Jaballi, S., Zrigui, S., Sghaier, M.A., Berchech, D., Zrigui, M.: Sentiment analysis of Tunisian users on social networks: overcoming the challenge of multilingual comments in the Tunisian dialect. In: Nguyen, N.T., Manolopoulos, Y., Chbeir, R., Kozierkiewicz, A., Trawiński, B. (eds.) Computational Collective Intelligence. ICCCI 2022. Lecture Notes in Computer Science, vol. 13501, pp. 176–192. Springer, Cham (2022). https://doi.org/10.1007/978-3-031-16014-1_15

13. Slimi, A., Hamroun, M., Zrigui, M., Nicolas, H.: Emotion recognition from speech using spectrograms and shallow neural networks. In: Proceedings of the 18th International Conference on Advances in Mobile Computing & Multimedia, pp. 35–39 (2022)
14. Bsir, B., Zrigui, M.: Bidirectional LSTM for author gender identification. In: Nguyen, N.T., Pimenidis, E., Khan, Z., Trawiński, B. (eds.) ICCCI 2018. LNCS (LNAI), vol. 11055, pp. 393–402. Springer, Cham (2018). https://doi.org/10.1007/978-3-319-98443-8_36
15. Bsir, B., Zrigui, M.: Enhancing deep learning gender identification with gated recurrent units architecture in social text. Computación y Sistemas **22**(3), 757–766 (2018)
16. Amari, R., Noubigh, Z., Zrigui, S., Berchech, D., Nicolas, H., Zrigui, M.: Deep convolutional neural network for Arabic speech recognition. In: Nguyen, N.T., Manolopoulos, Y., Chbeir, R., Kozierkiewicz, A., Trawiński, B. (eds.) Computational Collective Intelligence. ICCCI 2022. Lecture Notes in Computer Science, vol. 13501, pp. 120–134. Springer, Cham (2022). https://doi.org/10.1007/978-3-031-16014-1_11
17. Alhafidh, B.M.H., Daood, A.I., Alawad, M.M., Allen, W.: FPGA hardware implementation of smart home autonomous system based on deep learning. In: Georgakopoulos, D., Zhang, L.-J. (eds.) ICIOT 2018. LNCS, vol. 10972, pp. 121–133. Springer, Cham (2018). https://doi.org/10.1007/978-3-319-94370-1_9
18. Ayadi, R., Maraoui, M., Zrigui, M.: Intertextual distance for Arabic texts classification. In: 2009 International Conference for Internet Technology and Secured Transactions, (ICITST), pp. 1–6. IEEE (2009)
19. Mahmoud, A., Zrigui, M.: Deep neural network models for paraphrased text classification in the Arabic language. In: Métais, E., Meziane, F., Vadera, S., Sugumaran, V., Saraee, M. (eds.) NLDB 2019. LNCS, vol. 11608, pp. 3–16. Springer, Cham (2019). https://doi.org/10.1007/978-3-030-23281-8_1
20. Bassem, B., Zrigui, M.: Gender identification: a comparative study of deep learning architectures. In: Abraham, A., Cherukuri, A.K., Melin, P., Gandhi, N. (eds.) ISDA 2018 2018. AISC, vol. 941, pp. 792–800. Springer, Cham (2020). https://doi.org/10.1007/978-3-030-16660-1_77
21. Mounir, A.J., Mallat, S., Zrigui, M.: Analyzing satellite images by apply deep learning instance segmentation of agricultural fields. Periodicals Eng. Nat. Sci. **9**(4), 1056–1069 (2021)
22. Yoon, D.C., Mol, A., Benn, D.K., Benavides, E.: Digital radiographic image processing and analysis. Dent. Clin. **62**(3), 341–359 (2018)
23. Prados-Privado, M., Villalón, J.G., Martínez-Martínez, C.H., Ivorra, C.: Dental images recognition technology and applications: a literature review. Appl. Sci. **10**(8), 2856 (2020)
24. Majanga, V., Viriri, S.: Automatic blob detection for dental caries. Appl. Sci. **11**(19), 9232 (2021)
25. Zhang, X., et al.: Development and evaluation of deep learning for screening dental caries from oral photographs. Oral Dis. **28**(1), 173–181 (2022)
26. Anjum, A., Mythri, Pattar, S.Y.: Early identification of dental caries from IOPA images. https://www.ijrpr.com/. ISSN 2582: 7421
27. Sueishi, N., et al.: Quantification of dental plaque in oral cavity was enabled by a novel algorithm of image processing. J. Oral Biosci. **59**(3), 157–162 (2017)
28. Oliveira, J., Proença, H.: Caries detection in panoramic dental X-ray images. In: Tavares, J., Jorge, R. (eds.) Computational Vision and Medical Image Processing. Computational Methods in Applied Sciences, vol. 19, pp. 175–190. Springer, Dordrecht (2011). https://doi.org/10.1007/978-94-007-0011-6_10
29. Lakshmi, M.M, Chitra, P.: Classification of dental cavities from X-ray images using deep CNN algorithm. In: 2020 4th International Conference on Trends in Electronics and Informatics (ICOEI) (48184), pp. 774–779. IEEE (2020)

30. Latif, J., Xiao, C., Imran, A., Tu, S.: Medical imaging using machine learning and deep learning algorithms: a review. In: 2019 2nd International Conference on Computing, Mathematics and Engineering Technologies (iCoMET), pp. 1–5. IEEE (2019)
31. Ali, R.B, Ejbali, R., Zaied, M.: Detection and classification of dental caries in x-ray images using deep neural networks. In: International Conference on Software Engineering Advances (ICSEA), p. 236 (2016)
32. Tuan, T.M., Fujita, H., Dey, N., Ashour, A.S., Ngoc, V.T.N., Chu, D.-T.: Dental diagnosis from X-ray images: an expert system based on fuzzy computing. Biomed. Sig. Process. Control **39**, 64–73 (2018)
33. Prajapati, S.A., Nagaraj, R., Mitra, S.: Classification of dental diseases using CNN and transfer learning. In: 2017 5th International Symposium on Computational and Business Intelligence (ISCBI), pp. 70–74. IEEE (2017)
34. Sukegawa, S., et al.: Deep neural networks for dental implant system classification. Biomolecules **10**(7), 984 (2020)
35. Lakshmi, M.M., Chitra, P.: Tooth decay prediction and classification from X-ray images using deep CNN. In: 2020 International Conference on Communication and Signal Processing (ICCSP), pp. 1349–1355. IEEE (2020)
36. Geetha, V., Aprameya, K.S., Hinduja, D.M.: Dental caries diagnosis in digital radiographs using back-propagation neural network. Health Inf. Sci. Syst. **8**(1), 1–14 (2020)
37. Leo, L.M., Reddy, T.K.: Learning compact and discriminative hybrid neural network for dental caries classification. Microprocess. Microsyst. **82**, 103836 (2021)
38. Chen, H., Li, H., Zhao, Y., Zhao, J., Wang, Y.: Dental disease detection on periapical radiographs based on deep convolutional neural networks. Int. J. Comput. Assist. Radiol. Surg. **16**(4), 649–661 (2021)
39. Vasdev, D., et al.: Periapical dental X-ray image classification using deep neural networks. Ann. Oper. Res. 1–29 (2022)
40. Almalki, Y.E., et al.: Deep learning models for classification of dental diseases using orthopantomography X-ray OPG images. Sensors **22**(19), 7370 (2022)
41. He, K., Zhang, X., Ren, S., Sun, J. Deep residual learning for image recognition. In: Proceedings of the IEEE Conference on Computer Vision and Pattern Recognition, pp. 770–778 (2016)

Predicting Alzheimer's Disease Diagnosis Risk Over Time with Survival Machine Learning on the ADNI Cohort

Henry Musto[1(✉)], Daniel Stamate[1,2], Ida Pu[1], and Daniel Stahl[3]

[1] Data Science and Soft Computing Lab, Computing Department, Goldsmiths College, University of London, London, UK
hthom018@gold.ac.uk

[2] Division of Population Health, Health Services Research and Primary Care, School of Health Sciences, University of Manchester, Manchester, UK

[3] Institute of Psychiatry Psychology and Neuroscience, Biostatistics and Health Infomatics Department, King's College London, London, UK

Abstract. The rise of Alzheimer's Disease worldwide has prompted a search for efficient tools which can be used to predict deterioration in cognitive decline leading to dementia. In this paper, we explore the potential of survival machine learning as such a tool for building models capable of predicting not only deterioration but also the likely time to deterioration. We demonstrate good predictive ability (0.86 C-Index), lending support to its use in clinical investigation and prediction of Alzheimer's Disease risk.

Keywords: Survival Machine Learning · ADNI · Clinical Prediction Modelling

1 Introduction

One of the most pressing challenges for governments and healthcare systems is the rising number of people with dementia. More than 55 million people live with dementia worldwide, and there are nearly 10 million new cases yearly, with 60–70% of all dementias being of Alzheimer's Disease type (AD) [1]. Recently, attention has turned to Machine Learning (ML) as a tool for improving the predictive ability of clinical models concerning AD and addressing clinical challenges more widely. However, of the hundreds of clinical ML models that appear in scientific publications each year, few have thus far been successfully embedded into existing clinical practice [2]. One of the reasons for this is that most models only provide predictions for disease cases without quantifying the probability of disease occurrence. This limitation restricts clinicians' ability to accurately measure and communicate the probability of disease development over time with the patient. [3]. Also, in the context of predicting the progression of AD in particular, many studies that use ML methods employ a classification approach, whereby the outcome to be predicted is either a binomial or multinomial outcome within a specific timeframe [4, 5]. The datasets are often derived from longitudinal studies, whereby clinical marker data is collected from participants over months and years [6]. Thus, such

N. T. Nguyen et al. (Eds.): ICCCI 2023, LNAI 14162, pp. 700–712, 2023.
https://doi.org/10.1007/978-3-031-41456-5_53

data has a temporal element inherent to the methodology employed in the collection process. However, standard classification ML cannot consider the predictive power of time in conjunction with other predictors. Furthermore, classification models cannot handle drop-outs which are common in longitudinal studies.

With this in mind, a newly emerging field of exploration seeks to build on traditional time-dependent statistical models, such as survival analysis, to develop machine learning models which can predict the time-dependent risk of developing AD and go beyond simple classification. Survival analysis is a statistical method that aims to predict the risk of an event's occurrence, such as death or the emergence of a disease, as a function of time. A key aspect of survival analysis is the presence of censored data, indicating that the event of interest has not occurred while the subject was part of the study. The presence of censored data requires the use of specialised techniques. Traditionally, the Cox proportional hazards model [7] has been the most widely used technique for analysing data containing also censored records. However, the Cox model typically works well for small data sets and does not scale well to high dimensions [8]. ML techniques that inherently handle high-dimensional data have been adapted to handle censored data, allowing ML to offer a more flexible alternative for analysing high-dimensional, censored, heterogeneous data [8]. Furthermore, the ability to predict not only a binary or multinomial outcome but also the risk of such outcomes occurring at different timepoints provides clinicians and researchers with more information for the benefit of research and patients.

This work has several aims. First, it aims to build upon existing work demonstrating the utility of survival-based ML techniques in predicting the risk of deterioration at different time points in AD using the Alzheimer's Disease Neuroimaging Initiative (ADNI) database. Secondly, it aims to explore the predictive power of these techniques once the more physically intrusive biomarkers available in the dataset are removed. These predictors, such as ABETA, TAU and PTAU, which are established biomarkers for dementia, are collected via painful lumbar puncture procedures to sample cerebrospinal fluid (CSF). Recently efforts have been made to investigate alternative biomarkers such as blood metabolites which, in some studies, proved to have comparable predictive power to the established CSF-biomarkers [9].

The rest of the paper will be ordered as follows. First, it will review existing literature on survival-based ML as applied to clinical questions in general and AD prediction in particular. Next, the problem of interest will be defined. Then the proposed methodology will be outlined. Before the results are presented, the study design of the dataset will be described, including predictors and diagnostic criteria. A discussion of the implications of these results will then follow.

2 Related Work

Spooner et al. [8] systematically compared the performance and stability of ML algorithms and feature selection methods suitable for high-dimensional, heterogeneous, censored clinical data, in the context of cognitive ageing and AD, by predicting the risk of AD over time [8]. The authors assessed ten survival-based machine-learning techniques alongside the standard Cox proportional hazard model. The Sydney Memory and Aging Study (MAS) dataset and Alzheimer's Disease Neuroimaging Initiative (ADNI) dataset were utilised. All algorithms evaluated performed well on both data sets and outperformed the standard Cox proportional hazards model.

Another paper that explores the clinical utility of survival modelling within the domain of AD research comes from [10], which looked at the interaction between socioeconomic features and polygenic hazard scores on the timing of Alzheimer's diagnosis using Cox proportional hazard survival analysis. Only the standard Cox PH technique was used. The authors could demonstrate the clinical utility of using socioeconomic markers and the presence of the APOE4 gene expression to predict the time to AD diagnosis. Although a small study focusing on only one model, this work demonstrated the utility of survival-based models in AD prediction. However, more work was needed to build upon these results using ML methods. This was achieved in [11] using ML survival-based methods to predict the risk of developing AD in the English Longitudinal Study of Aging (ELSA) dataset. This work again found that Survival ML outperformed Cox methods.

On the other hand, [12] found the standard Cox regression and two ML models (Survival Random Forest and Extreme Gradient Boosting) had comparable predictive accuracy across three different performance metrics, when applied to the Prospective Registry For Persons with Memory Symptoms (PROMPT) dataset [13]. The authors concluded that survival ML did not perform better than standard survival methods.

In comparison, [14] found that multi-modal survival-based deep learning methods produced good results when applied to the ADNI dataset, comparable to [8]. In this context, our present work serves as an example of including neural network models, as these methods have hitherto seldom been explored in a survival context.

Despite the scarcity of survival modelling papers in relation to AD prediction, recent examples have shown promise in attempting to outperform the classic Cox proportional hazard model, using survival ML and survival neural networks/ deep learning on clinical datasets. This supports the continued exploration of survival ML as a predictive tool for clinical risk problems [11].

3 Problem Definition

This study uses survival-based ML methods to predict the risk of deterioration, defined as receiving a worse diagnosis at their final visit to the data collection centre before leaving the study, compared to baseline diagnosis. Furthermore, the study aims to build models to predict the risk of receiving a worse diagnosis within the data collection period using survival-based ML. These models will then be tested for stability, and two estimations of the general test error will be calculated based on C-Index and Calibration scores [15].

A secondary aim is to explore the predictive power of these models when predictors derived from invasive CSF collections are removed from the dataset.

4 Methodology

4.1 Data Description

Alzheimer's Disease Neuroimaging Initiative

The data used in this paper was derived from the Alzheimer's Disease Neuroimaging Initiative (ADNI) database [6]. This longitudinal case-control study was initiated in 2004 by the National Institute of Aging (NIA), The National Institute of Biomedical Imaging and Bioengineering (NIBIB), The Food and Drug Administration (FDA), as well as elements of the private and non-profit sectors. The initial protocol, ADNI1, was conducted over six years, recruiting 400 subjects diagnosed with Mild Cognitive Impairment (MCI), 200 subjects with Alzheimer's (AD), and 200 healthy controls (CN). The initial goal of the ADNI study was to test whether repeated collections of neuroimaging, biomarker, genetic, and clinical and neuropsychological data could be combined to contribute in an impactful way to research dementia [6].

Data for the present paper was downloaded on the 1st of October 2022 through the ADNIMERGE package in R. This package combines predictors from the different.

ADNI protocols. The final combined dataset contains 115 variables and 15,157 observations, which included multiple observations per participant. These observations represent data collection events where participants made up to 23 visits to study sites. The data used for this work is a subset of the full dataset, containing only information from the original ADNI2 study. After some initial cleaning, the resulting data contained 607 observations and 52 variables consisting of 50 input attributes, 1 time attribute (defined as the time in months until the participant visited the data collection centre for the last time), and 1 outcome attribute. The outcome attribute consisted of three diagnostic classes received at their final visit to the data collection centre: those who received a diagnosis of Cognitively Normal (CN), those who received a diagnosis of Mild Cognitive Impairment (MCI), and those who received a diagnosis of Alzheimer's Disease (AD) [4].

4.2 Predictors

- Baselines Demographics: age, gender, ethnicity, race, marital status, and education level were included in the original dataset.
- Neuropsychological test results, including those from the Functional Activities Questionnaire (FAQ), the Mini-Mental State Exam (MMSE), and Rey's Auditory Verbal Learning Test (RAVLT), were included in the data. This numeric data is well-validated as a tool for identifying cognitive impairment in general and AD-related cognitive impairment in particular. Full details of the tests included can be found at [16].
- Positron Emission Tomography (PET) measurements (FDG, PIB, AV45) are indirect measures of brain function using the Positron Emission Tomography neuroimaging modality.
- Magnetic Resonance Imaging (MRI) measurements (Hippocampus, intracranial volume (ICV), MidTemp, Fusiform, Ventricles, Entorhinal and WholeBrain) are structural measurements of a participant's brain derived from the Magnetic Resonance Imaging neuroimaging modality.

- APOE4 is an integer measurement representing the appearance of the epsilon 4 allele of the APOE gene. This allele has been implicated as a risk factor for AD [17]
- ABETA, TAU, and PTAU are cerebrospinal fluid (CSF) biomarker measurements. These biomarkers are collected via lumbar puncture. These predictors were removed from the model-building process for the second set of models.
- Last Visit is defined for this paper as the number of months from baseline data collection to the subject's last visit at a data collection centre. This variable was added to explicitly define a time predictor for survival-based ML modelling.

4.3 Data Preprocessing

Boolean variables were created, indicating the location of missing data for each predictor. Variables with missingness at 90% or greater of the total rows for that predictor were removed. All nominal predictors were dummy-coded.

The data was split into two groups to predict deterioration using survival-based ML. The first group contained only those diagnosed as cognitively normal (CN) on their first visit to the data collection centre. The second group contained only those diagnosed with Mild Cognitive Impairment (MCI) on their first visit to the data collection centre. Deterioration was defined as receiving a worse diagnosis on their final visit to the data collection centre. The resultant two datasets had 285 and 322 observations respectively and 98 variables with CSF-derived biomarkers included/92 without (See Tables 1, 2, 3).

Table 1. Those who received a cognitively normal (CN) diagnosis at baseline were the only group included. The models predicted the diagnoses these participants received at the final visit, defined here.

Outcome	Definition
CN	Those diagnosed with CN at baseline who received the same diagnosis at their last visit
MCI/AD	Those having received a diagnosis of CN at baseline *either* received a diagnosis of AD or MCI at their last visit

Table 2. Those diagnosed with Mild Cognitive Impairment (MCI) at baseline were the only group included. The models predicted the diagnoses these participants received at the final visit, defined here.

Outcome	Definition
CN/MCI	Those who had received a diagnosis of MCI at baseline either received the same diagnosis at their last visit or a more favourable diagnosis of CN
AD	Those diagnosed with MCI at baseline received a diagnosis of AD at their last visit

Table 3. The final dimensions of the two datasets after preprocessing.

Dataset	Variables	Observations
CN at baseline	98/92 (with/without CSF predictors)	285
MCI at baseline	98/92 (with/without CSF predictors)	322

4.4 Model Development

Model development, evaluation, and validation were carried out according to methodological guidelines outlined by [18]; results were reported according to the Transparent Reporting of a multivariable prediction model for Individual Prognosis or Diagnosis (TRIPOD) guidelines [19]. This paper explored three algorithms:

Cox Proportional Hazard Model (Cox PH) - The Cox model is expressed by the hazard function, which is the risk of an event occurring at time as follows:

$$h(t) = h_0(t) * exp(\beta_1 X_1 + \beta_2 X_2 + \beta_p X_p) \tag{1}$$

where t represents the survival time, $h(t)$ is the hazard function, $X_1, X_2, ...X_p$ are the values of the p covariates, $\beta_1, \beta_2 ...\beta_p$ are the coefficients that measure the effect of the covariates on the survival time and $h_0(t)$ is the baseline hazard function, which is unspecified. The regression coefficients are estimated by maximising the partial likelihood [8], and hence the model does not require tuning.

Survival Random Forest (SRF) - Random Forests seek to grow many trees using bootstrapped aggregation and splitting on a random subsection of predictors for each split point. The split points are chosen based on some criteria (such as entropy or purity of the node), which seeks to allocate classifications of one type within each terminal node. In a Survival Random Forest, the feature and split point chosen is the one that maximises the survival difference (in terms of the hazard function) between subsequent nodes [8, 20]. In the tuning grid for this model, the values of mtry varied between 1 and 20, with a step of 1, while the values for minimum node size in the grid were 10, 20, 30, 40, and 50. SRF comprised 1000 trees. The number of trees promotes model convergence (large is better) and generally is not tuned.

Survival Deep Hit Neural Networks (SNN) - Deep Hit is a multi-task neural network comprising a shared sub-network and K cause-specific sub-networks. The architecture differs from a conventional multi-task neural network in two ways. First, it utilises a single softmax layer as the output layer of Deep Hit to ensure that the network learns the joint distribution of K possible outcomes, not the marginal distributions of each outcome. Second, it maintains a residual connection from the input covariates into the input of each cause-specific sub-network. The full technical description of this model can be found in [21]. In the tuning grid for this model, the number of nodes was between 2 and 300, the epochs were between 10 and 400, and the batch sizes was 32. The learning rates were 0.001, and 0.01, the activation functions were 'relu', 'elu' and 'leakyrelu', and the optimisers were 'adam' and 'adamw'. 10% of the training dataset was held aside for validation in the early stopping procedure, with patience at either 10, or 150 epochs.

4.5 Nested Cross-Validation and Monte Carlo Simulation

A Nested Cross-Validation procedure was implemented to tune and evaluate the models so precise estimates of the model's performance of unseen cases (internal validation) could be gathered [4]. Nested Cross-Validation consisted of an outer 5-fold CV (model assessment) and an inner 5-fold CV (model tuning). We conducted a Monte Carlo procedure of 100 repetitions of the nested CV using different random splits per model to assess the models' stability. Performance statistics were recorded for each model produced by each iteration. Each performance statistic's mean and standard deviation across all iterations were recorded when the MC was complete. To ensure the representativeness of training and test samples in both procedures, the data splitting was stratified based on the AD cases variable.

4.6 Performance Metrics

To assess model performance, two statistics were recorded. Discrimination was assessed using the Concordance index or C-index [18]. This metric, also called Harrel's C-index, provides a global assessment of the model and can be considered a more general form of the AUCROC measure typically used in binary classification tasks. The C-index computes the percentage of comparable pairs within the dataset whose risk score was correctly identified by the model. Comparable pairs are defined as a selection of two observations, which can be compared in terms of survival time predicted by the model. If both are censored, then they are not included in the computation for this metric. A pair is considered concordant if the observation who experiences the earlier event is identified as having greater risk and discordant otherwise. Thus the total concordance score for a model is the ratio of concordant pairs within the dataset divided by the total number of observations [15].

Secondly, calibration was assessed using Van Houwelingen's Alpha Survival Measure of non-proportional hazards models [15]. This metric is defined as:

$$\alpha = \sum \delta / \sum H_i(t_i) \quad (2)$$

where δ is the true censoring indicator observed from the test data, H_i is the cumulative hazard predicted by the model, and t_i is the observed survival time. The model is well calibrated if the estimated α is equal or close to 1. Calibration is a formal comparison between the probability distribution and resultant survival instances observed in the test data and the probability distribution and resultant survival predictions generated by the model. A full exploration of this metric can be found in [22].

4.7 Software and Hardware

The data analysis was conducted using the R language [23]. Initial data cleaning was performed using base R functions and the Tidyverse R package [24]. The creation of dummy variables was performed using the Caret R package [25]. The nested cross-validation procedure, including training, tuning and evaluation, was performed on the Cox PH, SRF, and SNN models using the mlr3 R package [26]. The hardware consisted of 3 servers running Linux, with Xeon processors and 64 GB of RAM.

5 Results

The nested cross-validation C-index and Calibration performance for each model type is detailed below. Figures for the two groups' C-indexes, with CSF-derived biomarkers included in the models, can be found in Fig. 1 (Table 4).

Table 4. CN group with CSF-derived biomarkers included/removed.

Model	C-index CSF included/removed	Calibration CSF included/removed
Cox PH	0.71/0.59	0.01/0.01
SRF	0.84/0.86	0.80/1.02
SNN	0.80/0.70	0.64/0.60

The best-performing model for the CN group with CSF-derived biomarkers included was SRF, followed by SNN, followed by Cox PH model. Thus, the SRF and SNN outperformed the conventional statistical model Cox in the CN group with CSF-derived biomarkers included in the Calibration and the C-index metric.

Once the CSF-derived biomarkers were removed, for the CN group, both the Cox PH and the SNN reported worse predictive power. However, as the C-Index and Calibration estimated, the SRF retained its predictive ability, even significantly improving its calibration score (Table 5).

Table 5. MCI group with CSF-derived biomarkers included/removed.

Model	C-index CSF included/removed	Calibration CSF included/removed
Cox PH	0.78/0.78	0.29/0.25
SRF	0.84/0.84	0.98/0.99
SNN	0.83/0.77	1.16/0.91

When considering the C-index, the best-performing model for the MCI group, with CSF-derived biomarkers included, was SRF, followed by Cox PH model, followed by SNN. Calibration was again almost perfect for SRF followed by SNN and CoxPH.

Once the CSF-derived biomarkers were removed, for the MCI group, only the SNN reported worse predictive power, as measured by the C-Index. When considering calibration, however, the SNN and Cox PH models deteriorated when the CSF-derived biomarkers were removed, while SRF remained close to 1.

The datasets with the CSF-derived biomarkers removed were then taken forward for all models to undergo a Monte Carlo simulation with 100 iterations of the nested cross-validation procedure (Tables 6, 7 and 8).

The SRF model results on both the C-Index and Calibration proved the most stable upon repeated testing, with standard deviations at less than 0.03. The SNN model was

Table 6. Cox PH Monte Carlo at 100 iterations.

Group (Model)	Mean C-index (sd)	Mean Calibration (sd)
MCI (Cox PH)	0.78(0.02)	0.33(0.08)
CN (Cox PH)	0.59(0.06)	0.03(0.02)

Table 7. SNN Monte Carlo.

Group	Mean C-index (sd)	Mean Calibration (sd)
MCI (SNN)	0.77(0.02)	0.91(0.1)
CN (SNN)	0.7(0.06)	0.6(0.03)

Table 8. SRF Monte Carlo.

Group	Mean C-index (sd)	Mean Calibration (sd)
MCI (SRF)	0.84(0.008)	0.99(0.02)
CN (SRF)	0.83(0.01)	1.02(0.02)

less stable and reported less predictive power, as measured by both the C-Index and Calibration.

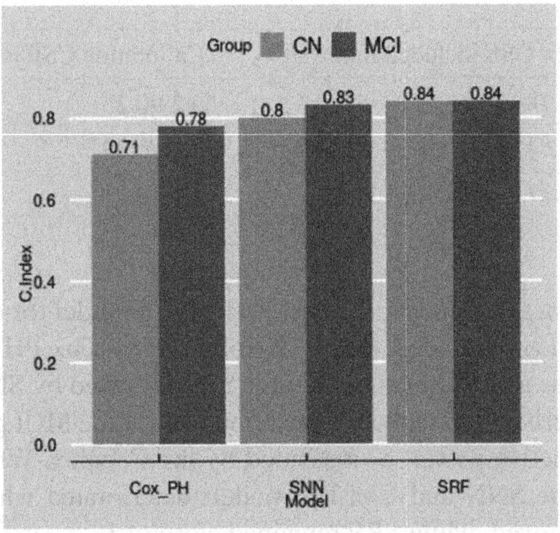

Fig. 1. C-indexes for models applied to the two groups with CSF-derived biomarkers included in the models.

6 Discussion

This study aimed to further explore the potential of survival-based ML as a tool for predicting time to AD diagnosis. This paper demonstrates the clear utility of such methods when predicting on the ADNI2 dataset. This provides further evidence for the continued exploration of the utility of survival ML in this context.

Several results reported here are worthy of note. Firstly, we demonstrated good predictive power for SRF with very good discrimination and excellent calibration, which was superior to both the standard Cox PH model and the SNN model. Good discrimination and calibration are essential in survival ML models to obtain accurate risk estimations at specific time periods of interest, which is not possible with traditional classification ML models. This allows for informed decision-making, personalised interventions, and timely allocation of resources for the prevention, early detection, or management of dementia. Our results support the work of [11] but disagrees with [20], which found that the standard Cox model was superior to tree-based ensemble methods. This is possibly due also to the way in which the Survival trees were constructed, with [18] using probabilities derived from a Cox model to construct a Random Forest. In comparison, the SRF presented here sought to create trees whose splits aimed to maximise the difference in survival between the resultant nodes. With the present study indicating strong results using this approach, it may be that the latter technique produces better models. However, we should note that these results were obtained on datasets other than the one used in this study, ADNI.

With the removal of the CSF-derived biomarkers, performance deterioration was seen for SNN but not SRF or the Cox PH. The choice to investigate an SNN was derived, in part, from the work of [14], whose best model achieved a C-index of 0.83 on the ADNI dataset. In comparison, the best model found by the present study, using SNN, achieved a C-index of 0.77. However, we should note that [13] did not provide a comparison between the Survival Neural Network models used and either a standard Cox PH model or any other survival ML algorithm. Another point of consideration is that the authors used a slightly different Neural Network algorithm to the one described here. Thus, an important next step would be directly comparing the DeepSurv model and the Deep Hit model described here.

SNN had worse stability than the SRF and Cox PH models, as measured by the standard deviations of the C-index and Calibration scores for these models. This would suggest that this algorithm produces unstable models with unreliable predictions. Neural Networks usually perform best in complex problems that require discovering hidden patterns in the data between a large number of interdependent variables. Furthermore, Neural Networks usually perform better on image and audio classification rather than tabular data, such as the dataset used in this study [27]. Therefore, it may be the case that a simpler model such as Random Forest might be better suited for the kind of limited datasets presented here. It may also be the case that the SNN model overfit the comparatively small dataset presented here.

Finally, the results in this work suggest that CSF-derived biomarkers did not have a clear contribution in this setting, for building models capable of accurately predicting the time to AD diagnosis on our considered ADNI sample. Although both the Cox PH and SNN models variously suffered from the removal of these predictors, the RSF model did not. This is important, as collecting biomarkers from CSF is an invasive and painful process for participants, which involves a lumbar puncture. Recent analyses conducted on EMIF-AD data [9] established that predictors such as metabolites in blood showed similar predictive power to the well-established but more invasive CSF biomarkers.

Despite the results obtained by this work, there are a number of limitations to the present paper that need to be considered. Firstly, the ADNI2 data is comparatively small, and future work is required to validate the models created here using external data. A related point is the lack of diversity within this data, which heavily skews towards white North-American participants. To validate the models created here, they must be tested on non-white, non-western participants such that evidence of model performance be gathered for a wider group of people.

A further limitation is that the choice of hyper-parameters for the grid search procedure for each model is finite. We were unable to conduct an exhaustive search over a larger set of combinations of hyperparameter values due to time constraints and computational cost. Therefore it is entirely possible that better results for these models can be found using hyperparameters not explored here.

7 Conclusion

This paper proposed a survival ML approach to predict the time to Alzheimer's Disease diagnosis accurately. It was compared with one of the most used statistical models for survival analysis, namely Cox PH. In our framework proposed by using the ADNI cohort, the Machine Learning based approach proved to be more accurate than the statistical approach, which was the case also in a recent study conducted on different clinical data [11].

Acknowledgements. Daniel Stahl was part funded by the NIHR Maudsley Biomedical Research Centre at South London and Maudsley NHS Foundation Trust and King's College London. This study represents independent research and views expressed are those of the author(s) and not necessarily those of the NIHR or the Department of Health and Social Care.

References

1. Dementia Statistics Hub | Alzheimer's Research UK. Dementia Statistics Hub. https://www.dementiastatistics.org/. Accessed 09 Aug 2022
2. Rittman, T.: Neurological update: neuroimaging in dementia. J. Neurol. **267**(11), 3429–3435 (2020). https://doi.org/10.1007/s00415-020-10040-0
3. Kelly, C.J., Karthikesalingam, A., Suleyman, M., Corrado, G., King, D.: Key challenges for delivering clinical impact with artificial intelligence. BMC Med. **17**(1), 195 (2019). https://doi.org/10.1186/s12916-019-1426-2
4. Musto, H., Stamate, D., Pu, I., Stahl, D.: A machine learning approach for predicting deterioration in alzheimer's disease. In: 2021 20th IEEE International Conference on Machine Learning and Applications (ICMLA), Pasadena, CA, USA, pp. 1443–1448 (2021). https://doi.org/10.1109/ICMLA52953.2021.00232

5. Stamate, D., et al.: Applying deep learning to predicting dementia and mild cognitive impairment. In: Maglogiannis, I., Iliadis, L., Pimenidis, E. (eds.) AIAI 2020. IAICT, vol. 584, pp. 308–319. Springer, Cham (2020). https://doi.org/10.1007/978-3-030-49186-4_26
6. ADNI | About. https://adni.loni.usc.edu/about/. Accessed 19 Feb 2023
7. Cox, D.R.: Regression models and life-tables. J. R. Stat. Soc. Ser. B Methodol. **34**(2), 187–202 (1972). https://doi.org/10.1111/j.2517-6161.1972.tb00899.x
8. Spooner, A., et al.: A comparison of machine learning methods for survival analysis of high-dimensional clinical data for dementia prediction. Sci. Rep. **10**(1), 20410 (2020). https://doi.org/10.1038/s41598-020-77220-w
9. Stamate, D., et al.: A metabolite-based machine learning approach to diagnose Alzheimer-type dementia in blood: results from the European medical information framework for Alzheimer disease biomarker discovery cohort. Alzheimers Dement. Transl. Res. Clin. Interv. **5**(1), 933–938 (2019). https://doi.org/10.1016/j.trci.2019.11.001
10. Ajnakina, O., Cadar, D., Steptoe, A.: Interplay between socioeconomic markers and polygenic predisposition on timing of dementia diagnosis. J. Am. Geriatr. Soc. **68**(7), 1529–1536 (2020). https://doi.org/10.1111/jgs.16406
11. Stamate, D., Musto, H., Ajnakina, O., Stahl, D.: Predicting risk of dementia with survival machine learning and statistical methods: results on the english longitudinal study of ageing cohort. In: Artificial Intelligence Applications and Innovations. AIAI 2022 IFIP WG 12.5 International Workshops, Cham, pp. 436–447 (2022). https://doi.org/10.1007/978-3-031-08341-9_35
12. Wang, M., et al.: Dementia risk prediction in individuals with mild cognitive impairment: a comparison of Cox regression and machine learning models. BMC Med. Res. Methodol. **22**(1), 284 (2022). https://doi.org/10.1186/s12874-022-01754-y
13. Sheikh, F., et al.: Prevalence of mild behavioral impairment in mild cognitive impairment and subjective cognitive decline, and its association with caregiver burden. Int. Psychogeriatr. **30**(2), 233–244 (2018). https://doi.org/10.1017/S104161021700151X
14. Mirabnahrazam, G., et al.: Predicting time-to-conversion for dementia of Alzheimer's type using multi-modal deep survival analysis. Neurobiol. Aging **121**, 139–156 (2023). https://doi.org/10.1016/j.neurobiolaging.2022.10.005
15. Longato, E., Vettoretti, M., Di Camillo, B.: A practical perspective on the concordance index for the evaluation and selection of prognostic time-to-event models. J. Biomed. Inform. **108**, 103496 (2020). https://doi.org/10.1016/j.jbi.2020.103496
16. Key ADNI tables merged into one table—adnimerge. https://adni.bitbucket.io/reference/adnimerge.html. Accessed 21 Feb 2023
17. Apostolova, L.G., et al.: ApoE4 effects on automated diagnostic classifiers for mild cognitive impairment and Alzheimer's disease. NeuroImage Clin. **4**, 461–472 (2014). https://doi.org/10.1016/j.nicl.2013.12.012
18. Steyerberg, E.W.: Clinical Prediction Models, 2nd edn. Springer, New York (2019). https://doi.org/10.1007/978-0-387-77244-8
19. Collins, G.S., Reitsma, J.B., Altman, D.G., Moons, K.G.M.: Transparent reporting of a multivariable prediction model for individual prognosis Or diagnosis (TRIPOD): the TRIPOD statement. Br. J. Surg. **102**(3), 148–158 (2015). https://doi.org/10.1002/bjs.9736
20. Shamsutdinova, D., Stamate, D., Roberts, A., Stahl, D.: Combining cox model and tree-based algorithms to boost performance and preserve interpretability for health outcomes. In: Maglogiannis, I., Iliadis, L., Macintyre, J., Cortez, P. (eds.) Artificial Intelligence Applications and Innovations: 18th IFIP WG 12.5 International Conference, AIAI 2022, Hersonissos, Crete, Greece, June 17–20, 2022, Proceedings, Part II, pp. 170–181. Springer International Publishing, Cham (2022). https://doi.org/10.1007/978-3-031-08337-2_15

21. Lee, C., Zame, W., Yoon, J., van der Schaar, M.: DeepHit: a deep learning approach to survival analysis with competing risks. In: Proceedings of AAAI Conference Artificial Intelligence, vol. 32, no. 1, Art no. 1 (2018). https://doi.org/10.1609/aaai.v32i1.11842
22. van Houwelingen, H.C.: Validation, calibration, revision and combination of prognostic survival models. Stat. Med. **19**(24), 3401–3415 (2000). https://doi.org/10.1002/1097-0258(20001230)19:24%3c3401::AID-SIM554%3e3.0.CO;2-2
23. R: The R Foundation. https://www.r-project.org/foundation/. Accessed 08 Mar 2023
24. Tidyverse packages. https://www.tidyverse.org/packages/. Accessed 08 Mar 2023
25. Kuhn, M.: The caret Package. https://topepo.github.io/caret/. Accessed 08 Mar 2023
26. Machine Learning in R - Next Generation. https://mlr3.mlr-org.com/. Accessed 08 Mar 2023
27. Borisov, V., Leemann, T., Seßler, K., Haug, J., Pawelczyk, M., Kasneci, G.: Deep neural networks and tabular data: a survey. IEEE Trans. Neural Netw. Learn. Syst., 1–21 (2022). https://doi.org/10.1109/TNNLS.2022.3229161

MEP: A Comprehensive Medicines Extraction System on Prescriptions

Ngoc-Thao Nguyen[1,2](✉), Duy Ha[1,2], Duc Nguyen[1,2], and Thanh Le[1,2]

[1] Faculty of Information Technology, University of Science, Ho Chi Minh City, Vietnam
hvduy37@gmail.com, {nnthao,lnthanh}@fit.hcmus.edu.vn
[2] Vietnam National University, Ho Chi Minh City, Vietnam

Abstract. Accurately identifying drug names from prescription images is essential for effectively processing and managing patient medical information. In order to enhance our previous approach, we have introduced a new version named Medicines Extraction on Prescription (MEP). This innovative approach employs heuristic rules and a Temporal Convolutional Network model to extract and classify proprietary medicines from prescription images captured by smartphones. Our model not only achieves a precision score of up to 0.94 on experimental datasets, but it also boasts impressive processing speed. The total drug name recognition and average extraction time is only 6.67 s per prescription, significantly faster than the 17.81 s average processing time of our previous model.

Keywords: Prescription Recognition · Optical Character Recognition · Medicines Classification · Fuzzy Matching

1 Introduction

Prescriptions are a common occurrence for individuals and organizations involved in the medical field, particularly for patients. They contain critical information such as the patient's identity, the doctor's name, the disease name, the current condition, and most importantly, the medication name and dosage. However, despite these details, prescriptions often fail to provide adequate information about the drug's origin, ingredients, and potential side effects, which can be dangerous. This lack of information has led to an increase in the number of patients experiencing poisoning or, in the worst-case scenario, death due to allergies or adverse reactions to some drug ingredients. Improper medication usage can also worsen chronic conditions, while certain medications can cause severe damage to vital organs such as the heart, liver, and kidneys. Depending on the drug administered, the body may recover or experience long-term physical harm. According to the National Center for Health Statistics (NCHS) [1], in 2020, 91,799 people in the US died from drug overdoses. Shockingly, recent federal data reveals that the overdose death rate in 2020 was over 31% higher than the rate in 2019.

N. T. Nguyen et al. (Eds.): ICCCI 2023, LNAI 14162, pp. 713–725, 2023.
https://doi.org/10.1007/978-3-031-41456-5_54

Currently, there are only a few studies that have investigated the processing of prescription tasks. Some studies have focused on supporting the extraction of information tasks. Hasan et al. [2] proposed a CNN (Convolutional Neural Network) model for drug prescription recognition. This is a mobile application that allows pharmacists and patients to receive digital prescriptions as well as information about drugs such as names and dosages. By using the CNN model, the accuracy of the model achieved was 70%. Ou [3] proposed an automated drug prescription recognition system. This system was developed to support the visual system of pharmaceutical robots, helping pharmacists identify medical information in prescriptions (drug names, usage, dosage, and usage instructions). By detecting the National Health Insurance code (each type of drug circulating in Taiwan has a different NHI code), the study achieved an accuracy rate of up to 92.4%.

In the previous study [4], we proposed an information extraction model for drug names applied to Vietnamese language using CRAFT and Tesseract OCR tools, along with fuzzy search based on the Levenshtein distance to retrieve drug names in the database collected from Drugbank Vietnam. However, the remaining problem with this system is the slow drug recognition speed and the small database size. Additionally, besides drug names, prescriptions also contain information such as disease names and names of hospitals providing the drugs. These pieces of information often cause noise and affect the speed and accuracy of the system. We address these issues by proposing an improved model for scoring higher performance.

To summarize, our main contributions are as follows:

- Designing a drug prescription recognition system named MEP that is capable of extracting drug names and related information.
- Integrating advanced text recognition models with a Medicine Classifier model and proposed Post-OCR methods.
- Through experiments on benchmark datasets, the proposed model achieves higher accuracy than baseline models while also reducing response time for results.

The remainder of this paper is organized as follows: Sect. 2 demonstrates the architecture of related techniques. The background technique and the proposed recognition system are described in Sect. 3 and Sect. 4, respectively. Experimental results on our datasets are presented in Sect. 5, and Sect. 6 provides conclusions and future work.

2 Related Work

The OCR (Object Character Recognition) system is a critical component for recognizing prescriptions, and it typically involves three main stages: text detection, text recognition, and extraction of drug names. In this section, we will provide a brief overview of the latest algorithms in each category and evaluate their suitability for our system.

2.1 Text Detection and Recognition

The process of text detection involves identifying and separating text from the background in an image. There are two primary methods for text detection: traditional and deep learning. Traditional methods like SIFT (Scale Invariant Feature Transform) and FAST (Features from Accelerated Segment Test) require manual extraction of text features, leading to complexity and errors with many rules that must be manually optimized. In contrast, recent advances in deep neural networks have allowed for deep learning techniques like semantic segmentation and object detection in images to be used. Semantic segmentation uses a segmentation map created by the FCN (Fully Convolutional Networks) to extract text blocks and then creates a bounding box through post-processing. Some popular algorithms utilizing this concept include TextSegNet [5] and WordDetNet [6].

Text recognition in images can also be accomplished by adopting an approach that is inspired by general object detection neural models. These methods focus on recognizing the text present in the scene by treating it as an object and predicting its bounding box. Several commonly used methods that implement this approach include CTPN [7] and CRAFT [8].

After the text has been detected, the next phase involves converting it into editable digital text, which can be achieved using recent text recognition methods that fall into two categories: segmentation-based and segmentation-free. Segmentation-based methods involve preprocessing and segmenting the text images before using a character classification model to recognize individual characters, which are then aggregated into lines. In contrast, segmentation-free methods recognize the entire line of text at once by using the encoder-decoder framework to convert the text image into an output text string. Some essential techniques for text recognition include CRF [9] and CRNN [10].

2.2 Post-OCR

The output of the OCR step includes all the information present in the prescription. Post-OCR methods have gained popularity in recent times and are extensively evaluated in a survey by Nguyen et al. [11]. As drug names are scientific terms that are context-independent and insignificant in terms of their position within the sentence, a dictionary of related terms is essential for extracting drug names from the OCR-generated text.

Karthikeyan et al. [12] proposed an OCR post-processing method for medical documents that utilizes a pre-trained natural language processing model and a deep neural network model called RoBERTa. Initially, the authors employed the Tesseract OCR tool to extract text from the documents. In the post-processing step, biomedical entities were eliminated using Named Entity Recognition (NER) from the ScispaCy model, which falls under the domain of natural language processing. After excluding specific entities, the model detects error words and non-vocabulary words using spell checkers. RoBERTa is then utilized to select the most similar candidates to the error words. This approach bears considerable similarity to the method proposed by Thompson et al. [13], which also uses spell checkers to identify error words. The main difference lies in the fact that Thompson's method adds medical terms to the spell checkers, while Karthikeyan's method takes advantage of a vast medical terminology database. However, the dataset used in this study is the UK NHS, which contains confidential patient information. According to the authors, the method achieves an accuracy of 81% without requiring further training on new datasets.

Moreover, Karthikeyan also proposed a post-processing approach that uses models in natural language processing. The Scispacy model used in this study can identify medical entities using Rxnorm, a database containing the active ingredients of drugs authorized for circulation in the United States. However, there is a distinction between the drug name and its active ingredient in the prescriptions that we have collected. While the drug name is the term given by the company that manufactured the drug, the active ingredient is usually the name of the chemical compound.

3 Background

3.1 CRAFT

In order to obtain information for the drug identification system, text recognition needs to be addressed. With the advent of deep learning, the CRAFT model has become one of the most popular methods for detecting text regions. It is capable of detecting individual character areas and the relationship among them. Specifically, CRAFT predicts two metrics for each character bounding box: (i) the region score, which is the probability that a given pixel is the center of a character, and (ii) the affinity score, which represents the probability that the space between adjacent characters represents a single word.

The process of label representation in CRAFT involves generating ground truths using bounding boxes that contain information about the pointers and combine to give the bounds of each word. Rather than using map segmentation binaries to label each pixel individually, a Gaussian heatmap is used to determine the encoding scale of the character center. In supervised learning, the characters detected are segmented into individual character sets for recognition. The images at the word level are cropped from the original image, and the affinity score for each region is calculated by the computational partitioning system. An algorithm is then applied to split the character regions, creating bounding boxes at the character level. Finally, the character's bounding box coordinates are returned to the origin.

3.2 TCN

To identify which texts in the database refer to medication, we can utilize text classification methods. While CNN-based models can accurately classify simple strings, they perform poorly when dealing with texts containing complex features or semantic ambiguity. To address this limitation, RNN-based models have been proposed. These models can capture hidden features in a sequence, allowing them to contextualize the text like the human brain does, leading to improved accuracy.

However, using RNNs (Recurrent Neural Networks) to process extensive data can be costly. To address this issue, Shaojie Bai et al. [14] introduced a new approach called Temporal Convolutional Network (TCN), which is a compact version of the CNN architecture. TCN uses causal convolutions, specifically dilated convolutions, which enable the model to efficiently learn information from past sequences. Each output $\mathbf{y}_t$ depends on a series of $\mathbf{x}$ inputs that are filtered by a parameter known as the *filter size*, with a range of *0, 1, 2, ..., t*. By adjusting two parameters, d (dilation factor) and k (filter size), the model can control its depth within the sentence. With dilation, TCN achieves a breakthrough that is similar to RNNs in terms of recurrence.

For prescription recognition, identifying medicine names requires classification, and these names may have distinct medical characteristics that set them apart from other types of text. Therefore, the TCN approach could be employed to address the task of drug name recognition, as outlined in the methods section.

4 The Prescription Medicine Extraction System

The proposed system (MEP) takes a prescription image as input and uses the detection model to identify the text region in the prescription. CRAFT is utilized to generate a word-by-word bounding box, which helps to maintain the accurate medicine name, as well as the tilt and skew of the input image, without adversely affecting the recognition results. Therefore, CRAFT is suitable for recognizing text in prescriptions. The detection output is then input into the recognition model to recognize the detected text. VietOCR is used for text recognition due to its minimal complexity, high accuracy, and faster processing time than popular models like Tesseract. Various methods such as regex and MergeOCRED lines are used to extract vital drug names and perform post-OCR procedures to maintain the accuracy of the medicine's text. The medicine classifier and correction approach are then used to obtain the precise name of the medicine in the prescription. Figure 1 illustrates the MEP drug name recognition system.

4.1 Craft-Text-Detector

While CTPN can detect an entire row of text and process images faster than CRAFT, it has a disadvantage in dealing with tilted and skewed images. Therefore, to overcome this limitation, we employ the craft-text-detector to detect the text area in our proposed system. This component groups words on the same line or region into an object based on the bounding boxes obtained from the conventional CRAFT architecture by applying thresholds. By doing so, it not only achieves the same effect as using CTPN but also retains the advantages of CRAFT.

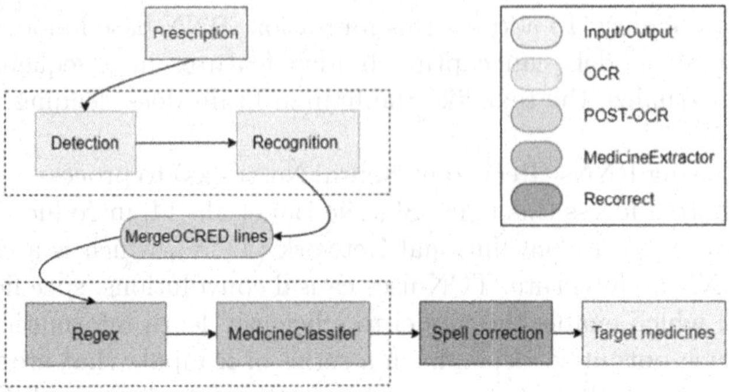

Fig. 1. The architecture of Medicines Extraction on Prescription (MEP) system

4.2 VietOCR

VietOCR is a Vietnamese text recognition model that is open-source and can be utilized for both print and handwriting recognition. Developed by Quoc Pham, the model has undergone continuous updates since its initial release in 2020. In this study, the Seq2Seq installation method is used instead of Transformer because of its faster detection time and comparable accuracy. VietOCR has achieved high accuracy even on new datasets. However, currently, VietOCR only supports recognition of text line by line, and thus, when presented with an image with multiple lines of text, additional techniques are required to split the text into individual lines. This is achieved in the craft-text-detector step by dividing the original image into smaller images containing the detected text areas, which are then passed into VietOCR to generate the resulting string.

4.3 Medicine Extractor

Prescriptions and receipts share common features, including the presentation of information in a systematic or semi-structured way. Drug names often appear in a consistent order and format. To extract medicine names from prescriptions, we employ two basic regular expressions:

- By adhering to a rule in which lines that begin with a number, followed by a brand-name drug and possibly an active component are considered to contain a drug name, we can extract the essential lines in a prescription while increasing the probability of including the drug names.
- Expanding the previous rule for prescription forms without numbering, we specify the line containing this structure to ensure the model's performance. While this technique may increase the number of unrelated lines that are matched, it serves as a backup step if the OCR step fails to recognize the number preceding the medicine name.

To avoid impacting the model's overall performance, we do not handle cases where medicine names and active components are spread across multiple lines,

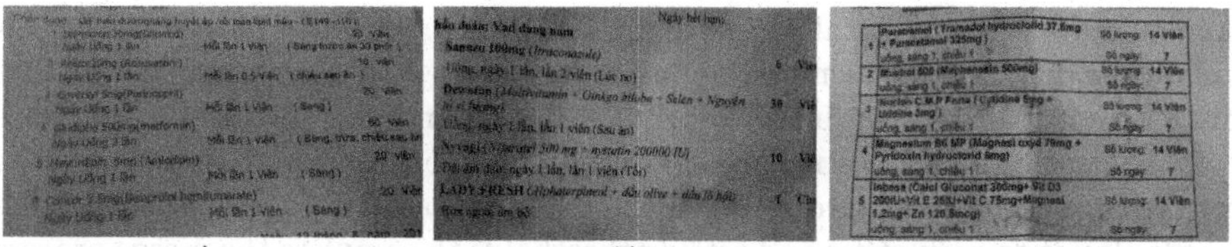

a) b) c)

Fig. 2. An example of prescription templates (a) Medicine lines start with number, followed by medicine and ingredient, (b) Medicine lines start without number, followed by medicine and ingredient, (c) Prescription with medicine in multi-line

even though it is a rare occurrence. Examples of such formats in prescriptions are illustrated in Fig. 2.

To reduce the matching cost as the size of the drug dictionary increases, in our previous work, the drug dictionary was matched with the entire output of the OCR. However, in this work, only the lines with a high likelihood of holding drug names are extracted and provided as input to the medicine classifier module.

4.4 MergeOCR

In order to ensure the accuracy of the medicine extractor's regular expression, it is necessary to bound lines containing drug names into boxes that include all necessary parts. However, if the image is blurry or noisy, the OCR process may not function properly and may generate multiple bounding boxes containing separate components instead of a single bounding box with all digits, drug names, and drug ingredients. This can cause the extract medicine step to fail as it may not match the regular expression. Skewed text is one of the challenges of the OCR task, as shown in Fig. 3a.

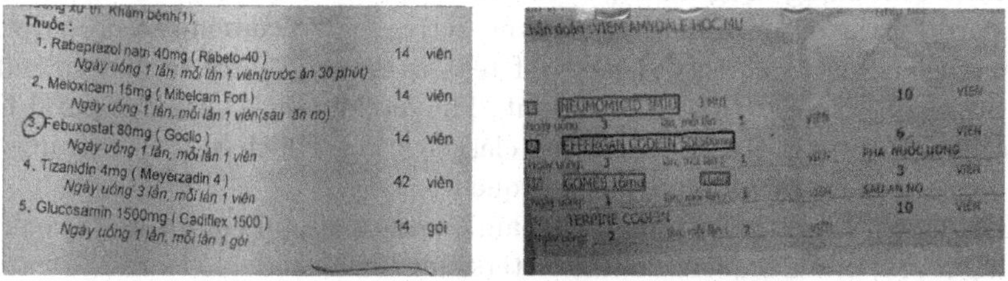

(a) (b)

Fig. 3. (a) An example show texts in prescription being skewed; (b) Result of MergeOCR, pieces of bounding box belong to a single line are merged correctly

An additional step called MergeOCR is proposed to address this issue by combining bounding boxes of text in the same line into a single line of text. The

Agglomerative Hierarchical Clustering (AHC) technique [15] is utilized to calculate the distance between two bounding cells based on their y-axis coordinate distance on the 2D coordinate system. AHC is beneficial in this case because it is efficient and requires no predetermined number of clusters, which is often referred to as the number of lines in the prescription. By prioritizing groups of words closest to each other and setting thresholds to complete the merge process quickly, the performance could be optimized. As the MergeOCR step occurs after the recognition process, the bounding boxes located on a line are still recognized separately, allowing for more effective recognition by VietOCR and preventing interference. After the MergeOCR step, strings corresponding to the bounding box could join the correct x-axis order on the 2D coordinate system. Figure 3b shows the result of MergeOCR when grouping bounding boxes.

4.5 Medicine Classifier

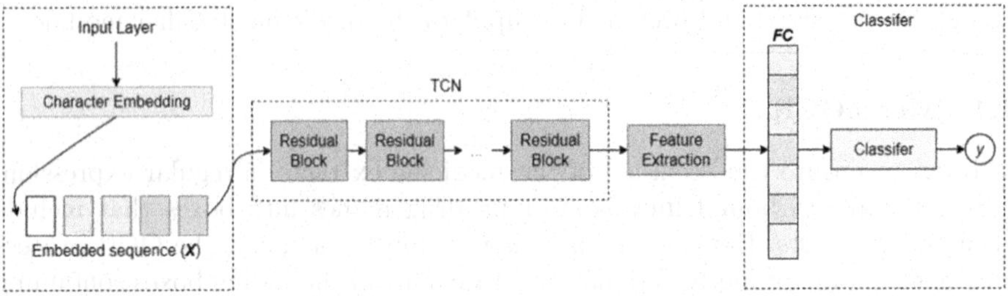

Fig. 4. Proposed medicine classifier architecture

The next paragraph describes the process of extracting the exact drug name from the lines containing drug names in the prescription. Since there is no common standard for the order of drug names and active ingredients in the prescription, the model needs to classify a piece of text as a drug name or not to reduce the processing time of the entire output. The model uses TCN (Temporal Convolutional Network) [14] for medicine classification, which aids in learning the features of the character embedding sequence.

The model structure includes two main parts: character embedding to convert the input text into a sequence of characters, and TCN model to learn the features of the character embedding sequence. The output of TCN is then sent to fully connected layers for classification into three categories: medicine names, active components, and others. The advantages of using TCN for this task are its ability to handle misspellings and its high performance in processing large amounts of data in a short time. Figure 4 shows the architecture of the medicine classifier model.

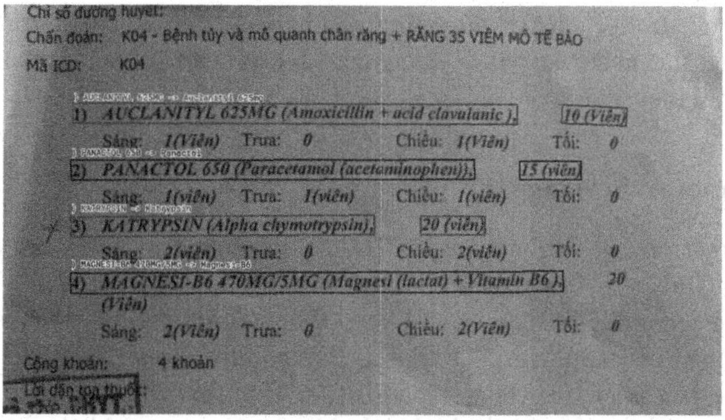

Fig. 5. Corrected output of proposed Prescription Recognition system

4.6 Context-Aware Spell Correction

The medicine classifier model distinguishes between drug names and ingredients, even though a drug name can sometimes also be an ingredient, and vice versa. The final step in the process involves filtering the remaining lines using a threshold to extract the most probable drug names. This is achieved by comparing each line with a limited medicine names dictionary and correcting any errors using an edit distance-based matching principle. Levenshtein, which was previously mentioned in [4], is an example of an edit distance algorithm used in many post-processing methods. The output of our overall system, which includes spell correction, is shown in Fig. 5.

5 Experiment

5.1 Datasets

The dataset used to evaluate our model consists of 1500 images containing over 10,000 distinct drug names. Each drug name is enclosed in a bounding box labeled with its corresponding name. These images were collected from various sources, including a Facebook group called "KHO DON THUOC"[1]. The group was created to gather prescriptions from around the world and the images were manually collected from hospitals, both large and small, in the area. To prevent duplication, a manual check was performed on the collected data.

In addition, despite being primarily written in Vietnamese, the drug names in this dataset often consist of scientific names and are therefore less impacted by Vietnamese punctuation and grammar. The prescription images in this dataset were captured using phone cameras and are subject to variations in brightness and tilt angle. While these conditions reflect real-world scenarios, they unintentionally present a significant challenge for text recognition models in accurately

[1] https://www.facebook.com/groups/392636900896314.

identifying text under such challenging conditions. Hence, this dataset is aimed at evaluating the accuracy and efficiency of prescription text recognition and detection systems.

5.2 Parameter Settings

For text detection, we adjusted the CRAFT parameters, with a text threshold of 0.7 and a link threshold of 0.4. We utilized the VGG sequence-to-sequence model in the recognition step of the VietOCR configuration. The sensitivity of the clustering process in MergeOCR was determined by a threshold of 0.016. In the medicine classifier, we set the padding size to 300, filter size to k = 2, and dilation factor to d = [1, 2, 4]. A threshold of 0.6 was established to confirm if the text could be considered a medicine in the classifier. Finally, the threshold for confirming and correcting medicines was set to 0.85.

5.3 Evaluation Metrics

In the experiment, precision and recall are the primary evaluation metrics used to measure the performance of the model. Additionally, we also use the H-mean metric to assess the overall accuracy of the model. The definitions of Precision, Recall, and H-mean are presented in Eqs. (1), (2), and (3), respectively.

$$Precision = \frac{|\{accurate\ drugs\} \cap \{retrieved\ drugs\}|}{|\{retrieved\ drugs\}|} \tag{1}$$

$$Recall = \frac{|\{accurate\ drugs\} \cap \{retrieved\ drugs\}|}{|\{accurate\ drugs\}|} \tag{2}$$

The average prescription recognition is as follows:

$$H - mean = \frac{\sum_{i=0}^{n} \frac{u}{U}}{N} \tag{3}$$

where u and U is the number of extracted drugs and labels, respectively; N is the number of samples.

5.4 Results and Analysis

To evaluate the performance of our proposed model, we chose to compare it with a baseline model, TrietPresc [4]. Although other models in Sect. 2 are related, they do not directly address the drug recognition problem, and they also do not disclose their datasets and source code, so a comparison cannot be conducted. The results of the experiment are presented in Table 1. The proposed approach exhibits better results in identifying drug names from the given dataset, achieving Precision and Recall scores of 0.94 and 0.73, respectively, indicating an increase of 0.4 and 0.56 in comparison to the baseline model. However, the Recall score of 0.73 suggests that the input data contains multiple errors. Additionally,

Table 1. Result Evaluation on previous and upgraded system

Model	@Precision	@Recall	@H-mean
TrietPresc	0.54	0.17	0.26
MEP	**0.94**	**0.73**	**0.82**

the efficiency of drug name extraction heavily influences the performance of the metrics. Thus, incorporating heuristic rules in future works can potentially enhance the extraction process.

In addition, Table 2 illustrates the more stability of MEP compared to the TrietPresc model. Specifically, both models effectively recognize the first medicine name "Alpovic" even when the input is misspelled, resulting in high confidence scores. However, when presented with the OCR output text "Eperison 50 mg (Macnir)", TrietPresc fails to correctly separate the drug name and ingredient before applying spell correction, resulting in a confidence score of only 0.6, below the configured threshold, and marking this text as non-drug. In contrast, MEP includes a new layer to precisely extract drug names from the OCR output, aided by the Medicine Classifier, regardless of the complexity of the OCRed text lines. Therefore, MEP effortlessly extracts "Macnir" and "Diovan 160 mg", passing them to the spell correction stage, and achieving excellent confidence scores.

Table 2. The performance of the proposed model and the baseline model

Model	OCRed text	MedicineExtractor	Spell correction	Output
TrietPresc	Allpovic	–	[Alpovic]@0.9	Alpovic
MEP	Allpovic	**Allpovic**	[Alpovic]@0.9	Alpovic
TrietPresc	Eperison 50mg (Macnir)	–	[Macnir]@0.6	–
MEP	Eperison 50mg (Macnir)	**Macnir**	[Macnir]@1.0	Macnir
MEP	Diovan 160mg (Valsartan)	**Diovan 160mg**	[Diovan 160]@0.94	Diovan 160

The proposed model not only achieves better performance but also faster processing time than TrietPresc. The processing time of the proposed system ranges from 1.38 s to 29.65 s, while the baseline model takes 3.81 s to 51.24 s to process. Figure 6 presents a comparison of the average processing time for each step of the prescription dataset between the two versions. Replacing Tesseract with VietOCR significantly reduces the average processing time from 15.84 s to 1.64 s, highlighting the importance of choosing appropriate character recognition models for each problem. Moreover, MEP reduces the matching time between the string and the dictionary, with only a 1.69 s average increase in matching time, despite having a lexicon over 100 times larger than TrietPresc.

In summary, the proposed system has shown remarkable improvement across various metrics. The total drug name recognition and average extraction time have been significantly improved, demonstrating the system's efficiency and

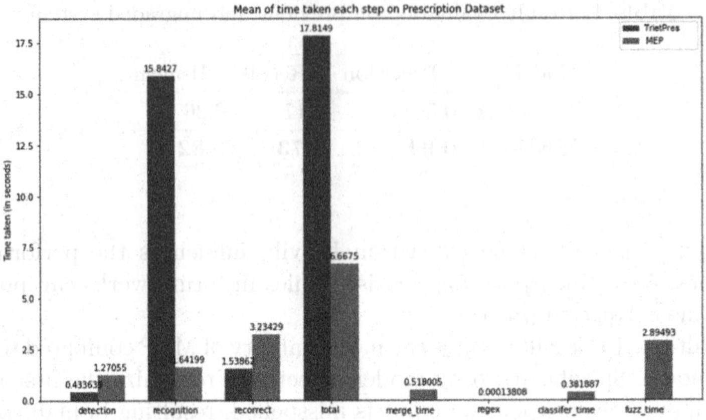

Fig. 6. Average processing time in stages

accuracy. Specifically, the proposed model achieved an average processing time of 6.67 s per prescription, which is substantially faster than the baseline model's average processing time of 17.81 s. These results demonstrate the effectiveness of the proposed model in solving the given problem with high efficiency and accuracy.

6 Conclusion

This paper describes the development of a prescription recognition system named MEP, which aims to improve medication safety by accurately identifying medicines and reducing the risk of errors. The system uses advanced models for text detection and recognition, as well as medicine classification and post-OCR approaches. Experimental results show that the model performs with high accuracy and efficiency on the given dataset. Future improvements include incorporating a prescription dictionary into the detection and identification process to increase accuracy and reduce operation time, as well as exploring new features such as advising patients on proper medication use and reminding them of dosage schedules.

Acknowledgements. This research is funded by Vietnam National University, Ho Chi Minh City (VNU-HCM) under grant number C2023-18-27.

References

1. Hedegaard, H., Miniño, A.M., Spencer, M.R., Warner, M.: Drug overdose deaths in the United States, 1999–2020 (2021)
2. Hassan, E., Tarek, H., Hazem, M., Bahnacy, S., Shaheen, L., Elashmwai, W.H.: Medical prescription recognition using machine learning. In: 2021 IEEE 11th Annual Computing and Communication Workshop and Conference (CCWC), pp. 0973–0979 (2021)

3. Ou, Y.-Y., Tseng, S.-P., Lin, J., Zhou, X.-P., Wang, J.-F., Kuan, T.-W.: Automatic prescription recognition system. In: 2018 International Conference on Orange Technologies (ICOT), pp. 1–4 (2018)
4. Nguyen, T.-T., Nguyen, D.-V.V., Le, T.: Developing a prescription recognition system based on CRAFT and tesseract. In: Nguyen, N.T., Iliadis, L., Maglogiannis, I., Trawiński, B. (eds.) ICCCI 2021. LNCS (LNAI), vol. 12876, pp. 443–455. Springer, Cham (2021). https://doi.org/10.1007/978-3-030-88081-1_33
5. Qin, S., Manduchi, R.: Cascaded segmentation-detection networks for word-level text spotting. In: 2017 14th IAPR international Conference on Document Analysis and Recognition (ICDAR), vol. 1, pp. 1275–1282 (2017)
6. Liu, X., Meng, G., Pan, C.: Scene text detection and recognition with advances in deep learning: a survey. Int. J. Doc. Anal. Recognit. (IJDAR) **22**, 143–162 (2019)
7. Tian, Z., Huang, W., He, T., He, P., Qiao, Yu.: Detecting text in natural image with connectionist text proposal network. In: Leibe, B., Matas, J., Sebe, N., Welling, M. (eds.) ECCV 2016, Part VIII. LNCS, vol. 9912, pp. 56–72. Springer, Cham (2016). https://doi.org/10.1007/978-3-319-46484-8_4
8. Baek, Y., Lee, B., Han, D., Yun, S., Lee, H.: Character region awareness for text detection. In: Proceedings of the IEEE/CVF Conference on Computer Vision and Pattern Recognition, pp. 9365–9374 (2019)
9. Tao, C., Filannino, M., Uzuner, Ö.: Prescription extraction using CRFs and word embeddings. J. Biomed. Inform. **72**, 60–66 (2017)
10. Fu, X., Ch'ng, E., Aickelin, U., See, S.: CRNN: a joint neural network for redundancy detection. In: 2017 IEEE International Conference on Smart Computing (SMARTCOMP), pp. 1–8 (2017)
11. Nguyen, T.T.H., Jatowt, A., Coustaty, M., Doucet, A.: Survey of post-OCR processing approaches. ACM Comput. Surv. (CSUR) **54**(6), 1–37 (2021)
12. Karthikeyan, S., de Herrera, A.G.S., Doctor, F., Mirza, A.: An OCR post-correction approach using deep learning for processing medical reports. IEEE Trans. Circ. Syst. Video Technol. **32**, 2574–2581 (2021)
13. Thompson, P., McNaught, J., Ananiadou, S.: Customised OCR correction for historical medical text. In: 2015 Digital Heritage, vol. 1, pp. 35–42. IEEE (2015)
14. Bai, S., Kolter, J.Z., Koltun, V.: An empirical evaluation of generic convolutional and recurrent networks for sequence modeling. arXiv preprint arXiv:1803.01271 (2018)
15. Garikapati, P.R., Balamurugan, K., Latchoumi, T.P., Shankar, G.: A quantitative study of small dataset machining by agglomerative hierarchical cluster and K-medoid. In: Marriwala, N., Tripathi, C.C., Jain, S., Mathapathi, S. (eds.) Emergent Converging Technologies and Biomedical Systems. LNEE, vol. 841, pp. 717–727. Springer, Singapore (2022). https://doi.org/10.1007/978-981-16-8774-7_59

New Approaches to Monitoring Respiratory Activity as Part of an Intelligent Model for Stress Assessment

Gonçalo Ribeiro[1,2](✉) and Octavian Postolache[1,2](✉)

[1] ISCTE-Instituto Universitário de Lisboa, Lisbon, Portugal
goncalo_tome_ribeiro@iscte-iul.pt, opostolache@lx.it.pt
[2] Instituto de Telecomunicações, Lisbon, Portugal

Abstract. Abnormal breathing patterns have been linked to many diseases and stress-related effect. Visually counting breaths per minute is the gold standard for measuring respiratory rate. In hospital research, most nurses recognize the physiological importance of respiratory rate however its measurement it is not considered mandatory. Current research studies offer viable options for continuous monitoring of respiratory activity, although with degraded performance due to artefact. This paper proposes five new respiratory rate estimation methods considering their strengths and drawbacks to determine the most suitable one for various activities. Photoplethysmography, accelerometry, infrared temperature and pressure sensors are therefore used to monitor respiratory activity. In addition, we present a method for estimating respiratory rate via thermographic video image processing. In terms of novelty and innovation, we highlight the intelligent algorithms developed for real-time respiratory rate extraction from Photoplethysmography signals, the mechanical sensor prototype based on pressure sensors, and the facial recognition, focus zone identification, and image pixel analysis algorithms for thermographic image processing. In addition, a multichannel sensing system characterized by distributed platform computation is utilized to extract physiological parameters forming the basis for the proposed Fuzzy Logic-based model to detect and classify stress levels. To validate the suggested approaches, an experimental protocol was established to monitor the volunteers' respiratory activity in a controlled setting, as well as health monitoring throughout the induction of thermal stress and its classification, yielding excellent indications of efficiency and accuracy.

Keywords: Contactless Health status Monitoring · Wearable Sensors · Infrared Temperature · Thermography · Digital Signal Processing · Fuzzy Logic · Photoplethysmography · Respiratory Rate · Stress Classification

1 Introduction

Respiratory Rate (RR) is a crucial physiological parameter that provides vital information about a patient's health [1], serving not only as a basis for the diagnosis of several respiratory diseases, but also as an evaluation parameter in other clinical settings, such

N. T. Nguyen et al. (Eds.): ICCCI 2023, LNAI 14162, pp. 726–740, 2023.
https://doi.org/10.1007/978-3-031-41456-5_55

as cardiac failure or metabolic emergencies [2, 3]. Despite its clinical significance, research indicates that respiratory rate is the most neglected vital sign in healthcare due to a lack of understanding regarding respiratory rate evaluation, nurses' perceptions of patient acuity, and a lack of time, even though the gold standard for measuring RR is manual counting the number of breaths for one minute [4].

Recent research on the sensory experience of breathing has also focused on breathing conditioning. It is crucial to understand daily conditioning and respiratory dysfunctions such as apnea and asthma. Such dysfunctions are brought on by emotional challenges. Because emotions affect respiration, diverse emotions are accompanied by distinct breathing patterns. Mental stress increases tidal volume and RR [5], therefore, monitoring stress is essential.

Concerning RR assessment, the challenge lies in the development of more efficient and user-friendly solutions. As a result, we propose five new methods for RR assessment based on Photoplethysmography (PPG) sensors, thermography, infrared-temperature sensors, pressure sensors, and accelerometers. A comparison between the proposed methods, based on their accuracy, sensitivity and specificity is also considered. In terms of novelty, a small, mechanical, pressure-sensor-based wearable device prototype is proposed for RR assessment. In terms of innovation, we propose a new method for RR assessment based on thermographic video acquisition and processing, the identification of highlighted areas, and the monitoring of the skin temperature oscillations in the face region using FLIR Tools and MATLAB.

Regarding stress assessment, most studies only detect the presence of stress, with few classifying it. As such, in this work we also propose a new Machine Learning (ML) model based on Fuzzy Logic to assess stress. Thus, we propose a Fuzzy Logic-based Machine Learning (ML) model to assess stress. We used a multichannel sensory system from the authors' previous work [6] to implement PPG signal processing and develop real-time algorithms for physiological parameter extraction, such as Heart Rate (HR), Heart Rate Variability (HRV), Blood Oxygen Saturation (SpO2), and RR. This multichannel sensor system also collects Galvanic Skin Response (GSR) data, a stress-related physio-logical parameter. The intelligent Fuzzy Logic model classifies each of the five physiological parameters and stress into five levels. This algorithm was also evaluated using data from the 5 proposed RR monitoring methods to determine the most suitable for RR monitoring and stress assessment.

This paper is organized as follows. Section 2 presented a brief literature review, for a better theoretical framework. Section 3 discusses the methodology adopted. Section 4 presents the results obtained, as well as some considerations and comparisons. Conclusion and future work follow in Sect. 5.

2 Related Work

In order to understand the aforementioned concerns and the proposed objectives of this study, this section addresses key concepts linked to the assessment of respiratory activity, as well as its relationship to stress, and stress levels assessment.

2.1 Respiratory Activity and Healthcare

RR has many clinical uses, such as, defining baselines for postoperative or comparative monitoring, identifying blood transfusion or drug reactions, and acid-base imbalance detection and compensation. Big RR variations may indicate health deterioration. An irregular RR can also predict other conditions such as organ failure. Yet, it's concerning because RR is the least measured vital sign in clinical settings [4].

RR values are expressed in Breaths Per Minute (BPM), and in the case of healthy resting adults, a normal RR can range between 12 and 20 BPM [7]. Manually counting chest wall movements and auscultation with a stethoscope is the gold standard for measuring RR [8], however, it's not very practical. Most hospital nurses understand the physiological necessity of RR, yet many believe they are enhancing patient outcomes by focusing on other tasks.

In Intensive Care Units (ICU), other more complex automated methods are used, such as Capnography, Impedance Plethysmography and Thermography [9]. Capnography ensures that anaesthetized patients obtain enough oxygen during surgery. The RR is estimated from the patient's gas (anesthesia) intake [9]. Regarding Impedance Plethysmography, this non-invasive method measures small relative changes in electrical resistance in different areas of the human body to determine blood vessel size or lung gas volume, which is used to estimate RR [9].

2.2 Solutions for Respiratory Assessment

There is a wide variety of proposed methods for RR assessment, as shown in Fig. 1.

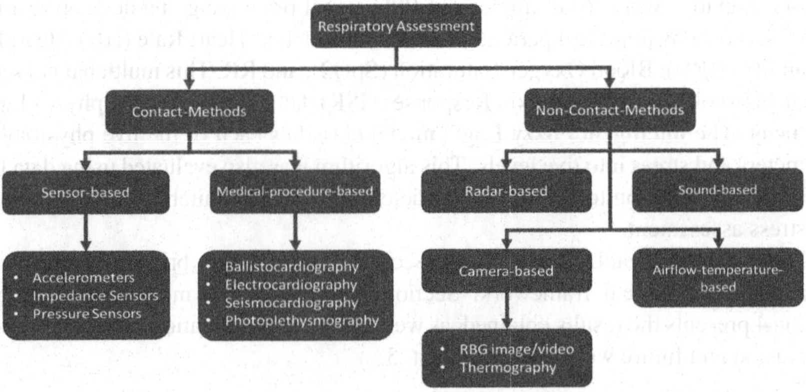

Fig. 1. Classification of Respiratory Assessment Methods

Breathing consists of two distinct movements, inspiration (thorax expands and abdomen rises) and expiration (thorax contracts and abdomen lowers). Using accelerometer and/or gyroscope sensors, the motions of the thoracic and/or abdominal cavities can be monitored to extract the RR [10]. Although several advantages, such as reduced size and low weight, these methods are susceptible to motion artefacts.

Through the monitoring of body posture based on impedance sensors, it is also possible to extract RR, considering different postures [11]. The problem lies in the fact that it is necessary to map all postures. With the introduction of intelligent algorithms and classifiers such as Support Vector Machine (SVM) the problem can be attenuated, however, this adds more complexity to the systems. In addition, accuracy can be affected by variations in body composition and clothing.

Regarding Ballistocardiography (BCG), it is a non-invasive technique based on the monitoring of body movement caused by blood ejection during cardiac cycle. BCG signals associated with cardiac activity are modulated by respiration, and as such, the RR can be extracted through BCG signal processing [12]. However, it's limited by noise artefacts, motion inhibition, and cannot be integrated into wearable devices.

Electrocardiography (ECG) measures heart electrical activity through repeated cardiac cycles, while PPG detects tissue blood volume changes in the microvascular bed. Both methods are used to monitor heart activity, such as HR, HRV, and SpO2 [6, 13]. Further investigation showed that respiratory activities modulate PPG signals in amplitude, frequency, and baseline shift [14, 15], which are used in RR estimation.

RGB cameras can capture chest and abdominal movements for RR estimation [16]. Nonetheless, body motion artefacts and even the subject's clothing can affect this method. Convolutional Neural Networks (CNNs) help training models to predict RR and reduce artefacts [17]. In the case of thermographic cameras, they estimate RR by measuring the airway's ambient temperature, which is usually lower than body temperature. When a person inhales, this air cools the airways. When a person exhales, body-temperature air leaves the airways, warming the airways [18]. These fluctuations in temperature observed by thermographic cameras correspond to the respiratory cycle, enabling the estimation of RR [19].

2.3 Stress and Respiration

Stress is a major health issue that affects many people regardless of age, environment, social standing, or other factors. It caused 51% of work-related illnesses in 2019/2020, according to the Labor Force Survey (LFS) [20]. These effects may cause fatigue or even worsen chronic conditions. Hence, early stress monitoring is crucial.

When confronted with a stressor, the autonomic nervous system releases hormones into the bloodstream, which affects various physiological parameters, including HR, RR, SpO2, Muscle Tension, among others. This autonomous response depends on the stressor's duration. Stress can lead to major health disorders such cardiovascular disease, respiratory disease, mental illness, diabetes, sleep disturbances, immune system degeneration, cancer, anxiety, and depression [21].

2.4 Stress Assessment

Currently, the monitoring of stress levels is not objective because it is primarily based on self-assessment questionnaires, such as the Perceived Stress Scale (PSS) [22], or even through the monitoring of brain activity via Electroencephalogram (EEG) [23], which is performed in controlled environments, such as laboratories, thereby limiting the applicability of these techniques in everyday life.

New promising studies address physiological stress employing vital signs monitoring from various methodologies. These works always include the GSR, which is strongly correlated with stress, although it cannot accurately measure stress alone. There are studies that propose the correlation of GSR with several physiological parameters like HRV [24], Blood Pressure (BP) [21] and Respiration [21], or even combining GSR with techniques like PPG [13], ECG [21], EEG [25], or Electromyography (EMG) [26], but most of them only detect stress and do not classify or quantify it. Because ECG and PPG can extract relevant physiological parameters from signal processing, they are one of the best solutions for stress assessment systems [21].

3 Materials and Methods

The proposed work aims at implementing an intelligent algorithm for assessing stress levels using the previously built multichannel system [6]. In this system, methods for estimating HR, HRV, RR, and SpO2 based on the capture and processing of PPG data are proposed. Since the RR method based on PPG signal presented an accuracy of 90.91%, to maximize the potential of the algorithm based on Fuzzy Logic presented for stress assessment, we first proceeded to study new and more accurate methods for estimating RR. As such, in this section, we will address the different new approaches proposed for RR estimation, the implementation of the novel Fuzzy Logic-based algorithm for stress assessment, and the experimental procedures.

3.1 Respiratory Rate Estimation

Five methods are proposed for RR estimation, using a PPG sensor, a 3D accelerometer, a pressure sensor, an infrared temperature sensor, and thermography.

Regarding the accelerometer-based RR estimation, it's a non-invasive and mechanical contact method, consisting of an ESP32 microcontroller, a BMA400 digital accelerometer, and an OLED LCD display. The used ESP32 microcontroller is characterized by Dual-Core 32-bit CPU, maximum Clock of 240 MHz, ROM memory of 448 Kbytes, RAM memory of 520 Kbytes, Flash memory of 4 MB, and is responsible for processing the data acquired by the accelerometer and applying the implemented algorithm for RR estimation. This estimation is then available through an OLED LCD display. The BMA400 accelerometer is a 3-axis, 12-bit digital accelerometer with intelligent chip and position-driven interrupt functions.

In this method, the accelerometer is attached to an elastic band, as can be seen in Fig. 2(a) below, which should be positioned on the person chest. This way, whenever the individual inhales, there is an increase in the volume of the rib cage, causing the three axes of the accelerometer to vary, which increases an implemented counter (bCounter). Knowing the time that has elapsed since the start of data acquisition (bTime) and bCounter, RR is then estimated based on Eq. (1), as shown in [6].

$$RR = (bCounter * 60)/bTime \quad (1)$$

Regarding the pressure sensor-based RR estimation, the mechanism of which the pressure sensor is part is contained inside a small module, as can be seen in Fig. 2(b) below, which must be positioned on the person chest. In this way, whenever the individual inhales, there is an increase in the volume of the rib cage, exerting pressure on the sensor through the mechanism. These pressure variations result also in the implemented counter (bCounter) increase, providing the RR estimation also through Eq. (1). This method is also classified as non-invasive and mechanical contact.

Fig. 2. Prototypes for RR Estimation. (a) BMA400 Accelerometer attached to an Elastic Band. (b) Proposed Prototype based on Pressure Sensor Mechanism.

The method based on PPG signal uses a MAX30102 PPG sensor, classified as a reflective sensor, i.e., it has two emitting LEDs, one of infrared light and the other of red light, which penetrate to a certain depth in the human tissue and are then reflected. This sensor has a photodetector LED, capable of acquiring both emitted lights, from which it is possible to monitor blood flow variations. After acquisition the signal is filtered and processed. Thus, a first-order low-pass filter is applied to reduce noise artifacts. With the filtered PPG signal, it is then possible to determine the signal maximum values, and through this, the developed algorithm estimates in real time the RR [6]. Note that this method is also classified as non-invasive and mechanical contact.

Infrared temperature-based RR estimation is a non-invasive and contactless method that consists of an ESP32 microcontroller, an MLX90614 infrared temperature sensor, and an OLED LCD display. The MLX90614 is a sensor designed for contactless temperature detection, which features a 17-bit internal Analogic Digital Converter (ADC) and high accuracy of 0,5 °C and measurement resolution of 0,02 °C. This sensor is factory calibrated in wide temperature ranges from −40 °C to 85 °C for ambient temperature, and from −70 °C to 382.2 °C for object temperature. In this method, the temperature of the nostrils is measured. When a person inhales, air at ambient temperature is inhaled, causing the nostril orifices to cool. In turn, when a person exhales, the exhaled air has the same temperature as the human body, and as such, an increase in temperature is visible in the nostril orifices. Our method can distinguish these temperature variations and account for them (bCounter), which in turn allows us to estimate the RR also using Eq. (1).

Regarding the estimation of RR based on thermography, this is a non-invasive and contactless method. For this estimation the FLIR E64501 thermographic camera was used (Fig. 3 below), capable of acquiring both thermographic images and videos, presenting a sample rate of 60Hz. This camera is capable of measuring temperatures up to a maximum of 650 °C, with an accuracy of ±2% and a sensitivity of 0.05 °C.

During the conducted experiment, the FLIR E64501 was used to acquire video, which was analyzed using the FLIR Tools platform provided by the manufacturer. As with the infrared temperature sensor method, each time a person inhales, a decrease

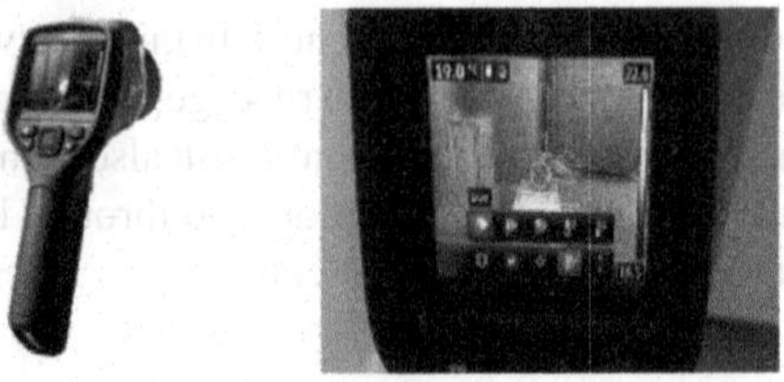

Fig. 3. FLIR E64501 Thermographic Camera

in temperature is visible at the nostrils, while when a person exhales, an increase in temperature is visible, as can be seen in Fig. 4 below. In the specific case of the experiment conducted, the temperature focus was the nostril orifices, and as such, in the graph of Fig. 5 below is an example of the wave corresponding to the temperature variation at that location and analyzed by FLIR Tools for a randomly chosen participant. Note that the data presented relate to the period of the experiment, that is, for 60 s, the period needed to estimate the RR.

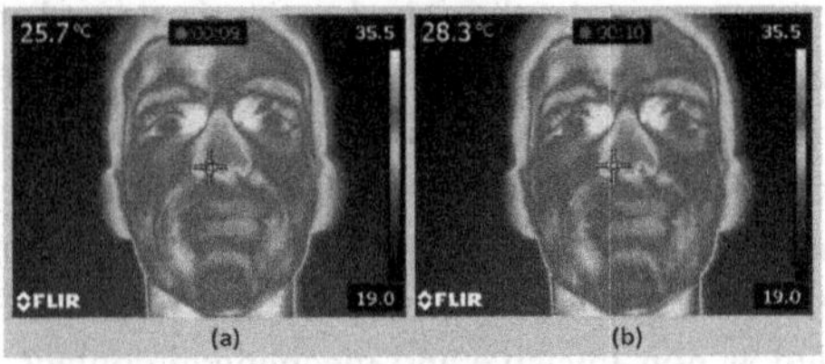

Fig. 4. Thermographic Image associated with Respiratory Cycle. In (a) it is possible to observe the com-ponent of the respiratory cycle regarding inspiration phase (nostril orifices cooling to a tempera-ture of 25.7 °C). In (b) it is possible to observe the component of the respiratory cycle regarding expiration phase (nostril orifices heating to a temperature of 28,3 °C).

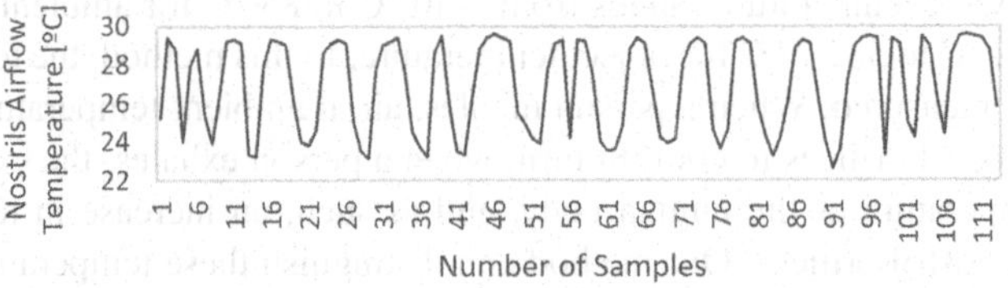

Fig. 5. Respiratory Activity extracted by the Thermography-based Method (70-year-old male volunteer).

As can be seen in the graph of Fig. 5, each minimum of the wave allows us to identify one breath. In this case, it is possible to identify that the participant presented a RR of 19 BPM. To automate the estimation process, the MATLAB platform is a great solution for working on video image processing, thus allowing not only facial recognition, but also to automatically recognize the region of interest for detecting temperature variations, such as the nostrils or the mouth region.

3.2 Intelligent Approach to Stress Assessment

The proposed algorithm for stress assessment is based on the acquisition of stress related physiological parameters, such as HR, PRV, RR, SpO2 and GSR. The classification of stress levels was performed through the implementation of Fuzzy Logic, where we defined for each physiological parameter its reference values (HR [27], PRV [28], RR [29], SpO2 [30], GSR [31]), the classification and the type of Membership Function, according to Table 1.

It is important to point out that in the case of HRV, the values tabulated for the approach employed Root Mean Square of Successive Differences (RMSSD) were considered, and as a result, Table 1 presents the range of potential values for all healthy age groups excluding children.

A Membership function for a Fuzzy set A on the universe of discourse X is defined as μA: X → [0, 1], where each element of X is mapped to a value between 0 and 1. This value, called membership value or degree of membership, quantifies the grade of membership of the element in X to the fuzzy set A.

Table 1. Physiological Parameters Treatment.

Parameter	Classification based on Parameter Reference Values				
	Very Low	Low	Normal	High	Very High
HR [beat-per-minute]	0–50	50–60	60–90	90–100	100–200
HRV [ms]	0–19	19–32	32–77	77–107	107–160
RR [breaths-per-minute]	0–10	10–12	12–18	18–22	22–30
SpO2 [%]	85–90	90–95	95–97	97–99	100
GSR [kOhm]	10–20	20–30	30–50	50–70	70–100

Based on previous Table 1, the Membership Functions used in the proposed model are categorised as Trapezoidal Function Type R for “Very Low”, defined in Eq. (2), Trapezoidal Function Type L for “Very High”, defined in Eq. (3), and Triangular Function for “Low”, “Normal” and “High”, defined in Eq. (4). According to physiological parameter classification based on the reference value ranges, the minimum value is “a”, the maximum value is “b”, and the average value is defined as “c”.

$$\text{Trapezoidal\_Type\_R} = \begin{cases} 0, & x > b \\ \frac{b-x}{b-a}, & a \le x \le b \\ 1, & x < a \end{cases} \tag{2}$$

$$\text{Trapezoidal\_Type\_L} = \begin{cases} 0, & x < a \\ \frac{x-a}{b-a}, & a \le x \le b \\ 1, & x > b \end{cases} \tag{3}$$

$$\text{Triangular\_Function} = \begin{cases} 0, & x \leq a \\ \frac{x-a}{c-a}, & a < x \leq c \\ \frac{b-x}{b-c}, & c < x < b \\ 0, & x \geq b \end{cases} \tag{4}$$

To assess the stress levels, five rules based on the investigated relationship between physiological parameters and stress [6] were established. These rules are presented below in Table 2. The quantification of stress is then given by Eq. (5).

Table 2. Classification of Stress Levels According to the Fuzzy Logic Algorithm.

Stress	Rules (R)	Stress Level (S)
Very Calm	R1 = VeryLow(HR) Λ VeryLow(HRV) Λ VeryLow(RR) Λ VeryHigh(SpO2) Λ VeryHigh(GSR)	S1 = R1 * 1
Calm	R2 = Low(HR) Λ Low(HRV) Λ Low(RR) Λ High(SpO2) Λ High(GSR)	S2 = R2 * 2
Normal	R3 = Normal(HR) Λ Normal(HRV) Λ Normal(RR) Λ Normal(SpO2) Λ Normal(GSR)	S3 = R3 * 3
Stressed	R4 = High(HR) Λ High(HRV) Λ High(RR) Λ Low(SpO2) Λ Low(GSR)	S4 = R4 * 4
Very Stressed	R5 = VeryHigh(HR) Λ VeryHigh(HRV) Λ VeryHigh(RR) Λ VeryLow(SpO2) Λ VeryLow(GSR)	S5 = R5 * 5

$$Stress = \frac{S1 + S2 + S3 + S4 + S5}{R1 + R2 + R3 + R4 + R5} \tag{5}$$

3.3 Experimental Procedure

In the scope of this work, two experiments were carried out, with 26 volunteers aged between 16 and 91 (mean age approximately 38, and age standard deviation approximately 20). All participants were informed about the experiments and gave their verbal consent. None of the participants reported any mental, cardiac, respiratory, or other disturbances.

In the experimental procedure implemented in this work two experiments were conducted. The first experiment was aimed at determining the feasibility of each proposed method for estimating RR. The second experiment was aimed at monitoring HR, HRV, RR, SpO2, and GSR during the thermal stress induction, to serve as a basis for the proposed model for stress levels assessment.

The first experiment was performed in a controlled environment. The duration of the experiment was 1 min, in which each participant was asked to remain seated and to avoid motions, thus facilitating data acquisition. Before the beginning of the experiment, each system relative to the 5 methods proposed in this paper was positioned, i.e., a PPG sensor was placed on the index finger of the participants, the device with the built-in pressure sensor and accelerometer was positioned on the chest of the participants, the participants were also asked to bring the infrared temperature sensor near the nasal orifice with their vacant hand, and the thermographic camera was also positioned in front of the participants, thus enabling facial capture. The considered acquisition rate was 2 samples per second, and each method generates about 120 samples per minute.

The second experiment was conducted at room temperature in a controlled environment. The participants remained seated and at rest during the entirety of the experiments. Participants were instructed to use their right to collect physiological parameters, and their left hand as the target of thermal stress induction (hot and cold). Limits were established to guarantee the participants physical integrity, being defined as low temperature 20 °C and high temperature 40 °C. This experiment has divided in 5 phases. Phase 1 lasted 5 min, in which only the physiological parameters were acquired, thus intended to establish a baseline for each participant. Phase 2 lasted 1 min, in which the participants physiological parameters were monitored when in contact with cold. Phase 3 lasted 10 min, the period necessary for the human body to recover from contact with cold. Phase 4 lasted 1 min, with the participants' physiological parameters being monitored when in contact with heat. Finally, phase 5 lasted 10 min, the period necessary for the human body to recover from the contact with the heat. At the end of each phase, each participant was asked to self-assess stress on a scale from 1 to 5, serving as reference values for model validation.

4 Results and Discussion

This section discusses the results and accuracy of the five proposed methods for RR estimation, also determining their sensitivity and specificity. In this section is also discussed the thermal stress induction study, and the validation of the algorithm for stress levels classification.

4.1 Assessment of the Proposed Methods for Estimating Respiratory Rate

A statistical analysis was performed according to the type A measurement of uncertainties, i.e., data collected from a series of observations and evaluated using statistical methods. To calculate the accuracy of the proposed methods each volunteer was asked to use a small counter during the experiments, that is, every time they took a breath, they had to press a small button that incremented the number of breaths, thus giving us a real breathing counter (reference values). Methods base on thermography, pressure sensor and infra-red temperature presented a mean relative error of 0,01%. Regarding accelerometer-based method, it presented a mean relative error of 10,79%. PPG-based method presented a mean relative error of 2,49%.

In addition, linear regression was also determined for each proposed method. Since methods based on thermography, infrared temperature and pressure sensor presented an accuracy of 99.99%, the linear regression is defined by $y = x$. For PPG and Accelerometer based methods, the respective linear regressions are presented below in Fig. 6.

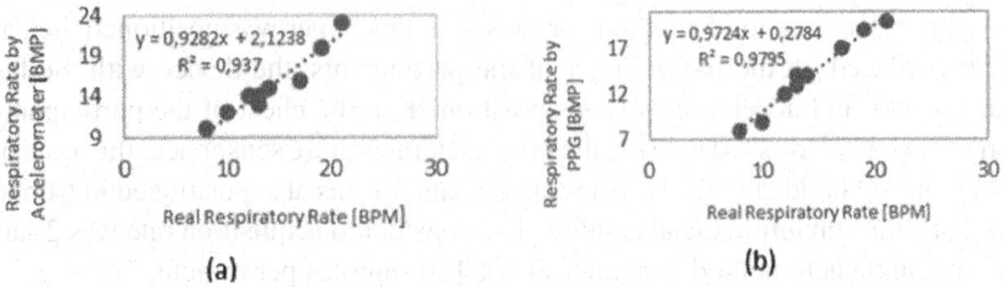

Fig. 6. PPG and Accelerometer based Methods Evaluation. (a) Linear Regression for Accelerometer-based Method. (b) Linear Regression for the Photoplethysmography-based Method.

The performance of the 5 proposed methods was evaluated using a multi-class confusion matrix and metrics such as sensibility and specificity were applied. Regarding the methods based on thermography, pressure sensor and infra-red temperature, the mean sensibility was 1 and the mean specificity was also 1. For accelerometer-based method, the mean sensibility was 0,99 and the mean specificity was 0,98. Regarding PPG-based method, the mean sensibility was 0,98 and the mean specificity was 0,99. In general, we can say that the proposed methods present satisfactory results, in that there are few false negatives and few false positives.

4.2 Thermal Stress Induction and Validation of Stress Level Classification

This experiment's main objective was to investigate the effects of temperature stressors on physiological parameters. In this instance, HR, HRV, RR, SpO2 and GSR are examined. The behavior of the acquired physiological parameters follows a pattern, in that the induction of thermal stress results in significant changes in the physiological parameters. During the recovery periods, however, physiological parameter values tend to stabilize at normal levels. To facilitate the data analysis, the average values of each physiological parameter obtained throughout the experiment were calculated. Figure 7 illustrates the RR and GSR averages of each participant, based on the PPG-based method. For better data comprehension, not all participants were considered.

In Fig. 7 (a) bellow, the induction of thermal stress, mainly with cold, generates direct changes in respiration, i.e., when stress is induced, RR typically increases. During recovery periods, the body attempts to normalize the levels, leading to a decrease in RR. In contrast to other physiological parameters such as HR, HRV, SpO2, and GSR, RR is the only parameter that can be controlled by the patient, such as by breathing exercises, decreasing the RR and consequently decreasing stress levels.

In the specific case of the GSR, after the first cold perturbation, there is a noticeable increase in the values, but in the recovery period, a large decrease in the values is not observed, as is the case with the other physiological parameters, leading us to believe that due to the strong relationship between the GSR and stress, it is affected for a longer period of time by the stressor. As seen in Fig. 7(b), another interesting aspect of the GSR is that the heat disturbance works as a technique to assist relax the participants rather than as a stressor.

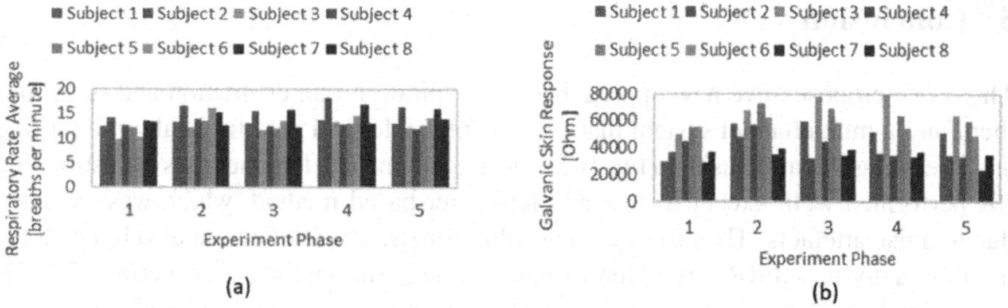

Fig. 7. Averages Values for each Participant. (a) RR Averages during each Testing Phase. (b) GSR Averages during each Testing Phase.

Age also affects how the body responds to the stressor. The time it takes the bodies of persons over 65 to recover is longer than that of persons younger than 65. Moreover, the response time to the stressor itself is lengthened. This is demonstrated in Fig. 8 by contrasting one of the randomly selected young participants (age criteria ranged from 16 to 30 years) with a randomly selected senior participant (age criteria ranged from 60 to 91 years). In addition, the male gender was a factor in the selection process (larger number of participants).

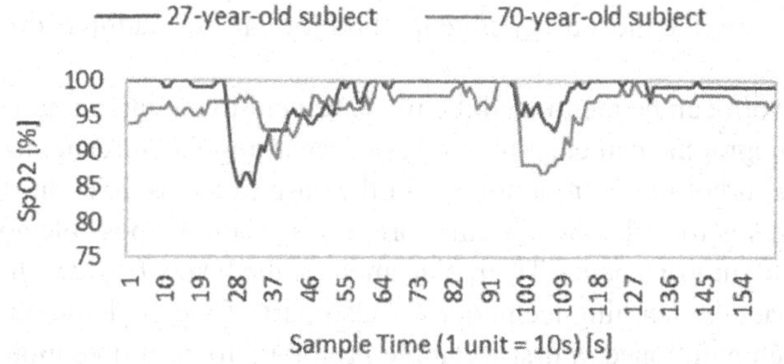

Fig. 8. Comparison between the SpO2 Values obtained by a 27-year-old Participant (highlighted in blue) and a 70-year-old Participant (highlighted in orange) throughout the duration of experiment 2 (Thermal Stress Induction).

To validate the Fuzzy Logic model for estimating stress levels, participants were given a slider button and asked to estimate their stress level on a scale from 0 to 5. After the experiments, the data were thoroughly analyzed using the Fuzzy Logic approach. This resulted in a rating of stress levels from 0 to 5 that was compared to the participants' self-assessment.

The suggested Fuzzy Logic methodology yields satisfactory results, evaluating the stress levels with precision. The self-classification done by the participants and the classification generated by Fuzzy Logic yielded identical findings.

5 Conclusion

This work proposes five new approaches for respiration rate estimation and integrates them into a multichannel system that extracts physiological data for health monitoring and stress classification using a Fuzzy Logic algorithm. The five methods for estimating RR performed well, except for the accelerometer-based method, which was expected due to noise artefacts. The proposed algorithm for stress classification also rejected the thermography-based RR estimation technique due to thermal stress induction. The RR estimation failed because the heat water container's vapor made thermographic detection impossible during thermal stress induction. Only pressure, infrared-temperature, and PPG sensor approaches were considered for RR estimation and stress classification. The infrared-temperature method was one of the most accurate for RR estimation, but it conditions breathing because it must be placed near a nasal orifice. In the case of the pressure sensor solution, this proves to be the most viable option. The fact that it is a wearable device with tiny dimensions makes it simple to operate, since it is quite accurate even during moderate motion. For stress classification, the physiological parameters extraction accuracy is essential; nevertheless, the tiny variation regarding accuracy between solutions based on PPG and pressure sensors does not translate into any difference in stress classification. In addition, the fact that the multichannel system already utilizes PPG to extract other physiological parameters makes RR estimation based on PPG more accessible. Thus, taking into consideration the methodology for stress classification, the most acceptable method for RR estimation is the one based on PPG.

As future work can be mentioned the improvement to the integration of the method based on thermographic cameras, for example, regarding facial recognition algorithms and multi-zone target region monitoring. In the case of stress assessment system, one of the challenges is to make the system more robust, with the possible addition of new mechanisms and improvements. The replacement of the Fuzzy Logic technique by other more robust machine learning techniques is also part of the goals. In addition to what has already been mentioned, a first wearable prototype for real time monitoring during daily life is under development.

References

1. Fusco, A. Locatelli, D., Onorati, F., Durelli, G.C., Santambrogio, M.D.: On how to extract breathing rate from PPG signal using wearable devices. In: IEEE Biomedical Circuits and Systems Conference on Engineering Health Minds Able Bodies, BioCAS 2015 - Proceedings, pp. 3–6 (2015). https://doi.org/10.1109/BioCAS.2015.7348369
2. Fie, J.F., Hendryx, M., Helms, C.M.: Respiratory rate predicts cardiopulmonary arrest for internal medicine Inpatients. J. Gen. Intern. Med. **8**(7), 354–360 (1990)
3. Yuill, G.M., Saroya, D., Yuill, S.L.: A national survey of the provision for patients with latex allergy. Anaesthesia **58**(8), 775–777 (2003). https://doi.org/10.1046/j.1365-2044.2003.03256.x
4. Elliott, M.: Why is respiratory rate the neglected vital sign? A narrative review. Int. Arch. Nurs. Heal. Care **2**(3), 2–5 (2016). https://doi.org/10.23937/2469-5823/1510050

5. Masaoka, Y., Homma, I.: Anxiety and respiratory patterns: their relationship during mental stress and physical load. Int. J. Psychophysiol. **27**(2), 153–159 (1997). https://doi.org/10.1016/S0167-8760(97)00052-4
6. Ribeiro, G., Postolache, O., Martín, F.F.: A practical approach to health status monitoring based on heart rate and respiratory rate assessment. In: 2022 IEEE International Symposium on Medical Measurements and Applications (MeMeA), Messina, Italy, pp. 1–6 (2022). https://doi.org/10.1109/MeMeA54994.2022.9856576
7. Flenady, T., Dwyer, T., Applegarth, J.: Accurate respiratory rates count: So should you! Australas. Emerg. Nurs. J. **20**(1), 45–47 (2017). https://doi.org/10.1016/j.aenj.2016.12.003
8. Nam, Y., Reyes, B.A., Chon, K.H.: Estimation of respiratory rates using the built-in microphone of a smartphone or headset. IEEE J. Biomed. Heal. Informatics **20**(6), 1493–1501 (2016). https://doi.org/10.1109/JBHI.2015.2480838
9. Birrenkott, D.A., Pimentel, M.A.F., Watkinson, P.J., Clifton, D.A.: A robust fusion model for estimating respiratory rate from photoplethysmography and electrocardiography. IEEE Trans. Biomed. Eng. **65**(9), 2033–2041 (2018). https://doi.org/10.1109/TBME.2017.2778265
10. Siqueira, A., Spirandeli, A.F., Moraes, R., Zarzoso, V.: Respiratory waveform estimation from multiple accelerometers: an optimal sensor number and placement analysis. IEEE J. Biomed. Heal. Informatics **23**(4), 1507–1515 (2019). https://doi.org/10.1109/JBHI.2018.2867727
11. Liu, G., Li, K., Zheng, L., Chen, W.H., Zhou, G., Jiang, Q.: A respiration-derived posture method based on dual-channel respiration impedance signals. IEEE Access **5**, 17514–17524 (2017). https://doi.org/10.1109/ACCESS.2017.2737461
12. Reinvuo, T., Hannula, M., Sorvoja, H., Alasaarela, E., Myllylä, R.: Measurement of respiratory rate with high-resolution accelerometer and EMFit pressure sensor. In: Proceedings of the 2006 IEEE Sensors Applications Symposium, no. February, pp. 192–195 (2006). https://doi.org/10.1109/sas.2006.1634270
13. Ribeiro, G., Postolache, O.: Sensors and mobile interfaces for stress level monitoring in people with diabetes. In: 12th International Symposium on Advanced Topics in Electrical Engineering, ATEE 2021 (2021). https://doi.org/10.1109/ATEE52255.2021.9425134
14. Karlen, W., Raman, S., Ansermino, J.M., Dumont, G.A.: Multiparameter respiratory rate estimation from the photoplethysmogram. IEEE Trans. Biomed. Eng. **60**(7), 1946–1953 (2013). https://doi.org/10.1109/TBME.2013.2246160
15. Charlton, P.H., Bonnici, T., Tarassenko, L., Clifton, D.A., Beale, R., Watkinson, P.J.: An assessment of algorithms to estimate respiratory rate from the electrocardiogram and photoplethysmogram. Physiol. Meas. **37**(4), 610–626 (2016). https://doi.org/10.1088/0967-3334/37/4/610
16. Lin, K.Y., Chen, D.Y., Tsai, W.J.: Image-based motion-tolerant remote respiratory rate evaluation. IEEE Sens. J. **16**(9), 3263–3271 (2016). https://doi.org/10.1109/JSEN.2016.2526627
17. Brieva, J., Ponce, H., Moya-Albor, E.: A contactless respiratory rate estimation method using a hermite magnification technique and convolutional neural networks. Appl. Sci. **10**(2), 607 (2020). https://doi.org/10.3390/app10020607
18. Kwon, H.M., Ikeda, K., Kim, S.H., Thiele, R.H.: Non-contact thermography-based respiratory rate monitoring in a post-anesthetic care unit. J. Clin. Monit. Comput. **35**(6), 1291–1297 (2021). https://doi.org/10.1007/s10877-020-00595-8
19. Takahashi, Y., Gu, Y., Nakada, T., Abe, R., Nakaguchi, T.: Estimation of respiratory rate from thermography using respiratory likelihood index. Sensors **21**(13), 1–12 (2021). https://doi.org/10.3390/s21134406
20. Health and Safety Executive. Work-Related Ill Health and Occupational Disease in Great Britain. https://www.hse.gov.uk/statistics/causdis/. Accessed 19 Sept 2022

21. Akmandor, A.O., Jha, N.K.: Keep the stress away with SoDA: stress detection and alleviation system. IEEE Trans. Multi-Scale Comput. Syst. **3**(4), 269–282 (2017). https://doi.org/10.1109/TMSCS.2017.2703613
22. Schmidt, P., Reiss, A., Duerichen, R., Van Laerhoven, K.: Introducing WeSAD, a multimodal dataset for wearable stress and affect detection. In: ICMI 2018 – Proceedings of the 2018 International Conference on Multimodal Interaction, pp. 400–408 (2018). https://doi.org/10.1145/3242969.3242985
23. Vanitha, V., Krishnan, P.: Real time stress detection system based on EEG signals. Biomed. Res. **2016**(Special Issue 2), S271–S275 (2016)
24. Giannakakis, G., et al.: Stress and anxiety detection using facial cues from videos. Biomed. Signal Process. Control **31**, 89–101 (2017). https://doi.org/10.1016/j.bspc.2016.06.020
25. Arsalan, A., Majid, M., Anwar, S.M., Bagci, U.: Classification of perceived human stress using physiological signals. In: Proceedings of Annual International Conference of the IEEE Engineering in Medicine and Biology Society, EMBS, pp. 1247–1250 (2019). https://doi.org/10.1109/EMBC.2019.8856377
26. Aigrain, J., Spodenkiewicz, M., Dubuiss, S., Detyniecki, M., Cohen, D., Chetouani, M.: Multimodal stress detection from multiple assessments. IEEE Trans. Affect. Comput. **9**(4), 491–506 (2018). https://doi.org/10.1109/TAFFC.2016.2631594
27. Healthy Lifestyle Fitness. What's a normal resting heart rate? https://www.mayoclinic.org/healthy-lifestyle/fitness/expert-answers/heart-rate/faq-20057979. Accessed 19 Sept 2022
28. EHRV. Normative HRV Scores by Age and Gender [Heart Rate Variability Chart]. https://elitehrv.com/normal-heart-rate-variability-age-gender. Accessed 19 Sept 2022
29. healthline. What Is a Normal Respiratory Rate for Adults and Children? https://www.healthline.com/health/normal-respiratory-rate. Accessed 19 Sept 2022
30. OnHealth. Safe, Normal, Low Blood Oxygen Levels: Pulse Oximeter Chart. https://www.onhealth.com/content/1/normal_low_blood_oxygen_pulse_oximeter_levels. Accessed 19 Sept 2022
31. Villarejo, M.V., Zapirain, B.G., Zorrilla, A.M.: A stress sensor based on galvanic skin response (GSR) controlled by ZigBee. Sens. (Switz.) **12**(5), 6075–6101 (2012). https://doi.org/10.3390/s120506075

An Adaptive Network Model for Anorexia Nervosa: Addressing the Effects of Therapy

Smruti Inamdar, Teresa Liberatore, and Jan Treur(✉)

Social AI Group, Department of Computer Science, Vrije Universiteit Amsterdam, Amsterdam, The Netherlands
{s.inamdar,t.liberatore}@student.vu.nl, j.treur@vu.nl

Abstract. This paper presents a potential model for understanding the development and maintenance of Anorexia Nervosa, a serious and potentially life-threatening eating disorder characterized by severe food intake restrictions, leading to extreme weight loss and a distorted body image. The proposed model is an adaptive temporal-causal network model that considers the complex interactions between multiple factors over time, and allows for the identification of potential perpetuating cycles that may maintain the disorder. Specifically, this work focuses on the perpetuating cycle between restrictive dieting and anxiety. The model suggests that initial states of low self-acceptance, adherence to the thin ideal, and perfectionism can lead to states of body dissatisfaction and feeling worthless, which in turn may drive individuals to engage in restrictive dieting behaviors. These behaviors can lead to weight loss, which can temporarily reduce anxiety levels, but ultimately perpetuate the cycle of anxiety and restrictive dieting. The potential impact of therapy on breaking this perpetuating cycle is discussed, as a form of improving self-acceptance, body satisfaction, and overall mental health. The potential strengths and limitations of this model are discussed, together with suggestions of possible directions for future research in this area. Overall, this proposed model offers a novel approach for understanding the complex interactions that contribute to the development and maintenance of Anorexia Nervosa, and the potential benefits of therapeutic interventions in addressing these underlying issues.

Keywords: Adaptive Network Model · Network Modeling · Social Artificial Intelligence · Anorexia Nervosa

1 Introduction

Anorexia Nervosa (AN) is an Eating Disorder occurring worldwide among females and males of all age groups, with a prevalence of adolescent and young adult females in Western Countries (van Eeden et al., 2021). An eating disorder is defined as a persistent disturbance of eating behavior leading to changes in the consumption of food that results in physiological and psychological impairments (Brytek-Matera and Czepczor, 2017). In particular, Anorexia Nervosa is characterized by self-starvation and compensatory behaviors, whilst being associated with low rates of recovery and the highest mortality

N. T. Nguyen et al. (Eds.): ICCCI 2023, LNAI 14162, pp. 741–752, 2023.
https://doi.org/10.1007/978-3-031-41456-5_56

rate of any psychiatric disorder (Godier and Park, 2014). Despite a proliferation of models of Eating Disorders, treatment for AN is limited and has not improved in the last 50 years, due to the incomplete comprehension of the basic mechanisms underlying this disorder (Haynos et al., 2022). In their paper, Mehta and Treasure highlight how establishing causality for AN has so far proven to be difficult, due to the sparsity of prospective longitudinal studies which makes it hard to establish causal relationships, whilst it is deemed to be possible to identify putative risk and perpetuating factors (Woerwag-Mehta and Treasure, 2008). For the sake of this study, the most known predisposing, precipitating, and perpetuating factors have been included in the model, where the model is an adaptation of the existing causal model for AN (Brytek-Matera and Czepczor, 2017; Vervaet et al., 2021; Treasure et al., 2005). The connectivity of the designed base network model can be seen in Fig. 1.

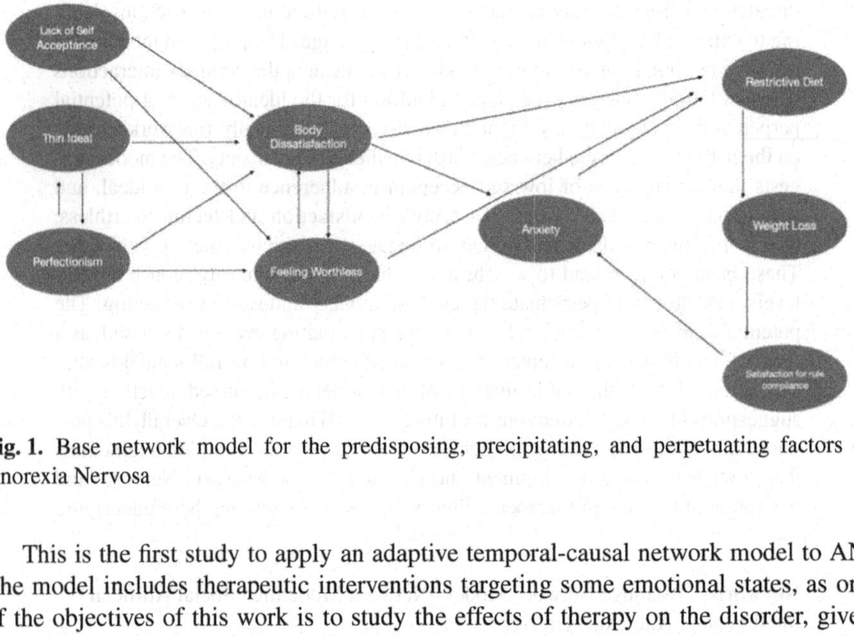

Fig. 1. Base network model for the predisposing, precipitating, and perpetuating factors of Anorexia Nervosa

This is the first study to apply an adaptive temporal-causal network model to AN. The model includes therapeutic interventions targeting some emotional states, as one of the objectives of this work is to study the effects of therapy on the disorder, given the modeling structure and the assumptions. This design choice has been made after this paper (van't Hof et al., 2020), where an adaptive network model has been applied to the study of Genito-Pelvic Pain/Penetration disorder, with a focus on the effects of therapy on the temporal causal model graph. The model has been designed in such a way that if the predisposing states are initialized to zero or they will be set with a speed different from zero, the precipitating states will not be activated and thus the AN loop will not be activated. On the other hand, if the predisposing factors are initialized as nonzero and a threshold is reached, the precipitating factors will be activated, and according to the perpetuating states threshold, the perpetuating cycle will be activated. The connections between the precipitating factors and therapy have been designed to allow for a decrease of their values over time if the therapy states are activated: the expectation is that therapy would bring a higher chance of exiting the perpetuating cycle. First, some background information is presented, after which the computational model is described. Next, simulation outcomes are reported and discussed.

2 Background

This section gives a comprehensive view of the Eating-disorders model to facilitate a better understanding of the network model. Eating disorders are characterized by a continuous disturbance of eating-related behavior that impacts the consumption or absorption of food. These further cause harm to physical or psychosocial beings. There are several disorders in the category - Anorexia Nervosa, Bulimia Nervosa, Binge-eating Disorder, Rumination Disorder, Pica, and Restrictive Intake Disorder. The above disorders have diagnostic criteria which have resulted in a mutually exclusive classification scheme. Only a single diagnosis can apply, and there is no overlap. In spite of having been caused by a substantial number of common social and psychological factors, every disorder differs in the clinical course, treatment, medication, and outcomes. Following are the potential prognostic factors leading to the development of Anorexia Nervosa:

- **Biological factors:** Individuals with first-degree biological relatives have a higher risk of being exposed to Anorexia. Signals such as gastrointestinal peptides tend to act on the central nervous system, which then influences eating behaviors, energy levels, and mood. Furthermore, interactions between cortisol, cytokine, and leptin could be accelerators in an ED onset.
- **Psychological factors:** Body dissatisfaction has been a prevalent risk factor for eating disorders. Another strong motivational factor is an individual's self-esteem. They tend to hinge their self-esteem on their appearance and body weight, which results in their pursuit of the supposed "thin ideal". It is an adaptive mechanism to mitigate negative emotions when there is a threat to their self-esteem (Grzelak et al., 2017).
- **Sociocultural factors:** Sometimes parents' own dissatisfaction with their bodies and dieting behavior is projected onto the children who then go on to develop eating disorders. Other factors include negative comments about weight, body shape, and pressure to lose weight have been associated with body dissatisfaction. Furthermore, parental control, hostility, societal norms about the "thin ideal", and peer influence specifically among adolescents accelerate the process of developing aforementioned disorders.

This paper focuses on the psychological and sociocultural factors for the simplicity of network modeling. Anxiety, Obsessive Compulsive Disorders, Bipolar, Depressive commonly co-occur with Anorexia Nervosa. In particular, Anxiety is strongly coupled with anorexia, or is a part of the onset of the eating disorder.

3 The Modeling Approach

In Sect. 4, the adaptive temporal-causal network model is presented. This computational model based on network-oriented modeling for adaptive networks (Treur, 2020) is a modeling approach that uses network concepts to represent the interactions between different components of a system. This modeling approach is a general framework that can be applied to a wide range of systems, including biological, social, and environmental systems. One key feature of the approach used here is its focus on adaptivity, or the ability of a system to change and evolve in response to external or internal stimuli as introduced in (Treur, 2020). In an adaptive computational model, the relationships between different components of a system may change as the system adapts to new conditions or inputs. The network characteristics specifying a network model are nodes and their connections (*connectivity characteristics*), combination functions (*aggregation characteristics*), and speed factors (*timing characteristics*). These characteristics are defined in the standard format of role matrices which allows a full specification of the model. The Base Connectivity role matrix **mb** defines the relationships between different nodes (also called states) in the network, specifying which nodes are connected to which other nodes, representing the structure of the network. In addition, in the **mcw** role matrix the weights of these connections are specified; they can be modified to capture changes in connectivity over time, for example, synaptic plasticity by Hebbian learning. The Aggregation role matrix **mcfw** for Combination Function Weights defines how the impacts from different nodes X_i on a given node Y in the network combine or interact with each other to form an aggregated impact on the given node Y. In addition, in the Aggregation role matrix **mcfp** for Combination Function Parameters the parameters of these functions are specified. The Speed Factor role matrix **ms** defines the rate at which different nodes in the network change over time based on the aggregated impact they receive. This matrix can be used to represent the relative speeds at which different nodes respond. In summary:

- **Connectivity:** The strength of a connection from state X to Y is represented by weight $\omega_{X,Y}$
- **Aggregation:** The aggregation of multiple impacts on state Y by combination function $\mathbf{c}_Y(..)$ and its parameters
- **Timing:** The timing of the effect of the impact on state Y by speed factor η_Y

Given initial values for the states (the nodes of the network), the network characteristics fully define the dynamics of the network, where *Y(t)* is the value of each state Y at time point t. The dynamics of the model is determined based on difference or differential equation defined in terms of the above network characteristics:

$$Y(t+\Delta t) = Y(t) + \eta_Y[\mathbf{aggimpact}_Y(t) - Y(t)]\Delta t$$
$$\text{or } \mathrm{d}Y(t)/\mathrm{d}t = \eta_Y[\mathbf{aggimpact}_Y(t) - Y(t)]$$
$$\text{with } \mathbf{aggimpact}_Y(t) = \mathbf{c}_Y\big(\omega_{X_1,Y}X_1(t), \ldots, \omega_{X_k,Y}X_k(t)\big) \quad (1)$$

where the X_i are all states from which state Y has incoming connections. In order to transform the conceptual design of the adaptive network into a numerical representation of the model, a dedicated software environment is available in MATLAB to be used for simulations. Each network structure characteristic can be made adaptive by adding self-model states (also called reification states) to the network (Treur, 2018, 2019, 2020): states $\mathbf{W}_{X,Y}$ for connection weights $\omega_{X,Y}$, states $\mathbf{C}_Y$ for combination functions $\mathbf{c}_Y$ (..), and states $\mathbf{H}_Y$ for speed factors η_Y. Self-model states get their own specific network structure to define their adaptive dynamics and they are usually depicted in 3D format at a higher level plane, as shown in Fig. 2. This kind of modeling allows, for example, to design the adaptation principle of Hebbian learning (Morris, 1999), which is a form of plasticity of the brain (*'neurons that fire together, wire together'*). In order to specify the effect of the impact on a state, different combination functions can be used, such as advanced logistic sum and Hebbian learning combination functions, which are defined as follows:

- the *advanced logistic sum* combination function with steepness σ and threshold τ

$$\mathbf{alogistic}_{\sigma,\tau}(V_1, \ldots, V_k) = [\frac{1}{1 + \mathrm{e}^{-\sigma(V_1 + \cdots + V_k - \tau)}} - \frac{1}{1 + \mathrm{e}^{\sigma\tau})](1 + \mathrm{e}^{-\sigma\tau}})$$

- the *Hebbian learning combination function* $\mathbf{hebb}_{\mu}(..)$ with persistence factor μ

$$\mathbf{hebb}_{\mu}(V_1, V_2, W) = V_1 V_2 (1 - W) + \mu W$$

with μ the persistence parameter, where V_1 stands for *X(t)*, V_2 for *Y(t)* and W for $\mathbf{W}_{X,Y}(t)$, where *X* and *Y* are the two connected states.

4 The Designed Computational Adaptive Network Model

The adaptive self-modeling network model introduced here to model Anorexia Nervosa consists of 14 nodes and 33 connections. The nodes are divided into 3 classes according to their role in the development and perpetuation of the disease:

- **Predisposing Factors:** Lack of self-acceptance, Thin Ideal, Perfectionism
- **Precipitating Factors:** Body Dissatisfaction, Feeling worthless, Anxiety
- **Perpetuating Factors:** Diet restriction, Weight loss, Satisfaction with rule compliance

The model represents physical or psychological states or reactions through nodes, with causal connections between them. For instance, a restrictive diet leads to weight loss, indicated by an arrow from the "diet" node to the "weight" node. Using this model, various spirals can be identified that demonstrate how psychological states associated with illnesses like "body dissatisfaction" and "feeling worthless" can create a closed loop, resulting in the continuation of a restrictive diet as a coping mechanism for these mental states, where this pattern can form a pathological reward system. This design approach is supported by the authors of (Haynos et al., 2022), who highlight how Anorexia Nervosa reflects an altered decision-making process that involves excessive goal pursuit. In this model, the goal pursuit is shaped into weight loss, which is achieved through a restrictive diet and compensatory behaviors. The satisfaction of achieving weight loss activates a sense of safety that reduces anxiety and reinforces the unhealthy behavior, perpetuating the cycle. The model includes only four states in the perpetuating cycle, and it should be noted that perpetuating factors, like all other states, have been simplified for modeling purposes.. The full specification of the network characteristics of the introduced model (connection weights $\omega_{X,Y}$, speed factors η_Y, and combination functions $\mathbf{c}_Y(..)$ and their parameters μ, τ and σ) and the initial values can be found in the role matrices document in the Appendix available as Linked Data. The graphical representation shown in Fig. 2 displays the overall connectivity of this network model. In Fig. 3 explanations of all states can be found.

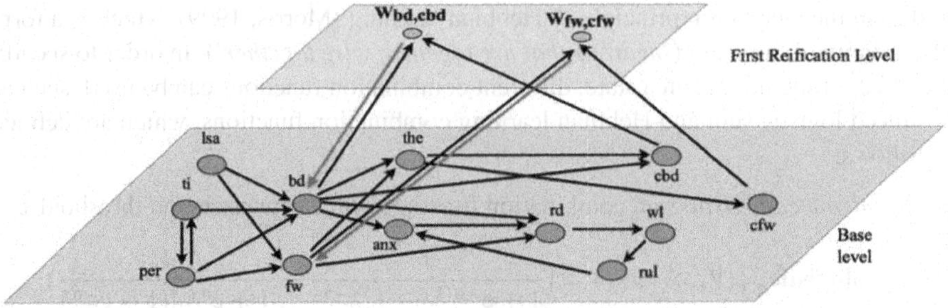

Fig. 2. Overview of the adaptive self-modeling network model: network architecture with base level (lower plane, pink) and self-model at the first reification level (upper plane, blue) and upward (blue) and downward causal connections (red) defining inter-level relations.

Most connection weights are positive, but three connections have negative weights: the connections from therapy to body dissatisfaction, from therapy to feeling worthless, and from satisfaction for rule appliance to anxiety. The connection from therapy should indeed decrease the likeability of perpetuating the disease and the connection for anxiety should, on the other hand, perpetuate the disorder cycle. For aggregation, the combination function $\mathbf{hebb}_{\mu}(..)$ is used for the two **W**-states X_{13} and X_{14} in the upper plane and $\mathbf{alogistic}_{\sigma,\tau}(..)$ for all other states in the base plane. The Hebbian function has been chosen for the W-states at the reification level to allow for plasticity according to the Hebbian learning principle (Morris, 1999 and Hebb, 1949). The values for the parameters σ, τ, μ for these combination functions can be found in role matrix **mcfp** in the Appendix; for example, $\mu = 0.99$, and the steepness σ mostly varies between 5 and 7, whilst the threshold τ varies between 0.4 and 0.6. The timing of the states is specified in the **ms** role matrix. For the sake of simplicity, all the states have been set to have a speed equal to 0.1 with the exception of X_4 which has been set to a higher speed factor of 0.9. For simulations where it has been assumed that the risk factors are constant over time, the speed factors of the risk factors have been set to 0. The states X_{11} and X_{12} are control states to address emotion regulation. Strengthening of emotion regulation by learning, and therapy to support that, is modeled by the **W**-states X_{13} and X_{14} at the reification level. The incorporated adaptive emotion regulation can be thus explained in the following way. An individual might experience body dissatisfaction or feelings of worthlessness, but may be able to consciously think and reason about this (e.g., 'I am not the only one feeling that way', 'It's temporary and I have support from my friends and family', etc.). The higher the activation of feeling worthless, the higher the activation of its control state.

Conversely, the higher the activity of the control state, the lower the activity of feeling worthless will become. So, by controlling the emotions and mental states one is experiencing, one can become less intense. The idea is that this process is adaptive in the sense that the strength of connection from feeling worthless to the control state can be 'trained' by interventions such as therapies; see also (van't Hof et al., 2020). It was found that a multimodal therapy should be implemented to treat Anorexia Nervosa (PhD and MA, 1985), and for that reason, multiple connections have been set to the therapy state. Here it can be mentioned that different types of therapies might target one

State	Abbr.	Description
X_1	lsa	Lack of Self Acceptance
X_2	ti	Thin Ideal
X_3	per	Perfectionism
X_4	bd	Body Dissatisfaction
X_5	fw	Feeling Worthless
X_6	anx	Anxiety
X_7	rd	Restricted Diet
X_8	wl	Weight Loss
X_9	rul	Satisfaction for Rule Appliance
X_{10}	the	Therapy
X_{11}	cbd	Control State for Body Dissatisfaction
X_{12}	cfw	Control State for Feeling Worthless
X_{13}	$\mathbf{W}_{bd,cbd}$	Self-model state for connection weight $\omega_{bd,cbd}$
X_{14}	$\mathbf{W}_{fw,cfw}$	Self-model state for connection weight $\omega_{fw,cfw}$

Fig. 3. Overview of all states used in the adaptive network model

or more states. As it is unclear which specific therapy targets which specific state(s), the term 'therapy' will be used to refer to a multimodal therapeutic approach to the disorder, which might include cognitive behavior therapy (with a focus on food re-education), individual therapy, and family therapy. The network model is thus adaptive in the sense that the weights of the incoming connections for the control states supporting emotion regulation can be adapted by learning. For example, if a healthy individual starts to feel worthless or dissatisfied with their body, it is likely that they will learn to control this state. The **W**-states are thus portrayed in the adaptation level, whilst therapy will positively affect (and thus decrease the values) one or more of the control states. In turn, the activation values of the feeling worthless state to the control state can strengthen or weaken the connection to the state and its control, where Hebbian learning is controlling this connection. The Hebbian combination function applied to the W-states indeed takes the values of the two connected states from the base level and of the weight itself and uses a persistence factor as a parameter. This parameter μ has been set to 0.8, meaning that every time unit the connection loses 20 percent of its strength.

5 Simulation Results

Using the computational model, simulations have been performed for different scenarios. The first scenario includes a healthy situation, where AN never develops, due to the low level of the risk factors. In the second scenario, the risk factors are activated and the individual develops AN over time as by entering the perpetuating cycle. In the third scenario therapies targeting both control states are included: both therapies strengthen the control state of the precipitating factors, with the idea that therapy helps people break the perpetuating cycle which is indeed caused by the precipitating factors. The simulations were run until an equilibrium was reached to see what the end state will be in the 3 different scenarios.

Scenario 1: No disorder. The first simulation shows a situation where the risk factors are set to be low and constant all equal to 0.2 and thus the individual does not develop AN. This situation is common for most of people, either at risk or not. Indeed, states such as lack of self-acceptance, thin ideal, and perfectionism are very common in western societies where social pressures have become a problem that often develops in those psychological states (Keel and Forney, 2013). The result of the simulation is shown below in Fig. 4: given initial states equal to 0.2 for the risk factors, the disorder will not occur as the AN cycle will not begin, whilst the factors have a low constant value over time.

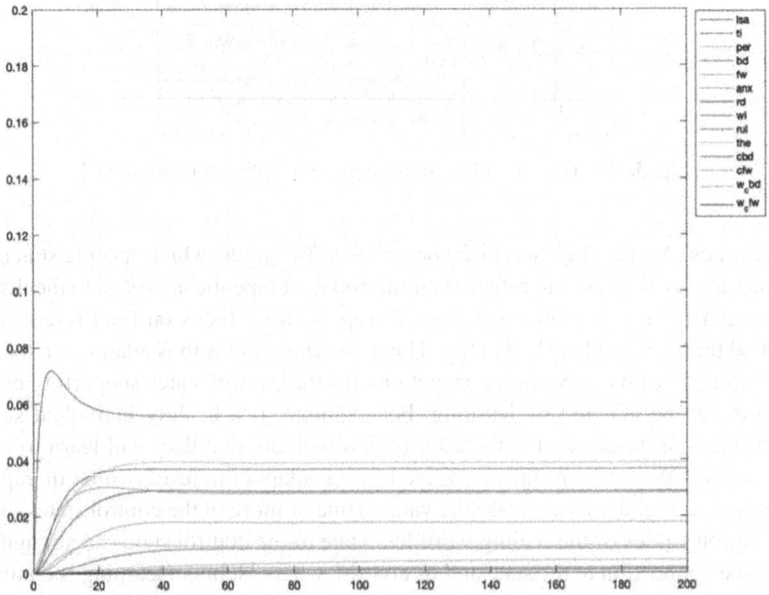

Fig. 4. Simulation of the ATCN with no development of the disease It is to be mentioned that many unhealthy states have non-zero values over time, but they don't pathologize: the individual will have some mental states badly affected, but not in a pathological way.

Scenario 2: AN and NO Therapy. The second simulation has been performed by leaving all the values of the network specification equal to the ones of the previous scenario, with the exception of the initial values for the risk states (Lack of self-acceptance, Body Dissatisfaction, and Thin Ideal), which has been set to be equal to 1 and constant over time. In this scenario, the individual would develop the disease pathologically as the perpetuating cycle would be activated. As it is shown in Fig. 5, there is a cycle of anxiety that gets perpetuated over time that keeps the AN cycle going on and thus reaching the extreme levels for what concerns the perpetuating states, being them at equilibrium at a value close to 1.

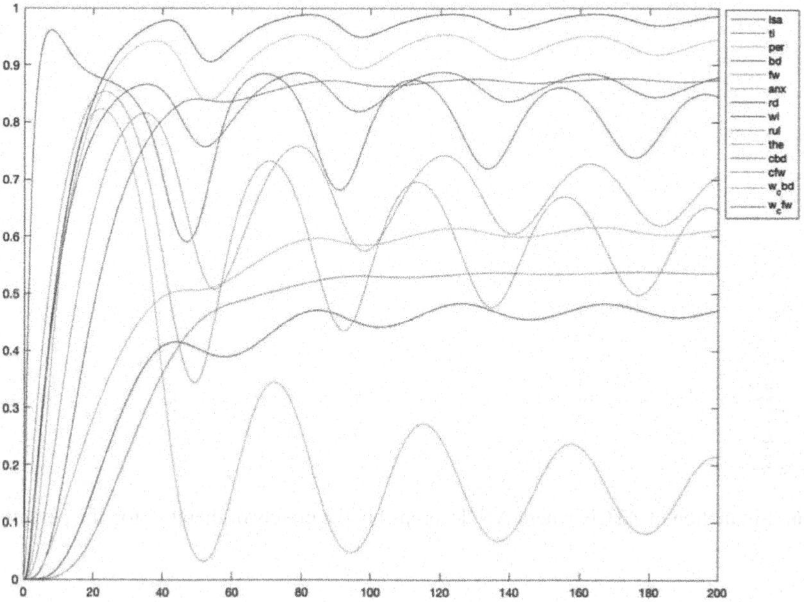

Fig. 5. Simulation of ATCN where AN develops in a perpetuating cycle.

Scenario 3: AN and Therapy. The next simulation focuses on the effects of therapy on this scenario. The model has control states embedded for the precipitating factors (body dissatisfaction and feeling worthless): the idea is that the individual can consciously think about those mental states and control them to some extent, with the help of friends and family. The activation of the control states thus negatively affects the precipitating states, where an adaptive weight connects the states to their control counterparts. In the model, the strength by which this happens is variable per person and situation and is positively affected by therapy. Indeed therapy was incorporated to target the strengths of the control states and thus weakening the precipitating factors, and hopefully breaking the cycle. Simulation results of therapy targeting the precipitating states are shown in Fig. 6. It can be seen that therapy alters the nature of the system, as the precipitating and perpetuating factors reach equilibrium at a lower level compared to the AN simulation. It is to be mentioned that many other factors do not significantly change in the Therapy scenario: this is due to the fact that Therapy directly affects the control states only, which then affect the precipitating factors Body Dissatisfaction and Feeling Worthless that influence the subsequent states, but Therapy has been modeled not to have a direct effect on all the states.

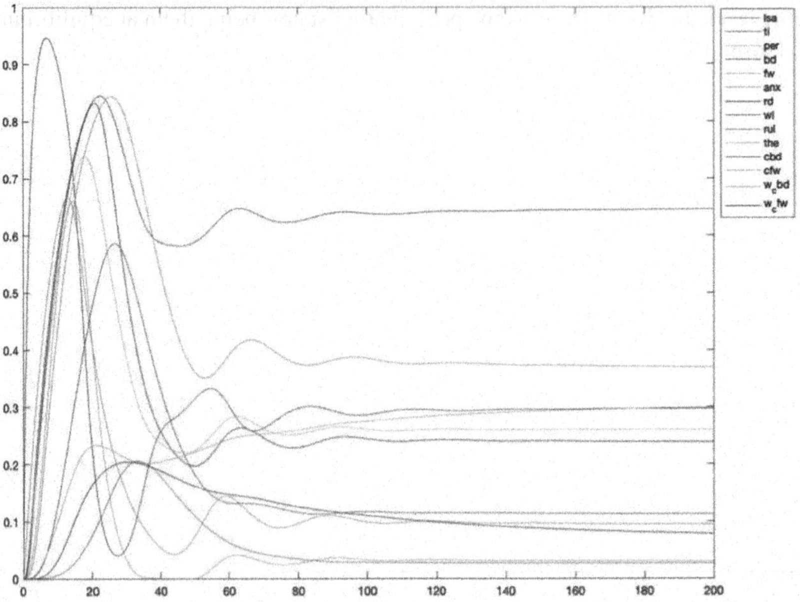

Fig. 6. Simulation of ATCN where AN develops but the effects of therapy stop the perpetuating cycle

6 Conclusion and Discussion

In this paper, a computational model for Anorexia Nervosa has been introduced. This was done by building a temporal-causal network based on the adaptive Network-Oriented Modelling Approach (Treur, 2020) described in Sect. 3. In this model, Anorexia Nervosa is classified as an eating disorder and characteristics from previous existing models have been incorporated by adding the perpetuating cycle component.

Characteristics of AN and interventions targeting the two modeled precipitating factors have been captured by creating an adaptive temporal-causal network model. Different therapeutic interventions can target different states of the model, where the type of therapy is highly influential in its effect on the outcome of the model. Indeed, simulations, where the effects of therapy are studied by varying the values of the parameters, show how a small variation can have a big impact on the outcome of the model. The thought process behind designing the model is based on identifying causal relations and (cyclic) causal pathways from the literature. The chosen modeling approach also uses this causal perspective and has been proven to be at least as general as any modeling approach based on (smooth) adaptive dynamical systems (Treur, 2021; Hendrikse, Treur, Koole, 2023).

We proved that in our simulation scenario if the predisposing factors do not activate over a certain threshold the disease will not develop, and as the model has been verified at the end time point with an obtained deviance significantly close to zero, we can claim that for the first scenario, the model is correctly specified. The third simulation studied the effects of therapy on the model where multiple further assumptions had to be made for the model. It would be interesting to research which states are exactly being targeted with different therapies and whether different kinds of therapies entail significantly different effects on the outcome of the model. Validation for our study made extensive use of empirical data, specifically (Schlegl, 2020). However, note that this computational model is a simplification and only provides some first steps of development of such a model. It is not meant to be used in daily medical practice in this form.

Future research could collect more empirical data and add more control states to create a more elaborate model that would be able to characterize different kinds of disease developments and therapies and thus increase the effectiveness of therapies for different kinds of individuals. Furthermore, more in depth statistical analyses of simulation experiments can be done.

Another future extension of the model would incorporate metaplasticity by making the learning speeds and the persisting factors adaptive so that a second-order adaptive network model would be obtained (Treur, 2019, 2020). This kind of modeling would be able to take into account the effect that circumstances have on a person's learning capabilities in the context of developing and healing from Anorexia Nervosa.

References

Brytek-Matera, A., Czepczor, K.: Models of eating disorders: a theoretical investigation of abnormal eating patterns and body image disturbance. Arch. Psychiatry Psychother. **19**, 16–26 (2017)

Godier, L.R., Park, R.J.: Compulsivity in anorexia nervosa: a transdiagnostic concept. Front. Psychol. **5**, 778 (2014)

Grzelak, T., Dutkiewicz, A., Paszynska, E., Dmitrzak-Weglarz, M., Slopien, A., Tyszkiewicz-Nwafor, M.: Neurobiochemical and psychological factors influencing the eating behaviors and attitudes in anorexia nervosa. J. Physiol. Biochem. **73**(2), 297–305 (2017)

Haynos, A.F., Widge, A.S., Anderson, L.M., Redish, A.D.: Beyond description and deficits: how computational psychiatry can enhance an understanding of decision-making in anorexia nervosa. Curr. Psychiatry Rep. **24**(1), 77–87 (2022)

Hebb, D.O.: The Organization of Behavior. Wiley, New York (1949)

Hendrikse, S.C.F., Treur, J., Koole, S.L.: Modeling emerging interpersonal synchrony and its related adaptive short-term affiliation and long-term bonding: a second-order multi-adaptive neural agent model. Int. J. Neural Syst. (2023). https://doi.org/10.1142/S0129065723500387

Keel, P.K., Forney, K.J.: Psychosocial risk factors for eating disorders. Int. J. Eat. Disord. **46**(5), 433–439 (2013)

Morris, R.G.: Hebb: The organization of behavior, Wiley: New York; 1949. Brain Res. Bull. **50**(5–6), 437 (1999)

PhD, E.J.O., Ma, C.C.: Multimodal therapy for anorexia nervosa. Psychother. Priv. Pract. **3**(2), 19–29 (1985)

Schlegl, S., Maier, J., Meule, A., Voderholzer, U.: Eating disorders in times of the COVID-19 pandemic—Results from an online survey of patients with anorexia nervosa. Int. J. Eat. Disord. **53**(11), 1791–1800 (2020)

Treasure, J., Tchanturia, K., Schmidt, U.: Developing a model of the treatment for eating disorder: using neuroscience research to examine the how rather than the what of change. Couns. Psychother. Res. **5**, 191–202 (2005)

Treur, J.: Network reification as a unified approach to represent network adaptation principles within a network. In: Fagan, D., Martín-Vide, C., O'Neill, M., Vega-Rodríguez, M.A. (eds.) TPNC 2018. LNCS, vol. 11324, pp. 344–358. Springer, Cham (2018). https://doi.org/10.1007/978-3-030-04070-3_27

Treur, J.: Multilevel network reification: representing higher order adaptivity in a network. In: Aiello, L., Cherifi, C., Cherifi, H., Lambiotte, R., Lió, P., Rocha, L. (eds.) COMPLEX NETWORKS 2018. Studies in Computational Intelligence, vol. 812, pp. 635–651. Springer, Cham (2019). https://doi.org/10.1007/978-3-030-05411-3_51

Treur, J.: Network-Oriented Modeling for Adaptive Networks: Designing Higher-Order Adaptive Biological, Mental and Social Network Models. Springer, Cham (2020). https://doi.org/10.1007/978-3-030-31445-3

Treur, J.: On the dynamics and adaptivity of mental processes: relating adaptive dynamical systems and self-modeling network models by mathematical analysis. Cogn. Syst. Res. **70**, 93–100 (2021)

Van Eeden, A.E., van Hoeken, D., Hoek, H.W.: Incidence, prevalence and mortality of anorexia nervosa and bulimia nervosa. Curr. Opin. Psychiatry **34**(6), 515–524 (2021)

van't Hof, S., Rydin, A., Treur, J., Enzlin, P.: An adaptive computational fear-avoidance model applied to genito-pelvic pain/penetration disorder. In: Mahmud, M., Vassanelli, S., Kaiser, M.S., Zhong, N. (eds.) BI 2020. LNCS (LNAI), vol. 12241, pp. 3–15. Springer, Cham (2020). https://doi.org/10.1007/978-3-030-59277-6_1

Vervaet, M., Puttevils, L., Hoekstra, R.H.A., Fried, E., Vanderhasselt, M.-A.: Transdiagnostic vulnerability factors in eating disorders: a network analysis. Eur. Eating Disord. Rev.: J. Eating Disord. Assoc. **29**(1), 86–100 (2021)

Woerwag-Mehta, S., Treasure, J.: Causes of anorexia nervosa. Psychiatry **7**(4), 147–151 (2008)

ReVQ-VAE: A Vector Quantization-Variational Autoencoder for COVID-19 Chest X-Ray Image Recovery

Nesrine Tarhouni[1(✉)], Rahma Fourati[1,2(✉)], Maha Charfeddine[1(✉)], and Chokri Ben Amar[1(✉)]

[1] REsearch Groups in Intelligent Machines, National Engineering School of Sfax, 3038 Sfax, Tunisia
{nesrine.tarhouni,maha.charfeddine,chokri.benamar}@enis.tn

[2] Faculty of Law, Economics and Management Sciences of Jendouba (FSJEGJ), University of Jendouba, Jendouba, Tunisia
rahma.fourati@ieee.org

Abstract. Nowadays, digital images have a valuable role in our daily life and can be used for a variety of applications like fingerprint recognition, video surveillance, etc. Sometimes, images mainly medical images get infected with attacks due to many reasons such as transmission in a noisy channel. Diagnosing an attacked medical image yields erroneous interpretation. So, to improve it for the right decision, the image must be recovered in advance. Therefore, there is a need for an efficient image recovering technique that helps to deal with medical attacked images. Image recovery is a process to realign the original image from the attacked image. In this paper, we propose an approach for chest X-Ray image recovery based on Vector Quantized Variational Autoencoder (VQ-VAE). The attacked images fed into the model to recover the images and get the original ones. The results of the SSIM show that our proposed model has produced better results than existing models.

Keywords: Self-supervised learning · Medical Image Recovering · VQ-VAE

1 Introduction

Medical imaging modalities generate massive amounts of volumetric medical data as images of internal organs. CT, MRI, and X-rays are common medical imaging techniques. Because medical data must be evaluated by a physician in order to reflect a life-saving scenario, the data must be recovered in case of alteration.

Supported by Tunisian Ministry of Higher Education and Scientific Research under the grant agreement number LR11ES48.

N. T. Nguyen et al. (Eds.): ICCCI 2023, LNAI 14162, pp. 753–765, 2023.
https://doi.org/10.1007/978-3-031-41456-5_57

The last few years have seen a significant increase in interest in machine learning. Around 2009, so-called deep artificial neural networks began to outperform other well-established models on a number of significant benchmarks, sparking the current boom [6]. Deep neural networks are currently the most advanced machine learning models in many fields, including image analysis and natural language processing, and they are widely used in both academia and industry. Medical imaging technology, medical data analysis, medical diagnosis, and healthcare, in general, all have enormous potential that is only now beginning to be fully realized. The goal of medical image reconstruction is to obtain high-quality medical images for use in a health context at the lowest possible cost and patient risk. Deep learning and its uses in medical imaging, particularly in image reconstruction, have received a lot of attention recently in the literature.

This article is divided into five sections. The first section introduces image recovery. Section two included a literature review. Section three presents the autoencoder (AE) and variational autoencoder (VAE). Section four describes the proposed approach for image recovery, including the description of VQ-VAE and the used network architecture. The experimental results in terms of SSIM are illustrated and discussed in section five. With Section six, this paper brings to a close and future perspectives on the proposed work.

2 Related Works on Image Recovery Based on Deep Learning

The main goal of this section is to review the current applications of deep learning in image processing, in particular for image reconstruction.

In the first simulation in [10] paper, the authors used a fully connected architecture with a six-layer encoder translating the 1024-dimensional input to a bottleneck layer of 256 units to train networks on tiny (32×32) pictures. The architecture's decoder mirror the encoder components. Through training, they developed two identical networks, one for MSE (Mean Square Error) optimization and the other for SSIM (Structure Similarity Index) optimization. The single-scale SSIM is appropriate since the images are so small; any greater downsampling would blur the content to the point where it would be difficult for humans to tell apart items in the image. Then, using a convolutional autoencoder architecture, they trained networks on larger images (96×96 pixels). Convolutional layers encode the input, while deconvolutional layers decode the feature representation in the latent space layer. The three convolutional layers of the convolutional network model each have a 5 as filter size and a 2 as stride. Again mirroring the convolutional layers, the deconvolutional layers. They utilized the MS-SSIM (Multiscale Structure Similarity Index) rather than the SSIM as their perceptual similarity metric for these larger images since they might have structure at various spatial scales. They have looked into what happens when perceptually-grounded loss functions, such as SSIM and MS-SSIM, are used in neural networks that reconstruct images in place of pixel-wise loss functions MSE and MAE (Mean Absolute Error). Over a variety of neural network models, human observers prefer SSIM-optimized images to PL-optimized images in terms of image quality. The architecture is very complicated even the results are good.

In [11], to conserve spatial information in the latent space, a fully convolutional VAE was created using PyTorch. The latent space was a $32 \times 4 \times 4$ multidimensional tensor whose size was optimized by comparing the visual quality of the reconstructed output. The voxelwise L2-loss function and a differentiable SSIM loss function were optimized as reconstruction loss functions. The findings show that using SSIM loss to train a VAE improves the perceptual visual quality of the reconstructed MRA compared to L2 loss.

The authors in [13] proposed two variational autoencoders (VAE) networks which are employed to do the spatial mapping in the first step. The mapping network's job is to convert deteriorated photographs back to the originals, to put it simply. In this article, it is possible to prohibit the network from using the pixels from the damaged area to repair it by using the scratch mask from the original old photo as input. The global information can be used to repair the input mask region if it is determined to be damaged; otherwise, the local feature information can be used, allowing the global branch and the local branch to be combined under the control of the input mask. This article's generator is made up of three components. The downsampling module is based on three convolution kernels of various sizes. A self-attention layer and a convolutional layer are both included in each little module that makes up the self-attention residual module, which is the second component. This module is made up of 16 identical self-attention residual blocks. The upsampling picture reconstruction module comes last. For pixel amplification, this portion primarily consists of two subpixel convolutional layers. In this article, a batch normalization layer is introduced to the discriminator network, the LeakyRelu activation function is utilized, and the discriminator network employs a deep convolutional neural network. The precise procedure is feeding the created image into a multilayer convolutional network to create a feature map, which is subsequently fed into a fully connected layer. Finally, to determine if the image is real or fake, the Sigmoid activation function performs two classifications of true and false. As of now, the generator and discriminator have been finished in terms of design, and they work together to produce high-resolution images through competitive optimization. PSNR and SSIM results demonstrate good results compared to two methods based on CNN and GAN respectively. However, there is still room for development, particularly when it comes to the restoration of damaged photographs, which is not good enough. In fact, the average of SSIM is 0.767 and PSNR is equal to 19.11.

In [5] paper, the authors presented an autoencoder model to recover CT and X-Ray images. An encoder plus a decoder make up an autoencoder. In addition to the batch normalization stage at the model's commencement, each of them has three layers. In the autoencoder, there are three convolutional layers and three convolution-transposed layers (ConvTrans). This autoencoder's main objective is to work on image denoising. A convolution autoencoder network with eight layers is used to achieve image denoising. The output image's dimensions are 224 × 224 × 32, while the input image's are 224 × 224 × 3. The output size of the decoder, which uses this output as its input, is 224 × 224 × 3. The batch normalization layer and the convolution layers make up the encoder in the proposed denoising autoencoder. Each layer's kernels are 3 × 3 in size, while layers 1, 2, and 3 have 128, 64, and 32 convolution filters, respectively. The decoder is composed of the ConvTrans layers and the output convolution layer, and layers 1, 2, and 3 have 32, 64, and 128 convolution filters, respectively. The convolution calculation's stride is 1. The padding process follows the same rules. Every ConvTrans and convolution layer uses the linear rectification unit (Relu) as the activation function. The experimental results present good results of PSNR and SSIM but without a comparison study.

The network architecture that is being proposed in [1] receives a degraded image as input and outputs a clean, enhanced image. Input layer, convolution layer, convolutional layer, deconvolution layer, and output layer are the main components of this model. The convolutional layer employs a number of compact and logically linked blocks known as convolutional denoising autoencoders (CDA). In order to correct the degradation in the input image, CDA attempts to learn it from the training images. Four internal layers make up the CDA block: a convolution layer, a pooling layer, a deconvolution layer, and an upsampling layer. The batch normalization and Parametric Rectified Linear Unit (PRelu) activation functions are used in this model, respectively, between the convolution layer and the pooling layer and the deconvolution layer and the upsampling layer. The input layer is the first layer in the proposed model architecture, followed by the convolution layer. The image is processed using a number of convolutional denoising autoencoders. Two deconvolutional layers are then used to restore the denoised image at the final result. To connect the input and output of the same denoiser autoencoder, skip connections are used. Ten blocks of the convolutional denoising autoencoder are used in this paper. The experiment's findings demonstrate that, in terms of PSNR, the suggested model outperformed more established technologies. But the model is tested only under gaussian attacks.

3 Background of AE, VAE

VQ-VAE is the acronym of Vector Quantized Variational Autoencoder, that's a lot of big words, so let's take a quick step back and go over the fundamentals first.

Before moving on to VQ-VAE, we will first define autoencoders, then, go over the fundamentals of variational autoencoders.

3.1 Autoencoders (AE)

An autoencoder is an unsupervised learning method that searches through a given data distribution for non-linear latent representations using neural networks. An encoder network $z = f(x)$ and a decoder network $g(z) = \hat{x}$ are the two components of the neural network. Here x represents the input data, z is the latent vector representation, and $\hat{x}$ is the "reconstruction" of x from the latent space. Both f(x) and g(z) are neural networks. When the two parts are combined, the entire model can be described by the relationship $\hat{x} = g(f(x))$ (see Fig. 1).

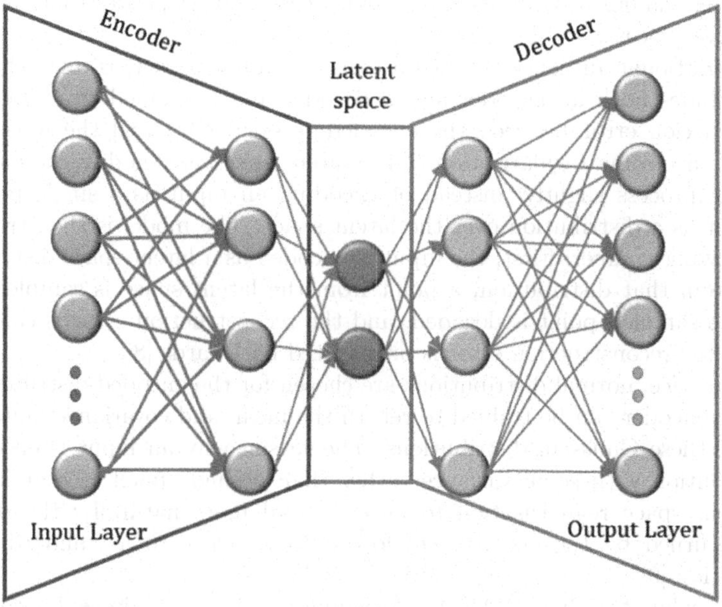

Fig. 1. Autoencoder architecture

The decoder should ideally be able to reconstruct the raw data from the encoder's latent representation. If the model can learn such a reconstruction, we can assume that our latent space accurately represents the data. To achieve this goal, we train the model with a reconstruction loss between x and $\hat{x}$ [7]. It's also worth noting that z should always have a smaller dimension than x. After all, the whole point is to encode a compressed representation of the data so that the algorithm is forced to find the most important components of the raw data.

This compressed, latent part of the autoencoder is also known as the network bottleneck because it compresses the data into a much smaller space.

The autoencoder is only trained to encode and decode with as little loss as possible, regardless of how the latent space is structured. Thus, if we are not careful in defining the architecture, during training, the network will take advantage of any overfitting possibilities to accomplish its task as well as it can, except if we consciously regularise it [2].

3.2 Variational Autoencoders (VAE)

So, in order to use our autoencoder's decoder for generative purposes, we must ensure that the latent space is regular enough. One approach to achieve such regularity is to include explicit regularisation during the training process. A variational autoencoder is an autoencoder whose training is regularised to avoid overfitting and ensure that the latent space has good properties that enable the generative process.

A variational autoencoder, like a standard autoencoder, is an architecture that includes both an encoder and a decoder and is trained to minimize the reconstruction error between the encoded-decoded data and the initial data. To introduce some regularisation of the latent space, we modify the encoding-decoding process slightly: instead of encoding an input as a single point, we encode it as a distribution over the latent space. The model is then trained in the following manner: First, the input is encoded as a latent space distribution. Then, from that distribution, a point from the latent space is sampled. After that, the sampled point is decoded, and the reconstruction error is calculated. Finally, the reconstruction error is propagated backwards [8].

In practice, normal distributions are chosen for the encoded distributions so that the encoder can be trained to return the mean and covariance matrix that describe these Gaussian distributions. The reason why an input is encoded as a distribution with some variance rather than a single point is that it allows the latent space regularisation to be expressed more naturally: the distributions returned by the encoder are forced to be close to a standard normal distribution [9].

Thus, when training a VAE, the loss function that is minimized is composed of a "reconstruction term" (on the final layer), which tends to make the encoding-decoding scheme as performant as possible, and a "regularisation term" (on the latent layer), which tends to regularise the organization of the latent space by making the distributions returned by the encoder close to a standard normal distribution [3].

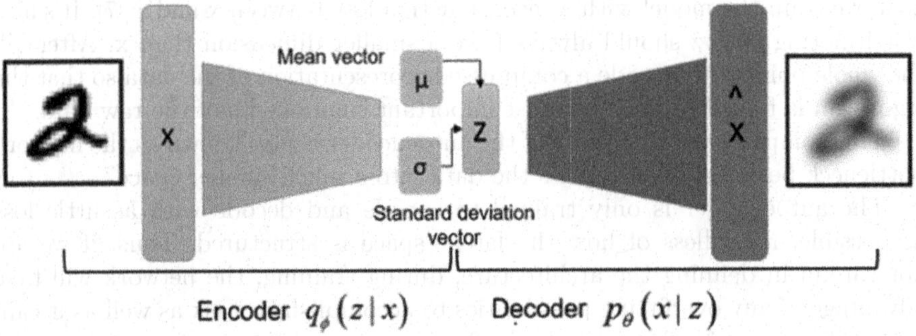

Fig. 2. The structure of Variational Autoencoder

4 Proposed Method of Image Recovery Based on VQ-VAE (ReVQ-VAE)

In this work, we explore the application of the Vector Quantised-Variational AutoEncoder (VQ-VAE) on image recovery using self-supervised machine learning algorithms. In this section, we introduce the VQ-VAE then we detail the network architecture used in image reconstruction. To our knowledge, we are the first who used VQ-VAE for image recovery. It is used usually for image generation [4].

4.1 Vector Quantized Variational Autoencoder (VQ-VAE)

As mentioned in the previous section, An encoder with a posterior distribution $q_\theta(z|x)$ and a prior distribution p (z), which are mapped using a Gaussian distribution with an acquired mean and standard deviation, and a decoder with a distribution $p_\theta(x|z)$ for the input data, are both included in the framework of a VAE (Fig. 2). Where x is the input data and z represents a discrete latent variable.

The VQ-VAE is based on the VAE structure. Instead of using Gaussian distributions to map the latent space, the VQ-VAE employs a vector quantization (VQ) procedure that converts the posterior and prior distributions into categorical distributions [4].

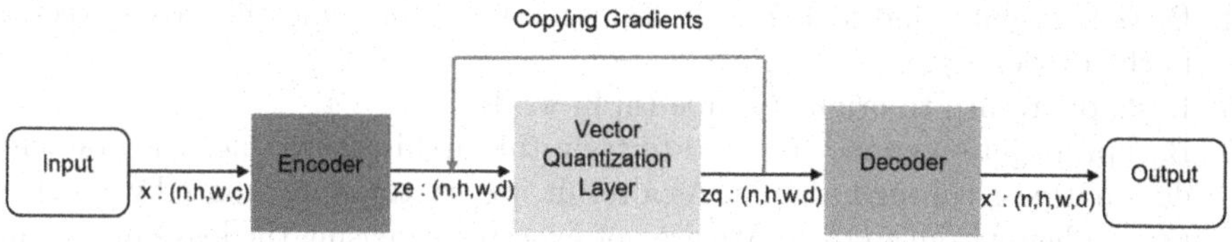

Fig. 3. VQ-VAE architecture

Figure 3 depicts various top-level components of the architecture, along with their dimensions at each stage. Assuming we run our model on image data. The operation can now be explained in the following steps: The encoder receives images x: (n, h, w, c) and outputs ze: (n, h, w, d). Then, the Vector Quantization layer takes ze and uses distance to select embeddings from a dictionary, producing zq. Finally, The decoder consumes zq and produces x'. Where n is the batch size, h is the image height, w is the image width, c is the number of channels in the input image and d represents the number of channels in the hidden state.

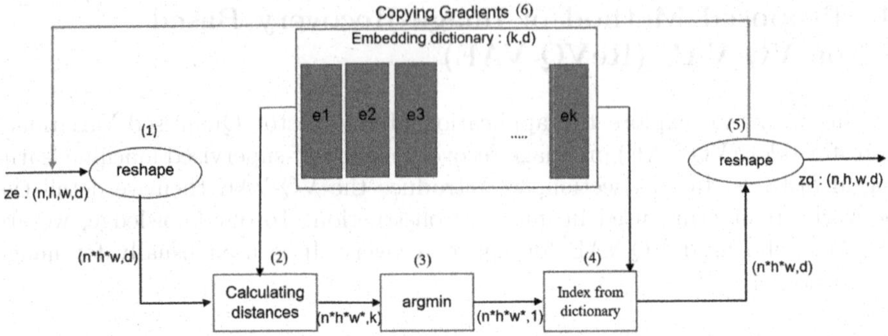

Fig. 4. Vector Quantization Layer

The operation of the VQ layer can be broken down into six parts, as shown in Fig. 4

1. Reshape: all dimensions except the final are combined into one, yielding n*h*w vectors of dimensionality d each.
2. Distances are calculated for each of the n*h*w vectors by subtracting the distance from each of the k vectors of the embedding dictionary, yielding a matrix of shape (n × h × w, k).
3. Argmin: we retrieve the index of the closest of the k vectors from the dictionary for each of the n × h × w vectors.
4. Dictionary entry index: For each of n × h × w vectors, find the closest vector in the dictionary.
5. Reshape: return to original shape (n, h, w, d)
6. Backpropagation cannot be used to train this architecture since the gradient does not pass through argmin. As a result, we try to approximate by copying the gradients from zq to ze. We are not exactly decreasing the loss function in this manner, but we are still able to pass some information back for training.

4.2 ReVQ-VAE Architecture

In this section, we detail the used architecture. As indicated in Fig. 5, the network takes an attacked image as input with size M × N and passes it through two 16×3 convolution layers, 2×2 pooling, two 32×3 convolution layers then 5×5 pooling, two 32 × 3 convolution layers, 3 × 3 pooling and finally latent_dimension × 1 convolution layer. These layers refer to the encoder. The encoder's output, ze(x), can be represented in the codebook by a combination of the indexes of different vectors, k. We can rebuild a distribution, zq (x), with the same structure as ze (x), but each pixel in zq (x) with the length of dimension, d, is quantized to one of the vectors in the codebook for the decoder's input. The codebook, ej, is represented by the 'Embedding dictionary' in Fig. 5. The decoder is composed of 3 × 3 upSampling, two 32 × 3 deconvolution layers, 5 × 5 upSampling, two

32×3 deconvolution layers, 2×2 upSampling and lastly two 16×3 deconvolution layers.

The VQ-VAE loss function is divided into three parts: reconstruction loss, codebook loss, and commitment loss. The reconstructed loss is calculated by comparing the decoder results to the original images. The codebook loss is used to make the chosen codebook, ej, approach the encoder output, ze (x), whereas the commitment loss is used to enable ze (x) to be similar to the selected codebook from the earlier epoch.

As a result, the loss function, L, for the VQ-VAE is as follows:

$$L = \log p(x|zq(x)) + \|sg[ze(x)] - e\|^2{}_2 + \beta\|ze(x) - sg[e]\|^2{}_2 \tag{1}$$

where sg denotes the stopgradient operator and β denotes the weight for the commitment loss. In our work, we used β= 0.25, as recommended by [12].

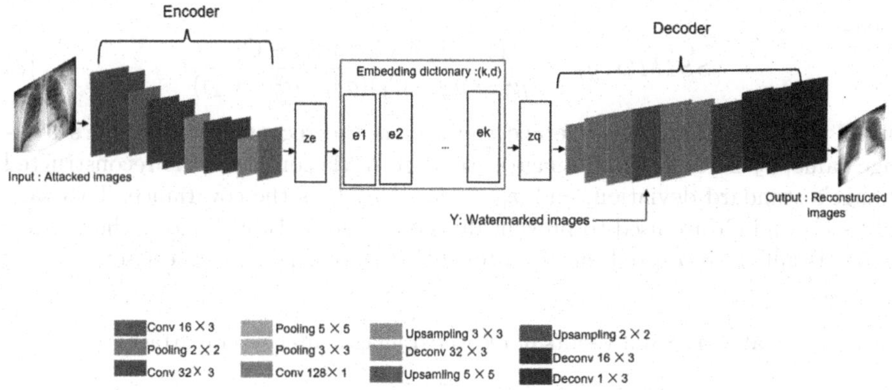

Fig. 5. General steps of the proposed ReVQ-VAE model

5 Experimental Results

The invisibility of the recovered images proposed by the model is analyzed in this section. Besides, a comparison with related works is also carried out. The performance tests are conducted using the COVID-19 chest X-ray dataset.

5.1 Dataset Description

To properly assess the performance of the proposed model, we used COVID-19 Chest X-ray images. The dataset can be accessed via the link in [14]. It consists of 3616 images of patients diagnosed with COVID-19. Before training, we applied several attacks to the 3616 original images such as text insertion, cropping, rotation, shearing, gaussian and also salt and pepper noises. We got finally 62054 images. We segmented them into 80% for training and 20% for testing. An example of original image and it's attacked versions are presented in Fig. 6.

5.2 Experimental Setup

To obtain accurate results, Adam's optimizer is used. The adaptive learning rate (LR) was set to 0.001. The proposed models' development and design are carried out using GPU machines for implementation, and the proposed structures are carried out using Vast AI that provides paid access to RTX A6000. TensorFlow and Keras are used as the deep learning backends, and Python 3.7 is used for simulation testing.

5.3 Recovery Results of ReVQ-VAE

Our recovery model is verified on the test set and evaluated based on SSIM (structural similarity Index) as shown in Eq. 2. SSIM is used to calculate the perceptual difference between the original image and the reconstructed image, when close to '1' indicates that the original image is similar to the reconstruction image.

$$SSIM(x,y) = \frac{(2\mu_x\mu_y + C_1)(2\sigma_{xy} + C_2)}{(\mu_x^2 + \mu_y^2 + C_1)(\sigma_x^2 + \sigma_y^2 + C_2))} \quad (2)$$

μ_x is the original image's average value, $\mu_y$is the reconstructed image's average value, σ_x is the original image's standard deviation, σ_y is the reconstructed image's standard deviation, and $\sigma_{xy} = \mu_{xy}$ - $\mu_x\mu_y$ is the covariance. Two variables C_2 and C_1 are used to prevent division by zero. Table 1 shows the average SSIM results of recovered images after different attacks on the test set.

Table 1. SSIM results of recovered images after several attacks

Attacks	SSIM
Cropping 1%	0.83
Cropping 10%	0.81
Cropping 25%	0.82
Cropping 50%	0.79
Rotation 15°	0.82
Shearing	0.83
Text insertion	0.83
Gaussian noise	0.88
Salt & Pepper	0.88

As shown in Table 1, for cropping attacks the SSIM values are 0.83, 0.81, 0.82 for cropping 1%, cropping 10% and cropping 25% respectively. Also for a very destructive attack such as cropping 50% of the image, the SSIM is equal to 0.79. In addition, for rotation 15°, the SSIM is 0.82 and 0.84 for gaussian noise and salt and pepper. The SSIM values are 0.83 for text insertion and shearing

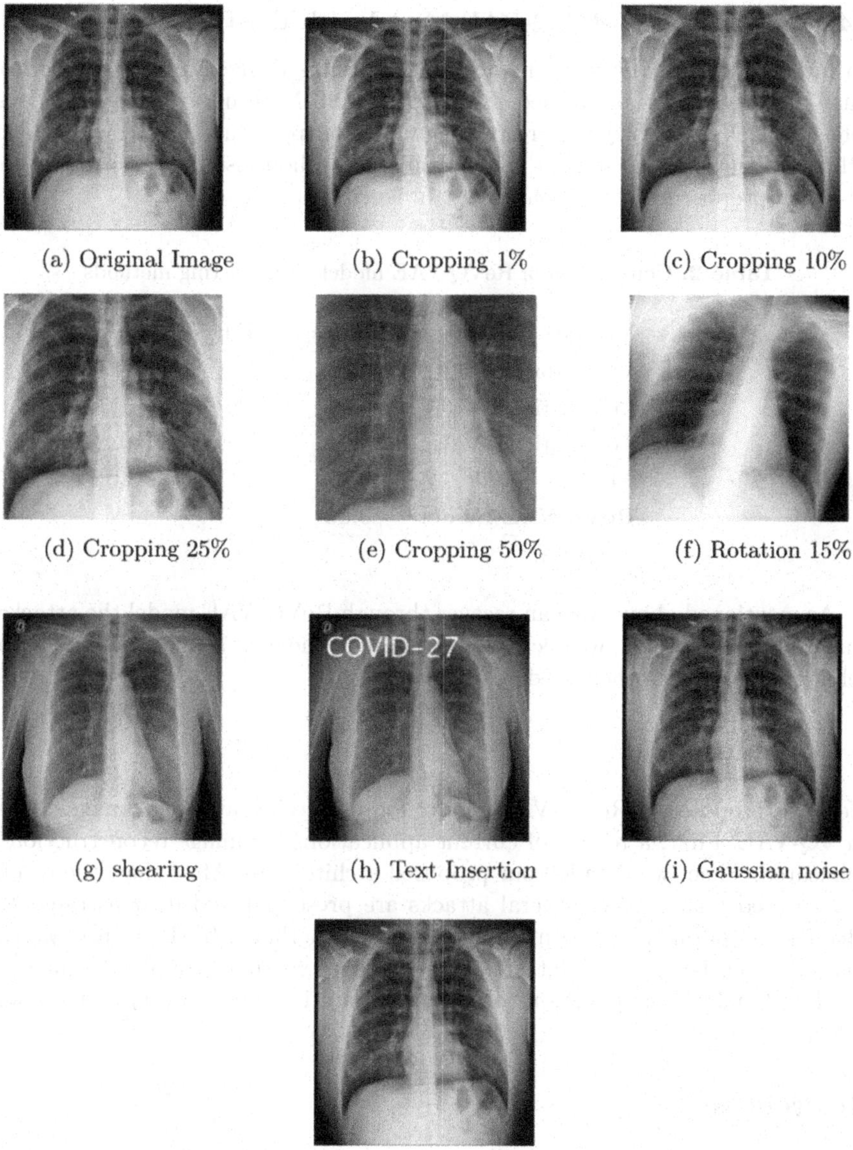

(a) Original Image (b) Cropping 1% (c) Cropping 10%

(d) Cropping 25% (e) Cropping 50% (f) Rotation 15%

(g) shearing (h) Text Insertion (i) Gaussian noise

(j) salt & pepper

Fig. 6. The original and attacked images

attacks. So, we can notice through the results presented in Table 1, the quality of the recovered images generated by ReVQ-VAE model are good after several attacks.

5.4 Comparison of ReVQ-VAE Model with Existing Architectures

To further validate the performance of the proposed algorithm, a comparison with four methods is performed. Based on the SSIM results in Table 2, we can conclude that our ReVQ-VAE recovering model outperforms the recovering algorithms using VAE [13] and [11]. The proposed method also outperforms [1] and [5] which proposed methods based on autoencoders.

Table 2. Comparison of ReVQ-VAE model with existing methods

Methods	Average SSIM
VAE+Mask [13]	0.767
Convolutional AE [1]	0.80
Convolutional VAE [11]	0.696
AE [5]	0.82
ReVq-VAE model	**0.83**

As mentioned above, we can recover through ReVQ-VAE model the attacked images. For this reason, we decided to propose in the next section an application helping doctors with their medical diagnoses.

6 Conclusion

We have proposed a ReVQ-VAE model for recovering attacked images based on VQ-VAE. First, a review of current applications for image reconstruction is delineated. Then, we detailed our proposed architecture. After that, the results of recovered images after several attacks are presented and demonstrated the effectiveness of our model compared to existing methods. In the future, we can deal with another type of dataset. This proposed method can also be incorporated with different applications like image inpainting and recovery of audio and video.

References

1. Bajaj, K., Singh, D.K., Ansari, M.A.: Autoencoders based deep learner for image denoising. Procedia Comput. Sci. **171**, 1535–1541 (2020)
2. Bank, D., Koenigstein, N., Giryes, R.: Autoencoders. arXiv preprint arXiv:2003.05991 (2020)
3. Cao, S., Li, J., Nelson, K.P., Kon, M.A.: Coupled VAE: improved accuracy and robustness of a variational autoencoder. Entropy **24**(3), 423 (2022)
4. Cohen, M., Quispe, G., Corff, S.L., Ollion, C., Moulines, E.: Diffusion bridges vector quantized variational autoencoders. In: Chaudhuri, K., Jegelka, S., Song, L., Szepesvari, C., Niu, G., Sabato, S. (eds.) Proceedings of the 39th International Conference on Machine Learning. Proceedings of Machine Learning Research, vol. 162, pp. 4141–4156. PMLR (2022)

5. El-Shafai, W., et al.: Efficient deep-learning-based autoencoder denoising approach for medical image diagnosis. CMC-Comput. Mater. Continua **70**(3), 6107–6125 (2022)
6. Lundervold, A.S., Lundervold, A.: An overview of deep learning in medical imaging focusing on MRI. Z. Med. Phys. **29**(2), 102–127 (2019)
7. Mahony, N.O., Campbell, S., Krpalkova, L., Carvalho, A., Walsh, J., Riordan, D.: Representation learning for fine-grained change detection. Sensors **21**(13), 4486 (2021)
8. Ok, C., Lee, G., Lee, K.: Informative language encoding by variational autoencoders using transformer. Appl. Sci. **12**(16), 7968 (2022)
9. Singh, A., Ogunfunmi, T.: An overview of variational autoencoders for source separation, finance, and bio-signal applications. Entropy **24**(1), 55 (2021)
10. Snell, J., Ridgeway, K., Liao, R., Roads, B.D., Mozer, M.C., Zemel, R.S.: Learning to generate images with perceptual similarity metrics. In: 2017 IEEE International Conference on Image Processing (ICIP), pp. 4277–4281. IEEE (2017)
11. Timmins, K.M., van der Schaaf, I.C., Ruigrok, Y.M., Velthuis, B.K., Kuijf, H.J.: Variational autoencoders with a structural similarity loss in time of flight MRAs. In: Medical Imaging 2021: Image Processing, vol. 11596, pp. 897–903. SPIE (2021)
12. Van Den Oord, A., Vinyals, O., et al.: Neural discrete representation learning. In: Advances in Neural Information Processing Systems, vol. 30 (2017)
13. Wang, R.: An old photo image restoration processing based on deep neural network structure. Wirel. Commun. Mob. Comput. **2022** (2022)
14. X-ray CC (2022). https://www.kaggle.com/code/timothy123oreilly/identification-of-covid-in-x-rays/data. Accessed 13 Sept 2022

Ensemble Models and Data Fusion

Credit Risk Scoring Using a Data Fusion Approach

Ayoub El-Qadi[1,3](✉), Maria Trocan[2], Patricia Conde-Cespedes[2], Thomas Frossard[3], and Natalia Díaz-Rodríguez[4]

[1] Sorbonne Université, Paris, France
ayoub.el_qadi_el_haouari@etu.sorbonne-universite.fr
[2] Institut Supérieur d'Électronique de Paris, Issy-les-Moulineaux, France
[3] Tinubu Square, Issy-les-Moulineaux, France
[4] DaSCI Institute, University of Granada, Granada, Spain

Abstract. Credit scoring is a vital task in the financial industry for assessing the creditworthiness of companies and mitigating credit risks. In recent years, machine learning algorithms have shown promising results in credit scoring by leveraging large amounts of tabular data. However, the traditional tabular data alone may not capture all the information relevant to credit scoring that is typically used by credit risk analysts. In this paper, we propose a novel approach for company credit scoring that integrates text and tabular data. Our method uses natural language processing techniques to extract key features from risk assessments made by credit risk experts which are then combined with financial data to predict the likelihood of default within a one-year horizon. We compare different Machine Learning based models for different text embedding techniques. Our results show that the fact of adding a textual feature improves the ability of the model to capture defaulted companies. More concretely, adding a categorical feature generated by the application of sentiment analysis over text risk assessments yields the best results.

Keywords: Natural Language Processing · Multimodal Credit Risk Scoring · Machine Learning

1 Introduction

Credit risk scoring algorithms play a critical role in the lending industry, helping financial institutions assess the likelihood of default by borrowers and make informed lending decisions [1]. Traditional credit scoring models primarily rely on tabular financial data, such as credit history, income, and debt-to-income ratio [2]. However, these models may not capture the full picture of a borrower's creditworthiness, especially when dealing with complex and dynamic markets.

Textual data, such as news articles, press releases, and social media posts, can provide valuable insights into potential risks that may impact a borrower's

N. T. Nguyen et al. (Eds.): ICCCI 2023, LNAI 14162, pp. 769–781, 2023.
https://doi.org/10.1007/978-3-031-41456-5_58

ability to repay a loan [3]. By combining these textual risk assessments with traditional financial data, financial institutions can improve the accuracy and reliability of credit risk scoring algorithms, leading to better lending decisions and reduced credit losses.

In this context, we propose a new framework that intends to leverage the non-structured information available in the comments made by risk analysts by combining it with tabular financial data. The paper is structured as follows: first, we present the previous research in the field of credit scoring and in Natural Language Processing (NLP). Then, we present our framework and the results yielded. Finally, we present the conclusion and potential hints for future work.

We compare the impact of adding the text feature using different Natural Language Processing techniques on the performance of several state-of-the-art models.

2 Related Work

2.1 Credit Scoring

Credit scoring is an important tool for financial institutions and is used to assess the creditworthiness of potential borrowers. Classical credit scoring models are based on statistical techniques such as Linear Discriminant Analysis, Logistic Regression [4,5].

Recently, there is a new wave of Machine Learning based algorithms that are used to estimate the probability of default. In [6], the authors have shown that high-level sub-symbolic algorithms outperform statistical-based models.

Recent works focus on the use of financial tabular data for predicting companies' future status (i.e., default/non-default). The authors in [2], center their efforts on predicting the default using a set of 81 financial features. They conclude that among all tested models, tree-based models are the best in terms of performance. In [9], the authors employed a similar approach for predicting the default of companies one year later after they published their financial sheets. An interesting different approach has been employed by the authors in [7]. They compare the output of a machine learning-based credit scoring model with the rating given by a credit risk company. The results show that the model distinguishes extremely rated companies.

A large number of works have shown that XGBoost [8], a boosting method, outperforms classical machine-learning-based methods (i.e., logistic regression, decision trees neural networks) for the task of predicting the default.

2.2 Natural Language Processing

There have been many significant advances in the field of natural language processing (NLP) in recent years. One of the most important developments has been the advancement of deep learning (DL) techniques [10], which have led to significant improvements in the accuracy and effectiveness of NLP models [11].

During the 1980s, the field of NLP experienced the first revolution with the introduction of statistical models such as Hidden Markov Models (HMM) [12] for speech recognition and N-grams models [13] for machine translation. Afterward, and as a result of the exponential growth of computational power, the deep learning models have rapidly gained interest for solving NLP tasks like Information Retrieval (IR) [14], Named Entity Recognition (NER) [15] or Text Classification [16].

Both Machine-Learning (ML) and DL models take as input numerical features. Two popular approaches are used in NLP for text representation and feature extraction. The methods employed for representing text and words in a numerical format (i.e., high-dimensional vectors) that aim to capture the meaning and context of the words are called Word Embeddings (WE). NLP researchers have adopted several methods for creating word embeddings (i.e., Word2vec [18], GLoVe [19], BERT [20]). More classical approaches like TF-IDF [17] represent the text as a sparse vector of word frequencies.

For the TF-IDF technique [17] the measurement of the importance of a word in a document is made by combining the term frequency (TF) and the inverse document frequency (IDF), which refers to how common or rare a word is across the entire document. Word2vec [18] is a WE-method that represents words in a continuous vector space in which words that have similar meanings are closer in the vector space. GloVe [19] is based on the idea of factorizing a large matrix of word-word co-occurrence counts, where the matrix is constructed from a large corpus of text. The co-occurrence information between words indicates how often they appear together in the corpus. BERT (Bidirectional Encoder Representations from Transformers) is a state-of-the-art natural language processing model developed by Google in 2018. It is a pre-trained language model that uses a deep neural network architecture called the transformer, which allows it to capture the context and dependencies of words in a sentence. Sentiment analysis has been used in several industries such as Marketing [24] or Finance [25]. For example in marketing, sentiment analysis is used to identify customer needs which triggers different strategies to improve customer satisfaction and retention. In finance, multiple different approaches have been adopted. In [26], the authors analyze the impact of social media opinion on different companies for stock market predictions. In credit scoring, few works have concentrated their efforts on the impact of textual data for default prediction. In [27], the authors found that a deep learning approach, based on the BERT model for default prediction using textual data, outperforms classical ML models (i.e., Logistic Regression and Random Forest). Other approaches that have been considered for the treatment of textual data for the default prediction focus on word embedding techniques to represent in a low-dimensional vector space the economic sector of the company [28].

3 Methodology

In this section, we present our proposed framework. First, we start by presenting the data and its characteristics. Then, we describe the different strategies we propose for dealing with the text feature. We show the preprocessing pipeline and the data-splitting strategy for the training stage. Finally, we compare the performance of different state-of-the-art machine learning models for the different text feature treatment strategies.

3.1 Data Overview

The dataset used in this work is provided by Tinubu, a company specializing in credit risk assessments. The original dataset contains 4951 credit assessments. For each assessment, we have 34 standard features that represent the companies information (e.g., creation year, the country in which it operates), its financial statements (e.g., net worth, current assets), and a text feature (e.g., risk analyst comments), that typically contains a description of the company, the business context, and its activities. Each data point corresponds to the year in which the company has been assessed by credit risk analysts. Word2vec [18,19].

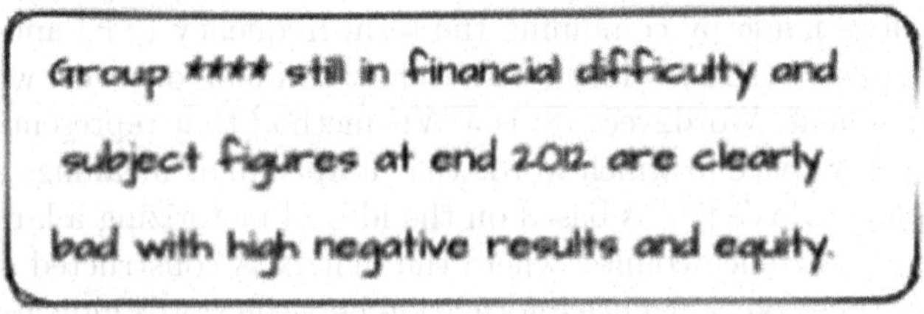

Fig. 1. Text assessment example generated by a risk analyst.

The target variable of our models is whether the company is in financial embarrassment[1] or being out of business. We create the default variable by setting it to 1 if the considered company is in financial embarrassment or out of business the year after the assessment and 0 otherwise.

3.2 Text Feature Treatment

The dataset contains a text feature in which the comments and opinions of the credit risk analysts are stored. The risk analysts' comments usually contain a summary of the industry trends and economic conditions that could impact the company as well as a description of the company and its activities.

The first step in the text feature pipeline is to remove stop words, punctuation, and other irrelevant information. Once the text has been preprocessed, we use an embedding algorithm to represent each word in the text as a vector in a lower dimensional space. For instance, in this work we employed two different word embedding techniques: Word2vec [18] and GLoVe [19].

[1] Financial embarrassment refers to a state of financial difficulty. Companies in financial embarrassment may have problems refunding their loans.

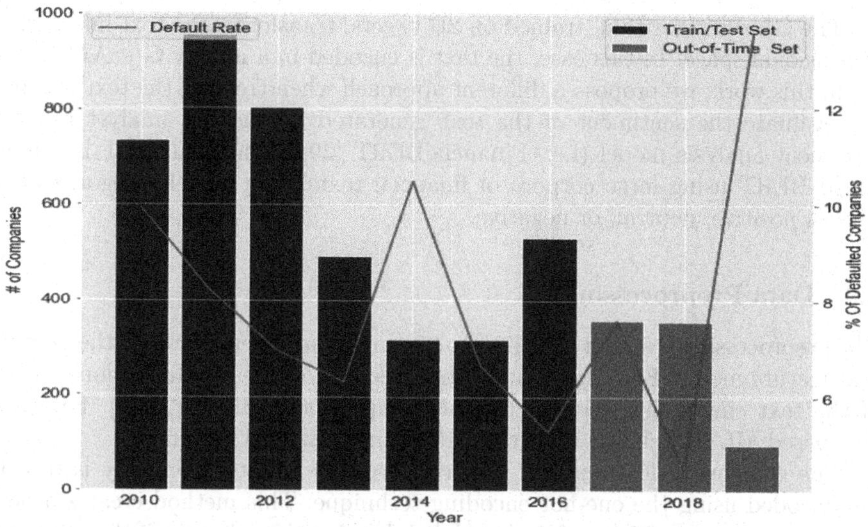

Fig. 2. Number of companies assessed each year. The default rate represents the percentage of companies that will experience financial difficulties the year after the assessment.

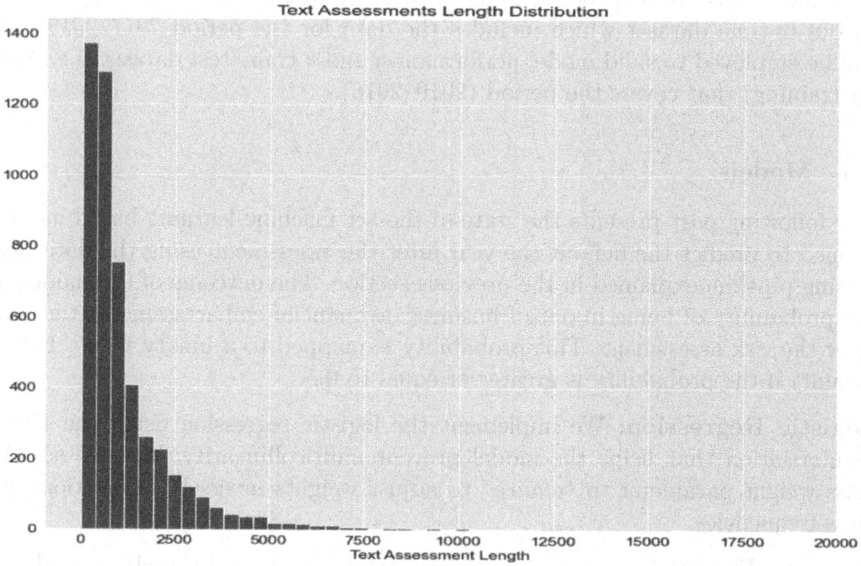

Fig. 3. Size distribution of the text assessment generated by the risk analysts.

We used the Word2Vec algorithm trained on the Google News dataset. The model contains 300-dimensional vectors for 3 million words and phrases. Each word in the text is represented in a 300-dimensional space. The text is encoded in a matrix $\mathbf{W} \in \mathcal{M}^{m,300}$ where m is the number of words in the text.

The GLoVe algorithm, trained on 2B tweets, transforms the text into a 200-dimensional space. In this case, the text is encoded in a matrix $\mathbf{G} \in \mathcal{M}^{m,300}$.

In this work, we propose a different approach when treating the text feature. We evaluate the sentiment of the text generated by the risk analyst using a sentiment analysis model (i.e., FinancialBERT [29]). FinancialBERT is a fine-tuned BERT using large corpora of financial texts. The model categorizes the text as positive, neutral, or negative.

3.3 Data Preprocessing

The preprocessing step can be split into two main parts depending on the applied text feature model. For GLoVe and Word2vec, we reduce the dimensional space of the text embedding using Principal Component Analysis [22,30]. For non-tree-based ML models, we scale the data using Standard Scaler [31].

The categorical features (i.e., the country in which the company is based) are encoded using the one-hot encoding technique. This method creates a new feature in the dataset for each feature label. It takes the value one if the company is based on the considered country. It is important to remark that the categorical feature derived from applying the Sentiment Analysis model to the text feature is also encoded using the same technique.

Finally, once we preprocessed our data, we split the dataset into three parts: an out-of-time dataset which includes the data for the period 2017–2019 that will be employed to valid model performance; and a train/test dataset (i.e., 70% for training) that covers the period (2010–2016).

3.4 Models

The following part presents the state-of-the-art machine learning-based models trained to predict the default the year after the assessment using the data processing pipeline explained in the previous section. The outcome of the models is the probability of being in out of business or financial embarrassments the year after the risk assessment. This probability is mapped to a binary value, 1 (i.e., default) if the probability is greater or equal to 0.5.

Logistic Regression: We implement the logistic regression using the Ridge regularisation that helps the model prevent multicollinearity. We also set the class weight parameter to *balanced* to adjust weights inversely proportional to class frequencies.

Random Forest: We set the number of trees to 100 and the class weight to *balanced* to deal with the imbalance in the target variable.

Support Vector Machine (SVM): In this case, we have set the hyperparameter *class_weight* = *'balanced'*. The other hyperparameters are the default ones.

XGBoost: This algorithm employs a sequential combination of 1000 weak learners. The hyperparameters of the xgboost are the follow: *n_estimators* = *1000*,

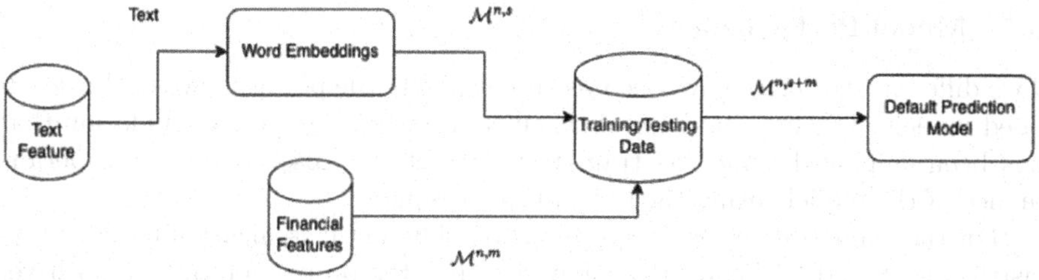

(a) Text processing using word embedding

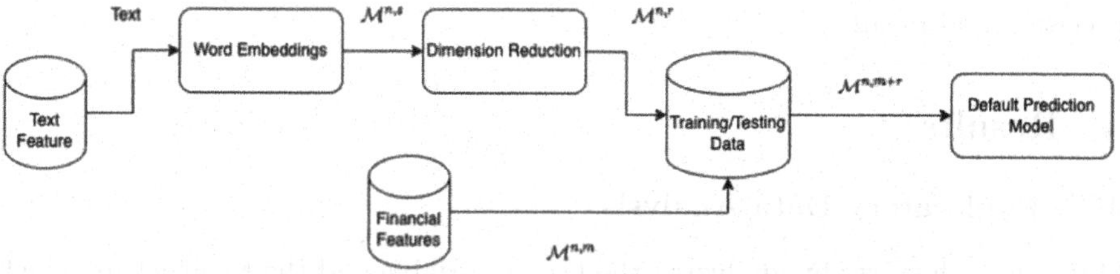

(b) Text processing using word embedding and dimension reduction

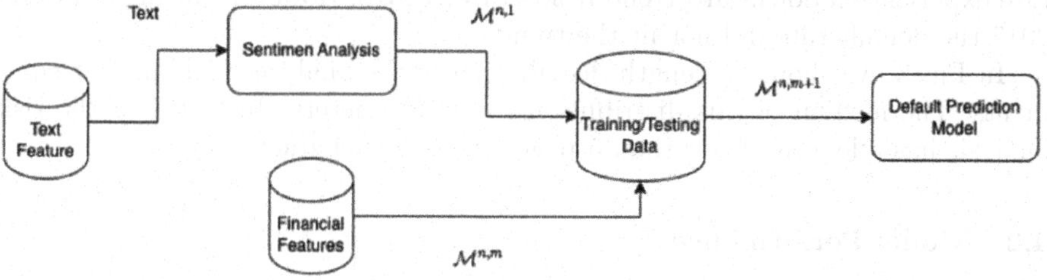

(c) Text processing using sentiment analysis

Fig. 4. Conceptual overview of the proposed framework. m, n represent respectively the number of assessments and the number of financial features available in the dataset. s represents the embedding dimension (i.e., s = 200 for GLoVe and s = 300 for Word2Vec). The variable r represents the word embedding space after the dimension reduction (i.e., r = 5).

learning_rate = 0.1 and *scale_pos_weight = 12*. The latter help the model with the imbalance dataset nad is usually set to $\frac{\#Positive\ Instances}{\#Negative\ Instances}$.

LightGBM: We set three different hyperparameters for this gradient boosting-based model: *n_estimators = 100*, *learning_rate = 0.1* and *class_weight = 'balanced'*.

Neural Network: We trained a neural network using stochastic gradient descent. The neural network is composed by 4 hidden layers with 128, 256, 512, and 128 neurons. The activation function is the *ReLU* function (Fig. 4).

3.5 Model Performance

Two different strategies have been used to evaluate the performance of the developed models. The first model evaluation comes from the 5 cross validation that has been employed using the train/test dataset. We also compare the performance of the models using the out-of-time sample.

For the train/test set, we employed three different classification metrics: precision, recall, and F1-Score. Precision measures the proportion of true positives among all predicted positives. Recall measures the proportion of true positives that were correctly identified. F1-Score is calculated as the harmonic mean of precision and recall.

4 Results

4.1 Exploratory Data Analysis

Our approach starts by analyzing the target variable and the text feature which is the risk analyst comments (e.g., see Fig. 1). As we can see in Fig. 2, the default rate experience a downward trend from 2010 to 2018. However, during 2014 and 2017 the default rate did not fit the trend.

In Fig. 3, we show the length distribution of the analyzed risk analyst comments. The median of this distribution is 693 characters. Just 10% of the risk analysis has a length bigger than 5 pages (i.e., 2600 characters).

4.2 Model Performance

For straightforward comparison, we employ the most commonly used classification evaluation metrics that lie in [0,1]. Higher values indicate superior performance. Table 2 display the accuracy of the different models with the different text embedding techniques. The overall performance of the models improves when we raw embed the text using Word2vec and GLoVe, especially for the logistic regression and the SVM.

The imbalanced characteristics of the dataset may bias the models to predict the most represented class (i.e., the non-defaulted class). In Table 3, we compare the precision of the models.

Table 2, we present the results using the approach described previously. In this work, we conducted 6 different experiences that related to the treatment of the textual feature. Tabular represents the model that has been trained just using the financial features. Tabular + Text (WE), we merged the financial features with the numerical representation generated by GLoVe and Word2Vec. In the WE + PCA experience, we performed a PCA to reduce the numerical representation from 200 and 300 respectively to 5 dimensions (i.e., these 5 dimensions represent 73.4 % of the variance). The SA represents the scenario in which we employ sentiment analysis to map the text to a categorical value.

In Table 1, we show the F1-Score for the models and the different text treatment configurations. Since we compute 5 cross-validations, we have the mean

F1-Score and the standard deviation. The table shows that both XGBoost and Logistic Regression models benefit from the addition of a text feature encoded using sentiment analysis.

The analysis of Table 3 shows that the reason behind the low values of the F1-Score (see Table 1) is the inability of the models to determine which companies will go into default. This is mainly due to the imbalanced characteristics of the dataset employed.

On the other hand, and regarding the F1-Score, we observe that Support Vector Machine and Neural Networks improve their performance by adding a significant number of features (i.e., the dimension of the word embeddings). This behavior is even more remarkable for Neural Networks.

In terms of the two embedding techniques proposed in this work, we see that there is no technique that improves the model performance for all the models (Table 4).

Table 1. F1 Score mean and standard deviation for the different strategies using 5-fold cross-validation. *WE* represent the dataset in which the text has been encoded using Word Embeddings. *SA* stands for Sentiment Analysis and is the dataset with the text categorically encoded using a sentiment analysis model. *PCA* is for the experience in which the dimensions of the numerical vector generated by the WE have been reduced using Principal Component Analysis.

	Tabular	Tabular + Text (WE)		Tabular + Text (SA)	Tabular + Text(WE+PCA)	
		GLoVe	Word2vec		GLoVe	Word2vec
Logistic Regression	0.208 ± 0.037	0.204 ± 0.023	0.196 ± 0.036	0.217 ± 0.040	0.209 ± 0.037	0.208 ± 0.036
SVM	0.210 ± 0.038	0.225 ± 0.042	0.235 ± 0.053	0.211 ± 0.038	0.209 ± 0.038	0.210 ± 0.037
Random Forest	0.012 ± 0.014	0.005 ± 0.009	0.010 ± 0.013	0.006 ± 0.011	0.010 ± 0.013	0.000 ± 0.000
XGBoost	0.124 ± 0.073	0.101 ± 0.038	0.081 ± 0.013	0.146 ± 0.061	0.117 ± 0.047	0.132 ± 0.077
LightGBM	0.164 ± 0.075	0.083 ± 0.033	0.096 ± 0.035	0.168 ± 0.072	0.163 ± 0.062	0.133 ± 0.067
MLP	0.000 ± 0.000	0.010 ± 0.021	0.006 ± 0.036	0.000 ± 0.000	0.000 ± 0.000	0.000 ± 0.000

Table 2. Accuracy Score mean and standard deviation for the different strategies using 5-fold cross-validation. *WE* represent the dataset in which the text has been encoded using Word Embeddings. *SA* stands for Sentiment Analysis and is the dataset with the text categorically encoded using a sentiment analysis model. *PCA* is for the experience in which the dimensions of the numerical vector generated by the WE have been reduced using Principal Component Analysis.

	Tabular	Tabular + Text(WE)		Tabular + Text (SA)	Tabular + Text(WE+PCA)	
		GLoVe	Word2vec		GLoVe	Word2vec
Logistic Regression	0.492 ± 0.149	0.684 ± 0.069	0.717 ± 0.042	0.550 ± 0.134	0.510 ± 0.139	0.717 ± 0.042
SVM	0.499 ± 0.152	0.718 ± 0.064	0.734 ± 0.059	0.511 ± 0.169	0.512 ± 0.141	0.734 ± 0.059
Random Forest	0.919 ± 0.017	0.922 ± 0.015	0.921 ± 0.015	0.920 ± 0.017	0.921 ± 0.015	0.922 ± 0.015
XGBoost	0.905 ± 0.023	0.916 ± 0.020	0.912 ± 0.018	0.907 ± 0.022	0.903 ± 0.020	0.912 ± 0.018
LightGBM	0.897 ± 0.022	0.914 ± 0.018	0.915 ± 0.017	0.899 ± 0.024	0.901 ± 0.023	0.915 ± 0.017
MLP	0.923 ± 0.015	0.923 ± 0.015	0.920 ± 0.015	0.923 ± 0.015	0.923 ± 0.015	0.923 ± 0.015

Table 3. Precision Score mean and standard deviation for the different strategies using 5-fold cross-validation. *WE* represent the dataset in which the text has been encoded using Word Embeddings. *SA* stands for Sentiment Analysis and is the dataset with the text categorically encoded using a sentiment analysis model. *PCA* is for the experience in which the dimensions of the numerical vector generated by the WE have been reduced using Principal Component Analysis.

	Tabular	Tabular + Text(WE)		Tabular + Text (SA)	Tabular + Text(WE+PCA)	
		GLoVe	Word2vec		GLoVe	Word2vec
Logistic Regression	0.119 ± 0.024	0.128 ± 0.019	0.126 ± 0.027	0.127 ± 0.026	0.120 ± 0.024	0.126 ± 0.027
SVM	0.121 ± 0.025	0.145 ± 0.032	0.154 ± 0.041	0.123 ± 0.025	0.121 ± 0.025	0.154 ± 0.041
Random Forest	0.135 ± 0.127	0.100 ± 0.200	0.067 ± 0.133	0.000 ± 0.000	0.340 ± 0.376	0.067 ± 0.133
XGBoost	0.209 ± 0.146	0.323 ± 0.085	0.221 ± 0.041	0.262 ± 0.081	0.278 ± 0.020	0.221 ± 0.041
LightGBM	0.219 ± 0.092	0.243 ± 0.051	0.319 ± 0.111	0.227 ± 0.072	0.242 ± 0.018	0.319 ± 0.111
MLP	0.000 ± 0.000	0.000 ± 0.000	0.000 ± 0.000	0.000 ± 0.000	0.000 ± 0.000	0.000 ± 0.000

Table 4. Accuracy score of the models using the out-of-time set. *WE* represents the dataset in which the text has been encoded using Word Embeddings. *SA* stands for Sentiment Analysis and is the dataset with the text categorically encoded using a sentiment analysis model. *PCA* is for the experience in which the dimensions of the numerical vector generated by the WE have been reduced using Principal Component Analysis.

	Tabular	Tabular + Text(WE)		Tabular + Text (SA)	Tabular + Text (WE + PCA)	
		GLoVe	Word2vec		GLoVe	Word2vec
Logistic Regression	0.695	0.762	0.743	0.701	0.847	0.743
SVM	0.706	0.770	0.748	0.706	0.853	0.748
Random Forest	0.930	0.932	0.932	0.931	0.965	0.930
XGBoost	0.921	0.928	0.924	0.923	0.899	0.924
LightGBM	0.927	0.929	0.929	0.924	0.949	0.929
MLP	0.931	0.931	0.931	0.931	0.965	0.931

5 Conclusions

In conclusion, this paper proposes a new approach to credit scoring that combines financial tabular data with credit risk textual assessment using word embedding techniques and sentiment analysis. Moreover, we addressed the problem of representing the text in a high dimensional space by using dimension reduction techniques (i.e., Principal Component Analysis).

Experimental results demonstrate that the addition of the textual feature slightly improves model performance. This suggests that incorporating credit risk textual assessment can provide additional information to financial institutions for more informed credit decisions. Furthermore, we experimentally demonstrate that the sentiment analysis approach tends to yield better results in comparison to the word embedding techniques. This is due to the fact that word embeddings, in essence, map words into a high-dimensional space where semantically similar words are placed closely together. However, these techniques focus primarily on individual words or at most, phrases. They do not inherently account for the larger syntactic or semantic context that extends beyond individual words and thus they might not adequately encapsulate the overall sentiment of a text, leading to a loss of crucial information.

In addition to improving model performance, a performant credit scoring system that combines financial tabular data with credit risk textual assessment can help credit risk analysts to focus on more critical cases, leaving the smaller cases to the system.

The framework proposed in this paper offers a promising approach for credit scoring and can be applied to other text classification tasks in finance and beyond. Future research should explore the use of more advanced techniques for sentiment analysis and word embedding (i.e. LSTM [32], GRU [33]), as well as the incorporation of other qualitative factors such as news articles and social media data to further improve model performance.

References

1. World Bank. Global Economic Prospects, June 2019: Heightened Tensions, Subdued Investment. World Bank, Washington, DC (2019). https://doi.org/10.1596/978-1-4648-1398-6
2. Addo, P., Guegan, D., Hassani, B.: Credit risk analysis using machine and deep learning models. Risks **6**(2), 38 (2018). https://doi.org/10.3390/risks6020038
3. Niu, B., Ren, J., Li, X.: Credit scoring using machine learning by combing social network information: evidence from peer-to-peer lending. Information **10**(12), 397 (2019). https://doi.org/10.3390/info10120397
4. Altman, E.I.: Financial ratios, discriminant analysis and the prediction of corporate bankruptcy. J. Financ. **23**(4), 589–609 (1968). https://doi.org/10.1111/j.1540-6261.1968.tb00843.x
5. Sohn, S.Y., Kim, D.H., Yoon, J.H.: Technology credit scoring model with fuzzy logistic regression. Appl. Soft Comput. **43**, 150–158 (2016). https://doi.org/10.1016/j.asoc.2016.02.025
6. Lessmann, S., Baesens, B., Seow, H.-V., Thomas, L.C.: Benchmarking state-of-the-art classification algorithms for credit scoring: An update of research. Eur. J. Oper. Res. **247**(1), 124–136 (2015)
7. El Qadi, A., Trocan, M., Dıaz-Rodr'ıguez, N., Frossard, T.: Feature contribution alignment with expert knowledge for artificial intelligence credit scoring. Signal Image Video Process. **17**, 427–434 (2022). https://doi.org/10.1007/s11760-022-02239-7
8. Chen, T., Guestrin, C.: XGBoost: a scalable tree boosting system. In: Proceedings of the 22nd ACM SIGKDD International Conference on Knowledge Discovery and Data Mining, pp. 785–794 (2016). https://doi.org/10.1145/2939672.2939785
9. Bussmann, N., Giudici, P., Marinelli, D., Papenbrock, J.: Explainable AI in fintech risk management. Front. Artif. Intell. **3** (2020). https://doi.org/10.3389/frai.2020.00026
10. Alzubaidi, L., et al.: Review of deep learning: concepts, CNN architectures, challenges, applications, future directions. J. Big Data **8**(1), 53 (2021). https://doi.org/10.1186/s40537-021-00444-8
11. Otter, D.W., Medina, J.R., Kalita, J.K.: A survey of the usages of deep learning in natural language processing. arXiv (2019). http://arxiv.org/abs/1807.10854. Accessed 10 Jan 2023

12. Rabiner, L.R.: A tutorial on hidden Markov models and selected applications in speech recognition. Proc. IEEE **77**(2), 257–286 (1989)
13. Brown, P.F., et al.: A statistical approach to machine translation. Comput. Linguist. **16**(2), 79–85 (1990)
14. Shen, Y., He, X., Gao, J., Deng, L., Mesnil, G.: Learning semantic representations using convolutional neural networks for web search. In: International Conference on World Wide Web, pp. 373–374 (2014)
15. dos Santos, C.N., Guimaraes, V.: Boosting named entity recognition with neural character embeddings. arXiv preprint arXiv:1505.05008 (2015)
16. Conde-Cespedes, P., Chavando, J., Deberry, E.: Detection of suspicious accounts on Twitter using word2vec and sentiment analysis. In: Choroś, K., Kopel, M., Kukla, E., Siemiński, A. (eds.) MISSI 2018. AISC, vol. 833, pp. 362–371. Springer, Cham (2019). https://doi.org/10.1007/978-3-319-98678-4_37
17. Berger, A., Lafferty, J.: Information retrieval as statistical translation. In: Proceedings of the 22nd Annual International ACM SIGIR Conference on Research and Development in Information Retrieval (SIGIR 1999), pp. 222–229. Association for Computing Machinery, New York (1999). https://doi.org/10.1145/312624.312681
18. Mikolov, T., Chen, K., Corrado, G., Dean, J.: Efficient estimation of word representations in vector space. arXiv (2013). http://arxiv.org/abs/1301.3781. Accessed 10 Jan 2023
19. Pennington, J., Socher, M., Richard, C.: Glove: global vectors for word representation. EMNLP **14**, 1532–1543 (2014). https://doi.org/10.3115/v1/D14-1162
20. Devlin, J., Chang, M.-W., Lee, K., Toutanova, K.: BERT: pre-training of deep bidirectional transformers for language understanding. arXiv (2019). http://arxiv.org/abs/1810.04805. Accessed 27 Feb 2023
21. Sivarajah, U., Kamal, M.M., Irani, Z., Weerakkody, V.: Critical analysis of big data challenges and analytical methods. J. Bus. Res. **70**, 263–286 (2017)
22. Raunak, V., Gupta, V., Metze, F.: Effective dimensionality reduction for word embeddings. In: Proceedings of the 4th Workshop on Representation Learning for NLP (RepL4NLP-2019), Florence, Italy, pp. 235–243. Association for Computational Linguistics (2019)
23. Agarwal, B., Mittal, N., Bansal, P., Garg, S.: Sentiment analysis using common-sense and context information. J. Comput. Intell. Neurosci. **9** (2015)
24. Rambocas, M., Pacheco, B.G.: Online sentiment analysis in marketing research: a review. JRIM **12**(2), 146–163 (2018). https://doi.org/10.1108/JRIM-05-2017-0030
25. Gupta, A., Dengre, V., Kheruwala, H.A., Shah, M.: Comprehensive review of text-mining applications in finance. Financ. Innov. **6**(1), 39 (2020). https://doi.org/10.1186/s40854-020-00205-1
26. Gupta, R., Chen, M.: Sentiment analysis for stock price prediction. In: 2020 IEEE Conference on Multimedia Information Processing and Retrieval (MIPR), Shenzhen, Guangdong, China, pp. 213–218 (2020). https://doi.org/10.1109/MIPR49039.2020.00051
27. Stevenson, M., Mues, C., Bravo, C.: The value of text for small business default prediction: a deep learning approach. Eur. J. Oper. Res. **295**(2), 758–771 (2021). https://doi.org/10.1016/j.ejor.2021.03.008
28. Provenzano, A.R., et al.: Machine learning approach for credit scoring. arXiv (2020). http://arxiv.org/abs/2008.01687. Accessed 11 Jan 2023
29. Hazourli, A.R.: FinancialBERT - a pretrained language model for financial text mining (2022). https://doi.org/10.13140/RG.2.2.34032.12803

30. Jolliffe, I.T., Cadima, J.: Principal component analysis: a review and recent developments. Phil. Trans. R. Soc. A **374**(2065), 20150202 (2016). https://doi.org/10.1098/rsta.2015.0202
31. Pedregosa, F., et al.: Scikit-learn: machine learning in Python. J. Mach. Learn. Res. **12**, 2825–2830 (2011)
32. Gers, F.A., Schmidhuber, J., Cummins, F.: Learning to forget: continual prediction with LSTM. Neural Comput. **12**(10), 2451–2471 (2000)
33. Chung, J., Gulcehre, C., Cho, K., Bengio, Y.: Empirical evaluation of gated recurrent neural networks on sequence modeling. arXiv (2014). http://arxiv.org/abs/1412.3555. Accessed 28 Feb 2023

Goal-Oriented Classification of Football Results

Szymon Głowania[1(✉)], Jan Kozak[1,2], and Przemysław Juszczuk[1]

[1] Faculty of Informatics and Communication, Department of Machine Learning, University of Economics in Katowice, 1 Maja 50, 40-287 Katowice, Poland
{szymon.glowania,jan.kozak,przemyslaw.juszczuk}@ue.katowice.pl

[2] Institute of Innovative Technologies EMAG Leopolda 31, 40-189 Katowice, Poland
jan.kozak@emag.lukasiewicz.gov.pl

Abstract. In this article, we propose identifying and analyzing the problem of relatively poor classification results related to a single decision class in sports data. First, we preprocess the data to obtain the decision class. Then, we implement a goal-oriented approach to the football data to improve the results for algorithms like ACDT (Ant Colony Decision Tree) and ACDF (Ant Colony Decision Forrest). The main difference in the case of the goal-oriented approach is the focus on particular classification measures like precision and recall. These measures are adapted to mentioned algorithms, and the whole approach is compared with the original algorithms based on the accuracy measure. Finally, numerical experiments are performed on the initially preprocessed real-world data set based on nine seasons of the German football Bundesliga.

Keywords: Ensemble methods · Classification · Sports data · Goal-oriented approach

1 Introduction

The still-increasing amount of data available to us leads to a situation in which complex algorithms are necessary to handle the available data. Such an approach is implemented in different fields of life, from scientific data to life logging, where various apps allow us to register our sports activity. Especially the last elements easily fit into the growing field of sports data, covering everything from well-known GPS data present in races to sports results and even gambling.

The last field related to various sports events is an exciting opportunity to investigate different machine learning algorithms instrumental in problems where the approximate solution could be sufficient. The machine learning techniques and methods were used in many domains like healthcare [1], finance [9], politic [17] or sport [23].

The subject analyzed in this paper fits into the above problem, where numerous algorithms were easily fit to different sports disciplines, including basketball,

N. T. Nguyen et al. (Eds.): ICCCI 2023, LNAI 14162, pp. 782–793, 2023.
https://doi.org/10.1007/978-3-031-41456-5_59

football, rugby, American football, or even javelin throw [10,16,25,26,28,29]. In this application, the proposed methods allowed not only to predict the result of the match or sports event, but also were used to estimate the results or even to select the best players proper for a team [20,25,28]. The last task can be transformed into choosing the subset of objects from a large set of available options, and can be generalized as the discrete knapsack problem with limitations.

Football is among the most popular sports when considering not only the number of fans but also the most popular sport-related scientific problems, which much attention is paid to using machine learning algorithms. Present works primarily focus on improving the overall quality of prediction [23,25]. One should know that football, in general, is not considered a problem as complex as, for example, algorithms for playing go and similar board games like AphaZero. However, the used methods lead to a significant limitation: the need for more confidence about the predicted result. Unfortunately, in the problems related to gambling, a single mistake in match betting leads to global loss; thus, despite the relatively small number of non-redundant data, it is still very challenging to find and fit the proper algorithm capable of achieving high-quality prediction.

One of the main existing problems related to sports results prediction is the relatively poor quality of prediction observed for specific decision classes. One should know that the problem is unrelated to the disturbed abundance of objects in decision classes. Such a problem is observed, for example, in financial data, where very few cases are related to specific decision classes [20]. In this case, we observe the poor classification quality for the draws between the two teams. The problem does not occur in situations where a decision indicates the winning of one of the teams. One possible explanation for this situation is the lack of unequivocal data on the advantage of a single team over another.

In this article, we propose a solution based on the goal-oriented prediction of the selected efficiency measure like precision or recall. Our assumption is to provide the methodology to prepare the initial sports data so that the decision table with several parameters is derived. Eventually, we use the ACDT (Ant Colony Decision Tree) and ACDF (Ant Colony Decision Forrest) to test our approach. We focus on different measures for data obtained from a real-world raw format.

Thus, our main contribution can be summarized as follows:

- we analyze and preprocess the real-world sports data related to football and represent it as the decision table with three possible decision classes;
- we implement and adjust the ACDT and ACDF algorithm to focus on the particular goal-oriented approach;
- we experimentally verify the goal-oriented approach focused on three well-known measures: recall, precision, and F1 score with the classical approach based on the accuracy measure.

The advantage of such an approach is the particular focus on the selected quality of classification measure, which can be crucial in situations where the overall results could be better. Moreover, this quality of classification is directly related to some particular class. This situation could be improved by adjusting the existing methods so that the initial accuracy measure is replaced by the measures favoring specific decision classes.

The article is organized as follows: in the next section, we describe the most popular algorithms from the literature. Section 3 derives the general description of the problem, while Sect. 4 presents the adapted algorithms with the goal-oriented approach. Section 5 includes numerical experiments and some observations, while the last section concludes.

2 Background

In this section, we start with the overall description of selected approaches for classification in sports data and machine learning methods. We also emphasize the role of machine learning methods in less popular sports. The next part of the section is devoted to the general description of the problem.

2.1 Related Works

Due to a large amount of data, sports prediction and human activity are interesting analysis subjects. Some papers are devoted to activity recognition and its relation to data obtained from various sensors. Articles like [30] focus on deep learning methods, where different activities like squats or pull-ups are recognized. While the more general survey focused, for example, on wearable equipment and multi-sensor data, can be found in [31].

The separate papers are strictly devoted to using neural networks in human activity and sports. In [35] authors describe the problem of match prediction using a neural network. In this article, the issue of overall team condition is also discussed. It is imperative in the context of the paper [34], where the problem is related to predicting injuries in sports. Sport-related problems focus not only on the machine learning methods but also include more complex analyses related, for example, to fuzzy methods [27]. At the same time, machine learning methods can be found in less popular sports like NFL [4].

More general papers on sports results prediction can be found in [8]. The authors emphasize the different problems related to sports results. First, we could discuss strictly numeric outcomes like the chance of winning. The number of attributes that can be collected is enormous, but it eventually can be reduced to calculating the chances of winning for a single team. This subject is covered in our article, as well as it was covered in numerous publications like [13]. One should know that this problem is analyzed not only in the most popular leagues like the English Premier League [3] and German league [33] but also less popular Iranian league [2]. At the same time, machine learning methods are not the only approach used for predictions. The statistical approach based on the Bayesian approach was introduced in [32]. While the Bayesian networks to predict the team results for the English Premier League were used in [19].

2.2 Problem Definition and Methods

Classification can be defined as follows. Let's assume that a set of objects X is given. Every object x can be described as a set of conditional attributes and a decision attribute (or decision class). We can define a pair (attribute, value) for every attribute, where the value can be numeric or symbolic. At the same time, the object has assigned a single value of the decision class. In the classification problem, we aim to estimate the class of the newly added object x. At the same time, the quality of classification can be measured based on well-known measures like accuracy, precision, recall, and F1 score.

The problem can be represented as the decision Table 1, in which rows correspond to the set of objects X. At the same time, columns are the attributes A, and the decision class c represents the label of objects representing the subset of X. The above definition can be summarized as follows:

$$DT = (X, A \cup \{c\}). \tag{1}$$

Table 1. Example of the decision table

	Conditional attribute						Decision
	a_1	a_2	a_3	a_4	a_5	a_6	class
x_1	1	9	1	9	1	0	0
x_2	2	12	3	8	3	0	1
x_3	2	9	3	7	3	0	1
x_4	3	1	7	11	3	4	1
x_5	3	10	4	9	6	−2	2
x_6	3	14	2	7	6	−4	2
x_7	3	18	1	15	2	−1	0

In the case of classical methods like the CART algorithm or the C4.5 algorithm are deterministic. This approach is sufficient in a simple problem where the number of objects and attributes is relatively small. On the other hand, for some issues, there is a need for an approximate solution that could derive the approximate classification for the set. The number of objects and attributes in the analyzed problem is not very large. Which initially could lead to using the deterministic approach. On the other hand, the proposed method based on the non-deterministic approach allows for freely modifying the goal of the classification, which in our case, will be the selected classification measure. Details will be presented in the following sections.

3 Proposed Solution

This section describes the raw data and the data preparation process leading to deriving the decision table. Next, we describe shortly the canonical versions of the ACDT and ACDF algorithms and their modifications based on the goal-oriented function. We aim to provide the tool to improve the classification quality for the selected measure without visibly decreasing overall algorithm quality. To do so, we use the classical efficiency measures like accuracy, precision, and recall modified and applied for the goal-oriented function.

3.1 Data Preparation and Preprocessing

We obtained the raw data from the [24]. The data concerned the German football Bundesliga and included nine seasons from 2010/2011 to 2018/2019. The data was transformed into a decision table. Additional attributes were included in the decision tables. For example, in the case of sports results where two or more teams are involved, there is a consensus to skip some initial matches between teams. It is essential for sports like football or basketball, where there are no good indicators of the strength of a given team at the beginning of the season, for example. Therefore, we excluded the first five rounds from each analyzed dataset to include these observations in our results. This approach is the same as in the article [23]. Next, the whole data was divided into training and testing sets.

Our full dataset included 1980 rows. We divide it as follows:

- the training set: 1827 rows– (9 seasons of 29 rounds with nine games each);
- the test set: 153 rows – (17 rounds of 9 games each).

The Fig 1 presents the division of objects belonging to different decision classes for both training and testing set.

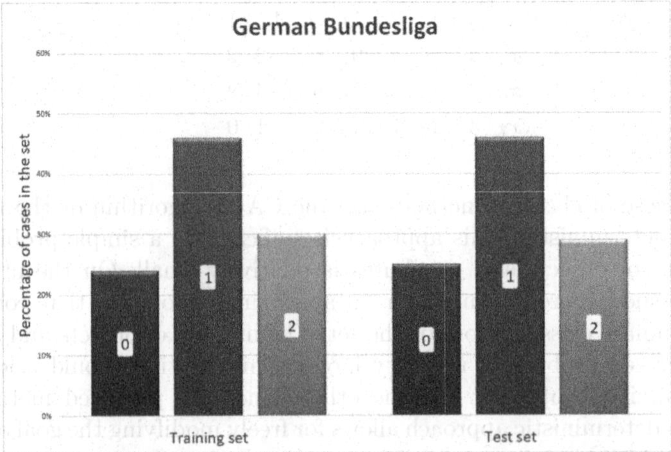

Fig. 1. Division of the training and test sets between decision classes

Eventually, we ended with six different conditional attributes, which were further used in the experiments:

- Round - the number of the current round;
- PositionHT - the current position of team 1 (home team) – in the league table;

- PositionVT - the current position of team 2 (visiting team);
- PointsHT - the number of points of team 1 (lose is equal 0, draw is equal to 1 point while winning is equal to 3 points);
- PointsVT - the number of points of team 2;
- Difference - the difference between the points of team 1 and team 2.

As one can see, we selected the relatively small, non-redundant set of attributes, which should lead to a good classification of results. The most crucial factor is measuring the difference in strength between two teams (home and visiting). To do so, we analyzed – the position in the table for both teams, the number of points - which is the essential element to identify the overall strength of the team, and finally – the difference (in points) between the two teams. An additional attribute Round is used to determine the actual round played. It is because matches in the league could be considered time-dependent data, where the first few matches are more random, while for the last matches in the season, less predictability could be observed. The summary of attribute ranges can be found in Table 2.

Table 2. Range of attribute values

No	Attribute	Training dataset		Test dataset	
		Min	Max	Min	Max
1	Round	6	34	18	34
2	PositionHT	1	18	1	18
3	PositionVT	1	18	1	18
4	PositionHT	0	102	0	102
5	PositionVT	0	102	0	102
6	Difference	−102	102	−102	102

An example fragment of the preprocessed data is presented in Table 3.

In our case, the decision class can be one of the following values: 1 – win for the HT (home team), 2 – win for the visiting team (VT), and 0 – draw. Thus, the decision for the problem can be one of three different values. We shouldn't expect considerable disproportions between the cardinality of each class. However, there exists a difficulty in prediction for class 0 (draw).

3.2 ACDT and ACDF Algorithms

The basic idea of the ACDT algorithm was taken from the original work of Marco Dorigo [11] and it is based on the construction of the decision tree. It also uses the concepts from the well-known CART algorithm and its splitting rule (explained in detail in [5]). The general ACDT formulation is as follows:

$$ACDT = \langle (DT, T(S), ants, p_{m,m_{L(i,j)}}(t), S \rangle. \quad (2)$$

Table 3. Sample set with values for the six objects

	Conditional attributes						Decision Target
	Round	PositionHT	PositionVT	PointsHT	PointsVT	Difference	
x_1	6	16	6	3	8	−5	2
x_2	6	13	6	4	8	−4	1
x_3	6	16	13	3	4	−1	0
x_4	9	8	16	12	5	7	0
x_5	9	3	1	15	21	−6	2
x_6	9	18	6	4	13	−9	1
...							
x_k	val_k^1	val_k^2	val_k^3	val_k^4	val_k^5	val_k^6	Dec_k^1

The above approach is based on constructing the whole decision tree $T(S)$ based on the learning data derived from the decision table DT. The selection of the splitting rule for the node is based on the heuristic function and the pheromone trail present in the original idea for the ACO approach. The split for analyzed nodes is calculated as follows:

$$p_{i,j} = \frac{\tau_{m,m_{L(i,j)}}(t) \cdot \eta_{i,j}^{\beta}}{\sum_i^a \sum_j^{b_i} \tau_{m,m_{L(i,j)}}(t) \cdot \eta_{i,j}^{\beta}} \tag{3}$$

where value for the single split for the i-th attribute and value j is $\eta_{i,j}$; t is the step of the algorithm; $\tau_{m,m_{L(i,j)}}$ is a pheromone value for the step t in arc connecting the m and $m_{L(i,j)}$ nodes; eventually the relative importance of the heuristic value is β. While the pheromone trail is used to estimate the strength of the connection between the tree node and its parent node (except the root). It can be calculated as follows:

$$\tau_{m,m_L}(t+1) = (1-\gamma) \cdot \tau_{m,m_L}(t) + Q(T), \tag{4}$$

where the γ parameter describes the evaporation rate of the pheromone, and as a default, it is set to 0.1. Eventually, the $Q(T)$ determines the evaluation function of decision tree:

$$Q(T) = \phi \cdot w(T) + \psi \cdot est(T, P), \tag{5}$$

where the size of the decision tree T is described as $w(T)$; while $est(T, P)$ is the quality of classification of the object P by the decision tree T. ϕ and ψ are constants.

The idea of the ACDT algorithm allows the generation of a decision tree (classifier) in a single algorithm run. Thus, its obvious extension is deriving the approach based on the ensemble methods. The first version of the ACDF algorithm (ant colony decision forest) was proposed in 2012 [22]. The idea for the ACDF was initially based on the possible adaptation of the Ant Colony Optimization (ACO) [11] to the ensemble methods. More details about the ACDF algorithm can be found in [22]. However, the general idea is based on the formulation:

$$ACDF = \langle DT, Result_{ACDT}, ants, p_{m,m_{L(i,j)}}(t), S \rangle, \tag{6}$$

where DT is the decision table, $Result_{ACDT}$ is the number of classifiers built based on the ACDT algorithm, *ants* is the number of ants used in the single iteration of the algorithms, $p_{m,m_{L(i,j)}}$ selection rule used in the decision process, while S is the set of acceptable object.

The probability of selecting the test in the node is not in the main scope of this article. However, its main idea is the same as in the ACDT approach.

3.3 Goal-Oriented Function

The evaluation function used in ACDT and ACDF algorithms is based on the accuracy measure. We can focus on different classification measures by modifying how this value is calculated. The above approach is sufficient for the case with binary decision class. However, for the multi-label decision classes, an additional extension is needed. First, the extended confusion matrix for more than two decision classes should be defined. Then, the whole process should be repeated for every single decision class. An example confusion matrix for the selected decision class can be defined as in 4.

Table 4. Confusion matrix – example for decision class '1'

	Predicted '1'	Predicted '0'	Predicted '2'
Examples '1'	True '1' (TP_1)	False '1' to '0' (FN_1)	False '1' to '2' (FN_1)
Examples '0'	False '0' to '1' (FP_1)	True '0' (TN)	False '0' to '2' (—)
Examples '2'	False '2' to '1' (FP_1)	False '2' to '0' (—)	True '2' (TN)

The accuracy measure for the multi-class approach leads to a simple methodology, where all correctly classified objects are summarized and divided by the number of all classified objects:

$$accuracy = \frac{\sum_{i=1}^{c} TP_i}{s}, \tag{7}$$

where s is the number of objects. For the multiclass approach, the precision and recall values should be calculated for each class separately, and eventually, the arithmetic mean of these values is derived:

$$macro\_precision = \frac{1}{c}\sum_{i=1}^{c} \frac{TP_i}{TP_i + FP_i}, \tag{8}$$

$$macro\_recall = \frac{1}{c}\sum_{i=1}^{c} \frac{TP_i}{TP_i + FN_i}, \tag{9}$$

where for both cases, c is the number of different decision classes. Thus, F1 score is the harmonic mean of the two above measures. Thus, we also decided to include it in our approach:

$$F1 = 2 \cdot \frac{macro\_precision \cdot macro\_recall}{macro\_precision + macro\_recall}. \tag{10}$$

4 Numerical Experiments

To test the performance of our solution, we derived a set of numerical experiments. Our goal was to experimentally verify the results' quality based on the goal-oriented ACDT and goal-oriented ACDF algorithms [21]. For this purpose, we used the previously described dataset and performed experiments (30 repetitions of each experiment).

For each of these algorithms, we made four settings:

1. the classical algorithm versions – accuracy is the goal (called $ACDT$ or $ACDF$).
2. An algorithm in which the macro recall measure is set as the target (called $ACDT_{rec}$ or $ACDF_{rec}$).
3. An algorithm in which the macro precision measure is set as the target (called $ACDT_{prec}$ or $ACDF_{prec}$).
4. An algorithm in which macro measure F1 is set as the target (called $ACDT_{F1}$ or $ACDF_{F1}$).

The algorithm parameters were as follows: the number of trees – 250; forest size – 10; the rest were set by default, according to [21]. Finally, the results of all the experiments were compared to the previous approach (see [23]) and presented in Table 5.

A heterogeneous ensemble of classifiers with simple voting was created, consisting of: Decision tree – maximum depth 3, algorithm CART (implementation [5,18]); Support vector machine – linear classifier (implementation [12]); AdaBoost (implementation [14,15]); Bagging (implementation [6]); Random forest – maximum depth of tree 3, 100 estimators (implementation [7]).

Table 5. Experimental results - measures to assess the quality of classification.

Approach	Accuracy	Macro recall	Macro precision	F1
$ACDT$	0.4039	0.3810	0.4579	**0.4013**
$ACDT_{rec}$	0.3906	0.3685	0.4444	0.3904
$ACDT_{prec}$	0.4525	0.3627	0.4614	0.3353
$ACDT_{F1}$	0.3978	0.3765	0.4465	0.3972
$ACDF$	0.4261	0.3834	0.4665	0.3880
$ACDF_{rec}$	0.4325	0.3896	0.4649	0.3918
$ACDF_{prec}$	0.4883	**0.3918**	**0.4805**	0.3502
$ACDF_{F1}$	0.4244	0.3824	0.4634	0.3857
heterogeneous*	**0.4976**	0.3886	0.3461	0.3661

* – heterogeneous classifier applied to this problem in the paper [23].

As can be seen, accuracy is the best for the previous approach (heterogeneous*). However, this work tried to improve the classification of other classes (above all "draw" class – 0, which was previously omitted), so attention should be paid to other measures. In this case, improvements are already possible, especially precision (it was deficient because draws were ignored entirely and with $macro_precision$ a 0 was included in the average value) and F1 score.

In the case of recall, the best result was obtained when running the $ACDF_{prec}$ algorithm, which interestingly was oriented towards the precision goal to assess classification quality. However, improving precision (again, this algorithm proved to be the best), in this case, was also associated with improving recall. It should be remembered that improving recall does not favor detecting all classes (those less numerous may be missed). In this case, enhancing precision influences each class to appear in the classification, and on top of that, the classification is as good as possible. Therefore, the goal set for precision affected the recalls. For recall, the difference between the worst and best approaches was insignificant at less than 3%, which also influenced this situation.

On the other hand, for precision, the algorithm for which precision was the goal was the best (as already presented) – $ACDF_{prec}$ (by the way, analyzing only $ACDT$, the precision goal was also the best here). It should be noted that with precision, the improvement was already considerable, amounting (compared to the baseline algorithm) to more than 11%.

When analyzing the F1 measure, the best results appeared for the classic $ACDT$ and $ACDF$ algorithms and when the goal was set to $F1$ or recall (this point has already been agreed). The best result ($ACDT$ allowed an improvement over the classical approach of more than 3%. However, it should also be noted that $ACDF_{prec}$, previously the best, is a much worse approach when analyzing the F1 score.

5 Conclusions and Future Works

In this article, we proposed the idea of the goal-oriented classification function related to the ACDT and ACDF algorithms to classify sports data. We used one major European league and obtained real-world data, which was initially preprocessed. The domain expert knowledge was used to obtain the most promising attributes, which were used in the classification process. Finally, the initial data were adapted to the decision table format and used in the ACDT algorithm.

We derived the general description of both algorithms, focusing on the goal-oriented function based on selected, well-known classification measures like precision and recall. We aimed to identify the problems related to the overall weak classification of the decision classes related to the draw between two teams.

We calculated the presented dataset divided for the training and learning set in the numerical experiments. We used two canonical versions of the algorithms: the ACDT and the ACDF approach. Next, we compared them with a goal-oriented approach, where the precision, recall, and F1 score replaced the initial evaluation function based on accuracy. Finally, the results were compared with those obtained in our previous article – indicated in the experimental sections as the heterogeneous approach.

Obtained results do not allow for a straightforward approach. However, it opens the way to a goal-oriented approach, in which the particular emphasis can be put on a specific measure or class indicated by the decision-maker (or selected automatically).

For future works, we aim to provide a large variety of additional attributes, which could allow identifying the crucial, non-dominated conditional attributes. Moreover, we want to focus on deriving the general schema for voting in the ensemble of methods, allowing for a more robust approach in the context of the ensemble methods.

References

1. Ahmad, M.A., Eckert, C., Teredesai, A.: Interpretable machine learning in healthcare. In: Proceedings of the 2018 ACM International Conference on Bioinformatics, Computational Biology, and Health Informatics, pp. 559–560 (2018)
2. Arabzad, S.M., Tayebi Araghi, M.E., Sadi-Nezhad, S., Ghofrani, N.: Football match results prediction using artificial neural networks: the case of Iran pro league. J. Appl. Res. Ind. Eng. **1**, 159–179 (2014)
3. Babota, R., Kaur, H.: Predictive analysis and modelling football results using machine learning approach for English premier league. Int. J. Forecast. **35**(2), 741–755 (2019)
4. Boulier, B.L., Stekler, H.O.: Neural network prediction of NFL football games. Int. J. Forecast. **19**(2), 257–270 (2003)
5. Breiman, L., Friedman, J., Stone, C., Olshen, R.: Classification and regression trees. Chapman & Hall, New York (1984)
6. Breiman, L.: Bagging predictors. Mach. Learn. **24**(2), 123–140 (1996). https://doi.org/10.1007/BF00058655
7. Breiman, L.: Random forests. Mach. Learn. **45**(1), 5–32 (2001). https://doi.org/10.1023/A:1010933404324
8. Bunker, R.P., Thabtah, F.: A machine learning framework for sport result prediction. Appl. Comput. Inform. **15**(1), 27–33 (2019)
9. De Prado, M.L.: Advances in Financial Machine Learning. Wiley, Hoboken (2018)
10. Delen, D., Cogdell, D., Kasap, N.: A comparative analysis of data mining methods in predicting NCAA bowl outcomes. Int. J. Forecast. **28**(2), 543–552 (2012). https://doi.org/10.1016/j.ijforecast.2011.05.002
11. Dorigo, M.: Optimization, learning and natural algorithms (in Italian). Ph.D. thesis, vol. 192, pp. 1573–1582 (1992)
12. Fan, R.E., Chang, K.W., Hsieh, C.J., Wang, X.R., Lin, C.J.: LIBLINEAR: a library for large linear classification. J. Mach. Learn. Res. **9**, 1871–1874 (2008). https://doi.org/10.1023/B:STCO.0000035301.49549.88
13. Fernandez, M., Ulmer, B.: Predicting soccer match results in the English premier league (2014)
14. Freund, Y., Schapire, R.E.: A decision-theoretic generalization of on-line learning and an application to boosting. J. Comput. Syst. Sci. **55**(1), 119–139 (1997). https://doi.org/10.1006/jcss.1997.1504
15. Freund, Y., Schapire, R.E., et al.: Experiments with a new boosting algorithm. In: ICML, vol. 96, pp. 148–156. Citeseer (1996)
16. Głowania, S., Kozak, J., Juszczuk, P.: New voting schemas for heterogeneous ensemble of classifiers in the problem of football results prediction. Procedia Comput. Sci. **207**, 3393–3402 (2022)

17. Hasan, A., Moin, S., Karim, A., Shamshirband, S.: Machine learning-based sentiment analysis for twitter accounts. Math. Comput. Appl. **23**(1), 11 (2018)
18. Hastie, T., Tibshirani, R., Friedman, J.H., Friedman, J.H.: The Elements of Statistical Learning: Data Mining, Inference, and Prediction, vol. 2. Springer, New York (2009). https://doi.org/10.1007/978-0-387-21606-5
19. Joseph, A., Fenton, N.E., Neil, M.: Predicting football results using Bayesian nets and other machine learning techniques. Knowl.-Based Syst. **19**(7), 544–553 (2006)
20. Juszczuk, P., Kozak, J., Dziczkowski, G., Głowania, S., Jach, T., Probierz, B.: Real-world data difficulty estimation with the use of entropy. Entropy **23**(12), 1621 (2021). https://doi.org/10.3390/e23121621
21. Kozak, J.: Decision Tree and Ensemble Learning Based on Ant Colony Optimization. SCI, vol. 781. Springer, Cham (2019). https://doi.org/10.1007/978-3-319-93752-6
22. Kozak, J., Boryczka, U.: Multiple boosting in the ant colony decision forest meta-classifier. Knowl.-Based Syst. **75**, 141–151 (2015)
23. Kozak, J., Głowania, S.: Heterogeneous ensembles of classifiers in predicting Bundesliga football results. Procedia Comput. Sci. **192**, 1573–1582 (2021). https://doi.org/10.1016/j.procs.2021.08.161
24. Kozak, J., Głowania, S.: Bundesliga football results (2021). https://www.ue.katowice.pl/index.php?id=20435
25. Maszczyk, A., Gołaś, A., Pietraszewski, P., Roczniok, R., Zając, A., Stanula, A.: Application of neural and regression models in sports results prediction. Procedia Soc. Behav. Sci. **117**, 482–487 (2014). https://doi.org/10.1016/j.sbspro.2014.02.249
26. McCabe, A., Trevathan, J.: Artificial intelligence in sports prediction. In: Fifth International Conference on Information Technology: New Generations (ITNG 2008), pp. 1194–1197. IEEE (2008). https://doi.org/10.1109/ITNG.2008.203
27. Men, Y.: Intelligent sports prediction analysis system based on improved gaussian fuzzy algorithm. Alex. Eng. J. **61**(7), 5351–5359 (2022)
28. Nguyen, N.H., Nguyen, D.T.A., Ma, B., Hu, J.: The application of machine learning and deep learning in sport: predicting NBA players' performance and popularity. J. Inf. Telecommun. **6**(2), 217–235 (2022)
29. Pai, P.F., ChangLiao, L.H., Lin, K.P.: Analyzing basketball games by a support vector machines with decision tree model. Neural Comput. Appl. **28**(12), 4159–4167 (2017). https://doi.org/10.1007/s00521-016-2321-9
30. Pająk, G., Krutz, P., Patalas-Maliszewska, J., Rehm, M., Pająk, I., Dix, M.: An approach to sport activities recognition based on an inertial sensor and deep learning. Sens. Actuators, A **345**(1), 113773 (2022)
31. Qiu, S., et al.: Multi-sensor information fusion based on machine learning for real applications in human activity recognition: state-of-the-art and research challenges. Physica A: Stat. Mech. Appl. **528**, 121461 (2019)
32. Rue, H., Salvesen, O.: Prediction and retrospective analysis of soccer matches in a league. J. Royal Stat. Soc. Ser. D (2000)
33. Schauberger, G., Groll, A., Tutz, G.: Modeling football results in the German Bundesliga using match-specific covariates. Technical report number 197 (2016)
34. Shen, H.: Prediction simulation of sports injury based on embedded system and neural network. Microprocess. Microsyst. **82**, 103900 (2021)
35. Zhang, Q., Zhang, X., Hu, H., Li, C., Lin, Y., Ma, R.: Sports match prediction model for training and exercise using attention-based LSTM network. Digi. Commun. Netw. **8**(4), 508–515 (2022)

Learning from Imbalanced Data Streams Using Rotation-Based Ensemble Classifiers

Ireneusz Czarnowski(✉)

Department of Information Systems, Gdynia Maritime University, Morska 83, 81-225 Gdynia, Poland

i.czarnowski@umg.edu.pl

Abstract. In this paper, the problem of learning from imbalanced data streams is considered. To solve this problem, an approach is presented based on the processing of data chunks, which are formed using over-sampling and under-sampling. The final classification output is determined using an ensemble approach, which is supported by the rotation technique to introduce more diversification into the pool of base classifiers and increase the final performance of the system. The proposed approach is called Weighted Ensemble with one-class Classification and Over-sampling and Instance selection (WECOI). It is validated experimentally using several selected benchmarks, and some results are presented and discussed. The paper concludes with a discussion of future research directions.

Keywords: Streaming Machine Learning · Data Stream · Imbalanced Data · Ensemble Learning · Rotation-Based Ensembles

1 Introduction

Nowadays, enormous amounts of data are generated by different devices, such as smartphones, wearables, computers, and Internet of Things (IoT) sensors, as well as by systems within businesses and corporations. These data have a massive character and are generated continuously, and can be seen as unbounded flows of data, which are known as data streams [1]. They can also be considered as a potential source of input to different systems, for example to support decision-making processes and in the use of machine learning algorithms for producing classifier models. However, such data streams pose challenges when used for machine learning.

One such challenge is to adapt the learning process to the presence of concept drift. Most of the data that are currently of interest have a non-stationary character and change over time, whereas traditional machine learning algorithms are not designed to monitor these changes. This means that machine learning tools are needed that can build models that evolve over time and are able to cope with concept drift in data. Thus, it is necessary to design machine learning algorithms that are able to adapt to these changes. In [5], it was highlighted that a data stream computational model can process only a small portion of the data, as it is not possible to keep and store all of the incoming data. In other words, the main challenge faced by machine learning algorithms is the ability to

N. T. Nguyen et al. (Eds.): ICCCI 2023, LNAI 14162, pp. 794–805, 2023.
https://doi.org/10.1007/978-3-031-41456-5_60

process these streams, as traditional approaches are based on processing in batch mode. Updating the classification model when new data are input poses a further challenge. An appropriate solution to this problem is the use of incremental or online learning. It should be also underlined that when processing data streams, attention needs to be paid to the class imbalance problem, which can have a very detrimental influence on the learning process [2]. In summary, the answer to these challenges is found in the domain of streaming machine learning [3] or online machine learning [5], where the main aim is to design machine learning models that are able to work with streaming data sources. This is currently a very hot topic, and is still open to research.

One potential approach that is of interest in the area of streaming machine learning is based on ensemble learning. The motivation for using ensemble learning was discussed in [11], where the authors very clearly showed that no single classifier is appropriate for all tasks, and that an ensemble approach to online learning may be suitable for dealing with the restrictions arising from drifting data, the class imbalance problem or the availability and character of the data stream. An ensemble learning method is resilient and adaptable to changes in data [11].

In this paper, the problem of learning from an imbalanced data stream is considered, and the classification problem forms the main area of interest of this research work. To solve this problem, a dedicated framework is considered, which was originally presented in [4]. This framework has features that make it suitable for processing streaming data, as mentioned above. The assumptions on which this dedicated and proposed framework is founded are as follows:

- The process of classifier learning is based on data chunks, which are formed from incoming instances. These data chunks are also updated over time and when new instances are input. The size of the data chunk is limited by the settings of the input parameters of the system.
- The classification problem considered here is based on the decomposition of a multi-class classification problem into a set of subproblems involving one-class classification. The final decision output is produced using a weighted ensemble classification model.
- The problem of imbalanced class distribution is eliminated through the use of over-sampling (i.e. synthetic instance generation) and under-sampling (i.e. instance selection) techniques. These techniques are applied to create the data chunks that are used in the next step to create an ensemble of classifiers.
- The system implemented based on this framework can be adapted to work with concept drift.

The approach summarised above, called Weighted Ensemble with one-class Classification and Over-sampling and Instance selection (WECOI), is based on ensemble learning. However, this paper extends the original approach and focuses on providing more diversity to the ensemble and improving the quality of the WECOI system. The research question addressed in this paper concerns the possibility of increasing the performance of the WECOI system by introducing a rotation-based technique to the stage in which the ensemble classifier is formed.

The remainder of this paper is organised as follows. In Sect. 2, a review of selected schemes in the literature is presented, and the motivation for this work is discussed.

A general framework for the WECOI approach is presented in Sect. 3. In Sect. 4, the rotation-based technique is introduced as an extension of WECOI. The results of computational experiments are presented and discussed in Sect. 5. Some conclusions and future directions for research are given in the final section.

2 Related Work and Motivation

The problem of streaming machine learning is very current one in the literature. A broad discussion of the more important aspects of streaming data processing is given in [6]; the paper also discusses current research opportunities, different courses of action and phenomena that are important with respect to the processing of data streams, and ways of improving the performance of this learning method. The aspects described in this paper include feature transformation (summarisation sketches, feature scaling, feature discretisation), dimensionality reduction, feature selection, ensemble learning, imbalanced learning, detection of concept drift, feature evolution, concept evolution, and the evolution of data sources. A fundamental discussion of the problem of streaming machine learning is presented.

The authors of [1] discussed the different types of streaming data with respect to concept drift. Different forms of concept drift were reviewed, and the speed of drift was discussed. Although the main research thread followed in this work was the generation of synthetic data in order to eliminate the phenomenon of class imbalance, these authors' research results clearly also show that learning from streaming data can be effective when ensemble learning is applied. Several different approaches for streaming machine learning were compared, and the one conclusion was that learning based on ensemble methods can help in eliminating the negative impacts of imbalanced classes in a data stream.

In general, it has been experimentally shown that better results from the machine learning process, as well as better classification performance, can be achieved by using multiple classification methods. The combination of multiple different sampling algorithms and types of classifiers results in a competitive heterogeneous ensemble classifier. When the learning process is merged with the perturbation of instances and classifiers, this provides more diversity to the final ensemble-based classifier. It has also been shown that the effects of increasing the quality of learning based on an ensemble approach can be especially crucial when the data are imbalanced with respect to the class distribution. A review and an extensive study of the different approaches to imbalanced data classification were included in [7], and different heterogeneous and multi-balancing ensemble architectures were discussed. The paper also considered a weighted selection of classification methods in which various classifier distributions were taken into account.

A weighted ensemble learning approach was proposed in [8] with the aim of balancing diversity and accuracy in ensemble learning. This approach was based on the use of the particle swarm optimisation (PSO) algorithm, with the aim of manipulating the datasets and input features and obtaining a set of individual learners with appropriate diversity. In an earlier paper, the authors of [9] considered the comparable problem of balancing accuracy and diversity in ensemble learning using an artificial bee colony approach.

A heuristic dataset modification to obtain a diverse classifier ensemble was considered in [10]. Through computational experiments using different strategies, including those based on artificially generated training samples, it was shown that it was possible to significantly increase the generalisation performance of the classification models.

A summary of different types of ensemble approaches for data stream classification was also presented in [11]. The authors underlined that although many important research results have been reported in the field of streaming machine learning, and approaches based on ensemble learning are promising and can eliminate most of the problems of streaming machine learning, there are still a number of open research problems and challenges for learning ensembles from data streams. Finally, potential directions for future research in this domain were formulated.

The present research work was undertaken in answer to new questions related to learning from data streams and with the aim of increasing the performance of WECOI through the diversification of ensemble classifiers, which represented some of the research challenges identified in [11]. Thus, the main motivation of the work was to increase the performance of WECOI by diversifying the ensemble classifiers and introducing a rotation technique at the learning stage.

3 The WECOI Approach to Learning from Imbalanced Data

The implementation, background and some initial evaluation results were discussed earlier in [4]. As mentioned above, WECOI is based on several assumptions, and involves the three components of data summarisation, learning, and classification.

In WECOI, data processing is carried out in the form of data chunks. These data chunks are formed from incoming instances, and are created independently for each decision class. The data summarisation step is responsible for forming the data chunks extracted from the classification component. This component is also responsible for continuous updating of the data chunks by selecting suitable instances (called prototypes) from the incoming data, memorising them and forgetting/removing other (non-informative) instances from current data chunks. It also generates synthetic instances when necessary.

The updating of each data chunk means that new instances covered by this new data chunk are directed to the learning component, which is responsible for creating a new base classifier for this data chunk. The learning process is carried out independently for each decision class of the problem.

In general, it is assumed that the size of the data chunks is limited, and is determined by a predefined threshold. When the number of instances in a data chunk is equal to this predefined threshold, all new incoming instances trigger a process of updating the data chunk, which is carried out by the data reduction module. From an algorithmic point of view, the data reduction process is applied to the instances from both the current data chunk and the new incoming instances. The aim of the data reduction step is to eliminate from the set of instances those that do not meet the reduction criterion [12]. A further aim is to obtain an acceptable level of data compression, which results in a target data chunk with a size equal to the defined threshold. In general, this process may result in the data chunk being updated by removing some old instances and adding to them the new incoming data. It is also possible that this process will not change the composition of the data chunk, if these new instances do not meet the quality criteria. In this step, various strategies for data reduction can be applied; for example, in [4], the condensed nearest neighbour (CNN) and edited nearest neighbour (ENN) algorithms were implemented[1].

When the size of the data chunk is smaller than the predefined threshold, all new instances corresponding to the decision class of the data chunk are allocated to it. However, one existing problem relates to completing a data chunk when the other data chunks are already complete. Without completing the data chunk, a situation arises where the learning process could proceed without finding a balance between the instances belonging to the considered classes, which is a feature of class imbalanced data. To obtain a more balanced distribution between the minority and majority instances, an oversampling procedure is applied, with the aim of generating a synthetic instances within the set of the instances belonging to the minority class. Various approaches to the oversampling procedure can be applied, including the well-known SMOTE algorithm and its different versions, including those dedicated to working with imbalanced data streams (see, for example, [1] and [7]). A new approach dedicated to the generation of synthetic instances for a chunk-based ensemble was presented in [4].

To sum up, the updating of each data chunk means that each newly formed data chunk is directed to the learning component, which carries out the process of induction of a new base classifier for such a new data chunk. The learning process is carried out independently for each decision class considered.

Data chunks represent collections of instances belonging to the different decision classes of the problem. Later data chunks are processed, merged, reduced and so on, to each decision class with the aim of inducing the base classifiers responsible for solving the given one-class classification problem. This process also aims to prepare suitable sets of instances, where one consists of positive instances and the other negative. The process is based on data reduction, and is applied to the negative instances with aim of compressing this subset to a level equal to that of the set of positive instances.

The learning component carries out continuous updating of a set of base classifiers. This also means that a base classifier is induced from each data chunk and that induction is carried out independently for each considered decision class. This approach was developed as a result of considering the single multi-class classification problem as a set of one-class classification problems. In other words, a multi-class classification problem is solved using an ensemble of single one-class classifiers, one for each target class. This also means that a pool of simple base classifiers is induced.

WECOI is also based on an ensemble of classifiers, consisting of base classifiers for the current step and base classifiers representing τ earlier steps, with respect to data chunks that no longer exist in the system and which have been forgotten. This also means that the ensemble consists of a fixed-size set of classifiers, depending on the value of τ, where τ is a WECOI parameter set by the user. The set of classifiers in WECOI (as originally described in [4]) can be denoted by the matrix Φ, consisting of $d \times \tau$ elements.

[1] In [4], it was shown that the use of ENN was superior to CNN, which held true for all of the datasets considered.

We have d one-class classifiers, one for each target class, which can be denoted as:

$$\Phi = \begin{bmatrix} \varphi_{t-\tau}^1 & \cdots & \varphi_{t-1}^1 & \varphi_t^1 \\ \vdots & \ddots & \vdots & \vdots \\ \varphi_{t-\tau}^d & \cdots & \varphi_{t-1}^d & \varphi_t^d \end{bmatrix}, \tag{1}$$

where t is the current step and the classifiers $\varphi_t^l (l = 1, \ldots, d)$ are induced from the set of positive instances included in the arriving data chunks.

The ensemble given above is updated each time a new data chunk arrives. Equation 1 clearly shows that classifiers induced earlier are forgotten, and only τ base classifiers are considered when forming a prediction result for new, incoming instances, which is done by the classification component.

The prediction result produced by the ensemble classifier is determined through a weighted majority vote, which can be expressed as:

$$\Phi(x) = \underset{l}{\operatorname{argmax}} \sum\nolimits_{i=1}^{\tau} \sum\nolimits_{l}^{d} w\left(\varphi_i^l\right)\left(\varphi_i^l(x) = c_l\right). \tag{2}$$

Here, $w(\varphi_i^l)$ are the weights assigned to each base classifier, which are calculated [13] as follows:

$$w\left(\varphi_i^l\right) = \frac{\Lambda(\varphi_i^l)}{\sqrt{z}}, \tag{3}$$

where $\Lambda(\varphi_i^l)$ are the values for the frequency of correct class predictions by the classifiers φ_i^l, and z ($z < \tau$) defines the number of iterations for which each φ_i^l stayed in the ensemble. The value of a classifier's weight increases if the classifier has been taking the correct decisions.

4 Rotation-Based Technique for WECOI

The aims of this paper are to extend WECOI and to improve the quality of its performance by introducing a rotation-based technique. This technique belongs to a family of methods for increasing the diversification of the ensemble. A rotation-based technique provides the possibility of combining several machine learning techniques into one prediction model [14, 15].

The main idea of a rotation-based ensemble is to transform a original dataset into a new feature space through feature extraction. In the first step, the original data are split into subsets, the number of which is defined as a parameter of the approach (referred to here as a rotation level). Splitting is carried out in a feature dimension. In the second stage, feature extraction is carried out to generate the various individual classifiers. The dataset is divided in to two subsets using a bootstrap method, where the larger one includes 75% of the instances from the original dataset. Classifiers are induced based on this larger subset, and the smaller one is used as a test set.

In the original description of the method, a rotation-based ensemble applied principal component analysis (PCA) for feature extraction. However, there are other approaches to feature extraction that can be applied to rotation-based ensembles, including maximum noise fraction (MNF), independent component analysis (ICA), and local Fisher discriminant analysis (LFDA) (see, for example, [16]).

This paper reports results obtained from using PCA and ICA. However, it should be noted that rotation is applied to data chunks that are adequately prepared for the induction of base classifiers and are well class-balanced.

Finally, an ensemble of classifiers, in which each base classifier is constructed using different training parameters (a set of instances diversified in a feature space), can be obtained. The procedure used for data processing within the data summarisation component for the current learning step is presented in Algorithm 1.

Algorithm 1. Rotation-based technique for WECOI

Input: $D_1, \ldots, D_d$ - data chunks with features described by a feature set A, where d, is a number of decision classes, and k is the value of the rotation level;
Output: φ_j^l- set of the base classifiers, where l=1,...,d and j=1,...,k;

Begin
For l=1 **to** d **do**
Let $D'_l = D - D_l$
Apply data reduction to D'_l and obtain the reduced set of instances D'_l
Let $T_l = D_l \cup D'_l$
Randomly partition the feature set A into k subsets to obtain subsets $T_l^1, \ldots, T_l^k$ of instances, each with identical numbers of features. These are smaller than the number of features in the original dataset, and are described by the feature sets $A_l^1, \ldots, A_l^k$.
For j=1 **to** k **do**
Generate the training set $T_l^{j'}$ through bootstrapping based on 75% of the original dataset, and create the testing set $T_l^{j''}$ from the remaining examples in the original set;
Apply **PCA** or **ICA** to the transformed $T_l^{j'}$ to produce new training datasets $rT_l^{j'}$, with features $A_l^{j'}$, using axis rotation;
Induce a base classifier φ_j^l based on $rT_l^{j'}$ and using a test set $T_l^{j''}$ described by a set $A_l^{j'}$.
End for
End for
Return φ_j^l, where l=1,...,d and j=1,...,k;
End

Algorithm 1 shows how the base classifiers φ_j^l are produced. However, WECOI is based on a pool of base classifiers, which are induced in the current step and in earlier steps, remembered over τ iterations. Thus, the final prediction result is produced based on the following expression (see also Eq. 3):

$$\Phi(x) = \underset{l}{\operatorname{argmax}} \sum\nolimits_{i=1}^{\tau} \sum\nolimits_{l}^{d} \sum\nolimits_{j}^{k} w\left(\varphi_{ij}^{l}\right)\left(\varphi_{ij}^{l}(x) = c_l\right). \quad (4)$$

5 Results of Computational Experiments

To validate the proposed approach, an computational experiment was carried out. The main goal was to answer the following question: can the rotation technique increase the performance of the WECOI approach, on average?

To assess the results reported in this section, the following versions of WECOI and other algorithms are compared:

- OLP (Online Learning based on Prototypes): This is the first version of the framework discussed in this paper. It is based on a simple ensemble model in which ensembles are updated by removing the oldest classifier; however, it is devoid of mechanisms for the decomposition of a multi-class classification problem into a set of subproblems involving one-class classification [17];
- WECU (Weighted Ensemble with one-class Classification and data chunk Updating): This is an earlier version of the framework discussed here, which is based on the use of an under-sampling procedure alone to form the data chunks [17];
- WECOI: This is earlier version of the proposed framework, based on a weighted ensemble with one-class classification, over-sampling and instance selection. An ENN-based instance selection approach was used in the under-sampling procedure [4];
- WECOI': This is an earlier version of the framework discussed here, which is based on an extended procedure for synthetic instance generation using a similarity-based approach for clustering and the ENN algorithm for under-sampling [18];
- WECOI$^{(1)}$: This an extended version of the WECOI'-based framework in which PCA is used for feature space rotation at the ensemble classifier formation stage (an approach proposed in this paper);
- WECOI$^{(2)}$: This is a WECOI'-based framework that was extended by using the ICA for feature space rotation at the ensemble classifier formation stage (an approach proposed in this paper);
- OUOB (over-sampling and under-sampling online bagging) [21];
- OB (online bagging) [20],
- The Learn + +.NIE algorithm[2] [22],
- AWE (accuracy weighted ensemble) [23],
- HOT (Hoeffding option tree) [19];
- iOVFDT (incrementally optimised very fast decision tree [19]).

In all versions of WECOI, a POSC4.5 algorithm was applied to generate the base classifiers. In the case of OLP, the C4.5 algorithm was applied to induce all the base models for the ensemble classifiers. All versions of WECOI were run with the number of nearest reference vectors (a parameter for synthetic instance generation) set to two, and the number of neighbours for ENN was set to three. The number of base classifiers and the rotation level were set to five. These values were set arbitrarily, using a trial and error procedure.

The computational experiment was performed using synthetic and real datasets. The data benchmarks containing real data streams are referred to as Electricity (45,312

[2] For OUOB, OB and Learn + +.NIE, the Hoeffding tree was used for the base classifiers, and the base classifier pool was set to 10.

instances, eight features, two classes); Airlines (539,383 instances, seven features, two classes); Ozone (2,534 instances, 72 attributes, two classes); and Gas sensor array (13,910 instances, 128 features, six classes). All of these datasets were taken from the UCI Machine Learning Repository and the IDA repositories. For the synthetic data, the MOA framework was used [19], and the following generators were applied: SEA (10% noise, sudden concept drift and no class balancing); HYPERPLANE (standard MOA parameters, rotation of the decision boundary, and the incremental concept drift set to 0.01); and AGRAWAL (sudden concept drift, and no class balancing). In the synthetic dataset, the number of instances was set to 10,000,000, with two decision classes, and the number of attributes was set to 10, with all attributes subject to drift. The threshold that defined the size of the data chunks for the synthetic data, electricity, airlines and gas sensor array sets was set to 1,000 instances, whereas for the ozone dataset it was set to 250.

The performance of the algorithms was compared with respect to the classification accuracy, and the results are shown in Table 1 as average values. The performance was evaluated using the test-then-train procedure. Average values were calculated after 30 repetitions on each data benchmark.

The results in Table 1 show that no one algorithm was the best for all of the benchmark datasets; however, it can be concluded that introducing more diversification between the base classifiers in the ensemble can yield promising results. In general, introducing the rotation technique to achieve this diversification resulted in an increase in the performance of WECOI. This conclusion was drawn from an analysis of the results obtained from different versions of the WECOI, including the versions denoted as WECOI$^{(1)}$ or WECOI$^{(2)}$. It should be also noted that PCA resulted in better accuracy.

It can be inferred that WECOI is competitive with the other algorithms in the literature that are suitable for use in learning from an imbalanced data stream.

Table 1. Average accuracy (in %)

ALGORITHM	ELECTRICITY	AIRLINES	OZONE	GAS	HYPERPLANE	AGRAWAL	SEA
OLP	70,52	60,58	78,92	80,08	75,48	82,5	80,67
WECU	75,31	65,42	80,56	82,61	83,46	88,67	83,22
WECOI	76,5	64,82	81,56	84,62	85,78	91,68	88,45
WECOI'	76,7	63,48	82,21	84,7	85,91	92,71	88,79
WECOI$^{(1)}$	*77,31*	*64,72*	***82,62***	*83,84*	***86,49***	92,54	*87,42*
WECOI$^{(2)}$	*76,54*	*63,43*	*82,46*	*83,15*	*85,78*	92,05	*86,9*
OUOB	75,42	65,42	82,31	83,42	72,27	92,48	86,69
OB	77,66	63,21	76,56	82	84,7	81,67	83,74

(continued)

Table 1. *(continued)*

ALGORITHM	ELECTRICITY	AIRLINES	OZONE	GAS	HYPERPLANE	AGRAWAL	SEA
LEARN++ NIE	70,7	66,8	82,1	83,5	84,51	92,42	89,3
AWE	71,06	63,4	66,54	82,42	70,15	80,2	77,81
HOT	74,02	62,34	81,03	82,6	80,07	94,99	88,03
IOVFDT	72,52	63,52	81,25	83,54	81,56	93,67	83,02

* The results presented on a gray background refer to the algorithms discussed in this paper

6 Conclusions

The main contribution of this paper is the presentation of a competitive approach to learning from imbalanced data streams. To address this problem, an approach was developed based on the processing of data chunks formed from incoming instances using over- and under-sampling. These procedures proved to be beneficial for the processing of imbalanced data. The proposed approach was also based on the assumption that the general problem could be solved by processing a set of independent one-class classification problems. The approach presented here can help in the recognition of concept drift, which is a challenge that arises when learning from data streams. The final output is calculated based on an ensemble approach, which in this study was extended by increasing the diversification between base classifiers by introducing a rotation in feature space in the data. This rotation offers benefits in terms of classification accuracy, as can be seen from a comparison of different alternative approaches to learning from data streams and earlier versions of the algorithm presented here.

The approach discussed here, called WECOI, needs to be further evaluated, particularly in terms of the influence of different parameters on its performance, including the rotation level. Important questions are also related to the impact of different rotation techniques on the performance of WECOI, and may provide directions for future research.

References

1. Bernardo, A., Valle, E.D.: An extensive study of C-SMOTE, a continuous synthetic minority oversampling technique for evolving data streams. Expert Syst. Appl. **196**, 116630 (2022). https://doi.org/10.1016/j.eswa.2022.116630
2. Khamassi, I., Sayed Mouchaweh, M., Hammami, M., Ghédira, K.: Discussion and review on evolving data streams and concept drift adapting. Evol. Syst. **9**(1), 1–23 (2018)
3. Shreya, S., Bernease, H., Aditya, G.P.: Rethinking streaming machine learning evaluation. arXiv (2022). https://doi.org/10.48550/arxiv.2205.11473
4. Czarnowski, I.: Weighted ensemble with one-class classification and over-sampling and instance selection (WECOI): an approach for learning from imbalanced data streams. J. Comput. Sci. **61**(1), 101614 (2022). https://doi.org/10.1016/j.jocs.2022.101614
5. Benczúr, A.A., Kocsis, L., Pálovics, R.: Online machine learning in big data streams. arXiv (2018). https://doi.org/10.48550/ARXIV.1802.05872

6. Gomes, H.M., Read, J., Bifet, A., Barddal, J.P., Gama, J.: Machine learning for streaming data: state of the art, challenges, and opportunities. ACM SIGKDD Explor. Newsl. **21**(2), 6–22 (2019). https://doi.org/10.1145/3373464.3373470
7. Ghaderi-Zefrehi, H., Altınçay, H.: Imbalance learning using heterogeneous ensembles. Expert Syst. Appl. **142**, 113005 (2020). https://doi.org/10.1016/j.eswa.2019.113005
8. You, G.-R., Shiue, Y.-R., Yeh, W.-Ch., Chen, X.-L., Chen, Ch.-M.: A weighted ensemble learning algorithm based on diversity using a novel particle swarm optimization approach. Algorithms **13**(10) 255 (2020). https://doi.org/10.3390/a13100255
9. Shiue, Y.-R., You, G.-R., Su, Ch..-T., Chen, H.: Balancing accuracy and diversity in ensemble learning using a two-phase artificial bee colony approach. Appl. Soft Comput. **105**, 107212 (2021). https://doi.org/10.1016/j.asoc.2021.107212
10. Jamalinia, H., Khalouei, S., Rezaie, V., Nejatian, S., Bagheri-Fard, K., Parvin, H.: Diverse classifier ensemble creation based on heuristic dataset modification. J. Appl. Stat. **45**(7), 1209–1226 (2018). https://doi.org/10.1080/02664763.2017.1363163
11. Krawczyk, B., Minku, L.L., Gama, J., Stefanowski, J., Woźniak, M.: Ensemble learning for data stream analysis: a survey. Inf. Fusion **37**, 132–156 (2017). https://doi.org/10.1016/j.inffus.2017.02.004
12. Czarnowski, I., Jędrzejowicz, P.: An approach to data reduction for learning from big datasets: integrating stacking, rotation, and agent population learning techniques. Complexity **7404627**, 1076–2787 (2018)
13. Wozniak, M., Cal, P., Cyganek, B.: The influence of a classifiers' diversity on the quality of weighted again ensemble. In: Nguyen, N.T., Attachoo, B., Trawinski, B., Somboonviwat, K. (eds.) ACIIDS 2014. LNAI, vol. 8398, pp. 90–99. Springer, Heidelberg (2014). https://doi.org/10.1007/978-3-319-05458-2_10
14. Adachi, K.: Rotation techniques. In: Adachi, K. (ed.) Matrix-Based Introduction to Multivariate Data Analysis, pp. 193–205. Springer, Singapore (2020). https://doi.org/10.1007/978-981-15-4103-2_13
15. Rodríguez, J.J., Alonso, C.J.: Rotation-based ensembles. In: Conejo, R., Urretavizcaya, M., Pérez-de-la-Cruz, J.-L. (eds.) CAEPIA/TTIA -2003. LNCS (LNAI), vol. 3040, pp. 498–506. Springer, Heidelberg (2004). https://doi.org/10.1007/978-3-540-25945-9_49
16. Xia, J.: Multiple classifier systems for the classification of hyperspectral data. Ph.D. thesis, University de Grenoble (2014)
17. Czarnowski, I., Jedrzejowicz, P.: Ensemble online classifier based on the one-class base classifiers for mining data streams. Cybern. Syst. **46**(1–2), 51–68 (2015). https://doi.org/10.1080/01969722.2015.1007736
18. Czarnowski, I., Martins, D.M.L.: Impact of clustering on a synthetic instance generation in imbalanced data streams classification. In: Groen, D., de Mulatier, C., Paszynski, M., Krzhizhanovskaya, V.V., Dongarra, J.J., Sloot, P.M.A. (eds.) ICCS 2022. LNCS, vol. 13351, pp. 586–597. Springer, Cham (2022). https://doi.org/10.1007/978-3-031-08754-7_63
19. Bifet, A., Holmes, G., Kirkby, R., Pfahringer, B.: MOA: massive online analysis. J. Mach. Learn. Res. **11**, 1601–1604 (2010)
20. Oza, N.C.: Online bagging and boosting. In: Proceedings of the 2005 IEEE International Conference on Systems, Man and Cybernetics, Waikoloa, HI, USA, 10–12 October 2005, vol. 2343, pp. 2340–2345 (2005)
21. Wang, S., Minku, L.L., Yao, X.: Dealing with multiple classes in online class imbalance learning. In: Proceedings of the 25th International Joint Conference on Artificial Intelligence (IJCAI 2016) (2016)

22. Ditzler, G., Polikar, R.: Incremental learning of concept drift from streaming imbalanced data. IEEE Trans. Knowl. Data Eng. **25**(10), 2283–2301 (2013). https://doi.org/10.1109/TKDE.2012.136
23. Wang, H., Fan, W., Yu, P.S., Han, J.: Mining concept-drifting data streams using ensemble classifiers. In: Proceedings of 9th ACM SIGKDD International Conference on Knowledge Discovery and Data Mining, pp. 226–235 (2003). https://doi.org/10.1145/956750.956778

DE-Forest – Optimized Decision Tree Ensemble

Joanna Grzyb(✉) and Michał Woźniak

Wrocław University of Science and Technology, Wrocław, Poland
{joanna.grzyb,michal.wozniak}@pwr.edu.pl

Abstract. Classifier ensembles are still in the spotlight due to their proven applications for many practical problems. One of the most interesting approaches is methods proposing the construction of such models based on learned classifiers using randomly selected attributes. Among the essential algorithms in this area is *Random Forest*, which uses decision trees as base classifiers. Although these methods obtain outstanding quality for many tasks, the random selection of attributes for individual base classifiers used above does not guarantee the optimal ensemble selection. In this paper, we proposed *DE-Forest* - an ensemble classifier learning method using evolutionary techniques to select non-random and optimized subsets. *Differential Evolution* was chosen as the optimization algorithm, selecting the best set of attributes to learn the individual base classifiers. The quality of the proposed method has been evaluated based on computer experiments performed on many benchmark datasets. The obtained results are promising and show the superiority of the proposed method over the benchmark solutions.

Keywords: Random Forest · classifier ensemble · classification · optimization

1 Introduction and Related Works

Classifier ensembles are one of the most promising directions in data classification [27]. The critical problem is to ensure an adequate diversity level of the base classifiers included in the ensemble. One of the most popular approaches is manipulating the base classifiers' input, i.e., vertical or horizontal partitioning. While horizontal partitioning does not yield good results, attribute selection is one of the most promising techniques [14]. Thus, this paper focuses on the learning base classifier algorithm based on selected features.

The most popular approach is random attribute selection proposed in *Random Subspace* [9] and further developed for *Random Forest* (RF) [3], where base classifiers were *Decision Trees* (DT). Additionally, they are trained on bootstrapped samples to boost the diversity of the individual predictors. The selection of classifiers for a pool, i.e., the attribute selection for each model, is random,

This work was supported by the Polish National Science Centre under the grant No. 2019/35/B/ST6/04442.

N. T. Nguyen et al. (Eds.): ICCCI 2023, LNAI 14162, pp. 806–818, 2023.
https://doi.org/10.1007/978-3-031-41456-5_61

which may lead to a poor-quality ensemble in a worst-case scenario. The random nature of the described approaches may also affect their stability.

Researchers have tried to improve the stability of the method [18] or by proposing methods based on a deterministic allocation of features to base classifiers [13]. It is also worth mentioning that the feature selection process for classifier ensemble has been considered, for example, by Canuto et al. [5] put *ReinSel* algorithm forward, that uses reinforcement learning for feature selection in the ensemble forming process. On the other hand, Nag and Pal [20] developed an algorithm for simultaneous feature selection and designing diverse classifiers using multi-objective genetic programming. Elyan and Gaber [8] proposed to use a *Genetic Algorithm* to set the best RF parameters and class decomposition. Similarly, Kaur et al. [12] focus on setting RF parameters for classification in medical applications.

Hence, it seems an attractive approach to propose a feature selection for each base classifier in the optimization process. It guarantees a qualitatively better choice than the random search, e.g., by *Random Forest.*

An important factor is the choice of the suitable optimization algorithm, and the selection is vast, from evolutionary algorithms to metaheuristics. Each algorithm has many modifications and improvements, and each has advantages and disadvantages for specific problems [28]. In our work, we use the *Differential Evolution* (DE) algorithm [26]. DE works on the differences between individuals from the population. It is a single-criterion algorithm that combines the advantages of local search and genetic algorithms. It uses classical crossover operators and search mechanisms typical for topological spaces. DE searches the continuous space. Hence the solution obtained from this algorithm is real numbers. DE is looking for new solutions close to the best in earlier iterations. However, it does not use a predefined scheme or distribution.

The main contributions of the work are:

- Proposition of the ensemble method based on optimized *Decision Trees* using the *Differential Evolution* algorithm to select a diverse subset of attributes intentionally.
- Analysis of the hyperparameter set of the proposed method obtained with *Sequential Model Algorithm Configuration* (SMAC).
- An extensive experimental study on a set of benchmark datasets evaluates the quality of *DE-Forest* compared to *Decision Tree* and the original implementation of *Random Forest* algorithm.

2 Proposition of *DE-Forest* Algorithm

The proposed method *DE-Forest* is the ensemble consisting of optimized *Decision Tree* classifiers using *Differential Evolution.* DE selects the best set of *Decision Trees* that uses chosen attributes. As the fitness function, any performance metric could be used, e.g., BAC, *Gmean*, or AUC. The choice of the metric is one of the *DE-Forest* parameters. The $f \times n$ dimensional vector PS represents a feature selection. f is the number of attributes and n stands for ensemble size.

Thus, the $PS[k]$ describes if the $\left(\lceil\frac{k}{f}\rceil\right)$th *Decision Tree* uses the $\left(k - \lfloor\frac{k}{f}\rfloor f\right)$th attribute.

The proposed algorithm can also employ data set bootstrapping to increase the diversity of the returned decision trees as well as classifier ensemble pruning techniques. The use of them is also *DE-Forest* parameter.

Figure 1 and Algorithm 1 present the *DE-Forest.* Let us shortly describe the main step of the proposed method. The ensemble uses base classifiers returned from the optimization process using the learning set $\mathcal{LS}$.

$$\mathcal{LS} = \{(x_1, i_1), (x_2, i_2), \ldots, (x_N, i_N)\} \tag{1}$$

If bootstrapping is disabled (step 2.), then there is additional *Repeated Stratified K-Fold (5 repeats x 2 splits) cross-validation* within the DE optimization. It ensures that the input data is split into training and test data to evaluate the classifiers properly. In contrast, cross-validation is no longer necessary with bootstrapping enabled (step 6.) because there are B subsets from the dataset randomly selected with replacement (step 7.).

Then, optimization using the DE algorithm is used (step 11). Each population in DE consists of $f \times n$ values. The algorithm searches for the population by crossover and evaluates it through the fitness function. Optimization runs until the maximum number of populations is reached and returns a solution (PS - a vector list). Because DE returns solutions represented by real numbers as shown in Fig. 2, we have to binarize them using simple thresholding (step 14.). In the step 12., j is a consecutive vectors, and in the step 13., m is a consecutive bit in the vector. The thresholding process changes values in the vector in such a way: if the value is greater than 0.5 for a given feature - it is selected, otherwise, the feature is not selected. After this process, a vector consisting of *True* and *False* values is partitioned into subspaces for each model in the ensemble. A single model is trained on the feature subspace (step 16.) and added to the ensemble (step 17.). An additional option is model pruning (step 20.). The BAC metric is calculated for each model and then added to the list M (step 21.), which is sorted descending–MS (step 22.). The p parameter determines the percentage of models removed from the ensemble from the end of the MS list. The output of the method is the ensemble classifier (step 23.).

To analyze the computational complexity of the proposed method, let us first introduce the complexity of the CART *Decision Tree* - $O(fN \times log_2 N)$, where f is the number of attributes, and N is the number of samples [24]. Thus, the computational complexity of training n decision trees is $O(nfN \times log_2 N)$. Additionally, since the computational complexity of *Differential Evolution* is $O(PDG_{max})$, where P–the population size, D–the dimension of the searched space, and G_{max} is the fixed number of generations [6]. Then, the overall computational complexity of the *DE-Forest* is $O(nfN \times log_2 N + PDG_{max})$.

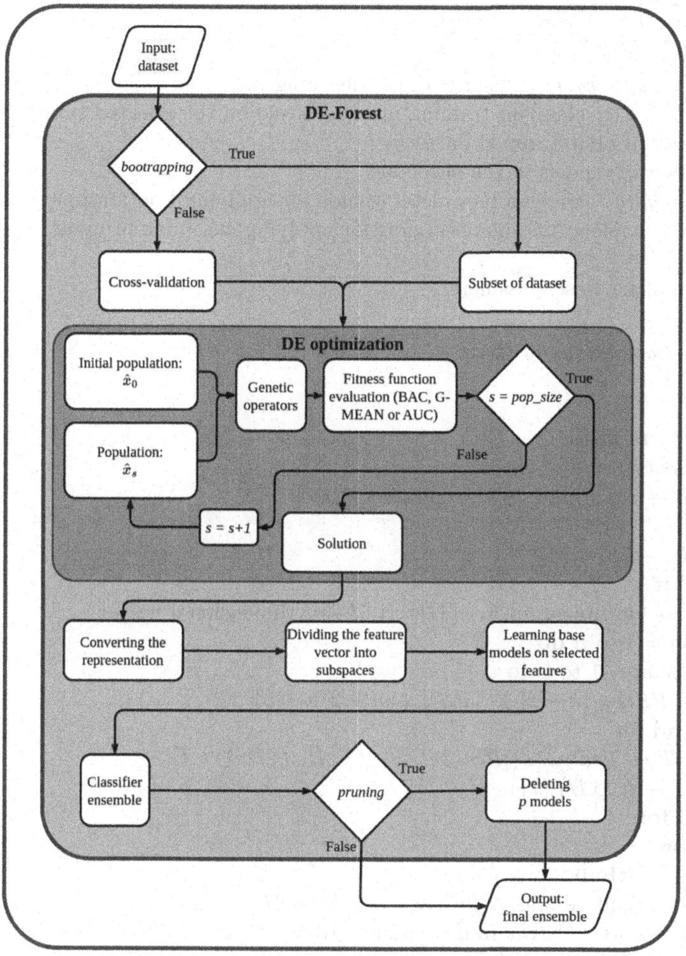

Fig. 1. The *DE-Forest* method diagram.

3 Experimental Evaluation

We performed a series of computer experiments to verify the quality of the proposed method. In the course of them, we intended to answer the following research questions:

RQ1: *What is the impact of hyperparameters on the proposed method and classification quality?*

RQ2: *How do various optimization criteria affect the DE-Forest method performance?*

RQ3: *Can the proposed algorithm outperform state-of-the-art methods?*

Algorithm 1. *DE-Forest* method

Require:

$\mathcal{LS} = \{(x_1, i_1), (x_2, i_2), \ldots, (x_N, i_N)\}$ – learning set
$TrainDT()$ – DT classifier training method based on the selected subset of features
k - number of bootstrapped datasets
n – number of models in the ensemble
Bootstrapping – boolean parameter stands for applying bootstrapping
Pruning – boolean parameter stands for applying ensemble pruning

Ensure:

Π – pool of DT base classifiers

$\Pi \leftarrow \emptyset$
if not *Bootstrapping* **then**
  $k \leftarrow 1$
end if
for $i = 1$ to k **do**
  if *Bootstrapping* **then**
    $S_i \leftarrow$ resampling with replacement from $\mathcal{LS}$
  else
    $S_i \leftarrow \mathcal{LS}$
  end if
  $PS \leftarrow$ Optimization(S_i) {}PS is $(f * n)$ dimensional vector
  for $j = 1$ to n **do**
    for $m = 1$ to f **do**
      $PS[j + m - 2] \leftarrow \lceil PS[j + m - 2] - 0.5 \rceil$
    end for
    $DT \leftarrow TrainDT([PS[(j-1) * f + 1], ..., PS[j * f]]$
    $\Pi \leftarrow \Pi \cup DT(\hat{x}_j)$
  end for
end for
if Pruning **then**
  $M \leftarrow$ calculate *metric* for each $DT(\hat{x})$ in Π
  $MS \leftarrow$ sort M array in descending order
  $\Pi \leftarrow \Pi - DT(\hat{x})$ {R}emove $p\%$ models with the worst *metric* based on MS
end if

3.1 Setup

This section provides a thorough overview of all the constituents needed to conduct reliable experiments. Thanks to this description, it is possible to reproduce the research.

Implementation. The implementation of methods and the experimental environment are done using the Python programming language and a few libraries: Pymoo [2], scikit-learn [23], Imbalanced-learn [15], Numpy [22], Matplotlib [10], Pandas [19]. Complete source code, sufficient to repeat the experiments, was

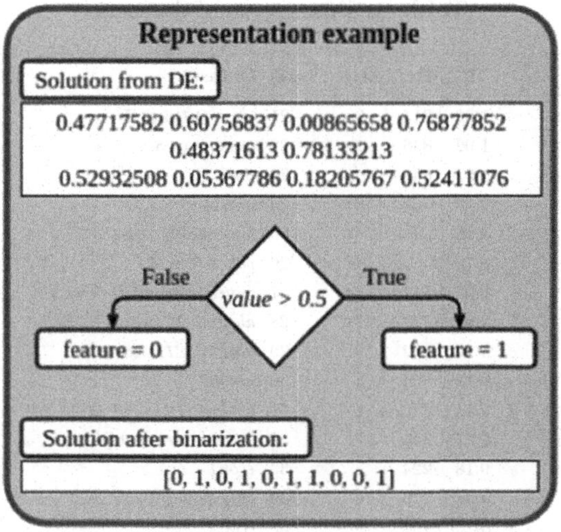

Fig. 2. The representation example.

made available at GitHub repository[1]. Additionally, we provided the complete results of the conducted experiments.

Datasets. All used datasets are obtained from Keel-dataset repository [1], presented in Table 1 sorted by the Imbalance Ratio. Columns in this table are as follows: *ID* - the number of datasets, *Dataset* - the name of the dataset, *IR* - Imbalance Ratio, *Ex.* - the number of instances, *Attr.* - the number of attributes. These are two-class problems. Datasets are used to relate to problems such as diseases, the quality of the wine, types of glass, and much more. The selection of these datasets is dictated by the problem of difficult, imbalanced data. The selected datasets have a wide range of parameters, in particular the *IR*, and are considered as benchmarks for this problem [21].

Methods. The methods, their abbreviations, and the parameters used in the experiments are presented below.

- DT–CART *Decision Tree Classifier* [4]. We used its *scikit-learn* implementation with default parameters such as:
  - *criterion of split–Gini impurity*
  - *maximum number of features–None* indicates no maximum value
- *DE-Forest–Differential Evolution Forest* ensemble with DT as the base classification model (the same default parameters as presented earlier). The experiment 1 set hyperparameters of *DE-Forest*: bootstrapping, metric's name, the number of classifiers, and population size. Another hyperparameter is pruning, but it was not used in the presented experiments.

[1] https://github.com/w4k2/DE-Forest.

Table 1. Description of datasets

ID	Dataset	IR	Ex.	Attr.	ID	Dataset	IR	Ex.	Attr.
1	*glass1*	1.82	214	9	21	*glass-0-1-6_vs_5*	19.44	184	9
2	*vehicle3*	1.92	846	18	22	*yeast-2_vs_8*	23.10	482	8
3	*vehicle1*	1.97	846	18	23	*flare-F*	23.79	1066	11
4	*haberman*	2.78	306	3	24	*yeast4*	28.10	1484	8
5	*yeast3*	8.10	1484	8	25	*winequality-red-4*	29.17	1599	11
6	*page-blocks0*	8.79	5472	10	26	*poker-9_vs_7*	29.50	244	10
7	*yeast-2_vs_4*	9.08	514	8	27	*winequality-white-9_vs_4*	32.60	168	11
8	*ecoli-0-6-7_vs_3-5*	9.09	222	7	28	*abalone-17_vs_7-8-9-10*	39.31	2338	8
9	*glass-0-1-5_vs_2*	9.12	172	9	29	*abalone-21_vs_8*	40.50	581	8
10	*yeast-0-3-5-9_vs_7-8*	9.12	506	8	30	*yeast6*	41.40	1484	8
11	*yeast-0-2-5-6_vs_3-7-8-9*	9.14	1004	8	31	*abalone-19_vs_10-11-12-13*	49.69	1622	8
12	*ecoli-0-1_vs_2-3-5*	9.17	244	7	32	*kr-vs-k-zero_vs_eight*	53.07	1460	6
13	*ecoli-0-2-6-7_vs_3-5*	9.18	224	7	33	*ecoli1*	63.75	336	7
14	*ecoli-0-6-7_vs_5*	10.00	220	6	34	*winequality-red-3_vs_5*	68.10	691	11
15	*glass-0-1-6_vs_2*	10.29	192	9	35	*ecoli2*	70.00	336	7
16	*ecoli-0-1-4-7_vs_2-3-5-6*	10.59	336	7	36	*abalone-20_vs_8-9-10*	72.69	1916	8
17	*glass-0-1-4-6_vs_2*	11.06	205	9	37	*kddcup-buffer_overflow_vs_back*	73.43	2233	41
18	*cleveland-0_vs_4*	12.31	173	13	38	*poker-8_vs_6*	85.88	1477	10
19	*page-blocks-1-3_vs_4*	15.86	472	10	39	*kddcup-rootkit-imap_vs_back*	100.14	2225	41
20	*abalone9-18*	16.40	731	8	40	*abalone19*	129.44	4174	8

- *RandomFS*–*Random Forest* native implementation on the basis of the original paper [3]. This implementation differs from the RF implementation from *scikit-learn*. One of the differences is prediction, *scikit-learn* RF combines classifiers by averaging their probabilistic prediction, but it used majority voting in the original idea. In *RandomFS*, the parameter *max features* is equal to $\sqrt{f}$, where f–the number of features. For each model, features are chosen randomly. DT (with the same default parameters as presented earlier) has been chosen. No bootstrapping has been applied.
- *RandomFS_b*–the method described above (*RandomFS*) with the bootstrapping option set to True.

Optimization. Optimization algorithm *Differential Evolution* (DE) that we used in our method based on Pymoo implementation, with the following parameters:

- *population size* is set during experiment 1
- *sampling* is *Latin Hypercube Sampling (LHS)*
- common *variant* is *DE/rand/1/bin*, where *rand* is selection individuals to be perturbed, *1* is the number of difference vector and *bin* is the crossover type
- *Crossover Constant* is $CR = 0.9$

Data Partitioning. Methods compared during experiments based on stratified datasets using *Repeated Stratified K-Fold (5 repeats x 2 splits) cross-validation* [7].

Metrics. We chose the widely used metrics to evaluate all methods: *Balanced Accuracy* (BAC), *Geometric Mean Score* (*Gmean*), *Recall*, *Specificity* and *Precision*. *Gmean* is based on *Precision* and *Recall* metrics.

Result Analysis. To summarize the results for all datasets, the Wilcoxon statistical rank-sum test at a significance level of 0.05 was chosen [25]. More accurate results for each dataset are shown in the repository linked in Sect. 3.1.

3.2 Results

The section presents the tuning of parameters in the experiment 1, and the experiment 2 comparing the proposed method and reference methods.

Experiment 1–Tuning Hyperparameters Using SMAC. Before proceeding with the main experiments comparing the proposed method and reference methods, it is necessary to select hyperparameters that will make the method obtain the best possible quality. For this purpose, the SMAC3 library version V2.0.0a1 was used [11,17]. This tool uses *Bayesian Optimization* and aggressive racing mechanism to optimize parameters. It can perform optimization in many instances. In the case of the experiment, the instances are five different datasets (*glass0*, *kddcup-rootkit-imap_vs_back*, *kr-vs-k-zero_vs_eight*, *page-blocks-1-3_vs_4*, *winequality-red-8_vs_6-7*). The method hyperparameters selected for optimization are listed in Table 2, which includes the range of each parameter and the value after using the SMAC algorithm. Only one of the values listed in the bootstrap and metric_name hyperparameters are selected. However, ranges are given in the other two hyperparameters, and SMAC independently selects numbers from this range. The number of classifiers in the ensemble is determined by a maximum value of 25 because a larger number of models does not indicate a significant improvement in the algorithm's quality, as noted by Lin et al. in the article [16] after conducting an experiment determining the number of models in the ensemble.

Table 2. Hyperparameters optimization

Hyperparameters	Range	Values
bootstrap	{True, False}	True
metric_name	{BAC, AUC, GM}	BAC
n_classifiers	[5, 25]	15
p_size	[100, 500]	107

Figure 3 shows the dependence of the four examined hyperparameters on the BAC metric in subsequent iterations of the SMAC algorithm. The algorithm searches the solution space in each iteration and selects a value for each parameter. As a result of the SMAC algorithm, those parameter values are selected to obtain the highest BAC metric value. In the case of this experiment, it is the seventh iteration, where $BAC = 0.858$. Comparing the second iteration, where the quality is very similar, the number of classifiers remains at a similar level (13 classifiers), but the remaining hyperparameters have entirely different values. Hence, the appropriate number of classifiers is significant in obtaining a high-quality metric. Other iterations did not improve the metric.

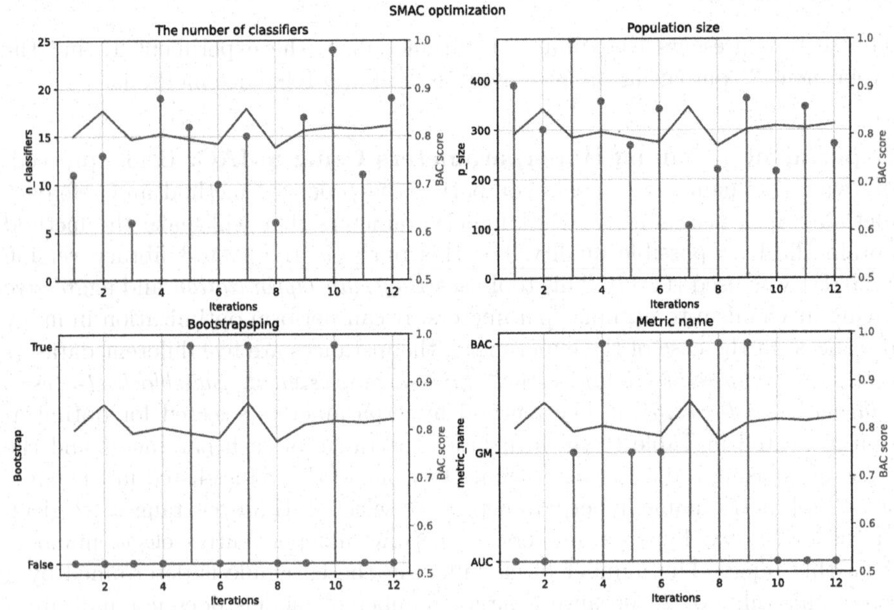

Fig. 3. SMAC optimization analysis.

Experiment 2–Comparative Study. The main experiment aimed to compare the quality of the proposed method in the version with constraints and without, a *Random Forest* classifier (*RandomFS*) with bootstrapping and without, and (DT) learned on all attributes. The exact tabular results can be found in the repository linked in Sect. 3.1. As an illustration, the individual fold scores for each dataset were averaged and presented using the *Wilcoxon rank-sum statistical test.* The proposed method is compared with three state-of-the-art methods whose names are on the left in each small figure. Green in the figure means that the *DE-Forest* method won against the method in a given row, yellow means a tie, and red means a loss. The black dashed vertical line indicates the level of statistical significance. The x-axis represents the number of datasets.

Figure 4 shows the results for the proposed method without any constraints within the DE optimization. After setting the hyperparameters in the previous experiment, the *DE-Forest* method has bootstrapping set to *True*. Comparing it with *RandomFS_b*, the BAC, *Specificity* and *Precision* metrics, the method achieves better results with statistical significance. Compared to the *RandomFS* method without bootstrapping, the proposed method wins for over half of all datasets. *DE-Forest* is better with static significance than the DT method for *Gmean*, *Recall*, and *Specificity* metrics.

On the other hand, high scores for some metrics of DT indicate favor towards the majority class, which is not desirable when classifying imbalanced data. The runtime for all methods based on this experiment is in the repository linked in Sect. 3.1. *DE-Forest* does not achieve the best times because optimization is time-consuming compared to other methods. Nevertheless, the DE algorithm searches for feature subspaces to build models that achieve the best possible results.

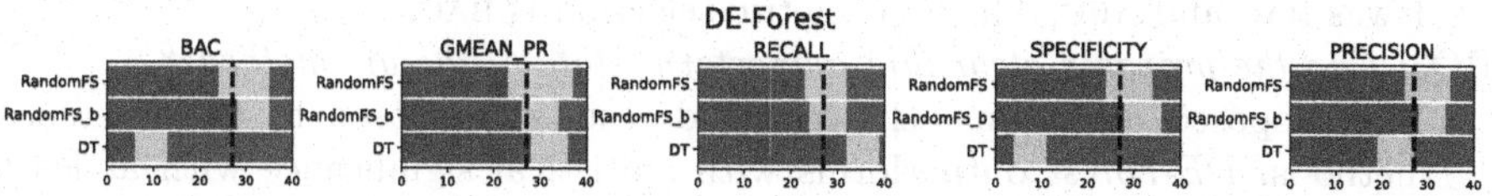

Fig. 4. The Wilcoxon test of *DE-Forest* method with reference methods (green–win, yellow–tie, red–loss).

The second tested case is the *DE-Forest* method having a constraint of the number of features to 50% of the original set of features within the DE optimization. Furthermore, the optimization does not search the entire subspace but is limited to half the features in advance. The advantage of this approach is the reduction of search time by the optimization algorithm, and the entire calculations are faster than *DE-Forest* without constraints. The reference methods and hyperparameters of the *DE-Forest* method are the same as in the previous case. Analyzing the individual metrics in Fig. 5, it can be concluded that the classification quality is not much worse than the unconstrained version of the method. For the *RandomFS* and *RandomFS_b* methods, the number of wins does not fall below 20 datasets for each metric. *DE-Forest* only wins against DT for *Recall* with statistical significance.

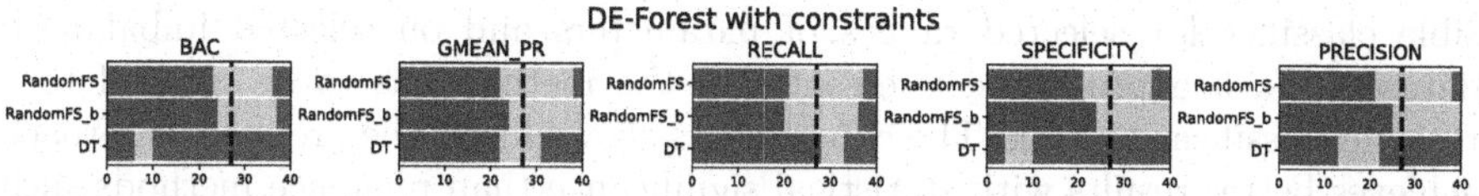

Fig. 5. The Wilcoxon test of *DE-Forest* method with constraints inside the optimization with reference methods (green–win, yellow–tie, red–loss).

3.3 Lesson Learned

Considering the presented results, let us answer the research questions.

RQ1: *What is the impact of hyperparameters on the proposed method and classification quality?*
Bayesian Optimization showed the dependence of hyperparameter values and the impact of settings on the final quality of the model. Depending on the input data, the proposed method may take different parameters. When testing the method on imbalanced data, specific hyperparameters were selected.

RQ2: *How do various optimization criteria affect the DE-Forest method performance?*
DE optimization tested three criteria metrics. Criteria–fitness function was one of the method's hyperparameters. The values were selected during experiment 1. The most common metric with the highest quality in the experiment 1 was BAC and AUC. The final metric selection is BAC.

RQ3: *Can the proposed algorithm outperform state-of-the-art methods?*
The proposed algorithm achieves good results compared to the reference methods. *DE-Forest* outperforms with statistical significance with at least one reference method for each metric. When designing our method, we wanted to obtain a good classification of imbalanced data, primarily a minority class, with which many classifiers do not cope well. The *DE-Forest* method obtains satisfactory results by analyzing the *Recall* metric reflecting the classification of the minority (positive) class.

4 Conclusion

This work proposed a novel classifier ensemble training method *DE-Forest*. Ensemble diversity was ensured by training each ensemble member on different attributes. Unlike algorithms known from the literature, such as *Random Forest*, the selection of the features was not random. Still, it resulted from an optimization algorithm based on *Differential Evolution* approach. Such an approach made it possible to build an ensemble of *Decision Tree* classifiers based on regularly searched subsets of features ensuring an appropriate diversity of the individual models.

A vital element of the experiments was tuning the hyperparameters of the *DE-Forest* using *Bayesian Optimization*, which allowed obtaining the best possible classifier for selected ranges of parameters and on selected imbalanced datasets. Such a procedure is essential if the method has to be applied to a real-life classification task. The experiments showed that the proposed approach achieves better results with statistical significance than reference methods such as *Decision Tree* and the native *Random Forest* implementation. The promising results encourage us to continue working on developing the proposed method. Despite *DE-Forest* receiving good quality classifiers, it should be mentioned that the proposed metadata is characterized by high computational complexity and thus requires significantly more computational resources than reference.

As the directions of further work, we may mention the use of other optimization methods, including multi-objective optimization. It would allow considering during a set of decision trees to learn their classification quality and diversity or the cost of building such trees (e.g., by differentiating possible choices of attributes according to their acquisition cost).

References

1. Alcalá-Fdez, J., et al.: Keel data-mining software tool: data set repository, integration of algorithms and experimental analysis framework. J. Multiple-Valued Logic Soft Comput. **17**, 255–287 (2011)
2. Blank, J., Deb, K.: Pymoo: multi-objective optimization in python. IEEE Access **8**, 89497–89509 (2020)
3. Breiman, L.: Random forests. Mach. Learn. **45**(1), 5–32 (2001)
4. Breiman, L., Friedman, J.H., Olshen, R.A., Stone, C.J.: Classification and regression trees. Routledge (2017)
5. Canuto, A.M., Vale, K.M., Feitos, A., Signoretti, A.: Reinsel: a class-based mechanism for feature selection in ensemble of classifiers. Appl. Soft Comput. **12**(8), 2517–2529 (2012)
6. Das, S., Suganthan, P.N.: Differential evolution: a survey of the state-of-the-art. IEEE Trans. Evol. Comput. **15**(1), 4–31 (2011). https://doi.org/10.1109/TEVC.2010.2059031
7. Demšar, J.: Statistical comparisons of classifiers over multiple data sets. J. Mach. Learn. Res. **7**, 1–30 (2006)
8. Elyan, E., Gaber, M.M.: A genetic algorithm approach to optimising random forests applied to class engineered data. Inf. Sci. **384**, 220–234 (2017)
9. Ho, T.K.: The random subspace method for constructing decision forests. IEEE Trans. Pattern Anal. Mach. Intell. **20**(8), 832–844 (1998). https://doi.org/10.1109/34.709601
10. Hunter, J.D.: Matplotlib: a 2D graphics environment. Comput. Sci. Eng. **9**(3), 90–95 (2007)
11. Hutter, F., Hoos, H.H., Leyton-Brown, K.: Sequential model-based optimization for general algorithm configuration. In: Coello, C.A.C. (ed.) LION 2011. LNCS, vol. 6683, pp. 507–523. Springer, Berlin Heidelberg, Berlin, Heidelberg (2011). https://doi.org/10.1007/978-3-642-25566-3_40
12. Kaur, M., Gianey, H.K., Singh, D., Sabharwal, M.: Multi-objective differential evolution based random forest for e-health applications. Mod. Phys. Lett. B **33**(05), 1950022 (2019). https://doi.org/10.1142/S0217984919500222
13. Koziarski, M., Krawczyk, B., WoźNiak, M.: The deterministic subspace method for constructing classifier ensembles. Pattern Anal. Appl. **20**(4), 981–990 (2017). https://doi.org/10.1007/s10044-017-0655-2
14. Kuncheva, L.I.: Combining Pattern Classifiers: Methods and Algorithms. Wiley, Hoboken (2014)
15. Lemaître, G., Nogueira, F., Aridas, C.K.: Imbalanced-learn: a python toolbox to tackle the curse of imbalanced datasets in machine learning. J. Mach. Learn. Res. **18**(17), 1–5 (2017)
16. Lin, W., Wu, Z., Lin, L., Wen, A., Li, J.: An ensemble random forest algorithm for insurance big data analysis. IEEE Access **5**, 16568–16575 (2017). https://doi.org/10.1109/ACCESS.2017.2738069

17. Smac3: a versatile Bayesian optimization package for hyperparameter optimization. J. Mach. Learn. Res. **23**(54), 1–9 (2022)
18. Liu, Z., Yang, Z., Liu, S., Shi, Y.: Semi-random subspace method for writeprint identification. Neurocomputing **108**, 93–102 (2013)
19. McKinney, W.: Data structures for statistical computing in python. In: van der Walt, S., Millman, J (eds.) Proceedings of the 9th Python in Science Conference, pp. 56–61 (2010)
20. Nag, K., Pal, N.R.: A multiobjective genetic programming-based ensemble for simultaneous feature selection and classification. IEEE Trans. Cybern. **46**(2), 499–510 (2016). https://doi.org/10.1109/TCYB.2015.2404806
21. Napierala, K., Stefanowski, J.: Types of minority class examples and their influence on learning classifiers from imbalanced data. J. Intell. Inf. Syst. **46**, 563–597 (2016)
22. Oliphant, T.E.: A guide to NumPy, vol. 1. Trelgol Publishing USA (2006)
23. Pedregosa, F., et al.: Scikit-learn: machine learning in python. J. Mach. Learn. Res. **12**, 2825–2830 (2011)
24. Sani, H.M., Lei, C., Neagu, D.: Computational complexity analysis of decision tree algorithms. In: Bramer, M., Petridis, M. (eds.) SGAI 2018. LNCS, vol. 11311, pp. 191–197. Springer International Publishing, Cham (2018). https://doi.org/10.1007/978-3-030-04191-5_17
25. Stapor, K., Ksieniewicz, P., García, S., Woźniak, M.: How to design the fair experimental classifier evaluation. Appl. Soft Comput. **104**, 107219 (2021)
26. Storn, R., Price, K.: Differential evolution-a simple and efficient heuristic for global optimization over continuous spaces. J. Global Optim. **11**(4), 341–359 (1997)
27. Woźniak, M., Graña, M., Corchado, E.: A survey of multiple classifier systems as hybrid systems. Inf. Fusion **16**, 3–17 (2014). special Issue on Information Fusion in Hybrid Intelligent Fusion Systems
28. Wu, G., Mallipeddi, R., Suganthan, P.N.: Ensemble strategies for population-based optimization algorithms - a survey. Swarm Evol. Comput. **44**, 695–711 (2019)

Mining Multiple Class Imbalanced Datasets Using a Specialized Balancing Algorithm and the Adaboost Technique

Joanna Jedrzejowicz[1] and Piotr Jedrzejowicz[2](✉)

[1] Institute of Informatics, Faculty of Mathematics, Physics and Informatics, University of Gdańsk, 80-308 Gdańsk, Poland
joanna.jedrzejowicz@ug.edu.pl

[2] Department of Information Systems, Gdynia Maritime University, Morska 83, 81-225 Gdynia, Poland
p.jedrzejowicz@umg.edu.pl

Abstract. In this paper, we propose an ensemble classifier extended from a specialized bicriterion balancing algorithm originally proposed by the authors for binary imbalanced classification. The approach uses two specialized criteria for oversampling - classification potential and distance from the borderline between minority and majority instances. For mining multiclass imbalanced datasets the bicriteria oversampling algorithm was adapted to the needs of the multiple class problems using the one-versus-one (OVO) approach and the Adaboost technique. To evaluate the performance of the proposed ensemble classifier we use several state of the art balancing algorithms. The computational experiment shows a very good performance of the proposed approach.

Keywords: multiple class classification · AdaBoost ensemble classifier · OVO strategy

1 Introduction

Learning from imbalanced datasets attracts a lot of research efforts since many real-world classification problems are inherently imbalanced, for example, medical diagnosis, fault detection, fraud detection, text classification, and many others. It is now generally accepted that dealing with imbalanced dataset mining requires specialized approaches as traditional machine learning algorithms produce biased results when dealing with imbalanced data. Methods used to construct classifiers able to effectively deal with imbalanced data can be broadly classified as data level, algorithm level, and hybrid ones [15]. Data-level approaches concentrate on transforming the available data before using a classifier. Such a transformation is usually based on rebalancing the data distribution by applying some resampling method. The algorithm-level approaches aim at constructing machine learning algorithms that tolerate skewed data distribution among

N. T. Nguyen et al. (Eds.): ICCCI 2023, LNAI 14162, pp. 819–831, 2023.
https://doi.org/10.1007/978-3-031-41456-5_62

classes, and, at the same time producing satisfactory results. Hybrid methods combine data-level and algorithm-level methods.

Mining imbalanced datasets get more complex in the case more than two classes are involved. In such cases, the problem is to deal with possibly multiple majority and minority classes. Several approaches to deal with mining multiple class imbalanced datasets have been recently proposed (see for example data level methods [1,2,15–17,20,24], and algorithm level methods [4,11]), but the search for effective methods of mining such datasets is still going on.

A promising direction of research efforts in the field of mining imbalanced multiclass datasets is constructing and using multiple classifier systems also known as ensemble classifiers. The idea is to combine a collection of, so-called, base classifiers and to use their outcomes to produce final classification decisions. Most of the ensemble classifiers are based on boosting, bagging, or stacking techniques. Boosting combines a set of weak learners into strong learners to minimize training errors. In boosting, a random sample of data is selected, fitted with a model, and then trained sequentially in the following iterations. Each subsequent model tries to compensate for the weaknesses of its predecessor. With each iteration, the weak rules from each base classifier are combined to form one, strong prediction rule. Bagging is a technique for reducing prediction variance by producing additional data for training from a dataset by combining repetitions with combinations to create multi-sets of the original data. Stacking or Stacked Generalization uses a meta-learning algorithm to learn how to best combine the predictions from two or more base classifiers.

Examples of using multiple classifier systems for mining imbalanced multiclass dataset can be found, for example, in [1,8,19,22,23,25].

In this paper, we propose an ensemble classifier constructed from a specialized balancing algorithm. It is an extension and modification of the bicriteria oversampling algorithm proposed originally in [12] for binary imbalanced classification. The approach uses two specialized criteria for oversampling - classification potential and distance from the borderline between minority and majority instances. The potential is to be maximized and the distance minimized. For mining multiclass imbalanced datasets the bicriteria oversampling algorithm was adapted to the needs of the multiple class problems using the one-versus-one (OVO) approach [5] and the Adaboost technique [7]. To evaluate the performance of the proposed ensemble classifier we have adapted similarly several state-of-the-art balancing algorithms which are used as reference algorithms in the subsequent computational experiment.

The rest of the paper includes Sect. 2 where balancing classifiers are described and Sect. 3 where our implementation of the OVO strategy and Adaboost approach are explained. Section 4 contains a description of the computational experiment plan and a discussion of the experiment results. Final Sect. 5 offers conclusions and ideas for future research.

2 Balancing Classifiers

Assume that $D \subset X \times Y$ is a multiclass training dataset with samples $(\mathbf{x_i}, y_i)$ for $i = 1, \dots, n$, where $\mathbf{x_i}$ is an instance (datarow) and y_i is the class identity label associated with it, Y contains K labels. In the first step of our approach, using one-vs-one (OVO) method the data is balanced. For each pair of labels c_1, c_2 the dataset $T(c_1, c_2)$ filtered from X is examined, and if imbalance ratio is above the threshold, then it is oversampled/undersampled to $T^*(c_1, c_2)$. It is shown as Algorithm 1 with the balancing method as an input parameter - the applied undersampling method is shown as Algorithm 2 and oversampling is one of 5 methods further described. In this paper, we evaluate the performance

Algorithm 1: Balancing training data

Input: Multiclass training dataset D, threshold α, balancing method $\mathcal{B}$
Output: Multiclass dataset D^*

$D^* \leftarrow \emptyset$;
foreach *pair of classes* $c_1, c_2 \in Y$ **do**
  `/* filtering training dataset to classes` c_1, c_2 `*/`
  $T(c_1, c_2) \leftarrow \{(\mathbf{x}, y) \in D: \ y = c_1 \vee y = c_2\}$;
  if *imbalance ratio of* $T(c_1, c_2)$ *is above* α **then**
    use algorithm $\mathcal{B}$ to transform $T(c_1, c_2)$ to $T^*(c_1, c_2)$;
    merge $T^*(c_1, c_2)$ to D^*;
  end
  else
    merge $T(c_1, c_2)$ to D^*;
  end
end
return D^*

Algorithm 2: Undersampling with minority class centroid

Input: data from majority class $majC$, data from minority class $minC$, parameter s - size of reduced majority class.
Output: reduced majority class $redMaj \subset majC$ of size s.

calculate centroid CN of $minC$
define distances of CN to majority instances
$DIST \leftarrow \{dist(x, CN) : \ x \in majC\}$
sort $DIST$ in ascending order $SORT = \{d_1, \dots, d_{|majC|}\}$
keep in reduced majority class instances whose distances are in the initial s segment of $DIST$
$redMaj \leftarrow \{x \in majC : \ dist(x, CN) \leq d_s\}$
return $redMaj$

of 5 oversampling methods. All of them have roots in binary imbalanced data classification methods, and all have been implemented by us, using the OVO approach to make them suitable for solving multiclass problems.

The list of algorithms implemented for mining multiclass imbalanced datasets follows:

- Adaptive synthetic sampling approach for imbalanced learning [10] – ADASYN.
- Local distribution-based adaptive minority oversampling [21] – LAMO.
- Combined synthetic oversampling and undersampling technique [13] – CSMOUTE.
- Feature-weighted oversampling approach [18] – FWSMOTE.
- Dominance-based oversampling approach [12] – DOMIN.

The first 4 algorithms are well known from literature and the description is omitted. In case of DOMIN which is based on our method suggested in [12] the relation of domination among instances is introduced and using the genetic algorithm (GA) in subsequent iteration steps the minority subset is oversampled with non-dominated members of GA population. The relation of domination uses two criteria. Assume majority objects $majC$, minority objects $minC$ fixed. The first criterion makes use of an approach suggested in [14] for oversampling strategies based on calculating real-valued potential of each instance. The potential is defined by a radial basis function based on a set of majority objects $majC$, minority objects $minC$ and parameter γ representing the spread of the function. For an instance x the potential is defined as:

$$\phi(x, majC, minC, \gamma) = \sum_{y \in majC} \exp^{-(\frac{dist(x,y)}{\gamma})^2} - \sum_{y \in minC} \exp^{-(\frac{dist(x,y)}{\gamma})^2}$$

For any two instances x, y we write:

$$x \prec_1 y \iff \phi(x, majC, minC, \gamma) < \phi(y, majC, minC, \gamma)$$

The second criterion makes use of an average distance of an instance to 25% of nearest neighbors from the majority instances. For a fixed instance x and fixed majority dataset $majC$, let $\{x_1, \dots, x_n\}$ stand for the 25% of nearest neighbors from $majC$. Define:

$$distMajority(x, majC) = \sum_{i=1}^{n} dist(x, x_i)/n$$

$$x \prec_2 y \iff distMajority(x, majC) < distMajority(y, majC)$$

Finally, x dominates y iff

$$x \prec y \iff x \prec_1 y \;\&\; x \prec_2 y$$

The genetic algorithm starts with random population of instances and fitness defined as level of domination. After each iteration members with lowest fitness are merged into the oversampled minority set. Details are in [12].

3 Implementation of OVO and Adaboost Strategies

The algorithm to learn the best possible classifier for training data transformed to $X^* = \sum_{c_1 \neq c_2} T^*(c_1, c_2)$ (see Algorithm 1) makes use of multiclass Adaboost introduced in [9] and Gene Expression Programming (GEP) [6] used as a weak classifier.

Gene Expression Programming (GEP) technique combines the idea of genetic algorithms and genetic programming and makes use of a population of genes. Each gene is a linear structure divided into two parts. The first part, the head, contains functions and terminals while the second part, the tail, contains only terminals. For this study terminals are of type (*oper*; *attr*; *const*), where the value of *const* is in the range of attribute *attr* and *oper* is a relational operator from $\{<, \leq, >, \geq, =, \neq\}$. Functions are from the set AND; OR; NOT; XOR; NOR. For a fixed instance x from the dataset, the value $g(x)$ of a gene g is Boolean and thus a gene can be treated as a binary classifier. Generating the multiclass classifier is performed in OVO mode which means that for each pair of class labels a respective gene is generated which if further merged to one denoted g_m (line 5 in Algorithm 3). The final g_m performs majority voting to establish the label for given datarow.

Adaboost algorithm is iterative. The datarows are given weights which are equal in the first iteration. The weak classifier is built. The error of the iteration step is calculated and weights for those datarows which are misclassified are increased (boosted) and have better chance to appear in the training set in the next iteration step. On the other hand in testing stage, classifiers with smaller error are stronger in the ensemble of weak classifiers - see line 12 in Algorithm 3.

4 Computational Experiment

4.1 Experiment Plan

Validating experiment involved 14 multiple-class imbalanced datasets from the Keel Dataset Repository [3] as shown in Tables 1–5. A detailed description of the datasets can be found in the above Repository. Each of the discussed balancing algorithms has been used in the experiment to produce synthetic minority examples followed by applying the binary GEP classifier under the OVO scheme and the Adaboost strategy, to obtain the confusion matrix from which values of the performance measures including accuracy (Acc.), index kappa (Kappa), balanced recall values (B.Rec.), the area under the roc curve (AUC), and geometric mean (Gmean) have been calculated using the standard formulas for the multiple class case. To obtain the average values we used a 5-CV scheme repeated 6 times.

In the reported experiment, for all considered balancing algorithms and datasets, the GEP classifier has been used with the following parameter value settings: population size - 100; the number of iterations - 200; probabilities of

Algorithm 3: Applying Adaboost

Input: multiclass dataset $Train \cup Test$, K - number of class labels, nIt-number of iterations.
Output: performance metrics.

```
/* initialize weights                                        */
for i ← 1 to n do
    w_i ← 1/n
for m ← 1 to nIt do
    generate dataset D_m using weights w_i
    apply GEP to generate classifier g_m for D_m
    compute err_m = Σ_{i=1}^n w_i · I(g_m(x_i) ≠ y_i) / Σ_{i=1}^n w_i
    compute α_m ← log((1−err_m)/err_m) + log(K − 1)
    /* modify weights                                        */
    for i ← 1 to n do
        w_i ← w_i · exp(α_m · I(g_m(x_i) ≠ y_i))
    normalize w_i
for x ∈ Test do
    C(x)=arg max_{k≤K} Σ_{m=1}^{nIt} α_m · I(g_m(x) = k)
return performance metrics
```

mutation, RIS transposition, IS transposition, 1-point and 2-point recombination - 0.5, 0.2, 0.2, 0.2, 0.2, respectively. For selection, the roulette wheel method has been used. Parameter values for oversampling algorithms have been set as in the original papers describing implementation for the binary classification task. The number of iterations for Adaboost was set to 10 (Tables 3, 4 and 5).

4.2 Experiment Results

In Tables 1–5 experiment results averaged over 6 runs of the 5 cross-validation scheme are shown.

To evaluate the results shown in Tables 1–5 we have performed the Friedman ANOVA by ranks test for each of the considered performance measures. The null hypothesis for the procedure is that the different algorithms produced statistically similar results i.e. produced samples drawn from the same population, or specifically, populations with identical medians. As it is shown in Table 6, summarizing the above test results, the null hypothesis for results measured using each of the considered performance measures, should be rejected at the significance level of 0.05. The Kendall concordance coefficient calculated for results produced using each of the performance measures shows a fair or poor agreement in the rankings of the variables among cases. The above findings tell us that there are statistically significant differences in the performance of the considered algorithms. To gain better knowledge of the performance of the considered balancing algorithms under the OVO scheme and the Adaboost strategy we have carried

Table 1. Average accuracy value obtained by the considered algorithms.

Dataset	Domin	Csmoute	FWSmote	Adasyn	Lamo
Balance	0.725	0.706	0.686	0.721	0.730
Contraceptive	0.492	0.359	0.446	0.485	0.481
Dermatology	0.940	0.923	0.931	0.935	0.945
Ecoli	0.785	0.630	0.686	0.791	0.815
Glass	0.588	0.499	0.437	0.548	0.573
Hayes-Roth	0.708	0.698	0.654	0.587	0.598
Lynphography	0.729	0.555	0.634	0.699	0.721
New Thyroid	0.281	0.250	0.453	0.283	0.789
Pageblocks	0.688	0.446	0.320	0.710	0.875
Penbased	0.873	0.874	0.848	0.879	0.887
Shuttle	0.620	0.448	0.716	0.577	0.833
Thyroid	0.233	0.125	0.209	0.257	0.831
Wine	0.910	0.864	0.840	0.910	0.928
Yeast	0.450	0.430	0.366	0.445	0.492
Average	0.644	0.557	0.587	0.630	0.750

Table 2. Average Kappa value obtained by the considered algorithms.

Dataset	Domin	Csmoute	FWSmote	Adasyn	Lamo
Balance	0.500	0.475	0.467	0.491	0.515
Contraceptive	0.239	0.082	0.192	0.228	0.219
Dermatology	0.924	0.903	0.912	0.918	0.930
Ecoli	0.706	0.527	0.564	0.706	0.746
Glass	0.420	0.307	0.223	0.366	0.400
Hayes-Roth	0.538	0.633	0.459	0.359	0.374
Lynphography	0.471	0.240	0.327	0.423	0.467
New Thyroid	0.117	0.078	0.245	0.116	0.475
Pageblocks	0.312	0.156	0.067	0.710	0.563
Penbased	0.859	0.859	0.831	0.865	0.874
Shuttle	0.273	0.134	0.232	0.224	0.374
Thyroid	0.022	0.004	0.013	0.030	0.155
Wine	0.863	0.793	0.756	0.861	0.889
Yeast	0.261	0.253	0.146	0.445	0.327
Average	0.464	0.389	0.388	0.482	0.522

Table 3. Average balanced recall value obtained by the considered algorithms.

Dataset	Domin	Csmoute	FWSmote	Adasyn	Lamo
Balance	0,533	0,524	0,533	0,525	0,515
Contraceptive	0,496	0,407	0,475	0,491	0,484
Dermatology	0,937	0,920	0,923	0,933	0,922
Ecoli	0,706	0,642	0,537	0,696	0,699
Glass	0,546	0,460	0,364	0,502	0,555
Hayes-Roth	0.734	0.421	0.691	0.606	0.628
Lynphography	0.663	0.605	0.581	0.643	0.674
New Thyroid	0.589	0.542	0.639	0.583	0.647
Pageblocks	0.583	0.577	0.513	0.610	0.640
Penbased	0.872	0.872	0.848	0.879	0.889
Shuttle	0.410	0.303	0.368	0.386	0.376
Thyroid	0.405	0.285	0.342	0.416	0.405
Wine	0.919	0.872	0.853	0.911	0.933
Yeast	0.335	0.345	0.240	0.362	0.395
Average	0.623	0.555	0.565	0.610	0.626

Table 4. Average AUC value obtained by the considered algorithms.

Dataset	Domin	Csmoute	FWSmote	Adasyn	Lamo
Balance	0.271	0.272	0.271	0.271	0.273
Contraceptive	0.311	0.277	0.305	0.312	0.309
Dermatology	0.398	0.388	0.424	0.394	0.399
Ecoli	0.248	0.242	0.226	0.249	0.346
Glass	0.359	0.330	0.288	0.338	0.359
Hayes-Roth	0.415	0.657	0.326	0.379	0.387
Lymphography	0.247	0.217	0.218	0.245	0.209
New Thyroid	0.333	0.295	0.307	0.322	0.378
Pageblocks	0.288	0.255	0.257	0.290	0.295
Penbased	0.379	0.375	0.384	0.377	0.379
Shuttle	0.216	0.204	0.185	0.203	0.215
Thyroid	0.276	0.255	0.264	0.273	0.283
Wine	0.440	0.425	0.432	0.438	0.446
Yeast	0.309	0.308	0.314	0.327	0.401
Average	0.321	0.321	0.300	0.315	0.334

Table 5. Average Gmean value obtained by the considered algorithms.

Dataset	Domin	Csmoute	FWSmote	Adasyn	Lamo
Balance	0.437	0.456	0.393	0.427	0.402
Contraceptive	0.311	0.293	0.442	0.479	0.470
Dermatology	0.932	0.912	0.917	0.926	0.911
Ecoli	0.791	0.656	0.638	0.775	0.778
Glass	0.626	0.554	0.458	0.536	0.604
Hayes-Roth	0.604	0.397	0.649	0.557	0.566
Lynphography	0.759	0.594	0.676	0.748	0.739
New Thyroid	0.352	0.318	0.507	0.370	0.673
Pageblocks	0.730	0.613	0.466	0.727	0.816
Penbased	0.865	0.867	0.840	0.873	0.884
Shuttle	0.267	0.287	0.232	0.293	0.363
Thyroid	0.276	0.238	0.292	0.273	0.300
Wine	0.916	0.855	0.841	0.905	0.930
Yeast	0.309	0.404	0.235	0.380	0.388
Average	0.584	0.532	0.542	0.591	0.630

Table 6. Summary of the Friedman ANOVA test results

Measure	Chi Sqr	p	Concordance
Accuracy	31.25714	0.00000	0.55816
Kappa	29.60000	0.00001	0.52857
B. recall	24.05714	0.00008	0.42952
AUC	21.11828	0.00030	0.37711
Gmean	14.17143	0.00677	0.25306

out a series of pairwise comparisons using the Wilcoxon matched pairs tests. The null hypothesis in such a case states that results produced by two different algorithms are drawn from samples with the same distribution. Test results are summarized in Table 7.

Table 7. Wilcoxon matched pair test results.

Measure	Compared algorithms		T	Z	p-value
Accuracy	Domin	Csmoute	1.000000	3.232989	0.001225
Accuracy	Domin	FWSmote	23.00000	1.851906	0.064040
Accuracy	Domin	Adasyn	34.00000	1.161365	0.245494
Accuracy	Domin	Lamo	23.00000	1.851906	0.064040
Kappa	Domin	Csmoute	10.00000	2.839809	0.004514
Kappa	Domin	FWSmote	11.00000	2.783013	0.005386
Kappa	Domin	Adasyn	50.00000	0.567962	0.570061
Kappa	Domin	Lamo	24.00000	1.789130	0.073595
B. recall	Domin	Csmoute	5.000000	2.981883	0.002865
B. recall	Domin	FWSmote	8.000000	2.793553	0.005214
B. recall	Domin	Adasyn	35.00000	1.098588	0.271948
B. recall	Domin	Lamo	48.00000	0.282494	0.777565
AUC	Domin	Csmoute	16.00000	2.291342	0.021944
AUC	Domin	FWSmote	13.00000	2.479671	0.013151
AUC	Domin	Adasyn	23.00000	1.851906	0.064040
AUC	Domin	Lamo	29.00000	1.475247	0.140147
Gmean	Domin	Csmoute	19.00000	2.103012	0.035465
Gmean	Domin	FWSmote	30.00000	1.412471	0.157812
Gmean	Domin	Adasyn	49.00000	0.219718	0.826091
Gmean	Domin	Lamo	33.00000	1.224141	0.220900

Data from Table 7 allow drawing the following observations valid at the significance level of 0.05:

- For the Accuracy measure, Domin, FWSmote, Adasyn, and Lamo, perform statistically equally well.
- For the Accuracy measure, Domin outperforms statistically Csmoute.
- For the Kappa index measure, Domin outperforms statistically Csmoute and FWSmote.
- For the Kappa index measure, Domin and Lamo perform statistically equally well.
- For the Balanced Recall measure, Domin outperforms statistically Csmoute and FWSSmoteA.
- For the Balanced Recall measure, Domin, Adasyn, and Lamo perform statistically equally well.
- For the AUC measure, Domin outperforms statistically Csmoute and FWSmote.
- For the AUC measure, Domin, Adasyn, and Lamo perform statistically equally well.
- For the Gmean measure, Domin outperforms statistically Csmoute.

- For the Gmean measure, Domin, Adasyn, and Lamo perform statistically equally well.

Based on the computational experiment results one may conclude that among considered balancing algorithms the proposed Domin and Lamo are the best performers when dealing with imbalanced, multiple-class datasets.

As a side experiment, we also analyzed the effect of introducing the Adaboost strategy to enhance the performance of the investigated classifiers. Performance comparisons for all considered measures are shown in Table 8. Values in Table 8 have been averaged over all 14 datasets. All results have been obtained using identical parameter settings and a 5-cross-validation scheme repeated 6 times.

Table 8. Performance of the balancing algorithm without and with applying Adaboost technique.

Method	Measure	Domin	Csmoute	FWSmote	Adasyn	Lamo
No Adaboost	Accuracy	0.559	0.362	0.548	0.522	0.355
Adaboost	Accuracy	0.644	0.557	0.587	0.630	0.750
No Adaboost	Kappa	0.393	0.257	0.345	0.362	0.190
Adaboost	Kappa	0.464	0.389	0.388	0.482	0.522
No Adaboost	B. recall	0.607	0.520	0.555	0.588	0.431
Adaboost	B.Recall	0.623	0.555	0.565	0.610	0.626
No Adaboost	AUC	0.345	0.315	0.329	0.352	0.258
Adaboost	AUC	0.321	0.321	0.300	0.315	0.334
No Adaboost	Gmean	0.584	0.419	0.483	0.548	0.410
Adaboost	Gmean	0.505	0.411	0.456	0.490	0.431

As it can be seen from Table 8, introducing ensemble strategy based on the Adaboost technique improves, in a majority of cases the classification results. For measures including area under curve (AUC) and geometric mean (G mean) such an improvement is relatively small or even not present. However for Lamo algorithm a substantial improvement can be observed for all considered performance measures.

5 Conclusion

The paper contributes by proposing an original balancing algorithm implementation for mining imbalanced multi-class datasets based on the Adaboost technique. As reference algorithms we have also implemented several state-of-the-art balancing algorithms including Csmoute, FWSmote, Adasyn and Lamo. Computational experiment has shown that among investigated approaches Domin, proposed by the authors, and Lamo have been the best performers while Csmoute the worst one. Introducing ensemble classification techniques like, for example

Adaboost enhances, in general, performance of the considered approaches but the improvement scale may vary between algorithms used. Future research will focus on improving, developing new or modifying the existing ensemble classification methods to better respond to the needs of multiple-class imbalanced datasets mining.

References

1. Abdi, L., Hashemi, S.: To combat multi-class imbalanced problems by means of over-sampling and boosting techniques. Soft. Comput. **19**(12), 3369–3385 (2015)
2. Agrawal, A., Viktor, H.L., Paquet, E.: SCUT: multi-class imbalanced data classification using smote and cluster-based undersampling. In: 2015 7th International Joint Conference on Knowledge Discovery, Knowledge Engineering and Knowledge Management (IC3K), vol. 01, pp. 226–234 (2015)
3. Alcalá-Fdez, J., et al.: KEEL: a software tool to assess evolutionary algorithms for data mining problems. Soft. Comput. **13**(3), 307–318 (2009)
4. Díaz-Vico, D., Figueiras-Vidal, A.R., Dorronsoro, J.R.: Deep mlps for imbalanced classification. In: 2018 International Joint Conference on Neural Networks, IJCNN 2018, Rio de Janeiro, Brazil, 8–13 July 2018, pp. 1–7. IEEE (2018)
5. Fernández, A., del Jesus, M.J., Herrera, F.: Hierarchical fuzzy rule based classification systems with genetic rule selection for imbalanced data-sets. Int. J. Approx. Reason. **50**(3), 561–577 (2009)
6. Ferreira, C.: Gene expression programming: a new adaptive algorithm for solving problems. Complex Syst. **13**(2) (2001)
7. Freund, Y., Schapire, R.E.: A desicion-theoretic generalization of on-line learning and an application to boosting. In: Vitányi, P. (ed.) EuroCOLT 1995. LNCS, vol. 904, pp. 23–37. Springer, Heidelberg (1995). https://doi.org/10.1007/3-540-59119-2_166
8. Haixiang, G., Yijing, L., Yanan, L., Xiao, L., Jinling, L.: BPSO-Adaboost-KNN ensemble learning algorithm for multi-class imbalanced data classification. Eng. Appl. Artif. Intell. **49**, 176–193 (2016)
9. Hastie, T.J., Rosset, S., Zhu, J., Zou, H.: Multi-class adaboost. Statist. Interface **2**, 349–360 (2009)
10. He, H., Bai, Y., Garcia, E., Li, S.A.: Adasyn: adaptive synthetic sampling approach for imbalanced learning. In: IEEE International Joint Conference on Neural Networks (IEEE World Congress on Computational Intelligence), IJCNN 2008, pp. 1322–1328 (2008)
11. Hoens, T.R., Qian, Q., Chawla, N.V., Zhou, Z.-H.: Building decision trees for the multi-class imbalance problem. In: Tan, P.-N., Chawla, S., Ho, C.K., Bailey, J. (eds.) PAKDD 2012. LNCS (LNAI), vol. 7301, pp. 122–134. Springer, Heidelberg (2012). https://doi.org/10.1007/978-3-642-30217-6_11
12. Jedrzejowicz, J., Jedrzejowicz, P.: Bicriteria oversampling for imbalanced data classification. In: Knowledge-Based and Intelligent Information & Engineering Systems: Proceedings of the 26th International Conference KES-2022, volume 207C of Procedia Computer Science, pp. 239–248. Elsevier (2022)
13. Koziarski, M.: CSMOUTE: combined synthetic oversampling and undersampling technique for imbalanced data classification. In: International Joint Conference on Neural Networks, IJCNN 2021, Shenzhen, China, 18–22 July 2021, pp. 1–8. IEEE (2021)

14. Koziarski, M.: Potential anchoring for imbalanced data classification. Pattern Recognit. **120**, 108114 (2021)
15. Koziarski, M., Krawczyk, B., Wozniak, M.: Radial-based oversampling for noisy imbalanced data classification. Neurocomputing **343**, 19–33 (2019)
16. Li, Q., Song, Y., Zhang, J., Sheng, V.S.: Multiclass imbalanced learning with one-versus-one decomposition and spectral clustering. Expert Syst. Appl. **147**, 113152 (2020)
17. Liu, X.Y., Wu, J., Zhou, Z.H.: Exploratory undersampling for class-imbalance learning. IEEE Trans. Syst. Man Cybern. Part B (Cybern.) **39**(2), 539–550 (2009)
18. Maldonado, S., Vairetti, C., Fernández, A., Herrera, F.: FW-SMOTE: a feature-weighted oversampling approach for imbalanced classification. Pattern Recognit. **124**, 108511 (2022)
19. Rodríguez, J.J., Díez-Pastor, J.F., Arnaiz-González, A., Kuncheva, L.I.: Random balance ensembles for multiclass imbalance learning. Knowl. Based Syst. **193**, 105434 (2020)
20. Sáez, J.A., Krawczyk, B., Wozniak, M.: Analyzing the oversampling of different classes and types of examples in multi-class imbalanced datasets. Pattern Recognit. **57**, 164–178 (2016)
21. Wang, X., Jian, X., Zeng, T., Jing, L.: Local distribution-based adaptive minority oversampling for imbalanced data classification. Neurocomputing **422**, 200–213 (2021)
22. Kaiyuan, W., Zheng, Z., Tang, S.: BVDT: a boosted vector decision tree algorithm for multi-class classification problems. Int. J. Pattern Recognit Artif Intell. **31**(05), 1750016 (2017)
23. Yijing, L., Haixiang, G., Xiao, L., Yanan, L., Jinling, L.: Adapted ensemble classification algorithm based on multiple classifier system and feature selection for classifying multi-class imbalanced data. Knowl.-Based Syst. **94**, 88–104 (2016)
24. Zhang, Z.-L., Luo, X.-G., García, S., Herrera, F.: Cost-sensitive back-propagation neural networks with binarization techniques in addressing multi-class problems and non-competent classifiers. Appl. Soft Comput. **56**, 357–367 (2017)
25. Zhang, Z., Krawczyk, B., García, S., Rosales-Pérez, A., Herrera, F.: Empowering one-vs-one decomposition with ensemble learning for multi-class imbalanced data. Knowl. Based Syst. **106**, 251–263 (2016)

Investigation and Prediction of Cognitive Load During Memory and Arithmetic Tasks

Patient Zihisire Muke, Adrianna Kozierkiewicz(✉), and Marcin Pietranik

Faculty of Information and Communication Technology, Wroclaw University of Science and Technology, Wybrzeze Wyspianskiego 27, 50-370 Wroclaw, Poland
{patient.zihisire,adrianna.kozierkiewicz,marcin.pietranik}@pwr.edu.pl

Abstract. The research presented in this paper aimed to study the effects of arithmetic and memory tasks (with two levels of difficulty: easy and hard) on human cognitive load using biometric eye tracking techniques. The experiment was conducted with thirty-one participants using iMotions' integrated biometric platform. In addition to the eye tracking technique, data was also collected by measuring the participants' performance to the tasks as well as two subjective type of questionnaires including the Single Ease Question (SEQ) and the National Aeronautics and Space Administration Task Load Index Scale (NASA-TLX Scale). A total of 16 metrics were extracted and evaluated, comprising two performance metrics, eight subjective metrics and six eye tracking metrics. Nonparametric Wilcoxon tests were used to find statistically significant differences between metrics at different level of difficulties. Relying on the obtained results from the psychophysiological measure, we concluded that eye tracking metrics can be helpful in analyzing cognitive load during arithmetic and memory recall tasks. At last, based on the overall results, a theoretical model for the prediction of the cognitive load adapted to machine learning techniques has been also proposed.

Keywords: cognitive load · prediction · NASA-TLX · eye tracking

1 Introduction

The theory of cognitive load (CLT) is essential in research on the human-computer interaction (HCI) domain. Non-invasive measurements of people's cognitive load, such as eye tracking and other biosensor techniques, are urgently needed. They can help interactive systems' developers avoid users overload while using those systems. Measuring cognitive load can enable a system to respond adequately to the need of the users, either by adapting mission-critical systems or by reducing or increasing task difficulty to the cognitive state of users [8].

Cognitive Load (CL) is a psychological concept that illustrates how learners' individual load constructs, processes, and stores (new) information from the sensory input throughout short-term and long-term memory. Therefore, Cognitive

N. T. Nguyen et al. (Eds.): ICCCI 2023, LNAI 14162, pp. 832–845, 2023.
https://doi.org/10.1007/978-3-031-41456-5_63

Load Theory (CLT) was developed precisely for situations where people must deal with high information processing loads. Thus it has effects on both training and practice. According to this theory, the link between short and long-term memory is the limited capacity of the human memory [10]. Therefore, the central role of working or short-term memory is to process new information acquired through attention and then understand, contrast, and organize that information in order to forward it to long-term memory, which in turn, gives meaning to the new information, organize and preserve it for future use [19].

The main contribution of this paper is twofold. Firstly, we explore the impact of various stimuli on participants' cognitive load by extracting and calculating metrics that can predict best the user's cognitive load from performance, subjective, and psychophysiological (eye tracking) measures. Secondly, we proposed a theoretical model for predicting cognitive load adapted to machine learning techniques. The experiment employed two types of tasks with two difficulty levels (Easy and Hard). The first task consisted of a Memory Recall Task similar to the digit span task, where a certain number of digits were displayed on the screen. The participant had to memorize them within the given period of time and reproduce them on the screen. Five tasks per level were prepared for this group of tasks. The second group of tasks was the arithmetical task, which consisted of 5 computational equations per difficulty level, comprising addition and subtraction operations.

Among psychophysiological measures, this study focused on Eye Tracking biosensor technology to examine to what extent biometric techniques are appropriate for measuring the human cognitive load. Because of the wide range of possible comparisons, the analysis was performed on measures including blink count, rate, fixation duration, saccade duration, saccade amplitude, and saccade peak velocity. In the second stage and future work, the most prominent cognitive load measures will be used to train the proposed theoretical ensemble learning model to predict cognitive load.

As part of this study, two master theses were completed containing detailed descriptions of the experiments presented in this work [2,12]. The study was approved by the Research Ethics Committee of the Wroclaw University of Science and Technology.

The remaining parts of this paper are organized as follows. Section 2 contains a short description of related works and background. Section 3 presents the experimental setup, extracted metrics, and results of the conducted experiments, where the essential measures that better assess participants' cognitive load are selected. Section 4 presents the basic notions for ensemble learning and specific instance. Conclusions are drawn in Sect. 5, as well as future research opportunities are also discussed.

2 Related Works

Cognitive load is related to the amount of information the brain can process at one time. There are two methods for assessing cognitive load: subjective and objective [16]. Subjective methods, based on self-report approaches, have online and spontaneous cognitive load evaluation limitations. NASA-TLX (NASA-Task Load Index) is one of the most commonly used subjective measures, which is a multidimensional scale focusing on different components of the workload. It has six dimensions: mental demand, physical demand, time pressure, mental effort, performance satisfaction, and frustration level [15]. Another measure of subjective rating scales, especially in usability testing and user experience is the Single Ease Question (SEQ). This is a 7 rating scale measuring the level of difficulty of a task [7]. However, the objective methods, including task performance, psychophysiological and behavioral approaches, have the advantage of continuously measuring cognitive load during cognitive tasks, especially the last two mentioned above [16].

These measurement methods have different applicable scenarios and characteristics. For example, subjective and task-performance approaches (time and task completion rate, error rate, etc.) are only captured after a person has completed or performed a task. In contrast, psychophysiological and behavioral measures can continuously and automatically monitor users' cognitive load [18].

Generally, physiological signals utilized for cognitive load measurement include electroencephalography (EEG), galvanic skin response (GSR), photoplethysmogram (PPG), electrocardiography (ECG), electromyography (EMG), facial expression, eye tracking analysis etc. [22]. The first five signals are acquired using wearable sensors but the last two which include eye tracking are non-invasive biosensor devices that enable the user to entirely focus his/her attention and cognitive resources on the task [5].

Numerous experimental types of research [6,11,17,18,21] have been carried out to examine and describe the impacts of eye-tracking metrics on measuring cognitive load. The first group of metrics is related to the blink, which is a semi-involuntary movement of quickly closing and reopening the eyelid(s) for 0.1 to 0.4 s average duration for a single blink. The blink-related features that provide information regarding a user's cognitive load in the literature include the blink rate, latency or velocity, frequency, and duration [11,18,21].

The second group of metrics is related to fixation, which happens when the eye stays focused on a particular target for a period of time (from 200–300 ms to a few seconds). Fixation count and duration are the two most used metrics regarding cognitive processing [18]. The third group of metrics is related to the Saccade, which happens when the eye moves voluntarily from one fixation point to another (30 to 80 ms). The most employed saccade movement features to measure CL are saccade rate and duration, saccadic velocity/amplitude, and the number of saccades [6,17,21]. Other metrics also involve pupil size and pupil diameter extracted from pupillometry.

Based on the literature, the decrease in Blink rate [21], Blink count [11], and saccade amplitude [6] is associated with higher cognitive load. On the contrary, in the literature, the increase in the fixation duration [18], saccade duration, and saccade velocity [6] is related to higher cognitive load.

To measure cognitive load (using some selected method), one needs to use a standardized task to stimulate the subject's brain. In the literature, two main trends can be found: memory recall tasks and arithmetic tasks. Memory recall tasks [14] are advantageous for simulating tasks requiring different cognitive load levels. They can be applied in several domains, such as education, device operation, driving, user experience, etc. It is a well-known task used in cognitive psychology research to study the effects of information overload on short-term memory and its capacity. It may have multiple different forms. For example, in [20], authors propose that a participant memorizes a string of digits, holding it in short-term memory for a few seconds, and then retrieves back the information considering that the proposed digit can range from within to beyond an individual's capacity limit depending on the difficulty level. Multiple developments of this basic approach can be found in the literature [3,13].

The second type of task used to stimulate people to measure their cognitive load is the mental arithmetic tasks, considered a standardized stress testing protocol and commonly used in cognitive load research [19,23]. For instance, in [4] and [5], metrics extracted from the eye-tracking biosensor including pupillary responses, showed clear patterns in a task incorporating multiplication of two numbers with three difficulty levels. They also discussed the properties of pupillary responses when performing arithmetic tasks and their connection with different phases of cognitive processes. The results in their works shown that pupils' size increased with the increase in task difficulty and prove the feasibility of a relatively fine-grained approach to measuring cognitive load in a dynamic workplace environment using this non-invasive technique.

In the literature, a plethora of additional cognitive load measures can be found. A broad survey is provided in [9]. The main contribution of this article is to analyze the characteristics of those measures to select those which can most reliably indicate whether the cognitive load of some person is approaching too high level.

3 Experimental Design, Selected Metrics, and Results

3.1 Experimental Setup

The main goal of the performed experiment comes down to three questions:

1. What are the best metrics among performance, subjective, and eye-tracking measures that relate significantly to the experienced cognitive load while performing arithmetic and memory tasks on web applications?
2. Are there statistical differences in individual performance and subjective and psychophysiological measures between easy and difficult task loads while performing arithmetic and memory tasks?
3. Based on the results, what is the appropriate theoretical model, adapted to machine learning techniques, can better predict cognitive load during arithmetic and memory tasks performed on web applications?

In order to answer the above questions, thirty-one volunteer participants participated in the experiment. The participants ranged between 18 and 50 years, and the average age was 34. All participants had at least a high school degree. Thus it was more straightforward for them to understand the requirements of the tasks. All were equipped with appropriate biometric sensors, and the Tobii X3-120 Eye Tracker was set. The stimuli displayed on the PC monitor were embedded in a web-based application, working on the localhost server, and developed in Python, Conda environment with Flask[1] framework. The application was then synchronized with the iMotions software version 8.1 [24].

At the beginning of the experiment and at each level of difficulty per group of tasks, participants were presented with a basic information page with task descriptions, followed by a 1-minute baseline rest period. After each difficulty level in each task group, participants took the SEQ and NASA TLX questionnaires. The experiment time for one participant is approximately 40 min. Participants were faced with two types of tasks: memory tasks and arithmetic tasks. For memory recall tasks, we induced an exercise for the participants to memorize a randomly generated set of numbers displayed on the screen and to reproduce the same in a text box. The time to complete each task in the easy level was 60 s, of which 10 s were spent on memorizing a set of two bunch of three digits' numbers (e.g., 123-123) displayed and 50 s for indicating memorized numbers. 60 s were allocated for completing each task in the difficult level, of which 15 s were for memorizing three bunches of 4 digits' numbers (e.g., 1234-1234-1234) displayed and 45 s for indicating a memorized set of numbers. In the rest of the paper, memory tasks on the easy level will be denoted *MemE*, and hard tasks will be marked *MemH*.

Regarding the mental calculation arithmetical tasks, to avoid the same question per task for all participants, the developed web application generated digits randomly based on the level of difficulty for each participant employing the following algorithm format: "Argument1 + Argument2 + Argument3 - Argument4 + Argument5 - Argument6 =". For each argument, a one-digit number from 1 to 9 was randomly selected for easy-level tasks and two digits' numbers from 11 to 99 for hard-level tasks. In the rest of the paper, arithmetic tasks on the easy level will be denoted *AriE*, and hard tasks will be marked *AriH*. The time to complete each easy task was 60 s, and hard tasks were 120 s.

3.2 Metrics Extraction

Based on the collected data, in total 16 metrics were extracted and calculated including 2 performance, 8 subjective and 6 psychophysiological (eye tracking) metrics, which are summarized in Table 1. Their values were calculated as the mean of five tasks at the same difficulty level. The performance metrics included the task completion rate (Tcr) and the task completion time (Tct).

For subjective measurement, we used two types of self-report questionnaires, which participants filled out after completing each group of tasks. This study

[1] https://flask.palletsprojects.com/.

Table 1. Metrics used to measure cognitive load

Type	Metrics	Denotation
Performance Metrics	Task completion rate	Tcr
	Task completion time	Tct
Subjective Metrics	Task difficulty (SEQ)	Seq
	NASA-TLX - Overall	NXo
	NASA-TLX - Complexity	NXc
	NASA-TLX - Physical demand	NXp
	NASA-TLX - Time pressure	NXt
	NASA-TLX - Performance satisfaction	NXs
	NASA-TLX - Mental effort	NXm
	NASA-TLX - Frustration	NXf
Eye Tracking Metrics	Blink count	Ybc
	Blink rate	Ybr
	Fixation duration	Yfd
	Saccade duration	Ysd
	Saccade amplitude	Ysa
	Saccade peak velocity	Ysv

used a modified version of the NASA TLX questionnaire, as we did not use a weighting scheme to calculate the total score. Also, instead of the original scale, we applied a Likert 7-point scale to rate each question. This scale could help participants to make a more reliable assessment in less time. The second questionnaire was the Single Ease Question (SEQ). SEQ is a 7-point rating scale used to determine how difficult the participants perceived the task. Eye tracking metrics were computed using R notebook algorithms in the iMotions platform [24, 25]. Six EyeTracking measures were considered, including Blink count *Ybc*, Blink rate *Ybr*, Fixation duration *Yfd*, Saccade duration *Ysd*, Saccade amplitude *Ysa*, and Saccade peak velocity *Ysv*.

To compute the participants' blink-related features (*Ybc* and *Ybr*), the algorithm first tags all instances of missing values as blinks. The algorithm only considers instances with consistent missing values in the participant's left and right eye. Hereafter, the algorithms re-evaluate the tagged blinks, retaining only the tags that likely represent actual blinks. The remaining tags are counted as blinks and are used to compute the blink rate (i.e., the number of blinks per minute). The defaults parameter was set as follows: Min duration: 20 ms, Max duration: 500 ms, Min duration between two blinks: 70 ms.

To compute the Fixation and saccade-related metrics (*Yfd*, *Ysd*, *Ysa*, and *Ysv*), the I-VT (velocity-threshold identification) filter was used. The Fixation duration is the fixation duration calculated in milliseconds (ms) as the time difference between the fixation's start and end times of each difficulty level. The saccade duration is the saccade duration calculated in milliseconds (ms) as the time difference between the saccade's start and end times of each level of difficulty for each participant. The saccade amplitude, calculated in degree (°), is the saccade amplitude, i.e., the angular distance that the eyes traveled from the start point to the end point of each difficulty level for each participant. The saccade peak velocity, calculated in degrees per second (°/s), is the peak velocity of the saccade, i.e., the maximal speed of the eyes during each saccade of each level of difficulty for each participant.

3.3 Analysis of the Results

The analysis of the mean and median value results for individual performance and subjective measures presented in Fig. 1 as well as eye tracking measures presented in Fig. 2 allows us to draw some interesting conclusions.

Among the performance metrics, the mean and median of the task completion rate (*Tcr*) decreased significantly with the increasing task difficulty in both

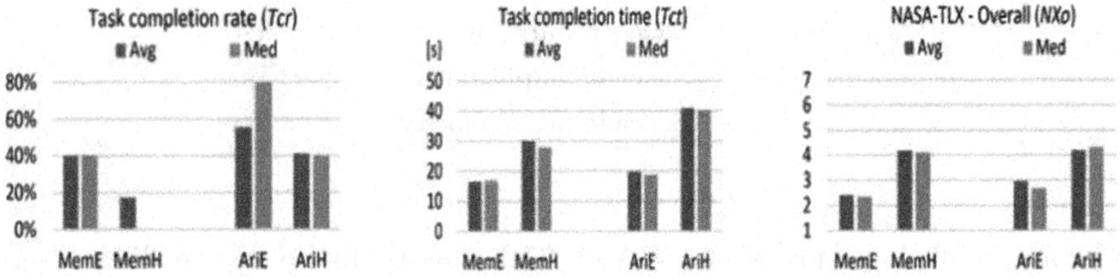

Fig. 1. Results of performance and subjective (average NASA-TLX score) metrics

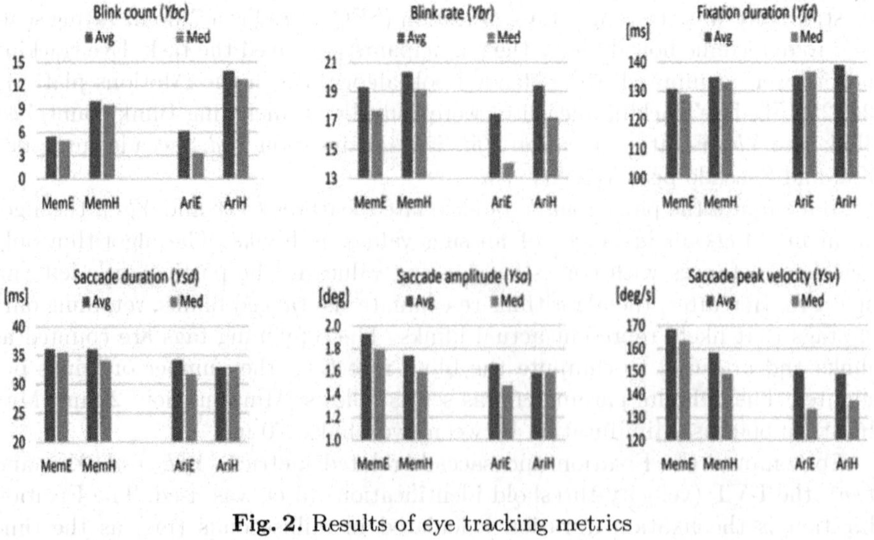

Fig. 2. Results of eye tracking metrics

arithmetical and memory recall tasks. In turn, the mean and median of the task completion time (*Tct*) increased significantly with increasing task difficulty in both arithmetic and memory recall tasks. In line with performance metrics, similar conclusions were also drawn in [1].

Concerning subjective metrics, in both group of tasks, the mean and median values of seven metrics including Single Easy Question (*Seq*), Ovarall NASA-TLX (*Nxo*), Task complexity (*NXc*), Task physical demand (*NXp*), Task time pressure (*NXt*), Task mental effort (*NXm*), and Task frustration (*NXf*) were increasing with the increase of task difficulty in both arithmetic and memory recall tasks. The remaining metric Task performance satisfaction (*NXs*) mean and median values were decreasing with the increase of difficulty in both group of tasks. NASA-TLX results also confirm differences in task difficulty levels.

Regarding eye tracking psychophysiological measures, the mean values for Blink count (*Ybc*), Blink rate (*Ybr*), and Fixation duration (*Yfd*) metrics were increasing with increase of task difficulty for both arithmetic and memory recall tasks, while the mean values for Saccade duration (*Ysd*), Saccade Amplitude (*Ysa*) and Saccade peak velocity (*Ysv*) were decreasing with the increase of task difficulty in both group of tasks. Only the Fixation duration (*Yfd*), and saccade amplitude (*Ysa*) metrics reflect conclusions done in the literature [6,18]. Thus, the two are significant in relation to the cognitive load experienced by both groups of tasks.

Statistical analysis was carried out for a reliable assessment of the obtained results. In accordance with the performed statistical Shapiro-Wilk test, larger part of results from performance, subjective, and psychophysiological measures were not normally distributed. Hence, for the comparison between variables in terms of significant differences, a nonparametric Wilcoxon test was applied. The null hypothesis assumes that there are no significant differences in the values of the individual metrics between tasks. 0.05 was set as the significance level for rejecting the null hypothesis.

Table 2 shows the Wilcoxon test results for each metrics between Easy Difficulty and Hard Difficulty in the two groups of tasks. 0.000 means a very small p-value, close to 0. Therefore, for memory recall tasks, the level of difference between easy and difficult tasks was only statistically significant for *Tcr, Tct, Seq, NXo, Nxc, NXp, NXt, NXm, NXf, Ybc*, and *Ysa*. In turn, for arithmetic tasks, the level of difference between easy and difficult tasks was only statistically significant for *Tct, Seq, NXo, Nxc, NXp, NXt, NXm, NXf* and *Ybc*. The remaining measures of arithmetic and memory tasks showed that the differences between easy and difficult tasks were not statistically significant, apart from one observation, where *Yfd* was very close to the significance level for rejecting the null hypothesis of 0.05 in both groups of tasks. Thus, it can also be considered among the metrics that best differentiate the difficulty level in both groups of tasks. Measures that statistically significantly differentiate difficult and easy tasks were adapted to the cognitive load prediction model in the Sect. 4.

Table 2. Results of the Wilcoxon test for the comparison of metrics in terms of p-values (significant differences are shown in bold)

Type	Metrics	MemE vs MemH	Metrics	AriE vs AriH
Performance Metrics	Tcr	0.027	Tcr	0.170
	Tct	0.000	Tct	0.000
Subjective Metrics	Seq	0.000	Seq	0.002
	NXo	0.000	NXo	0.000
	NXc	0.000	NXc	0.000
	NXp	0.000	NXp	0.007
	NXt	0.000	NXt	0.000
	NXs	0.060	NXs	0.203
	NXm	0.000	NXm	0.008
	NXf	0.001	NXf	0.005
Eye Tracking Metrics	Ybc	0.000	Ybc	0.000
	Ybr	0.485	Ybr	0.123
	Yfd	0.077	Yfd	0.094
	Ysd	0.506	Ysd	0.426
	Ysa	0.002	Ysa	0.858
	Ysv	0.149	Ysv	0.088

4 Cognitive Load Prediction Model

This section contains an overview of our CLPELM2 (*Cognitive Load Predication Ensemble Learning Meta Model*) framework presented in Fig. 3. Initially, the mathematical foundations will be described which include all of the formal definitions and how they are structured together. On this basis an overview of a concrete materialisation of the model using the selected cognitive load measures is provided.

4.1 Basic Notions

By DI we denote a finite set of raw, unprocessed data inputs:

$$DI = \{d_1, d_2, d_3, ..., d_n\} \tag{1}$$

Each d_i ($i \in [1, n]$) can be understood as a domain of data collected from selected sensors (e.g. eye tracking). However, such raw and unprocessed data require initial preprocessing, which may include such operations as feature extractions, normalisation, etc. Elements of selected domain after preprocessing form entirely new domain, which will be further denoted as $\widetilde{d_i}$. A set of all domain created by preprocessing original domains will be denoted as $\widetilde{DI}$:

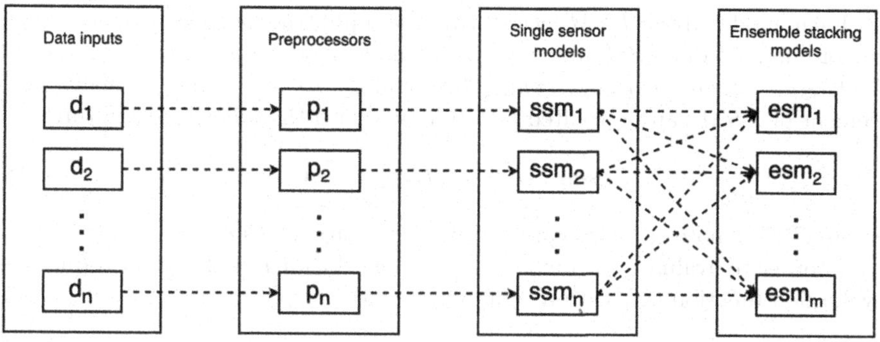

Fig. 3. The general architecture of ensemble learning method of cognitive load prediction

$$\widetilde{DI} = \{\widetilde{d_1}, \widetilde{d_2}, \widetilde{d_3}, ..., \widetilde{d_n}\} \tag{2}$$

Obviously there can be no single preprocessing method, but data type must have a dedicated preprocessor. The set of preprocessors P is defined as follows:

$$P = \{p_1, p_2, p_3, ..., p_n\} \tag{3}$$

Each p_i $(i \in [1, n])$ has a following signature:

$$p_i : d_i \rightarrow \widetilde{d_i} \tag{4}$$

By *SSM* we denote a set of single sensor models used to classify preprocessed data into one of preselected classes. Analogously to preprocessors each data input has a complementary single sensor model:

$$SSM = \{ssm_1, ssm_2, ssm_3, ..., ssm_n\} \tag{5}$$

The output of each of the above single sensor models in one of the classification classes from the set $CO = \{co_1, co_2, ..., co_p\}$. Moreover, each model accepts a model optimiser - an auxiliary element which is used to tune the model in order to increase its performance. Each model ssm_i from *SSM* has its own dedicated optimiser o_i. A set of all model optimiser will be denoted as $MO_{SSM} = \{osm_1, osm_2, ..., osm_n\}$.

Assuming the above notations, we can treat each element of *SSM* as a function with a signature as follows:

$$ssm_i : \widetilde{d_i} \times MO_{SSM} \rightarrow CO \tag{6}$$

The final element of the proposed approach is the ensemble learning stage. We distinguish a finite set of ensemble stacking models denoted as ESM:

$$ESM = \{esm_1, esm_2, esm_3, ..., ssm_m\} \tag{7}$$

Each model from ESM accepts as an input the outputs of each single sensor model from SSM along with ensemble model optimiser from the set $MO_{ESM} = \{oem_1, oem_2, ..., oem_n\}$ (by analogy to MO_{SSM}). Formally, each element of ESM can be treated as a function with the following signature:

$$esm_i : CO^n \times MO_{ESM} \rightarrow CO \tag{8}$$

where CO^n denotes a n-ary cartesian power of the set CO.

In order to evaluate the output of ensemble stacking model we introduce the evaluation function evh with a signature:

$$evh : ESM \rightarrow CLP \tag{9}$$

where $CLP \in \mathbb{N}$, which is a finite set of classes describe the level of cognitive load. For example, in the next section $CLP = [0, 1]$ which represents two classes: High and Low cognitive load.

Having the above, the main task introduced in Sect. 1 can be formally defined as *find an ensemble stacking model denoted as* esm^* *from the set ESM which meets the condition:* $esm^* = argmax_{esm \in ESM} evh(esm)$.

4.2 Ensemble Learning Model for Cognitive Load Prediction

This paper proposes an ensemble learning model which combines expert knowledge to pre-process collected data coming from different cognitive load measurement modalities including performance, subjective and eye tracking sensor metrics. Classic Machine Learning algorithms should be incorporated and used to enable the classification of users' CL by fusioning extracted metrics from different CL measurement methods or modalities to create a single ensemble model.

The model presented in Fig. 4 includes (i) The features extracted and selected based on overall experimental results from individual modalities which constitute CL set of measures; (ii) Cross-validation, data preprocessing (identifying outliers and handling missing values), normalization of features data; (iii) development of individual CL classification model from each modality using classical machine learning algorithm where only the best algorithm will be selected and optimized; (iv) a fusion of outputs from the best algorithms of each modality will take place to constitute the stacking ensemble model using classical machine learning algorithms where the optimization and robustness testing of the best algorithm model(s) will take place to improve the final prediction(s) accuracy.

By utilizing diverse modalities, modeling human cognitive load and psychophysiological states, in general, is more accurate as various modalities ensure deep involvement into the memory processes of subjects. Furthermore, incorporating various modalities and models enhances the system's ability to tolerate noise in data. Ultimately, the ensemble learning approach facilitates performance personalization, optimization, and the ability to consider temporal dependencies in data, thereby improving cognitive load state monitoring.

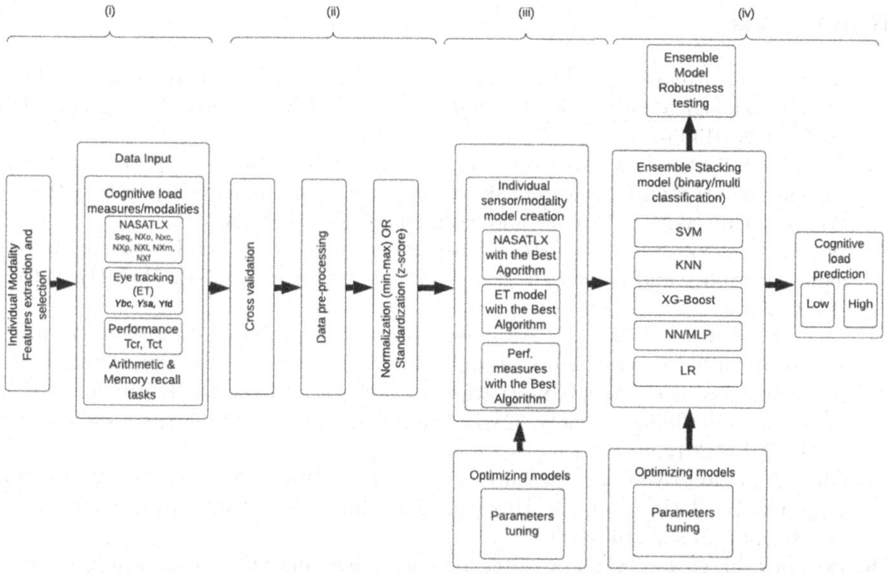

Fig. 4. Example instance of ensemble learning method for cognitive load prediction setup

5 Future Works and Summary

The main goal of this article was to determine the impact of the difference level of difficulties of the two group of tasks on all used cognitive load measurements and to compare employed metrics in terms of statistical differences related to the task difficulties.

Our study proved the effectiveness of both Memory recall and Arithmetic tasks as cognitive tasks stimuli and the usefulness of performance, subjective, and psychophysiological metrics used to measure cognitive load. As observation, the level of differences between easy and hard tasks for both groups of tasks were statistically significant in most of subjective and performance metrics while very less in psychophysiological metrics. The following metrics are significantly in relation with the cognitive load experienced by participants during the performance of memory recall and arithmetic tasks: *Tcr, Tct, Seq, NXo, NXc, NXp, NXt, NXs, NXf, NXm, Ybc, Ysa*, and *Yfd*.

We have also proposed an ensemble learning method for cognitive load prediction based on selected measures. In our future work, we are planning to verify the performance of the proposed method in terms of accuracy measures. Additionally, future research will target to differentiate cognitive load from overload levels by employing machine learning algorithms that use as input not only metrics from performance, subjective and eye tracking sensor measures but also other sensor data like EEG, GSR and facial expression should be considered and included to offer deep insights into different aspects of the nervous system and achieve high classification rates.

References

1. Ahmad, M.I., Keller, I., Robb, D.A., et al.: A framework to estimate cognitive load using physiological data. Pers. Ubiquit. Comput. (2020). https://doi.org/10.1007/s00779-020-01455-7
2. Babu, D.K.: Study of cognitive load during human-computer interaction using galvanic skin response measurement and facial expression analysis. Master's thesis. Wroclaw University of Science and Technology, Wrocław (2021)
3. Berka, C., et al.: EEG correlates of task engagement and mental workload in vigilance, learning, and memory tasks. Aviat. Space Environ. Med. **78**(5 II), B231–B244 (2007)
4. Chen, S., Epps, J., Chen, F.: An investigation of pupil-based cognitive load measurement with low cost infrared webcam under light re- flex interference. In: Proceedings of the Annual International Conference of the IEEE Engineering in Medicine and Biology Society, EMBS, pp. 3202–3205 (2013). https://doi.org/10.1109/EMBC.2013.6610222
5. Chen, F., et al.: Eye-based measures. In: Chen, F., et al. (eds.) Robust Multimodal Cognitive Load Measurement. HIS, pp. 75–85. Springer, Cham (2016). https://doi.org/10.1007/978-3-319-31700-7_4
6. De Cock, L., et al.: Taking a closer look at indoor route guidance; usability study to compare an adapted and non-adapted mobile prototype. Spat. Cogn. Comput. **22**(1–2), 51–73 (2021). https://doi.org/10.1080/13875868.2021.1885411
7. Gibson, A., et al.: Assessing usability testing for people living with dementia. In: REHAB 2016: Proceedings of the 4th Workshop on ICTs for improving Patients Rehabilitation Research Techniques, pp. 25–31 (2016). https://doi.org/10.1145/3051488.3051492
8. Krejtz, K., Duchowski, A.T., Niedzielska, A., Biele, C., Krejtz, I.: Eye tracking cognitive load using pupil diameter and microsaccades with fixed gaze. PLoS ONE **13**(9), 1–23 (2018). https://doi.org/10.1371/journal.pone.0203629
9. Krieglstein, F., Beege, M., Rey, G.D., Ginns, P., Krell, M., Schneider, S.: A systematic meta-analysis of the reliability and validity of subjective cognitive load questionnaires in experimental multimedia learning research. Educ. Psychol. Rev. **34**(4), 2485–2541 (2022)
10. Leppink, J., van Gog, T., Paas, F., Sweller, J.: Cognitive load theory: Researching and planning teaching to maximise learning. Res. Med. Educ. 207–218 (2015). https://doi.org/10.1002/9781118838983.ch18
11. Morton, J., et al.: Danger, high voltage! Using EEG and EOG measurements for cognitive overload detection in a simulated industrial context. Appl. Ergon. **102**, 103763 (2022). https://doi.org/10.1016/j.apergo.2022.103763
12. Ojha, S.: Study of cognitive load during human-computer interaction using pupillometry and photopletysmography (PPG). Master's thesis. Wroclaw University of Science and Technology, Wrocław (2021)
13. Pavlov, Y.G., Kasanov, D., Kosachenko, A.I., Kotyusov, A.I., Busch, N.A.: Pupillometry and electroencephalography in the digit span task. Sci. Data **9**(1), 1–6 (2022). https://doi.org/10.1038/s41597-022-01414-2
14. Ramakrishnan, P., Balasingam, B., Biondi, F.: Cognitive load estimation for adaptive human-machine system automation. In: Learning Control, pp. 35–58. Elsevier (2021). https://doi.org/10.1016/B978-0-12-822314-7.00007-9
15. Rubio, S., Diaz, E., Martin, J., Puente, J.M.: Evaluation of subjective mental workload: a comparison of SWAT, NASA-TLX, and workload profile methods. Appl. Psychol. **53**(1), 61–86 (2004). https://doi.org/10.1111/j.1464-0597.2004.00161

16. Sarailoo, R., Latifzadeh, K., Amiri, S.H., Bosaghzadeh, A., Ebrahimpour, R.: Assessment of instantaneous cognitive load imposed by educational multimedia using electroencephalography signals. Front. Neurosci. **16**(August), 1–16 (2022). https://doi.org/10.3389/fnins.2022.744737
17. Skaramagkas, V., et al.: Review of eye tracking metrics involved in emotional and cognitive processes. IEEE Rev. Biomed. Eng. 1–19 (2021). https://doi.org/10.1109/RBME.2021.3066072
18. Tong, S., & Nie, Y.: Measuring designers cognitive load for timely knowledge push via eye tracking. Int. J. Hum.-Comput. Interact. 1–14 (2022). https://doi.org/10.1080/10447318.2022.2057898
19. Wang, C.C., Cheng, P.K.H., Wang, T.H.: Measurement of extraneous and germane cognitive load in the mathematics addition task: an event-related potential study. Brain Sci. **12**(8), 1036 (2022). https://doi.org/10.3390/brainsci12081036
20. Wong, H.K., Epps, J.: Pupillary transient responses to within-task cognitive load variation. Comput. Methods Programs Biomed. **137**, 47–63 (2016). https://doi.org/10.1016/j.cmpb.2016.08.017
21. Zagermann, J., Pfeil, U., Reiterer, H.: Measuring cognitive load using eye tracking technology in visual computing. In: ACM International Conference Proceeding Series, 24 October 2016, pp. 78–85 (2016). https://doi.org/10.1145/2993901.2993908
22. Zihisire Muke, P., Trawinski, B.: Concept of research into cognitive load in human computer interaction using biometric techniques. In: Proceedings of the PP-RAI 2019 Conference, Wrocław, Poland, pp. 78–83 (2019)
23. Zyma, I., et al.: Electroencephalograms during mental arithmetic task performance. Data **4**(1), 14 (2019). https://doi.org/10.3390/data4010014
24. iMotions Biometric Research Platform (8.1), iMotions A/S, Copenhagen, Denmark (2021)

Author Index

N. T. Nguyen et al. (Eds.): ICCCI 2023, LNAI 14162, pp. 847–849, 2023.
https://doi.org/10.1007/978-3-031-41456-5

Printed in the United States
by Baker & Taylor Publisher Services